Law School Publications

of

WEST PUBLISHING COMPANY

St. Paul 2, Minnesota

ACCOUNTING

Shannon's Accounting and the Law, 604 pages, 1957.

Shannon's Legal Accounting, 366 pages, 1951.

ADMINISTRATIVE LAW

Davis' Cases, 592 pages, 1959.

Davis' Text, 617 pages, 1959.

Davis' Cases, Text and Problems, 609 pages, 1960.

Merrill's Cases, 720 pages, 1954.

ADMIRALTY

Robinson's Text, 1025 pages, 1939.

Sprague and Healy's Cases, 859 pages, 1950.

AGENCY

Seavey and Hall's Cases, 431 pages, 1956.

Seavey's Studies, 451 pages, 1949.

Steffen's Cases, 2nd Ed., 902 pages, 1952.

Tiffany's Text, 2nd Ed., 485 pages, 1924.

AGENCY AND PARTNERSHIP

Seavey, Reuschlein & Hall's Cases, 599 pages, 1962.

BANKRUPTCY

MacLachlan's Text, 500 pages, 1956.

Nadler's Cases on Creditor-Debtor Relations, 698 pages, 1956.

Nadler's Supp., 233 pages, 1959.

Sturges' Cases on Debtors' Estates, 4th Ed., 1291 pages, 1949.

See Creditors' Rights.

BILLS AND NOTES

Aigler and Steinheimer's Cases, 670 pages, 1962.

Britton's Text, 2nd Ed., 794 pages, 1961.

CODE PLEADING

Clark's Cases on Modern Pleading, 1042 pages, 1952.

Clark's Text, 2nd Ed., 874 pages, 1947.

Cleary's Cases on Pleading, 2d Ed., 434 pages, 1958.

Elliott & Karlen's Cases, 441 pages, 1961.

COMMON LAW PLEADING

McBaine's Cases, Introduction to Civil Procedure, 399 pages, 1950.

Shipman's Text, 3rd Ed., 644 pages, 1923.

COMMUNITY PROPERTY

Burby's Cases, 4th Ed., 342 pages, 1955.

Huie's Texas Cases on Marital Rights, 781 pages, 1955.

Verrall's Cases, California Community Property, 320 pages, 1960.

CONFLICT OF LAWS

Ehrenzweig's Text, 824 pages, 1962.

Goodrich's Text, 3rd Ed., 662 pages, 1949.

Lorenzen's Cases, 6th Ed., 918 pages, 1951.

Selected Readings, 1151 pages, 1956.

Stumberg's Cases, 497 pages, 1956.

CONSTITUTIONAL LAW

Dodd's Cases, 5th Ed., 1438 pages, 1954.

Dodd's Cases, 5th Ed., Shorter Ed., 969 pages, 1954.

Dodd's Supplement.

Forrester's Cases, 879 pages, 1959.

Forrester's Supplement.

Rottschaefer's Text, 982 pages, 1939.

Selected Essays, 971 pages, 1963.

CONTRACTS

Corbin's Cases, 3rd Ed., 1381 pages, 1947, and 1953 Supplement, 36 pages.

Corbin's Text, Student Edition, 1224 pages, 1952.

Fuller's Cases, 994 pages, 1947.

Simpson's Cases, 592 pages, 1956.

Simpson's Text, 692 pages, 1954.

CORPORATIONS

Henn's Text, 735 pages, 1961.

Stevens & Larson's Cases, 2nd Ed., 741 pages, 1955.

Stevens' Text, 2nd Ed., 1125 pages, 1949.

CREDIT TRANSACTIONS

Maxwell & Riesenfeld's California Cases on Security Transactions, 371 pages, 1957.

Maxwell & Riesenfeld's Supplement, 68 pages, 1963.

Sturges' Cases, 4th Ed., 599 pages, 1955.

CREDITORS' RIGHTS

Nadler's Cases on Creditor and Debtor Relations, 698 pages, 1956.

Nadler's Supplement, 233 pages, 1959.

Sturges' Cases, Debtors' Estates, 4th Ed., 1291 pages, 1949.

CRIMINAL LAW

Hall & Glueck's Cases, 2d Ed., 699 pages, 1958.

Miller's Text, 649 pages, 1934.

Stumberg's Texas Cases, 505 pages, 1954.

DAMAGES

Crane's Cases, 3rd Ed., 337 pages, 1955.

McCormick's Text, 811 pages, 1935.

DICTIONARIES

Black's, one volume.

Bouvier's, two volumes.

DOMESTIC RELATIONS

Compton's Cases, 638 pages, 1951.

Huie's Texas Cases, 781 pages, 1955.

Madden's Text, 748 pages, 1931.

DRUGS AND DRUGGISTS

Arthur's Text, 4th Ed., 399 pages, 1955.

ENGINEERING LAW

Simpson & Dillavou's Text, 4th Ed., 506 pages, 1958.

EQUITY

Cook's Cases, 4th Ed., 1192 pages, 1948.

McClintock's Text, 2nd Ed., 643 pages, 1948.

Van Hecke's Cases on Equitable Remedies, 651 pages, 1959.

EVIDENCE

McCormick's Cases, 3rd Ed., 663 pages, 1956.

McCormick's Text, 774 pages, 1954.

Selected Writings, 1232 pages, 1957.

FEDERAL ANTI-TRUST LAWS

Oppenheim's Cases, 1188 pages, 1959.

FEDERAL JURISDICTION AND PROCEDURE

Bunn's U. S. Courts, Text, 5th Ed., 408 pages, 1949.

Forrester & Currier's Cases, 906 pages, 1962.

Wright's Text, Federal Courts, 634 pages, 1963.

FRAUD AND MISTAKE

Keeton's Cases, 514 pages, 1954.

FUTURE INTERESTS
Gulliver's Cases, 624 pages, 1959.
Powell's Cases, 3rd Ed., 621 pages, 1961.
Simes' Text, 495 pages, 1951.

INSURANCE
Keeton's Basic Insurance Law, 655 pages, 1960.
Vance's Cases, 4th Ed., 994 pages, 1952.
Vance's Text, 3rd Ed., 1290 pages, 1951.

INTERNATIONAL BUSINESS
Ebb's Cases, about 800 pages, 1964.

INTERNATIONAL LAW
Hudson's Cases, 3rd Ed., 770 pages, 1951.

INTRODUCTION TO LAW
Bowman's Text, 307 pages, 1929.
Smith's Text, 2nd Ed., 468 pages, 1939.
See Legal Method.

JUDICIAL REMEDIES
Cribbet's Cases, 762 pages, 1954.

JURISPRUDENCE
Simpson and Stone's Cases, Law and Society, Book I, Law and Society in Evolution, 692 pages, 1948. Book II, Law in Modern Democratic Society, 902 pages, 1949. Book III, Law, Totalitarianism and Democracy, 796 pages, 1949.
Wu's Cases, 719 pages, 1958.

LABOR LAW
Handler & Hays' Cases, 4th Ed., 916 pages, 1963.

LANDLORD AND TENANT
Jacobs' Cases, 2nd Ed., 815 pages, 1941.

LEGAL ACCOUNTING
See Accounting.

LEGAL BIBLIOGRAPHY
How to Find the Law, 5th Ed., 207 pages, 1957.

LEGAL ETHICS
Pirsig's Cases on the Legal Profession, 211 pages, 1957.
Selected Readings Legal Profession, 565 pages, 1962.

LEGAL HISTORY
Radin's Text, 612 pages, 1936.

LEGAL METHOD
Fryer and Benson's Legal Method and Legal System, 1 volume Ed., 843 pages, 1950.

LEGAL WRITING STYLE
Weihofen's Text, 323 pages, 1961.

LEGISLATION
Nutting & Elliott's Cases, 3rd Ed., 414 pages, 1964.

MILITARY LAW
Schiller's Cases, 590 pages, 1952.

MORTGAGES
Osborne's Cases, Property Security, 2nd Ed., 725 pages, 1954.
Osborne's Text, 1117 pages, 1951.
Sturges' Cases, Credit Transactions, 4th Ed., 599 pages, 1955.

MUNICIPAL CORPORATIONS
Stason and Kauper's Cases, 3rd Ed., 692 pages, 1959.

NATURAL RESOURCES
Martz's Cases, 1124 pages, 1951.

OIL AND GAS
Huie, Walker and Woodward's Cases, 848 pages, 1960.
Kulp's Cases, 3rd Ed., 910 pages, 1947. Supplement, 1953.

PARTNERSHIP
Crane's Text, 2d Ed., 655 pages, 1952.
Seavey, Reuschlein and Hall's Cases on Agency and Partnership, 599 pages, 1962.

LAW SCHOOL PUBLICATIONS—Continued

PERSONAL PROPERTY

Aigler, Smith and Tefft's Cases on Property, 2 Vols., 1339 pages, 1960.

Bigelow's Cases, 3rd Ed., 500 pages, 1942.

Fryer's Readings, 3rd Ed., 1184 pages, 1938.

PLEADING

See Code Pleading.

See Common Law Pleading.

PRESS, LAW OF

Hale's Text, 3rd Ed., 691 pages, 1948.

PROPERTY SECURITY

Osborne's Cases, 2nd Ed., 725 pages, 1954.

See also Mortgages.

PUBLIC UTILITIES

Auerbach & Nathanson's Cases on Federal Regulation of Transportation, 1223 pages, 1953.

QUIZZERS

Ballantine's Problems.

Burby's Law Refreshers.

Smith's How to Answer Law Examinations.

Smith's Reviews for Law Examinations.

REAL PROPERTY

Aigler, Smith and Tefft's Cases on Property, 2 Vols., 1339 pages, 1960.

Burby's Text, 2nd Ed., 758 pages, 1954.

Horack and Nolan's Land Use Controls, 240 pages, 1955.

Jacobs' Cases, Landlord and Tenant, 2nd Ed., 815 pages, 1941.

Moynihan's Introduction, 254 pages, 1962.

Smith's Survey, 370 pages, 1956.

REMEDIES

Wright's Cases, 498 pages, 1955.

RESTITUTION

Keeton's Cases, (Fraud and Mistake) 514 pages, 1954.

Thurston's Cases, 964 pages, 1940.

RIGHTS IN LAND

Aigler, Smith and Tefft's Cases on Property, 2 Vols., 1339 pages, 1960.

SALES

McCurdy's Cases, 727 pages, 1959.

Vold's Cases, 3rd Ed., 860 pages, 1960.

Vold's Supplement, 118 pages, 1962.

Vold's Text, 2nd Ed., 611 pages, 1959.

STATUTES

Selected Statutes, 5th Ed., 373 pages, 1944.

See Legislation.

SURETYSHIP AND GUARANTY

Osborne's Cases, 65 pages, 1955.

Simpson's Cases, 538 pages, 1942.

Simpson's Text, 569 pages, 1950.

Sturges' Cases, Credit Transactions, 4th Ed., 599 pages, 1955.

TAXATION

Bruton and Bradley's Cases, 808 pages, 1955.

Hellerstein's Cases on State and Local Taxation, 2nd Ed., 669 pages, 1961.

Lowndes and Kramer's Text, 951 pages, 1962.

TITLES

Aigler, Smith and Tefft's Cases on Property, 2 Vols., 1339 pages, 1960.

TORTS

Green, Malone, Pedrick & Rahl's Cases on Injuries to Relations, 544 pages, 1959.

Green, Malone, Pedrick & Rahl's Cases, 855 pages, 1957.

Hepburn's Cases, 3rd Ed., 540 pages, 1954.

Prosser's Text, 2nd Ed., 952 pages, 1955.

Seavey, Keeton and Keeton's Cases on Torts, 768 pages, 1957.

TRADE REGULATION

See Federal Anti-Trust Laws.
See also Unfair Trade Practices.

TRIAL PRACTICE

Karlen's Cases, 439 pages, 1961.

TRUSTS

Bogert's Text, 4th Ed., 528 pages, 1963.
Powell's Cases, Trusts and Wills, 639 pages, 1960.
Smith's Survey, 167 pages, 1949.

UNFAIR TRADE PRACTICES

Oppenheim's Cases, 1534 pages, 1950.
Oppenheim's Supp., 389 pages, 1960.

WILLS

Atkinson's Text, 2nd Ed., 975 pages, 1953.
Turrentine's Cases, 2nd Ed., 483 pages, 1962.

WORKMEN'S COMPENSATION

Malone and Plant's Cases, 622 pages, 1963.

HANDBOOK

OF THE

LAW OF EVIDENCE

BY

CHARLES T. McCORMICK
LATE PROFESSOR OF LAW, UNIVERSITY OF TEXAS

HORNBOOK SERIES

ST. PAUL, MINN.
WEST PUBLISHING CO.
1954

McCormick Evidence HB

To My Wife

*

PREFACE

That part of the law of procedure known as evidence law has not responded in recent decades to the need for simplification and rationalization as rapidly as other parts of procedural law. Writers and teachers, such as Wigmore and Morgan, have laid the groundwork for modernization, and presumably judges, legislators and lawyers will increasingly in the next few years lend their efforts toward improving the structure. In this brief treatise I have attempted not only to picture the existing practice in respect to the topics considered but also where the rules seem defective to give my views as to the changes needed for the better administration of justice. Some directions in which as it seems to me improvement may be sought are the following:

The relaxation or abandonment, in trials before the judge without a jury, of the exclusionary rules, apart from the rules of privilege.

The simplification and liberalization of the exceptions to the rule against hearsay.

The modification of the rules of privilege for confidential communications so as to empower the judge to require the disclosure of the communication when it appears that the withholding of the evidence will probably result in a miscarriage of justice.

The re-shaping of the rules to recognize the superior value of statements made by a witness, near in time to the event described by him, as compared with his sworn, cross-examined statements made months or years later at the trial. Recognition of the findings of psychology and common sense in this regard would require the modification of some present restrictions upon the use of prior inconsistent statements, memoranda of past recollection, and former testimony.

The implementation by statute or rule of the court's common-law power to seek the aid of impartial experts.

The lessening of surprise by the determination, where feasible, of anticipated evidence questions at pre-trial hearings, and by the service upon the adversary in advance of trial of copies of documents which it is proposed to introduce, except where there is good cause for failure to do so.*

Increasing the simplicity and accessibility of the law of evidence by the adoption in the federal and state jurisdictions of the Uniform Rules of Evidence. These Rules embrace only a few of the foregoing suggestions, proposed as directions of future development, but they do represent a fair embodiment of the current opinions of progressive judges, lawyers and writers

---

* Compare The Recommendations of the Conference on Administrative Procedure, 15 F.R.D. 217, 221 (1953).

as to the "better view" upon evidence questions, where the courts are at variance. Rules of evidence should not be unchanging, and the study of experience under the Uniform Rules should be continuous, and should lead to their improvement as needs emerge.

The doctrines of evidence and the decisions on evidence questions are as the sands of the sea. The reader will soon discover that the treatment in this book, both as to topics and cases, is highly selective, with no pretensions to completeness. The purpose is to give the student a preliminary view of some of the important areas, and to furnish the lawyer or the judge with a starting point on some of his evidence problems. As keys to further search I have provided references to the legal periodicals, the digests and encyclopedias, the Uniform Rules, and above all to the Wigmore treatise.

CHARLES T. McCORMICK

The University of Texas
November, 1954

SUMMARY OF CONTENTS

SUMMARY OF CONTENTS

TITLE 8.   WRITINGS

TITLE 9.   THE HEARSAY RULE AND ITS EXCEPTIONS

TABLE OF CONTENTS

TITLE 1. INTRODUCTION

Chapter 1. Preparing and Presenting the Evidence

TITLE 2. EXAMINATION OF WITNESSES

Chapter 2. The Form of Questions on Direct: The Judge's Witnesses: Refreshing Memory

Chapter 3. The Requirement of First-Hand Knowledge: The Opinion Rule: Expert Testimony

Chapter 4. Cross-Examination and Subsequent Examinations

Chapter 5. Impeachment and Support

TABLE OF CONTENTS

TITLE 3. ADMISSION AND EXCLUSION

Chapter 6. The Procedure of Admitting and Excluding Evidence

TITLE 4. COMPETENCY

Chapter 7. The Competency of Witnesses

TITLE 5. PRIVILEGE

Chapter 8. The Scope and Effect of Evidentiary Privileges

TABLE OF CONTENTS

TABLE OF CONTENTS

Chapter 29. Dying Declarations

Chapter 30. Spontaneous Declarations

TOPIC 1. DECLARATIONS OF BODILY CONDITION

TOPIC 2. DECLARATIONS OF MENTAL STATE

TOPIC 3. EXCITED UTTERANCES

TOPIC 4. DECLARATIONS OF PRESENT SENSE IMPRESSIONS

TOPIC 5. RES GESTAE

TOPIC 6. SELF-SERVING DECLARATIONS

Chapter 31. Records of Past Recollection

TABLE OF CONTENTS

TABLE OF CONTENTS

HANDBOOK
ON THE
LAW OF EVIDENCE

TITLE 1

INTRODUCTION

CHAPTER 1

PREPARING AND PRESENTING THE EVIDENCE

Sec.
1. Planning and Preparation of Proof as Important as the Rules of Evidence
2. Preparation for Trial on the Facts Without Resort to the Aid of the Court
3. Invoking the Aid of the Court in Preparing for Trial
4. The Order of Presenting Evidence at the Trial

1. Planning and Preparation of Proof as Important as the Rules of Evidence.

The law of Evidence is the system of rules and standards by which the admission of proof at the trial of a lawsuit is regulated. It is apparent, however, that this stage, when proof is offered and the rules of evidence come into play, is a late stage in a long process. It is appropriate at the outset to emphasize this, lest the student, in his absorption in the rules of evidence, lapse into the assumption that his concern, in the handling of litigation, will chiefly be directed to the learning and application of those rules. He should be conscious throughout that every case which will be encountered, dealing with a dispute over a rule of evidence or its application, presents a situation in which the lawyers concerned have been required to shoulder many other tasks in the planning and production of testimony, long before the question of evidence-law could be presented to the court. It will

be useful, as a reminder, to mention some of these earlier stages in the problem of proof.

2. Preparation for Trial on the Facts, Without Resort to the Aid of the Court.[1]

The client must be interviewed to ascertain the facts, and these interviews should in-

[1] There is much dross in the professional writing on this subject, but also much of value. See the following trial practice pamphlets of the Practising Law Institute, all published in 1946: Bodin, Marshalling the Evidence; Dawson, Examinations before Trial in State Courts; Bodin, Final Preparation for Trial. Stimulating general suggestions will be found in addresses such as Martin F. Conboy, The Preparation of a Case for Trial, 11 Am.Bar Asso.J. 310 (1925); Emory R. Buckner, The Trial of Cases, 15 Am.Bar Asso.J. 271, 273 (1929); Louis Nizer, The Art of Jury Trial, 32 Corn.L.Q. 59 (1946); and in B. K. and W. F. Elliott, The Work of the Advocate, Ch. I, 2d ed., 1912. See also Francis L. Wellman, Success in Court (1941). For detailed practical suggestions, see F. X. Busch, Law and Tactics in Jury Trials, §§ 200–216 (1949), and I. Goldstein, Trial Technique, Ch. I, 1935; Wm. A. Stern II, Getting the Evidence, Pt. II, 1936; S. C. Schweitzer, Trial Manual for Negli-

x

clude a tactful cross-examination to overcome the client's natural tendency to confine the story to the facts favorable to himself. The witnesses who have first-hand knowledge of the transaction in controversy must likewise be interviewed, and where possible, their written statements taken. Apart from the ordinary eye-witnesses, it becomes today increasingly necessary to arrange for the employment of technical experts, such as physicians in personal injury cases, chemists and physicists in patent litigation, engineers and architects in controversies over construction contracts, alienists in criminal cases, and handwriting experts in disputes over the genuineness of documents. To prepare himself to testify, and to give to counsel the information he will need to frame his questions at the trial, the expert must usually be furnished by the lawyer with a detailed request for an investigation and report upon specific questions.[2] Then it will often be necessary to assemble such documentary evidence as is available, such as contracts, letters, receipts, and loose-leaf records, in commercial litigation, and deeds and certified copies of conveyances and of judgments and decrees, in land litigation. Other physical evidence, such as the revolver of the attacker and the perforated coat of the victim, in a murder case, or a sample of the goods in an action for breach of warranty, should be inquired for, and preserved for use at the trial. The lawyer, moreover, must be fertile in planning for the production of all those aids to the senses which quicken the jury's interest in and understanding of the testimony, such as photographs, motion picture films, x-ray photographs, plats, diagrams, and models. Where practicable, the task of proof should be lightened by securing written stipulations from opposing counsel of the existence of facts not in controversy, such as the execution of documents, or the ownership of a vehicle, or of premises, involved in the suit. If it is anticipated that the terms of a document in the possession of the adversary will need to be proved by use of a copy, written notice to produce the original at the trial must be given to opposing counsel.

Manifestly, all of this preparation must be planned, and the plan will develop as new information is disclosed, but as the trial approaches, a definite program must be formulated. Each fact involved in the claim or defence should be listed, with the witnesses and documents by which it will be proved.[3] This may well be supplemented by a list of the witnesses in the order in which it is expected to call them, and the subjects upon which they will be examined. Finally, and most important, at the last minute before the witnesses are to go on the stand, the counsel who calls them must talk to each to ascertain what he is prepared to swear, and cause him to refresh his memory, if necessary, by reading his signed statement, and warn him of the probable line of the adversary's cross-examination.

3. Invoking the Aid of the Court in Preparing for Trial: Motions for Particulars; Requests for Admissions; Discovery and Depositions; Pre-Trial Conferences.[1]

Most of the preparation of proof, outlined above, must under modern conditions be made before the process of settling the plead-

gence Actions, 2d ed., Ch. I, 1941. W. J. Hornaday, Some Suggestions on the Investigation of Facts, 15 Ind.L.J. 499 (1940), deals with the interviewing of witnesses. See also B. A. Bowman, How to Make an Investigation, 21 Okl.B.A.J. 1346 (1950), 19 Ins. Counsel J. 23 (1952).

2. See Carr, Pre-Trial Preparation of the Medical Evidence, 20 U.Kan. City L.Rev. 103 (1952); Cecil, Preparation and Presentation of Medical Evidence, 19 Ins.Counsel J. 380 (1952).

3. For a good example of such a diagram, see Goldstein, Trial Technique, § 74 (1935).

1. A convenient chart which lists the various kinds of pre-trial proceedings for securing evidence, with citations to statutes and decisions in each state, is found in Stern, Getting the Evidence, at p. 425 (1936). See also Burns, Fact Finding Devices before Trial, 9 S.D.Bar J. 98 (1940).

ings upon which the parties will go to trial has been finally completed. In most jurisdictions, amendments are allowed with fair liberality until the eve of trial. The pleadings serve to identify the transaction in controversy, but if it was ever true that they served to define the exact issue so as to enable a party to limit his preparation of proof to such issue, it is not true today.[2] Despite the requirements of the pleading codes designed to elicit a full disclosure of the contentions upon which the parties will rely, and to eliminate the need of proving matters which are not genuinely contested, a party will frequently face the apparent necessity of preparing to prove facts about which he thinks there is no real dispute.

There are, however, certain proceedings which can be taken before trial which may avoid this necessity. A motion for particulars under the common law practice, or a motion to require the adversary to make his allegation more definite and certain, under the Code practice, may result in narrowing the need for proof. In some states,[3] a convenient code-provision permits one to call upon the opposite party to admit the genuineness of a paper which one intends to use in evidence. In a few states,[4] and under the new Federal Rules,[5] he may call for an admission of any fact. In either event, if the admission is refused, and if it appears at the trial that the refusal was unreasonable, the expense of making the proof will be assessed against the adversary. But more help to this end can usually be found in the use of the process of Discovery.[6] By this device, the adversary can be required to make disclosures which will serve the other party as proof, and which will have the even more important effect of holding the adversary to a particular ground of contention from which he cannot shift. One type of discovery proceeding permits a party to secure an order requiring the adversary to exhibit for inspection by the party applying, the documents, books, papers, and other physical evidence in his hands. Similarly, in nearly half the states, the defendant in a personal injury case may procure an order requiring the claimant to submit to a bodily examination by physicians.[7] If the condition of premises in possession of the adversary is involved in the controversy, the party in some states may apply for an order to permit him to inspect such premises.[8]

Moreover, a still more sweeping inquisition is permitted. The party is permitted to address questions to the adversary about the facts of the case. The traditional method is by framing written interrogatories. This is often ineffective, as it is hard to phrase questions so that they cannot be evaded. Consequently, the practice in nearly half the states has come to permit a party to subject his opponent to an oral examination, conducted by counsel, before an officer of the court. The oral examination may be made far more

---

[2] See George Ragland, Jr., Discovery before Trial, (1932), Ch. I, Inadequacy of Pleading as a Basis of Preparation for Trial.

[3] E. g., S.H.A.Ill. ch. 110, § 259.18(1); Mass.G.L.(Ter. Ed.) c. 231, § 69; N.Y. Civil Practice Act, § 322 as amended L. 1941, c. 254; Ohio, R.C. § 2317.31; Wis. St.1953, § 327.22(1) (a).

[4] S.H.A.Ill. ch. 110, § 259.18(2); Mass. G.L.(Ter.Ed.) c. 231, § 69; N.Y. Civil Practice Act, § 322 as amended L. 1941, c. 254; Wis.St.1953, § 327.22(1) (b).

[5] Fed.Rules Civ.Proc. rule 36, 28 U.S.C.A., and see 4 Moore, Federal Practice, ch. 36 (2d ed. 1950).

[6] A comprehensive treatment of discovery from the viewpoint of its value in the administration of justice is to be found in Ragland, Discovery before Trial (1932). This valuable work collects the statutory provisions on the subject in each state. Descriptions of the procedure from the viewpoint of its practical value to the party litigant are presented in Stern, Getting the Evidence, Part III (1936), and Goldstein, Trial Technique, secs. 124–166a (1935).

[7] See 8 Wigmore, Evidence, § 2220, Ragland, cited above, ch. 22.

[8] And so also as to chattels. Wigmore, cited above, § 2221.

searching than the written, since the questioner may pursue new and unlooked-for lines of inquiry opened up by the answers. Where the oral examination is permitted, the statute may require that an application and showing be made to the court for an order for such examination. In the greater number of states, the result is attained more simply and conveniently, and usually without order of court, by giving notice to take the party's deposition under the general statute authorizing the testimony of a witness to be given by deposition.

Apart from this use as a vehicle of discovery, by examination of the adverse party, and the similar use in examining adverse witnesses who will not give a voluntary statement, the deposition is even more frequently employed as the means of recording and preserving the testimony of witnesses favorable to the party who takes the deposition.[9] One who is preparing a case for trial will wish to take the depositions of those witnesses whose attendance at the trial is doubtful, such as travelers or sick or aged persons, or those persons living at a distance from the place of trial who are unwilling to attend, or whose attendance is not so essential as to warrant the client in defraying the expense of the trip. It may be desirable to take the deposition of a vital witness on a disputed point, as a safeguard in case of his death or disappearance. It is even possible that some witnesses are likely to do the party who calls them more harm than good when placed on the stand before a jury. But in the usual case, counsel will plan to call in person at the trial all witnesses whose testimony is vital, and will rely on the colorless reading of a deposition only for the proof of facts not likely to be disputed, or as a last resort when it is impracticable to bring in the witness himself.

The proceedings incident to the taking of a deposition vary greatly in detail from state to state. Usually, the party taking the deposition may choose to have the witness answer written interrogatories, or to have him examined orally. The former is much cheaper, and is well adapted for making proof of simple matters by experienced witnesses, as where a book-keeper is called upon to identify an entry in his books. If the matter is more complex, as where an eye-witness is to be asked to describe an automobile collision, the oral examination would usually be preferable. Under the better modern statutes, the only step prerequisite to the taking of the deposition, is the serving of a notice upon the other party. If the deposition is upon written interrogatories, a copy of these is attached to the notice, and the adversary has a fixed time in which to serve cross-interrogatories. These last, it may be added, are frequently futile, since they must be framed before the witness's answers to the questions on direct can be known. If an oral examination is desired, the notice will state the time and place. If the deposition, whether upon written or oral examination, is to be taken in another state, it will usually be necessary to procure the issuance of a commission authorizing an officer to conduct the examination. This officer may be some person specially designated by the court as a commissioner for the purpose, or more usually the statute permits the duty to be performed by any notary public, justice of the peace, or judge.

If the deposition is taken upon commission, rather than upon the simpler practice of mere service of notice, the officer executing the commission will have the duty of fix-

---

9. A good short description of depositions and their use is found in Goldstein, Trial Technique, §§ 146–165 (1935). See also Abbott's Civil Jury Trials, ch. X, 5th ed. by P. W. Viesselman (1935); Stern, Getting the Evidence, Part III (1936); 4 Jones, Commentaries on the Law of Evidence, ch. 20, (2d ed. 1926).

For the detailed rules of course the statutes and rules of court of the various jurisdictions must be consulted. In the Federal courts in civil actions, the matter is regulated by Rules 26–33. See 4 Moore, Federal Practice, chs. 26–33 (2d ed. 1950).

ing a time and place and notifying the witness and the parties. If the questions are written, the officer writes down the witness's answers to the questions, and causes him to sign and swear to the answers. An oral examination, on the other hand, closely resembles the examination of a witness in court. The officer swears the witness, and superintends the hearing; a stenographer is present to take down the questions and answers; and counsel for both sides are at hand to examine and cross-examine. Objections to the form of the questions asked, as that the question is leading, are required to be stated at the hearing or they will be waived. Such objections of form as well as those relating to the manner of conducting the examination, must be promptly called to the court's attention in advance of trial by motion to strike particular answers or to suppress the whole deposition. If not, these defects of form are waived. Upon completion of the examination, when the answers have been transcribed and the witness has read and signed his testimony, the officer certifies to its authenticity and returns it into court. Nevertheless, the deposition can only become part of the evidence at the trial if one of the parties actually offers it as such during the hearing of the case, and is permitted to read it in evidence. In most but not all the states the rule is adopted that the party at whose instance the deposition is taken cannot read it in evidence until he makes preliminary proof that the witness is not available to be placed on the stand in person, by reason of death, disability, or absence from the jurisdiction. When the deposition is offered at the trial, objection to the competency of the witness may be made, and objections likewise to particular questions and answers, when they go to the substance, as it is said, and not the form merely, may be urged.

Within the last decade in this country another and most effective device for narrowing the need of proof has been imported. This is the pre-trial hearing or conference.

When the case is approaching the time for trial, usually two or three weeks before the date set, the judge summons the counsel for both sides, and sometimes the parties, and seeks to settle all preliminary questions of pleading, to ascertain the scope of the dispute, and to secure agreements as to the facts not really at issue. The Federal Rule [10] mentions, as among the objects of the hearing:

"(1) The simplification of the issues;

. . .

"(3) The possibility of obtaining admissions of fact and of documents which will avoid unnecessary proof;

"(4) The limitation of the number of expert witnesses;

"(5) The advisability of a preliminary reference of issues to a master for findings to be used as evidence when the trial is to be by jury;"

As this procedure becomes more widely used, a good many difficult problems of proof will be solved by agreement at the pre-trial stage.

A final step that should be mentioned before concluding the description of ways in which the aid of the court is invoked in the preparation for trial on the facts, is the procurement of the issuance and service of writs of subpena for the witnesses who are to be used at the trial. In the case of a document or other physical evidence held by another, the party who desires its production at the trial may secure a subpena duces tecum addressed to the possessor commanding him to attend the trial as a witness and to bring with him the document or other object.

[10]. Rule 16, Federal Rules of Civil Procedure, and see 3 Moore, Federal Practice, ch. 16 (2d ed. 1948). The pre-trial hearing came to us from Scotland via England. Sunderland, Theory and Practice of Pre-Trial Procedure, 21 J.Am.Jud.Soc. 125, (1937). Readable descriptions by trial judges of how it works: Delehant, The Pre-Trial Conference in Practical Employment, 28 Neb.L.Rev. 1 (1948); Suggs, Pre-Trial Technique, 6 Tex.Bar J. 61, 81 (1943); 12 id. 17 (1949); Laws, Pre-Trial Procedure, 1 F.R.D. 397 (1940); Fisher, Judicial Mediation, 10 Univ.Chi.L.Rev. 453 (1943).

4. The Order of Presenting Evidence at the Trial.

Under the usual order of proceeding at the trial, the plaintiff, who has the burden of establishing his claim, will first introduce the evidence to prove the facts necessary to enable him to recover,[1] e. g., the making of the contract sued on, its breach, and the amount of damages. At this stage the plaintiff will bring forward successively all the witnesses on whom he will rely to establish these facts, together with the documents pertinent for this purpose, which will be offered when they have been authenticated by the testimony of the witnesses. During this stage each witness of the plaintiff will first be questioned by the plaintiff's counsel, upon direct examination, then cross-examined by opposing counsel, and these may be followed by re-direct and re-cross examinations. When all of the plaintiff's witnesses to his main case have been subjected, each in turn, to this process of questioning and cross-questioning, the plaintiff signifies the completion of his case in chief by announcing that he rests.

Then the defendant presents the witnesses (and also the documents and other tangible evidence) in support of his case. At this stage the defendant will produce evidence not only in denial of the plaintiff's claim, such as evidence that a contract sued on was never actually agreed on, or in a negligence case that some bodily injury was not permanent as claimed by the plaintiff, but also in support of any affirmative defenses which the defendant has pleaded, such as the defense of fraud in the procurement of a contract sued on, or the making of a release of a personal injury claim. Here again each witness's story on direct examination is subject to be tested by cross-examination and supplemented on re-direct, etc., before he leaves the stand. When the defendant has thus completed the presentation of his proof of affirmative defenses, if any, and his evidence in denial of the plaintiff's claims, the defendant announces that he rests.

The plaintiff is now entitled to another turn at bat. He may now present his case in rebuttal. The plaintiff is not entitled to present at this stage witnesses who merely support the allegations of the complaint, but is confined to testimony which is directed to refuting the evidence of the defendant, unless the court in its discretion permits him to depart from the regular order of proof. The plaintiff's witnesses in rebuttal may be new ones, but he may often recall witnesses who testified for him on the case in chief, to answer some point first raised by the defendant's witnesses. In this, as in the other stages, the witness may not only be examined on direct, but cross-examined and re-examined. When the plaintiff's case in rebuttal is finished, he closes his case. If new points are brought out in the plaintiff's rebuttal-evidence, the defendant may meet them by evidence in rejoinder, otherwise he

---

1. This is the usual order, since the plaintiff has the "burden of proof," in the sense of the duty of first proceeding with evidence to establish the facts pleaded in the complaint. But this burden of opening the evidence usually carries with it the compensating advantage called the "right to open and close," that is, the privilege of having the first and the last word in the argument to the jury. To get this advantage, the defendant will occasionally admit the plaintiff's cause of action, and rest solely on some affirmative defense in the answer, and thus assume the burden of proceeding with the evidence first, along with the right to open and close the argument. The order of presenting evidence and the right to open and close are clearly described in

Abbott, Civil Jury Trials, chs. V and VI, 5th ed., 1935. See also 6 Wigmore, Evidence, § 1866 (a helpful chart showing the stages in presenting evidence, and in examining the individual witness), § 1867 (discussing the power of the trial judge to permit variations from the usual order). As will appear in Chapter 37 herein, the sufficiency of the proof to meet the requirements of claim or defense is often a turning-point in the case. Preparation for this test is essential, and practical suggestions for various types of cases are to be found in Spellman, How to Prove a Prima Facie Case, rev. ed., 1939; Spellman, How to Prove a Prima Facie Defense (1941).

closes his case at once. When both parties have announced that they have closed, the hearing on the facts comes to an end and the trial proceeds with the argument of counsel and the court's instructions to the jury.

To sum up: The stages of the hearing of the facts are

(1) the plaintiff's main case, or evidence in chief,

(2) the defendant's case or evidence in defense,

(3) the plaintiff's evidence in rebuttal, and

(4) the defendant's evidence in rejoinder.

In each of these stages, all of the witnesses to the facts appropriate at the particular period will be called by the party, and the examination of each witness may pass through these steps:

(1) the direct examination, conducted by the party who calls the witness,

(2) the cross-examination by the adversary,

(3) re-direct, and

(4) re-cross.

TITLE 2
EXAMINATION OF WITNESSES

CHAPTER 2

THE FORM OF QUESTIONS ON DIRECT: THE JUDGE'S WITNESSES: REFRESHING MEMORY

Sec.
5. The Form of Questions: (a) Questions Calling for a Free Narrative versus Specific Questions
6. —— (b) Leading Questions
7. —— (c) Misleading and Argumentative Questions
8. The Judge May Examine and Call Witnesses
9. Refreshing Recollection

5. The Form of Questions: (a) Questions Calling for a Free Narrative versus Specific Questions.

The art of direct examination, of telling a composite story from the mouths of your own witnesses, is far more important, though perhaps less difficult, than the art of cross-examination.[1] One of the problems of tactics is whether the information which the particular witness will give can best be elicited by a succession of questions about specific facts and happenings or will be brought out more effectively by a general question. In the latter case the attention of the witness will be directed to the incident in litigation by asking him whether he was on the scene at the time and then requesting him to tell what he saw and heard on that occasion. Ordinarily, the former method, the specific interrogation, is less effective. The narrative seems to come from the counsel rather than the witness. If the witness has any skill of speech, the spontaneous telling of his own story is more interesting and impressive, though occasionally the witness may be so over-speaking that it is unwise to trust him with a loose rein. Scientific tests have indicated that the spontaneous narrative is more accurate (because less influenced by suggestion) while the fully interrogated testimony is, naturally, more complete in its representation of the facts.[2] The moral, then, is clear. In most cases it will be best to ask the witness to tell his story, and after he has done so, to have him supplement the narrative by answers to specific questions about omitted facts.

There is, it is believed, under the prevailing view, no rule of law requiring or preferring either form of questioning. Courts have emphasized the danger that when asked to tell his story the witness will include hearsay or other incompetent testimony,[3] but a proper caution by court or counsel, on the adversary's request, will usually prevent this. True, if the improper statement comes out

1. See B. K. and W. F. Elliott, The Art of the Advocate, Ch. VII (2d ed., 1911) and numerous similar works cited 3 Wigmore, Evidence, § 768, n. 1.

2. D. S. Gardner, The Perception and Memory of Witnesses, 18 Corn.L.Q. 391, 404 (1923), citing W. M. Marston, Studies in Testimony, 15 J.Crim.Law and Criminology, 1–31 (1924); Wigmore, The Science of Judicial Proof, § 264 (3d ed., 1937).

3. State v. Allemand, 153 La. 741, 96 So. 552, 553, syl. 1 (1923) (better practice is to ask definite questions but here no prejudice); State v. Sullivan, 159 La. 589, 105 So. 631, syl. 9 (1925) (witness volunteered incompetent evidence in course of story which jury were instructed to disregard; no prejudice); 70 C.J. 504,

in the story, there is only the remedy of striking out that part of the evidence. But the need for eliciting what the witness knows in the most vivid and accurate way is an interest to be balanced against the need of the adversary for a fair opportunity to object. The guiding principle is that the trial judge has a discretion, not reviewable except for abuse,[4] to control the form of examination,[5] to the end that the facts may be clearly and expeditiously presented, and hence he may permit either of the methods discussed.[6] It is believed, however, that for the reasons given above the more expedient method both in the interest of the examining party and of the accurate disclosure of the truth, is the free narrative, and that the use of this method will seldom be curbed by enlightened judges, and will become more widespread as the process of proof looks more to the ascertainment of truth and less to the technique of admissibility.

6. The Form of Questions: (b) Leading Questions.

We have discussed in the preceding section the advantages and disadvantages of the free and unguided narrative of the witness. The danger of the opposite method, the method of drawing out the testimony by specific questions, is the danger that the witness may acquiesce in a false suggestion. The suggestion itself may plant the belief in its truth. The psychologists have verified the convictions of the judges that this danger is greater than one who has had no experience with trials would suppose.[1]

A leading question then is one which suggests to the witness the answer desired by the examiner. One who seeks to prove a set of facts instinctively shapes his questions in this suggestive fashion, and the first task of the beginning advocate is to harness his tongue to the neutral form. Nor is it wholly a matter of form. The question which contains a phrase like "Did he not?" is obviously and invariably leading, but almost any other type of question may be leading or not, dependent upon the content and context. It is sometimes supposed that a question which can be answered yes or no is by that fact marked as leading, and the beginner finds it helpful to couch his inquiries in the form of a neutral alternative ("State whether or not . . . .") to escape the charge of leading, but quite often the former kind of question will not be leading and equally often the latter kind will be.[2] The whole is-

---

4. Pumphrey v. State, 84 Neb. 636, 122 N.W. 19, 21, syl. 6 (1909).

5. Ewing v. People, 87 Colo. 6, 284 Pac. 341, syl. 1 (1930); State v. Larsen, 42 Idaho 517, 246 Pac. 313, 314, syl. 4 (1926); Dec.Digests, Witnesses, § 226; Am.L.Inst.Model Code of Evidence, Rule 105 (1942); 5 Jones, Commentaries, § 2315 (2d ed., 1926).

6. Northern P. R. Co. v. Charless, 51 Fed. 562, 570, syl. 4 (C.C.A.Wash.1892, reversed on other grounds, 162 U.S. 359, 16 S.Ct. 848) (leading case permitting free narrative in court's discretion); Mobile, J. & K. C. R. Co. v. Hawkins, 163 Ala. 565, 51 So. 37, 44, syl. 17 (1909); People v. Davis, 6 Cal.App. 229, 91 Pac. 810, syl. 2 (1907); Kinkaide v. Cavanagh, 198 Mass. 34, 84 N.E. 307, syl. 1 (1908) (within court's discretion to permit counsel to place statement of account before witness and ask her generally to explain each item); State v. Bengal, 124 S.W.2d 687, syl. 9 (Mo.App.1939); Hendricks v. St. Louis Transit Co., 124 Mo.App. 157, 101 S.W. 675, 676, syl. 1 (1907) (deposition); Pumphrey v. State, 84 Neb. 636, 122 N.W. 19, 21, syl. 6 (1909) (in court's discretion to require specific questions); Call v. Linn, 112 Ore. 1, 228 Pac. 127, 130, syl. 3 (1924) (question should have been limited to time and place, but since answer so limited no harm); 3 Wigmore, Evidence, § 767 (1940); 3 Jones, Commentaries on Evidence, § 2312 (2d ed., 1926). See also Ward v. City of Pittsburgh, 353 Pa. 156, 44 A.2d 553, syl. 1 (1945), where it was held not improper for judge to permit witness, whose power of speech had been affected by a stroke, to give his testimony by a written statement, where he was present and could have been cross-examined.

1. D. S. Gardner, The Perception and Memory of Witnesses, 18 Corn.L.Q. 391, 405 (1933), citing statements of psychologists and judges.

2. A question which may be answered yes or no is not on that account leading unless it suggests the answer wanted. Harward v. Harward, 173 Md. 339, 196 Atl. 318, syl. 6 (1938); State v. Scott, 20 Wash. 2d 696, 149 P.2d 152, syl. 2 (1944). And it has been

sue is, would an ordinary man get the impression that the questioner desired one answer rather than another? The course of the previous questioning may combine with this question to indicate the desire, but the most important circumstance is the extent of the particularity of the question itself. If the question describes an incident in detail and asks if this happened, the natural inference is that the questioner expects an affirmative answer. Or if one alternative branch of the question is concrete and detailed and the other vague ("Was the sound like the scream of a woman in fear or was it otherwise?") the impression is that the first alternative is suggested. On the other hand, if the question is sufficiently neutral ("At what time did this occur?") or sufficiently balanced ("Was the water hot or cold?") it is not leading. Obviously, a question may suggest a subject or topic, as distinguished from an answer, without offending.[3]

As we have seen, the normal practice is for the careful lawyer to interview in advance all witnesses whom he expects to call for direct examination to prove his own case. This practice is entirely proper, but it does create a probability that the lawyer and the witness will have reached an *entente* which

will make the witness especially susceptible to suggestions from the lawyer as to what the facts were. On the other hand, normally when counsel cross-examines a witness called by the adversary, he has had no opportunity to talk to the witness before, and there is no likelihood that any friendly understanding between them about the facts has been reached. Hence the practice: the judge will ordinarily, if objection is made, forbid leading questions on direct examination; he will ordinarily permit them on cross-examination. But the entire matter of the allowability of leading questions is discretionary,[4] and the judge's action will nowadays not be reviewed unless it is charged that it amounted to, or contributed to, the denial of a fair trial.[5]

When the normal assumption about the relation between the witness and the examining counsel or his client appears unfounded, the usual practice is reversed. If, on direct, the witness appears hostile to the examiner, the danger of suggestion disappears and the judge will permit leading questions,[6] and conversely, if on cross-examination the witness appears to be biassed in favor of the cross-examining party, the counsel may be prohibited from leading.[7]

said that prefacing a question by "whether or not" seldom removes its leading character. State v. Murphy, 216 S.C. 44, 56 S.E.2d 736, syl. 4 (1949). For illustrative cases see 3 Wigmore, Evidence, §§ 769–772; 5 Jones, Commentaries, §§ 2324–2326; Decennial Digests, Witnesses, ☞240(3–5).

3. People v. Hodge, 141 Mich. 312, 104 N.W. 599 (1905).

4. See, e. g., Stahl v. United States, 144 F.2d 909, syl. 2 (C.C.A. 8, 1944); People v. Merritt, 367 Ill. 521, 12 N.E.2d 7, syl. 2 (1938); Comm. v. Sheppard, 313 Mass. 590, 48 N.E.2d 630, syl. 10 (1943); Am.L.Inst. Model Code of Evidence, R. 105(g) ("The judge . . . in his discretion determines . . . to what extent and in what circumstances a party calling a witness shall be permitted, and a party not calling him shall be forbidden, to put to the witness questions suggesting the desired answers."); Dec. Dig., Witnesses, ☞240(2).

5. Sometimes the formula is that the ruling is discretionary and not reviewable. McKay v. Bullard,

219 N.C. 589, 14 S.E.2d 657, syl. 5 (1941). Sometimes that the abuse must be palpable and prejudicial. Hawthorne v. Pope, 51 Ga.App. 498, 180 S.E. 920 (1935). Or, that the trial judge's control is practically absolute and will be reversed only for gross abuse of power resulting in miscarriage of justice. Usher v. Eckhardt, 176 Minn. 210, 222 N.W. 924 (1929). See Dec.Dig., Appeal and Error, ☞971 (5); Witnesses, ☞240(2).

6. People v. Gallery, 336 Ill. 580, 168 N.E. 650, syl. 4, 5 (1929) (questions by prosecutor to unwilling state's witness; permissible to refresh memory, not to impeach); Bresch v. Wolf, 243 Mich. 638, 220 N.W. 737, syl. 2, 3 (1928); McNeill v. Fidelity & Cas. Co. of New York, 336 Mo. 1142, 82 S.W.2d 582, syl. 5 (1935) (plaintiff's examination of witness employed in agency of defendant insurance company); Dec. Dig., Witnesses, ☞244; Note, 117 A.L.R. 328.

7. Rush v. French, 1 Ariz. 99, 25 Pac. 816, 828 (1874) (court in discretion may forbid cross-examiner to lead if witness biassed in his favor); Moody v. Row-

As to matters merely preliminary, such as the name and occupation of the witness, or matters not substantially in dispute, the danger of *false* suggestion is absent, and leading is customary and timesaving.[8] Other relaxations are grounded in necessity. Thus, the judge, when need appears, will ordinarily permit leading questions to children, or to witnesses so ignorant, timid, weak-minded, or deficient in the English language, that they cannot otherwise be brought to understand what information is sought.[9] It is recognized, especially as to children,[10] that in these cases the danger of false suggestion is at its highest, but it is better to face that danger than to abandon altogether the effort to get what the witness knows. Similarly, when a witness has been fully directed to the subject by non-leading questions without securing from him a complete account of what he is believed to know, his memory is said to be "exhausted" and the judge may permit the examiner to ask questions which by their particularity may revive his memory but which of necessity may thereby suggest the answer desired.[11] Necessity, again, and necessity alone justifies the court, where coun-

sel has planted a suggestion by an improper leading question and then withdraws the question, in permitting him to pursue the inquiry thereafter by proper questions.[12]

There appears to be a long-standing practice in some jurisdictions to permit leading questions to a witness by whom it is sought to prove, for impeachment purposes, that another witness has made a previous statement inconsistent with his testimony at the present trial.[13] Necessity again is urged to justify this. It is said that it might otherwise be impossible to call his attention to the subject of his testimony.[14] Of course, the judge's discretion if not abused should control the matter, but it may well be doubted whether the usual safeguards are not specially needed here.[15] Impeaching evidence relates only to a secondary, and not the main, issue, and testimony as to conversations heard long ago has little reliability at best, and this is not enhanced when suggestion is permitted.

7. The Form of Questions: (c) Misleading and Argumentative Questions.

The examiner may not ask a question which calls for no new fact but merely invokes the

---

ell, 17 Pick. (Mass.) 490, 498 (1835); 3 Wigmore, Evidence, § 773; 5 Jones, Commentaries § 2336.

8. Southern Ry. Co. v. Hall, 209 Ala. 237, 96 So. 73, syl. 4 (1923) (introductory questions identifying time and place of incident in suit). So also as to preliminary matters triable to the court in the absence of the jury. State v. Castelli, 92 Conn. 58, 101 Atl. 476, 479, syl. 6 (1917) (question whether threats were made or inducements given to secure confession); Dec.Dig., Witnesses, ☞241.

9. State v. Tenney, 137 Wash. 47, 241 Pac. 669, syl. 2 (1925) (child 12 years old, prosecuting witness in rape); Campion v. Lattimore, 70 Neb. 245, 97 N.W. 290, syl. 2 (1903) (ignorant, dull person); Nelson v. Jadrijevics, 68 F.2d 631, syl. 2 (C.C.A.Canal Zone, 1934) (foreigner who did not understand English); Dec.Dig., Witnesses, ☞243.

10. See Coon v. People, 99 Ill. 368, 370 (1879).

11. Gray v. Kelley, 190 Mass. 184, 76 N.E. 724, syl. 1 (1906); O'Hagan v. Dillon, 76 N.Y. 170, 173 (1879); Born v. Rosenow, 84 Wis. 620, 54 N.W. 1089, syl. 4 (1893); 3 Wigmore, Evidence, § 777; Dec.Dig., Witnesses, ☞242. And where a hostile witness sur-

prises the examiner by testimony contrary to his earlier statement before trial, the examiner may ask leading questions about the former statement, not to discredit but to refresh his recollection. People v. Gallery, 336 Ill. 580, 168 N.E. 650, syl. 4 (1929); Malone v. State, 192 Wis. 379, 212 N.W. 879, syl. 5 (1927).

12. Allen v. Hartford Life Ins. Co., 72 Conn. 693, 45 Atl. 955, 956 (1900) (. . . "This result is an incident of that imperfection attaching to all that man does, and from which even judicial procedure cannot be kept free. The only remedy is a preventive one, and lies in the power of trial courts to regulate the conduct of counsel at the bar.").

13. Swanson v. McDonald, 58 S.D. 119, 235 N.W. 118, syl. 1 (1935) (citing authorities); Dec.Dig., Witnesses, ☞391.

14. 3 Wigmore, Evidence, § 779.

15. See Swoboda v. Union P. R. Co., 87 Neb. 200, 127 N.W. 215, 220, 221 (1910), and Norton v. Parsons, 67 Vt. 526, 32 Atl. 481, 482 (1895), which recognize, but deprecate, the practice.

witness's assent to the questioner's inferences from or interpretations of the facts proved or assumed. Such a question is subject to objection as "argumentative"[1] but the trial court has a wide range of discretion in enforcing the rule, particularly on cross-examination, the more frequent occasion for such questions. A still more common vice is for the examiner so to couch the question that it assumes as true matters to which the witness has not testified, and which are in dispute between the parties.[2] The danger here is two-fold. If the examiner is putting the question to a friendly witness, the recitation of the assumed fact may suggest the desired answer, and secondly, whether the witness is friendly or hostile, the answer is likely to be misleading. Oftentimes, the question will be so far separate from the assumption that if the witness answers the question without mentioning the assumption, you cannot tell whether he ignored the assumption or affirmed it.

8. The Judge May Examine[1] and Call[2] Witnesses.

Under the Anglo-American trial system, the parties and their counsel have the primary responsibility for finding, selecting and presenting the evidence. This is often characterized as the contentious or adversary system, in contrast with the inquisitorial system which prevails in some European countries, under which the judge has a wider responsibility for investigating the facts and presenting the proofs.[3] Nevertheless, our system of party-presentation is not exclusive or all-sufficient. It is but a means to the end of disclosing truth and administering justice, and for reaching this end the judge has the over-all responsibility. When the party-presentation is incomplete and fails to elicit some material fact the judge not only may, but seemingly owes a duty[4] to supply the omission by further examination.

Accordingly the judge in his discretion may examine any witness to bring out need-

1. Questions held argumentative: Pettus v. Louisville & N. R. Co., 214 Ala. 187, 106 So. 807, syl. 11 (1926) ("If you had not been burning off the grass and weeds . . . on the right of way, it was still there?"); Johnson v. Wilmington City Ry. Co., 23 Del. 5, 76 Atl. 961, syl. 4 (1905) ("Was there any other force of any kind, other than the suction created by the rapidly moving car, that would cause the rope to become entangled in the gearing?"); White v. State, 22 Okl.Cr. 131, 210 Pac. 313, syl. 5 (1922) (in mayhem prosecution, question, "Isn't it a fact that [defendant's] mouth is so small that he could not reach up and get it wide enough open to get [complainant's] ear in there?", argumentative where both mouth and ear were visible to jury); 70 C.J., Witnesses, 508, § 676.

2. See, e. g., for questions held objectionable: Haithcock v. State, 23 Ala.App. 460, 126 So. 890, syl. 5 (1930) (questions on cross-examination of defendant's witness, as to how long defendant was making liquor); Price v. Rosenberg, 200 Mass. 36, 85 N.E. 887, syl. 9 (1908) (in action for price of goods, question to plaintiff as to how he knew that goods delivered were goods called for in contract, improper as assuming that the goods delivered were those called for); Reardon v. Boston Elev. Ry. Co., 311 Mass. 228, 40 N.E.2d 865, syl. 5 (1942) (question as to how many years water used to come through walls, bad as assuming that it had come through at

all in the past); Central Radiator Co. v. Niagara Fire Ins. Co., 109 N.J.L. 48, 160 Atl. 342, syl. 4 (1932) (questions as to what the custom is, without any previous testimony that any custom about the matter exists); Kirschman v. Pitt Pub. Co., 318 Pa. 570, 178 Atl. 828, 100 A.L.R. 1062 (1935), annotated on this point (affirmative answer to question assuming disputed fact is no evidence of the fact assumed); Dec.Dig., Witnesses, ☞237; 70 C.J., Witnesses, 547, §§ 706, 707; 3 Wigmore, Evidence, §§ 771, 780. But the questioner may properly assume the truth of a disputed fact previously testified to by the same witness. State v. Marshall, 105 Iowa 38, 74 N.W. 763, syl. 7 (1898); Graham v. McReynolds, 90 Tenn. 673, 18 S.W. 272, syl. 9 (1891) (question by court).

1. Wigmore, Evidence, III, § 784, IX, § 2484; 70 C.J., Witnesses, §§ 718–722; Note, Judge's Questions in Criminal Cases, 84 A.L.R. 1172; Dec.Dig., Witnesses, ☞246.

2. 9 Wigmore, Evidence, § 2484, note 1; 70 C.J., Witnesses, § 723; Dec.Dig., Witnesses, ☞246(2).

3. See 9 Wigmore, Evidence, § 2483.

4. "He enjoys the prerogative, rising often to the standard of a duty, of eliciting those facts he deems necessary to the clear presentation of the issues. Pariser v. City of New York, 2 Cir., 146 F.2d 431." C. E. Clark, J., in United States v. Brandt, 196 F.2d 653, 655 (C.A.2, 1952). But see n. 13, infra.

ed facts which have not been elicited by the parties.[5] In those states—the great majority —which have shorn the judge of his common law power to comment on the weight of the evidence, the judge's questioning must be cautiously guarded so as not to constitute an implied comment.[6] The policy against leading questions by counsel, namely, that of avoiding false testimony elicited by partisan suggestion,[7] has no application in general to judges,[8] whose office is to be impartial, to hold the balance even. But the leading question in suggesting the desired answer may often strongly imply that the judge believes that the answer desired is the truth, and thus may offend the rule against comment.[9] Similarly, questions which are aimed at discrediting or impeaching the witness, though allowable for counsel, when asked by the judge may often—not always—intimate the

judge's belief that the witness has been lying, and thus be an implied comment on the weight of his testimony.[10]

In the federal courts and in the few states where the common law power to comment is retained, these restrictions on leading questions and impeaching questions have no place. Nevertheless, even in those enviable jurisdictions, the judge, though he has a wide power to examine witnesses, must avoid such extreme exercises of the power to question, just as he must avoid extreme exercises of the power to comment. He must not assume the role of an advocate or of a prosecutor.[11] If his questions are too partisan or even if they are too extensive, he faces the risk that the appellate court will find that he has crossed the line between judging and advocacy.[12]

---

5. Griffin v. United States, 164 F.2d 903, syl. 2, 3 (C.A.D.C.1947); Simon v. United States, 123 F.2d 80, 83, syl. 5–8 (C.C.A. 4); State v. Keehn, 85 Kan. 765, 118 Pac. 851, syl. 4 (1911); McLaughlin v. Municipal Court, 308 Mass. 397, 32 N.E.2d 266, 271, syl. 11 (1941).

Jurors, with the judge's leave, may question the witnesses. White v. Little, 131 Okl. 132, 268 Pac. 221 (1928); Stamp v. Commonwealth, 200 Ky. 133, 253 S.W. 242 (1923); 70 C.J. 567, § 724; Note, 159 A.L.R. 347. See O'Nellion v. Haynes, 122 Cal.App. 329, 9 P.2d 853 (1932), where a juror asked the defendant "You carry liability insurance, don't you?" and was answered, "Yes," before objection could be made. The privilege of permitting jurors to ask questions of witnesses should be granted only when in sound discretion of court it appears that it will aid a juror in understanding a material issue involved, and ordinarily when some juror has indicated that he wishes such a point clarified. State v. Anderson, 108 Utah 130, 158 P.2d 127, 159 A.L.R. 340 (1945).

6. People v. De Lordo, 350 Ill. 148, 182 N.E. 726, 730, 731 (1932); Dennis v. McArthur, 23 Wash.2d 33, 158 P.2d 644, syl. 4 (1945); Note, 84 A.L.R. 1181–1192.

7. See § 6, above.

8. Comm. v. Galavan, 9 Allen (Mass.) 271 (1864); Connor v. Township of Brant, 31 Ont.L.Rep. 274 (1913). Instances wherein particular leading questions by the judge were held necessary and within his discretion: Stinson v. State, 125 Ark. 339, 189 S.W. 49, syl. 4 (1916) (carnal abuse, questions to

victim); Driscoll v. People, 47 Mich. 413, 11 N.W. 221, 223 (1882).

9. See, e. g., People v. Bowers, 79 Cal. 415, 21 Pac. 752 (1889); Anderson v. State, 83 Tex.Cr.R. 261, 202 S.W. 944, syl. 4 (1918); State v. Crotts, 22 Wash. 245, 60 Pac. 403, syl. 2–4 (1900).

10. State v. Allen, 100 Iowa 7, 69 N.W. 274, syl. 2 (1896) (error to ask defendant's witness if he had conversed with defendant's counsel before trial); State v. Drew, 213 S.W. 106, syl. 2 (Mo.1919) (questions indicating a purpose to discredit defendant and one of his witnesses). But it seems that not all questions bearing on credibility would show an adverse opinion, even though the answer might happen to be discrediting. Thus, neutral questions about knowledge or interest seemingly might be needed and desirable. See Cusmano v. United States, 13 F.2d 451, syl. 6 (C.C.A. 6, 1926) (questions disclosing witness's absence of knowledge, proper). Accordingly, the view of the court in State v. Perry, 231 N.C. 467, 57 S.E.2d 774, syl. 2 (1950) that "it is improper for a trial judge to ask questions for the purpose of impeaching" may need qualification.

11. United States v. Lee, 107 F.2d 522, 529, syl. 10 (C.C.A. 7, 1939); State v. Winchester, 166 Kan. 512, 203 P.2d 229, 233, syl. 5 (1949).

12. See United States v. Brandt, 196 F.2d 653, syl. 1–4 (C.A.2d 1952) (conviction set aside where judge asked more than 900 questions during eight-day trial and cross-examined accused and defense witnesses with apparent purpose of emphasizing incon-

Not only may the judge examine witnesses called by the parties, he may also, for the same purpose of bringing out material facts that might not otherwise be elicited, call witnesses himself whom the parties might not have chosen to call.[13] It is of course a matter of discretion, and is perhaps most often exercised when the prosecution expects that a necessary witness will be hostile and desires to escape the necessity of calling him and being cumbered by the rule against impeaching one's own witness. He may then invoke the court's discretion to call the witness,[14] in which event either party may cross-examine and impeach him. Another use of the power, implemented by statute in some jurisdictions, is to mediate the battle of partisan expert witnesses employed by the parties, through the court's resumption of its ancient power to call an expert of his own choosing, or one agreed upon by the parties, to give impartial testimony to aid the court or jury in resolving the scientific issue.[15] But the judge's power of calling witnesses in aid of justice is general and not limited to meeting these particular needs.

9. Refreshing Recollection.[1]

It is abundantly clear from every-day observation that the latent memory of an experience may be revived by an image seen, or a statement read or heard. It is a part of the group of phenomena which the classical psychologists have called the law of association. The recall of any part of a past experience tends to bring with it the other parts that were in the same field of awareness, and a new experience tends to stimulate the recall of other like experiences.[2] The effect of a reminder, encountered in reading a newspaper or in the conversation of a friend, which gives us the sensation of recognizing as familiar some happening which we had forgotten, and prompts our memory to bring

---

sistencies in defence and discrediting defence witnesses; instructive opinion by C. E. Clark, J.).

13.   Coulson v. Disborough, [1894] 2 Q.B. 316 (Ct.App.) (but in recent English decisions the right has unfortunately and inexplicably been limited to criminal cases: In re Enoch, [1910] 1 K.B. 327, 332 approved in Rex v. Harris, [1927] 2 K.B. 587); Marin Water & Power Co. v. R. R. Comm., 171 Cal. 706, 154 Pac. 864, 867, syl. 5 (1916) (commission as a judicial tribunal may call witnesses); Merchants Bank v. Goodfellow, 44 Utah 349, 140 Pac. 759, syl. 3 (1914) (suit on bill of exchange, court called last endorser).

There has been some support for the suggestion that in some cases, in the interest of justice the judge may have the duty as well as the power to call witnesses and hence may be reversed for a failure to do so. See Moore v. Sykes' Estate, 167 Miss. 212, 149 So. 789, syl. 7 (1933); Frankfurter, J., dissenting, in Johnson v. United States, 333 U.S. 46, 54, 68 Sup.Ct. 391, 395, 92 L.Ed. 468 (1948); Note, Judge's Duty to Call Witnesses, 58 Yale L.J. 183. But efforts at reversal on this ground have usually been unavailing, e. g., Steinberg v. United States, 162 F.2d 120, syl. 7 (C.C.A. 5, 1947); United States v. Pape, 144 F.2d 778, syl. 12 (C.C.A.2d 1944); Halloran-Judge Trust Co. v. Carr, 62 Utah 10, 218 Pac. 138, syl. 3 (1923). And Wigmore denies the existence of a duty. 9 Wigmore, Evidence, § 2484, p. 267.

14.   See, e. g., Young v. United States, 107 F.2d 490, syl. 15, 16 (C.C.A. 5, 1939) (sole surviving eye-witness of homicide who had made inconsistent statements to prosecution); People v. Shelton, 388 Ill. 56, 57 N.E.2d 473, syl. 4, 5 (1944) (rape of girl under age, court called joint indictee for whose integrity prosecution could not vouch).

15.   See, e. g., Citizens State Bank v. Castro, 105 Cal. App. 284, 287 Pac. 559, syl. 3 (1930) (handwriting expert, under Code Civ.Proc. § 1871); Christina v. Cusimano, 125 La. 1056, 52 So. 157, 158 (1910) (same, under Code Pract. art. 442; power recognized but here improperly exercised); State v. Horne, 171 N.C. 787, 88 S.E. 433, syl. 1 (1916) (alienist in murder case: "expert witnesses . . . were originally regarded as amici curiae and were called generally by the court," citing 3 Chamberlayne, Evidence, §§ 2376, 2552).

For further discussion see § 17, herein.

1.   General references: Wigmore, Evidence, §§ 758–765; 5 Jones, Commentaries, §§ 2378–2394 (2d ed. rev., 1926); 70 C.J., Witnesses, §§ 742–771; Dec. Dig., Witnesses, ☜253–260; Note, Refreshment of Recollection by Use of Memoranda and Other Writings, 125 A.L.R. 19; Notes, 18 Ore.L.Rev. 136 (1939); 15 Wash.L.Rev. 257 (1940).

2.   These are the principles of contiguity and similarity. See Gardner, The Perception and Memory of Witnesses, 18 Corn.L.Q. 390, 392 (1933); 2 Encyc. Brit., title, Association (14th ed., 1929).

back associated experiences, is a familiar process.

As we have seen,[3] the interviewing of witnesses by counsel who will examine them in court is a necessary step in preparing for trial. It is at this stage that the memory of the witness can best be refreshed about the facts of the case, by giving him the opportunity to read his own written statements previously made, or the letters, maps, or other documents in the case. It is only when this review of the data is insufficient to enable the witness to recall the facts while testifying that refreshing his memory on the stand is advisable. If it is matter which a jury would suppose he should remember unaided, the use of a crutch lessens their confidence in the testimony.

Nevertheless, the practice has long been established that in interrogating a witness counsel may hand him a memorandum to inspect for the purpose of "refreshing his recollection," and that when he speaks from a memory thus revived, his testimony is what he says, not the writing[4] This is the process of *refreshing recollection,* in the strict and accurate sense. But when this simple but helpful expedient had become established, it was natural for counsel to seek to carry it a step further. If the witness, being shown the writing, states that his memory is revived thereby, he may testify, as we have seen, from his refreshed recollection. But it may happen that the witness cannot go so far. He may say that, on looking at the writing, he recognizes it as a memorandum made by him when the facts were fresh in his mind, and *therefore,* though he has no present memory of the transaction described, he is willing to testify that the facts were as recited in the memorandum. Under the guidance of Wigmore, we now recognize this as quite a different process. In the one instance, the witness stakes his oath on his present memory; in the other, upon his written recital of things remembered in the past.[5]

The procedure of tendering a memorandum to the witness is alike in both cases, and it was convenient to justify the new extension by the old and approved phrase, "refreshing recollection." But the underlying justification in the new situation is quite different. It rests on the reliability of a writing which the witness swears is a *record of his past recollection.* Appropriate safeguarding rules have been developed for this latter kind of memoranda, requiring that they must have been written by the witness or examined and found correct by him, and that they must have been prepared so promptly after the events recorded that these must have been fresh in the mind of the witness when the record was made or examined and verified by him. We have treated such memoranda separately, as an exception to the hearsay rule.[6]

Apparently the earlier English cases of genuine refreshment of recollection imposed no restriction upon the use of memoranda to refresh.[7] These were not required to have been written by the witness or under his direction, nor to have been made near in time to the event. In the later-developed practice of using records of past recollection these restrictions, with good reason, were imposed. Since, however, the old name of "refreshing recollection" was given to both practices, it was natural that the restrictions developed for one kind of memoranda should be applied to the other. Which is the wiser practice, the rule of the older cases, championed by Wigmore and by a good many present-day courts, to the effect that any memorandum, without restriction of authorship, time, or correctness, may be used when the purpose is to revive mem-

3. See § 2, herein.

4. Henry v. Lee, 2 Chitty 124 (1810), cited 3 Wigmore, Evidence, § 758.

5. See Jewett v. United States, 15 F.2d 955, 956 (C.C. A. 9th, 1926).

6. See Ch. 31, infra.

7. Henry v. Lee, supra n. 4; Rex v. St. Martin's, 2 Ad. & El. 210, 111 Eng.Rep. 81 (K.B.1834).

ory, or the rule requiring that the memorandum to refresh must meet the same tests as the record of past recollection? Even if the latter requirement is a historical or analytical blunder, it will be none the worse for that, if it is a safeguard needed in the search for truth.

It is true that any kind of stimulus, "a song, or a face, or a newspaper item," [8] may produce the "flash" of recognition, the feeling that "it all comes back to me now." But the genuineness of the feeling is no guaranty of the correctness of the image recalled. The danger that the mind will "remember" something that never happened is at least as great here as in the case of leading questions. "The problem is complicated by the deceptive certainty of the recognizer. This certainty is a direct function of the similarity of the material. As a result it has an eccentric relation to objective accuracy. . . . It will be objected that, although the foregoing criteria may be interesting as far as recognition is concerned, a present refreshed recollection is based only in part on recognition. Granting this inaccuracy, is there any proof that recall, stimulated by that recognition, and supposed to 'function independently thereof,' is also inaccurate? A recent experiment answers the objection decisively. In a class lecture the instructor made certain unequivocal statements about the results of a series of experiments. A well-meaning, but none

too thoughtful, reporter on the local student paper printed an entirely erroneous account of the lecture. On the routine examination at the end of the week, after the usual questions, each student was asked to indicate on his paper whether or not he had read the press account. Most of those who had read it 'recognized' it as accurate, and on the examination paper remembered what they had erroneously recognized. Those who had not read the article reported the lecture with their customary accuracy."[9] "Imagination and suggestion are twin artists ever ready to retouch the fading daguerrotype of memory." [10]

The substantial number of decisions which import into the realm of refreshing memory the requirements developed for memoranda of past recollection recorded, namely, the requirement that the witness must have made the writing or have recognized it as correct, and that such making or recognition must have occurred at the time of the event or while it was fresh in memory,[11] have therefore a plausible basis in expediency.

Nevertheless, it is probable that most courts today when faced with the clear distinction between the two uses of the memoranda, will adhere to the "classical" view that any memorandum or other object may be used as a stimulus to present memory, without restriction by rule as to authorship, guaranty of correctness, or time of making.[12]

8. See Jewett v. United States, supra, n. 5.

9. Hutchins and Slesinger, Some Observations on the Law of Evidence—Memory, 41 Harv.L.Rev. 860, 868, 869 (1928). See also the telling passage quoted from Bentham, 3 Wigmore, Evidence, § 758.

10. Gardner, The Perception and Memory of Witnesses, 18 Corn.L.Q. 390, 401 (1933).

11. See, e. g., Putnam v. United States, 162 U.S. 687, 695, 16 Sup.Ct. 923 (1896) (transcript of prior testimony by witness not allowed to be used to refresh, because not contemporaneous with events testified about); State v. Patton, 255 Mo. 245, 164 S.W. 223, syl. 3 (similar to last; "the ease with which, as Prof. Muensterberg tells us, the human mind is influenced by suggestion would seem to form an in-

superable psychological objection to the use of data for this purpose, of the correctness of which the witness is ignorant"); Farmers' Elev. Co. v. Gt. Northern R. Co., 131 Minn. 152, 154 N.W. 954, 956 (1915) (dictum).

These requirements create special difficulties in respect to the use of a transcript of the witness's own prior testimony. Hale, The Use by a Witness of His Own Prior Testimony for the Purpose of Refreshing His Recollection, 15 St. Louis L.Rev. 137, 146 (1930).

12. Henowitz v. Rockville Savings Bank, 118 Conn. 527, 173 Atl. 221, 222 (1934) (photograph of stairway excluded from evidence because not fairly representative. allowed to be used to refresh); People v. Griswold, 405 Ill. 533, 92 N.E.2d 91, syl. 8, 9 (1950);

On balance, it would seem that this liberality of practice is the wiser solution, since there are other safeguards which seem sufficient. The first safeguard is the power of control by the trial judge. It is a preliminary question for his decision whether the memorandum actually does refresh and from the nature of the memorandum and the witness's testimony he may find that it does not.[13] Moreover, as in the case of leading questions, he may decline to permit the use of the aid to memory, where he regards the danger of undue suggestion as outweighing the probable value, in the exercise of his discretion to control the manner of the examination.[14]

The second safeguard is the rule which entitles the adverse party, when the witness seeks to resort to the memorandum, to inspect the memorandum so that he may object to its use if ground appears,[15] and to have the memorandum available for his reference in cross-examining the witness.[16] With the memorandum before him, the cross-examiner has a good opportunity to test the credibility of the witness's claim that his memory has been revived, and to search out any discrepancies between the writing and the testimony. This right to demand inspection has usually been limited to writings used by the witness on the stand,[17] but the reasons seem equally applicable to writings used by the witness to refresh his memory before he testifies. Doubtless the courts have thought that to require inspection of such papers may unduly encourage prying into the opponent's file, but the public interest in the full disclosure of the source of a witness's testimony seems a weightier consideration, and there are decisions taking this view.[18]

Comm. v. McDermott, 255 Mass. 575, 152 N.E. 704, syl. 2 (1926) (any paper though not contemporaneous and not made by witness); State v. Hale, 85 N.H. 403, 160 Atl. 95, syl. 7 (1932); Copeland Co. v. Davis, 125 S.C. 449, 119 S.E. 19, syl. 4 (1923); Sagers v. International Smelting Co., 50 Utah 423, 168 Pac. 105, syl. 1–3 (1917); and see State v. Bradley, 361 Mo. 267, 234 S.W.2d 556, 560, syl. 9–11 (1950); Wigmore, Evidence, § 761; 70 C.J., Witnesses, § 763, p. 592, notes 43–46. Compare People v. Betts, 272 App.D. 737, 74 N.Y.S.2d 791, syl. 1–4 (1947), noted 23 N.Y.U.L.Q. 529, 34 Va.L.Rev. 607. There the court held that a policeman who had destroyed the notes taken by him during a conversation with accused, and also his transcript from those notes, to avoid their use on cross-examination, was improperly allowed to refresh his memory from another version of his transcript embodied in the complaint.

13. The statement of the witness is not conclusive, when the circumstances show that his memory is not revived. Weigel v. Powers Elevator Co., 49 N.D. 867, 194 N.W. 113, 120 (1923). Compare an important recent case where the judge's finding was upheld that the memory of witnesses who testified while consulting a lengthy list of articles was actually refreshed. United States v. Riccardi, 174 F.2d 883, syl. 8, 9 (C.A. 3, 1949) (instructive opinion by Kalodner, J.).

14. The element of discretion is recognized in United States v. Lonardo, 67 F.2d 883, syl. 3 (C.C.A.N.Y. 1933); Farmers Elev. Co. v. Great Northern R. Co., 131 Minn. 152, 154 N.W. 954, syl. 2 (1915); State v. Bradley, 361 Mo. 267, 234 S.W.2d 556, syl. 10 (1950);

Myers v. Weger, 62 N.J.L. 432, 42 Atl. 280, 283 (1899); Dec.Digests, Witnesses, ☞255; 70 C.J., Witnesses, § 742, notes 53, 54, § 746, note 96; 5 Jones Evidence, (2d ed., 1926), § 2378; Model Code, R. 105(i).

15. Morris v. United States, 149 Fed. 123, syl. 2 (C.C.A.Tex., 1907). See also State v. Gadwood, 342 Mo. 466, 116 S.W.2d 42, 51, syl. 6 (1938) (in trial judge's discretion whether inspection postponed to time of cross-examination).

16. Little v. United States, 93 F.2d 401, syl. 1–5 (C.C.A.Mo., 1937); Green v. State, 53 Tex.Crim. 490, 110 S.W. 920, syl. 1, 22 L.R.A.,N.S., 706 (1908); Dec.Dig., Witnesses, ☞256; Note, 125 A.L.R. 194–199; 3 Wigmore, Evidence (3d ed., 1940) § 762. Compare United States v. Socony Vacuum Oil Co., 310 U.S. 150, 233, 60 Sup.Ct. 811, 848 (1940), where it was held (reversing the Circuit Court of Appeals) that where a transcript of prior testimony was not shown to the witness, but the judge read from it to refresh the witness, the opposing counsel was not entitled of right to inspect it, but under these conditions the matter was in the judge's discretion.

17. Lennon v. United States, 20 F.2d 490, syl. 3 (C.C.A.Minn., 1927); Star Mfg. Co. v. Atlantic Coast Line R. Co., 222 N.C. 330, 23 S.E.2d 32, syl. 7 (1942); State v. Paschall, 182 Wash. 304, 47 P.2d 15, syl. 4, 5 (1935) (transcript of prior testimony, in hands of state's counsel, in court) and cases collected in Note, 125 A.L.R. 200; 70 C.J., Witnesses, § 769, p. 598, note 36.

18. The Alpha, 44 F.Supp. 809, 815, syl. 13 (E.D.Pa. 1942); State v. Deslovers, 40 R.I. 89, 100 Atl. 64, 69,

Not only may the adversary inspect the memoranda, but he may submit them to the jury for their examination,[19] but the party offering the witness may not do so,[20] and the cardinal rule is that they are not evidence, but only aids in the giving of evidence. Consequently, a copy may be used without accounting for the original.[21]

The line between using the writing as an aid to memory and basing one's testimony upon it as a correct record of past memory is sometimes shadowy. Must it be shown that the witness has no present recollection of the matters embodied in the memorandum before he can use it as an aid to memory? It is usually said that this must appear,[22] but it is believed that this requirement is unsound. The witness may believe that he remembers completely but on looking at the memorandum he would be caused to recall additional facts. As the Chinese proverb has it, "The palest ink is clearer than the best memory." On the other hand, there is here the ever-present danger that a suggestible witness may think that he remembers a fact because he reads it. It seems eminently a matter for discretion, rather than rule. Similarly, it would seem that a witness may recognize from present memory the correctness of successive facts set out in a memorandum, but that he may be unable, despite this recognition, to detail those facts from memory without continuing to consult the writing. Accordingly, the statement that a witness once refreshed[23] must speak independently of the writing [23] seems too inflexible, and it is believed that the matter is discretionary and that the trial judge may properly permit the witness to consult the memorandum as he speaks, especially where it is so lengthy and detailed that even a fresh memory would be unable to recite all the items unaided.[24]

---

syl. 6 (1917), both relying on Wigmore, Evidence, § 762. See also Goldman v. United States, 316 U.S. 129, 132, syl. 1, 62 Sup.Ct. 993 (1942), where a refusal of the judge to order the witness' memoranda, which were part of the government's files, to be submitted to the defendant for inspection, was sustained as being within his discretion, which was not abused. If the memorandum is not in court or immediately available, the court should have a discretion whether to require its production. Comm. v. Lannan, 13 Allen (Mass.) 563, 569 (1866).

19. Smith v. Jackson, 113 Mich. 511, 71 N.W. 843 (1897); Note, 125 A.L.R. 78. When so submitted by the adversary it would seem that he may place it in evidence, to let the jury compare it with the testimony. Riley v. Fletcher, 185 Ala. 570, 64 So. 85, 87 (1913). But see, contra, Comm. v. Ponzi, 256 Mass. 159, 152 N.E. 307, syl. 2 (1926), and compare Capodilupo v. F. W. Stock & Sons, 237 Mass. 550, 130 N.E. 65 (1921).

20. Luse v. United States, 49 F.2d 241, syl. 2, 3 (C.C. A.Calif., 1931); Shear v. Rogoff, 288 Mass. 357, 193 N.E. 63, syl. 4 (1934); Miller v. Borough of Exeter, 366 Pa. 336, 77 A.2d 395, syl. 11 (1951); Dec.Dig., Witnesses, ☞257; Note, 125 A.L.R. 65.

21. Atlanta, etc., R. Co., v. Ewing, 112 Fla. 483, 150 So. 586, syl. 3; Comm. v. Levine, 280 Mass. 83, 181 N.E. 851, syl. 7, 8 (1932); Dec.Dig., Witnesses, ☞255(5); Note, 125 A.L.R. 50. See also Notes, 17 Ore.L.Rev. 78 (1937); 13 Wash.L.Rev. 61 (1938). Compare Jewett v. United States, 15 F.2d 955 (1927), where the court considered that the witness who testified from copied memoranda was not actually refreshed, and that it was error, therefore, to allow use of a copy.

22. People v. Kraus, 377 Ill. 539, 37 N.E.2d 182, syl. 3 (1941); Battle Creek Food Co. v. Kirkland, 298 Mich. 515, 299 N.W. 167, syl. 5 (dictum); Dec.Dig., Witnesses, ☞254; 70 C.J., Witnesses, § 748; Note, 125 A.L.R. 27. These references, however, mix in cases of past recollection recorded without discrimination.

23. Roll v. Dockery, 219 Ala. 374, 122 So. 630, 65 A.L. R. 1473, 1476 (1929) (dictum); 70 C.J., Witnesses, § 767, p. 595, note 3.

24. See Ward v. Morr Transfer & Storage Co., 119 Mo.App. 83, 95 S.W. 964, syl. 7 (itemized list of goods lost); World Fire & Marine Ins. Co. v. Edmondson, 244 Ala. 224, 12 So.2d 754, syl. 6 (similar); People v. Allen, 47 Calif.App.2d 735, 118 P.2d 927, syl. 3 (1941) (aged witness' prior testimony read to her and she assented to its correctness).
But the witness must swear that he is genuinely refreshed. Wolf v. Mallinckrodt Chem. Wks., 336 Mo. 746, 81 S.W.2d 323, syl. 10 (1935). Freeland v. Peltier, 44 S.W.2d 404, syl. 3–5 (Tex.Civ.App.1931). And cannot be allowed to read the writing in the guise of refreshment, as a cloak for getting in evidence an inadmissible document. Freeland v. Peltier, supra; S. W. Bridges & Co. v. Caudland, 88 Utah 373, 54 P.2d 842, 846, 847 (1936) (clear statement by Wolfe, J.). When the writing satisfies the requirements of past recollection recorded of course the witness may read from it. Guiffre v. Carapezza, 298 Mass. 458, 11 N.E.2d 433, 125 A.L.R. 1 (1937).

CHAPTER 3

THE REQUIREMENT OF FIRST-HAND KNOWLEDGE: THE OPINION RULE: EXPERT TESTIMONY

10. The Requirement of Knowledge from Observation.[1]

The common law system of proof is exacting in its insistence upon the most reliable sources of information. This policy is apparent in the Opinion rule, the Hearsay rule and the Documentary Originals rule. One of the earliest and most pervasive manifestations of this attitude is the rule requiring that a witness who testifies to a fact which can be perceived by the senses must have had an opportunity to observe, and must have actually observed the fact.[2] The same requirement, in general, is imposed upon declarations coming in under exceptions to the hearsay rule, that is, the declarant must so far as appears have had an opportunity to observe the fact declared.[3]

The burden of laying a foundation by showing that the witness had an adequate opportunity to observe is upon the party offering the testimony.[4] By failing to object the adversary waives the preliminary proof, but not the substance of the requirement, so that if it later appears that the witness lacked opportunity, or did not actually observe the

---

1. 2 Wigmore, Evidence, §§ 650–670; 58 Am.Jur., Witnesses, §§ 113, 114; Dec.Dig., Witnesses, ⟐37.

2. Barnett v. Aetna Life Ins. Co., 139 F.2d 483, syl. 3 (C.C.A.N.J.1943); Fredricksen v. Fullmer, 258 P.2d 1155, syl. 3 (Idaho 1953) (requirement applied to witness who testifies to signature of written instrument).

See Uniform Rules of Evidence, Rule 19: *"Prerequisites of Knowledge and Experience.* As a prerequisite for the testimony of a witness on a relevant or material matter, there must be evidence that he has personal knowledge thereof, or experience, training or education if such be required. Such evidence may be by the testimony of the witness himself. The judge may reject the testimony of a witness that he perceived a matter if he finds that no trier of fact could reasonably believe that the witness did perceive the matter. The judge may receive conditionally the testimony of the witness as to a relevant or material matter, subject to the evidence of knowledge, experience, training or education being later supplied in the course of the trial."

3. 2 Wigmore, Evidence. § 670, and see the discussion herein of the various exceptions. There are some instances, however, in which the requirement is not applied, e. g., admissions of a party-opponent, see § 240, herein. And where reputation is used as hearsay evidence of a fact (see § 299), while the witness who testifies to the reputation must know the reputation the community-talk itself need not be shown to be based on knowledge, though the reputation is limited to that in the locality where people would presumably know the reputed fact.

4. Cleveland, T. & V. Co. v. Marsh, 63 Oh.St. 236, 58 N.E. 821, syl. 1 (1900) (error to admit evidence, over objection without proof of knowledge); State v. Prescott, 70 R.I. 403, 40 A.2d 721, syl. 1 (1944) (no error to exclude evidence where foundation not laid). But the judge has a discretion to admit the evidence, deferring the proof of knowledge to a later stage. Sofas v. McKee, 100 Conn. 541, 124 Atl. 380, syl. 4 (1924).

fact, his testimony will be stricken.[5]   If under the circumstances proved, reasonable men could differ as to whether the witness did or did not have adequate opportunity to observe, then the testimony of the witness should come in, and the jury will appraise his opportunity to know in evaluating the testimony.[6]

In laying this foundation of knowledge, it is allowable for the examiner to elicit from the witness the particular circumstances which led him to notice or observe or remember the fact.[7]

While the law is exacting in demanding first-hand observation, it is not so impractical as to insist upon preciseness of attention by the witness in observing, nor certainty of recollection in recounting the facts. Accordingly, when a witness uses such expressions as "I think," "My impression is," or "In my opinion," this will be no ground of objection if it appears that he merely speaks from an inattentive observation, or an unsure memory,[8] though it will if the expressions are found to mean that he speaks from conjecture or from hearsay.[9]

One who has no knowledge of a fact except what another has told him cannot, of course, satisfy the present requirement of knowledge from observation. When the witness, however, bases his testimony partly upon first-hand knowledge and partly upon the accounts of others, the problem is one which calls for a practical compromise. Thus when he speaks of his own age,[10] or of his kinship with a relative,[11] the courts will allow the testimony. And in business or scientific matters when the witness testifies to facts that he knows partly at first hand and partly from reports, the judge, it seems, should admit or exclude according to his view of the need for and the reasonable reliability of the evidence.[12]

---

5. City Nat. Bank v. Nelson, 218 Ala. 90, 117 So. 681, 61 A.L.R. 938, 944 (1928); Sofas v. McKee, next preceding note; 2 Wigmore, Evidence, § 654.

6. Jack Cole, Inc. v. Walker, 240 Ala. 682, 200 So. 768, syl. 5, 6 (1941) (opportunity in brief time to judge speed of truck); Senecal v. Drollette, 304 N.Y. 446, 108 N.E.2d 602 (1952) (error to exclude testimony of 12-year-old boys as to speed and make of automobile, based on brief glance); Humphries v. Louisiana Ry. & Irr. Co., 291 S.W. 1094, syl. 1 (Tex.Comm.App.1927) (speed of train); Uniform Rule 19, note 2, above. But compare Davidson v. Beacon Hill Taxi Service, 278 Mass. 540, 180 N.E. 503, syl. 2 (1932), which seems to treat a similar question of opportunity to estimate speed as a preliminary question for the judge.

7. Cole v. Lake Shore & M. S. Ry. Co., 105 Mich. 549, 63 N.W. 647, syl. 2 (1895) (witness could say that he remembered that the wind was so high because "we spoke about it"); Brown v. Chicago B. & Q. R. Co., 88 Neb. 604, 130 N.W. 265, syl. 5 (1911) (witness may state that his attention was called to approaching vehicle by remark of his little boy). Similarly the expert witness may explain the grounds of his opinion. Leslie v. Granite Ry. Co., 172 Mass. 468, 52 N.E. 542, syl. 5, 6 (1899); State v. Young, 210 N.C. 452, 187 S.E. 561 (1936) (handwriting expert).

8. Auerbach v. United States, 136 F.2d 882, syl. 3, 4 (C.C.A. 6, 1943) (witness testified to identity of man he saw, "to the best of my belief" but acknowledg-ing he might be mistaken, allowed); People v. Palmer, 351 Ill. 319, 184 N.E. 205, syl. 4 (1932) ("I believe"); E. F. Enoch Co. v. Johnson, 183 Md. 327, 37 A.2d 901, syl. 3 (1944) ("It looked like that truck . . . swung in"); Tews v. Bamrick, 148 Neb. 59, 26 N.W.2d 499, syl. 6 (1947) ("I guess," as to speed of car); 2 Wigmore, Evidence, § 658.

9. Lovejoy v. Howe, 55 Minn. 353, 57 N.W. 57, syl. 4 (1893) ("impression"); State v. Thorp, 72 N.C. 186 (1875) ("my best impression").

10. Antelope v. United States, 185 F.2d 174, syl. 1 (C.C.A. 10, 1950) (statutory rape: victim may testify to her age and date of birth). So as to the age of a near relative. Hancock v. Supreme Council, 69 N.J.L. 308, 55 Atl. 246, syl. 1 (1903) (elder brother).

11. Brown v. Mitchell, 88 Tex. 350, 31 S.W. 621, 623, syl. 4 (1895) (witness testified that he was son of decedent, based on fact that she called him son and on other facts).

12. The evidence was admitted in Hunt v. Stimson, 23 F.2d 447, syl. 12, 13 (C.C.A.Ky.1928) (sales manager of lumber yard testified to amount of lumber on hand, based on his estimates from inspection and tallies made by other employees); Gresham v. Harcourt, 75 S.W. 808, syl. 1 (Tex.Civ.App.1903) (witness, present when sheep were counted, testified to the number; she heard the two men who did the counting call out the numbers, and she at the time

THE OPINION RULE [1]

11.　The Evolution of the Rule against Opinions.

The opinion rule, though it developed from practices and expressions of the English courts, seems to be emphasized more generally and enforced far more inflexibly here than in the mother country.[2]　In the first place a rule against "opinions" may have had a different meaning for the English judge. We are told that in English usage of the 1700's and earlier, "opinion" had the primary meaning of "notion" or "persuasion of the mind without proof or certain knowledge."[3] It carried an implication of lack of grounds, which is absent from our present-day meaning of the term "opinion" in this country. We use the word as denoting a belief, inference or conclusion without suggesting that it is well- or ill-founded.

The requirement that witnesses must have personal knowledge, already discussed, was a very old rule, having its roots in medieval law,[4] which demanded that they speak only "what they see and hear."[5]　The classic dictum of Coke in 1622, that "It is no satisfaction for a witness to say that he 'thinketh' or 'persuadeth himself' "[6] and Mansfield's statement in 1766, "It is mere opinion, which is not evidence"[7] are to be understood as condemning testimony when not based upon personal knowledge.　Statements founded only on hearsay or conjecture would fall under this ban.　But as Wigmore interprets the historical evidence, there was not until the 1800's any recognition of an opinion rule which would exclude inferences by witnesses possessing personal knowledge.[8]

By the middle of the 1800's [9] the disparagement of "mere opinion" in the sense of a no-

put them down in a book); Dick v. Puritan Pharmaceutical Co., 46 S.W.2d 941, 946 (Mo.App.1932) (owner-manager of business testified that samples and letters were mailed to his customers, though he did not personally mail them, but supervised the mailing); Schooler v. State, 175 S.W. 664, syl. 16 (Tex.Civ.App.1943) (geologist's testimony as to structure and oil prospects of land based on inspection and on reports of other geologists).　Cases are collected and acutely discussed in Maguire and Hahesy, Basis for Expert Opinion, 5 Vand.L.Rev. 432 (1952).　See also § 15, herein.

1. 7 Wigmore, Evidence, §§ 1917–2028; 3 Jones, Commentaries on Evidence, §§ 1241–1375 (2d ed., 1926); Decennial Digests, Crim.Law, ☞448–494; Evidence, ☞470–574; 32 C.J.S., Evidence, §§ 438–575; King and Pillinger, Opinion Evidence in Illinois (1942) (a work valuable in any jurisdiction for its original analysis and creative ideas).

2. See for example the brief treatment of opinion evidence in Phipson, Evidence, ch. 36 (9th ed., 1952). The chapter heading is Reputation, Opinion, Inference, Belief.

3. Samuel Johnson's Dictionary (1st ed., 1755) cited in King and Pillinger, *op. cit.* n. 1, at p. 8.

4. 9 Holdsworth, Hist.Eng.L. 211 (1926).

5. In 1349 it was held that witnesses were not challengeable "because the verdict will not be received from them, but from the jury; and the witnesses are to be sworn 'to say the truth,' without adding 'to the best of their knowledge,' for they should

testify nothing but what they . . . know for certain, that is to say what they see and hear." Anon.Lib.Ass. 110, 11 (1349), quoted in Phipson, *op. cit.* at p. 398.

6. Adams v. Canon, Dyer 53b, quoted 7 Wigmore, Evidence, p. 2.

7. Carter v. Boehm, 3 Burr. 1905, 1918 (1766) quoted 7 Wigmore, Evidence, p. 7.

8. 7 Wigmore, Evidence, § 1917; King and Pillinger, op. cit. n. 1, at p. 7.　The latter work cites Peake on Evidence, an English work published in 1801 as the source of the first statement that witnesses generally must state "facts" rather than "opinion."

9. See, e. g., Donnell v. Jones, 13 Ala. 490, 511 (1848) (opinion of one acquainted with business whether levy of attachment had destroyed credit and forced business into assignment, excluded. "The general rule requires, that witnesses should depose only to facts, and such facts too as come within their knowledge.　The expression of opinions, the belief of the witness, or deductions from the facts, however honestly made, are not proper evidence as coming from the witness; and when such deductions are made by the witness, the prerogative of the jury is invaded."); Hartford Protection Ins. Co. v. Harmer, 2 Oh.St. 452, 456 (1853).　It is notable, however, that even in the 1850's, the Illinois court states the matter thus hesitantly, "It is true, probably, that mere opinions, as opinions, when offered in evidence, should be confined to experts in the questions of skill or science as such, which are open

tion or conjecture not rooted in observation had emerged into a much more questionable canon of exclusion. This is the doctrine that witnesses generally must give the "facts" and not their "inferences, conclusions, or opinions." [10]

This classic formula, based as it is on the assumption that "fact" and "opinion" stand in contrast and hence are readily distinguishable, has proven the clumsiest of all the tools furnished the judge for regulating the examination of witnesses. It is clumsy because its basic assumption is an illusion. The words of the witness by no possibility can "give" or recreate the "facts," that is, the objective situations or happenings about which the witness is testifying. Drawings, maps, photographs, even motion pictures, would be only a remote and inaccurate portrayal of those "facts" and how much more distant approximations of reality are the word pictures of oral or written testimony. There is no conceivable statement however specific, detailed and "factual," that is not in some measure the product of inference and reflection as well as observation and memory. The difference between the statement, "He was driving on the left-hand side of the road" which would be classed as "fact" under the rule, and "He was driving carelessly" which would be called "opinion" is merely a difference between a more concrete and specific

form of descriptive statement and a less specific and concrete form. The difference between so-called "fact," then, and "opinion," is no difference between opposites or contrasting absolutes, but a mere difference in degree with no recognizable line to mark the boundary.[11]

If you give the trial judge the task of applying one rule to writings and another to oral speech, or one rule to testimony in court and another to hearsay, these are clear-cut distinctions. You can demand that they be accurately and uniformly applied. If you give him, however, the task of distinguishing on the spur of the moment between "fact" and "opinion" you give him a task in which it would be impossible over a wide range of cases to expect two judges, acting independently on the same questions to reach the same results. True it is that there are many familiar problems that have often recurred and as to which customs have arisen, as we shall see, to call one statement "fact" and another "opinion," but there will constantly in a changing world be presented a myriad of new statements to which the judge must apply the distinction. For these reasons, good sense demands that the trial judge be accorded a wide range of discretion in classifying evidence as "fact" or "opinion," as well as in admitting evidence even where found to constitute opinion.[12]

---

to that kind of proof, and for want of better." Butler v. Mehrling, 15 Ill. 488, 491 (1854). And Greenleaf in the 6th edition of his treatise, issued in 1852, when he deals with opinions in § 440 cites no cases for his statement that "the opinions of witnesses are in general not evidence" but devotes his numerous citations in the main to cases where opinions were received.

10. Among the leading cases discussing and applying the rule, in addition to the cases in the next preceding note, are Baltimore & O. R. Co. v. Schultz, 43 Ohio 270, 1 N.E. 324 (1885) (opinion of observer that fence not fit to keep stock off, excluded); Graham v. Pennsylvania Co., 139 Pa. 149, 21 A. 151, 12 L.R.A. 293 (1891) (opinion of architect who had seen defendant's platform, for alighting passengers, that because of construction and lighting it was unsafe, excluded).

11. For a masterly exposition of this view, see 7 Wigmore, Evidence, § 1919. Another discussion, with vivid illustrative material, is King & Pillinger, Opinion Evidence in Illinois, 1–6, 21–23 (1942).

12. Fred J. Keisel & Co. v. Sun Ins. Office, 88 F. 243, 249 (C.C.A.Utah, 1898)—"The trial court sees and hears each witness, and in doubtful cases is far better qualified than the court of appeals to determine whether a witness should be confined to the facts, or should be allowed to state his conclusions"; Farish v. Madison Distributing Co., Inc., 37 F.2d 455, syl. 8 (C.C.A.N.Y., 1930); Dersis v. Dersis, 210 Ala. 308, 311, 98 So. 27, syl. 6 (1923). "A certain discretion is rightly vested in the trial courts in directing the search for the truth by this class of evidence, and their action should not be disturbed unless it is apparent some right of a party has been invaded or suppressed. We think a man sitting

The recognition of the impossibility of administering the opinion-standard as a mandatory rule, however, has come but slowly. The alleviation of the strictness of the standard was justified at first as the recognition of exceptions limited to cases of strict necessity.[13] This doubtless remains as the "orthodox" view of the many courts who depend only on the encyclopedias which repeat the formulas of the older cases. The actual practice in the trial of cases is becoming, if indeed it has not always been, far more liberal than the older formulas,[14] and might more accurately be reflected in a formula which would sanction the admission of opinions on grounds of "expediency" or "convenience" rather than "necessity."

It is believed that the standard actually applied by the trial judges of today approaches more nearly the principle espoused by Wigmore, namely that the opinion should be rejected only when it is superfluous in the sense that it will be of no value to the jury.[15] In the view of the present writer the prevailing practice in respect to the admission of the opinions of non-expert witnesses may best be described, not as a rule excluding opinions but as a rule of preference. The more concrete description is preferred, to the more abstract. Moreover, it seems that the principal impact of the rule is upon the form of examination. The questions, while they cannot suggest the particular details desired, else they will be leading, must nevertheless call for the most specific account that the witness can give. For example, he must not be asked, "Did they agree?" but "What did they say?" When recognized as a matter of the form of the examination rather than the substance of the testimony—again, a difference

---

up all night with a sick man, or one grievously wounded in the head may form an opinion whether he is conscious or unconscious, which may be given to the jury for what it is worth"; Grismore v. Consolidated Products, 232 Ia. 328, 5 N.W.2d 646, syl. 17 (1942) "The courts and other authorities uniformly agree that the receipt of opinion evidence, whether lay or expert, and the extent to which it will be received in any particular case, are matters resting largely in the administrative discretion of the court."; McDuffie v. Root, 300 Mich. 286, 1 N.W.2d 544, syl. 7, 9 (1942); Dowling v. L. H. Shattuck, Inc., 91 N.H. 234, 17 A.2d 529, 532, syl. 1, 2 (1941); Cover v. Hershey Transit Co., 290 Pa. 551, 139 A. 266, syl. 6 (1927) (whether expert opinion allowable upon question whether child after fracture of skull was unconscious, discretionary); and see other cases collected in 32 C.J.S., Evidence, § 449, p. 86.

13. See, e. g., the following passage from a leading case: "A few general propositions are submitted, which, it is believed, fairly reflect the current of authority on the subject of the admissibility of the opinions of witnesses as evidence. (1) That witnesses shall testify to facts and not opinions is the general rule. (2) Exceptions to this rule have been found to be, in some cases, necessary to the due administration of justice. (3) Witnesses shown to be learned, skilled, or experienced in a particular art, science, trade, or business may, in a proper case, give their opinions upon a given state of facts. This exception is limited to experts. (4) In matter more within the common observation and experience of men, non-experts may, in cases where it is not practicable to place before the jury all the primary facts upon which they are founded, state their opinions from such facts, where such opinions involve conclusions material to the subject of inquiry. (5) In such cases the witnesses are required, so far as may be, to state the primary facts which support their opinions." Baltimore & O. R. Co. v. Schultz, 43 Ohio 270, 1 N.E. 324, 331 (1885).

14. A long-established "exception" to the opinion-rule in some states is the practice of admitting "opinions" where they can be justified as "shorthand renditions" of a total situation, or as "statements of collective facts": "Dulaney v. Burns, 218 Ala. 493, 513, 119 So. 21, 24, syl. 8, 1928, ('Did you ever say anything to influence him about not leaving anything to his kinfolks?'); Pollard v. Rogers, 234 Ala. 92, 173 So. 881, syl. 17–19, 1937, ('He looked like he was dying'; opinion has extensive discussion); City of Beaumont v. Kane, 33 S.W.2d 234, 241, 242, syl. 12, Tex.Civ.App., 1930, ('The situation at the end of Pearl Street presented such an appearance that a stranger on a rainy night would be liable to drive off into the river.'); Horn v. State, 12 Wyo. 80, 148, 73 P. 705, 721–723, 1903 (a witness who overheard, but did not see, defendant and another person in conversation was allowed to state whether defendant's admission of killing was "sincere" or "joshing"; an extremely picturesque case).

This so-called exception certainly seems to savor of a principle of mere convenience rather than of necessity.

15. 7 Wigmore, Evidence, § 1918.

of degree—the opinion rule, like other regulations of form, such as the control over leading questions and questions calling for a free narrative and over the order of proof is seen to fall naturally in the realm of discretion. Furthermore, it seems that this habit and tradition of Anglo-American lawyers to examine about specific details is a valuable heritage. The problem is to preserve this scientific habit of approach but yet to curb the time-wasting quibbling over trivial objections on the ground of "opinion" which may still be heard occasionally in those courts which attempt a literal application of the older formulas.

Perhaps the prediction may be ventured that this core of value will be preserved and the quibbling discarded, by the evolution of the Opinion Rule into a rule prescribing that the trial judge in his discretion may require that a witness, before giving testimony in terms of inference or general description, shall first give the concrete details upon which the inference or description is founded, so far as feasible.[16]

Many critics of the opinion rule, however, would doubtless believe that to preserve even such a vestige as that just suggested would do more harm than good.[17] They would contend that the all-sufficient substitute for requiring the proponent to elicit his testimony by specific questions, is the power of the adversary on cross-examination to inquire as he will into specific details. As has been pointed out,[18] however, this is not quite the same. The impression from the general description or inference has already been made by the examination. Moreover, every careful trial lawyer is slow to cross-examine unless he has reason to hope for helpful answers, which he seldom does. The professional habit of inquiry into the concrete particulars of the principal facts will probably be much weakened if the power of the trial judge to require it be taken away.

12. The Relativity of the Opinion Rule: Opinions on the Ultimate Issue.

As we have pointed out in the next preceding section, the terms "fact" and "opinion" denote merely a difference of degree of concreteness of description or a difference in nearness or remoteness of inference. The opinion rule operates to prefer the more concrete description to the less concrete, the direct form of statement to the inferential. But there is still another variable in the equation. The purpose of the testimony will have an effect on the degree of concreteness required. In the outer circle of collateral facts, near the rim of relevancy, evidence in general terms will be received with relative freedom, but as we come closer to the hub of

---

16. The Uniform Rules of Evidence so provide in Rule 57: "The judge may require that a witness before testifying in terms of opinion or inference be first examined concerning the data upon which the opinion or inference is founded."

But this is preceded by Rule 56 which maintains a general limitation upon opinion-evidence with a leeway, however, for liberal administration under subsec. (1) (b). Its provisions follow. Rule 56: "(1) If the witness is not testifying as an expert his testimony in the form of opinions or inferences is limited to such opinions or inferences as the judge finds (a) may be rationally based on the perception of the witness and (b) are helpful to a clear understanding of his testimony or to the determination of the fact in issue.

"(2) If the witness is testifying as an expert, testimony of the witness in the form of opinions or inferences is limited to such opinions as the judge

finds are (a) based on facts or data perceived by or personally known or made known to the witness at the hearing and (b) within the scope of the special knowledge, skill, experience or training possessed by the witness.

"(3) Unless the judge excludes the testimony he shall be deemed to have made the finding requisite to its admission.

"(4) Testimony in the form of opinions or inferences otherwise admissible under these rules is not objectionable because it embraces the ultimate issue or issues to be decided by the trier of the fact."

17. See 7 Wigmore, Evidence, § 1929 (The Future of the Opinion Rule); Bozeman, Suggested Reforms of the Opinion Rule, 13 Temple U.L.Q. 296 (1939).

18. King and Pillinger, Opinion Evidence in Illinois, 337 (1942).

the issue, the courts are more careful to call for details instead of inferences. This is clearly pointed out in the following passages:

"The rule seems to be that inference, conclusion, or understanding of the witness is admissible when it relates to a fact which is collateral or relatively unimportant, but is inadmissible when the purpose is to establish an issue upon which the case turns." Speer, J., in Crawford v. El Paso Sash and Door Co., 288 S.W. 169, 171 (Tex.Com.App., 1926).

"There are many degrees of generality of statement. In comparison with the next broader statement, each statement may be said (and is said) to be a statement of fact. Thus, in comparison with the statement 'X was not mentally competent to execute a will' the statement 'X was insane' is a statement of fact. In comparison with the statement 'X was insane' the statement 'X acted peculiarly' is a statement of fact. In comparison with the statement 'X acted peculiarly' the statement 'X had a vacant stare' is a statement of fact. · · ·

· · · · · · · · · · · · · ·

"But there is always one statement that, for our purposes, is an opinion and not a statement of fact. If a witness says, 'X should win this law suit' that is an opinion. · · ·

"But the question arises: How specific shall we compel the witness to be? If we allow him to testify that 'defendant owes plaintiff $500' he is merely reiterating that plaintiff should win. If he testifies, 'I heard defendant agree to pay plaintiff $500' he is a bit more specific but he is still testifying in substance that plaintiff should win. We then say to him, 'Just what was said— you must give the substance of it, but you are not required to give the exact words.' When he gives the substance of the conversation he is obviously stating his conclusion, but it is a conclusion that satisfies us provided he does not use the words 'agreed,' 'promised,' 'assented,' 'consented' or similar words unless such words were used by the parties. These words mark the line where the witness begins to give his opinion on ultimate issues.

"In other words, we always have many degrees of decisiveness shading back from the decisive statement that 'The plaintiff (or defendant) should prevail.' As against these degrees of decisiveness we have many degrees of generality of statement. The admissibility of any opinion depends upon two factors: (1) its degree of generality and (2) its decisiveness of the case. King and Pillinger, Opinion Evidence in Illinois, 10–12 (1942).

These considerations lead to the recognition that the trial judge may be more liberal in the use of his discretion to admit opinions and inferences as to collateral matters and should be sedulous to see that the concrete details are brought out as to more crucial matters. Is it expedient to go further and to tie his hands by a rule forbidding opinion-evidence as to these "ultimate" matters?

Undoubtedly there is a kind of statement by the witness which amounts to little more than an expression of his belief as to how the case should be decided or as to the amount of damages which should be given or as to the credibility of certain testimony. Such extreme expressions as these all courts, it is believed, would exclude.[1] There is no necessity for such evidence, and to receive it would tend to suggest that the judge and jury may shift responsibility for decision to the witnesses.

A very substantial number of courts, however, have gone far beyond this common-sense reluctance to listen to the witness's views as to how the judge and jury should exercise their functions and have announced the general doctrine that witnesses will not

1. See, e. g., Duncan v. Mack, 59 Ariz. 36, 122 P.2d 215, syl. 4 (1942) (whether public convenience would be served by transfer of license): Grismore v. Consolidated Products, 232 Ia. 328, 5 N.W.2d 649, syl. 28, 29 (1942) (opinions as to guilt, negligence, testamentary capacity, reasonable cause—dictum).

be permitted to give their opinions or conclusions upon an ultimate fact in issue.[2]

The reason is sometimes given that such testimony "usurps the function"[3] or "invades the province"[4] of the jury. Obviously these expressions are not intended to be taken literally, which would render them absurd,[5] but merely to suggest the danger that the jury may forego independent analysis of the facts and bow too readily to the opinion of an expert or otherwise influential witness.

It is believed, however, that this general rule is unduly restrictive, is pregnant with close questions of application, and often unfairly obstructs the party's presentation of his case. Even the courts which profess adherence to the rule fail to apply it with consistency. All such courts, for example, disregard the supposed rule, usually without explanation as to why it should not be applied, when value, sanity, handwriting and identity are in issue.[6]

The opposite view would entirely discard the rule that mere coincidence with an ultimate issue is a ground for exclusion of a witness's opinion or conclusion. It is doubt-ful if any court has found it expedient to go so far,[7] but this is the view of Wigmore[8] and is the one embodied in the Uniform Rules.[9] Probably Wigmore would have conceded that the extreme instances mentioned above of opinions as to how the case should be decided, and the like, should be excluded as impolitic and superfluous, and there is little doubt that a judge trained in the common law tradition, in a state which had adopted the Uniform Rules, would exclude such opinions under Rule 45, on the ground that their value is outweighed by a "substantial danger of undue prejudice, or of confusing the issues or of misleading the jury."

There are other lines of decision departing from the strict rule of exclusion, but with varying degrees of liberalization. Under one view, the doctrine which prohibits opinions upon an ultimate issue is held to be qualified by the same principle of necessity which has been the orthodox justification for receiving any kind of opinion evidence.[10] Accordingly it is held by these courts that where it is necessary in order that the trier of fact may intelligently determine an issue, for the opinion on that issue of an expert[11] or even of a

---

2. United States v. Spaulding, 293 U.S. 498, 506, 55 S.Ct. 273, 79 L.Ed. 617 (1935); State v. Carr, 196 N.C. 129, 144 S.E. 698 (1928) and cases collected in Dec.Digests, Evidence, ⊝472 and 506, Criminal Law, ⊝450; 32 C.J.S. 74, 75, title Evidence, § 446; and see Notes, 7 N.C.L.Rev. 320 (1928), 16 Id. 180 (1938); 26 Ia.L.Rev. 819 (1941).

3. Chicago & Alton R. Co. v. Springfield & N. W. R. Co., 67 Ill. 145 (1873).

4. De Groat v. Winter, 261 Mich. 660, 247 N.W. 69, 71 (1933).

5. Wigmore calls them "empty rhetoric." 7 Evidence, § 1920.

6. These and other instances where the rule is honored in the breach are pointed out in Grismore v. Consolidated Products, 232 Ia. 328, 5 N.W.2d 646, 656 (1942) (a masterly and exhaustive opinion by Bliss, J.) and in Note, 16 N.C.L.Rev. 180, 182. See likewise the subsequent sections of this chapter in which particular kinds of opinion-evidence are discussed.

7. Perhaps as near as any to this position is Grismore v. Consolidated Products, supra, wherein the

Court said: "In view of the numerous decisions of this court and of other courts and of the pronouncements of eminent authorities, we think there can no longer be any question of the soundness of the rule that if the matter before the tribunal for determination is one in which opinion testimony, either lay or expert, is necessary or proper, the witness may express his opinion either as to the possibility, probability, or actuality of the matter of fact about which he is interrogated, and the answer will not be an invasion or usurpation of the province or function of the jury, even though it passes upon an ultimate fact which the jury must determine."

8. 7 Evidence, §§ 1920, 1921.

9. Rule 56(4), set out in § 11, n. 16, supra.

10. See n. 13, supra.

11. Grismore v. Consolidated Products, 232 Ia. 328, 5 N.W.2d 646, syl. 21 (1942) (opinion of experienced turkey-raiser, based on facts assumed in question, as to what caused death of turkeys held admissible); National Life & Accident Ins. Co. v. Follett, 168 Tenn. 647, 80 S.W.2d 92, syl. 2 (1935) (doctor's

layman speaking from his first-hand knowl-edge,[12] to be heard, such opinion may be received. Some courts are more liberal and possibly more realistic when they say that such opinions are to be admitted whenever they are calculated to aid the jury appreciably in reaching a right conclusion.[13]

Some courts have intimated that the form of the witness' testimony may be significant, in that a direct statement of the fact in issue may be inadmissible while a mere statement that it is the witness' opinion that the fact is so, would be allowable.[14] This has been rightly called a mere quibble.[15] The two forms of statement are both mere expressions of belief and should be treated alike. The degree of positiveness should make no difference in admissibility.

A more substantial distinction is made between those questions which merely call for an opinion as to an ultimate fact in issue, and those which have the additional feature that they are expressed in terms of some legal standard which though familiar to lawyers may not be understood, or not be understood in the same sense, by the witness and the jury. A court which does not ban opinions on the ultimate issue as such may nevertheless condemn a question phrased in terms of a legal criterion not adequately defined by the questioner so as to be correctly understood by laymen.[16] The problem has arisen most often in relation to testimony on the issue of capacity to make a will. Thus a court taking the view last mentioned would approve a question, "Did X have mental ca-

---

opinion, on hypothetical question, as to cause of death, admissible.

And in malpractice cases it appears that testimony by experts on the ultimate issue is not only permitted but often may be required. Pedigo v. Roseberry, 340 Mo. 724, 102 S.W.2d 600, syl. 7, 8 (1937); Hall v. Nagel, 139 Oh.St. 265, 39 N.E.2d 612, syl. 3 (1942); Note, 141 A.L.R. 5.

12. Weber v. Chicago R. I. & P. R. Co., 175 Ia. 358, 151 N.W. 852, 859, L.R.A.1918A., 626 (lay opinion testimony as to whether spikes holding rails had been pulled with a crowbar, admissible) cited and discussed in Grismore v. Consolidated Products, 232 Ia. 328, 5 N.W.2d 646, 662 (1942).

13. United States Smelting Co. v. Parry, 166 F. 407, 410, 411, syl. 2, 3 (C.C.A.Utah, 1908, opinion by Vandevanter, J.) (testimony by an experienced brick-mason and builder, as to whether a scaffold was dangerous, allowed); John V. Schaefer, Jr. v. Ely, 84 Conn. 501, 80 A. 775, syl. 7 (testimony of architect as to whether work done was according to plans and specifications, admissible); Patrick v. Treadwell, 222 N.C. 1, 21 S.E.2d 818, syl. 9 (1942) (exception recognized but particular testimony held improvidently admitted).

See also the following cases where expert testimony on the ultimate issue was held admissible without specifying any limitation: Cropper v. Titanium Pigment Co., 47 F.2d 1038, syl. 9, 10, 78 A.L.R. 737 (C.C.A.Mo.1931) (doctor's evidence as to cause of plaintiff's condition); Svenson v. Mutual Life Ins. Co., 87 F.2d 441, syl. 8, 9 (C.C.A., S.D., 1937) (doctor's opinion as to cause of death); Federal Underwriters' Exchange v. Cost, 132 Tex. 299, 123 S.W.2d 332, syl. 5–7 (1938) (doctor's opinion that plaintiff unable

to secure and retain employment and to perform usual tasks of a workman).

14. State v. Steffen, 210 Ia. 196, 230 N.W. 536, 78 A.L.R. 748 (1930) (expert may not testify that two fingerprints made by same person); Re Harris, 247 Mich. 690, 226 N.W. 661 (1929) (handwriting expert improperly allowed to testify, "I find that the signature is not written by the same hand").

15. Note, 78 A.L.R. 755, 758.

16. See the enlightening opinions by Smedley, C. in Federal Underwriters' Exchange v. Cost, 132 Tex. 299, 123 S.W.2d 332, 334, 335 (1938), and by Bliss, J. in Grismore v. Consolidated Products, 232 Ia. 328, 5 N.W.2d 646, 663 (1942). In the latter case the court said: "No witness should be permitted to give his opinion directly that a person is guilty or innocent, or is criminally responsible or irresponsible, or that a person was negligent or not negligent, or that he had capacity to execute a will, or deed, or like instrument, or, as held by us in Halligan v. Lone Tree Farmers Exchange, 230 Iowa 1277, 1283, 300 N.W. 551, respecting whether a county attorney had probable cause to believe the plaintiff was guilty of the crime charged. But the reason is that such matters are not subjects of opinion testimony. They are mixed questions of law and fact. When a standard, or a measure, or a capacity has been fixed by law, no witness whether expert or non-expert, nor however qualified, is permitted to express an opinion as to whether or not the person or the conduct, in question, measures up to that standard. On that question the court must instruct the jury as to the law, and the jury must draw its own conclusion from the evidence." See also Kinney, A Reexamination of the Ultimate Issue Rule, 32 U.Cin.L. Rev. 161 (1953).

pacity sufficient to understand the nature and effect of his will?" [17] but would frown on the question, "Did X have sufficient mental capacity to make a will?" [18] because the latter question may be incorrectly understood by the witness and the jury if they do not know the law's definition of "capacity to make a will." But a court which prohibits generally opinions on the ultimate issue would condemn both forms of questions,[19] or even one where the questioner breaks down "testamentary capacity" into its factual elements as legally defined.[20] Similar problems may arise in respect to such issues as undue influence, total and permanent disability, negligence and the like. On the whole, it is thought that the danger that these questions phrased in terms of "legal conclusions" will be misunderstood is very slight, since they will seldom be asked except when the popular meaning is approximately the same as the legal. In a jurisdiction where there is no general rule against opinions on the ultimate issue, it seems that a request by the adversary that the questioner define his terms should be the only recourse.

13. Expert Witnesses:[1] Qualifications.[2]

An observer is qualified to testify because he has firsthand knowledge which the jury does not have of the situation or transaction at issue. The expert has something different to contribute. This is a power to draw inferences from the facts which a jury would not be competent to draw. To warrant the use of expert testimony, then, two elements are required. First, the subject of the inference must be so distinctively related to some science, profession, business or occupation as to be beyond the ken of the average layman,[3] and second, the witness must have such skill, knowledge or experience in that

---

17. See Scalf v. Collin County, 80 Tex. 514, 16 S.W. 314 (1891) (capacity to understand nature and effect of deed); McDaniel v. Willis, 157 S.W.2d 672 (Tex. Civ.App.1941, error ref'd.) (opinion that testator mentally incapable of transacting business). But see Pickering v. Harris, 23 S.W.2d 316 (Tex.Comm. App., 1930) and White v. White, 168 S.W.2d 324 (Tex. Civ.App.1943) both *contra*, and both, it is believed, decided under a mistaken analysis. The decision in the latter case was reversed, however, without explicitly passing on this question. 141 Tex. 328, 172 S.W.2d 295 (1943). *See* Note (1930) 8 Texas Law Review 589.

18. Brown v. Mitchell, 88 Tex. 350, 31 S.W. 621, 36 L.R.A. 64 (1895).

19. See In re Jahn's Will, 184 Ia. 416, 165 N.W. 1021 (1918) ("able to comprehend transactions involving disposition of property by will or otherwise"); Baker v. Baker, 202 Ill. 595, 67 N.E. 410 (1903) ("whether he was able understandingly to execute a will"); Schneider v. Manning, 121 Ill. 376, 12 N.E. 267 (1887) ("Had he mental capacity to dispose of his property by will or deed?") and see King & Pillinger, Opinion Evidence in Illinois, 225–228 (1942).

20. Hann v. Hann, 202 Ia. 807, 812, 211 N.W. 495 (1926); Baddeley v. Watkins, 293 Ill. 394, 127 N.E. 725, syl. 4 (1920); King & Pillinger, op. cit. 226; and in Pickering v. Harris (cited supra, n. 17) a similar question was condemned (groundlessly, it is submitted) in a state which has no general rule against opinions on the ultimate issue.

1. There is an interesting body of professional literature on the subject. See Ladd, Expert Testimony, 5 Vand.L.Rev. 414 (1952); Buescher, Use of Experts by the Courts, 54 Harv.L.Rev. 1105 (1941); Moodie, Expert testimony—its past and its future, 11 Aust. L.J. 210 (1937); Bomar, Compensation of Expert Witnesses, 2 Law & Cont.Prob. 510 (1935); Yankwich, On the Use of Experts, 26 A.B.A.Jour. 736 (1940); Experts in Patent Causes, 22 J.Pat.Off.Soc. 639 (1940); Fouts, Medical Experts, 19 Neb.L.B. 213 (1940); May, The Engineer as an Expert Witness, 13 Okl. B.A.J. 204 (1942); Stichter, Use of Exhibits and Expert Testimony, 8 Oh.St.L.J. 295 (1942); Ploscowe, The Expert Witness in Criminal Cases in France, Germany and Italy, 2 Law & Cont.Prob. 504 (1935); Osborn, Cooperation of Attorney and Expert, 21 A.B.A.J. 151 (1935).

2. Dec.Dig., Crim.L ☞477–481, Evidence, §§ 537–546; 32 C.J.S., Evidence, §§ 456–458; 7 Wigmore, Evidence, §§ 1923, 1925.

3. Admissible: Manhattan Oil Co. v. Mosby, 72 F.2d 840, syl. 12, 14 (C.C.A.Mo.1934) (effects of drinking salt water by cattle; how much weight cattle should gain on certain range); Bank of Vance v. Crowder, 194 N.C. 331, 139 S.E. 604, syl. 2 (1927) (explanation of entries in books of bank cashier). Inadmissible: First Trust Co. v. Kansas City Life Ins. Co., 79 F.2d 48, syl. 12 (C.C.A.Minn.1935) (legibility of printed application by man of 51); Equitable Life Assur. Soc. v. Davis, 231 Ala. 261, 164 So. 86 (1935) (ability of man who has lost use of left arm to perform manual labor); Goodrich v. May, 121 Ore. 418,

field or calling as to make it appear that his opinion or inference will probably aid the trier in his search for truth.[4] The knowledge may in some fields be derived from reading alone, in some from practice alone, or as is more commonly the case, from both.[5] While the court may rule that a certain subject of inquiry requires that a member of a given profession, as a doctor, an engineer or a chemist, to be called, usually a specialist in a particular branch within the profession will not be required.[6] The practice, however, in respect to experts' qualifications has not for the most part crystallized in specific rules, but is recognized as a matter for the trial judge's discretion reviewable only for abuse.[7]

14. Hypothetical Questions.[1]

If an expert witness has firsthand knowledge of material facts, as when a physician has examined an injured plaintiff, naturally he may describe what he has seen, and give his expert inferences therefrom, such as his opinion as to the cause or the probable duration of the condition. In these circumstances, it is unnecessary to couch the question in hypothetical form[2] and it would certainly weaken the effect of the testimony to do so. We have assumed that the expert witness has first specified the data gleaned from observation on which he founds his inferences. Is this required? Some courts insist that this be done,[3] so that the jury may know the

---

255 P. 464, syl. 1–3 (1927) (inferences from examination of wheel, in evidence, as to which car struck the other); Dec.Dig., Evidence, ⚖505–534; Jones, Commentaries on Evidence, § 1312 (2d ed., 1926).

4. Pennsylvania Threshermen, etc. Ins. Co. v. Messenger, 181 Md. 295, 29 A.2d 653, syl. 2 (1943) (professor of science may give computation of distances); Bebont v. Kurn, 348 Mo. 501, 154 S.W.2d 120, syl. 5 (1941) (one with long experience in railroad work as brakeman and otherwise could testify as to distance required for stopping train, though he had never been engineer); State v. Killeen, 79 N.H. 201, 107 A. 601, syl. 2 (1919) (experienced clerk who checks delivery orders may give opinion as to signatures).
Sometimes the expert testimony is excluded because the court takes judicial knowledge that the observed data upon which the inference is founded are insufficient. Wisniewski v. Weinstock, 130 N.J.L. 58, 31 A.2d 401, syl. 1 (1943) (inference of speed from examining tire skid marks on pavement).

5. Empire Oil & Ref. Co. v. Hoyt, 112 F.2d 357, syl. 1 (C.C.A.Mich.1940); Carter v. Marble Products Inc., 179 Ga. 122, 175 S.E. 480, syl. 1 (1934); Pennsylvania Threshermen, etc. Ins. Co. v. Messenger, 181 Md. 295, 29 A.2d 653, syl. 3, 4 (1943); Dowling v. L. H. Shattuck, Inc., 91 N.H. 234, 17 A.2d 529, syl. 6 (1941).

6. Drucker v. Philadelphia Dairy Products Co., 5 W. W.Harr. 437, 166 A. 796, syl. 2 (Del.Super.1933) (general physician, as to heart condition); Kabai v. Majestic Collieries Co., 293 Ky. 783, 170 S.W.2d 357, syl. 5 (1943) (general physician, as to brain injury); Pridgen v. Gibson, 194 N.C. 289, 139 S.E. 443, syl. 5, 8, 9 (1927) (general physician, as to proper treatment of injury to eye); Decennial Dig., Evidence ⚖537. Contra: In re Lindon's Will, 241 App.Div.

819, 270 N.Y.S. 771 (1934) (only alienist may testify as to testator's capacity to make will).

7. Cohen v. Travelers' Ins. Co., 134 F.2d 378, syl. 6, 7 (C.C.A., Ill., 1943); Smith v. Arrow Drilling Co., 191 Okl. 381, 130 P.2d 95, syl. 6 (1942); Dec.Dig., Evidence, ⚖546. The judge's ruling that a retired physician from another state was not qualified on a question of surgery in a malpractice case was reversed as clearly erroneous in Carbone v. Warburton, 11 N.J. 418, 94 A.2d 680 (1953), noted 14 Oh.St.L. 335.

1. 2 Wigmore, Evidence, §§ 672–686; 32 C.J.S. §§ 549–560; Dec.Dig.Crim.Law, ⚖482–489, Evidence, ⚖547–557; King & Pillinger, Opinion Evidence in Illinois, ch. 14 (1942).

2. Langenfelder v. Thompson, 179 Md. 502, 20 A.2d 491, syl. 9, 11 (medical expert, whether accident could have caused; but where facts voluminous and evidence conflicting court in discretion may require hypothetical presentation); Hester v. Horton Motor Lines, 219 N.C. 743, 14 S.E.2d 794, syl. 4 (1941) (medical expert, cause of injury) and see, for form of question, Note, E. W. Cole, Jr., 20 N.C.L.Rev. 100 (1941); Foott v. Lindstrom, 143 Ore. 309, 22 P.2d 321, syl. 1, 2 (1933) (amount of shrinkage of building material); Independent School Dist. No. 35 v. A. Heidenberg & Co., 214 Minn. 82, 7 N.W.2d 511, syl. 13 (1943) (error to require hypothetical presentation based on testimony of others); Note, 82 A.L.R. 1338. Contra: Van Deusen v. Newcomer, 40 Mich. 90, 119 (1879) (examining physician, cause of condition); Southern Iron & E. Co. v. Smith, 257 Mo. 226, 165 S.W. 804 (1914) (condition of engines) and cases cited 2 Wigmore, Evidence, § 675, n. 1.

3. Raub v. Carpenter, 187 U.S. 159, 161, 23 S.Ct. 72, 47 L.Ed. 119 (1902) (opinion as to sanity "from all you know about him yourself," properly excluded),

premises before they hear the conclusions. Others say that it is not essential since the opponent is free to elicit the grounds on cross-examination.[4] The wisest view, it seems, is to leave to the trial court's discretion whether this shall be required.[5]

When the expert has no firsthand knowledge of the situation at issue, and has made no investigation of the facts for himself, then the most convenient way of securing the benefit of his scientific skill is to ask him to assume certain facts and then to give his opinions or inferences in view of such assumptions. These are known as hypothetical questions, and the rules regulating the form and content of such questions have been evolved with perhaps more of logical rigor than of practicality.

In many jurisdictions, it seems customary to have the expert witnesses in court during the taking of testimony, and then when the expert is himself called as a witness, simplify the hypothetical question by asking the expert to assume the truth of the previous testimony, or some specified part of it.[6] This practice has some advantages, and some limi-tations. Two obvious requirements are that the facts that the witness is assuming must be clear to the jury, and that the data assumed must not be conflicting. A question which asks the witness to assume the truth of one previous witness' testimony will usually meet these requirements,[7] but as the range of assumption is widened to cover the testimony of several witnesses,[8] or all the testimony for one side[9] the risk of infraction is increased, and when it covers all the testimony in the case, the question would manifestly be approved only when the testimony on the issue is not conflicting and is brief and simple enough for the jury to recall its outlines without having them recited.[10] In framing these hypothetical questions in which the witness is asked to assume the truth of previous testimony, one difficulty may be overlooked. What if part of the previous testimony is itself the inference (as to the cause or the probable consequences of an injury, for example) of a previous expert? Of course, it will often be apparent that the witness is being asked only to accept the objective descriptions given by the previous

---

Brown v. Mobile Electric Co., 207 Ala. 61, 91 So. 802, syl. 4 (1921); Note, 82 A.L.R. 1338, 1340.

4. Morrow v. National Masonic Acc. Ass'n, 125 Ia. 633, 101 N.W. 468, syl. 8 (1904) (attending physician, error to require detailing of grounds); Comm. v. Johnson, 188 Mass. 382, 74 N.E. 939, 940 (1905) (dictum); People v. Youngs, 151 N.Y. 210, 45 N.E. 460, syl. 5 (1896); People v. Faber, 199 N.Y. 256, 92 N.E. 674, syl. 5, 520 Ann.Cas. 879 (1910); Note, 82 A.L.R. 1338, 1342. And it has been held that if the facts are too voluminous they need not be stated. Grison Oil Corp. v. Corporation Comm., 186 Okl. 548, 99 P. 2d 134, syl. 6 (1940).

5. See People v. Youngs, 151 N.Y. 210, 218, 45 N.E. 460, 462 (1896).

6. See 3 Wigmore, Evidence, § 681; Note, 82 A.L.R. 1460.

7. Burdick v. Mann, 60 N.D. 710, 236 N.W. 340, 82 A.L.R. 1443, 1452 (1931) (claim for legal services, witness' opinion of value based on plaintiff's testimony, approved).

8. Damm v. State, 128 Md. 665, 97 A. 645, syl. 4 (1916) (abortion: opinion of doctor based on evidence of at-tending and examining doctors, approved); Cornell v. State, 104 Wis. 527, 80 N.W. 745, syl. 7 (1899) (murder: defense, insanity: opinion of doctor based on 40 or 50 pages of testimony of other witnesses, approved on ground testimony not conflicting and whether too voluminous and complicated was in trial judge's discretion).

9. State v. Eggleston, 161 Wash. 486, 297 P. 162, 82 A.L.R. 1439, 1441 (1931) (murder: defense, insanity: "assuming all of the testimony given by the defendant's witnesses is true . . . what is your opinion as to whether the defendant was sane . . .?" approved).

10. Shouse v. Consol. Flour Mills Co., 132 Kan. 108, 294 P. 657, syl. 1, 2 (1931) (opinion as to value of legal services, from all the testimony, disapproved, testimony conflicting); State v. Reilly, 25 N.D. 339, 141 N.W. 720, 734, syl. 16 (1913) (discussing the practice). But compare State v. Carroll, 52 Wyo. 29, 69 P.2d 542, 550–552, syl. 7–10 (1937) where the court suggests that more consideration should be given to the fact that the cross-examiner has a complete opportunity to clear up any ambiguity in the hypothesis flowing from the conflict in the testimony.

experts, not their inferences or conclusions, and then there can be no objection.[11] And it might be arguable, that since the expert in giving a private opinion would certainly take into account previously expressed opinions of other experts on the same question, he should be allowed to do so on the stand. But on the stand he is not asked merely to take them into account, but to assume them to be true, and if he does this his own opinion may then be but an academic echo. It is held that such a question, which asks the witness to assume the truth of testimony which itself includes expert opinions is improper.[12] It is apparent, however, that the line between observed "fact" and inferential "opinion" is here, as always, a shadowy one and the trial judge should be allowed a wide latitude of good sense in passing on such an objection.

The type of hypothetical questions just discussed, namely those based on other testimony in the case, have the advantage of satisfying the requirement imposed upon all hypothetical questions that the facts assumed must be supported by evidence in the case.[13] This requirement is based on the notion that if the answer is founded on premises of fact which the jury, for want of evidence, cannot find to be true, then they are equally disabled from using the answer as the basis for a finding. Direct testimony supporting the fact assumed is not required. It is sufficient if it is fairly inferable from circumstances proved.[14] Moreover, the supporting evidence need not have been already adduced if the interrogating counsel gives assurance that it will be.[15] And of course, it is no objection that the supporting evidence is controverted.[16] The proponent is entitled to put his side of the case to the witness for his opinion.

In doing this, however, there is danger that by omitting some of the facts, he may present an unfair and inadequate picture to the expert, and that the jury may give undue weight to the answer, without considering its faulty basis. What safeguards should be supplied? Some courts have required that all facts material to the question should be embraced in the hypothesis,[17] but this seems

11. Howland v. Oakland Consol. St. Ry. Co., 110 Calif. 513, 42 P. 983, syl. 2 (1895) ("assuming statement made by Dr. D to be true" means assuming the truth of facts stated as to character of injury, not Dr. D's opinion as to cause of condition); Cody v. Toller Drug Co., 232 Ia. 520, 5 N.W.2d 824, syl. 13, 14 (1942) (question which asked expert witness to assume truth of testimony of previous witness, a chemist, as to the results of tests made by him, proper).

12. Corrigan v. United States, 82 F.2d 106, syl. 1 (C. C.A., Idaho, 1936) (error to ask question based on assumption of truth of another doctor's diagnosis); Mt. Royal Cab Co. v. Dolan, 168 Md. 633, 179 A. 54, 98 A.L.R. 1106 (1935) (previous testimony including expert's opinion as to cause of symptoms); Wise v. State Ind. Acc. Comm., 148 Ore. 461, 35 P.2d 242, syl. 6–9 (1934) (assuming truth of diagnosis of another doctor); Note, 98 A.L.R. 1109; 32 C.J.S. 356, n. 95.

13. As to this requirement, see, e. g., Troutman v. Mutual Life Ins. Co., 125 F.2d 769, syl. 2, 3 (C.C.A. Ky.1942); Takoma Park Bank v. Abbott, 179 Md. 249, 19 A.2d 169, syl. 17, 18; 32 C.J.S.Evidence, § 552, n. 33.

14. Krug v. Mutual Life Ins. Co., 149 S.W.2d 393, syl. 6, 7 (Mo.App., 1941); Teeters v. Frost, 145 Okl. 273, 292 P. 356, 71 A.L.R. 179, 188 (1930); Carruthers v. Phillips, 169 Ore. 636, 131 P.2d 193, syl. 11 (1942) (may include scientific inferences deducible from the facts); Dec.Dig., Evidence, ☞553(3).

15. Proechel v. United States, 59 F.2d 648, syl. 8 (C.C. A.Minn.1932).

16. Fidelity & Casualty Co. v. McKay, 73 F.2d 828, syl. 3 (C.C.A.Tex.1934) (jury should be instructed to disregard answer if they find facts assumed are not true); Enyart v. Orr, 78 Colo. 6, 238 P. 29, syl. 20 (1925); Fairview Fruit Co. v. H. P. Boydon & Bro., 85 W.Va. 609, 102 S.E. 231, syl. 1 (1920); Opp v. Pryor, 294 Ill. 538, 128 N.E. 580, syl. 7 (1920) (must not ignore material undisputed facts).

17. Hicks Adm'x. v. Harlan Hospital, 231 Ky. 60, 21 S.W.2d 125, syl. 6 (1929) (substantially all facts relating to matter as to which opinion is sought); Mathieson Alkali Works, Inc. v. Redden, 177 Md. 560, 10 A.2d 699, syl. 2 (1940) (every material fact in evidence essential to a rational opinion); In re Scherrer's Estate, 242 Wis. 211, 7 N.W.2d 848, syl. 2 (1943) (all the facts necessary to be considered in arriving at a correct answer); Dec.Dig., Evidence, ☞553(2).

undesirable as likely to multiply disputes as to the sufficiency of the hypothesis, and as tending to cause counsel, out of abundance of caution, to propound questions so lengthy as to be wearisome and almost meaningless to the jury.[18] The more expedient and more widely prevailing view is that there is no rule requiring that all material facts be included.[19] The safeguards are that the adversary may on cross-examination supply omitted facts and ask the expert if his opinion would be modified by them,[20] and further that the trial judge if he deems the original question unfair may in his discretion require that the hypothesis be reframed to supply an adequate basis for a helpful answer.[21]

15. Expert's Opinion Based on Reports of Others.

We have seen that if an expert has first-hand knowledge of a situation, as where a physician has examined and treated an injured person, he may give his inferences or opinions positively and directly, rather than in the muffled, abstract form of an answer based on a hypothesis. The question calling for the direct opinion is so much simpler and more effective that a party may desire to use it when the expert's acquaintance with the material facts is not derived from obser-vation, but from statements made by third persons. Often these statements are of a highly reliable kind such as a report of an examination by another physician, or hospital charts and records showing the symptoms, treatment and progress of a patient. The prevailing view, however, is that a question calling for the witness' opinion on the basis of such reports (without reciting their contents as hypotheses, to be supported by other evidence as their truth) is improper.[1] The essential objection seems to be that since the question is not hypothetical in form, the jury is asked to accept as evidence the witness' inference, based upon some one else's hearsay assertion of a fact which is, presumably, not supported by any evidence at the trial and which therefore the jury has no basis for finding to be true. Moreover, the objection may be asserted of want of the knowledge-qualification. Should these objections still prevail when the witness is asked to give a similar direct (not hypothetical) opinion, on the basis not merely of such reports, but of such reports supplemented by the witness' own observation of the person or situation in question? Probably the majority of courts would apply the same reasoning, and exclude the evidence,[2] but there are

---

18. See, e. g., Treadwell v. Nickel, 194 Calif. 243, 228 P. 25, 35 (1924) where the court refers to a question "contained in some 83 pages of typewritten transcript, and an objection involved in 14 pages more of the record."

19. Napier v. Greenzweig, 256 F. 196, syl. 5 (C.C.A. N.Y.1919); Virginia Beach Bus Line v. Campbell, 73 F.2d 97, syl. 5 (C.C.A.N.C.1934) (reviewing prior decisions); United States v. Aspinwall, 96 F.2d 867, syl. 3 (1938); Forbis v. Holzman, 5 Calif.2d 407, 55 P.2d 201, syl. 4 (1936); Godfrey v. Western Carolina Power Co., 190 N.C. 24, 128 S.E. 485, syl. 8 (1925); Carruthers v. Phillips, 169 Ore. 636, 131 P. 2d 193, syl. 11, 12 (1942); Shuffield v. Taylor, 125 Tex. 601, 83 S.W.2d 955, syl. 6 (1935); 2 Wigmore, Evidence, § 682; Dec.Dig., Evidence, ⊂⟩553(2); 32 C.J.S.Evidence, § 551, notes 82 and 91.

20. See authorities cited in n. 19, supra.

21. See authorities cited in n. 19, supra.

1. Equitable Life Assur. Soc. v. Kazee, 257 Ky. 803, 79 S.W.2d 208, syl. 3, 4 (1935) (opinion based on X-ray picture and reports from others); Howarth v. Adams Express Co., 269 Pa. 280, 112 A. 536, (syl. 6) (1921) ("From what you have been told and what you have heard in court and what you have gotten from the doctor and the history of the case, would you say that her condition is due to the accident?"); Pecos & N. T. R. Co. v. Coffman, 160 S.W. 145, syl. 11 (Tex.Civ.App.,1913) (opinion based on depositions of two other experts); Note, 98 A.L.R. 1109, 1112; Dec.Dig., Evidence, ⊂⟩555.

2. People v. Black, 367 Ill. 210, 10 N.E.2d 801, syl. 1 (1937) (physician in charge of department of mental and nervous diseases of house of correction testified as to his opinion of sanity of defendant based on report of investigation of social workers in his department and his own observation of defendant); People v. Keough, 276 N.Y. 141, 11 N.E.2d 570, syl. 1, 2 (1937) (on insanity defence in murder trial, alienists gave their opinion based on personal observation

strong expressions of a contrary view.[3] It seems arguable that an expert in a science is presumably competent to judge of the reliability of statements made to him by other investigators or technicians.[4] He seems just as competent indeed to do this as a judge and jury are to pass upon the credibility of an ordinary witness on the stand. If the statements, then, are attested by the expert as the basis for a judgment upon which he would act in the practice of his profession, it seems that they should ordinarily be a sufficient basis even standing alone for his direct expression of professional opinion on the stand, and this argument is reinforced when the opinion is founded not only upon such reports but also in part upon the expert's firsthand observation. The data of observation will usually enable the expert to evaluate the reliability of the statement.

16. Should the Hypothetical Question Be Retained?

The hypothetical question is an ingenious and logical device for enabling the jury to apply the expert's scientific knowledge to the facts of the case. Nevertheless, it is a failure in practice and an obstruction to the administration of justice. If we require that it recite all the relevant facts, it becomes intolerably wordy. If we allow, as most courts do, the interrogating counsel to select such of the material facts as he sees fit,[1] we tempt him to shape a one-sided hypothesis. Those expert witnesses who have given their views seem to agree that this partisan slanting of

---

of defendant and on testimony which they had heard as members of lunacy commissions which had considered defendant's sanity); State v. David, 222 N.C. 242, 22 S.E.2d 633, syl. 6 (1942) (murder by gas poisoning: opinion of toxicologist based partly on examination of organs of deceased by witness and partly upon findings of doctor who performed autopsy); Hunt v. State, 9 Tex.Cr.App. 166, syl. 1, 2 (1880) (murder: doctor gave opinion as to which wound was first inflicted, from what others had told him); Dec.Dig., Evidence, ⊂⇒555, Crim.Law, ⊂⇒486; Note, 98 A.L.R. 1109, 1112.

3. Schooler v. State, 175 S.W.(2d) 664, syl. 16 (1943) (geologist testifies to opinion as to prospects for oil in a certain region, based on his own inspection and upon geological reports); Sundquist v. Madison Rys. Co., 197 Wis. 83, 221 N.W. 392, syl. 4, 5 (1928) (opinion of doctor who treated plaintiff, based in part upon reports of examinations made by hospital technicians).

Moreover, most courts will admit the opinion of a physician who has treated and examined the patient, though his opinion is based in part upon the "history" given him by the patient. Kansas City Southern R. Co. v. Clinton, 224 F. 896, syl. 5 (C.C.A.1915); Block v. Milwaukee St. Ry. Co., 89 Wis. 371, 61 N.W. 1101, 1102, 27 L.R.A. 365 (1895); 2 Wigmore, Evidence, § 680; Note, 65 A.L.R. 1217, 1223. Many courts, however, have refused to admit opinions so based when the physician-witness examined the patient not for purposes of treatment but solely to prepare himself to testify. Nashville C. & St. L. R. Co. v. York, 127 F.2d 606, syl. 9 (C.C.A.Tenn.1942); Southern Underwriters v. Blair, 144 S.W.2d 641, syl. 14 (Tex.Civ.App.1940); Note, 65 A.L.R. 1217, 1219. And at least one court has even held that

the doctor examining only to prepare himself to testify cannot base his opinion in part upon any reactions or movements of the patient during the examination which could have been simulated. Greinke v. Chicago City R. Co., 234 Ill. 564, 85 N.E. 327, syl. 6 (1908). Such restrictions on the testimony of an expert called to testify seem unjustified. They assume that the greater number of plaintiffs will give an untrue history to the doctor called to testify and that the majority of such doctors will rely on such untrue statements. They assume further that the existence of an interest to falsify is a sufficient reason for exclusion of testimony, which is the philosophy, now discredited, of the common law disqualification of witnesses for interest. See 3 Wigmore, Evidence, § 688, n. 2; Rossman, J., in Reid v. Yellow Cab Co., 131 Ore. 27, 279 P. 635, 67 A.L.R. 1, 7 (1929).

A similar distinction has been made as to the admissibility of evidence of the statements themselves made by the patient to the doctor, as to which see §§ 266, 267, herein.

4. "In making a diagnosis for treatment, physicians must of necessity consider many things that do not appear in sworn proof on the trial of a lawsuit—things that mean much to the trained eye and touch of a skilled medical practitioner. This court has held that it will not close the doors of the courts to the light which is given by a diagnosis which all the rest of the world accepts and acts upon, even if the diagnosis is in part based upon facts which are not established by the sworn testimony in the case to be true." Stevens, J. in Sundquist v. Madison Rys. Co., cited n. 3, supra.

1. See § 14, n. 19, supra.

the hypothesis is the fatal weakness of the practice.[2] The legal writers who have studied the problem seem equally agreed in condemnation.[3] What is the remedy? It seems hardly practicable to require the trial judge to undertake such a preliminary study of the case as would be necessary to enable him to make the selection of the significant facts to be included. It would probably be feasible for such questions to be framed by both counsel in conference with the judge, either at a pre-trial hearing or during the trial, with the jury excluded.[4] But this is wasteful of time and effort. The only remaining expedient is the one generally advocated, namely, that of dispensing with the requirement that the question be accompanied by a recital of an hypothesis, unless the proponent elects to use the hypothetical form, or unless the trial judge in his discretion shall require it.[5] It will be for the cross-examiner to bring out if he so desires, the bases for the expert's opinion.[6] Manifestly, this does not lessen the partisanship of the question or the answer, but it does greatly simplify the examination, and removes the occasion for imperiling the judgment by mistakes in the form of hypothetical questions.

17. Proposals for Improvement of the Practice Relating to Expert Testimony.[1]

In common law countries we have the contentious, or adversary, system of trial, where the opposing parties, and not the judge as in other systems, have the responsibility and initiative in finding and presenting proof.[2] Advantageous as this system is in many respects, its present application in the pro-

---

2. See, e. g., Dr. Wm. A. White, Insanity and the Criminal Law, 56 (1923) ("in a large experience, I have never known a hypothetical question, in a trial involving the mental condition of the defendant, which in my opinion offered a fair presentation of the case"); Dr. Harold S. Hulbert, Psychiatric Testimony in Probate Proceedings, 2 Law & Contemp. Prob. 448, 455 (1935) ("But the present practice of misusing the hypothetical question as restatement of the case to re-impress the jury is bad strategy, though good tactics; bad strategy because it is so unfair, confusing and degrading that it does not clarify the issue nor help achieve justice").

3. See, e. g., 2 Wigmore, Evidence, § 686 ("It is a strange irony that the hypothetical question, which is one of the truly scientific features of the rules of Evidence, should have become that feature which does most to disgust men of science with the law of Evidence."); Judge Learned Hand, New York Bar Association Lectures on Legal Topics, 1921–1922, ("the most horrific and grotesque wen on the fair face of justice").

4. See Hulbert, op. cit., n. 2, who states that the Michigan courts follow this practice.

5. Uniform Rules of Evidence, Rule 58: "Questions calling for the opinion of an expert witness need not be hypothetical in form unless the judge in his discretion so requires, but the witness may state his opinion and reasons therefor without first specifying data on which it is based as an hypothesis or otherwise; but upon cross examination he may be required to specify such data." See also Uniform Act on Expert Testimony, Sec. 9, which is similar.

6. One commentator argues that if the cross-examiner is free, as apparently he would be, to ask hypothetical questions as a means of procuring the expert to "specify" the "data" upon which his inferences were based, all the evils of the hypothetical question are retained. He seems to suggest that the hypothetical form be forbidden on cross-examination, and continues: "If the cross-examiner, in turn, desires an opinion from the expert, the question may be asked in general, non-hypothetical form, leaving the opponent to uncover the propositions upon which the opinion is based. The net effect of such a reform would be to transfer from lawyer to expert the initiative of explaining the opinion, yielding an expression of the expert's opinion upon the living material of the case, rather than upon a hypothetical set of facts, and a probable decrease in confusion of experts by cross-examination —hence, a decrease in confusion of the jury."— Note, The Uniform Expert Testimony Act, 38 Col. L.Rev. 368, 374 (1938).

1. The most comprehensive discussions are to be found in 2 Wigmore, Evidence, § 563; Second Annual Report, New York Law Revision Commission, 795–910 (1936); Expert Testimony (a series of several articles) 2 Law and Contemporary Problems, 401–527 (1935).

2. See R. W. Millar, Legal Procedure, 12 Encyc.Soc. Sc. 439, 450 (1934) where the two principles of party-prosecution and judicial prosecution are contrasted, but it is pointed out that most systems of procedure make use of both principles in some degree.

curement and presentation of expert testimony is widely considered a sore spot in judicial administration. There are two chief points of weakness. The first is the choice of experts by the party, who will naturally be interested in finding, not the best scientist, but the "best witness." As an English judge has said:

> ". . . the mode in which expert evidence is obtained is such as not to give the fair result of scientific opinion to the Court. A man may go, and does sometimes, to half-a-dozen experts . . . He takes their honest opinions, he finds three in his favor and three against him; he says to the three in his favor, 'will you be kind enough to give evidence?' and he pays the three against him their fees and leaves them alone; the other side does the same . . . I am sorry to say the result is that the Court does not get that assistance from the experts which, if they were unbiased and fairly chosen, it would have a right to expect." [3]

The second weakness is that the adversary method of eliciting scientific testimony, by direct and cross-examination in open court, frequently upon hypothetical questions based on a partisan choice of data, is ill-suited to the dispassionate presentation of technical data, and results too often in over-emphasizing conflicts in scientific opinions which a jury is incapable of resolving.[4]

The remedy for the first weakness is not far to seek. It lies simply in using the trial judge's common law power to call experts. Cases are recorded as early as the 14th century—before witnesses were heard by juries —of the summoning of experts by the judges to aid them in determining scientific issues.[5] The existence of the judge's power to call witnesses generally and expert witnesses particularly seems fairly well recognized in this country.[6] It has been declared by statutes in a substantial number of states empowering the trial judge to summon expert witnesses of his own choosing.[7] Some of these statutes apply to scientific issues in any case, civil or criminal,[8] some are limited to criminal cases [9] and a good many to issues of sanity in criminal cases.[10] The principle is implemented in the carefully drafted Model Expert Testimony Act approved in 1937 by

---

3. Jessel, M. R., in Thorn v. Worthington Skating Rink Co., L.R. 6 Ch.D. 415, 416 (1876), note to Plimpton v. Spiller, 6 Ch.D. 412 (1877). See also similar criticisms by Grier, J., in Winans v. N. Y. & Erie R. R., 21 How. 88, 101 (U.S.1858); Henshaw, J., in In re Dolbeer's Estate, 149 Cal. 227, 243, 86 P. 695, 702 (1906) and Cartwright, C. J. in Opp v. Pryor, 294 Ill. 545, 128 N.E. 580 (1920).

4. See criticism cited in notes 1 and 3, supra.

5. Rosenthal, The Development of the Use of Expert Testimony, 2 Law & Contemp.Prob. 403, 406–411 (1935).

6. Kamabalo v. Coelho, 24 Hawaii 689 (1919) (handwriting expert); Fullerton v. Fordyce, 144 Mo. 519, 44 S.W. 1053, syl. 1 (1898) (physician); State v. Horne, 171 N.C. 787, 88 S.E. 433, syl. 1 (1916); 9 Wigmore, Evidence, § 2484; Contra, In re Enoch, [1910] 1 K.B. 337, 332 (denying power of judge to call witnesses in civil cases); People v. Scott, 326 Ill. 327, 157 N.E. 247, 255, syl. 20 (1927) (court's appointment of alienist to examine accused improper); People v. Dickerson, 164 Mich. 148, 129 N.W. 199, syl. 2 (1910) (holding invalid a statute empowering court to appoint alienist-witness in homicide case).

7. See collections of statutes in 2 Wigmore, Evidence, § 563; Note, 38 Col.L.Rev. 369, 370, n. 9. In both these collections are included in addition statutes which provide merely for appointment of experts to examine and report, without authorizing them to testify.

A similar practice has been provided in non-jury cases by rule of court in England since 1934. Rules of Supreme Court, Order 37a (providing that the Court or Judge may appoint, but only on application of a party, a "court expert" to inquire and report upon any question of fact or opinion). The rule has seldom been used. Ann.Prac.1954, 673.

8. Calif.St.1925, c. 156, p. 305 (now C.C.P. § 1871); Rhode Island, Gen.Laws 1938, c. 537, § 20.

9. Florida, Laws 1937, May 17, c. 18412, p. 1347, F.S. A. § 932.30 (felony trials); Wisconsin St.1953, § 357.27.

10. Calif.Penal Code, § 1027; La.Acts 1932, No. 136, LSA–R.S. 15:267 to 15:269; Ohio, R.C. § 2945.40; North Dakota, Laws 1933, c. 216, § 3.

the Commissioners on Uniform State Laws,[11] and embodied in abbreviated form in the Uniform Rules of Evidence.[12] The substance of these proposals, it seems, should be included in the procedural rules of the State and Federal systems.[13]

The Act provides that in any case the court, upon request or of his own motion, may after notice appoint an expert or experts to testify at the trial. It is wisely provided that if the parties agree upon an expert, the Court shall appoint him. The important concession is made to the adversary tradition that the parties, if they give notice, may call additional experts of their own selection. But the jury is to be apprised that the court's expert was so appointed, and it may be expected that his testimony will usually carry decisive weight. This fact, and the substantial expense of employing a private expert not taxable as costs as is the expense of the official expert, make it likely that parties will seldom avail themselves of this power. Nevertheless, it stands as a wise safeguard against arbitrary or mistaken opinions of the court's witness.

It is not only essential to reduce the partisan element in the selection of experts, but it is equally important that the contentious character of the presentation of the results of the expert's investigation be modified. Otherwise, the "battle of experts" might merely evolve into a battle of examiner and cross-examiner in the interrogation of the official expert at the trial. Experience has shown that in some kinds of controversies a well-devised plan of scientific investigation and report can operate to reduce greatly the need for contested trials in court.[14] The Uniform Act, accordingly, provides that at the request of the court or a party, the experts shall make such inspection and examination of the person or subject matter involved in the case as may be necessary, and that each expert may be required to file a report under oath, which shall be subject to inspection. Furthermore, it is provided that the court may require a conference of the experts, whether chosen by the court or the parties, so that they may as far as possible resolve together, in the light of the knowledge and observations of all of them, their differences of view and their difficulties in interpreting the data. Often this may result in a complete agreement which may practically settle the issue for the parties. If not, it will at least make clear the area of agreement and may narrow the controversy within manageable limits. Two or more experts,

---

11. The Act, is set out in 1937 Handbook, Nat'l. Conf.Com'rs on Unif.St.Laws, pp. 339–348 and in 9 Unif.L.Ann. 427.

12. Rule 59: "If the judge determines that the appointment of expert witnesses in an action may be desirable, he shall order the parties to show cause why expert witnesses should not be appointed, and after opportunity for hearing may request nominations and appoint one or more such witnesses. If the parties agree in the selection of an expert or experts, only those agreed upon shall be appointed. Otherwise the judge may make his own selection. An expert witness shall not be appointed unless he consents to act. The judge shall determine the duties of the witness and inform him thereof at a conference in which the parties shall have an opportunity to participate. A witness so appointed shall advise the parties of his findings, if any, and may thereafter be called to testify by the judge or any party. He may be examined and cross-examined by each party. This rule shall not

limit the parties in calling expert witnesses of their own selection and at their own expense." This rule is based on Rule 28 of the Federal Rules of Criminal Procedure. See also Model Code of Evidence, Rules 402–410.

13. The Model Act has been adopted in South Dakota by Supreme Court Rule, Order No. 5, 1942, 9 Unif.L.Ann. 427.

14. This has been conspicuously illustrated in respect to the insanity issue in criminal cases. In states where the statutes provide for the examination by psychiatrists of persons charged with serious crimes, the tendency has been for the prosecution, the defendant and the court to acquiesce in the expert's conclusions. See Weihofen, An Alternative to the Battle of Experts: Hospital Examination of Criminal Defendants Before Trial, 2 Law & Contemp.Prob. 419, 422, (1935); Overholser, The History and Operation of the Briggs Law of Massachusetts, 2 id. 436, 444.

it is provided, may join in a single report. At the trial, moreover, the individual report of the expert witness, or a joint report, may be read to the court and jury as a part of his testimony, and he may be cross-examined thereon. As previously stated,[15] the Act dispenses with the requirement of the use of the hypothetical question.

The Act likewise endeavors to protect the impartiality of the court's expert by providing that his fees shall be fixed by the court and taxed as costs and by prohibiting the payment to him of additional compensation. Court-appointed experts in criminal cases are to be paid by the public authority. The compensation of the party's expert in any case is to be defrayed by the party and is not taxable as costs.

There are other features of the common law procedure not dealt with in the Uniform Act which greatly hamper the effectiveness of expert testimony. Among these are, first, the unsuitability of the jury, a body of twelve laymen usually required to be unanimous, as a tribunal for appraising scientific evidence; second, the rules of privilege, especially the physician-patient privilege and the privilege against self-crimination,[16] and third, the occasional employment by the courts of standards of liability, which do not accord with the scientific standards which the experts are accustomed to use as criteria, as in the case of the "understanding of right and wrong" test of responsibility of insane persons.[17]

Finally, it should be borne in mind that the need for better employment by the courts of the resources of technicians and scientists goes beyond the use of expert witnesses. A judge has said:

"The methods of courts might well be supplemented by the use of well tested examples of administrative tribunals, of expert investigators acting for the court—engineers, scientists, physicians, economic and social investigators, as needed—in addition to, not in substitute for, similar experts acting for the parties . . .

"Why should not judge and jury in cases involving multitudinous scientific exhibits, or scientific questions, have the benefit of the assistance of those competent to organize such data and analyze such questions? Why should not courts have adequate fact finding facilities for all kinds of cases? Boards of directors do. Administrative tribunals do. The parties, and in a large sense the public, have an interest in the decision of cases on whole truth, not on partial understanding. The machinery and expert staffs developed by the interstate commerce commission, state public service commissions, and workmen's compensation boards have values for fact finding which may profitably be studied in reference to judicial reorganization . . ."[18]

The judicial tradition has known an abundance of procedures which are well adapted to the utilizing of the services and knowledge of experts. Most important is the power, often regulated by statute but in any event presumably one of the latent, "inherent" judicial powers,[19] namely, that of referring a question to a master, referee, auditor or simi-

---

15. See § 16, n. 5.

16. See Morgan, Suggested Remedy for Obstructions to Expert Testimony by Rules of Evidence, 10 U. Chi.L.Rev. 284, 286 (1943).

17. Weihofen, Insanity as a Defense in Criminal Law, 64–68, 409–418 (1933).

18. Mr. Justice Harold M. Stephens, What Courts can Learn from Commissions, 21 Am.Bar Asso.J. 141, 142 (1933).

19. See the statesmanlike opinion of Brandeis, J. in Ex parte Peterson, 253 U.S. 300, 312, 40 S.Ct. 543, 64 L.Ed. 919 (1919) (District Court may appoint auditor with provision that his report shall be used in evidence. "Courts have (at least in the absence of legislation to the contrary) inherent power to provide themselves with appropriate instruments required for the performance of their duties. Compare Stockbridge Iron Co. v. Cone Iron Works, 102 Mass. 80, 87–90. This power includes authority to appoint persons unconnected with the court to aid judges in the performance of specific judicial duties, as they may arise in the progress of a cause.")

lar officer, standing or special. The reference may contemplate merely an investigation and report, or a hearing followed by a report or a preliminary decision.[20] In England, moreover, the judge has long been empowered in admiralty cases to sit with assessors, who may be experts, who will advise him as to technical questions.[21] A recent writer has urged that these traditional procedures be more widely used and more effectively prescribed by statute.[22] He suggests likewise with much force that the courts make wider use of the technical resources of the sister branch of the government, the administrative commissions.[23] It may be predicted that all of these opportunities of the courts for using expert knowledge less clumsily than in a duel before the jury will be more widely employed in the future. They will not merely be useful as aids to a more intelligent final trial of the issue, but they will more and more often render such trial unnecessary.

18. Application of the Opinion Rule to Out of Court Statements.

Does the opinion rule apply to statements made out of court, and offered in court under some exception to the hearsay rule? The question has received little consideration by the textwriters and by the courts. If we accept the traditional view[1] that the opinion rule is a categorical rule of exclusion, rejecting a certain clearly definable type of evidence, it is natural to assume that if this kind of evidence is excluded when elicited from a witness on the stand, it should also be rejected when offered in the form of the repetition in court of what some narrator has said out of court. Consequently, most of the decisions simply discuss the admissibility of opinions contained in hearsay declarations as if they had been given by a witness on the stand, and reject or admit them accordingly,[2] although common sense doubtless has an unspoken influence toward a more liberal treatment of the out-of-court opinions. If on the other hand we adopt the view to which the courts seem now to be tending, namely, that the opinion rule is not an absolute rule of exclusion, but rather a relative rule for the examination of witnesses, preferring when it is feasible the more concrete form of examination to the more general and inferential,[3] then it becomes obvious that it has no sensible application to statements made out of court. Sustaining an objection to counsel's question to a witness as calling for an "opinion" is usually not a serious matter since counsel can in most cases easily reframe the question to call for the more concrete statement. But to reject the statement of the out-of-court narrator of what he observed, made in a dying declaration, for example, on the ground that it is too general in form to meet the courtroom rules of interrogation mistakes the function of the opinion rule and may shut out altogether a valuable item of proof. Some of the cases, and Mr. Wigmore, have taken this view as to admissions,[4] and

---

20. Beuscher, The Use of Experts by the Courts, 54 Harv.L.Rev. 1105, 1111–1120 (1941). A doctor has suggested that there should be a routine reference to a medical master of all personal injury and other cases having medical issues, for investigation and report. The report would be received as evidence at the trial. Koerner, Diagnosis and Treatment of Legal Congestion, 22 J.Am.Jud.Soc. 168 (1939).

21. Beuscher, op. cit., at p. 1108–1111. See Rules Supreme Court, Order 36, R. 2, Ann.Prac.1954, 589, making this method of trial available in any case tried without a jury.

22. Beuscher, op. cit., at p. 1126.

23. Id. at 1123.

1. See § 11, supra.

2. E. g., Philpot v. Comm., 195 Ky. 555, 242 S.W. 839, syl. 2, 3, 25 A.L.R. 1367 (1922), with note, dying declarations involving an opinion or conclusion; Pendleton v. Comm., 131 Va. 676, 109 S.E. 201, syl. 5 (1929) (dying declaration); Henry v. Seattle Elec. Co., 55 Wash. 444, 104 P. 776, syl. 5 (1909) (spontaneous declaration after accident, "This motorman is green at the business" excluded).

3. See §§ 11, 12, supra.

4. Swain v. Oregon Motor Lines, 160 Ore. 1, 82 P.2d 1084, 118 A.L.R. 1225 (1938) (statement by injured

it is believed that it will prevail as to the other classes of declarations coming in under exceptions to the hearsay rule.[5]

Of course, the speciously similar question of the want of personal knowledge of the declarant should be distinguished. If it appears that the out-of-court declarant had not observed at first hand the fact declared, this goes not to form but to substance and is usually fatal to admissibility if the statement is offered to prove the fact.[6]

---

party after collision that he considered driver of other car to blame) with note, admissions involving matters of opinion; 4 Wigmore, Evidence, § 1053(3), and see § 241, herein. Compare the similar problem presented in respect to evidence of inconsistent statements to impeach, see § 35, infra.

[5] As to dying declarations see § 262, herein.

[6] See §§ 262, 277, and 286.

CHAPTER 4

CROSS–EXAMINATION AND SUBSEQUENT EXAMINATIONS

19. The Right of Cross-Examination:[1] Effect of Deprivation of Opportunity to Cross-Examine.

The common law judges and lawyers for two centuries have regarded the opportunity of cross-examination as an essential safeguard of the accuracy and completeness of testimony,[2] and they have insisted that cross-examination is a right[3] and not a mere privilege.[4] This right is available, of course, upon the taking of depositions, as well as on the examination of witnesses at the trial.[5]

This premise that the opportunity of cross-examination is an essential safeguard is the principal justification for the exclusion generally of hearsay statements,[6] and for the admission as an exception to the hearsay rule of reported testimony taken at a former hearing when the present adversary was afforded the opportunity to cross-examine.[7] Similarly, the constitutional provisions guaranteeing to the accused the right of confrontation have been interpreted as merely codifying this right of cross-examination.[8]

---

1. As to cross-examination, generally, see Wigmore, Evidence, vol. 5, §§ 1390–1394, vol. 6, §§ 1884–1894; Dec.Dig. Witnesses, ☞266–284; 70 C.J., Witnesses, §§ 779–850; 58 Am.Jur., Witnesses, §§ 609–673.

2. See 5 Wigmore, Evidence, § 1367. See also Hungate v. Hudson, 353 Mo. 944, 185 S.W.2d 646, syl. 6, 157 A.L.R. 598 (1945).

3. Alford v. United States, 282 U.S. 687, 691, 51 S. Ct. 218, syl. 1, 75 L.Ed. 624 (1931).

4. Resurrection Gold Min. Co. v. Fortune Gold Min. Co., 129 F. 668, 674 (C.C.A.Col. 1904).

5. State v. Guardian Realty Co., 237 Ala. 201, 186 So. 168, syl. 9, 121 A.L.R. 634 (1939).

6. See § 224.

7. See §§ 230, 231.

8. State v. Crooker, 123 Me. 310, 122 A. 865, syl. 3, 33 A.L.R. 821 (1923) (confrontation right does not mean merely that accused shall see the witness, but the right to cross-examine) and see § 231.

What are the consequences of a denial or failure of the right? There are several common situations.[9] First, when a party testifying on his own behalf unjustifiably refuses to answer questions necessary to a complete cross-examination. Here it is generally agreed that the adversary is entitled to have the direct testimony stricken out,[10] and this seems clearly warranted. Second, a non-party witness similarly refuses to be cross-examined, or to answer proper questions of the cross-examiner. Here the case is a little less clear, but the expressions of judges and writers seem to sanction the same remedy of excluding the direct.[11] This minimizes the temptation for the party to procure the witness's refusal, a collusion which is often hard to prove, but perhaps a better rule would be to exclude unless the party calling the witness can clearly satisfy the judge that he did not induce the refusal.[12] Third, the witness becomes, or purports to become, sick or otherwise physically or mentally incapacitated, before cross-examination is begun or completed. Many of such cases arouse suspicion of simulation, particularly when the witness is a party, and as to the party-witness the remedy of excluding the direct is generally allowed.[13] In the case of the non-party witness, the same result is usually reached,[14] but it seems that it should be qualified so that the judge would exclude unless he is clearly convinced that the incapacity is genuine in which event he should let the direct testimony stand,[15] but should be authorized to explain to the jury the weakness of such un-cross-examined evidence.[16] The fourth situation is that of the death of the witness before the cross-examination. Here again it is usually said that the party thus deprived of cross-examination is entitled to have the direct testimony stricken,[17] unless, presumably, the death occurred during a postponement of the cross-examination consented to or procured by him.[18] In case of death there seems no adequate reason for excluding the direct

---

9. See the analyses of these problems in 5 Wigmore, Evidence, § 1390, and in Notes, 27 Col.L.Rev. 327 (1927), 35 Calif.L.Rev. 299.

10. People v. McGowan, 80 Cal.App. 293, 251 P. 643, syl. 3 (1926) (direct testimony of accused to an alibi stricken when on cross-examination he refused to answer question as to name of person who was with him at the time); Aluminum Industries, Inc. v. Egan, 61 Ohio App. 111, 22 N.E.2d 459, syl. 7 (direct testimony of party-witness, refusing to answer pertinent cross-questions on unjustified ground of privilege); 70 C.J. Witnesses, § 789; Dec.Dig. Witnesses, ⚓284. Seemingly the cross-examiner could invoke the court's action to compel the witness to answer, but is not required to do so.

11. State v. Davis, 236 Iowa 740, 19 N.W.2d 655, syl. 4 (1945) (but here held that full opportunity was later accorded); Hadra v. Utah Nat. Bank, 9 Utah 412, 414, 35 P. 508, syl. 2 (1894) (deposition properly excluded for witness's refusal to answer material cross-question); 5 Wigmore, Evidence, § 1391; 70 C.J. Witnesses, § 789.

12. Or it may be desirable simply to leave it to the judge's discretion. See Stephan v. United States, 133 F.2d 87, syl. 17, 18 (1943) (refusal to answer only a few of the cross-questions, judge in discretion properly refused to strike direct testimony); Moormeister v. Golding, 84 Utah 324, 27 P.2d 447 (1933) (whether deposition should be excluded for

witness's failure to answer a question under notary's prompting, in judge's discretion).

13. See, e. g., Louisville & N. R. Co. v. Gregory, 284 Ky. 297, 144 S.W.2d 519, syl. 1–4 (1940) (plaintiff suing for personal injuries testified from a cot and on cross-examination professed to be unable to proceed; judge refused to strike direct but offered to let defendant use cross-examination taken at former trial, which the defendant declined to do; held error to refuse to strike).

14. Wray v. State, 154 Ala. 36, 45 So. 697, syl. 3 (1908); People v. Cole, 43 N.Y. 508, 512 (1871).

15. Unless of course the incapacity is temporary in which event a mistrial or adjournment might be an available expedient.

16. This is suggested in the Note, 27 Col.L.Rev. 327 (1927).

17. Kemble v. Lyons, 184 Iowa 804, 169 N.W. 117, syl. 1, 2 (1918); Sperry v. Moore's Estate, 42 Mich. 361, 4 N.W. 13 (1880) (death during continuance procured by direct examiner); State v. Bingham, 133 S.C. 491, 131 S.E. 603, syl. 10 (1926); In re Sweeney's Estate, 248 Wis. 607, 22 N.W.2d 657, syl. 3 (1946) (right of cross-examination specially reserved by judge); 70 C.J. Witnesses, § 788.

18. See 5 Wigmore, § 1390, n. 5. The cases cited there, however, are cases of disabilities other than death.

testimony. It has been suggested that exclusion of the direct should be discretionary [19] but no matter how valuable cross-examination may be, common sense tells us that the half-loaf of direct testimony is better than no bread at all.[20] This was the accepted practice in equity.[21] It is submitted that the judge should let the direct testimony stand but should be required on request to instruct the jury in weighing its value to consider the lack of opportunity to cross-examine.

It has been held where the incapacity is temporary, that the cross-examiner may not insist upon immediate exclusion of the direct testimony, but must be content with the offer of a later opportunity to cross-examine even when this makes it necessary for him to submit to a mistrial.[22] It has been assumed in the preceding paragraphs that though some cross-questions may have been answered, a failure to secure a complete cross-examination would be treated as if cross-examination had been wholly denied. It seems, however, that a cross-examination though cut off before it is finished may yet under the circumstances be found to have been so substantially complete as to satisfy the requirement of opportunity to cross-examine,[23] or failing that it may be regarded in the particular situation as having been sufficient cross-examination as to part of the direct testimony so that such part may stand though the rest must be stricken.[24]

The infringement of the right of cross-examination, however, may come, not from the refusal or inability of the witness, but from the action of the judge. The judge, as we shall see, has wide discretionary control over the *extent* of cross-examination upon particular topics, but the denial of cross-examinations altogether, or its arbitrary curtailment, upon a proper subject of cross-examination will be ground for reversal [25] if the ruling appears to have been substantially harmful.[26]

20. Form of Interrogation

In contrast with direct examination, the form of questions upon cross-examination is usually and properly leading.[1] The cross-examiner's purpose in the main is to weaken the effect of the direct testimony and the witness is usually a more or less uncooperative one, and consequently the danger of undue acquiescence in the examiner's suggestions is not ordinarily present. When it appears that the witness is biased in favor of the cross-examiner, and likely to be unduly yielding to the suggestions of leading ques-

---

19. 5 Wigmore, Evidence, § 1390, p. 110 ("But the true solution would be to avoid any inflexible rule, and to leave it to the trial judge to admit the direct examination so far as the loss of cross-examination can be shown to him to be not in that instance a material loss") quoted approvingly in Kubin v. Chicago Title and Trust Co., 307 Ill.App. 12, 29 N.E.2d 859, 863 (1940) (ruling excluding direct examination affirmed in absence of showing of prejudice), Notes, 29 Ill.B.J. 29, 19 Chi-Kent L.Rev. 190.

20. See Note, 27 Col.L.Rev. 327 (1927) which points out that the testimony is more trustworthy than evidence admitted under many of the established hearsay exceptions.

21. See Scott v. McCann, 76 Md. 47, 24 A. 536, syl. 2 (1892).

22. Gale v. State, 135 Ga. 351, 69 S.E. 537, syl. 2 (1910) (where witness collapsed on defendant's cross-examination, no error in refusing to strike out the evidence when defendant declined to consent to mistrial).

23. Fuller v. Rice, 70 Mass. (4 Gray) 343 (1855).

24. See Curtice v. West, 50 Hun 47, 48, 2 N.Y.S. 507, syl. 2 (1888) and compare In re Mezger's Estate, 154 Misc. 633, 278 N.Y.S. 669, syl. 1, 2 (1935).

25. Alford v. United States, 282 U.S. 687, 51 S.Ct. 218, 75 L.Ed. 624 (1931) (refusal to permit cross-examination of government witness about his present residence); Fahey v. Clark, 125 Conn. 44, 3 A.2d 313, syl. 4-6 (1938) (refusal to permit cross-examination of plaintiff about prior injury).

26. State v. Talamante, 50 N.M. 6, 165 P.2d 812, syl. 5, 6 (1946) (erroneous restriction here not prejudicial).

1. Ewing v. United States, 135 F.2d 633, syl. 8 (App. D.C.1943); In re Mitgang, 385 Ill. 311, 52 N.E.2d 807, syl. 9 (1944); 3 Wigmore, Evidence, § 773; Dec.Dig.Witnesses, ⬤➞282.

tions the judge may restrain the asking of such questions,[2] and in those jurisdictions where the scope of cross-examination is limited, if the examiner goes beyond the proper field of cross-examination he may be required to refrain from leading the witness.[3]

21. Scope of Cross-Examination: Restriction to Matters Opened up on Direct: The Various Rules [1]

The practice varies widely in the different jurisdictions on the question whether the cross-examiner is confined in his questions to the subjects testified about in the direct examination, and if so to what extent.

The traditional rule of wide-open cross-examination. In England and in about one-fifth of the states, the simplest and freest practice prevails. In these jurisdictions, the cross-examiner is not limited at all to the topics which the direct examiner has chosen to open,[2] but is free to cross-examine about any subject relevant to any of the issues in the entire case, including if he chooses facts relating solely to the cross-examiner's own case or affirmative defence.

The "restrictive" rule, in various forms, limiting cross-examination to the scope of the direct. The Federal courts and the majority of the states agree in the general view that the cross-examination must be limited to the matters testified to on the direct examination.[3] This doctrine can be employed narrowly to restrict the cross-questions to

---

2. Moody v. Rowell, 34 Mass. 490, 498 (1835) ("So a judge may, in his discretion, prohibit certain leading questions from being put to an adversary's witness, where the witness shows a strong interest or bias in favor of the cross-examining party, and needs only an intimation, to say whatever is most favorable to that party."); 3 Wigmore, Evidence, § 773. See Tolomeo v. Harmony Short Line Motor Transport Co., 349 Pa. 420, 37 A.2d 511, syl. 3 (1944) (in collision case where plaintiff called defendant's bus driver to show defendant's ownership, court improperly permitted defendant to cross-examine driver by leading questions on negligence). But it is a matter of discretion. Lauchheimer v. Jacobs, 126 Ga. 261, 55 S.E. 55, syl. 2 (1906); Westland Housing Corp. v. Scott, 312 Mass. 375, 44 N. E.2d 959, syl. 13 (1942). Both are cases of a party called by his adversary and cross-examined by his own counsel.

3. People v. Melone, 71 Cal.App.2d 291, 162 P.2d 505, syl. 9 (1945).

1. See 6 Wigmore, Evidence, §§ 1886–1891; Dec. Dig. Witnesses, ☞269; 70 C.J. Witnesses, §§ 818–827; Notes, general, 37 Col.L.Rev. 1373 (1937), 24 Iowa L.Rev. 564 (1939); local, 2 Ark.L.Rev. 212 (1948), 30 Ky.L.J. 317 (1942), 32 Ill.L.Rev. 71 (1937), 10 Tulane L.Rev. 294 (1936).

2. Mayor and Corporation of Berwick-on-Tweed v. Murray, 19 L.J.Ch. 281, 286 (V.C., 1850); Morgan v. Brydges, 2 Stark. 314, 171 Eng.Rep. 657 (N.P.1818) (witness called by plaintiff for formal proof, may be cross-examined by defendant, his employer, on the whole case); Carter v. State, 191 Ala. 3, 67 So. 981, syl. 4 (1915); Ariz. Rules of Civil Procedure, rule 43(b), A.C.A.1939, § 21–922 ("Any witness may be cross-examined on any matter material to the case"); Podol v. Jacobs, 65 Ariz. 50, 173 P.2d 758, 764 (1946) ("This [Code 1939, § 21–922] now commits us to the English rule"); Ficken v. Atlanta, 114 Ga. 970, 41 S.E. 58, syl. 1 (1902); LSA–R.S. 15:376 (a witness who "has testified to a single fact . . . may be cross-examined upon the whole case"); King v. Atkins, 33 La.Ann. 1057, 1064 (1881); Falmouth v. Windham, 63 Me. 44 (1873); Moody v. Rowell, 34 Mass. 490 (1835) (leading case, opinion by Shaw, C. J.); Mask v. State, 32 Miss. 405 (1856); State v. West, 349 Mo. 221, 161 S.W.2d 966, syl. 2–4 (1942) (citing statutes permitting cross-examination "on the entire case" except in case of cross-examination of the accused, or the spouse of accused, in a criminal case); State v. Huskins, 209 N.C. 727, 184 S.E. 480, syl. 1 (1936); State v. Howard, 35 S.C. 197, 14 S.E. 481, syl. 2 (1892); Sands v. Southern Ry. Co., 108 Tenn. 1, 64 S.W. 478, syl. 2 (1901); Grocers' Supply Co. v. Stuckey, 152 S.W.2d 911, syl. 2 (Tex.Civ.App.1941, error refused); Wentworth v. Crawford, 11 Tex. 127, 132 (1853); and cases cited 70 C.J. 661, note 89. Recent Michigan opinions seem also to approve this "wide-open" liberty of cross-examination. See, e. g., Spillman v. Weimaster, 279 Mich. 93, 271 N.W. 564 (as applied to adversary's employee called by plaintiff for cross-examination under statute); Waller v. Sloan, 225 Mich. 600, 196 N.W. 347, syl. 3 (1923) (same). But Michigan is sometimes classed as espousing a slightly more restrictive practice halting at the cross-examiner's own case or defense. 6 Wigmore, Evidence, §§ 1889, 1890; Note, 24 Iowa L.Rev. 564 (1939).

3. Among the leading cases which served to introduce this innovation upon common law practice were Ellmaker v. Buckley, 16 S. & R. 72, 77 (Pa., 1827), People v. Horton, 4 Mich. 67, 82 (1856), and Phil-

those relating only to the same acts or facts,[4] and, perhaps, those occurring or appearing at the same time and place. The doctrine is most frequently formulated in a way to suggest this meaning. Thus, the cross-examination is said to be limited to "the same points" brought out on direct,[5] to the "matters testified to,"[6] to the "subjects mentioned,"[7] and the like. Slightly more expansive is the extension to "facts and circumstances connected with" the matters stated on direct,[8] but this still suggests the requirement of identity of transaction, and proximity in time and space. Seemingly a much wider extension is accomplished by another variation of the formula. This is the statement that the cross-examination is limited to the matters opened in direct and to facts tending "to explain, contradict, or discredit the testimony given in chief,"[9] and even more widely, facts tending to rebut any "inference or deduction" from the matters testified on direct.[10] There is little consistency in the use of particular formulas or their variations.[11] All express criteria too vague to be employed with precision.

All of these limiting formulae have a common escape-valve, namely, the notion that where part of a transaction, "res gestæ," contract or conversation has been revealed on direct, the remainder may be brought out on cross-examination.[12] The fact that this is

adelphia & Trenton R. Co. v. Stimpson, 14 Pet. 448, 461, 10 L.Ed. 535 (1840, by Story, J.).

4. See, e. g., State v. Guilfoyle, 109 Conn. 124, 145 A. 761, syl. 11 (1929) (doctor testified to general description of wound, cross-examination as to opinion whether wound caused by near or far shot properly excluded); Wheeler & Wilson Mfg. Co. v. Barrett, 172 Ill. 610, 50 N.E. 325, syl. 1 (1898) (plaintiff testified she bought and paid for sewing machine from defendant, cross-examination designed to show she took possession under written lease contract properly excluded); McNeely v. Conlon, 216 Iowa 796, 248 N.W. 17, syl. 2-6 (1933) (eye-witness described accident, prejudicial error to permit defendant on cross to elicit that witness just after and at scene said to defendant, "It was not your fault").

5. Carey v. City of Oakland, 44 Cal.App.2d 503, 112 P.2d 714, syl. 1 (1941).

6. McAden v. State, 155 Fla. 523, 21 So.2d 33, syl. 4 (1945); Nadeau v. Texas Co., 104 Mont. 558, 69 P. 2d 586, syl. 22 (1937).

7. State v. Bagley, 339 Mo. 215, 96 S.W.2d 331, syl. 11 (1936).

8. Story, J., in Philadelphia & Trenton R. Co. v. Stimpson, 14 Pet. 448, 461, 10 L.Ed. 535 (1840); Austin v. State, 14 Ark. 555, 563 (1854); Williams v. State, 32 Fla. 315, 317, 13 So. 834 (1893). ". . . but if he [defendant] offers himself as a witness, he may be cross-examined by the counsel for the people as to all matters about which he was examined in chief . . . ." Cal.Pen.Code (Deering, 1931) § 1323; Ariz.Rev.Code Ann. (Struckmeyer, 1928) § 5179; Nev.Comp.Laws (Hillyer, 1929) § 11253; N.C.Code Ann. (Michie, 1935) § 1799; Va.Code (Michie, 1936) § 4778; Utah Rev.Stat.Ann. (1933) § 105–45–5; Wash.Rev.Stat.Ann. (Remington, 1932) § 2148; W.

Va.Code (1931) § 57–3–6. Note, 37 Col.L.Rev. 1373, 1380, n. 51 (1937).

9. Krametbauer v. McDonald, 44 N.M. 473, 104 P.2d 900, syl. 7 (1940); Thompson v. State, 73 Okl.Cr. 72, 118 P.2d 269, syl. 3, 4 (1941).

10. A leading case for this view is Conley v. Mervis, 324 Pa. 577, 188 A. 350, 108 A.L.R. 160 (1936) (suit for damages for injury caused by a truck; defendant denies ownership; plaintiff calls defendant as witness and proves on direct that defendant owned license-plates on truck; held, error to refuse to permit defendant to be cross-examined by his own counsel to show the plates were taken from his place of business without his knowledge or consent; this was allowable to rebut the inference of ownership of the truck and agency of the driver which would be derived from ownership of the plates). So also Crosby v. Deland District, 367 Ill. 362, 11 N.E.2d 937, syl. 3 (1937); State v. Harvey, 130 Iowa 394, 106 N.W. 938, syl. 4 (1906); Eno v. Adair County Mutual Ins. Ass'n, 229 Iowa 249, 294 N.W. 323, syl. 1 (1940); and cases cited in Note, 108 A.L.R. 167.

11. See Note, 37 Col.L.Rev. 1373, 1375, 1381 (1937).

12. Gilmer v. Higley, 110 U.S. 47, 3 S.Ct. 471, 28 L.Ed. 62, syl. 1 (1884) (transaction); Hatfield v. Levy Bros., 18 Cal.2d 798, 117 P.2d 841, syl. 24, 25 (1941) (conversation); Ah Doon v. Smith, 25 Ore. 89, 34 P. 1093, syl. 1 (1893) (transaction); Glenn v. Philadelphia & W. C. Traction Co., 206 Pa. 135, 139, 55 A. 860, syl. 3 (1903) (conversation); Smith v. Philadelphia Traction Co., 202 Pa. 54, 51 A. 345, syl. 2 (1902) (res gestæ); Vingi v. Trillo, 77 R.I. 55, 73 A.2d 43, syl. 3 (1950) (conversation); Note, 37 Col.L.Rev. 1373, 1376 (1937); Dec.Dig., Witnesses, ⊜268(3). But see In re Campbell's Will, 100 Vt. 395, 138 A. 725, 726 (1927) (will-contest: proponents placed wit-

substantially a mere statement of the converse of the limiting rule itself does not detract from its usefulness as an added tool for argument.

The half-open door: cross-examination extends to any matters except cross-examiner's affirmative case. A third view as to the scope of cross-examination takes a middle course between the two extremes. Under this view the cross-examiner may question the witness about any matters relevant to any issue in the action, except facts relating only to the cross-examiner's own affirmative case, such as defendant's affirmative defences or cross-claims, or in case of a plaintiff, his new matter in reply.[13] This rather liberalized standard has in some instances served as a half-way house, for a time, for courts which later have turned to the "wide-open" practice.[14] It has the merit, as compared with the restrictive practice, of lessening dispute

by widening the ambit of examination. Its drawback is that it is often difficult to determine, particularly under the liberal pleading rules of today, whether the matter inquired about does relate solely to the examiner's "distinct grounds of defense or avoidance."[15]

22. Cross-Examination to Impeach not Limited to the Scope of the Direct

One of the main functions of cross-examination is to afford an opportunity to elicit answers which will impeach the veracity, capacity to observe, impartiality and consistency of the witness. This, of course, is for the purpose of shaking the credibility of his direct testimony, but the direct could seldom be expected to touch explicitly on the points to which impeachment is directed. Accordingly, the rule prevails, even in jurisdictions adopting the restrictive practice, that cross-examination to impeach is not, in general,

---

ness on stand who testified that Mrs. Campbell told her that instrument claimed to be will was in trunk; contestants were allowed to bring out on cross-examination that Mrs. Campbell told her on same occasion that she wanted her husband to destroy the instrument; held, error, but harmless. "The fact that the proponents had, in effect, put in evidence a part of a statement of Mrs. Campbell, did not, of itself, entitle the contestants to put in all of that statement. The latter could give in evidence whatever Mrs. Campbell then said that tended to qualify, explain, or contradict what Mrs. Stevens had testified to, but no more."). See Williams v. Graff, 194 Md. 516, 71 A.2d 450, 453, syl. 3, 4, 6 (1950) (officer testifying on direct to observation at scene of accident, including pool of blood, could be cross-examined about skid-marks, which were not mentioned on direct. "Where a general subject has been entered upon in the examination in chief, the cross-examining counsel may ask any relevant questions on the general subject.")

13. Legg v. Drake, 1 Ohio St. 286, 290 (1853) (party may cross-examine "as to all matters pertinent to the issue on the trial; limited, however, by the rule that a party cannot, before the time of opening his own case introduce his distinct grounds of defense or avoidance" by cross-examination); Smith v. State, 125 Ohio St. 695, syl. 1 (1932); Dietsch v. Mayberry, 70 Ohio App. 527, 47 N.E.2d 404, syl. 5 (1942). Ohio seems to be the principal, if not the only, present-day stronghold of this practice,

The objection that the cross-examination elicits matter proper only to the cross-examiner's own case is often given as a ground of decision in states that follow the more restrictive practice limiting the cross to the scope of the direct. See, e. g., Haines v. Snedigar, 110 Cal. 18, 42 P. 462, syl. 1 (1895), and cases cited, 5 Jones, Evidence, § 2342 (2d ed. 1926). But even under the more restrictive view, if the matter is opened in direct, it may be followed up in cross-examination, though this may happen to sustain the cross-examiner's affirmative claim or defense. Garlich v. Northern Pac. Ry. Co., 131 F. 837, syl. 1 (C.C.A.Minn.1904); Jones, as cited above.

14. See, e. g., Allison v. Chandler, 10 Mich. 460, 476 (1862) where this standard is perhaps first adumbrated, when Campbell, J., in sustaining the propriety of cross-questions said, "They were designed to determine the real character of the transaction in issue. They did not relate to matter in avoidance of it. . . ." See also Rush v. French, 1 Ariz. 99, 139, 140, 25 P. 816, 828 (1874) (witness may be cross-examined "upon all matters pertinent to the case of the party calling him, except exclusively new matter; and nothing shall be deemed new matter except it be such as could not be given under a general denial"). Michigan and Arizona now seem to adopt the "wide-open" practice, see cases cited in note 2, above.

15. See discussion in Note, 37 Col.L.Rev. 1373, 1382 (1937).

limited to matters brought out in the direct examination.[1]

23. Practical Consequences of the Restrictive Rules: Effect on Order of Proof: Side-Effects

It is sometimes asserted that the only "essential" difference between the "wide-open" and the restrictive rules as to scope of cross-examination is in the time or stage at which the witness may be called upon to testify to the facts inquired about.[1] Thus under the "wide-open" rule the witness may be questioned on the new matter on cross-examination, whereas under the restrictive rules the cross-examiner can merely postpone the questions until his own next stage [2] of putting on proof, and then call him and prove the same facts.[3] This is, of course, a substantial difference, but a mere postponement of the questions is probably not the usual result of a ruling excluding a cross-question as not in the scope of the direct. Most often, unless the question is vital and he is fairly confident of a favorable answer, the cross-examiner will not call the adversary's wit-

ness at a later stage as his own, but will abandon the inquiry. Getting concessions from the opponent's witness while his story is fresh is worth trying for. To call the perhaps unfriendly witness later when his first story is stale is usually a much less effective expedient.

A ruling excluding questions as not within the scope of the direct is not, however, the only consequence of the restrictive rule. There are many collateral effects. Thus the courts adopting the restrictive practice, often say that if the cross-examiner, perhaps without objection, cross-examines on new matter he makes the witness his own.[4] This being so, he is normally forbidden to ask leading questions about such new matter,[5] and under the traditional rule against impeaching one's own witness[6] is precluded from impeaching the witness as to such facts.[7] Furthermore, the application of the restrictive rule so as to exclude unfavorable testimony from the plaintiff's witness which could otherwise be elicited on cross-examination, may save the plaintiff from a directed verdict at the close of his case in chief.[8] This is usually a tacti-

---

[1.] Chicago City Ry. Co. v. Carroll, 206 Ill. 318, 324, 69 N.E. 523, 525 (1903) (cross-question to doctor as to who paid him); Dickey v. Wagoner, 160 Kan. 216, 160 P.2d 698, syl. 10 (1945) (discretionary to permit impeaching cross-examination upon matters not touched in direct); Kennamer v. State, 59 Okl.Cr. 146, 57 P.2d 646, 659 (1936) (cross-examination about prior contradictory statements); Dayton v. Fenno, 99 Ore. 137, 195 P. 154, syl. 3 (1921) (rule stated, not applicable on the facts); Beck v. Hood, 185 Pa. 32, 38, 39 A. 842, 843 (1898) (that witness had talked at previous trial with foreman of jury); 6 Wigmore, Evidence, § 1891; 70 C.J. 804, n. 74, 867, n. 13.

[1.] Valliant, J., in Ayers v. Wabash R. Co., 190 Mo. 228, 88 S.W. 608, 609 (1905); 6 Wigmore, Evidence, § 1895.

[2.] As to the order of proof, by stages, of the respective parties, see sec. 4, herein.

[3.] If party avails himself of the opportunity to call the witness at a later stage, he cannot complain on appeal of a restriction on cross-examination. Clucas v. Bank of Montclair, 110 N.J.L. 394, 166 A. 311, 315, 88 A.L.R. 302, syl. 10 (1933); and see State v. Savage, 36 Ore. 191, 61 P. 1128 (1900) (same questions asked on re-call).

[4.] Longini Shoe Mfg. Co. v. Ratcliff, 108 F.2d 253, 257 (C.C.P.A.1939); State v. Spurr, 100 W.Va. 121, 130 S.E. 81, syl. 3 (1925); 3 Wigmore, Evidence, § 914.

[5.] People v. Court of Oyer and Terminer, 83 N.Y. 436, 459 (1881). But this result rests upon an assumption of a hard-and-fast rule that leading questions are always permissible in the proper field of cross-examination and never in the proper area of direct. 3 Wigmore, Evidence, § 915. The criterion is whether the witness is probably willing or unwilling to yield to suggestion, and as to this there is usually no difference in the attitudes of the witness, when the question is, or is not, within the scope of the direct. See § 6, herein.

[6.] This rule, however, has now been much liberalized in many jurisdictions. See § 38, herein.

[7.] Pollard v. State, 201 Ind. 180, 166 N.E. 654, syl. 8, 84 A.L.R. 779 (1929); 3 Wigmore, Evidence, § 914; Dec.Dig., Witnesses, ⊂⊃325.

[8.] Seemingly this was the result in the trial court of the judge's ruling limiting the cross-examination, in Conley v. Mervis, described in § 21, n. 10, above. See also Ah Doon v. Smith, 25 Ore. 89, 34 P. 1093

cal advantage, as affording the plaintiff a wider possibility for strengthening his case from his opponent's witnesses, even though the unfavorable testimony of the cross-examined witness may be later elicited by the defendant in the course of his own case in defense, and standing undisputed may thus ultimately result in a directed verdict, anyway. Finally, in one situation, the restrictive rule may become a rule of final exclusion, not a rule of postponement. This is the situation where the witness has a privilege not to be called as a witness by the cross-examiner. Thus, the privilege of the accused, and of the spouse of the accused, not to be called by the state in a criminal case will prevent the prosecutor from eliciting the new facts at a law stage, if he cannot draw them out on cross-examination.[9]

24. The Scope of the Judge's Discretion under the Wide-Open and Restrictive Rules.

When Gibson, C. J.[1] and Story, J.[2] introduced the innovation upon the orthodox "wide-open" cross-examination, by suggesting that questioning about new matter was not proper at the stage of cross-examination, they thought of their admonitions as relating solely to the order of proof. Traditionally the order of proof[3] and the conduct and extent of cross-examination[4] have been said

to be specially subject to discretionary control by the trial judge.

Accordingly the earlier[5] and even many of the recent cases[6] in jurisdictions adopting the restrictive rule in any of its forms, emphasize the power of the trial judge to allow deviations in his discretion. It has been said, indeed, that both the courts following the wide-open and those adopting the restrictive practice "recognize the discretionary power of the trial court to allow variations from the customary order and decline ordinarily to consider as an error any variation sanctioned by the trial court."[7] If this statement were fully true, the hazards of injustice at the trial or of reversals on appeal, in the administration of either rule would be insubstantial. But the statement paints too bright a picture. Trial courts and lawyers in the states adopting "the scope of the direct" test tend to find it easier to administer it as a rule than as a flexible standard of discretion. Appellate courts, though often giving lip-service to discretion, reverse a large number of cases for error in the application of the test, almost as many for excessive liberality by the judge, as for excessive strictness.[8]

As to courts following the traditional wide-open view, there seems to have been, from the first recognition of the rule, little tendency to apply here the general notion that the

---

(1893) where the judge's ruling permitting the cross-examination as to alleged new matter exposed the plaintiff to a dismissal of the action at the close of his testimony.

9. See §§ 25, 26, below.

1. In Ellmaker v. Buckley, 16 Sarg. & Rawles 72, 77 (Pa. 1827).

2. In Philadelphia & Trenton R. Co. v. Stimpson, 14 Pet. 448, 461, 10 L.Ed. 535 (1840).

3. See 6 Wigmore, Evidence, §§ 1867, 1885, 1886.

4. See 3 Wigmore, Evidence, §§ 944, 983(2).

5. See, e. g., Chicago & R. I. Ry. Co. v. Northern Illinois C. & I. Co., 36 Ill. 60 (1864); Glenn v. Gleason, 61 Iowa 28, 32, 15 N.W. 659 (1883); Blake v. People, 73 N.Y. 586 (1878); Kaeppler v. Red River Nat. Bank, 8 N.D. 406, 410, 79 N.W. 869 (1899); Schnable

v. Doughty, 3 Pa.St. 392, 395 (1846); State v. Bunker, 7 S.D. 639, 642, 65 N.W. 33 (1895); Lueck v. Heisler, 87 Wis. 644, 58 N.W. 1101 (1894).

6. See, e. g., United States v. Minuse, 142 F.2d 388, 389 (C.C.A.2d 1944); St. Louis, I. M. & S. Ry. Co. v. Raines, 90 Ark. 398, 119 S.W. 665, 668 (1909); People v. Andrews, 327 Ill. 162, 158 N.E. 462 (1927); Crawfordsville Trust Co. v. Ramsay, 178 Ind. 258, 98 N.E. 177 (1912); Black v. Bank, 96 Md. 399, 54 A. 88 (1903); Wrabek v. Suchomel, 145 Minn. 468, 177 N.W. 764 (1920); State v. Fisher, 94 N.J.L. 12, 110 A. 124 (1920); Goodbody v. Margiotti, 323 Pa. 529, 187 A. 425 (1936).

7. St. Louis, I. M. & S. Ry. Co. v. Raines, 90 Ark. 398, 119 S.W. 665, 668 (1909).

8. See Note, 37 Col.L.Rev. 1373, 1381 (1937) giving the results of a study of 810 decisions.

order of proof is discretionary. The tradition has not been shaped in terms of order of proof, but in the language of a right to cross-examine upon the whole case.[9] The situation which puts the most strain upon the wide-open rule is the one where a party, usually the plaintiff, finds himself compelled at the outset in order to make out his case to call from the adversary's camp either the party himself or some ally or employee to prove up some formal fact not substantially in dispute. Shall the adversary be allowed to disrupt the proponent's case at this stage by cross-examining the willing witness about matters of defense unrelated to the direct examination? This is an appealing situation for the exercise of a discretion to vary from the wide-open practice and to require the cross-examiner to call the witness for these new matters when he puts on his own case. So far, however, as the decisions examined reveal, such power seems not to be sanctioned in the "wide-open" jurisdictions.[10]

There is an even more unfortunate instance of unwillingness to use the doctrine that order of proof and scope of cross-examination are subject to variation in the judge's discretion. This is the refusal of the courts following the restrictive practice to permit the cross-examination of the accused in a criminal case beyond the scope of the direct. This permits the accused by confining his testimony to some formal and limited matter, such as his age, or alibi, to confine cross-examination to this narrow point and escape a searching inquisition on the entire charge.[11] Surely it would have been wise administration to recognize a discretion in the judge to permit the cross-examination to extend to the whole case. A refusal to do so unjustifiably converts the practice of limited cross-examination, always rationalized as a mere discretionary control of the *order* of proof, into a privilege of the accused to remain silent altogether, though he has voluntarily taken the stand, about relevant matters bearing on the charge against him.

25. Application of Wide-Open and Restrictive Rules to the Cross-Examination of Parties—(a) Civil Parties.[1]

Here two situations are to be distinguished, namely, the hostile cross-examination by the adversary of a party who calls himself as a witness in his own behalf, and the friendly cross-examination by the counsel of a party who has been called as an adverse witness by his opponent. In the first situation, in jurisdictions following the restrictive rules it is usually held that while the range of discretion to permit the relaxation of the restrictive practice is wider,[2] yet the general limitation to the "scope of

---

9. See Morgan v. Brydges, 2 Stark. 314, 171 Eng.Rep. 657 (N.P.1818) (witness called by plaintiff for formal proof, may be cross-examined by defendant, his employer, on the whole case); Cowart v. Strickland, 149 Ga. 397, 100 S.E. 447, 7 A.L.R. 1110, 1114 (1919) ("The rule in this state is that 'when a witness is called and examined, even to only a formal point, by one party, the other party has the right to cross-examine him as to all points.'")

10. O'Connell v. Dow, 182 Mass. 541, 66 N.E. 788, syl. 2 (1903) (subscribing witness); State v. Brady, 87 Mo. 142, syl. 2 (1885) ("adverse party could cross-examine the witness as to all matters involved in the case, no matter how formal or unimportant the examination in chief"); 5 Jones, Evidence, § 2341, note 8 (2d ed. 1926).

Of course, courts following some form of the restrictive rule easily control this type of cross-examination of the witness called to a formal point. See,

e. g., Finch v. Weiner, 109 Conn. 616, 145 A. 31, syl. 5 (1929) (automobile collision; plaintiff calls defendant's driver, to prove his employment and identify accident report: held, abuse of discretion to permit defendant to cross-examine on negligence); First National Bank v. Smith, 8 S.D. 101, 65 N.W. 439 (1895) (witness called by plaintiff to prove signature on note cannot be cross-examined about consideration); Jones, op. cit., § 2341.

11. See § 26.

1. 6 Wigmore, Evidence, § 1890; 58 Am.Jur. Witnesses, § 648; 70 C.J. Witnesses, §§ 822, 823; Dec.Dig., Witnesses, ⊂⇒275(5), 275(8).

2. California Fruit Canners' Ass'n v. Lilly, 184 F. 570, 572, syl. 1 (C.C.A.Wash.1911); Tawzer v. McAdams, 134 Kan. 596, 7 P.2d 516, syl. 2 (1932); Ward v. Thompson, 146 Wis. 376, 131 N.W. 1006, syl. 5 (1911).

the direct," based on the maintenance of the normal order of proof is still applicable.[3] A few courts, however, without much discussion of reasons have said that upon the hostile cross-examination of a party, the limitation to the scope of the direct will not be applied.[4] Of course, in the "wide-open" states the usual freedom from the restriction is accorded here without question.

When a party calls the adverse party as a hostile witness, it is usually provided by statute or rule[5] that he may question him "as upon cross-examination," i. e., he may ask leading questions, and that he is not "bound" by the answers of the adverse witness, which means chiefly that he may impeach the testimony by showing inconsistent statements. When this examination, savoring so nearly of a cross-examination, is concluded, some states give no right to the party to be further examined immediately by his own counsel, but give the judge a discretion to permit it or to require that his examination be deferred until the witness-party's own "case" is put on.[6] Most states however permit the immediate further examination by his own

counsel.[7] Presumably upon request the trial judge would forbid leading questions, and there is no tendency here in the restrictive states to relax for this cross-examination of a friendly witness, the usual restrictions limiting the questions to the scope of the direct,[8] and precluding the cross-examiner from examining about his own affirmative case.[9]

26. Application of Wide-Open and Restrictive Rules to the Cross-Examination of Parties—(b) The Accused in a Criminal Case.[1]

As a means of implementing the prescribed *order* of producing evidence by the parties, the restrictive rules limiting cross-examination to the scope of the direct or to the proponent's case are burdensome, but understandable. The cross-examiner who has been halted has at least a theoretical remedy. He may call the witness to answer the same questions when he puts on his own next stage of evidence. But the Federal courts and the states following the restrictive practice have applied these confining rules to the cross-examination of the accused by the prosecution.[2] Thus, the accused may limit his direct examination to some single aspect of the

---

3. See, e. g., Farmers' Fertilizer Co. v. Lillie, 18 F.2d 197, syl. 4, 5, 52 A.L.R. 552, 557 (C.C.A.Ohio, 1927) (applying restrictive rule without discussion); Brownlie v. Brownlie, 327 Ill. 117, 191 N.E. 268, 93 A.L.R. 1041, syl. 6 (1934) (similar).

4. Merrihew v. Goodspeed, 102 Vt. 206, 147 A. 346, 66 A.L.R. 1109, syl. 3 (1929); Ingles v. Staley, 85 W.Va. 155, 158, 101 S.E. 167, 168 (1919); Cuddy v. Foreman, 107 Wis. 519, 83 N.W. 1103, 1105, syl. 3 (1900). See, however, Felsenthal Co. v. Northern Assur. Co., 284 Ill. 343, 351, 120 N.E. 268, syl. 6 (1918) where a more liberal view is expressed.

5. See e. g., Federal Rules of Civil Procedure, Rule 43(b): *"Scope of Examination and Cross-Examination.* A party may interrogate any unwilling or hostile witness by leading questions. A party may call an adverse party or an officer, director, or managing agent of a public or private corporation or of a partnership or association which is an adverse party, and interrogate him by leading questions and contradict and impeach him in all respects as if he had been called by the adverse party, and the witness thus called may be contradicted and impeached by or on behalf of the adverse party also, and may

be cross-examined by the adverse party only upon the subject matter of his examination in chief."

6. See, e. g., Davis v. Wright, 194 Ga. 1, 21 S.E.2d 88, syl. 2 (1942); Miller v. Carnes, 95 Minn. 179, 103 N.W. 877, syl. 1 (1905); O'Day v. Meyers, 147 Wis. 549, 133 N.W. 605, syl. 9 (1911).

7. See, e. g., Peters v. Shear, 351 Pa. 521, 41 A.2d 556, syl. 4 (1945) and cases cited therein, and in 70 C.J. Witnesses, § 780, note 55.

8. Blum v. Getz, 294 Ill.App. 432, 13 N.E.2d 1019, syl. 3 (1938); Womochil v. Peters, 226 Iowa 924, 285 N.W. 151, syl. 2 (1939).

9. Podol v. Jacobs, 65 Ariz. 50, 173 P.2d 758, syl. 9, 10 (1946).

1. 6 Wigmore, Evidence, § 1890, 8 id. §§ 2276(d), 2278; Dec.Dig. Witnesses, ⊂⊃277(4); 70 C.J. Witnesses, §§ 824, 825; 58 Am.Jur. Witnesses, §§ 649–652. Note, Privilege of Criminal Defendant and Scope of Cross-Examination, 5 Univ. of Chi.L.Rev. 117 (1937).

2. Tucker v. United States, 5 F.2d 818, syl. 3–5 (C.C.A.8, 1925); Madden v. United States, 20 F.2d 289, syl. 6 (C.C.A.1927); Simon v. United States, 123 F.2d

case, such as age, sanity or alibi, and then invoke the court's ruling that the cross-examination be limited to the matter thus opened.[3] Surely the according of a privilege to the accused to select out a favorable fact and testify to that alone, and thus get credit for testifying but escape a searching inquiry on the whole charge, is a travesty on criminal administration. It is supposed to be necessitated by the principle that by taking the stand the accused subjects himself to cross-examination "as any other witness." Seemingly at least two escapes are available. First, the rule limiting the cross-examination has always been professedly subject to variation in the judge's discretion, and the fact that the cross-examiner cannot call the witness is a ground for exercising the discretion to permit cross-examination on any relevant fact.[4] Second, the accused might reasonably be held to have waived altogether his right not to be compelled to be a witness against himself, by taking the stand in his own behalf. Consequently, the prosecution could later call the accused as state's witness, and the one-sided effect of limiting the cross-examination would be mitigated.[5] In jurisdictions following the wide-open practice there is of course no obstacle to cross-examining the accused upon any matters relevant to any issue in the entire case.[6]

27. Merits of the Systems of Wide-Open and Restricted Cross-Examination [1]

The only virtue ever claimed for the restrictive rules is that they tend to require the parties to present their *facts* in due order, first the facts on which the plaintiff has the burden, then those which the defendant must prove, and so on following the prescrib-

80, syl. 17 (C.C.A.4, 1941); State v. Ragona, 232 Iowa 700, 5 N.W.2d 907, 909, syl. 4 (1942) (I.C.A. § 781.13, requiring cross-examination to be "strictly confined" to matters testified to in chief, largely left in application to judge's discretion); State v. Ewing, 174 Ore. 487, 149 P.2d 765, syl. 11 (1944) (limited under ORS 139.310 to facts given on direct and those germane thereto).

3. Except of course that cross-examination to impeach is not confined to the direct (see § 22, above). State v. Shipman, 354 Mo. 265, 189 S.W.2d 273, syl. 7 (1945) (may be cross-examined about prior convictions). And defendants are prone on direct to testify to their past records, which may open the door even wider to cross-examination on misconduct than the ordinary rule of impeachment would allow. See, e. g., Ivey v. State, 132 Fla. 36, 180 So. 368, syl. 1 (1938); State v. Hargraves, 62 Idaho 8, 107 P.2d 854, syl. 3 (1941).

4. The New Jersey cases seem to take this position. Disque v. State, 49 N.J.L. 250, 8 A. 281, syl. 1 (1887) (since passage of statutes permitting civil and criminal parties to testify "it has been the general practice . . . to permit such testifying party to be cross-examined as to the whole case" and such action being discretionary is not subject to review); State v. Grover, 104 N.J.L. 10, 139 A. 417, syl. 4, 5 (1927) (reaffirming rule).

5. Compare the practice of permitting the state after the defense has rested to recall the accused for additional cross-examination, recognized as permissible in discretion. See, e. g., People v. Searing, 20 Cal.App.2d 140, 66 P.2d 696, syl. 5 (1937); Bailey v.

Comm., 312 Ky. 764, 229 S.W.2d 767, syl. 4 (1950); Dec.Dig., Witnesses, ⚛277(7).

6. Clarke v. State, 78 Ala. 474, 480, 56 Am.Rep. 45 (1885) ("cross-examination relating to any matter connected with the transaction, or pertinent to the issue, and impeachment . . ."); State v. McGee, 55 S.C. 247, 33 S.E. 353, syl. 3 (1899); Brown v. State, 38 Tex.Cr. 597, 44 S.W. 176 (1898). In Missouri, however, where the wide-open practice prevails in civil cases, (see § 21, note 2, supra) the legislature has misguidedly enacted that the accused and his spouse shall be shielded from cross-examination except upon matters referred to in the examination in chief. V.A.M.S. § 546.260, construed in State v. Davit, 343 Mo. 1151, 125 S.W.2d 47, syl. 8, 13, 16 (1939).

1. See 6 Wigmore, Evidence, §§ 1887, 1888 (marshaling arguments pro and con, including judicial views and favoring "wide-open" practice); 5 Jones, Evidence, §§ 2339, 2340 (2d ed. 1926) (contra); Maguire, Evidence: Common Sense and Common Law, 45–49 (1947) (something for both sides). Some notewriters favor the wide-open practice. Notes, 37 Col.L.Rev. 1373, 1381 et seq. (1937) (semble—at least he passes the ammunition); 2 Ark.L.Rev. 212, 220 (1948). Contra: Note, 30 Ky.L.J. 317, 320 (1942). The compilers of the Model Code of Evidence made no clear choice. Rule 105(h) would leave to the judge's discretion "to what extent and in what circumstances a party cross-examining a witness may be forbidden to examine him concerning material matters not inquired about on a previous examination by the judge or by an adverse party".

ed stages.[2]　This avoids the danger, mentioned in section 24, supra, that one party's plan of presenting *his* facts will be interrupted by the interjection on cross-examination of new and damaging matters which constitute his adversary's case.　This interjection lessens the impact and persuasiveness of the proponent's facts.　The nice case which he planned to lay out fact by fact has been muddled and complicated during its very presentation by new and doubt-raising facts drawn out in cross-examination of the proponent's own witnesses.　The regular order of presenting the two parties' "cases" by separate stages is thus modified.　The "case," formerly a single melody, becomes convertible to counter-point.

It must be remembered, however, that like all rules of order, the common law order of proof by "cases" or stages, is to some extent arbitrary.　Two witnesses cannot be allowed to speak at once, so some rules must be worked out as to who shall call the witnesses and in what order.　A further rule, however, that a witness who knows many facts about the case shall be allowed to tell only certain ones at his first appearance, and as to others must be called later, seems even more artificial. The freer system obtaining under the wide-open practice, by which on the direct examination the regular order of proof of the "cases" of the respective parties is maintained but on the cross-examination the adversary is free to draw out all the damaging facts, has a natural order of its own.　The procedure by which each witness successively may be caused to tell all he knows about the case, is a system which would be followed spontaneously in any informal investigation untrammeled by rules.　It serves the convenience of witnesses and is accepted by the jury as a natural way of developing the facts.　Moreover, to the objection that diversion into new paths upon cross-examination lessens the unity and persuasiveness of the direct examiner's presentation of his

case, we may raise the doubt whether the direct examiner is in justice entitled to the psychological advantage of presenting his facts in this falsely simple and one-sided way.[3]　Is he in justice entitled to this clear impact on the jury's mind, to this favorable first impression which, though to be answered later, is so hard to dislodge?

The foregoing considerations favoring the wide-open or restrictive rules may well be thought to be fairly evenly balanced.　There is another factor, however, which seems to swing the balance overwhelmingly in favor of the wide-open rule.　This is the consideration of economy of time and energy.　Obviously, the wide-open rule presents little or no opportunity for dispute in its application.[4] The restrictive practice in all its forms, on the other hand, is productive in many court rooms, of continual bickering over the choice of the numerous variations of the "scope of the direct" criterion, and of their application to particular cross-questions.　These controversies are often reventilated on appeal, and reversals for error in their determination are frequent.[5]　Observance of these vague and ambiguous restrictions is a matter of constant and hampering concern to the cross-examiner.　If these efforts, delays and misprisions were the necessary incidents to the guarding of substantive rights or the fundamentals of fair trial, they might be worth the cost.　As the price of the choice of an obviously debatable regulation of the order of evidence, the sacrifice seems misguided. The American Bar Association's Committee

---

2.　See § 4, herein.

3.　This query was first suggested to me by Professor Clarence Morris.

4.　A glance at Fifth Dec.Dig., Witnesses, ⊂⇒269 demonstrates the almost entire absence of appellate dispute over the application of the wide-open practice, and the large number of such questions from the federal courts and the states following the restrictive practice.

5.　See Note, 37 Col.L.Rev. 1373, 1381 (1937).

for the Improvement of the Law of Evidence for the year 1937–38 said this:

> " 'The rule limiting cross-examination to the precise subject of the direct examination is probably the most frequent rule (except the Opinion rule) leading in trial practice today to refined and technical quibbles which obstruct the progress of the trial, confuse the jury, and give rise to appeal on technical grounds only. Some of the instances in which Supreme Courts have ordered new trials for the mere transgression of this rule about the order of evidence have been astounding.
>
> " 'We recommend that the rule allowing questions upon any part of the issue known to the witness . . . be adopted. . . .' " [6]

The statement and the recommendation seem well sustained by reason and experience.

28. Cross-Examination About Witness's Inconsistent Past Writings: Must Examiner Show the Writing to the Witness before Questioning About Its Contents.

The fatal weakness of swindlers, crooks and perjurers is letter writing. Such betraying letters are often inspired by mere boastfulness, sometimes by greed for the greater gain of the "double-cross." Properly used they have destroyed many a fraudulent witness.[1] An eminent trial lawyer makes these suggestions to the attacking cross-examiner:

> ". . . There is an art in introducing the letter contradicting the witness' testimony. The novice will rush in. He will obtain the false statement and then quickly hurl the letter in the face of the witness. The witness, faced with it, very likely will seek to retrace his steps, and sometimes do it skillfully, and the effect is lost.
>
> "The mature trial counsel will utilize the letter for all it is worth. Having obtained the denial which he wishes, he will, perhaps, pretend that he is disappointed. He will ask that same question a few moments later, and again and again get a denial. And he will then phrase—and this requires preparation—he will then phrase a whole series of questions not directed at that particular point, but in which is incorporated the very fact which he is ready to contradict—each time getting closer and closer to the language in the written document which he possesses, until he has induced the witness to assert not once, but many times, the very fact from which ordinarily he might withdraw by saying it was a slip of the tongue. Each time he draws closer to the precise language which will contradict the witness, without making the witness aware of it, until finally, when the letter is sprung, the effect as compared with the other method is that, let us say, of atomic energy against a fire-cracker." [2]

However, there is a rule which is an obstacle in the way of this effective method. This is the rule in Queen Caroline's Case, pronounced by the English judges in an advisory opinion in 1820.[3] The significant part of the opinion for present purposes is the

---

6. See 6 Wigmore, Evidence, § 1888, p. 545, where the relevant part of the Committee's report is set out in full.

1. Probably the most famous instance is the demolition by Sir Charles Russell of the witness Richard Pigott before the Parnell Commission in 1888, described in ch. 20 of Wellman, The Art of Cross-Examination (4th ed. 1936), and set out in Busch, Law and Practice in Jury Trials, § 350 (1949). This and many other striking instances are detailed in 4 Wigmore, Evidence, § 1260.

2. Nizer, The Art of Jury Trial, 32 Corn.L.Q. 59, 68 (1946). An instructive, similar suggestion as to the technique of "exposure by document" is found in Love, Documentary Evidence, 38 Ill.Bar J. 426, 429–30 (1950).

3. 2 B. & B. 284, 286–90, 129 Eng.Rep. 976, 11 Eng. Rul.C. 183 (1820) (The House of Lords put the question to the judges: "First, whether, in the courts below, a party on cross-examination would be allowed to represent in the statement of a question the contents of a letter, and to ask the witness whether the witness wrote a letter to any person with such contents, or contents to the like effect, *without having first shown* to the witness the letter, and having asked that witness whether the witness wrote that

pronouncement that the cross-examiner cannot ask the witness about any statements made by the witness in writing, or ask whether the witness has ever written a letter of a given purport, without *first* producing the writing or letter and exhibiting it to the witness, and permitting the witness to read the writing or such part of it as the cross-examiner seeks to ask him about. In vain is the trap laid before the eyes of the bird. While reading the letter the shifty witness will be warned by what he sees not to deny it and will be swiftly weaving a new web of explanation.

The rule that the writing must first be shown to the witness before he can be questioned about it was thought by the judges to be an application of the established practice requiring the production of the Original Document *when its contents are sought to be proved*.[4] This was a misconception, in at least two respects. First, the cross-examiner

is far from seeking to prove *at this stage* the contents of the writing by the answers of the witness. On the contrary his zealous hope is that the witness will deny the existence of the letter. Second, the Original Documents rule is a rule requiring the production of the document to the judge and jury, not to the witness, as proof of its contents.[5] So obstructive did the powerful Victorian cross-examining barristers find the rule in the Queen's case that they secured its abrogation by Parliament in 1854.[6]

This practice requiring exhibition to the witness has been usually accepted without question by American courts[7] and occasionally by legislators.[8] It is believed that its actual invocation in trials is relatively infrequent in most states, and that the generality of judges and practitioners are unaware of this hidden rock in the path of the cross-examiner.

letter and his admitting that he wrote such letter? . . ." Abbott, C. J., for the judges, answered the first question in the negative).

4. This rule, also called the Best Evidence Rule, is developed in Ch. 23, herein.

5. For these and other refutations of the theory of the Queen's case, see the masterly discussion in 4 Wigmore, § 1260.

6. St. 17 & 18 Vict. c. 125, § 24 ("A witness may be cross-examined as to previous statements made by him in writing or reduced into writing, relative to the subject-matter of the cause, without such writing being shown to him; but if it is intended to contradict such witness by the writing, his attention must, before such contradictory proof can be given, be called to those parts of the writing which are to be used for the purpose of so contradicting him; providing always that it shall be competent for the judge, at any time during the trial, to require the production of the writing for his inspection, and he may thereupon make such use of it for the purposes of the trial as he shall think fit").

7. See, e. g., Kennedy v. State, 240 Ala. 89, 196 So. 884, syl. 2 (1940) (cross-examination of accused as to statement signed by him, must be shown before questioning about contents); Glenn v. Gleason, 68 Iowa 28, 33, 15 N.W. 659 (1883) (whole letter must be read, relying on 1 Greenleaf on Evidence, § 463, which popularized the rule in this country before

judges here became aware that it had been abrogated in England); McDonald v. Bayha, 93 Minn. 139, 100 N.W. 679, syl. 2 (1904), and cases collected, 4 Wigmore, § 1263; Dec.Dig., Witnesses, ☞271(2) (4), 277(6); 70 C.J. Witnesses, § 816, note 41; 58 Am. Jur. Witnesses, § 643.

The rule is often applied to cross-examination of parties about what they have written, see Kennedy v. State, supra, but if the Original Documents principle is the basis, it has no application, as a party's oral admission of what he has written is a recognized exception to that rule, see § 208, herein.

It is arguable that the rule is applicable to a signed deposition which may be looked on as a writing, and it is sometimes applied to them, though this seems an inconvenient practice. See 4 Wigmore, Evidence, § 1262. But most courts have distinguished from depositions transcripts of oral testimony at a former trial, as to which the "show-me" rule is not applicable. Toohey v. Plummer, 69 Mich. 345, 349, 37 N.W. 297, syl. 2 (1888) (reporter's notes); Couch v. St. Louis Pub. Service Co., 173 S.W.2d 617, 622, syl. 5 (Mo.App.1943); Charles v. McPhee, 92 N.H. 111, 26 A.2d 30, syl. 7 (1942). Contra: Meadors v. Comm., 281 Ky. 622, 136 S.W.2d 1066, syl. 4 (1940).

8. See, e. g., Ark.Stats. § 28–708; Calif. C.C.P. § 2052; Georgia, Code 1933, § 38–1803; Idaho, I.C. § 9–1210; Montana, R.C.M.1947, § 93–1901–12; ORS 45–610. On the other hand, New Mexico's legislature has followed England's in abrogating the rule. 1941 Comp. § 20–201.

So far we have discussed the rule as it works in the situation where the cross-examiner is seeking to uncover in dramatic and devastating fashion the perjury of a witness who is a calculating villain. It seems to blunt the counsel's sharpest weapon of exposure. But the weapon may be misdirected. Innocent and well-meaning witnesses write letters and forget their contents and later testify mistakenly to facts inconsistent with the assertions in the letters. Their forgetfulness may need to be revealed, and their present testimony thus discredited to that extent. They should not, however, be invited by subtle questioning to widen the gap between their present statements and their past writings, and then be devastated by a dramatic exposure. Exhibiting the letter to such a witness before questioning him about its contents, or at least before proving the actual terms of the writing, will serve the purpose of the requirement that before impeaching a witness by showing his prior inconsistent statement he must be asked specifically whether he made such a statement and be given an opportunity to deny or explain it. The right treatment for the crook is not the right one for the mistaken seeker after truth. Who is to say whether the witness is of the one kind or the other? Probably the trial judge is most likely to pass on this impartially. In the light of this opinion, he should be vested with the discretion to permit the questioning about the writing without requiring its exhibition to the witness, or on the other hand to require that it be shown to the witness, or that the witness be asked so specifically about the letter as to time, addressee, and contents as to refresh his memory and give him a chance to deny or explain.[9]

29. The Standard of Relevancy as Applied on Cross-Examination:[1] Trial Judge's Discretion [2]

There are three main functions of cross-examination: (1) to shed light on the credibility of the direct testimony; (2) to bring out additional facts related to those elicited on direct,[3] and (3) in states following the "wide-open" rule,[4] to bring out additional facts which tend to elucidate any issue in the case. As to cross-examination designed to serve the second or third of these functions, there seems to be no reason why the usual standard of relevancy as applied to testimony offered on direct examination should not equally be applied to facts sought to be elicited on cross-examination.[5]

---

9. The suggested practice, or something near it, seems to prevail in the federal courts. The Charles Morgan, 116 U.S. 69, 77, 5 S.Ct. 1172, 29 L.Ed. 316, syl. 4 (1884) ("If the contradictory declaration is in writing, questions as to its contents, without the production of the instrument itself, are ordinarily inadmissible; and a cross-examination for the purpose of laying the foundation of its use as impeachment would not, except under special circumstances, be allowed, until the paper was produced and shown to the witness while under examination. Circumstances may arise, however, which will excuse its production. All the law requires is that the memory of the witness shall be so refreshed by the necessary inquiries as to enable him to explain, if he can and desires to do so."); United States v. Dilliard, 101 F.2d 829, 837 (C.C.A.2d 1938) (Learned Hand, J.: "Fairness usually does require that the witness shall be told when and where he made the putatively contradictory statement; but that is really all that the Supreme Court has ever exacted, and we think more is not necessary.") Compare

Model Code of Evidence, Rule 106(1) (2) which provides in part that the cross-examiner "need not in examining [a witness] as to a statement made by him in writing inconsistent with any part of his testimony, show or read to him any part of the writing," but that "(2) The judge in his discretion may exclude extrinsic evidence of a written or oral statement of the witness offered under Paragraph (1) unless the witness was so examined while testifying as to give him an opportunity to deny or explain the statement."

1. 5 Jones, Evidence, § 2352; Dec.Dig., Witnesses, ⊂⊃270; 58 Am.Jur. Witnesses, §§ 623–626; 70 C.J. Witnesses, §§ 809, 1010.

2. 5 Jones, Evidence, §§ 2348–2351; Dec.Dig., Witnesses, ⊂⊃267; 58 Am.Jur. Witnesses, §§ 623–626; 70 C.J. Witnesses, §§ 837, 1008.

3. See § 21, supra.

4. See § 21, supra.

5. See, e. g., Moulton v. State, 88 Ala. 116, 6 So. 758, 759 (1889) (cross-examination must relate to

As to the first function, that of evaluating the credibility of the evidence given on direct, the object and purpose is contrastingly different. Here the test of relevancy is not whether the answer sought will elucidate any of the main issues, but whether it will to a useful extent aid the court or jury in appraising the credibility of the witness and assessing the probative value of the direct testimony. There are many recognized lines of questioning for this purpose, none of which are commonly relevant to the main issues. A familiar type is the question or series of questions, often used as preliminary questions on cross-examination, inquiring as to residence and occupation, designed to place the witness in his setting.[6] Another is the testing or exploratory type of question. In asking this kind of questions the cross-ex-

aminer (who it will be remembered seldom has the advantage of having previously interviewed the witness) will ask disarming questions often remote from the main inquiry, which are designed to test by experiment the ability of the witness to remember detailed facts of the nature of those which he recited on direct, or his ability accurately to perceive such facts, or his willingness and capacity to tell the truth generally, without distortion or exaggeration.[7] This is part of the tradition and of the art of cross-examination and many of the famous instances of dramatically devastating cross-examinations are of this type.[8] The courts recognize that a rule limiting questions to those relevant to the main issues would cripple the usefulness of this kind of examination.[9] A final instance of evaluative cross-examination is

---

facts in issue, except that irrelevant questions which tend to test credibility may sometimes be asked); Yadkin Valley Motor Co. v. Home Ins. Co., 220 N.C. 168, 16 S.E.2d 847, syl. 6 (1941) (dictum: right to cross-examine on subject of direct is limited to matters "germane to the controversy"); 58 Am.Jur. Witnesses, § 623, note 12.

6. A leading case is Alford v. United States, 282 U.S. 687, 691, 51 S.Ct. 218, 219, 75 L.Ed. 624 (1931) where Stone, J., held for the court that it was an abuse of discretion for the trial judge to refuse to allow cross-examination of the government's witness respecting his residence where the accused suspected that the witness was detained in custody of federal authorities, and said: "Cross-examination of a witness is a matter of right. * * * Its permissible purposes, among others, are that the witness may be identified with his community so that independent testimony may be sought and offered of his reputation for veracity in his own neighborhood * * * that the jury may interpret his testimony in the light reflected upon it by knowledge of his environment * * *" Compare the questionable holding in Hungate v. Hudson, 353 Mo. 944, 185 S.W.2d 646, 157 A.L.R. 604 (1945) that while a foreign plaintiff, in a personal injury action, could be asked on cross-examination where he lived, it was prejudicial error to cross-examine him as to his motive in suing away from home.

7. For opinions approving this type of examination, see, e. g., Kervin v. State, 254 Ala. 449, 48 So.2d 204, syl. 3 (1950) (wide latitude to test recollection of witness is permitted subject to judge's dis-

cretion); Louette v. State, 152 Fla. 495, 12 So.2d 168, syl. 16 (1943) (one object of cross-examination to test recollection, veracity or prejudice of the witness); People v. Sorge, 301 N.Y. 198, 93 N.E.2d 637, syl. 4, 5 (1950) (proper for district attorney in cross-examining accused about other offenses, to persist after denial, "in the hope of inducing the witness to abandon his negative answers" and "on the chance that he may change his testimony"). See also the statement of Stone, J., in Alford v. United States, 282 U.S. 687, 692, 51 S.Ct. 218, 219, 75 L.Ed. 624 (1931): "Counsel often cannot know in advance what pertinent facts may be elicited on cross-examination. For that reason it is necessarily exploratory; and the rule that the examiner must indicate the purpose of his inquiry does not, in general, apply." An enlightening discussion of the technique of the "testing" cross-examination, with examples, is found in Busch, Law and Tactics in Jury Trials, § 303 (1949).

8. For instructive examples, see Wellman, Art of Cross-Examination, ch. 26 (4th ed. 1936) (by Martin W. Littleton); Reed, Conduct of Law Suits, §§ 423–439 (2d ed.1912); Kiendl, Some Aspects of Cross-Examination, 51 Case and Comment, No. 6, pp. 27–30 (1946); Busch, Law and Tactics in Jury Trials, § 303 (1949).

9. Accordingly, they point out that the rules of relevancy are not applied with the same strictness on cross-examination as on direct: State v. Smith, 140 Me. 255, 37 A.2d 246, syl. 17 (1944); O'Sullivan v. Simpson, 123 Mont. 314, 212 P.2d 435, syl. 4 (1949); Grocers Supply Co. v. Stuckey, 152 S.W.2d

the direct attack by impeaching questions seeking to show such matters as bias, inconsistent statements, or conviction of crime.[10]

As to all of the lines of inquiry mentioned in the next preceding paragraph, designed to shed light on the credibility of the witness and his direct testimony, the criteria of relevancy are vague, and the purpose of the cross-examiner is often experimental. Accordingly too tight a rein upon the cross-examiner may unduly curb the usefulness of the examination. On the other hand, dangers of undue prejudice to the party or the witness and of waste of time from extended exploration are apparent. Consequently, the trial judge has a recognized discretionary power to control the extent of such examination.[11] It is said that the exercise of such discretion will only be reviewed for abuse resulting in substantial harm to the complaining party.[12] The writer's examination of a large number of these cases leaves the impression that in practice such abuse is more often found when complaint is made that the judge has unduly curbed the examination than when undue extension of the discretion to permit the questioning is charged.[13]

30. The Cross-Examiner's Art

The following suggestions, gleaned from the prolific writing on the subject,[1] are not rules. As admonitions they must all be disobeyed on occasion. But they serve to raise in the mind of the beginning advocate questions about choices he might have taken for

---

911, syl. 2, 3 (Tex.Civ.App.1941, error refused) (on cross-examination any fact bearing on credit of witness is relevant).

10. See ch. 5, herein, dealing with impeachment of witnesses.

11. Alford v. United States, 282 U.S. 687, 694, 51 S.Ct. 218, 220, syl. 5, 75 L.Ed. 624 (1931) ("The extent of cross-examination with respect to an appropriate subject of inquiry is within the sound discretion of the trial court. It may exercise a reasonable judgment in determining when the subject is exhausted"; but here, excluding inquiry as to place of residence of witness held an abuse of discretion); Hider v. Gelbach, 135 F.2d 693, syl. 2 (C.C.A.S.C.1943) (judge properly exercised discretion to curb repetitious cross-examination); Trammell v. State, 193 Ark. 21, 97 S.W.2d 902, syl. 6, 7 (1936) (court did not abuse discretion in limiting defendant's cross-examination of state's witness as to time spent in jail); Guiffre v. Carapezza, 298 Mass. 458, 11 N.E.2d 433, syl. 7, 8 (1937) (in action for conversion of 49 items of goods, exclusion on cross of question as to value of other goods, to test knowledge, not abuse); Dec.Dig. Witnesses, ⊜267. But it is only after the party has had an opportunity substantially to exercise his right of cross-examination that the discretion becomes operative. Lindsey v. United States, 133 F.2d 368, syl. 2 (Ct.App.D.C.1942) (curtailment of defendant's cross-examination of government's alienists held improper, Edgerton, Circ. J., dissenting).

12. Bates v. Chilton County, 244 Ala. 297, 13 So.2d 186, syl. 6 (1943); Conley v. Mervis, 324 Pa. 577, 188 A. 350, syl. 4, 108 A.L.R. 160 (1936).

13. For notable and instructive instances of holdings of abuse in curbing the cross-examination of government witnesses by the accused, see Alford v. United States, 282 U.S. 687, 51 S.Ct. 218, 75 L.Ed. 624 (1931); District of Columbia v. Clawans, 300 U.S. 617, 57 S.Ct. 660, 81 L.Ed. 843 (1937).

1. For a hundred years lawyers have been fascinated with the topic and have developed practical maxims and gathered dramatic instances. Begin with Wigmore's section on the "Theory and Art" in his Treatise, § 1368. Most helpful and practical are the hints and examples in Busch, Law and Tactics in Jury Trials, Ch. 15 (1949) and in Goldstein, Trial Technique, Ch. XI, 1935. See also Reed, Conduct of Lawsuits, 2d ed., 1912; Elliott, The Work of the Advocate, 2d ed., 1912; Wellman, The Art of Cross-Examination, 4th ed., 1936; Stryker, The Art of Advocacy, Chs. 4, 5 (1954); Wrottesley, The Examination of Witnesses in Court, Ch. 3, 2d ed., 1926; and the ironic comments of Lord Darling in Scintillae Juris, 61–70 (1914). Among numerous readable articles, these are choice: W. A. Henderson, The High Art of Cross-Examination, 19 Case and Comment, 594, 1913; Judge C. A. Steeves, The Art of Cross-Examination, 38 Can. Law Times 97, quoted in The Dangers of Cross-Examination, 86 Cent.L.J. 206, 1918; C. J. Ramage, A Few Rules for Cross-Examination, 91 Cent.L.J. 354, 1920; T. Kiendl, Some Aspects of Cross-Examination, Case and Comment, Nov.–Dec., 1946, p. 25; Nizer, The Art of Jury Trial, 32 Corn.L.Q. 59 (1946).

granted, and to bring him some of the wisdom which other lawyers have harvested from hard knocks.

Preparation is the golden key. Movie-goers and readers of detective fiction are likely to suppose that successful cross-examination is the product of intuition, inspiration, and flashes of telepathic insight. The cross-examiner's art, they think, is a native gift for black magic, and one was either born with this gift or without it. A great Victorian advocate, Montagu Williams, seemed to share this view when he said, "I am by trade a reader of faces and minds." [2] Today the stress is upon thorough preparation, not upon sudden sallies of inspiration.[3] Improvisation is often necessary but its results are small compared to those from planned questions based on facts dug out before trial. The first task of the lawyer directing the preparation is to find out the names and addresses of the witnesses he will have to cross-examine. Some of the sources of information are his own client and his own witnesses. Often eye-witnesses are listed in reports of accidents made by employees in cases of injuries caused by railways and busses. Next, he will try to find out what these prospective adverse witnesses will testify. If important, he may take their oral depositions. In other cases, he will seek to interview them. In addition, he will try to learn any facts about the adverse witness which might show bias, inconsistent statements or a criminal record.[4] Not all these steps can be taken as to all adverse witnesses—there will always be surprise witnesses. Nor can every case bear the expense of such preparation. Nevertheless preparation before trial is the only soil from which, in the day-to-day run of cases, successful cross-examination can grow.[5] At the trial this preparation of the cross-examiner should be continued by his giving the closest attention to the witness's answers and demeanor on both direct and cross-examinations. Notes in preparation for later questions should be made by an associate or by the client, rather than by the examiner. Oral suggestions to the examiner in court should be avoided.[6]

No cross-examination without a purpose. As we have seen, these purposes may be, first, to elicit new facts, qualifying the direct, or in some states bearing on any issue in the case—a friendly purpose; second, to test the story of the witness by exploring its details and implications, in the hope of disclosing inconsistencies or impossibilities, and third, to prove out of the mouth of the witness, impeaching facts known to the cross-examiner such as prior contradictory statements, bias and conviction of crime—a hostile purpose. In considering any of these objectives, but particularly the latter two, the cross-ex-

---

2. Quoted Elliott, op.cit. 231.

3. See especially the works of Busch and Goldstein, and the articles of Kiendl and Nizer, cited above, n. 1. Nizer says at p. 68: "Most lawyers who will tell you of brilliant cross-examination will not confess this: We are entranced by a brilliant flash of insight which broke the witness, but the plain truth of the matter is, as brother to brother, that ninety-nine per cent of effective cross-examination is once more our old friend 'thorough preparation,' which places in your hands a written document with which to contradict the witness. That usually is the great gift of cross-examination."

4. These steps in preparation are discussed in Busch, Law and Practice in Jury Trials, §§ 286–290 (1949).

5. That most of the famous, devastating cross-examinations were grounded in pre-trial preparation

is illustrated by such celebrated instances as the cross-examination of Richard Pigott by Sir Charles Russell before the Parnell Commission, see Wigmore, op. cit. n. 1, supra, and Wellman, op. cit., ch. 22. It is even more clearly evident in that store-house of great cross-examinations, Aron Steuer, Max D. Steuer, Trial Lawyer (1950), especially in the account of People v. Gardner in the second chapter.

6. Another phase of preparation that is often neglected is the cautioning of one's own witnesses about the probable line of cross-examinations, and especially warning them of such pit-fall questions as "Whom have you talked to about this case?" and "When did you first know you would be called as a witness?" Goldstein, Trial Technique, §§ 572, 573 (1935).

aminer must be conscious that the odds are slanted against him. An unfavorable answer is more damaging when elicited on cross-examination. It is hard for a cross-examiner to win his case on cross-examination; it is easy for him to lose it. Accordingly, if the witness has done your case no harm on direct examination, a cross-examination for the second or third purpose is usually ill-advised. Do not be afraid when such a witness is tendered for cross-examination, to say "No questions." There remains the witness whose direct testimony has been damaging, or even threatens to be destructive of your case if the jury believes it. Him you will usually need to cross-examine, and whether your object shall be a skirting reconnaissance distant from the crucial issues, or a frontal attack on the story or the credit of the witness, will depend on the availability of impeaching material disclosed by your preparation and on your judgment of the risks and advantages of the holding defence or the counter-attack.[7]

A question directed to a crucial or critical fact on which the outcome of the case depends should seldom be asked an adverse witness unless you are reasonably confident the answer will be favorable. Similarly, broad questions which open the door for an eager witness to reinforce his direct testimony with corroborating circumstances, e. g., "How do you explain?" or "How did it happen?" are usually ill-advised.[8] If you have drawn out a discrepant fact on cross-examination it is often better to wait and stress the inconsistency in argument than to press the witness with it. If there is an explanation, it is the responsibility of the proponent's counsel to elicit this on re-direct.

In conducting a testing or exploratory examination, for obvious reasons it is inadvisable to follow the order of the witness's direct testimony. "If the witness is falsifying, jump quickly with rapid-fire questions from one point of the narrative to the other, with-

out time or opportunity for a connected narrative: backward, forward, forward, backward from the middle to the beginning, etc."[9]

Cross-examine for the jury not for your client. It is often a temptation to the cross-examiner to display his wit and skill before his client, or to feed the vengeful feelings of the latter toward opposing witnesses by tripping and humiliating them upon cross-examination.[10] Frequently such small victories upon collateral inquiries are easy to secure. The odds between the experienced advocate and the witness, nervous in new surroundings, are not even. The cross-examiner needs constantly to remind himself that the jury is keenly aware of this inequality of position, and that each juror is prone to imagine himself in the shoes of the witness. Better results with the witness, and a better impression upon the jury will usually flow from tact and consideration than from bulldozing and ridicule. The cloak falls more easily in the sunshine than in the hurricane. In the rare case when you are convinced that a crucial witness is dishonest and that you can demonstrate it, the attack must be pressed home to the jugular. But the cross-examiner should always be mindful of his duty to use his skills and weapons justly and fairly, and also of the need so to conduct him-

---

7. See the enlightening discussion in Kiendl, Some Aspects of Cross-Examination, 51 Case and Comment, No. 6, p. 25 (1946).

8. Goldstein, Trial Technique, § 565 (1935).

9. Ramage, A Few Rules for the Cross-Examination of Witnesses, 91 Cent.L.J. 354 (1920). For illustrative instances see Reed, Conduct of Law-Suits, 307–312 (2d ed. 1912).

10. "The object of cross-examination is not to produce startling effects, but to elicit facts which will support the theory intended to be put forward. Sir William Follett asked the fewest questions of any counsel I ever knew; and I have heard many cross-examinations from others listened to with rapture from an admiring client, each question of which has been destruction to his case." Sergeant Ballantine's Experiences, 1st Am.ed., 106, quoted in Reed, Conduct of Lawsuits, 278 (2d.ed. 1912).

self that the jury, with its latent sympathy for witnesses, will be impressed with his fairness.[11]

Make one or two big points; end on a high note. When you have led up to and secured an important admission, do not dull the edge of the effect by too many explanatory details, nor risk a recantation by calling for a repetition. Pass on to another important point if you have one, and end the examination when your last big point is made. "When you have struck oil stop boring." [12]

31. Cross-Examination Revalued

Early Victorian writers on advocacy exaggerated the strategic significance of cross-examination as affecting the outcome of trials. One of them wrote, "There is never a cause contested, the result of which is not mainly dependent upon the skill with which the advocate conducts his cross-examination." [1] This stands in contrast with the view of Scarlett, a great "leader" of a later day, who said, "I learned by much experience that the most useful duty of an advocate is the examination of witnesses, and that much more mischief than benefit generally results from cross-examination. I therefore rarely allowed that duty to be performed by my colleagues. I cross-examined in general very little, and more with a view to enforce the facts I meant to rely upon than to affect the witness's credit,—for the most part a vain attempt." [2] Reed, one of our most sensible American writers on trial tactics, expresses

the modern informed opinion when he says, "Sometimes a great speech bears down the adversary, and sometimes a searching cross-examination turns a witness inside out and shows him up to be a perjured villain. But ordinarily cases are not won by either speaking or cross-examining." [3] Thus, to the advocate of today cross-examination has become principally the means of gleaning additional facts from the opponent's witnesses. As a weapon of attack upon the credit of the direct testimony or of destroying the witness in the jury's eyes it is regarded as a two-edged sword, sparingly and cautiously employed. In either aspect it no longer looms large as a determinant of victory.

In the appraisal of policies upon which the modernizing of the existing system of evidence rules must be based, it seems that a similar revaluation of cross-examination as an engine for discovering truth will be called for. The present assumption is that the statement of a declarant or witness, if opportunity for cross-examination is not afforded, is so fatally lacking in reliability as not even to be worth hearing in a court of justice, and that the opportunity for cross-examination is indispensable. Now obviously cross-examination is a useful device to secure greater accuracy and completeness for the witness's testimony as a whole, and in the hands of a skilful advocate will often—not always—expose fraud or honest error in the witness. But it has its own hazards of producing errors.[4] It is, in truth, quite doubt-

---

11. These points are especially well made by Kiendl, op. cit., 51 Case & Comment, No. 6, pp. 24, 32 (1946). See also Goldstein, Trial Technique, § 558 (1935).

12. Credited to Josh Billings in Steeves, The Dangers of Cross-Examination, 86 Cent.L.J. 206, 207 (1918). "If you have made a home run do not run around the bases twice." Ramage, A Few Rules, 91 Cent.L.J. 354, 356 (1920).

1. Quoted from Cox, The Advocate, 434 in Reed, Conduct of Lawsuits, 277 (2d ed. 1912).

2. Memoir of Lord Abinger, 75, quoted in Reed, op. cit. 278.

3. Reed, op. cit. 276.

4. For some accounts of staged experiments attempting to show some comparative results as to accuracy and completeness of free narrative, direct examination and cross-examination see Marston, Studies in Testimony, 15 J.Crim.Law & Criminology, 1 (1924); Cady, On the Psychology of Testimony, 35 Am.J.Psych. 10 (1924); Weld and Danzig, Study of Way in Which a Verdict is Reached by a Jury, 53 Am.J.Psych. 518 (1940) (effect of cross-examinations upon jurors during progress of simulated trial); Snee and Lush, Interaction of the Narrative and Interrogatory Methods of Obtaining Testimony, 11 Am.J.Psych. 229 (1941) and the conclu-

ful whether it is not the honest but weak or timid witness, rather than the rogue, who most often goes down under the fire of a cross-examination.[5] Certainly every witness in judicial proceedings should in fairness be made available for cross-examination by the opponent wherever possible. But the premise that where cross-examination is not possible, as in the case of out-of-court statements, or as in the case of a witness who dies before cross-examination, the statement or testimony should generally be excluded for that reason alone, seems ill-founded. Cross-examination, it is submitted, should be considered as useful but not indispensable as an agency of discovering truth, and absence of opportunity to cross-examine should only be one factor to be weighed in determining whether the statement or testimony should be received. Such an approach to hearsay problems might lead us to conclude that when opportunity to cross-examine a witness is permanently cut off without fault of either party, the direct testimony should nevertheless be received[6] and that hearsay statements should be admitted if the statement was made by the declarant on personal knowledge, and reported by the witness at first hand, and the declarant is now dead or unavailable for cross-examination or perhaps in the case of written statements wherever production for cross-examination can fairly be dispensed with.[7]

32. Redirect and Subsequent Examinations [1]

One who calls a witness is normally required to elicit on his first examination, the direct, all that he wishes to prove by him. This norm of proving everything so far as feasible at the first opportunity is manifestly in the interest of fairness and expedition. Whether the cross-examiner is limited to answering the direct is, as we have seen, a matter as to which our jurisdictions are divided, with the greater number favoring the restrictive rule.[2] As to the redirect, however, and all subsequent examinations, there is no such division and the practice is uniform that the party's examination is normally limited to answering any new matter drawn out in the next previous examination of the adversary. It is true that the judge under his general discretionary power to vary the normal order of proof may permit the party who through oversight has failed to elicit on direct some matter relevant to his case or defense, to bring it out on redirect.[3] But the reply to new matter drawn out on cross-examination is the normal function of the redirect, and examination for this purpose is a matter of right,[4] though its extent is subject to control in the judge's discretion.[5]

A skillful re-examiner may often draw the sting of a lethal cross-examination.[6] The reply on redirect may take the form of explanation, avoidance or qualification of the

sions thereon in Gardner, The Perception and Memory of Witnesses, 18 Corn.L.Q. 391, 404 (1933) and Burtt, Legal Psychology, 147 (1931) ("It appears that when we really go after the observer in a rigorous fashion we tend to introduce some errors, perhaps through the mechanism of suggestion. . . .").

5. Elliott, The Work of the Advocate, 235 (2d ed. 1911).

6. Compare § 19, supra.

7. Compare § 305, herein.

1. See 6 Wigmore, Evidence, §§ 1896, 1897; 6 Jones, Evidence, §§ 2459–2463; Dec.Dig. Witnesses, ⊙ 285–291; 70 C.J. Witnesses, §§ 851–868.

2. See § 21, supra.

3. State v. Conner, 97 N.J.L. 423, 118 A. 211, syl. 2 (S.Ct.1922); 70 C.J. 712, note 44.

4. Villeneuve v. Manchester St. R. Co., 73 N.H. 250, 60 A. 748, syl. 6, 7 (1905) (when inconsistent statement out of court proved on cross, witness and party have right that witness be permitted to explain on redirect); Gray v. Metropolitan St. R. Co., 165 N.Y. 457, 59 N.E. 262 (1901); Martin's Adm'r v. Richmond F. & P. R. Co., 101 Va. 406, 44 S.E. 695, syl. 1 (1903).

5. People v. Kynette, 15 Cal.2d 731, 104 P.2d 794, syl. 15 (1940); Comm. v. Galvin, 310 Mass. 733, 39 N.E.2d 656, syl. 13 (1942).

6. An interesting example is the examination by Sir Edward Carson quoted in 6 Wigmore, Evidence, § 1896.

new substantive facts or matters of impeachment elicited by the cross-examiner.[7] The approach direct, such as "What did you mean by"[8] or "What was your reason for"[9] a statement made by the witness on cross-examination, may often be proper, but a mere reiteration of assertions previously made on the direct or cross-examination is not usually sanctioned.[10]

The rule of completeness[11] permitting, when part of a transaction, conversation or writing has been proven by the adversary, the proof of the remainder,[12] so far as it re-lates to the same subject-matter,[13] is often invoked by the re-examiner. Moreover, the principle of Curative Admissibility,[14] under which evidence that is irrelevant or otherwise incompetent may sometimes be allowed to be answered by the adversary, is likewise frequently resorted to by the examiner on redirect.[15]

Re-cross-examination, following the rule of first opportunity mentioned above, is normally confined to questions directed to the explanation or avoidance of new matter brought out on redirect.[16]

---

7. State v. Bengal, 124 S.W.2d 687, syl. 5 (Mo.App. 1939) (function of redirect to enable witness "to explain or avoid the effect of new matter brought out on cross-examination, or to rebut the discrediting effect of damaging statements or admissions elicited from him on cross-examination"). Illustrative cases: Myers v. Rose, 27 Cal.App.2d 87, 80 P.2d 527, syl. 1, 2 (1938) (where defendant inquired as to plaintiff driver's instructions from employer on cross-examination, plaintiff entitled to pursue subject further on redirect "to correct or repel any false impressions"); Johnson v. Minihan, 355 Mo. 1208, 200 S.W.2d 334, syl. 1–6 (1947) (where in collision case plaintiff's witness, driver of car in which plaintiff was guest, admitted signing, without reading, damaging statements on cross-examination, abuse of discretion to deny redirect examination about fact that witness signed statement in order to secure settlement from defendant of witness's own claim); Long v. F. W. Woolworth Co., 232 Mo.App. 417, 109 S.W.2d 85, syl. 11 (1937) (proper to allow plaintiff, asked on cross if she had consulted doctor, to explain on redirect that she had not, because she could not pay); Long v. Crystal Refrigerator Co., 134 Neb. 44, 277 N.W. 830, syl. 10 (1938) (plaintiff who was asked on cross-examination about statement signed by her, allowed to explain circumstances of statement as having been procured by agent of defendant's insurer; seemingly approved on appeal, though sufficiency of defendant's objections denied); Crowell v. State, 147 Tex.Cr. 299, 180 S.W.2d 343, syl. 8 (1944) (in prosecution for keeping bawdy house, where deputy sheriff on cross-examination admitted that he said he wanted to run defendant out of town, proper for him to explain on redirect that it was because of citizens' complaints against defendant).

Whether a witness who admits a conviction on cross-examination is allowed on redirect to explain the circumstances of the conviction, is a moot question. Yes. Chappel v. State, 136 Tex.Cr. 538, 126 S.W.2d 984, syl. 4, 5 (1939). No. Lebak v. Nelson, 62 Idaho 96, 107 P.2d 1054, syl. 3 (1940).

8. People v. Buchanan, 145 N.Y. 1, 39 N.E. 846, 853 (1895) (dictum); 70 C.J. 704, note 74.

9. State v. Kaiser, 124 Mo. 651, 28 S.W. 182, syl. 4 (1894); 70 C.J. 705, note 84.

10. Moore-Handley Hardware Co. v. Williams, 238 Ala. 189, 189 So. 757, syl. 14 (1939) (question calling for summation of witness's theory of accident as already given on direct and cross, properly excluded in judge's discretion). But where witness on cross-examination was confronted with her written statement contradicting her story on direct, it was proper to ask her on redirect whether her testimony on direct was true. Grayson v. United States, 107 F.2d 367, syl. 2 (C.C.A.8, 1939).

11. See § 56, herein.

12. Richardson v. State, 237 Ala. 11, 186 So. 580, syl. 2, 3 (1938).

13. White v. Comm., 292 Ky. 873, 166 S.W.2d 873, syl. 9, 10 (1942).

14. See § 57, herein.

15. Barrett v. United States, 82 F.2d 528, syl. 3 (C.C.A.7, 1936); United States v. Maggio, 126 F.2d 155, syl. 10 (C.C.A.3, 1942).

16. Where no new matter was opened on redirect the trial court's action in denying a recross was approved in Faulk v. State, 47 Ga.App. 804, 171 S.E. 570, syl. 3, 4 (1933) and in Atlantic & Danville R. Co. v. Rieger, 95 Va. 418, 28 S.E. 590, syl. 4 (1897). But a recross, though not in reply to new matter on redirect may be allowed in the court's discretion. Maryland Wrecking and Equipment Co. v. News Pub. Co., 148 Md. 560, 129 A. 836, syl. 2 (1925).

CHAPTER 5

IMPEACHMENT AND SUPPORT

33. Introductory: The Stages of Impeachment and the Lines of Attack.

The main lines of attack upon the credibility of a witness are six. The first, and probably the most effective and most frequently employed, is by proving that the witness on a previous occasion has made statements inconsistent with his present testimony.[1] Second, by showing that the witness is biased, by reason of emotional influences such as kinship for one party or hostility to another, or motives of pecuniary interest, whether legitimate or corrupt. Third, by attacking the character of the witness. Fourth, by showing a defect of capacity in the witness to observe, remember or recount the matters testified about. Fifth, by showing specific error, that is, proving by other witnesses that material facts are otherwise than as testified to by the witness under attack. Sixth, by proving a lack of the reli-

gious belief which would give the fullest traditional sanction to the obligation to speak the truth. This last ground we shall see is obsolescent.

There are two stages at which the process of impeachment may be employed. First, by eliciting out of the witness's own mouth, upon cross-examination, the facts discrediting the witness or his testimony. Certain kinds of attack are limited to this stage. As to them, "you must take his answer." Second, by extrinsic evidence, that is, the assailant waits until the time for putting on his own case in rebuttal, and then proves by a second witness or by documentary evidence,

---

1. Of course, the same effect is produced by eliciting on cross-examination statements from the witness contradictory to his own statements on direct or in other parts of the cross-examination. The practice of asking exploratory or testing questions designed to elicit such self-contradictions is described in §§ 29, 30, supra.

the facts discrediting the testimony of the witness attacked.

There is a cardinal rule of impeachment. Never launch an attack which implies that the witness has lied deliberately, unless you are convinced that the attack is justifiable, and is essential to your case. Almost never is it desirable to assail a witness whose evidence is not crucial. An assault which fails often produces in the jury's mind an indignant sympathy for the intended victim. Evidence of bad reputation, especially, may often produce an unexpected reaction among the triers, if they gain the impression that malice is prompting a neighbor to "swear a man's character away."

It is believed that, in general, the emphasis in trials has shifted away from impeachment of witnesses, and that the elaborate system of rules regulating the practice and scope of impeachment which has been developed in the past is likely to be applied in future with less strictness and to be simplified by confiding the control less to rules and more to judicial discretion. Accordingly, the treatment of the subject herein is selective rather than complete and is designed to give only the larger outlines of the field.

34. Prior Inconsistent Statements:[1] Degree of Inconsistency Required.[2]

When a witness has testified to facts material in the case, it is provable by way of impeachment that he has previously made statements relating to these same facts which are inconsistent with his present testimony.[3] The making of these previous statements may be drawn out in cross-examination of the witness himself, or if on such cross-examination the witness has denied making the statement, or has failed to remember it,[4] the making of the statement may be proved by another witness. This form of impeachment, sometimes loosely called "contradiction," is to be distinguished from evidence of Specific Error, also and more properly termed "contradiction," which consists merely in producing evidence as to material facts conflicting with the evidence of the assailed witness. It is discussed in a later section.[5]

The theory of attack by prior inconsistent statements is not based on the assumption that the present testimony is false and the former statement true but rather upon the notion that talking one way on the stand and another way previously is blowing hot and cold, and raises a doubt as to the truthfulness of both statements.[6] To create this doubt, what is the degree of inconsistency required? The language of some of the cases seems over-strict in suggesting that a contradiction must be found,[7] and under the more widely accepted view any material variance between the testimony and the previous

---

1. 3 Wigmore, Evidence, §§ 1017–1046; 6 Jones, Evidence, §§ 2398–2414; Hale, Prior Inconsistent Statements, 10 So.Cal.L.R. 135 (1937); Dec.Dig. Witnesses, ☞379–397; 70 C.J., Witnesses, §§ 1219–1338, 58 Am.Jur.Witnesses, §§ 767–781.

2. 3 Wigmore, Evidence, §§ 1040–1043; Dec.Dig.Witnesses, ☞386; 70 C.J.Witnesses, § 1241.

3. Any form of statement is acceptable. It may have been made orally, may have been taken as testimony at another trial or by deposition, or in writing, as a letter, accident-report or witness-statement or affidavit, or in any other form. Conduct, likewise, evincing a belief inconsistent with the facts asserted on the stand is usable on the same principle. Thus in accident litigation a witness who testifies to facts exculpating one party, may be shown to have asserted a claim of negli-

gence against that party. Missouri Pac. Transp. Co. v. Norwood, 192 Ark. 170, 90 S.W.2d 480, syl. 3 (1936); Dec.Dig.Witnesses, ☞347. Compare Bratt v. Western Air Lines, 169 F.2d 214, syl. 5 (1948), Note, Forney, 27 Tex.L.Rev. 555.

4. As to this, see § 37, below.

5. See § 47, below.

6. Compare the discussion in 3 Wigmore, Evidence, § 1017.

7. See, e. g., Sanger v. Bacon, 180 Ind. 322, 328, 101 N.E. 1001, 1003 (1913) (must be contradictory construing the statement most favorably to the witness); State v. Bowen, 247 Mo. 584, 153 S.W. 1033, 1038, syl. 7 (1913) ("must be such as, either in their substance or their general drift, contradict"); 70 C.J. 1054, note 89.

statement would suffice.[8] Accordingly if the former statement fails to mention a material circumstance presently testified to, which it would have been natural to mention in the prior statement, this is sufficient.[9] Again, an earlier statement by the witness that he had no knowledge of facts now testified to, should be provable.[10] Seemingly the test should be, could the jury reasonably find that a witness who believed the truth of the facts testified to would have been unlikely to make a prior statement of this tenor? Accordingly if the previous statement is ambiguous and according to one meaning would be inconsistent with the testimony, it should be admitted for the jury's consideration.[11] In applying the criterion of material inconsistency reasonable judges will be likely to differ, and a fair range of discretion should be accorded to the trial judge. Moreover, it is to be hoped that instead of restricting the use of prior statements by a mechanical use of the test of inconsistency, the courts may lean toward receiving such statements in case of doubt, to aid in evaluating the testimony. The statements, indeed, having been made when memory was more recent and when less time for the play of influence has elapsed, are often inherently more trustworthy than the testimony itself.[12]

8. Leinbach v. Pickwick Greyhound Lines, 135 Kan. 40, 10 P.2d 33, 39, syl. 7–9 (1932) (in action for injury due to collision with defendant's bus; on stand witness testified to negligent conduct of bus driver; held, error to exclude as impeaching statement witness's answer in accident report that he considered driver of third car involved in collision "to blame for accident," quoting Wigmore's test, "On a comparison of the two utterances, are they in effect inconsistent? Do the two expressions appear to have been produced by inconsistent beliefs?"); Comm. v. West, 312 Mass. 438, 440, 45 N.E.2d 260 (1942) ("And it is not necessary that there should be a contradiction in plain terms. It is enough if the proffered testimony, taken as a whole, either by what it says or by what it omits to say, affords some indication that the fact was different from the testimony of the witness whom it is sought to contradict."); O'Neill v. Minneapolis St. Ry. Co., 213 Minn. 514, 7 N.W.2d 665, 669, syl. 8 (1942) ("Whether a prior statement does in fact impeach a witness does not depend upon the degree of inconsistency between his testimony and his prior statement. If there is any variance between them, the statement should be received and its effect upon the credibility of the witness should be left to the jury." Statement held not to meet the test.). Illustrative cases where no material variance was found: Bosell v. Rannstad, 226 Minn. 413, 33 N.W.2d 40, syl. 16 (1948); Calley v. Boston and Maine R. Co., 93 N.H. 359, 42 A.2d 329, syl. 4 (1945).

9. Carroll v. Krause, 295 Ill.App. 552, 15 N.E.2d 323, syl. 5, 6 (1938) (witness on stand testified that automobile in which plaintiff was riding had only one headlight; statement of witness at coroner's inquest mentioning automobile but failing to mention single headlight, held provable to impeach even though was not specifically asked about headlights at inquest); Erickson v. Erickson & Co., 212 Minn. 119, 2 N.W.2d 824, syl. 6, 7 (1942) (workmen's compensation automobile accident claimant testified on stand that his trip was for two purposes, one individual, the other for the employer; held, his prior statements to adjuster mentioning only the individual purpose admissible to impeach). Contra: Hall v. Phillips Petroleum Co., 358 Mo. 313, 214 S.W.2d 438, syl. 1 (semble) (1948).

10. Hoagland v. Canfield, 160 F. 146, 171, syl. 16 (Circ.Ct.S.D.N.Y.1908); In re Olson's Estate, 54 S. D. 184, 223 N.W. 41, syl. 7; 70 C.J. 1057, note 6. Similarly, it seems that a previous statement denying recollection of facts testified to should be provable, but see Hancock v. Bevins, 135 Kan. 195, 9 P.2d 634, syl. 4 (1932), a debatable holding to the contrary.

11. State v. Kingsbury, 58 Me. 238, 242 (1870); Town of Concord v. Concord Bank, 16 N.H. 26, 32 (1844); 70 C.J. 1058, note 7. But there are recent contrary decisions. State v. Bush, 50 Idaho 166, 295 P. 432, syl. 11 (1930), and cases cited.

12. See the comment by Davis, J. for the court in Judson v. Fielding, 227 App.Div. 430, 237 N.Y.S. 348, 352 (1929): "In considering the evidence so sharply in dispute, the jury was entitled to know the contrary views the witness had expressed when the incident was fresh in his mind, uninfluenced by sympathy or other cause. Very often by calm reflection a witness may correct inaccurate observations or erroneous impressions hastily formed. But the jury should have all the facts in making an appraisement of the value and weight to be given the testimony."

35. Inconsistent Statements in Opinion Form.[1]

If a witness, such as an expert, testifies in terms of opinion, of course all courts will permit impeachment by showing a previous expression by the witness of an inconsistent opinion.[2] More troublesome is the question which arises when the witness testifies to specific facts and then is sought to be impeached by prior inconsistent expressions of opinion. In a collision case the plaintiff's witness testifies to particular facts inculpating the driver of a bus involved in the accident. Proposed impeachment: that the witness said just after seeing the collision, "The bus was not to blame."[3] In a will-contest, a physician testifies that the testator was sane when the will was signed. Proposed impeachment: that he said after the will was made that "it was not worth a snap of the fingers."[4] Prosecution for larceny of mules. Defendant's father testified to facts tending to show innocence. Proposed impeachment that the witness said "he thought defendant had taken the mules."[5]

Should the opinion rule be applied to exclude such impeaching statements? The early American tradition of a tight rule against opinions has been much relaxed in recent trial administration.[6] It is now seen that what was supposed to be a difference in kind between fact and opinion is a difference in degree only.[7] Wigmore considers that the rule goes no further than to exclude opinion as superfluous when more concrete statements could be resorted to.[8] The Model Code would leave the preference to the judge's discretion.[9] Seemingly the only practical value of the opinion rule is as a regulation of trial practice requiring the examining counsel to bring out his facts by more specific questions if practicable, before resorting to more general ones. Thus it seems a mistake of policy to apply it to any out-of-court statements whatsoever, since no such controls are possible.[10] Moreover, when as here the out-of-court statement is not offered at all as evidence of the fact asserted, but only to show the asserter's inconsistency the whole purpose of the opinion rule, to improve the objectivity and hence reliability of testimonial assertions, is quite inapplicable. Hence, though many earlier decisions, influenced perhaps by a statement in Greenleaf [11] and a casual English holding at *nisi prius*,[12] excluded impeaching statements in opinion

---

1. 3 Wigmore, Evidence, § 1051; 6 Jones, Evidence, § 2401 (2d ed.1926); Decennial Digests, Witnesses, ☞384; 70 C.J. §§ 1239, 1252; 58 Am.Jur. Witnesses, § 768; Notes, 66 A.L.R. 289, 158 A.L.R. 820.

2. McGrath v. Fash, 244 Mass. 327, 139 N.E. 303, syl. 5 (1923) (doctor who testified to moderate injuries, impeached by his statement after examining plaintiff that "this was the worst accident case he handled in the last ten years"); In re County Ditch, 150 Minn. 69, 184 N.W. 374, syl. 5 (1921) (value-witness impeached by his report on value as viewer); 3 Wigmore, Evidence, § 1051, note 3; 70 C.J. 1052, 1053.

3. Judson v. Fielding, 227 App.Div. 430, 237 N.Y.S. 348, syl. 5 (1929) (impeachment allowed).

4. Beaubien v. Cicotte, 12 Mich. 460, 487 (1864) (allowed, perhaps under principle of cases in note 2, supra).

5. State v. Nave, 283 Mo. 35, 222 S.W. 744, syl. 1 (1920) (excluded as opinion).

6. See §§ 11, 12, 17, supra.

7. See §§ 11, 12, supra.

8. 7 Wigmore, Evidence, § 1918.

9. Model Code of Evidence, R. 401(b). Uniform Rule 56 (quoted in § 17, herein) is less liberal but purports to apply only to the testimony of witnesses, not to out-of-court statements.

10. See § 18, herein.

11. 1 Greenleaf, Evidence, § 449 (3d ed.1846).

12. Elton v. Larkins, 5 Car. & P. 385, 172 Eng.Rep. 1020 (1832) (suit on marine policy; the broker who effected policy for the plaintiff, called as witness for defendants, testified to facts showing material concealment; plaintiff sought to show by extrinsic evidence after witness denied it, that witness had said that "the underwriters had not a leg to stand on," excluded by Tindal, C. J. as "only a contradiction on a matter of judgment").

form,[13] the trend of recent holdings is in accord with the common sense view that if a substantial inconsistency appears the form of the impeaching statement is immaterial.[14]

36. The Subject-Matter of the Inconsistent Statements.

On cross-examination we have seen that strict rules of relevancy are relaxed,[1] and generally the trial judge in his discretion may permit the cross-examiner to inquire about any previous statements inconsistent with assertions, relevant or irrelevant, which the witness has testified to on direct or cross. At this stage, there is no requirement that the previous impeaching statements must not deal with "collateral" matters.[2] But as appears in the next paragraph, if the inquiry

on cross-examination is as to inconsistent statements about "collateral" matters, the cross-examiner must "take the answer"—he cannot bring on other witnesses to prove the making of the alleged statement.[3]

At this latter stage, of extrinsic evidence, that is, the production of attacking witnesses, for obvious reasons of economy of time and attention, the range of impeachment by inconsistent statements is sharply narrowed. The tag, "You cannot contradict as to collateral matters," applies, and here the meaning is that to impeach by extrinsic proof of prior inconsistent statements, such statements must have as their subject (1) facts relevant to the issues in the cause, or (2) facts which are themselves provable by extrinsic evidence to discredit the witness.[4] Facts

13. See, e. g., City Bank v. Young, 43 N.H. 457, 460 (1862); Morton v. State, 43 Tex.Crim. 533, 67 S.W. 115, syl. 5 (1902), and see cases cited Note, 158 A.L.R. 820, 821, from which it appears that this view persists in Missouri, Ohio, Oklahoma, Tennessee, and Texas.

14. See, e. g., Atlantic Greyhound Corp. v. Eddins, 177 F.2d 954, syl. 4, 5 (C.A.S.C.1949); Leinbach v. Pickwick Greyhound Lines, 135 Kan. 40, 10 P.2d 33, syl. 7, 8 (1932); Judson v. Fielding, 227 App.Div. 430, 237 N.Y.S. 348, syl. 3–5 (1929); and see the description of the trend and the collections of cases in Note, 158 A.L.R. 821–824.

1. See § 29, supra.

2. Howard v. City Fire Ins. Co., 4 Denio 502, 506 (S. Ct.N.Y.1847); Dane v. MacGregor, 94 N.H. 294, 52 A.2d 290, syl. 6, 7 (1947); 3 Wigmore, Evidence, § 1023.

3. That a denial on cross-examination of a statement relating to a "collateral" matter cannot be disputed by extrinsic evidence, see Marcum v. Comm., 282 Ky. 799, 140 S.W.2d 387, syl. 4 (1940); State v. Wellmon, 222 N.C. 215, 22 S.E.2d 437, syl. 7 (1942) and cases cited Dec.Dig. Witnesses, ⊚⇒383.

4. The classic statement of the test of "collateralness" is in the opinions in Attorney-General v. Hitchcock, 1 Exch. 91, 99, 154 Eng.Rep. 38 (1847). That case was an information under the revenue laws. A witness for the plaintiff was asked on cross-examination if he had not said he had been offered 20 pounds to testify by officers of the Crown, which he denied. Held, the defendant could not call a witness to testify that the first witness had made the alleged statement. Pollock, C. B. said: "A distinction should be

observed between those matters which may be given in evidence by way of contradiction as directly affecting the story of the witness touching the issue before the jury, and those matters which affect the motives, temper, and character of the witness, not with respect to his credit, but with reference to his feelings towards one party or the other. It is certainly allowable to ask a witness in what manner he stands affected toward the opposite party in the cause . . . and whether he has not used expressions importing that he would be revenged on some one or that he would give such evidence as might dispose of the cause in one way or the other. If he denies that, you may give evidence as to what he said,—not with the view of having a direct effect on the issue, but to show what is the state of mind of that witness in order that the jury may exercise their opinion as to how far he is to be believed." Another illuminating discussion is the opinion of Rutledge, J. in Ewing v. United States, 135 F.2d 633, 640–642, syl. 9–14 (Ct.App.D.C.1942). Here a witness for the defendant accused of rape swore to facts which if believed made it impossible to believe complainant's story. Over the witness's denial, the government was (it was held) properly allowed to prove that the witness had said (1) I believe the defendant guilty but (2) he is facing the electric chair and I must be on his side. The court rejected the test of collateralness used in some cases (see, e. g., Butler v. State, 179 Miss. 865, 176 So. 589, syl. 2 (1937)) whether the party would have been entitled to prove the matter "as part of his case," and approved Wigmore's statement of the test as follows: "Could the fact as to which the prior self-contradiction is predicated have been shown in evidence for any purpose independently of the self-contradiction?" 3 Wig-

showing bias or interest,[5] and presumably facts showing that the witness had no opportunity to know the material matters testified to,[6] would fall in the second class.

A distinct but somewhat cognate notion is the view that if a party interrogates a witness about a fact which would be favorable to the examiner if true, and receives a reply which is merely negative in its effect on examiner's case, the examiner may not by extrinsic evidence prove that the first witness had earlier stated that the fact was true as desired by the enquirer.[7] An affirmative answer would have been material and subject to be impeached by an inconsistent statement, but a negative answer is not damaging to the examiner, but merely disappointing, and may not be thus impeached. In this situation the policy involved is not the saving of time and confusion, as before, but the protection of the other party against the hear-

say use by the jury of the previous statement.

37. Prior Inconsistent Statements: Requirement of Preliminary Questions on Cross-Examination as "Foundation" for Proof by Extrinsic Evidence.[1]

In 1820 in the answers of the judges in Queen Caroline's case, it was announced: "If it be intended to bring the credit of a witness into question by proof of anything he may have said or declared touching the cause, the witness is first asked, upon cross-examination, whether or no he has said or declared that which is intended to be proved." [2] Thus was crystallized a practice which was previously occasional and discretionary only. Only later and gradually has it been accepted in this country.[3] The purposes of the requirement are (1) to avoid unfair surprise to the adversary, (2) to save time, as an admission by the witness may make the extrinsic proof unnecessary, and (3) to give the wit-

more, Evidence 692 (3d ed. 1940). This seems to be equivalent to saying that the fact which is the subject of the previous statement must be (1) relevant to an issue, or (2) provable under impeachment practice by extrinsic evidence. Of course, the second previous statement in the Ewing case is not a prior inconsistent statement but is a direct expression of bias, and provable as such for impeachment regardless of self-contradiction. Somewhat similar is State v. Sandros, 186 Wash. 438, 58 P.2d 362, syl. 2–5 (1936), where, despite his denials, the state was allowed to prove that defense witness, claimed to be an accomplice with accused in forging a will, had (1) said that he had carried the will in his pocket for three weeks (which was material as tending to show it could not have been made at the time it was dated) and (2) made efforts to persuade a person to testify falsely to the genuiness of the signature. The court approved the Wigmore test, as given above.

See also King v. State, 233 Ala. 198, 171 So. 254, syl. 1, 2 (1937) (prior statement regarding whereabouts of one not a participant or witness, collateral); Luke v. State, 184 Ga. 551, 192 S.E. 37, syl. 3 (1937) (rape, during absence of husband, who testified that he was away on a stated mission: held, he could not be impeached by testimony that he had stated he had gone for a different purpose—collateral); Crabtree v. Kurn, 351 Mo. 628, 173 S.W.2d 851, syl. 8 (1943) (personal injury to brakeman; held, prior

contradictory statement of witness as to whether engineer was on the ground or in cab just before injury in switching operation, held material as bearing on opportunity to signal, and not collateral).

5. See, e. g., the Ewing and Sandros cases in the next preceding note.

6. See 3 Wigmore, Evidence, § 1022.

7. Miller v. Comm., 241 Ky. 818, 45 S.W.2d 461, syl. 1 (1932) (witness for defense who denied she heard defendant say he was going to kill deceased, improperly allowed to be impeached by proof that she had said she had heard such threats); Woodroffe v. Jones, 83 Me. 21, 21 A. 177 (1890) (suit by wife for sprained ankle due to defective sidewalk; defense, plaintiff negligent in wearing high-heeled shoes; husband, as witness, denied on cross-examination that he had spoken to his wife about her high heels; held proof by another witness that he had said "that he told his wife about wearing such high heeled boots" improperly admitted to impeach his denial which was merely negative and without probative significance).

1. 3 Wigmore, Evidence, §§ 1025–1039; 6 Jones, Evidence, §§ 2402–2413; Hale, Inconsistent Statements, 10 So.Cal.L.R. 135–147 (1937); Dec.Dig. Witnesses, ☞388, 389; 70 C.J. Witnesses, §§ 1275–1300; 58 Am.Jur. Witnesses, §§ 776–780.

2. 2 Brod. & Bing. 284, 313, 129 Eng.Rep. 976 (1820).

3. 3 Wigmore, Evidence, § 1026.

ness, in fairness to him, a chance to explain the discrepancy.[4] On the other hand, the requirement may work unfairly for the impeacher. He may only learn of the inconsistent statement after he has cross-examined and after the witness by leaving the court has made it impracticable to re-call him for further cross-examination to lay the foundation belatedly. It is moreover a requirement which can serve as a trap since it must be done in advance before the final impeachment is attempted and is supremely easy to overlook.

The requirement applies not only to oral inconsistent statements but also to those in writing. Its application to writings is discussed in an earlier section.[5]

To satisfy the requirement the cross-examiner will ask the witness whether he made the alleged statement, giving its substance, and naming the time, the place and the person to whom made.[6] The purpose of this particularity is, of course, to refresh the memory of the witness as to the supposed statement by reminding him of the accompanying circumstances.

If the witness denies the making of the statement, or fails to admit it, but says "I don't know" or "I don't remember" then the requirement of "laying the foundation" is satisfied and the cross-examiner, at his next stage of giving evidence, may prove the making of the alleged statement.[7] If, however, the witness unequivocally admits the making of the supposed statement, may the cross-examiner still choose to prove it again by another witness? Wigmore suggests that he may,[8] but probably the prevailing view is to the contrary[9] and this seems the more expedient practice. It saves time and minimizes the calling of witnesses upon what is only a side-issue.[10]

The trial situation to which the requirement of the preliminary question typically applies, is of course the situation where the witness attacked is on the stand in the present trial. What if he is not present, but his testimony given in this or some other case, by

---

4. If he is not accorded the opportunity on cross-examination, as he ordinarily would be, the other counsel should elicit any explanation he has on redirect.

5. See § 28, supra.

6. This is the usual formula. See, e.g., Angus v. Smith, Moo. & M. 473, 474, 173 Eng.Rep. 1228 (1829) ("you must ask him as to time, place, and person . . . it is not enough to ask him the general question whether he has ever said so and so"); Robinson v. United States, 144 F.2d 392, 405 (C. C.A. 6, 1944); State v. Jones, 62 Idaho 552, 113 P. 2d 1106, syl. 4 (1941).

7. People v. Perri, 381 Ill. 244, 44 N.E.2d 857, syl. 4 (1942) (denial); Blackford v. Kaplan, 135 Oh.St. 268, 20 N.E.2d 522 (1939) ("I don't know"); McGehee v. Perkins, 188 Va. 116, 49 S.E.2d 304, syl. 3 (1948) ("I don't recall"), noted, 2 Vand.L.Rev. 317; Dec.Dig., Witnesses, ⊕389.

8. Evidence, vol. 3, § 1037, note 4. A recent case supporting this view is People v. Schainuck, 286 N.Y. 161, 36 N.E.2d 94, syl. 3, 4 (1941) (arson: prosecution witness admitted on cross-examination that in investigation-hearing by Fire Marshal he said he knew nothing about cause of fire; held, error to refuse request of defense counsel to inspect hearing-record with a view to proving statements of witness).

9. Babbitt v. Say, 120 Oh.St. 177, 165 N.E. 721, syl. 2 (1929) (written statement: exclusion not prejudicial: "it would not contradict him . . . any more than his admissions would do"); Burckhalter v. Vann, 59 Okl. 114, 157 P. 1148, syl. 3 (1916) (former testimony); Lyon v. Rhode Island Co., 38 R. I. 252, 94 A. 893, syl. 3 (1915) (former testimony); Sloan v. State, 129 Tex.Cr. 131, 84 S.W.2d 484, syl. 2 (1935) (written statement); State v. Buffone, 65 Utah 92, 234 P. 539, syl. 4 (1925) (oral statements; "If the witness' attention is called to the conflicting statements he may admit them, and may perhaps make a satisfactory explanation why he made them. If he admits the statements, whether he explains them or not, that ends the inquiry"); and decisions collected in 70 C.J. Witnesses, § 1298.

10. It is arguable however that in respect to inconsistent writings signed by the witness, or even possibly in the case of recorded testimony, the production of the writing or the reading of the record, adds substantially to the impressiveness of the impeachment without requiring the calling of an additional witness. Even in these situations most courts adhere to the practice of excluding the proof, see next preceding note.

deposition or at a trial, is used as evidence in the present trial? Will the impeachment by inconsistent statements be excluded unless the impeacher at the former hearing asked the preliminary question?[11] Most of the decisions forbid the impeachment for want of the "foundation" without discrimination.[12] It seems, however, that in the case of a deposition taken upon written interrogatories when the cross-questions must be propounded before the answers to the direct can usually be known, the foundation should not be required. Even more clearly it seems that when the inconsistent statement was made after the testimony was given, and when the witness is now dead or unavailable, the foundation should be dispensed with.[13]

A similar question has been raised with respect to the impeachment by inconsistent statements of declarants whose hearsay declarations have been admitted under exceptions to the hearsay rule. But here the declarant has never been on the stand, and thus the opportunity for the preliminary question has never been afforded. Accordingly the courts are generally agreed that inconsistent statements of the makers of dying declarations[14] and declarations against interest[15] and of attesting witnesses,[16] and presumably of the makers of other hearsay declarations, may be proven to impeach, despite the want of a foundation.

If one of the parties to the suit takes the stand as a witness, and the adversary desires to use against him his prior statements inconsistent with his testimony, such statements are receivable in two aspects, first, as the admissions of an opposing party,[17] and second, as inconsistent statements to impeach a witness. If offered as admissions it is almost universally held that the requirement of the preliminary question is inapplicable.[18] In the case of the party there is less danger of unfair surprise than in the case of the ordinary witness, and the party will have ample opportunity for denial or explanation aft-

---

11. In the converse case when the witness now on the stand is sought to be impeached by inconsistent statements contained in previous testimony of the witness at a former hearing or trial, the need for the preliminary question, to give opportunity for explanation is usually conceded. See, e.g., Umemoto v. McDonald, 6 Cal.2d 587, 58 P.2d 1274, syl. 5 (1936) (under Code Civ.Proc. § 2052) and cases cited 3 Wigmore, Evidence, § 1035; Dec.Dig., Evidence ⊂388(8); 70 C.J. Witnesses, § 1284.

12. Mattox v. United States, 156 U.S. 237, 29 S.Ct. 337, syl. 4, 39 L.Ed. 409 (1895) (witness for government in murder case dies after first trial, and his testimony was read at second trial: defendant offered evidence that after first trial witness said his testimony was secured by duress and was untrue; held, three judges dissenting, properly excluded for want of foundation); Doe v. Wilkinson, 35 Ala. 453, syl. 2 (1860) (written deposition); Gregory v. Cheatham, 36 Mo. 155, 161 (1865) (letter written after deposition taken); Nagi v. Detroit United Ry., 231 Mich. 452, 204 N.W. 126, syl. 3 (1925) (on motion for new trial, defendant offers evidence that witness for plaintiff, who committed suicide after the trial, wrote a letter confessing that plaintiff had paid him $500 for testifying falsely: held, excluded), and cases cited 3 Wigmore, Evidence, §§ 1031, 1032.

13. People v. Collup, 27 Cal.2d 829, 167 P.2d 714, 718, syl. 4–6 (1946) (prosecution for rape: testimony of state's witness, at preliminary hearing read at trial; held, error to exclude evidence of subsequent inconsistent statements of witness, now absent from state; "the goal of all judicial proceedings is to bring before the trier of fact all pertinent evidence. Hence the rule allowing the use of former testimony is a salutary expedient . . . But it is equally clear that by reason of the same principle the impeaching evidence should be admitted for what it is worth"). See approving Note, 20 So.Calif.L.Rev. 102.

14. Carver v. United States, 164 U.S. 694, 17 S.Ct. 228, syl. 4, 41 L.Ed. 602 (1897) (two judges dissenting); State v. Debnam, 222 N.C. 266, 22 S.E.2d 562, syl. 3, 4 (1942).

15. 3 Wigmore, Evidence, § 1033.

16. Mobley v. Lyon, 134 Ga. 125, 67 S.E. 668, syl. 4 (1910). Contra: Craig v. Wismar, 310 Ill. 262. 141 N.E. 766, syl. 4 (1923).

17. See ch. 27, herein.

18. Howe v. Messimer, 84 Mont. 304, 275 P. 281, syl. 1 (1929); McDaniel v. Farlow, 132 Neb. 273, 271 N.W. 905, syl. 3 (1937) and cases cited 4 Wigmore, Evidence, § 1051; Dec.Dig. Witnesses, ⊂388(3); 70 C. J. Witnesses § 1277.

er the inconsistent statement is proved. Occasionally, the courts inadvertently assume that the requirement applies to the party-witness.[19] Sometimes they impose it if the proponent offers the statement only for impeachment,[20] and in one state the judge has discretion to impose the requirement as prerequisite to proof of a party-witness's admission.[21] These niggling qualifications seem hardly worth their salt and the sensible practice is the simple one of dispensing with the "foundation" entirely in respect to parties' admissions.

The preliminary question requirement when complied with conduces to fairness and economy of time. When overlooked by the impeacher, as it often is, then it seems that the judge should have a discretion to consider such factors as whether the impeaching counsel knew of the inconsistent statement when he cross-examined, the importance or unimportance of the testimony under attack, and the practicability of re-calling the witness for denial or explanation, and in the light of these circumstances, to permit the impeachment without the foundation if it seems fairer to do so.[22]

38. Prior Inconsistent Statements: Rule against Impeaching One's Own Witness.[1]

The common law rule forbidding a party to impeach his own witness is of obscure origin but probably is a late manifestation of the evolution of the common law trial procedure from an inquisitorial to a contentious or adversary system.[2] The prohibition is general applying to all forms of impeachment, not only by inconsistent statements but by attack on character, or by a showing of bias, interest or corruption. It does not, however, forbid the party to bring other evidence to dispute the facts testified to by his witness.[3]

Among the reasons, or rationalizations, found for the rule are, first, that the party by calling the witness to testify vouches for his trustworthiness, and second, that the power to impeach is the power to coerce the witness to testify as desired, under the implied threat of blasting his character if he does not. The answer to the first is that, except in a few instances such as character witnesses or expert witnesses, the party has little or no choice. He calls only those who happen to have observed the particular facts in controversy. The answers to the second are (a) that it applies only to two kinds of impeachment, the attack on character and the showing of corruption, and (b) that to forbid the attack by the party calling leaves the party at the mercy of the witness and his adversary. If the truth lies on the side of the calling party, but the witness's character is bad, if he tells the truth he may be at-

---

19. See, e.g., Wiggins v. State, 27 Ala.App. 451, 173 So. 890, syl. 2, 3 (1937); Finn v. Finn, 195 S.W.2d 679, syl. 1 (Tex.Civ.App. 1946).

20. Washington & O. D. Ry. Co. v. Smith, 53 App. D.C. 184, 289 F. 582, syl. 7 (1923); Malia v. Seeley, 89 Utah 262, 57 P.2d 357, syl. 2 (1936); 70 C.J. 1087, note 33.

21. Giles v. Valentic, 355 Pa. 108, 49 A.2d 384, syl. 1, 2 (1946).

22. The Model Code of Evidence, Rule 106(2) leaves the enforcement of the requirement to the judge's discretion.

1. 3 Wigmore, Evidence, §§ 896–918; 6 Jones Evidence, §§ 2423–2433 (2d ed. 1926); Ladd, Impeachment of One's Own Witness—New Developements, 4 Univ. of Chi.L.Rev. 69 (1936); Schatz, Impeach-

ment of One's Own Witness: Present New York Law and Proposed Changes, 27 Corn.L.Q. 377 (1942); Hauser, Impeaching One's Own Witness, 11 Oh.St.L.J. 364 (1950); Dec.Dig. Witnesses, ⊂⊃ 320–325; 70 C.J. Witnesses, §§ 991–999, 1147, 1224–1236.

2. Ladd, article cited in preceding note, at p. 70.

3. Vondrashek v. Dignan, 200 Minn. 530, 274 N.W. 609, syl. 1 (1937) (principle recognized, but court refused to apply it to permit party to contradict by other witnesses his own testimony that he was not drunk—a picturesque case of behind the scenes conflict between the party and his insurer); Talley v. Richart, 353 Mo. 912, 185 S.W.2d 23, syl. 5–8 (1945) (to contradict is not to impeach); Dec. Dig. Witnesses, ⊂⊃400–402.

tacked by the adversary: if he tells a lie the adversary will not attack him, and the calling party, under the rule, cannot. Certainly it seems that if the witness has been bribed to change his story, the calling party should be allowed to disclose this to the court.

The most important, because most effective, kind of impeachment, however, is by inconsistent statements and nearly all the cases applying the rule are of this type. It is hard to see any justification for prohibiting this sort of showing as to the reliability of a witness who has testified contrary to his previous assurances. It is believed that the underlying reason for the opposition to change is not that this type of impeachment is unjustified as impeachment, but the fear that the previous statement will be considered by the jury as substantive evidence of the facts asserted. How far this fear is justified, will be discussed in the next section.

The principal impact of the common law prohibition, then, is in preventing impeachment by previous contradictory statements. The principal means of escape from the prohibition, where it still persists, is by resort to questioning of the witness by the calling party about the previous statement not avowedly to discredit but to refresh his memory, or as it is sometimes more urgently phrased, "to awaken his conscience." [4]

Who is the party's own witness within the prohibitory rule? It is not the mere calling but the eliciting of testimony that makes him the party's witness.[5] In the case of deposition testimony it is the introduction of the deposition in evidence, not the taking of the deposition, that constitutes the adoption of the witness as the party's own.[6] The calling and examining of an attesting witness,[7] or other witness required by law to be called,[8] is not such adoption.[9] When a party calls an adverse party as a witness, the reasons for the prohibition, such as they are, seem inapplicable, and the Federal Rule [10] and a few other regulations,[11] expressly permit the calling party to impeach. In the absence of such provision, most courts mechanically apply the prohibition.[12] When the same witness is called twice, first by A and then by B,

4. People v. Michaels, 335 Ill. 590, 167 N.E. 857, syl. 1 (1929). Or "for the purpose of probing his recollection, recalling to his mind the statements he has previously made and drawing out an explanation of his apparent inconsistency." Bullard v. Pearsall, 53 N.Y. 230, 231 (1873). Or to show why the proponent called the witness. Meyerson v. State, 181 Md. 105, 28 A.2d 833, syl. 1 (1942); Morton v. Hood, 105 Utah 484, 143 P.2d 434, syl. 3, (1943).

5. Fall Brook Coal Co. v. Hewson, 158 N.Y. 1, 52 N. E. 1095, syl. 1 (1899).
Moreover, in some jurisdictions restricting the cross-examination to the scope of the direct, if the cross-examiner elicits new matter he makes the witness his own as to such testimony. State v. Wheaton, 149 Kan. 802, 89 P.2d 871, syl. 2 (1939); 3 Wigmore, Evidence, § 914; Dec.Dig. Witnesses, ⬤325.

6. Chicago College of Osteopathy v. Littlejohn, 234 Mich. 528, 208 N.W. 691, syl. 3, 4 (1926); Rule 26, Federal Rules of Civil Procedure; 3 Wigmore, Evidence, §§ 912, 913.

7. Whitman v. Morey, 63 N.H. 448, 456, 2 A. 899, syl. 4 (1886).

8. People v. Connor, 295 Mich. 1, 294 N.W. 74, syl. 5 (1940) (prosecutor can impeach witness endorsed on indictment and called by him at defendant's insistence).

9. 3 Wigmore, Evidence, § 917; Dec.Dig. Witnesses, ⬤322.

10. Rule 43(b), Federal Rules of Civil Procedure, and the corresponding rules bearing the same number, in the Rules of Arizona, Colorado and New Mexico.

11. See, e.g., N. H. R. L. c. 392, § 24. So. Dak. SDC 36.0208.

12. Price v. Cox, 242 Ala. 568, 7 So.2d 288, syl. 6 (1942) (can contradict but not impeach); Tullis v. Tullis, 235 Iowa 428, 16 N.W.2d 623, syl. 1 (1944) (same). But see Lovinger v. Anglo-Calif. Nat. Bank, 243 P.2d 561, syl. 20 (Cal.App. 1952) (permitting impeachment by felony conviction, construing Code Civ.Proc. § 2055), critically noted 26 So.Cal.L.Rev. 105; Brown v. Meyer, 137 Kan. 553, 21 P.2d 368, syl. 3 (1933) (impeachment by inconsistent statement permissible in court's discretion in interest of justice). See 3 Wigmore, Evidence, § 916; 70 C.J. 796, § 994; Dec.Dig. Witnesses, ⬤324.

the courts have been troubled.[13] The most practical solution would be to hold that the prohibitory rule does not apply at all, and both A and B may freely impeach.[14] Next most sensible is to say, as some courts do, that either A or B may impeach, at least by inconsistent statements, as to the testimony elicited on the other's call of the witness.[15] The majority view that the witness is the witness of A, and A at any event is precluded,[16] has less to commend it. Surely the worst solution is to hold, as some states do, that both parties have adopted the witness and neither may impeach.[17]

Some of the inconveniences and puzzles of the prohibitory rule have been swept away by reforming statutes. A provision in the draft of the Field Code of Civil Procedure in 1849 found fruit in the English Common Law Procedure Act of 1854, as follows: "St. 17 & 18 Vict. c. 125, § 22: '[1] A party producing a witness shall not be allowed to impeach his credit by general evidence of bad character; [2] but he may, in case the witness shall in the opinion of the judge prove adverse, [3]

contradict him by other evidence, [4] or by leave of the judge prove that he has made at other times a statement inconsistent with his present testimony.'" This has been copied in Florida, New Mexico, Vermont and Virginia.[18] Eleven other states, following the example of Massachusetts in 1869 have adopted the English statute except for omitting the troublesome condition that the witness must have proved "adverse." [19] New York, in opening the door to impeachment of one's own witness by prior inconsistent statements limits them to statements in writing or under oath.[20]

These statutes open the door to the most important type of impeachment of one's own witness, namely, prior inconsistent statements, and some courts have reached this result without the aid of statute.[21] But whether the extension is derived from statute or decision, two troublesome qualifications have been imposed on the reform by many courts. The first is that the party seeking to impeach must show that he is surprised at the testimony of the witness.[22] The second is that

---

13. See decisions collected 3 Wigmore, Evidence, § 913; 70 C.J. 797, § 995.

14. Perhaps the nearest decision is one which leaves impeachment in this situation to the judge's discretion. Avery v. Howell, 102 Kan. 527, 171 P. 628, syl. 6 (1918).

15. See, e.g., People v. Van Dyke, 414 Ill. 251, 111 N.E.2d 165, syl. 1 (1953), noted 1953 U.Ill.L.F. 296; Arnold v. Manzella, 186 S.W.2d 882, syl. 10 (Mo. App. 1945); 70 C.J. 797, note 81.

16. Smith v. Provident Savings Life Ins. Co., 65 F. 765, 772, syl. 7 (C.C.A. Ohio, 1895) (contradiction); Hanrahan v. New York Edison Co., 238 N.Y. 194, 144 N.E. 499, syl. 4 (1924) (conviction).

17. Re Campbell, 100 Vt. 395, 138 A. 725, syl. 4, 54 A.L.R. 1369 (1927), with note collecting cases.

18. Fla. F.S.A. § 90.09; N.M. 1941 Comp. § 20-204; Vt.V.S. § 1743; Va.Code 1950, § 8-292.

19. Ark. Stats. § 28-706; Cal.Code Civ.Proc. § 2049; Idaho, I.C. § 9-1207; Ind. Burns' Ann. St. § 2-1726; Ky.Civ.Code Proc. § 596; Ore. ORS 45-590; Texas, Vernon's Ann.C.C.P. art. 732; Wyo. WCS 1945 § 3-2606; N.Y. Code Cr.Proc. § 8-a.

20. N.Y. Civil Practice Act, § 343-a; Code Cri.Proc. § 8-a. See Comment, 27 Corn.L.Q. 377, 386 (1942), and see this lead followed in Wisconsin, St.1945, Aug. 17, c. 535 (for criminal cases).

21. See, e. g., London Guarantee & Accident Co. v. Woelfle, 83 F.2d 325, syl. 2-9 (C.C.A.Mo.1936) (cross-examination of evasive witness about prior statements, allowable in discretion: previous Federal decisions reviewed by Sanborn J.); Nuzum v. Springer, 97 Kan. 744, 156 P. 704, syl. 2 (1916) (proof by extrinsic proof of conflicting affidavit, allowable in interest of justice); Lindquist v. Dixon, 98 Minn. 369, 107 N.W. 958, syl. 4 (1906) (similar to last). See cases in 3 Wigmore, Evidence, § 905.

22. Young v. United States, 97 F.2d 200, syl. 3-9 (C.C.A. 5th 1938) (error to admit prior statement where prosecutor knew before placing witnesses on the stand that they would recant); Missouri Pac. R. Co. v. Sullivan, 197 Ark. 360, 122 S.W.2d 947, syl. 8 (1938) (surprise; allowed); Anthony v. Hobbie, 85 Cal.App.2d 798, 193 P.2d 748, syl. 4-6 (1948) (no surprise: excluded); Fjellman v. Weller, 213 Minn. 457, 7 N.W.2d 521, syl. 21 (1942) (surprise: allowed).

he cannot impeach unless the witness' testimony is positively harmful to his cause, reaching further than a mere failure ("I do not remember," "I do not know") to give expected favorable testimony.[23] These limitations are explainable only as attempts to safeguard the hearsay policy by preventing the party from proving the witness' prior statements in situations where it appears that its only value to the proponent will be as substantive evidence of the facts asserted. The rule against such use of the statements, and the soundness of its policy is the theme of the next section.

As to the prohibitory rule itself the Uniform Rule proposes that it be abandoned.[24] Surely the power to attack the character of one's own witness can be of little practical value to the attacker, and is of little moment to the administration of justice; but it seems that the rule against the showing of the pri-

or statements of one's own witness, to aid in evaluating his testimony, is a serious obstruction to the ascertainment of truth.

39. Previous Statements Not Usable as Substantive Evidence of the Facts Stated.

When a witness has changed sides and altered his story or forgets or claims to forget some fact, and his previous statement is received for impeachment purposes, what effect shall be given to the statement as evidence? Under the generally accepted doctrine the statement is not usable as substantive evidence of the facts stated.[1] The adversary if he so requests is entitled to an instruction to that effect,[2] and, more important, if the only evidence of some essential fact is such a previous statement, the party's case fails.[3]

Only two escapes from the lethal effect of this doctrine, where the sole witness to a

---

23. Mitchell v. Swift & Co., 151 F.2d 770, syl. 3, 4 (C.C.A.Tex.1945); Martin v. Los Angeles R. Corp., 75 Cal.App. 744, 171 P.2d 511, syl. 2–5 (1946) (lack of surprise and damage); Roe v. State, 152 Tex. Cr.R. 119, 210 S.W.2d 817, syl. 1–3 (1948); Virginia Elec. & Power Co. v. Hall, 184 Va. 382, 34 S.E.2d 382, syl. 3, 4 (1945). But see People v. Le Beau, 39 Cal.2d 146, 245 P.2d 302, syl. 3 (1952) and Bassett v. Crisp, 113 Cal.App.2d 295, 248 P.2d 171, syl. 9 (1952), which seem to allow impeachment by inconsistent statement even where the witness' response is merely negative, when under the circumstances the response would create a damaging impression. See note, 62 Yale L.J. 650.

24. Uniform Rules of Evidence, Rule 20.

1. Decisions are collected in 3 Wigmore, Evidence, § 1018; Dec.Dig., Witnesses, ☞397; Note 133 A.L.R. 1454 (1941); 70 C.J., Witnesses, § 1339. See also my article, The Turncoat Witness, 25 Tex.L.Rev. 573 (1947); Notes, Pantzer, 8 Mont.L.Rev. 39 (1947); 56 Yale L.J. 583 (1947).

Though the question arises less frequently, the agreed view is that prior consistent statements of the witness are similarly precluded from use as "substantive" evidence of the facts stated, by the rule against hearsay. See, e. g., Dyer v. Dyer, 141 Neb. 685, 4 N.W.2d 731, syl. 12, 13 (1942) (divorce suit; trial judge admitted in evidence written report of investigator appointed by court under requirement of statute, purporting to give statements of parties (who apparently testified in cause)

and of others: judge offered opportunity to counsel on both sides to cross-examine investigator and persons giving information to him: held, error, report was "hearsay"); Grand Forks Bldg. & Development Co. v. Implement Dealers Mut. Fire Ins. Co., 75 N.D. 608, 31 N.W.2d 495, syl. 3, 4 (1948) (where defendant's investigator testified, error to receive in evidence his detailed written report to defendant); 4 Wigmore, Evidence, § 1132. See also Kaminski v. State, 63 So.2d 339, syl. 1 (Fla.1953) (where state allowed to rehabilitate witness by showing he had taken a lie detector test prior to the trial, conviction reversed), noted 6 Stanford L.Rev. 172 (1953).

Accordingly, prior inconsistent statements must be limited to the function of supporting or sustaining the credibility of the witness after attack, under such restrictions as exist in the particular jurisdiction upon the use of consistent statements for this latter purpose. See § 49, herein.

2. Winchester & Partridge Mfg. Co. v. Creary, 116 U.S. 161, 6 S.Ct. 369, 371, 29 L.Ed. 591 (1885); Ritter v. People, 130 Ill. 255, 22 N.E. 605, syl. 2 (1889); Medlin v. Board of Education, 167 N.C. 239, 83 S.E. 483, syl. 3, Ann.C.1916E, 300 (1914).

3. Bridges v. Wixon, 326 U.S. 135, 150, 65 S.Ct. 1443, syl. 11, 89 L.Ed. 2103 (1945); United States v. Biener, 52 F.Supp. 54, syl. 4 (D.C.Pa.1943); State v. Baltimore Const. Co., 177 Md. 1, 6 A.2d 625, syl. 3 (1939), Note, 4 Md.L.Rev. 193; Selden v. Metropolitan Life Ins. Co., 157 Pa.Super. 500, 43 A.2d 571, syl. 21, 23 (1945).

vital fact has turned coat, are revealed by the cases. The first is the rule that when the hostile witness is an adverse party to the present action, his former inconsistent statement has two faces. As an impeaching statement it would not be substantive evidence, but as the admission of a party opponent it comes in under an exception to the rule excluding hearsay and as such is evidence of its truth.[4] Other recent cases have revealed the success of a stratagem. If the turncoat's prior statement was in writing, it can be presented to him before the conflict between it and his present story is high-lighted; and if he is asked whether his signed statement is true, he will naturally often state that it is. If he does, the prior statement is thereby incorporated in his present testimony and may be used substantively even though the witness later tells a contrary story.[5] This merely creates a conflict, and the jury is entitled to base its finding on either of the conflicting stories.

The reason for the orthodox view that a previous statement of the witness, though admissible to impeach, is not evidence of the facts stated, is clear and obvious. When used for that purpose, the statement is hearsay. Its value rests on the credit of the declarant, who was not under oath nor subject to cross-examination, when the statement was made.

Nevertheless, there are reasons for a contrary view, that the statements should be received as "substantive" evidence of their truth. These reasons are not so obvious. They depend upon judgments as to the balancing of values, but the more maturely they are considered, the more impressive they seem.[6]

The two safeguards of the truth of testimony on the stand are the oath, with its accompanying liability to punishment for perjury, and the probe of cross-examination. It is only the former, the oath and its accompanying liability, that are lacking when the previous statement of a witness now on the stand or available in court, is offered in proof of the facts stated. Probably most trial lawyers and most students in the field of evidence would now agree that the oath and the penalties of perjury, though of substantial value, are not the principal safeguard of the trustworthiness of testimony.[7] In the common law tradition the affidavit, under oath as it is, does not gain admission as evidence at a plenary trial. Moreover, of all the fifteen or so instances when hearsay evidence is admitted exceptionally, only one exception requires that the hearsay to come in must have been under oath. That instance, namely prior testimony, can moreover probably best be understood as a situation where the policy of the hearsay rule has been satisfied rather than as an exception to its requirements.[8]

It would doubtless be generally agreed among courts and lawyers, and among writers in the evidence field, that by all odds the major safeguard of the veracity of testimony and its main factor of superiority to out-of-court statements is its subjection to the test of cross-examination.[9]

4. See, e. g., Hill v. Small, 129 Conn. 604, 30 A.2d 387, syl. 1 (1943); Olson v. Hodges, 236 Iowa 212, 19 N.W.2d 676, syl. 7 (1945); Scoggins v. Miller, 80 S.W.2d 724, syl. 4 (Mo.App.1935).

5. Stewart v. Baltimore & Ohio R. Co., 137 F.2d 527, syl. 3 (C.C.A.2d, 1943); Zimberg v. United States, 142 F.2d 132, syl. 10 (C.C.A.1st, 1944).

6. Witness the conversion of our greatest scholar in this field, who after expressing the view that such statements should be received as substantive evidence adds: "The orthodox view was approved in the first edition of this Treatise. Further reflection, however, has shown the present writer that the natural and correct solution is the one set forth in the text above." 3 Wigmore, Evidence (3d ed.1940) § 1018, n. 2.

7. See 6 Wigmore, op. cit., § 1827, collecting numerous discussions of the value of the oath, and § 1831 for similar references on the efficiency of the perjury-penalty.

8. 5 Wigmore, op. cit., § 1370.

9. See 5 Wigmore, op. cit., § 1362 (Theory of the Hearsay Rule); § 1367 (Cross-Examination as a

If the prior statement of the witness is contradictory of his present story on the stand, the opportunity for testing the veracity of the two stories by the two parties through cross-examination and re-examination is ideal. Too often the cross-examiner of a dubious witness is faced by a smooth, blank wall. The witness has been able throughout to present a narrative which may be false, yet is consistent with itself and offers no foothold for the climber who would look beyond. But the witness who has told one story aforetime and another today has opened the gates to all the vistas of truth which the common law practice of cross-examination and re-examination was invented to explore. It will go hard, but the two questioners will lay bare the sources of the change of face, in forgetfulness, carelessness, pity, terror or greed, and thus reveal which is the true story and which the false. It is hard to escape the view that evidence of a previous inconsistent statement, when the declarant is on the stand to explain it if he can, has in high degree the safeguards of examined testimony.

Accordingly, if we look to the procedural guaranties of truth of the prior statement and of the present testimony of the same witness, we can only conclude that they stand approximately equal, since they both are subject to the same test of cross-examination, the main invention and reliance of the common law system of proof. But there is another factor which bears even more crucially upon the comparison, and may reasonably persuade us that prior statements are not merely of equal reliability with the witness's testimony, but are *superior* in trustworthiness. This is the obvious truth, which the voluble readiness of witnesses tends to obscure, that memory hinges upon recency. The prior statement is always nearer and usually very much nearer to the event than is the testimony. The fresher the memory, the fuller and more accurate it is. The rule as to memoranda of past recollection, permitting their use only when made while the matter recorded is fresh in memory,[10] is based precisely on this principle.

The courts themselves often stress the importance of recency of memory in appraising conflicting statements.[11] The following passage gives a psychologist's view as to the relative values of a statement made near to the event and subsequent testimony:

"Other things being equal, a memory is most accurate when recall is made immediately following the observation. The effect of time interval

---

Distinctive and Vital Feature of Our Law); § 1368 (Theory and Art of Cross-Examination,—a mine of examples of triumphs and disasters of cross-examiners).

10. 3 Wigmore, op. cit. § 745.

11. See, e. g., State Bank v. McGuire, 14 Ark. 530, 536 (1854) ("The two letters to McGuire, written by Drew while the transactions were recent, are so inconsistent with his statements made nine years afterwards, as to raise a violent presumption, that he was mistaken in his recollection of every material fact touching the pinch of the case. . . ."); Adams Express Co. v. Ten Winkel, 44 Colo. 59, 96 Pac. 818, syl. 2 (1908) (discrepancies in testimony of witness given at different trials should be resolved in favor of the earlier testimony, the transaction being then fresher in mind); The Douglass, 7 Fed.Cas. 974, No.4,031, syl. 3 (E.D.Mich.1863) ("It is safer to trust to the narrative of a sailor, made when all the incidents were fresh in his memory, than condemn on testimony given a year subsequent, and after appliances brought to bear upon him, probably superinducing a contrary statement."); and other cases cited 23 C.J., Evidence, § 1764, notes 78, 80. This argument is marshaled directly in support of the admissibility of prior inconsistent statements as substantive evidence in Pulitzer v. Chapman, 337 Mo. 298, 85 S.W.2d 400, 411, syl. 7 (1935) ("But the former statements are entitled to some weight as establishing the facts stated— that is why they tend to discredit the witness— and the jury have the undoubted right in the light of all the evidence to find which version of the facts is correct. With reference to the actual probative force of such conflicting statements (made by an honest witness), it is said in 22 C. J., Evidence, § 533, that 'any discrepancy in the testimony of a witness testifying on different trials of a cause should be resolved in favor of the earlier testimony, the transaction then being fresher in his mind.' ").

on the error of report has been shown by Dallenbach to increase from 14 per cent errors on the day of the observation to 22 per cent errors after an interval of forty-five days. It would be fortunate indeed if testimony could be taken soon after observations were made. Long delays of weeks and months between the time an observation was made and the time the witness is called for testimony are often made necessary by crowded court dockets, preparation of cases, etc. Meanwhile testimony during a coroner's inquest, newspaper reports, discussion with friends, and the modification constantly occurring through recall and imagination all serve to distort the original observation. The process of cross-examination may sift out many of the fallacies in testimony, but also may confuse some memories which are already relatively correct." [12]

Manifestly, this is not to say that when a witness changes his story, the first version is invariably true and the later is the product of distorted memory, corruption, false suggestion, intimidation, or appeal to sympathy. No, but the time-element plays an important part, always favoring the earlier statement, in respect to all of these hazards. The greater the lapse of time between the event and the trial, the greater the chance of exposure of the witness to each of these influences. A *priori,* the probability that the earlier statement has been so influenced is always less. All in all, in view of these considerations, and after reading hundreds of illustrative cases, the writer believes that as a class prior inconsistent statements, when they are so verified that their actual making is not in doubt, are more reliable as evidence of the facts than the later testimony of the same witnesses.[13]

12. Whitmer, Psychology in Law, c. 9, Gray et al., Psychology in Use (2d ed.1951) at 242. Other valuable discussions of memory, recency and the rate of forgetting, in their bearing upon the evaluation of testimony: Gardner, The Perception and Memory of Witnesses, 18 Corn.L.Q. 391, 392–4 (1933); Hutchins and Slesinger, Some Observations on the Law of Evidence—Memory, 41 Harv.L.R. 860, 864–7 (1928).

13. The writer requested from several able and experienced Texas district judges their opinion on this question and received these replies:

(a) "Should the prior statement have been given under oath or should [it] be in writing, then it often would be entitled to be given more credibility than the statement given on the trial."

(b) "Where there is no doubt that the prior statement was made, it is my opinion that such statement is more likely to be true than the present testimony."

(c) "It is my experience where a witness gives a statement under oath shortly after the occurrence of the event or where he makes a written statement and signs same and there is no coercion or undue persuasion used on the witness at the time of making the first statement, such statement is more likely to be true than the later testimony contradictory of said earlier statement. This is particularly true where the witness, after making the first statement, is approached by a lawyer or by a friend who is an interested party and against whose interest the first statement would tend to be. In this case, where the testimony given on

the stand is favorable to his friend or to the attorney who has used his persuasive powers on the witness, and is contradictory to the first statement which the witness unquestionably has made, I ordinarily would place more credence in the first statement made by the witness.

"Often, however, persons, especially shy, timid persons, who are not accustomed to being witnesses, are taken advantage of by hardened and experienced claim agents of insurance companies and other concerns, and are caused to sign written statements that really do not represent their true notions of the occurrence about which they have made statements. When there is an issue in court as to whether or not this has happened, then we have to take all the facts and circumstances of the particular matter under consideration, and more often than not the subsequent statement of the witness is more reliable."

An interesting case, illustrative of the situations where the probability of truth of the prior statement is overwhelming and the proof clearly reveals the influences which caused the change of story, is Young v. United States, 97 F.2d 200 (C.C.A. 5th, 1938) (Murder of revenue officer in the woods, near an illicit still; written statement of boy who was eyewitness shortly after killing, charging defendant, owner of still, with having instructed the killer to act as guard and "shoot it out" with any officers that might come; boy on stand denied truth of his statement; held, trial judge failed sufficiently to warn jury against using prior statement as substantive evidence). Compare also Bartholomew v. Impastato,

The rule against the use of prior statements substantively, then, is basically misguided, it is believed, in attempting to deny such statements the full probative effect to which they are reasonably entitled. But the attempt is in most cases ineffectual, and in the minority of cases where it is given practical effect, the incidence of the rule is harsh and haphazard. It is usually ineffectual because ordinarily the party who proves the prior statements will have some other "substantive" first-hand testimony of like purport with the impeaching statements to support him on the issue, and consequently the issue will be submitted to the jury for their decision on the conflicting "substantive" evidence. The only available sanction for our rule is an instruction that the jury must not consider the prior statements of the witness as substantive evidence on the main issue, but solely as bearing on the credibility of the witness. Such an instruction, as seems to be generally agreed, is a mere verbal ritual.[14] The distinction is not one that most jurors would understand.[15] If they could understand it, it seems doubtful that they would attempt to follow it. Trial judges seem to consider the instruction a futile gesture.[16] If the prior statement and the present testimony are to be considered and compared, what is the purpose? The intuitive good sense of laymen and of lawyers seems to agree that the only rational purpose is not merely to weigh the credibility of the testimony, but to decide *which of the two stories is true.*[17] To do this is ordinarily to decide the substantive issue.

12 So.2d 700, 705 (La.App.1943) (". . . where the prior unsworn statement of a witness contradicts sworn testimony later given on the stand, the court may, in the light of the facts, regard the prior statement as conclusive impeachment of, and entitled to greater credence than, the testimony given in open court.").

14. ". . . If a jury is not to be trusted to evaluate hearsay evidence properly, it may be doubted that it could consider it for one purpose but avoid being influenced by it for another purpose.

"Jurors normally reach a decision as a spontaneous reaction to the incidents of the trial as a whole, the conduct of the witnesses, the parties, the court, and counsel. They do not, and ordinarily could not, add to the scales of their deliberation each item of evidence, assigning to each fragment its due legal value, and then reach a decision by merely ascertaining which side preponderates. Opinions are not formed in any such manner; belief or disbelief is not a voluntary process, controllable with the precision of a scientific instrument. The impression that testimony makes upon the minds of the jury can never be entirely removed or controlled by instructions from the court, no matter how conscientiously the jury may try to follow the instructions. It is a very difficult matter to control our own psychological reactions. We cannot take a drug for its salutary properties without receiving at least a part of its poison." Note, 133 A.L.R. 1454, 1466 (1941).

15. "The distinction between the two is not easily appreciated by a jury." Clark, C. J., in Medlin v. County Board of Education, 167 N.C. 239, 241, 83 S. E. 483, 484 (1914).

16. All five of the Texas district judges who answered my inquiry agreed on this, see note 13, supra. One of their comments follows: "It is my opinion that an instruction to the jury advising that 'the prior inconsistent statement can only be considered for impeachment purposes,' is not understood by the average jury, and even a jury composed of lawyers would have difficulty in drawing such a fine distinction."

17. See, e. g., Young v. United States, 97 F.2d 200, 204 (C.C.A.5th, 1938) ("The Court: You offer these letters in evidence for the purpose of impeachment of this witness? The District Attorney [W. R. Smith, Jr.]: Yes, sir, to shed what light they may as to which of four different statements made by the witness are true.") People v. Ferraro, 293 N.Y. 51, 56, 55 N.E.2d 861, 863 (1944); Note, 30 Corn.L.Q. 511 (1945). (Trial judge charging jury: "The District Attorney claims that some of the witnesses have testified during this trial somewhat differently than when before the Grand Jury; he claims also that the testimony differs substantially to the statements given to the police after the shooting. . . . It is for you to determine when there is such a difference as claimed whether you are to believe the testimony given in this trial or believe the statements made by the same witness testifying differently before the Grand Jury."); Rex v. Francis, 23 Sask.L.R. 517 523, [1929] 3 D.L.R. 593, 600 (Sask., Canada 1929) (Trial judge addressing the jury upon inconsistencies between witness's previous statements and his testimony: "However, it is for you, observing and seeing what has occurred, how he made these statements which have been put in evidence, and how he took them back; to conclude what is the true view of the

The distinction between using a previous statement as evidence of its truth, and as evidence that the declarant in testifying differently is lying or mistaken, is surely a most artificial one. Unless the statement *may* be true, it does not have the effect of shaking the credibility of the testimony; and that it *may* be true is about all one means by accepting a statement as evidence of its truth. The notion that the judge and the jury may only say, "We know not which story is true; we only say that the witness blows hot and cold, and hence is not to be believed in either," demands a finical neutrality alien to the atmosphere of jury trial.

Moreover, as suggested above, the incidence of the rule that previous statements are not substantive is arbitrary and indiscriminate. In the first place, it is practically without effect where the impeaching party does not have the burden of producing evidence on the issue to which the statement relates. If the state's only witness to a material fact in a criminal case or the plaintiff's sole witness in a personal injury case is attacked by showing his previous statement giving a different story of the alleged crime

or collision, it is immaterial to the defendant whether the statement is substantive or merely impeaching. In either event, the jury can use it to cancel the effect of the witness's testimony. Thus, the impeaching statement, though not "substantive," may be a sufficient basis for a verdict for the defendant,[18] while in the reverse situation the state or a civil plaintiff could not go to the jury at all on the issue if the impeaching statement of the defendant's witness were all he had.[19] The argument seems persuasive that if the previous statement and the circumstances surrounding its making are sufficiently probative to empower the jury to disbelieve the story of the witness on the stand, they should be sufficient to warrant the jury in believing the statement itself.

These arguments in favor of using prior statements as substantive evidence seem weighty enough either to cause the courts to bring forward answering arguments supporting the orthodox rule, or to abandon it. The reasons have not lacked for respectable sponsors since they have been voiced most strongly by the greatest judge of our day [20] and by the greatest legal writer in our his-

---

facts and in what weight in the scale of justice he should be placed.")

In each of these cases the appellate court held that these expressions were erroneous, but the question is whether the lawyer and trial judges were not expressing a more reasonable and natural attitude and one more consonant with the practicalities of jury trial, than that of the appellate courts. If so, then any rule which runs counter to this reasonable way of regarding the impeaching statements will always be a source of friction in the gears of justice, resulting in improvident nonsuits and directed verdicts, new trials, and reversals.

18. Ricks v. State, 70 Ga.A. 395, 28 S.E.2d 303, syl. 11 (1943) (in view of impeaching statement jury may reject testimony of impeached witness); Portland Cattle Loan Co v. Gemmel, 41 Idaho 756, 242 Pac. 798, syl. 5 (1925) (while impeaching statement is not substantive, it may have effect of rendering nugatory the witness's testimony); In re Calich's Estate, 214 Minn. 292, 8 N.W.2d 337, syl. 4 (1943) (testimony of proponent and his witness, though otherwise uncontradicted, could be disregarded in

view of proponent's prior inconsistent statements); Dec.Digest, Witnesses, ☞397.

19. See, e g., Rashaw v. Cent. Vt. Ry., 133 F.2d 253, syl. 3 (C.C.A.2d, 1943) (error to submit plaintiff's allegation where only evidence in support was prior statement of defendant's witness who denied fact on stand); United States v. Biener, 52 F.Supp. 54 (E.D.Pa.1943); State v. Carroll, 143 Tex.Crim.Rep. 269, 158 S.W.2d 532 (1942); Smith v. Pelz, 384 Ill. 446, 51 N.E.2d 534, syl. 7 (1943); Jeffries v. Jodawelky, 304 Mich. 421, 8 N.W.2d 121, syl. 5 (1943); Dec. Digests, Witnesses, ☞397. See especially the holdings in automobile injury cases that where the defendant's driver testifies that he was on a frolic of his own, proof that he said shortly after the accident that he was on an errand of the employer does not warrant submitting the issue to the jury. Frick v. Bickel, 115 Ind.A. 114, 54 N.E.2d 436, syl. 7 (1944); Schwartz v. Lawrence, 214 App.Div. 559, 212 N.Y.Supp. 494, syl. 5 (1st Dep't 1925).

20. Learned Hand, Circuit Judge, in his opinions in DiCarlo v. United States, 6 F.2d 364, 368 (C.C.A.2d, 1925) ("The possibility that the jury may accept

tory.[21] But so far as I can find, only two reported cases, one in Missouri [22] and the other in Montana,[23] have clearly espoused the principle contended for, and the Missouri court

as the truth the earlier statements in preference to those made upon the stand is indeed real, but we find no difficulty in it. If, from all that the jury see of the witness, they conclude that what he says now is not the truth, but what he said before, they are none the less deciding from what they see and hear of that person and in court. There is no mythical necessity that the case must be decided only in accordance with the truth of words uttered under oath in court.") and United States v. Block, 88 F.2d 618, 620 (C.C.A.2d, 1937) (Reversal because prosecutor read to the jury the grand jury testimony of government's turncoat witness: "Perhaps the rule against hearsay ought to be discretionary, dependent upon how far the party against whom it is used has effective protection. In a case like this for instance, there seems to be no good reason why the prosecution should be held to what it can extract from such a witness on the stand; he confronts the accused, and if he retracts, the accused gets whatever benefit that may be. In other affairs such a statement would be accepted as evidence to be weighed against the retraction, and nobody would think it an injustice to make use of it. But we are not free so to make over the law; we cannot sustain a conviction based upon unsworn evidence.").

Another eminent judge of the same circuit (Swan, J.) is even more forthright in United States v. Corsi, 65 F.2d 564, 565 (C.C.A.2d, 1933) (Court holds that the Board of Inquiry in an immigration case can consider as evidence in support of its decision of exclusion, the previous sworn statement of a witness. "If the board were to proceed on strict common-law principles of evidence, the prior record could be used merely to discredit. . . . That is an artificial doctrine. Practically, men will often believe that if a witness has earlier sworn to the opposite of what he now swears to, he was speaking the truth when he first testified. These administrative boards are not bound by common-law rules of evidence, and we see no reason why they should not be permitted to accept a witness' prior testimony as affirmative proof of the fact then asserted, provided it is thought worthy of credence."). The holding in the last case is overruled in Bridges v. Wixon, 326 U.S. 135, 150 (1945); see note 3, supra.

21. "It does not follow, however, that Prior Self-Contradictions, when admitted, are to be treated as having no *affirmative testimonial* value, and that any such credit is to be strictly denied them in the mind of the tribunal. The only ground for doing so would be the Hearsay rule. But the theory of the Hearsay rule is that an extrajudicial statement is rejected because it was made out of Court by an absent person not subject to cross-examination. Here, however, by hypothesis the wit-

ness is present and subject to cross-examination. There is ample opportunity to test him as to the basis for his former statement. The whole purpose of the Hearsay rule has been already satisfied. Hence there is nothing to prevent the tribunal from giving such testimonial credit to the extrajudicial statement as it may seem to deserve. Psychologically of course, the one statement is as useful to consider as the other; and everyday experience outside of court-rooms is in accord." 3 Wigmore, Evidence (3d ed. 1940) § 1018(b) quoted with approval in Chicago, St. P., M. & O. Ry. v. Kulp, 102 F.2d 352, 358 (C.C.A. 8th, 1939).

22. Pulitzer v. Chapman, 337 Mo. 298, 315–320, 85 S. W.2d 400, 409–412 (1935). This was a will-contest and a question on appeal was whether there was evidence of undue influence justifying the trial judge in setting aside the verdict sustaining the will. Judge Cave, the scrivener of the will and an attesting witness, testified for the proponents, but on cross-examination he admitted the making of certain statements in a deposition given by him in the case which were inconsistent with his testimony and tended to show activity by the proponents in procuring the signing of the will. The court in a masterly opinion by Ellison, J., marshals the arguments for the general proposition that prior inconsistent statements may be used as substantive evidence, but limits its conclusion as follows: "We shall not attempt to lay down a rule going beyond the facts of this case. But we do hold that prior inconsistent sworn statements made by a witness in a deposition in the same case, and used to impeach his testimony at the trial, may be accepted as substantive proof of the facts stated, so far as they are competent and have probative value." See the interesting analysis and discussion of this case in Note, 21 St. Louis L.Rev. 122 (1936).

23. State v. Jolly, 112 Mont. 352, 355, 116 P.2d 686, 687 (1941) (Appeal from conviction for receiving stolen property, on ground of insufficiency of the evidence of knowledge. Prosecution relied on fact brought out on cross-examination of a witness, Dees, that the witness had stated in affidavit that when he helped defendant install the stolen equipment, defendant said it was "hot" and they would have to be careful. "The argument on appeal is limited almost entirely to the effect of evidence of prior conflicting statements of a party's own witness under section 10666, Revised Codes, and the circumstances here shown; whether it is limited to the purpose of impeachment, or whether it constitutes affirmative evidence of the fact stated. . . . While the weight of authority would limit such evidence to the impeachment of the witness' subsequent testimony on the stand (2 Wigmore on

has since retreated from its pioneer position.[24]

There has been advance in other areas. The English Evidence Act of 1938 clearly provides for the admission, as evidence of the fact stated, of any previous *written* statement made by a person who had personal knowledge and who is called as a witness.[25] The Model Code [26] and the Uniform Rule [27] go the whole distance and admit any statement, oral or written, of a person who is present at the trial and subject to cross-examination.

The course of decision, however, as noted above, has not yet been appreciably affected by the criticism of the prevailing rule. If, as we may believe, the courts should be rela-

tively flexible in their willingness to modify procedural as contrasted with substantive doctrine, there is little evidence of such an attitude in the treatment of this problem.[28] In the opinion [29] which contains the most extensive recent discussion of the question, the able judge devoted his entire consideration to an acute analysis of the previous decisions for the purpose of demonstrating that the Wigmore "heresy" was unsupported by authority. He made no examination or even any mention of the arguments which might justify reconsideration of the expediency of the practice. So far as I have discovered, in the hundreds of decisions on the question, only one judge—Stone, J., in State v. Sapor-

---

Evidence, 2nd Ed., 459, § 1018), the better reasoning would seem to support the other view (3 Wigmore on Evidence, 3rd Ed., 687, § 1018), since the prior statement is not properly subject to objection as hearsay, the witness being present in court for cross-examination concerning it." One judge dissented from this view. The court concluded, however, that under the circumstances the making by the defendant of the alleged statement was so improbable that it could not sustain the conviction.)

24. In Hammond v. Schuermann, 352 Mo. 418, 177 S.W.2d 618, syl. 5, 6, 9 (1944), the court says that Pulitzer v. Chapman, 337 Mo. 298, 85 S.W.2d 400 (1935) is not authority for giving substantive effect to impeaching statements since it was concerned only with a deposition taken in the same case, and holds that extrajudicial impeaching statements are not substantive evidence, and cites other recent Missouri cases to like effect. See also Hertzman, Prior Inconsistent Statements as Substantive Evidence, 12 Mo.Bar.J. 83 (1941).

25. Evidence Act, 1938, 1 & 2 Geo. VI, c. 28, § 1:

1. "(1) In any civil proceedings where direct oral evidence of a fact would be admissible, any statement made by a person in a document and tending to establish that fact shall, on production of the original document, be admissible as evidence of that fact if the following conditions are satisfied, that is to say—

"(i) if the maker of the statement either—

  "(a) had personal knowledge of the matters dealt with by the statement; or

  "(b) [made the statement as part of a business record] ; and

"(ii) if the maker of the statement is called as a witness in the proceedings. . . ."

26. "Rule 503. Admissibility of Evidence of Hearsay Declaration.

"Evidence of a hearsay declaration is admissible if the judge finds that the declarant

  "(a) is unavailable as a witness, or

  "(b) is present and subject to cross-examination."

27. Uniform Rules of Evidence, Rule 63, sub. 1, admits as an exception to the hearsay rule "a statement previously made by a person who is present at the hearing and available for cross examination with respect to the statement and its subject matter, provided the statement would be admissible if made by declarant while testifying as a witness."

28. See the illuminating review of the trend of decision on the question in Morgan, The Law of Evidence 1941–1945, 59 Harv.L.Rev. 481, 545 (1946), and a later expression of the same writer's views urging that previous statements should no longer be classified as hearsay, Hearsay Dangers, 62 Harv.L. Rev. 177, 192 (1948).

29. Ellis v. United States, 138 F.2d 612, 616–621 (C.C. A. 8th, 1943), opinion by Delehant, District Judge. The case was a prosecution of two brothers for transporting two high school girls in interstate commerce for immoral purposes. One of the girls made a statement of the immoral conduct to the district attorney and testified to the same effect before the grand jury, resulting in the indictment. At the trial, however, she denied all immorality, and testified that she made the previous statements but they were false. The convictions were reversed because there was no substantial evidence of immorality. The court seemed to have no doubt of guilt, and the facts present, in the writer's view, a striking illustration of the actual probative value of previous statements.

en [30]—has examined the criticisms and has undertaken to answer them. His opinion presents the orthodox position impressively, but seems to the writer not adequately to meet the main argument of Wigmore that the opportunity of cross-examination on the two conflicting stories is a sufficient safeguard. The points of Stone, J., may be summarized, and the counter-argument briefly indicated.

First, the oath and liability to punishment for perjury are wanting.

This must be granted, and the question is whether the want is fatal in view of (1) the fact that the prior statement was nearer to the event, and hence fresher in memory, than the present testimony and (2) the opportunity to cross-examine.

Second, the "principal virtue" of cross-examination "is in its immediate application of the testing process." There was no *immediate* opportunity of cross-examination of the previous statement.

But another virtue of cross-examination is in its opportunity to require the witness to explain the discrepancies of conflicting statements, and when this process is afforded, it seems that the earlier statement should at least stand equal with the later.

Third, the unrestricted use as evidence of impeaching statements would "increase both temptation and opportunity for the manufacture of evidence." [31]

But it must be remembered that this temptation exists almost equally under the orthodox rule, since the statements will come in to impeach and will be considered by the jury as evidence, regardless of contrary instructions, if there is an issue of fact to submit.

Fourth, if the hearsay rule is satisfied as to prior contradictory statements, it is equally so as to statements consistent with his testimony, and would lead to their admission as substantive evidence, and this, presumably, he would argue, would still further open the

door to the evil last mentioned, that of manufacturing evidence, by securing successive statements from the witnesses.

To this it may be answered that the extension suggested seems a logical one, and it is accepted in the provisions of the English Evidence Act of 1938 and the Uniform Rule. Such an extension may encourage further the early taking of written statements from the witnesses, and the securing so far as possible of additional statements on fact-questions later revealed in the progress of investigation. These practices, however, are precisely those followed by diligent parties and counsel under the present system. [32] It is hard to see how the present inducements to unscrupulous parties to put pressure upon crucial witnesses to change their stories will be materially increased. If witnesses are induced by such an extension more often to put in writing their recollection of the facts, even though prodded thereto by interested parties, and if the statements are given consideration more nearly equal with the later testimony, it seems probable that on the whole the interests of truth will be served.

If this be so, how far should we go in modifying the present practice? It may be suggested that we need go no further, in the first step, than to concede substantive value to statements admissible to discredit under the existing rules for impeachment by prior inconsistent statements. This solution, however, as Stone, J., suggests, could not be logically supported. If they are to be given substantive effect upon the main issues because their trustworthiness is adequately safeguarded, we can hardly confine this con-

---

30.   205 Minn. 358, 361–363, 285 N.W. 898, 900, 901 (1939).

31.   This objection is vividly presented and acutely discussed in Maguire, Evidence: Common Sense and Common Law (1947) 59–63.

32.   An instance of conflicting statements secured by the opposing parties from a driver involved in a fatal collision is Sweazey v. Valley Transport, Inc., 6 Wash.2d 324, 107 P.2d 567 (1940).

cession to statements which would come in on the minor and secondary issue of credibility. Moreover, such a limitation would keep alive the present restrictions upon impeaching one's own witness. These restrictions usually consist of requirements that the party must show that he has been surprised by the turncoat testimony, and that he has not merely been disappointed by a failure of the witness to testify beneficially as expected, but has been positively damaged by the purport of the testimony.[33] These restrictions, confining the use of such statements to circumstances where there is a practical need for discrediting the witness, make sense only as safeguards of the rule that impeaching statements are not to be used as substantive evidence. When that rule falls, the retention of these limitations serves no purpose. Accordingly, it seems that the framers of the English Evidence Act and of the Model Code provision took the wise course in admitting evidence of previous statements when relevant to the issues regardless of their admissibility to impeach.

There is a hazard which is ignored by the Model Code provision referred to, and which is ignored generally by our rules which admit hearsay under the established exceptions. That is the hazard of error or falsity in the reporting of oral words. The memory of a witness for words spoken in his presence by another is peculiarly faulty and fleeting.[34] If the court has the task of determining what were the words of an oral contract or of a defamatory statement, where these are in issue, obviously this special risk of error in reporting oral words must be taken. But in the case of the offer of previous oral statements by a witness to shake or supplement his present testimony, the necessity is by no means so strong. We may well be justified in placing a special safeguard upon the use of such supplemental evidence if we believe that the risk of mistransmission outweighs the probable value of the evidence.

This hazard of error is very much lessened in the case of previous written statements. Modern methods of detecting and establishing forgery or alteration are highly effective. Similarly, if the words of a witness are taken down by a stenographer at an official hearing and later transcribed, the trustworthiness of the report of the words is of high degree. Moreover, if the witness whose oral statement is sought to be used, admits on the stand that he made the statement, the risk again is much reduced.

In the light of all these considerations, I submit the following suggested statute, as at least a halfway house on the road of progress:

"A statement made on a former occasion by a declarant having an opportunity to observe the facts stated, will be received as evidence of such facts, notwithstanding the rule against hearsay if

"(1) the statement is proved to have been written or signed by the declarant, or to have been given by him as testimony in a judicial or official hearing, or the making of the statement is acknowledged by the declarant in his testimony in the present proceeding, and

"(2) the party against whom the statement is offered is afforded an opportunity to cross-examine the declarant."

40. Bias.[1]

The law recognizes the slanting effect upon human testimony of the emotions or feelings of the witness toward the parties or the self-

---

33. See, e. g., Young v. United States, 97 F.2d 200 (C.C.A. 5th, 1938); Ellis v. United States, 138 F.2d 612 (C.C.A. 8th, 1943); Selden v. Metropolitan Life Ins. Co., 157 Pa.Super. 500, 43 A.2d 571 (1945), all cited in previous footnotes herein.

34. Wigmore, The Science of Judicial Proof (3d ed. (1937) §§ 208, 215.

1. 3 Wigmore, Evidence, §§ 943–969; 6 Jones, Evidence, §§ 2438, 2439; Dec.Dig. Witnesses, ☞363–378; 70 C.J. Witnesses, §§ 1143–1218; 58 Am.Jur. Witnesses, §§ 706–722.

interest of the witness in the outcome of the case. Any such partiality, proceeding from any acts, relationships or motives, may be proven to impeach credibility. The sources of partiality are too infinitely varied to be here reviewed, but a few of the common instances may be mentioned. *Favor* or friendly feeling toward a party may be evidenced by family [2] or business [3] relationship, by employment by a party [4] or his insurer,[5] or by sexual relations,[6] or by particular conduct or expressions by the witness evincing such feeling.[7] It is commonly held in colli-

sion cases that when a witness appears for defendant the fact that he has made a claim against the defendant and has been paid a sum in settlement tends to show bias in favor of defendant.[8] Similarly, *hostility* toward a party may be shown by the fact that the witness has had a fight or quarrel with him,[9] or has a law-suit pending against him,[10] or has contributed to the defense [11] or employed special counsel to aid in prosecuting the party.[12] In criminal cases, the feeling of the witness toward the victim sheds light on his feeling toward the charge.[13] *Self-interest* of

---

2. Christie v. Eager, 129 Conn. 62, 26 A.2d 352, syl. 2 (1942) (in suit by guest against motorist, duty of jury in weighing testimony of motorist and wife to consider fact the plaintiff is brother of motorist's wife, and that insurance company is the real defendant); 3 Wigmore, Evidence, § 949; 70 C.J. 950, §§ 1151, 1152.

3. Curry v. Fleer, 157 N.C. 16, 72 S.E. 626, syl. 3 (1911) (that witness for party had sold his land to him at big price, admissible); 70 C.J. 951, § 1153.

4. Arnall Mills v. Smallwood, 68 F.2d 57, syl. 2 (C.C.A.Ga.1933) (witnesses' employment by defendant may be considered on credibility but is not, by itself, sufficient ground for disregarding their testimony); Dec.Dig. ☞369, 70 C.J. 951, § 1154.

5. It is usually held that the relevancy of the showing that the witness is an employee of defendant's liability insurer outweighs the danger of prejudice in disclosing the fact of insurance. Westgate Oil Co. v. McAbee, 181 Okl. 487, 74 P.2d 1150, syl. 3 (1937) and see numerous decisions, pro and con, collected in Note, 4 A.L.R.2d 779–781.

6. Tla-Koo-Yellee v. United States, 167 U.S. 274, 17 S.Ct. 855, 856, 42 L.Ed. 166 (1897) (murder: error to exclude evidence that witness was living with other government witness); Dec.Dig. Witnesses, ☞370(5); 70 C.J. 949, 956.

7. State v. McKee, 131 Kan. 263, 291 P. 950, syl. 6 (1930) (witness for accused may be cross-examined as to furnishing appearance bond and advancing attorneys' fees for him); 3 Wigmore, Evidence, § 950.

8. Joice v. Missouri-Kansas-Texas Co., 354 Mo. 439, 189 S.W.2d 568, syl. 19, 161 A.L.R. 383 (1945); Rynar v. Lincoln Transit Co., 129 N.J.L. 525, 30 A.2d 406, syl. 1–10 (1943) (judge may admit for this purpose, in discretion, though inadmissible as implied admission of liability); Hyde v. Marks, 138 S.W.2d 619, syl. 3–7 (Tex.Civ.App.1940) (court on re-

quest will instruct jury to consider for impeachment only).

9. Fields v. State, 46 Fla. 84, 35 So. 185, 186 (1903) (error to exclude cross-examination of state's witness as to "personal difficulty" with defendant); 3 Wigmore, Evidence, § 950.

In Jacek v. Bacote, 135 Conn. 702, 68 A.2d 144, syl. 9 (1949) a question asking whether witness was prejudiced against negroes, to which race defendant belonged, was held proper. See Note, 19 U.Cin. L.Rev. 392 which collects cases on inquiries about race, religion, and politics and suggests that to lessen the danger of jury-prejudice such questions should not be permitted unless the witness has first given some affirmative manifestation of this type of prejudice.

10. State v. Michelske, 66 N.D. 760, 268 N.W. 713, syl. 3 (1936) (in prosecution for manslaughter by automobile, held defendant entitled to show that state's witnesses had civil actions against defendant arising from same collision, on far-fetched ground that conviction would be admissible to impeach defendant in civil actions). But, on similar facts, the evidence was excluded in State v. Lawson, 128 W.Va. 136, 36 S.E.2d 26, syl. 3 (1945) and this was held a proper exercise of discretion. Cases are collected in 6 Wigmore, Evidence, § 949, notes 5, 6; 70 C.J. 985, § 1189; Dec.Dig. Witnesses, ☞ 370(3).

11. State v. Cerar, 60 Utah 208, 207 P. 597, syl. 10 (1922); 70 C.J. 953.

12. Brogden v. State, 33 Ala.App. 132, 31 So.2d 144, syl. 2 (1947); State v. Wray, 217 N.C. 167, 7 S.E.2d 468, syl. 1–3 (1940) (court assumes fact relevant on bias, but upholds exclusion as being discretionary and not shown prejudicial).

13. Richardson v. State, 91 Tex.Cr. 318, 239 S.W. 218, syl. 2, 20 A.L.R. 1249 (1922) (witness for defense said deceased "was dead in hell, where he ought to be").

the witness is manifest when he is himself a party,[14] or a surety on the debt sued on.[15] It may be shown likewise as reflecting on his interest that he is being paid by a party to give evidence, even though such payment beyond regular witness fees may as in the case of an expert be entirely proper.[16] So also in a criminal case when the witness testifies for the state and it is shown that an indictment is pending against him,[17] or that he is an accomplice or co-indictee in the crime on trial.[18] Such self-interest in extremest form may be manifested in *corrupt* activity by the witness, such as seeking to bribe another witness,[19] or by taking or offering to take a bribe to testify falsely,[20] or by the making of other similar charges on other occasions without foundation.[21]

Preliminary question.[22] A majority of the courts impose here the same requirement as in the case of impeachment by prior inconsistent statements, that before the witness

14. Accordingly, it is held in some jurisdictions that the court, on request, must charge that the jury in weighing the party's testimony are to bear in mind his interest in the outcome. Denver City Tramway Co. v. Norton, 141 F. 599, 608, syl. 7 (C.C.A.Colo. 1905); 70 C.J. Witnesses, §§ 1145, 1146.

15. Southern Ry. Co. v. Bunnell, 138 Ala. 247, 36 So. 380, 383 (1903) (question whether employee witness had given indemnity bond to employer defendant, proper).

16. Grutzki v. Kline, 252 Pa. 401, 43 A.2d 142, syl. 4 (1945); 3 Wigmore, Evidence, § 961, note 2. A medical witness may be asked if the payment of his fee depends on the outcome of the case. Volpe v. Perruzzi, 122 N.J.L. 57, 3 A.2d 892, 894 (S.Ct.1939) (question should have been allowed in discretion, but refusal not harmful). A witness as to value may be asked how much he has received from the defendant city for similar testimony in the past year. City of Chicago v. Van Schaack Bros. Chem. Works, 330 Ill. 264, 161 N.E. 486, syl. 8 (1928).

17. People v. Dillwood, 106 Cal. 129, 39 P. 438, syl. 3 (1895) (as a circumstance to show that his testimony may be actuated by desire to seek favor of court and prosecutor by aiding in convicting defendant); 3 Wigmore, Evidence, § 967, note 2.
But the pressure to curry favor with the prosecutor is not present in a civil suit, and in a collision suit where plaintiff introduced as witness the driver of one of the cars, it was held error to permit the defendant to impeach him by showing that he had been indicted for driving while intoxicated on the occasion in question and that the indictment was pending because of its liability to misuse as evidence of his guilt. Holden v. Berberich, 351 Mo. 995, 174 S.W.2d 791, syl. 5, 149 A.L.R. 929 (1943), annotated on this point. But if it had appeared that plaintiff had instigated and was controlling the prosecution of the criminal case a different result might be warranted.

18. People v. Dail, 111 P.2d 723, syl. 1–3 (Cal.App. 1941) (error to charge that credibility of accomplice

to be judged by same standard as other witnesses); People v. Simard, 314 Mich. 624, 23 N.W.2d 106, syl. 3 (1946) (defendant should have been allowed to ask state's witness if she had not been arrested for participation in same crime); 3 Wigmore, Evidence, § 967.

19. People v. Alcalde, 24 Cal.2d 177, 148 P.2d 627, syl. 2, 3 (1944); 3 Wigmore, Evidence, § 960. Or writing a letter designed to intimidate another witness into giving perjured testimony. State v. Moore, 180 Ore. 502, 176 P.2d 631, syl. 3 (1947).

20. See Martin v. Barnes, 7 Wis. 239, 241, 242 (1858) (bargain between doctor-witness and plaintiff that she should pretend to be injured from fall, and they should share recovery); 3 Wigmore, Evidence, § 961.

21. But the cases are conflicting. See 3 Wigmore, Evidence, § 963, note 2. Among those supporting this kind of impeachment are People v. Evans, 72 Mich. 367, 40 N.W. 473, syl. 1 (1888) (rape upon daughter: other false charges by daughter against other men, allowed: such charges may also evidence mental abnormality, see § 45, below); Larson v. Russell, 33 N.D. 45, 176 N.W. 998, 1012, syl. 7 (1920) (action for personal injuries in which the plaintiff claims paralysis due to traumatic neurosis; error to exclude impeachment on ground plaintiff's witnesses had given testimony in a bankruptcy, "a big fortune suit," which the judge in the former suit found to be perjured). Compare cases involving the question whether a plaintiff may be cross-examined about the previous institution of other suits and claims to show "claim-mindedness." Mintz v. Premier Cab Ass'n, Inc., 75 App.D.C. 389, 127 F.2d 744, syl. 3 (1942) (yes); Dent v. Monarch Life Ins. Co., 231 Mo.App. 283, 98 S.W.2d 123, syl. 5 (1936) (not where no other evidence present suit fraudulent).

22. 9 Wigmore, Evidence, § 963; 6 Jones, Evidence, § 2439 (2d ed. 1926); Notes, 39 Yale L.J. 129 (1929), 13 Iowa L.Rev. 482 (1927), 20 Wash.L.Rev. 168 (1945), 16 A.L.R. 991; Dec.Dig. ⚬➜ 373; 70 C.J. 995, § 1201.

can be impeached by calling other witnesses to prove acts or declarations showing bias, the witness under attack must first have been asked about these facts on cross-examination.[23] A substantial minority decline to impose this requirement.[24] Fairness to the witness is most often given as the reason for the requirement, but the saving of time by making unnecessary the extrinsic evidence seems even more important. Some courts, adhering to the analogy of inconsistent statements, make a difference between declarations and conduct evidencing bias, requiring the preliminary question as to the former and not as to the latter.[25] But as suggested in a leading English case, words and conduct are usually intermingled in proof of bias, and "nice and subtle distinctions" should be avoided in shaping this rule of trial practice.[26] Better require a "foundation" as to both or neither. It seems that jurisdictions recognizing the requirement should recog-

nize also a discretion in the judge to dispense with it when mere matters of indisputable relationship, such as kinship, are concerned, or where the foundation was overlooked and it is not feasible to recall the witness, or where other exceptional circumstances make it unfair to insist on the prerequisite.

Cross-examination and extrinsic. We have seen that in most states the impeacher must inquire as to the facts of bias on cross-examination as the first step in impeachment. It seems that if the witness fully admits the facts claimed to show bias, the impeacher should not be allowed to repeat the same attack by calling other witnesses to the admitted facts.[27] And it is held that when the main circumstances from which the bias proceeds have been proven, the trial judge has a discretion to determine how far the details, whether on cross-examination or by other witness, may be allowed to be brought out.[28]

---

23. Louisville & N. R. Co. v. Courson, 234 Ala. 273, 174 So. 474, syl. 3 (1937) (existence of unfriendly feeling); State v. Harmon, 21 Wash.2d 581, 152 P.2d 314, syl. 3, 4 (1944) (threats). The Note, 16 A.L.R. 984, lists cases supporting this view from Arkansas, California, Delaware, Idaho, Illinois, Indiana, Iowa, Kentucky, Minnesota, Mississippi, Missouri, Nebraska, North Carolina, Oregon, Texas, Vermont, Virginia, and Wisconsin.

As in the case of inconsistent statements, the preliminary question as to declarations showing bias should call attention to time, place, and persons involved. See Wright v. State, 133 Ark. 16, 201 S.W. 1107, syl. 12 (1918); State v. Harmon, supra.

24. Kidd v. People, 97 Colo. 480, 51 P.2d 1020, syl. 3 (1935) (witness' threat to "pin something on" another witness unless he testified for the state); People v. Michalow, 229 N.Y. 325, 128 N.E. 228, syl. 4, 5 (1920). In the Note, 16 A.L.R. 991, cases from Florida, Georgia, Louisiana, Maine, New Hampshire, New York, and South Dakota are cited for this view.

25. See, e. g., Martin v. Barnes, 7 Wis. 239, 243 (1858) (proof of medical witness' corrupt bargain with plaintiff without preliminary question, being conduct, "not like conversations"); Smith v. State, 106 Tex.Cr. 202, 291 S.W. 544, syl. 5 (1927). But the civil courts in Texas reject the distinction, see e. g., Good v. Texas & P. R. Co., 166 S.W. 670, syl. 3

(Tex.Civ.App.1914, error refused) (payment received by expert witness).

26. See the excerpt from the opinion of Abbott, C.J. in the Queen's Case, 2 Brod. & B. 284, 129 Eng.Rep. 976 (1820) as quoted in Note, 16 A.L.R. 989.

27. This is the prevailing holding as to inconsistent statements, see § 37, above and similar reasons apply here.

28. People v. Fleming, 166 Cal. 357, 136 P. 291, syl. 13 (1913) (law-suit between witness and party, inquiry into details unduly curbed); State v. Malmberg, 14 N.D. 523, 105 N.W. 614, 616 (1905) (village political rivalry; proof of main facts, matter of right; extent of proof of details, discretionary; here unduly curbed); State v. Burkett, 33 N.M. 159, 262 P. 532, syl. 1 (1928) (similar to last); Brink v. Stratton, 176 N.Y. 150, 68 N.E. 148 (1903) (similar); 3 Wigmore, § 951, note 2; 70 C.J. 990, § 1197. A few courts have held that if the witness admits bias in general terms this precludes further inquiry. See, e. g., Walker v. State, 74 Ga.App. 48, 39 S.E.2d 75, 77, syl. 1 (1946); 3 Wigmore, Evidence, § 951, note 3. Contra: Newton v. State, 32 Ala.App. 640, 29 So.2d 353, 355 (1947) (admission of bias does not close door to showing of extent or cause, but exclusion here not erroneous in view of all the evidence); Glass v. Bosworth, 113 Vt. 303, 34 A.2d 113, 115 (1943) (disapproving earlier contrary holding).

After all, impeachment is not a central matter, and the trial judge, though he may not deny a reasonable opportunity at either stage to prove the bias of the witness, has a discretion to control the extent to which the proof may go.[29] He has the responsibility for seeing that the side-show does not take over the circus. On the other hand, if the witness on cross-examination denies or does not fully admit the facts claimed to show bias, the attacker has the right to prove those facts by extrinsic evidence. In courtroom parlance, facts showing bias are not "collateral," [30] and the cross-examiner is not required to "take the answer" of the witness,[31] but may call other witnesses to prove them.[32]

41. Character: In General.

Obviously the character of a witness for truthfulness or mendacity is material circumstantial evidence on the question of the truth of particular testimony of the witness. The discussion of the rules which have developed as to character-impeachment will reveal certain general questions of balancing policies. Among them are these: How far in any particular situation does the danger of unfair prejudice against the witness and the party calling him from this type of impeachment outweigh the probable value of the light shed on credibility? Again, should the field of character-impeachment be limited so far as practicable to attack on the particular character-trait of truthfulness or should it extend to "general" character for its undoubted though more remote bearing upon truthfulness, on the notion that the greater includes the less?

It seems probable, moreover, that the tendency, particularly in civil cases, is to use this form of attack more and more sparingly. It was part of the melodrama of the pioneer trial to find "the villain of the piece." It fits less comfortably into the more business-like atmosphere of the present court-room. Moreover, as a method of advocacy, the danger

to the attacker if such an attack fails of its mark, or if it is pressed too far, comes more to be realized and emphasized. Finally, judges and lawyers are more and more conscious of their duty of fairness to witnesses. The following quotations from a ruling of the English Bar Council on November 6, 1950, show the trend:

> "On 6th November, 1950, the council approved the following ruling of professional etiquette with regard to cross-examination:
>
> "'. . . 1. In all cases it is the duty of the barrister to guard against being made the channel for questions which are only intended to insult or annoy either the witness or any other person, and to exercise his own judgment both as to the substance and the form of the questions put.
>
> . . .
>
> "'4. Questions which affect the credibility of a witness by attacking his character, but are not otherwise relevant to the actual inquiry, ought not to be asked unless the cross-examiner has reasonable grounds for thinking that the imputation conveyed by the question is well-founded or true.
>
> . . .
>
> "'7. Such questions should only be put if, in the opinion of the cross-examiner, the answers would or might materially affect the credibility of the witness; and if the imputation conveyed by the question relates to matters so remote in time or of such a character that it would not materially

29. Glass v. Bosworth, 113 Vt. 303, 34 A.2d 113, syl. 3 (1943) (wide scope on cross-examination, in court's discretion); People v. Lustig, 206 N.Y. 162, 99 N.E. 183, 186, syl. 5 (1912) (extent of testimony by other witnesses in court's discretion).

30. State v. Day, 339 Mo. 74, 95 S.W.2d 1183, 1184, syl. 2–5 (1936); Smith v. Hockenberry, 146 Mich. 7, 109 N.W. 23, 24 (1906).

31. Helwig v. Laschowski, 82 Mich. 623, 46 N.W. 1033, 1034 (1890); 6 Wigmore, Evidence, § 1005(b) (c).

32. People v. Lustig, 206 N.Y. 162, 99 N.E. 183, syl. 4 (1912); 6 Wigmore, Evidence, § 943; 70 C.J. 995, § 1200, note 33.

affect the credibility of the witness, the question should not be put.'"

42. Character: Misconduct, Not the Subject of Criminal Conviction.[1]

The English common law tradition of "cross-examination to credit," permits the counsel to inquire into the associations and personal history of the witness, including any particular misconduct which would tend to discredit his character, though not the subject of conviction for crime.[2] Apparently, the courts trust usually to the disciplined discretion of the bar, to avoid abuses, though restraint by the court by informal intervention is not unknown.[3]

In this country, the danger of victimizing witnesses and of undue prejudice to the parties, has led most of our courts to recognize that this kind of cross-examination, though permitted, is subject to a discretionary control by the trial judge.[4] Some of the factors, in addition to those of undue humiliation and unfair prejudice, already mentioned, which may, it seems, sway discretion, are (1) whether the testimony of the witness under attack is crucial or unimportant, (2) whether the misconduct inquired into is relevant to truthfulness,[5] such as false swearing, fraud and swindling, or bears only on "general bad character"[6] such as acts of violence or

1. 3 Wigmore, Evidence, §§ 981–987; Dec.Dig. Witnesses, ⊕344, 349; 70 C.J.Witnesses, §§ 1084–1100.

2. 3 Wigmore, Evidence, §§ 983, 986; Phipson, Evidence, 470 (8th ed. 1942).

3. See Rules quoted in next preceding section; quotations from Stephen and Birkenhead in 3 Wigmore, Evidence, § 983; and 13 Halsbury's Laws of England, Evidence, § 836 (2d ed. 1934) ("There are, also, certain limits, which must be determined by the discretion of the judge to the questions which may be asked affecting a witness's credit . . .").

4. Simon v. United States, 123 F.2d 80, syl. 13–15, 18 (C.C.A. 4th 1941) (accused as witness properly subjected to inquiry as to false swearing in application for visa and tax return: trial judge has discretion as to extent of cross-examination on misconduct); Pullman Co. v. Hall, 55 F.2d 139, syl. 6–8 (C.C.A. 4th 1932) (trial court excluded inquiry as to plaintiff's having filed false pauper's affidavit, held, error, discretion applied only to the extent to which such examination should be pursued: the particular result is right but surely the formula announced is an unwise curtailment of discretion); Niemeyer v. McCarty, 221 Ind. 688, 51 N.E.2d 365, syl. 17, 154 A.L.R. 115 (rule of discretion as in last case); People v. Sorge, 301 N.Y. 198, 93 N.E.2d 637, syl. 1, 3, 8 (1950) (in abortion prosecution, accused properly cross-examined as to previous abortions; manner and extent in judge's discretion); State v. Neal, 222 N.C. 546, 23 S.E.2d 911, syl. 4 (1943) (accused in murder case properly asked about previous cutting affrays, larceny, vagrancy, nuisance and violation of the prohibition law, in judge's "sound discretion").

A comprehensive collection of decisions is found in 3 Wigmore, Evidence, § 987, covering 45 pages. Torrance, J. gives an enlightening discussion of

the various views, in Shailer v. Bullock, 78 Conn. 65, 61 A. 65 (1905).

5. Some courts limit the inquiry to misconduct indicating lack of veracity. State v. Schutte, 97 Conn. 462, 117 A. 508, syl. 8 (1922) (living in adultery properly excluded); Nelson v. State, 99 Fla. 1032, 128 So. 1, syl. 2, 3 (1930) (use of opium, at other than relevant times, properly excluded); State v. Knox, 98 S.C. 114, 82 S.E. 278, syl. 2 (1914) (previous cutting scrapes should have been excluded); 70 C.J. 869, § 1088.

6. Some decisions admit misconduct which either bears directly on veracity or indicates such moral depravity "as would likely render him insensible to the obligations of an oath." Coulston v. United States, 51 F.2d 178, 181 (C.C.A. 10th 1931) (morphine transactions, excluded); Miller v. Territory, 149 F. 330, 338 (C.C.A. 8th, 1906). To meet this test the conduct need not be criminal. People v. Johnston, 228 N.Y. 332, 127 N.E. 186, syl. 5 (1920) (sending money to an accused prisoner for him to buy witnesses). The fact that the witness has been dishonorably discharged from the army was held so doubtful in its implications as to "moral character" as to warrant the judge, in discretion, to exclude the inquiry. Kelley v. State, 226 Ind. 148, 78 N.E.2d 547, syl. 14 (1948).

Another theory, akin to but distinguishable from misconduct as showing character, is the theory that on cross-examination the examiner is entitled to place the witness in his setting by showing his residence and occupation. See § 29, supra. A recent leading case has greatly revived the vogue of this theory. Alford v. United States, 282 U.S. 687, 51 S.Ct. 218, syl. 2, 75 L.Ed. 624 (1931). Under this theory, it may be shown that a witness is or has been engaged in a disreputable occupation. Sweeney v. State, 161 Ark. 278, 256 S.W. 73, syl

unchastity,[7] (3) the nearness or remoteness of the misconduct to the time of trial,[8] and (4) whether the matter inquired into is such as to lead to time-consuming and distracting explanations on cross-examination or re-examination.[9]

A minority of jurisdictions in this country, including Massachusetts,[10] Pennsylvania,[11] Texas,[12] and California [13] and the states following its Code,[14] avoid the dangers of cross-examination as to particular misconduct not the subject of convictions, solely to discredit, by forbidding such cross-examination altogether.[15]

In the formative period of Evidence law, there came to be recognized, as a sort of vague corollary of the privilege against self-incrimination, a privilege of a witness not to answer questions calling for answers which would degrade or disgrace him, provided such questions were not material to the issues in the case.[16] The privilege, though sporadically recognized from time to time during the 1800s,[17] has in the present century been generally abandoned,[18] except as it is encysted in the Codes of a few states.[19] The practical protection to the witness is not so effective as that given by courts which prohibit

---

6 (1923); Fowler v. State, 8 Okl.Cr. 130, 126 P. 831, syl. 3 (1912) (boot-legger); 3 Wharton's Criminal Evidence, § 1317 (11th ed. 1935). And this theory is employed in some states which prohibit cross-examination as to misconduct. People v. Lain, 57 Cal.App.2d 123, 134 P.2d 284, syl. 12, 13 (gambler); Roberts v. State, 83 Tex.Cr. 139, 201 S.W. 998, syl. 11 (1918) (employee of disorderly house). Cases pro and con are collected in Dec.Dig. Witnesses, ⊆344(4); Note, 1 A.L.R. 1402.

7. See, e. g., Robinson v. Atterbury, 135 Conn. 517, 66 A.2d 593, syl. 6, 7 (1949) (acts of immorality, judge properly excluded in discretion); State v. Whipkey, 358 Mo. 563, 215 S.W.2d 492, syl. 8, 11 (1948) (murder: cross-examination as to unchaste conduct, properly excluded, in discretion); Frank v. State, 150 Neb. 745, 35 N.W.2d 816, syl. 13 (1949) (assault to rape; cross-examination and extrinsic evidence of unchaste conduct of prosecutrix admissible on credibility and consent); Riddle v. State, 92 Okl.Cr. 397, 223 P.2d 379, syl. 5–7 (1950) (female witness cannot be impeached by questions as to immoral conduct); Note, 65 A.L.R. 410.

8. Shailer v. Bullock, 78 Conn. 65, 61 A. 65, 67 (1905); 70 C.J. 871, § 1091.

9. See Robinson v. Atterbury, 135 Conn. 517, 66 A.2d 593, syl. 8 (1949).

10. So held in Comm. v. Schaffner, 146 Mass. 512, 16 N.E. 280, syl. 6 (1888), but later cases seem to recognize the rule of discretion. See Campbell v. Ashler, 320 Mass. 475, 70 N.E.2d 302, syl. 5 (1946); 3 Wigmore, Evidence, p. 592.

11. Berliner v. Schoenberg, 117 Pa.Super. 254, 178 A. 330, syl. 4 (1935).

12. Gulf, C. & S. F. Ry. Co. v. Johnson, 83 Tex. 628, 19 S.W. 151, syl. 6 (1892); Burns v. State, 127 Tex.Cr. 599, 78 S.W.2d 956, syl. 2 (1935); McCormick and Ray, Texas Law of Evidence, § 311 (1937).

13. In re Gird's Estate, 157 Cal. 534, 108 P. 499, 505, syl. 9 (1910).

14. Code Civ.Proc. § 2051 (witness may not be impeached "by evidence of particular wrongful acts, except that it may be shown by the examination of the witness, or the record of the judgment, that he has been convicted of a felony").

15. This view seems to be accepted in Uniform Rules of Evidence, R. 22(d), which provides that "evidence of specific instances of his conduct relevant only as tending to prove a trait of his character, shall be inadmissible."

16. See 3 Wigmore, Evidence, §§ 984, 986(3).

17. See 3 Wigmore, Evidence, §§ 986(3) note 13, 987.

18. Among decisions rejecting the privilege, see, e. g., Wallace v. State, 41 Fla. 547, 26 So. 713, 722, syl. 14 (1899); State v. Pfefferle, 36 Kan. 90, 92, 12 P. 406, 408 (1886) (degrading character of question factor for judge's discretion); Carroll v. State, 32 Tex. Cr. 431, 24 S.W. 100 (1893).

19. Calif.Code of Civ.Proc. § 2065 (privilege not to give "an answer which will have a direct tendency to degrade his character, unless it be to the very fact in issue, or to a fact from which the fact in issue would be presumed" and must answer to a conviction for felony); Georgia, Code 1933, §§ 38–1205, 38–1711 (facts "which shall tend to bring infamy or disgrace or public contempt upon himself or any member of his family"); Iowa, I.C.A. §§ 622.14, 622.-15 (answers which would "expose him to public ignominy," with exceptions); Montana, R.C.M.1947 § 93–2101–2 (like Calif., supra); Nebraska, R.S.1943. §§ 25–1210, 25–1214 (like Iowa, supra); Nevada, N.C. L.1929, § 8984 (like Calif., supra); Oregon, ORS 44–070 (like Calif., supra); Utah, U.C.A.1953, 78–24–9 (like Calif., supra).

such cross-examination altogether, since the prohibitory rule will be invoked by counsel or by the court of its own motion, whereas the privilege must be claimed by the witness, and such a claim is almost as degrading as an affirmative answer.

The final curb on character-impeachment by proof of misconduct not the subject of convictions is the important and accepted rule that it is limited to cross-examination. Thus, if the witness denies the alleged misconduct, the examiner must "take his answer," not in the sense that he may not further cross-examine to extort an admission,[20] but in the sense that he may not call other witnesses to prove the discrediting acts.[21]

43. Character: Conviction of Crime.[1]

At common law the conviction of a person for treason or any felony, or for a misdemeanor involving dishonesty (*crimen falsi*), or the obstruction of justice, rendered the convicted person altogether incompetent as a witness. These were said to be "infamous" crimes.[2] By statutes which are practically universal in the common law world, this primitive absolutism has been abandoned and the disqualification for conviction of crime has been abrogated, and by specific provision or by decision has been reduced to a mere ground of impeachment of credibility. Just as the common law definition of disqualifying crimes was not very precise, so also the abrogating statutes are correspondingly indefinite,[3] and the resulting definitions of

---

20. People v. Sorge, 301 N.Y. 198, 93 N.E.2d 637, syl. 4, 5 (1950) (when witness denies, examiner in good faith may question further in hope of inducing witness to change answer).

21. United States v. Sager, 49 F.2d 725, syl. 6, 7 (C.C. A.2d 1931, opinion by Manton, J.) (accused on cross-examination denied he was forced to resign as Assistant Attorney General; held error to allow government to call Attorney General to contradict this); Coulston v. United States, 51 F.2d 178, syl. 11, 14 (C.C.A. 10th, 1931); State v. Herson, 84 N.H. 433, 152 A. 276, syl. 2, 4 (1930) (error to allow state to prove after defendant's denial on cross, that defendant had intercourse with girl under age); State v. Bowman, 232 N.C. 374, 61 S.E.2d 107, syl. 5 (1950) (improper for state to attack credibility of defendant's witness by calling other witnesses to testify to her acts of misconduct); 3 Wigmore, Evidence, § 979; 70 C.J. 897, § 1099.

1. 3 Wigmore, Evidence, §§ 980, 980a, 985–987; 6 Jones, Evidence, §§ 2440, 2441 (2d ed. 1926); Ladd, Credibility Tests, 89 U.Pa.L.Rev. 166, 174 (1940) (excellent); Dec.Dig. Witnesses, ☜345; 70 C.J. Witnesses, §§ 1052–1063; 58 Am.Jur. Witnesses, §§ 734–753.

2. Greenleaf, Evidence, § 373 (1842); 2 Wigmore, Evidence, § 520.

3. See, e. g., England, St. 6 & 7 Victoria, c. 85 (". . . no person offered as a witness shall hereafter be excluded by reason of incapacity from crime . . .") followed in 1865, by the Criminal Procedure Act, sec. 6, which provided: "A witness may be questioned as to whether he has been convicted of any felony or misdemeanor, and upon being so questioned, he either denies or does not ad-

mit the fact, or refuses to answer, it shall be lawful for the cross examining party to prove such conviction; and a certificate containing the substance and effect only (omitting the formal part) of the indictment and conviction for such offense, purporting to be signed by the clerk of the court or other officer having the custody of the records of the court where the offender was convicted, or by the deputy of such clerk or officer, (for which certificate a fee of five shillings and no more shall be demanded or taken,) shall, upon proof of the identity of the person, be sufficient evidence of the said conviction, without proof of the signature or official character of the person appearing to have signed the same."; Alabama, Code 1940, Tit. 7, § 434 ("No objection must be allowed to the competency of a witness because of his conviction for any crime, except perjury or subornation of perjury; but if he has been convicted of a crime involving moral turpitude, the objection goes to his credibility"); California, Code Civ.Proc. § 1879 ("All persons, without exception, otherwise than is specified in the next two sections, who, having organs of sense, can perceive, and, perceiving, can make known their perceptions to others, may be witnesses. Therefore, neither parties nor other persons who have an interest in the event of an action or proceeding are excluded; nor those who have been convicted of crime; nor persons on account of their opinions on matters of religious belief; although in every case the credibility of the witness may be drawn in question, . . ."); Connecticut, Gen.Stat.1949, (§ 7868 "No person shall be disqualified as a witness in any action by reason of his interest in the event of the same as a party or otherwise, or of his disbelief in the existence of a Supreme Being, or of his conviction of crime; but

crimes for which a conviction[4] shall be ground of impeachment vary widely among the states.

A few jurisdictions seem to adhere to the loose common law definition, described above, of "infamous crimes."[5] The California Code[6] and codes modeled upon it, adopt the limitation to "felonies," which is at least simple to apply. Similarly easy of administration is the English description "any felony or misdemeanor."[7] This last seems to be the construction which some of the courts place upon the statutes worded in terms of "crime" or "any crime."[8] But most courts, oversensitive perhaps to the feelings of witnesses, have been unwilling to accept such simple mechanical tests, and have read into such general statutes the requirement that as to misdemeanors at least, the offense must be one involving "moral turpitude."[9] Thus

---

such interest or conviction may be shown for the purpose of affecting his credit"); Iowa, I.C.A. (§ 622.1: "Every human being of sufficient capacity to understand the obligation of an oath is a competent witness in all cases, except as otherwise declared"; § 622.2: "Facts which have heretofore caused the exclusion of testimony may still be shown for the purpose of lessening its credibility"); Minnesota, M.S.A. (§ 610.49: "Every person convicted of crime shall be a competent witness in any civil or criminal proceeding, but his conviction may be proved for the purpose of affecting the weight of his testimony, either by the record or by his cross-examination, upon which he shall answer any proper question relevant to that inquiry; and the party cross-examining shall not be concluded by his answer thereto"), and other statutes collected in 2 Wigmore, Evidence, § 488.

4. Conviction, of course, is the present requirement, and though it was once thought otherwise, an accusation, though official, as an arrest, indictment, or information, cannot be inquired of. State v. Christopharo, 70 R.I. 57, 37 A.2d 163, syl. 5, 7 (1944) (arrest); State v. Goodwin, 29 Wash.2d 276, 186 P.2d 935, syl. 1–3 (1947) (indictment); 3 Wigmore, Evidence, § 980a. Contra: State v. Guillory, 201 La. 52, 9 So.2d 450, syl. 7 (1942) (accused taking stand properly cross-examined as to prior arrests and indictments). In criminal cases in Texas, such examination was formerly allowed, but this practice was abrogated by Tex.Gen.Laws 1951, ch. 458, p. 814, Vernon's Ann.C.C.P. art. 732a and note. In collision cases, proof is often sought to be made, under guise of impeachment, that one of the drivers has been arrested for negligent driving at the time of the collision. It may have a remote bearing upon bias, but its prejudicial use by the jury as hearsay evidence of guilt is an overweening danger, and the courts usually exclude it. See Holden v. Berberich, 351 Mo. 995, 174 S.W.2d 791, syl. 5 (1943) (cross-examination of driver as to indictment for driving while intoxicated at time of collision); and see Paul v. Drown, 108 Vt. 458, 189 A. 144, 146, syl. 6, 109 A.L.R. 1085 (1937) (offer by defendant in collision to show that defendant was not arrested, requires reversal).

5. National Labor Relations Board v. Baldwin Locomotive Works, 128 F.2d 39, syl. 15 (C.C.A. 3d, 1942) (trial examiner properly limited impeachment to convictions for felony or misdeameanors amounting to crimen falsi); United States v. Montgomery, 126 F.2d 151, syl. 12, 13 (C.C.A. 3d. 1942) (same, criminal case); People v. Thomas, 393 Ill. 573, 67 N.E. 2d 192, syl. 8, 9 (1946) ("record of an infamous crime" to be considered on credibility); Kornreich v. Industrial Fire Ins. Co., 132 Oh.St. 78, 5 N.E.2d 153, syl. 3 (1936); Comm. v. Kostan, 349 Pa. 560, 37 A.2d 606, syl. 10 (1944) (treason, felony or crimen falsi: inquiry as to 26 convictions for "drunk and disorderly" properly excluded).

6. See note 3, supra.

7. See note 3, supra.

8. See, e. g., State v. Cioffe, 128 N.J.L. 342, 26 A.2d 57, 65, syl. 32 (1942) ("any crime"); State v. Carter, 750 Ohio App. 545, 58 N.E.2d 794, syl. 1 (1944) ("crime," error to hold permits only proof of conviction of felony); Coslow v. State, 83 Okl.Cr. 378, 177 P.2d 518, syl. 10 (1947) ("conviction of crime" not limited to offences involving moral turpitude). But a mere violation of a city ordinance would not be included. Koch v. State, 146 Wis. 470, 106 N.W. 531, syl. 4 (1906).

9. Sparks v. State, 32 Ala.App. 450, 27 So.2d 508, syl. 1 (1946) (dictum, "crime involving moral turpitude"); State v. Jenness, 143 Me. 380, 62 A.2d 867, syl. 1–6 (1948) (R.S.1944, c. 100, § 128 as amended by Pub.L.1947, c. 265, "felony, any larceny or any other crime involving moral turpitude" does not extend to illegal possession and sale of liquor); Gantt v. Columbia Coca-Cola Co., 204 S.C. 374, 29 S.E.2d 488, syl. 3 (1944) (illicit distilling to defraud federal government is a felony involving "moral delinquency"); Rylee v. State, 131 Tex.Cr. 127, 96 S.W.2d 988, syl. 1 (1936) (conviction must be of felony or of misdemeanor involving moral turpitude); Burford v. Comm., 179 Va. 608, 20 S.E.2d 508, syl. 7, 9, 10 (1942) (conviction in federal court for removal of non-tax paid liquor not provable to impeach, though a federal felony, because corresponding offense not a felony under state law, and does not

does the serpent of uncertainty crawl into the Eden of trial administration. Still more uncertain is the situation in the states which leave to the trial judge's discretion whether the particular conviction substantially affects the credibility of the witness.[10] It seems questionable whether the creation of a detailed catalog [11] of crimes involving "moral turpitude" and its application at the trial and on appeal is not a waste of judicial energy in view of the size of the problem. Moreover, it seems that shifting the burden to the judge's discretion is inexpedient, since only in a minority of cases will the judge have adequate information upon which to exercise such discretion. A clear certain rule like the English one is preferable, despite its somewhat arbitrary cast. Perhaps better still is the proposal of the Uniform Rules to limit impeachment to conviction of crimes "involving dishonesty or false statement," [12] a fairly definite, but not arbitrary criterion.

Convictions in another state [13] or in the federal court [14] are usable to impeach. Though a judgment against a lawyer of suspension or disbarment for criminal misconduct is not technically a conviction, it has been held to be provable to impeach.[15] In statutes relating to proceedings in juvenile courts it is frequently provided that an adjudication of delinquency shall not be used in evidence against the child in any other court and shall not be deemed a "conviction." Such statutes are usually construed as precluding such a finding from being used as a conviction to impeach credibility.[16]

A pardon does not prevent the use of the conviction to impeach,[17] but most courts hold that lapse of time may have this effect, and that a conviction too remote in time may be excluded by the judge if in his discretion he finds that under the circumstances it lacks probative value.[18]

involve moral turpitude; so also state conviction for assault and battery, no turpitude).

10. Burgess v. State, 161 Md. 162, 155 A. 153, syl. 12–15, 75 A.L.R. 1471 (1931) ("in the sound discretion of the trial court"; admitting evidence of conviction for simple assault not abuse of discretion); Zimmerman v. Goldberg, 277 Mich. 134, 268 N.W. 837, syl. 1 (1936) (in judge's discretion to admit or exclude convictions for misdemeanors; but error here to exclude, in collision case, conviction of defendant for reckless driving at time of this accident, because it was based on plea of guilty and hence admission).

11. For an example, see Drazen v. New Haven Taxicab Co., 95 Conn. 500, 111 A. 861, 863 (1920).

12. Uniform Rules of Evidence, R. 21: "Evidence of the conviction of a witness for a crime not involving dishonesty or false statement shall be inadmissible for the purpose of impairing his credibility. . . ."

13. City of Boston v. Santosuosso, 307 Mass. 302, 30 N.E.2d 278, syl. 27 (1940); State v. Velsir, 61 Wyo. 476, 159 P.2d 371, syl. 4 (1945).

14. See Burford v. Comm., 179 Va. 752, 30 S.E.2d 509, syl. 7 (1942) where it was assumed that the federal conviction would be admissible if it met the Virginia standard of felony or misdemeanor affecting credibility. A state conviction may be proved in the

federal court. United States v. Skidmore, 123 F.2d 604, syl. 24 (C.C.A. 7th, 1941) (semble).

15. Lansing v. Michigan Central Ry. Co., 143 Mich. 48, 106 N.W. 692, syl. 4 (1906); 6 Jones, Evidence 4836, note 2 (2d ed. 1926).

16. Thomas v. United States, 121 F.2d 905, syl. 4 (Ct.App.D.C.1941); State v. Kelly, 169 La. 753, 126 So. 49, syl. 2 (1930); Burge v. State, 96 Tex.Cr. 32, 255 S.W. 754, syl. 4 (1923); 70 C.J. 853, note 23. But compare the views expressed in 3 Wigmore, Evidence, §§ 924a, 980(7). He collects the statutes in § 196, note 5.

17. Richards v. United States, 192 F.2d 602, syl. 4 (C.A.D.C.1951) (one judge dissenting); Vedin v. McConnell, 22 F.2d 753, syl. 1 (C.C.A. 9th, 1927); 70 C.J. 857, note 84; Note, 59 A.L.R. 1480, 1489. As to the effect of the pendency of an appeal from the conviction see United States v. Empire Packing Co., 174 F.2d 16, 20 (C.A. 7th, 1949), but compare Campbell v. United States, 176 F.2d 45, syl. 6 (Ct.App. D.C.1949).

18. Fire Ass'n of Philadelphia v. Weathered, 62 F.2d 78, syl. 4, 5 (C.C.A.Tex., 1932) (court in discretion properly excluded convictions 30 and 50 years old); Goddard v. United States, 131 F.2d 220, syl. 4, 5 (1942) (not abuse of discretion to admit conviction of felony 12 years before when witness was only 15). Compare a Texas case where the element of discretion is not mentioned and the question treat-

The general rule is that proof of an official record must if feasible be made by the use of a certified or examined copy, in preference to oral testimony of its contents.[19] The rule was applied in England to proof of records of conviction, so as to preclude the cross-examiner from asking about convictions.[20] This practice still lingers in a few states,[21] but the inconvenience of such a requirement, and the obvious reliability of the answer of a witness acknowledging his own conviction, have lead most jurisdictions, by either statute or decision, to permit the proof to be made either by production of the record or a copy, or by the oral statement of the convicted witness himself.[22] Here the cross-examiner need not "lay a foundation" for proof by copy or record,[23] nor is he bound to "take the answer" if the witness denies the conviction, but may prove it by the record.[24]

How far may the cross-examiner go in his inquiries about convictions? He may ask about the name of the crime committed,[25] as murder or embezzlement, and the punishment awarded.[26] It will certainly add to the pungency of the impeachment where the crime was an aggravated one if he may ask about the circumstances, such as in a conviction of murder whether the victim was a baby, the niece of the witness.[27] And it is argued that since proof by record is allowable, and the record would show many of these circumstances, the cross-examination should at least be permitted to touch all the facts that the record would.[28] On the whole, however, the more reasonable practice, minimizing prejudice and distraction from the issues, is the one generally prevailing that beyond the name of the crime,[29] the time and place of conviction,[30] and the punishment, further details such as the name of the vic-

---

ed seemingly as one for the upper court *de novo.* Gill v. State, 147 Tex.Cr. 392, 181 S.W.2d 276, syl. 1–3 (1944) (error to exclude conviction 18 years old where followed by other convictions as recent as 7 years before trial). Decisions are collected, 70 C.J. 854, § 1057.

19. See, e. g., Jones v. Melindy, 62 Ark. 203, 208, 36 S.W. 22, syl. 2 (1896), and discussion § 207, herein, and 4 Wigmore, Evidence, § 1269.

20. R. v. Castell Careinion, 8 East 77, 79, 103 Eng. Rep. 273 (K.B.1806).

21. See, e. g., Corley v. State, 64 Ga.App. 841, 14 S.E. 2d 121, syl. 4 (1941); People v. Grizzle, 381 Ill. 278, 44 N.E.2d 917, 922, syl. 13 (1942); Comm. v. Walsh, 196 Mass. 369, 82 N.E. 19, syl. 1 (1907).

22. See, e. g., State v. English, 132 Conn. 573, 46 A.2d 121, syl. 6 (1946); Smith v. Comm., 182 Va. 585, 30 S.E.2d 26, syl. 11 (1944) and the provisions of the English and Minnesota statutes, note 3, this sec., above. Authorities are collected in 4 Wigmore, Evidence, § 1270, note 5.

23. State v. Hougenson, 91 Utah 351, 64 P.2d 229, syl. 7 (1936) (dictum); State v. Beard, 148 Wash. 701, 269 P. 1051, syl. 1 (1928).

24. See MacKnight v. United States, 263 F. 832, syl. 8 (C.C.A. 1st, 1920) (where witness denies he was same person who served term in penitentiary, impeacher may prove he was inmate by men who saw

him there); Ivey v. State, 132 Fla. 36, 180 So. 368, syl. 2 (1938) (by statute).

25. Hadley v. State, 25 Ariz. 23, 212 P. 458, syl. 12, 13 (1923); People v. Romer, 218 Cal. 449, 23 P.2d 749, syl. 2 (1933); State v. Crawford, 60 Utah 6, 206 P. 717, syl. 7 (1922); 70 C.J. 854, § 1053.

26. See, e. g., Reid v. State, 100 Tex.Cr. 512, 271 S.W. 625, syl. 3 (1925) (payment of fine as prostitute); Finch v. State, 103 Tex.Cr. 212, 280 S.W. 597, syl. 1 (1926) (permissible to ask if he has not served a term in penitentiary).

27. Choice v. State, 54 Tex.Cr. 517, 521, 114 S.W. 132, 133 (1908) (properly excluded).

28. See State v. Green, 167 Wash. 266, 9 P.2d 62, syl. 2 (1932) (permitting "further interrogation as to the nature of the crime," extent not shown); Note, 7 Wash.L.Rev. 303. See also State v. Rodia, 132 N.J. L. 199, 39 A.2d 484, syl. 1, 2. ("Were you ever convicted of the crime of atrocious assault and battery by cutting," approved over objection that "by cutting" was improper, on ground that the charge of cutting would have been shown by the record of conviction).

29. See note 25, supra.

30. Hadley v. State, 25 Ariz. 23, 212 P. 458, 462 (1923) ("Were you ever convicted of a felony in Oklahoma," approved).

tim[31] and the aggravating circumstances may not be inquired into.[32]

It may be thought that if the impeacher is precluded from showing details and circumstances of aggravation, the witness should similarly be cut off from explaining or extenuating the conviction or denying his guilt. Certainly it is impractical and forbidden to re-try the case on which the conviction was based. And many courts forbid any explanation, extenuation or denial of guilt even by the witness himself on re-direct.[33] This is a logical consequence of the premise of conclusiveness of the judgment. It does not, however, satisfy our feeling that some reasonable outlet for the instinct of self-defense by one attacked should be conceded, if it can be done without too much damage to the business at hand. Accordingly a substantial number of courts, while not opening the door to a re-trial of the conviction, do permit the witness himself to make a brief and general statement in explanation, mitigation, or denial of guilt,[34] or recognize a discretion in the trial judge to permit it.[35] Wigmore aptly terms it a "harmless charity to allow the

witness to make such protestations on his own behalf as he may feel able to make with a due regard to the penalties of perjury."[36]

The sharpest and most prejudicial impact of the practice of impeachment by conviction (as is true also of cross-examination as to misconduct, see § 42, above) is upon one particular type of witness, namely, the accused in a criminal case who elects to take the stand. If the accused is forced to admit that he has a "record" of past convictions, particularly if they are for crimes similar to the one on trial, the danger is obvious that the jury, despite instructions, will give more heed to the past convictions as evidence that the accused is the kind of man who would commit the crime on charge, or even that he ought to be put away without too much concern with present guilt, than they will to its legitimate bearing on credibility. This places the accused, who has a "record" but who thinks he has a defense to the present charge, in a grievous dilemma. If he stays off the stand his silence alone will prompt the jury to believe him guilty. If he elects to testify, his "record" becomes provable to impeach

31. Stevens v. State, 138 Tex.Cr. 59, 134 S.W.2d 246, syl. 6 (1939).

32. Powers v. State, 156 Miss. 316, 126 So. 12, syl. 1 (1930) ("You are under suspended sentence for beating your wife and son?", improper); White v. State, 202 Miss. 246, 30 So.2d 894, syl. 3 (1947) (inquiry whether conviction for wilful trespass followed a withdrawn plea of guilty of burglary, improper); State v. Mount, 73 N.J.L. 583, 64 A. 124, syl. 1 (1906) (error to inquire of accused about particulars of prior assault for which he was convicted, such as size of the man assaulted and weapon used); Finch v. State, 103 Tex.Cr. 212, 280 S.W. 597, syl. 2 (1926) (hit-and-run; proof of details of prior offense with a car for which accused convicted, error); 70 C.J. 854, § 1054.

33. Mayo v. State, 32 Ala.App. 264, 24 So.2d 769, syl. 2, 3 (1946) (acused-witness not allowed to show he was given probation for offence for which convicted); Lamoureux v. New York, N. H. & H. R. Co., 169 Mass. 338, 47 N.E. 1009, syl. 3 (1897) (witness's extenuation properly excluded; leading opinion, by Holmes, J.); State v. Lapan, 101 Vt. 124, 141 A. 686, syl. 24 (1928) (extensive discussion, following preceding case).

34. Hopper v. State, 151 Ark. 299, 236 S.W. 595, syl. 2 (1922) (that he was only 19 and was persuaded by another to commit a robbery); Perry v. State, 146 Fla. 187, 200 So. 525, syl. 6 (1941) (witness may testify he has been paroled or pardoned); State v. Oxendine, 224 N.C. 825, 32 S.E.2d 648, syl. 3 (1945) (explanation of conviction for assault); Remington v. Judd, 186 Wis. 338, 202 N.W. 679, syl. 2 (1925) (witness should be permitted to state in a general way the nature of the offense, not to re-try, but to enable jury to judge "impeaching power" of conviction); 4 Wigmore, Evidence, § 1117, note 3.

35. Donnelly v. Donnelly, 156 Md. 81, 143 A. 648, syl. 7–9 (1928) (witness may not deny guilt, but judge in discretion may permit him to explain and extenuate); United States v. Boyer, 80 App.D.C. 202, 150 F.2d 595, syl. 1, 2 (1945) (witness, in discretion, may be allowed to extenuate or to assert innocence; fine discussion by Edgerton, J.), noted approvingly, 37 J.Crim.Law 515, 19 So.Cal.L.Rev. 129, and annotated in Note, Explaining Former Conviction, 166 A.L.R. 211.

36. 4 Evidence, § 1117, p. 191.

him, and this again is likely to doom his defense. Where does the balance of justice lie? Most prosecutors would say with much force that it would be unfair to permit the accused to appear as a witness of blameless life, and this argument has generally prevailed. But in England [37] and in Pennsylvania [38] the accused who takes the stand is shielded, under certain circumstances, from inquiry or proof as to misconduct or conviction of crime when offered to impeach. Similarly the Uniform Rule [39] provides that if the accused does not offer evidence supporting his own credibility the prosecution shall not be allowed, on cross-examination or otherwise, to prove for impeachment purposes his commission or conviction of crime. On balance it seems that to permit, as these provisions do, one accused of crime to tell his story without incurring the overwhelming prejudice likely to ensue from disclosing past convictions, is a more just, humane and expedient solution than the prevailing practice.

44. Character: Impeachment by Proof of Bad Reputation.[1]

There is a third way in which the character of the witness may be attacked. The impeacher brings on another witness, and in most states questions him like this:

> "Do you know the general reputation at the present time of William Witness in the community in which he lives, for truth and veracity?"
> "Yes."
> "What is that reputation?"
> "It is bad."

This routine is the distillation of traditions which have become established in a majority of American courts. These are the result of choices between alternative solutions, some wise, some seemingly misguided.

Misguided it seems is the first choice we shall mention. The majority doctrine is that this attack on character for truth must be in the abstract, debilitated form of proof of reputation. By what is apparently a misreading of legal history,[2] the American courts have generally prohibited the proof of character to be made by having the witness describe his belief or opinion of the character of the witness under attack based upon his experience with the man and observation of his conduct.[3] The limitation to reputation has been defended on the ground that

---

37. The Criminal Evidence Act, 1898 (61 & 62 Vict. c. 36), subs. 1(f) provides: "A person charged and called as a witness in pursuance of this Act shall not be asked, and if asked shall not be required to answer, any question tending to show that he has committed or been convicted of or been charged with any offence other than that wherewith he is then charged, or is of bad character, unless—(i) the proof that he has committed or been convicted of such other offence is admissible evidence to show that he is guilty of the offence wherewith he is then charged; or (ii) he has personally or by his advocate asked questions of the witnesses for the prosecution with a view to establish his own good character, or has given evidence of his good character, or the nature or conduct of the defence is such as to involve imputations on the character of the prosecutor or the witnesses for the prosecution; or (iii) he has given evidence against any other person charged with the same offence." See analysis and discussion, 1 Wigmore, Evidence, § 194a.

38. Act of July 3, 1947, P.L. 1239 (amending Act of March 15, 1911, Purdon's Pa.Stat.Ann. tit. 19, § 711),

discussed in 1 Wigmore, Evidence, § 194b, and pocket part.

39. Uniform Rules of Evidence, R. 21: ". . . If the witness be the accused in a criminal proceeding, no evidence of his conviction of a crime shall be admissible for the sole purpose of impairing his credibility unless he has first introduced evidence admissible solely for the purpose of supporting his credibility."

1. See 3 Wigmore, Evidence, §§ 920–930; 6 Jones, Evidence, §§ 2415–2422 (2d ed. 1926); Ladd, Credibility Tests, 89 U.Pa.L.Rev. 166, 171 (1940); Ladd, Techniques of Character Testimony, 24 Iowa L.Rev. 498 (1939); Dec.Dig., Witnesses, ☞333–343 356–358; 70 C.J. Witnesses, §§ 1032–1042; 58 Am.Jur. Witnesses, §§ 725–732.

2. See 7 Wigmore, Evidence, §§ 1981, 1982, and further discussion herein, § 153.

3. Sisson v. State, 168 Ark. 1005, 272 S.W. 674, syl. 3 (1925); Gifford v. People, 148 Ill. 173, 176, 35 N.E. 754, (dictum) (1893); State v. Steen, 185

to let in opinion from observation would provoke distracting side-issues over disputes about specific conduct of the witness attacked, since the impeaching witness may be cross-examined about the grounds of his opinion.[4] This danger undoubtedly exists and such controversies would need to be held to reasonable limits by the judge, but the question is whether the choice of reputation instead of experience and observation has not eliminated most of the objectivity from the attempt to appraise character, and has not encouraged the parties to select those who will give voice, under the guise of an estimate of reputation, to prejudice and ill-will. The hand is the hand of Esau, but the voice is the voice of Jacob.

The courts also have faced here another choice—a recurrent one in various phases of character-impeachment—namely, shall the inquiry be as to "general character," or as to other specific types of bad traits such as sexual immorality, or shall it be directed solely and specifically to the trait of veracity? Surely it is clear that in this elusive realm of opinion as to reputation as to character it is best to reach for the highest degree of relevancy that is attainable. Fortunately the great majority of our courts have taken this view and limit the inquiry to "reputation for truth and veracity."[5] Only a few open the door, in addition, to reputation for "general character"[6] or "general moral character"[7] and fewer still permit proof of reputation for specific traits other than veracity.[8]

The crucial time when the character of the witness under attack has its influence on his

---

N.C. 768, 117 S.E. 793, syl. 1 (1923); State v. Polhamus, 65 N.J.L. 387, 47 A. 470 (S.Ct.1900).

Many courts, however, perhaps conscious of the weakness of evidence limited strictly to reputation, have compromised by permitting the injection of personal opinion by such questions as these: (after proving bad reputation) "From that reputation, would you believe him on oath?" Burke v. Zwick, 299 Ill.App. 558, 20 N.E.2d 912 (1939). Or an even more curious straddle: "From your association with W. and from what you know about his reputation . . . do you believe him entitled to credit under oath?" See Bowles v. Katzman, 308 Ky. 490, 214 S.W.2d 1021, syl. 5 (1941).

4. See Willard Bartlett, J. in People v. Van Gaasbeck, 189 N.Y. 408, 82 N.E. 718, 721 (1907) (discussing the analogous problem as to character-evidence offered by the accused on the issue of guilt). The contrary argument of policy is powerfully presented in 7 Wigmore, Evidence, § 1986.

5. Pandula v. Fonseca, 145 Fla. 395, 199 So. 268, syl. 6 (1941) (confined to veracity and may not extend to general character or particular traits); Hoffman v. State, 93 Md. 388, 49 A. 658, syl. 2 (1901) (reputation for veracity exclusively); State v. Kahner, 217 Minn. 574, 15 N.W.2d 105, syl. 12, 13 (1944) (reputation for truth but not "moral character"); Schueler v. Lynam, 80 Ohio App. 325, 75 N.E.2d 464, syl. 3 (1947) (confined to veracity, does not extend to "general moral character"); 70 C.J. 826, notes 95, 96; 7 Wigmore, Evidence, § 923; Dec.Dig. Witnesses, ⊂➞342.

The California Code extends the inquiry to allied traits. Code Civ.Proc. § 2051 ("general reputation for truth, honesty or integrity"). So also Uniform Rules of Evidence, R. 22: "As affecting the credibility of a witness . . . (d) evidence of specific instances of his conduct relevant only as tending to prove a trait of his character, shall be inadmissible."

6. Grammar v. State, 239 Ala. 633, 19 So. 268, 272 (1940).

7. Indiana, Burns' Ann.St. §§ 2–1724, 9–1608; State v. Teager, 222 Iowa 391, 269 N.W. 348, syl. 7–9 (1936) (under I.C.A. § 622.18, general moral character may be shown, but proponent not precluded from showing veracity-reputation); New Mexico, 1941 Comp. § 20–204 ("general evidence of bad moral character not restricted to his reputation for truth and veracity"); 70 C.J. 825, note 93, 826, note 94.

8. Among decisions excluding the evidence are Calkins v. Ann Arbor Ry. Co., 119 Mich. 312, 78 N.W. 129, syl. 1 (1899) (honesty); State v. Colson, 193 N.C. 236, 136 S.E. 730, 732 (1927) (reputation as a boot-legger); Chatham v. State, 65 Okl.Cr. 240, 84 P.2d 804, syl. 1–3 (1938) (same as last). Most of the cases admitting the evidence are cases of prosecutions for sexual offences where the reputation for chastity of the prosecutrix is assailed. McGehee v. State, 162 Ark. 560, 258 S.W. 358, syl. 6 (1924) (carnal knowledge). Contra: State v. Stimpson, 78 Vt. 124, 62 A. 14, syl. 2 (1905) (rape under age, character as prostitute excluded); State v. Detweiler, 60 W.Va. 583, 55 S.E. 654 (1906) (rape). In this class of cases, it seems to be a psychological fact that the sexual experiences and propensities of

truth-telling is the time when he testifies.[9] But obviously reputation takes time to form and is the resultant of earlier conduct and demeanor, so that it does not precisely reflect character at a later date. The practical solution is to do what most courts actually do, that is, (1) to permit the reputation-witness to testify about the impeachee's "present" reputation, as of the time of the trial, if he knows it,[10] and (2) to permit testimony as to reputation (which is usually a settled, continuing condition) as of any time before trial which the judge in his discretion finds is not too remote to be significant.[11]

As to place,[12] the traditional inquiry is as to general reputation for veracity "in the community where he lives." The object of this limitation of place is obviously to restrict evidence of repute, to reputation among the people who know him best. This limitation was appropriate for the situation in England (and less so in America) before the Industrial Revolution, when most people lived either in small towns or in rural villages. But as an exclusive limitation it would not be appropriate in this country today, where a man may be little known in the suburb or city neighborhood where he lives, but well known in another locality where he spends his work-days or in several localities where he does business from time to time. Today accordingly it is generally agreed that proof may be made not only of the reputation of the witness where he lives, but also of his repute, so it be "general" and established, in any substantial community of people among whom he is well known,[13] such as the group with whom he works,[14] does business[15] or goes to school.[16] The trial judge has a reasonable meed of discretion to determine

the complainant do have great significance in respect to the probable truth of her complaints. See 3 Wigmore, Evidence, § 924a, citing the views of eminent psychiatrists as to the prevalence, and the abnormal motivations, of groundless complaints of sexual crime. Compare Redmon v. State, 150 Neb. 62, 33 N.W.2d 349 (1948) (trial judge should have permitted cross-examination of complainant as to previous acts of unchastity, quoting from the above section of Wigmore).

9. See State v. Sprague, 64 N.J.L. 419, 45 A. 788, syl. 1, 2 (S.Ct.1900) (when accused proves good character on issue of guilt, it is reputation at the time of act that counts, but if his credibility as a witness is in question, it is reputation at the time of trial that is proved).
Decisions as to time are collected in 3 Wigmore, Evidence, § 928; Dec.Dig. Witnesses, ⊜343; 70 C.J. Witnesses, §§ 1041, 1042.

10. Carter v. State, 226 Ala. 96, 145 So. 814, syl. 2 (1933) (time to which the character relates is "the time of trial and prior thereto"). But compare Frith v. Comm., 288 Ky. 188, 155 S.W.2d 851, syl. 4 (1941) (manslaughter: held impeachment by showing reputation for bad moral character as of time of trial ordinarily proper but error to admit where witness impeaching witness testifies bad reputation was due to the homicide).

11. Snow v. Grace, 29 Ark. 131, 136 (1874) (character seven years before properly received); Shuster v. State, 62 N.J.L. 521, 41 A. 701, syl. 3 (1898) (reputation 18 years before, properly excluded);

State v. Thomas, 8 Wash.2d 573, 113 P.2d 73, syl. 7, 12 (1941) (sodomy, evidence that prosecuting witness 13 years old had bad reputation for truth two years before trial, held, exclusion, in view of child's age, not abuse of discretion; careful opinion by Driver, J.).

12. See 9 Wigmore, Evidence, § 930; Dec.Dig. Witnesses, ⊜343, 70 C.J. 831, § 1043; Note, 112 A.L.R. 1020.

13. Craven v. State, 22 Ala.App. 39, 111 So. 767, syl. 4 (1927).
The question of place is often essentially a matter of the time when the reputation was acquired, discussed in the preceding paragraph. See, e g., Lee v. State, 179 Miss. 122, 174 So. 85, syl. 1 (1937) (reputation in place where witness lived six months before trial, provable).

14. Hamilton v. State, 129 Fla. 219, 176 So. 89, syl. 15, 112 A.L.R. 1013 (1937) (reputation could be proved by fellow-employees at hotel where accused worked).

15. Hubert v. Joslin, 285 Mich. 337, 280 N.W. 780, syl. 7 (1938) (reputation in locality 15 miles away from home, where he owned a farm, visited frequently and had many business dealings); State v. Henderson, 29 W.Va. 147, 1 S.E. 225, 240 (1886).

16. People v. Colantone, 243 N.Y. 134, 152 N.E. 700, 702, syl. 4, 5 (1926) (error to exclude evidence of reputation of ex-soldier, by instructors at vocational school, members of his company in army, and member of disabled veterans' post of 250 men. "The

whether the reputation sought to be proved among the group in question meets these standards.[17]

45. Defects of Capacity, Sensory or Mental.[1]

Any deficiency of the senses, such as deafness, or color-blindness or defect of other senses which would substantially lessen the ability to perceive the facts which the witness purports to have observed, should of course be provable to attack the credibility of the witness, either upon cross-examination or by producing other witnesses to prove the defect. Probably the limits and weaknesses of human powers of perception should be studied more widely by judges and lawyers in the interest of a more accurate and objective administration of justice. Moore[2] presents a valuable compendium of judicial empirical wisdom on the subject. Wigmore[3] gives a wealth of examples from the recorded cases and comments of the older school of psychologists. Burtt[4] and Gardner[5] and Elon Moore[6] present the findings of the newer group of psychologists.

As to the mental qualities of intelligence and memory, we must discriminate between attacks on competency[7] and attacks on credibility, with which latter we are now concerned. Sanity is not the test of competency and an insane person may testify if he is able to report correctly the matters he will be called to testify and understands the duty to speak the truth.[8] Manifestly, however, the fact of insanity or mental "abnormality" either at the time of observing the facts or at the time of testifying will be provable, on cross or by extrinsic evidence, as bearing on credibility.[9] What of defects of mind within the range of normality, such as a slower than average mind or a poorer than usual memory? These qualities reveal themselves in a testing cross-examination by a skilled questioner.[10] May they be proved by other wit-

determining factor is whether the community in which the defendant has lived his life is sufficiently large for the persons to become acquainted with his character and to form a general opinion of it. This we call general reputation. The cases are quite right which exclude evidence of reputation among such a small class of persons or business associates, as to make it, not a general reputation, but rather the evidence of individual and independent dealings."). Compare Williams v. United States, 168 U.S. 382, 18 S.Ct. 92, 97, 42 L.Ed. 509 (1897), (error to permit evidence of reputation of immigration inspector "in the custom house"; evidence as to his reputation "among the limited number of people in a particular public building" was inadmissible).

17. Ulrich v. Chicago, B. & Q. Ry. Co., 281 Mo. 697, 220 S.W. 682, 684, syl. 3, 4 (1920) (judge did not abuse discretion in admitting evidence of plaintiff's reputation at time of trial in locality where he formerly lived and continued to do business).

1. See 3 Wigmore, Evidence, §§ 931–935, 989–995; 70 C.J. Witnesses, §§ 922–932, 1021, 1024; Note, Impeachment by expert evidence of mental defects, 15 A.L.R. 932.

2. C. C. Moore, A Treatise on Facts (1908), v. I, ch. 5 (Sound and Hearing); ch. 6 (Light and Sight); ch. 7 (Taste, Smell and Touch); ch. 8 (Distance); ch. 9 (Speed), v. II, ch. 14 (Observation).

3. Principles of Judicial Proof (3d ed. 1937), ch. 22 (Perception).

4. Legal Psychology (1940), ch. 2 (Perception), ch. 3 (Attention).

5. The Perception and Memory of Witnesses, 18 Corn. L.Q. 391 (1933).

6. Elements of Error in Testimony, 28 Ore.L.Rev. 293 (1949).

7. See § 62, herein.

8. See, e. g., State v. Wildman, 145 Oh.St. 379, 61 N. E.2d 790, syl. 3 (1945); Dec.Dig., Witnesses, ☞41, and § 62, herein.

9. People v. La Rue, 62 Cal.App. 276, 216 P. 627, syl. 9 (1923) (incipient paresis, producing insanity); State v. Hayward, 62 Minn. 474, 65 N.W. 63, 69, syl. 13 (1895) (distinguishing issue of competency from credibility). There are contrary cases, but they often mistakenly treat the question as one of competency; see e. g., Metropolitan Life Ins. Co. v. James, 228 Ala. 383, 153 So. 759, syl. 24 (1934). Cases are collected in 3 Wigmore, Evidence, § 932, note 1; 70 C.J. 763, § 922, notes 71, 72.

10. That a cross-examination to test intelligence is allowable, see dicta in Blanchard v. People, 70 Colo. 555, 203 P. 662, syl. 2 (1922) and Henry v. State, 6 Okl.Cr. 430, 119 P. 278, syl. 1 (1911).

nesses? The decisions are divided.[11] It seems eminently a case for discretion. The trial judge would determine whether the crucial character of the testimony attacked and the evaluative light shed by the impeaching evidence over-balance the time and distraction involved in opening this side-dispute. The development of standardized tests for intelligence and for various aptitudes, and their widening use in business, government and the armed forces, suggest that they may come to serve as useful aids in the evaluation of testimony.[12]

Abnormality, we have seen, is a horse of a different color. It is a standard ground of impeachment.[13] One form of abnormality is that of being under the influence of drugs or drink. If the witness was under such influence at the time of the happenings which he reports in his testimony or is so at the time he testifies, this of course is provable, on cross or by extrinsic evidence, to impeach.[14] Habitual addiction stands differently. Under a tradition arising perhaps when three-bottle men were more frequently encountered, it is generally held that the mere fact of chronic alcoholism is not provable on credibility.[15] On the other hand, as to drug-addiction to which more social odium has been attached, many decisions allow it to be shown to impeach, even without evidence that it did in the particular case affect truth-telling,[16] while an equal number, absent a particular showing of effect on the witness's veracity, would exclude it.[17] In respect to both addictions the excluding courts seem to have the better of the arguments. It can hardly be contended that there is such scientific agreement as to warrant judicial notice that addiction of itself usually affects

11. Admitted. Isler v. Dewey, 75 N.C. 466, syl. 1 (1876) (evidence of impeaching witness that memory of impeached witness is weak). Excluded. Blanchard v. People, 70 Colo. 555, 203 P. 662, syl. 1 (1922) (forgery: witness for defendant testified that interlineation was made before instrument signed; held, error to permit witnesses to testify that he was of low intelligence). Decisions are collected in 3 Wigmore, Evidence, § 935, note 1.

12. See Hutchins and Slesinger, The Competency of Witnesses, 37 Yale L.J. 1017, 1019 (1928); Gardner, op.cit., 18 Corn.L.Q. 391, 409 (1933).

13. See note 9, above.

14. Drink. Walker's Trial, 23 How.St.Tr. 1157 (1794) ("Do you know whether he had drunk any [liquor]?" "He had had a little; he knew what he was saying and doing." "Just as much as he knows now?" "He was not half so much in liquor then as he is now."); Olstad v. Fahse, 204 Minn. 118, 282 N.W. 694, syl. 3 (1938) (that the witness had been drinking beer at the time of the accident, and was under influence, extrinsic evidence allowable); 3 Wigmore, Evidence, § 933; 70 C.J. 864, § 924.
Drugs. Wilson v. United States, 232 U.S. 563, 34 S. Ct. 347, syl. 5, 15 L.Ed. 728 (1914) (witness having admitted addiction, and that she had taken a dose in the morning before testifying, was asked how often she used it and whether she had with her the "implements"; held, proper, to show whether at the moment of testifying she was under its influence); State v. Smith, 103 Wash. 267, 174 P. 9, syl. 3 (1918) (In prosecution for selling morphine

without a physician's prescription where evidence showed that prosecuting witness was under the influence of morphine at the time of the alleged sale, expert testimony as to the effect of morphine upon the mind and memory of its user was admissible); Note, 15 A.L.R. 912; 70 C.J. 765, § 926.

15. Lanham v. Lanham, 62 Tex.Civ.App. 431, 146 S. W. 635, syl. 10 (1912); 3 Wigmore, Evidence, § 933, note 2; 70 C.J. 859, § 1070, note 25. But it seems that where general moral character may be shown to impeach (see § 44, above), habitual drunkenness is let in. State v. Wright, 152 Mo.App. 510, 133 S.W. 664, syl. 2 (1911).

16. See, e. g., State v. Fong Loon, 29 Idaho 248, 158 P. 233, syl. 1–3 (1916); Beland v. State, 86 Tex.Cr. 285, 217 S.W. 147, syl. 1 (1920), and see the valuable descriptions and analyses of the cases in Hale, Comment, 16 So.Calif.L.Rev. 333 (1943), and discussion and citations in 3 Wigmore, Evidence, § 934; Rossman, The Testimony of Drug Addicts, 3 Ore. L.Rev. 81 (1924); Note, 15 A.L.R. 912; 70 C.J. 862, § 1080.

17. See e. g., Kelly v. Maryland Casualty Co., 45 F. 2d 782 (W.D.Va.1929) (scholarly and comprehensive opinion by McDowell, J.), affirmed 45 F.2d 788 (C. C.A. 4, 1930) without passing on this question, on the ground that the evidence offered did not show excessive use; State v. Gleim, 17 Mont. 17, 41 P. 998, syl. 8 (1895), and see general references, next preceding note.

credibility.[18]   Certainly it is pregnant with prejudice.

In recent decades with the growth in importance of psychiatry, the testimony of psychiatrists upon issues of sanity in cases of wills and crimes has become familiar to judges. Naturally, the use of psychiatric testimony as to mental disorders and defects suggests itself as a potential aid in determining the credibility of crucial witnesses in any kind of litigation. In one type of case, namely that of sex offenses, the indispensible value of this kind of testimony has been urged by Wigmore,[19] and other commentators,[20] and such testimony has been widely received by the courts.[21] An earlier leading case [22] excluded such evidence, but failed to discriminate between the question of competency and that of credibility, and misconceived the attack as one on character rather than on mental capacity for truth-telling, as it was. This case would probably not be followed today. There is special danger of sympathy swaying judgment on credibility in sex cases, but the need exists for appraising the testimony with all the resources of psychiatric science in every case where there is ground for believing that a witness on whom the issue depends is subject to some mental abnormality which might significantly affect his credibility.[23] In that remarkable state trial, the Hiss case,[24] this need was recognized. A psychiatrist as a witness for the defendant was permitted, over objection, to testify to his diagnosis (formed from court-room observation) that the star witness for the government was a psychopathic personality with "a tendency towards making false accusations." [25] Doubt-

---

18. In the Kelly case, in the next preceding note, Judge McDowell marshals the medical opinions pro and con (45 F.2d 782, 784, 785). In Weaver v. United States, 111 F.2d 603, 606 (C.C.A. 8, 1940) the court holding correct the refusal of an instruction that the jury might consider on credibility the fact that a witness was an habitual user of morphine sulphate said, "There was no evidence, expert or otherwise, to the effect that the use of morphine affects the credibility of a witness; and, if it be true that its use does have such an effect, that fact is not so generally true that courts would be warranted in taking judicial notice of it."

19. Evidence, § 934a.

20. Note, Psychiatric Aid in Evaluating Credibility of Rape-Complainant, 26 Ind.L.J. 98 (1950) (arguing with force and originality that clinical examination be required where no substantial confirmation of complainant's story: splendid collection of references to psychiatric literature); Note, Machtinger, Psychiatric Impeachment in Sex Cases, 39 J.Crim.L. 750 (1949).

21. People v. Cowles, 246 Mich. 429, 224 N.W. 387 (1929) (evidence of doctors that the girl was a pathological liar and nymphomaniac received without objection); State v. Wesler, 137 N.J.L. 311, 59 A.2d 834, syl. 3 (1948) (testimony of doctors that girls are psychopaths and immoral and that psychopaths are prone to be untruthful did not require rejection of girls' stories); Miller v. State, 49 Okl.Cr. 133, 295 P. 403 (1930) (testimony of superintendent of insane hospital that girl, said to be nymphomaniac, was normal, admissible on credibility);

Rice v. State, 195 Wis. 181, 217 N.W. 697, syl. 3 (1928) (indecent liberties with child; conviction set aside, relying on testimony of doctor that girl "had a mental condition calculated to induce unreal and phantom pictures in her mind").

22. State v. Driver, 88 W.Va. 479, 107 S.E. 189, syl. 2, 3, 15 A.L.R. 917 (1921) (judge properly refused to appoint commission to examine complainant and report on her competency and credibility, also properly excluded testimony of experts who from observation in court would testify that girl was moron and prone to tell lies).

23. These are classified and described in an enlightening comment, Psychiatric Evaluation of the Mentally Abnormal Witness, 59 Yale L.J. 1324, 1326 (1950) as (a) Disorders, including psychoses (psychotics are the groups which lawyers call the "insane"; they include paranoiacs, and other types), neuroses and psychopathic personalities; (b) Defects (mental defectives, the "feebleminded" are classed as idiots, imbeciles, and morons). The comment is notable for its wealth of information from, and references to, the literature of psychiatry.

24. United States v. Hiss, 88 F.Supp. 559 (S.D.N.Y. 1950) (memorandum opinion of Goddard, J., limited to the question of the admissibility of psychiatric testimony as to credibility).

25. Comment, cited above, 59 Yale L.J. 1324, at p. 1339.

The emptiness of the term "psychopathic personality" is stressed in an article by Philip Q. Roche, M. D., Truth Telling, Psychiatric Expert Testimony, and the Impeachment of Witnesses, 22 Pa.B.A.Q. 140,

less most courts today would accept the principle that psychiatric evidence should be received, at least in the judge's discretion, when its value outweighs the cost in time, distraction, and expense. The value seems to depend first upon the importance of the appraised witness's testimony, and second upon the opportunity of the expert to form a reliable opinion. An opinion based solely upon a hypothetical question seems almost valueless here. Only slightly more reliable is an opinion derived from the subject's demeanor and his testimony in the court-room. Most psychiatrists would say that a satisfactory opinion can only be formed after the witness has been subjected to a clinical examination.[26] It seems that a discretionary power should be recognized in the judge upon application before trial, to order such an examination, subject to the consent of the witness, and to limit the psychiatric evidence in the other forms to cases where a clinical examination has not been feasible.[27]

46. "Lie-Detectors" and "Truth Serums."

These devices offer interesting possibilities for the appraisal of the credibility of testimony—possibilities which have been widely realized in out-of-court investigations, and which may to some extent in the future be directly utilized by the courts. They are discussed in the chapter on Experimental and Scientific Evidence.[1]

47. Impeachment by "Contradiction": Disproving the Facts Testified to by the First Witness.[1]

Statements are elicited from Witness One who has testified to a material story of a contract, crime, or conveyance, to the effect that at the time he witnessed these matters the day was windy and cold and he the witness was wearing his green sweater. Let us suppose these latter statements about the day and the sweater to be "disproved." This may happen in several ways. Witness One on direct or cross-examination may acknowledge that he was in error. Judicial notice may be taken that at the time and place it could not have been cold and windy, e. g., in Tucson in July. But most commonly disproof or "contradiction" is accomplished by calling Witness Two to testify to the contrary, i. e., that the day was warm and Witness One was in his shirt-sleeves. It is in this sense that we shall use the term "contradiction."[2]

What impeaching value would the contradiction have in this situation? It merely tends to show—for One may be right and Two may be mistaken—that one has erred or falsified as to certain particular facts, and therefore is capable of error or lying, and this should be considered negatively in weighing his other statements. But all humans have this capacity and all testimony should be discounted to some extent for this weakness. It is true that the trial judge in his discretion may permit the cross-examiner to

---

148, 152 (1951) (". . . there has been no agreement among psychiatrists as to what a psychopath is . . . Perhaps our psychopathic personality is the heretic or witch in modern guise."). See also Note, 30 Neb.L.Rev. 513, 516–519 (1951).

26. Comment, 59 Yale L.J. 1324, at p. 1339 (1950); Note, 30 Neb.L.Rev. 513, 519 (1951).

27. Compare the recommendations in the Comment, above cited, 59 Yale L.J. 1324, 1340, 1341 (1950).

1. See § 174, herein.

1. 3 Wigmore, Evidence, §§ 1000–1007; Dec.Dig. Witnesses, ☞308–409; 70 C.J. Witnesses, §§ 1340–1364.

The Massachusetts decisions are collected and classified in Rosenthal, Note, 33 Mass.L.Q. 28 (Oct.1948).

2. In the court-room and in the cases "contradiction" is loosely extended to include impeachment by proof of a prior inconsistent statement of the first witness. See, e. g., Calley v. Boston & M. R. Co., 92 N.H. 455, 33 A.2d 227, syl. 15 (1943). Because of the requirement of a preliminary question, see § 37, above, the proof by a second witness of the prior inconsistent statement usually entails a contradiction too, but it is the witness's inconsistency that is the heart of the attack.

conduct a general test of the power of Witness One to observe, remember and recount facts unrelated to the case, to "test" or "explore" these capacities.[3] To permit a dispute, however, about such extraneous facts material only for "testing" the witness, by allowing the attacker to call other witnesses to disprove them, is unpractical. Dangers of surprise, of confusion of the jury's attention,[4] and of time-wasting[5] are apparent.

So as to "collateral" facts the courts maintain the safe-guarding rule that a witness may not be impeached by producing extrinsic evidence to "contradict" the first witness's assertions about such facts.[6] If the fact is elicited, as it usually is, on cross-examination, this is often expressed by saying that the answer is conclusive or that the cross-examiner must "take the answer."[7] By the better view, if the "collateral" fact happens to have been drawn out on direct, the rule against contradiction should still be applied.[8] The danger of surprise is lessened, but waste of time and confusion of issues stand as objections.

What is to be here regarded as within this protean word of art, "collateral"? This will best be answered by inquiring as to what facts are not within the term, and thus finding the escapes from the prohibition against contradicting upon collateral facts. The classical approach is that facts which would have been independently provable regardless of the contradiction are not "collateral."[9]

Two general kinds of facts meet this test. First, of course, facts which are relevant to the substantive issues in the case.[10] It may

---

3. See § 29, supra.

4. ". . . Witnesses are not expected to come prepared to sustain all the statements they have made upon subjects not involved in the controversy, and because its admission would involve the trial of too many issues as to the truth of the statements the determination of which would at last have little effect upon the decision of the cause." Williams, J., in Gulf, C. & S. F. R. Co. v. Matthews, 100 Tex. 63, 93 S.W. 1068, 1070 (1906).

5. "If we lived for a thousand years, instead of about sixty or seventy, and every case were of sufficient importance, it might be possible and perhaps proper to throw a light on matters in which every possible question might be suggested, for the purpose of seeing by such means whether the whole was unfounded, or what portion of it was not, and to raise every possible inquiry as to the truth of the statements made. But I do not see how that could be; in fact, mankind find it to be impossible. Therefore, some line must be drawn." Rolfe, B. in Attorney General v. Hitchcock, 1 Exch. 104, 154 Eng. Rep. 38 (1847).

6. Consolidated Beef & Provision Co. v. Witt & Co., 184 Md. 105, 40 A.2d 295, syl. 1, 2 (1945); Klein v. Keresey, 307 Mass. 51, 29 N.E.2d 703, syl. 2, 3 (1940); 70 C.J. 1161, § 1345, note 3.

7. State v. Silvers, 230 Minn. 12, 40 N.W.2d 630, syl. 4 (1950); Latham v. State, 152 Neb. 113, 40 N.W.2d 522, syl. 9 (1949); 70 C.J. 1162, note 5.

8. Lambert v. Hamlin, 73 N.H. 138, 59 A. 941, syl. 3 (1905); State v. Price, 92 W.Va. 542, 115 S.E. 393, 405, syl. 21 (1922); 3 Wigmore, Evidence, § 1007. But many courts hold to the contrary. See, e. g., Howell v. State, 141 Ark. 487, 217 S.W. 457, syl. 2 (1920) (carnal knowledge; testimony of complainant on direct that she had never had intercourse with anyone but defendant should have been allowed to be contradicted, distinguishing situation where brought out on cross-examination) and cases cited Wigmore, ibid. and 70 C.J. 1164, note 20.

9. State v. Kouzounas, 137 Me. 198, 17 A.2d 147, syl. 1 (1941); State v. Kritzer, 21 Wash.2d 710, 152 P.2d 967, syl. 8 (1944); 3 Wigmore, Evidence, § 1003; 70 C.J. 1165, note 27.

The same test of "collateralness" of subject-matter is applied to impeachment by prior inconsistent statements, see § 36, supra; 3 Wigmore, Evidence, § 1020.

10. Examples: Louisville Taxicab & Tr. Co. v. Tungent's Adm'r, 313 Ky. 1, 229 S.W.2d 985, syl. 2 (1950) (In action for death of one riding in truck struck by defendant's taxicab at street intersection, testimony as to decedent's and truck driver's drunkenness at time of collision was admissible as bearing on questions of negligence and credibility of such driver, who testified that neither she nor decedent drank any liquor during morning before collision); Thompson v. Walsh, 203 Okl. 453, 223 P.2d 357, syl. 4 (1950) (In action for injury to and death of cattle from drinking salt water negligently permitted to escape from defendants' oil lease testimony that salt water was seen running from defendants' wells into creek on day before trial was permissible to impeach the testimony of a defendant that salt water never escaped from the lease into the creek).

seem strained to call such proof of relevant facts by the name of "contradiction" or "impeachment." But it does have the dual aspect of relevant proof and of reflecting on the credibility of contrary witnesses,[11] and the "contradiction" theory has at least one practical consequence, namely, it permits contradicting proof, which without the contradiction would be confined to the case in chief, to be brought out in rebuttal.[12] Second, facts which would be independently provable, by extrinsic evidence, apart from the contradiction, to impeach or disqualify the witness.[13] Among these are facts showing bias, interest,[14] conviction of crime,[15] and want of capacity or opportunity for knowledge. Extraneous misconduct of the witness (for which no conviction has been had) is not within this last class, but is collateral, and if denied on cross-examination cannot be proved to contradict.[16]

A witness has told a story of a transaction crucial to the controversy. To prove him wrong in some trivial detail of time, place or circumstance is "collateral." But to prove untrue some fact recited by the witness that if he were really there and saw what he claims to have seen, he could not have been mistaken about, is a convincing kind of impeachment that the courts must make place for, despite the fact that it does not meet the test of admissibility apart from the contradiction. To disprove such a fact is to pull out the linchpin of the story. So we may recognize this third type of allowable contradiction, namely, the contradiction of any part of the witness's account of the background and circumstances of a material transaction, which as a matter of human experience he would not have been mistaken about if his story were true.[17] This test is of necessity a vague one, as it must meet an indefinite

---

11. Thus, the limitation upon impeaching one's own witness does not prevent a party from contradicting his own witness by adducing contrary proof as to a material fact. Talley v. Richart, 353 Mo. 912, 185 S.W.2d 23, syl. 5–7 (1945); Dec.Dig. Witnesses, ⊂⇒400, and see § 38, above.

12. Hensley v. Comm., 264 Ky. 718, 95 S.W.2d 564, syl. 4 (1936) (wounding with intent to kill: where defendant said, on cross, that he did not remember whether he made a threat, evidence that he did threaten admissible, not only in chief, but in rebuttal, to contradict); State v. Prater, 26 S.C. 198, 2 S.E. 108, syl. 3 (1887).

13. 3 Wigmore, Evidence, § 1005.

14. State v. Kouzounas, 137 Me. 198, 17 A.2d 147, syl. 1, 2, 4 (1941) (accused in arson prosecution, who had been charged by witness with offering money to get him to change his testimony, denied on cross-examination that he visited lawyer with this witness; held, state may contradict this denial by evidence of lawyer that accused came to his office with witness).

15. Storer v. State, 84 Okl.Cr. 176, 180 P.2d 202, syl. 4 (1947).

16. People v. Rosenthal, 289 N.Y. 482, 46 N.E.2d 895, syl. 7 (1943) (accused was asked on cross-examination about other like crimes, and denied them, held state cannot produce other witnesses to contradict); State v. Broom, 222 N.C. 324, 22 S.E.2d 926 (1942) (similar).

17. See, e. g., East Tennessee R. Co. v. Daniel, 91 Ga. 768, 18 S.E. 22, syl. 1 (1893) (witness of alleged killing of mule at crossing accounted for his presence by saying he left home to get some tobacco, going to a certain store and getting the tobacco on credit, and on his way home he saw the accident; adversary offered evidence of store-keeper that witness did not buy tobacco at that time, held, erroneously excluded, "it was indirectly material because it contradicted the witness as to the train of events which led him to be present"); Stephens v. People, 19 N.Y. 549, 572 (1859) (murder by poisoning with arsenic; defendant's witnesses testified the arsenic was administered to rats in cellar where provisions kept; held proper for state to prove by another witness that no provisions were kept in cellar, "not strictly collateral"); Gulf C. & S. F. Ry. Co. v. Matthews, 100 Tex. 63, 93 S.W. 1068, 1070, syl. 2 (1906) (suit for death of M., run over by train; controverted issue was whether M. was sober and walking or drunk and lying on tracks; A., a hotel clerk, crucial witness for plaintiff, said M. left hotel early in morning, sober: foul play in the death of M. was publicly suspected; A. said on cross-examination that he had never mentioned M.'s presence and departure from hotel except a couple of times to one W.; defendant offered evidence that A. when he gave above testimony by deposition believed W. was dead, and produced W. and offered proof by him that A. had never told him about M.'s presence in the hotel; held, exclusion of defendant's evidence was error. "Evidence there-

variety of situations, and consequently in its application a reasonable latitude of discretionary judgment must be accorded to the trial judge.[18]

Of course, the contradicting witness may simply state the facts as he asserts them, without reference to the prior testimony which is being contradicted. It seems, however, that where appropriate the contradiction may be more direct. Thus it would seem acceptable to recite in the question the pertinent part of the prior testimony of the first witness, and inquire, "What do you say as to the correctness of this statement? "[19]

48. Beliefs Concerning Religion.[1]

As we shall see,[2] the common law required as a qualification for taking the oath as a witness, the belief in a God who would pun-

ish untruth. This rule grew up in a climate of custom and assumptions which today seem primitive and archaic. It has quite generally been abandoned in most common law jurisdictions. General provisions like that in the Illinois constitution to the effect that "No person shall be denied any civil or political rights, privilege or capacity on account of his religious opinions"[3] have been construed in many states to abrogate the rule of incompetency to take the oath.[4]

The general tendency, as we know, has been to convert the old grounds of incompetency to testify, such as interest and infamy, into grounds of impeaching credibility, and this principle of conversion is sometimes expressly enacted in constitutional provisions and in statutes.[5]

---

fore which bears upon the story of a witness with sufficient directness and force to give it appreciable value in determining whether or not that story is true cannot be said to be addressed to an irrelevant or collateral issue. . . . The effort of the defendant was . . . to maintain its contention that he had never told any one; and that fact being relevant, the defendant had the right, we think, to meet his apparent effort to break its force." Able opinion by Williams, J.).

18. The cases dealing with discretion in the field of contradiction seem to go further than the text. Some imply that the trial judge has a discretion to decide what is and is not "collateral." Radio Cab, Inc. v. Houser, 128 F.2d 604, syl. 10 (App.D.C.1942). Others suggest that even if "collateral" the judge has a discretion to permit the contradiction. Salem News Co. v. Caliga, 144 F. 965, syl. 1 (C.C.A.Mass. 1906); Todd v. Bradley, 99 Conn. 307, 122 A. 68, syl. 9, 10 (1923); Lizotte v. Warren, 302 Mass. 317, 19 N.E.2d 60, syl. 2 (1939) (self-contradiction by party). See cases collected in 70 C.J. 1169, note 89.

19. See Uhlman v. Farm Stock & Home Co., 126 Minn. 239, 148 N.W. 102, syl. 5 (1914) and compare Scoggins v. Turner, 98 N.C. 135, 3 S.E. 719, 723, syl. 3 (1887). Cases are collected in 70 C.J. 1168, § 1351.

1. See Wigmore, Evidence, § 518 (competency), § 936 (impeachment), § 2213 (privilege), and the excellent comment by Prof. J. H. Chadbourn on State v. Beal, 199 N.C. 278, 154 S.E. 604, 1930, 9 N.C.L.Rev. 77 (1930); Note, Religious Belief as Affecting Credibility, 95 A.L.R. 723; Swancara, Impeachment of Non-Religious Witnesses, 13 Rocky Mt.L.Rev. 336 (1941). See also 5 Jones, Evidence, § 2347 (3d ed. 1926);

Dec.Dig. Witnesses, ⊛340(2); 70 C.J. Witnesses, § 1077.

2. See § 63.

3. Quoted in Starks v. Schlensky, 128 Ill.App. 1, 4 (1906).

4. See the constitutional and statutory provisions, and decisions interpreting them, from twenty-four states, compiled in 70 C.J. 98, 99, note 76, and see § 63, supra. A compilation of specific references to the articles and sections of the constitutions dealing with Witnesses appears in 3 Constitutions, 1813 (1938) published by N. Y. State Const. Committee. Forty jurisdictions are listed as having abolished by statute or constitutional provision the requirement for witnesses of religious belief. Torpey, Judicial Doctrines of Religious Rights, 278 (1948).

5. "N.M.Ann.Stat. § 2165 provides: 'Hereafter in the courts of this state no person shall be disqualified to give evidence on account of any disqualification known to the common law, but all such common law disqualifications may be shown for the purpose of affecting the credibility of any such witness and for no other purpose. . . .' A legitimate construction would be that want of religious belief was not a testimonial disqualification and is thus not covered by the statute. However, the express wording of the following unfortunate statutes would have to be disregarded to prevent impeachment by religious belief: Nev.Rev.Laws § 5419 ('. . . Facts which by the common law would cause the exclusion of witnesses may still be shown for the purpose of affecting their credibility. . . .'); Neb.Comp.Stat. (1922) § 8845; Iowa Code (1927) § 3637, State v. Elliott, 45 Iowa 486 (1877); Searcy

Should the principle be applied so as to permit the credibility of a witness to be attacked by showing that he is an atheist or an agnostic and does not believe in Divine punishment for perjury? The greater number of courts that have answered the question at all have said no, either by interpreting general provisions [6] such as that quoted above from the Illinois constitution, or by mandate of specific constitutional or statutory language.[7] A minority, either reasoning from the principle of conversion or following specific provisions, allows this ground of impeachment.[8] It is to be observed, however, that the common law analogy would not extend to permit inquiry into particular creeds, faiths or affiliations except as they shed light on the witness's belief in a God who will punish untruth.[9]

The history of modern Europe whence our people come is the history of religious persecution. From this derives a strong common feeling of revulsion against interrogation of a man about his religious beliefs. Often in our history have such inquiries been the aftermath of the rack and the prelude to the flaming faggot. There is a feeling also that such inquiries into faith offend against the dignity of the individual. Moreover, the disclosure of atheism or agnosticism, or of affiliation with some new strange or unpopular sect, will often in many communities be fraught with intense prejudice. For all these reasons many states recognize a privilege of the witness not to be examined about his own religious faith or beliefs, except so far as the judge in his discretion [10] finds that the relevance of the inquiry upon some substantive issue in the case outweighs the interest of privacy and the danger of prejudice.[11]

There is a strong reason why the legislatures and courts should, in addition to recog-

---

6. See, e. g., McClellan v. Owens, 335 Mo. 884, 74 S.W. 2d 570, 576, syl. 11 (1934) and cases from California, Illinois, Kansas, Kentucky, Louisiana, Maine, Michigan, Missouri, New Hampshire, New York, Pennsylvania and Texas in Note, 95 A.L.R. 724. To like effect is Darby v. Ouseley, 1 H. & N. 1, 156 Eng.Rep. 1093 (1856).

7. A constitutional provision (Ariz.Const. Art. 2, § 12) forbids the questioning of a witness "touching his religious belief . . . to affect the weight of his testimony." This was held to forbid counsel, when a particular church is interested as a legatee in the outcome of the suit on trial, to ask a witness if he is a member of that church. Tucker v. Reil, 51 Ariz. 357, 77 P.2d 203, 1938. See State v. Estabrook, 162 Or. 476, 91 P.2d 838, syl. 18–21, 1939, where a similar Oregon provision was held to forbid cross-examining a witness who has testified to the good reputation of the accused, as to whether she is a Christian Scientist and hence believes no evil of anyone.

8. Allen v. Guarante, 253 Mass. 152, 148 N.E. 461, syl. 6 (1925) and decisions cited from Georgia, Indiana, Iowa, Massachusetts, Mississippi, and Ohio in Note, 95 A.L.R. 726. Most of the cases, however, are old, and we may assume that the decent restraint of lawyers leaves this field of impeachment to lapse into dormancy.

9. "The credibility of witnesses can be affected only by evidence of their disbelief in the existence of

v. Miller, 57 Iowa 613, 10 N.W. 912 (1881)." Chadbourn, op. cit., 9 N.C.L.Rev. 78, n. 5.

God. . . . Adherence to any particular sect is no basis for argument in this respect." Allen v. Guarante, 253 Mass. 152, 148 N.E. 461, 462 (1925).

10. Searcy v. Miller, 57 Ia. 613, 621, 10 N.W. 912, 916 (1881) ("He is not to be questioned as to his religious belief . . ."); Comm. v. Burke, 82 Mass. 33 (1860) (improper to question witness about his beliefs on voir dire or on cross-examination, despite statute permitting impeachment on this ground); Free v. Buckingham, 59 N.H. 219, 225 (1879) ("This is not because the inquiry might tend to disgrace him, but because it would be a personal scrutiny into the state of his faith and conscience, contrary to the spirit of our institutions"); 8 Wigmore, Evidence, § 2213.

11. Examples of situations where relevancy did outweigh: McKim v. Philadelphia Transp. Co., 364 Pa. 237, 72 A.2d 122, syl. 2 (1950) (under statute recognizing privilege judge properly permitted cross-examination of personal injury plaintiffs to show they were ministers in Jehovah's Witnesses sect and what their duties were, on issue of damages); Ft. Worth & D. C. Ry. Co. v. Travis, 45 Tex.Civ.App. 117, 99 S.W. 1141, syl. 2, 3 (1907) (personal injury plaintiff could be cross-examined as to her beliefs as Christian Scientist, as to suffering, and as to whether her faith caused her not to take medicine prescribed). But compare cases where inquiry into the plaintiff's faith as Christian Scientist was found not to be sufficiently relevant to the substantive issues. City of Montgomery v. Wyche, 169 Ala.

nizing the privilege of a witness not to answer to his own religious beliefs, forbid the party to impeach by bringing other witnesses to attack the faith of the first one. This reason of course is that there is no basis for believing that the lack of faith in God's avenging wrath is today an indication of greater than average untruthfulness. Without such basis, the evidence of atheism is simply irrelevant upon the question of credibility.[12]

A Pennsylvania statute is a model of clarity and settles most of the questions left unsettled in other states: "No witness shall be questioned, in any judicial proceeding, concerning his religious belief; nor shall any

evidence be heard upon the subject, for the purpose of affecting either his competency or credibility."[13]

49.　Supporting the Witness.

Impeachment is not a dispassionate study of the capacities and character of the witness, but is regarded in our tradition as an *attack* upon his credibility. Under our adversary system of trials the opponent must be given an opportunity to meet this attack by evidence sustaining or rehabilitating the witness. One principle we find at the outset, namely, that in the absence of an attack upon credibility no sustaining evidence is allowed.[1] Another truism that finds constant applica-

---

181, 53 So. 786, syl. 10 (1910); Adams v. Carlo, 101 S.W.2d 753, syl. 4, 5 (Mo.App.1937).

12. "Unorthodox religious convictions, even though they extend to the extremes of agnosticism and atheism, may quite often exist because of honest intellectual doubts. It is untenable to argue that there is a correlation between this kind of unorthodoxy and inveracity. That correlation which may exist between what Pope calls 'blind unbelief' and untruthfulness is so slight that the value of the evidence is outweighed by the possibilities for prejudice with which it is pregnant." Chadbourn, op. cit., 9 N.C.L.Rev. 81.

13. 28 P.S. § 313, quoted and interpreted in McKim v. Philadelphia Transp. Co., 364 Pa. 237, 72 A.2d 122 (1950).

1. Woey Ho v. United States, 109 F. 888, syl. 1 (C.C.A. 9th 1901) (petitioner resisting deportation properly refused permission to support her witnesses, who were Chinese, by evidence of their good character, there being no attack); State v. Harmon, 278 S.W. 733, syl. 2 (Mo., 1925) (testimony offered to support unimpeached character for truth of accused as witness, properly excluded); Notes, Unimpeached Witness, Admissibility of Evidence of Good Reputation, 15 A.L.R. 1065, 33 id. 1220. The exclusion of character-support, in the absence of attack, is frequently explained as the corollary of a presumption that the character of the witness is good. See, e. g., Johnson v. State, 129 Wis. 146, 108 N.W. 55, 58 (1906); 3 Jones, Evidence, § 2446 (3d ed. 1926). Wigmore v. 3, § 1104) says that the character is simply unknown.

Nor can the party bolster his witness by proof, in the case in chief, that the witness has previously told the same story that he tells on the stand. Mellon v. United States, 170 F.2d 583, syl. 1, 2 (C.C.A.

5th 1948) (bribing public officer; officer testified, in chief, that he reported payment of bribe-money to his superior, held, error); Newton v. State, 147 Tex.Cr. 339, 180 S.W.2d 946, syl. 1–3 (1948) (prosecuting witness in attempted murder, where issue is identity of assailant, allowed to recite his report to guests of identity of telephone caller on night of attack, held error). 4 Wigmore, Evidence, § 1124. This can be justified on grounds of saving of time, by avoiding a defense of the witness before a need for one appears. But when the principal fact to which this "bolstering" evidence is addressed is later denied by the adversary's witness (as in the two cases cited above), does this furnish the "attack" and convert the present point into one of mere order of proof? See the next to last paragraph in this section.

Acts done by the witness which are consistent with his testimony about the main fact, have been held admissible, even in the absence of attack, as corroborating the testimony—and the line between conduct and statements may be an elusive one. See the subtle and ingenious opinion of Allen, J., in State v. Slocinski, 89 N.H. 262, 197 A. 560, syl. 3–7, 10, 1938 (witness to arson threat, allowed to testify that he reported the threat to the police and to his own lawyer, at the time it was made). On this or another theory, should evidence be admitted in criminal cases of disputed identity, that the complainant pointed out the accused as the man, on some earlier occasion? For other theories favoring admissibility, see Wigmore, Evidence, § 1130, followed in People v. Slobodian, 31 Cal.2d 555, 191 P.2d 1, syl. 3 (1948) (rebutting implication of recent contrivance); State v. Buschman, 325 Mo. 553, 29 S.W.2d 688, 70 A.L.R. 904, 909 (1930) (seeing assailant day after crime and identifying shows opportunity for careful observation and fixing features in

tion is that when there has been evidence of impeaching facts the proponent may bring contradictory evidence asserting the untruth of the alleged impeaching facts. Such a denial is always relevant and generally allowable.[2]

The more common form of sustaining evidence is the confession and avoidance, which tends to refute or explain away the inferences which the attacker seeks to derive from the impeaching facts. Usually it is in respect to this kind of rehabilitating proof that the problems arise. More concretely, the questions commonly encountered are whether particular kinds of impeachment will warrant support in the form of evidence of good character, or in the form of prior consistent statements of the witness. The

general approach to the solution of these questions is that the supporting fact must not merely be logically relevant to explain or refute the impeaching fact, but it must meet the attack with relative directness. The wall, attacked at one point, may not be fortified at another.[3] Credibility is a side-issue and the circle of relevancy here may well be narrowly drawn. How narrowly is a question of degree as to which reasonable courts differ, and a solution reached in a particular state soon becomes part of the local "cake of custom."

When may the party supporting the witness offer evidence of his good character for truth? Certainly attacks by evidence of bad reputation,[4] conviction of crime,[5] or eliciting

---

mind, giving better basis for witness's identifying accused in court-room). The majority of courts have come to this result. Note, 70 A.L.R. 910, 911. Contra: Thompson v. State, 223 Ind. 39, 58 N.E.2d 112, syl. 2 (1944) (that complainant had selected defendant's photograph from pictures shown her by police, erroneously admitted); Note, 70 A.L.R. 910, 915.

2. Thus, evidence of bad character to impeach may be rebutted by evidence of good character. See, e. g., Prentiss v. Roberts, 49 Me. 127, 137 (1860); 4 Wigmore, Evidence, § 1105. Some courts at least permit a summary denial or explanation by the witness of guilt where he has been impeached by conviction. See § 43, notes 34, 35, above. Facts showing bias may of course be denied (4 Wigmore, Evidence, § 1119), as well as the making of an alleged prior inconsistent statement. Tri-State Transfer Co. v. Nowotny, 198 Minn. 537, 270 N.W. 684, syl. 4 (1936) (rebutting witness may testify that complaint introduced as inconsistent statement of former witness, was not drawn by him but by attorney).

3. The approach is illumined by the opinion of Holmes, J., in Gertz v. Fitchburg R. Co., 137 Mass. 77, 78 (1884). In holding that the plaintiff, impeached as a witness by conviction of crime, could give evidence of his good reputation for truth, he said: "We think that the evidence of his reputation for truth should have been admitted, and that the exception must be sustained. There is a clear distinction between this case and those in which such evidence has been held inadmissible, for instance, to rebut evidence of contradictory state-

ments; Russell v. Coffin, 8 Pick. 143; Brown v. Mooers, 6 Gray, 451; or where the witness is directly contradicted as to the principal fact by other witnesses. Atwood v. Dearborn, 1 Allen, 483.

"In such cases, it is true that the result sought to be reached is the same as in the present,—to induce the jury to disbelieve the witness. But the mode of reaching the result is different. For, while contradiction or proof of contradictory statements may very well have the incidental effect of impeaching the character for truth of the contradicted witness in the minds of the jury, the proof is not directed to that point. The purpose and only direct effect of the evidence are to show that the witness is not to be believed in this instance. But the reason why he is not to be believed is left untouched. That may be found in forgetfulness on the part of the witness, or in his having been deceived, or in any other possible cause. The disbelief sought to be produced is perfectly consistent with an admission of his general good character for truth, as well as for the other virtues; and until the character of a witness is assailed, it cannot be fortified by evidence.

"On the other hand, when it is proved that a witness has been convicted of a crime, the only ground for disbelieving him which such proof affords is the general readiness to do evil which the conviction may be supposed to show."

4. See note 2, supra.

5. See note 3, supra. See likewise Derrick v. Wallace, 217 N.Y. 520, 112 N.E. 440, syl. 1 (1916) and 4 Wigmore, Evidence, § 1106.

from the witness on cross-examination acknowledgment of misconduct not the subject of conviction,[6]—these will all open the door to character-support. Moreover, a slashing cross-examination may carry strong accusations of misconduct and bad character, which the witness's denial will not remove from the jury's mind. If the judge considers that fairness requires it, he may permit evidence of good character, a mild palliative for the rankle of insinuation.[7] Corrupt conduct of a witness of a sort to show bias should seemingly be regarded as including an attack on veracity-character and as warranting character support,[8] but an impeachment for bias or interest by facts not involving corruption, such as proof of family relationship,[9] have no such effect.

Two other situations, first where the witness has been impeached by prior inconsistent statements, and second, where his evidence of a certain fact has been met by evidence adduced by the adversary denying the fact, provoke controversy among the courts as to whether they so far constitute attacks on character as to admit character-support. Probably the greater number of courts would say yes as to the first,[10] no as to the second.[11] Convenient as automatic answers to these minor trial questions may be, surely it is unrealistic to handle them in this mechanical fashion. The view of the Kansas court seems sensible, that the judge shall consider in each case whether the particular impeachment for inconsistency and the conflict in testimony,[12] or either of them, amounts in net effect to an attack on character for truth and shall

---

6. First Nat. Bank v. Blakeman, 19 Okl. 106, 91 P. 868 (1907) ("when the witness has been impeached by evidence of particular acts of criminal or moral misconduct, either on cross-examination or by record of conviction," citing cases); 4 Wigmore, Evidence, § 1106.

7. Harris v. State (1906) 49 Tex.Cr.R. 338, 94 S.W. 227 (syl. 5) (most rigid cross-examination, in a manner tending to bring witness into disrepute before jury and indirectly attack his testimony). See also Comm. v. Ingraham, 7 Gray (Mass.) 46, 49 (1856) which sanctions proof of good character after a mere abortive attempt to prove the witness's bad character.

8. People v. Ah Fat, 48 Calif. 61, 64 (1874) (evidence that state's witness had offered to identify killer "if there was any coin in it").

9. Lassiter v. State, 35 Ala.App. 323, 47 So.2d 230, syl. 2 (1950), Note, 3 Ala.L.Rev. 206.

10. Dickson v. Dinsmore, 219 Ala. 353, 122 So. 437, syl. 1 (1929); Turner v. State, 112 Tex.Cr. 245, 16 S.W.2d 127, syl. 3 (1929). Contra: State v. Hoffman, 134 Iowa 587, 112 N.W. 103, syl. 5 (1907). See 4 Wigmore, Evidence, § 1108; 70 C.J. 1146, § 1334; Note, 6 A.L.R. 862.

11. Louisville & N. R. Co. v. McClish, 115 F. 268, syl. 1 (C.C.A.Tenn.1902, opinion by Day, J.) (witness who testified he saw decedent pass along railway track shortly before train passed, contradicted by witness who testified first witness was not at the scene but was in opera house at the time; held error to admit character-support, though contradiction "admits of no reconciliation . . . upon any theory of

honest mistake or failure of memory"); Whaley v. State, 157 Fla. 593, 26 So.2d 656, syl. 5 (1946) (murder: material conflict between testimony of accused and of officers as to terms of alleged oral confession, does not warrant admission of defendant's good reputation for truth). Contra: Franklin Sugar Ref. Co. v. Luray Supply Co., 6 F.2d 218, syl. 1 (C.C.A. Va.1925) (held admissible as matter of local Virginia law). See 4 Wigmore, Evidence, § 1109; 6 Jones, Evidence, § 2455 (2d ed. 1926); 70 C.J. 1177, § 1363. Wigmore, ubi supra, suggests that the argument for supporting character here is weaker than in the case of impeachment for inconsistency. This may be so when viewed from the requirement of an attack on character, but from the view of the administration of justice can one imagine a greater need for the jury to know "what manner of man" the witness is than in these cases of irreconcilable conflicts? It is only a pity that the minority who admit character support, have nothing better to avail themselves of than the feeble aid of "reputation for truth." Surely it is here that progress is needed so that courts may use an observer's opinion from observation of the witness's character, see § 41, above; results of deception-tests, see § 46, above; and results of tests for capacity to perceive and remember, see § 45, above.

12. In most cases both the inconsistency and the conflict are available. The proof by the second witness of an inconsistent statement by the first, after the witness has denied on cross-examination making the inconsistent statement, always involves a conflict, and in general whenever a witness is impeached for inconsistency his substantive story will be contradicted.

exercise his discretion accordingly to admit or exclude the character-support.[13]

What kind of attack upon the witness opens the door to the other favorite form of "bolstering" evidence, namely, evidence of prior statements by the witness consistent with his present story[14] on the stand? When the attack takes the form of impeachment of character, by showing misconduct, convictions or bad reputation, it is generally agreed that there is no color for sustaining by consistent statements.[15] The defense does not meet the assault. If the attacker has charged bias, interest, corrupt influence, contrivance to falsify, or want of capacity to observe or remember, the applicable principle is that the prior consistent statement has no relevancy to refute the charge unless the consistent statement was made before the source of the bias, interest, influence or incapacity originated.[16]

There is much division of opinion on the question whether impeachment by inconsistent statements opens the door to support by proving consistent statements.[17] A few courts hold generally that it does.[18] This has the merit of easy application in the court room. Most courts, since the inconsistency remains despite all consistent statements, hold generally that it does not.[19] But certain exceptions should be recognized. If the attacked witness denies the making of the inconsistent statement then the evidence of consistent statements near the time of the alleged inconsistent one, is relevant to fortify his denial.[20] Again, if in the particular situ-

---

13. Colvin v. Wilson, 100 Kan. 247, 164 P. 284, syl. 1, 6 A.L.R. 859 (1917, opinion by Porter, J.). See likewise the stress placed upon discretion by Sibley, J. in Outlaw v. United States, 81 F.2d 805, 808 (C. C.A. 5th 1936) and by Burford, C. J. in First Nat. Bank v. Blakeman, 19 Okl. 106, 91 P. 868, 871 (1907).

14. It will be noted that when the sole purpose of introducing the prior statement is to support the credibility of the witness, it is not "substantive" evidence. Townsend v. United States, 106 F.2d 273, syl. 1 (C.C.A.3d 1939) (dictum); 4 Wigmore, Evidence, § 1132.

15. Stanford v. State, 34 Tex.Cr. 89, 29 S.W. 271 (1895) (bad reputation); 4 Wigmore, Evidence, § 1125; Note, 140 A.L.R. 21, 34.

16. Excluded on this ground: Kipp v. Silverman, 25 Mont. 296, 64 P. 884, 887, syl. 4 (1901) (recent fabrication); Abernathy v. Emporia Mfg. Co., 122 Va. 406, 95 S.E. 418, syl. 13 (1918) (corrupt offer by witness to sell testimony: consistent statement not shown to have been before the corrupt intent arose, improperly received); Sweazey v. Valley Transport, 6 Wash.2d 324, 354, 107 P.2d 567, syl. 2, 5, 140 A.L.R. 1 (1940) (impeachment by inconsistent statement implying recent contrivance; held, improper to bolster witness with consistent statement made after impeaching statement on solicitation of party calling the witness, and not before the influence or contrivance originated). Admitted where statement was made before the alleged influence arose. People v. Kynette, 15 Cal.2d 731, 104 P.2d 794, syl. 22, 23 (1940). See Note, 140 A.L.R. 21, 117–128.
If the witness's accuracy of memory is challenged, it seems clear common sense that a consistent statement made shortly after the event and before he had time to forget, should be received in support. ". . . The accuracy of memory is supported by proof that at or near the time when the facts deposed to have transpired, and were fresh in the mind of the witness, he gave the same version of them that he testified to on the trial." Smith, C. J. in Jones v. Jones, 80 N.C. 246, 250 (1879). See also Cross v. State, 118 Md. 660, 86 A. 223, 227, syl. 4 (1912). But some courts seem to reject this view. Note, 140 A.L.R. 21, 48.

17. See decisions collected in 4 Wigmore, Evidence, § 1126; Note, 140 A.L.R. 21, 49–77; Dec.Dig.Witnesses, ☞395, 414(2).

18. See, e. g., Cross v. State, 118 Md. 660, 86 A. 223, syl. 4 (1912); Piehler v. Kansas City Pub. Service Co., 360 Mo. 12, 226 S.W.2d 681, syl. 4 (1950); State v. Bethea, 186 N.C. 22, 118 S.E. 800, syl. 1 (1923) (allowable after any form of impeachment).

19. See, e. g., Ellicott v. Pearl, 10 Pet. (U.S.) 412, 439, 9 L.Ed. 475, 486 (1836) (opinion by Story, J.); Comm. v. Jenkins, 10 Gray (Mass.) 485, 488 (1858).

20. Stewart v. People, 23 Mich. 63, 74 (1871) (opinion by Cooley, J.); Parker v. State, 183 Ind. 130, 108 N.E. 517, syl. 3 (1915) (rule recognized); Twardosky v. New England Tel. & Tel. Co., 95 N.H. 279, 62 A.2d 723, syl. 8 (1948); Donovan v. Moore McCormack Lines, 266 App.Div. 406, 42 N.Y.S.2d 441 (1943). Contra: Burks v. State, 78 Ark. 271, 93 S.W. 983 (1906). See also Comm. v. White, 340 Pa. 139, 16 A.2d 407, syl. 2–4 (1940) which suggests that where the witness denies the inconsistent statement the admission of the supporting statement is in the judge's discretion.

ation, the attack by inconsistent statement is accompanied by, or interpretable as, a charge of a plan or contrivance to give false testimony, then proof of a prior consistent statement *before* the plan or contrivance was formed, tends strongly to disprove that the testimony was the result of contrivance. Here all courts agree.[21] It is for the judge to decide whether the impeachment amounts to a charge of contrivance,—ordinarily this is the most obvious implication—and it seems he is entitled to have an avowal one way or another from counsel. If it does not, then it may often amount to an imputation of inaccurate memory. If so the consistent statement made when the event was recent and memory fresh should be received in support.[22] Recognition of these exceptions would leave it still open to these courts to exclude most statements procured after the

inconsistent statement, and thus to discourage pressure on witnesses to furnish successive counter-statements.[23]

There are some special situations where native common sense and early tradition attached probative value to statements or conduct consonant with a later litigated claim. In some instances this tradition, somewhat mangled, has survived the relatively modern acceptance of the hearsay rule, which has been thought to be an obstacle to the use of consistent statements.[24] The most important instance is the use of the victim's complaint in rape cases.[25] Under the presently prevailing practice the state may prove the fact of complaint, made within a reasonable time,[26] to rebut the inference which might otherwise be drawn, unfavorable to the complainant's testimony, if complaint were not mentioned.[27] Note however that it is only

21. Affronti v. United States, 145 F.2d 3, syl. 7, 9 (C.C.A. 8th 1944) (rule recognized; discretionary); Coates v. People, 106 Colo. 483, 106 P.2d 354, syl. 9, 10 (1940); People v. Singer, 300 N.Y. 120, 89 N.E.2d 710, syl. 4–6 (1949), noted 35 Cornell L.Q. 867. In the last case the court points out that though the common phrase is "recent" fabrication or contrivance, the "recent" is misleading. It is not required to be recent as regards the trial, but only that the contrivance be more recent than the consistent statement. See cases collected 4 Wigmore, Evidence, § 1129; Note, 140 A.L.R. 21, 93–128.

22. See note 16, supra.

23. Such after-statements have usually been excluded. See, e. g., United States v. Sherman, 171 F.2d 618, syl. 3, 4 (C.C.A.2d, 1948, opinion by L. Hand, J.); Crawford v. Nilan, 289 N.Y. 444, 46 N.E.2d 512, syl. 2–4 (1943) (consistent statement procured from witness on morning of trial, held improperly admitted); Sweazey v. Valley Transport, 6 Wash.2d 324, 107 P.2d 567, syl. 5, 6, 140 A.L.R. 1 (1940) (described in note 16, supra). The last two cases exemplify the stresses of the race for statements in accident controversies. See Maguire, Evidence: Common Sense and Common Law, 63 (1947). We know that pressures by investigators of defendants and insurance companies often secure from witnesses one-sided statements in defendants' favor, and if the witness's testimony diverges in plaintiff's favor, these come in as inconsistent statements. The obviously needed opportunity to counter such statements comes in the witness's opportunity to deny or explain on cross-examination

and re-direct. And in a recent New York case where the plaintiff raised doubts as to the accuracy of his signed inconsistent statement written by defendant's investigator and said that he "talked him into giving it," the court admitted the plaintiff's consistent statement made five days later to plaintiff's employer and not for the purpose of the action, as bearing on the issue as to the accuracy of the inconsistent statement. One judge dissented in a vigorous opinion. Donovan v. Moore-McCormack Lines, 266 App.Div. 406, 42 N.Y.S.2d 441 (1943).

24. For the argument that the hearsay rule should be considered inapplicable to out-of-court statements of witnesses now present for cross-examination, see § 39.

25. See 4 Wigmore, Evidence, §§ 1134–1140; Dec. Dig., Rape, ⊂⇒48; 52 C.J., Rape, §§ 90–92.

26. Reg. v. Lillyman, [1896] 2 Q.B. 167; Curtis v. State, 167 Tenn. 430, 70 S.W.2d 363, syl. 3 (1932).

27. Powell v. State, 195 Miss. 161, 13 So.2d 622, syl. 3 (1943); State v. Lynch, 94 N.H. 52, 45 A.2d 885, syl. 1 (1946). The courts frequently say that the evidence comes in solely to support the credibility of the victim, not as "substantive" evidence of guilt. See, e. g., State v. Lynch, supra, and People v. Scott, 407 Ill. 301, 95 N.E.2d 315, syl. 7 (1950). Doubtless this is a modern sophistication designed to reconcile the admission of this ancient evidence of "hue and cry" with the modern ban upon hearsay. To say that prompt complaint does not substan-

the *fact* of complaint of ravishment (including time, place and person to whom made [28]) that may be proven but not the "details," as they are called, that is, the purport of the story,[29] nor even the name of the person charged.[30] There are two other theories [31] to which the prosecutor may resort on occasion, which do let in the "details," so much more stirring than the bare fact of complaint. The complaint if made while the victim is still under the immediate excitement of the outrage, may be admitted as a spontaneous exclamation, sometimes called "res gestae." [32] For this purpose, it comes in as substantive evidence under an exception to the hearsay rule. Again, if the prosecutrix is impeached as a witness the complaint may come in to support credibility as a prior consistent statement, subject to the limitations already set out in this section, upon that form of support.[33]

50. Changes in Existing Law Proposed by the Uniform Rules.

One who has read the description of the present practice of impeachment and support, in the preceding sections, will have marveled at the archaic and seemingly arbitrary character of many of the rules. He will also have observed with regret the laggard pace of the law in taking advantage of the techniques and knowledge which are afforded by the modern sciences of physiology and psychology in appraising the perception, memory and veracity of witnesses. Two principal retarding influences are apparent, namely, an undue distrust by the judges of the capacity of jurors, and an over-emphasis upon the adversary or contentious aspect of our trial tradition.

The drafters of the Uniform Rules of Evidence in the proposed Rules dealing with credibility [1] have moved in the direction of

---

tively strengthen the state's case runs counter to common sense.

28. Cape v. State, 61 Okl.Cr. 173, 66 P.2d 959, syl. 11 (1937); State v. Smith, 3 Wash.2d 543, 101 P.2d 298, syl. 1 (1940). And the condition and appearance of the complainant. Jackson v. State, 77 Okl.Cr. 160, 140 P.2d 606, syl. 15 (1943).

29. Wright v. Comm., 267 Ky. 441, 102 S.W.2d 376, syl. 5 (1937); State v. Saccone, 7 N.J.Super. 263, 72 A.2d 923, syl. 1 (1950); State v. Shults, 43 N.M. 71, 85 P.2d 591, syl. 9 (1938). But compare Glover v. Callahan, 299 Mass. 55, 12 N.E.2d 194, syl. 3 (1937) which seems to sanction the admission of details.

30. Lee v. State, 246 Ala. 69, 18 So.2d 706, syl. 8 (1944). But this will usually not be prejudicial unless identity of the other participant is disputed. Jump v. State, 146 Neb. 501, 20 N.W.2d 375, syl. 2 (1945) (intercourse admitted, claimed to be voluntary).

31. The three are marshaled in State v. Bragg, 141 Me. 157, 40 A.2d 1, syl. 6 (1944).

32. Complaints of rape admitted under this theory: Luke v. State, 184 Ga. 551, 192 S.E. 37, syl. 2 (1937); Terrill v. State, 133 Tex.Cr. 584, 112 S.W.2d 734, syl. 3 (1938); State v. Linton, 36 Wash.2d 67, 216 P.2d 761, syl. 1, 2 (1950), and cases collected Dec.Dig. Crim. Law, ☞366(1). See generally as to this doctrine, § 272, herein.

33. This theory is recognized in the following cases, but the local requirement that the witness must

have been impeached was held not to be satisfied. State v. Fleming, 354 Mo. 31, 188 S.W.2d 12, syl. 5, 7 (1945); State v. Saccone, 7 N.J.Super. 263, 72 A.2d 923, syl. 3 (1950).

1. Rule 20. "Subject to Rules 21 and 22, for the purpose of impairing or supporting the credibility of a witness, any party including the party calling him may examine him and introduce extrinsic evidence concerning any conduct by him and any other matter relevant upon the issues of credibility."

Rule 21. "Evidence of the conviction of a witness for a crime not involving dishonesty or false statement shall be inadmissible for the purpose of impairing his credibility. If the witness be the accused in a criminal proceeding, no evidence of his conviction of a crime shall be admissible for the sole purpose of impairing his credibility unless he has first introduced evidence admissible solely for the purpose of supporting his credibility."

Rule 22. "As affecting the credibility of a witness (a) in examining the witness as to a statement made by him in writing inconsistent with any part of his testimony it shall not be necessary to show or read to him any part of the writing provided that if the judge deems it feasible the time and place of the writing and the name of the person addressed, if any, shall be indicated to the witness; (b) extrinsic evidence of prior contradictory statements, whether oral or written, made by the witness, may in the discretion of the judge be excluded unless the witness was so examined while testifying as to

simplifying and modernizing the practice. The following changes, among others, are proposed:

1. The prohibition against impeaching one's own witness [2] is abandoned.

2. The rule of the Queen's Case requiring the cross-examiner to exhibit a writing, about which he is questioning,[3] to the witness is abolished as a rule, but the judge may require the examiner to give the identifying facts about the writing.[4]

3. Similarly the requirement of a preliminary "foundation" question as a condition upon extrinsic impeachment by inconsistent statements is made discretionary.[5]

4. Extrinsic evidence of character does not extend to "general" character but is limited to the traits of honesty and veracity.[6] Accordingly convictions offered to impeach no longer extend to all serious crimes,[7] but are limited to crimes involving dishonesty or false statement.

5. Proof of particular acts, by extrinsic evidence and seemingly by cross-examining the witness, where relevant only to show the witness's character (as distinguished from acts showing bias, interest or want of power to perceive) is excluded.[8]

6. The accused in a criminal case who elects to testify in his defense is shielded from impeachment by evidence of his conviction of another crime unless he has offered evidence in support of his credibility.[9]

---

give him an opportunity to identify, explain or deny the statement; (c) evidence of traits of his character other than honesty or veracity or their opposites, shall be inadmissible; (d) evidence of specific instances of his conduct relevant only as tending to prove a trait of his character, shall be inadmissible."

2. See R. 20, above.

3. See § 28.

4. See R. 22(a), above.

5. See R. 22(b), above.

6. See R. 22(c), above.

7. See R. 21, above.

8. See R. 22(d), above.

9. See R. 21, above.

TITLE 3

ADMISSION AND EXCLUSION

CHAPTER 6

THE PROCEDURE OF ADMITTING AND EXCLUDING EVIDENCE

51. The Offer of Evidence.[1]

It may be said at the outset that the rules of practice about offers of evidence and about objections are slanted so as to make it incumbent upon counsel on both sides, who are familiar with the facts and issues in the case, to present clearly to the judge, who when the case is called has never heard of it before, the proffered evidence, its bearing on the issues, and any questions which arise as to admissibility.

How is an offer of evidence made?

In the case of tangible things, such as writings, depositions, photographs, bullets, articles of clothing or the like, the counsel for the introducing party (after having produced witnesses to identify or authenticate the writing or other object) submits it to opposing counsel for inspection, and when this has been done, presents it to the judge, with the statement, "We offer this (document or object, describing it) in evidence." In a jury trial it is customary then in case of a writing for counsel to read it to the jury.[2]

The normal way of offering—and eliciting—oral testimony is of course by placing a witness on the stand and asking him a question or a series of questions. The sufficiency of the offer, however, ordinarily comes into question only if the court sustains an objection, and thus prevents the witness from answering. In such event the question itself may so specifically indicate the purport of the expected answer that it is regarded as completing the offer.[3] Usually, however, it

1. 1 Wigmore, Evidence, § 17; 6 Jones, Evidence, § 2526 (2d ed. 1926); Dec.Dig., Trials, ⊗39, 40, 44–48; 64 C.J. Trial, §§ 119–126, 139–154; Busch, Law and Tactics in Jury Trials, § 490 (1949).

2. For descriptions of the method of offering documents, see Virgie v. Stetson, 73 Me. 452, 461 (1882); 64 C.J., Trial, §§ 119–126.

3. Hartnett v. Boston Store, 265 Ill. 331, 106 N.E. 837, syl. 6 (1914); Marshall v. Marshall, 71 Kan. 313, 80 P. 629, 630 (1905) (". . . the question itself may be, and often is, of such character that, in connection with the other proceedings, it clearly indicates the materiality of the answer sought, and renders superfluous any statement as to what it is expected to be," a dictum); Patterson-Stocking v,

will be necessary, and always it will be safer, for counsel to state to the court for inclusion in the record "what he expects to prove by the answer of the witness." [4] This offer, proffer, or avowal as it is variously known will usually be required by the court to be made out of the hearing of the jury.

This method of producing a witness, asking a question, and stating the expected answer is the normal way of making and completing an offer of testimony. Suppose, however, there are several witnesses who are available, but not in court, to prove a line of facts, and the judge's rulings on the law have indicated that he will probably exclude this line of testimony. Must the party produce each of these witnesses, question them, and on exclusion, state the purport of each expected answer? A few decisions have said that this must be done, before an effective ruling can be secured.[5] Obviously it would often be a wasteful performance which witnesses, counsel and judge would desire to avoid. The prevailing view is that it is not invariably essential, but that a sufficient offer of proof may be made without producing the witnesses, if it is sufficiently specific,[6] and if there is nothing in the record to indicate a want of good faith or inability to produce the proof.[7]

We have seen, then, that whether a witness be produced and questioned or whether the offer be made without the witness, a statement of the purport of the expected evidence is required. The reason for the requirement is that the judge must be fairly in-

---

Dunn Bros. Warehouses, 201 Minn. 308, 276 N.W. 737, syl. 2 (1938).

4. Federal Rules of Civil Procedure, Rule 43(c): "Record of Excluded Evidence. In an action tried by a jury, if an objection to a question propounded to a witness is sustained by the court, the examining attorney may make a specific offer of what he expects to prove by the answer of the witness. The court may require the offer to be made out of the hearing of the jury. The court may add such other or further statement as clearly shows the character of the evidence, the form in which it was offered, the objection made, and the ruling thereon. In actions tried without a jury the same procedure may be followed, except that the court upon request shall take and report the evidence in full, unless it clearly appears that the evidence is not admissible on any ground or that the witness is privileged."

For cases stating the requirement of an offer of proof, see e. g., Petition of Mackintosh, 268 Mass. 138, 167 N.E. 273, syl. 1 (1929); Philadelphia Record Co. v. Sweet, 124 Pa.Super. 414, 188 A. 631, syl. 3, 4 (1936) (reversible error to refuse counsel opportunity of making offer).

On cross-examination, however, the examining counsel will not ordinarily have an advance opportunity to know what the witness will answer, and the requirement of an offer will not usually be applied. Cohen v. Cohen, 196 Ga. 562, 27 S.E.2d 28, 30 (1943); Higgins v. Pratt, 316 Mass. 700, 56 N.E.2d 595, syl. 16 (1944). But even on cross-examination the court in its discretion may require counsel to hint his purpose far enough to show the materiality of the answer hoped for. Fahey v. Clark, 125 Conn. 44,

3 A.2d 313, syl. 7, 120 A.L.R. 517 (1938) (court here required too strong an assurance); Cox v. Norris, 70 Ga.App. 580, 28 S.E.2d 888, syl. 8 (1944).

5. Chicago City Ry. Co. v. Carroll, 206 Ill. 318, 68 N.E. 1087, syl. 8 (1903); Eschbach v. Hurtt, 47 Md. 61, 66 (1877) ("If the defendant had at the trial witnesses who could have proved . . . it was his duty to have called them or one of them to the stand and propounded appropriate questions. . . .").

6. It would seem wise to name the witness or witnesses and to indicate the particulars of what each would prove.

7. Scotland County v. Hill, 112 U.S. 183, 186, 5 S.Ct. 93, 95, 28 L.Ed. 692 (1884) ("If the trial court has doubts about the good faith of an offer of testimony, it can insist on the production of the witness, and upon some attempt to make the proof, before it rejects the offer; but it does reject it, and allows a bill of exceptions which shows that the offer was actually made and refused, and there is nothing else in the record to indicate bad faith, an appellate court must assume that the proof could have been made. . . ."); Missouri Pac. Ry. Co. v. Castle, 172 F. 841, syl. 3 (C.C.A. Neb.1909); Garvey v. Chicago Rys. Co., 339 Ill. 276, 171 N.E. 271, 274, 275 (1930) (Offer of evidence on motion for new trial without producing witness held sufficient, distinguishing Carroll case in next preceding note); Witt v. Voight, 162 Wis. 568, 156 N.W. 954, syl. 3 (1916) (counsel said he had witnesses in court who would testify to certain facts, whereon court said such evidence would not be received, held a sufficient offer).

formed of the basis for the proponent's claim of admissibility and the appellate court may understand the scope and effect of his ruling. To this end the statement must be reasonably specific,[8] must state the purpose of the proof offered unless that is apparent,[9] and where the offered facts suggest a question as to their materiality or competency the offer must show the facts on which relevancy [10] or admissibility [11] depends.

We have seen that a party in case of doubt must specify the purpose for which the evidence is offered.[12] If he specifies a purpose

for which it is inadmissible and the judge excludes, he cannot complain of the ruling though for another purpose it could have been rightly admitted.[13]

If part of the evidence offered, as in the case of a deposition, a letter, or a conversation, is admissible and a part is not, it is incumbent on the offeror, not the judge, to select the admissible part. If he offers both good and bad together, like a barrel of apples some good, some rotten, and the judge rejects the entire offer, the offeror may not complain.[14]

---

8. Kane v. Carper-Dover Merc. Co., 206 Ark. 674, 177 S.W.2d 41, syl. 1, 2 (1944) ("we offer to prove . . . that C. D. is not the proper plaintiff for recovery or damage": too indefinite: must be so specific as to give the opportunity to court to rule on particular testimony); Douillard v. Wood, 20 Cal.2d 665, 128 P.2d 6, syl. 11 (1942) (counsel for defendant offered to show by defendant and "by other witnesses" that the plaintiffs took positions inconsistent with asserted agreement, too general); Ostmo v. Tennyson, 70 N.D. 558, 296 N.W. 541, syl. 7 (1941) (must show what facts are sought to be introduced, so that court may see whether they have any bearing); Bailey v. Victoria Bank & Trust Co., 114 S.W.2d 920, syl. 2 (Tex.Civ.App.1938) (offer to prove, in malicious prosecution case that particular member of grand jury "procured" the indictment, bad as a "general conclusion"). Compare Moran v. Levin, 318 Mass. 770, 64 N.E.2d 360, syl. 1 (1945) (deceit for sale of dairy cows, one of which was alleged not to produce milk because diseased, plaintiff's offer to show by plaintiff and wife "certain representations made by defendant with reference to the condition, the health of these cows, as to whether they were milk producers" held, sufficient though a "summary" or "abstract" of the proposed evidence).

9. Brothers v. Adams, 152 Kan. 675, 107 P.2d 757, syl. 13 (1941) (recognizing requirement); Holman v. Kemp, 70 Minn. 422, 73 N.W. 186, 188 (1897) (counsel asked plaintiff if he did not drink a good deal before the accident, excluded; appellant claimed this was relevant to explain plaintiff's physical condition at time of trial; held, insufficient offer. "If such was the real purpose of the evidence, it was not apparent upon the record, and the trial court's attention should have been specifically called to the object of the evidence."); Matter of Bateman, 145 N.Y. 623, 40 N.E. 10, syl. 2 (1895) and cases cited 64 C.J. 125, § 144, note 26.

10. Braman v. Wiley, 119 F.2d 991, syl. 8 (C.C.A.Ind. 1941) (collision; there was evidence that defendant

was drunk; defendant offered a witness to testify to a conversation with defendant soon after; on appeal defendant contended this was material to negative drunkenness; held, not relevant to the purpose stated); Taylor v. Henderson, 112 Vt. 107, 22 A.2d 318, syl. 23, 24 (1941) (must point out evidentiary relation to the issue on which offered). Unless relevancy must have been apparent. Joslin v. Idaho Times Pub. Co., 60 Idaho 235, 91 P.2d 386, syl. 2 (1939); Creighton v. Elgin, 387 Ill. 592, 56 N. E.2d 825, syl. 9, 10 (1944) (question itself showed purposes and materiality).

11. Smith v. Pine, 234 Iowa 256, 12 N.W.2d 236, syl. 21 (1943) (failure to prove time of making of statement offered as "res gestae"); Emery v. F. P. Asher, Jr. & Sons, 196 Md. 1, 75 A.2d 333, syl. 13 (1950) (collision: trial court properly refused to permit plaintiff to prove by expert witness the normal reaction time, the stopping distance on highway involved and other scientific deductions, where proffer did not take into consideration fact that accident occurred at night on highway with which plaintiff was unfamiliar, and that plaintiff did not know whether his headlights were depressed or shining full distance ahead.); Deaton & Son v. Miller Well Servicing Co., 231 S.W.2d 944, syl. 4–6 (Tex. Civ.App.1950) (party offering evidence which would ordinarily be hearsay—here declarations of an agent—must show facts bringing it under some exception).

12. See note 9, above.

13. Dietrich v. Kettering, 212 Pa. 356, 61 A. 927, syl. 1 (1905).

14. Dorsey v. Dorsey, 189 Ga. 662, 7 S.E.2d 273, syl. 6 (1940) (evidence of declarations of decedent); Morris v. E. I. DuPont de Nemours & Co., 346 Mo. 126, 139 S.W.2d 984, syl. 7 (1940) (motion picture, in part irrelevant); Garneau v. Garneau, 63 R.I. 416, 9 A.2d 15, syl. 6, 7, 131 A.L.R. 450 (1939) ("Even if this rule might be too strict, where proof of only a few related facts is offered, it should, in our judg-

On the other hand, if evidence offered is admissible upon one issue, but not upon another or if admissible as against one adverse party, but not against another, and the legitimate purpose is reasonably apparent, the offer is not defective for the proponent's failure to limit it to the particular issue [15] or party. [16] The adversary must request the judge to give a limiting instruction.[17]

When an offer is made, it may of course be withdrawn before the evidence is received. If a party has introduced evidence which is not objected to and which turns out to be favorable to the adversary, it has sometimes been intimated that the offering party may withdraw the evidence as of right.[18] The accepted rule seems, however, to be that such a withdrawal is not of right, but the adversary is entitled to have the benefit of the testimony as it bears in his favor,[19] unless the special situation makes it fair for the judge in discretion to permit the withdrawal.[20] If, however, the evidence is admitted over the adversary's objection, and the proponent later decides to yield to the objection, and asks to withdraw the evidence the court may revoke his ruling and permit the withdrawal.[21]

52.   Objections.[1]

If the administration of the exclusionary rules of evidence is to be fair and workable the judge must be promptly informed by a party, who contends that evidence should be rejected, of his contention and the reason therefor.   The initiative is placed on the party not on the judge.   The approach, accordingly, is that a failure to object to an offer of evidence at the time the offer is made, assigning the grounds, is a waiver of any ground of complaint against its admission.

Time of Making: Motions to Strike.   The cardinal point is that counsel are not allowed to gamble upon the possibility of a favorable answer,[2] but the objection must be made as soon as the ground becomes apparent.[3]   Usually this will be as soon the question is asked, assuming that the question shows that it calls for inadmissible evidence.   Then counsel must, if opportunity affords as it usually does, state his objection before the witness answers.[4]   But sometimes this is not feasi-

ment, be applied to such a single offer of proof of a mass of largely unrelated facts as was made in this cause   .   .   ."); Texas Reciprocal Ins. Ass'n v. Stadler, 140 Tex. 96, 166 S.W.2d 121, syl. 13 (Comm., 1943).

15.   Hammond v. Schuermann Bldg. & Realty Co., 352 Mo. 418, 177 S.W.2d 618, syl. 4 (1944); Rynar v. Lincoln Transit Co., 129 N.J.L. 525, 30 A.2d 406, syl. 4 (1943); Blum Milling Co. v. Moore-Seaver Grain Co., 277 S.W. 78, syl. 4–7 (Tex.Comm.1925).

16.   Miller v. Minhinnette, 185 Ga. 490, 195 S.E. 425, syl. 2 (1938).

17.   See cases in note 15, above.

18.   See Young v. United States, 97 F.2d 200, 205, syl. 6 (C.C.A.5th 1938), and comment on this point in Note, 17 Tex.L.Rev. 373, 374 (1939).

19.   Alabama Great Southern Ry. Co. v. Hardy, 131 Ga. 238, 62 S.E. 71, syl. 2 (1908) enlightening discussion by Evans, P. J.); Page v. Payne, 293 Mo. 600, 240 S.W. 156, syl. 12 (1922) (defendant had no right to withdraw parts of documents introduced by him); National Newark Banking Co. v. Sweeney, 88 N.J.L. 140, 96 A. 86, syl. 3 (1915); 1 Wigmore,

Evidence, § 17c, Dec.Dig. Trials, ⊙58, 64 C.J. 144, § 168, note 72.

20.   Maas v. Laurson, 219 Minn. 461, 18 N.W.2d 233, 235, syl. 7, 158 A.L.R. 215 (1945) (discretionary, may be allowed if evidence irrelevant, or if favorable only to withdrawing party; court here did not err in denying withdrawal).

21.   Alabama Great Southern Ry. Co. v. Hardy, 131 Ga. 238, 62 S.E. 71, 72 (1908); McCarty v. Bishop, 231 Mo.App. 604, 102 S.W.2d 126, syl. 11 (1937) (may be withdrawn in court's discretion, despite objection of opposing party.)

1.   Wigmore, Evidence, § 18; 6 Jones, Evidence, §§ 2517–2530 (2d ed. 1926); Dec.Dig. Trial, ⊙73–97; 64 C.J. Trial, §§ 185–229; 53 Am.Jur. Trial, §§ 132–155.

2.   Hastings v. Serieto, 61 Cal.App.2d 672, 143 P.2d 956, syl. 15 (1943).

3.   Cheffer v. Eagle Discount Stamp Co., 348 Mo. 1023, 156 S.W.2d 591, syl. 5 (1941).

4.   Stark's Adm'r v. Herndon's Adm'r, 292 Ky. 469, 166 S.W.2d 828, syl. 9 (1942) (question asked by

ble. A forward witness may answer before he had a chance to object.[5] A question which is not objectionable may be followed by an unresponsive answer, which is.[6] Or, after the evidence is received, a ground of objection to this evidence is disclosed for the first time in the later course of the trial.[7] In all these cases an after-objection may be stated as soon as the ground appears, and in proper technique, such after-objection is phrased as a motion to strike out the objectionable evidence, and for an instruction to the jury to disregard it. Counsel, of course, makes his way easier by calling his after-objection by its proper name, but it seems that any phraseology which directs the judge's attention to the grounds as soon as they appear and asserts the objection should be sufficient.[8]

As to the time when objections must be made to questions asked and answers given in the taking of depositions, written or oral, this is a matter variously regulated by rules and statutes in the different jurisdictions.[9] Usually objections going to the "manner and form" of the questions or answers, such as the objection to leading questions or unresponsive answers—sometimes opinions and secondary evidence are put in this class—must be made at the time of taking the deposition and disposed of upon motion before the trial.[10] Objections going to the "substance," such as relevancy and hearsay, may usually be urged for the first time when the deposition is offered in evidence at the trial.[11] Excerpts from the Federal rules illustrate the complexity of these regulations.[12]

juror); Doherty v. St. Louis Butter Co., 339 Mo. 996, 98 S.W.2d 742, syl. 8, 9 (1936).

5. A motion to strike should be made. Wightman v. Campbell, 217 N.Y. 479, 112 N.E. 184, syl. 1 (1916) (but in the particular situation an objection sufficed); Sorenson v. Smith, 65 Ore. 78, 129 P. 757, syl. 3, 131 P. 1022 (1913).

6. Wallace v. American Toll Bridge Co., 124 Ore. 179, 264 P. 351, syl. 3 (1928) (proper question, improper answer, approved practice is motion to strike.)

The mere fact that the answer is unresponsive is not an objection available to the opponent. Rowe v. Alabama Power Co., 232 Ala. 257, 167 So. 324, syl. 1 (1936). But only to the questioner, who may move to strike. Davidson v. State, 211 Ala. 271, 100 So. 641, syl. 12 (1924).

7. Manley v. Combs, 197 Ga. 768, 30 S.E.2d 485, syl. 8 (1944) (diagnosis testified to by doctor on direct, disclosed on cross-examination to have been possibly based on hearsay: held, objection at time of later disclosure insufficient, should have made motion to rule out the earlier testimony).

8. See Hackenson v. City of Waterbury, 124 Conn. 679, 2 A.2d 215, syl. 4–9 (1938) (where plaintiff-witness "jumped the gun" and answered a question before defendant objected, and court sustained the objection; held, sufficient to eliminate evidence from jury's consideration, though there was no motion to strike); Wightman v. Campbell, 217 N.Y. 479, 112 N.E. 184, syl. 1 (1916) (where first question in series in proving the making by witness of a survey of land was answered before objection, and

objection then made "to all that proof," and overruled; held, objector has benefit of his exception without motion to strike).

9. See the references to statutes compiled in 1 Wigmore, Evidence, § 18, note 6. Decisions are collected in notes 7–15, same section, and in Dec.Dig., Depositions, ☞105–111, and 26 C.J.S. Depositions, §§ 101–105.

10. 1 Wigmore, Evidence, § 18, notes 7–14; 26 C.J.S., Depositions, § 101, pp. 947–949.

11. See references next preceding note.

12. Rules of Civil Procedure, Rule 26(e) *Objections to Admissibility*. Subject to the provisions of Rule 32(c), objection may be made at the trial or hearing to receiving in evidence any deposition or part thereof for any reason which would require the exclusion of the evidence if the witness were then present and testifying.

Rule 30(c) *Record of Examination; Oath; Objections.* . . . All objections made at the time of the examination to the qualifications of the officer taking the deposition, or to the manner of taking it, or to the evidence presented, or to the conduct of any party, and any other objection to the proceedings, shall be noted by the officer upon the deposition. Evidence objected to shall be taken subject to the objections. . . .

Rule 32(c) (1) Objections to the competency of a witness or to the competency, relevancy, or materiality of testimony are not waived by failure to make them before or during the taking of the deposition, unless the ground of the objection is one

If evidence is introduced at the first trial of a case, and an available objection is waived by failure to assert it, may the same evidence when tendered at a second trial of the same case be effectively objected to then for the first time? It is usually held that when the objection is to the competency of the witness under the Dead Man's Statute,[13] or is a claim of privilege for confidential communications,[14] the failure to object at the first trial operates as a waiver even for the second trial. The dubious policy of the Dead Man's Acts which leads the courts to say they should be strictly confined,[15] and the fact that a confidential communication once made public has lost its secrecy forever, justify these holdings. In the absence, however, of special considerations such as these, it seems that an objection to admissibility of evidence [16] or to the competency of a witness,[17] based on substance rather than form, should be assertable at the second trial though it was available and not asserted at the first. This assumes that the enforcement generally of the substantial rules of evidence and competency will make for the better administration of justice. The widening of waiver would be justified upon the opposite assumption.

General and Specific Objections.[18] The precept constantly urged in the opinions is that objections must be accompanied by a reasonably definite statement of the grounds.[19] The purposes of the requirement are that the judge may understand the question raised and that the adversary may have an opportunity to remedy the defect, if possible.[20] The "venom" of this requirement is the doctrine that if the judge *over-rules* the general objection the objecting party may not complain of the ruling on appeal by urg·ing a valid ground not mentioned when the objection was made.[21] To this three excep-

which might have been obviated or removed if presented at that time.

(2) Errors and irregularities occurring at the oral examination in the manner of taking the deposition, in the form of the questions or answers, in the oath or affirmation, or in the conduct of parties and errors of any kind which might be obviated, removed, or cured if promptly presented, are waived unless seasonable objection thereto is made at the taking of the deposition.

(3) Objections to the form of written interrogatories submitted under Rule 31 are waived unless served in writing upon the party propounding them within the time allowed for serving the succeeding cross or other interrogatories and within 3 days after service of the last interrogatories authorized.

13. Faden v. Midcap's Estate, 112 Colo. 573, 152 P.2d 682, syl. 3–5 (1944); Billingsley v. Gulick, 256 Mich. 606, 240 N.W. 46, syl. 1, 79 A.L.R. 166 (1932); Collins v. Collins' Estate, 104 Vt. 506, 162 A. 361, syl. 1 (1932). Note, 79 A.L.R. 176.

14. Green v. Crapo, 181 Mass. 55, 62 N.E. 956, syl. 5 (1902) (attorney-client; Holmes, C. J., "The privacy for the sake of which the privilege was created was gone by the appellant's own consent . . ."); Elliott v. Kansas City, 198 Mo. 593, 96 S.W. 1023, syl. 2 (1906) (patient's privilege); People v. Bloom, 193 N.Y. 1, 85 N.E. 824 (1908) (same). Contra: Maryland Casualty Co. v. Maloney, 119 Ark. 434, 178 S.W. 387, syl. 3 (1915). See

Note, 79 A.L.R. 176, 179; 1 Wigmore, Evidence. § 18(3), 53 Am.Jur.Trial, § 145.

15. Lucas v. Hamilton Realty Corp., 70 App.D.C. 277, 105 F.2d 800, syl. 5 (1939); Dec.Dig.,Witnesses, ☞126.

16. State v. Kelleher, 224 Mo. 145, 123 S.W. 551, syl. 2 (1909) (dying declaration not confined to facts attending the act of killing); Meekins v. Norfolk & S. R. Co., 136 N.C. 1, 48 S.E. 501, syl. 1 (1904) (hearsay).

17. Young v. State, 122 Ga. 725, 50 S.E. 996, syl. 1 (1905) (want of knowledge of nature and sanctity of oath by witness, child of 12 years).

18. 1 Wigmore, Evidence, § 18(c) (1) (2); Dec.Dig. Trials, ☞81–84; 64 C.J. Trials, §§ 203–213; 23 C.J.S., Criminal Law, §§ 1062, 1063.

19. See, e. g., Forest Preserve Dist. v. Lehmann Estate, 388 Ill. 416, 58 N.E.2d 538, syl. 20 (1945); Craig v. Citizens Trust Co., 217 Ind. 434, 26 N.E.2d 1006, syl. 17 (1940).

20. Jackson v. Chesapeake & O. Ry. Co., 179 Va. 642, 20 S.E.2d 489, syl. 8 (1942).

21. See, e. g., United States v. Sessin, 84 F.2d 667, syl. 2 (C.C.A. 10th, 1936) ("I object," too general to present reviewable question,) and see 4 C.J.S., Appeal and Error, §§ 247, 253.
Similarly, the overruling of an objection based on an untenable ground, will not be overturned on appeal on the basis that there was a tenable ground for ex-

tions have been stated. The first is that if the ground for exclusion was obvious to judge and opposing counsel without stating it, the want of specification is immaterial.[22] This exception is clear good sense, and is acted upon constantly by trial judges who sustain the bare, "I object," without waiting for the needless reason why. It has also been said that if the evidence is not admissible for any purpose, the general objection may be sufficient.[23] But if the ground is not apparent, it seems there is still need for specification. It has likewise been suggested that if the omitted ground was one that could not have been obviated, the general objection may serve.[24] This overlooks, it is believed, the consideration that though the objection to the particular evidence could not have been obviated, yet if the ground of objection had been stated the judge and adverse counsel might have appreciated its force, and the offer might have been excluded or withdrawn, and the adversary might have secured other evidence to fill the gap.[25]

We have discussed the effect of overruling a general objection. Usually the trial judge's action will be supported on appeal. If the trial judge *sustains* the general objection, the upper court is again charitable toward his ruling. "When evidence is *excluded* upon a mere general objection, the ruling will be upheld, if any ground in fact existed for the exclusion. It will be assumed, in the absence of any request by the opposing party or the court to make the objection definite, that it was understood, and that the ruling was placed upon the right ground." [26]

General objections have been termed "sheet-lightning" [27] objections and might be

clusion which could have been urged. Kroger Grocery & Baking Co. v. Harpole, 175 Miss. 227, 166 So. 335, syl. 12 (1936).

22. Stylblo v. McNeil, 217 Ill.App. 316, 45 N.E.2d 1011, syl. 5 (1943) ("An objection, except where it is obvious, should be stated in such a manner as to inform the court of the point being urged"); Floy v. Hibbard, 227 Iowa 149, 287 N.W. 829, syl. 3 (1939) (general objection sufficient, "where the grounds of the objection are discernible"); Hungate v. Hudson, 353 Mo. 944, 185 S.W.2d 646, syl. 5, 157 A.L.R. 598 (1945) (when evidence "self-evidently wholly incompetent" or obviously prejudicial, general objection of irrelevancy sufficient). See also People v. Bob, 29 Cal.2d 321, 175 P.2d 12, syl. 7 (1946) where the evidence offered was hearsay but the opponent did not specifically make that objection, the court said that where it was obvious from the colloquy that an objection specifying hearsay would have been overruled, the lack of precision in the objection would not render it ineffective. See Note, 35 Calif. L.Rev. 456.

23. Louisville & N. R. Co. v. Scott, 232 Ala. 284, 167 So. 572, syl. 17 (1936) (if illegal for any purpose, and incurable by other evidence or by reframing question); Scally v. Flannery, 292 Ill.App. 349, 11 N.E.2d 123, syl. 12 (1937); Carroll v. Missouri Power & Light Co., 231 Mo.App. 265, 96 S.W.2d 1074, syl. 16 (1936) (exception recognized).

24. Louisville & N. R. Co. v. Scott, next preceding note; Floy v. Hibbard, 227 Iowa 149, 287 N.W. 829,

syl. 3 (1939); Smith v. Fine, 351 Mo. 1179, 175 S.W. 2d 761, syl. 13 (1943).

25. See Campbell v. Paschall, 132 Tex. 226, 121 S.W. 2d 593, syl. 1 (1938).

26. Tooley v. Bacon, 70 N.Y. 34, 37 (1877). To like effect: Morgan Hill Paving Co. v. Pratt City Sav. Bank, 220 Ala. 686, 127 So. 501, syl. 5 (1930); White v. Hasburgh, 124 S.W.2d 560, syl. 11 (Mo.App. 1939); Luckenbach v. Sciple, 72 N.J.L. 476, 63 A. 244, syl. 1 (1906) (discretionary in trial judge to sustain objection on ground not stated by counsel); 64 C.J.Trial, § 204, note 93; 1 Wigmore, Evidence, § 18, note 26. If the offering counsel, however, requests of the objector and the judge the reason for objection, and the request is denied when if the grounds had been furnished they could have been obviated, the ruling can be attacked. Colburn v. Chicago, St. Paul, M. & O. Ry. Co., 109 Wis. 377, 85 N.W. 354, syl. 3 (1901).

If a specific objection is made on an untenable ground and sustained, it seems that if there were another valid ground for exclusion, the ruling should be upheld unless it appears that the true objection if stated could have been obviated, or if incurable the gap could have been filled by other testimony. Compare, however, Bloodgood v. Lynch, 293 N.Y. 308, 56 N.E.2d 718, syl. 5 (1944) where the court intimates that where the evidence is excluded on a specific objection, the appellate court will not consider the availability of a different ground.

27. Sherwood, P. J. in State v. Bartlett, 170 Mo. 658, 71 S.W. 148, 152 (1902).

called "masked battery" objections. Examples of general objections are "I object," [28] objections on the ground that the evidence is "inadmissible," [29] "illegal" [30] or "incompetent," [31] or is not proper testimony for the jury,[32] or "on all the grounds ever known or heard of"![33] One of the most overworked forms is an objection on the ground that the evidence is "incompetent, irrelevant and immaterial." Its rhythm and alliteration have seduced some lawyers to employ it as a routine and meaningless ritual, a "vain repetition." This has caused courts frequently to treat it as equivalent merely to the general objection,[34] "I object." The word "incompetent" as applied to evidence means no more than inadmissible, and thus cannot be said to state a ground of objection. "Irrelevant and immaterial," however, do state though in general terms a distinct and substantial ground for exclusion.[35] A requirement that the objector state specifically wherein the evidence, as applied to the particular issues, is irrelevant or immaterial, as the courts seem to demand, seems in many situations unduly burdensome. It would be far more practical to entertain the irrelevancy objection in this general form, and for the judge if he has any doubt of relevancy to call upon the proponent to explain the purpose of the proof.[36] If relevancy is adequately challenged, it seems that it is not essential to specify in addition that the evidence is "prejudicial" in the sense of arousing undue hostility against the party.[37] Prejudice is a mere factor in weighing relevancy, i. e., in determining whether the evidence has sufficient probative value to outweigh its liabilities.

Objections are required to be specific not only in respect to the statement of grounds, but also in respect to a particular part of the offer. If the offer consists of several statements or items tendered as a unit, e. g., a deposition, a letter, a conversation, a transcript of testimony or the like, and it is objected to as a whole, and parts are subject to the objection made and parts are not, the judge will not be put in error for overruling the objection.[38] His answer to the objec-

28. Semkin v. Hollander, 82 N.J.L. 485, 81 A. 980, syl. 2 (1911); 64 C.J.Trial, § 206, note 30.

29. Fowler v. Wallace, 131 Ind. 347, 31 N.E. 53, syl. 1 (1892).

30. Johnston v. Johnston, 174 Ala. 220, 57 So. 450, syl. 3 (1912).

31. Minchen v. Hart, 72 F. 294 syl. 1 (C.C.A. Iowa, 1896); 64 C.J. 187, note 97.

32. Itasca Lumber Co. v. Martin, 230 F. 584, syl. 1 (C.C.A.Minn.1916).

33. Johnston v. Clements, 25 Kan. 376, syl. 4 (1881).

34. Cook-O'Brien Const. Co. v. Crawford, 26 F.2d 574, syl. 2 (C.C.A.Ariz.1928) (no effect to present a ground of objection "not discernible"); Goldfoot v. Lofgren, 135 Ore. 533, 296 P. 843, syl. 1 (1931); Dec. Dig.Trial, ☞83(2); 64 C.J. 187, note 13; 53 Am. Jur.Trial, §§ 138, 139.

35. See ch. 16, herein.

36. Compare the practice, under a statute in Oklahoma which makes an objection to evidence on the ground that it is incompetent, irrelevant, and immaterial cover all matters ordinarily embraced within such objections, and makes it unnecessary "to specify further the grounds of such objections or to state the specific reasons whereby the question is so objectionable," unless the court or opposing counsel inquire of the objector wherein the question is so objectionable, and thereupon the objector shall state specifically his reasons or grounds for such objection. McDonald v. Strawn, 78 Okl. 271, 190 P. 558, 562, 1920.

37. Hungate v. Hudson, 353 Mo. 944, 185 S.W.2d 646, syl. 4, 5, 157 A.L.R. 598, 602, 1945, and Luechtefeld v. Marglous, 151 S.W.2d 710, 713, syl. 1–4, Mo., 1941, wherein the court said: "Of course a party objecting to evidence under the general assignment that it is irrelevant may on appeal show its prejudicial effect, though not specifically pointed out to the trial court, but such prejudice must be of the character naturally to be expected from the admission of such evidence." The contrary holding in McEwen v. Texas & P. Ry. Co., 92 S.W.2d 308, syl. 1–4 (Tex.Civ.App.1936) seems difficult to support.

38. People v. Lang Transp. Corp., 43 Cal.App.2d 134, 110 P.2d 464, syl. 6 (1941) (report of proceedings at a meeting); Brown & Root v. Haddad, 142 Tex. 624, 180 S.W.2d 339, syl. 4, 5 (1944) (objection to highway patrolman's report of accident on ground that it contained hearsay statements without pointing them out, insufficient); Jacobson v. Bryan, 244 Wis.

tor [39] is that it is not the judge's duty to sever the bad parts if some are good. Obviously such a rule should be administered by the appellate courts not stiffly but with due concession, if need be, to the realities of the particular trial situation.

Even more clearly, if evidence offered is properly admissible on a particular issue,[40] but not upon some other, or is admissible against one party but not against another,[41] an objector who asks that this evidence be excluded altogether, though he assigns grounds, cannot complain if his objection be overruled. He should have asked that the admission of the evidence be limited to the particular purpose or party.[42]

Repetition of Objections. A offers testimony by one witness which his adversary, B, thinks is incompetent. He objects, and the objection is *sustained.* In such event, if A offers similar testimony by the same or another witness, B must of course repeat his objection if he is to complain of the later evidence.[43] Suppose, however, the first objection is *overruled.* Must B then repeat his objection when other like evidence similarly objectionable is offered? A few decisions intimate that he must,[44] a practice which places B in the invidious semblance of a contentious obstructor, and conduces to waste of time and fraying of patience. Most courts hold that B is entitled to assume that the judge will continue to make the same ruling and that he need not repeat the objection.[45] It seems that the consequence of this view should be, not only that the first objection is not waived, but that the reach of this objection extends to all similar evidence subject to the same objection. It seems that in any jurisdiction where the practice in this respect is at all doubtful, it is a wise precaution for objecting counsel to ask the judge to have the record show that it is understood that the objection goes to all other like evidence, and when later evidence is offered, to have it noted that the earlier objection applies.

The Exception.[46] Closely associated with the objection but distinct from it in the classic common law practice is the exception. Taking an exception includes two steps. After the judge's adverse ruling excluding his evidence or overruling his objection, the party's counsel says, "We except." This is a protest against the correctness of the ruling and a statement that the party does not acquiesce

---

359, 12 N.W.2d 789, syl. 4, 5 (1944) (traffic officer's report of accident partly based on personal knowledge, partly not; objection to whole report, insufficient); Dec.Dig.Trial, ☞85; 64 C.J.Trial, § 214.

39. As it is to the proponent if he decides to sustain the objection, see § 51, above.

40. Amos v. State, 209 Ark. 55, 189 S.W.2d 611, syl. 5 (1945); Curtin v. Benjamin, 305 Mass. 489, 26 N.E.2d 354, syl. 5, 129 A.L.R. 433 (1940); Dec.Dig. Trial, ☞86.

41. Solomon v. Dabrowski, 295 Mass. 358, 3 N.E.2d 744, syl. 2, 3, 106 A.L.R. 464 (1936); Utt v. Herold, 127 W.Va. 719, 34 S.E.2d 357, syl. 3 (1945) (in civil action, plea of guilty by one defendant in previous criminal prosecution; overruling other defendant's general objection was not error). Dec.Dig., Trial, ☞87.

42. Solomon v. Dabrowski, next preceding note.

43. Wagner v. Jones, 77 N.Y. 590 (semble) (1879); Frost v. Goddard, 25 Me. 414, syl. 3 (1845).

44. See, e. g., Crowther v. Hirschmann, 174 Md. 100, 197 A. 868, syl. 2 (1938) (here the question objected to was not answered); Shelton v. Southern Ry. Co., 193 N.C. 670, 139 S.E. 232, syl. 5 (1927).

45. Tucker v. Reil, 51 Ariz. 357, 77 P.2d 203, syl. 13–15 (1938); Metropolitan National Bank v. Commercial Savings Bank, 104 Iowa 682, 691, 74 N.W. 26, 29 (1898); Louisville & N. R. Co. v. Rowland's Adm'r, 215 Ky. 663, 286 S.W. 929, syl. 2 (1926); State v. Taylor, 130 W.Va. 74, 42 S.E.2d 549, syl. 11, 12 (1947); Dec.Dig.Trial, ☞79, 64 C.J.Trial, § 201; 53 Am.Jur.Trial, § 146, and see an excellent discussion in Ladd, Common Mistakes in the Technique of Trial, 22 Iowa L.Rev. 609, 612–617 (1937).

46. 1 Wigmore, Evidence, § 20; Dec.Dig.Trial, ☞99–105; 64 C.J. Trial §§ 235–238; 53 Am.Jur. Trial, §§ 154, 155.

in it.[47] Following this the party aggrieved will request that "a bill of exception be allowed," and the terms of this may then be briefly agreed on between judge and counsel. This bill of exceptions will recite (1) the evidence admitted, when the ruling overrules the objection, or (2) the evidence expected or proffered, if the ruling excludes, (3) the objection, (4) the ruling, and (5) the fact that the protestation was made and the bill requested and allowed.[48] The bill of exceptions when finally signed by the judge becomes part of the record for the reviewing court by the terms of the ancient Statute of Westminster the Second.[49]

This procedure is clumsy and burdensome. The policy of requiring counsel to protest against the court's rulings when the party's position is already clear from the terms of his offer or objection is of dubious wisdom. Moreover, the modern practice of having a stenographer in attendance who records in his notes all of the matters embodied in the ancient bill of exceptions makes it unnecessary to halt the proceedings to recite the terms of a bill. Indeed, it dispenses with the need of separate bills of exception in the record or of any memorial beyond the stenographer's transcript of the testimony, offers, objections, and rulings. Accordingly, the Federal rules and the practice in many progressive states have dispensed with exceptions,[50] and have provided that for all purposes formerly served thereby, "it is sufficient that a party at the time the ruling or order of the Court is made or sought, makes known to the Court the action which he desires the court to take or his objection . . . and his grounds therefor."[51]

The Tactics of Objecting. One who comes to the trial of cases fresh from the course in Evidence in law school tends to assume that whenever the adversary offers proof that is inadmissible, the right thing to do is to object. Experience will soon convince a sensible learner that this attitude of automatic objecting is wrong. One must remember that the rules of exclusion are numerous and far-reaching so that any case offers an infinity of opportunities for plausible objecting. One learns also that the jury does not look upon a trial as a lawyer's game of which objecting is one of the moves. They want to know the facts and they look upon objections as attempts to hide the facts, and successful objections as the actual suppression of facts.[52] If this description of the jury's attitude is sound, then certain consequences as to desirable tactics seem to follow.

In the first place, no objections should be made unless you have reason to believe that the making of the objection will do your case more good than harm. If the objection has little chance of being sustained, at the trial or on appeal, it should usually be waived. It has been pointed out that objections to

47. The two functions of the exception are lucidly described by Harris, J., in State v. Laundy, 103 Ore. 443, 206 P. 290, 291 (1922).

48. Compare the requirements of the bill of exceptions in Connecticut under the Practice Book (1908), see Leahy v. Cheney, 90 Conn. 611, 98 A. 132, syl. 6 (1916) (a finding stating the objection, the exception, and the answer).

49. 1285, St. 13 Edw. I, Westminster Second, c. 31, quoted 1 Wigmore, Evidence, § 20, note 1. The note also has references to the history of the early practice.

50. Among states and territories which have followed the Federal lead are Arizona, Colorado, Missouri, Nevada, New Jersey, New Mexico, Puerto Rico, and Texas. 1 Wigmore, Evidence, § 20, suppl.

51. The quoted language is found in Federal Rules of Civil Procedure, Rule 46, and Federal Rules of Criminal Procedure, Rule 51. The former is to be read with Federal Rules of Civil Procedure, Rule 43(c) discussed in the next preceding section, which provides that when an objection to evidence is sustained the examining attorney "may make a specific offer of what he expects to prove by the answer of the witness."

52. Trial judges likewise, while they usually are tolerant of objections when based on reasonable grounds and not too numerous, soon become disapproving of persistent objections upon trivial grounds. Goldstein, Trial Technique, § 422 (1935).

leading questions or to opinion-evidence frequently result in strengthening the examiner's case by requiring him to elicit his testimony in more concrete and convincing form.[53] In general, your objections should be few and should be directed only to evidence which if admitted will be substantially harmful, and as to which you think you can get a favorable ruling at the trial or on appeal.[54]

Finally, the manner of the objector and the terms of the objection, when made as they usually are in the jury's presence, are important. Here the cardinal aim is that the jury be made to see that the objection is based not on a mere technical rule, but on reason and fairness.[55] Thus, an objection to a copy should not be stated solely in terms of "secondary evidence" but also grounded upon the safer reliability of the original writing. "Hearsay," again, should be expanded by an explanation of the need, in justice and fairness, for producing the original informant so that the jury may see him, and his sources of knowledge may be explored.

53. Preliminary questions of Fact Arising on Objections.[1]

The great body of the law of evidence consists of rules which, based on long-term policies derived from experience, operate to exclude relevant evidence.[2] This is the effect, for example, of the hearsay rule, the rule preferring original writings, and the various rules of privilege for confidential communica-

tions. These exclusionary rules are all "technical" in the sense that they have been developed by a special professional group, namely judges and lawyers, and in the further sense that for long-term ends they sometimes obstruct the ascertainment of truth in the particular case. Many if not most of these technical exclusionary rules, and the exceptions thereto, are in terms expressed to be conditioned upon the existence of certain facts. Thus the copy of a writing will not be received unless the original is lost, destroyed, or otherwise unavailable.[3] A book-entry is not admissible to prove the facts recited unless it was recorded at or near the time of the transaction.[4] Suppose, in the first example, a copy is offered and there is conflicting evidence as to whether the original is destroyed or intact, or in the second, the entry is offered and the evidence is in dispute as to whether it was made on the day of the sale or a week later. The judge of course ascertains and announces the rule of evidence law setting up the criterion of admission or exclusion, but who is to decide these preliminary questions of fact upon which hinges the *application* of the rule of evidence law?

Issues of fact are usually left to the jury, but there are strong reasons here for not doing so. If the special question of fact were submitted to the jury when objection is made, this would be cumbersome and raise awkward problems about unanimity. If the judge admits the evidence (the copy and the book-entry as above) to the jury and directs them

53. Ladd, Common Mistakes in the Technique of Trial, 22 Iowa L.Rev. 609, 617 (1937).

54. Goldstein, Trial Technique, § 422 (1935).

55. See the very practical discussion with examples of objections, in Busch, Law and Tactics in Jury Trials, §§ 488, 492 (1949).

1. 9 Wigmore, Evidence, § 2550; Maguire, Evidence: Common Sense and Common Law, 211–230 (1947); Maguire and Epstein, Preliminary Questions of Fact, 40 Harv.L.Rev. 392 (1927); Morgan, Functions of Judge and Jury in Preliminary Questions, 43 Harv.L.Rev. 165 (1929); Morgan and Maguire, Cases on Evidence, 875–884 (3d ed. 1951); Barnhart,

Preliminary Facts in Arkansas Courts, 2 Ark.L.Rev. 1 (1947); Note, Province of Judge and Jury in Preliminary Questions in New York, 23 N.Y.U.L.Q.Rev. 472 (1948); Dec.Dig.Trial, ⊜138; 64 C.J. Trial, § 316.

2. "And chiefly it [the law of evidence] determines as among probative matters . . . what classes of things shall not be received. This excluding function is the characteristic one in our law of evidence." Thayer, Preliminary Treatise on Evidence, 264 (1898).

3. See § 196, herein.

4. See § 285, herein.

to disregard it unless they find that the disputed fact exists, the aim of the exclusionary rule is likely to be frustrated, for two reasons. First, the jury will often not be able to erase the evidence from their minds, if they find that the conditioning fact does not exist. They could not if they would. Second, the average jury will not be interested in performing this intellectual gymnastic of "disregarding" the evidence. They are intent mainly on reaching their verdict in this case in accord with what they believe to be true, rather than in enforcing the long-term policies of evidence law.

Accordingly, the traditional view and the accepted principle is that the trial judge decides with finality those preliminary questions of fact upon which depends the admissibility of an item of evidence which is objected to under an exclusionary rule of evidence.[5] The same practice extends to the determination of preliminary facts conditioning the application of the rules as to the competency [6] and privileges [7] of witnesses. On all these preliminary questions the judge, on request, will hold a hearing in which each side may produce evidence.[8]

---

5. Bartlett v. Smith, 11 M. & W. 483, 152 Eng.Rep. 895 (Exch., 1843) (question whether bill drawn in London or Dublin, on which depended its admissibility under the Stamp Act, should have been decided by judge instead of leaving to jury); De Graffenreid v. Thomas, 14 Ala. 681, syl. 1–3 (1848) (declarations of persons who were claimed to be in possession of slave, but this was doubtful; court let in the declarations but instructed the jury to consider only such as were made by persons in possession; held, error; able exposition of the principle by Collier, C. J.); Runels v. Lowell Sun Co., 318 Mass. 466, 62 N.E.2d 121, syl. 8 (1945) (declarations admissible against party only if made in course of conspiracy; held, existence of conspiracy question of fact for judge preliminary to admission of declaration, and his decision conclusive in absence of error of law); W. A. Manda, Inc. v. City of Orange, 82 N.J.L. 686, 82 A. 869, syl. 2 (1912) (eminent domain: evidence of prices paid for other properties, admissible if substantially similar property, which is to be decided by judge); State v. Maynard, 184 N.C. 653, 113 S.E. 682, syl. 3 (1922) (admissibility in criminal case of former testimony of witness, held judge properly decided and refused to submit to jury, preliminary question whether witness absent by defendant's procurement); Blue v. City of Union, 159 Ore. 5, 75 P.2d 977, syl. 22 (1938) (whether offer to accept sum was intended as compromise was question of fact of intention, for the judge). Uniform Rules of Evidence, R. 8: "When the qualification of a person to be a witness, or the admissibility of evidence, or the existence of a privilege is stated in these rules to be subject to a condition, and the fulfillment of the condition is in issue, the issue is to be determined by the judge, and he shall indicate to the parties which one has the burden of producing evidence and the burden of proof on such issue as implied by the rule under which the question arises. The judge may hear and de-

termine such matters out of the presence or hearing of the jury, except that on the admissibility of a confession the judge, if requested, shall hear and determine the question out of the presence and hearing of the jury. But this rule shall not be construed to limit the right of a party to introduce before the jury evidence relevant to weight or credibility."

6. Bell v. State, 164 Ga. 292, 138 S.E. 238, syl. 3 (1927) (competency of nine-year-old boy as witness, for judge, error to submit to jury); Moosbrugger v. Swick, 86 N.J.L. 419, 92 Atl. 269 (1914) (whether assignor of claim sued on had assigned in good faith and hence escaped incompetency under Dead Man's Act, for judge); Meiselman v. Crown Heights Hospital, 285 N.Y. 389, 34 N.E.2d 367, syl. 10 (1941) (whether doctor qualifies as expert, for judge, reviewable only for serious mistake, error of law, or abuse of discretion; here error to exclude on ground that his training and practice were abroad).

7. Robinson v. United States, 144 F.2d 392, syl. 21 (C.C.A. 6th 1944) (attorney and client's communications); but if there is a charge of fraudulent purpose of client in consulting attorney, and evidence from which the jury could so find, the judge does not pass on this, but admits the communication; Williams v. Williams, 108 S.W.2d 297, syl. 7 (Tex. Civ.App.1937); Phelps Dodge Corp. v. Guerrero, 273 Fed. 415, syl. 2 (1921) (physician-patient privilege); Dwelly v. McReynolds, 6 Cal.2d 128, 56 P.2d 1232, syl. 3 (1936) (statutory privilege for reports of accident to officers). The last two cases hold that the burden of proof of the facts of privilege is on the asserter of the privilege.

8. Should the exclusionary law of evidence, "the child of the jury system" in Thayer's phrase, be applied to this hearing before the judge? Sound sense backs the view that it should not, and that the judge should be empowered to hear any relevant evidence, such as affidavits or other reliable

Such is the orthodox principle, but there are qualifications to be noted, and a distinction.

First, many courts, out of a supposed tenderness for persons accused of crime, in cases wherein confessions and dying declarations are offered in evidence have given to the jury some share in passing upon the preliminary questions respectively of the voluntariness of the confession and of the existence in the declarant of a settled, hopeless expectation of death.[9] It may be doubted whether this sharing with the jury of the responsibility of enforcing these conditions has enured to the benefit of defendants.

A second group of cases has placed a strain upon the practice of giving decisive power to the judge over preliminary facts. These are the cases in which it happens that the preliminary fact-question on which competency of evidence or witness depends is also one of the ultimate disputed fact-issues which the jury would normally decide. Examples are the cases of prosecution for bigamy where the first marriage is disputed, the second wife is offered as a state's witness, and the defendant objects under the statute disqualifying the wife to testify against her husband.[10] Another example is the situation where the plaintiff sues on a lost writing; the defendant contends that it was not lost because it was never in existence. When the plaintiff offers as secondary evidence a copy of the alleged writing, logically it seems that to decide the preliminary question of loss, the judge would have to decide the ultimate issue of whether there was an original.[11] Some of the decisions even in these cases of coincidence with an ultimate issue, steadfastly ad-

hearsay. Wigmore states this as the law, without citing supporting authority. 5 Evidence, § 1385. English texts and scattered cases give some color to this view. American authorities are scattered and inconclusive but suggest that the judges trial and appellate give primacy here to habit rather than to practical adaptation to the situation, and tend to require the observance of jury-trial rules of evidence. These are principally cases holding affidavits inadmissible on such hearings. Valenzuela v. State, 30 Ariz. 458, 248 Pac. 36, syl. 1 (1926); Becker v. Quigg, 54 Ill. 390, syl. 1 (1870); Poignand v. Smith, 8 Pick.(Mass.) 272, 277 (1829); Viles v. Moulton, 13 Vt. 510, 515 (1841). One realistic short-cut, however, is generally allowed, in that the trial judge is permitted to consider as part of the evidence on the hearing, the testimony of the challenged witness. James v. Fairall, 168 Iowa 427, 434, 148 N.W. 1029, syl. 8 (1914) (interest). Or the hearsay declaration, the admissibility of which is being disputed. Armour & Co. v. Industrial Commission, 78 Colo. 569, 243 Pac. 546 (1926) (whether declaration by engineer, since deceased, as to fall was "spontaneous"; statement itself seemingly considered). Decisions admitting the declarations as spontaneous without direct proof of the shocking event are sometimes explainable on the ground that there is sufficient circumstantial evidence of the happening of the event. See, e. g., Insurance Co. v. Mosley, 8 Wall. 397, 19 L.Ed. 437 (1869). Other cases presenting the problem are Collins v. Equitable Life Ins. Co., 122 W. Va. 171, 8 S.E.2d 825, 1940, noted in 47 W.Va.L. Q. 340, 130 A.L.R. 287; Stewart v. Baltimore &

Ohio R. Co., 137 F.2d 527, syl. 4 (C.C.A.N.Y.1943); Preferred Accident Ins. Co. of New York v. Combs, 76 F.2d 775, syl. 2 (C.C.A.Neb.1935); Johnston v. W. S. Nott Co., 183 Minn. 309, 236 N.W. 466, syl. 1, 2 (1931); National Life & Accident Ins. Co. v. Hedges, 233 Ky. 840, 27 S.W.2d 422, syl. 1, 2 (1930); Industrial Commission v. Diveley, 88 Colo. 190, 192, 193, 294 Pac. 532 (1930).

The best discussion of the topic is Maguire and Epstein, Rules of Evidence in Preliminary Controversies as to Admissibility, 36 Yale L.J. 1101 (1927).

9. See for discussion and citations, §§ 111, 112, as to confessions, and § 259, as to dying declarations.

10. See, e. g., Matz v. United States, 81 App. D.C. 326, 158 F.2d 190, syl. 7, (1946) (for the judge to decide whether first marriage established).

11. Stowe v. Querner, L.R. 5 Exch. 155 (1870) (suit on insurance policy, defense: denial of issuance of policy; plaintiff offered a copy of the policy, with evidence that it was furnished by defendant's broker; defendant at that point requested a hearing on whether copy admissible and offered evidence that there was no policy; the trial judge refused, and admitted the copy; held, no error, "where the objection goes to show that the very substratum and foundation of the cause of action is wanting, the judge must not decide . . . but receive the copy and leave the main question to the jury.") See discussion of this case in Maguire, Evidence: Common Sense and Common Law, 228–230 (1947) and see Uniform Rules of Evidence, R. 70.

here to the traditional view, that the judge decides finally the preliminary fact.[12] Others have adopted what is probably a more acceptable accommodation of powers of judge and jury. In these cases of coincidence they direct the judge if he finds that the offering party has given evidence on the preliminary question from which a jury could reasonably find in his favor, to admit the offered evidence or witness.[13]

We have been discussing situations wherein *competency* of evidence or witnesses is in question, that is, shall relevant data be kept out under a "technical" exclusionary rule.[14] Here if a dispute about a preliminary conditioning fact is not reserved for the judge, but is left to the jury, the exclusionary rule is likely to be disregarded. We have seen that the hearsay rule, the original documents rule, all the rules disqualifying witnesses, and all the rules of privilege are examples of this class. The *competency* cases are to be sharply marked off from another type of situations. These are the cases where the *relevancy* of a fact offered in evidence depends on the existence of another conditioning fact.[15] Questions of authenticity of writings, that is, whether a writing, offered as the writing of A, was actually signed by him, are usually of this sort. So likewise are questions of the authority of an agent, when the acts of A are offered as proof of a tort or contract of B. On the other hand, if hearsay declarations of A are offered as the admissions of B, because made in the course of an agency for B, or because made in B's presence and adopted by silence, then a "technical" rule, the hearsay rule, is at stake, and the preliminary facts of agency or adoption should be for the judge. When the conditioning fact determines merely the relevancy of the offered fact there is no need for any special safeguarding procedure, for relevancy is a mere matter of probative pertinence which the jury understands and is willing to observe. Accordingly, where the fact conditions relevancy merely, the judge will not permit the adversary to raise a prelim-

---

12. Matz v. United States, note 8, supra; State v. Lee, 127 La. 1077, 54 So. 356, syl. 2 (1911) (murder by Mack Lee conceded, but defendant claims he is not Mack Lee; defense offers as a witness the wife of Mack Lee, who presumably would have testified defendant was not her husband; trial judge, after preliminary hearing rejected witness under statute forbidding wife to testify for husband, on the ground that he was satisfied that the accused was Mack Lee; held, no error, general rule applies).

13. Thus when declarations of one party to an alleged conspiracy, the existence of which is part of the issue, are offered against another, most cases hold that the judge should require prima facie proof only (not necessarily proof convincing to him) of the existence of common design. Conn. Mutual Life Ins. Co. v. Hillmon, 188 U.S. 208, 217, 23 S.Ct. 294, syl. 4, 47 L.Ed. 446 (1903); Budd v. Morgan, 187 Cal. 741, 745–9, 203 P. 754, syl. 2 (1922); Cooke v. Weed, 90 Conn. 544, 97 A. 765, syl. 1 (1916); Rowley v. Braly, 286 S.W. 241, syl. 6 (Tex.Civ.App. 1926); State v. Wappenstein, 67 Wash. 502, 507, 121 P. 989, syl. 2 (1912). And when in a suit on a writing, the making of the writing is in issue, and the plaintiff offers secondary evidence of the terms of the writing, the plaintiff is usually required to produce prima facie proof only, not to convince the judge, of the execution of the original. Stowe v. Querner, note 11, supra; St. Croix Co. v. Seacoast Canning Co., 114 Me. 521, 96 A. 1059, syl. 4 (1916); Uniform Rules, R. 70. The foregoing and other authorities are cited and discussed in Maguire and Epstein, Preliminary Questions, 40 Harv. L.Rev. 392, 415–420 (1927).

Where the declarations or the copy of a writing are thus admitted upon a mere prima facie showing of conspiracy or of execution of the writing, shall the judge instruct the jury to disregard the evidence unless they find that the conspiracy, or the writing, exists? The more logical and practical view is that he should not. See Rowley v. Braly, supra, and the incisive dicta of Learned Hand, J., in United States v. Dennis, 183 F.2d 201, 230, 231 syl. 34 (C.A.2d, 1950).

14. These rules "assume relevancy and then under special circumstances apply an extra safeguard to meet special dangers." 4 Wigmore, Evidence, § 1171, quoted and discussed in McElroy, Note, 21 Tex.L.Rev. 778, 779 (1943).

15. The best discussion of this distinction, and of the cases applying and failing to apply it, is in Morgan, Functions of Judge and Jury in Preliminary Questions of Fact, 43 Harv.L.Rev. 164, especially 164–175 (1929).

inary dispute upon it, but will merely require the proponent to bring forward evidence from which the jury could find it to be true, upon which the conditionally relevant fact will be admitted. At his next stage of proof, the adversary may bring disputing evidence, and the dispute will in the end be for the jury, not the judge, to resolve.[16]

54. Availability as Proof of Evidence Admitted without Objection.

A failure to make a sufficient objection to evidence which is incompetent waives as we have seen any ground of complaint of the admission of the evidence.[1] But it has another effect, equally important. If the evidence is received without objection, it becomes part of the evidence in the case, and is usable as proof to the extent of whatever rational persuasive power it may have.[2] The fact that it was inadmissible does not prevent its use as proof so far as it has probative value. Such incompetent evidence, unobjected to, may be relied on in argument,[3] and alone or in part may support a verdict or finding.[4] This principle is almost universally accepted,[5] and it applies to any ground of incompetency under the exclusionary rules. It

---

16. Patton v. Bank of Lafayette, 124 Ga. 965, 53 S. E. 664, syl. 5 (1906) (suit on note, execution denied; held, note admissible when evidence offered from which it could be found to be genuine); Coleman v. McIntosh, 184 Ky. 370, 211 S.W. 872, syl. 3 (1919) (breach of promise; defendant offered in evidence a purported letter from plaintiff to another man; plaintiff denied she wrote it and judge excluded; held, error, there being some evidence of genuineness, letter should have been admitted and authenticity left to jury); Winslow v. Bailey, 16 Me. 319 (1839) (defense to note on ground of fraudulent misrepresentation; defendant offered as evidence of the false statement, a certificate of a third person as to the amount of timber on a tract; held, judge properly ruled that he should not determine whether the certificate was used as an inducement to plaintiff, but should only require prima facie evidence of this, before admitting the certificate); Coghlan v. White, 236 Mass. 165, 128 N.E. 33, syl. 5 (1920) (whether required statutory written notice was delivered to defendant was not for judge as fact preliminary to admitting notice in evidence, but for jury on conflicting testimony). But the distinction is one over which the courts occasionally stumble. Gila Valley, Globe & No. Ry. v. Hall, 232 U.S. 94, 34 S.Ct. 229, syl. 5, 58 L.Ed. 521 (1914) (there was issue whether plaintiff knew of defect in appliance; defendant offered evidence of remark about defect made when plaintiff less than 20 yards away: on objection judge excluded on ground not proved to have been heard by plaintiff: held, no error, preliminary question for judge); Dexter v. Thayer, 189 Mass. 114, 75 N.E. 223, syl. 1, 2 (1905) (whether agreement between parties alleged to have been made for one by purported agent, was authorized, preliminary fact for judge); Dunklee v. Prior, 80 N.H. 270, 116 A. 138, syl. 1, 2 (1922) (prior contradictory statement in writing, denied by witness, offered to impeach; trial judge finding on conflicting testimony of witness himself that it was not made

by him, excluded it; held, proper though judge might in his discretion have admitted it and left the question of its making to the jury).

1. See § 52, above.

2. Keeler v. Sears Roebuck Co., 121 Conn. 56, 183 A. 20, syl. 3 (1936) (hearsay); Vilas v. Vilas, 153 Fla. 102, 13 So.2d 807, syl. 2, 3 (1943).

3. Birmingham Elec. Co. v. Wildman, 119 Ala. 547, 24 So. 548, syl. 4 (1898); Chicago & E. I. Ry. Co. v. Mochell, 193 Ill. 208, 61 N.E. 1028, syl. 4 (1901); 64 C.J. 226, note 25.

4. Nelson v. Fernando Nelson & Sons, 5 Cal.2d 511, 55 P.2d 859, syl. 8 (1936); Indianapolis Blue Print & Mfg. Co. v. Kennedy, 215 Ind. 409, 19 N.E.2d 554, syl. 4 (1939); J. R. Watkins Co. v. Brown, 134 Me. 473, 188 A. 212, syl. 1 (1936); Dafoe v. Grantski, 143 Neb. 344, 9 N.W.2d 488, syl. 2 (1943) (hearsay standing alone may sustain a finding), and see decisions collected in Dec.Dig. ⊕105, 64 C. J. Trial, §§ 239–244; 53 Am.Jur., Trial, § 135.

5. See references in next preceding note. In one state, Texas, the opposite principle, that competent evidence only can be counted in support of a verdict or finding, has been announced and has been applied to hearsay. Texas Co. v. Lee, 138 Tex. 167, 157 S.W. 2d 628, syl. 8 (1941). And to incompetent opinion evidence. Casualty Underwriters v. Rhone, 134 Tex. 50, 132 S.W.2d 97, syl. 3 (1939). But not to testimony of an incompetent witness. Walker v. Fields, 247 S.W. 272, syl. 3 (Comm.App.1923). Or to secondary evidence of a writing. Brown v. Lessing, 70 Tex. 544, 7 S.W. 783, syl. 4 (1888). This wrong turning seems to be founded upon an untenable assumption that incompetent evidence is generally without probative force. See McElroy, Comment, Incompetent Evidence Admitted without Objection, 21 Tex.L.Rev. 778 (1943), a penetrating discussion of the Texas holdings. This assumption finds sporadic expression in a few opinions of other

is most often invoked in respect to hearsay,[6] but it has been applied to evidence vulnerable as secondary evidence of writings,[7] opinions,[8] evidence elicited from incompetent witnesses [9] or subject to a privilege,[10] or subject to objection because of the want of authentication of a writing,[11] of the lack of knowledge-qualification of a witness,[12] or of the expertness-qualification.[13] Relevancy and probative worth, however, stand on a different footing. If the evidence has no probative force, or insufficient probative value to sustain the proposition for which it is offered, the want of objection adds nothing to its worth [14] and it will not support a finding. It is still irrelevant or insufficient. However, the failure to object to evidence related to the controversy but not covered by the pleadings, may often amount to the informal framing of new issues.[15] When this is held to have been the result, the failure to object on the ground that the evidence is not material to any issue raised by the pleadings is waived,[16] and the

courts, particularly as to hearsay. See, e.g., Higgins v. Trentham, 186 Ga. 264, 197 S.E. 862, syl. 1 (1938) ("Ordinarily hearsay . . . is not only inadmissible but wholly without probative value . . ."); Shaw v. McKenzie, 131 Me. 248, 160 A. 911, syl. 6 (1932) ("Hearsay evidence has no probative force and will not sustain a verdict lacking other support.").

6. Ventromile v. Malden Elec. Co., 317 Mass. 132, 57 N.E.2d 209, syl. 5 (1944) (statement of plaintiff after accident made in presence of defendant's employee); De Moulin v. Retheli, 354 Mo. 425, 189 S.W. 2d 562, syl. 3 (1945) (statement by manager of defendant's grocery store after plaintiff's fall); Barlow v. Verrill, 88 N.H. 25, 183 A. 857, syl. 3, 104 A.L.R. 1126. The Note, Hearsay Evidence Taken without Objection, 104 AL.R. 1130, collects numerous cases.

7. Sublett v. Henry's Turk & Taylor Lunch, 21 Cal. 2d. 273, 131 P.2d 369, syl. 3 (1943); Morgan v. Bell, 189 Ga. 432, 5 S.E.2d 897, syl. 8 (1940); Glover v. Mitchell, 319 Mass. 1, 64 N.E.2d 648, syl. 6 (1946) (federal price regulations); Dec.Dig. Trial, ⊂⇒105 (5).

8. Burns v. Blythwood, 28 Ala.App. 335, 184 So. 346, syl. 9, cert. den. (1938) (mechanic's estimate of damage to car); Dieter v. Scott, 110 Vt. 376, 9 A.2d 95, syl. 2 (1939) (testimony of defendant that he acted as agent of lessee is a conclusion, but not objected to, it is entitled to consideration if not in conflict with underlying facts regarding the relationship); Dec.Dig. Trial, ⊂⇒105(3). But the Georgia court weakens when the opinion is on the ultimate issue. Morgan v. Bell, 189 Ga. 432, 5 S. E.2d 897, syl. 10 (1940) (mental capacity to make will).

9. Walker v. Fields, 247 S.W. 272, syl. 3 (Tex.Comm. App. 1923) (testimony of interested survivor, not objected to, "not without probative force").

10. Gruner v. Gruner, 165 S.W. 865, syl. 5 (Mo.App. 1914) (marital communications).

11. Collins v. Streitz, 95 F.2d 430, syl. 21 (C.C.A. Ariz. 1938); Elswick v. Charleston Transit Co., 128 W.Va. 241, 36 S.E.2d 419, syl. 3 (1946) (city ordinance: failure to object waives proof of existence and authenticity); Dec.Dig. Trial, ⊂⇒105(4).

12. See Winsor v. Hawkins, 130 Conn. 669, 37 A.2d 222, syl. 5 (1944) (plaintiff's testimony, received without objection, that she had neuritis and water on the knee, though she probably had it secondhand from doctor, could be given such weight as it deserved).

13. McGuire v. Baird, 9 Cal.2d 353, 70 P.2d 915, syl. 4 (1937) (malpractice: defendant by not objecting admitted qualifications of plaintiff's doctor to testify to skill ordinarily exercised in that community); Woods v. Siegrist, 112 Colo. 257, 149 P.2d 241, syl. 1 (1944) (evidence of chiropractor-witness, whose qualifications were not objected to, sustains findings though contradicted by qualified neurologists); Dec.Dig. Trial, ⊂⇒105(3).

14. Danahy v. Cuneo, 130 Conn. 213, 33 A.2d 132, syl. 2 (1943); Craig v. Citizens' Trust Co., 217 Ind. 434, 26 N.E.2d 1006, syl. 8 (1940); DeLong v. Iowa State Highway Commission, 229 Iowa 700, 295 N.W. 91, 97, syl. 7 (1941) (but here the court goes on to adopt the untenable view that hearsay, standing alone, can never have sufficient probative worth to support a finding).

15. Phillips v. New Amsterdam Cas. Co., 193 La. 314, 190 So. 565, syl. 1, 2 (1939) (evidence in support of defense not pleaded "enlarges the pleadings and must be considered by court"); Thompson v. Porter, 21 Wash.2d 449, 151 P.2d 433, syl. 3 (1944) (inadmissible evidence not objected to, helps to make the issues); Ludwig v. Wisconsin Power & Light Co., 242 Wis. 434, 8 N.W.2d 272, syl. 3 (1943) (complaint considered amended to include negligent acts testified to without objection).

16. Atlanta Enterprises v. James, 68 Ga.App. 773, 24 S.E.2d 130, syl. 8, 9 (1943).

evidence will support the proponent's side of the new informal issue.[17]

The application of these principles to cases involving the Parole Evidence Rule presents special problems the discussion of which can best be deferred to the chapter on that subject.[18]

55. Waiver of Objection.

We have seen that a failure to assert promptly and specifically an objection is a waiver.[1] What other conduct is a waiver?

Demand for inspection of a writing. One party, D, gives notice to his opponent, O, to produce a document, and O does produce it at the trial, and thereupon in open court D asks to inspect it, and is allowed to do so. The document if offered by O would be inadmissible, except for the notice, production, and inspection. Do these facts preclude D from objecting when the document is offered by O? England, Massachusetts and a half-dozen other states say yes, D is precluded from objecting.[2] This result was based at first upon the notion that it would be unconscionable to permit the demanding party to examine the private papers of the producing party without being subjected to some corresponding risk on his own part.[3] A later case, however, has justified the result on the ground that the party who is called on in open court before a jury to produce a writing for inspection may be suspected of evasion or concealment unless he is given the privilege of introducing the writing.[4] Cases from Connecticut and New York and a scattering from other states recognize that the older policy against compelled disclosure to his adversary of relevant writings in possession of a party is now outmoded[5] and that the prevailing policy is just the opposite, namely, that of exerting pressure for full disclosure except for privileged matter. Accordingly these states reject the rule,[6] refuse to penalize the demanding party and permit him to as-

---

17. Wood v. Claxton, 199 Ga. 809, 35 S.E.2d 455, syl. 3 (1945) (can be considered by jury).

18. See § 213, n. 2, herein.

1. See § 52, above.

2. Wharem v. Routledge, 5 Esp. 235, 170 Eng.Rep. 797 (Nisi prius, 1805, Lord Ellenborough); Calvert v. Flower, 7 Car. & P. 386, 173 Eng.Rep. 172 (1836); United States Fidelity and G. Co. v. Continental Baking Co., 172 Md. 24, 190 A. 768, syl. 3–6 (1937) (witness-statement, but when admitted it only bears on credibility and does not "prove the fact"); Clark v. Fletcher, 1 Allen (Mass.) 53 (1861) (leading case); Leonard v. Taylor, 315 Mass. 580, 53 N.E.2d 705, syl. 1, 2, 151 A.L.R. 1002 (1944); Decker v. George W. Smith & Co., 88 N.J.L. 630, 96 A. 915, syl. 12 (1916), and cases cited from Delaware, Georgia, Maine, Mississippi, and New Hampshire, in Note, 151 A.L.R. 1006, 1012. See also Evidence, ⊕368(14).
But the rule does not apply when the writing is used by one party to refresh the memory of his witness: the other party is entitled to inspect the writing without being penalized by being required to permit its introduction in evidence. Clearly the supposed reason of the rule does not apply. Nussenbaum v. Chambers & Chambers, 322 Mass. 419, 77 N.E.2d 780, syl. 8 (1948).

3. Clark v. Fletcher, next preceding note, at p. 57, quoted 151 A.L.R. 1013.

4. Leonard v. Taylor, note 2, above. This shifting of ground, however tenuous the new justification may seem, at least implies that the rule should be restricted to the limits of the new reason, namely, to jury trials where request for inspection is made in the jury's presence.

5. See the vigorous criticism of the rule in 7 Wigmore, Evidence, § 2125.

6. Kane v. New Idea Realty Co., 104 Conn. 508, 133 A. 686, syl. 6 (1926) (party called on to produce may not require that demanding party promise to put writing in evidence, before surrendering it for inspection); Smith v. Rentz, 131 N.Y. 169, 30 N.E. 54, 56, syl. 2 (1892) ("The party who has in his possession books or papers which may be material to the case of his opponent has no moral right to conceal them from his adversary. . . . The party calling for books and papers would be subjected to great hazard if an inspection merely, without more, would make them evidence in the case. That rule tends rather to the suppression than the ascertainment of truth, and the opposite rule is, as it seems to us, better calculated to promote the ends of justice."); Summers v. McKim, 12 Serg. & R. (Pa.) 405, 411, syl. 4 (1825); Ellis v. Randle, 60 S.W. 462, 465, syl. 3 (Tex.Civ.App. 1900).

sert any pertinent objection if the producing party offers the writing.

Failure to object to earlier like evidence. A party has introduced evidence of particular facts without objection. Later he offers additional evidence, perhaps by other witnesses or writings, of the same facts or a part thereof. May the adversary now object, or has he waived his right by his earlier quiescence? It is often summarily stated in the opinions that he is precluded from objecting.[7] But in opinions where the question is carefully discussed it is usually concluded that the mere failure to object to other like evidence is not a waiver of objection to new incompetent evidence.[8] Of course, an overruling of this new objection will frequently not be prejudicial, but that is a different question.[9] The practice of the best advocates of withholding objection unless it is clear that the evidence would be damaging is in the interest of dispatch of business and would be encouraged by the non-waiver rule. On the other hand, when the evidence of the fact, admitted without objection, is extensive,[10] and the fact though incompetent has some probative value, the trial judge should be conceded a discretion to find that the objector's conduct has amounted to a waiver.

The Offering of Like Evidence by the Objector. If it happens that a party who has objected to evidence of a certain fact himself produces evidence from his own witness of the same fact, of course he has waived his objection.[11] However, when his objection was made and overruled he was required and entitled to treat this ruling as the "law of the trial" and to explain or rebut, if he can, the evidence which has come in over his protest. Consequently, it will not be a waiver if he cross-examines the adversary's witness about the matter,[12] even though the cross-examina-

---

7. Boston Woven-hose & Rubber Co. v. Kendall, 178 Mass. 232, 59 N.E. 657, syl. 3 (1901) (intimation rather than a holding); Shrimpton v. Philbrick, 53 Minn. 366, 55 N.W. 551, syl. 3 (1893) (no prejudicial error in overruling the objection); Shelton v. Southern Ry. Co., 193 N.C. 670, 130 S.E. 232, syl. 5 (1927) (benefit of exception ordinarily lost if same evidence admitted earlier or later without objection —an arguendo statement); Perry v. New England Transp. Co., 71 R.I. 352, 45 A.2d 481, syl. 7 (1946). Decisions pro and con are collected in 64 C.J. Trial, § 192. See also 6 Jones, Evidence, § 2524, note 9.

But no court would hold that because earlier evidence was subject to an objection under a particular exclusionary rule, e. g., hearsay, and was received without objection, that this would preclude the adversary to assert this ground of objection against new evidence. See, e. g., New York Life Ins. Co. v. Neasham, 250 F. 787, syl. 3 (C.C.A.Nev.1918) (consent to use transcript of testimony of one witness at coroner's hearing, not waiver of right to object to transcript of testimony of another witness at same hearing).

8. Lowery v. Jones, 219 Ala. 201, 121 So. 704, syl. 10, 64 A.L.R. 553 (1929) ("If these [later] objections had been sustained, the force of the former testimony would probably have been weakened in the minds of the jury"); Slocinski v. Radwan, 83 N.H. 501, 144 A. 787, syl. 9 (1929); Bobereski v. Insurance Co. of Pa., 105 Pa.Super. 585, 161 A. 412, 415, syl. 9 (1932) (". . . the fact that incompetent, irrelevant, and

9. As pointed out by Phillips, C. J. in Slayden v. Palmo, 103 Tex. 413, 194 S.W. 1103, 1104 (1917).

immaterial evidence may be introduced on a trial by one party, without objection from the other party, because he may deem it of no importance and harmless, does not prevent the latter from objecting to the further introduction and elaboration of such evidence when he is of opinion that it is both important and harmful. The principle of estoppel does not apply in such case."); McLane v. Paschal, 74 Tex. 27, 11 S.W. 837, 839, syl. 4 (1889).

10. Of course, evidence and counter-evidence may make the fact material, though not pleaded. See, e. g., Sweazey v. Valley Transport, 6 Wash.2d 324, 107 P.2d 567, syl. 9 (1940), and see § 54, note 15, above.

11. Trouser Corp. v. Goodman & Theise, 153 F.2d 284, syl. 9 (C.C.A.Pa.1946) (recognizing principle: but not clear here whether was elicited in effort to rebut); Gale v. Shillock, 4 Dak. 182, 29 N.W. 661, 665, syl. 5 (1886) (stating rule); Ryder v. Board of Health, 273 Mass. 177, 173 N.E. 580, syl. 1 (1930); In re Forsythe's Estate, 221 Minn. 303, 22 N.W.2d 19, syl. 10 (1946) (other letter from same person giving similar but more prejudicial facts, a waiver); and cases in 1 Wigmore, Evidence, § 18, note 35; 6 Jones, Evidence, § 2524, note 8; 64 C.J.Trial, § 193.

12. Barker v. St. Louis I. M. & S. Ry. Co., 126 Mo. 143, 28 S.W. 866, 867, syl. 2 (1894); Shelton v. Southern Ry. Co., 193 N.C. 670, 139 S.E. 232, syl. 4 (1927);

tion entails a repetition of the fact,[13] or if he meets the testimony with other evidence which under the theory of the objection would be incompetent.[14]

Exclusion by Judge in Absence of Objection. A party's failure to object usually waives the objection and precludes the party from complaining if the evidence is let in.[15] But such failure by the party does not of itself preclude the trial judge from excluding the evidence on his own motion if the witness is disqualified for want of capacity or the evidence is incompetent, and he considers that the interests of justice require the exclusion of the testimony.[16] There is much evidence, however, such as reliable affidavits or copies of writings, which though incompetent under the technical exclusionary rules, may be valuable in the particular situation and which the trial judge in the absence of objection would not be justified in excluding. It is only when the evidence is irrelevant, unreliable, misleading, or prejudicial, as well as incompetent, that the judge should exercise his discretionary power to intervene. Privileged evidence, such as confidential communications between husband and wife, are in different case. The privileges protect the outside interests of the holders, not the interest of the parties in securing justice in the present litigation, and the tendency today is to confine their application.[17] Accordingly, in case privileged matter is called for, and the holder is present, the judge may if necessary explain the privilege to the holder, but will not assert it of his own motion; but if the holder is absent the judge has a discretionary power to assert it in his behalf.[18]

Mitchell v. Koch, 193 Okl. 342, 143 P.2d 811, syl. **5** (1943); Cathey v. Missouri, K. & T. Ry. Co. of Texas, 104 Tex. 39, 133 S.W. 417, syl. 2 (1911). There are sporadic holdings to the contrary, see e. g., Hutto v. Am. Fire & Casualty Co., 215 S.C. 90, 54 S.E.2d 523, syl. 12 (1949).

Similarly, when the evidence objected to is elicited on cross-examination, the objector may seek to explain or refute on redirect without a waiver. Tucker v. Reil, 51 Ariz. 357, 369, 77 P.2d 203, syl. 17 (1938).

13. See, e. g., the Barker and Cathey cases in next preceding note. While calling for a repetition is a permissible part of a testing or exploratory cross-examination, as a tactical matter such repetition should be held to a minimum.

14. Salt Lake City v. Smith, 104 F. 457, 470, syl. 9 (C.C.A.Utah 1900) (lucid discussion by Sanborn, J.); Chicago City Ry. Co. v. Uhter, 212 Ill. 174, 72 N.E. 195, 197, syl. 5 (1904) (meeting hearsay with like hearsay); State v. Beckner, 194 Mo. 281, 91 S.W. 892, 896, syl. 2 (1906) (accused did not waive objection to evidence of his bad character by meeting it with evidence of good character).

15. See § 52.

16. Bodholdt v. Garrett, 122 Cal.App. 566, 10 P.2d 533, syl. 2 (1932) (truckdriver's unexcited statement that broken spring was cause of collision, excluded by judge: held, no error. "The court on its own motion in the interest of justice may exclude. . . ." Query, whether the ruling was in the interest of justice); South Atlantic S. S. Co. v. Munkacsy, 37 Del. 580, 187 A. 600, syl. 15–17 (1936) (suit by seaman for injury: opinion of boatswain as to safe character of work, excluded by judge; held, no error; "the trial judge is something more than a mere umpire"; careful exposition of judge's authority); City of Detroit v. Porath, 271 Mich. 42, 260 N.W. 114, syl. 14 (1935) (irrelevant picture); Electric Park Amusement Co. v. Psichos, 83 N.J.L. 262, 83 A. 766, syl. 1, 2 (1912) (judge upheld in excluding opinion of expert of inadequate qualification, distinguishing case of disqualification for interest which parties may effectively waive; extensive discussion by Kalisch, J.); Wisniewski v. Weinstock, 130 N.J.L. 58, syl. 3 (1943) (truckdriver's testimony as to speed from tire-tracks excluded for lack of qualification); Best v. Tavenner, 189 Ore. 46, 218 P.2d 471, syl. 2, 3 (1950) (where witness died from stroke after direct testimony partly completed, judge had discretion to withdraw testimony from jury on own motion, or declare mistrial). Cases are collected in Trial, ⊂⟹105(6) and in 64 C.J. Trial, § 245.

It is even sometimes said that the judge at the close of the case may of his own motion withdraw incompetent evidence from the jury though not objected to when received. See, e. g., American Workmen v. Ledden, 196 Ark. 902, 120 S.W.2d 346, 120 A.L.R. 201, 204 (1938). But an opposite result is advocated "to prevent unfairness, in that, if the counsel offering the testimony were made aware of the objection to the testimony at the time, he would have had an opportunity to cure it." Electric Park Amusement Co. v. Psichos, supra, 83 A. 766, 768.

17. See §§ 72, 81.

18. People v. Atkinson, 40 Cal. 284 (1870) (where witness, an attorney, on examination was unable to

56. The Effect of the Introduction of Part of a Writing or Conversation.[1]

Two important considerations come into play when a party offers in evidence a portion only of a writing, or of an oral statement or conversation. The first is the danger of wresting a part of such a body of expressions out of its context. "The fool hath said in his heart, there is no God,"[2] where the last phrase only is quoted, and, "Topknot, come down," another Biblical excerpt,[3] are examples of the possibilities of distortion. This danger, moreover, is not completely averted by a later, separate, supplying of the relevant omitted parts. The distorted impression may sometimes linger, and work its influence at the subconscious level. The other danger is that of waste of time and attention by cumbering the trial and the record, in the name of completeness, with passages and statements which have no bearing on the present controversy.

In the light of these policies is one who seeks to give in evidence part of a writing or statement required to offer it in entirety, or at least all of it that is relevant to the facts sought to be proved? The cases are not consistent, but the prevailing practice seems to permit the proponent to prove any relevant part that he desires.[4] It seems, however, that to guard against the danger where it exists of an ineradicable false first impression, the adversary should be permitted to invoke the court's discretion to require the proponent to prove so much as relates to the fact sought to be proved, that is, all that

---

say whether communications from client were public or private, judge, over defendant-client's objection admitted the evidence, held error, and by way of dictum that the court should have excluded on its own motion); Hodges v. Mullikin, 1 Bland Ch. (Md.) 503, 509 (1828) ("and if the client be no party . . . the lips of his attorney must remain closed and the Court cannot allow him to speak. . . ."); see 70 C.J. Witnesses, § 618; Model Code of Evidence, R. 105(e) (The judge . . . in his discretion determines . . . (e) whether to exclude, of his own motion, evidence which would violate a privilege of a person who is neither a party nor the witness from whom the evidence is sought if the privilege has not been waived or otherwise terminated, or which would be excluded on appropriate objection by an adverse party").

1. 7 Wigmore, Evidence, §§ 2094–2125; Evidence, ☞155(8), 155(10); 31 C.J.S. Evidence, § 190, 32 C.J.S. Evidence, § 774.

2. The oft-repeated, classic illustration, see 7 Wigmore, Evidence, § 2094, pp. 472, 477.

3. "The setting of a word or words gives character to them, and may wholly change their apparent meaning. A notable instance of such practice is that of the minister, displeased with the manner of hairdressing used by the women of his congregation, who preached from the text, '*Topknot come down!*' which was found to be the latter part of the scriptural injunction, 'Let them that are upon the *housetop not come down.*'" Lattimore, J., in Weathered v. State, 129 Tex.Cr. 514, 89 S.W.2d 212, 214 (1935).

4. See, e. g., Gencarella v. Fyfe, 171 F.2d 419, syl. 1, 3 (C.C.A.R.I.1948) (plaintiff wished to introduce part of police officer's report of highway accident giving measurements of scene without introducing part reporting statements of by-standers as to who was to blame, held, error for trial judge to prevent him from introducing part, which was severable); Melnick v. Melnick, 154 Pa.Super. 481, 36 A.2d 235, syl. 2 (1944) (plaintiff could offer a part of the petition and admission in corresponding paragraph of answer without including other matters in that paragraph by way of avoidance or defense); and see People v. Adamson, 27 Cal.2d 478, 165 P.2d 3, syl. 2 (1946) (witness may testify to part of conversation where that is all he heard and it is intelligible); 7 Wigmore, Evidence, § 2099, p. 489. But there seems to be a tendency where a conversation is one which creates or transfers rights, such as a contract or a notice, to require the whole, so far as material. See, e. g., Flood v. Mitchell, 68 N.Y. 507, 511 (1877); 7 Wigmore, Evidence, § 2099, p. 491. And a special rule has grown up for testimony at a former trial. It requires that all that was testified to on the particular subject, on direct and cross, be given, in substance. Bennett v. State, 32 Tex.Cr. 216, 22 S.W. 684, syl. 1 (1893). Foley v. State, 11 Wyo. 464, 72 P. 627, syl. 9 (1903); 7 Wigmore, Evidence, § 2098, note 4, § 2099(4). Compare the practical and flexible rule for depositions, in the Federal Rules of Civil Procedure, Rule 26(d) (4): "If only part of a deposition is offered in evidence by a party, an adverse party may require him to introduce all of it which is relevant to the part introduced, and any party may introduce any other parts."

is relevant to explain or is needed in interpreting the part proved.

As to the adversary's other alternative the cases are much clearer and more consistent. He may wait until his own next stage of presenting proof, and then merely by reason that the first party has introduced a part, he has the right to introduce the remainder of the writing, statement, correspondence, former testimony, or conversation so far as it relates to the same subject-matter and hence tends to explain and shed light on the meaning of the part already received.[5] This is subject to the qualification that where the remainder is incompetent, not merely as to form as in the case of secondary evidence or hearsay, but because of its prejudicial character then the trial judge should exclude if

he finds that the danger of prejudice outweighs the explanatory value.[6]

57. Fighting Fire with Fire: Inadmissible Evidence as Opening the Door.[1]

One party offers evidence which is inadmissible. Because the adversary fails to object, or because he has no opportunity to do so, or because the judge erroneously overrules an objection, the incompetent evidence comes in. Is the adversary entitled to answer this evidence, by testimony in denial or explanation of the facts so proven? Most of the courts seem to say generally that "one who induces a trial court to let down the bars to a field of inquiry that is not competent or relevant to the issues cannot complain if his adversary is also allowed to avail himself of the opening." [2]

---

5. Calif.Code Civ.Proc. § 1854: "When part of an act, declaration, conversation, or writing is given in evidence by one party, the whole on the same subject may be inquired into by the other; when a letter is read, the answer may be given; and when a detached act, declaration, conversation, or writing is given in evidence, any other act, declaration, conversation, or writing which is necessary to make it understood may also be given in evidence"; White v. Comm., 292 Ky. 416, 166 S.W.2d 873, 877, syl. (1942) (conversation); Trammell v. State, 145 Tex.Cr. 224, 167 S.W.2d 171, syl. 6 (1942) (oral statement by accused).

It is sometimes said that this type of "remainder"-evidence is a mere aid in interpreting the evidence already received or in appraising credibility, and is not itself substantive evidence. People v. Schlessel, 196 N.Y. 476, 90 N.E. 44, syl. 4 (1909); 7 Wigmore, Evidence, § 2113, p. 524. But in another place, Wigmore has properly termed this "an artificial doctrine tending to a quibble." Student Text-book on Evidence, 322 (1935).

6. Socony Vacuum Oil Co. v. Marvin, 313 Mich. 528, 21 N.W.2d 841, syl. 6 (1946) (when part of transcribed interview between plaintiff's investigator and defendant was introduced by plaintiff, defendant not entitled to offer remaining part stating his poor financial condition and that he was not insured); Jeddeloh v. Hockenhull, 219 Minn. 541, 18 N.W.2d 582, syl. 14, 15 (1945) (where part of conversation after accident proved, door not opened to proof of part showing defendant insured); State v. Skaug, 63 Nev. 59, 161 P.2d 708, syl. 1–3 (1945) (separable part of confession showing commission of other unconnected crimes should have been excluded).

1. The best discussions are in 1 Wigmore, Evidence, § 15 (Curative Admissibility) and in Vogt, Note, 35 Mich.L.Rev. 636 (1937). See also 1 Jones, Evidence, § 172 (4th ed., 1938); Abbott, Civil Jury Trials, § 204 (5th ed. 1935); Dec.Dig. Evidence ⊜155(5); 31 C.J.S., Evidence, § 190a; 20 Am.Jur. Evidence, § 274.

2. Warren Live Stock Co. v. Farr, 142 F. 116, 117 (C.C.A.Colo.1905). To like effect, see, e. g., Bogk v. Gassert, 149 U.S. 17, 25, 13 Sup.Ct. 738, 37 L.Ed. 631 (suit to declare a deed a mortgage; defendant having given evidence of conversations when deed delivered, has no right to object to plaintiff's giving his version of same conversations); United States v. Regents of New Mexico School of Mines, 185 F.2d 389, syl. 3–5 (C.A. 10th, 1950) (eminent domain; when government asked witness about a particular offer made for the land, it could not complain that court allowed owner to go further into circumstances of offer); Mobile & B. Ry. Co. v. Ladd, 92 Ala. 287, 9 So. 169, syl. 1 (1891) (meeting immaterial evidence that night was dark by evidence that moon was shining); Perkins v. Hayward, 124 Ind. 449, 24 N.E. 1033, 1034 (1890) (citing cases); Sisler v. Shafer, 43 W.Va. 769, 28 S.E. 721, syl. 1 (1897) ("strange cattle having wandered through a gap made by himself, he cannot complain").

Some courts, however, have, at least occasionally, expressed the view that admission of incompetent evidence does "not open the door" to answering inadmissible evidence. People v. McDaniel, 59 Cal. App.2d 672, 140 P.2d 88, syl. 5 (1943); Candler v. Byfield, 160 Ga. 732, 129 S.E. 57, syl. 6 (1925).

Such pronouncements, however, do not settle the questions as to how the trial judge should deal with the problem, nor as to whether the adversary is entitled as of right to introduce the answering evidence. Because of the many variable factors affecting the solution in particular cases, the decisions do not lend themselves easily to generalizations, but the following conclusions, having some support in the decisions, are submitted as reasonable:

(1) If the incompetent evidence sought to be answered is immaterial and not prejudice-arousing, the judge to save time and to avoid distraction of attention from the issues should refuse to hear answering evidence.[3]

(2) If the evidence, though inadmissible, is relevant to the issues and hence probably damaging to the adversary's case, or though irrelevant is prejudice-arousing to a material degree, and provided the adversary has seasonably objected or moved to strike, then the adversary should be entitled to give answering evidence as of right.[4] By objecting he has done his best to save the court from mistake, but his remedy by assigning error to the ruling is not an adequate one.[5] He needs a fair opportunity to win his case at the trial by refuting the damaging evidence.

(3) If again the first incompetent evidence is relevant, or though irrelevant is prejudice-arousing, but the adversary has failed to object or to move to strike out, where such an objection might apparently have avoided the harm, then the allowance of answering evidence should rest in the judge's discretion.[6] He will weigh the probable influence of the first evidence, the time and distraction incident to answering it, and the possibility and effectiveness of an instruction to the jury to disregard it.

(4) In the last situation, if the incompetent evidence, or even the inquiry eliciting it, were so prejudice-arousing that an objection or motion to strike could not have erased the harm, then it seems that the adversary should be entitled to answer it as of right.[7]

It will be noted that the question discussed in this section as to rebutting incompetent evidence, is a different one from whether a party's introduction of evidence incompetent under some exclusionary rule (such as hear-

---

3. But if he does seemingly under the prevailing view, the party opening the door would have no standing to complain. See note 2, supra.

4. Budd v. Meriden Elec. Co., 69 Conn. 272, 37 A. 683, syl. 6 (1897); Bremhorst v. Phillips Coal Co., 202 Iowa 1251, 211 N.W. 898, 904, syl. 22 (1927) ("It was the duty of the court to give both parties the benefit of the same rules of evidence."); Lake Roland Elec. Ry. Co. v. Weir, 86 Md. 273, 37 A. 714, 715 (1897) (a considered dictum); Mattechek v. Pugh, 153 Ore. 1, 55 P.2d 730, syl. 7, 8, 168 A.L.R. 725 (1936). Contra: Buck v. St. Louis Union Trust Co., 267 Mo. 644, 185 S.W. 208, 213 syl. 15 (1916) (". . . his objection will save him on appeal and he needs no other protection"). For other cases see Note, 35 Mich.L.Rev. 636, 637 (1937).

5. See Note, 35 Mich.L.Rev. 636, 637 (1937). Wigmore takes the opposite view. Evidence, § 15.

6. Crosby v. Keen, 200 Miss. 590, 28 So.2d 322, syl. 5 (1946); Biener v. St. Louis Pub. Service Co., 160 S.W.2d 780, syl. 6 (Mo.App.1942) (semble); Franklin Fire Ins. Co. v. Coleman, 87 S.W.2d 537, syl. 2 (Tex.Civ.App.1935) (suit on fire policy, defense, arson; defendant's witness volunteered statement that he arrested plaintiff after the fire; held, permitting defendant to show that complaint on which he was arrested was dismissed was discretionary). Massachusetts, however, draws the line between answering immaterial testimony which is discretionary and answering material evidence which is of right. Comm. v. Wakelin, 230 Mass. 567, 575, 576, 120 N.E. 209 (1918).

7. Thus, in State v. Witham, 72 Me. 531, 535 (1881) the birth of a child to an unmarried woman was improperly admitted as evidence of defendant's adultery, and counter-evidence of other men's intercourse was received to rebut it. The court said: "The introduction of immaterial testimony to meet immaterial testimony on the other side is generally within the discretion of the presiding judge. But if one side introduces evidence irrelevant to the issue, which is prejudicial and harmful to the other party, then, although it come in without objection, the other party is entitled to introduce evidence which will directly and strictly contradict it." It seems that the situation in the Franklin Fire Insurance Co. case in the next preceding note would have warranted the same holding.

say or secondary evidence of writings) gives license to the adversary to introduce other evidence incompetent under the same exclusionary rule.[8] While such a practice would have some arguments of fairness to support it, apparently the doctrine of "opening the door" has not been extended so far.

58. Admissibility of Evidence Dependent on Proof of Other Facts: "Connecting Up." [1]

Very often the relevancy or admissibility of evidence of a particular fact hinges upon the proof of other facts. Thus, proof that a swaying automobile passed a given spot at a certain time,[2] or that a conversation was had by the witness at a given time and place with an unidentified stranger,[3] will become relevant and significant only when the automobile is identified as the defendant's, or the stranger is shown to be the deceased for whose death the plaintiff is suing. So evidence of acts and declarations may not become material or admissible until shown to be those of an agent of the other party,[4] and a copy of a writing may not become competent evidence until the original is proven to be lost or destroyed.[5] Some of these missing facts may be thought of, in terms of the logic of pleading or argument, as preliminary to the fact offered, some as co-ordinate with it. It matters not. In either event, often

only one fact can be proven at a time or by a given witness, and the order of convenience in calling witnesses or of clear presentation may not in a particular case be the order of logical statement.[6]

Who decides the order of facts? In the first instance, the offering counsel does so by making his offer. The court in its general discretionary supervision of the order of proof,[7] may, to avoid a danger of prejudice or confusion, require that the missing fact be proved first. But he seldom does, and the everyday method of handling the situation when the adversary objects to the relevancy or the competency of the offered fact is to permit it to come in conditionally, upon the assurance, express or implied, of the offering counsel that he will "connect up" the tendered evidence by proving, in the later progress of his case, the missing facts.[8]

In a long trial, however, where the witnesses are many and the facts complex, it is easy for the offering counsel to forget the need for making the required "connecting" proof, and for the judge and the adversary to fail to observe this gap in the evidence. Who invokes the condition subsequent, upon such breach? The burden is placed upon the objecting party to renew the objection and invoke the condition.[9] By the majority view this is to be done by a motion to strike out

---

8. The distinction is acutely discussed by Hughes, P. J. in Longmire v. Diagraph-Bradley Corp., 237 Mo.App. 553, 176 S.W.2d 635, 646 (1944).

1. Wigmore, Evidence, I, § 14, VI, § 1871; Note, Failure to Object to Evidence Admitted on Condition, 32 Ill.L.Rev. 882 (1938); Dec.Dig. Trial, ⊙—51, 79, 90; 64 C.J., Trial, §§ 157, 172, 173.

2. State v. Freeman, 93 Utah 125, 71 P.2d 196, syl. 21 (1937).

3. Atlanta & W. P. Ry. Co. v. Truitt, 65 Ga.App. 320, 16 S.E.2d 273, syl. 6–9 (1941).

4. Smith v. Ohio Millers' Mutual Fire Ins. Co., 320 Mo. 146, 6 S.W.2d 920, syl. 12 (1928); 64 C.J. 150, § 173.

5. See ch. 23, herein.

6. See the remarks of Miller, J. in a conspiracy case: "The logical sequence of events—from agreement in

a common purpose to perpetration of an act designed to carry it out—does not require that introduction of the evidence must follow that same rigorous sequence." McDonald v. United States, 77 D.C.App. 33, 133 F.2d 23 (1942).

7. Matz v. United States, 81 App.D.C. 326, 58 F.2d 190, syl. 2, 3 (1946) (order of prosecution's evidence in a bigamy case); and see 6 Wigmore, Evidence §§ 1867, 1871.

8. For decisions approving the practice see, e. g., Parrish v. Thurman, 19 Cal.App. 523, 65 P.2d 932, syl. 1 (1937) and Wickman v. Bohle, 173 Md. 694, 196 A. 326, syl. 9 (1938).

9. Webb v. Biggers, 71 Ga.App. 90, 30 S.E.2d 59, syl. 2 (1944); Dec.Dig. Trial, ⊙—79.

the evidence conditionally received,[10] when the failure of condition becomes apparent. It seems that it does become apparent when the offering party completes the particular stage of his case in which the evidence was offered,[11] and that when he "rests" without making the missing proof, the adversary should then move to strike, failing which, he cannot later claim as of right to invoke the condition. Some weight should be given, however, to the duty assumed by the offering party in promising to furnish the connecting proof, and recognition of this can best be given by according the trial judge a discretion to allow the adversary to invoke the condition, if the continuing availability of the missing proof makes it fair to do so, at any time before the case is submitted to the jury or before final judgment in a judge-tried case.[12] Though some courts have considered the difference in form material, it seems that a motion to strike, a motion to withdraw the fact from the jury, or a request that the jury be instructed to disregard the evidence should each be regarded as a sufficient invocation of the condition.

To be distinguished from the practice described above of conditional admission pending further proof, is the custom of some judges of admitting evidence provisionally where objection is made, subject to a later ruling on the objection in the light of further consideration when the case has been more amply developed. Here again the objecting counsel, to preserve the objection must renew the objection before the case is concluded.[13] The practice seems appropriate enough in a judge-tried case [14] but where the trial is with a jury there is danger that letting the evidence in, even provisionally, may make an impression that a later ruling of exclusion may not erase [15]—a danger that here seems unnecessary to incur. Accordingly this practice, though doubtless in the realm of discretion, has frequently been criticised by reviewing courts.[16]

59. Evidence Admissible for One Purpose, Inadmissible for Another: "Multiple Admissibility." [1]

An item of evidence may be logically relevant in several aspects, as leading to distinct

10. Little Klamath Water Ditch Co. v. Ream, 27 Ore. 129, 39 P. 998, syl. 2 (1895); State v. Freeman, 93 Utah 125, 71 P.2d 196, syl. 21 (1937) (motion to strike necessary; request for instruction to disregard, at close of case, insufficient: full discussion, one judge dissenting). Other courts have thought that a motion for an instruction to disregard the evidence is the proper recourse. See, e. g., Kolka v. Jones, 6 N.D. 461, 71 N.W. 558, 564, syl. 9, 10 (1897). Decisions are collected in 6 Wigmore, Evidence, § 1871, note 6 and in 64 C.J. 206, note 41.

Normally, it is assumed when evidence is improperly received, or is not "connected up," an instruction to disregard is a sufficient corrective. But the evidence may be so prejudicial that an instruction does not cure the harm. National Cash Register Co. v. Kay, 119 S.W.2d 437, syl. 3–5, Mo.App., 1938. "Human nature does not change merely because it is found in the jury box. The human mind is not a slate, from which can be wiped out, at the will and instruction of another, ideas and thoughts written thereon." People v. Deal, 357 Ill. 634, 192 N.E. 649, 652 (1934.)

11. In Keber v. American Stores Co., 116 N.J.L. 437, 184 A. 795, syl. 2, 3 (1936) this was said to be the

proper time and that an earlier motion was premature. See also Note, 32 Ill.L.Rev. 882, 883 (1938).

12. See Note, 32 Ill.L.Rev. 882, 884 (1938).

13. Snow v. Snow, 71 Ga.App. 316, 30 S.E.2d 823, syl. 2 (1944).

14. Its advantages are pointed out by Sanborn, Circ. J., in Builders' Steel Co. v. Commissioner, 179 F.2d 377, 379 (C.A. 8, 1950). But compare Kovacs v. Szentes, 130 Conn. 229, 33 A.2d 124, syl. 2–5 (1943) applying a statute forbidding the practice.

15. McKee v. Bassick Mining Co., 8 Colo. 392, 8 P. 561 (1885). As applied to jury-tried cases this practice is often condemned. Missouri Pac. Transp. Co. v. Beard, 179 Miss. 450, 176 So. 156, syl. 16 (1937); Dec.Dig., Trial ⊕51. It is forbidden by statute in Connecticut even in judge-tried cases. Gen.St.1949, § 7960, construed in Kovacs v. Szentes, 130 Conn. 229, 33 A.2d 124, syl. 3–5 (1943).

16. See, e. g., Missouri Pac. Transportation Co. v. Beard, 179 Miss. 764, 176 So. 156 (1937); Trial ⊕ 51.

1. 1 Wigmore, Evidence § 13; Dec.Dig., Trial ⊕48; 64 C.J.Trial § 151.

inferences or as bearing upon different issues. For one of these purposes it may be competent, but for another incompetent. In this frequently arising situation, the normal practice is to admit the evidence.[2] The interest of the adversary is to be protected, not by an objection to its admission,[3] but by a request at the time of the offer for an instruction that the jury is to consider the evidence only for the allowable purpose.[4] Such an instruction may not always be effective, but admission of the evidence with the limiting instruction is normally the best available reconciliation of the respective interests. It seems, however, that in extreme situations, where the danger of the jury's misuse of the evidence for the incompetent purpose is great, and its value for the legitimate purpose is slight or the point for which it is competent can readily be proved by other evidence, the judge's power to exclude the evidence altogether would be recognized.[5]

Similarly, evidence may frequently be competent as against one party, but not as against another, in which event the practice is to admit the evidence, with an instruction, if requested, that the jury are to consider it only as to the party against whom it is competent.[6]

---

2. Sprinkle v. Davis, 111 F.2d 925, syl. 13–18 (C.C.A. Va.1940) (suit for injury to highway workman, plaintiff, by defendant's automobile: court erred in excluding defendant's evidence that plaintiff had been compensated by Highway Department; not admissible on issue of liability or damages but was, to show bias of witnesses who were highway employees); Williams v. Milner Hotels Co., 130 Conn. 507, 36 A.2d 20, syl. 1, 2, 4, 5 (1944) (guest, suing hotel for having been bitten by rat while lying in bed, could prove that rat-holes in room were later closed by tin patches; inadmissible as admission of fault, admissible to show control, existence of rat-holes, and to corroborate guest's evidence); Millman v. United States Mortgage & Title Guaranty Co., 121 N.J.L. 28, 1 A.2d 265, syl. 5, 6 (1938) (action by tenant for injury on stairs; evidence of subsequent repairs, inadmissible on negligence, admissible to show defect).

It seems, however, that the proponent, to complain of the judge's exclusion of evidence inadmissible in one aspect must have stated the purpose for which it is competent. Archer v. Sibley, 201 Ala. 495, 78 So. 849, syl. 2 (1918). Unless the admissible purpose is plainly apparent. Kansas City Southern Ry. Co. v. Jones, 241 U.S. 181, 36 S.Ct. 513, 60 L.Ed. 943 (1916). See 64 C.J. Trial, § 151, notes 27, 28.

3. Scott v. Missouri Ins. Co., 361 Mo. 51, 233 S.W.2d 660, syl. 8, 9 (1950) (action on life policy; defendant offered report of its investigators on the death; plaintiff objected as hearsay, and judge excluded; held error to exclude, should have admitted with limiting instruction, if requested).

4. Hatfield v. Levy Bros., 18 Cal.2d 798, 117 P.2d 841, syl. 20 (1941) (opponent, not having requested instruction, waived right thereto); Bouchard v. Bouchard, 313 Mass. 531, 48 N.E.2d 161, syl. 10 (1943); Rynar v. Lincoln Transit Co., 129 N.J.L. 525, 30 A.2d 406, 409, syl. 4 (1943) (". . . The party . . . may summon the court's assistance by request to charge or other appropriate means."); Lundberg v. Baumgartner, 5 Wash.2d 619, 106 P.2d 566, syl. 3 (1940) (death action; plaintiff objected to evidence of decedent's habits of insobriety; held, she cannot complain of failure to instruct that evidence could only be used in mitigation in absence of request).

5. See the persuasive statement to this effect, which may have been a dictum, by Olney, J. in Adkins v. Brett, 184 Cal. 252, 193 P. 251, 254 (1920) (in husband's action for alienation, evidence of wife's statement as to parties with and gifts from defendant, though would ordinarily be competent to show wife's feelings, might be excluded if danger great that jury would use it as evidence of defendant's conduct). See also Shepard v. United States, 290 U.S. 96, 103, syl. 4, 54 S.Ct. 22, 78 L.Ed. 196 (1933); Uniform Rules of Evidence, R. 45: ". . . The judge may in his discretion exclude evidence if he finds that its probative value is substantially outweighed by the risk that its admission will (a) necessitate undue consumption of time, or (b) create substantial danger of undue prejudice or of confusing the issues or of misleading the jury, or (c) unfairly and harmfully surprise a party who has not had reasonable opportunity to anticipate that such evidence would be offered."

6. Nash v. United States, 54 F.2d 1006, syl. 2 (C.C.A. 2d 1932) (written statement of one of several defendants properly admitted under instruction confining its use to him; L. Hand, J.: "If we were to reframe the law of evidence and were still to preserve the hearsay rule, it might be better to keep out all such, for the practice, though well settled, is an evasion, and evasions are discreditable. There is no reason why the prosecution, if it chooses to indict several defendants together, should not be confined to evidence admissible

60. Admission and Exclusion of Evidence in Trials without a Jury.

Thayer considers that our law of evidence is a "product of the jury system . . . where ordinary untrained citizens are acting as judges of fact."[1] It might have been more expedient if these rules had been, at least in the main, discarded in trials before judges. Their professional experience in valuing evidence greatly lessens the need for exclusionary rules. Such has not, however, been the approach, but rather the traditional starting-point is that in general the jury-trial system of evidence governs in trials before the judge as well.[2] Nevertheless the feeling of the inexpediency of these restrictions as applied to the hearing has caused courts to say that the same strictness will not be observed in applying the rules of evidence in judge-trials as in trials before a jury.[3]

The most important influence in encouraging in trial judges this attitude toward evidence rules in non-jury cases is a rule of pre-

sumption obtaining in most appellate courts. These courts have said that in reviewing a case tried without a jury the admission of incompetent evidence over objection will not ordinarily be a ground of reversal if there was competent evidence received sufficient to support the findings, since the judge will be presumed to have disregarded the inadmissible and relied on the competent evidence.[4] If he errs, however, in the opposite direction, by excluding evidence which he ought to have received his ruling if substantially harmful to the losing party will of course be subject to reversal.[5]

These contrasting attitudes of the appellate courts toward errors in receiving and those in excluding evidence seem to support the wisdom of the practice adopted by many experienced trial judges in non-jury cases of provisionally admitting all evidence which is objected to if he thinks its admissibility is debatable,[6] with the announcement that all questions of admissibility will be reserved un-

---

against all, and if real injustice were done, the result would be undesirable. In effect, however, the rule probably furthers, rather than impedes, the search for truth, and this perhaps excuses the device which satisfies form while it violates substance; that is, the recommendation to the jury of a mental gymnastic which is beyond, not only their powers, but anybody's else."); Chesapeake & O. Ry. Co. v. Boyd's Adm'r, 290 Ky. 9, 160 S.W. 2d 342, syl. 10 (1942) (statement of engineer, codefendant, admissible against him, if not against railway; general objection without request to limit the evidence, ineffective); Ft. Worth Hotel Co. v. Waggoman, 126 S.W.2d 578, syl. 9 (Tex.Civ.App. 1939) (evidence admissible against one of defendants, joint tort-feasors, not subject to objection by other defendant; his only relief is a request to have it limited).

1. Preliminary Treatise on Evidence, 509 (1898).

2. See, e. g., Stewart v. Prudential Ins. Co., 147 Pa. Super. 296, 24 A.2d 83, syl. 3 (1942).

3. See e. g., Weisenborn v. Rutledge, 233 Mo.App. 464, 121 S.W.2d 309, 313, syl. 6 (1938); and numerous cases collected in Dec.Dig. Trial, ☞377(1); 64 C.J. Trial § 1009, note 74.

4. Stewart v. American Life Ins. Co., 89 F.2d 743, syl. 10 (C.C.A.Kan.1937); Hiatt v. Lee, 48 Ariz. 320, 61 P.2d 401, syl. 7, 107 A.L.R. 444 (1936); Smyers

v. Raleigh, 189 Okl. 32, 113 P.2d 363, syl. 2 (1941); Victory v. State, 138 Tex. 285, 158 S.W.2d 760, syl. 17 (1942); Herbert A. Neiman & Co. v. Holton Co., 248 Wis. 324, 21 N.W.2d 637, syl. 4 (1946); 6 Jones, Evidence, § 2534 (2d ed. 1926); Dec.Dig. Appeal & Error, ☞931(6); 5 C.J.S. Appeal and Error § 1564e; Maguire & Epstein, Preliminary Questions of Fact, 36 Yale L.J. 1100, 1115 (1927). From these references the qualifications and conditions upon the rule will fully appear.

But a few courts decline to apply the presumption when the evidence was objected to and the objection overruled. Farish v. Hawk, 241 Ala. 352, 2 So.2d 407, syl. 6 (1941); In re Conner's Estate, 240 Iowa 479, 36 N.W.2d 833, syl. 3 (1949) (judge is presumed to have considered it); Weibert v. Hanan, 202 N.Y. 328, 95 N.E. 688, syl. 3 (1911) (referee). In Kansas to obviate the presumption the complaining counsel must not only object but move to strike. Walker v. Anderson, 160 Kan. 461, 163 P. 2d 359, syl. 6, 7 (1945).

5. Examples of reversals where the exclusion was found prejudicial: LaFon v. Grimes, 86 F.2d 809, syl. 3, 109 A.L.R. 156 (C.C.A.Tex. 1936); Reynolds v. Vroom, 132 Conn. 53, 42 A.2d 336, syl. 8 (1945). See Dec.Dig. Appeal and Error, ☞1056(5); 5 C.J. S. Appeal and Error § 1746, notes 13, 14.

6. Builders Steel Co. v. Commissioner, 179 F.2d 377, 379, syl. 1, 2 (C.A. 8th 1950) (valuable discussion by

til the evidence is all in. In considering the objections if renewed by motion to strike at the end of the case, he will lean toward admission rather than exclusion[7] and at the end will seek to find clearly admissible testimony on which to base his findings.[8] This practice will lessen the time spent in arguing objections and will ensure that the appellate court will have in the record the evidence that was rejected as well as that which was received. This will often help them to make an end of the case.[9] It will readily be seen, however, that this practice of hearing everything first and deciding upon its competency later creates an atmosphere which muffles the impact and de-emphasizes the importance of the exclusionary rules of evidence.

Sanborn, J.); Powell v. Adams, 98 Mo. 598, 12 S.W. 295, 297 (1889); Degginger v. Martin, 48 Wash. 1, 92 P. 674, syl. 7 (1907); Holendyke v. Newton, 50 Wis. 635, 638, 7 N.W. 558, syl. 2 (1880) (referee or judge should be very careful in rejecting evidence, and where there is reasonable doubt though he thinks it inadmissible, should receive it subject to objections); 64 C.J., Trial, § 1009, notes 81–84.

But occasionally appellate courts (misguidedly it is believed) disapprove. See Kovacs v. Szentes, 130 Conn. 124, 33 A.2d 124, syl. 4, 5 (1943) (based on Gen.St.1949, § 7960 forbidding court to admit evidence subject to objection unless parties agree; "A judge has not such control over his mental faculties that he can definitely determine whether or not inadmissible evidence he has heard will affect his mind . . .")); Holcombe v. Hopkins, 314 Mass. 113, 49 N.E.2d 722, syl. 7 (1943) (semble); Dec.Dig. Trial, ⬦51, 379.

7. See Powell, Degginger and Holendyke cases in next preceding note.

8. As in Hatch v. Calkins, 21 Cal.App.2d 364, 122 P. 2d 126, syl. 7 (1942) where the judge in his memorandum decision recited that his decision was based on the competent portion of certain affidavits.

9. As pointed out in the decisions cited in the first paragraph of note 6, supra.

TITLE 4

COMPETENCY

CHAPTER 7

THE COMPETENCY OF WITNESSES

61. In General.[1]

The common-law rules of incompetency have been undergoing, for a century, a process of piecemeal revision by statutes, so that today most of the former grounds for excluding a witness altogether have been converted into mere grounds of impeaching his credibility.

Since the disqualification of witnesses for incompetency is thus dwindling in importance, and since the statutory modifications vary substantially from state to state, a development of the law in the different jurisdictions is not justified.[2] The following summary of the common-law grounds of incom-

---

1. The subject is covered in detail in Wigmore, Evidence, §§ 483–721. Its history is fully treated in 9 Holdsworth Hist.Eng.Law, 177–197, 1926, and briefly sketched in Rowley, The Competency of Witnesses, 24 Iowa L.Rev. 482 (1939). Good discussions of local rules: Barnhart, Testimonial Competency and Privilege, 4 Ark.L.Rev. 377 (1950); Slough, Competency of Witnesses, 18 Kan.Bar A.J. 220 (1950).

The rules regulating the competency of witnesses (as well as admissibility of evidence generally) in the Federal Courts are as follows:

Rules of Civil Procedure for the District Courts of the United States, Rule 43(a): Form and Admissibility. In all trials the testimony of witnesses shall be taken orally in open court, unless otherwise provided by these rules. All evidence shall be admitted which is admissible under the statutes of the United States, or under the rules of evidence heretofore applied in the courts of the United States on the hearing of suits in equity, or under the rules of evidence applied in the courts of general jurisdiction of the state in which

the United States court is held. In any case, the statute or rule which favors the reception of the evidence governs and the evidence shall be presented according to the most convenient method prescribed in any of the statutes or rules to which reference is herein made. The competency of a witness to testify shall be determined in like manner.

Rules of Criminal Procedure for the District Courts of the United States, Rule 26: In all trials the testimony of witnesses shall be taken orally in open court, unless otherwise provided by an act of Congress or by these rules. The admissibility of evidence and the competency and privileges of witnesses shall be governed, except when an act of Congress or these rules otherwise provide, by the principles of the common law as they may be interpreted by the courts of the United States in the light of reason and experience.

2. Fortunately, a convenient compilation of the statutes on competency, for each state, is available in Wigmore, Evidence, § 488. This will give a rapid access to the local changes, and may be supple-

petency, and the general lines of statutory change, will suffice.

62.   Mental Incapacity [1] and Immaturity.[2]

There is no rule which excludes an insane person as such,[3] or prohibits a child of any specified age from testifying,[4] but in each case the test is whether the witness has intelligence enough to make it worth while to hear him at all and whether he feels a duty to tell the truth.[5] Is his capacity to observe, remember, and recount, such that he can probably bring added knowledge of the facts? This is frequently phrased, in traditional language as a requirement that the witness must have intelligence enough to "understand the nature and obligation of an oath." [6] This, manifestly, is inappropriate. It confounds a religious with a mental standard, and if literally applied, the most intelligent witness could hardly meet the test, much less a child or an insane person. Such liberalization as has been accomplished in the practice has come by liberalization in judicial custom, as the statutes have seldom purported to change the common-law standard. Disqualification for mental incapacity or immaturity seems to have more reason behind it, than any of the other rules of incompetency. Nevertheless, even this rule would doubtless have long since been abandoned, except for the presence of the jury as the trier of facts. The judges distrust a jury's ability to assay the words of a small child or of a deranged person. Conceding the jury's deficiencies, the remedy of exclud-

---

mented by searching the annotated statutes of the state for the leading decisions.

1. 2 Wigmore, Evidence, §§ 492–501; 70 C.J.Witnesses, § 123; Dec.Dig., Witnesses, ⊂⇒39–41; Notes, 8 Ark.L.Rev. 100 (1953), 39 Va.L.Rev. 358 (1953).

2. 2 Wigmore, Evidence, §§ 505–509; 70 C.J., Witnesses, § 122; Dec.Dig., Witnesses, ⊂⇒40, 45.

3. District of Columbia v. Armes, 107 U.S. 519, 2 S.Ct. 840, 27 L.Ed. 618 (1883) (feeble-minded man competent); Truttman v. Truttman, 328 Ill. 365, 159 N.E. 775, syl. 1, 2 (1927) (mental defective, competent); State v. Wildman, 145 Oh.St. 379, 61 N.E.2d 790, syl. 3 (1945) (imbecile girl competent). And a witness who suffers from insane delusions that he is possessed by spirits but is not prevented thereby from giving a rational account of the matters he testifies to, is not incompetent. Regina v. Hill, 5 Cox Crim.C. 259, 5 Eng.Law & Eq.Rep. 547 (Ct.Crim.App.1851).

4. Radiant Oil Co. v. Herring, 146 Fla. 154, 200 So. 376, 377 (1941) ("not an arbitrary age but the degree of intelligence . . . is the test . . ."); Rueger v. Hawks, 150 Neb. 834, 36 N.W.2d 236, 244 (1949) ("There is no precise age which determines the question of a child's competency"); Cargill v. State, 25 Okl.Cr. 314, 220 Pac. 64, 65 (1923) ("intelligence, not age, is the vital criterion").

5. State v. Segerberg, 131 Conn. 546, 41 A.2d 101, 102, syl. 2, 157 A.L.R. 1335 (1945) ("The principle . . . is that the child shall be sufficiently mature to receive correct impressions by her senses, to recollect and narrate intelligently and to appreciate the moral duty to tell the truth"); Burnam v. Chicago Great Western Ry. Co., 340 Mo. 25, 100 S.W.2d 858, syl. 2 (1936) (child, 5 at time of injury,

8 at time of trial, competent though had been held incompetent at earlier trial); Hancock v. Hallman, 229 Wis. 127, 281 N.W. 703, syl. 3 (1938) (feeble-minded girl held not competent under this test).

The judge will ordinarily conduct an interrogation of the witness to ascertain and test his capacity. See, e. g., Commonwealth v. Tatisos, 238 Mass. 322, 130 N.E. 495 (1921), and the interesting comparison of the judge's examination in that case with the standard psychological intelligence-tests, in Hutchins and Schlesinger, The Competency of Witnesses, 37 Yale L.J. 1017, 1928.

6. Examples of decisions in which the court recites this as one of the tests are Bielecki v. State, 140 Tex.Cr. 355, 145 S.W.2d 189, syl. 3 (1945), and Mullins v. Comm., 174 Va. 472, 5 S.E.2d 499, syl. 1 (1939). The more modern approach is illustrated in Hill v. Skinner, 81 Oh.App. 375, 377, 79 N.E.2d 787, 789 (1947). There a child of four was held competent. He testified that if he didn't tell the truth God wouldn't love him. The court said: "The nature of his conception of the obligation to tell the truth is of little importance if he shows that he will fulfill the obligation to speak truthfully as a duty which he owes a Deity or something held in reverence or regard, and if he has the intellectual capacity to communicate his observations and experiences."

Canadian provincial statutes which provide that when the judge finds that the child does not understand the nature of an oath, his evidence may be received without an oath, offer useful precedents. Alberta, St.1944, c. 8, The Child Welfare Act, Part I, § 14(6); Brit.Columbia, St.1943, c. 5, Protection of Children Act, § 37(1).

ing such a witness, who may be the only person available who knows the facts, seems inept and primitive. Though the tribunal is unskilled, and the testimony difficult to weigh, still it would be better to let the evidence come in for what it is worth, with cautionary instructions to the jury. As has already been seen,[7] mental derangement, where calculated to affect at all the ability of the witness to observe, remember, and recount, may always be proved as impeaching credibility.

63. Religious Belief.[1]

Belief in a Divine Being who, in this life or hereafter, will punish false swearing was a prerequisite at common law to the capacity

to take the oath.[2] The Jew or the Mohammedan, as well as the Christian, could meet the test, but the atheist or agnostic could not. This ground of incapacity has fortunately been abandoned in most jurisdictions,[3] either by explicit constitutional or statutory provisions,[4] or by expansive interpretation of provisions forbidding deprivation of rights for religious beliefs,[5] or by changing the common law "in the light of reason and experience."[6] Inquiry into the religious opinions of the witness for impeachment purposes is discussed in another place.[7]

64. Conviction of Crime.[1]

The common law disqualified altogether the witness who had been convicted of trea-

---

7. See § 45, herein.

1. 2 Wigmore, Evidence, § 518, 6 id. §§ 1816–1829; Hartogensis, Denial of Rights to Religious Minorities and Non-Believers, 39 Yale L.J. 659, 666–671 (1930); 58 Am.Jur., Witnesses, §§ 125–128; 70 C.J., Witnesses, § 128; Dec.Dig., Witnesses, ⊕44, 227.

2. Attorney-General v. Bradlaugh, [1885], L.R. 2 Q.B. D. 697; 6 Wigmore, Evidence, § 1817.

3. See the constitutional and statutory provisions listed and described in 6 Wigmore, Evidence, § 1828, note 1.

4. E. g., Calif., Const.1879, art. I, § 4 ("No person shall be rendered incompetent to be a witness or juror on account of his opinions on matters of religious belief"); New York, Const.1895, Art. I § 3 (similar to last, as to witnesses); Texas, Const. 1876, Art. I, § 5 ("No person shall be disqualified to give evidence in any of the courts of this state on account of his religious opinions or for want of any religious belief . . ."); Penn., P.S. 1930, tit. 28, § 312 ("The capacity of any person who shall testify in any judicial proceeding shall be in no wise affected by his opinions on matters of religion."

5. E. g., Hronek v. People, 134 Ill. 139, 152, 24 N.E. 861, syl. 7 (1890) (under Const. Art. 2, § 3, S.H.A. Ill., which provides that "no person shall be denied any civil or political right, privilege or capacity on account of his religious opinions" a witness is qualified though he lacked the religious belief required at common law); and see State v. Levine, 109 N.J.L. 503, 162 Atl. 909, syl. 2–5 (1932), noted 33 Col.L.Rev. 539 (under Art. 1, § 5 of New Jersey Constitution, N.J.S.A., providing that no person shall be denied enjoyment of civil rights because

of religious principles, it was error to deny accused privilege of affirming as a witness on account of his want of religious belief, even though he was allowed to tell his story to the jury).

6. See Gillars v. United States, 182 F.2d 962, 969, 970 (C.A.D.C., 1950). In that case it was held proper to allow a witness to "affirm" and testify though he did not believe in divine punishment for perjury and though the D.C.Code, Title 14, sec 101 provides that "all evidence shall be given under oath according to the forms of the common law," except that a witness with conscientious scruples against an oath may affirm. Fahy, J., said for the court: "The early common law rule, and therefore the rule which at an earlier period would have prevailed under the Code might well have rendered Schnell incompetent. But the Code must now be read with Rule 26 of the Federal Rules of Criminal Procedure, 18 U.S.C.A., which provides, *inter alia:* '. . . competency and privileges of witnesses shall be governed, except when an act of Congress or these rules otherwise provide, by the principles of the common law as they may be interpreted by the courts of the United States in the light of reason and experience.'

"A fair reading together of the Code and the Rule leads to the conclusion that the common law rule in the District of Columbia is to be interpreted now in the light of reason and experience. This brings into the area of competence witnesses who were under disability under the older criteria."

7. See § 48, herein.

1. 2 Wigmore, Evidence, §§ 488, 519–524; 70 C.J., Witnesses, §§ 132–143; 58 Am.Jur., §§ 137–148; Dec.Dig., Witnesses, ⊕48, 49.

son, felony, or a crime involving fraud or deceit.[2] In England and in most of the states during the last hundred years, this disqualification has been swept away by legislation.[3] In 1917, the Supreme Court of the United States determined that "the dead hand of the common law rule" of disqualification should no longer be applied in criminal cases in the federal courts.[4] In a few states, however, it has been retained for conviction of perjury and subornation thereof, and in a few others the disqualification is continued for criminal cases only. In one state, Tennessee, it apparently has not been abandoned or even liberalized but maintained in a form "more inflexible and broader in scope" than the common law rule.[5] Doubtless the course of legal evolution in the next few decades will see the complete extinction of this archaic and obstructive disqualification.

65. Parties and Persons Interested: The Dead Man Statutes.[1]

By far the most drastic of the rules of incompetency was that which excluded from testifying in any case, civil or criminal, the parties to the lawsuit and all persons having a direct interest, of a pecuniary or proprietary kind, in the outcome. In effect this imposed a disability upon the party to testify in his own behalf and conferred on him a privilege not to be used as a witness against himself by the adversary. The disability had the specious justification of preventing self-interested perjury: the privilege had not even a specious excuse. The intolerable absurdity of the rule of disqualification for interest makes it almost unbelievable that it could have continued in force in England until the middle of the 19th century, and in this country until the English reform was accepted in the various states, as it was within the next few decades. In England, fortunately, the reform was sweeping, and no shred of disqualification in civil cases remains.

In this country, however, a compromise was forced upon the reformers, by some ingenious objector, and this compromise has bred injustice and uncertainty ever since. The objection was raised that if parties and interested persons were admitted to testify, this would work harshly in controversies over contracts or other transactions where one party to the transaction has died and the other survives. The survivor could testify though the adverse party's lips would be sealed in death. This is a seductive argument. It was accepted in nearly all the early statutes, at a time when the real dispute was whether the general disqualification should be abolished or retained, and this concession for survivors' cases seemed a minor one. But the concession has now become so ingrained a part of judicial and professional habits of thinking that it is as hard to dislodge by argument as was the original disqualification of parties generally.

The statutes, accordingly, in most states now provide that the common-law disqualification of parties and interested persons is abolished, except that such persons remain disqualified to testify concerning a transaction or communication with a person since deceased in a suit prosecuted or defended by the executor or administrator of such decedent.[2] It is usually provided, however, that the surviving party or interested person may

2. 2 Wigmore, Evidence, §§ 519, 520.

3. See the statutes collected in 2 Wigmore, Evidence, § 488.

4. Rosen v. United States, 245 U.S. 467, 38 S.Ct. 148, syl. 1, 62 L.Ed. 406 (1917).

5. Halliday, Infamy as a Ground of Disqualification in Tennessee, 22 Tenn.L.Rev. 544, 547 (1952).

1. 2 Wigmore, Evidence, §§ 488, 575–580; 58 Am. Jur., Witnesses, §§ 159–174, 214–362; 70 C.J., Witnesses, §§ 260–496; Dec.Dig., Witnesses, ⊜80–183½.

2. This is the most common form, but there are variants. See Note, 31 Ill.L.Rev. 218, at 222 (1936). A fairly representative statute is the Texas Dead Man's Act, Vernon's Ann.Civ.St., art. 3716: "In actions by or against executors, administrators, or

testify if called by the adversary, i. e., by the executor or administrator, thus abrogating the privilege feature of the common law rule. The practical consequence of such statutes is that a survivor who, without an outside witness, has rendered services, furnished goods or lent money to a man whom he trusted, and from whom he took no written agreement, is helpless if the other dies and the representative of his estate declines to pay. The survivor's mouth may even be closed in an action arising from a fatal automobile collision,[3] or where he seeks to defend a suit upon a note or an account which he has paid in cash without taking a receipt.

Most commentators agree that here again the expedient of refusing altogether to listen to the survivor is, in the words of Bentham, a "blind and brainless" technique. In seeking to avoid injustice to one side, the statute-makers have ignored the equal possibility of injustice to the other. The temptation to the survivor to fabricate a claim or defense is obvious enough, so obvious indeed that any jury will realize that his story must be cautiously heard. A searching cross-examination will usually, in case of fraud, reveal discrepancies inherent in the "tangled web"

of deception. In any event, the survivor's disqualification is more likely to balk the honest than the dishonest survivor. One who would not stick at perjury will hardly hesitate at suborning a third person, who would not be disqualified, to swear to the false story.

Slowly, the law-makers are being brought to see the blindness of the traditional survivors' evidence Acts, and liberalizing changes are being adopted. A few states have provided that the survivor may testify, but his testimony will not support a judgment, unless corroborated by other evidence. Others authorize the trial judge to permit the survivor to testify when it appears that this is necessary to prevent injustice. Both of these solutions have drawbacks which are reasonably apparent, and these are avoided by the third type of statute. This sweeps away the disqualification entirely and permits the survivor to testify without restriction, but seeks to minimize the danger of injustice to the decedent's estate by admitting any writings of the deceased or evidence of oral statements made by him, bearing on the controversy, both of which would ordinarily be excluded as hearsay.[4]

---

guardians, in which judgment may be rendered for or against them as such, neither party shall be allowed to testify against the others as to any transaction with, or statement by, the testator, intestate or ward, unless called to testify thereto by the opposite party; and the provisions of this article shall extend to and include all actions by or against the heirs or legal representatives of a decedent arising out of any transaction with such decedent." The variations in the statutes are summarized and graphically charted in Vanderbilt, Minimum Standards of Judicial Administration, 334–341 (1949).

3. This has been a trouble-point recently; see, e. g., Sankey v. Interstate Dispatch, 339 Ill.App. 420, 90 N.E.2d 265, syl. 1, 2 (1950), Note, 45 Ill.L.Rev. 685; Andreades v. McMillan, 256 S.W.2d 477 (Tex.Civ. App.1953) (collision is a transaction and in action against administrator of the man killed the survivor is disqualified); Cox, Troublesome Evidence Rules, 14 Tex.Bar J. 61, 94 (1951); Atkins, Can an Accident Be a Transaction? 20 Ins.Counsel J. 106 (1953).

4. This solution was recommended by the American Bar Association in 1938, as follows: "That the rule excluding testimony of an interested party as to transactions with deceased persons, should be abrogated by the adoption of a statute like that of Connecticut, which removes the disqualification of the party as a witness and permits the introduction of declarations of the decedent, on a finding by the trial judge that they were made in good faith and on decedent's personal knowledge." Only six states, Connecticut, Louisiana, Massachusetts, Oregon, Rhode Island and South Dakota, have such statutes. Vanderbilt, op. cit. 334, 338. For valuable discussion of the entire problem and the alternative solutions, see Wigmore, Evidence, § 578; Morgan and others, The Law of Evidence, Some Proposals for Its Reform, Ch. III (1927); Ladd, The Dead Man Statute, 26 Iowa L.Rev. 201 (1941); Note, Qualifying the Interested Survivor as a Witness, 46 Harv.L.Rev. 834 (1933); Note, Evidence by Survivors in Illinois, 31 Ill.L.Rev. 89, 218 (1936).

Interest, then, as a disqualification in civil cases has been discarded, except for the fragmentary relic retained in the survivors' evidence statutes. The disqualification of parties defendant in criminal cases which at common law prevented the accused from being called as a witness by either side has been abrogated in England and in this country so far as it disabled the defendant to testify in his own behalf, but it survives to the extent that the prosecution cannot call him. In this form, it is a rule of privilege, and constitutes one aspect of the privilege against self-incrimination, treated in a later section.[5]

While the disqualification of parties and persons interested in the result of the lawsuit has thus been almost entirely swept away, the same fact of interest of the witness, whether as a party or otherwise, is by no means disregarded. The fact of interest may be proved as a ground of impeaching credibility,[6] and in most jurisdictions the court will instruct that a party's testimony may be weighed in the light of his interest.[7]

66. Husbands and Wives of Parties.[1]

Closely allied to the disqualification of parties, and even more arbitrary and misguided,

was the disqualification of the husband or wife of the party. This prevented the party's husband or wife from testifying either for or against the party in any case, civil or criminal.[2] Doubtless we should classify the disability of the husband or wife as a witness to testify *for* the party-spouse as a disqualification, based upon the supposed infirmity of interest, and the rule enabling the party-spouse to prevent the husband or wife from testifying *against* the party as a privilege.[3] This privilege even at common law was withheld from the husband in criminal prosecutions against him for wrongs directly against the person of the wife.[4] In the majority of jurisdictions statutes have made the husband or wife fully competent to testify for or against the party-spouse in civil cases. In criminal cases, while generally the disqualification of the husband or wife to testify for the accused has been removed, it is generally provided that the prosecution may not call the spouse, without the consent of the accused, thus preserving for criminal cases the privilege of the accused to keep the spouse off the stand altogether. Usually the common law exception to the privilege has been

---

5. See § 122, herein.

6. See § 40, herein.

7. See, e. g., Hancheft v. Haas, 219 Ill. 546, 76 N.E. 845, syl. 5 (1906); Lovely v. Grand Rapids & I. Ry. Co., 137 Mich. 653, 100 N.W. 894, syl. 2 (1904); 64 C.J., Trial, § 475.

1. 2 Wigmore, Evidence, §§ 488 (statutes), 600–620 (marital disqualification to testify for the spouse), 8 id., §§ 2227–2245 (privilege of party-spouse to prevent other spouse from testifying against the party); 70 C.J., Witnesses, §§ 145–231; 58 Am. Jur., Witnesses, §§ 175–207; Dec.Dig., Witnesses, ⊜51–65.

2. See authorities in next preceding note. A good survey of the present law in the various American jurisdictions is the Note, W. I. T., Jr., Competency of One Spouse to Testify against the Other in Criminal Cases: Modern Trend, 38 Va.L.Rev. 359 (1952).

3. In probably the majority of states, not only is the party-spouse privileged to keep the spouse-

witness off the stand, but the latter has a privilege also to refuse to testify against the party though he consents. United States v. Mitchell, 137 F.2d 1006, 1008 (C.C.A.2d 1943) (Dictum: ". . . clearly the better view is that the privilege is that of either spouse who chooses to claim it"); State v. Dunbar, 360 Mo. 788, 230 S.W.2d 845, 849, syl. 1–5 (1950) (prosecution of husband for shooting wife in arm, so that it had to be amputated, held under statute that wife though competent was not compellable to testify, reversing defendant's conviction because she was required to testify; but this ignores the principle that a party cannot complain of the infringement of a witness's privilege, see § 73, herein), but see contra, Shores v. United States, 174 F.2d 838, syl. 1 (C.A.8, 1949) (dictum, wife cannot refuse to testify against husband prosecuted for transporting her for prostitution, under Mann Act, 18 U.S.C.A. §§ 2421–2423); 8 Wigmore, Evidence, § 2241.

4. 1 Blackstone, Commentaries, 443 (1765); 8 Wigmore, Evidence, § 2239.

broadened to cover any "crime committed by one against the other." [5]

The privilege has sometimes been defended, after the manner in which we find reasons for inherited customs generally, as protecting family harmony. But family harmony is nearly always past saving when the spouse is willing to aid the prosecution. The privilege, in truth, is an archaic survival of a mystical religious dogma [6] and of a way of thinking about the marital relation, which are today outmoded.[7] So generally is this recognized [8] that one may expect the federal courts in the future to follow the lead of some forward-looking judges [9] by declaring that the privilege has no place in common

law as interpreted by present-day courts "in the light of reason and experience." [10] Thus far the greater number of lower federal courts have declined to take this step.[11]

Both this privilege, and the ancient disqualification, must be clearly distinguished from another privilege which has a somewhat sounder justification. This is the privilege against disclosure of confidential communications between husband and wife. It is developed in another place.[12]

67. Incompetency of Husband and Wife to Give Testimony on Non-Access.[1]

In 1777, in an ejectment case where the issue of the legitimacy of the claimant was

5. 2 Wigmore, Evidence, § 488, 8 id., § 2240. And the statutes frequently go further and expressly except particular crimes (aside from crimes against the person or property of the spouse) such as bigamy, adultery, rape, crimes against the children of either or both, and abandonment. Note, 38 Va.L. Rev. 359, 364, 365 (1952); 8 Wigmore, Evidence, § 2240.

6. Coke, Commentary on Littleton, 6b, ". . . a wife cannot be produced either for or against her husband, *"quia sunt duae animae in carne una,"* 1628 ("for they are two souls in one flesh").

7. See Hutchins and Slesinger, Some Observations on the Law of Evidence: Family Relations, 13 Minn.L.Rev. 675, 678 (1929), but compare Note, 17 U.Chi.L.Rev. 525, 530, note (1950). See also Note, 15 U.Pitt.L.Rev. 318 (1954).

8. See the criticisms of the privilege collected in 8 Wigmore, Evidence, § 2228, ranging from the phillipic by Jeremy Bentham in 1827 to the recommendation for its abolition by the Committee on the Improvement of the Law of Evidence of the American Bar Association in 1937.

9. McDermott, J. in Yoder v. United States, 80 F.2d 665 (C.C.A.10, 1935), and C. E. Clark, J., dissenting in United States v. Walker, 176 F.2d 564, 569 (C.A.2, 1949). See also the liberal opinion of Levin, J. in United States v. Graham, 87 F.Supp. 237 (E.D. Mich.1949).

10. This phrase was used by Stone, J. in Wolfle v. United States, 291 U.S. 7, 12, 54 S.Ct. 279, 78 L. Ed. 617 (1934), as descriptive of the standard employed in Funk v. United States, 290 U.S. 371, 54 S.Ct. 212, 78 L.Ed. 369 (1933) where Sutherland, J. for the court held that the disqualification of the wife to testify for the husband was no longer

a part of the modern common law administered in the federal courts. This criterion was codified in 1940 in Rule 26 of the Federal Rules of Criminal Procedure: "The admissibility of evidence and the competency and privileges of witnesses shall be governed, except when an act of Congress or these rules otherwise provide, by the principles of the common law as they may be interpreted by the courts of the United States in the light of reason and experience."

11. See, e. g., United States v. Walker, 176 F. 564, syl. 6 (C.A.2, 1949), certiorari denied, noted 17 U.Chi.L.Rev. 525; Brunner v. United States, 168 F.2d 281, syl. 2 (C.C.A.6, 1948); Paul v. United States, 79 F.2d 561, syl. 2 (C.C.A.3, 1935). In a recent case in the highest court, however, the court said "it is open to us to say whether we shall go further and abrogate the common law rule disqualifying one spouse from testifying in criminal cases against the other spouse." But the marriage there was held to be a sham with no intent by the parties to assume a genuine marital relationship and the court concluded: "The light of reason and experience do not compel us to so interpret the common law as to disqualify these ostensible spouses from testifying in this case." Three justices dissented. Lutwak v. United States, 344 U.S. 604, 73 S.Ct. 481, 487, 488, syl. 4–6, 97 L.Ed. 593 (1953), noted 31 N.C.L.Rev. 520, 101 U. Pa.L.Rev. 700.

12. See ch. 9, herein.

1. 7 Wigmore, Evidence, §§ 2063, 2064; 70 C.J., Witnesses, §§ 176, 177; Dec.Dig., Witnesses, ☞57; discussions of local decisions: Bell, article, 21 Temp. L.Q. 217 (1948), note, 3 Md.L.Rev. 79 (1938); Notes, 60 A.L.R. 380, 68 id. 421, 89 id. 911.

raised, Lord Mansfield delivered a pronouncement which apparently was new-minted doctrine, "that the declarations of a father or mother cannot be admitted to bastardize the issue born after marriage . . . it is a rule founded in decency, morality and policy, that they shall not be permitted to say after marriage that they have had no connection and therefore that the offspring is spurious. . . . ." [2] This invention of the great jurist though justly criticised by Wigmore as inconsistent, obstructive and pharisaical,[3] has been followed by later English decisions [4] until recently abrogated by statute,[5] and has been generally accepted in this country.[6] A few courts have wisely rejected it by construing the general statutes abolishing the incompetency of parties and of spouses as abolishing this eccentric incompetency also,[7]

but most courts have not yielded to this argument.[8] The points of controversy in the application of the rule are (a) whether it is limited strictly to evidence of non-access,[9] or whether it extends to other types of evidence showing that some one other than the husband is the father,[10] (b) whether the rule is limited to proceedings wherein legitimacy is in issue [11] or extends to suits for divorce where the question is adultery rather than the legitimacy of the child,[12] and (c) whether it is confined to prohibiting the testimony of husband and wife on the stand,[13] or extends to excluding evidence of the previous admissions or declarations of the spouse.[14] In view of the impolicy of the rule it is believed that in all these instances the more restrictive application is to be preferred.

2. Goodright v. Moss, 2 Cowp. 291, 98 Eng.Rep. 1257 (1777).

3. Evidence, § 2064.

4. See, e. g., Russell v. Russell, [1924] App.C. 687 (H.L.)

5. St.1949, 12, 13, and 14 Geo. 6, ch. 100, Law Reform (Miscellaneous Provisions) Act, 1949, § 7 ("evidence of a husband or wife shall be admissible in any proceedings to prove that marital intercourse did or did not take place between them during any period . . . husband or wife shall not be compellable in any proceeding to give evidence of the matters aforesaid"). Similar provisions are contained in St.1950, 14 Geo. 6, ch. 25, Matrimonial Causes Act, 1950, § 32.

6. See authorities cited in f. n. 1, above. The realistic opinion of Smith, C. J., writing for the court in Moore v. Smith, 178 Miss. 383, 172 So. 317 (1937) is one of the few which reject outright the reasoning in Goodright v. Moss, supra.

7. In re McNamara's Estate, 181 Cal. 82, 183 Pac. 552, 7 A.L.R. 313, 325, syl. 14 (1919); State v. Soyka, 181 Minn. 533, 233 N.W. 300, syl. 2 (1930); Loudon v. Loudon, 114 N.J.Eq. 242, 168 Atl. 840, syl. 1, 2, 89 A.L.R. 904 (Ct.Errors & App. 1933) (extensive discussion by Perskie, J.)

8. See, e. g., Hubert v. Cloutier, 135 Me. 230, 194 Atl. 303, syl. 6–8 (1937); Harward v. Harward, 173 Md. 339, 196 Atl. 318, syl. 7–9 (1938).

Specific statutes, however, often limit or abrogate the rule in particular proceedings. See, e. g., the

statutes described in Sayles v. Sayles, 323 Mass. 66, 80 N.E.2d 21, 22 (1948) (statutes permitting spouses testimony to non-access in prosecutions for non-support and in illegitimacy proceedings); People on complaint of D——— v. C———, 194 Misc. 94, 85 N.Y.S.2d 751, syl. 1 (Children's Ct.1949) (Sec. 126 Domestic Relations Law changes common law rule so as to allow spouses to testify to nonaccess).

9. As held in Hall v. State, 176 Md. 488, 5 A.2d 916, syl. 4, 5 (1939); Comm. v. Gantz, 128 Pa.Super. 97, 193 Atl. 72, syl. 2 (1937).

10. As in Grates v. Garcia, 20 N.M. 158, 148 Pac. 493, syl. 1 (1915); U. S. Fid. & Guaranty Co. v. Henderson, 53 S.W.2d 811, syl. 2, 3 (Tex.Civ.App. 1932).

11. The reasoning, if not the holding, in Sayles v. Sayles, 323 Mass. 66, 80 N.E.2d 21 (1948) supports the view that a suit for divorce for adultery is not within the rule. Monahan v. Monahan, 142 Me. 72, 46 A.2d 706, syl. 9 (1946) seems a square holding to that effect.

12. As in Harward v. Harward, 173 Md. 339, 196 Atl. 318, syl. 7 (1938).

13. As held in Sayles v. Sayles, 323 Mass. 66, 80 N.E.2d 21, syl. 1, 2, 6, 7 (1948).

14. As in Zakrzewski v. Zakrzewski, 237 Mich. 459, 212 N.W. 80, syl. 2 (1927) (wife's admission that child not her husband's excluded under the rule); Schmidt v. State, 110 Neb. 504, 194 N.W. 679, 681 (1923) (wife's declarations); West v. Redmond, 171 N.C. 742, 88 S.E. 341, syl. 3 (1916).

68. Judges [1] and Jurors.[2]

A judicial officer called in a case in which he is not sitting as a judge is of course not disqualified by his office from testifying.[3] But when a judge in a trial before him is called as a witness, the role is manifestly inconsistent with the attitude of impartiality which he is sworn to maintain.[4] Nevertheless, under the older view he was in general regarded as a competent witness,[5] though he might have a discretion to decline to testify,[6] and this view is preserved in some state statutes.[7] A second view is that the judge is disqualified from testifying to material, disputed facts, but may testify to matters merely formal and undisputed.[8] This is not an easy line to draw, and formal matters nearly always can be proved by other witnesses. Accordingly the third view, for which support is growing, that a judge is incompetent to testify in a case which he is trying,[9] seems the most expedient one.

Some of the same danger to the impartial position of the tribunal from the judge's taking the stand is present when a juror sitting in the case is called as a witness, and it may well be that he should be held incompetent.[10] But the traditional common law and present-

---

1. 6 Wigmore, Evidence, § 1909; 70 C.J., Witnesses, § 237; 58 Am.Jur., Witnesses, § 150; Dec.Dig., Witnesses, ⊕68–70; Note, Judge as a Witness in a Cause on Trial before Him, 157 A.L.R. 315.

2. 6 Wigmore, Evidence, § 1910; 8 id., §§ 2345–2356; 70 C.J., Witnesses, § 242, 66 C.J.S., New Trial, § 169; 58 Am.Jur., Witnesses, § 151; Dec.Dig., Witnesses, ⊕73, New Trial, ⊕141–143.

3. Thus, it is not uncommon for judges to testify about matters occurring in former trials in which they presided. See, e. g., Woodward v. City of Waterbury, 113 Conn. 457, 155 Atl. 825, syl. 15 (1931); State v. Hindman, 159 Ind. 586, 65 N.E. 911, syl. 6 (1903).

4. "The two characters are inconsistent with each other and their being united in one person is incompatible with the fair and safe administration of justice." Parker, J., in Morss v. Morss, 11 Barb. (N.Y.) 510, 511 (1851).

5. See examples in the English practice in the 1600s and 1700s, described in 6 Wigmore, Evidence, § 1909, note 1.

6. See O'Neill & Hearne v. Bray's Adm'x, 262 Ky. 377, 90 S.W.2d 353, syl. 11 (1936); O'Neal v. State, 106 Tex.Cr. 158, 291 S.W. 892, syl. 4, 5 (1927).

7. See, e. g., La.Rev.L.1897, § 3192 (judge not incompetent for "being a material witness in the case in favor of either party") and similar statutes in Tennessee and Texas described in 6 Wigmore, Evidence, § 1909, note 5. The most wide-spread form of statute is that embodied in Calif.Code Civ.Proc., § 1883 ("The judge himself, or any juror, may be called as a witness by either party; but in such case it is in the discretion of the Court or judge to order the trial to be postponed or suspended, and to take place before another judge or jury"). Similar provisions are found in Idaho, Iowa, Kentucky, Montana, Nebraska, North Dakota, Oregon, and Utah. Wigmore, loc. cit.

8. See, e. g., Wingate v. March, 117 Fla. 104, 157 So. 421, syl. 1 (1934) (testimony as to formal matter did not constitute the judge a "material" witness under disqualifying statute). This view seems to be advocated by Wigmore. See Evidence, § 1909, p. 592. A similar line is drawn in Model Code of Evidence, R. 302 ("If the judge testifies concerning a disputed material matter, he shall not continue as a judge in the action against . . . objection. . ."). Compare 28 U.S.C.A. § 455, as amended June 25, 1948 ("Any justice or judge of the United States shall disqualify himself in any case in which . . . he is or has been a material witness. . . .").

9. See the general statements of the rule of disqualification, or of the impropriety of testimony by the judge, in State v. Sandquist, 146 Minn. 322, 178 N. W. 883, 885 (1920); Brashier v. State, 197 Miss. 237, 20 So.2d 65, 157 A.L.R. 311, 313 (1944); Maitland v. Zanga, 14 Wash. 92, 44 Pac. 117 (1896). See Report of a Special Committee on the Propriety of Judges Appearing as Witnesses, 36 A.B.A.J. 630, 633 (1950) ("The modern rule is that a judge is not a competent witness in a case in which he is presiding, unless there is a statute permitting it."). See also Uniform Rules of Evidence, Rule 41: "Against the objection of a party, the judge presiding at the trial may not testify in that trial as a witness."

Nevertheless, even though the judge may be incompetent, his testimony, if not harmful, may not be ground of reversal. See, e. g., McCaffrey v. State, 105 Oh.St. 508, 138 N.E. 61, 63 (1922), and cases cited in Note, 157 A.L.R. 315, 319, 320.

10. This view is embodied in Uniform Rules of Evidence, R. 42, as follows: "A member of a jury sworn and empanelled in the trial of an action, may not testify in that trial as a witness."

day practice holds him competent generally to testify.[11] There is one limitation upon this competency, namely, the doctrine that a juror is incompetent to testify in impeachment of his verdict.[12] In that form the doctrine has been much criticized, but retains wide currency in the decisions.[13] Though arbitrary in its limits, in that it disqualifies jurors but not officers and eavesdroppers who may gain knowledge of misconduct,[14] it does serve to protect in some measure the finality of verdicts, and it is this policy that has doubtless led to its survival. Other courts would abandon the rule of disqualification, and would permit jurors to testify to misconduct and irregularities which are ground for new trial.[15] For protection of finality they would trust to a doctrine which excludes, as immaterial, evidence as to the expressions and arguments of the jurors in their deliberations and evidence as to their own motives, beliefs, mistakes and mental operations generally, in arriving at their verdict.[16] To be distinguished from these rules

---

11. Statutes frequently so provide. See e. g., State v. Cavanaugh, 98 Iowa 688, 68 N.W. 452, syl. 3 (1896) (juror may testify, under I.C.A. § 780.17). They are collected in 6 Wigmore, Evidence, § 1910.

12. Like the rule forbidding parents to bastardize their issue, see § 67, supra, this dogma was an innovation introduced by Lord Mansfield. The parent case was Vaise v. Delaval, 1 T.R. 11, 99 Eng.Rep. 944, (K.B. 1785). There affidavits of jurymen that their verdict was based on chance was rejected and Lord Mansfield said: "The Court cannot receive such an affidavit from any of the jurymen themselves, in all of whom such conduct is a very high misdemeanor; but in every such case the Court must derive their knowledge from some other source, such as some person having seen the transaction through a window or by some such other means". The weaknesses of this position are pointed out in 8 Wigmore, Evidence, §§ 2352, 2353.

13. See, e. g., McDonald v. Pless, 238 U.S. 264, 35 S. Ct. 783, syl. 2, 59 L.Ed. 1300 (1915) (affidavits as to quotient verdict excluded); Hoffman v. City of St. Paul, 187 Minn. 320, 245 N.W. 373, syl. 7 (1932) (same) and cases collected in 8 Wigmore, Evidence, § 2354 and in Dec.Dig., New Trial, ⟨key⟩142, 143.

Some courts which follow the dogma of the juror's incompetency to impeach his verdict limit the disqualification to testimony about matters occurring within the jury room, and allow the juror to testify to irregularities occurring outside. Pierce v. Brennan, 83 Minn. 422, 86 N.W. 417, syl. 1 (1901) (jurors' affidavits as to their privately viewing the scene); and see Welshire v. Bruaw, 331 Pa. 392, 200 Atl. 67, syl. 1–3 (1938) (while jurors cannot testify to misconduct among themselves in jury room, can testify as to misconduct there of outsiders—here a drunken tipstaff puts pressure on them for a verdict by remarks in jury room). The disqualification to "impeach" the verdict does not preclude the juror from testifying in support of the verdict, when it is attacked by testimony of outsiders. Morakes v. State, 201 Ga. 425, 40 S.E.2d 120, 127, syl. 11 (1946);

Iverson v. Prudential Ins. Co., 126 N.J.L. 280, 19 A.2d 214, syl. 14 (Ct.E. & A. 1941).

The various problems are acutely analyzed and the lines of decision indicated in Morgan and Maguire, Cases on Evidence 333–336 (3d ed. 1951); see also valuable notes, 47 Col.L.Rev. 1373 (1947), 10 Oh.St.L. J. 262 (1949).

14. Reich v. Thompson, 346 Mo. 577, 142 S.W.2d 486, 129 A.L.R. 795, 802, 803 (1940), annotated on this point. In the cited case testimony of the clerk, who overheard from adjoining room statements made in the jury room, was held admissible.

15. Some leading opinions favoring this view: Whyte, J., in Crawford v. State, 2 Yerg. (Tenn.) 60, 67 (1821); Cole, J., in Wright v. Telegraph Co., 20 Iowa 195, 210 (1866); Brewer, J., in Perry v. Bailey, 12 Kan. 539, 544. For later decisions and statutes in the various jurisdictions, see 8 Wigmore, Evidence, § 2354, note 2. It is matter of doubt whether the federal courts have abandoned the disqualification, see the discussion by L. Hand, J., in Jorgenson v. York Ice Machinery Corp., 160 F.2d 432, 435 (C.C.A.2d 1947). In Texas, misconduct of the jury may be proven in civil cases by testimony of a juror and in criminal cases by his "voluntary affidavit." Rules of Civil Procedure, Rule 327 (Franki, 1948); Vernon's Ann.C.C.P., art. 753. Many states copy Calif.Code Civ.Proc., § 657, permitting the affidavits of jurors to prove that the verdict was determined by chance. Seemingly, this curious provision was a legislative overruling of Vaise v. Delaval, note 12, supra, but limited to the particular form of misconduct there involved.

16. See, e. g., Davis v. United States, 47 F.2d 1071, syl. 1, 2 (C.C.A.5, 1931) (testimony of some jurors that defendant's failure to take stand was discussed as indicating guilt and that this was given weight, excluded); Caldwell v. E. F. Spears & Sons, 186 Ky. 64, 216 S.W. 83, syl. 5 (1919) (that jury misunderstood instructions); Collings v. Northwestern Hospital, 202 Minn. 139, 277 N.W. 910, syl. 3 (1938) (same as last); State v. Best, 111 N.C. 638, 15 S.E.

of incompetency and exclusion, is the doctrine which has the support of Wigmore [17] and of some judicial expressions,[18] to the effect that each juror has a privilege against the disclosure in court of his communications to the other jurors during their retirement.

69. First-Hand Knowledge and Expertness.

Two other rules, already considered, may be brought into view again to round out the picture. These are the requirement that a witness testifying to objective facts must have had means of knowing them from observation,[1] and the rule that one who would testify to his inference or opinion in matters requiring special training or experience to understand, must be qualified as an expert in the field.[2] It will be noted that unlike most of the other rules of competency, which go to the capacity of the witness to speak at all, these last are directed to his capacity to speak to a particular matter.

70. The Procedure of Disqualification.[1]

Under the earlier common-law practice, the witness was not sworn until he was placed upon the stand to begin his testimony. Before the oath was administered the adversary had an opportunity to object to his competency and the judge or counsel would then examine the witness touching upon his qualifications, before he was sworn as a witness. This was known as a voir dire examination. The matter is now handled more informally. Ordinarily, all the witnesses in attendance at the beginning of the trial are administered the oath in mass. But the practice still requires that when the witness is first called to the stand to testify, the opponent must then challenge his competency, if grounds of challenge are then known to him.[2] If not then known, and the cause for disqualification is disclosed in the testimony the challenge may

---

930, syl. 2 (1892) (affidavit of five jurors that they assented to verdict of guilty on belief that recommendation to mercy would save accused from death penalty). Such matters are said to "inhere in the verdict." Schindler v. Mulhair, 132 Neb. 809, 273 N.W. 217, syl. 4 (1937). Decisions are collected in 8 Wigmore, Evidence, § 2349; Dec.Dig., New Trial, ⬉143(4, 5).

While such expressions and mental operations are thus no ground of attack upon the verdict, it seems that when an allowable attack is made for misconduct, such as an unauthorized view, evidence of the jurors as to whether the misconduct actually influenced their finding (and this evidence would usually support the verdict) should be received. Caldwell v. Yeatman, 91 N.H. 150, 15 A.2d 252, syl. 1 (1940) (semble). But Wigmore and some decisions are to the contrary. Evidence, § 2349(2); and see, e. g., People v. Stokes, 103 Cal. 193, 37 Pac. 207, 209 (dictum) (1894); City of Houston v. Quinones, 142 Tex. 282, 177 S.W.2d 259, syl. 14 (1944). But as to the influence on the jurors of erroneous instructions, improper arguments of counsel, etc., as distinguished from misconduct of the jurors, the considerations may well be different and the test may be, not were the jurors influenced, but was the instruction or the argument calculated to mislead. See e. g., People v. Duzan, 272 Ill. 478, 112 N.E. 315, syl. 8 (1916) (error in refusing instruction, jurors' evidence that they did not notice that instruction was marked refused, rejected).

17. 8 Evidence, § 2346.

18. In Clark v. United States, 289 U.S. 1, 12-14, 53 S. Ct. 465, 468, 469, 77 L.Ed. 993 (1933), on appeal from a conviction of a juror for contempt in giving false answers, Cardozo, J., for the court said: "The books suggest a doctrine that the arguments and votes of jurors, the media concludendi, are secrets, protected from disclosure unless the privilege is waived. . . . Freedom of debate might be stifled and independence of thought checked if jurors were made to feel that their arguments and ballots were to be freely published to the world. The force of these considerations is not to be gainsaid. . . . Assuming that there is a privilege which protects from impertinent exposure the arguments and ballots of a juror while considering his verdict, we think the privilege does not apply where the relation giving birth to it has been fraudulently begun or fraudulently continued." The privilege was held inapplicable because of such fraudulent conduct.

1. See § 10, herein.

2. See § 13, herein.

1. 2 Wigmore, Evidence, §§ 483–487; Dec.Dig., Witnesses, ⬉76–79, 121–124, 180–183.

2. People v. Stewart, 107 Cal.App., Supp. 757, 286 Pac. 57, syl. 9 (1930); Texas Employers' Ins. Ass'n v. Eubanks, 240 S.W.2d 811, syl. 6, 7 (Tex.Civ.App. 1951); 2 Wigmore, Evidence, § 586.

then be made.[3] If the challenge goes to incompetency generally, as for mental incapacity, the burden rests on the objector to show by examination of the challenged witness, or by other evidence, that the disqualification exists.[4] With respect to knowledge or expertness, the offering party must first prove, usually by questioning the witness himself, that he is qualified.

If the question of fact is disputed or doubtful on the evidence, the trial judge sitting with a jury does not submit this question of fact to the jury. As with all similar issues of fact arising in the determination of the admissibility of evidence[5] the judge himself decides the preliminary issue and sustains or rejects accordingly the challenge to the witness or the objection to evidence.[6]

71. Probable Future of the Rules of Competency.

The rules which disqualify witnesses who have knowledge of relevant facts and mental capacity to convey that knowledge are serious obstructions to the ascertainment of truth. For a century the course of legal evolution has been in the direction of sweeping away these obstructions. Rule 101 of the Model Code of Evidence seems to represent the goal toward which legislators and rulemakers should press. It provides: "Every person is qualified to be a witness as to any material matter unless the judge finds that (a) the proposed witness is incapable of expressing himself concerning the matter so as to be understood by the judge and jury either directly or through interpretation by one who can understand him, or (b) the proposed witness is incapable of understanding the duty of a witness to tell the truth."

3. Nunn v. Slemmons' Adm'r, 298 Ky. 315, 182 S.W. 2d 888, syl. 2 (1944).

4. State v. Barker, 294 Mo. 303, 242 S.W. 405, syl. 4 (1922); Batterton v. State, 52 Tex.Cr. 381, 107 S.W. 826, syl. 1 (1908); 2 Wigmore, Evidence, §§ 484, 497.

5. See § 53, herein.

6. De Silvey v. State, 245 Ala. 163, 16 So.2d 183, syl. 8 (1944); State v. Teager, 222 Iowa 391, 269 N.W. 348, syl. 14 (1936); 2 Wigmore, Evidence, § 487; Dec.Dig., Witnesses, ⊛79(1).

TITLE 5

PRIVILEGE

CHAPTER 8

THE SCOPE AND EFFECT OF EVIDENTIARY PRIVILEGES

72. Distinction between Rules of Privilege and Rules of Incompetency—[1](a) Difference in Purpose.

In our offhand thinking about evidential privileges as distinguished from rules of exclusion, we are apt to assume that the difference is that a privilege may be claimed or waived at some one's election, whereas a rule of exclusion operates automatically to keep evidence out. A moment's reflection will cause us to abandon this view. We would recall that the rule of exclusion, no less than

the privilege, will also be waived ordinarily, if it is not promptly claimed,[2] and only in rare instances will the trial judge of his own motion interpose to enforce the rule.

If we call to mind the subjects of the two groups of rules, the underlying distinction becomes apparent. Among the rules of exclusion the most prominent are the hearsay rule, the opinion rule, the rule rejecting proof of bad character as evidence of crime, and the rule excluding secondary evidence until the original document is shown to be unavail-

1. As to the basis of privileges see 8 Wigmore, Evidence, §§ 2192, 2197, and 2285 and the opinion by Learned Hand, Circuit Judge, in McMann v. Securities and Exchange Commission, 87 F.2d 377, 378 (1937), in which he says in denying the claim of a customer to a privilege against disclosure of his broker's records relating to his trading account: "The suppression of truth is a grievous necessity at best, more especially when as here the inquiry concerns the public interest; it can be justified at all only when the opposed private interest is supreme." See also Donnelly, The Law of Evidence: Privacy and Disclosure, 14 La.L.Rev. 361 (1954); Barnhart,

Theory of Testimonial Competency and Privilege, 4 Ark.L.Rev. 377 (1950); Note, Privileged Communications—Some Recent Developments, 5 Vand.L.Rev. 590 (1952).

As to availability of the common law privileges in administrative hearings, see Davis, Administrative Law, 144 (1951); Note, 133 A.L.R. 732.

2. Diaz v. United States, 223 U.S. 442, 32 S.Ct. 250 (1911) (hearsay); Hill v. Baylor, 23 Tex. 261 (1859) (objections to evidence not taken at trial cannot be urged on appeal); 1 Wigmore, Evidence, § 18, n. 1, and see §§ 52, 55, herein.

able. On the other hand the privileges which come most familiarly to mind are the one which protects a witness against self-crimination, and those which give their shield to confidential communications between husband and wife, attorney and client, and in some jurisdictions to those between priest and penitent, and physician and patient.

Manifestly the first group have as their common purpose to facilitate the ascertainment of the facts by guarding against evidence which is unreliable or is calculated to prejudice or mislead. Equally obviously, the second group of rules is devised for no such end. They do not in any wise aid the ascertainment of truth, but rather they shut out the light. Their sole warrant is the protection of interests and relationships which, rightly or wrongly, are regarded as of sufficient social importance to justify some incidental sacrifice of sources of facts needed in the administration of justice.[3]

We may doubt today whether these aims and interests, the encouragement of full and free disclosure between the husband and the wife, and by the client to the attorney, by the penitent to the confessor, and by the patient to the doctor, and the liberty of silence about one's misdeeds, really need this sort of protection bought at such a price. There can be little doubt, however, that the rules extending such protection stand apart from the rules which segregate and exclude classes of evidence as unreliable or prejudicial.

73. Distinction between Rules of Privilege and Rules of Incompetency—(b) Who May Assert?[1]

This difference in origin of the two groups of rules manifests itself in another line of cleavage, which may be of value in aiding to classify a rule in the one group or the other. The rule of exclusion or preference, being designed to make the trial more efficient as a vehicle of fact-disclosure, may be invoked, as of right, only by the person whose interest in having the verdict follow the facts is at stake in the trial. Thus, when evidence condemned by one of these rules is offered, only the adverse party may object, unless the judge elects to interpose. But by contrast, if the evidence is privileged, the right to object does not attach to the opposing party as such, but to the person vested with the outside interest or relationship fostered by the particular privilege.[2] True, other persons present at the trial, including the adverse party,[3] may call to the court's attention the existence of the privilege, or the judge may choose to intervene of his own accord to protect it, but this is regarded as having been done on behalf of the owner of the privilege.[4]

The right to complain on appeal is a more crucial test. If the court erroneously recognizes an asserted privilege and excludes proffered testimony on this ground, of course the adverse party has been injured in his capacity as litigant and may complain on appeal. But if a claim of privilege is wrongly denied,

---

3. The same discrimination may be made between privileges of witnesses not to testify, such as the privilege of the wife not to testify against the husband, or the privilege of the accused not to be called as a witness, and the rules declaring witnesses incompetent, as for mental incapacity, or as being an interested survivor in litigation with an estate of a decedent. The present discussion, however, is chiefly confined to privileges attaching to evidence by reason of its subject-matter.

1. See Redwine, Article, 34 Ky.L.J. 213 (1946); Note, 20 U.Cin.L.Rev. 76 (1951); Note, Privilege—Who May Invoke? 2 A.L.R.2d 645; 58 Am.Jur., Witnesses, § 368; Dec.Dig., Witnesses, ☞217.

2. State v. Knight, 204 Iowa 819, 216 N.W. 104 (1927) (self-disgracing testimony); Ingersoll v. McWillie, 87 Tex. 647, 30 S.W. 869 (1895) (self-crimination); 8 Wigmore, Evidence, § 2196. See also San Francisco v. Superior Court, 37 Cal.2d 227, 231 P.2d 26, syl. 6, 25 A.L.R.2d 1418 (1951) (only patient, not physician, may claim).

3. Dalton v. People, 68 Colo. 44, 189 Pac. 37 (1920) (wife's privilege asserted by prosecution); O'Brien v. New England Mutual Life Ins. Co., 109 Kan. 138, 197 Pac. 1100 (1921) (absent client's privilege asserted, apparently by lawyer-witness or by adverse party); Comment (1930) 30 Col.L.Rev. 686, 690.

4. Ex parte Lipscomb, 111 Tex. 409, 415, 239 S.W. 1101 (1922) (attorney-client privilege).

and the privileged testimony erroneously let in, the distinction which we have suggested between privilege and rule of exclusion would seem to be material. If the adverse party to the suit is likewise the owner of the privilege, then, while it may be argued that the party's interest *as a litigant* has not been infringed,[5] most courts decline to draw so sharp a line, and permit him to complain of the error.[6]

Where, however, the owner of the privilege is not a party to the suit, it is somewhat difficult to see why this invasion of a third person's interest should be ground of complaint for the objecting party, whose only grievance can be that the overriding of the outsider's rights has resulted in a fuller fact-disclosure than the party desires. In view of the usual willingness of trial courts of their own motion to safeguard the privileges, it can hardly be necessary to afford this extreme sanction to prevent a breakdown in their protection.[7] In at least two classes of privileges, the privileges against self-crimination[8] and against the use of evidence secured by unlawful search or seizure,[9] this distinction has been clearly perceived and the party is quite consistently denied any ground for reversal. The results in cases of erroneous denials of other privileges are more checkered, but a considerable number of the older cases seem to allow the party to take advantage of the error on appeal.[10] Uniform Rule 43 is clearcut. It provides: "A party may predicate error on a ruling disallowing a claim of privilege only if he is the holder of the privilege."

74. Rules Which Should be Classed as Rules of Privilege—(a) Evidence Illegally Obtained.[1]

Building upon this premise that an exclusionary rule is one which safeguards against unreliable evidence and may be invoked as of right only by a party to the suit, and that a rule of privilege is one which may not be invoked by a party as such, but only by one

---

5. 8 Wigmore, Evidence, § 2196.

6. People v. Werner, 225 Mich. 18, 195 N.W. 697 (1923) (privilege not to have husband testify); Garrett v. State, 118 Neb. 373, 224 N.W. 860 (1929) (same); People v. Brown, 72 N.Y. 571, 28 Am.Rep. 183 (1878) (self-disgracing testimony); Ex parte Lipscomb, 111 Tex. 409, 239 S.W. 1101 (1922) (where attorney refuses to testify as to communications with client, in a suit to which the client is a party, the attorney when committed for contempt cannot test by habeas corpus the propriety of the denial of the privilege; appeal by the client is the proper remedy); Comment (1930) 30 Col.L.Rev. 686, 693, n. 41, citing additional cases.

7. But see the vigorous expression of an opposing view by the dissenting judges in State v. Snook, 94 N.J.Law 271, 109 Atl. 289, 290 (1920).

8. Regina v. Kinglake, 11 Cox Cr.Cas. 499 (1870); State v. Cassady, 67 Ariz. 48, 190 P.2d 501, 509, syl. 14 (1948); Beauvoir Club v. State, 148 Ala. 643, 42 So. 1040, 121 Am.St.Rep. 82 (1907); Samuel v. People, 164 Ill. 379, 45 N.E. 728 (1896); State v. Crisinger, 197 Iowa 613, 195 N.W. 998 (1923); State v. Hanley, 249 Wis. 399, 24 N.W.2d 683, syl. 3 (1946); Comment (1930) 30 Col.L.Rev. 686, 694, n. 43. Contra: Chesapeake Club v. State, 63 Md. 446 (1895).

9. See cases cited infra note 4, § 74.

10. Many of the cases are explainable by the fact that the question of the party's capacity to raise the point was not noticed, e. g., Bell v. State, 88 Tex. Crim.Rep. 64, 224 S.W. 1108 (1920) (marital communications; witness' privilege denied; defendant allowed to assign as ground of error on appeal). In other cases the court assumes that the evidence usually classified as privileged is "unlawful" or incompetent, e. g., State v. Jolly, 20 N.C. 108, 32 Am.Dec. 656 (1838) (privilege against disclosure of facts learned by spouse confidentially). A few opinions in cases permitting the party to complain place it expressly on ground of public policy. State v. Barrows, 52 Conn. 323 (1884) (client's privilege); Bacon v. Frisbie, 80 N.Y. 394, 36 Am.Rep. 627 (1880) (client's privilege). The more recent cases where the point is considered seem to be coming around, under the influence of the Wigmore treatise (§ 2196) to the contrary holding. Martin v. State, 203 Miss. 187, 33 So.2d 825, 2 A.L.R.2d 640 (1948) (marital communications); Luick v. Arends, 21 N.D. 614, 132 N.W. 353, 362 (1911) (marital communications); Coles v. Harsch, 129 Ore. 11, 276 Pac. 248, 255 (1929) (marital communications); State v. Snook, 93 N.J.Law 29, 107 Atl. 62 (Sup.Ct.1919), *aff'd by equally divided court*, 94 N.J.Law 271, 109 Atl. 289 (1920) (client's privilege). The cases pro and con are collected in Comment (1930) 30 Col.L.Rev. 686, 694, n. 44; Note, 2 A.L.R.2d 645.

1. See Ch. 14, herein.

who claims an interest other than a stake in the outcome of the trial, we may be led to classify some rules as rules of privilege which have not always been recognized as such. Thus, the objection to evidence obtained as the fruit of a search or seizure made in violation of constitutional immunities has apparently usually been thought of as invoking a rule of exclusion.[2] Manifestly, however, the rule allowing the objection is not designed to protect the parties against unreliable evidence. Quite the contrary. The constitution-makers looked back to the protection of the person, the home, and the owner's effects, against unreasonable official interference. If the court rejects the evidence, it is not because it would shed a false light on the issues, but only because its exclusion may serve to discourage future unlawful seizures and raids. The objection, then, seems properly classed as a claim of privilege.[3] If this conclusion is sound, the losing party as such would not be entitled to complain on appeal of an erroneous refusal to exclude the evidence. Such is the actual practice of the courts. If a party is on trial, and weapons, contraband liquor, incriminating books and documents, or the like, are admitted as evidence against him, despite the fact that they had been seized by officers without warrant or reasonable cause, he has no ground of complaint on appeal, unless it appears that the premises invaded were owned or occupied by him or the articles seized belonged to him or were in his custody.[4] Invasion of a third person's interests will not suffice.

75. Rules Which Should be Classed as Rules of Privilege—(b) Do the Rules about Confessions Fall in This Class? [1]

Less clear is the case of confessions. In some features the cluster of doctrines relating to confessions bears the aspect of a regulation which safeguards the discovery of

---

2. It is classed in Wigmore among the rules of extrinsic policy, but as a rule of absolute exclusion rather than as a privilege. See 8 Wigmore, Evidence, § 2175.

3. See the interesting case of McMann v. Securities and Exchange Commission, 87 F.2d 377 (C.C.A.2d, 1937), cert. denied 301 U.S. 684, 57 S.Ct. 785 (1937), opinion by L. Hand, Circ. J., in which is discussed the basis of evidential privileges, and the conclusion reached that there is no privilege for communications between client and stockbroker. The suit was by the client to enjoin the broker from disclosing information to the Commission, in response to a subpoena issued by it, regarding the client's account. The court said, further, that if the subpoena had been so sweeping as to constitute an unreasonable search, the immunity would have been personal to the brokers and probably would not extend to the client.

4. Lagow v. United States, 159 F.2d 245, syl. 2, 3 (C.C.A.2d 1946) (sole stockholder cannot complain of evidence secured by wrongful seizure of corporation's documents); Connolly v. Medalie, 58 F.2d 629, syl. 1, 2 (C.C.A.2d 1932) (opinion by L. Hand, Circ. J.); Remus v. United States, 291 Fed. 501, 511 (C.C.A.6th, 1923), cert. denied 263 U.S. 717, 44 S.Ct. 180 (1924); Walker v. State, 194 Ind. 402, 142 N.E. 16 (1924); Craft v. State, 107 Tex.Crim.Rep. 130, 295 S.W. 617 (1927); Thomason v. State, 128 Tex.Crim. Rep. 490, 81 S.W.2d 704 (1935), and see Dec.Dig., Criminal Law, ⊂⇒393, 691.

United States v. Jeffers, 342 U.S. 48, 72 S.Ct. 93, 96 L.Ed. 59 (1951) has cast a cloud on this doctrine but may not have been so intended. There the accused secreted bottles of narcotics in a box on a shelf in the hotel room rented by his aunts. He had permission to use the room, but was not an occupant. Officers entered without a warrant in the absence of the occupants and seized the narcotics. Held, though 21 U.S.C.A. § 174 denies "ownership" in contraband narcotics, yet "it being his property for purposes of the exclusionary rule, he was entitled on motion to have it suppressed as evidence on his trial."

The privilege extends to one who occupies and controls a room, wrongfully invaded, on premises owned by another, Davis v. State, 144 Miss. 551, 110 So. 447 (1926), to the owner's wife having joint possession with him, Brewer v. State, 142 Miss. 100, 107 So. 376 (1926), and to one whose papers are unlawfully seized on the premises of another, Pielow v. United States, 8 F.2d 492 (C.C.A.9th, 1925). A recent case denied protection to one whose baggage was wrongfully opened by an officer, and held that he could not object to the introduction in evidence of papers seized therefrom, on the ground that the papers belonged to another. Lewis v. United States, 92 F.2d 952 (C.C.A.10th, 1937). The result seems questionable.

1. See ch. 12, herein, for a fuller discussion of the confession rules.

truth by keeping away from the jury a kind of evidence because of its special untrustworthiness. Wigmore strongly champions this view as regards the rule regulating admissibility [2] and substitutes for the usual statement that a confession procured by force, fear, or promise of benefit is excluded, the general principle that they are rejected wherever procured by any influence calculated to induce a false confession. [3]

Other rules, obtaining in most states, demand confirmation of the guilt confessed. Thus some courts make a general requirement that the confession, to sustain a conviction, be corroborated; [4] others, specifically, that the state furnish independent proof of the *corpus delicti*. [5] These requirements point again to the desire to protect the interest of safeguarding the search for truth.

Nevertheless, there is an insistent recurrence in the decisions on confessions of language which savors of privilege. Thus most courts, as a shorthand expression, customarily say that the confession, to be admitted, must have been "voluntary." [6] Wigmore,

perceiving the inaptness of this term to voice a principle of trustworthiness, condemns it, [7] but eminent judges have continued to use it. [8] It well may be that the adherence of the courts to this form of statement of the confession-rule in terms of "voluntariness" is prompted not only by a liking for its convenient brevity, but also by a recognition that there is an interest here to be protected closely akin to the interest of a witness or of an accused person which is protected by the privilege against compulsory self-crimination.

It may be conceded that in time of origin the confession-rule and the self-crimination rule were widely separated, [9] and certainly Chief Justice White's language in Bram v. United States [10] to the effect that the fifth amendment guaranteeing the privilege "was but a crystallization of the doctrine as to confessions" is an historical blunder. Nevertheless, the kinship of the two rules is too apparent for denial. It is significant that the shadow of the rack and the thumbscrew was part of the background from which each rule emerged. [11] Today this same black shadow,

---

2. 3 Wigmore, Evidence, § 822. See also the opinion of Lattimore, J., in Parker v. State, 91 Tex.Crim. Rep. 68, 238 S.W. 943, 948 (1922), on rehearing.

3. 3 Wigmore, Evidence, § 824.

4. Daeche v. United States, 250 Fed. 566 (C.C.A.2d, 1918); and see People v. Lytton, 257 N.Y. 310, 178 N.E. 290 (1931); (1932) 45 Harv.L.Rev. 587; (1932) 32 Col.L.Rev. 378; 7 Wigmore, Evidence, §§ 2070, 2071, and see § 110, herein.

5. See McGregor v. State, 121 Tex.Crim.Rep. 419, 49 S.W.2d 818 (1932); Mills v. State, 123 Tex.Crim. Rep. 395, 59 S.W.2d 147 (1933); 7 Wigmore, Evidence, § 2071, n. 4, and see § 110, herein.

6. Wilson v. United States, 162 U.S. 613, 623, 16 S. Ct. 895, 899 (1896); 3 Wigmore, Evidence, § 896.

7. 3 Wigmore, Evidence, § 843.

8. For example, Brandeis, J., in Ziang Sung Wan v. United States, 266 U.S. 1, 14, 45 S.Ct. 1, 3 (1924), a murder case, where the judgment was reversed because based on a confession elicited after prolonged examination of accused, while suffering with severe spastic colitis. The court said: "The court of appeals appears to have held the prisoner's statements

admissible on the ground that a confession made by one competent to act is to be deemed voluntary, as a matter of law, if it was not induced by a promise or a threat; and that here there was evidence sufficient to justify a finding of fact that these statements were not so induced. In the federal courts, the requisite of voluntariness is not satisfied by establishing merely that the confession was not induced by a promise or a threat. A confession is voluntary in law if, and only if, it was, in fact, voluntarily made." See also State v. Perry, 212 N. C. 533, 193 S.E. 727 (1937); Matura v. State, 132 Tex.Crim.Rep. 106, 103 S.W.2d 152 (1937).

9. The privilege against self-crimination gained recognition in the Commonwealth period, in the middle of the seventeenth century. 9 Holdsworth, History of English Law (1926) 199; 4 Wigmore, Evidence, § 2250. The first clear enunciation of the confessions-rule was over a hundred years later, in Warickshall's Case, 1 Leach C.C. 135 (1783); 3 Wigmore, Evidence, § 819.

10. 168 U.S. 532, 542, 18 S.Ct. 183, 186 (1897).

11. Torture as a mode of compelling an accused to confess appears not to have been sanctioned by the

changed only in reflecting subtler and more secret methods of torture, falls upon the pages of the opinions of judges relating to confessions.[12] The unlicensed barbarity of the practice, which is almost a routine in some parts of the country, of torturing prisoners to extort confessions,[13] is in some aspects more dangerous than the medieval judicial torture, which was carefully regulated by law and administered only upon the order of a responsible authority.[14]

Certainly the right to be immune in one's person from the secret violence of the police seems to be even more deserving of judicial protection than the constitutional immunity from searches and seizures. The courts and the legislatures have increasingly come to believe that a privilege to have the fruits of such a search or seizure suppressed as evidence, is needed as a discourager of the practice.[15] The reason for extending to the person from whom a confession has been wrung

by torture, a similar privilege, whether the confession be true or false, is even stronger.[16] Such policy as modern writers are able to discover as a basis for the self-crimination privilege—and it is feeble and inadequate at best—pales to a flicker beside the flaming demands of justice and humanity for protection against extorted confessions.

It may be objected, however, that the actual practice excludes not only confessions extorted by force or fear, but those induced by promise of leniency, and that for these last no outside interest which should be protected by privilege could be claimed. This is quite true, and the exclusion of confessions of this kind must rest on untrustworthiness, not on privilege. Still, the cases where force or fear are claimed today are legion, and the evil they point to furnishes the main justification of the confessions-rules, whereas the danger that confessions induced by promises of leni-

---

traditional common law before the 16th century. Then it was borrowed as part of the French inquisitional criminal procedure, imitated in England under the Tudors and Stuarts. It was finally condemned as unlawful by resolution of the judges in Felton's case, Lit. 237 (1628). The disappearance of torture and the recognition of the privilege were victories in the same political struggle. 5 Holdsworth, op. cit. supra note 22, 184–187 (1924); Lowell, The Judicial Use of Torture (1897) 11 Harv.L.Rev. 220, 290, 292–295. The term "confession" was first most commonly applied to pleas of guilty in open court. Sixteenth century treason statutes anticipated the phrasing of the modern confession-rule in requiring two witnesses for conviction of treason unless the party "shall *willingly without violence* confess the same." 1 Edw. VI, c. 12, § 22 (1547); 5 & 6 Edw. VI, c. 11, § 8 (1554). Confessions extorted by the rack were admitted without scruple in the 1600s and the confessions-rule does not find expression until a century later. 3 Wigmore, Evidence, § 818. But it can hardly be doubted that a memory of the old abuses of torture and a desire to protect against them were present in the minds of the judges who shaped the rule excluding involuntary confessions. See Hinton's Cases on Evidence (2d ed. 1931) 405, n. 2.

12. State v. Garrison, 59 Ore. 440, 444, 117 Pac. 657, 658 (1911)—"To go further . . . is to put a premium on the unscrupulous methods of overzeal-

ous detectives, and to take a step backward towards the thumbscrew and the rack as a means of procuring testimony"; Brown v. State, 173 Miss. 542, 574, 161 So. 465, 470 (1935)—"Further details of the brutal treatment to which these helpless prisoners were subjected need not be pursued. It is sufficient to say that in pertinent respects the transcript reads more like pages torn from some medieval account than a record made within the confines of a modern civilization which aspires to be an enlightened constitutional government," per Griffith, J., dissenting; case reversed, 297 U.S. 278 (1936), see note 29, infra; and see People v. Cope, 345 Ill. 278, 285, 178 N.E. 95, 99 (1931); People v. Barbato, 254 N.Y. 170, 172 N.E. 458, 461 (1930); People v. Mummiani, 258 N.Y. 394, 180 N.E. 94 (1932); and cases currently appearing in Decennial, Current, and General Digests, Criminal Law, ⬿522. See also Note (1923) 24 A.L. R. 703.

13. See § 109, herein.

14. See title on Torture, 22 Encyclopedia Brittanica (14th ed. 1929) 311, 312.

15. The clearest exposition of this view is given in an article by Atkinson, Admissibility of Evidence Obtained through Unreasonable Searches and Seizures (1925) 25 Col.L.Rev. 11, and see Ch. 14, herein.

16. See, for the development of the doctrine that a state conviction upon an "involuntary" confession is a denial of federal due process, § 117, herein.

ency may be untrue seems slight and of lesser concern.

Other features of the rules about "involuntary" confessions give some additional support to the privilege theory. If the sole basis for exclusion is untrustworthiness, we should expect to see them excluded in civil actions, at the instance of the party against whom they are offered. But the prevailing view is to the contrary.[17] The objection to the confession as improperly induced, which rules it out in a criminal case, is a mere matter of fact to be proved in explanation, by the civil party.

Still another inference in favor of privilege may be drawn from the rule, supported by the decisions generally, but altered in Texas by statute, relating to the confirmation of the confession by external facts disclosed by the confession and verified by later investigation. If untrustworthiness were the only obstacle, an adequate circumstantial voucher, such as the discovery of the empty cartridges at the place where the murderer confesses he shot from ambush, or the finding of the stolen money in the place of hiding, might well be deemed to remove the obstacle to admitting the confession. But the courts let in only the external confirming facts, with evidence that they were discovered as a result of the disclosures in the confession, or at most the particular parts of the confession leading to the discovery.[18]

In truth, do we not invite delusion when we frame the issue whether the purpose of the confessions-doctrine is to protect an outside interest or to safeguard the truth? Can we not best understand the entire course of decisions in this field as an application to confessions both of a privilege against evidence illegally obtained—a privilege more clearly emerging in the decisions as the courts more clearly perceive the hidden iniquities of torture—and of an overlapping rule of incompetency which excludes the confessions when untrustworthy?

76. Rules Which Should be Classed as Rules of Privilege—(c) Offers of Compromise.[1]

Another rule which lies close to the border between privilege and incompetency is that which excludes proof that the adverse party has made an offer of compromise, when sought to be used as an admission of liability. Courts and writers have classed this as a mere application of the requirement of relevancy.[2] They advance the argument that if you offer to pay one-third of the amount of a claim against you, this is not relevant to show that you believed that the claim had merit, for it can just as convincingly be accounted for on the supposition that you thought the claim unfounded but considered nevertheless that it would be expedient to avoid litigation at that cost.

I am not persuaded. In the first place, the requirement that circumstantial evidence

---

17. Riggs v. State, 217 Ala. 102, 115 So. 1 (1927); Fidler v. McKinley, 21 Ill. 308, 309, 316, 318 (1859); Newhall v. Jenkins, 2 Gray 562 (Mass. 1854), and other cases cited in 3 Wigmore, Evidence § 815, n. 1.

True, this may be reconciled with the trustworthiness theory by the suggestion that a factor of unreliability may not be so crucial that it cannot be suffered, and discount made for it, in a civil case, and yet may be serious enough to be decisive in a criminal case, where the defendant's freedom or life is at hazard.

18. See Baughman v. Commonwealth, 206 Ky. 441, 267 S.W. 231 (1924); State v. Garrison, 59 Ore. 440, 117 Pac. 657 (1911) and other cases collected in 3 Wigmore, Evidence §§ 856–859.

In Texas the statute, Tex.Vernon's Ann.C.C.P. art. 727, provides that when thus confirmed the whole confession, and not merely the part specifically corroborated, comes in. Snow v. State, 106 Tex.Crim. Rep. 222, 291 S.W. 558 (1927); McClure v. State, 100 Tex.Crim.Rep. 545, 272 S.W. 157 (1925).

1. See the valuable article, Bell, Admissions Arising out of Compromise—Are They Irrelevant? 31 Tex. L.Rev. 239 (1953). For a general treatment of evidence of compromise, see § 251, herein.

2. Sullivan v. Missouri, K. & T. Ry. of Texas, 110 Tex. 360, 220 S.W. 769 (1920); Jones v. Jernigan, 29 N.M. 399, 223 Pac. 100 (1924); 4 Wigmore, Evidence, § 1061(c); 31 C.J.S. 1041, notes 25–27.

must be explainable only, or most convincingly, upon the inference relied on by the proponent, is not one usually applied by the courts in testing relevancy. A moment's survey of familiar types of circumstantial evidence (*e. g.*, evidence of threats and opportunity to commit an act, as evidence of its commission) will show that no such test for a particular item of proof is customarily required for its admission. It may look both ways, but it is for the adversary to argue its contrary bearing to the jury. All that is required for admission is that the item offered, taken alone or in conjunction with other evidence in the case, might suggest the inference proposed to a reasonable man, not that the judge must believe that the inference is more probable than not.[3] Sufficiency, of course, is another story.

For another reason the argument fails. The reason offered is not coextensive with the rule. The reason is applicable only to such offers as might ordinarily be made to one asserting an unfounded claim or defense. If the defendant offers to pay nine-tenths of the asserted claim, it is unlikely in the highest degree that he believes the claim unfounded, but the rule applies to that offer just as it does to the proposal to pay one-tenth.

The privilege theory here seems more convincing. To a jury any substantial offer of compromise would be quite persuasive that the one who made the offer believed that the adversary's claim had substantial merit. There is nothing unreasonable in this inference, neither does it conduce to confusion of issues, undue prejudice, or unfair surprise. There is no threat to the search for truth at the trial in such evidence. The courts are protecting an interest which goes further back. If one contemplating an offer of settlement, or his attorney, knew that the offer, if refused, could be used against him, he would as a practical matter weigh this danger in the balance, and it would often turn the scale of decision against making the offer. This view that the rule excluding offers of compromise is a rule of privilege designed to encourage the settlement of disputes out of court, and not a rule of competency, is fortified by a substantial number of judicial pronouncements.[4] If the rule excluding compromise-offers as evidence is a rule of privilege, the adverse party is allowed to object because otherwise he would suffer prejudice from having sought to avoid litigation. This reason would still obtain if the objecting party's offers or compromises of similar claims with third persons are sought to be used against him.[5] But a compromise in which the party now objecting was not involved would not be privileged on this ground. The persons who made the settlement are not imperiled by any evidence that may be received in the present litigation. A recent case presenting this latter situation admits the evidence.[6] This seems sustainable only on the privilege theory.

---

3. See also § 152, herein.

4. The reason of policy, to encourage settlement of litigation, as distinguished from the relevancy-argument is stressed in Moffitt-West Drug Co. v. Byrd, 92 Fed. 290, 292 (C.C.A.8th, 1899); Dickinson v. Dickinson, 9 Metc. 471, 474 (Mass. 1845); Eckhardt v. Harder, 160 Wash. 207, 211, 294 Pac. 981 (1931); and cases noted in 22 C.J. 308, nn. 73–75; 31 C.J. S. 1040, notes 22–24.

In numerous cases the policy-argument and the relevancy-argument are both relied on. T. M. Deal Lumber Co. v. Jones, 137 Kan. 480, 21 P.2d 933, 935, 936 (1933); Gagne v. New Haven Road Construction Co., 87 N.H. 163, 175 Atl. 818 (1934) (illuminating opinion by Woodbury, J.).

5. Such evidence is usually excluded, and would be inadmissible on either theory. Hawthorne v. Eckerson Co., 77 F.2d 844 (C.C.A.2d 1935); Carpenter v. Boston & Maine R. R., 295 Mass. 103, 3 N.E.2d 184 (1936); Svea Fire & Life Ins. Co. v. Spokane, P. & S. Ry., 175 Wash. 622, 28 P.2d 266 (1933).

6. Huntley v. Snider, 86 F.2d 539 (1936), rehearing denied 88 F.2d 335 (C.C.A.1st, 1937) (objection by trustee in bankruptcy to bankrupt husband's discharge on ground of fraudulent concealment of assets of estate; held, evidence that bankrupt's wife surrendered a portion of the property alleged to have been concealed, by way of compromise with trustee, admissible on trustee's behalf). Compare Esser v. Brophey, 212 Minn. 194, 3 N.W.2d 3 (1942),

77. Rules Which Should be Classed as Rules of Privilege—(d) Remedial Measures after an Accident.

A closely allied question presents itself in respect to evidence of repairs and improvements after an accident. When offered as evidence of negligence, it is excluded.[1] This result has been justified on grounds of relevancy.[2] Yet, according to ordinary standards applied to admissions by conduct, it seems relevant (though rebuttable, of course) as a circumstance tending to show consciousness that the situation called for additional safety-precautions. The dominant motive for exclusion, it seems clear, is the reason

often relied on in the opinions;[3] namely, the policy against discouraging the taking of steps to remove a danger. Manifestly, this is an external policy, not looking to the trial and truth-finding, but to the interest of public safety. If so, then according to the analysis suggested herein, the rule is one of privilege.[4]

78. Rules Which Should be Classed as Rules of Privilege—(e) Reports Made by an Agent to His Principal.

Another highly debatable question at the cross-roads of competency and privilege relates to the admissibility in evidence against a principal of a report made by an agent to

---

where the plaintiff suing for injury in a collision in which three drivers were involved placed the third driver (not a party) on the stand who testified to defendant's negligence. Defendant sought to show that the witness had paid defendant a sum in compromise of defendant's suit based on the negligence of the witness in the same accident. The court (Peterson, J.) surveyed the various theories for excluding compromises, but held that this evidence was not admissible to impeach because "not relevant to show either an admission of liability or the witness's hostility to defendant." It seems, however, that it should have come in to impeach as prior inconsistent conduct (see § 34, herein).

Such evidence may, however, be objectionable as hearsay. Ray v. State, 88 Tex.Crim.Rep. 196, 225 S.W. 523 (1920); and see § 229, herein.

1. Morse v. Minneapolis & St. L. Ry. Co., 30 Minn. 465, 16 N.W. 358 (1883) and cases cited in Note, 170 A.L.R. 7, 65 C.J.S., Negligence, § 225, Dec.Dig., Negligence, ☞131. Uniform Rule 51: "When after the occurrence of an event remedial or precautionary measures are taken, which, if taken previously would have tended to make the event less likely to occur, evidence of such subsequent measures is not admissible to prove negligence or culpable conduct in connection with the event."

Evidence of changes in rules or methods, Stevens v. Boston Elev. R. Co., 184 Mass. 476, 69 N.E. 338 (1904), and evidence of the discharge of the employee involved in the accident, Armour & Co. v. Skene, 153 Fed. 241 (C.C.A.Mass.1907), are excluded on the same principle.

An analogous doctrine is applied when a person concerned in an accident gives aid to the victim. "The defendant, not knowing whether it was liable or not, had the humanity to take plaintiff, who was struck by its engine, to a hospital in Danville, and employed Dr. Miller to attend him. It was an act

of mercy which no court should hold in any respect was an implied admission or circumstance tending to admit liability. If a court should so hold, it would tend to stop, instead of encourage, one injuring another from giving aid to the sufferer." Barber v. Southern Ry. Co., 193 N.C. 691, 138 S.E. 17, 19 (1927).

2. "To improve the condition of the injury-causing object is therefore to indicate a belief merely that it has been *capable of causing such an injury*, but indicates nothing more, and is equally consistent with a belief in injury by mere accident, or by contributory negligence, as well as by the owner's negligence." 2 Wigmore, Evidence, § 283; Columbia & Puget Sound R. R. v. Hawthorne, 144 U.S. 202, 207, 12 S.Ct. 591, 593 (1892).

3. Hodges v. Percival, 132 Ill. 53, 23 N.E. 423, 424 (1890); Texas Trunk R. R. v. Ayres, 83 Tex. 268, 271, 18 S.W. 684 (1892); Terre Haute & I. R. R. v. Clem, 123 Ind. 15, 18, 23 N.E. 965, 7 L.R.A. 588 (1889); Note, 170 A.L.R. 7, 25.

4. True, the privilege if it be one is unusual in its scope in that the evidence is not excluded for all purposes, but only when offered to show negligence. Bixby v. Thurber, 80 N.H. 411, 118 Atl. 99, 103 (1922); 4 Tex.L.Rev. 120 (1935). Thus, where defendant disputes that he was in control, repairs by him may be shown. Slattery v. Marra Bros., 186 F.2d 134, syl. 9, 10 (C.C.A.2, 1951). And if the defendant is so incautious as to introduce evidence that it was not feasible to undertake particular precautionary measures, the plaintiff may rebut by showing that the defendant actually did later adopt such measures. Cincinnati, H. & D. R. Co. v. Van Horne, 69 Fed. 139, C.C.A.Ohio (1895); Reynolds v. Maine Mfg. Co., 81 N.H. 421, 128 Atl. 329, syl. 1 (1925); Jefferson v. City of Raleigh, 194 N.C. 479, 140 S.E. 76 (1927).

the principal himself, or to some other agent in the same organization, in the course of the business. Typical instances are the railway conductor's report of a wreck or accident, or a letter to the home office from a manager of a branch office of a bank. Under a familiar application of the agency principle that the words and acts of the agent in the scope of his authority are treated as if they were the words and acts of the principal, it is held that the statements of an agent made in the scope of authority, and made to a third person, are admissible against the principal, just as the principal's own statement would be.[1]

But if the agent's statement thus offered against the principal as an admission, though plainly made in the scope of authority, was a statement made to the principal himself, many courts refuse to admit it.[2] An equal number let such a statement come in.[3] The issue is usually assumed to be this: are such reports competent as admissions? This leads to the question, does the agent speak for the principal in such a report? No, it is answered, the doctrine of *respondeat superior*

does not apply to transactions between the agent and the principal.[4] This statement is doubtless intended to suggest that some analogies, not specified, in the rules of substantive liability of principals should be controlling. But why other analogies, such as instances of statements made by a party himself not intended for the outside world, as where he is overheard talking to himself, or where he makes entries in a secret diary, should not be equally available, is not apparent. It seems clear that such latter statements and entries would be received against him as admissions.

Such analogies are helpful as make-weight arguments to support a choice already made. But the decision whether such reports should be used as evidence ought to be guided by more practical considerations. First, do such reports as a class have the degree of trustworthiness required to counterbalance the hazards of hearsay? While slightly less reliable as a class than the agent's authorized statements to outsiders, intra-organization reports are generally made as a basis for some action, and when this is so, they share

1. See § 244, herein.

2. E. g., Swan v. Miller [1919], 1 Ir.R. 151 (C.A.) (reviewing English authorities); Lever Bros. Co. v. Atlas Assur. Co., 131 F.2d 770, 776, syl. 7 (C.C.A.Ind.1942) (report of investigating engineers on explosion); United States v. United Shoe Machinery Corp., 89 F.Supp. 349, syl. 1–8 (D.Mass.1950) (intracorporate letters and reports: principle and authorities ably discussed by Wyzanski, D. J., recognizing that they may come in as admissions if adopted by directors). Carroll v. East Tennessee, V. & G. Ry., 82 Ga. 452, 10 S.E. 163, 6 L.R.A. 214 (1889) (written report of accident, made after investigation, by conductor to superintendent); Atchison, T. & S. F. Ry. v. Burks, 78 Kan. 515, 96 Pac. 950, 18 L.R.A. N.S. 231 (1908) (reports of car-inspectors as to defective coupler, inadmissible against railway company as admissions, unless adopted by company; extensive review of principles and authorities by Burch, J.); Warner v. Maine Central R. R., 111 Me. 149, 88 Atl. 403, 47 L.R.A.,N.S. 830 (1913) (station-agent's report to general manager about fire); Bell v. Milwaukee Electric Ry. & Light Co., 169 Wis. 408, 172 N.W. 791 (1919) (written report of accident made by street-car conductor, at end of his run); Restatement, Agency, § 287.

3. E. g., The Solway, 10 P.D. 137 (1885) (letter by master of ship to owners); Chicago, St. P. M. & O. Ry. Co. v. Kulp, 102 F.2d 352, syl. 6, 7, 133 A.L.R. 1445 (C.C.A.Minn.1939) (conductor's report to employer as to cause of injury to brakeman); Hilbert v. Spokane International Ry., 20 Idaho 54, 116 Pac. 1116 (1911) (section foreman's written report to company about a fire); Lemen v. Kansas City Southern Ry., 151 Mo.App. 511, 515, 132 S.W. 13 (1910) (oral report by conductor to station-agent, "Better send your section gang up the road. I think we set something on fire there."); Metropolitan Life Ins. Co. v. Moss, 109 S.W.2d 1035 (Tex. Civ.App.1937) (medical examiner's report to insurance company of state of health of applicant); Supreme Lodge, Knights of Honor v. Rampy, 45 S.W. 422 (Tex.Civ.App.1898, writ of error refused) (report by officers of local lodge to supreme lodge concerning good standing of member). Cases pro and con are collected in 47 L.R.A.,N.S., 830 (1914), and earlier notes there referred to.

4. Morgan, The Rationale of Vicarious Admissions, 42 Harv.L.Rev. 461, 463 (1929).

the reliability of business records.[5] They will only be offered against the principal when they admit some fact disadvantageous to the principal, and such statements by an agent are likely to be true. No special danger of surprise, confusion, or prejudice from the use of the evidence is apparent. There seems little basis, then, for shaping our rule of competency of admissions to exclude this type of statements.

If we consider the possibility of conceding a privilege to the principal for these intra-organization reports, we come nearer the core of the practical. In some situations, it seems that business will be facilitated, if the manager of the enterprise can, as a guide for action, call for an agent to make an investigation and report all the facts, favorable and unfavorable, and still be assured that he does this without danger of making evidence for a possible adversary in a law-suit. Is this danger so unlikely to be present to the mind of the manager, that it would have no practical deterrent effect? If it is likely to be a substantial obstruction, does this outweigh the desirability of the fullest use of reliable evidence of the facts? If a privilege is to be conceded for intra-company reports, should

it be for all, or only for some limited class, such as accident-reports or investigation-reports?

Without considering these questions most courts have brushed aside privilege as a possible theory, and have, to my mind, obscured the essential problem by stating the issue as one of competency. It is interesting to observe, however, that another question of the use of this same class of evidence has been discussed almost exclusively in terms of privilege. This is the question whether the adversary, in a suit against the principal, may secure an order for discovery before trial, of reports made to the principal by an agent. The solution worked out by the courts in England, and followed in some American decisions, is to allow discovery of agents' reports generally but to recognize here a privilege not peculiar to agent's reports—the privilege against disclosure of papers made or compiled by or for a litigant or his counsel as part of the special preparation for trial of a lawsuit.[6] In this view a routine accident-report or other communication by the agent would be unprivileged, but a special report made in preparation for actual or threatened litigation would be protected.[7] It is submit-

---

5. This special trustworthiness is pointed out by Professor Morgan in the article referred to in the next preceding note (42 Harv.L.Rev. at 463, n. 4), but he contends that this furnishes no reason for using the representation-formula in this situation as a theory of admissibility.

6. Skinner v. Great Northern Ry., L.R. 9 Ex. 298 (1874) (report of officials in course of ordinary duties is subject to discovery, but not the report of medical examiner after claim made); Anderson v. Bank of British Columbia, 2 Ch.D. 644 (1876) (letter from manager of branch in Oregon to general manager of bank in London in reply to latter's request, as to transaction in which litigation had been threatened; held, not privileged, since not written directly and solely for purpose of placing before solicitors); Southwark & Vauxhall Water Co. v. Quick, 3 Q.B. 315 (C.A.1878) (notes of interviews by officers of company with employees, held privileged as having been prepared for use of solicitors); Birmingham & Midland Motor Omnibus Co. v. London & N. W. Ry. [1913], 3 K.B. 850 (C.A.) (action for destruction

of hay by fire; defendant's affidavit of documents claims privilege for a bundle of forty-five documents; claim sustained by trial judge as to those dated after claim, denied as to others; held, error, the line is not drawn at the date of claim, but the question is whether the particular documents were obtained for the solicitors). See 5 Wigmore, Evidence §§ 2319, 2320, and also the cases cited in next footnote.

7. Dulanskey v. Iowa-Illinois Gas & Elec. Co., 10 F.R.D. 146, syl. 5 (S.D.Iowa 1950) (routine report of bus-driver about accident, discovery allowed); Wise v. Western Union Tel. Co., 6 Harr. 456, 178 Atl. 640 (Del.Super.Ct.1935) (discovery of agent's report allowed; opinion draws line clearly between reports in ordinary course and those prepared for use of counsel in suit); Carlton v. Western & A. R. R., 81 Ga. 531, 7 S.E. 623 (1888) (*dictum* that conductor's accident report would be subject to discovery); Davenport Co. v. Pennsylvania R. R., 166 Pa. 480, 31 Atl. 245 (1895) (special report of agent relative to delay of freight prepared **after**

ted that this line should also be drawn at the trial, with the result that the agent's reports and statements made in the scope of authority would be competent against the principal unless privileged as materials specially prepared for use in litigation.

79. Limitations on the Effectiveness of Privileges—(a) Risk of Eavesdropping and of Interception of Letters.

On some points, the decisions reveal a surprising unwillingness to extend the benefit of a privilege to the full measure of protection which one would expect. This is a distortion which probably results from straining toward conflicting ends, the end of truth and the end of furthering the outside interest. The re-

luctance is manifested in the cases which hold that an eavesdropper may testify to privileged confidential communications,[1] and that a letter, confidential and privileged, is not protected if it is purloined or intercepted before reaching the addressee, or otherwise secured without the addressee's connivance.[2] Perhaps these incidental hazards may be thought so remote as not to be likely to discourage disclosure. But the chariness of these cases stands in contrast to the indifference of the courts to the fact that a confidential communication has already been disclosed to third persons by the recipient and has thus lost in fact the veil of secrecy. It is still protected at the trial.[3] A glaring in-

---

claim made, for submission to counsel held privileged); Robertson v. Comm., 181 Va. 520, 25 S.E.2d 352, syl. 15, 16, 146 A.L.R. 966 (1943) (motorman's routine report of collision, in hands of employer's counsel, discoverable, distinguishing special report for benefit of counsel: extensive discussion); Notes, (1907) 6 L.R.A.,N.S., 325; 146 A.L.R. 977; 70 C.J. 378; Dec.Dig., Fed.Civil Proc. ⊂⇒1590. Compare, however, the decision in Ex parte Schoepf, 74 Ohio St. 1, 77 N.E. 276, 6 L.R.A.,N.S., 325 (1904), which holds that a routine report of accident by a street-car conductor and motorman was privileged as confidential and that, on the taking of the deposition of the company's claim agent, he was not compellable to produce them. Other cases denying discovery of apparently routine reports without consideration of the distinction between those made with a view to litigation, and those made in ordinary course: Powell v. Northern Pac. R. R., 46 Minn. 249, 48 N.W. 907 (1891) (would be hearsay); State ex rel. Missouri Pac. Ry. v. Hall, 325 Mo. 102, 27 S.W.2d 1027 (1930) (attempt to pry into defense, and hearsay).

1. This seems to be the holding even when the overhearing was not due to carelessness on the part of the confidants. Commonwealth v. Griffin, 110 Mass. 181 (1872) (conversation in jail of husband and wife, overheard by officers in concealment); Commonwealth v. Wakelin, 230 Mass. 567, 120 N.E. 209 (1918) (dictograph hidden in cell of husband and wife); Clark v. State, 261 S.W.2d 339, syl. 3–5 (Tex.Cr.1953) (conversation of accused with attorney over long-distance telephone reported by operator who eavesdropped in violation of company rule); Notes (1911) 33 L.R.A.,N.S., 477, 485, (1929) 63 A.L.R. 107; 58 Am.Jur. 216; Dec.Dig., Witnesses, ⊂⇒ 206.

2. Intercepted letters, admitted: Hammons v. State, 73 Ark. 495, 84 S.W. 718, 68 L.R.A. 234 (1905); People v. Dunnigan, 163 Mich. 349, 128 N.W. 180, 31 L.R.A.,N.S., 940 (1910); Commonwealth v. Smith, 270 Pa. 583, 113 Atl. 844 (1921). Testimony of person who saw letters without recipient's connivance, admitted: Harris v. State, 72 Tex.Crim.Rep. 117, 161 S.W. 125 (1913). But a conflicting view excludes the letters, whether secured with or without the addressee's consent. McKie v. State, 165 Ga. 210, 140 S.E. 625 (1927) (letters of wife to husband, produced at trial of wife for husband's murder, by temporary administrator appointed during trial to secure the letter from husband's deposit-box offered by state, held inadmissible. "If the privilege cannot be destroyed by collusion between a spouse and a third party, it should not be permitted to be destroyed by some one surreptitiously and wrongfully obtaining letters from the possession of the spouse to whom they were written. The purpose of the law in excluding communications between husband and wife is to produce perfect trust and confidence between them, which cannot be secured if the communications can be disclosed either by the party to whom they were made or by third parties who surreptitiously or otherwise obtain the letters containing them from the spouse to whom they were addressed." Id. at 218, 140 S.E. at 629. In the opinion in the last-named case the authorities are collected and discussed. See also 8 Wigmore Evidence §§ 2325, 2326, 2329(2), 58 Am.Jur., Witnesses, § 366.

3. Mercer v. State, 40 Fla. 216, 24 So. 154, 157, 74 Am.St.Rep. 135 (1898); McCoy v. Justice, 199 N.C. 602, 155 S.E. 452, 458 (1930); 8 Wigmore Evidence § 2339, n. 2.

stance of this sort of facing both ways appears in a Massachusetts decision. In this case the court permitted a wife, over objection, to testify that she had a private conversation with her husband, and that as a result of this conversation, she disregarded a citation that had been served upon her in her husband's divorce suit, and the upper court approved a finding based chiefly on this testimony, that in the conversation the husband had fraudulently told her that he had discontinued the suit.[4] The case seems to stand alone, however, in sanctioning this device for avoiding the privilege by indirection.

80. **Limitations on the Effectiveness of Privileges—(b) Adverse Arguments and Inferences from Claiming the Privileges.**

The underlying conflict comes most clearly in view in the decisions relating to the allowability of an adverse inference from the assertion of privilege. Plainly, such an inference may not be made against a party when a witness for such party claims a privilege personal to the witness, for this is not a matter under the party's control.[1] But where the party himself suppresses evidence by invoking a privilege given to him by the law, should an adverse inference be sanctioned? The question may arise in various forms, for example, whether an inquiry of the witness, or of the party, calling for information obviously privileged, may be pressed for the pointed purpose of forcing the party to make an explicit claim of the privilege in the jury's hearing, or again,

whether the inference may be drawn in argument, and finally, whether the judge in the instructions may mention the inference as a permissible one.

Under familiar principles an unfavorable inference may be made against a party not only for destroying evidence, but for the mere failure to produce witnesses or documents within his control.[2] No showing of wrong or fraud seems to be required as a foundation for the inference that the evidence if produced would have been unfavorable. Why should not this same conclusion be drawn from the party's active interposing of a privilege to keep out the evidence? A leading case for the affirmative is Phillips v. Chase,[3] where the court said:

> "It is a rule of law that the objection of a party to evidence as incompetent and immaterial, and insistence upon his right to have his case tried according to the rules of law, cannot be made a subject of comment in argument. . . . On the other hand, if evidence is material and competent except for a personal privilege of one of the parties to have it excluded under the law, his claim of the privilege may be referred to in argument and considered by the jury, as indicating his opinion that the evidence, if received, would be prejudicial to him." [4]

An oft-quoted statement by Lord Chelmsford gives the contrary view:

> "The exclusion of such evidence is for the general interest of the community, and therefore to say that when

---

[4] Sampson v. Sampson, 223 Mass. 451, 458, 112 N.E. 84 (1916). The result, it seems, could have been more persuasively sustained upon the principle, often applied in the cases of confidences between attorney and client, that a communication made for the purpose of effecting a fraud or crime is not privileged. Fraser v. United States, 145 F.2d 139, syl. 11–13 (C.C.A.Tenn.1945); Uniform Rules of Evidence, Rule 28 (2) (e).

[1] Bales v. Evans, 182 Mich. 383, 148 N.W. 790 (1914) (witness produced by plaintiff claimed privilege against self-crimination against answering question

on cross-examination; claim sustained; held, error to permit defendant's counsel to argue inference that witness was guilty). See also Andrews v. Frye, 104 Mass. 234 (1870) (dictum).

[2] Wilkerson v. State, 113 Tex.Crim.Rep. 591, 23 S.W. (2d) 731 (1929); 2 Wigmore Evidence §§ 285–291; 4 id. § 2273.

[3] 201 Mass. 444, 87 N.E. 755, 758 (1909), writ of error dism'd 216 U.S. 616, 30 S.Ct. 577 (1910).

[4] Id. at 450, 87 N.E. at 758.

a party refuses to permit professional confidence to be broken, everything must be taken most strongly against him, what is it but to deny him the protection which, for public purposes, the law affords him, and utterly to take away a privilege which can thus only be asserted to his prejudice?" [5]

It may be doubted whether either of these arguments is controlling. As to the first, it is based upon an unfounded distinction between incompetent and privileged evidence, namely, a supposition that the privilege can be waived and the incompetency cannot.[6] As we have seen, both may be waived with equal facility. As to the second, it is hardly true that permitting the inference "utterly takes away" the privilege. A privilege has its chief practical benefit when it enables a party to exclude from the record a witness, document, or line of proof which is essential to the adversary's case, lacking which he cannot get to the jury at all on a vital issue. The inference does not supply the lack of proof.[7] Except for the benefit accruing in this situation, the privilege is usually of dubious value at best, for if it is used to exclude evidence which is not essential to the adversary, the objector knows that the jury (whatever is or is not told them by judge or lawyer) may draw a damaging conclusion from the concealment.

81. Attitude of the Courts: New Statutory Privileges: The Future of Privilege.

Some opinions on this question of inference confine themselves to the particular privilege in question, while others discuss it as a problem of trial policy common to privileges generally.[1] It may be most expedient to differentiate, and to permit the inference

5. Wentworth v. Lloyd, 10 H.L.Cas. 589, 591 (1864).

6. See § 72 supra.

7. St. Louis & S. F. R. R. v. Finley, 122 Tenn. 127, 118 S.W. 692, 18 Ann.Cas. 1141 (1909) (where plaintiff fails to show negligence, no inference can be drawn from defendant's failure to call witnesses); Cooper v. Upton, 65 W.Va. 401, 64 S.E. 523 (1909) (similar to last); Gayle v. Perryman, 6 Tex.Civ. App. 20, 24 S.W. 850 (1894) (failure to produce deed on notice does not prove contents); Galveston, H. & S. A. Ry. v. Landeros, 264 S.W. 524 (Tex.Civ. App. 1924) (defendant's failure to offer evidence is not proof of plaintiff's claim); 1 Jones, Commentaries on Evidence (2d ed. 1926) § 97.

1. The following is a sampling of the cases pro and con. Permitting the adversary to force the party to claim the privilege: State v. Booth, 121 Iowa 710, 97 N.W. 74 (1903) (no error for state to put defendant's physician on the stand, thus forcing defendant to claim privilege); McCooe v. Dighton S. & S. St. Ry., 173 Mass. 117, 53 N.E. 133 (1899) (plaintiff's lawyer on stand claims privilege for communications with plaintiff, held, no error for judge to ask plaintiff personally if he objects to the disclosure). Permitting the inference: Phillips v. Chase, 201 Mass. 444, 87 N.E. 755 (1909), writ of error dism'd 216 U.S. 616, 30 S.Ct. 577 (1910) (attorney-client); Andrews v. Frye, 104 Mass. 234 (1870) (defendant in civil case claims self-crimination privilege); Deutschmann v. Third Avenue Ry., 87 App.Div. 503, 84 N.Y.Supp. 887 (1st Dep't 1903) (physician-patient: reasoning would apply to all privileges); New York Produce Exch. Bank v. Twelfth Ward Bank, 162 App.Div. 13, 147 N.Y.Supp. 278 (1st Dep't 1914) (where plaintiff declined to consent to chemical demonstration in open court as to whether check was raised, defendant entitled to argue inference from this claim of privilege—but query whether this was a matter of privilege, or rather one of the trial court's exercise of discretion?).

Cases which seem to frown on the inference: Pennsylvania R. R. v. Durkee, 147 Fed. 99, 8 Ann.Cas. 790, 792, with annotation on this point (C.C.A.2d, 1906) (held, trial judge properly instructed jury that no inference could be drawn against plaintiff for claiming the statutory privilege for information confided to physician; declining to follow the Deutschmann case, supra; McConnell v. Osage, 80 Iowa 293, 45 N.W. 550, 8 L.R.A. 778 (1890) (error to permit defendant to ask plaintiff on cross-examination whether she was willing to have her physician disclose conversation; distinguished in State v. Booth, supra); Carne v. Litchfield, 2 Mich. 340 (1852) (civil action for false imprisonment; defendant declined to answer question on ground of self-crimination; held, error to refuse instruction that they could not draw inference; the annotation criticizes the ruling on the ground that the jury should consider this as they do other demeanor, and they will, anyway); People v. Werner, 225 Mich. 18, 195 N.W. 697 (1923) (prosecution called husband of accused, in presence of jury, and thus forced accused to object; trial judge instructed that no inference could be drawn; held, error not cured by the instruction); Thomas v. Bryon Township, 168 Mich. 593, 134 N.W. 1021, 38 L.R.A.,N.S., 1186 (1912) (persistent repetition of questions to physician about privileged matters,

where the policy behind the particular privilege is conceived to be weak, and to suppress the comment when a privilege is asserted which is thought to be backed by strong reasons. The tendency, however, in a given jurisdiction will be to handle the different privileges alike.

The courts often say that privileges, since they curtail the truth from disclosure, should be strictly construed.[2] One may go further, and believe that the privileges are never sufficiently helpful in protecting the outside interests they purport to foster, to justify their obstructive effect in cloaking the facts. In this view, opening the door to the cold wind of adverse inference in respect to all the privileges may be the most feasible way of devitalizing them.

If, on the other hand, one conceives that some of the privileges answer an effective demand that will persist, and thus that the main cost of keeping out crucial facts essential to a case or defense will continue to be paid, then the small change of inference had better be sacrificed also, in the interest of practical trial administration. The pull-and-

haul of argument about why the blinders were put on the horse will divert time and attention that the jury could better spend in considering the evidence that did get in.

Perhaps in conclusion a glance toward the horizon is permitted. The development of judge-made privileges halted a century ago. The manifest destiny of evidence law is a progressive lowering of the barriers to truth. Seeing this tendency, the commentators who take a wide view, whether from the bench, the bar, or the schools, seem generally to advocate a narrowing of the field of privilege. However, some of the old privileges give real or fancied shelter or prestige to special groups of people. If, for example, the privilege of the accused to remain silent were taken away, it would be very hard for lawyers in a large proportion of criminal cases to put up any fight worthy of a fee. A proposal to do away with the various privileges for professional confidences would be stoutly resisted by the professions concerned. Correspondingly, newer crafts and professions whose secret communications with their patrons are not privileged are exerting pressure from

---

forcing plaintiff to object repeatedly, reversible error); Norwood v. State, 80 Tex.Cr. 552, 192 S.W. 248 (1917) (comment on claim of privilege for marital communications). This is the more widely prevailing view. See Notes, Comment on Claim Privilege, 116 A.L.R. 1170, Right to Insist that Claim of Privilege Be Made before Jury, or to Ask Adversary if He is Willing to Waive, 144 A.L.R. 1007. Under the Uniform Rules of Evidence comment on the exercise of privileges is in general forbidden. Rule 39. But comment on the failure of the accused in a criminal case is permitted. Rule 23(4). The latter topic is treated separately herein, see § 132. Under the Texas statute, Vernon's Ann.C.C.P. art. 714, the accused may call his wife as a witness, but the state cannot call her. Though phrased in language of competency, the net effect would seem to create a privilege to keep her off the stand. It is held that the state may comment on the failure of the accused to call his wife, if it appears that she had firsthand knowledge of the facts. Gomez v. State, 75 Tex. Crim.Rep. 239, 170 S.W. 711 (1914); Cole v. State, 92 Tex.Crim.Rep. 368, 243 S.W. 1100 (1922). But, rather

surprisingly, the court refuses to allow the state to offer the wife as a witness, and thus force the accused to claim the privilege expressly. Eads v. State, 74 Tex.Crim.Rep. 628, 170 S.W. 145 (1914). Curiously, under a like statute, California forbids the comment on the failure to call the wife, but permits the State to call her and thus force the husband to object. People v. Klor, 32 Cal.2d 658, 198 P.2d 705, syl. 5, 6 (1948).

Where what the physician knows would be subject to the patient's privilege, a comment on the patient's failure to call him has been considered a comment on the exercise of the privilege. Howard v. Porter, 240 Iowa 153, 35 N.W.2d 837 (1949). But the question is arguable, see 8 Wigmore, Evidence, § 2386, note 6.

2. Hyman v. Grant, 102 Tex. 50, 112 S.W. 1042 (1908) (attorney-client); Foster v. Hall, 12 Pick. 89, 22 Am.Dec. 400 (Mass.1831) (attorney-client); Southwest Metals Co. v. Gomez, 4 F.2d 215, 39 A.L.R. 1416 (C.C.A. 9th, 1925) (physician-patient); Dec.Dig. title Witnesses ⬤185.

time to time for new statutory privileges. This has resulted in the legislative creation of a number of new privileges.[3] The most widespread are the privilege of journalists to withhold their sources of information,[4] and the privilege for communications between accountants and their clients.[5] Moreover, the privilege for communications between penitent and priest, the existence of which was doubtful at common law, has been sanctioned by the legislatures of a substantial majority of the states.[6]

One may hazard a guess, however, that in a secular sense privileges are on the way out. Perhaps the route they will take is the path from rule to discretion.[7] If the trial judge is permitted a lee-way, he can prevent those disclosures of marital or professional secrets which needlessly shock our feelings of delicacy, but at the same time he can override these minor amenities when it appears necessary in order to secure the facts essential to do justice in the case before him. This modification has been proposed, by a group which

3. These are discussed in 8 Wigmore, Evidence, § 2286; Vanderbilt, Minimum Standards of Judicial Administration, 344–348 (1949); Note, 5 Vand.L. Rev. 590, 601 (1952).

4. The legislatures in twelve states (Alabama, Arizona, Arkansas, California, Indiana, Kentucky, Maryland, Michigan, Montana, New Jersey, Ohio and Pennsylvania) have created the privilege. Alabama has extended it to include radio newsmen. Arkansas and Maryland include radio and television newsmen. The statutes are cited and analyzed in 8 Wigmore, Evidence, § 2286, note 13, and in Note, 36 Va. L.Rev. 61 (1950) (excellent study of the history of the privilege, with conclusion adverse to the policy of the statutes).

5. Nine states (Colorado, Georgia, Florida, Illinois, Iowa, Kentucky, Louisiana, Michigan, New Mexico) and Puerto Rico have conferred this privilege by statutes, which are cited and summarized in 8 Wigmore, § 2286, note 14 and 1953 Supp. See Note, 5 Vand.L.Rev. 590, 603 (1952).

6. Wigmore considered that the privilege never became established as part of the common law, but that there were adequate reasons of policy for its recognition. 8 Wigmore, Evidence, §§ 2394, 2396. He cites and summarizes the statutes in id. § 2395. Several jurisdictions have been added to the roster since 1940. Id., Supp.1953. The privilege is codified in Uniform Rules of Evidence, Rule 29, as follows: "(1) As used in this rule, (a) "priest" means a priest, clergyman, minister of the gospel or other officer of a church or of a religious denomination or organization, who in the course of its discipline or practice is authorized or accustomed to hear, and has a duty to keep secret, penitential communications made by members of his church, denomination or organization; (b) "penitent" means a member of a church or religious denomination or organization who has made a penitential communication to a priest thereof; (c) "penitential communication" means a confession of culpable conduct made secret-

ly and in confidence by a penitent to a priest in the course of discipline or practice of the church or religious denomination or organization of which the penitent is a member.
(2) A person, whether or not a party, has a privilege to refuse to disclose, and to prevent a witness from disclosing a communication if he claims the privilege and the judge finds that (a) the communication was a penitential communication and (b) the witness is the penitent or the priest, and (c) the claimant is the penitent, or the priest making the claim on behalf of an absent penitent."

7. Precedents, statutory and court-made, for the introduction of this factor of discretion into the administration of evidential privileges are not wanting. Examples of such qualified privileges: (a) The privilege recognized in some jurisdictions to decline to answer questions calling for information bringing disgrace on the witness, 3 Wigmore, Evidence §§ 983(2), 984; 4 id. § 2215; (b) the privilege for trade secrets, Willson v. Superior Court, 66 Cal.App. 275, 225 Pac. 881 (1924), 8 Wigmore Evidence § 2212; (c) the privilege for religious opinions, 8 Wigmore Evidence § 2213; (d) 35 C.S.A. Ch. 177, § 9, subd. 5: "A public officer shall not be examined as to communications made to him in official confidence, when the public interests in the judgment of the court, would suffer by the disclosure"; (e) N.C.G.S. § 8–53, creates the privilege for information confided to a physician, but concludes "provided that the presiding judge of a superior court may compel such a disclosure if in his opinion the same is necessary to the proper administration of justice."

Compare the criterion for the application of the privilege prescribed in Jackson v. Pillsbury, 380 Ill. 554, 44 N.E.2d 537, 547: "The resulting injury to the relation by the disclosure of the communications must be greater than the benefit thereby gained for the correct disposal of the litigation." See also Shafer v. Utica Mut. Ins. Co., 248 App.Div. 279, 289 N.Y.Supp. 577 (4th Dep't 1936), and Comment (1937) 46 Yale L.J. 703.

speaks with authority,[8] in respect to the statutory privilege for information confided to physicians. For most privileges it offers the best compromise of those conflicting demands which, as we have seen, the law of privilege is constantly straining to reconcile.

8. Report of Committee on Improvements in the Law of Evidence, American Bar Ass'n, Section on Judicial Administration (Report of March 15, 1938) Pt. III, § 12; Vanderbilt, Minimum Standards of Judicial Administration, 342 (1949).

CHAPTER 9

THE PRIVILEGE FOR MARITAL COMMUNICATIONS[1]

82. History and Background and Kindred Rules.[2]

We are dealing here with a late offshoot of an ancient tree. The older branches are discussed in another chapter.[3] These earlier rules, to be sharply distinguished from the present doctrine, are first, the rule that the spouse of a party or person interested is disqualified from testifying for the other spouse, and second, the privilege of a party against having the party's husband or wife called as an adverse witness. These two former rules forbid the calling of the spouse as a witness at all, for or against the party, regardless of the actual testimony to be elicited, whereas the privilege presently discussed is limited to a certain class of testimony, namely communications between the spouses or more broadly in some states, information gained on account of the marital relation.

The movement for procedural reform in England in the first half of the 1800s found expression in the evidence field in the agitation for the break-up of the system of disqualification of parties and spouses. One of the auxiliary reasons which had been given to justify the disqualification of spouses was that of preserving marital confidences.[4] As to the disqualification of spouses the reform was largely accomplished by the Evidence Amendment Act, 1853. On the eve of this legislation, Greenleaf writing in this country in 1842, clearly announced the existence of a distinct privilege for marital communications, and this pronouncement was echoed in England by Best in 1849,[5] though seemingly there was little or no support for such a view in the English decisions.[6] Moreover, the Second Report of 1853 of the Commissioners on Common Law Procedure, after rejecting the arguments for the outmoded rules of disqualification, calls attention to the special danger of "alarm and unhappiness occasioned to society by . . . compel-

1. 8 Wigmore, Evidence, §§ 2332-2341, 5 Jones, Evidence, §§ 2143-2148 (2d ed. rev. 1926); Dec.Dig. Witnesses, ☞187-195; 70 C.J., Witnesses, §§ 508-531; 58 Am.Jur., Witnesses, §§ 375-400.

2. 8 Wigmore, Evidence, § 2332-2334.

3. See § 66, herein.

4. See 8 Wigmore, Evidence, § 2333; Taylor, Evidence, 899 (1848) (recounting this as a reason given but rejecting it as "too large"), quoted Shenton v. Tyler, L.R. 1939 Ch. D. 620, 634.

5. See the citations to these early editions of Greenleaf and Best in Shenton v. Tyler, L.R. 1939 Ch. D. 620, 633, 634.

6. The English decisions before 1853 are carefully dissected in the opinion of Greene, M.R. in Shenton v. Tyler, supra.

ling the public disclosure of confidential communications between husband and wife . . ." and declares that "[a]ll communications between them should be held to be privileged." [7]

However, though the policy supporting a privilege for marital communications had thus been distinctly pointed out, there had been little occasion for its judicial recognition, since the wider disqualifications of the spouses of parties left small possibility for the question of the existence of such a privilege to arise.[8]

Nevertheless, the English Act of 1853, mentioned above, after it abolished the disqualification of husbands and wives of the parties, enacted that "no husband shall be compellable to disclose any communication made to him by his wife during the marriage, and no wife shall be compellable to disclose any communication made to her by her husband during the marriage." [9] Moreover, nearly all of the states in this country, in their statutes making spouses competent to testify have included provisions disabling them from testifying to communications between them.[10]

In the light of this history the Court of Appeal in England has denied that there was any common law privilege for marital communications.[11] In this country, however, the courts have frequently said that the statutes protecting marital communications from disclosure are declaratory of the com-

---

7. See quotation from this report, 8 Wigmore, Evidence, § 2332.

8. See Wigmore, Evidence, § 2333.

9. St. 16 & 17 Vict. c. 83, § 3.

10. Typical provisions are the following: Calif. Code Civ.Proc. § 1881 "There are particular relations in which it is the policy of the law to encourage confidence and to preserve it inviolate; therefore, a person cannot be examined as a witness in the following cases: 1. A husband cannot be examined for or against his wife, without her consent, nor a wife for or against her husband, without his consent; nor can either, during the marriage or afterwards, be, without the consent of the other, examined as to any communication made by one to the other during the marriage; but this exception does not apply to a civil action or proceeding by one against the other, nor to a criminal action or proceeding for a crime committed by one against the other, or in an action brought by husband or wife against another person for the alienation of affections of either husband or wife; or in an action for damages against another person for adultery committed by husband or wife"; Kansas, G.S. 1949, § 60–2805, "The following persons shall be incompetent to testify. . . . Third, husband and wife, for or against each other, concerning any communication made by one to the other during the marriage, whether called while that relation subsisted or afterward"; Minnesota, M.S.A. § 595.02, "Every person of sufficient understanding, including a party, may testify in any action or proceeding, civil or criminal, in court or before any person who has authority to receive evidence, except as follows: 1. A husband cannot be examined for or against his wife without her consent, nor a wife for

or against her husband without his consent, nor can either, during the marriage or afterward without the consent of the other, be examined as to any communication made by one to the other during the marriage. But this exception does not apply to a civil action or proceeding by one against the other, nor to a criminal action or proceeding for a crime committed by one against the other, nor to an action or proceeding for abandonment and neglect of the wife or children by the husband."; New York, Civil Practice Act, § 349" . . . A husband or wife shall not be compelled, or, without the consent of the other if living, allowed to disclose a confidential communication made by one to the other during marriage. In an action for criminal conversation, the plaintiff's wife is not a competent witness for the plaintiff, but she is a competent witness for the defendant, as to any matter in controversy; except that she cannot, without the plaintiff's consent, disclose any confidential communication had or made between herself and the plaintiff".

Statutes on this topic are compiled in 2 Wigmore, Evidence, § 488. See also the excellent survey and analysis of the various statutes in the opinion of Harris, J., in Pugsley v. Smyth, 98 Ore. 448, 194 Pac. 686, 694, 695 (1921).

11. Shenton v. Tyler, L.R. 1939 Ch. D. 620, and see Notes, 55 Law Q.Rev. 329; Holdsworth, 56 id. 137. In this case the court held that the English statute, cited note 9, supra, providing that "husbands" and "wives" shall not be compellable to testify to communication, did not apply to exempt a surviving widow from interrogation as to conversations with her husband claimed to have created a secret trust in favor of the plaintiff, a third person.

mon law.[12] This approach may well be justifiable even if no common law decision can be found sanctioning the privilege in advance of a statute. The principle upon which the privilege is founded was clearly recognized, as we have seen, by leading law writers before the statutes. The statutes all derive from a common source in this previously recognized principle, and in this country they have usually been treated despite minor variations in phrasing as expressions of a common policy. This attitude probably makes for a broader and juster development and application of the privilege than would an attitude of concentration on local variations of phraseology with little regard to the conclusions of other courts under cognate statutes.

83. What is Privileged? Communications Only, or Acts and Facts? [1]

Greenleaf arguing in 1842 for a privilege distinct from marital incompetency, and fur-

nishing the inspiration for the later statutes by which the privilege was formally enacted, spoke only of "communications" and "conversations." [2] Those later statutes themselves (except one or two [3]) sanctioned the privilege for "communications" and for nothing beyond.[4] Accordingly it would seem that the privilege should be limited to *expressions* intended by one spouse to convey a meaning or message to the other. These expressions may be by words, oral, written or in sign-language, or by expressive acts, as where the husband opens a trunk before his wife and points out objects therein to her. Moreover, the protection of the privilege will shield against indirect disclosure of the communication,[5] as where a husband is asked for his wife's whereabouts which he learned only from her secret communication.[6] It seems, nevertheless, that logic and policy should cause the courts to halt with communications as the furthest boundary of the privilege,

---

12. Hopkins v. Grimshaw, 165 U.S. 342, 17 Sup.Ct. 401, 403, 41 L.Ed. 739 (1897); Hagerman v. Wigent, 108 Mich. 192, 194, 65 N.W. 756 (1896); Gjesdahl v. Harmon, 175 Minn. 414, 221 N.W. 639, 641 (1928); 70 C.J. 379, note 90(b).

1. 8 Wigmore, Evidence, § 2337; Note, Marital Communications Privilege as Including Knowledge of Acts, 10 A.L.R.2d 1389; Notes, Kaman, 35 Corn. L.Q. 187 (1949) (excellent), 34 Minn.L.Rev. 257 (1950), 3 Vand.L.Rev. 656 (1950), 35 Va.L.Rev. 1111 (1949).

2. See next preceding section.

3. Ohio, R.C. § 2317.02 ("communication made by one to the other, or an act done by either in the presence of the other, during coverture unless . . . in the known presence or hearing of a third person competent to be a witness"); Tenn., Code 1932, § 9777 (". . . neither husband nor wife shall testify to any matter that occurred between them by virtue of or in consequence of the marital relation").

4. See the statutes compiled in 2 Wigmore, Evidence, § 488.

5. See by analogy Quarfot v. Security Nat. Bank & Trust Co., 189 Minn. 451, 453, 249 N.W. 668, syl. 1 (1933) (In action against executor to recover note

alleged to constitute gift, plaintiff's testimony stating reason why he left note in decedent's possession held inadmissible as conclusion and as concerning conversation with deceased (M.S.A. § 595.04). In Sampson v. Sampson, 223 Mass. 451, 112 N.E. 84, syl. 8–10 (1916), a proceeding to vacate a divorce for fraud of the husband, the wife testified, without objection, that as a result of a talk with the husband she did nothing about the pending divorce suit of her husband. The court held (1) that the fact of a communication is not privileged, and (2) that the trial judge could properly find from this testimony that the husband made fraudulent representations. It seems that this result can best be justified on the ground of waiver, or of absence of privilege for fraudulent statements.

6. Blau v. United States, 340 U.S. 332, 71 Sup.Ct. 301, syl. 2–5, 95 L.Ed. 306 (1951) (witness's wife was hiding out to avoid service of subpoena in connection with Communist investigation; held, since witness got his knowledge of his wife's whereabouts from what she "secretly told" him, he could refuse to disclose). But the mere fact that a transaction involving marital property happened during the marriage is insufficient to show that the husband's knowledge was derived from communications made by his wife. Petition of Fuller, 63 Nev. 26, 159 P.2d 579, syl. 10 (1945).

and a substantial number have held steadfast at this line.[7]

An equal or greater number of courts, however, have construed their statutes which say "communications" to extend the privilege to acts, facts, conditions and transactions not amounting to communications at all. One group seems to announce the principle that acts done privately in the wife's presence amount to "communications."[8] Another would go even further and say that any information secured by the wife as a result of the marital relation and which would not have been known in the absence of such relation is protected.[9] Some at least of this latter group would hold that information secured by one spouse through observation during the marriage as to the health,[10] or intoxication, habitual or at a particular time,[11] or the mental condition [12] of the other spouse, would be protected by the privilege.

All extensions beyond communications seem unjustified. The acts thus protected are frequently acts done in furtherance of a crime or fraud,[13] and thus under the principle developed for the cognate privilege for attorney client communications,[14] should not be protected from disclosure even by direct communication. Moreover, the confidence which the court relies on in these cases is

---

7. United States v. Mitchell, 137 F.2d 1006, syl. 6 (C.C.A.2, 1943) (prosecution for transporting wife in interstate commerce for purpose of prostitution; held, wife's testimony as to husband's act of taking money from her not privileged); Posner v. New York Life Ins. Co., 56 Ariz. 202, 106 P.2d 488, syl. 4 (1940) (former husband's testimony that he purchased insulin for plaintiff and saw her make tests of her urine, not privileged); Shanklin v. McCracken, 140 Mo. 348, 41 S.W. 898 (1897) (widow may testify she saw deeds delivered to her husband); Note, 35 Corn.L.Q. 187, 189 n. 27 (1949).

8. People v. Daghita, 299 N.Y. 194, 86 N.E.2d 172, 10 A.L.R.2d 1385 (1949) (husband charged with theft, wife's testimony as to the husband's acts in her presence of bringing in the loot and hiding it under the bed and in the basement held violation of statutory privilege for "confidential communication"); Menefee v. Comm., 189 Va. 900, 55 S.E.2d 9, syl. 2, 3 (1949) noted 34 Minn.L.Rev. 257 (wife's testimony as to husband's leaving home before robbery, as to time of returning, as to his placing pistol on mantle-piece, and as to her driving with him near where stolen safe was hid, held privileged as "communication privately made"). Perhaps the reductio ad absurdum of the "acts" cases is State v. Robbins, 35 Wash.2d 389, 213 P.2d 310, syl. 2–4 (1950). There the husband was charged with automobile theft, and evidence of his former wife that when she was presenting application for license for the stolen car at the office her husband was waiting outside in an automobile was a "communication" and privileged. The court said, "It is obvious that he would not have waited in the automobile had he not relied on the confidence between them by reason of the marital relation."

9. Prudential Ins. Co. v. Pierce's Adm'x, 270 Ky. 216, 109 S.W.2d 616, syl. 2 (1917) (formula held to apply to knowledge gleaned by the wife from the entry of husband's birth in his family Bible).

10. Griffith v. Griffith, 162 Ill. 368, 44 N.E. 820, syl. 3 (1896) (impotence); Willey v. Howell, 168 Ky. 466, 182 S.W. 619, syl. 1 (1916) (venereal disease). But it has been held that testimony as to the general condition of health, accessible to other persons, would not be privileged. Supreme Lodge v. Jones, 113 Ill.App. 241 (1903), and see Note, 10 A.L.R.2d 1397–1400.

11. Monaghan v. Green, 265 Ill. 233, 106 N.E. 792, syl. 4, 5 (1914). Contra: In re Van Alstine's Estate, 26 Utah 193, 72 Pac. 942, syl. 2 (1903) (privilege does not cover testimony as to facts learned from observation). See Note, 10 A.L.R.2d 1389, 1400.

12. McFadden v. Welch, 177 Miss. 451, 170 So. 903, syl. 1 (1936). Contra: Lanham v. Lanham, 62 Tex.Civ.App. 431, 146 S.W. 635, syl. 1, 2 (1912) (husband's demeanor in wife's presence on train); Note, 10 A.L.R.2d 1389, 1401.

13. See, e. g., the cases cited in note 8, supra.

14. See §§ 99, herein. The application of this limitation, so clearly justified in policy, is suggested in Fraser v. United States, 145 F.2d 139, 143, 144, syl. 11 (1944) (citing cases); People v. Coleman, [1945] Irish Rep. 237, 247; 70 C.J., Witnesses, § 530; and is embodied in the Uniform Rules of Evidence, R. 28(2): "Neither spouse may claim such privilege (a) in an action by one spouse against the other spouse, or . . . (e) if the judge finds that sufficient evidence, aside from the communication, has been introduced to warrant a finding that the communication was made, in whole or in part, to enable or aid anyone to commit or to plan to commit a crime or a tort."

more often a general family confidence, which is concededly unprivileged, not specifically a confidence reposed in the wife alone. The attitude of the courts in these cases seems in effect a reaching back toward the old common law principle of preserving family harmony by disqualifying a spouse from testifying for or against the other. A different attitude it is believed would be wiser, namely, that of accepting the view that all privileges, in general, and this privilege for marital confidences in particular, are inept and clumsy devices to promote the policies they profess to serve, but are extremely effective as stumbling-blocks to obstruct the attainment of justice. Accordingly the movement should be toward restriction, and not toward expansion, of these mechanisms for concealment of relevant facts.

84. The Communication Must be Confidential.[1]

Most statutes expressly limit the privileges to "confidential communications."[2] However, even where the words used are "any communication" or simply "communications," the notion that the privilege is born of the "common law" and the fact that the pre-statutory descriptions of the privilege had clearly based it upon the policy of protecting confidences,[3] have actuated most courts to read into such statutes the requirement of confidentiality.[4] Communications in private between husband and wife are assumed to be confidential unless the subject of message or the circumstances show to the contrary.[5] It is confidential if it was expressly made so, or if the subject is such that the communicating spouse would probably desire that the matter be kept secret, either because its disclosure would be embarrassing or for some other reason.[6] If a third person (other than a child of the family) is present to the knowledge of the communicating spouse, this stretches the web of confidence beyond the marital pair, and the communication is unprivileged.[7] If children of the family are present this likewise deprives the conversa-

---

1. 8 Wigmore, Evidence, § 2336; Decennial Digests, Witnesses, ⊙=192, 193, 70 C.J., Witnesses, §§ 511–519.

2. See statutes compiled in 2 Wigmore, Evidence, § 488.

3. See § 82, supra, this chapter.

4. New York Life Ins. Co. v. Mason, 272 Fed. 28, syl. 2, 3 (C.C.A.Mont.1921) ("any communications" in R.C.M.1947, § 93–701–3 should be interpreted as limited to confidential statements); Shepherd v. Pacific Mut. Life Ins. Co., 230 Iowa 1304, 300 N.W. 556, syl. 5 (1941); Thayer v. Thayer, 188 Mich. 261, 154 N.W. 32, 35 (1915); 70 C.J. 382, note 31. Contra: Pugsley v. Smyth, 98 Ore. 448, 194 Pac. 686, syl. 12 (1921) (reviewing statutes and decisions in various states); 70 C.J. 381, note 25.

5. Blau v. United States, 340 U.S. 332, 71 Sup.Ct. 301, 95 L.Ed. 306 (1951).

6. For general discussions, see e. g., Parkhurst v. Berdell, 110 N.Y. 386, 393, 18 N.E. 123, 127 (1888) ("such communications as are expressly made confidential, or such as are of a confidential nature, or induced by the marital relation"); Mitchell v. Mitchell, 80 Tex. 101, 15 S.W. 705 (1891) ("determined by the subject-matter of the communication or the circumstances under which it was made or both").

Threats of bodily harm, though in secret, being a violation of marital duty, should not, it seems, be privileged. People v. Zabijak, 285 Mich. 164, 280 N.W. 149, syl. 11, 13 (1938). Contra: O'Neil v. O'Neil, 264 S.W. 61, syl. 10, 11 (Mo.App.1924) (private threats privileged, unless accompanied by violence).

Where the husband left a note for the wife, at their home, written on a large cardboard, the message was held not to be confidential. Yoder v. United States, 80 F.2d 665, syl. 4, C.C.A.Okl., 1935.

7. United States v. Mitchell, 137 F.2d 1006, syl. 6 (1943) (threats against wife in presence of others); Shepherd v. Pacific Mut. Life Ins. Co., 230 Iowa 1304, 300 N.W. 556, syl. 5, 6 (1941) (negotiations between husband, wife, and her father); Dec.Dig. Witnesses, ⊙=193, 70 C.J., Witnesses, § 525.

A letter from a prisoner to his wife, dictated by him to a stenographer, is not privileged. "Normally husband and wife may conveniently communicate without stenographic aid, and the privilege of holding their confidences immune from proof in court may be reasonably enjoyed and preserved without embracing within it the testimony of third persons to whom such communications have been voluntarily revealed. . . . The privilege suppresses relevant testimony, and should be allowed only when it is plain that marital confidence cannot

tion of protection unless the children are too young to understand what is said.[8] The fact that the communication relates to business transactions tends to show that it was not intended as confidential.[9] Examples are statements about business agreements between the spouses,[10] or about business matters transacted by one spouse as agent for the other,[11] or about property [12] or conveyances.[13] Usually such statements relate to facts which are intended later to become

publicly known. To cloak them with privilege when the transactions come into litigation would be productive of special inconvenience and injustice.

85. The Time of Making the Communication.[1]

The privilege is created to encourage marital confidences and is limited to them. Consequently, communications between the husband and wife before they were married,[2] or

---

otherwise reasonably be preserved. Nothing in this case suggests any such necessity." Wolfle v. United States, 291 U.S. 7, 16, 17, 54 Sup.Ct. 279, 78 L.Ed. 617 (1934) (Stone, J.)

8. Freeman v. Freeman, 238 Mass. 150, 130 N.E. 220, syl. 4 (1921) (in presence of children, the oldest nine years old, held, for the judge to determine whether old enough to pay attention and understand); Fuller v. Fuller, 100 W.Va. 309, 130 S.E. 270, syl. 2 (1925) (in presence of 13 year old daughter, not privileged); 70 C.J. 393, notes 79–81.

9. "So, too, it cannot be that the rule of privilege must be held to extend so far as to exclude all communications between husband and wife having reference to business relations existing either as between them directly, or as between them—one or both—and others. Certainly as to business relations existing between husband and wife directly, there can be no adverse consideration of public policy. Quite to the contrary, public policy, as reflected by statute and by our decisions, permits of such relations to the fullest extent. And it would be shocking to say that a contract thus made, or rights or liabilities thus accruing, could not be enforced because, forsooth, a communication between the parties having relation thereto, and essential to proof, was privileged. The cases are almost unanimously against such a conclusion." Bishop, J. in Sexton v. Sexton, 129 Iowa 487, 105 N.W. 314, 316 (1905). See 70 C.J., Witnesses, § 515; Note, Conversations between Husband and Wife Relating to Property or Business, 4 A.L.R.2d 835.

10. Appeal of Spitz, 56 Conn. 184, 14 A. 776, syl. 3 (1887) (claim of wife against insolvent estate of husband: held, wife's testimony as to husband's promises and representations which induced her to advance money, not privileged; "they were no more privileged than a promissory note would have been, if he had made his contract in that form"); Brooks v. Brooks, 357 Mo. 343, 208 S.W.2d 279, 4 A.L.R.2d 826, 832 (1948) (wife sues husband for proceeds of joint adventure. "In actions between a husband and wife involving property rights the

rule excluding relevant conversations . . . yields to the necessity of the situation for the prevention of injustice. . . ."); Bietman v. Hopkins, 109 Ind. 177, 9 N.E. 720, syl. 1 (1887) (in suit by husband's creditor to set aside husband's deed to wife, plaintiff objects to wife's testimony that deed given to repay advances—seemingly could be based on ground that the plaintiff is not the holder of the privilege); Ward v. Oliver, 129 Mich. 300, 88 N.W. 631 (1902) (similar to last).

11. Schmied v. Frank, 86 Ind. 250, 257 (1882) (wife's testimony that she authorized husband to buy note as her agent, not privileged: such authority "is intended to be known and would be worthless unless known"); Lurty's Curator v. Lurty, 107 Va. 466, 59 S.E. 405, syl. 10 (1907) (husband's account of money due wife on sale of their joint property not privileged).

12. Hagerman v. Wigent, 108 Mich. 192, 65 N.W. 756 (1896) (wife's delivery of mortgage to husband with instructions to give to plaintiff after wife's death, not privileged, as it was expected to be disclosed); Parkhurst v. Berdell, 110 N.Y. 386, 18 N.E. 123, syl. 2 (1888) (husband's conversation with wife as to securities in his hands belonging to third person, not privileged; "they were ordinary conversations, relating to matters of business, which there is no reason to suppose he would have been unwilling to hold in the presence of any person").

13. Eddy v. Bosley, 34 Tex.Civ.App. 116, 78 S.W. 565, syl. 5 (1903) (communication by husband to second wife preceding his deed to her advising her of the interest of his children in the property will be received to show notice to her; claim of privilege overruled on ground that the conveyance "if accomplished would operate as a fraud" upon the children).

1. 70 C.J.Witnesses, § 510.

2. United States v. Mitchell, 137 F.2d 1006, syl. 5 (C.C.A.2d, 1943); Forshay v. Johnston, 144 Neb. 525, 13 N.W.2d 873, syl. 5 (1944) (agreement establishing a common law marriage not a "communication between husband and wife"); Dec.Dig.Witnesses, ⊜194.

after their divorce[3] are not privileged. A communication made during a purported marriage, later annulled for fraud, by the victim of the fraud, has been held to be privileged.[4] What of husband and wife living apart? It has been said that the privilege "should not apply when the parties are living in separation and especially, as in this case, so living under articles of separation, and the one making the communication is actively hostile to the other." [5] In other circumstances when the separation has not been sanctioned by contract or decree and the communication has been made in hope of reconciliation, it might well be found to be a privileged confidence.[6]

86. Hazards of Disclosure to Third Persons against the Will of the Communicating Spouse.[1]

The weight of decision seems to support the view that the privilege does not protect against the testimony of third persons who have overheard (either accidentally or by eavesdropping) an oral communication between husband and wife,[2] or who have secured possession or learned the contents of a letter from one spouse to another by interception,[3] or through loss or misdelivery by the custodian.[4] There is one important qualification which many if not most of the cases announce, namely that the privilege will not be lost if the eavesdropping,[5] or the delivery or disclosure of the letter [6] be due to the betrayal or connivance of the spouse to whom the message is directed. Just as that spouse would not be permitted, against the will of the communicating spouse, to betray the confidence by testifying in court to the message, so he or she may not effectively destroy the privilege by out-of-court betrayal.

The first-mentioned doctrine that the eavesdropper, or the interceptor of the letter,

---

3. Yoder v. United States, 80 F.2d 665, syl. 2 (C.C.A. 10th 1935).

4. People v. Godines, 17 Cal.App.2d 721, 62 P.2d 787, syl. 8 (1936) (hearing denied by Supreme Court), noted 25 Col.L.Rev. 619.

5. Holyoke v. Holyoke's Estate, 110 Me. 469, 87 Atl. 40, syl. 4 (1913). See also McEntire v. McEntire, 107 Oh.St. 510, 140 N.E. 328, syl. 2 (1923) (communications about property settlement between spouses who had been separated under oral agreement for several months), and cases cited 70 C.J. 381, note 20.

6. This seems to be assumed without discussion in McCoy v. Justice, 199 N.C. 637, 155 S.E. 452, syl. 14 (1930).

1. 8 Wigmore, Evidence, § 2339; Note, Third Person's Overhearing or Seeing Marital Communication, 63 A.L.R. 107.

2. Comm. v. Everson, 123 Ky. 330, 96 S.W. 460 (1906) (eavesdropper); Nash v. Fidelity Phenix Fire Ins. Co., 106 W.Va. 672, 146 S.E. 726, 63 A.L.R. 101, 104 (1929) (same).

3. Batchelor v. State, 217 Ark. 340, 230 S.W.2d 23, syl. 5 (1950) (letter to wife intercepted by jailer); Connella v. Terr., 16 Okl. 365, 86 Pac. 72, syl. 2 (1906) (letter from defendant to his wife, sent by messenger; letter came in hands of sheriff); People v. Dunnigan, 163 Mich. 349, 128 N.W. 180, syl. 1 (1910) (spy entering prisoner's cell ostensibly to cut his hair promises to take letter to wife but gives it to sheriff).

4. Hammons v. State, 73 Ark. 495, 84 S.W. 718, syl. 2 (1905) (letter to wife from defendant in jail delivered by messenger to wife's father: two judges dissenting); O'Toole v. Ohio German Fire Ins. Co., 159 Mich. 187, 123 N.W. 795, syl. 3 (1909) (letter from wife to husband, dropped and lost by husband).

5. Hunter v. Hunter, 169 Pa.Super. 498, 83 A.2d 401, syl. 3–8 (1951) (husband suing wife for divorce offers wire-recordings of their conversation in bed: the wire-recorder having been set up by plaintiff's son, with plaintiff's connivance without wife's knowledge, held privileged), Notes, 1 Buff.L.Rev. 314, 50 Mich.L.Rev. 933.

6. Wilkerson v. State, 91 Ga. 729, 17 S.E. 990, syl. 2 (1893) (letter from husband to wife delivered by her to paramour, inadmissible against husband); Scott v. Comm., 94 Ky. 511, 23 S.W. 219, syl. 1 (1893) (letter to wife voluntarily surrendered by her); McCoy v. Justice, 199 N.C. 637, 155 S.E. 452, syl. 14 (1930) (husband's letters disclosed by wife to third persons).

Nevertheless, there are a substantial number of cases which disregard this element of betrayal and hold the privilege not applicable. See, e. g., People v. Swaile, 12 Cal.App. 192, 107 Pac. 134, syl. 5–7 (1909) (prisoner sends wife letter by police officer: she gives it back to officer at his request); State

may testify to the confidential message is sometimes supported on the ground that the particular statute is phrased in terms of incompetency of the spouses to testify to the communication, and should not be extended to disqualify third persons.[7] Perhaps it may be better sustained on the more general view that since the privilege has as its only effect the suppression of relevant evidence, its scope should be confined as narrowly as is consistent with reasonable protection of marital communications.

In this latter view, it seems, since the communicating spouse can ordinarily take effective precautions against overhearing, he should bear the risk of a failure to use such precautions.[8] Moreover, if he sends a messenger with a letter, he should ordinarily assume the risk that the chosen emissary may lose or misdeliver the message.[9] But if a prisoner in jail speaks to his wife with all the secrecy that his poor cell affords, it seems unduly harsh to forfeit the privilege if by wire-recorder or by eavesdroppers in the next cell his confidences are overheard.[10] He has done what he could. Similarly, it seems that when one sends a written message to his wife by an agent there are no practical precautions that sender or agent can use

against forcible seizure, and if the letter is so taken it should still be privileged.[11]

If the spouse to whom the letter is addressed dies and it is found among the effects of the deceased, may the personal representative be required or permitted to produce it in court? Here is no connivance or betrayal by the deceased spouse, and on the other hand this is not a disclosure against which the sender could effectively guard. If the privilege is to be held, as most courts do,[12] to survive the death of one of the spouses, it seems that only a court which strictly limits the effect of the statute to restraining the spouses themselves from testifying, could justify a denial of the privilege in this situation.[13]

87. Who Is the Holder of the Privilege? Enforcement and Waiver.

Greenleaf in 1842 in foreshadowing the protection of marital communications, wrote of the projected rule as a "privilege" based on "public policy." Many legislatures, however, when they came to write the privilege into law phrased the rule simply as a survival in this special case of the ancient incompetency of the spouses, which the same statutes undertook to abolish or restrict. So it

---

v. Sysinger, 25 S.D. 110, 125 N.W. 879, syl. 5. (1910) (prisoner's letter to wife, delivered by her to State's attorney); Note, 63 A.L.R. 107, 124.

7. See, e. g., Comm. v. Wakelin, 230 Mass. 567, 120 N.E. 209, 212 (1918); Connella v. Terr., 16 Okl. 365, 86 Pac. 72, 75 (1906).

8. Comm. v. Everson, 123 Ky. 330, 96 S.W. 460, 461 (1906) (likened to attorney-client privilege as to which "it has been said that if persons wish the communications they have with their attorneys to be kept secret, they should be careful not to talk in the hearing of others"); 8 Wigmore, Evidence, §§ 2339(1), 2326.

9. See Hammons and O'Toole cases, supra note 4.

10. But thus far the scanty authority seems to deny the privilege in this situation. Comm. v. Wakelin, 230 Mass. 567, 120 N.E. 209, syl. 19, 20 (1918) (dictograph planted in cell where husband and wife were held), and cases cited therein.

11. See Ward v. State, 70 Ark. 204, 66 S.W. 926, syl. 1 (1902) (letter to wife and enclosure to third person given by husband in jail to wife and seized from her by officers, held, the former privileged, the latter not).

12. See § 89, below.

13. Privilege applied. Bowman v. Patrick, 32 Fed. 368 (Circ.Ct.Mo.1887) (forcible opinion by Miller, J.); McKie v. State, 165 Ga. 210, 140 S.E. 625, syl. 1, 2 (1927) (trial of wife for murder of husband; wife's letter to husband, produced by his temporary administrator, held improperly admitted, two judges dissenting), noted critically, 37 Yale L.J. 669. Privilege denied. Dickerson v. United States, 65 F.2d 824, syl. 3 (C.C.A. 1st 1933) (trial of husband for murder of wife; letter to wife found by third person among her effects, held admissible).

is often provided that the spouses are "incompetent" to testify to marital communications. Consequently, the courts frequently overlook this "common law" background [1] of privilege, and permit any party to the action to claim the benefit of the rule by objection. Doubtless counsel often fail to point out that privilege, not incompetency, is the proper classification, and that the distinctive feature of privilege is that it can only be claimed by the holder or beneficiary of the privilege, not by a party as such.[2] Nevertheless, some courts have clearly announced and acted upon this latter principle.[3]

Who is the holder? Wigmore's argument, that the policy of encouraging freedom of communication points to the communicating spouse as the holder,[4] seems convincing. Under this view, in the case of a unilateral oral message or statement, of a husband to his wife, only the husband could assert the privilege, where the sole purpose is to show the expressions and attitude of the husband. If the object, however, were to show the wife's adoption of the husband's statement by her silence, then the husband's statement and her conduct both become her communication and she can claim the privilege. Similarly, if a conversation or an exchange of correspond-

ence between them is offered to show the collective expressions of them both, either it seems could claim privilege as to the entire exchange.

A failure by the holder to assert the privilege by objection, or a voluntary revelation by such holder of the communication on the stand,[5] or of a material part, is a waiver. The judge, however, may in his discretion protect the privilege [6] if the holder is not present to assert it, and objection by a party not the holder may serve the purpose of invoking this discretion, though the party may not complain [7] if the judge fails to protect this privilege, belonging to the absent spouse.

88. Controversies in Which the Privilege Is Inapplicable.[1]

The common law privilege against adverse testimony of a spouse was subject to an exception in cases of prosecution of the husband for acts of violence to the wife.[2] When nineteenth century statutes in this country limited and regulated this privilege and the incompetency of spouses as witnesses and defined the new statutory privilege for confidential communications the common law exception above mentioned was usually incorporated and extended, and frequently other

---

1. See § 82, above.

2. See § 73, herein.

3. Luick v. Arends, 21 N.D. 614, 132 N.W. 353, 362, 363, syl. 10 (1911) (statutory phrase, "nor can either be . . . without consent of the other examined as to any communication" creates a privilege, not a disqualification, which only a spouse can assert, and the defendant in the alienation suit here, cannot assert the privilege or complain on appeal of its denial); Coles v. Harsch, 129 Ore. 11, 276 Pac. 248, 253–255, syl. 9 (1929) (alienation action, plaintiff's wife having later married defendant; defendant, not being the holder of the privilege, could not object at the trial or on appeal to plaintiff's disclosure of marital communications); Patterson v. Skoglund, 181 Ore. 167, 180 P.2d 108, syl. 15 (1947) (only husband or wife, not the defendant, can assert the privilege).

4. 8 Wigmore, Evidence, § 2340(1). This view is approved in Fraser v. United States, 145 F.2d 139, syl.

14 (C.C.A. 6th, 1944). But see Hagedorn v. Hagedorn, 211 N.C. 175, 189 S.E. 507, syl. 5 (1937) which construed a statute which said that no spouse "shall be compellable" to disclose communications to mean that either could disclose, though the other objects. See critical Note, 15 N.C.L.Rev. 282.

5. Patterson v. Skoglund, note 3, above, syl. 16.
It is suggested in Fraser v. United States, 145 F.2d 139, 144, syl. 15 (C.C.A.6th 1945) that when the husband claims the privilege on the stand, but answers when ordered by the court to do so, this is a waiver, but this conclusion seems questionable.

6. Coles v. Harsch, 129 Ore. 11, 276 Pac. 248, 255 (1929); Model Code of Evidence, Rule 105(e).

7. See decisions cited note 3, above.

1. 8 Wigmore, Evidence, § 2338; 70 C.J., Witnesses, §§ 527–529; 58 Am.Jur., Witnesses, §§ 396, 398; Model Code of Evidence, Rule 216.

2. See § 66, herein, and 8 Wigmore, Evidence, § 2239.

exceptions were added. Under these statutes [3] it is not always clear how far the exceptions are intended to apply only to the provisions limiting the competency of the spouses as witnesses, or whether they apply also to the privilege for confidential communications. Frequently, however, in the absence of a contrary decision, it is at least arguable that the exception does have this latter application, and in some instances this intent is clearly expressed.

The types of controversies in which the marital communication privilege is made inapplicable vary, of course, from state to state. They may be derived from express provision, from statutory implication, or from decisions based upon common law doctrine.[4] They may be grouped as follows: [5]

1. Prosecutions for crimes committed by one spouse against the other or against the children of either. Besides statutes in general terms, particular crimes, most frequently family desertion and pandering, are often specified, and as to these latter the withdrawal of the privilege for communications is usually explicit.

2. Actions by one of the spouses against an outsider for an intentional injury to the marital relation. Thus far this exception has been applied, sometimes under statutes, sometimes as a continuation of common law tradition, chiefly in actions for alienation of affection or for criminal conversation.[6] It is usually applied to admit declarations expressive of the state of affection of the alienated spouse.[7]

3. Actions by one spouse against the other. Some of the statutes are in this broader form. Some apply only to particular kinds of actions between them, of which divorce suits are most often specified. This exception for controversies between the spouses,[8] which should extend to controversies between the representatives of the spouses, seems worthy of universal acceptance. In the analogous case of clients who jointly consult an attorney, the clients are held to have no privilege for such consultation in controversies between themselves.[9] So here it seems that husband and wife, while they would desire that their confidences be shielded from the outside world, would ordinarily anticipate that if a controversy between themselves should arise in which their mutual conversations would shed light on the

---

3. See the compilation of such statutes in 2 Wigmore, Evidence, § 488.

4. See e. g., United States v. Walker, 176 F.2d 564, 568 (C.A.2d 1949) (L. Hand, C. J.: "We do not forget that a wife from the earliest times was competent to testify against her husband, when the crime was an offense against her person. . . . The same exception probably extends to the privilege against the admission of confidential communications"); People v. McCormack, 278 App.D. 191, 104 N.Y.S.2d 139, 143, syl. 10 (1951) (common law exception for testimony as to assaults on wife is to be read into statute creating privilege, though exception not mentioned).

5. Compare Uniform Rules of Evidence, R. 28(2): "Neither spouse may claim such privilege (a) in an action by one spouse against the other spouse, or (b) in an action for damages for the alienation of the affections of the other, or for criminal conversation with the other, or (c) in a criminal action in which one of them is charged with a crime against the person or property of the other or of a child of either, or a crime against the person or property of a third person committed in the course of committing a crime against the other, or bigamy or adultery, or desertion of the other or of a child of either, or (d) in a criminal action in which the accused offers evidence of a communication between him and his spouse. . . ."

6. Stocker v. Stocker, 112 Neb. 565, 199 N.W. 849, syl. 1, 36 A.L.R. 1063 (1924); Hafer v. Lemon, 182 Okl. 578, 79 P.2d 216, syl. 4 (1938). Contra: Gjesdal v. Harmon, 175 Minn. 414, 221 N.W. 639, syl. 2 (1928); McKinnon v. Chenoweth, 176 Ore. 74, 155 P.2d 944, syl. 15 (1945). Cases are collected in Note, Alienation of Affection and Confidential Communications, 36 A.L.R. 1068.

7. Note, 36 A.L.R. 1068, 1070.

8. See statutes of Arizona, California, Colorado, Idaho, Minnesota, Montana, Nevada, Oregon, South Dakota, Utah, Wisconsin, and Wyoming, quoted from in 2 Wigmore Evidence, § 488.

9. See § 95, herein.

merits, the interests of both would be served by full disclosure.

4. A criminal prosecution against one of the spouses in which a declaration of the other spouse made confidentially to the accused would tend to justify or reduce the grade of the offense.[10]

89. If the Communication Was Made During the Marriage, Does Death or Divorce End the Privilege?[1]

The incompetency of husband or wife to testify for the other, and the privilege of each spouse against adverse testimony are terminated when the marriage ends by death or divorce.[2] The privilege for confidential communications of the spouses, however, was based (in the mind of its chief sponsor, Greenleaf) upon the policy of encouraging confidences and its sponsor thought that such encouragement required not merely temporary but permanent secrecy.[3] The courts in this country have accepted this need for permanent protection[4]—though it is obviously a most unrealistic assumption—and about one-half of our statutes codifying the privilege explicitly provide that it continues after death or divorce.[5] It is probably in these cases where the marital tie has been severed, that the supposed policy of the privilege has the most remote and tenuous relevance, and the possibilities of injustice in its application are most apparent. Wigmore points out that in this area, "there must arise occasional instances of hardship where ample flexibility should be allowed in the relaxation of the rule."[6]

In the famous recent English case of Shenton v. Tyler,[7] the court was faced with one of those instances of hardship. The plaintiff sued a widow and alleged that her deceased husband had made an oral secret trust, known to the widow, for the benefit of plaintiff, and sought to interrogate the widow. The widow relied on sec. 3 of the Evidence Amendment Act, 1853, as follows: " . . . no wife shall be compellable to disclose any communication made to her during the marriage." The court rejected the Greenleaf theory of a common-law privilege for communications surviving the end of the marriage, and was "unable to find any warrant for extending the words of the section by construc-

---

10. Texas Vernon's Ann.C.C.P. art. 714 recognizes an exception, "where one spouse is prosecuted for an offense and a declaration by one or the other goes to extenuate or justify the offense for which either is on trial." Wigmore argues for such an exception. Evidence, § 2338(4). And he calls attention to the "cruel absurdity" of excluding the communication in these circumstances in Steeley v. State, 17 Okl.Cr. 252, 187 Pac. 820, syl. 2 (1920) (defendant charged with murder of wife's paramour could not testify to wife's communications to him disclosing deceased's conduct in debauching her) and other cases cited. This view is adopted in Model Code of Evidence, Rule 216 (d) and Comment.

1. 8 Wigmore, Evidence, § 2341; 5 Jones, Evidence, § 2147 (2d ed. rev. 1926); 70 C.J. Witnesses, § 531; 58 Am.Jur., Witnesses, § 379; Dec.Dig., Witnesses, ☞195.

2. See § 66, herein.

3. "The happiness of the married state requires that there should be the most unlimited confidence between husband and wife; and this confidence the law secures by providing that it shall be kept forever inviolable; that nothing shall be extracted from the bosom of the wife which was confided there by the husband. Therefore, after the parties are separated, whether it be by divorce or by the death of the husband, the wife is still precluded from disclosing any conversations with him . . . ." 1 Greenleaf, Evidence, 296 (13th ed. 1876).

4. Rance v. Hutchinson, 131 Fla. 460, 179 So. 777, syl. 1 (1938) (divorced wife of decedent may not testify to communications between herself and husband during marriage, about conveyance by spouses to husband in trust for children); In re Osbon's Estate, 205 Minn. 419, 286 N.W. 306, syl. 4 (1939) (in will contest, trial judge properly refused to permit divorced wife of testator to testify to their conversations during marriage); Pace v. State, 61 Tex.Cr. 436, 135 S.W. 379, syl. 2 (1911) (confession of husband to wife that he killed a man).

5. See the compilation of such statutes, 2 Wigmore, Evidence, § 488.

6. 8 Wigmore, Evidence, § 2341.

7. L.R. [1939] Ch.Div. 620 (C.A.).

tion so as to include widowers and widows and divorced persons." [8] However debatable may be the court's position that there was no common law privilege for marital communications,[9] it seems clear that the actual holding that the privilege for communications ends when the marriage ends is far preferable in policy to the contrary result reached under American statutes and decisions.

90. Policy and Future of the Privilege.[1]

The most substantial argument that present-day judges and writers advance in support of the privilege is that the privilege against court-room disclosure is needed for the encouragement of marital confidences, which confidences in turn promote harmony between husband and wife. Freedom of marital confidences to a reasonable extent at least is desirable, but this freedom is generally a result rather than a cause of marital harmony. The main answer to the argument of policy, however, is that the contingency of court-room disclosure would almost never (even though the privilege did not exist) be in the minds of the parties in considering how far they should go in their secret conversations. What encourages them to fullest frankness is not the assurance of court-room privilege, but the trust they place in the loyalty and discretion of each other. If the secrets are not told outside the court-room there will be little danger of their being elicited in court. In the lives of most people appearance in court as a party or a witness is an exceedingly rare and ususual event, and the anticipation of it is not one of those factors which materially influence in daily life the degree of fullness of marital disclosures.[2] Accordingly, we must conclude that, while the danger of injustice from suppression of relevant proof is clear and certain,[3] the probable benefits of the rule of privilege in encouraging marital confidences and wedded harmony, is at best doubtful and marginal.

Probably the policy of encouraging confidences is not the prime influence in creating and maintaining the privilege. It is really a much more natural and less devious matter. It is a matter of emotion and sentiment. All of us have a feeling of indelicacy and want of decorum in prying into the secrets of husband and wife. It is important to recognize that this is the real source of the privilege. When we do, we realize at once that this motive of delicacy, while worthy and desirable, will not stand in the balance with the

8. L.R. [1939] Ch.Div. 620, 652 (by Luxmoore, L. J.).

9. See § 82, above.

1. 8 Wigmore, Evidence, § 2332, 70 C.J., Witnesses, § 508, 58 Am.Jur., Witnesses, § 375, Dec.Dig., Witnesses, ☞188(1). The foregoing give the supporting arguments of policy. Two law review articles criticize with much penetration the soundness of these reasons. Hutchins and Slesinger, Some Observations on the Law of Evidence: Family Relations, 13 Minn.L.Rev. 675, 682 (1929), Hines, Privileged Testimony of Husband and Wife in California, 19 Calif.L.Rev. 390, 410–414 (1931).

2. ". . . Very few people ever get into court, and practically no one outside the legal profession knows anything about the rules regarding privileged communications between spouses. As far as the writers are aware (though research might lead to another conclusion) marital harmony among lawyers who know about privileged communications is not vastly superior to that of other professional groups." Hutchins and Slesinger, op. cit., p. 682.

3. Examples of cases where the possibilities of injustice seem conspicuous are In re DeNeef, 42 Cal. App.2d 691, 109 P.2d 741, syl. 4 (1941) (wife sues on life insurance policy taken out in her favor by deceased husband. Defense: fraudulent representations by husband as to his health. Held, wife cannot be interrogated as husband's statements to her as to his physical condition. "We are not concerned with the reason for the rule or its effect on the administration of justice"); McKie v. State, 165 Ga. 210, 140 S.E. 625, syl. 1, 2 (1927) (wife's conviction for murder of husband because of admission of wife's letters to husband, found in his effects after he was killed); Todd v. Barbee, 271 Ky. 381, 111 S.W.2d 1041, syl. 6 (1938) (excluding husband's testimony that he gave wife money to pay rent) and People v. Daghita, 299 N.Y. 194, 86 N.E. 2d 172, syl. 3, 4 (1949) (error to allow wife to testify in prosecution of husband for grand larceny, that she saw him bringing stolen property into their home and hiding it under his bed).

need for disclosure in court of the facts upon which a man's life, liberty, or estate may depend.

This feeling of disproportion between the interest of delicacy and the interest of justice has doubtless swayed the courts in limiting the privilege in groups of cases where injustice in its application was most apparent,[4] in the illogical permission to the third party intercepting or overhearing the message to make disclosure,[5] and in the oft-repeated admonition that the scope of the privilege should, in case of doubt, be strictly confined.[6] Seemingly all of these limiting practices are

paths leading to and converging in a wider solution. This solution is to recognize, by statute, rule of court or decision, that the privilege is not an absolute but a qualified one, which must yield if the trial judge finds that the evidence of the communication is required in the due administration of justice.[7] The judge could then protect the marital confidence when it should be protected, namely, when the material fact sought to be established by the communication is not substantially controverted and may be proven with reasonable convenience by other evidence.

---

4. See § 88, above.

5. See § 86, above.

6. " 'The policy of the law is to require the disclosure of all information by witnesses in order that justice may prevail. The granting of a privilege from such disclosure constitutes an exception to that general rule.' People ex rel. Mooney v. Sheriff of New York County, 269 N.Y. 291, 295, 199 N.E. 415, 416, 102 A.L.R. 769. 'The suppression of truth is a grievous necessity at best.' McMann v. Securities and Exchange Commission, 2 Cir., 87 F.2d

377, 378. And apropos of the particular question of privilege before us, we have it on the authority of Wolfle v. United States, 291 U.S. 7, at pages 14, 17, 54 S.Ct. 279, at pages 280–281, 78 L.Ed. 617, that:

" '. . . The privilege suppresses relevant testimony and should be allowed only when it is plain that marital confidence cannot otherwise reasonably be preserved.' " People v. McCormack, 278 App.D. 191, 104 N.Y.S.2d 139, 144 (1951).

7. See a similar suggestion for all privileges for confidential communications, § 81, herein.

CHAPTER 10

THE CLIENT'S PRIVILEGE: COMMUNICATIONS BETWEEN CLIENT AND LAWYER

91. Background and Policy of the Privilege.

The notion that the loyalty owed by the lawyer to his client disables him from being a witness in his client's case is deep-rooted in Roman law.[1] This Roman tradition may or may not have been influential in shaping the early English doctrine of which we find the first traces in Elizabeth's time, that the oath and honor of the barrister and the attorney protect them from being required to disclose, upon examination in court, the secrets of the client.[2] But by the eighteenth century in England the emphasis upon the code of honor had lessened and the need of the ascertainment of truth for the ends of justice loomed larger than the pledge of secrecy. So a new justification for the lawyer's exemption from disclosing his client's secrets was found. This was the theory that claims and disputes which may lead to litigation can most justly and expeditiously be handled by practised experts, namely lawyers, and that such experts can act effectively only if they are fully advised of the facts by the parties whom they represent.[3] Such full disclosure will be promoted if the client knows that what he tells his lawyer cannot, over his objection, be extorted in court from the lawyer's lips.

The proposition is that the detriment to justice from a power to shut off inquiry to pertinent facts in court, will be outweighed by the benefits to justice (not to the client) from a franker disclosure in the lawyer's office. Wigmore who supports the privilege, acknowledges that "Its benefits are all indirect and speculative; its obstruction is plain and concrete."[4]

The tendency of the client in giving his story to his counsel to omit all that he suspects will make against him, is matter of

1. See Radin, The Privilege of Confidential Communication between Lawyer and Client, 16 Calif. L.Rev. 487, 488 (1928).

2. 8 Wigmore, Evidence, § 2290 (3d ed. 1940) (history of the privilege).

3. " . . . An increase of legal business, and the inabilities of parties to transact that business themselves, made it necessary for them to employ . . . other persons who might transact that business for them; that this necessity introduced with it the necessity of what the law hath very justly established, an inviolable secrecy to be observed by attornies, in order to render it safe for clients to communicate to their attornies all proper instructions. . . ." Mounteney, B. in Annesley v. Earl of Anglesea, 17 How.St.Tr. 1225 (1743) quoted in 8 Wigmore, Evidence, § 2291 (3d ed. 1940) (policy of the privilege).

4. Wigmore, op.cit. § 2291, p. 557.

181

everyday professional observation. It makes it necessary for the prudent lawyer to cross-examine his client searchingly about possible unfavorable facts. Perhaps in criminal cases the accused if he knew the lawyer could be compelled to repeat the facts disclosed might be induced by fear of this to withhold an acknowledgement of guilt. He knows that the prosecution cannot compel him, the accused, to testify. And in civil cases, before the mid-nineteenth century statutes making parties compellable to testify, the party might have feared to give damaging facts to his counsel if the latter could have been called to disclose these admissions in court. Now, however, when the party knows that he himself can be called as a witness by the adversary, the danger from disclosure to counsel is less important.

Perhaps we need not yield fully to the force of Bentham's slashing argument that the privilege is not needed by the innocent party with a righteous cause or defense, and that the guilty should not be given its aid in concerting a false one.[5] Wigmore in answer points out that in lawsuits all is not black and white but a client's case may be one where there is no clear preponderance of morals and justice on either side, and he may mistakenly think a fact fatal to his cause, when it is not, and thus be impelled, if there were no privilege, to forego resort to counsel for advice in a fair claim.[6] Yet it must be acknowledged that the existence of the privilege may often instead of avoiding litigation upon unfounded claims, actually encourage such litigation. A rascally client consults one lawyer who tells him that certain facts disclosed are fatal to his case. The client then goes to another attorney and tells the story differently, so that a claim may be supported—a course which in the absence of the privilege would be much more dangerous.[7]

If one were legislating for a new commonwealth, without history or customs, it would be hard to maintain that a privilege for lawyer-client communications would facilitate more than it would obstruct the administration of justice. But we are not writing on a blank slate. Our adversary system of litigation casts the lawyer in the role of fighter for the party whom he represents. A strong sentiment of loyalty attaches to the relationship, and this sentiment would be outraged by an attempt to change our customs so as to make the lawyer amenable to routine examination upon the client's confidential disclosures regarding professional business. Loyalty and sentiment are silken threads, but they are hard to break. Accordingly, confined as we are by this "cake of custom," it is unlikely that enough energy could now be generated to abolish the privilege, particularly since its obstructive effect has been substantially lessened by the development of liberal doctrines as to waiver and as to denial of the privilege in case of consultation for unlawful ends. Nevertheless, some progress toward liberalization of the practice, some better reconciliation of the conflicting pulls of sentiment and delicacy on the one hand and of the need, on the other, for full ascertainment of the crucial facts by a tribunal of justice, seems possible. It is suggested that

1. The lawyer's duty to maintain out of court the secrecy of his client's confidential disclosures be retained intact. This assurance furnishes to most clients having a good faith claim or defense all the security (and hence encouragement to full disclosure) for which they would feel any need.

2. The present privilege against disclosure of such communications in judicial proceedings, should be made subject to the exception that the trial judge may require a

---

5. See Bentham, Rationale of Judicial Evidence, b. IX, pt. IV, c. 5 (1827), passages quoted Wigmore, op.cit., § 2291.

6. Wigmore, op.cit., § 2291, p. 555.

7. Radin, op.cit., 16 Calif.L.Rev. at 490. See also Morgan, Foreword, Model Code of Evidence, 19, 20 (pamphlet ed., 1942).

particular disclosure if he finds that it is necessary in the administration of justice.[8] Notwithstanding such a change, the present reluctance of lawyers to call an opposing counsel for routine examination on his client's case would continue as a restraining influence. The duty to the client of secrecy would still be recognized and protected in the ordinary course, but the lawyer's duty as an officer of the court to lend his aid in the last resort to prevent a miscarriage of justice would be given the primacy which a true balancing of the two interests would seem to demand.

A clear statement of the presently accepted scope of the privilege is embodied in the Uniform Rules.[9]

92. The Professional Relationship.

The privilege for communications of a client with his lawyer hinges upon the client's belief that he is consulting a lawyer in that capacity and his manifested intention to seek such professional advice.[1] It is sufficient if he reasonably believes that the person con-

---

8. Compare Gen.Stats.N.C.1943, § 8–53, which after directing that physicians shall not be required to disclose information acquired in attending a patient, adds "Provided, that the presiding judge of a superior court may compel such disclosure, if in his opinion the same is necessary to a proper administration of justice." See also the court's language regarding the attorney-client privilege in Jackson v. Pillsbury, 380 Ill. 554, 44 N.E.2d 537, 547 (1942): "The resulting injury to the relation by the disclosure of the communications must be greater than the benefit thereby gained for the correct disposal of the litigation." For a suggestion that the probable and desirable course of evolution for all the privileges is the path from rule to discretion, see McCormick, The Scope of Privilege in the Law of Evidence, 16 Tex.L.Rev. 447, 469 (1938).

9. Uniform Rules of Evidence, R. 26: "(1) *General Rule*. Subject to Rule 37 [as to waiver] and except as otherwise provided by Paragraph 2 of this rule communications found by the judge to have been between lawyer and his client in the course of that relationship and in professional confidence, are privileged, and a client has a privilege (a) if he is the witness to refuse to disclose any such communication, and (b) to prevent his lawyer from disclosing it, and (c) to prevent any other witness from disclosing such communication if it came to the knowledge of such witness (i) in the course of its transmittal between the client and the lawyer, or (ii) in a manner not reasonably to be anticipated by the client, or (iii) as a result of a breach of the lawyer-client relationship. The privilege may be claimed by the client in person or by his lawyer, or if incompetent, by his guardian, or if deceased, by his personal representative. The privilege available to a corporation or association terminates upon dissolution.

"(2) *Exceptions*. Such privileges shall not extend (a) to a communication if the judge finds that sufficient evidence, aside from the communication, has been introduced to warrant a finding that the legal service was sought or obtained in order to enable or aid the client to commit or plan to commit a crime or a tort, or (b) to a communication relevant to an issue between parties all of whom claim through the client, regardless of whether the respective claims are by testate or intestate succession or by *inter vivos* transaction, or (c) to a communication relevant to an issue of breach of duty by the lawyer to his client, or by the client to his lawyer, or (d) to a communication relevant to an issue concerning an attested document of which the lawyer is an attesting witness, or (e) to a communication relevant to a matter of common interest between two or more clients if made by any of them to a lawyer whom they have retained in common when offered in an action between any of such clients.

"(3) *Definitions*. As used in this rule (a) 'Client' means a person or corporation or other association that, directly or through an authorized representative, consults a lawyer or the lawyer's representative for the purpose of retaining the lawyer or securing legal service or advice from him in his professional capacity; and includes an incompetent whose guardian so consults the lawyer or the lawyer's representative in behalf of the incompetent, (b) 'communication' includes advice given by the lawyer in the course of representing the client and includes disclosures of the client to a representative, associate or employee of the lawyer incidental to the professional relationship, (c) 'lawyer' means a person authorized, or reasonably believed by the client to be authorized to practice law in any state or nation the law of which recognizes a privilege against disclosure of confidential communications between client and lawyer."

1. See Note, Nature of Professional Relationship Required under Privilege Rule, 24 Ia.L.Rev. 538 (1939).

sulted is a lawyer, though in fact he is not.[2] Communications in the course of preliminary discussion with a view to employing the lawyer are privileged though the employment is in the upshot not accepted.[3] The burden of proof (presumably in both senses) rests on the person asserting the privilege to show that the consultation was a professional one.[4]

Payment or agreement to pay a fee, however, is not essential.[5] But where one consults an attorney not as a lawyer but as a friend[6] or as a business adviser[7] or negotiator,[8] or where the communication is to the attorney acting as a "mere scrivener"[9] or as an attesting witness to a will or deed,[10] or as

2. People v. Barker, 60 Mich. 277, 27 N.W. 539, syl. 7 (1886) (confession to detective pretending to be an attorney).
A student in a law office would not come within the privilege except as he might be acting as a clerk or agent for the lawyer. Wartell v. Novograd, 48 R.I. 296, 137 A. 776, syl. 8 (1927).

3. In re Dupont's Estate, 60 Cal.App.2d 276, 140 P.2d 866, syl. 11, 12 (1943) (preliminary negotiations fall within language of Code Civ.Proc. sec. 1881, subd. 2, conferring privilege to communications, "in the course of professional employment", "no person could ever safely consult an attorney for the first time . . . if the privilege depended on the chance of whether the attorney after hearing the statement of the facts decided to accept the employment or decline it"); Denver Tramway Co. v. Owens, 20 Colo. 107, 36 P. 848, syl. 8 (1894); Keir v. State, 152 Fla. 389, 11 So.2d 886, syl. 8 (1943) (letters). Of course, statements made after the employment is declined are not privileged. McGrede v. Rembert N. Bank, 147 S.W.2d 580, syl. 4 (Tex.Civ.App.1941) (citing authorities).

4. McGrede v. Rembert N. Bank, 147 S.W.2d 580, syl. 5 (Tex.Civ.App.1941); McKnew v. Superior Court, 23 Cal.2d 58, 142 P.2d 1, syl. 2 (1943).

5. Matters v. State, 120 Neb. 404, 232 N.W. 781, syl. 9 (1930) (citing authorities); Hodge v. Garten, 116 W.Va. 564, 182 S.E. 582, syl. 1 (1935).

6. Modern Woodmen v. Watkins, 132 F.2d 352, syl. 6, 7 (C.C.A.Fla.1942) (disclosure of suicidal intent); Solon v. Lichtenstein, 39 Cal.2d 75, 244 P.2d 907, syl. 2, 3 (1952); Lifsey v. Mims, 193 Ga. 780, 20 S.E.2d 32, syl. 1 (1942) (lawyer drawing deed as a "friendly act"); In re Conner's Estate, 33 N.W.2d 866, syl. 5 (1948) (modified on other grounds, 240 Ia. 479, 36 N.W.2d 833 (1949) (divulging grandson's illegitimacy, to secure friend's help in telling boy).

7. United States v. United Shoe Machinery Corp., 89 F.Supp. 357, syl. 6-8 (1950) (a communication soliciting business advice, not privileged, and attorney-client privilege does not extend to attorneys employed in a department of corporation which functions as a business branch, but does exist between corporation and attorneys in its legal department who perform substantially the same service as outside counsel); United States v. Vehicular Parking,

52 F.Supp. 751, syl. 1-3 (D.Del.1943) (business advice and directions by attorney who was promoter, director and manager of corporation concerned); Clayton v. Canida, 223 S.W.2d 264, syl. 2 (Tex.Civ. App.1949) (attorney acting as accountant, income tax return).

8. Myles E. Rieser Co. Inc. v. Loew's Inc., 194 Misc. 119, 81 N.Y.S.2d 861 (S.Ct.Sp.T.1948) (attorneys acting both as lawyers and as negotiators; communications in latter capacity not privileged). Henson v. State, 261 P.2d 916, syl. 7-9 (Okla.Crim.1953) (communication between defendant and attorney sharing office and secretary with defendant's attorney, not privileged and no attorney-client relationship existed where defendant knew attorney represented another and attorney tried to settle differences between his client and defendant).

9. The phrase is often used as a justification for denying the privilege, see e. g., Benson v. Custer, 236 Ia. 345, 17 N.W.2d 889, syl. 6 (1945); Sparks v. Sparks, 51 Kan. 195, 201, 32 P. 892, syl. 3 (1893). The distinction is usually drawn between instances where the lawyer is employed merely to draft the document and cases where his advice is sought as to terms and effect. Mueller v. Batcheler, 131 Ia. 650, 652, 109 N.W. 186, 187 (1906) (conveyances); Dickerson v. Dickerson, 322 Ill. 492, 153 N.E. 740, syl. 9 (1926) (deed); Wilcox v. Coons, 359 Mo. 52, 220 S.W. 2d 15, syl. 2, 3 (1949); Shelley v. Landry, 97 N.H. 27, 79 A.2d 626, syl. 7 (1951). Usually it will be found that an attorney asked to draw a will, is not a mere-scrivener, but is acting professionally. Booher v. Brown, 173 Ore. 464, 146 P.2d 71, syl. 4 (1944). And the strict view of privilege in respect to the employment of lawyers as conveyancers seems somewhat inconsistent with the bar's present-day emphasis upon the importance of this as a lawyer's function. See Houck, Real Estate Instruments and the Bar, 5 Law and Contemporary Problems 66 (1938).

10. Jones v. Smith, 266 Ga. 162, 56 S.E.2d 462, syl. 11-13 (1949) (lawyer may testify as to client's mental condition, his knowledge of the contents and other pertinent facts attending execution of contract, prepared and attested to by him); In re Heiler's Estate, 288 Mich. 49, 284 N.W. 641, syl. 4 (1939) (lawyer attesting will could testify to what he learned in his capacity as witness); Larson v. Dahlstrom, 214 Minn. 304, 8 N.W.2d 48, syl. 2, 3 (1943) (lawyer at-

an executor [11] or as agent,[12] the consultation is not professional nor the statement privileged. The privilege does not extend to communications between a client and administrative practitioners who are not attorneys.[13] Traditionally, the relationship sought to be fostered by the privilege has been that between the lawyer and a private client and the policy that of encouraging the client to make full disclosure, so far as appears relevant, of facts affecting his private interests. This tradition and policy seem inapplicable when the attorney is consulted as a lawyer for the public, though other considerations may justify the creation of some distinct privilege. Thus, disclosures to the public prosecuting attorney by an informer are not within the attorney-client privilege,[14] but an analogous policy of protecting the giving of such information has led to the recognition of a privilege against the disclosure of the identity of the informer, unless the trial judge finds that such disclosure is necessary in the interests of justice.[15] Communications to an attorney appointed by the court to serve the interest of a party are of course within the privilege.[16] A communication by a lawyer to a member of the Board of Governors of the state bar association, revealing a fraudulent conspiracy in which he had been engaged and expressing his desire to resign from the practice of law was held not privileged.[17] In a recent case the question was raised whether a letter from the state auditor to the attorney general relating to litigation pending against the auditor in his official capacity was privileged and the court without discussion held that the privilege applied, as in the case of a private litigant.[18] This seems debatable, since the need for secrecy to encourage full disclosure by the official is not apparent and the policy favoring publicity of official acts may well be thought preponderant.

Wigmore argues for a privilege analogous to the lawyer-client privilege for "confessions or similar confidences" made privately by persons implicated in a wrong or crime to the judge of a court.[19] As to judges generally there seems little justification for such a privilege if the policy-motive is the furtherance of the administration of justice by encouraging a full disclosure.[20] Unlike the lawyer the judge needs no private disclosures

---

testing deed could testify to statements made by client at time of execution as bearing on mental condition); Anderson v. Thomas, 108 Utah 252, 159 P. 2d 142, syl. 9, 10 (1945) (deed; attesting lawyer may testify to conversations at time of execution).

11. Peyton v. Werhane, 126 Conn. 382, 11 A.2d 800, syl. 10 (1940).

12. Banks v. United States, 204 F.2d 666, syl. 8 (C.C.A. 8, 1953) (attorney acting also in capacity of agent in negotiations with Internal Revenue Officer); Pollock v. United States, 202 F.2d 281, syl. 8, 9 (C.C. A. 5, 1953) (money deposited with attorney to be applied on purchase of real estate); Palatini v. Sarian, 15 N.J.Super. 34, 83 A.2d 24, syl. 7, 10 (1951).

13. Falsone v. United States, 205 F.2d 734, syl. 10 (C.C.A. 5, 1953) (certified public accountant having the same rights as an enrolled attorney under Treasury Department regulations); United States v. United Shoe Machinery Corp., 89 F.Supp. 357, syl. 8 (1950) (patent solicitors not members of bar employed in corporation's patent department); Kent Jewelry Corp. v. Kiefer, 113 N.Y.S.2d 12, syl. 2 (1952)

(patent agent authorized to practice before the United States Patent Office).

14. Fite v. Bennett, 142 Ga. 660, 83 S.E. 515, syl. 2 (1914); Cole v. Andrews, 74 Minn. 93, 76 N.W. 962, syl. 2 (1898); Application of Heller, 184 Misc. 75, 53 N.Y.S.2d 86, syl. 4 (1945).

15. Wilson v. United States, 59 F.2d 390, syl. 2–4 (C. C.A. 3, 1932); 8 Wigmore, Evidence, §§ 2374, 2375 (3d ed.1940).

16. Jayne v. Bateman, 191 Okl. 272, 129 P.2d 188, syl. 3, 4 (1942) (lawyer appointed as guardian ad litem of incompetent party apparently expected to act as attorney also).

17. Steiner v. United States, 134 F.2d 931, syl. 7, 8 (C.C.A.La.1943).

18. Rowley v. Ferguson, 48 N.E.2d 243, syl. 8 (Ct. App.Ohio, 1942).

19. Evidence, § 2376.

20. Authority is scanty. People v. Pratt, 133 Mich. 125, 94 N.W. 752, 67 L.R.A. 923 (1903) tends to support the privilege. Of opposite tendency are,

in advance of trial to enable him to perform his functions. In fact such revelations would ordinarily embarrass rather than aid him in carrying out his duties as a trial judge.[21] The famous case of Lindsey v. People,[22] however, raised the question whether the judge of a juvenile court does not stand in a special position with regard to confidential disclosures by children who come before him. The majority of the court held that when a boy under promise of secrecy confessed to the judge that he had fired the shot that killed his father the judge was compellable, on the trial of the boy's mother for murder, to divulge the confession. The court pointed out that a parent who had received such a confidence would be compellable to disclose. In the case of this particular court the need for encouraging confidences is clear, but in most cases the most effective encouragement will come from the confidence-inspiring personality of the judge, even without the aid of assurances of secrecy. The court's conclusion that the need for secrecy for this type of disclosure does not outweigh the sacrifice to the administration of justice from the suppression of the evidence seems justifiable.

93. Subject-Matter of the Privilege—(a) Communications.

The modern justification of the privilege, namely, that of encouraging full disclosure by the client for the furtherance of the administration of justice,[1] gives no foundation for extending the privilege beyond communications of the client or his agents [2] to the lawyer or his clerk.[3] In the main it seems that, in keeping with the policy of restricting rather than extending privileges which shut out relevant evidence,[4] the courts should in states where the question is open confine the privilege to such communications. There are statutes [5] and decisions [6] however which extend the protection to advice given by the lawyer to the client. If offered to show circumstantially the client's own communications,[7] or as an admission of the client by his failure to object, there is color, particularly in the former instance, for considering them as implied communications of the client, and extending the shield.[8] Some statutes like-

---

People v. Sharac, 209 Mich. 249, 176 N.W. 431, syl. 2 (1920); Agnew v. Agnew, 52 S.D. 472, 218 N.W. 633, syl. 2 (1928), and Lindsey v. People, cited in note 17.

21. Prichard v. United States, 181 F.2d 326, syl. **3** (C.C.A. 6th 1950), aff'd 339 U.S. 974, 70 Sup.Ct. 1029 (communications between judge and attorney seeking legal advice concerning his conduct which was to be investigated by a grand jury called by the judge to investigate election frauds, not privileged and attorney-client relationship did not arise).

22. 66 Colo. 343, 181 P. 531, syl. 4–8, 16 A.L.R. 768 (1919) (three judges dissenting), discussed in 33 Harv.L.Rev. 88, 35 id. 693, 29 Yale L.J. 356, 4 Minn.L.Rev. 227; State v. Bixby, 27 Wash.2d 144, 177 P.2d 689, syl. 26–28 (1947).

Cases recognizing the application of the informer's privilege for information given to judges (see cases pro and con collected in Note, 59 A.L.R. 1555) are to be distinguished.

1. See § 91, supra.

2. Anderson v. Bank of British Columbia, [1876] L.R. 2, Ch.D. 644 (Ct.App.); Wheeler v. Le Marchant [1881] L.R. 17 Ch. D. 675 (Ct.App.); Notes on Com-

munications by Clients' Agents, 139 A.L.R. 1250, 1943 Wis.L.Rev. 424.

3. State v. Krich, 123 N.J.L. 519, 9 A.2d 803, syl. 3, 4 (S.Ct.N.J.1939) (communication to attorney's secretary); Wigmore, Evidence, § 2301 (3d ed. 1940).

4. See §§ 81, 90, supra.

5. See, e.g. the Arkansas, California, Indiana, Kentucky, Missouri and Ohio statutes set out in 8 Wigmore, Evidence, § 2292 n. 2 (3d ed. 1940).

6. United States v. United Shoe Machinery Corp., 89 F.Supp. 357, syl. 4 (1950); Sovereign Camp W. O. W. v. Ward, 196 Ala. 327, 71 So. 404, syl. 5 (1916); Missouri, K. and T. Ry. Co. v. Williams, 43 Tex. Civ.App. 549, 96 S.W. 1087, syl. 3 (1906).

7. As would have been the effect in the cases cited in the next previous note.

8. A recent English decision recognized the privilege for a defamatory statement made by the lawyer in declining employment and sought to be proved solely as a basis for an action against the lawyer for slander. Minter v. Priest, [1929] 1 K.B. 655. It is criticized as unwarranted by the policy of the privilege in a Note, 43 Harv.L.Rev. 134.

wise draw the curtain over matters generally of which the attorney has gained knowledge by reason of the relationship.[9] This seemingly carries the obstructive effect of the privilege far beyond any justification in present-day policy, and is probably a carry-over from the days when the privilege was thought of as primarily for the protection of the honor of the profession. Probably, in the absence of statute, most courts would not support such an extension.[10]

A confidential disclosure may be made by acts as well as by words, as if the client rolled up his sleeve to show the lawyer a hidden scar, or opened the drawer of his desk to show a revolver there. Certainly the fact of the client's disclosure, if in confidence,[11] and presumably the facts so disclosed, would be privileged, provided in the latter case such facts would not have been apparent to the lawyer in the absence of any effort by the client to reveal them.[12]

The application of the privilege to writings presents practical problems requiring discriminating analysis. A professional communication in writing, as a letter from client to lawyer for example, will of course be privileged.[13] These written privileged communi-

---

Communications upon the client's business between co-counsel have been said to be within the privilege. In re Felton, 60 Idaho 540, 94 P.2d 166, syl. 3 (1939); 70 C.J., Witnesses, § 543. And this seems justifiable when one counsel acts for the client in communicating with the other.

See, e.g. Missouri, K. & T. Ry. Co. v. Williams, 43 Tex.Civ.App 549, 96 S.W. 1087, syl. 3 (1906) (general counsel of railway writes to local attorney). United States v. United Shoe Machinery Corp., 89 F.Supp. 357, syl. 4, 8 (privilege extends to communications to and from corporation's outside counsel or general counsel and staff and employees in its patent department); Gen. Acc. Fire & Life Assur. Corp. v. Mitchell, 259 P.2d 862, syl. 7 (Colorado, 1953) (order for production of all correspondence between home office and local counsel and local agents and all telegrams and written memoranda between home office, its attorneys and agents and insured, should have been denied on ground of privilege).

9. See, e.g., the Alabama, Georgia, and Louisiana statutes quoted in 8 Wigmore, Evidence, § 2292, n. 2, and Texas, Vernon's Ann.C.C.P. art. 713.

10. "The rule of privileged communications arose in order that a party might with safety completely inform his attorney as to the matters in which he is employed to the end that the attorney might act with full understanding of them. The limits of the rule, however, are well defined, and as its tendency is to stifle a full disclosure of the truth, courts have been careful to confine it within its legitimate scope, and so it has been held that the rule does not apply to the discovery of facts within the knowledge of an attorney which were not communicated by a client, though he became acquainted with such facts while engaged as attorney for the client. Crosby v. Berger, 11 Paige (N.Y.) 377, 42 Am.Dec. 177." Tutson v. Holland, 50 F.2d 338, 340 (Ct.App.D.C. 1931). See also Hawley v. Hawley, 114

F.2d 745, syl. 11, 12 (Ct.App.D.C. 1940) (attorney's knowledge of client's handwriting, though gained while in employ, not privileged); Kerr v. Hofer, 347 Pa. 356, 32 A.2d 402, syl. 8 (1943) (information about accident obtained by lawyer, not from client, not privileged); Burton v. McLaughlin, 117 Utah 483, 217 P.2d 566, syl. 1 (1950) (facts observed by attorney as to services rendered client when attorney visited client in his home to draw up will and on subsequent visits as a friend); and see 70 C.J., Witnesses, § 556.

11. City and County of San Francisco v. Superior Ct., 37 Cal.2d 227, 231 P.2d 26, syl. 10 (1951); State v. Douglass, 20 W.Va. 770, syl. 2–5 (1882) (Counsel's testimony that he received pistol from client, privileged).

12. Clark v. Skinner, 334 Mo. 1190, 70 S.W.2d 1094, syl. 8 (1934) (attorney's knowledge of client's mental capacity and of want of any and that deeds were delivered, undue influence not privileged); State v. Fitzgerald, 68 Vt. 125, 34 A. 429, syl. 1 (1896) (attorney's testimony to client's intoxication, observable by all, not privileged); 8 Wigmore, Evidence, § 2306 (3d ed. 1940).

Of course, where the client calls in the attorney as a witness to a transaction with a third person, though the client desires that the attorney keep secret the details of the transaction, there is no privilege. McKnew v. Superior Court, 23 Cal.2d 58, 142 P.2d 1 (1943) (attorney asked by client to witness client's making deposit of money in bank, so that attorney could verify deposit to enable client to secure credit, with understanding attorney not to reveal name of bank, held no privilege for latter fact); Note, 17 So.Calif.L.Rev. 410.

13. Peyton v. Werhane, 126 Conn. 382, 11 A.2d 800, syl. 12 (1940).

An interesting case presented the question whether confidential letters of the client were usable, not as evidence of their contents but as specimens for

cations are to be steadily distinguished from other pre-existing documents or writings, such as deeds, wills, and warehouse receipts, not in themselves constituting communications between client and lawyer. As to these pre-existing documents two notions come into play. First, the client may make communications about the document by words or by acts, such as sending the document to the lawyer for perusal or handing to him and calling attention to its terms. Such communications, and the knowledge of the terms and appearance of the documents which the lawyer gains thereby are privileged from disclosure by testimony in court.[14] Second: on a different footing entirely stands the question, shall a lawyer who has been entrusted with the possession of a document by his client be subject to an order of court requiring him to produce the document at the trial or in pre-trial discovery proceedings whether for inspection or for use in evidence? The policy of encouraging full disclosure does of course apply to encouraging the client to apprise his lawyer of the terms of all relevant documents, and the disclosure itself and the lawyer's knowledge gained thereby as we have seen is privileged. It is true also that placing the documents in the lawyer's hands is the most convenient means of disclosure. But the next step, that of adding to the privilege for communications a privilege against production of the pre-existing documents themselves, would be an intolerable obstruction to justice. To prevent the court's gaining access to a relevant document a party would only have to send it to his lawyer. So here the principle is controlling: if a document would be subject to an order for production if it were in the hands of the client it will be equally subject to such an order if it is in the hands of his attorney.[15] An opposite conclusion would serve the policy of encouraging the client to make full disclosure to his lawyer right enough, but reasonable encouragement is given by the privilege for communications about documents, and the price of an additional privilege would be intolerably high. There are other doctrines which may impel a court to recognize a privilege against production of a pre-existing document,[16] but not the doctrine of privilege for lawyer-client communications.

94. Subject-Matter of the Privilege—(b) Fact of Employment and Identity of the Client.

When a client consults an attorney for a legitimate purpose, he will seldom, but may occasionally, desire to keep secret the very fact of consultation or employment of the lawyer. Nevertheless, such consultation and employment are something more than a mere private or personal engagement. They are the calling into play of the services of an officer licensed by the state to act in cer-

---

comparison by expert witnesses with an anonymous letter charged to have been written by the client. People v. Smith, 318 Ill. 114, 149 N.E. 3, syl. 4 (1925) (not privileged against use for this purpose).

14. Wheatley v. Williams, 1 M. & W. 533, 150 Eng. Rep. 546, (Exch. 1836) (attorney not required to testify whether paper shown him by client bore a stamp); Arbuckle v. Templeton, 65 Vt. 205, 25 A. 1095, syl. 3 (1892) (whether note exhibited to lawyer by client bore an endorsement); 70 C.J. Witnesses, § 572.

But the act of the execution of a document by the client in the lawyer's presence is not ordinarily intended as a confidential communication and thus is usually not privileged. Chapman v. Peebles, 84 Ala. 283, 4 So. 273, syl. 4 (1888). *A fortiori*, when the attorney signs as a witness and takes the ac-

knowledgment of the client as a notary. McCaw v. Hartman, 190 Okl. 264, 122 P.2d 999, syl. 1 (1942).

15. Falsone v. U. S., 205 F.2d 734, syl. 6 (C.A.5, 1953); Sovereign Camp v. Reed, 208 Ala. 457, 94 So. 910, syl. 13 (1922); Andrews v. Railway Co., 14 Ind. 169, 174 (1860); Palatini v. Sarian, 15 N. J.Super. 34, 83 A.2d 24, syl. 6 (1951); Pearson v. Yoder, 39 Okl. 105, 134 Pac. 421, syl. 3, 48 L.R.A. N.S., 334 (1913); 8 Wigmore, Evidence, § 2307 (3d ed. 1940).

And as a necessary incident the attorney may be required to testify whether he has possession of such a document of the client. Guiterman, Rosenfield & Co. v. Culbreth, 219 Ala. 382, 122 So. 619, syl. 1 (19-29).

16. See § 100, infra.

tain ways in furtherance of the administration of justice, and vested with powers of giving advice on the law, of drafting documents, and of filing pleadings and motions and appearing in court for his client, which are limited to this class of officers.

Does the privilege for confidential communications, extend to the fact of consulting or employing such an officer, when intended to be confidential? The weight of authority denies the privilege for the fact of consultation or employment,[1] including the component facts of the identity of the client,[2] such identifying facts about him as his address [3] and occupation,[4] the identity of the lawyer,[5] and the scope or object of the employment.[6]

Some reasons have been advanced which are sufficient for the particular situation but which should not be understood as limitations on the doctrine. Among these are: (1) that the fact of employment is not a confidential communication,—but we have seen that it may be the product of such a communication; (2) "the mere fact of the

[1.] See authorities collected in 8 Wigmore, Evidence, § 2313 (3d ed.1940); 70 C. J. Witnesses, § 562; Note, Disclosure of name, identity, address, occupation or business of client as violation of attorney-client privilege, 114 A.L.R. 1321. Magida v. Continental Can Co., 12 F.R.D. 74, syl. 7 (1951) (the fact of the existence of a retainer, not privileged, but the terms of the retainer within privilege).

[2.] Tomlinson v. United States, 68 App.D.C. 106, 93 F.2d 652, syl. 8–10, 114 A.L.R. 1315 (1937) (Robbery: one of the defendants, a lawyer, testified on direct, that a co-defendant was brought into his office by "a client," held, he was properly required on cross-examination to identify the client); Mauch v. Commissioner of Internal Revenue, 113 F.2d 555, syl. 2 (C.C.A. 3, 1940) (attorney who claimed bank deposits in his name were for clients required to disclose their identity); United States v. Pape, 144 F.2d 778, syl. 13 (C.C.A.2d, 1944) (prosecution for violation of White Slave Traffic Act; lawyer-witness properly allowed to be asked by prosecution whether accused employed him to represent the woman whom he was charged with transporting and himself; Learned Hand, Circ. J., dissenting); In re Illidge, 162 Ore. 303, 91 P.2d 1100, syl. 1 (1939) (attorney accused in disbarment proceedings properly compelled to testify as to identity and residence of client for whom he had entered appearance as counsel in a lawsuit); People ex rel. Vogelstein v. Warden of County Jail, 150 Misc. 714, 270 N.Y.S. 362 (S.Ct.Sp.T.1934, affirmed without opinion, 242 App.Div. 611, 271 N.Y.S. 1059) (attorney who entered appearance for fifteen defendants charged with violation of gambling laws, required in Grand Jury investigation to testify as to whether one person, the man behind the scene, had not employed him to act for all these defendants; opinion by Shientag, J., is the best on the question).

Contra: Ex parte McDonough, 170 Calif. 230, 149 P. 566, L.R.A. 1916C, 593, Ann.C.1916E, 327 (facts similar to People v. Warden, supra; court reviews the authorities elaborately; dissenting opinion by Lawlor, J.)

[3.] United States v. Lee, 107 F. 702 (Circ.Ct.E.D.N.Y. 1901); Note, 114 A.L.R. 1328. Falkenhainer v. Falkenhainer, 198 Misc. 29, 97 N.Y.S.2d 467, syl. 1, 2 (S.Ct.1950).

[4.] Tomlinson v. United States, supra Note 2.

[5.] Goddard v. United States, 131 F.2d 220, syl. 2 (C.C.A. 5th, 1942).

[6.] Upon an issue as to whether some act done by the attorney was authorized, the attorney may testify as to the terms of employment. Sachs v. Title Ins. & Trust Co., 305 Ky. 153, 202 S.W.2d 384, syl. 2 (1947) (on question whether defendant in prior judgment was before court attorney who appeared for her can testify to employment to defend suit); Kentucky-Virginia Stages v. Tackett, 298 Ky. 78, 182 S.W.2d 226, syl. 6 (1944) (whether one of attorneys in instant case was authorized to file motion for new trial); Coley v. Hall, 206 Ark. 419, 175 S.W.2d 979 syl. 3 (1943) (client claimed attorney who filed suit was unauthorized); Falkenhainer v. Falkenhainer, 198 Misc. 29, 97 N.Y.S.2d 467, syl. 1, 2 (Sup.Ct.1950).

It may be, however, that when the object of the employment is not directly in issue but only circumstantially relevant, the testimony would be limited to a more general statement of purpose. See Chirac v. Reinicker, 11 Wheat. (U.S.) 820, 6 L.Ed. 474 (1826) (in action for mesne profits, court intimated that attorney could be asked whether he appeared in former ejectment suit for one of present defendants, but questioned whether he could be asked if they were employed by him to conduct the suit for him as landlord of the premises); Stephens v. Mattox, 37 Ga. 289 (1867) (similar, whether employed by plaintiff to sue for him individually or in his right as administrator). These particular holdings are probably too narrow to be followed today, but seemingly the right to show the purpose of the employment should not be usable as a pretext for detailed disclosure of communications when scope of authority is not in issue.

engagement of counsel is out of the rule [of privilege] because the privilege and duty of being silent do not arise until that fact is ascertained";[7] (3) that a party to legal proceedings is entitled to know the identity of his adversary who is putting in motion or staying the machinery of the court,[8] and to know the authority of counsel appearing in adverse interest; but the rule should not be limited to employment in litigation,[9] and is carried further by the next theory; (4) that the fact of employment should be disclosed where the employment is for a purpose of performing acts which would affect the rights of third persons; [10] this would seem to cover most employments but it is questionable whether even this should be imposed as a limitation. Finally, it has been suggested, (5) that where the fact of employment is relevant for other purposes it may be shown, but not where it is offered as evidence of an acknowledgment of guilt or of an admission of liability of the client.[11] This limitation would negative much of the effect of the rule of disclosure, and it is not generally accepted.[12]

The rule exempting the fact of employment, and the component facts such as the identity of the client, from the curtain of the privilege, seems to be based upon a judicial consideration of the balance of conflicting policies.[13] One who reviews the cases in this area will be struck with the prevailing flavor of chicanery and sharp practice pervading most of the attempts to suppress the proof of professional employment, and the broader solution of a general rule of disclosure seems the one most consonant with the preservation of the high repute of the lawyer's calling.[14]

95. The Confidential Character of the Communications.

It is of the essence of the privilege that it is limited to those communications as to which the client either expressly made confidential or which he could reasonably assume under the circumstances would be understood by the attorney as so intended. This common law requirement seems to be read into those statutes which codify the privilege without mentioning the confiden-

---

7. Shientag, J. in People v. Warden, 270 N.Y.S. at 369, cited note 2, supra. But the party propounding the question as to the identity of the client may state and assume that the relationship exists, so that there is no need to establish it. In re Shawmut Mining Co., 94 App.Div. 156, 87 N.Y.S. 1059, 1062 (1904).

8. "Every litigant is in justice entitled to know the identity of his opponents." 8 Wigmore, Evidence, § 2313, (3d ed. 1940).

9. Compare Neugass v. Terminal Cab Corporation, 139 Misc.Rep. 699, 249 N.Y.S. 631, 634 (S.Ct. 1931) (action by occupant of taxicab injured in collision with another taxicab; plaintiff seeks order requiring attorney for owner of taxicab in which he was riding to disclose name of owner of other cab, for whom he was also acting as attorney for casualty company; motion denied. "His client is not seeking to use the courts, and his address cannot be disclosed on that theory. . . .").

10. In re Shawmut Mining Co., 94 App.Div. 156, 87 N.Y.S. 1059, 1063 (1904).

11. Ex parte McDonough, supra note 2, 149 P. at p. 568; In re Shawmut Mining Co., supra note 9.

12. See, e. g. United States v. Pape, In re Illidge, and People v. Warden, supra note 2 and cases cited in Note, 114 A.L.R. 1322-1325.

13. See discussion of Clark, Circ. J. in Mauch v. Commissioner of Internal Revenue, 113 F.2d 555, 556 (C.C.A.3d, 1940).

14. "The conclusion reached would seem to be inevitable, if we are to maintain the honor of the profession, and make an officer of the court an agency to advance the ends of justice, rather than to be used as an instrument to subvert them. The identity of an employer or client who retains a lawyer to act for him or for others in a civil or criminal proceeding should not be veiled in mystery. The dangers of disclosure are shadowy and remote; the evils of concealment are patent and overwhelming. As between the two social policies competing for supremacy, the choice is clear. Disclosure should be made if we are to maintain confidence in the bar and in the administration of justice." Shientag, J. in People v. Warden, supra note 2, 270 N.Y.S. at p. 371.

tiality requirement.[1] A mere showing that the communication was from client to attorney does not suffice, but the circumstances indicating the intention of secrecy must appear.[2] Wherever the matters communicated to the attorney are intended by the client to be made public or revealed to third persons, obviously the element of confidentiality is wanting.[3] Similarly, if the same statements have been made by the client to third persons on other occasions this is persuasive that like communications to the lawyer were not intended as confidential.[4]

Questions as to the effect of the presence of other persons than the client and the law-

yer often arise. At the extremes answers would be clear. Presumably the presence of a casual disinterested third person within hearing to the client's knowledge would demonstrate that the communication was not intended to be confidential.[5] On the other hand if the help of an interpreter is necessary to enable the client to consult the lawyer his presence would not deprive the communication of its confidential and privileged character.[6] Moreover, in cases where the client has one of his agents attend the conference,[7] or the lawyer calls in his clerk [8] or

---

1. See, e. g., the Alabama, Arkansas, Georgia, Minnesota, Missouri, Nebraska, Ohio, Oklahoma, Tennessee, Wisconsin, and West Virginia statutes, privileging "communications" generally, quoted in 8 Wigmore, Evidence, § 2292, note 2 (3d ed. 1940).

2. Gardner v. Irvin, L.R.Exch.Div 49, 53 (1878); Hiltpold v. Stern, 82 A.2d 123, syl. 8, 9 (D.C.1951).

3. Himmelfarb v. United States, 175 F.2d 924, syl. 32–4 (C.C.A. 9th 1949) (disclosures to accountant by attorney, impliedly authorized by client under special circumstances of previous meetings with accountant concerning income taxes and client's knowledge of accountant's employment with attorney); Hill v. Hill, 106 Colo. 492, 107 P.2d 597, syl. 3 (1940) (letters by wife to attorney giving data on alimony in arrears, with intention that he should present the information to delinquent husband); Spencer v. Burns, 413 Ill. 420, 108 N.E.2d 413, syl. 2, 3 (1952) (statement of true marital status made by client for purpose of transmission to seller and examiner of title to property client wished to purchase); Clayton v. Canida, 223 S.W.2d 264, syl. 2 (Tex.Civ.App. 1949) (information given to attorney for use in preparing income tax return for transmittal to Internal Revenue Department); Anderson v. Thomas, 108 Utah 252, 159 P.2d 142, syl. 12 (1945) (suit to cancel deed of deceased for mental incapacity, testimony of deceased's attorney asked him to arrange for bank not to cash his checks without attorney's approval, not privileged. Good discussion of confidentiality-requirement by Wolfe, J.).

4. Solon v. Lichtenstein, 39 Cal.2d 75, 244 P.2d 907, syl. 4 (1952); Bryan v. Barnett, 205 Ga. 94, 52 S.E.2d 613, syl. 8 (1949); Travelers Indemnity Co. v. Cochrane, 155 Ohio St. 305, 98 N.E.2d 840, syl. 9 (1951).

5. Mason v. Mason, 231 S.W. 971, syl. 5 (Mo.1921); Re Quick's Estate, 161 Wash. 537, 297 P. 198, syl.

6 (1931) and cases collected in 8 Wigmore, Evidence, § 2311, note 6, 70 C.J. Witnesses, § 583, Note, Privilege as affected by the Presence of Third Parties, 36 Mich.L.Rev. 641 (1938).

In the case of persons overhearing without the knowledge of the client, it seems that the more reasonable view if there is to be any privilege at all, would protect the client against disclosure, unless he has failed to use ordinary precautions against overhearing, but the cases permit the eavesdropper to speak. Van Horn v. Commonwealth, 239 Ky. 833, 40 S.W.2d 372, syl. 2 (1931), and see Perry v. State, 4 Idaho 224, 38 P. 655, syl. 1 (1894) (court mentions want of precaution).

6. Du Barre v. Linette, Peake 108, 170 Eng.Repr. 96 (N.P.1791); State v. Loponio, 85 N.J.L. 357, 88 A. 1045, syl. 2 (1913).

7. In re Busse's Estate, 332 Ill.App. 258, 75 N.E. 36, 38 (1947) (client's agent who was nurse and business caretaker present at conference with attorney); Foley v. Poschke, 137 Oh.St. 593, 31 N.E.2d 845, syl. 2 (1941) (detective employed by divorce plaintiff to investigate husband's conduct present at conference with lawyer).

Of course, the presence of additional counsel to participate in the consultation does not detract from confidentiality. Dickerson v. Dickerson, 322 Ill. 492, 153 N.E. 740, syl. 6 (1926).

8. Sibley v. Wopple, 16 N.Y. 180 (1857); Hunt v. Taylor, 22 Vt. 556 (1850); Note, 53 A.L.R. 369, 370.

A substantial number of state statutes provide that communications to the employees of the attorney are privileged. See statutes collected and quoted, 8 Wigmore, Evidence, § 2292, note 2. And disclosures to a physician employed by the client's attorney to examine the client have been held subject to the attorney-client privilege. City & County

confidential secretary,[9] the presence of these intermediaries will be assumed not to militate against the confidential nature of the consultation, and presumably this would not be made to depend upon whether the presence of the agent, clerk or secretary was in the particular instance reasonably necessary to the matter in hand.[10] It is the way business is generally done and that is enough. As to relatives and friends of the client, the results of the cases are not consistent,[11] but it seems that here not only might it be asked whether the client reasonably understood the conference to be confidential but also whether the presence of the relative or friend was reasonably necessary for the protection of the client's interests in the particular circumstances.[12]

When two or more persons, each having an interest in some problem or situation, jointly consult an attorney, their confidential communications with the attorney, though known to each other, will of course be privileged in a controversy of either or both of the clients with the outside world, that is, with parties claiming adversely to both or either of those within the original charmed circle.[13] But it will often happen that the two original clients will fall out among themselves and become engaged in a controversy in which the communications at their joint consultation with the lawyer may be vitally material. In such a controversy it is clear that the privilege is inapplicable. In the first place the policy of encouraging disclosure by holding out the promise of protec-

---

of San Francisco v. Superior Court, 37 Cal.2d 227, 231 P.2d 26, syl. 12–14 (1951).

A law student in the office is not within the rule, unless he acts as clerk. Wartell v. Navograd, 48 R.I. 296, 137 A. 776, 53 A.L.R. 365 (1927).

9. Taylor v. Taylor, 179 Ga. 691, 693, 177 S.E. 582, syl. 1–2 [all] (1934) ("Under modern practice of law the business of an attorney in most offices cannot be conducted without such an assistant"; Ga. Code, § 38–419, however, expressly extended privilege to communications to attorney "or his clerk"). A Texas case, however, would seemingly give the privilege only when the secretary or stenographer is the medium of communication. Otherwise, the court suggests "it could as well be claimed that the rule would extend to the employee, who swept the attorney's floor." Morton v. Smith, 44 S.W. 683, 684, syl. 3 (Tex.Civ.App. 1898) (stenographer allowed to testify to statements made by client to attorney).

10. But compare Morton v. Smith, supra, and Himmelfarb v. United States, 175 F.2d 924, syl. 29–30 (C.C.A.9th 1949) (testimony of accountant employed as attorney's agent, not privileged where his presence at conference with client was not indispensably necessary to communication between attorney and client).

11. Cafritz v. Koslow, 167 F.2d 749, syl. 7 (C.A.D.C. 1948) (sister accompanies brother, client, to attorney's office; "There was no identity of interest between [brother and sister] nor can it be said that [sister] stood in relation of agent to [brother]"); Baldwin v. Commissioner of Internal Revenue, 125 F.2d 812, syl. 3–5 (C.C.A.9th 1942) (son accompanied mother to conferences with her attorney over proposed transfer of some of her property to

son, held presence of son did not destroy privilege but chiefly on ground that it was joint consultation in which son was interested); Smith v. State, 204 Ga. 184, 47 S.E. 579, syl. 2 (1948) (murder prosecution, evidence of what was said in conference with attorney by wife of defendant, when deceased was present, held privileged, without discussion); Bowers v. State, 29 Oh.St. 542, 546 (1876) (prosecution for seduction of girl under eighteen; girl's statements at conference with attorney consulted about bastardy proceedings against defendant held privileged despite presence of girl's mother).

12. Compare the remarks of the court in Bowers v. State, in the preceding note: "We think it is only a dictate of decency and propriety to regard the mother in such a case as being present and acting in the character of confidential agent of her daughter. The daughter's youth and supposed modesty would render the participation of her mother appropriate and necessary." 29 Oh.St. at 546.

13. People v. Abair, 102 Cal.App.2d 765, 228 P.2d 336, syl. 5 (1951); In re Selser, 27 N.J.Super. 259, 99 A.2d 313, syl. 2 (1953); State v. Archuleta, 29 N.M. 25, 217 Pac. 619, syl. 3 (1923) and cases cited in note, 141 A.L.R. 562 (communication privileged as against the state in a criminal case, although parties fall out and one acts as witness against others); Minard v. Stillman, 31 Ore. 164, 49 Pac. 976 (1897); Vance v. State, 190 Tenn. 521, 230 S.W.2d 987, cert. den. 339 U.S. 988, 70 Sup.Ct. 1010, syl. 5 (1950) (communications at conference between co-defendants and their separate counsel in preparation of joint defense, privileged as against the state in a criminal case, but not privileged where one defendant makes no defense).

tion seems inapposite, since as between themselves neither would know whether he would be more helped or handicapped, if in any dispute between them, both could invoke the shield of secrecy. And secondly, it is said that they had obviously no intention of keeping these secrets from each other, and hence as between themselves it was not intended to be confidential. In any event, it is a qualification of frequent application [14] and of even wider potentiality, not always recognized. Thus, in the situation mentioned in the previous paragraph where a client calls into the conference with the attorney one of the client's agents, and matters are discussed which bear on the agent's rights against the client, it would seem that in a subsequent controversy between client and agent, the limitation on the privilege accepted in the joint consultation cases should furnish a controlling analogy.[15]

One step beyond the joint consultation where communications by two clients are made directly in each other's hearing is the situation where two parties separately in-terested in some contract or undertaking as in the case of borrower and lender or insurer and insured, engage the same attorney to represent their respective interests, and each communicates separately with the attorney about some phase of the common transaction. Here again it seems that the communicating client, knowing that the attorney represents the other party also, would not ordinarily intend that the facts communicated should be kept secret from him.[16] Accordingly, the doctrine of limited confidentiality has been applied to communications by the insured under a liability insurance policy to the attorney employed by the insurance company to represent both the company and the insured. A confidential statement made by the insured to the attorney would thus be privileged if sought to be introduced at the trial of the injured person's action against the insured,[17] but not in a controversy between the insured, or one claiming under him, and the company itself over the company's liability under the policy.[18]

---

14. Grand Trunk Western R. Co. v. H. W. Nelson Co., 116 F.2d 823, syl. 29, rehearing denied 118 id. 252 (C.C.A.Mich.1941); Re Bauer, 79 Cal. 304, 21 Pac. 759, syl. 2 (1889); Luthy v. Seaburn, 242 Iowa 184, 46 N.W.2d 44, syl. 4 (1951); Benson v. Custer, 236 Iowa 345, 17 N.W.2d 889, syl. 5 (1945); Thompson v. Cashman, 181 Mass. 36, 62 N.E. 976, syl. 3 (1902); Wahl v. Cunningham, 320 Mo. 57, 6 S.W.2d 576, syl. 7, 67 A.L.R. 489 (1928); Jenkins v. Jenkins, 151 Neb. 113, 36 N.W.2d 635, syl. 1–3 (1949); Hurlburt v. Hurlburt, 128 N.Y. 420, 28 N.E. 651, syl. 1, 26 Am.St.Rep. 482 (1891); Emley v. Selepchak, 76 Ohio App. 257, 63 N.E.2d 919, syl. 4 (1945); and cases cited in 8 Wigmore, Evidence, § 2312 (3d ed. 1940); Note, 141 A.L.R. 553.

It has been held that the beneficiary of a contract made by the jointly consulting clients at the conference or discussed thereat, stands in the shoes of the parties and is entitled to disclosure. Allen v. Ross, 199 Wis. 162, 225 N.W. 831, syl. 2, 64 A.L.R. 180 (1929). So also as to personal representatives and others in privity. Hurlburt v. Hurlburt, supra (action by administrator of one client against administratrix of the other). Query as to judgment creditors, but seemingly they should be in like case. Note, 141 A.L.R. 558.

15. But in the only cases encountered in which this situation was presented the analogy was not discussed and the privilege was sustained against the agent. In re Busse's Estate and Foley v. Poschke, cited and described in note 7, supra. The Busse case is criticized on this point in Note, 61 Harv. L.Rev. 717, and on another point in Note, 15 U. Chi.L.Rev. 989.

16. See, e. g., Gottwald v. Mettinger, 257 App.Div. 107, 12 N.Y.S.2d 241, syl. 3 (1939) (in suit on bond where attorney originally represented borrower and lender in arranging loan, statement of borrower to attorney of amount owed, not privileged.)

17. See In re Klemann, 132 Oh.St. 187, 5 N.E.2d 492, syl. 1 (1936) (in suit of injured person, written statement made by insured to insurance company for transmittal to attorney held privileged).

18. Klefbeck v. Dous, 302 Mass. 383, 19 N.E.2d 308, syl. 12 (1939) (suit by injured party after judgment to subject policy to payment of judgment, defended by insurer on ground automobile not legally registered in state of issuance; held, plaintiff, claiming under insured, entitled to use letter of attorney, acting for both, to insurer); Travelers Indemnity Co. v. Cochrane, 155 Ohio St. 305, 98 N.E.2d 840, syl. 8, 10 (1951); Shafer v. Utica Mut.

The weight of authority seems to support the view that when client and attorney become embroiled in a controversy between themselves, as in an action by the attorney for compensation or by the client for damages for the attorney's negligence, the seal is removed from the attorney's lips.[19] Though sometimes rested upon other grounds [20] it seems that here again the notion that as between the participants in the conference the intention was to disclose and not to withhold the matters communicated offers a plausible reason.[21] As to what is a controversy between lawyer and client the decisions do not limit their holdings to litigations between them, but have said that whenever the client, even in litigation between third persons, makes an imputation against the good faith of his attorney in respect to his professional services, the curtain of privilege drops so far as necessary to enable the lawyer to defend his conduct.[22] Perhaps the whole doctrine that in controversies between attorney and client the privilege is relaxed, may best be based upon the ground

of practical necessity that if effective legal service is to be encouraged the privilege must not stand in the way of the lawyer's just enforcement of his rights to be paid a fee and to protect his reputation. The only question about such a principle is whether in all cases the privilege ought not to be subject to the same qualification, that it should yield when the evidence sought is necessary to the attainment of justice.

96. The Client as the Holder of the Privilege: Who may Assert, and Who Complain on Appeal of Its Denial? [1]

A rule regulating the *competency* of evidence or of witnesses—a so-called "exclusionary" rule—is normally founded on the policy of safe-guarding the fact-finding process against error, and it is assertable by the party against whom the evidence is offered. The ear-marks of a *privilege,* as we have seen, are first, that it is not designed to protect the fact-finding process but is intended to protect some "outside" interest, other than the ascertainment of truth at the trial, and second, it cannot be asserted by the ad-

---

Ins. Co., 248 App.Div. 279, 289 N.Y.S. 577, syl. 7 (1936) (action by injured party after judgment to subject policy to payment of judgment contested by company on ground of failure of insured to co-operate; held, company entitled to prove statements of insured to joint attorney); Hoffman v. Labutzke, 233 Wis. 365, 289 N.W. 652, syl. 7, 8 (1940) (on motion to set aside verdict against automobile liability insurer for damages to injured party, on ground of non-cooperation by insured, statement of insured to joint attorney not privileged).

19. Mave v. Baird, 12 Ind. 318 (1859) (suit by client for negligence); Weinshenk v. Sullivan, 100 S.W. 2d 66, syl. 1, 2 (Mo.App.1937) (attorney's suit for compensation); Stern v. Daniel, 47 Wash. 96, 91 P. 552, syl. 2 (1907) (lawyer's suit for fee; client's letters to lawyer not privileged though it discloses client's improper conduct. "They would have been privileged, no doubt as between either of the parties to this suit and third parties; but as between the attorney and client the rule of privilege will not be enforced where the client charges mismanagement of his cause by the attorney, as was the case here, and where it would be a manifest injustice to allow the client to take advantage of the

rule of privilege to the prejudice of the attorney, or when it would be carried to the extent of depriving the attorney of the means of obtaining or defending his own rights."); State v. Markey, 259 Wis. 527, 49 N.W.2d 437, syl. 1 (1951).

20. As that a contract for compensation is not a communication from the client, and is "collateral" to the professional relation. Strickland v. Capital City Mills, 74 S.C. 16, 54 S.E. 220, 7 L.R.A.,N.S., 426 (1906).

21. Minard v. Stillman, 31 Ore. 164, 49 Pac. 976 (1897); see 8 Wigmore, Evidence, § 2312(2) (3d ed. 1940).

22. United States v. Monti, 100 F.Supp. 209, syl. 5 (1951); Pierce v. Norton, 82 Conn. 441, 74 Atl. 686, syl. 2 (1909); Hyde v. State, 70 Ga.App. 823, 29 S.E.2d 820, syl. 9, 10 (1944); Moore v. State, 231 Ind. 690, 111 N.E.2d 47, syl. 7 (1953); Doll v. Loesel, 288 Pa. 527, 136 Atl. 796, syl. 7 (1927); Chase v. Chase, 78 R.I. 278, 81 A.2d 686, syl. 1 (1951).

1. See 8 Wigmore, Evidence, § 2321 (3d ed. 1940); Note, Persons Entitled to Waive or Claim Privileges, 30 Col.L.Rev. 686 (1930); 58 Am.Jur. Witnesses, § 519.

verse party as such, but only by the person whose interest the particular rule of privilege is intended to safe-guard.[2] While once it was conceived that the privilege was set up to protect the lawyer's honor, we know that today it is agreed that the basic policy of the rule is that of encouraging clients to lay the facts fully before their counsel. They will be encouraged by a privilege which they themselves have the power to invoke. To extend any benefit or advantage to someone as attorney, or as party to a suit, or to people generally, will be to suppress relevant evidence without promoting the purpose of the privilege.

Accordingly it is now generally agreed that the privilege is the client's and his alone.[3] It is thought that this would be recognized even in those states which, before modern notions of privilege and policy were adequately worked out, codified the rule in terms of inadmissibility of evidence of communications, or of incompetency of the attorney to testify thereto.[4] These statutes

are generally held not to be intended to modify the common law doctrines.[5]

It is not surprising that the courts, often faced with statutes drafted in terms of obsolete theories, and reaching these points rarely and usually incidentally, have not worked out a consistent pattern of consequences of this accepted view that the rule is one of privilege and that the privilege is the client's. It is believed that the applications suggested below are well grounded in reason and are supported by some authority, whether of text or decision.

First, it is clear that the client may assert the privilege even though he is not a party to the cause wherein the privileged testimony is sought to be elicited.[6] Second, if he is present at the hearing whether as party, witness, or bystander he must assert the privilege personally or by attorney, or it will be waived.[7] Third, if he is not present at the taking of testimony, nor a party to the proceedings, the privilege may be called to the court's attention by anyone present, such as the attorney[8] for the absent client, or a party in the

---

2. See the discussion in §§ 72, 73, supra, of the distinction between competency and privilege.

3. Among the many cases where this is recognized are Minter v. Priest, [1930] A.C. 558, 579 (By Lord Atkin: "But the right to have such communications so protected is the right of the client only. In this sense it is a 'privilege', the privilege of the client"); Abbott v. Superior Court, 78 Cal.App.2d 19, 177 P.2d 317, syl. 3, 4 (1947) (where client has no privilege because of his illegal purpose, attorney has none); Foster v. Hall, 12 Pick. (Mass.) 89 (1931); Russell v. Second National Bank, 136 N.J.L. 270, 55 A.2d 211, syl. 9 (1947); Ex parte Lipscomb, 111 Tex. 409, 239 S.W. 1101, syl. 1 (1922).

4. See the statutes collected and quoted in 8 Wigmore, Evidence, § 2292, note 2.

5. See e. g. In re Young's Estate, 33 Utah 382, 94 P. 731, 732 (1908) where the court said: "Subdivision 2 of section 3414, Rev.St.1898, so far as material to the present inquiry, provides as follows: 'An attorney cannot, without the consent of his client, be examined as to any communication made by the client to him, or his advice given therein in the course of professional employment.' It will be observed that, under the foregoing provision, the

privilege therein given, as at common law, is purely personal, and belongs to the client. If the client waives the privilege, neither the attorney nor any one else may invoke it. It is likewise apparent that the privilege given by the statute is simply declaratory of that existing at common law. Without this statute, therefore, in view of section 2488, Rev.St.1898, in which the common law of England is adopted, the privilege would exist and be in force in this state. The mere fact that the common-law privilege is declared in statutory form does not extend the scope of its operation."

6. See Ex parte Martin, 141 Oh.St. 87, 47 N.E.2d 388, syl. 9 (1943) (client who was a witness whose testimony by deposition was sought, allowed to test question of privilege).

7. Steen v. First National Bank, 298 F. 36, syl. 2–4 (C.C.A.8th, 1924) (client's testimony on preliminary hearing to conversation with lawyer, a waiver); Hill v. Hill, 106 Colo. 492, 107 P.2d 597, syl. 2 (1940) (client as witness asked for production of documents to refresh her memory, waiver of privilege, if any, for documents).

8. Chicago Great Western Ry. Co. v. McCaffrey, 178 Ia. 1147, 160 N.W. 818, syl. 4 (1917) (attorney for railway, party to present suit, asked to produce

case,[9] or the court of its own motion may protect the privilege.[10] Fourth: While if an asserted privilege is erroneously sustained, the aggrieved party may of course complain on appeal of the exclusion of the testimony, the erroneous denial of the privilege can only be complained of by the client whose privilege has been infringed. This opens the door to appellate review by the client if he is a party and suffers adverse judgment.[11]

If he is not a party, the losing party in the cause, by the better view is without recourse.[12] Relevant, competent testimony has come in, and the privilege was not created for his benefit. But the witness, whether he is the client or his attorney, may refuse to answer and suffer a commitment for contempt and may, in some jurisdictions at least, secure release on habeas corpus if the privilege was erroneously denied.[13] This remedy, however, is calculated to interrupt and often disrupt progress of the cause on trial. Does a lawyer on the witness stand who is asked to make disclosures which he thinks may constitute an infringement of

his client's privilege, owe a duty to refuse to answer and if necessary to test the judge's ruling on habeas corpus? It seems clear that, unless in a case of flagrant disregard of the law by the judge, the lawyer's duty is merely to present his view that the testimony is privileged, and if the judge rules otherwise, to submit to his decision.[14]

97. Waiver.[1]

Since as we have seen, it is the client who is the holder of the privilege, the power to waive it is his, and he alone, or his attorney or agent acting with his authority, may[2] exercise this power. Waiver includes, as Wigmore points out, not merely words or conduct expressing an intention to relinquish a known right, but conduct, such as a partial disclosure, which would make it unfair for the client to insist on the privilege thereafter.[3]

By the prevailing view, which seems a reasonable one, the mere voluntary taking the stand by the client as a witness in a suit to which he is party and testifying to facts

---

correspondence with client properly claimed privilege).

9. O'Brien v. New England Mutual Life Ins. Co., 109 Kan. 138, 197 P. 1100, syl. 3 (1921) (absent client's privilege asserted, apparently by lawyer-witness or by party).

10. Tingley v. State, 16 Okl.Cr. 639, 184 P. 599, syl. 3 (1919). And the judge may advise the witness of the privilege. See State v. Madden, 161 Minn. 132, 134, 201 N.W. 297, 298 (1924).

11. Ex parte Lipscomb, 111 Tex. 409, 239 S.W. 1101, 1105 (1922) (attorney for one of the parties when required by judge to testify to transaction with client, refused and sought to raise question of privilege on habeas corpus; held, writ denied because of client's adequate remedy by appeal).

12. Schaibly v. Vinton, 338 Mich. 191, 61 N.W.2d 122, syl. 3, 4 (1953); Dowie's Estate, 135 Pa. 210, 19 A. 936, syl. 2 (1890).

13. Ex parte Martin, 141 Oh.St. 87, 47 N.E.2d 388, syl. 10 (1943); Elliott v. United States, 23 App. D.C. 456 (1904); 39 C.J.S. Habeas Corpus § 37, Note 77. But not if the client is a party and so has an adequate remedy by appeal. Ex parte Lipscomb, note 11, supra.

14. Compare the remarks of Shaw, C. J., in Foster v. Hall, 12 Pick. (Mass.) 89, (1831): "Mr. Robinson [an attorney-witness] very properly submitted it to the court to determine, on the facts disclosed, whether he should answer or not, having no wish either to volunteer or withhold his testimony. The rule in such case is, that the privilege of confidence is the privilege of the client, and not of the attorney, and, therefore, whether the facts shall be disclosed or not, must depend on the just application of the rule of law, and not upon the will of the witness."

1. See 8 Wigmore, Evidence, §§ 2327–2329 (3d ed. 1940); Note, Waiver of Attorney-Client Privilege, 16 Minn.L.Rev. 818 (1932); Dec.Dig., Witnesses, ☞ 219(3); 58 Am.Jur., Witnesses, §§ 522–530.

2. Wilcox v. Coons, 359 Mo. 52, 220 S.W.2d 15, syl. 4 (1949) (either personal representative or devisee of deceased may waive); In re Selser, 27 N.J. Super. 257, 99 A.2d 313, syl. 5, 6 (1951) (personal representative of deceased client); Yancy v. Erman, 99 N.E.2d 524, syl. 8–10 (Oh.App.1951) (guardian of an incompetent client may waive his privilege).

3. 8 Wigmore, Evidence, § 2327 (3d ed. 1940).

which were the subject of consultation with his counsel is no waiver of the privilege for secrecy of the communications to his lawyer.[4] If on direct examination, however, he testifies to the privileged communications, in part, this is a waiver as to the remainder of the privileged consultation or consultations about the same subject.[5]

What if the client is asked on cross-examination about the communications with his lawyer, and he responds without asserting his claim of privilege? Is this a waiver? Unless there are some circumstances which show that the client was surprised or misled, it seems that the usual rule that the client's failure to claim the privilege when to his knowledge testimony infringing it is offered,[6] would apply here,[7] and that the decisions treating such testimony on cross-examination as being involuntary and not constituting a waiver [8] are hardly supportable.

How far does the client waive by calling the attorney as a witness? If the client elicits testimony from the lawyer-witness as to privileged communications this obviously would waive as to all consultations relating to the same subject,[9] just as the client's own testimony would.[10] It would seem also that by calling the lawyer as a witness he opens the door for the adversary to impeach him by showing his interest.[11] And it seems reasonable to contend as Wigmore does [12] that if the client uses the lawyer to prove matter which he would only have learned in the course of his employment this again should be considered a waiver as to related priv-

---

4. Magida v. Continental Can Co., 12 F.R.D. 74, syl. 6 (1951); Bigler v. Reyher, 43 Ind. 112 (1873); Barker v. Kuhn, 38 Iowa 392 (1874); State v. White, 19 Kan. 445, 27 Am.Rep. 137 (1877); Shelly v. Landry, 97 N.H. 27, 79 A.2d 626, syl. 6 (1951). An early Massachusetts decision is to the contrary. Woburn v. Henshaw, 101 Mass. 193, 200 (1869). But there is some inconsistency in later opinions, see Spalding, The Uncertain State of the Law as to Waiver of Professional Confidences, 20 Mass. L.Q.N. 3, p. 16 (May, 1935). So also decisions under statutes, in Ohio and Oregon. Spitzer v. Stillings, 109 Ohio 297, 142 N.E. 365, syl. 1–3 (1924) (in civil cases, under R.C. § 2317.02; Note, 33 Yale Law J. 782; Sitton v. Peyree, 117 Ore. 107, 241 Pac. 62, syl. 7 (1925) (under ORS 44–040).

5. Steen v. First National Bank, 298 Fed. 36, syl. 3 (C.C.A.8, 1924); Kelly v. Cummens, 143 Iowa 148, 121 N.W. 540, syl. 3, 20 Ann.C. 1283 (1909); Chase v. Chase, 78 R.I. 278, 81 A.2d 686, syl. 1 (1951); Rodriguez v. State, 130 Tex.Cr. 438, 94 S.W.2d 476, syl. 6, 7 (1936). Similarly, if the party-client introduces part of his correspondence with his attorney, the production of all the correspondence could be demanded. Kunglig Jarnvagsstyrelson v. Dexter & Carpenter, 32 F.2d 195, syl. 16 (C.C.A. N.Y.1929). But the waiver extends only to so much of the privileged communications as relates to the matter testified to. People v. Gerold, 265 Ill. 448, 107 N.E. 165, syl. 18, Ann.C.1916A, 636.

6. See, e. g., Rock v. Keller, 312 Mo. 458, 278 S.W. 759, syl. 4 (1926); Weisser v. Preszler, 62 N.D. 75, 241 N.W. 505, syl. 4 (1932).

7. Steen v. First National Bank, 298 F. 36, 43, syl. 4, 5 (C.C.A.Mo. 1924) (persuasive opinion by Sanborn,

Circ. J.); Raleigh and C. Ry. Co. v. Jones, 104 S.C. 332, 88 S.E. 896, 898 (1916) (failure to object on cross-examination entitles other party to call attorney); Pinson v. Campbell, 124 Mo.App. 260, 101 S.W. 621, syl. 2 (1907) (Similar). It is clear, of course, that the party-witness may claim the privilege during the cross-examination. Ex parte Bryant, 106 Ore. 359, 210 P. 454, syl. 5 (1922).

8. Seaboard Air Line Ry. Co. v. Parker, 65 Fla. 543, 62 So. 589, syl. 4 (1913); Lauer v. Banning, 140 Iowa 319, 118 N.W. 446, 450 (1908), on later appeal, 152 Iowa 99, 131 N.W. 783, syl. 4 (1911); Foley v. Poschke, 66 Oh.App. 227, 32 N.E.2d 858, 861 (1940), affirmed 137 Oh.St. 593, 31 N.E.2d 845 (1941); State v. James, 34 S.C. 49, 12 S.E. 657, syl. 7 (1891). In none of these opinions is there any discussion of why the usual rule of waiver from failure to object does not apply. In most of them, however, the testimony on cross-examination consisted of a denial of having made to the attorney the statement inquired about, and it is arguable that a layman might not realize when he anticipated making such an answer, that there was any occasion to claim privilege.

9. Brooks v. Holden, 175 Mass. 137, 55 N.E. 802, syl. 3 (1900); 8 Wigmore, Evidence, § 2327 (3d ed. 1940).

10. See cases cited note 5, supra.

11. Conyer v. Burckhalter, 275 S.W. 606, syl. 9 (Tex. Civ.App., 1925) (error to exclude cross-examination as to attorney's fee-interest in outcome of suit); Moats v. Rymer, 18 W.Va. 642, syl. 1–5, 41 Am.Rep. 703 (1881).

12. See reference, note 9, supra.

ileged communications.[13] But merely to call the lawyer to testify to facts known by him apart from his employment should not be deemed a waiver of the privilege. That would attach too harsh a condition on the exercise of the privilege.[14] Unless the lawyer-witness is acting as counsel in the case on trial, there is no violation of the Canon,[15] and if he is, it recognizes that his testifying may be essential to the ends of justice. Moreover, these are matters usually governed not by the client but by the lawyer, to whom the ethical mandate is addressed.

When at an earlier trial or stage of the case the privilege has been waived and testimony as to the privileged communications elicited without objection, the prevailing view is that this is a waiver also for any subsequent hearing of the same case.[16] In the words of Holmes, J., "the privacy for the sake of which the privilege was created was gone by the appellant's own consent, and the privilege does not remain in such circumstances for the mere sake of giving the client an additional weapon to use or not at his choice." [17] The same reasons seem to apply where the waiver was thus publicly made upon the trial of one case, and the privilege later sought to be asserted on the hearing of another cause.[18] How far does this argument of once published, permanently waived, apply to out-of-court disclosures made by the client or with his consent? Authority is scanty, but it seems that if the client makes public disclosure, this should clearly be a waiver,[19] and even where privately revealed

---

13. This view seems supported by the result in Jones v. Marble Co., 137 N.C. 237, 49 S.E. 94, syl. 2 (1904) (action for attorney's fees; defendant called attorney formerly associated with plaintiff in employment for which fee is claimed, to testify that fee claimed, is excessive, held, this waived defendant's right to object to plaintiff's introducing letter from witness during pendency of employment which would otherwise have been privileged).

But there is authority for the view that if the lawyer's testimony does not relate to the privileged communications themselves, there is no waiver. Drayton v. Industrial Life & Health Ins. Co., 205 S.C. 98, 31 S.E.2d 148, syl. 16 (1944).

14. See 8 Wigmore, § 2327 (3d ed. 1940); Note, 16 Minn.L.Rev. 818, 827 (1932). But see Martin v. Shaen, 22 Wash.2d 508, 156 P.2d 681, 685, syl. 7 (1945) where attorney-executor testified that he received a certain deed from the deceased client, and the court said that when he "voluntarily took the stand and testified upon a vital issue in the case, he waived the privilege of withholding his testimony as to all matters relevant to that issue" including communications between lawyer and client at the time the deed was placed in the lawyer's hands.

15. Canons of Professional Ethics, Canon 19: "Appearance of lawyer as witness for his client. When a lawyer is a witness for his client, except as to merely formal matters, such as the attestation or custody of an instrument and the like, he should leave the trial of the case to other counsel. Except when essential to the ends of justice, a lawyer

should avoid testifying in court in behalf of his client." 62 Reports, American Bar Assoc. 1112 (1937).

16. Green v. Crapo, 181 Mass. 55, 62 N.E. 956, 959, syl. 5 (1902) (waiver at probate court hearing, effective at subsequent hearing on appeal); In re Whiting, 110 Me. 232, 85 A. 79, syl. 2 (1913) (similar); 8 Wigmore, Evidence, § 2328 (3d ed. 1940); Note, 16 Minn.L.Rev. 818, 829 (1932). See also discussions of the question as applied to waiver of objections generally by waiver at an earlier trial: 58 Am.Jur. Witnesses § 373; Note, 79 A.L.R. 176.

17. Green v. Crapo, supra, 62 N.E. 956, 959.

18. Thus in Steen v. First National Bank, 298 F. 36 (C.C.A.Mo.1924) it was held that a failure to object to questions to the client's representative about privileged matter at the preliminary hearing in a criminal prosecution, prevented assertion of the privilege at the trial of an action for malicious prosecution. Compare Alden v. Stromsem, 347 Ill. App. 439, 106 N.E.2d 837, syl. 9 (1952) (in suit for engineering fees communications disclosed by both parties at previous trial for attorney fees, not privileged). But see Matison v. Matison, 95 N.Y.S.2d 837 (1950) (in action by third party, communications between attorney and client were privileged, though attorney had testified thereto in previous action by him for attorney fees).

19. In re Burnette, 73 Kan. 609, 85 P. 575, 583, syl. 10 (1906) (procured stranger to read, published contents in newspaper interview, and spread substance on record of a court in a pleading).

to a third person,[20] or authorized to be revealed [21] it should have the same effect, by analogy to the cases which deny privilege when a third person is present at the consultation. The Uniform Rule [22] accepts this view for all privileges, with a comment stating that the principle is generally recognized for confidential communications.

The question as to who may waive the privilege after the death of the client will be considered in the next section.

98. The Effect of the Death of the Client.[1]

The accepted theory is that the protection afforded by the privilege will in general survive the death of the client.[2] But under various qualifying theories the operation of the

privilege has in effect been nullified in the class of cases where it would most often be asserted after death, namely, cases involving the validity or interpretation of a will, or other dispute between parties claiming by succession from the testator at his death. this result has been reached by different routes. Wigmore argues, as to the will-contests, that communications of the client with his lawyer as to the making of a will are intended to be confidential in his life-time but that this is a "temporary confidentiality" not intended to require secrecy after his death [3] and this view finds approval in some decisions.[4] Other courts say simply that where all the parties claim under the client the privilege does not apply.[5] The distinction

20. Holland v. State, 17 Ala.App. 503, 86 So. 118, syl. 2 (1920) (oral disclosure by defendant to witness of advice given him by lawyers); and see Seeger v. Odell, 148 P.2d 901, 906, syl. 8 (Cal.App.1944).

21. Phillips v. Chase, 201 Mass. 444, 87 N.E. 755, syl. 7, 131 Am.St.Rep. 406 (1909) (deceased client had requested attorney to communicate facts disclosed to him, to her brothers after her death.); Halloran v. Tousignant, 230 Minn. 399, 41 N.W.2d 874, syl. 6 (1950) (arrangement of insurance carriers to exchange statements of their insured, as waiver of privilege).

22. Uniform Rules of Evidence, Rule 37: A person who would otherwise have a privilege to refuse to disclose or to prevent another from disclosing a specified matter has no such privilege with respect to that matter if the judge finds that he or any other person while the holder of the privilege has (a) contracted with anyone not to claim the privilege or, (b) without coercion and with knowledge of his privilege, made disclosure of any part of the matter or consented to such a disclosure made by any one.

1. See 8 Wigmore, Evidence, §§ 2314, 2329 (3d ed. 1940); Model Code of Evidence, Rule 213 (2); Note, 64 A.L.R. 184; 58 Am.Jur., Witnesses, § 505.

2. In re Busse's Estate, 332 Ill.App. 258, 75 N.E.2d 36, syl. 3 (1947); Martin v. Shaen, 22 Wash.2d 505, 156 P.2d 681, syl. 2 (1945); 8 Wigmore, Evidence, § 2323 (3d ed. 1940).

3. 8 Wigmore, Evidence, § 2314 (3d ed. 1940).

4. See, e. g., Dickerson v. Dickerson, 322 Ill. 492, 153 N.E. 740, syl. 11 (1926) (communications between client and attorneys concerning deed, intended to be confidential during client's lifetime only);

Hecht's Admr. v. Hecht, 272 Ky. 400, 114 S.W. 2d 499, syl. 7 (1938) (death removes the pledge of secrecy); Snow v. Gould, 74 Me. 540, 543 (1883).

5. Russell v. Jackson, 9 Hare 387, 392, 68 Eng. Rep. 558, 560 (V.C.1851) ("The disclosure in [testamentary] cases can affect no right or interest of the client. The apprehension of it can present no impediment to the full statement of his case to his solicitor. . . . In the cases of testamentary dispositions the very foundation on which the rule proceeds seems to be wanting . . . ."); Glover v. Patten, 165 U.S. 394, 406, 17 Sup.Ct. 411, 41 L.Ed. 760 (1897) (bill by devisees to construe will and to charge estate with claims); Clark v. Turner, 183 F.2d 141, syl. 3 (C.A.D.C.150) (in suit to establish lost will, testimony as to existence of will); Olsson v. Pierson, 237 Iowa 1342, 25 N.W.2d 357, syl. 8 (1946) (suit to set aside conveyance of deceased for constructive fraud and mental incapacity); In Re Kemp's Will, 236 N.C. 680, 73 S.E.2d 906, syl. 4 (1953) (will contest—mental capacity); Gaines v. Gaines, 207 Okl. 619, 251 P.2d 1044, syl. 12 (1953) (in action to construe written assignment of deceased, testimony of attorney and his stenographer as to statements of deceased concerning his intentions); Pierce v. Farrar, 60 Tex.Civ.App. 12, 126 S.W. 932, syl. 3 (1910) (will-contest, undue influence); In re Young's Estate, 33 Utah 382, 94 Pac. 731, syl. 3, 17 L.R.A., N.S., 108 (1908) (will-contest, undue influence); Re Healy, 94 Vt. 128, 109 Atl. 19, syl. 4 (1920) (will-contest, mental capacity); Note, 64 A.L.R. 185–189. Contra: In re Coon's Estate, 154 Neb. 690, 48 N.W. 2d 778, syl. 5–8 (1951). See also Uniform Rules of Evidence, R. 26(2) (b), which provides that the privilege shall not extend "to a communication

is taken that when the contest is between a "stranger" and the heirs or personal representatives of the deceased client, the heirs or representatives can claim privilege,[6] and they can waive it.[7] Even if the privilege were assumed to be applicable in will-contests, it could perhaps be argued that since those claiming under the will and those claiming by intestate succession both equally claim under the client, each should have the power to waive.[8]

This doctrine that the privilege is ineffective, on whatever ground, when both litigants claim under the deceased client has been applied to suits by the heirs or representatives to set aside a conveyance by the deceased for mental incapacity[9] and to suits for the enforcement of a contract made by the deceased to make a will in favor of plaintiff.[10] The cases encountered where the party is held to be a "stranger" and hence not entitled to invoke this doctrine are cases where the party asserts against the estate a claim of a promise by the deceased to pay, or make provision in his will for payment,

for services rendered.[11] It may well be questioned whether the deceased would have been more likely to desire that his attorneys lips be sealed after his death in the determination of such claims than in the case of a controversy over the validity of the will. The attorney's offered testimony would seem to be of more than average reliability. If such testimony supporting the claim is true, presumably the deceased would have wanted to promote, rather than obstruct the success of the claim. It would be only a short step forward for the courts to apply here the notion that the privilege is "personal" to client, and to hold that in all cases death terminates the privilege. This could not in any substantial degree lessen the encouragement for free disclosure which is the purpose of the privilege.

99. Consultation in Furtherance of Crime or Fraud.[1]

Since the policy of the privilege is that of promoting the administration of justice, it would be a perversion of the privilege to ex-

---

relevant to an issue between parties all of whom claim through the client, regardless of whether the respective claims are by testate or intestate succession or by inter vivos transaction."

6. Doyle v. Reeves, 112 Conn. 521, 152 A. 882, syl. 2 (1931) (claim of servant against estate for value of services to deceased); In re Busse's Estate, 332 Ill.App. 258, 75 N.E.2d 36, syl. 6 (1947) (similar); Runnels v. Allen's Adm'r, 169 S.W.2d 73, syl. 2 (Mo.App.1943) (similar); Note, 64 A.L.R. 191. In Doyle v. Reeves, supra, the plaintiff seems to have relied on a promise by decedent to make provision in his will for payment for the services.

7. Phillips v. Chase, 201 Mass. 444, 87 N.E. 755, syl. 5 (1909) (in controversy with stranger, either personal representative or heir may waive—dictum).

8. See Wilcox v. Coons, 359 Mo. 52, 220 S.W.2d 15, syl. 4 (1949) (privilege of deceased client accrues to his personal representatives and may be waived either by his grantees under deed or his devisees under will).

9. Olsson v. Pierson, 237 Iowa 1342, 25 N.W.2d 357, syl. 8 (1946).

10. Eicholtz v. Grunewald, 313 Mich. 666, 21 N.W. 2d 914, syl. 2–6 (1946) (suit by children to enforce

contract of parents to make mutual wills and to set aside conveyance by father); Cummings v. Sherman, 16 Wash.2d 88, 132 P.2d 998, syl. 7 (1943) (similar); Allen v. Ross, 199 Wis. 162, 225 N.W. 831, 64 A.L.R. 180, syl. 1 (1929) (similar). But see, In re Smith's Estate, McGlone v. Fairchild, 263 Wis. 441, 57 N.W.2d 727 (1953 (in suit against estate based upon breach of contract by testatrix in making her last will, attorney's testimony privileged on ground that claimants were not claiming through testatrix but asserting adverse claim against the estate).

11. See the cases cited in note 6 supra.

1. 8 Wigmore, Evidence §§ 2298, 2299 (3d ed. 1940); Decennial Digest, Witnesses, ☞201(2); 70 C.J. Witnesses, § 560; 58 Am.Jur. Witnesses, §§ 516, 517; Note, 125 A.L.R. 508.

Uniform Rules of Evidence, Rule 26(2). Such privileges shall not extend (a) to a communication if the judge finds that sufficient evidence, aside from the communication, has been introduced to warrant a finding that the legal service was sought or obtained in order to enable or aid the client to commit or plan to commit a crime or a tort. . . ."

tend it to the client who seeks advice to aid him in carrying out an illegal or fraudulent scheme. Advice given for such a purpose would not be a professional service but participation in a conspiracy. Accordingly, it is settled under modern authority that the privilege does not extend to communications between attorney and client where the client's purpose is the furtherance of a future intended crime or fraud.[2] Advice secured in aid of a legitimate defense by the client against a charge of past crimes or past misconduct, even though he is guilty, stands on a different footing and such consultations are privileged.[3]

If the privilege is to be extended, it will be the client's not the attorney's and if it is to be denied on the ground of unlawful purpose, the client's guilty intention will be ground for denying the privilege, though the attorney may have acted innocently and in good faith.[4]

Must the judge, before denying the claim of privilege on this ground find as a fact, after a preliminary hearing if contested, that the consultation was in furtherance of crime or fraud? This would be the normal procedure in passing on such a preliminary fact, on which the admissibility of evidence depends, but such a procedure would probably facilitate too far the use of the privilege as a cloak for crime, and the courts have cast the balance in favor of disclosure, by requiring only that the one who seeks to avoid the privilege, bring forward evidence from which the existence of an unlawful purpose could reasonably be found.[5]

---

2. Queen v. Cox, 14 Q.B.D. 153 (C.C.R. 1884) (prosecution for conspiracy to defraud judgment creditor by transfer of debtor's property; communications between debtor and solicitor in respect to preventing collection of judgment by transfer of assets, not privileged); United States v. Bob, 106 F.2d 37, syl. 3-5, 125 A.L.R. 502 (C.C.A.2d, 1939) (conspiracy for fraudulent sale of mining stock through use of mails); Standard Fire Ins. Co. v. Smithhart, 183 Ky. 679, 211 S.W. 441, syl. 5-7, 5 A.L.R. 972 (1919) (communications by insured in fire policy tending to show arson and fraudulent claim); Gebhardt v. United Rys. Co. 220 S.W. 677, 679, 9 A.L.R. 1076 (Mo.Sup.1920) (client asserting personal injury on street car, discloses to attorney that she was not on car; "The law does not make a law office a nest of vipers in which to hatch out frauds and perjuries"); Ott v. State, 87 Tex.Cr. 382, 222 S.W. 261, syl. 5 (1920) (husband consults attorney as to what punishment would probably be incurred if he killed his wife).

A leading case recognizes the rule, but places a seemingly unjustifiable restriction upon it in holding that the client may assert the privilege in a case when he is sued or prosecuted for a different crime from the one involved in the consultation. Alexander v. United States, 138 U.S. 353, 11 S.Ct. 350, 34 L.Ed. 954 (1891) (client on trial for murder of his partner; error to admit communications to lawyer asserted to show plan to convert murder-victim's property).

If the client consults the lawyer about a proposed course of action, about the legality of which he is doubtful and is advised that it would be unlawful and then desists, it can not be said that the consultation was in furtherance of wrong. Cummings

v. Commonwealth, 221 Ky. 301, 298 S.W. 943, syl. 6 (1927). But a case which on this ground holds privileged a consultation about the effect of altering a deed in the client's favor, where the deed was later actually altered by someone, seems a misapplication. Williams v. Williams, 108 S.W.2d 297, syl. 6 (Tex.Civ.App.1937). The client could hardly have supposed that such an alteration could be innocent and the inquiry is itself strong circumstantial evidence that the client participated in the alteration.

3. "The privileged communications may be a shield of defense as to crimes already committed, but it cannot be used as a sword or weapon of offense to enable persons to carry out contemplated crimes against society." Gebhardt v. United Rys. Co., 220 S.W. 677, 699, 9 A.L.R. 1076 (Mo.Sup.1920). Clark v. State, 261 S.W.2d 339, syl. 13, 14 (Tex.Cr.1953), cert. den. 346 U.S. 855, 74 Sup.Ct. 69.

4. Queen v. Cox, 14 Q.B.D. 153 (C.C.R.1884); In re Selser, 27 N.J.Super. 257, 99 A.2d 313, syl. 3 (1953); Orman v. State, 22 Tex.App. 604, 3 S.W. 468, syl. 1 (1886); Note, 125 A.L.R. at 520. A converse question is raised in State v. Clark, next preceding note. The accused called his lawyer and told him that he had just killed his former wife. Though seemingly the call was for counsel in his defence, the lawyer volunteered advice that he should get rid of the fatal weapon. Apparently this advice was taken, as the weapon was not found. The court held that "the conversation was admissible as not within the realm of legitimate professional counsel and employment" (p. 347).

5. O'Rourke v. Darbishire, [1920] App.C. 581, 604, 614, 622 (H.L.) (evidence and not mere pleading of

Questions arise fairly frequently under this limitation upon the privilege in the situation where a client has first consulted one attorney about a claim, and then employs other counsel and brings suit. At the trial the defense seeks to have the first attorney testify to disclosures by the client which reveal that the claim was fabricated or fraudulent. This of course may be done,[6] but if the statements to the first attorney would merely reveal variances from the client's later statements or testimony, not sufficient to evidence fraud or perjury, the privilege would stand.[7]

It may be questioned whether the traditional statement of the area of the limitation, that is, in cases of communications in aid of crime or fraud is not itself too limited. It seems, as Wigmore argues, that the privilege should not be accorded to communications in furtherance of any deliberate scheme to deprive another of his rights by tortious or unlawful conduct.[8] Stricter requirements such as that the intended crime be *malum in se* or that it involve "moral turpitude", suggested in some of the older decisions,[9] seem out of place here where the only sanction proposed

is that of opening the door to evidence concededly relevant upon the issue on trial.

100. Protective Rules Relating to Materials Collected for Use of Counsel in Preparation for Trial: Reports of Employees, Witness-Statements, Experts' Reports, and the Like.

A heavy emphasis on the responsibility of counsel for the management of the client's litigation is a characteristic feature of the adversary or contentious system of procedure of the Anglo-American tradition. The privilege against disclosure in court of confidential communications between lawyer and client as we have seen, is supported in modern times upon the policy of encouraging free disclosure by the client in the attorney's office to enable the lawyer to discharge that responsibility.[1] The need for such encouragement is understood by lawyers because the problem of the guarded half-truths of the reticent client is familiar to them in their day-to-day work.

Closely allied to this felt need of promoting a policy of free disclosure by the client to enable the lawyer to do the work of managing his affairs most effectively in the inter-

---

fraud required); Clark v. United States, 289 U.S. 1, 14, 53 Sup.Ct. 465, 77 L.Ed. 993 (1933) ("There must be a showing of a prima facie case sufficient to satisfy the judge that the light should be let in"); United States v. Bob, 106 F.2d 37, 125 A.L.R. 502, 506 (C.C.A. 2, 1939); Pollock v. United States, 202 F.2d 281, syl. 10 (C.A. 5, 1953) (communication not privileged, where communication was made in furtherance of crime of which client was charged and evidence had been introduced giving color to the charge); Securities & Exchange Commission v. Harrison, 80 F.Supp. 226, syl. 5, 6, 10 (1948) (requisite prima facie showing of fraud to pierce attorney-client privilege, not made where circumstances not such as to justify verdict of wrong doing); Uniform Rules of Evidence, Rule 37(2), quoted note 1, supra.

Of course, the inference of the client's wrongful intent will often be a circumstantial one. See, e. g., Sawyer v. Stanley, 241 Ala. 39, 1 So.2d 21, syl. 4 (1941) where a will was contested for forgery and evidence of an attorney was admitted that the purported beneficiary asked him whether decedent had left a will, without disclosing existence of purported will.

6. In re Koellen's Estate, Willie v. Lampe, 167 Kan. 676, 208 P.2d 595, syl. 9 (1949) (client admitted to first lawyer that he had forged will which he later sought to probate, not privileged); Standard Fire Ins. Co. v. Smithhart, 183 Ky. 679, 211 S.W. 441, 5 A.L.R. 972 (1919) (client sought first lawyer to sue on fire policy, disclosing that she had connived in burning her house; not privileged); Gebhardt v. United Rys. Co., 220 S.W. 677, 9 A.L.R. 1076 (Mo.Sup.1920) (fabricated personal injury claim: no privilege).

7. Nadler v. Warner Co. 321 Pa. 139, 184 A. 3, syl. 3, 4 (1936); (offer to show statement of personal injury claimant, merely inconsistent with present position but not claimed to show fraud, rejected); Thomas v. Jones, 105 W.Va. 46, 141 S.E. 434, syl. 2 (1928) (inconsistency not such as to show fraud).

8. 8 Wigmore, Evidence, § 2298, p. 579 (3d ed. 1940).

9. Bank of Utica v. Mersereau, 3 Barb.Ch. 528, 598 (1848) (limited to felony or malum in se); Hughes v. Boone, 102 N.C. 137, 9 S.E. 286, 292 (1889) (similar dictum).

1. See § 82, supra.

ests of justice, is a feeling by lawyers of a need for privacy in their work and for freedom from interference in the task of preparing the client's case for trial. Certainly if the adversary were free at any time to inspect all of the correspondence, memoranda, reports, exhibits, trial briefs, drafts of proposed pleadings, and plans for presentation of proofs, which constitute the lawyer's file in the case, the attorney's present freedom to collect for study all the data, favorable and unfavorable, and to record his tentative impressions before maturing his conclusions, would be cramped and hindered.

The natural jealousy of the lawyer for the privacy of his file, and the courts' desire to protect the effectiveness of the lawyer's work as the manager of litigation, have found expression, not only as we have seen in the evidential privilege for confidential lawyer-client communications, but in rules and practices about the various forms of pre-trial discovery. Thus, under the chancery practice of discovery, the adversary was not required to disclose, apart from his own testimony, the evidence which he would use, or the names of the witnesses he would call in support of his own case.[2] The same restriction has often been embodied in, or read into, the statutory discovery-systems.[3] And under the Illinois rule of court it is provided that the right to discovery of documents "shall not apply to memoranda, reports or documents prepared by or for either party in preparation for trial, or to any communication between any party or his agent and the attorney for such party."[4]

Counterbalancing this need for privacy in preparation, of course, is the very need from which the discovery devices spring, namely, the need to make available to each party the widest possible sources of proof as early as may be so as to avoid surprise and facilitate preparation.[5] The present trend is manifestly in the direction of the wider recognition of this latter need, and the taboo against the "fishing expedition"[6] is yielding to a realization that the ends of justice require a wider availability than in the past of the various devices for discovery,[7] such as interrogatories to the adverse party, demands for admissions, oral and written depositions of parties and witnesses, and orders for production and inspection of writings, and the like. In this country, the greatest influence in this development is the example of the liberal discovery procedures provided in the Federal rules.[8] How far has the interest in privacy of preparation been submerged by the tide flowing toward a wider scope of discovery?

In the first place, of course, it is recognized that if the traditional privilege for attorney-client communications applies to a particular writing which may be found in a lawyer's file, the privilege exempts it from pre-trial

---

2. 6 Wigmore, Evidence § 1856 (3d ed. 1940). As to the application of the restriction in the United States, and the departures from it in some states, see Ragland, Discovery before Trial, ch. 15, May a Party be required to Disclose Evidence of his own Case? (1932); Decennial Digests, Discovery, ⊂ 8. For a criticism of the requirement, see Sunderland, Scope and Method of Discovery before Trial, 42 Yale L.J. 862, 866 (1933).

3. Wigmore, op. cit. §§ 1856a, 1856b; Ragland, ubi supra, note 2.

4. Revised Rules of Supreme Court, Rule 17(1) (1941).

5. 2 Moore, Federal Practice, § 26.01 (1938); Holtzoff, New Procedure in the Federal Courts, 70 (published by the American Bar Association, 1940); Goodrich,

Circ.J. in Hickman v. Taylor, 153 F.2d 212, 217 (C.C.A.3d, 1945). Equally important is the need to supplement the inadequacy of the pleadings as a vehicle for disclosing what points are really in dispute. Moore, section cited above; Sunderland, The Theory and Practice of Pre-trial Procedure, 36 Mich.L.Rev. 215, 216 (1937).

6. See Sunderland, Foreword, Ragland, Discovery before Trial, p. iii (1932).

7. See the enlightening discussion and citations, in the opinion of Goodrich, Circ.J. at p. 217 in Hickman v. Taylor, cited note [5], supra, and see the Section of Moore, cited in the same note, at footnote 9.

8. Federal Rules of Civil Procedure, Rules 26–37.

discovery proceedings,[9] such as orders for production or questioning about its contents in the taking of depositions. On the other hand, if the writing has been in the possession of the client or his agents and was there subject to discovery, it seems axiomatic that the client cannot secure any exemption for the document by sending it to an attorney to be placed in his files.[10]

How do these distinctions apply to a report made by an agent to the client of the results of investigation by himself or another agent of facts pertinent to some matter which later becomes the subject of litigation, such as a business dispute or a personal injury. It is usually held that an agent's report to his principal though confidential is not privileged as such,[11] and looked on as a mere pre-existing document it would not become privileged when sent by the client-principal to his lawyer for his information when suit is brought or threatened.[12] The problem frequently arises in connection with proceedings for discovery of accident-reports by employees, with lists of eye-witnesses, and in connection with signed statements of witnesses attached to such reports or secured separately by investigators employed in the client's claim department or by an insurance company with whom the client carries insurance against liability.[13]

Since a statement made by the client's agent, on behalf of the client to the latter's attorney would be privileged,[14] it is an easy step to treat in the same way a report secured by the client from his employee for the purpose of submitting it to counsel in connection with an actual or anticipated claim or suit. Most of the decisions treat such special reports as privileged from discovery under the privilege for attorney-client communications.[15] On the other hand, rou-

---

9. Leonia Amusement Corp. v. Loew's Inc., 13 F.R.D. 438, syl. 3 (1952) (communications from attorney to client, privileged); Wise v. Western Union Telegraph Co., 178 Atl. 640, syl. 3 (Del.Super.1935); Ragland, Discovery before Trial, 146 (1932); Decennial Digests, Discovery, Key No. 90; 17 Am. Jur., Discovery, § 28.

10. See § 93, supra.

11. Southwark & V. Water Co. v. Quick, 3 Q.B.D. 315, 9 Eng.Rul.Cas. 587 (C.A.1878); Schmitt v. Emery, 211 Minn. 547, 2 N.W.2d 413, 416, 139 A.L.R. 1242 (1942); Note, 146 A.L.R. 977, 978.

12. See § 93, supra.

13. Cases involving the claim of privilege for such reports and statements are collected in Notes, 26 Minn.L.Rev. 744 (1942); 108 A.L.R. 510, 146 A.L.R. 977.

14. See § 95, supra.

15. Lafone v. Falkland Islands Co., 4 K. & J. 34, 70 Eng.Rep. 14 (V.C.1857) (agent's report secured for purpose of communication to attorney); Cossey v. London, Brighton & South Coast R. Co., L. R. 5 C.P. 146 (1870) (medical officer's report made after claim and with a view to litigation); Skinner v. Great Northern R. Co., L.R. 9 Exch. 298 (1874) (similar to last); Adams Steamship Co. v. London Assurance Co. [1914] 3 K.B. 1256 (special reports by agents of marine insurance to salvage association in anticipation of litigation); Schmitt v. Emery, 211 Minn. 547, 2 N.W.2d 413, syl. 3, 139 A.L.R.

1242, annotated (1942) and noted 26 Minn.L.Rev. 744 (statement from bus driver, co-defendant with bus company in personal injury action, obtained by bus company's claim agent and delivered by him to attorney for both defendants; privilege asserted by bus company discussed and sustained, but apparently privilege was also asserted by driver, as to whom it was even more clearly sustainable); State ex rel. Terminal R. Ass'n of St. Louis v. Flynn, 257 S.W. 2d 69, syl. 9-14 (Mo.1953) (photographs taken immediately after accident by defendant's employee and in possession of defendant's claim agent, privileged as work product prepared with a view to litigation); Davenport Co. v. Penn. R. Co., 166 Pa. 480, 31 Atl. 245 (1895) (report of local agent of railway to superior officer relating to shipment of fruit for which claim of damage had been made, for express purpose of submission to counsel); Note, 146 A.L.R. 977, 987; 8 Wigmore, Evidence, §§ 2318, 2319 (3d ed. 1940).

A confidential report made at the client's instance by one of his agents directly to the attorney would be privileged manifestly, just as the client's own communications would. Lalance and Grosjean Mfg. Co. v. Haberman Mfg. Co., 87 F. 563, syl. 2 (C.C.S.D.N.Y. 1898) (communication between attorney and scientific expert employed by client); Woolley v. North London R. Co., L.R. 4 C.P. 602 (1869) (similar); Note, 139 A.L.R. 1256. Apparently the same result is reached when the report is made at the attorney's instance, though theoretically the same principle would only apply if the reporter acted as an agent

tine reports of employees made in the regular course of business, before suit is brought or threatened, have usually, though not always, been treated as pre-existing documents which not being privileged in the client's hands do not become so when delivered into the possession of his attorney.[16] It must be admitted, however, that these classifications are not quite mutually exclusive and that some cases will fall in a doubtful borderland.[17] And the law is in the making on the question whether a report of accident or other casualty by a policy-holder or his agents to a company insuring the policy-holder against liability, is to be treated as privileged when the insurance company passes it on to the attorney who will represent both the company and the insured.[18] Probably the insurance company may reasonably be treated as an intermediary to secure legal representation for the insured, by whom the confidential communications can be transmitted as through a trusted agent. Routine reports of the insured or his agents before suit or threat of suit should not be privileged, but a confidential report made after suit filed or under circumstances indicating a high probability of litigation, and intended for the use of counsel, might reasonably be embraced within the privilege.

Another approach to the problems of discovery of materials contained in the files of

---

for the client. If he acted as the attorney's agent or assistant, it would seem necessary to resort to a privilege for materials constituting part of the lawyer's preparation for trial. See Lalance and Grosjean Mfg. Co. v. Haberman Mfg. Co., supra; Webb v. Francis J. Lewald Coal Co., 214 Cal. 142, 4 P.2d 532, syl. 3 (1931) (report to plaintiff's attorney by doctor who made examination of plaintiff: does not appear whether doctor retained at lawyer's instance or client's, but court treated the report as privileged as a communication of client's agent). Similarly, reports secured by the lawyer from third persons by correspondence can again not be brought within the privilege for attorney client communications (Wigmore, op. cit. § 2319, sub. 3) and can only be exempted from discovery, if at all, on some theory of privilege for preparatory materials, or the "lawyer's work product".

16. Woolley v. North London R. Co., L.R. 4 C.P. 602 (1869) (court allowed inspection of reports of accident by guard of train, an inspector, and the locomotive superintendent to the general manager; significant question was not time of reports nor whether confidential, but whether made in ordinary course of duty); Anderson v. Bank of British Columbia, L.R. 2 Ch.Div. 644 (C.A.1876) (letter from manager of branch bank to head office in response to telegram, reporting on transfer of funds from one account to another, written before suit filed though litigation then probable, not privileged against production, since there was no suggestion in the telegram that the report was for submission to counsel); Hurley v. Connecticut Co., 118 Conn. 276, 172 A. 86, syl. 11 (1934) (motorman's report of accident subject to inspection; mere fact that it was made for preparation against possibility of litigation not sufficient for privilege); Wise v. Western Union Telegraph Co., 178 A. 640, syl. 12, 13 (Del.Super.

1935) (report from one branch office to another, at latter's request, upon complaint of patron that forged telegram transmitted in his name; held not privileged from discovery in absence of clear showing that document was prepared with bona fide intention of laying before attorney); Robertson v. Commonwealth, 181 Va. 520, 25 S.E.2d 352, syl. 17, 146 A.L.R. 966 (1943) (motorman's report of accident made in course of ordinary duty before suit brought or threatened required to be produced at trial by counsel from his files); 8 Wigmore, Evidence § 2319, (3d ed. 1940); Note, 146 A.L.R. 977, 980.

In Ohio, however, and perhaps in some other states, an accident report, made in ordinary course but in anticipation of the possibility of litigation, is when transmitted to counsel, privileged from discovery. Ex parte Schoepf, 74 Oh.St. 1, 77 N.E. 276, syl. 3, 6 L.R.A.,N.S., 325 (1906); In re Hyde, 149 Oh.St. 407, 79 N.E.2d 224, syl. 1 (1948) (but other routine records, such as names of operators of cars, and times of operation, not privileged).

17. See e. g. The Hopper No. 13, [1925] Prob. 52 (shipmaster's report required by general rule, of a collision, on a printed form headed "confidential report . . . in view of anticipated litigation," sent to solicitors; held, privileged); Note, Attorney-Client Privilege for Documents Originating with Client's Agent, 88 U.Pa.L.Rev. 467, 469 (1940).

18. Privilege denied: Virginia-Carolina Chem. Co. v. Knight, 106 Va. 674, 680, 56 S.E. 725, 727 (1907); Brown v. Meyer, 137 Kan. 553, 21 P.2d 368, syl. 1 (1933). Privilege accorded: In re Klemann, 132 Oh.St. 187, 5 N.E.2d 492, syl. 1, 108 A.L.R. 505 (1936) and note; New York Casualty Co. v. Superior Court, 30 Cal.App.2d 130, 85 P.2d 965, syl. 3 (1938); Notes, 26 Minn.L.Rev. 744, 745 (1941); 88 U.Pa.L. Rev. 467, 470 (1940).

counsel is furnished by the decisions interpreting the Federal rules regulating discovery.[19] In the leading case of Hickman v. Taylor,[20] suit was brought for the death of a member of the crew of a tug, who with four others was drowned when the tug sank in the course of towing a car-float across the Delaware River. About three weeks later a public hearing was held by the United States Steamboat Inspectors, at which the four surviving crew members were examined, and their testimony was made available to the parties interested. A few days later, before suit was brought, an attorney employed by the tug owners to defend against possible suits, interviewed the four survivors and took their signed statements, and likewise interviewed other persons believed to have information about the accident, and in some cases made memoranda (apparently not signed by the informants) of what they told him. After suit brought in the Federal court, the plaintiff filed interrogatories asking for copies of any written statements taken by the defendant and for disclosure of the terms of any oral statements or of any memoranda relating to the accident. The defendants and their counsel declined to furnish the information on the ground that it called "for privileged matter obtained in preparation for litigation" and was "an attempt to obtain indirectly counsel's private files." The trial court ordered the production of the written statements, the disclosure by counsel of relevant

facts learned from oral statements, and the submission of his memoranda to the court to determine which of them might be revealed to the plaintiff. The counsel persisted in refusal, was adjudged in contempt [21] and an appeal was taken from this judgment. In the Court of Appeals, the judgment was reversed on the ground that the information sought was part of the "work product of the lawyer" and hence within the exemption in the Rules for "privileged" matter.[22]

The Supreme Court heard the case on certiorari, discussed extensively the questions involved and affirmed the decision, but with a somewhat different *rationale*. Apparently restricting the exception in the Rules [23] for "privileged" matter, so far as here relevant, to the traditional privilege for attorney-client communications, they held that the information called for was not within the "privilege." But, as reflected in the following passages from the court's opinion, it seems to have recognized what might be termed a qualified privilege for some of the materials constituting the lawyer's preparation for trial. The court said: "Proper preparation of a client's case demands that he [the lawyer] assemble information, sift what he considers to be the relevant from the irrelevant facts, prepare his legal theories and plan his strategy without undue and needless interference. . . . This work is reflected, of course, in interviews, statements, memoranda, correspondence, briefs, mental

---

19. The five principal methods of discovery under the Federal Rules are (1) depositions oral or written of the parties, and of other witnesses (Rules 26–32); (2) interrogatories to parties (Rule 33); (3) production of documents for inspection or copying (Rule 34); (4) physical and mental examination of persons (Rule 35); and (5) requests for admission of facts (Rule 36). See Note, 31 Minn. L.Rev. 712, 714 (1947). The parts of the Rules most pertinent to the present discussion have been summarized as follows: "Rule 26 provides that either party may, on notice to adverse parties, take the deposition of any person on any relevant matter not privileged; Rule 30(b) authorizes the trial court to issue such orders as are neces-

sary to protect the interrogated person from hardship; Rule 33 provides that any party may put written interrogatories to his adversary respecting any material matter in issue: Rule 34 provides that, on motion of any party and good cause shown therefor, the trial court may order the production of any document which constitutes or contains evidence." Note, 62 Harv.L.Rev. 269, n. 2.

20. 329 U.S. 495, 67 S.Ct. 385, 91 L.Ed. 451 (1947).

21. 4 F.R.D. 479 (1945).

22. 153 F.2d 221 (C.C.A.3d, 1945, enlightening opinion by Goodrich, Circ. J.).

23. Rule 26(b) and Rule 34.

impressions, personal beliefs, and countless other tangible and intangible ways—aptly though roughly termed by the Circuit Court of Appeals in this case as the 'work product of the lawyer.' Were such materials open to opposing counsel on mere demand, much of what is now put down in writing would remain unwritten. An attorney's thought, heretofore inviolate, would not be his own. Inefficiency, unfairness and sharp practices would inevitably develop in the giving of legal advice and in the preparation of cases for trial. The effect on the legal profession would be demoralizing. And the interests of the clients and the cause of justice would be poorly served.

"We do not mean to say that all written materials obtained or prepared by an adversary's counsel with an eye toward litigation are necessarily free from discovery in all cases. Where relevant and non-privileged facts remain hidden in an attorney's file and where production of those facts is essential to the preparation of one's case, discovery may properly be had. Such written statements and documents might, under certain circumstances, be admissible in evidence or give clues as to the existence or location of relevant facts. Or they might be useful for purposes of impeachment or corroboration. And production might be justified where the witnesses are no longer available or can be reached only with difficulty. . . . But the general policy against invading the privacy of an attorney's course of preparation is so well recognized and so essential to an orderly working of our system of legal procedure that a burden rests on the one who would invade that privacy to establish adequate reasons to justify production through a subpoena or court order. That burden, we believe, is necessarily implicit in the rules as now constituted." [24]

Applying these standards, the court concluded that since there was no showing by the plaintiff of necessity for the written statements, the witnesses so far as appears being still available to plaintiff for interviewing, there was no ground for the exercise of discretion to order production, and as to the oral statements, the court said, " . . . we do not believe that any showing of necessity can be made under the circumstances of this case so as to justify production. Under ordinary conditions, forcing an attorney to repeat or write out all that witnesses have told him and to deliver the account to his adversary gives rise to grave dangers of inaccuracy and untrustworthiness. No legitimate purpose is served by such production. The practice forces the attorney to testify as to what he remembers or what he saw fit to write down regarding witnesses' remarks. Such testimony could not qualify as evidence; and to use it for impeachment or corroborative purposes would make the attorney much less an officer of the court and much more an ordinary witness. The standards of the profession would thereby suffer." [25]

While the Hickman case was pending, the Advisory Committee on Federal Rules submitted a proposed amendment to Rule 30(b) which seemed to foreshadow the qualified privilege approach adopted in the opinion and which went further in specifying the types of material which would be exempt, or qualifiedly privileged, from discovery as part of the preparation for trial.[26] The court, evi-

[24]. 329 U.S. 511, 512.

[25]. 329 U.S. 512, 513.

[26]. "The court shall not order the production or inspection of any writing obtained or prepared by the adverse party, his attorney, surety, indemnitor, or agent in anticipation of litigation or in preparation for trial unless satisfied that denial of production or inspection will unfairly prejudice the party seeking the production or inspection in preparing his claim or defense or will cause him undue hardship or injustice. The court shall not order the production or inspection of any part of the writing that reflects an attorney's mental impressions, conclusions, opinions, or legal theories or except as provided in Rule 35, the conclusion of an expert." Report of Proposed Amendments to Rules of Civil Procedure for District

dently preferring to lead the way by its own decision to a case-by-case development of the practice, failed to adopt the proposed amendment.

The test of "good cause" [27] laid down by the court, may be satisfied, it has been suggested, "(1) whenever production of witness's statements was necessary to forestall a failure of proof, or (2) whenever such statements might be admissible as evidence or give clues to relevant evidence not otherwise available or be useful for impeachment or corroboration, or (3) whenever the witness who gave the statement was no longer available." [28] As we have seen, this privilege for preparatory materials is qualified by a power in the trial judge to draw aside the curtain if in the particular case the demands of justice so require, that is, if the applicant's need for access to the sources of proof outweighs the policy of encouraging thorough

preparation by protecting the lawyer's creative contribution against intrusion. The indefiniteness of this standard of "good cause" makes it clear that it reposes wide discretion in the trial judge.[29]

Since the standard is a discretionary one, the types of materials used in preparation for trial cannot be classified as subject, or not subject, to discovery. It seems probable, however, that in order of facility of showing "good cause," the materials might be arranged in the following sequence, from a first group of which discovery would be granted with relative facility, to the last in which the necessary showing could almost never be made. First, routine reports of employees about the accident or other transaction, made in the usual course of business, without the intervention of counsel, at or near the time of the accident or transaction.[30] An important decision subsequent to the Hickman case

Courts of the United States, Rule 30(b) (1946) 5 F.R.D. 433, 456–457. See also Discovery Procedure Symposium, (1946) 5 F.R.D. 403; Note, 31 Minn.L. Rev. 712, 735, 736 (1947).

27. "Good cause" in Rule 30(b) is a requirement not for granting but for refusing discovery, whereas in Rule 34, the showing of "good cause" is a requirement for obtaining an order to a party to produce documents. But the court finds a showing of "good cause" an implicit requirement for discovery of preparatory materials under any of the various forms of discovery. See Hickman v. Taylor, 329 U.S. 495, 512, 67 S.Ct. 385, 394, 91 L.Ed. 451 (1947).

28. Note, The Attorney's Trial Preparations and Pre-Trial Discovery under the Federal Rules: Hickman v. Taylor, Two Years After, 62 Harv.L.Rev. 269, 275 (1948). The most comprehensive and illuminating treatment is in 4 Moore, Fed.Practice, §§ 26.23–26.25 (2d ed. 1950, and supplements). Another valuable discussion is Paine, Discovery of Trial Preparation in the Federal Courts, 50 Col.L.Rev. 1026 (1950). See also Speck, Use of Discovery in United States Courts, 60 Yale L.J. 1132 (1951) (a statistical survey); Note, Discovery—The Federal Rules, 31 Minn. L.Rev. 712 (1948); The Discovery Procedure Symposium, 5 F.R.D. 403 (1946) (counsel in Hickman case and other lawyers discuss its problems).

29. Some of the decisions discussing and applying the "good cause" requirement: Safeway Stores, Inc. v. Reynolds, 12 Fed.Rules Serv. 34.411 Case 3 (C.A., D.C.1949) (plaintiff seeks discovery of own state-

ment taken by defendant's claim agent before plaintiff employed counsel, plaintiff's counsel says he needs to ascertain whether plaintiff has changed version of facts, held, insufficient: a mechanical opinion); Martin v. Capital Transit Co., 170 F.2d 811, syl. 1–4 (C.A.D.C.1948) (employee's report of accident, motion for discovery denied; movant must show in motion and affidavit grounds of "good cause"); Newell v. Capital Transit Co., 7 F.R.D. 732, 11 Fed.Rules Serv. 34.411 Case 2 (1948) (Dist. Ct.D.C.1948) (plaintiff's motion for discovery of witness-statements taken by defendant's investigators; fact that plaintiff unconscious after accident and his lawyers unable to locate witnesses is good cause); Lauritzen v. Atlantic Greyhound Corp., 8 F.R.D. 237, 11 Fed.Rules Serv. 34.411 case 6 E.D. Tenn., 1948) (plaintiffs sue for death of son in bus accident and seek discovery, list of witnesses and statements, sufficient); Lindsay v. Prince, 8 F.R.D. 233, 11 Fed.Rules Serv. 34.411 case 5 (N.D.Oh.1948) (defendant in personal injury, sued belatedly after plaintiff had sued other person, was not present at accident and made no investigation, sufficient). For a convincing and liberal view of "good cause" for requiring discovery of witness-statements (including those signed by the moving party, see 4 Moore, Fed.Practice, § 26.23[8], pp. 1141–1149 (2d ed. 1950).

30. See, e. g. Smith v. Washington Gas. Light Co., 11 Fed.Rules Serv. 34.411 case 3 (D.C.1948) (repairman's report); Morrone v. Southern Pacific Co., 7 F.R.D. 214 (S.D.Cal.1947) (report of train crew). Such routine reports as a matter of practical ad-

makes clear that the requirement of a showing of good cause applies to the discovery of witness-statements taken by claim-adjusters and investigators, regardless of whether they happen to be lawyers, and is not limited to statements taken by counsel employed in the litigation.[31] This would include lists of eye-witnesses [32] and statements taken from such witnesses by the employees under general instructions.[33] Second, reports made and witness-statements taken by employees at the request of counsel after claim asserted or suit brought.[34] Third, photographs of places or objects directly involved in the accident, such as the scene of the accident, the wrecked automobile, the car-step from which the injured party fell, and the like.[35] Fourth, witness-statements taken by the lawyer in writing and signed by the witness.[36] Fifth, the lawyer's memoranda of his recollection, or his unaided memory of oral statements of witnesses interviewed by him.[37] Sixth, reports of experts employed at the lawyer's suggestion, about questions directly at issue in the litigation.[38] Seventh, reports of experiments performed by experts, under plans formulated by the lawyer, and photographs and exhibits prepared in connection with such experiments.[39] Eighth, the lawyer's memoranda of his thought-processes,[40] findings and

---

ministration should be discoverable without the consumption of time necessary to decide upon the existence of good cause, and this is the practice in at least one district. Hen Ray Food Products, 12 Fed.Rules Serv. 34.81 case 2 (1949), and see Hayman v. Pullman Co., 8 F.R.D. 238, 11 Fed.Rules Serv. 33.351 case 2 (1948). But compare Martin v. Capital Transit Co. cited in next preceding note, and Alltmont v. United States, cited in next following note.

31. Alltmont v. United States, 177 F.2d 971 (C.A. 3, 1949), certiorari denied (action for personal injury due to explosion on government vessel; order for production of copies of statements of witnesses taken by agents of Federal Bureau of Investigation held erroneous in absence of showing of good cause, that is, circumstances making it essential for the plaintiffs to see the statements). The decision and the problems radiating from it are lucidly discussed in 4 Moore, Fed.Practice, § 26.23[8].

32. See, e. g. Lauritzen v. Atlantic Greyhound Corp., 8 F.R.D. 237, 11 Fed.Rules Serv. 34.411 case 6 (E. D.Tenn.1948); Silvetti v. United States, 8 F.R.D. 558, 12 Fed.Rules Serv. 34.13 case 5 (1949) (death injury; discovery allowed); Hayman v. Pullman Co., next preceding note.

33. Lauritzen v. Atlantic Greyhound Corp., next preceding note, Newell v. Capital Transit Co., 7 F.R.D. 732, 11 Fed.Rules Serv. 34.411 case 2 (1948); Lindsay v. Prince, 8 F.R.D. 233, 11 Fed.Rules Serv. 34.411 case 5, (N.D.Ohio, 1948).

34. Compare the decisions cited in note 15, supra.

35. See Shields v. Sobelman, 64 F.Supp. 619 (E.D. Pa.1946) (photograph of winch involved in accident, taken under direction of attorney, ordered to be produced by him). Compare Reeves v. Pennsylvania R. Co., 80 F.Supp. 107 (1948) (order against party to produce X-ray photographs denied because in doctor's not party's control).

36. Hickman v. Taylor, 329 U.S. 495, 512, 67 S.Ct. 385, syl. 14, 91 L.Ed. 451 (1947).

37. Hickman v. Taylor, 329 U.S. 495, 512, 513, 67 S.Ct. 385, syl. 15, 91 L.Ed. 451 (1947). But the facts learned by the attorney may be discoverable when the witness-statements would not be. Gaynor v. Atlantic Greyhound Corp., 11 Fed.Rules Serv. 26b.211 case 6 (1948).

38. See United States v. 300 Cans of Black Raspberries, 7 F.R.D. 36, syl. 6 (N.D.Oh.1947) (discovery allowed of government's records of tests and analyses); Bergstrom Paper Co. v. Continental Insurance Co., 7 F.R.D. 548, syl. 4, 11 Fed.Rules Serv. 26b.411 case 1 (E.D.Wis.1947) (taking deposition of adversary's expert as to conclusions as to cause and situs of explosion, allowed). See Note, 62 Harv.L. Rev. 269, 272 (1948) advocating liberal discovery of experts' reports, and discussing arguments that such reports are lawyers' work-product and that discovery would result in unjust enrichment. See also 4 Moore, Fed.Practice, § 26.24 (2d ed. 1950).

39. See Lewis v. United Air Lines, 32 F.Supp. 21, syl. 2 (W.D.Pa.1940) (order to expert to answer questions as to tests of cylinder involved in accident, made by him under attorney's instruction, denied); Cold Metal Process Co. v. Aluminum Co., 7 F.R.D. 684, syl. 2 (D.Mass.1947) (patent infringement, plaintiff seeks disclosure by expert in deposition of X-ray examination of products alleged to infringe, denied because reports of expert privileged as those of lawyer's assistant); Cold Metal Process Co. v. Aluminum Co., 7 F.R.D. 425 (N.D.Oh.1947) affirmed sub nom. Sachs v. Aluminum Co., 167 F.2d 570 (C.C.A. 6th 1948) (similar to last, questions as to expert's findings, but not as to his methods, required to be answered). See also cases in next preceding note.

40. Hickman v. Taylor, supra, passim.

plans, such as his memoranda as to the facts to be proved and the witnesses he will use to prove them,[41] and his memoranda as to available legal theories.

In criminal cases, while the remedy of discovery on behalf of the accused seems to be gaining wider recognition, a similar unwill-ingness to require the prosecuting attorney to disclose in advance of trial his own memoranda and the statements taken from witnesses, constituting his work as a lawyer in preparation for trial, is reflected in the decisions.[42]

---

41. McNamara v. Erschen, 8 F.R.D. 427, 12 Fed. Rules Serv. 33.316 case 1 (D.Del.1948); Aktiebolaget Vargos v. Clark, 8 F.R.D. 635 (D.Ct.D.C.1949) (both cases deny discovery of witnesses to be used at trial, distinguishing discovery of names of persons who have knowledge of facts, see note 32, supra). See also note, 32 Neb.L.Rev. 495 (1953).

42. See State v. Rhoads, 81 Oh.St. 397, 91 N.E. 186, syl. 1, 27 L.R.A.,N.S., 558 (1910) (accused not entitled to inspect at trial stenographic report of interview with prosecution witness of city solicitor later delivered to prosecuting attorney: court discussed amenability to inspection of prosecutor's notes, memoranda and plans made in preparation for trial); People ex rel. Lemon v. Supreme Court, 245 N.Y. 24, 156 N.E. 84, syl. 1, 52 A.L.R. 200 (1927) (murder by poisoning; application by accused for inspection before trial of statements made by accomplice to district attorney, reports by experts on results of post mortem examination, and reports of chemical analyses of parts of body of deceased; held, in opinion by Cardozo, C. J., question of availability of discovery in criminal cases left open, but if available, does not extend to papers here sought to be inspected, since they are not admissible as evidence but "merely mnemonic instruments whereby the prosecutor may be better able to elicit evidence hereafter"). As to extent of availability of discovery in criminal cases, see Notes, 60 Yale L.J. 626 (1951); 42 J.Crim.L. 774 (1952), 38 id. 249 (1947), 52 A.L.R. 207; 6 Wigmore, Evidence, §§ 1859g, 1863; Dec.Dig., Crim.Law, ⟊627½. Federal Rules of Criminal Procedure, Rule 16, allows discovery of writings and objects in the hands of the prosecution only where "obtained from or belonging to the defendant or obtained from others by seizure or by process." This narrow limitation is not applicable to Rule 17(c) which permits the issuance of a subpoena against the government requiring the production of papers and objects for inspection before trial, if they are of such character as to be prima facie admissible in evidence. Bowman Dairy Co. v. United States, 341 U.S. 214, 71 Sup.Ct. 675, 95 L.Ed. 879 (1951). Under this rule the defendant is entitled to inspection of his own written statement in the hands of the prosecution. Fryer v. United States, 207 F.2d 134, syl. 1 (C.A.D.C. 1953, certiorari denied) (one judge dissenting). Similarly, at the trial itself, the court is bound under its common law powers to order, at defendant's request, production of a prior inconsistent statement in the government's hands of a crucial witness for the prosecution. Gordon v. United States, 344 U.S. 414, 73 Sup.Ct. 369, 97 L.Ed. 447 (1953). See also Note, 156 A.L.R. 345.

CHAPTER 11

THE PRIVILEGE FOR CONFIDENTIAL INFORMATION SECURED IN THE COURSE OF THE PHYSICIAN-PATIENT RELATIONSHIP

101. The Statement of the Rule and Its Purpose.[1]

The common law knew no privilege for confidential information imparted to a doctor. When a physician raised the question before Lord Mansfield whether he was required to disclose professional confidences, the great Chief Justice drew the line clear: "If a surgeon was voluntarily to reveal these secrets, to be sure, he would be guilty of a breach of honor and of great indiscretion; but to give that information in a court of justice, which by the law of the land he is bound to do, will never be imputed to him as any indiscretion whatever."[2]

The pioneer departure from the common law rule was the New York provision of 1828 which in its original form was as follows: "No person authorized to practice physic or surgery shall be allowed to disclose any information which he may have acquired in attending any patient, in a professional character, and which information was necessary to enable him to prescribe for such patient as a physician, or to do any act for him as a surgeon."[3]

Another early Act which has been widely copied is the following provision of the Cali-fornia Code of Civil Procedure of 1872: § 1881, par. 4, "A licensed physician or surgeon cannot, without the consent of his patient, be examined in a civil action as to any information acquired in attending the patient which was necessary to enable him to prescribe or act for the patient." These two ground-breaking statutes indicate the general scope and purport of this legislative privilege which in some form has been enacted in nearly two-thirds of the states.[4] Seventeen states maintain the common law position denying any privilege for information disclosed to medical practitioners.[5]

1. See, in general, 8 Wigmore, Evidence, §§ 2380–2391; 5 Jones, Evidence, §§ 2183–2200 (2d ed.rev. 1926); Model Code of Evidence, Rules 220–223 and commentary; 70 C.J. Witnesses §§ 588–613; Dec. Dig. Witnesses, ☞208–214, 217, 219(4–6), 220–223. See also Hammelmann, Professional Privilege: a Comparative Study, 28 Can.Bar Rev. 750 (1950); Freedman, Medical Privilege, 32 id. 1 (1954).

2. The Duchess of Kingston's Trial, 20 How.St.Trials 573 (1776).

3. Rev.Stats. 1829, vol. II, Part III, c. 7, Tit. 3, art. eight, § 73.

4. The statutes are compiled and quoted in 8 Wigmore, Evidence, § 2380, note 5.

5. These are listed in Chafee, Is Justice Served by Closing the Doctor's Mouth, 52 Yale L.J. 607 (1943)

It seems that the only purpose that could possibly justify the suppression in a law suit of material facts learned by the physician is the encouragement of freedom of disclosure by the patient so as to aid in the effective treatment of disease and injury.[6] To attain this objective, the immediate effect of the privilege is to protect the patient against the embarrassment and invasion of privacy which disclosure would entail.[7] But if this were the only interest involved it is hard to suppose that the desire for privacy would outweigh the need for complete presentation of the facts in the interest of justice. A fuller discussion of the policy of the privilege is reserved for a later section.[8]

102. Relation of Physician and Patient.

The first requisite for the privilege is that the patient must have consulted the physician[1] for treatment or for diagnosis looking toward treatment.[2] If consulted for treatment it is immaterial by whom the doctor is employed.[3] Usually, however, when the doctor is employed by one other than the patient, treatment will not be the purpose and the privilege will not attach. Thus, when a doctor is appointed by the court[4] or the prosecutor[5] to make a physical or mental examina-

---

as follows: Alabama, Connecticut, Delaware, Florida, Georgia, Illinois, Maine, Maryland, Massachusetts, New Hampshire, New Jersey, Rhode Island, South Carolina, Tennessee, Texas, Vermont, and Virginia.

6. Thus the New York Commissioners on Revision in justifying the new privilege said, "unless such consultations are privileged men will be incidentally punished by being obliged to suffer the consequences of injuries without relief from the medical art." N.Y.Rev.Stats.2d ed. vol. III, p. 737 (1836). See also Metropolitan Life Ins. Co. v. Ryan, 237 Mo.App. 464, 172 S.W.2d 269, 272, syl. 4 (1943).

7. This is stated as the aim of the privilege in Falkinburg v. Prudential Ins. Co., 132 Neb. 831, 273 N.W. 478, syl. 4 (1937) (to enable patient to secure medical service without fear of betrayal); Woernle v. Electromatic Typewriters, 271 N.Y. 228, 2 N.E.2d 638, syl. 1 (1936) (to prevent physician from disclosing matters which might humiliate the patient).

8. See § 108, below.

1. The statutes usually specify "physician" or "physician or surgeon," and sometimes require that they be "licensed" or "authorized." Accordingly, the decisions usually deny the privilege for communications to other practitioners, such as dentists. Gulf, Mobile & N. Ry. Co. v. Willis, 171 Miss. 732, 157 So. 899, syl. 2 (1934). Druggists. Brown v. Hannibal & St. J. Ry. Co., 66 Mo. 588, 597 (1877). Chiropractors. S. H. Kress & Co. v. Sharp, 156 Miss. 693, 126 So. 650, 68 A.L.R. 167, 173 (1930) (dictum). See Notes, Persons within term "Physician" in rule as to privilege, 68 A.L.R. 176; 70 C.J. 442, 443. An intern may be a "physician" though not yet licensed to practice. Eureka-Maryland Assur. Co. v. Gray, 121 F.2d 104, syl. 5 (C.A.D.C.1941). As to nurses, assistants and technicians see § 104, below.

2. Burgdorf v. Keeven, 351 Mo. 1003, 174 S.W.2d 816, syl. 2 (1943); People v. Austin, 199 N.Y. 446, 93 N.E. 57, syl. 4 (1910); Dec.Dig. Witnesses, ⊜210. The examination contemplated remedial measures if possible, in Bassil v. Ford Motor Co., 278 Mich. 173, 270 N.W. 258, 107 A.L.R. 1491, 1493 (1936) (husband and wife consult doctor to ascertain why child was not born of their union).

3. Russell v. Penn Mutual Life Ins. Co., 70 Oh.App. 113, 41 N.E.2d 251, syl. 5 (1941) (doctors who attended insured, apparently employed by life insurance company). See also Malone v. Industrial Comm., 140 Oh.St. 292, 43 N.E.2d 266, syl. 14 (1942) (privilege for communications to plant physician to whom employee was taken while in semi-conscious condition for examination and treatment). And when a patient goes, or is taken unconscious, to a hospital for care or treatment, the hospital doctors who are charged with the duties of examination, diagnosis, care or treatment are within the purview of the privilege statute. Smart v. Kansas City, 208 Mo. 162, 105 S.W. 709, syl. 4–7 (1907); Notes, 72 U.S.L.Rev. 619 (1938), 22 A.L.R. 1217. So also if the doctor, though employed by the defendant, examines the plaintiff in the hospital under circumstances causing the patient to believe that the examination is part of the hospital's care. Ballard v. Yellow Cab Co., 20 Wash.2d 67, 145 P.2d 1019, syl. 3 (1944).

4. Keeton v. State, 175 Miss. 631, 167 So. 68, syl. 11 (1936) (to ascertain sanity of accused); Smiecek v. State, 243 Wis. 439, 10 N.W.2d 161, syl. 6 (1943) (same).

5. People v. Austin, 199 N.Y. 446, 93 N.E. 57, syl. 5 (1910) (sanity); Leard v. State, 30 Okl.Cr. 191, 235 Pac. 243, syl. 3 (1925).

tion, or is employed for this purpose by the opposing party,[6] or is selected by a life insurance company to make an examination of an applicant for a policy [7] or even when the doctor is employed by plaintiff's own lawyers in a personal injury case to examine plaintiff solely to aid in preparation for trial,[8] the information secured is not within the present privilege. But when the patient's doctor calls in a consultant physician to aid in diagnosis or treatment, the disclosures are privileged.[9]

If the patient's purpose in the consultation is an unlawful one, as to secure an illegal abortion,[10] to obtain narcotics in violation of law,[11] or as a fugitive from justice to have his appearance disguised by plastic surgery,[12] the law withholds the shield of privilege.

After the death of the patient the relation is ended and the object of the privilege can

no longer be furthered. Accordingly, it seems the better view that facts discovered in an autopsy examination are not privileged.[13]

103. Subject-Matter of the Privilege: Information Acquired in Attending the Patient and Necessary for Prescribing.

Although a considerable number of the statutes speak of "communications," most of them follow the lead of the pioneer New York and California provisions [1] in extending the privilege to all "information," secured by the doctor through his observation or examination [2] or by explicit communication from the patient, so far as "necessary to enable him to prescribe or act for the patient." [3]

While the information secured by the physician may be privileged the fact that he has

---

6. Heath v. Broadway & S. A. Ry. Co., 8 N.Y.S. 863, syl. 1 (Super.Ct.Gen.T.,1890). But when the patient supposes that the doctor is a hospital specialist acting on his behalf, the privilege has been held to apply. Arizona & N. M. Ry. Co. v. Clark, 207 F. 817, syl. 5 (C.C.A.Ariz.1913).

7. McGinty v. Brotherhood of Railway Trainmen, 166 Wis. 83, 164 N.W. 249, syl. 4 (1917); 70 C.J. 441, n. 94. And so of an examination by employer's physician of an applicant for employment. Montzoukos v. Mutual Ben. Health & Accident Ins. Co., 69 Utah 309, 254 Pac. 1005, syl. 2 (1927).

8. City and County of San Francisco v. Superior Court, 37 Cal.2d 227, 231 P.2d 26, syl. 5 (1951) (but held in acute opinion by Traynor, J., that the communications were privileged under the attorney-client privilege), noted 25 So.Cal.L.Rev. 237, 13 U.Pitts.L.Rev. 428.

9. Leonczak v. Minneapolis, St. P. & S. S. M. Ry. Co., 161 Minn. 304, 201 N.W. 551, syl. 5 (1924); 70 C.J. 441, note 97.

10. Seifert v. State, 160 Ind. 464, 67 N.E. 100, syl. 4 (1903); Sticha v. Benzick, 156 Minn. 52, 194 N.W. 752, 753 (1923).

11. The rule is codified in Uniform Narcotic Drug Act (1932), § 17, par. 2, provides that information given to a doctor "in an effort unlawfully to procure a narcotic drug" shall not be privileged.

12. Compare Model Code of Evidence, Rule 222: "No person has a privilege under Rule 221 if the judge finds that sufficient evidence, aside from the communication, has been introduced to warrant

a finding that the services of the physician were sought or obtained to enable or aid anyone to commit or to plan to commit a crime or a tort, or to escape detection or apprehension after the commission of a crime or a tort."

13. Eureka-Maryland Assur. Co. v. Gray, 121 F.2d 104, syl. 7 (C.A.D.C.1941); Cross v. Equitable Life Assur. Soc., 228 Iowa 800, 293 N.W. 464, syl. 7 (1940). Decisions pro and con are cited in 8 Wigmore, Evidence, § 2382, note 11, and in an excellent Note, 12 Minn.L.Rev. 390 (1928).

1. See § 101, above.

2. This result is reached both in states which have "communication" statutes. E. g., Heuston v. Simpson, 115 Ind. 62, 17 N.E. 261 (1888) (knowledge gained from words or by observation); Burns v. Waterloo, 187 Iowa 922, 173 N.W. 16, syl. 2 (1919) (intoxication, observed by doctor); McKee v. New Idea, 44 N.E.2d 697, syl. 7 (Oh.App.1942) (submission to examination is "communication"). And of course in the states having "information" statutes. Smoot v. Kansas City, 194 Mo. 513, 92 S.W. 363, 367, syl. 4 (1906) (information acquired from inspection, examination or observation, after the patient has submitted to examination); Hansen v. Sandvik, 128 Wash. 60, 222 Pac. 205 (X-ray photograph taken by attending doctor, privileged). Probably information which is apparent to everyone should not be regarded as privileged. People v. De France, 104 Mich. 563, 570, 62 N.W. 709, 711 (1895).

3. Instances of disclosures not necessary for treatment: Cook v. People, 60 Colo. 263, 153 Pac. 214,

been consulted by the patient and has treated him,[4] and the number and dates of his visits,[5] are not within the shelter of the privilege.

The extent to which the privilege attaches to the information embodied in hospital records is discussed in the chapter on Business Records.[6]

104. The Confidential Character of the Disclosure: Presence of Third Persons and Members of Family: Information Revealed to Nurses and Attendants: Public Records.

We have seen that the statutes existing in many states codifying the privileges for marital communications and those between attorney and client usually omitted the requirement that to be privileged such communications must have been made in confidence. Nevertheless, the courts have read this limitation into these statutes, assuming that the legislatures must have intended this common law requirement to continue.[1] The statutes giving the patient's privilege for information gained in professional consultations again omit the adjective "confidential."[2] Should it none the less be read in, not as a continuation of a common law requirement, but as an interpretative gloss, spelled out from policy and analogy? Certainly the policy-arguments are strong. First, the policy of holding all privileges within reasonable bounds since they cut off access to sources of truth. Second, the argument that the purpose of encouraging those who would otherwise be reluctant, to disclose necessary facts to their doctors, will be adequately served by extending a privilege for only such disclosures as the patient wishes to keep secret.

This principle of confidentiality[3] is supported by those decisions which hold that if a casual third person is present with the acquiescence of the patient at the consultation, the disclosures made in his presence are not privileged,[4] and thus the stranger, the patient and the doctor may be required to divulge them in court.

Under this view, however, if the third person is present as a needed and customary participant in such consultation, the circle of confidence may be reasonably extended to include him and the privilege will be maintained. Thus the presence of one sustaining a close family relationship to the patient

---

syl. 3 (1915) (defendant refused to allow physician to remove bullet from wound or tell how it was received); Meyers v. State, 192 Ind. 592, 137 N.E. 547, syl. 7, 24 A.L.R. 1196 (1922) (patient's threats, overheard by doctor, to kill his wife); Griffith v. Continental Casualty Co., 299 Mo. 426, 253 S.W. 1043, syl. 2 (1923) (patient's statement that life not worth living, might as well jump in river); see 70 C.J. Witnesses, § 508. It may well be debatable in a particular case whether the patient's statement as to how an accident happened, for which he is being treated, is information necessary for the treatment. See Raymond v. Burlington, C. R. & N. Ry. Co., 65 Iowa 152, 21 N.W. 495, syl. 1 (1884) (privileged); Green v. Metropolitan St. Ry. Co., 171 N.Y. 201, 63 N.E. 958 (1902) (not privileged: three judges dissenting). And whether the privilege attaches to the doctor's observation, when called to treat one injured by a collision or assault, that the patient shows signs of liquor, has been made to turn on this question. State v. Aguirre, 167 Kan. 266, 206 P.2d 118, syl. 6, 7 (1949) (not privileged); Perry v. Hannagan, 257 Mich. 120, 241 N.W. 232, 79 A.L.R. 1127 (1932) (same: two judges dissenting). But other decisions sustaining

the privilege without discussing the question of "necessity" are cited in a Note, 79 A.L.R. 1131.

4. In re Albert Lindley Lee Memorial Hospital, 209 F.2d 122 (C.A.2d 1953) (names of patients not privileged in investigation of doctor's income tax liability), noted 67 Harv.L.Rev. 1272; Cross v. Equitable Life Assur. Soc., 228 Iowa 806, 293 N.W. 464, syl. 6 (1940).

5. Polish Roman Catholic Union v. Palen, 302 Mich. 557, 5 N.W.2d 463, syl. 7 (1942).

6. See § 290, herein.

1. See §§ 84, 95.

2. See § 101, herein.

3. See 8 Wigmore, Evidence, § 2381; 70 C.J. Witnesses, § 596; Dec.Dig. Witnesses, ☞213.

4. Horowitz v. Sacks, 89 Cal.App. 336, 265 Pac. 281, syl. 10 (1928) (several members of family present); In re Swartz, 79 Okl. 191, 192 Pac. 203, 16 A.L.R. 450, 453 (1920) (citing authorities); Notes, Barney, 16 Neb.L.Bull. 206 (1937), 96 A.L.R. 1419; 70 C.J. 449.

should not curtail the privilege.[5] And the nurse present as the doctor's assistant during the consultation or examination, or the technician who makes tests or X-ray photographs under the doctor's direction, will be looked on as the doctor's agent in whose keeping the information will remain privileged.[6]

Many courts on the other hand do not analyze the problems in terms of whether the communications or disclosures were confidential and professional, but rather in terms of what persons are intended to be silenced as witnesses. This seems to be sticking in the bark of the statute, rather than looking at its purpose. Thus, these courts if casual third persons were present at the consultation will still close the mouth of the doctor but allow the visitor to speak.[7] And if nurses or other attendants or technicians gain information necessary to treatment they will be allowed by these courts to speak (unless the privilege statute specifically names them) but the physician may not.[8]

When the attending physician is required by law to make a certificate of death to the public authority, giving his opinion as to the cause, the certificate should be provable as a public record, despite the privilege. The duty to make a public report overrides the general duty of secrecy, and in view of the availability of the record to the public, the protection of the information from general knowledge, as contemplated by the privilege, cannot be attained. Accordingly, under the prevailing view, the privilege does not attach.[9]

---

5. Bassil v. Ford Motor Co., 278 Mich. 173, 270 N.W. 258, 107 A.L.R. 1491, 1493 (1936) (husband and wife consult doctor about their childlessness: but the principle of joint consultation could have been relied on); Denaro v. Prudential Ins. Co., 154 App. Div. 840, 139 N.Y.S. 758, 761 (1913) ("when a physician enters a house for the purpose of attending a patient, he is called upon to make inquiries, not alone of the sick person, but of those who are about him and who are familiar with the facts, and communications necessary for the proper performance of the duties of a physician are not public, because made in the presence of his immediate family or those who are present because of the illness of the person").

6. Mississippi Power & Lt. Co. v. Jordan, 164 Miss. 174, 143 So. 483, syl. 5 (1932) (knowledge gained by nurse in assisting doctor to treat patient privileged); Culver v. Union Pac. Ry. Co., 112 Neb. 441, 199 N.W. 794, 797, syl. 2 (1924) (question to nurse as to doctor's taking blood specimen from patient in her presence and directing her to send the specimen for a test, and the results thereof privileged, as she acted as agent of doctor); and cases cited in Notes, Taay, 22 Marq.L.Rev. 22 (1938), 39 A.L.R. 1421, 169 A.L.R. 678, 679.

The patient-privilege statutes in a few states, e. g., Arkansas and New York, specifically include information given to nurses within the scope of the privilege. See 8 Wigmore, Evidence, § 2380, note 4.

7. Iwerks v. People, 108 Colo. 556, 120 P.2d 961, syl. 5 (1942) (deputy sheriff present at doctor's examination of injured prisoner may testify as to what examination disclosed and prisoner's statements to doctor); Springer v. Byram, 137 Ind. 15, 36 N.E. 361, 363, syl. 3 (1894) (ambulance drivers could testify to accident-victim's statements to doctor); Indiana Union Tr. Co. v. Thomas, 44 Ind.App. 468, 88 N.E. 356, 359, syl. 4, 5 (1909) (patient privileged not to disclose communications with doctor, though in presence of daughter and friend); Leeds v. Prudential Ins. Co., 128 Neb. 395, 258 N.W. 672, 96 A.L.R. 1414, 1418 (1935) (bringing friend to consultation does not waive privilege); Note, 96 A.L.R. 1419, 70 C.J. 449, notes 73, 76.

And, as in the case of the other privileges for confidential communications, the eavesdropper is permitted to testify to what he overhears. Ryan v. Industrial Comm., 72 N.E.2d 907, syl. 2 (Oh.App. 1946) (dictum).

8. First Trust Co. v. Kansas City Life Ins. Co., 79 F.2d 48, 52, syl. 5–8 (C.C.A.Minn.1935) (nurse and dietician could testify as to information gained in carrying out doctors' instructions for care of patient); Weis v. Weis, 147 Oh.St. 416, 72 N.E.2d 245, syl. 12, 13, 169 A.L.R. 668 (1947) (similar to last); Prudential Ins. Co. v. Kozlowski, 226 Wis. 641, 276 N.W. 300, syl. 1–4 (1937) (testimony of nurse and X-ray operator received); Notes, 22 Marq.L.Rev. 211 (1938), 169 A.L.R. 678.

9. Polish Roman Catholic Union v. Palen, 302 Mich. 557, 5 N.W.2d 463, syl. 1 (1942); Randolph v. Supreme Liberty Life Ins. Co., 359 Mo. 251, 221 S.W.2d 155, syl. 1–3 (1949) and cases cited 8 Wigmore, Evidence, § 2385a. Contra: Davis v. Su-

105. Rule of Privilege Not Incompetency: Privilege Belongs to the Patient, Not to an Objecting Party as Such: Effect of the Patient's Death.

As has been pointed out in the discussion of privileges generally,[1] the rule which excludes disclosures to physicians is not a rule of incompetency of evidence serving the end of protecting the adverse party against unreliable or prejudicial testimony. It is a rule of privilege protecting the extrinsic interest of the patient and designed to promote health not truth. It encourages free disclosure in the sick-room by preventing such disclosure in the courtroom. The patient is the person to be encouraged and he is the holder of the privilege.[2]

Consequently, he alone during his lifetime has the right to claim or to waive the privilege. If he is in a position to claim it and does not, it is waived[3] and no one else may assert it.[4] If he is not present and so far as known is unaware of the proposed disclosure, the judge in his discretion may enforce the privilege of his own motion.[5] Accordingly, if the judge at the suggestion of a party or counsel or the physician-witness, enforces the privilege, this is not to be understood as the assertion of a right by the party or counsel or witness but as an informal invocation of discretion. The adverse party as such has no interest to protect if he is not the patient, and thus cannot object as of right,[6] and should have no right to complain on appeal if the patient's privilege is erroneously denied.[7]

The whole supposition of the patient-privilege legislation, that the patient's fear of revelation in court of the information he gives the doctor will be such as to discourage free disclosure, is highly speculative. To think that he is likely to be influenced by fear that such revelations may occur after his death seems particularly fanciful. A rule that the privilege terminated with the patient's death would have reached a common-sense result which would have substantially lessened the obstructive effect of the privilege. The courts, however have not taken this tack but hold that the privilege continues

---

preme Lodge, 165 N.Y. 159, 58 N.E. 891 (1900) (two judges dissenting). Compare the similar question about the records of public hospitals, discussed in 8 Wigmore, Evidence, § 2382(c).

1. See § 72, herein.

2. Metropolitan Life Ins. Co. v. Kaufman, 104 Colo. 13, 87 P.2d 758, syl. 2 (1939) (physician compelled to give testimony where privilege had been waived by patient. "Privileged communications are personal to the patient only."); Maas v. Laursen, 219 Minn. 461, 18 N.W.2d 233, syl. 3, 158 A.L.R. 213 (1945) (dictum, privilege belongs to patient and can be waived only by him); 8 Wigmore, Evidence, § 2386; Dec.Dig. Witnesses, ⊂⇒217.

3. People v. Bloom, 193 N.Y. 1, 85 N.E. 824 (1908) (patient who fails to claim privilege against testimony of his physicians, at first trial, a civil case, waives permanently and cannot object to similar testimony at his later trial for perjury).

4. See State v. Thomas, 1 Wash.2d 298, 95 P.2d 1036, syl. 7 (1939) (defendant charged with carnal knowledge of child, could not object to physician's testimony where child and mother did not; but here physician made examination at instance of county and doctor-patient relation probably did not exist).

5. Model Code of Evidence, Rule 105, "The judge . . . in his discretion determines . . . (e) whether to exclude, of his own motion, evidence which would violate a privilege of a person who is neither a party nor the witness from whom the evidence is sought if the privilege has not been waived or otherwise terminated. . . ."

6. Thus, after the death of the patient, in a suit on an insurance policy, the insurer cannot assert the privilege. Olson v. Court of Honor, 100 Minn. 117, 110 N.W. 374, 377, syl. 2 (1907); Hier v. Farmers Mut. Fire Ins. Co., 104 Mont. 471, 67 P.2d 831, syl. 11–13, 110 A.L.R. 1051 (1937). Contra: Westover v. Aetna Life Ins. Co., 99 N.Y. 56, 1 N.E. 104 (1885). See Note, Who may invoke privileges? 2 A.L.R.2d 645, 658.

7. See Vance v. State, 143 Miss. 121, 108 So. 433, 45 A.L.R. 1348 (1926). In that case the defendant charged with murder objected to the testimony of the physician who examined the victim, and this was overruled. Ethridge, J. held that "if it was error to admit the evidence it is error of which he [the accused] cannot complain." Two judges concurred in affirmance on another ground. Three judges dissented.

after death.[8] Nevertheless, in contests of the survivors in interest with third parties, e. g., actions to recover property claimed to belong to the deceased, actions for the death of the deceased, or actions upon life insurance policies, the personal representative, heir or next of kin, or the beneficiary in the policy may waive the privilege,[9] and by the same token, the adverse party may not effectively assert the privilege.[10] In contests over the validity of a will, where both sides—the executor on the one hand and the heirs or next of kin on the other—claim under and not adversely to the decedent, the assumption should prevail that the decedent would desire that the validity of his will should be determined in the fullest light of the facts.[11] Accordingly in this situation either the executor or the contestants may effectively waive the privilege without the concurrence of the other.[12]

106. What Constitutes a Waiver of the Privilege?

Except in two states[1] it is agreed that a contractual stipulation waiving the privilege, such as is frequently included in applications for life or health insurance, or in the policies themselves, is valid and effectual.[2]

How far does the patient's testifying waive the privilege? Doubtless, if the patient on direct examination testifies to,[3] or adduces

---

8. Bassil v. Ford Motor Co., 278 Mich. 173, 270 N.W. 258, syl. 4, 107 A.L.R. 1491 (1936).

9. Aetna Life Ins. Co. v. McAdoo, 106 F.2d 618, syl. 4 (C.C.A.Ark.1939) (beneficiary under life policy); Harvey v. Silber, 300 Mich. 510, 2 N.W.2d 483, syl. 5 (1942) (administrator suing for death due to defendants' alleged malpractice); Industrial Comm. v. Warnke, 131 Oh.St. 140, 2 N.E.2d 248 (1936) (widow suing for compensation for death of husband); Colwell v. Dyer, 35 N.E.2d 789, syl. 9 (Oh.App.1941) (administrator, plaintiff in death action). A recent statute in Ohio codifying this result is discussed in Ball, Legislative Note, 14 Oh. St.L.J. 432 (1953).

10. See cases cited note 6, above.

11. "If he did not have testamentary capacity, then the paper was not his will, and it is not the policy of the law to maintain such an instrument. It is undoubtedly the policy of the law to uphold the testamentary disposition of property, but not until it is ascertained whether such a disposition has been made. . . . And no one can be said to represent the deceased in that contest, for he could only be interested in having the truth ascertained, and his estate can only be protected by establishing or defeating the instrument as the truth so ascertained may require. The testimony of the attending physician is usually reliable, and often controlling, and to place it at the disposal of one party to such a proceeding and withhold it from the other would be manifestly partial and unjust." Ladd, J., in Winters v. Winters, 102 Iowa 53, 71 N.W. 184, 185 (1897).

12. Hyatt v. Wroten, 184 Ark. 847, 43 S.W.2d 726, syl. 4 (1931) (heirs); Marker v. McCue, 50 Idaho 462, 297 Pac. 401, syl. 1 (1931) (executor); Winters v. Winters, supra (heir); Gorman v. Hickey, 145

Kan. 54, 64 P.2d 587, syl. 1 (1937) (heir contesting the will could waive though executor opposed the waiver); Notes, 31 A.L.R. 167, 126 A.L.R. 380. It seems that suits attacking conveyances made by the deceased on grounds of incapacity are within the same principle. See Calhoun v. Jacobs, 79 App. D.C. 29, 141 F.2d 729, syl. 3 (1944) (heir may waive, despite grantee's invocation of the privilege); Schornick v. Schornick, 25 Ariz. 563, 220 Pac. 397, 31 A.L.R. 159 (1923) (same).

1. In Michigan such an agreement to waive is held invalid as against public policy. Gilchrist v. Mystic Workers of the World, 196 Mich. 247, 248, 163 N.W. 10, 11, syl. 1 (1917). The New York statute provides that a waiver "must be made in open court, on the trial of the action or proceeding, and a paper executed by a party prior to the trial . . . shall be insufficient." L.1935, amending C.P.A. § 354 (quoted in 8 Wigmore, Evidence, p. 807).

2. New York Life Ins. Co. v. Taylor, 79 U.S.App.D.C. 66, 147 F.2d 297, syl. 7 (1945); Murphy v. Mut. L. Ins. Co., 62 Idaho 362, 112 P.2d 993, 994, syl. 1 (1941); Templeton v. Mut. Life Ins. Co., 177 Okl. 94, 57 P.2d 841, syl. 1 (1936); 1 Wigmore, Evidence, § 7a; Note, Schiller, Waiver Clauses in Insurance Applications, 16 N.C.L.Rev. 53 (1938) (excellent); Note, 54 A.L.R. 412; Dec.Dig. Witnesses, ⊜219(6). But occasionally a court by an eccentric interpretation may emasculate the waiver. Noble v. United Ben. Life Ins. Co., 230 Iowa 471, 297 N.W. 881, syl. 2 (1941) (consent to doctor's furnishing to insurer information gained in attending patient is not waiver of privilege as to doctor's testimony in court.)

3. Nolan v. Glynn, 163 Iowa 146, 142 N.W. 1029, syl. 2 (1913) (plaintiff in breach of promise case

other evidence of,[4] the communications exchanged or the information furnished to the doctor consulted this would waive in respect to such consultations. When, however, the patient in his direct testimony does not reveal any privileged matter respecting the consultation, but testifies only to his physical or mental condition, existing at the time of such consultation, then one view is that, "where the patient tenders to the jury the issue as to his physical condition, it must in fairness and justice be held that he has himself waived the obligation of secrecy."[5] This view has the great merit of curtailing the scope of an obstructive privilege, but there is some logic in the position of the larger number of courts which hold that the patient's testimony as to his condition without disclosure of privileged matter is not a waiver.[6] If the patient reveals privileged matter

on cross-examination, without claiming the privilege, this is usually held not to be a waiver of the privilege enabling the adversary to make further inquiry of the doctors, on the ground that such revelations were not "voluntary."[7] The counter-argument, that the failure to assert the privilege should be a complete waiver, seems persuasive.

If the patient examines a physician as to matters disclosed in a consultation, or course of treatment, of course this is a waiver and opens the door to the opponent to examine him about any other matters then disclosed.[8] And if several doctors participated jointly in the same consultation or course of treatment the calling of one to disclose part of the shared information waives objection to the adversary's calling any other of the joint consultants to testify about the consultation, treatment or the results thereof.[9] Liberal

---

testifying as to consultation of doctor about pregnancy and abortion, waived as to such consultation, but not as to earlier, distinct ones); Epstein v. Pennsylvania R. Co., 250 Mo. 1, 156 S.W. 699, syl. 3 (1913) (". . . since plaintiff had himself voluntarily gone upon the stand, and in his case in chief, as a witness for himself, laid bare for lucre's sake all of the secrets of his sickroom, since he had told and retold what Dr. Elston, his physician, said to him, and what he said to Elston, since he had told the precise nature of his alleged hurts as he said Elston found them, and since he had also voluntarily related the treatment professionally given to him by Elston, he waived the competency of other physicians, also there present, having knowledge of the identical facts."); Note, 114 A.L.R. 798, 802.

4. Buckminster's Estate v. Commissioner of Internal Revenue, 147 F.2d 331, syl. 4 (C.C.A.2, 1944) (executrix introducing statements and diagnosis of physician who attended decedent waived privilege).

5. Andrews, J. in Hethier v. Johns, 233 N.Y. 370, 135 N.E. 603 (1922). To like effect see O'Brien v. Gen. Accident, etc. Corp., 42 F.2d 48, 53 (C.C.A. Neb.1930) (under 1925 amendment to Nebraska privilege statute, beneficiary waives "by offering any testimony touching the physical or mental condition of the insured"); Moreno v. New Guadalupe Mining Co., 35 Cal.App. 744, 170 Pac. 1088, syl. 6 (1918); Freisen v. Reimer, 124 Neb. 620, 247 N.W. 561, syl. 1 (1933) (under specific provision of Nebraska statute); 8 Wigmore, Evidence, § 2389(2).

6. Arizona & N. M. Ry. Co. v. Clark, 235 U.S. 669, 35 Sup.Ct. 210, syl. 2, 59 L.Ed. 415 (1915) (plaintiff testified as to his injury and called nurse as witness, held no waiver under Arizona statute which provides that it is waiver if patient testifies as "to such communications," Hughes and Day, J.J., dissenting); Harpman v. Devine, 133 Oh.St. 1, 10 N.E.2d 776, syl. 2, 3, 114 A.L.R. 789 (1937) (two judges dissenting), critically noted 51 Harv.L.Rev. 931; Clawson v. Walgreen Drug Co., 108 Utah 577, 162 P.2d 759, syl. 9 (1945) (no waiver when patient testified concerning nature and extent of injury, but did not give evidence of what doctors told him nor of details of treatment; Noelle v. Hoquiam Lumber & Shingle Co., 47 Wash. 519, 92 Pac. 372, syl. 2 (1907) (forceful dissent by Root, J., joined by Hadley, C.J.); Green v. Nebagamain, 113 Wis. 508, 89 N.W. 520, syl. 2 (1902), and cases cited in Note, 114 A.L.R. 798, Dec.Dig. Witnesses, ☞219 (5).

7. Johnson v. Kinney, 232 Iowa 1016, 7 N.W.2d 188, syl. 9, 10, 144 A.L.R. 997 (1943); Harpman v. Devine, 133 Oh.St. 1, 10 N.E.2d 776, syl. 1, 114 A.L.R. 789 (1937) and cases cited in Note, 114 A.L.R. 798, 806.

8. Maas v. Laursen, 219 Minn. 461, 18 N.W.2d 233, syl. 4, 158 A.L.R. 215 (1945); Demonbrunn v. McHaffie, 348 Mo. 1120, 156 S.W.2d 923, syl. 1, 2 (1942).

9. Doll v. Scandrett, 201 Minn. 319, 276 N.W. 281, syl. 4 (1937) (three judges dissenting), noted 22 Minn.L.Rev. 580; Morris v. New York, O. & W. R.

courts go further and hold that calling by the patient of one doctor and eliciting privileged matter from him opens the door to the opponent's calling other doctors consulted by the patient at other times to bring out any facts relevant to the issue on which the privileged proof was adduced.[10] It is not consonant with justice and fairness to permit the patient to reveal his secrets to several doctors and then when his condition comes in issue to limit the witnesses to the consultants favorable to his claims.[11] But a substantial number of courts balk at this step.[12]

A failure by a patient to object to the testimony of one of his physicians called by the adversary seems generally to be given the same effect, in respect to waiver, that the particular court would give to the patient's calling and examination of the doctor as his own witness.[13]

A shrinking from the embarrassment which comes from exposure of bodily disease or abnormality is human and natural. It is arguable that legal protection from such exposure is justified to encourage frankness in consulting physicians. But it is neither human, natural, nor understandable to claim protection from such exposure by asserting a privilege for communications to doctors, at the very same time when the patient is parading before the public the mental or physical condition as to which he consulted the doctor, by bringing an action for damages arising from such condition. This in the oft-repeated phrase is to make the privilege not a shield only, but a sword. Consequently, the California statute provides that "where any person brings an action to recover damages for personal injuries, such action will be deemed to constitute a consent by the person bringing such action that any physician who has prescribed for or treated such person . . . shall testify," with a similar provision as to

---

Co., 148 N.Y. 88, 42 N.E. 410 (1895). Contra: Jones v. Caldwell, 20 Idaho 5, 116 Pac. 110, syl. 7 (1911). See Note, 62 A.L.R. 680, 684, 685.

10. Weissman v. Wells, 306 Mo. 82, 267 S.W. 400, syl. 1 (1924) (personal injury plaintiff who claimed nervous state due to injury, by calling doctor to testify to her condition after injury waived objection to defendant's proving by other doctor her same condition before injury); Steinberg v. New York Life Ins. Co., 263 N.Y. 45, 188 N.E. 152, syl. 2 (1933) (plaintiff suing on disability policy puts doctor on stand to prove that he has had disability from tuberculosis since time of claim: held this warrants defendant in proving by another doctor that plaintiff had same disease several years before, in support of its plea of misrepresentation); McUne v. Fuqua, 42 Wash.2d 65, 253 P.2d 632, syl. 15 (1953) (lucid discussion by Hamley, J.); and cases cited in Note, 62 A.L.R. 680, 685, 686.

Compare the provision in Rule 35(b) (2) of the Federal Rules of Civil Procedure to the effect that if a person who has been examined by a physician under order of court, requests and obtains a copy of the doctor's report, he "waives any privilege he may have . . . regarding the testimony of every other person who has examined or may thereafter examine him in respect of the same mental or physical condition."

11. "A litigant should not be allowed to pick and choose in binding and loosing; he may bind or he may loose. . . . He may choose a serviceable and mellow one out of a number of physicians to fasten liability upon the defendant, and then, presto! change! exclude the testimony of those not so mellow and serviceable, to whom he has voluntarily given the same information and the same means of getting at a conclusion on the matter already uncovered by professional testimony to the jury. There is no reason in such condition of things, and where reason ends the law ends." Lamm, J. in Smart v. Kansas City, 208 Mo. 162, 105 S.W. 709, 722 (1907).

12. No waiver as to doctors consulted separately. Mays v. New Amsterdam Cas. Co., 40 App.D.C. 249, 46 L.R.A.,N.S., 1108, 1112 (1913); Acme-Evans Co. v. Schnepf, 214 Ind. 394, 14 N.E.2d 561, syl. 7 (1938); Johnson v. Kinney, 232 Iowa 1016, 7 N.W.2d 188, syl. 8, 144 A.L.R. 997 (1942); United States Nat. Life & Cas. Co., 148 Okl. 274, 298 Pac. 619 (1931) and cases cited in Notes, 62 A.L.R. 680, 681, 90 A.L.R. 646, 58 Am.Jur. Witnesses, § 458, Dec. Dig. Witnesses, ⊜219(5).

13. See, e. g., Captron v. Douglass, 193 N.Y. 11, 85 N.E. 827, syl. 2 (1908) (malpractice; failure of plaintiff to object to testimony of one of two doctors who treated him after defendant did, was waiver as to other also).

actions for injuries resulting in death.[14] Up to this time, however, the courts, unaided by statute have been unwilling to take this step,[15] though it seems a thoroughly justifiable holding under a statute which, like most of them, does not attempt to specify what shall constitute a "consent" or waiver. The Model Code of Evidence withdraws the privilege "in an action in which the condition of the patient is an element or factor of the claim or defense of the patient or of any party claiming through or under the patient or claiming as a beneficiary of the patient through a contract to which the patient is or was a party." [16] This broad and equitable result should be reached by the march of decision. As Chief Justice Lamm said in respect to another phase of waiver of the patient's privilege, "The scandals in beating down the truth arising from a too harsh and literal interpretation of this law (if unaided and unrelieved by waiver) every one of us knows by experience and observation in the courtroom." [17]

107. Kinds of Proceedings Exempted from the Application of the Privilege.[1]

Two broad fields of litigation and administrative proceedings are frequently withdrawn by statute from the operation of the privilege, namely, criminal prosecutions generally [2] and workmen's compensation proceedings.[3] Other types of controversies in which the privilege is occasionally withheld or curtailed in the statutes are actions for malpractice,[4] prosecutions for homicide,[5] lunacy proceedings [6] and will-contests.[7] Whenever the issue turns upon the diagnosis and treatment of attending physicians and their assistants, then the application of the privilege closes the main source of knowledge and can end only in frustration and injustice. Thus, in New York City the City Council under statutory authority provided for a Committee with subpoena powers to investigate charges of maladministration of Lincoln Hospital. The Committee called upon the Commissioner of Hospitals to produce the records of treatment of certain patients. It was held, however, that the privilege forbade such pro-

14. C.C.P. § 1881 as amended May 26, 1917. It has not been too liberally interpreted. See Hirschberg v. Southern Pac. Co., 180 Cal. 774, 183 Pac. 141, syl. 2 (1919) (ban of privilege not waived as to information acquired by doctor several years before injury sued for), noted 8 Calif.L.Rev. 104; Webb v. Lewald Coal Co., 214 Cal. 182, 4 P.2d 532, syl. 2 (1931) (provision that suit for personal injuries shall give consent does not apply to physician employed only to examine the plaintiff for benefit of her counsel), noted, 20 Calif.L.Rev. 302, 5 So.Calif.L.Rev. 446.

15. Federal Mining & Smelting Co. v. Dalo, 252 Fed. 356, 359 (C.C.A.Idaho, 1918); Smart v. Kansas City, 208 Mo. 162, 105 S.W. 709, 714, but see dissent by Lamm, J. at 722 (1907).

16. Rule 223, subs. 3.

17. Epstein v. Pennsylvania R. Co., 250 Mo. 1, 156 S.W. 699, 711 (1913).

1. 70 C.J. Witnesses, §§ 608–613; 58 Am.Jur. Witnesses, §§ 432–434; Dec.Dig. Witnesses, ☜208(2).

2. The California Code provision, C.C.P. § 1881, par. 4, is limited to "a civil action," and this limitation has been followed by many states which have taken over that Code, e. g., Idaho, Oregon, South Dakota and Washington. Pennsylvania has a similar limitation. See the statutes as compiled in 8 Wigmore, Evidence, § 2380, note 5. Most states apart from specific provision seem to deny the accused the power to assert the privilege as to information given by the victim of a crime to a physician. Note, 45 A.L.R. 1357.

3. More than half the states which have the privilege provide that it shall not apply in Workmen's Compensation proceedings. See the statutes compiled in 8 Wigmore, Evidence, § 2380, note 6.

4. As in the Colorado, Michigan and Wisconsin statutes. 8 Wigmore, Evidence, § 2380, note 5. And even in the absence of specific provision, it is sometimes held that in such a suit the defendant, despite the privilege, must be permitted to testify to the facts necessary to his defence. Cramer v. Hurt, 154 Mo. 112, 55 S.W. 258, syl. 1 (1900). See § 95, above.

5. As in the District of Columbia and in Wisconsin. See statutes compiled in 8 Wigmore, Evidence, § 2380, note 5.

6. As in Wisconsin.

7. As in California. And see § 105, above.

duction.[8] Here it seems strongly arguable that the very policy of promoting better medical care, which is the purpose of the privilege, should lead the court to open the door for this investigation.[9]

108. The Policy and Future of the Privilege.[1]

Some statements of Buller, J., in 1792 in a case involving the application of the attorney-client privilege seem to have furnished the inspiration for the pioneer New York statute of 1828 on the doctor-patient privilege. He said: "The privilege is confined to the cases of counsel, solicitor, and attorney. . . . It is indeed hard in many cases to compel a friend to disclose a confidential conversation; and I should be glad if by law such evidence could be excluded. It is a subject of just indignation where persons are anxious to reveal what has been communicated to them in a confidential manner. . . . There are cases to which it is much to be lamented that the law of privilege is not extended; those in which medical persons are obliged to disclose the information which they acquire by attending in their professional characters." [2]

These comments reveal attitudes which have been influential ever since in the spread of statutes enacting the doctor-patient privilege. One attitude is the shrinking from forcing anyone to tell in court what he has learned in confidence. It is well understood today, however, that no such sweeping curtain for disclosure of confidences in the courtroom could be justified. Another is the complete failure to consider the other side of the shield, namely, the loss which comes from depriving the courts of any reliable source of facts necessary for the right decision of cases.

Perhaps the main burden of Justice Buller's remarks, however, is the suggestion that since the client's disclosures to the lawyer are privileged, the patient's disclosures to the doctor should have the same protec-

---

8. New York City Council v. Goldwater, 284 N.Y. 296, 31 N.E.2d 31, 133 A.L.R. 728 (1940) (two judges dissenting).

9. See Note, 26 Corn.L.Q. 482, 484. For other notes, see 4 U.Detroit L.J. 173, 54 Harv.L.Rev. 705, 16 Ind.L.J. 592, 39 Mich.L.Rev. 1258, 89 U.Pa.L.Rev. 961.

1. There is a wealth of cogent discussion of the policy of the privilege. All that I have seen are adverse. Wigmore's scalpel cuts deepest. 8 Evidence, § 2380a. Other excellent discussions: Chafee, Is Justice Served by Closing the Doctor's Mouth?, 52 Yale L.J. 607 (1943); Purrington, An Abused Privilege, 6 Col.L.Rev. 388 (1906) (historical, comparative, critical); Notes, 33 Ill.L.Rev. 483 (1939), 12 Minn.L.Rev. 390 (1928). See also for worthwhile treatments: Welch, Another Anomaly— the Patient's Privilege, 13 Miss.L.J. 137 (1941) (emphasis on local decisions); Curd, Privileged Communications between Doctor and Patient—an Anomaly, 44 W.Va.L.Q. 165 (1938).

2. Wilson v. Rastall, 4 Term Rep. 753, 759, 100 Eng.Rep. 1287 (K.B.1792).

The Revisers who drafted the New York statute, supported it in their report as follows: "In 4 Term, Rep. 580, Buller, J. (to whom no one will attribute a disposition to relax the rules of evidence), said it was 'much to be lamented' that the information specified in this section was not privileged. Mr. Phillips expresses the same sentiment in his treatise on evidence, p. 104. The ground on which communications to counsel are privileged, is the supposed necessity of a full knowledge of the facts, to advise correctly, and to prepare for the proper defense for prosecution of a suit. But surely the necessity of consulting a medical adviser, when life itself may be in jeopardy, is still stronger. And unless such consultations are privileged, men will be incidentally punished by being obliged to suffer the consequences of injuries without relief from the medical art and without conviction of any offense. Besides, in such cases, during the struggle between legal duty on the one hand, and professional honor on the other, the latter, aided by a strong sense of the injustice and inhumanity of the rule, will in most cases furnish a temptation to the perversion or concealment of truth, too strong for human resistance. In every view that can be taken of the policy, justice or humanity of the rule, as it exists, its relaxation seems highly expedient. It is believed that the proposition in the section is so guarded, that it cannot be abused by applying it to cases not intended to be privileged." Original Reports of Revisers, vol. 5, p. 34, quoted Purrington, op. cit., 6 Col.L.Rev. 392, 393.

tion. This analogy has probably been more potent than any other argument, particularly with the lawyers in the legislatures. They would be reluctant to deny to the medical profession a recognition which the courts have themselves provided for the legal profession. Manifestly, however, the soundness of the privilege may not be judged as a matter of rivalry of professions, but by the criterion of the public interest. It has been persuasively urged that the same need for the protection of the patient's confidences as in the case of the client's communications does not exist.[3] As the client considers what he shall reveal to his lawyer he will often have in mind the possibility of the exposure of his statements in court, for the lawyer's office is the very ante-room to the courthouse. The patient, on the other hand, in most instances, in consulting his doctor will have his thoughts centered on his illness or injury and his hopes for betterment or cure, and the thought of some later disclosure of his confidences in the courtroom would not usually be a substantial factor in curbing his freedom of communication with his doctor. Accordingly, the justification in the need for encouraging the frank disclosure of information to the doctor seems to have slight relevancy to the actual play of forces upon the average patient.

Doubtless the willingness of the doctors to support the adoption of privilege-statutes is in large part due to their esteem for the tradition, dignity and honor of the profession. The tradition of respect for the confidences of the patient is an ancient and honorable one. But the Hippocratic oath does not enjoin absolute secrecy on all occasions,[4] and doubtless the modern oaths of secrecy could well be understood as being subject to justified departure for the saving of life or in conformity with the requirements of law in the interest of justice. Actually, this practice of the physician in his every-day walks of abstaining from gossiping about his patients, of which the doctor's honor, and not the law, is the guardian, is a far more important factor in inspiring frankness in the patient than any courtroom privilege can be.[5]

Nor does the privilege in fact usually operate to protect against public exposure of humiliating facts. Usually the facts are not shameful, save as they may disclose falsehood in the patient's claims, and the various contentions as to what the facts are, are fully and publicly made known in the pleadings, the opening statements and the other testimony.[6]

If actually the chief effect of the privilege is to enable the patient to tell on the witness-

---

3. See especially the discussions of Wigmore and Chafee, cited in note 1, supra. Compare, however, recent suggestions, supported by a trial court decision, that confidences to a psychiatrist stand on a special footing and should be privileged even though a general patient's privilege is not recognized. Notes, Guttmacher and Weihofen, 28 Ind.L.J. 32 (1952); 47 N.W.U.L.Rev. 384 (1952).

4. See Purrington, op. cit., 6 Col.L.Rev. at 395, and see the discussion of the scope and effect of this oath in Morrison v. Malmquist, 62 So.2d 415 (Fla. 1953) and in the able article, Dewitt, Medical Ethics and the Law, 5 West.Reserve L.Rev. 5, 7 (1953).

5. Purrington calls attention to art. 378 of the French Code Pénal which makes the doctor's disclosure of a medical secret, *except under compulsion of law,* punishable by fine and imprisonment, and he adds this comment: "Litigation is too uncommon an

incident in the life of the average man for the anticipation of it to prove a deterrent. Gossip, on the other hand, and the desire to publish scientific, or pseudo-scientific papers are constant temptations to violation of confidence. Yet the physician is left free under our law to prattle at will of his patient's condition and affairs, subject in remote contingencies to a civil action for damages, and is forbidden to speak of them only when the interests of justice demand disclosure of that truth which the patient, it may be, is suppressing or misrepresenting in court." 6 Col.L.Rev. at pp. 394, 396, 397.

6. See 8 Wigmore, Evidence, § 2380a, p. 812, where he says: "From asthma to broken ribs, from ague to tetanus, the facts of the disease are not only disclosable without shame, but are in fact often publicly known and knowable by everyone—except the appointed investigators of truth."

stand a story of his ailment, injury or state of health, without contradiction from his physician whose testimony would prove the first story to be untrue, does such a privilege, and such enforced silence, promote the honor and dignity of the medical profession?

In a rare case, one will read between the lines a situation in which a doctor, after examining or treating a patient, will for mercenary motives betray his secrets before litigation to the defendant who has injured the patient, or to a life-insurance company against whom the patient's family has a claim. Such rare cases, however, lend little support to the privilege. Despite his disloyalty the testimony of such a doctor may be true, and a judge or jury when his motives have been exposed will not be inclined to give undue weight to his story.

It may happen, also, that the privilege will occasionally work in the interest of justice by defeating a life insurance company's defense of misrepresentation by the patient in answering questions as to the past state of his health. Such answers may be of trivial significance and may have been made in good faith. While the privilege which keeps the insured's physician from testifying may happen to obstruct such an unjust defense, the more effective remedy is an enlightened doctrine as to the materiality of the representation, or the requirement of a comprehensive incontestable-clause of reasonably short duration.[7]

So much for the benefits which the privilege is supposed to furnish. After the description in the preceding sections of the actual working of the statutes, no detailed recital of the evil results of the privilege is needed. They may be summed up in general terms:

1. The suppression of what is ordinarily the best source of proof, namely, the physician who examined and treated the patient, upon what is usually a crucial issue, namely, the physical or mental condition of the patient.

2. The one-sided view of the facts upon which the court must act when it hears the story of the patient and some doctors selected by him but allows the patient to close the mouth of another doctor whom he has consulted, who would contradict them.

3. The complexities and perplexities which result from a statute which runs against the grain of justice, truth and fair dealing. These perplexities inevitably produce a spate of conflicting and confusing appellate decisions, and encrust the statutes with numerous amendments, reaching for but never attaining the reconciliation of the privilege with the needs of justice.

Among the practicable remedies for the evils of the privilege the following should be considered.

First, the adoption of the provisions of the Uniform Rules of Evidence [8] which seem to

---

7. See 8 Wigmore, Evidence, § 2389(b).

8. R. 27: "(1) As used in this rule, (a) "patient" means a person who, for the sole purpose of securing preventive, palliative, or curative treatment, or a diagnosis preliminary to such treatment, of his physical or mental condition, consults a physician, or submits to an examination by a physician; (b) "physician" means a person authorized or reasonably believed by the patient to be authorized, to practice medicine in the state or jurisdiction in which the consultation or examination takes place; (c) "holder of the privilege" means the patient while alive and not under guardianship or the guardian of the person of an incompetent pa-

tient, or the personal representative of a deceased patient; (d) "confidential communication between physician and patient" means such information transmitted between physician and patient, including information obtained by an examination of the patient, as is transmitted in confidence and by a means which, so far as the patient is aware, discloses the information to no third persons other than those reasonably necessary for the transmission of the information or the accomplishment of the purpose for which it is transmitted.

"(2) Except as provided by paragraphs (3), (4), (5) and (6) of this rule, a person, whether or not a party, has a privilege in a civil action or in a prosecution

eliminate the principal abuses of the privilege. This would be a great advance upon any of the existing statutes but these provisions are detailed and complex calling for much judicial labor in their interpretation, and the drafters being human have not been able to foresee and provide against all the possibilities of injustice.

Second, the modification of the privilege-statute by adding a clause, as in the North Carolina Code, "Provided, that the presiding judge . . . may compel such disclosure, when, in his opinion, the same is necessary to a proper administration of justice." [9] A clear-eyed and courageous judiciary, trial and appellate, with an apprecia-

tion of the need for truth and a fear of its suppression, could draw the danger of injustice from the privilege, under this provision. A judiciary with the sentimental attitude of Buller, J., would administer the mixture as before.

Third, the retention or the re-establishment of the common law practice which makes accessible to the court the facts which the physician learns from consultation and examination. More than a century of experience with the statutes has demonstrated that the privilege in the main operates not as the shield of privacy but as the protector of fraud. Consequently the abandonment of the privilege seems the best solution.

for a misdemeanor to refuse to disclose, and to prevent a witness from disclosing, a communication, if he claims the privilege and the judge finds that (a) the communication was a confidential communication between patient and physician, and (b) the patient or the physician reasonably believed the communication to be necessary or helpful to enable the physician to make a diagnosis of the condition of the patient or to prescribe or render treatment therefor, and (c) the witness (i) is the holder of the privilege or (ii) at the time of the communication was the physician or a person to whom disclosure was made because reasonably necessary for the transmission of the communication or for the accomplishment of the purpose for which it was transmitted or (iii) is any other person who obtained knowledge or possession of the communication as the result of an intentional breach of the physician's duty of nondisclosure by the physician or his agent or servant and (d) the claimant is the holder of the privilege or a person authorized to claim the privilege for him.

"(3) There is no privilege under this rule as to any relevant communication between the patient and his physician (a) upon an issue of the patient's condition in an action to commit him or otherwise place him under the control of another or others because of alleged mental incompetence, or in an action in which the patient seeks to establish his competence or in an action to recover damages on account of conduct of the patient which constitutes a criminal offence other than a misdemeanor, or (b) upon an issue as to the validity of a document as a will of the patient, or (c) upon an issue between parties claiming by testate or intestate succession from a deceased patient.

"(4) There is no privilege under this rule in an action in which the condition of the patient is an element or factor of the claim or defense of the patient or of any party claiming through or under the patient or claiming as a beneficiary of the patient through a contract to which the patient is or was a party.

"(5) There is no privilege under this rule as to information which the physician or the patient is required to report to a public official or as to information required to be recorded in a public office, unless the statute requiring the report or record specifically provides that the information shall not be disclosed.

"(6) No person has a privilege under this rule if the judge finds that sufficient evidence, aside from the communication has been introduced to warrant a finding that the services of the physician were sought or obtained to enable or aid anyone to commit or to plan to commit a crime or a tort, or to escape detection or apprehension after the commission of a crime or a tort.

"(7) A privilege under this rule as to a communication is terminated if the judge finds that any person while a holder of the privilege has caused the physician or any agent or servant of the physician to testify in any action to any matter of which the physician or his agent or servant gained knowledge through the communication."

These provisions are the same as Model Code of Evidence, Rules 220–223.

9. N.C.G.S. § 8–53. Such a proviso was recommended for enactment by other states by Committee on the Improvement of the Law of Evidence of the American Bar Association for 1937–38. 8 Wigmore, Evidence, p. 815.

CHAPTER 12

CONFESSIONS

109. Are Confessions Trustworthy? Dangers of Mistake, Hallucination, Coercion.

Our greatest writer on evidence viewed the elaborate system of common law rules restricting the admission of confessions, as a system of special safeguards against *false* confessions.[1] Is this species of evidence so particularly unreliable as to need special restrictions?

Obviously it has some characteristics which make for verity. One who states that he has committed a crime is ordinarily as conscious as other people are of the moral duty to speak the truth, and the likelihood that he has done so is somewhat enhanced by the fact that it is easier for most people to tell what they believe to be true than to invent. Contrariwise, there are factors of unreliability common to all forms of human testimony, such as the possibility of error in observation or memory.[2] These last, however, must surely be reduced to the minimum in respect to confessions, since the narrator professes to have been himself the chief participant in the incident he recounts.

To some extent, also, the confession, like other statements, is subject to the hazard that the confessor may have been deliberately lying. Conceivably, it has been suggested, he may confess to shield the real culprit, or more often to secure a real or supposed advantage for himself.[3] A man having com-

[1] 3 Wigmore, Evidence (3d ed. 1940) § 822.

[2] Of course, confessions share all the risks of out-of-court statements generally in respect to the danger of fabrication, or of error in reporting the terms of the statement. These dangers and errors are greatest, manifestly, in respect to alleged oral confessions, and the Texas statute guards against this by requiring statements of persons under arrest to be written and signed if they are to be admitted. Tex. Vernon's Ann.C.C.P. art. 727.

[3] Gross, Criminal Psychology (2d ed. 1905, published in translation in 1911 as one of the volumes in the Modern Criminal Science Series) § 8, pp. 30–36. This passage is one of the classical discussions of

mitted a murder may confess to a burglary which occurred at the same hour in a distant part of the city.[4] And it may occasionally happen that even an innocent accused, to whom the prosecution's case seems unbeatable, consents to confess and plead guilty in return for a promise of leniency.

The possibility, again, that the declarant's statement may be the product of an abnormal mind is an infirmity to which all testimony is susceptible. Is there a substantial *special* danger here in respect to confessions? Possibly there may be. No adequate scientific study of the question seems to have been made, but the literature on psychiatry at the lawyers' level indicates that persons suffering with melancholia have a recognizable tendency toward self-accusation,[5] which conceivably might be so exaggerated as to lead to a false confession of crime. Terror and excitement over an accusation may be so shocking as to cause a state of abnormal suggestibility, and a delusion of guilt. So Munsterberg explains the confessions of the poor creatures who were burned as witches at Salem.[6] Experienced police officers, moreover, have said that a brutal and notorious crime often brings an aftermath of false con-

fessions by half-wits.[7] Dr. William Healy in his detailed study of pathological lying and accusation includes "mendacious self-impeachment" as its most striking form,[8] but his case-histories do not indicate that it is a very frequent one. In sum, then, one gets the impression from the brief and casual discussion of the instances of abnormal self-accusation by these writers, and from a lawyer's general observation, that these cases are much more often encountered by the doctors than by the police; and that when they do come before the police, they are usually, though not always, recognizable as abnormal by experienced officers. On the whole they can hardly be said to present a substantial special danger of untrustworthiness peculiar to confessions.[9]

Over and against all these possibilities of mistake, falsehood, and hallucination, common sense urges the insistent and ever-present force of self-interest.[10] In ordinary circumstances a man will not acknowledge the commission of a crime carrying serious penalties, even if he is guilty, and this motive of self-protection will operate a hundred times more strongly to prevent his acknowledging a crime of which he is innocent.

the dangers of false confessions and the precautions to be taken by the investigator.

4. Burtt, Legal Psychology (1940) c. 8, Confessions, at p. 174.

5. Arnold, Psychology Applied to Legal Evidence (2d ed. 1913) 336. Jacoby, The Unsound Mind and the Law (1918) 236; Burtt, op.cit. supra note 4, 173. For other references to the danger of pathological confessions see Inbau, Lie Detection and Criminal Interrogation (1942) 113, 114 and Healy, The Individual Delinquent (1915) § 349, pp. 749 et seq.; Healy and Healy, Pathological Lying, Accusation, and Swindling (1926) 203, 224, 233. The most comprehensive discussion and collection of materials upon the motivation and trustworthiness of confessions is to be found in Wigmore, The Science of Judicial Proof (3d ed. 1937) §§ 273–277. An extensive discussion in rather popular vein is the essay entitled "Untrue Confessions" in Munsterberg, On The Witness Stand. Essays in Psychology and Crime (1909) pp. 135–172.

6. Munsterberg, op. cit. supra n. 5, pp. 145–148.

7. Wensley, Detective Days (1931) 54, 263, cited Wigmore, Science of Judicial Proof (3d ed. 1937) 621.

8. The Individual Delinquent (cited n. 5, supra) pp. 729 et seq.

9. For a contrary view see the able Note, Voluntary False Confessions, 28 Ind.L.J. 374 (1953).

10. These striking over-statements make the point: "Love, loyalty, honesty, religion and patriotism, though firm as a rock, may lapse and fall. A man might have been counted on for one of these qualities ten times with safety, and on the eleventh, he might collapse like a house of cards. Count on egoism and laziness a hundred or a thousand times and they are as firm as ever. More simply, count on egoism—for laziness and conceit are only modifications of egoism. The latter alone then should be the one human motive to keep in mind when dealing with men. . . . Egoism is the best criterion of the presence of veracity." Gross, Criminal Psychology (1905) 27, 28.

Manifestly the gravest special danger of untrustworthiness in the use of confessions in the prosecution of crime is none of those we have mentioned. It is the danger of duress, of such pressure that the victim's reluctance to make a confession which in the long run will lose him life or liberty is converted to a willingness to accept this hazard whose consequence is deferred, in order to escape a more terrifying immediate evil.[11]

The pressure has most commonly in the past consisted in the use of stark physical violence,[12] such as the blow of a fist on the jaw,[13] striking with a whip,[14] a club,[15] or a rubber hose,[16] the application of the water-cure,[17] hanging,[18] or the "mild" use of the electric chair.[19] Indirect methods of torture may be preferred. They leave no trace, but they can often be just as effective to break the will. Such are threats of assault by officers,[20] threats of mob violence,[21] the confrontation of an ignorant, superstitious person with the corpse of the victim or similar grisly exhibits,[22] the withholding from an addict of his drug until he consents to confess,[23] and torturing compulsion exerted by extended questioning of a weak or sick person.[24]

11. Compare the following statement of Lord Sumner in Ibrahim v. The King, [1914] A.C. 599, 610, 611: "Even the rule which excludes evidence of statements made by a prisoner, when they are induced by hope held out, or fear inspired, by a person in authority, is a rule of policy. 'A confession forced from the mind by the flattery of hope or by the torture of fear comes in so questionable a shape, when it is to be considered as evidence of guilt, that no credit ought to be given to it:' Rex v. Warwickshall [Warickshall] (1783), 1 Leach, 263 [168 E.R. 234]. It is not that the law presumes such statements to be untrue, but from the danger of receiving such evidence judges have thought it better to reject it for the due administration of justice: Reg. v. Baldry (1852), 2 Den.Cr.C. 430, at p. 445."

12. The two most enlightening discussions of third degree practices are Hopkins, Our Lawless Police (1931) (See especially c. 3, "Club, Blackjack, and Gun") and National Commission on Law Observance and Enforcement, Report No. 11, Lawlessness in Law Enforcement (1931) (the "Wickersham Report"). See also Lavine, the Third Degree (1930) (a superficial but lively account by a New York police reporter); Barnes and Teeters, New Horizons in Criminology (1944) 276–282 (an excellent brief discussion of the evil and suggested remedies). See also Kutz, Trial by Torture (1938) 72 U.S.L.Rev. 316 (brief, cogent analysis of the problem); Booth, Confessions, and Methods Employed in Procuring Them (1930) 4 So.Calif.L.Rev. 83 (gives results of questionnaire addressed to California officers as to practices in securing confessions).

Decisions involving extorted confessions are collected and discussed in Notes, (1922) 8 Va.L.Rev. 527; (1930) 43 Harv.L.Rev. 617; (1938) 18 Boston U.L. Rev. 630. See Decennial Digests, Criminal Law, Key no. 522 (threats and fear).

13. White v. State, 93 Tex.Cr. 532, 248 S.W. 690 (1923) (also whipping, and threat of "shocking machine").

14. Dickson v. Commonwealth, 210 Ky. 350, 275 S.W. 805 (1925); Thompson v. State, 124 Tex.Cr. 440, 63 S.W.(2d) 849 (1933).

15. State v. Nagle, 326 Mo. 661, 32 S.W.(2d) 596 (1930).

16. Rowe v. State, 98 Fla. 98, 123 So. 523 (1929).

17. Fisher v. State, 145 Miss. 116, 110 So. 361 (1926); White v. State, 129 Miss. 182, 187, 91 So. 903 (1922).

18. Brown v. Mississippi, 297 U.S. 278 (1936).

19. N. Y. Times, Nov. 23, 1929, cited Note, (1930) 43 Harv.L.Rev. 617, 619, n. 21 (incident in Arkansas); Hopkins, op. cit. supra note 10, 220 (use of "electric monkey" in Dallas before 1925, discontinued since that time).

20. People v. Spranger, 314 Ill. 602, 145 N.E. 706, 710 (1924).

21. Rice v. State, 204 Ala. 104, 85 So. 437 (1920); Thomas v. State, 169 Ga. 182, 149 S.E. 871 (1929).

22. Davis v. United States, 32 F.(2d) 860 (C.C.A. 9th, 1929) (indian suspected of murder was taken to morgue and questioned there at side of corpse of victim); People v. Lipsczinska, 212 Mich. 484, 180 N.W. 617 (1920) (illiterate Polish woman, arrested for the murder of a nun, taken to a cell, lighted by candles, where the skeleton of the victim, arranged so that it could be manipulated, was placed; conviction affirmed).

23. See State v. Woo Dak San, 35 N.M. 105, 290 Pac. 322 (1930) (conviction affirmed because it did not appear that defendant was so confirmed an addict that deprivation would be compulsive).

24. Ziang Sung Wan v. United States, 266 U.S. 1 (1924) (extended questioning of suspect who was suffering with spastic colitis); People v. Clark, 55 Cal.App. 42, 203 Pac. 781 (1921) (woman questioned

Finally, the subtlest and the most laborious form of indirect pressure is the cumulative suggestive force of mere protracted questioning alone.[25] Practically always the interrogation is conducted by a battery of questioners operating in relays, and usually the questioning is continuous, or nearly so, for such time as to deprive the victim of normal sleep. Formerly, the hypnotic torture of a bright light shining in the prisoner's eyes was frequently an added feature,[26] and the suspect was often denied food[27] during the interrogation so that the pangs of hunger were likewise added to the other pressures. These aids seem now less often resorted to. Prolonged and insistent questioning alone seems effective to shatter the resistance of at least the average casual suspect who is not a professional criminal.[23] Obviously, this form of pressure can usually only be carried out by denying the prisoner his right to communicate with friends and counsel.

How prevalent in this country is the practice of subjecting suspected persons to these various direct and indirect pressures? The only thoroughgoing investigation that has been made of the practice throughout the country was that conducted on behalf of the Wickersham Committee in 1930–1931 under the direction of Professor Zechariah Chafee, Jr., of the Harvard Law School and Messrs. Walter H. Pollak and Carl S. Stern. They studied the published discussions, analyzed the reported decisions for a ten-year period, examined the statutes, surveyed a mass of newspaper accounts, sent questionnaires to officials and bar associations in many parts of the country, and conducted a field investigation in fifteen representative cities.[29]

Their conclusions are clear-cut:

"The third degree—the inflicting of pain, physical or mental, to extract confessions or statements—is widespread throughout the country. . . . Physical brutality is extensively practiced. . . . The method most commonly employed is protracted questioning. . . . At times such questioning is the only method used. At times the questioning is accompanied by blows or by throwing continuous straining light upon the face of the suspect. At times the suspect is kept standing for hours, or deprived of food or sleep, or his sleep is periodically interrupted to resume questioning. . . . Methods of intimidation adjusted to the age or mentality of the victim are frequently used alone or in combination with other practices. The threats are usually of bodily injury. . . . Prolonged illegal detention is a common practice. The law requires prompt production of a prisoner before a magistrate. In a large majority of the cities we have investigated this rule is constantly violated."[30]

No similar survey has since been made, but we would tend to assume that as we become more civilized, and as we select and train policemen more discriminatingly, this practice of extorting confessions by torture is disappearing. Perhaps it is, but the super-

---

during two-week period, though she was in such condition, mentally and physically, that she had to be assisted into the room, and have her head covered with wet towels, in order to answer questions).

25. People v. Vinci, 295 Ill. 419, 129 N.E. 193 (1920) (interrogation almost continuous for four nights and three days); State v. Doyle, 146 La. 973, 84 So. 315 (1920) (questioned forty hours out of fifty-three), and other cases cited in Note, (1930) 43 Harv.L.Rev. 617, 621, n. 42. The most striking recent instance is Ashcraft v. Tennessee, 322 U.S. 143, 64 Sup.Ct. 921, 88 L.Ed. 1192 (1944) (officers in relays questioned prisoner almost continuously for thirty-six hours).

26. Commonwealth v. Jones, 297 Pa. 326, 146 Atl. 905 (1929).

27. State v. Ellis, 294 Mo. 269, 242 S.W. 952 (1922).

28. But this is questioned, in the light of recent medical experiments, in Marx, Psychosomatics and Coerced Confessions, 57 Dickinson L.Rev. 1, 14–23 (1952).

29. The Wickersham Report (cited n. 12, supra), Report No. 11 on Lawlessness in Law Enforcement (1931) 22–24.

30. Id. at 153.

ficial evidence of the appellate reports does not sustain this cheerful assumption. The digests for the twenty-year period 1926–1945 reveal 94 appeals in which the appellant claimed force or threats in securing a confession. The number of cases by years varies from 1 to 8. There was 1 in 1927, and there were 8 in each of the years 1930 and 1939, and surprisingly there were likewise 8 in the first half year of 1945. The number of these cases in which a reversal is granted varies from 1 to 4 annually and recent years have seen no lessening of reversals.

So far, then, as we can assess probabilities upon such limited data, it seems probable that third degree practices are still prevalent in many parts of the country.[31] They constitute a betrayal and a mockery of those principles of respect for the worth of the individual citizen upon which our religious ideas, our constitution, and our philosophy of government rest.[32]

If we revert, however, to our first inquiry as to whether the danger of false confessions is substantial enough, beyond the danger of untruth in out-of-court statements generally, to warrant the special rules restricting the admissibility of confessions, the answer certainly cannot be a confident "yes." It may well be doubted whether confessions of guilt, even where they are extorted by pressure of force or fear, are not reasonably trustworthy. Dangers of mistake and delusion in confessions, though existent, have never been thought to be such as to require any special exclusionary rule to protect against them. Some slight evidence that confessions generally are not so untrustworthy as to constitute a frequent cause of miscarriage of justice may be found in Professor Borchard's compilation of such cases, Convicting the Innocent.[33] This selection was a random, and we may presume a fairly representative, group of sixty-five criminal convictions where convincing proof later appeared of the innocence of the accused. In only seven of these cases was there evidence of a confession.[34] Accordingly, it seems clear that while the policy on which all rules of *competency* are founded, the policy of safeguarding the trustworthiness of evidence admitted, has had an ancillary role in shaping the rules restricting the admission of confessions, the predominant motive of the courts has been that of protecting the citizen against the violation of his *privileges* of immunity from bodily manhandling by the police, and from the other undue pressures, described above, of the "third degree."[35]

110. **Existing Safeguards—(a) Corroboration.**[1]

The English courts and text writers have warned that, in homicide cases, it is dangerous to convict upon a confession alone without some additional evidence such as the

31. The President's Committee on Civil Rights reported in 1947 that "the use of third degree methods to extort confessions" was "widespread." To Secure These Rights: The Report of the President's Committee on Civil Rights (1947).

32. New England seems to be the only section where evidence of the evil does not appear in the appellate reports. Wickersham Report, op. cit. supra n. 10, at 53.

33. Borchard, Convicting the Innocent (1932).

34. These are the cases of the Boorn brothers (Borchard, op. cit. supra n. 30, pp. 14, 17), J. B. Brown (32, 36, but accused denied making the confession), John A. Johnson (110, 112, confession due to fear of mob violence), Ernest Lyons (144, 146, confession aft-

er conviction), Stielow and Green (241, 243, oral confession in presence of several officers, accused denied making it), Thorvik and Hughes (276, 277, perjured evidence by officer as to confession), and James Willis (359, 360, untrue plea of guilty). See Borchard's comments on these cases (371, 372).

35. See the writer's discussion of the distinction between competency and privilege, The Scope of Privilege in the Law of Evidence (1938) 16 Texas Law Review 447, 451, and see Ch. 5, herein.

1. See 7 Wigmore, Evidence §§ 2070–2073; Notes (1940) 31 J.Crim.L. 457; (1940) 29 Georgetown L.J. 247; (1940) 54 Harv.L.Rev. 335; (1942) 17 Temp. U.L.Q. 189; (1943) 29 Va.L.Rev. 1070; **43** J.Crim.L. 214 (1952); 33 Neb.L.Rev. 495 (1954).

finding of the body, and in such cases, and perhaps in bigamy and larceny cases, the judges may well require some independent confirming evidence or caution the jury against accepting the confession too lightly.[2] This rather flexible practice has, in most American courts, hardened into a rigid rule based upon the premise that confessions generally are an unreliable class of evidence.[3] This premise, as suggested above, seems to be quite unfounded,[4] and the cases applying the rule give for the most part the impression of measuring the proof according to a mechanical yardstick, rather than by a standard aimed at preventing the conviction of the innocent.[5]

The most widely prevailing form of the American rule is that in a prosecution for any crime where the state relies on a confession, it must also produce evidence independent of the confession tending to establish the *corpus delicti*, that is, the fact that the crime charged has been committed.[6]

Conceivably this doctrine might involve some or all of three elements: first, the harm or injury embraced in the particular crime, such as the death in a murder case or the loss of property in a larceny charge; second, the criminal origin of the harm or injury; and, third, the criminal participation of the accused himself. Most courts hold that the requirement embraces the first two elements only.[7] Of these the second, the pro-

---

2. See 7 Wigmore § 2070; Phipson, Evidence (8th ed., 1942) 249; Halsbury's Laws of England, title Criminal Law & Proc., pars. 268, n.(g), 291, n.(n).

3. See the elaboration of this premise in State v. Johnson, 95 Utah 572, 83 P.2d 1010, 1014, 1015 (1938).

4. In addition to the discussion herein above, see the quotations pro and con from cases and textwriters collected in 3 Wigmore § 866.

5. See the remarks of Judge Learned Hand in Daeche v. United States, 250 Fed. 566, 571 (C.C.A. 2d, 1918) ("That the rule [requiring corroboration of confessions] has in fact any substantial necessity in justice, we are much disposed to doubt . . . it seems to us that such evils as it corrects could be much more flexibly treated by the judge at trial. . . .").
It is submitted that hard-and-fast rules requiring corroboration are as likely to obstruct the punishment of the guilty as they are to safeguard the innocent. Much more effective in protecting the innocent would be the abolition of the rule that the court on appeal in a criminal case cannot consider the justice of the conviction if there is evidence to support it. An adequate power of review on the facts and on the justice of the result would lessen the urge to resort to such mechanical rules as grounds for reversing an unjust conviction.

6. Daeche v. United States, 250 Fed. 566, syl. 5 (C.C.A.2d 1918) (conspiracy to destroy merchant vessels in war-time by planting bombs); Iowa, I.C.A. § 782.7 ("The confession of the defendant, unless made in open court, will not warrant a conviction, unless accompanied with other proof that the offense was committed"); Minn. M.S.A. § 634.03 (confession not "sufficient to warrant his

conviction without evidence that the offense charged has been committed"); N.Y.Code Crim.Proc. § 395 (similar to last); People v. Cuozzo, 292 N.Y. 85, 54 N.E.2d 20, syl. 1 (1944); and cases collected, 7 Wigmore, op. cit. supra § 2071, **n. 4**; Decennial Digests, Crim.L. ⊂⇒535.
In a few states, seemingly, or at least in some sporadic decisions, a more flexible doctrine, resembling the English practice, is announced requiring merely that some facts be proven outside the confession which under the circumstances give it reasonable corroboration. Logue v. State, 198 Ga. 672, 673, 32 S.E.2d 397, 399 (1944) (infanticide, "Corroboration of the confession in any material particular satisfies the requirements"); State v. Geltzeiler, 101 N.J.L. 415, 128 Atl. 240, syl. 2 (1925) ("Evidence corroborating some fact or facts in the confession itself," enough), and cases and statutes collected in 7 Wigmore § 2071, n. 3.
It is to be noted that even under the stricter requirement generally prevailing of evidence of the *corpus delicti*, it is not demanded that the outside proof be sufficient standing alone. Daeche v. United States, supra ("Independently they need not establish the truth of the corpus delicti at all, neither beyond a reasonable doubt nor by a preponderance of proof."); United States v. Kertess, 139 F.2d 923, syl. 4 (C.C.A.2d 1944); State v. Lyle, 353 Mo. 386, 182 S.W.2d 530, syl. 4 (1944) ("full proof" of corpus delicti not required). It is sufficient if the outside proof, together with the confession, satisfies the jury of guilt beyond a reasonable doubt. Jordan v. United States, 60 F.2d 4, (C.C.A. 4th, 1932); Phillips v. State, 196 Miss. 194, 16 So.2d 630, syl. 2 (1944).

7. Murray v. United States, 53 App.D.C. 119, 288 Fed. 1008, syl. 7 (1923); Messel v. State, 176 Ind.

duction of evidence tending to show that the death, loss or injury was due to a crime, causes the most difficulty. It is, for example, a frequent stumbling-block to the prosecution in cases of infanticide where the accused confesses the killing, but the infant's body is found under circumstances which are consistent with accident.[8]

111. Existing Safeguards—(b) The requirement that the Confession Must not Have Been Induced by Force, Threats, or Promise of Leniency, but Must Have Been "Voluntary." [1]

By the fifties of the last century the test of the admissibility of confessions had been formulated in a two-branched statement. First, it was said that a confession would not be received if induced by force, threat of force, or promise of leniency,[2] on the

---

214, 95 N.E. 565, syl. 2 (1911); Lacey v. Commonwealth, 251 Ky. 419, 65 S.W.2d 61, syl. 5 (1933); State v. Gillman, 329 Mo. 306, 44 S.W.2d 146, syl. 2, 4 (1931); People v. Cuozzo, 292 N.Y. 85, 54 N.E. 2d 20, syl. 4 (1944); Commonwealth v. Turza, 340 Pa. 128, 16 A.2d 401, syl. 2 (1940); 7 Wigmore § 2072, n. 4.

The condition of the body, in a homicide case, may be sufficient to show the criminal origin of the death. People v. Cuozzo, supra, syl. 2.

May admissions of the accused serve to corroborate a confession? If made voluntarily and not as a part of the confession itself, they would certainly seem to give persuasive confirmation of the truth of the confession. It is submitted that they should be regarded, where they tend to prove the corpus delicti, as sufficient. This view finds support in State v. McLain, 208 Minn. 91, 292 N.W. 753 (1940) (statutory rape, defendant's written confession held sufficiently corroborated by his subsequent admission of guilt at preliminary hearing before magistrate), but see adverse comment in Note, (1940) 54 Harv.L.Rev. 335. Contra: Gulotta v. United States, 113 F.2d 683, syl. 9 (C.C.A. 8th, 1940) (false representation by accused, in registration for voting, that he was United States citizen, not sufficiently corroborated, as to falsity, by statement in declaration of intention to become a citizen that he was born in Italy, and by his delivery of a passport reciting the same fact), and see critical comment, (1940) 31 J.Crim.L. 456.

There have been expressions by judges in some opinions which might suggest that even the third element also, namely the connection of the defendant with the crime, must be shown by evidence apart from the confession, but there seems to be no substantial support in the decisions for this view. State v. Bass, 251 Mo. 107, 157 S.W. 782 (1913) explained and discredited in State v. Hawkins, 165 S.W.2d 644, syl. 6, 7 (Mo.Sup.1942); and see Nicholson v. State, 20 S.W.2d 762 (Tex.Cr.1929) (doubting), Wigmore § 2072, n. 4; but the trend of decision in Texas supports the prevailing view. McGinty v. State, 134 Tex.Cr. 539, 116 S.W.2d 713, syl. 4 (1938) and cases cited therein. The first view would relegate the confession, even though satis-

factorily proved to have been voluntarily made, to a minor role indeed. A recent Texas decision, however, seems to go even beyond this doctrine in holding, in an embezzlement case against a receiver, in which the accused made a full confession in his receiver's report, that the state failed because it did not prove, outside the confession, that the embezzlement occurred within the period of limitation. East v. State, 146 Tex.Cr. 396, 175 S.W.2d 603, syl. 10 (1943).

8. E. g., State v. Johnson, 95 Utah 572, 83 P.2d 1010 1938) (extended discussion of the medical testimony as to condition of child's body, relied on to corroborate mother's confession that she strangled child, held insufficient). Other such cases in which the corroboration was held sufficient: Warmke v. Commonwealth, 297 Ky. 649, 180 S.W.2d 872 (1944); Commonwealth v. Lettrich, 346 Pa. 497, 31 A.2d 155 (1943), noted in (1943) 29 Va.L.Rev. 1070.

1. Uniform Rules of Evidence, Rule 63(6): "In a criminal proceeding as against the accused, a previous statement by him relative to the offense charged [is admissible] if, and only if, the judge finds that the accused when making the statement was conscious and was capable of understanding what he said and did, and that he was not induced to make the statement (a) under compulsion or by infliction or threats of infliction of suffering upon him or another, or by prolonged interrogation under such circumstances as to render the statement involuntary, or (b) by threats or promises concerning action to be taken by a public official with reference to the crime, likely to cause the accused to make such a statement falsely, and made by a person whom the accused reasonably believed to have the power or authority to execute the same."

2. The courts show a tendency to construe statements such as "You had better tell the truth," made to a prisoner by one in authority, as being promises of leniency, and as such, grounds for exclusion. 3 Wigmore, Evidence, § 838. But see Commonwealth v. Mabey, 299 Mass. 96, 12 N.E.2d 61 (1937), Note, 37 Mich.L.Rev. 315.

ground that such influences made the confession untrustworthy, and second, as an alternative form of statement, it was said that the confession must be "voluntary." [3] As commonly understood, however, the two requirements are not coextensive. A confession induced by assurance of lenience would not ordinarily be thought involuntary, and, conversely, other pressures than threats or force might overcome the will. Occasionally courts have spoken as if "voluntary" was intended to have an additional effect and to require that the confession be a spontaneous outpouring of the conscience with no outside prompting or suggestion,[4] but such expressions are departures from the accepted view.[5] The prevailing doctrine, on the contrary, limits "voluntary" to the special content of freedom from physical force or threats thereof and absence of offers of leniency and takes no account of other forms of pressure.[6]

Under this generally accepted practice, accordingly, a confession extorted by a threat to arrest a companion is unobjectionable.[7] Procurement of a confession by trick or deception does not vitiate it, unless the deception is calculated to prompt the victim to confess falsely.[8] A confession impelled by the results of an actual interrogation under the lie-detector, voluntarily submitted to, will be admitted.[9] The mere facts of arrest, custody and questioning by officers, though these circumstances in themselves place strong pressure on the ordinary man to talk, do not render the confession inadmissible.[10]

---

3. See, e. g., Campbell, L.C.J., in Scott's Case, 1 D. & B. 47, 58, 169 Eng.Rep. 909, 914 (1856); "It is a trite maxim that the confession of a crime, to be admissible against the party confessing, must be voluntary; but this only means that it shall not be induced by improper threats or promises, because, under such circumstances, the party may have been influenced to say what is not true, and the supposed confession cannot be safely acted upon." And other passages quoted in 3 Wigmore, Evidence §§ 822–826.

4. See, e. g., Parker v. State, 46 Tex.Cr. 461, 470, 80 S.W. 1008 (1904) (where accused while under arrest was questioned by the county attorney, his consequent statement was held inadmissible, because elicited by "a severe cross-examination"). Compare the statement by Lehman, J., in People v. Mummiani, 258 N.Y. 394, 397, 180 N.E. 94, 95 (1932): "Whatever the rule may be in other jurisdictions (Bram v. United States, 168 U.S. 532, 18 S.Ct. 183), our law does not require that a confession to be admissible shall be a spontaneous utterance made by a defendant to relieve his conscience."

5. See, e. g., People v. Shelton, 388 Ill. 56, 63, 57 N.E.2d 473, 477 (1944) where the court quoted approvingly from an earlier case as follows: "A confession is regarded as voluntary when it is made of the free will and accord of the accused without fear of any threat of harm or without promise or inducement by hope of reward. It need not be spontaneous and it is not necessary that it be wholly made upon the suggestion of the accused." See also 3 Wigmore, Evidence §§ 825, 826.

6. See, e. g., Brown v. State, 208 Ark. 28, 184 S.W.2d 805, syl. 3 (1945) (illiterate laborer's confession re-

ceived where no showing of force, threats, or promised leniency, though accused testified—it is not clear whether the upper court accepted it as true—that the officers "cussed him" and thus put him in fear).

7. Ruhl v. United States, 148 F.2d 173 (C.C.A. 10th, 1945) (accused claimed such a threat was made; officers denied it; court held, if made, incredible that under the circumstances it would cause him to confess).

8. 3 Wigmore, Evidence, § 841; Commonwealth v. Hipple, 333 Pa. 33, 3 A.2d 353, syl. 6 (1939) (officers placed lie-detector attachment on defendant's arm, and told him, "You can lie to us, but you cannot lie to this machine"). But see People v. Leyra, 302 N.Y. 353, 98 N.E.2d 553, syl. 5 (1951), where a confession extorted by phychiatrist employed by state, who assumed the role of defendant's confidential physician was held involuntary. The case is noted in 52 Col.L.Rev. 423, 36 Minn.L.Rev. 274.

9. See Commonwealth v. Jones, 341 Pa. 541, 548, 19 A.2d 389 (1941); State v. DeHart, 242 Wis. 562, 8 N.W.2d 360, syl. 2 (1943); Note, 1943 Wis.L.Rev. 430; Note, 23 A.L.R.2d 1310. But not if the prisoner is compelled to submit to the lie-detector. People v. Sims, 395 Ill. 69, 69 N.E.2d 336, syl. 1, 2 (1946.) In proving the confession elicited by the lie-detector care must be taken not to disclose to the jury the result of the test. Leeks v. State, 245 P.2d 764, syl. 15 (Okl.Cr.1952).

10. Gray v. United States, 9 F.2d 337, syl. 8 (C.C.A. 9th, 1926); People v. McFarland, 386 Ill. 122, 53 N.E.2d 844, syl. 4 (1944); State v. Seminary, 165 La. 67, 115 So. 370, syl. 6 (1928); Commonwealth

Moreover, the accepted doctrine, at least in the state courts, has not accounted the fact that the confessor was in custody under illegal arrest,[11] or that the confessing prisoner was not allowed access to family, friends or counsel,[12] or that the confession was elicited by prolonged and persistent questioning by officers,[13] sufficient as grounds of exclusion. It was also fairly well settled in the state courts (and in federal prosecutions as well until the decision in the McNabb case, discussed in a later paragraph) that the fact that the confession was secured while the prisoner was being illegally held in violation of the law requiring his prompt production before a committing magistrate, does not invalidate it as evidence.[14]

112. Danger That Confession, though Involuntary, may Actually be Received and Considered.

In practice the requirement of "voluntariness" as above described has the conspicuous weakness that it does not in fact prevent the successful use of confessions in many instances when there is strong ground to believe that they were extorted by force or by other compulsive third degree methods. In the first place, the extorted confession is often the white flag of surrender, followed by a plea of guilty. Or even though not usable in evidence, it may serve to uncover other sources of information and the identity of witnesses by whom the case can be proved without the confession. But the rule of exclusion does not in practical administration close the door to the prosecution's hope that the confession itself though "involuntary" may be used in evidence.

The hope, of course, arises from the possibility that the judge or jury, despite the actual extortion by pressure, will find the confession voluntary. Why such a hope? First, because an officer who is willing to use methods which he knows are unlawful is frequently (by no means always) willing to deny the wrong under oath. The end justifies the perjury if it justifies the brutality. Second, the judge or jury if there is a conflict in the evidence as to pressure will often be more interested in punishing the crime with which the prisoner is charged, than in protecting the civil rights of a probably guilty man by disregarding the extorted confession.

This last danger is much enhanced in the states, apparently a majority, in which the jury is given a share in deciding whether the confession is admissible.[1] In some of

---

v. Szczepanek, 235 Mass. 411, 126 N.E. 847, syl. 2 (1920); State v. Haskins, 327 Mo. 313, 36 S.W.2d 909, syl. 3, 4 (1931).

"The mere questioning of a suspect while in the custody of police officers is not prohibited either as a matter of common law or due process." Lyons v. Oklahoma, 322 U.S. 596, 601, 64 S.Ct. 1208, 1211, 1212 (1944) (State court conviction attacked for want of due process, affirmed).

11. People v. Klyczek, 307 Ill. 150, 138 N.E. 275, syl. 4 (1923) (citing cases); State v. Haskins, 327 Mo. 313, 36 S.W.2d 909, syl. 3 (1931).

12. People v. Nagle, 25 Cal.2d 216, 153 P.2d 344 (1944); People v. McFarland, 386 Ill. 122, 53 N. E.2d 884, syl. 4 (1944).

13. State v. Wickman, 39 N.M. 198, 43 P.2d 933, syl. 5 (1935); People v. Doran, 246 N.Y. 409, 159 N. E. 379, syl. 5 (1927); O'Neil v. State, 38 Okl.Cr. 391, 262 Pac. 218, syl. 3 (1927); Commonwealth v.

Cavalier, 284 Pa. 311, 131 Atl. 229, syl. 1 (1925) (14-year-old boy questioned for 4 hours).

14. People v. Nagle, 25 Cal.2d 216, 153 P.2d 344 (1944) (prisoner held incommunicado for three days before making statement); Cahill v. People, 111 Colo. 29, 137 P.2d 673, syl. 15 (1943); Cates v. State, 118 Tex.Cr. 35, 37 S.W.2d 1031, syl. 3 (1930); and cases cited in Decennial Digests, Crim.Law, ☞519(8); Note, (1935) 94 A.L.R. 1036.

Most state courts, moreover, since the McNabb case have declined to adopt its doctrine so as to invalidate confessions taken by state officers before arraignment. See, e. g., State v. Browning, 206 Ark. 791, 178 S.W.2d 77 (1944); Finley v. State, 153 Fla. 394, 14 So.2d 844 (1943); State v. Collett, 58 N.E.2d 417, 425 (Oh.App.1944), and see Comment, (1944) 22 Texas Law Review 473, 479. Note, Delay in Arraignment, 19 A.L.R.2d 1331.

1. See 3 Wigmore, Evidence, § 861; Note, Voluntariness of Confession Admitted by Court as Question for Jury, 85 A.L.R. 870 (1933), where the states are

these the judge is required if he believes, on conflicting testimony, that the confession was involuntary to exclude it altogether, but if he finds it voluntary to admit it with an instruction to the jury to disregard it if they think it involuntary.[2] This may seem a sufficient safeguard, but in practice it may seriously weaken the judge's responsibility. He is reluctant to brand the officers who took the confession as liars and he is encouraged to admit a doubtful confession by the rule which says that if he admits it the jury must pass on the same question. Of course, the administration of the rule of exclusion is least effective and the probability of securing a conviction on an extorted confession is most substantial, in those states where the whole question of voluntariness, if the evidence is conflicting, is for the jury.[3] In these states, even though the judge may believe that the confession was secured by brutality, yet if the officers deny it the confession presumably would nevertheless be admitted with a direction to the jury to disregard if they find it was involuntary. Seemingly, the best system of administration if the aim is the exclusion of involuntary confessions, is the practice, obtaining in a substantial minority of the states,[4] which gives entire responsibility to the judge for deciding the question of admissibility, and leaves to the jury only its credibility.[5]

113. Possible Escapes from the Common Law Restrictions on the Use of Coerced Confessions: (a) The Doctrine That Mere Admissions Are Not Confessions.[1]

A confession is a complete acknowledgment of guilt of the crime on trial.[2] An admission is any other statement of a fact, relevant to the charge, made by the accused and offered against him as evidence of the fact.[3] Such an admission has been termed a little brother of a confession.[4] It is frequently said that the distinctive rules relating to confessions are inapplicable to mere admissions, but the courts have seldom faced the crucial question, will an admission be received in evidence when it has been induced

---

classified; Dec.Dig., Crim.Law, ⬅532. An able review of the various practices, with a realistic discussion of the problems and dangers involved, is Meltzer, Involuntary Confessions: The Allocation of Responsibility between Judge and Jury, 21 U.Chi. L.Rev. 317 (1954).

2. See, e. g., Davis v. State, 182 Ark. 123, 30 S.W. (2d) 830 (1930); State v. Hubbard, 351 Mo. 143, 171 S.W.(2d) 701, 705 (1943).

3. Illustrative cases: People v. Doran, 246 N.Y. 409, 159 N.E. 379 (1927); Commonwealth v. Weiss, 284 Pa. 105, 130 Atl. 403 (1925); Gipson v. State, 147 Tex.Cr.R. 428, 181 S.W.(2d) 76, syl. 2 (1944); Newman v. State, 148 Tex.Cr.R. 645, 187 S.W.(2d) 559, syl. 12 (1945).

4. E. g., Moss v. State, 19 Ala.App. 85, 96 So. 451 (1923) (improper to charge jury to disregard confession if they find it involuntary); Reedy v. State, 246 Ala. 363, 20 So.(2d) 528, syl. 6 (1945); People v. Fox, 319 Ill. 606, 150 N.E. 347 (1925) (competency not to be submitted to jury); State v. Compo, 108 N.J.L. 499, 158 Atl. 541 (Errors and Appeals, 1932); Wynn v. State, 181 Tenn. 325, 181 S.W.(2d) 332, syl. 1 (1944).

In 1942 Kentucky adopted this practice by an amendment to its so-called Anti-Sweating Act providing

that "The trial judge shall determine the competency and admissibility of any alleged confession under the provisions of this section from evidence heard by him, independent of and without the hearing of the jury trying the case." KRS, § 422.110, Laws of 1942, c. 141, § 2.

5. Upon which they may consider evidence as to voluntariness. People v. Fox, supra; Hauk v. State, 148 Ind. 238, 264, 47 N.E. 465 (1897).

1. 3 Wigmore, Evidence, § 821; Strock, Validity of the Admission-Confession Distinction as to Admissibility, 39 J.Crim.L. 743 (1949); 20 Am.Jur., Evidence, § 478; Dec.Dig., Crim.L., ⬅ 516.

2. Gulotta v. United States, 113 F.2d 683, syl. 6 (C.C. A. 8, 1940); People v. Allen, 413 Ill. 69, 107 N.E.2d 826, syl. 10 (1952); Comm. v. Dascalakis, 243 Mass. 519, 137 N.E. 879, syl. 1 (1923).

3. Ford v. State, 181 Md. 303, 29 A.2d 833, syl. 2 (1943); Whomble v. State, 143 Neb. 667, 10 N.W.2d 627, syl. 5 (1943). The term also includes admissions by conduct. See, e. g., Cortes v. State, 135 Fla. 589, 185 So. 323 (1939) (offer to bribe officers). In a wider sense, confessions are merely one species of admissions.

4. Strock, op.cit., 39 J.Crim.L. 743.

by the pressure of threats, force or promises which would ban a confession? Of course, admissions range from those which are as persuasive of guilt as a confession itself would be [5] and those which merely acknowledge subordinate facts not crucial to the state, which could usually find other evidence of the fact. Some courts seem to apply the requirement of voluntariness to the former, the seriously incriminating admission.[6]

In a case in which the accused was charged with procuring one Ware to kill his wife, the accused after prolonged interrogation amounting to coercion confessed. At his trial the prosecution introduced only his statement (made earlier in the interrogation and under the same pressure) that he had seen the killer ride away with the victim, which was highly incriminating to the accused. The Supreme Court held that a conviction based on this admission violated the due process requirement.[7]

Under the usual practice, when the state offers a confession, a complete acknowledgment of guilt, the defendant may object on the ground that it has not been shown to have been voluntary, and if he does,[8] the state has the duty of producing proof of voluntariness [9] in a preliminary hearing on which the accused may offer counter-evidence. This is a time-consuming procedure, but one which is appropriate in determining the admissibility of a confession, as to which the likelihood of undue pressure is substantial. It is less appropriate to the offer of an admission, usually less damaging to the accused and generally less likely to have been induced by undue pressure. As to admissions therefore it seems practical, if the accused objects on the ground of involuntariness, to place on him the burden of producing evidence of undue pressure.[10] Conceding

---

5. See, e. g., Ashcraft v. Tennessee, 327 U.S. 274, 66 Sup.Ct. 544, 90 L.Ed. 667 (1946) (on second appeal) (husband, charged with procuring one Ware to kill his wife, after first denying he knew who killed her, admits he saw his wife forced by Ware to drive off with him, just before the killing); People v. Wynekoop, 359 Ill. 124, 194 N.E. 276, syl. 1–3 (1934) (murder: exculpatory statement by accused giving different explanation of the circumstances of death from the one she had previously given); Comm. v. Haywood, 247 Mass. 571, 141 N.E. 571 (1923) (incest with niece; statements acknowledging intercourse with niece on other occasions, and pleading guilty to adultery at time charged with committing incest, not confessions).

6. McGuire v. State, 299 Ala. 315, 194 So. 815, syl. 9 (1940) (murder in execution of conspiracy to rob: defendant's statement, offered by state, that there had been discussion among the conspirators as to a robbery was an inculpatory admission in nature of confession, and entitled defendant to preliminary hearing as to voluntariness); Lovette v. State, 152 Fla. 495, 12 So.2d 168, syl. 5 (1943) (as to "admission of an incriminating fact or facts, from which guilt may be inferred" rules are similar to those as to confessions); Winchester v. State, 163 Miss. 462, 142 So. 454, syl. 3 (1932) (record did not show tenor of statement, and court said that on another trial, if the statement "has a direct bearing on his guilt" state should be required to show that it was volun-

tary); State v. Durkee, 68 R.I. 73, 26 A.2d 604, 607, syl. 3, 4 (1942) ("admissions . . . not amounting to a confession but from which an inference of guilt may reasonably be drawn, are admissible . . . if such admissions are voluntarily made").

7. Ashcraft v. Tennessee, 327 U.S. 274, 66 Sup.Ct. 544, 90 L.Ed. 667 (1946) (second appeal).

8. If he fails to object, the question is waived. People v. Leving, 371 Ill. 448, 21 N.E.2d 391, syl. 3 (1944).

9. People v. Crowl, 28 Cal.App.2d 299, 82 P.2d 507, 513, syl. 18 (1938); Coker v. State, 199 Ga. 20, 33 S.E.2d 171, syl. 3 (1945); Stagemeyer v. State, 133 Neb. 9, 273 N.W. 825, 829, syl. 1 (1937); Dec.Dig., Crim.Law, ⟐ 517(3).

10. Perhaps the courts mean no more than this when they say that the admission need not be proved to have been made voluntarily. State v. Braathen, 77 N.D. 309, 43 N.W.2d 202, syl. 10 (1950). Or that the court need not hold a preliminary hearing on voluntariness when an admission is offered. People v. Wynekoop, 359 Ill. 124, 194 N.E. 276, syl. 3 (1934); Comm. v. Haywood, 247 Mass. 16, 141 N.E. 571, syl. 2, 4 (1923). But there are occasional statements that go further, see, e. g., People v. Trawick, 78 Cal. App.2d 604, 178 P.2d 45, 48, syl. 6 (1947) (mere admissions "admissible . . . irrespective of their voluntary character"). And even holdings that coerced admissions are competent evidence. State

the reasonableness of such a distinction in allocation of the burden of producing evidence, it is believed that it is unreasonable to make a difference in the ultimate rule of exclusion for involuntary confessions and involuntary admissions [11] and that the Supreme Court's interpretation of the due process clause requires that both be excluded.[12]

114. Possible Escapes from the Common Law Restrictions: (b) The Doctrine That a Second Confession, Following a Confession Induced by Undue Pressure, is Competent if Voluntary.

When a confession has once been extorted from a prisoner by force, threats or the pressure of prolonged questioning, the securing of a second like confession, even without any overt menace, becomes relatively easy. As shrewdly suggested by Jackson, J., "after an accused has once let the cat out of the bag by confessing, no matter what the induce-

ment, he is never thereafter free of the psychological and practical disadvantages of having confessed. He can never get the cat back in the bag. The secret is out for good. In such a sense, a later confession always may be looked upon as fruit of the first. But this Court has never gone so far as to hold that making a confession under circumstances which preclude its use, perpetually disables the confessor from making a usable one after those conditions have been removed." [1]

How is the temptation to undue pressure in securing a confession, in the hope of breaking the prisoner's resistance to giving a later "voluntary" confession, to be lessened? Some safeguarding effect is afforded by the presumption, recognized by most courts, that a subsequent confession, following one that was improperly induced, was also induced by the same influence, unless it appears from lapse of time or other facts

---

v. Romo, 66 Ariz. 174, 185 P.2d 757, syl. 2, 11, 14 (1947) (evidence that admissions were procured by threats and violence properly rejected); State v. Pittman, 137 S.C. 75, 134 S.E. 514, syl. 5 (1926) (admissions not improperly admitted even if made under duress).

11. See the statement arguendo that when coerced they are both to be excluded. Gullotta v. United States, 113 F.2d 683, 686, syl. 8 (C.C.A. 8, 1940), and see the cases cited in note 6, above, and the conclusion in 22 C.J.S., Crim.Law, § 732. Uniform Rule 63(6), quoted above, § 111, note 1, so provides.

12. Ashcraft v. Tennessee, 327 U.S. 274, 66 Sup.Ct. 544, 90 L.Ed. 667 (1946) (second appeal). See, however, a statement which casts a cloud on this holding without mentioning the prior decision. Stein v. New York, 346 U.S. 156, 163, note 5, 73 Sup.Ct. 1077, 1082, 97 L.Ed. 1522 (1953).

1. United States v. Bayer, 331 U.S. 532, 540, 67 Sup. Ct. 1394, 1398, 91 L.Ed. 1654 (1947). This was a federal prosecution. While illegally detained the defendant, an army officer, confessed that he accepted bribes. Six months later, no longer imprisoned but merely restricted to the base, he made a second confession, after due warning. The court held that the trial judge was not in error in finding that the second confession was voluntary. Whether the use of such a second confession was a denial of due process was presented in Lyons v.

Oklahoma, 322 U.S. 596, 64 Sup.Ct. 1208, 88 L.Ed. 1481 (1944). In that case, a tenant farmer, his wife and a child were killed and the house burned to conceal the crime. Lyons, a young Negro of 21 or 22, was arrested and held in custody without arraignment. He was questioned, with conflicting testimony as to mistreatment, for two hours when arrested. Eleven days later he was given "the works." He was examined in the county prosecutor's office from 6:30 in the evening until some time between 2:00 and 4:00 in the morning. Eleven or twelve officers were in and out of the office during the night. Lyons testified that he was assaulted. Some of the participants denied the mistreatment. It was not disputed that a pan of the victim's bones were placed in Lyons' lap to prompt the confession. He confessed. This confession, however, was not introduced. Later, after having been taken to the scene of the crime and there questioned, Lyons was lodged in the penitentiary and there, twelve hours after his first confession, he signed another acknowledgment of guilt. This second confession was introduced, was found by court and jury to have been made voluntarily, and on it the conviction rested. The majority opinion, in affirming the conviction, said, "The Fourteenth Amendment does not provide review of mere error in jury verdicts, even though the error concerns the voluntary character of a confession."

that this pressure was no longer operative.[2] This is as far as the decisions have gone, but it has been well suggested that the courts should consider the possibility of prescribing as one of the facts necessary to rebut the presumption, that the officer must have advised the prisoner that the earlier confession cannot be used in evidence against him.[3]

115. State Statutory Regulations Attempting to Safeguard the Use of Confessions.

There are numerous statutes in various states, as well as Acts of Congress, regulating the conduct of officers toward their prisoners which afford incidental protection against third-degree practices in securing confessions.[1] Examples are the statutes obtaining in nearly every state, and similar enactments by Congress, requiring that persons arrested be taken promptly before a magistrate for examination.[2] Similar in purpose are statutes which require jailers, under penalty, to allow access to prisoners of counsel, relatives, or friends.[3] Numerous other statutes forbid and penalize brutal treatment generally by officers toward prisoners under their care.[4]

A substantial number of enactments specifically forbid violent, oppressive, or coercive practices designed to secure a confession.[5] Others in effect simply enact the common law doctrine that confessions induced by threats or fear are inadmissible.[6]

Probably the most detailed legislative attempts, however, to prevent abuses in securing confessions or in their use are the Texas and Kentucky statutes. The Texas statute was enacted in its present form in 1907. It is set out in a footnote.[7] It applies

---

2. People v. Jones, 24 Cal.2d 601, 150 P.2d 801, syl. 6, 7 (1944) (first confession induced by beatings); State v. Moore, 210 N.C. 686, 188 S.E. 421, syl. 6 (1936); Abston v. State, 132 Tex.Cr. 130, 102 S.W. 2d 428, syl. 3 (1937); Dec.Dig., Crim.Law, ☞ 519(2), 531(1).

3. Hobbs, Note, 26 Tex.L.Rev. 536, 538 (1948). Such failure to advise the prisoner was considered in People v. Jones, 24 Cal.2d 601, 150 P.2d 801, 805 (1944) as one of the reasons for excluding the second confession.

1. See compilation, Statutes directed against the Third Degree or Related Evils, in Lawlessness in Law Enforcement, app. III, 113 (1931) cited note 12, § 109 supra.

2. E. g., Tex. Vernon's Ann.C.C.P. arts. 233, 234, 235, and other statutes cited in McNabb v. United States, 318 U.S. 332, 342, 63 S.Ct. 608, 613 (1943).

3. Calif. Pen. Code, § 825 (attorney); Colorado, '35 C.S.A. c. 48, § 560 (attorney); Nevada, N.C.L.1929, § 10488 (friends or attorney); New Hampshire, R.L. c. 423, § 8 (relatives, friends, and attorney); Ohio, R.C. §§ 2935–16, 2935–17 (attorney); Tex. Vernon's Ann.P.C. art. 1176 (counsel).

4. Ariz.A.C.A.1939, § 44–143 (willful inhumanity or oppression); Calif. Pen. Code, § 147 (same as last); Colorado, '35 C.S.A. c. 48, § 152 (same); Ga.Code, § 77–104 (same); Idaho, I.C. § 18–704 (same); Vermont, V.S. § 8262 (1917) § 6829 (unnecessary cruelty or failure to provide with food, etc.); Wis. S.1953, § 340.58 (abuse, neglect or ill-treatment).

5. Colorado, '35 C.S.A. c. 48, § 153 (makes it a felony); Ill.S.H.A. ch. 38, § 379 (assaulting or imprisoning to induce confession), § 383 (threats of violence); Ind. Burns' Ann.St. §§ 10–404, 10–405 (violence, threats, deprivation of food or sleep); La. LSA–R.S. 15:452 (treatment designed by effect on body or mind to compel confession); V.A.M.S. § 558.360 (frightening by threat, torture, or attempt to torture); Montana R.C.M. 1947, §§ 94–3918, 94–3919 (similar to last); Nevada, N.C.L.1929, § 10488 (violence, intimidation, indignity, or threats); Wash.RCW 9.33.030. (similar to last).

6. These are compiled and summarized in 3 Wigmore, Evidence § 831, n. 2.

7. Tex. Vernon's Ann.C.C.P. art. 727:
"The confession shall not be used if, at the time it was made, the defendant was in jail or other place of confinement, nor while he is in the custody of an officer, unless made in the voluntary statement of accused, taken before an examining court in accordance with law, or be made in writing and signed by him; which written statement shall show that he has been warned by the person to whom the same is made: First, that he does not have to make any statement at all. Second, that any statement made may be used in evidence against him on his trial for the offense concerning which the confession is therein made; or, unless in connection with said confession he made statements of facts or circumstances that are found to be true, which conduce to establish his guilt, such as the finding of secreted or stolen property, or the

only to confessions of persons in custody. Its most distinctive restrictions are, first, the confession must be *in writing* unless taken by an examining court in accordance with law, and second, the prisoner must be *warned* that he does not have to make a statement and that if he does it may be used against him, and the giving of the warning must be recited. As would be expected, the statute requires that the confession be "voluntary." As would not be expected, it provides that when a confession not complying with the statute is taken and the prisoner's statements lead the officers to uncover confirmatory evidence such as the stolen property or the fatal weapon, the confession itself and not merely the confirmatory evidence is admitted.[8] On the other hand, the court's definition of "confession" is equally surprising. Any statement offered against the accused, whether an acknowledgment of the crime or any other statement, is included.[9] Even evidence of conduct of the prisoner while under arrest has been held to come within the term,[10] though it is hard to find rational warrant for this. On the other hand if the

words used however confessory will satisfy the requirements for so-called *res gestae*, e. g., spontaneous exclamations made excitedly immediately after arrest, the statute is deemed not to apply.[11] The requirement of writing probably is a substantial clog on the activities of unscrupulous officers in taking confessions. At least they must do more than merely invent and swear to an imaginary oral confession. But neither the writing, nor the warning, are of much value in preventing the extortion of confessions by force or fear. If a man is tortured or afraid, he will sign as readily as he will talk, and the inclusion in the writing that he signs of a statement that he has been warned is hardly a substantial safeguard. Since Texas is one of the states in which the largest number of cases of charges of undue pressure in securing confessions appear in the appellate reports,[12] the effectiveness of the statute as a preventive of third-degree methods has been limited.

The Kentucky Anti-Sweating Act, originally passed in 1912, and amended in 1942, is copied below.[13] It goes beyond the common

---

instrument with which he states the offense was committed. If the defendant is unable to write his name, and signs the statement by making his mark, such statement shall not be admitted in evidence, unless it be witnessed by some person other than a peace officer, who shall sign the same as a witness. O.C. 662; Acts 1907, p. 219."

8. The entire confession, moreover, and not merely the part confirmed, comes in, Torres v. State, 145 Tex.Cr. 365, 168 S.W.2d 265, syl. 1 (1943).

9. Silver v. State, 110 Tex.Cr. 512, 8 S.W.2d 144, syl. 6 (1928).

10. Riojas v. State, 102 Tex.Cr. 258, 277 S.W. 640, syl. 3 (1925) (attempt to bribe an officer); Beachem v. State, 144 Tex.Cr. 272, 162 S.W.2d 706 (syl. 4) (1942) (prisoner required to talk for purpose of comparison).

11. Stout v. State, 142 Tex.Cr. 537, 155 S.W.2d 374, syl. 6 (1941) (burglar, surprised by officers in the act, says, "You have got me cold turkey this time.").

12. See National Commission on Law Observance and Enforcement, Report No. 11, Lawlessness in Law Enforcement (1931) pp. 52, 202. Results are there

given of a study of appellate cases from 1920 to 1930 in which third-degree methods were charged. Sixty-seven cases were found in which such methods were established, and 39 in which the evidence was contradictory or doubtful. Of these 106 cases, 10 arose in Texas, a larger number than in any other state except Illinois, in which there were 16.

13. Ky. KRS § 422.110: "(1) No peace officer or other person having lawful custody of any person charged with crime, shall attempt to obtain information from the accused concerning his connection with or knowledge of crime by plying him with questions, or extort information to be used against him on his trial by threats or other wrongful means, nor shall the person having custody of the accused permit any other person to do so.

"(2) A confession obtained by methods prohibited by subsection (1) is not admissible as evidence of guilt in any court. The trial judge shall determine the competency and admissibility of any alleged confession under the provisions of this section from evidence heard by him, independent of and without the hearing of the jury trying the case. (1942, c. 141, § 2)."

law rule of exclusion of involuntary confessions in two significant particulars. First, it forbids peace officers to attempt to obtain information from the accused "by plying him with questions" and excludes confessions so obtained. This, however, has not been construed to ban questioning about the crime altogether, after arrest, as the English do, but only to forbid questions so persistent, so repeated, or so accompanied by threats or force, as to amount to duress.[14] Second, by the amendment of 1942, the statute adopts the practice, sanctioned by common law tradition, but abandoned in a majority of states, placing the full responsibility of determining whether it has in fact been complied with, and hence whether the confession is competent, upon the trial judge. Naturally the statute has not abolished third-degree methods in Kentucky,[15] but it is more consistent within itself than the Texas statute and perhaps somewhat better adapted, therefore, as a text for the education of peace officers in respect for civil rights of persons under arrest.

116. The present English Practice in Respect to Questioning Prisoners.

As we have seen, the mere fact that a confession has been elicited from a person in custody is not regarded as a ground of exclusion in this country, in the absence of other pressure, such as threats, violence, promise of leniency or such other influence as may in the particular jurisdiction be considered improper.[1] Actual police practice in this country is based on the assumption that questioning of prisoners by the police is a necessary and ethical procedure provided there is no undue pressure and no deceit or overreaching.[2] This seems likewise to be the standard police practice in Western Europe.[3] In England, however, in the last half-century the evolution of police customs and traditions in this particular has taken a surprising turn. In the 1600's torture as an investigation procedure is still common, but goes out with that century; in the 1700's the rejection of confessions secured by threats and promises begins; and in the 1800's stress is laid on the "voluntariness" of the prisoner's statement and the sufficiency of the warning given him.[4]

In the latter half of the 1800's there began a series of *dicta* and dissents which expressed disapproval of police questioning.[5] Thus, in 1863 a judge in admitting a statement of the accused taken by the police, said: "I entirely

14. Collins **v.** Commonwealth, 296 Ky. 564, 178 S.W.2d 9, syl. 1 (1944), sheriff asked only a few questions; McClain v. Commonwealth, 284 Ky. 359, 144 S.W.2d 816, syl. 5, 6 (1940) (county attorney visited jail with stenographer and asked 160 questions; no violation of prohibition against "plying with questions," which prohibits persistent questioning carried to such extent that prisoner feels under irresistible pressure).

15. Among the 106 third-degree cases during a ten-year period, mentioned in note 12, supra, 4 were in Kentucky.

1. See note 10, § 111 supra.

2. See e.g., Perkins, Elements of Police Science (1942) p. 45, pars. 15, 16 (questioning of suspects); Inbau, Lie Detection and Criminal Interrogation (1942) Part II.

3. See, e.g., Fosdick, European Police Systems (1916) 309 (German practice of interrogating suspects, contrasted with English); Gross, Criminal Investigation (3d ed. by N. Kendal, 1934) 74 (examination of accused; the author was the professor of criminology in the University of Prague); Keedy, The Third Degree and Legal Interrogation of Suspects (1937) 761, 767 (legal powers of interrogation in France).

4. This evolution is fully recounted in 3 Wigmore, Evidence §§ 817–820, 842–47.

5. Reg. v. Kerr, 8 C. & P. 176, 173 Eng.Rep. 449 (1837) (holding confession admissible though secured by police questioning, but expressing disapproval of the practice: by Park, J.); R. v. Thornton, 1 Moody C. C. 27, 168 Eng.Rep. 1171 (1824) (statement held admissible, but three judges dissented); R. v. Wild, 1 Moody C.C. 452, 168 Eng.Rep. 1341 (1835) (similar to Reg. v. Kerr, supra; Reg. v. Gavin, 15 Cox Crim. C. 656 (n.p., 1885) (A. L. Smith, J.: "When a prisoner is in custody, the police have no right to ask him questions. Reading a statement over, and then

disapprove of the system of police officers examining prisoners." [6]

In later cases, the judges, both in England and Canada, have for the most part repeated the expressions condemnatory of police questioning of prisoners but they have declined to hold that statements which are the fruit of such questioning are inadmissible.[7] Nevertheless, they seem to recognize a judicial discretion to exclude.[8] This judicial attitude evidently led to some tendency among the police to look for their guide to the judges' deeds rather than their words, for in 1912 the Home Secretary requested the judges of the King's Bench Division to draw up some rules for police officers on this subject of questioning. This in itself seems a strange extension of the judicial function, but the judges consented and pronounced the following:

(3) "Police Enquiries.
"Memorandum by H. M. Judges of the King's Bench Division
"1. When a police officer is endeavouring to discover the author of a crime there is no objection to his putting questions in respect thereof to any person or persons whether suspected or not from whom he thinks that useful information can be obtained.
"2. Whenever a police officer has made up his mind to charge a person with a crime he should first caution such person before asking any ques-

tions or any further questions as the case may be.
"3. Persons in custody should not be questioned without the usual caution being first administered.
"4. If the prisoner wishes to volunteer any statement the usual caution should be administered. It is desirable that the last two words of such caution should be omitted, and that the caution should end with the words 'be given in evidence.'

"Alverstone, C. J.
October, 1912." [9]

It is apparent, however, that paragraph (3) of these rules touches the allowability of questioning only by implication. Moreover, the implication, contrary to the previous judicial expressions, which the police might reasonably have drawn was that questioning would be proper if a caution was given.

In 1928 the sensational case of Miss Savidge [10] again raised the question of the propriety of the interrogation of persons under arrest. A Royal Commission on Police Powers and Procedure made a forthright recommendation as follows:

[After Arrest]

"Questioning of Persons in Custody. (xlviii) a rigid instruction should be issued to the Police that no questioning of a prisoner, or a 'person in custody, about any crime or offence with which he is, or may be, charged, should be permitted. This does not exclude

saying to him, 'What have you to say?' is cross-examining the prisoner and therefore I shut it out.")

6. Regina v. Mick, 3 F. & F. 822, 823, 176 Eng.Rep. 376 (n.p., 1863).

7. See, e.g., Ibrahim v. The King, [1914] A.C. 599, 610, 611; R. v. Stein, [1928] 3 D.L.R. 792, 806–812 (Ct. App., Man.) (Opinion of Trueman, J. reviews prior cases). Other cases are collected in 3 Wigmore, Evidence § 847, n. 10.

8. R. v. Voisin, [1918] 1 K.B. 531; Phipson Evidence (9th ed. 1952) 268.

9. [1918] 1 K.B. 531 at 539; 3 Wigmore, Evidence 294. In 1918 five additional rules were added by the judges including the following: "(7) A prisoner making a voluntary statement must not be cross-

examined, and no questions should be put to him about it except for the purpose of removing ambiguity in which he has actually said. For instance, if he has mentioned an hour without saying whether it was morning or evening, or has given a day of the week and a day of the month which do not agree, or has not made it clear to what individual or what place he intended to refer in some part of his statement, he may be questioned sufficiently to clear up the point." 1 Taylor, Evidence (12th ed. 1931) 557, 558.

10. See the accounts of this incident in National Commission on Law Observance and Enforcement, Report No. 11, Lawlessness in Law Enforcement 259. See also Howard, Criminal Justice in England (1931) 229–231.

questions to remove elementary and obvious ambiguities in voluntary statements, under No. (7) of the Judges' Rules, but the prohibition should cover all persons who, although not in custody, have been charged and are out on bail while awaiting trial. . . ." [11]

Apparently, this represents the governing policy and practice in England today.[12]

117. Federal Control of State Administration of the Safeguarding Doctrines about confessions.[1]

We have seen that in 1931 the Wickersham Commission reported that there was much evidence that the extortion of confessions by the police by undue pressure was a widespread practice. It was apparent that appellate review in the state courts of convictions thus secured had not sufficed to eliminate the practice. In 1936 the Supreme Court of the United States, in Brown v. Mississippi,[2] was presented with the question whether through the due process clause of the Federal Constitution additional protection could be afforded against the abuses of the third degree. Extensions of the scope of control of state criminal processes, through the use of the due process clause, to avoid a mob-dictated conviction,[3] to pass upon the adequacy of the opportunity to be represented by counsel,[4] and to declare that a conviction secured by known perjury would be invalid,[5] were matters of recent history. In the Brown case

three negroes were charged with murder. They were tried one week after the killing and were represented by appointed counsel. On the basis of the evidence of confessions they were convicted. It appeared, without substantial dispute, that a deputy sheriff, accompanied by other persons, took one of the defendants to the scene and accused him of the crime. "Upon his denial they seized him, and with the participation of the deputy they hanged him by a rope to the limb of a tree, and having let him down, they hung him again, and when he was let down the second time, and he still protested his innocence, he was tied to a tree and whipped, and still declining to accede to the demands that he confess, he was finally released and he returned with some difficulty to his home, suffering intense pain and agony. The record of the testimony shows that the signs of the rope on his neck were plainly visible during the so-called trial." [6] A day or two later, two deputies whipped him until he confessed. The other two "defendants were made to strip and they were laid over chairs and their backs were cut to pieces with a leather strap with buckles on it, and they were likewise made by the said deputy definitely to understand that the whipping would be continued unless and until they confessed, and not only confessed, but confessed in every matter of detail as demanded by those present; and in this manner the defendants confessed the crime." [7] The state supreme court affirmed

11. Quoted, 3 Wigmore, Evidence 295.

12. See Phipson, Evidence, 268–270 (9th ed.1952). A late case in which the question of admissibility is touched obliquely shows the present disfavor of police questioning. R. v. Treacey, [1944] 2 All Eng.L.R. 229, syl. 3 (Ct.App.).

1. Among the important articles in this field are Inbau, The Confession Dilemma in the Supreme Court, 43 Ill.L.Rev. 442 (1948); Scott, Federal Restrictions on Evidence in State Criminal Cases, 34 Minn.L.Rev. 489 (1950); Wicker, Some Developments in the Law Concerning Confessions, 5 Vand. L.Rev. 507 (1952); Matherne, Pre-Trial Confessions —a New Rule, 22 Tenn.L.Rev. 1011 (1953).

On the problem of confessions secured through the commitment of suspects as material witnesses, see Comment, 17 U.Chi.L.Rev. 706 (1950).

2. 297 U.S. 278, 56 Sup.Ct. 461, 80 L.Ed. 682 (1936).

3. Moore v. Dempsey, 261 U.S. 86, 43 Sup.Ct. 265, 67 L.Ed. 543 (1923).

4. Powell v. Alabama, 287 U.S. 45, 53 Sup.Ct. 55, 77 L.Ed. 158 (1932).

5. Mooney v. Holohan, 294 U.S. 103, 55 Sup.Ct. 340, 79 L.Ed. 791 (1935).

6. Brown v. Miss., 297 U.S. 278, 281, 56 Sup.Ct. 461, 80 L.Ed. 682 (1936).

7. Id. at 282.

the conviction, on the ground among others that the objection made to one of the confessions, before the evidence as to the brutal treatment came in, should have been renewed by a motion to exclude the confessions after the evidence showed their inadmissibility. Two justices courageously dissented in forthright opinions. These dissents were probably influential in causing the grant of certiorari. In reversing the convictions, the court, through Hughes, Chief Justice, said that a trial "is a mere pretense where the state authorities have contrived a conviction resting solely upon confessions obtained by violence," and answering the contention that the objection to the confession was insufficient, "the trial court was fully advised by the undisputed evidence of the way in which the confessions had been procured. The trial court knew that there was no other evidence upon which conviction and sentence could be based. Yet it proceeded to permit conviction and to pronounce sentence. The conviction and sentence were void for want of the essential elements of due process, and the proceeding thus vitiated could be challenged in any appropriate manner." [8]

The Brown case thus established the principle. It was marked, however, by two features that made the result easy to accept. First, the conviction rested solely on the confession, and second, there was no substantial dispute as to the fact that the confessions were coerced. These circumstances suggest questions as to the "reach" of the decision. Upon this the later cases shed some light.

Chambers v. Florida,[9] decided in 1940, went far to set the pattern for the application of the new doctrine. Four young negro men were convicted of murder upon proof of their confessions. Again there was a dissent when the state court affirmed. The Supreme Court of the United States, in considering whether due process had been denied by conviction upon forced confessions, was faced at the outset by the fact that the evi-

dence as to coercion had twice been submitted to juries who had found that the confessions were voluntary.[10] Mr. Justice Black, who wrote the opinion for the court, met this objection squarely. "Since petitioners have seasonably asserted the right under the federal Constitution to have their guilt or innocence of a capital crime determined without reliance upon confessions obtained by means proscribed by the due process clause of the Fourteenth Amendment, we must determine independently whether petitioners' confessions were so obtained, by review of the facts upon which that issue necessarily turns." [11]

Nevertheless, overturning a jury's finding upon disputed evidence is uncomfortable business for judges bred in the common law tradition. Accordingly, he searched for undisputed facts upon which to rest his conclusion. He found that the prisoners were arrested without warrant, and held in jail without communication with family and friends, while they were almost continually questioned by officers for six days before they confessed.

The conclusion follows:

> "Here, the record develops a sharp conflict upon the issue of physical violence and mistreatment, but shows, without conflict, the dragnet methods of arrest on suspicion without warrant, and the protracted questioning and cross questioning of these ignorant young colored tenant farmers by state officers and other white citizens, in a fourth floor jail room, where as prisoners they were without friends, advisers or counselors, and under circumstances calculated to break the strongest nerves and the stoutest resistance. Just as our decision in Brown v. Mississippi was based upon the fact that the confessions were the result of com-

8. Id. at 287, 288.

9. 309 U.S. 227, 60 Sup.Ct. 472, 84 L.Ed. 716 (1940).

10. Id. at 227, 228 n. 2.

11. Id. at 228, 229,

pulsion, so in the present case, the admitted practices were such as to justify the statement that 'The undisputed facts showed that compulsion was applied'." [12]

The final passage is an eloquent answer to the argument of convenience:

"We are not impressed by the argument that law enforcement methods such as those under review are necessary to uphold our laws. The Constitution proscribes such lawless means irrespective of the end. . . . Due process of law, preserved for all by our Constitution, commands that no such practice as that disclosed by this record shall send any accused to his death. No higher duty, no more solemn responsibility, rests upon this Court, than that of translating into living law and maintaining this constitutional shield deliberately planned and inscribed for the benefit of every human being subject to our Constitution—of whatever race, creed or persuasion." [13]

The same technique, that is, the recitation of the disputed claim of brutality, but the reliance upon undisputed objective facts as constituting a deprivation of due process, is exemplified in two Texas cases, in which convictions were reversed. [14]

A dissent appears for the first time in a case from California, [15] where the petitioner was described as having little education, but as being intelligent and experienced in business. It was charged that the accused conspired with one Hope to murder his wife and to collect from an insurance company double indemnity as for an accident, and that after Hope at the instigation of the accused had several times caused her to be bitten by rattlesnakes without the desired fatal results, the accused drowned her in a fishpond. The accused, convicted with the death penalty, charged that the use in evidence of his confession denied due process. It appeared without dispute that he was arrested on Sunday, April 19, and that from Sunday night

until Tuesday morning without arraignment he was "repeatedly and persistently questioned at intervals" [16] by officers and an Assistant District Attorney, and was once slapped by an officer. He charged beating also, but this was denied, and dubious under all the evidence; but the admitted detention without production before a magistrate was a violation of local law. [17] As yet, however, there was no confession. Eleven days later, on May 2d, Hope, the accomplice had confessed and a new interrogation of the accused began. He was taken to the District Attorney's office in the afternoon. His request to have an attorney was denied. He was questioned about Hope's statements by the District Attorney until suppertime, when coffee was served, and thereafter the questioning was continued by other officers until midnight. He and the officers and a friend of the latter adjourned to a public cafe for a meal, after which the accused was taken to the District Attorney's office again, where he made a full confessory statement. He testified at the trial that he made this statement because of threats of beating made before the dinner by the officer who had previously slapped him, but who apparently was not present at the dinner or at the time of the statement. The State's evidence was to the effect that the statement was voluntary, and the trial judge admitted it subject to the jury's finding that it was voluntarily made.

12. Id. at 238, 239. It is significant that in a footnote to this passage Mr. Justice Black, in a brief and pointed discussion of the social effects of third-degree practices, repeatedly cites and relies upon the Wickersham Commission's Report on Lawless Enforcement of the Law.

13. 309 U.S. 240, 241.

14. White v. Texas, 310 U.S. 530, 60 Sup.Ct. 1032, 84 L.Ed. 1342 (1940); Ward v. Texas, 316 U.S. 547, 62 Sup.Ct. 1139, 86 L.Ed. 1663 (1942).

15. Lisenba v. California, 314 U.S. 219, 62 Sup.Ct. 280, 86 L.Ed. 166 (1941).

16. Id. at 230.

17. Id. at 234.

The high court, in a long opinion by Roberts, J., affirmed the conviction. The following passages show the court's difficulty in defining the effect it should give to a jury's finding on voluntariness:

"Where the claim is that the prisoner's statement has been procured by such means [threats or promises], we are bound to make an independent examination of the record to determine the validity of the claim. The performance of this duty cannot be foreclosed by the finding of a court, or the verdict of a jury, or both. If the evidence bearing upon the question is uncontradicted, the application of the constitutional provision is unembarrassed by a finding or a verdict in a state court. . . .

"Here, judge and jury passed on the question whether the petitioner's confessions were freely and voluntarily made. . . . Our duty, then, is to determine whether the evidence requires that we set aside the finding of two courts and a jury, and adjudge the admission of the confessions so fundamentally unfair, so contrary to the common concept of ordered liberty, as to amount to a taking of life without due process of law.

". . . On the facts as we have endeavored fairly to set them forth, and in the light of the findings in the state courts, we cannot hold that the illegal conduct in which the law enforcement officers of California indulged, by the prolonged questioning of the prisoner before arraignment, and in the absence of counsel, or their questioning on May 2, coerced the confessions, the introduction of which is the infringement of due process of which the petitioner complains." [18]

Black, J., joined by Douglas, J., dissented on the ground that he believed that the confession was secured by coercion.

As the crude practices of Brown v. Mississippi,[19] namely, hanging and beating, become outmoded, and more subtle pressures such as the protracted interrogation and the prepara-

tory terror with deferred examination, are resorted to, doubt and dissent increase. Thus in Ashcraft v. Tennessee,[20] where the accused, a well-to-do, respectable white man was charged with having hired a negro to murder the former's wife, the accused was grilled from 7:00 Saturday evening until 11:-00 Monday morning. At the latter time, several prominent citizens were called in to hear the alleged confession, and they testified that Ashcraft was cool and collected, with no outward signs of being tired or sleepy. The jury found the confession voluntary. Black, J., for the court, said: "This treatment of the confessions by the two state courts, the manner of the confessions' submission to the jury, and the emphasis upon the great weight to be given confessions make all the more important the kind of 'independent examination' of petitioners' claims which, in any event, we are bound to make. Lisenba v. California, 314 U.S. 219, 237–238, 62 S.Ct. 280, 290–291. Our duty to make that examination could not have been 'foreclosed by the finding of a court, or the verdict of a jury, or both.'
. . .

"We think a situation such as that here shown by uncontradicted evidence is so inherently coercive that its very existence is irreconcilable with the possession of mental freedom by a lone suspect against whom its full coercive force is brought to bear." [21] But Jackson, J., wrote a long dissent which is a powerful exercise in advocacy, and Justices Roberts and Frankfurter joined.

From 1944, when Ashcraft was decided, down to 1953 these themes of the duty of "independent examination" to determine whether under the undisputed facts the cir-

---

18. Id. at 237–240.

19. 297 U.S. 278, 56 Sup.Ct. 461, 80 L.Ed. 682 (1936).

20. 322 U.S. 143, 64 Sup.Ct. 921, 88 L.Ed. 1192 (1944). A similar result was reached on a subsequent appeal. Ashcraft v. Tennessee, 66 Sup.Ct. 544, 327 U. S. 274, 90 L.Ed. 667 (1946).

21. Id. at 147, 148, 154.

cumstances were "inherently coercive" were on the whole the dominant strains in the confessions decisions, and of the convictions in which certiorari was granted a considerable number were reversed for denial of due process.[22] Moreover, in several cases the court declared that if a confession, found under these tests to have been involuntary, was admitted in evidence the conviction would be reversed even though there were other evidence sufficient to convict.[23] Nevertheless, there were a mounting number of dissenters who were disposed to give controlling weight to the deference due to the findings of state judges and juries, upon conflicting evidence, that the confession was voluntary. And the majority of the court have steadily rejected the argument that the securing of the confession during a period when the prisoner's detention was illegal because of failure to produce him promptly for a preliminary hearing is of itself a sufficient basis for overturning the conviction on due process grounds.[24]

In a recent important case,[25] there were undisputed circumstances in the taking of the confessions, which might have led the court, in the days of Ashcraft, to find them upon "independent examination" to have been "inherently coercive." The prisoners confessed only after about twelve hours of intermittent questioning, stretched out over a thirty-two hour period, with intervals for eating and sleeping. They were illegally detained without arraignment. When examined by a doctor after arraignment, they bore bruises which could have been caused by beatings administered during their detention. There were, however, countervailing circumstances,[26] and the court, emphasizing the primary responsibility of state jurors and judges for weighing the facts and protecting the fairness of the trial, concluded that the jury could reasonably have found that the confessions were voluntary. Three justices dissented. The tone if not the tenor of the opinion may portend a somewhat greater reluctance in the future than in the recent past to overturn convictions based on confessions where there is substantial but disputed evidence of coercion.[27]

---

22. Reversed: Malinski v. New York, 324 U.S. 401, 65 Sup.Ct. 781, 89 L.Ed. 1029 (1945) (four justices dissenting); Ashcraft v. Tennessee, second appeal, 327 U.S. 274, 66 Sup.Ct. 544, 90 L.Ed. 667 (1946); Haley v. Ohio, 332 U.S. 596, 68 Sup.Ct. 302, 92 L.Ed. 224 (1948) (four justices dissenting); Lee v. Mississippi, 332 U.S. 742, 68 Sup.Ct. 300, 92 L.Ed. 330 (1948); Watts v. Indiana, 338 U.S. 49, 69 Sup.Ct. 1347, 93 L.Ed. 1801 (1949) (three justices dissenting); Turner v. Pennsylvania, 338 U.S. 62, 69 Sup.Ct. 1352, 93 L.Ed. 1810 (1949) (four justices dissenting); Harris v. South Carolina, 338 U.S. 68, 69 Sup.Ct. 1354, 93 L.Ed. 1815 (1949) (three justices dissenting).
Affirmed: Lyons v. Oklahoma, 322 U.S. 143, 64 Sup.Ct. 921, 88 L.Ed. 1192 (1944) (three justices dissenting) (second confession); Gallegos v. Nebraska, 342 U.S. 55, 72 Sup.Ct. 141, 96 L.Ed. 86 (1951) (held by four justices that conviction based on confession obtained during period of unlawful detention not a deprivation of due process, two concurring justices doubted that detention was unreasonable, two dissented); Stroble v. California, 343 U.S. 181, 196, 197, 72 Sup.Ct. 599, 96 L.Ed. 872 (1952) (three justices dissenting); Brown v. Allen, 344 U.S. 443, 475, 476, 73 Sup.Ct. 397, 416, 417, 97 L.Ed. 469 (1953) (if coerced confession received in evidence, the resulting conviction denies due process, even though there

was other evidence sufficient to convict; but the fact that the confession was secured during a period of detention illegal because of delay in arraignment, not of itself a ground for holding that conviction denied due process).

23. Malinski v. New York, Brown v. Allen, next preceding note.

24. Gallegos v. Nebraska, Brown v. Allen, note 22 above.

25. Stein v. New York, 346 U.S. 156, 73 Sup.Ct. 1077, 97 L.Ed. 1522 (1953). See comment, 67 Harv.L.Rev. 118, and an interesting analysis of the decision and its implications by Prof. Robert W. Miller, 5 Syracuse L.Rev. 53 (1953). See likewise the able article, Paulsen, the Fourteenth Amendment and the Third Degree, 6 Stan.L.Rev. 411 (1954).

26. Thus, as to one prisoner it appeared that before he confessed he successfully bargained for exemption of his brother from prosecution for parole violation. The prisoners did not testify to having been beaten—they did not testify at all—and the police on the stand denied any brutality. The doctor who examined the prisoners testified that the bruises might have ante-dated arrest.

27. The opinion may be thought to cast doubt on the doctrine that if a confession which the Supreme

118. The Federal Doctrine of the Inadmissibility in Federal Trials of Confessions Secured While the Accused is Unlawfully Detained.[1]

Perhaps as a result of the court's observation, in its review of state cases, of the evils of third-degree practices, the Supreme Court of the United States, in two cases decided together in 1943, announced a new policy in respect to the use of confessions in Federal criminal trials. In the McNabb [2] case the defendants were five members of a clan of Tennessee mountaineers who made and sold illicit whiskey. An informer led revenue officers at night to a rendezvous in a graveyard near the McNabb settlement. There they found the whiskey which was to be delivered, but the McNabbs disappeared in the darkness. One of the officers going too far in pursuit was shot and killed. The next day, Thursday, several of the McNabbs were arrested by the Federal officers, brought to Chattanooga and placed in a detention room, and finally in jail. They were questioned intermittently but extensively, separately and together, until the following Saturday, and three of them made incriminating statements. During this time, so far as the record showed,[3] they were not brought before a United States commissioner or judge, and were not given access to family, friends, or counsel. They were prosecuted in the Federal court for murder of an officer engaged in the performance of duty, and the three who confessed were convicted, principally on the evidence of these statements. The opinion of the Court for reversal, written by Frankfurter, J., leaves wide scope for differing interpretations. It stresses at the outset the distinction between the power of the federal Supreme Court to maintain "civilized standards of procedure and evidence" in federal tribunals and the more limited review of state convictions under the due process clause. The opinion then refers to the federal statutes requiring the prompt production of a person arrested before the nearest judicial officer for hearing commitment or bail,[4] points out that their purpose is the prevention of secret interrogation and third-degree practices, and refers to the English

Court concludes was coerced is admitted at the trial, this is ground for reversal though there was other evidence sufficient to convict. See note 23, above. This doctrine is an important safeguard and its abandonment would be unfortunate. But the doctrine was put to a distorted use by the defense, who asked for an instruction at the trial, that if the jury found the confessions were involuntary, they must acquit, though in fact there was ample other evidence from which they could find guilt. This was refused, and the Supreme Court held that there was no constitutional error in such refusal. If a coerced confession is admitted, with instruction to the jury that they may consider it on the issue of guilt, this is constitutional error. But the remedy, as the Court held, is not an instruction to acquit. It is the granting of a new trial below or in a reviewing court for the use in evidence of a confession that could not reasonably have been found to be voluntary, followed by a conviction. It is believed that the holding here is not an abandonment of the former doctrine as to the effect of admitting a coerced confession where there is other evidence. See the acute discussion in Meltzer, Comment on Stein v. People, 21 U.Chi.L.Rev. 317, 344–354 (1954). See also Bennett, The Decade of Change since the Ashcraft Case, 32 Tex.L.Rev. 429 (1954).

1. See Inbau, The Confession Dilemma in the Supreme Court, 43 Ill.L.Rev. 442 (1948); Wicker, Some Developements in the Law Concerning Confessions, 5 Vand.L.Rev. 507 (1952).

2. McNabb v. United States, 318 U.S. 332, 63 Sup.Ct. 608, 87 L.Ed. 819 (1943). Among numerous comments, the following are especially discriminating: (1943) 56 Harv.L.Rev. 1008 (critical); J. B. Waite (1944) 42 Mich.L.Rev. 679, 909 (critical); (1943) 28 Minn.L.Rev. 73 (favorable); H. Pressley (1944) 22 Texas Law Review 473 (favorable); 1945 Wis.L. Rev. 105; (1944) 53 Yale L.J. 758.

3. "It is interesting to add that in the McNabb case the Supreme Court decision actually rested on a misapprehension as to facts. The McNabbs were in fact arraigned in timely fashion, though the record did not show that the arraignment had occurred. There has since been a retrial with the confessions admitted by the trial court under the McNabb rule and convictions of manslaughter duly returned." Testimony of Attorney General Biddle, p. 29, Hearings on H. R. 3690, Serial No. 12 (Government Printing office 1944).

4. Fed.Rules Crim.Proc. rule 5(a), 18 U.S.C.A.; 18 U.S.C.A. §§ 3052, 3107.

rules, hereinabove discussed, relating to the interrogation of prisoners. It concludes:

> "The record leaves no room for doubt that the questioning of the petitioners took place while they were in the custody of the arresting officers and before any order of commitment was made. Plainly, a conviction resting on evidence secured through such a flagrant disregard of the procedure which Congress has commanded cannot be allowed to stand without making the courts themselves accomplices in willful disobedience of law. Congress has not explicitly forbidden the use of evidence so procured. But to permit such evidence to be made the basis of a conviction in the federal courts would stultify the policy which Congress has enacted into law." [5]

Does this mean that the fact that the statements were taken at a time when the detention was illegal because of the delay in arraignment was sufficient to require their exclusion, or were the additional pressures of protracted questioning and denial of access to friends and counsel essential to that result?

The Anderson case [6] was similar, except that the detention was by state officers,

seemingly acting at the instance of federal officers, who conducted the questioning. The federal offense was damage to government property by union miners on strike. The court held that the failure to produce the prisoners for commital, as required by the Tennessee statute, coupled with the circumstances of unlawful arrest, protracted questioning by federal agents, and the holding of the prisoners *incommunicado* required the exclusion of the confessions.

The Mitchell case,[7] decided in 1944, marked out one clear and needed limitation upon the McNabb doctrine, namely that delay in arraignment occurring after the confession will not be a reason for exclusion, where the confession was voluntarily made after the arrest but before the time for prompt arraignment had elapsed. A still more important decision in 1948 answered the question, mentioned above, whether other forms of pressure such as protracted questioning or holding *incommunicado* must combine with the mere illegal detention to render the confession incompetent. This was Upshaw v. United States, a five-to-four decision, wherein the majority interprets the former rulings as meaning "that a confession is inadmissible if

---

5. 318 U.S. 332 at 344, 345, 63 Sup.Ct. 608, 87 L.Ed. 819 (1943).

6. Anderson v. United States, 318 U.S. 350, 63 Sup. Ct. 599, 87 L.Ed. 829 (1943).

7. United States v. Mitchell, 322 U.S. 65, 64 Sup.Ct. 896, 88 L.Ed. 1140 (1944). The defendant was convicted for housebreaking and larceny in the District of Columbia. The Court of Appeals reversed on account of the admission of his confession, and the Government secured certiorari. The following passages from the opinion (Frankfurter, J.,) disclose the facts and holding: "In August and early October 1942, two houses in the District of Columbia were broken into and from each property was stolen. The trail of police investigation led to Mitchell who was taken into custody at his home at 7 o'clock in the evening on Monday, October 12, 1942, and driven by two police officers to the precinct station. Within a few minutes of his arrival at the police station, Mitchell admitted guilt, told the officers of various items of stolen property to be found in his home and consented to their going to his home to recover the property. It is

these admissions and that property which supported the convictions, and which were deemed by the court below to have been inadmissible. * * * "But the circumstances of legality attending the making of these oral statements are nullified, it is suggested, by what followed. For not until eight days after the statements were made was Mitchell arraigned before a committing magistrate. Undoubtedly his detention during this period was illegal. . . . But in any event, the illegality of Mitchell's detention does not retroactively change the circumstances under which he made the disclosures. These, we have seen, were not elicited through illegality. Their admission, therefore, would not be use by the Government of the fruits of wrongdoing by its officers. Being relevant, they could be excluded only as a punitive measure against unrelated wrongdoing by the police. Our duty in shaping rules of evidence relates to the propriety of admitting evidence. This power is not to be used as an indirect mode of disciplining misconduct." 322 U.S. 65 at 69, 70, 71.
Black, J., dissented without opinion; Douglas, J., Rutledge, J., and Reed, J., concurred in the result.

made during illegal detention due to failure promptly to carry a prisoner before a committing magistrate, whether or not the 'confession is the result of torture, physical or psychological. . . .' " [8] But the mere fact that the confession was made before arraignment does not invalidate it, if it was not made during an "unnecessary delay." [9] Thus, if the prisoner voluntarily confesses, under moderate questioning, while the police are awaiting the time when the Commissioner's office will be open, [10] or while they are momentarily checking the leads given by the prisoner's voluntary statements, [11] the detention may not be illegal. Moreover, if the prisoner is lawfully arrested, promptly taken before the magistrate and held for trial, on one charge, he may while so held be moderately questioned about another crime. [12] Since he is lawfully detained on the previous committal there is no obstacle to proper questioning. Doubtless the court might reach a different result if the first charge were a mere pretext designed solely to create an op-

portunity to question the prisoner about another crime.

119. The Future of Confessions.

The decisions which condemn convictions in state courts on involuntary confessions as denials of due process have declared doctrines which are binding on state courts and state legislatures as well. Already they have made their impress on state decisions. For example, we now find some state courts reversing convictions on the ground that the confession was secured by protracted questioning. [1]

What of the future of the doctrine of the McNabb case which excludes a confession secured by federal officers during an unlawful delay in arraignment? Will this rule be abrogated by legislation or will its domain be extended to prosecutions in state courts? The McNabb case was greeted with a fiercer critical barrage than any other recent federal decision in the field of criminal procedure. The Hobbs bill [2] was drafted to repeal the

---

8. Upshaw v. United States, 335 U.S. 410, 413, 69 Sup.Ct 170, 172, 93 L.Ed. 100 (1948). Here the prisoner was arrested without a warrant on suspicion of larceny and was held, without commital, for thirty hours, during which time he confessed. The only purpose in holding him was for questioning. Black, J., for the majority said that "the plain purpose of the requirement that prisoners should promptly be taken before committing magistrates was to check resort by officers to 'secret interrogation of persons accused of crime.' " (p. 412). The opinion of Reed, J., for the minority is a powerful argument for the more limited interpretation of the McNabb holding.

Compare a recent opinion which would similarly limit the holding in Upshaw v. United States by interpreting it to invalidate confessions obtained during illegal detention, only when the confession was actually produced by the detention. Purce v. United States, 197 F.2d 189, syl. 1 (C.A.D.C.1952) (the court also held that the detention was not unreasonable). This test sets a task of proof which it would be impracticable for the defendant to meet, except in cases of prolonged detention.

9. Haines v. United States, 188 F.2d 546, syl. 5–8 (C.A. 9, 1951) (defendant has burden of showing delay unnecessary), noted 100 U.Pa.L.Rev. 136, 25 So. Cal.L.Rev. 215.

10. Garner v. United States, 174 F.2d 499, syl. 2–4 (C.A.D.C.1949) (one judge dissenting), noted 48 Mich. L.Rev. 1028.

11. United States v. Leviton, 193 F.2d 848, syl. 4–6 (C.A.2, 1951) (lucid opinion by C. E. Clark, Circ. J. and strong dissent by Frank, Circ. J.), ably noted by Steely, 31 Tex.L.Rev. 212.

12. United States v. Carignan, 342 U.S. 36, 72 Sup.Ct. 97, 96 L.Ed. 48 (1951), noted 36 Minn.L.Rev. 271, 3 Stan.L.Rev. 727, 60 Yale L.J. 1228. The last note makes the constructive suggestion that Fed.R.Crim. Proc. 5 be amended to provide for a limited rearraignment of a prisoner before questioning on another offense, so as to secure (a) a statement of the charge, (b) explanation of his right not to answer, and (c) advice as to his right to counsel.

1. Coker v. State, 199 Ga. 20, 33 S.E.(2d) 171, syl. 7 (1945); People v. Goldblatt, 383 Ill. 176, 49 N.E.2d 36, syl. 8 (1943).

2. This bill as amended and favorably reported, May 24, 1944, by the Judiciary Committee of the House of Representatives reads:

"The failure to observe the requirement of law as to the time within which a person under arrest must be brought before a magistrate, commissioner or court shall not render inadmissible any evidence that is otherwise admissible." Hearings cited note

doctrine. An attempt to embody the holding in the new Federal Rules of Criminal Procedure failed.[3] The existence of a genuine need in law enforcement for a brief period of private interrogation of suspected persons by the police has been suggested.[4] But the McNabb doctrine as limited and applied in the Mitchell case[5] does not forbid such questioning in the interval between arrest and prompt compliance with the arraignment statute. Under the state statutes which require production of the prisoner "immediately" or "forthwith," any detention for interrogation, however brief, may be questioned. Probably the interests of civil liberty and of effective investigation of crimes can best be balanced by a relaxing of the require-

ment for "immediate" production. "Within a reasonable time," suggested by Attorney General Biddle[6] seems to leave too wide a discretion in the arresting officer. "Without unnecessary delay," the provision of the present Rule 5(a) of the Federal Rules of Criminal Procedure, gives flexibility, without too great latitude for abuse.[7] Possibly a specific limit, of say, twenty-four hours, as in the English statute,[8] would be a desirable safeguard.

Though the court in the McNabb case was careful to point out that it was announcing a rule only for federal prosecutions, some state decisions have already acknowledged the persuasive force of the precedent.[9] The

---

115 supra; Report No. 1509 to accompany H.R. 3690, 78 Cong.2d session, p. 1 (May 24, 1944).

3. In the preliminary draft, Rule 5(a) required production before the commissioner "without unnecessary delay" and 5(b) was as follows: "Exclusion of Statement Secured in Violation of Rule. No statement made by a defendant in response to interrogation by an officer or agent of the government shall be admissible in evidence against him if the interrogation occurs while the defendant is held in custody in violation of this rule." Prel.Draft, Fed. Rules Crim. Proc. (1943) 11, and a carefully documented argument in support of the proposed rule was presented. Id., at 11–16. In the Second Preliminary Draft, Rule 5, p. 10, 1944, the quoted section of the rule was omitted, and so in the Rules of Criminal Procedure, Rule 5 (1946).

4. Note (1944) 53 Yale L.J. 758, 765; and see 3 Wigmore, Evidence § 851, pp. 318, 319.

Moreover, it is urged that an even wider need for holding a prisoner without a hearing stems from the danger that a hearing of one suspect, in cases of gang crime, will give the alarm to the others and prevent or impede their capture. See letter of J. Edgar Hoover to Secretary, Advisory Committee on Federal Rules of Criminal Procedure, opposing proposed Rule 5(b), quoted by Waite (1944) 42 Mich.L. Rev. 679–691 (referring to cases of espionage, kidnapping, and bank robbery). See also the testimony of Attorney General Biddle: "In the saboteurs' cases Mr. Hoover called me, I think it was Thursday night when the first saboteur was arrested. The last one was not arrested until 8 or 9 days later. If we had arraigned the first one immediately, that would have forewarned the other seven who were in possession of these dangerous implements. Therefore, I specifically had to disre-

gard the law requiring me to arraign all of them immediately, for the preservation of the country." Hearings, cited note 3, § 118, supra, at pp. 35, 36. The case referred to was Ex Parte Quirin, 317 U.S. 1, 63 Sup.Ct. 1, 87 L.Ed. 3 (1942). Procedures such as "investigatory imprisonment" and "prison arraignment" in cases of special danger have been suggested to meet these needs. Note (1944) 53 Yale L.J. 758, 769 et seq.

5. United States v. Mitchell, 322 U.S. 65, 64 Sup.Ct. 896, 88 L.Ed. 1140 (1944).

6. Hearings, cited note 3, § 118 supra, at p. 35. This suggestion is embodied in the report of the Judiciary Committee on H. R. 43, the successor to the Hobbs Bill, which recommends that the federal statutory provisions for preliminary hearing be so amended. Report N. 245, 79th Congress, 1st Session, pp. 7, 8 (March 2, 1945).

7. The phrase appears in some state statutes; e. g., Calif.Penal Code, § 849; Idaho, I.C. §§ 19–515, 19–615.

8. Summary Jurisdiction Act, 42 and 43 Vict. c. 49, § 38 (1879) cited Note (1944) 53 Yale L.J. 758, 767 n. 56. California has a limit as follows, "in any event, within two days after his arrest, excluding Sundays and holidays." Penal Code, § 825.

9. See, e. g., the following cases, none of which, however, turned on delay in arraignment: Palmore v. State, 244 Ala. 227, 12 So.(2d) 854 (1943) (cites McNabb case, but reverses for other coercive pressures in securing confession); State v. Behler, 65 Idaho 464, 146 P.2d 338, 340 (1944) (cites with apparent approval but holds no "unnecessary delay" shown); State v. Ellis, 207 La. 812, 22 So.(2d) 181 (1945) (promise of leniency); State v. Collett, 58 N.E.(2d)

groundwork may have been laid in judicial thinking for a future holding that due process of law demands the suppression of statements taken under the pressure of illegal detention.[10]

Nevertheless, even when confined to the brief period before a prompt arraignment, the secret questioning by the police of a person in custody is still subject to dangers of pressure and abuse. England, schooled in a long tradition of law-abidingness, has been able to go further as we have seen, and to require as the normal practice at least that questioning of suspects by the police be conducted before arrest.[11] In Scotland the rule is even more clear-cut. "Interrogations of arrested persons by the police are forbidden and confessions and admissions obtained in this way are inadmissible in evidence." [12] Desirable as such a reform would be in the interest of liberty of the citizen, it could only be maintained in a community where the crime rate

is relatively low, where the police are highly efficient and trained to a strong sense of professional ethics, and where the community has a regard for civil rights so strong that it will insist upon the maintenance of these rights even in favor of the "least of these,"— the disreputable and the outcast.

The Wickersham Commission in 1931 reported that probably the best remedy for the evils of the third degree "would be the enforcement of the rule that every person arrested charged with crime should be forthwith taken before a magistrate, advised of the charge against him, given the right to have counsel and then interrogated by the magistrate. His answers should be recorded and should be admissible in evidence against him in all subsequent proceedings. If he choose not to answer, it should be permissible for counsel for the prosecution and for the defense, as well as for the trial judge, to comment on his refusal." [13] Doubtless he should

---

417, 425, 426 (Oh.App., 1944) (recognizes persuasive effect of McNabb case but distinguished on ground delay did not cause confession); Foster v. State, 79 Okl.Cr. 183, 152 P.(2d) 929, syl. 6 (1944) (emphasizes need for caution in taking statements before defendant has counsel or hearing); Cavazos v. State, 146 Tex.Cr. 144, 172 S.W.(2d) 348, 350 (1943) (refers to holding in McNabb case with seeming approval but reverses conviction because of protracted questioning inducing confession).

Other cases announce their unwillingness to follow the McNabb doctrine, e. g., Hall v. State, 209 Ark. 180, 189 S.W.(2d) 917, syl. 1 (1945); Bryant v. State, 197 Ga. 641, 30 S.E.(2d) 259, 263 (1944); State v. Smith, 158 Kan. 645, 149 P.(2d) 600, 604 (1944).

10. For a forceful brief argument for this view, see Comment, Illegal Delay and Confessions—a "Civilized Standard," 1 Catholic Univ.L.Rev. 1 (1950). The prevalence of statutes requiring prompt arraignment in England and in nearly all American jurisdictions is some evidence that due process requires it. It is another step to say that due process requires the exclusion of confessions under pressure of illegal detention, but the following passage from the opinion (Loring, C. J.) in State v. Schabert, 218 Minn. 1, 15 N.W.2d 585, 587, 588 (1944) suggests that the step is a short one: "While in this state we have no statute such as the Federal statute, or such as most states have, requiring that the arrested accused be immediately taken before a judge

or magistrate, where, of course, he would be entitled to counsel . . . we believe that fundamental fairness to the accused requires that he should with reasonable promptness be taken before a magistrate in order to prevent the application of methods approaching what is commonly called the 'third degree.' 'Fundamental fairness' prohibits the secret inquisition in order to obtain evidence. Certainly, delay in arraignment is a circumstance to be considered with other facts tending to show that the accused was subjected to pressure to obtain a confession."

11. See notes 7–12, § 116, supra, and see also the references to the English practice in Prel.Draft, Fed.Rules Crim.Proc. (1943) 15, 16, and in Note (1944) 53 Yale L.J. 758, 767, 768.

12. Keedy, Criminal Procedure in Scotland (1913) 16, 17, 18 cited Prel.Draft, Fed.Rules Crim.Proc. (1943) 14.

13. National Commission on Law Observance and Enforcement, Report No. 11, Lawlessness in Law Enforcement (1931) 5. Among the eminent lawyer members of the commission was Dean Roscoe Pound, who further supported this reform in an article, Legal Interrogation of Persons Accused or Suspected of Crime (1934) 24 J.Crim.L. and Criminology 1014 (1934). See also 3 Wigmore, Evidence § 851, p. 320; Kauper, Judicial Examination of the Accused—A Remedy for the Third Degree (1932) 30 Mich.L.Rev. 1224.

be informed also that he is not required to answer.[14] Even so, it has been suggested that the procedure would infringe the constitutional privilege against self-incrimination.[15] There are decisions which support this view.[16] It is believed, however, that the courts as they become more conversant with the history of the privilege will see that it is a survival that has outlived the context that gave it meaning, and that its application today is not to be extended but is to be kept within the limits of realism and common sense.[17] Thus tested, the procedure of judicial interrogation safeguarded as suggested above might well secure eventual sanction by the courts.

This procedure would remove some of the present pressure felt by the police to resort to the abuses of the third degree, by giving a legal opportunity for extended examination not now afforded. Nevertheless it would not be a cure-all.[18] A resolute suspect having the benefit of counsel is much less likely to give incriminating information in a judicial hearing than under the pressure of police questioning. Abstention from third-degree abuses will still depend on the ability of the police to protect society without resort to them.[19]

Science can be a substitute for cruelty Interrogation accompanied by measurement of emotional responses has proved its value, when professionally conducted and interpreted.[20] Other methods of scientific proof, apart from examination of suspects, may likewise make extorted confessions unnecessary. Examples are fingerprint, handwriting, and typewriting identification; firearms identification by the use of the comparison microscope; the blood-grouping tests for paternity; and blood-tests to determine intoxication.[21] Manifestly, the full use of these resources for the protection of society against crime can only be accomplished by a well-selected, professionally-trained body of law enforcement officers. Notable examples prove that such a service can furnish a career attractive to young men of integrity, talent, and public spirit. A general demand for higher standards of personnel and more humane methods of interrogation, for officers who can respect individual rights and at the same time defend the community, will come with the widening of popular understanding of the problem. To lead in creating this understanding is the duty and the opportunity of lawyers.

14. See the rule proposed by Prof. J. B. Waite, a member of the Advisory Committee, Prel.Draft, Fed.Rules Crim.Proc. (1943) 249. It was rejected by the Committee. Id. at 253.

15. It was suggested by the Committee that Prof. Waite's proposed rule (see note 140 supra) in providing for interrogation violated the privilege though it stipulated that he was not required to answer and that his refusal to answer could not be used against him. Id. at 253.

16. Interrogation at preliminary hearing as violation. State v. Smith, 56 S.D. 238, 228 N.W. 240 (1929). Compare 8 Wigmore, Evidence § 2268 (2), n. 6. Comment on silence as compulsion to testify. State v. Wolfe, 64 S.D. 178, 266 N.W. 116 (1936); In Re Opinion of the Justices, 300 Mass. 620, 15 N.E.

(2d) 662 (1938). See the cogent dissenting opinions in each case, and the acute discussion of the cases by D. M. Swope (1939) 37 Mich.L.Rev. 777 (1939).

17. 8 Wigmore, Evidence §§ 2250, 2251, esp. pp. 304, 319.

18. Thus, Prof. Keedy found evidence that in France, where preliminary judicial examination is authorized, the abuses of the third degree were not unknown. The Third Degree and Legal Interrogation of Suspects (1937) 85 U.Pa.L.Rev. 761.

19. See Warner's excellent article, How Can the Third Degree be Eliminated (1940) 1 Bill of Rights Review 24.

20. See § 174, herein.

21. See Ch. 20, herein.

CHAPTER 13

THE PRIVILEGE AGAINST SELF-INCRIMINATION [1]

120. History.[2]

The privilege not to answer questions as to one's own criminal acts is so surprising, and runs so counter to any rational system of investigation, that we instinctively turn to history for an explanation. The facts as yet have been only incompletely garnered.

The mystical and emotional atmosphere of the privilege may be partly accounted for by the fact that the procedure from which the outcry of protest arose and the maxim, no man shall be compelled to accuse himself, took their origin in the canons of the medieval church.

In 1236 there was instituted in the ecclesiastical courts in England a new procedure by which a party might be required to answer specific questions asked him by the judge, under an oath to speak the truth (de veritate dicenda).[3] This stood in contrast with the older procedure of compurgation, later known as wager of law. Under this, the party took an oath, it is true, but the oath sworn by him

and his oath-helpers was a ritual, upon the correct pronouncing of which the decision of the case turned.[4] Under the old ritual there was no questioning by the judge; under the new there was the thrust of the judge's

---

1. 8 Wigmore, Evidence, §§ 2250-2284; Decennial Digests, Witnesses ⊖292–310, Criminal Law, ⊖ 393, 721; Corwin, The Supreme Court's Construction of the Self-Incrimination Clause, 29 Mich.L. Rev. 1, 191 (1930).

2. 8 Wigmore, Evidence, § 2250 (a brilliant but occasionally over-confident exposition); Mary Hume Maguire, Attack of the Common Lawyers on the Oath Ex Officio, in Essays in History and Political Theory in Honor of C. H. McIlwain, 199 (Harv. Univ. Press. 1936); Pittman, The Colonial and Constitutional History of the Privilege against Self-Incrimination in America, 21 Va.L.Rev. 763 (1935); Riesenfeld, Law-Making and Legislative Precedent in American Legal History, 33 Minn.L.Rev. 103, 115–120 (1949); Morgan, The Privilege against Self-Incrimination, 34 Minn.L.Rev. 1–23 (1950). All of these will be cited throughout this section simply by the authors' names.

3. Wigmore, 278.

4. Wigmore, 279–281.

sharp questions [5] and the uncomfortable consciousness of one's oath to tell the whole truth.

Like so many reforms it was feared and disliked. In about 1326 a statute prescribed that the royal officers should not permit any persons in their districts to come together for any "recognitions" to be taken on their oaths, except in matrimonial and testamentary causes—the traditional fields of civil jurisdiction of the church courts.[6] This famous statute was probably as much the expression of a firm intent to hold in narrow channels the business of the foreign-dominated church courts as of a desire to limit the use of the new and efficient practice of oath and inquisition.

As the church courts, and the newly created special King's courts of High Commission and Star Chamber using the same procedure, reach out to punish heresy and sedition, the effectiveness of the inquisitional procedure begins to pinch tighter and tighter, and the dissenters tend more and more to urge restrictions upon the use of the oath and interrogation. Perhaps the actual association of this procedure with the use of torture may have largely contributed both to its effectiveness and to the increasing odium with which it was regarded.[7] The canonists had always laid down certain safeguarding conditions upon the use of the inquisitional oath, though their scope was ill-defined and open to debate at the time of the English controversies under the Tudors and Stuarts. There was at least support for the view that before the inquisitional oath could be administered to a party there must have been some form of specific accusation, either by a private person or a public accuser, or if that were lacking and the judge were to act on his own initiative (*ex officio mero*) then he must show "common report" or "notorious suspicion" of the guilt of the party.[8] The controversy in England centered around this last, the *ex officio* oath—at first, over the precedent conditions and latterly, over the question, was it lawful at all in penal proceedings? But until the final demolition stage, the assumption always was that if the required form of accusation had first been made, the interrogation under oath about the charges would be lawful.

When the maxim, no man shall be compelled to accuse himself, which in various forms goes far back in patristic [9] and canonist [10] writings, comes first to be used in these English controversies, it seems to have acquired this meaning last described, namely, that no man without a prior specific charge shall be compelled to submit to a "fishing" interrogation about his crimes. No man shall be compelled to make the *first charge* against himself.[11]

---

5. Compare Cotton Mather's advice to one of the judges before the Salem Witch Trials, "Now first a credible confession of the guilty wretches is one of the most hopefull wayes of coming at them . . . . I am farr from urging the Un-English method of torture . . . but whatever hath a tendency to put the witches into confusion is likely to bring unto confession. . . . Here Crosse & Swift Questions have their use." Pittman, 782.

6. This was the statute De Articulis Cleri. Wigmore, 286.

7. Compare Morgan, 14, 15.

8. Wigmore, 283.

9. "Its roots can probably be traced to a statement of St. Chrysostomous (ca. 400) in his commentary to St. Paul's Epistle to the Hebrews. Said he:

'Non tibi dico ut ea tamquam pompam in publicum proferas, neque ut apud alios te accuses' (I don't tell you to display that [your sin] before the public like a decoration, nor to accuse yourself in front of others)." Riesenfeld, 118.

10. "This rule was incorporated into Gratian's celebrated Decretum, which was a restatement of early canon law, in the following form: 'Non tibi dico, ut te prodas in publicum, neque apud alios accuses' (I don't tell you to incriminate yourself publicly or to accuse yourself before others)." Riesenfeld, 118. 7 Enc. Soc. Sc. titl. Gratian, 156 (1932). But see the view of Corwin that the maxim was not derived from any text of canon law. Op. cit. 29 Mich.L.Rev. 1, 3.

11. See Morgan, 8, 9.

By the second decade of the 1600s the opposition of Coke and the non-conformists to high-handed methods in heresy hunts had established the doctrine that the ex officio oath and interrogation, without formal accusation, was unlawful for the ecclesiastical courts (including the Court of High Commission) in any punitive proceeding. But this still fell far short of acceptance of any general prohibition against requiring a man to speak about his crimes. The Star Chamber was specifically empowered by statute to examine the accused on oath in criminal cases, without mention of the canon law safeguards.[12] Up to the eve of the Commonwealth period its arrogant practices aroused resentment in the popular party, and the *ex officio* oath was the symbol if not the chief means of its offending.

John Lilburn, a libertarian as obdurate as the Court was high-handed, brought its downfall. He was formally charged in the Star Chamber with printing or importing certain heretical and seditious books. After arrest, he was examined by the Attorney General and denied these charges. Then he was interrogated about other like matters. Mark his answer. "I am not willing to answer you to any more of these questions, because I see you go about by this examination to ensnare me; for, seeing the things for which I am imprisoned cannot be proved against me, you will get other matter out of my examination; and therefore, if you will not ask me about the thing laid to my charge, I shall answer no more . . ." Later before the Court he said ". . . if I had been proceeded against by a bill, I would have answered." For his "boldness in refusing to take a legal oath" he was whipped and pilloried. Three years later, when the Long Parliament met he laid before them his complaint of this treatment, and after four years more, the Lords set aside his conviction, "it being contrary to the laws of God, nature and the Kingdom for any man to be his own ac-

cuser."[13] In the same year, bills were passed abolishing the courts of High Commission and Star Chamber, and forbidding all ecclesiastical courts to administer any oath, ex officio or otherwise, whereby the party may be obliged to accuse himself of any crime. When Charles II came in this last provision was re-enacted in strengthened form.[14] By 1700, as Wigmore concludes, professional opinion was agreed that those courts had lost all power to exact an oath from a person about matters which might subject him to punishment or forfeiture.[15]

Down to the dramatic aftermath of Lilburn's case, there was little evidence of any general prohibition applicable in common law courts against requiring an accused to incriminate himself. Thus under a general, and many special statutes, it was provided that persons charged with crime should be examined by justices of the peace, or other officers, upon a preliminary hearing and the examination recorded and preserved for use at the trial.[16] So far as appears this practice, which recognized no privilege of refusal to answer, was not challenged until the middle 1700s. Not until 1848 was it modified by Sir John Jervis's Act which provided that the accused should not be questioned but could make a statement after being warned that he need not do so.[17] Moreover, during all the period of agitation against the inquisitional oath of the ecclesiastical courts, down to the time of Lilburn's case, it was the unchallenged practice of the common law judges in criminal trials to question the accused and

12.   Wigmore, 289, Coke, as a member of the Star Chamber, consented to the practice there. Id. 290 note 64.

13.   Wigmore, 291, summarizes the report of Lilburn's Trial, 3 How.St.Tr. 1315 (1637–1645).

14.   Wigmore, 292.

15.   Wigmore, 292.

16.   Wigmore, 294.

17.   Morgan, 14.

bully him to admit his guilt.[18] It is true, he was not under oath, for he was then incompetent as a witness, but there was no thought that he could not be called on to incriminate himself. By 1641, as an aftermath of Lilburn's case, defendants began to claim, and judges to be persuaded, that an accused on trial was not to be compelled to disclose his guilt.[19] Here again by the early 1700s, the revolution was complete and the general principle becomes accepted that in all proceedings civil as well as criminal not only parties but witnesses as well [20] are privileged against compulsion to testify to facts subjecting them to punishment or forfeiture.

Why did this transformation come about? The maxim which once meant that no man shall be questioned until he has been first accused comes to mean that no man shall ever be required to answer about his crimes. The best explanation seems to be that of Bentham. It is, he says, a result of the association of ideas.[21] The ecclesiastical courts and the High Commission and Star Chamber had a practice, under conditions, of examining an accused about his crimes. These same courts were the efficient vehicles of the power of foreign Popes, of bigoted prelates persecuting religious dissent, of dictatorial Tudor and Stuart kings. The practice markedly contributed to these courts' success in these hated objectives. Therefore the practice is to be condemned generally. The hatred of the end is visited upon the means.

The notion of a general privilege against being compelled to incriminate oneself was never embodied in any of the great English charters, either Magna Charta, the Petition of Right (drafted by Coke) or even the Bill of Rights of 1689.[22] The notion was in process of gradual acceptance and checkered application in England in the period 1640–1700, and had not then come to be regarded as a "fundamental" right. Nevertheless, in this same period, one of active colonization in America, the new expanded principle seems to have won early and widespread recognition over here.[23] It must have had an appeal to the persecuted dissenters who fled to New England and to the sturdy veterans of Cromwell's army who emigrated as indentured servants to Virginia. The scope of the privilege troubled Deputy Governor Bellingham of Massachusetts in 1642, when he wrote as a part of his inquiry into the laws, "quest. (2): How farr a magistrate may extracte a confession from a delinquente, to accuse himselfe of a capitall crime, seeing *nemo tenetur prodere seipsum*." [24] The Massachusetts Body of Liberties of 1641 had not given any direct support to the privilege, but had struck at the kindred evil of torture by a guardedly qualified prohibition.[25]

To keep alive the demand for protection against arbitrary inquisitions without specific charges, there were famous acts of oppression by the Royal Governors. Governor Berkeley in Virginia by "the indiscriminate giving of oath and tortures" was able to convict the leaders of Bacon's Rebellion. In 1677 the House of Burgesses enacted: "Upon a motion from Accomac County, sent by their burgesses, it is answered and declared that the law has provided that a witness summoned against another ought to answer upon oath, but noe law can compel a man to sweare against himself in any matter wherein he is lyable to corporal punishment." [26] One of the grievances against Governor An-

---

18. Wigmore, 295, describing Udall's and Garnet's cases, in 1590 and 1606.

19. Wigmore, 298, 299, Morgan, 9.

20. Wigmore, 299.

21. Bentham, Rationale of Judicial Evidence, b. IX, pt. IV, ch. III (Bowring's ed. v. VII, 456, 460) quoted and discussed in Wigmore, 300, 301.

22. Wigmore, 301.

23. Pittman, 775–783.

24. Quoted Wigmore, 301, note 112, Pittman, 777.

25. Pittman, 776, where some of the provisions are quoted.

26. Pittman, 781.

dros of Massachusetts in 1689 was that he called people from remote counties before the Governor and Council in Boston, for examinations that "were unreasonably strict and rigorous and very unduely ensnaring." [27] When William Bradford in Pennsylvania was bold enough to print copies of the Penn charter, he was hauled before the Governor and Council. The colloquy shows that the privilege not to be forced to "accuse" oneself was strongly asserted.[28] On the eve of the Revolution Governor Dunmore in Virginia evoked a resolution of protest from the Burgesses by his inquisitorial examinations in Council of those accused of forging paper currency.[29]

In the light then of these incidents (which might be multiplied) and especially of the constant association in the mind of the reformers of the evils of free-lancing inquisition and of torture, it is not too surprising to find this right against self-incrimination, which in England was still new and ill-defined, embodied in the constitutions or bills of rights of seven American states before 1789.[30] It since has spread, though slowly,[31] to find place in all the state constitutions except those of Iowa and New Jersey.

In the debates in the Virginia Convention on the Federal Constitution, Patrick Henry voiced his fears, "Congress may introduce the practice of the civil law . . . They may introduce the practice . . . of torturing

to extort confessions of the crime. . . . They will tell you . . . that they must have a criminal equity, and extort confessions by torture, in order to punish with still more relentless severity." [32] To answer these misgivings Virginia and three other states proposed amendments which included the language "in all criminal prosecutions" and a phrase protecting one against being compelled to give evidence against himself.[33] Before these were considered by the House of Representatives, Madison presented a version of his own. It was included not in a section specially devoted to criminal trials, but in one dealing generally with protection of individuals against arbitrary Federal action. It read: "No person shall . . . be compelled to be a witness against himself. . . ." John Lawrence of New York "thought it ought to be confined to criminal cases" and his amendment to that effect was adopted without reported discussion.[34] Was that interpolation intended to confine it literally to criminal cases, thus giving it a narrower scope than the English privilege? Or was it due rather to a fear that Madison's original language would have the undesired effect of preventing the examination of a party by his adversary in a civil case as was commonly done in chancery? Under the latter supposition the words interpolated must have been a clumsy effort to limit the privilege to wit-

---

27. Pittman, 784.

28. See Pittman, 785, where these excerpts appear:
"Gov. (Blackwell) * * * I desire to know from you, whether you did print the charter or not, and who set you to work?"

"Bradford—Governor, it is an impractible thing for any man to accuse himself, thou knows it very well."

"Governor—Well, I will not press you to it, but if you were so ingenious as to confess, it should go the better with you."

"Bradford—Governor, I desire to know my accusers; I think it is very hard to be put upon accusing myself."

. . .

"Bradford—. . . if anything be laid to my charge, let me know my accusers. I am not bound to accuse myself."

29. Pittman, 786.

30. In order beginning in 1776, ending 1784. Virginia, Pennsylvania, Maryland, North Carolina, Vermont, Massachusetts and New Hampshire. Pittman, 765, Wigmore, 303.

31. South Carolina and Georgia had no such provision until after the Civil War. Morgan, 23.

32. 3 Elliott's Debates, 447, 448 (1876); Pittman, 789.

33. Note, Applicability of Privilege to Legislative Investigations, 49 Col.L.Rev. 87, 91 (1949).

34. Op. cit. 49 Col.L.Rev. 91.

nessing about incriminating facts. The historical evidence on the question as to which was the purpose of Congress has been said to be inconclusive,[35] but the Supreme Court has left no doubt as to its interpretation. It rejects the literal meaning which would confine the privilege to criminal trials.[36]

121. Privilege Not Imposed on the States by Federal Constitutional Provisions.

A series of decisions beginning more than a hundred years ago determined that the Federal Bill of Rights, including the Fifth Amendment protecting against self-incrimination, was binding only on the Federal government, not upon the states.[1] About fifty years ago the same court decided that the Fourteenth Amendment had not imposed the privilege against self-incrimination upon the states under the privileges and immunities clause, and that they are not required to recognize the privilege as a requirement of a fair trial under the due process clause of the same amendment.[2] A recent notable decision of the same court, by a five to four vote, has reaffirmed these holdings.[3]

122. The Two Branches: The Privilege of the Accused and the Privilege of a Witness.[1]

The generations that saw the acceptance on both sides of the Atlantic of the notion that a man could not be compelled to give in-criminating evidence against himself had long been familiar with another rule, that an accused in an ordinary prosecution in the common law courts could not be called as a witness against himself. But that rule was not due to any privilege against incriminating oneself. The accused was incompetent as a witness, either for or against himself, and this incompetency continued until after the middle of the 1800s.[2] Nevertheless, the language of the constitutional provisions, generally that no one in a criminal case shall be compelled to be a witness (or to give evidence) against himself,[3] seemed to fit perfectly the case of an accused. Thus when the statute removed his disqualification, and the legislatures provided, as they generally did, that he could be called "at his own request and not otherwise," [4] this legislative privilege not to be called or to be required to testify was naturally assimilated to the constitutional privilege. Accordingly, it is usually assumed that the constitutional provisions, though not at all necessary, when adopted, to guard the accused against being called, were intended to preserve that result of the incompetency from being abrogated by legislation.[5]

The incompetency, however, gave a wider protection than the privilege did. The accused was exempt from being called at all as a

---

35. Op. cit. 49 Col.L.Rev. 94.

36. See § 123, infra.

1. Barron v. Baltimore, 7 Pet. 243, 8 L.Ed. 672 (1833); Brown v. Walker, 161 U.S. 591, 606, 16 S. Ct. 644, 40 L.Ed. 819 (1895); Feldman v. United States, 322 U.S. 487, 490, 64 S.Ct. 1082, 88 L.Ed. 1408 (1943).

2. Twining v. New Jersey, 211 U.S. 78, 29 S.Ct. 14, 53 L.Ed. 97 (1908) (masterly opinion by Moody, J., discussing the history and policy of the privilege: Harlan, J., dissenting).

3. Adamson v. California, 332 U.S. 46, 67 S.Ct. 1672, 91 L.Ed. 1903 (1947) (appeal from murder-conviction under California law permitting comment on failure of accused to take the stand; four judges dissenting on ground that the Fourteenth Amendment imposes upon the states all the

provisions of the Federal Bill of Rights); Notes, 33 Iowa L.Rev. 666, 46 Mich.L.Rev. 372, 58 Yale L.J. 268.

1. 8 Wigmore, Evidence, § 2268; Note, 29 Iowa L. Rev. 373 (1944).

2. See § 65, herein.

3. The various constitutional provisions are quoted in 8 Wigmore, Evidence, § 2252, note 3. Some of them, e. g., Conn., Del., Fla., Texas are phrased in terms of "the accused" rather than "no person."

4. These statutes are set out in 2 Wigmore, Evidence, § 488, note 2.

5. See United States v. Housing Foundation, 176 F. 2d 665 (C.A. 3, 1949) (error to compel accused to testify at request of co-defendant: privilege of accused as well as that of ordinary witness protected by the Fifth Amendment).

witness; the ordinary witness was only privileged against incriminating questions. This difference persists under the present statutory practice by which the accused in a criminal prosecution has a privilege not to be called or sworn as a witness [6] at the State's instance. His is a privilege to stay off the stand. The ordinary witness, that is, any witness except such an accused, has no such broad exemption. He must submit to be called and sworn by either party and to answer all questions except incriminating ones.[7] The practical difference is substantial, since the ordinary witness has the burden, generally, of sifting out the incriminat-

ing questions and claiming privilege as to them—no easy task.

Who is "the accused in a criminal prosecution"? Under the better and prevailing view it is one against whom a punitive criminal proceeding has been specifically directed,[8] as by an indictment, an information upon which a criminal trial can be based, or contempt proceedings where the purpose is predominantly punitive, not remedial.[9] Under this view an investigation into the circumstances and authorship of an alleged crime for the purpose of determining whether a prosecution shall be instituted is not itself a criminal prosecution.[10] Under this view, a

---

6. State v. Smith, 56 S.D. 238, 228 N.W. 240, syl. 17–23 (1929) (applied to suspect summoned to testify at John Doe investigation, where witness was himself suspected); Blair v. Comm., 166 Va. 715, 185 S.E. 900 (1936) (attempted rape: after evidence completed, juror asked if they "could have the benefit of defendant's testimony"; defendant then testified, without his being advised of his rights, held, error); 8 Wigmore, Evidence, § 2268, n. 6; Model Code of Evidence, Rule 201(1): "Every person has a privilege not to be called as a witness and not to testify in any criminal action in which he is an accused." So also Uniform Rule 23(1).

7. The contrast between the rights of the accused and the ordinary witness is clearly drawn by Spence, J., in In re Lemon, 15 Cal.App.2d 82, 59 P.2d 213 (1936).

A proceeding for the enforcement of professional discipline is not a criminal prosecution. State v. Barlow, 132 Neb. 166, 271 N.W. 282, syl. 4 (1937) (privilege of accused not extended to respondent in disbarment proceedings).

8. See the statement of Gray, J., in Post v. United States, 161 U.S. 583, 587, 16 S.Ct. 611, 613, 40 L.Ed. 816, 817 (1894): "Criminal proceedings cannot be said to be brought or instituted until a formal charge is openly made against the accused, either by indictment presented or information filed in court, or, at the least, by complaint before a magistrate. . . . The submission of a bill of indictment by the attorney for the government to the grand jury, and the examination of witnesses before them, are both in secret, and are no part of the criminal proceedings against the accused, but are merely to assist the grand jury in determining whether such proceedings shall be commenced. . . ." There the question as to when the pro-

ceedings were commenced affected the jurisdiction of the court.

9. Root v. McDonald, 260 Mass. 344, 157 N.E. 684, 54 A.L.R. 1422, 1434 (1927), annotated. Contra: State v. Barlow, 132 Neb. 166, 271 N.W. 282, syl. 4 (1937).

10. Mulloney v. United States, 79 F.2d 566, 578, syl. 29 (C.C.A. 1, 1935) (defendant had been questioned before grand jury, held no violation of constitutional privilege); O'Connell v. United States, 40 F.2d 201, syl. 13 (C.C.A.2, 1930) (contempt for refusal to answer questions before grand jury: defendant's contention that he was "accused" because the investigation was intended to disclose crimes committed by him, insupportable); United States v. Price, 163 Fed. 904 (C.C.S.D.N.Y.) (motion to quash indictment because testimony taken from defendant in grand jury investigation, held unfounded in acute opinion by Hough, J.); In re Lemon, 15 Cal.App.2d 82, 59 P.2d 213 (1936) (grand jury investigation of graft in San Francisco police department; witness, police captain refused to be sworn; held, he is not an "accused"; able opinion by Spence, J.); Ex Parte Barnes, 73 Tex.Cr. 583, 166 S.W. 728, syl. 3 (1914) (witness presumed that grand jury was going to question her about incest with her father, and refused to be sworn; "This furnishes no excuse for refusing to be sworn to answer such questions as might be propounded to her by the grand jury. After being sworn, if such questions were propounded, then, and not until then, would she be justified in refusing to answer such questions.") Compare State v. McDaniel, 336 Mo. 656, 80 S.W.2d 185, syl. 7 (1935) where the court holds that it is allowable to question the suspect at a coroner's hearing, when he has been warned that he need not answer and consents to talk.

grand jury investigation, or a coroner's inquest, or a preliminary hearing by a magistrate where no information has been filed on which a trial could be had, is not a prosecution, and there is no accused. In such a proceeding no witness (however strongly suspected he might be) would have this privilege of staying off the stand altogether and refusing all cooperation in the inquiry. A minority view would give the privilege of an "accused" of staying off the stand to one summoned to testify in such an investigation if the person is suspected of criminal complicity by the officers directing the investigation.[11] The line between those suspected and those not suspected is an elusive one, and the view which entitles everyone who may be suspected to stand mute in a lawful inquiry, even though no incriminating question is asked, seems to ignore the origin of the protection of the accused, and to impede unduly the investigation of crime.

123. The Witness-Privilege: Proceedings in Which Applicable.[1]

Despite the language of the Federal Fifth Amendment and many similar state provisions, purporting to limit the protection to criminal cases, it is clear that the privilege of a witness not to answer incriminating questions extends to all judicial or official hearings, investigations or inquiries where persons are called upon formally to give testimony.[2] A witness has this protection accordingly in a judicial trial in a civil[3] or criminal[4] case, or in any deposition[5] or hearing therein, or in an investigation or hearing by a grand jury,[6] a legislative committee,[7] or an administrative official or board.[8]

124. Incrimination under the Laws of Another Sovereign.[1]

Is the danger that his answer will subject the witness to punishment *in another coun-*

---

11. State v. Allison, 116 Mont. 352, 153 P.2d 141, syl. 3–6 (1944) (error for county attorney at inquest to question person whom he suspected of murder, without first advising him of his right to refuse to testify); People v. Gillette, 126 App.Div. 665, 111 N.Y.S. 133, 135 (1908) (John Doe investigation before grand jury; witness, a suspect, gave answers for which he was indicted for perjury: held, investigation was a "criminal case" and oath was not legally administered); State ex rel. Poach v. Sly, 63 S.D. 162, 257 N.W. 113, syl. 4–8 (1934) (stating that rule of text applies to make the questioning a violation of suspect's privilege even though he be told that he need not answer where to do so would incriminate him).

1. 8 Wigmore, Evidence, § 2252; Dec.Dig. Witnesses, ☞293½.

2. For similar broad statements of the principle see United States v. Goodner, 35 F.Supp. 286, 290, syl. 2 (D.Colo.1940); In re West, 348 Mo. 30, 152 S.W. 2d 69, syl. 4 (1941).

3. Ex parte Senior, 37 Fla. 1, 19 So. 652, syl. 2, 3 (1896) (election contest); Karel v. Conlon, 155 Wis. 221, 144 N.W. 266, syl. 3 (1913) (action for libel).

4. Counselman v. Hitchcock, 142 U.S. 547, 562, 12 S.Ct. 195, 35 L.Ed. 1110 (1892) (dictum, privilege not limited in criminal cases to the accused but extends to other witnesses); People v. Hockley, 24 N.Y. 74, 83 (1861).

5. Phleps v. Phleps, 133 N.J.Eq. 392, 32 A.2d 81, syl. 5 (1943).

6. Counselman v. Hitchcock, supra; State v. Kemp, 126 Conn. 60, 9 A.2d 63, syl. 14, 15 (1939) (applies but extends only to immunity from answering incriminating questions).

7. United States v. Di Carlo, 102 F.Supp. 597, syl. 13 (1952) (Congressional Committee on Organized Crime; witnesses privileged against disclosing acts criminal under state law); Doyle v. Hofstader, 257 N.Y. 244, 177 N.E. 489, 496, syl. 16 (1931); In re Hearing Before Joint Legislative Committee, 187 S.C. 1, 196 S.E. 164, 167, syl. 6 (1938). See Liacos, Rights of Witnesses before Congressional Committees, 33 B.U.L.Rev. 337, 370 (1953); Note, Applicability of Privilege against Self-Incrimination to Legislative Investigations, 49 Col.L.Rev. 87 (1949).

8. Smith v. United States, 337 U.S. 137, 150, 69 S. Ct. 1000, 93 L.Ed. 1264 (1949) (testimony given before an examiner of Office of Price Administration under subpena); Comm. v. Prince, 313 Mass. 223, 46 N.E.2d 755, syl. 6 (1943) (information called for by school attendance supervisor); State v. Gensmer, 235 Minn. 72, 51 N.W.2d 680, syl. 5 (1952) (investigation by public examiner).

1. 8 Wigmore, Evidence, § 2258; Notes, Privilege as Extending to Prosecution in Another State or Country, 59 A.L.R. 895, 82 A.L.R. 1380, Privilege as to Testimony Compelled in Another Jurisdiction, 154 A.L.R. 994.

try a valid ground for refusal? Among the considerations against conceding the privilege here are the difficulty of ascertaining the scope of liability under foreign law, and the fact that the danger of such prosecution is usually (but by no means always) remote. In the light of these considerations the first English judge to pass on the question, laid down the general rule "that the rule of protection is confined to what may tend to subject a party to penalties by our own laws."[2] A somewhat later English opinion declared that the privilege would be accorded when the foreign law subjecting the witness to penalty was admitted or proved.[3] These two divergent approaches are reflected in the American holdings, but the influence of the earlier negative pronouncement has been the more pervasive. Many decisions, however, which proclaim the negative rule, mention as significant the fact that in the particular situation the actual danger of foreign prosecution is remote.

In our system of dual sovereignties, the problem arises in several forms, and the various situations differ in respect to the probable nearness or remoteness of the danger of prosecution under the law of the other jurisdiction. The cases, which predominantly reflect the negative view, may be grouped as follows: (a) A witness in state or Federal court claims danger of incrimination under the law of a foreign country;[4] (b) A witness in a state court claims incrimination under the laws of another state;[5] (c) A witness in a state court claims incrimination under Federal law;[6] (d) A witness in the Federal court claims incrimination under state law.[7]

---

2. King of the Two Sicilies v. Willcox, 1 Sim., N.S., 301, 61 Eng.Rep. 116, 128 (V.C.1851) (suit by the King against Sicilian revolutionary agents who had used revolutionary funds to buy ships, for recovery of ships and for order to produce documents; latter order resisted on ground of incrimination under Sicilian law; order for production granted).

3. United States of America v. McRae, L.R. 3 Ch. App. 79, 85 (L.Ch.1867) (bill by United States for accounting and discovery of money received by Confederate agent: defendant pleaded terms of law of United States making his property subject to confiscation and pendency there of proceedings to confiscate; held, discovery denied. "The plea . . . sets out the Act of Congress . . . That being admitted, it is the same as if it were proved as a fact in the case").

4. Republic of Greece v. Koukouras, 264 Mass. 318, 164 N.E. 345, syl. 3, 59 A.L.R. 891 (1928) (privilege denied: protection only against self-incrimination under laws of this jurisdiction).

5. Privilege denied. In re Werner, 167 App.D. 384, 152 N.Y.S. 862 (1915) (extensive discussion by Scott, J., no "real and substantial danger" here; one judge dissenting); State v. Wood, 99 Vt. 490, 134 Atl. 697, syl. 6, 48 A.L.R. 985 (1926). Privilege granted. State v. Doran, 215 La. 151, 39 So.2d 894, 897, syl. 6 (1949) (habeas corpus by former wife against former husband to secure custody of their child: defendant, who had been indicted for abduction of child in California, privileged against disclosure about facts of abduction).

6. Privilege denied. Jack v. Kansas, 199 U.S. 372, 26 S.Ct. 73, 50 L.Ed. 234 (1905) (prosecution in state court for violation of state anti-trust laws; defendant refused to answer though questioned only about state transactions and given immunity under state law, because no immunity under Federal law; adjudged in contempt by state court; held, no Federal right violated; no real danger of Federal prosecution); Ex parte Copeland, 91 Tex.Cr. 549, 240 S.W. 314, 318 (1922) (no real danger). Privilege granted. People v. Den Uyl, 318 Mich. 645, 29 N.W.2d 284, syl. 1–4 (1947) (facts inquired about related to Federal crime for which prosecution was then pending).

7. Privilege denied. Brown v. Walker, 161 U.S. 591, 606, 16 S.Ct. 644, 40 L.Ed. 819 (1896) (witness before Federal grand jury investigating violation of Interstate Commerce Act refuses to answer on ground, inter alia, that immunity does not protect against state prosecution, held, Congress can grant such immunity, it apparently has done so here, and if not, the danger of prosecution here is not "real and substantial"); Hale v. Henkel, 201 U.S. 43, 26 S.Ct. 371, syl. 4, 50 L.Ed. 652 (1906) (witness before Federal grand jury investigating anti-trust violations, held, relying on prior cases, fact that immunity statute does not protect against state prosecution does not give witness privilege to refuse); United States v. Murdock, 284 U.S. 141, 148, syl. 3, 52 S.Ct. 63 (1932) (prosecution for wilful failure to supply to Federal revenue agent information about payments claimed in defendant's income tax return: defense, that he had declined for fear of state prosecution for such payments, presumably made

A related problem here is that of the effectiveness of immunity granted by the law of the forum jurisdiction, and the admissibility in another jurisdiction of testimony given under such a grant of immunity.[8] Presumably the Federal government could grant immunity from prosecution in the state courts for answers given in a Federal investigation[9] when such allowance of immunity may reasonably be considered as in furtherance of a granted Federal power.[10] Doubtless the state governments are devoid of any power to grant immunity from prosecution under Federal law.[11] The highest court has held that a state court may constitutionally require a witness to answer though his state-granted immunity affords no protection against Federal prosecution,[12] and conversely that the Federal court may validly require an answer though the immunity under Federal law offers no protection against state prosecution.[13] The same court has likewise decided that answers actually given by a witness in a state proceeding, under a state immunity statute, are receivable against the witness as admissions in a subsequent federal prosecution for the acts inquired about.[14]

Certainly there is nothing in the language nor in the history of the Constitutional provisions which dictates an answer either way upon the question whether the protection should extend to prosecution under "foreign" law. Judges who consider that the policy[15] behind the privilege is so salutary that the range of its application should be extended, will be inclined to accord protection when the danger of "foreign" prosecution is clear. The argument based on the difficulty in ascertaining the scope of the "foreign" law has lost much of its force with the widening of the reach of judicial notice.[16]

The paramount argument for confining the privilege to incrimination under the laws of

for gambling protection; "The plea does not rest upon any claim that the inquiries were being made to discover evidence of crime against state law. Nothing of state concern was involved. The investigation was under federal law in respect of federal matters. . . . As appellee at the hearing did not invoke protection against federal prosecution, his plea is without merit. . . . ").
Privilege upheld: United States v. Di Carlo, 102 F. Supp. 597, syl. 17–21 (D.C.N.D. Ohio, 1952) (prosecution for refusal by witness before Congressional Committee Investigating Organized Crime, to answer on ground of incrimination under state law; held, refusal justified, because where Congress is investigating state crime as incident to its power to regulate commerce it must secure to witnesses the protection against self-incrimination they are accorded under state law, distinguishing United States v. Murdock, supra, as a case where the investigation was solely a matter of Federal concern; the justness of the distinction seems debatable, and certainly more one of degree than of kind). The last case is ably and critically reviewed in the Note, 4 Stanford L.Rev. 594.

8. See § 135, which deals generally with the grant of immunity.

9. Brown v. Walker, described in note 7, supra.

10. McCulloch v. Maryland, 4 Wheat. 316, 421, 423, 4 L.Ed. 579 (1819); Interstate Commerce Comm. v.

Brimson, 154 U.S. 447, 472, 14 S.Ct. 1125, 38 L.Ed. 1047 (1894).

11. See statements to this effect in Feldman v. United States, 322 U.S. 487, 493, 64 S.Ct. 1082, 88 L.Ed. 1408 (1944); Dunham v. Ottinger, 243 N.Y. 423, 154 N.E. 298, 302 (1926).

12. Jack v. Kansas, described in note 6, supra.

13. Brown v. Walker, supra, note 7 (semble); Hale v. Henkel, supra, note 7.

14. Feldman v. United States, 322 U.S. 487, 64 S.Ct. 1082, 88 L.Ed. 1408 (1944), noted 30 Corn.L.Q. 255, 39 Ill.L.Rev. 184, 53 Yale L.J. 364. Though three justices dissented, it is hard to see how any different holding could be justified. The testimony was not contended to have been wrongly secured under the law of New York. Its procurement did not violate the Federal constitution which imposes no duty on the states to enforce the privilege against self-incrimination, see § 121, supra. Nor was there any showing that he was falsely assured of Federal immunity. The most that could be supposed was that he was acting under a mistake as to such immunity. But this was not injurious since he was bound to answer without such immunity. Jack v. Kansas, supra, note 6; Dunham v. Ottinger, 243 N.Y. 423, 154 N.E. 298, syl. 6 (1926).

15. See § 136, herein.

16. See § 326, herein.

the forum is based upon the undesirability of a wholesale extension of this already burdensome obstruction upon the judicial investigation of facts. Moreover, apart from collusion between the law enforcement agencies of state and Federal governments, there is little incentive for the enforcement officers of one government to seek to require a witness to inculpate himself under the laws of another jurisdiction. When such collusion does occur then the "foreign" government is participating in the compulsion, and its own constitutional provision forbidding it to compel the testimony should be applied.[17]

125. Corporations and Associations and Their Agents.[1]

The history of the evolution of the privilege in England and America before its embodiment in our constitutions is the history of protest against pressure on flesh-and-blood witnesses.[2] Those constitutions purport to give protection against compulsion "to be a witness" or "to give evidence" against oneself. Such language seems to point to a prohibition against exerting pressure upon individuals. Accordingly, it has been generally agreed by American courts that a corporation has no privilege against self-incrimination, but must submit to the visitorial power of state and Federal governments to examine its books, records and transactions even though this discloses criminal acts by the corporation.[3] Consequently no agent of a corporation having actual custody of its records and papers can object to producing them upon judicial order on the ground of a supposed privilege of the corporation against self-incrimination. Moreover, the visitorial power of investigation of the corporation's affairs could not be effectively exercised if such agent whose criminality was exposed by the corporation's records could assert a privilege of his own, and it is held that he cannot.[4]

The highest court in 1944 took a bold forward step in this field when it applied by analogy these doctrines of the denial of privilege and the compellability of agents to produce records incriminating them, to unincorporated associations, in the case of a trade union.[5]

By a further analogy, it might well be determined that the agent of a corporation or association could be compelled to disclose by his oral testimony any acts performed for the principal, though incriminating the

---

17. See the analogy drawn to the cases of searches and seizures in Feldman v. United States, 322 U.S. 487, 492, 64 S.Ct. 1082, 88 L.Ed. 1408 (1944).

1. 8 Wigmore, Evidence, §§ 2259a, 2259b; Note, Privilege as Available to Member or Officer of Unincorporated Association, 152 A.L.R. 1208.

2. See § 120, herein.

3. Hale v. Henkel, 201 U.S. 43, 26 S.Ct. 370, 379, syl. 6, 50 L.Ed. 652 (1906); Wilson v. United States, 221 U.S. 361, 377, 31 S.Ct. 538, 544, 55 L.Ed. 771 (1911) (leading opinion by Hughes, J.); Ex parte Bott, 146 Oh. 511, 66 N.E.2d 918, 922, syl. 4 (1946). But in England corporations have the privilege. Triplex Safety Glass Co. v. Lancegaye Safety Glass Co. [1939] K.B. 935 (Ct.App.).

In Oklahoma Press Pub. Co. v. Walling, 327 U.S. 186, 208, 66 S.Ct. 494, 90 L.Ed. 614 (1946), Rutledge, J., after reviewing the decisions on the applicability of the self-incrimination and search-and-seizure privileges to orders against corporations to produce documents, said ". . . the Fifth Amendment affords no protection by virtue of the self-incrimination provision, whether for the corporation or for its officers; and the Fourth, if applicable, at the most guards against abuse only by way of too much indefiniteness or breadth in the things required to be 'particularly described,' if also the inquiry is one the demanding agency is authorized by law to make and the materials specified are relevant." See also United States v. Morton Salt Co., 338 U.S. 632, 652, 70 S.Ct. 357, 94 L.Ed. 401 (1950).

4. Wilson v. United States, 221 U.S. 361, 382, 31 S.Ct. 538, 55 L.Ed. 771 (1911); Essgee Co. v. United States, 262 U.S. 151, 158, 43 S.Ct. 514, 67 L.Ed. 917 (1923).

5. United States v. White, 322 U.S. 694, 699, 64 S.Ct. 1248, 1251, 88 L.Ed. 1542, 1546 (1944); noted, 20 N.Y.U.L.Q.R. 364. Compare In re Subpena Duces Tecum, 81 F.Supp. 418, 430 (D.Ct.N.D.Calif.1948), where the court said that the doctrine of United States v. White is inapplicable to a "small family partnership."

agent. The courts seem as yet not to have settled this question.[6] Broader doctrines may evolve in this area. Thus, one distinguished judge has made the statement that "The claim of privilege against self-incrimination has no application to the contemnor's refusal to produce books held by him in a representative capacity."[7] And as a radiation from the cases requiring a bankrupt to deliver to the trustee his incriminating records and papers,[8] the Uniform Rules of Evidence propose that the privilege against self-incrimination shall not apply to protect one from being compelled to produce an incriminating paper or chattel if some other person has a superior right to its possession.[9]

126. What is Meant by Compulsion to be a Witness or to Give Evidence? [1]

The first and most appropriate test is historical.[2] The privilege, as it emerged in England and as it was expressed in our constitutions was against being compelled to "be a witness" or "to give evidence" against oneself. Compulsion to be a witness or to give evidence was compulsion to do those things

---

6. The cases thus far encountered have dealt only with the production of records except United States v. Austin-Bagley Corp., 31 F.2d 229, 233, syl. 6 (C.C.A. 2, 1929) where the court permitted several defendants, officers of the corporate defendant, to be called to authenticate the corporation's papers: this was sustained on appeal in an opinion by L. Hand, J., who said: " . . . we think that the greater includes the less and that since the production can be forced, it may be made effective by compelling the producer to declare that the documents are genuine." But does this consideration apply here to defendants who have the privilege of accused persons to stay off the stand altogether? See also United States v. Daisart, 169 F.2d 856, 861, syl. 6, 7 (C.A.2d, 1948) which implies that compelled oral testimony, beyond identifying the records, would be privileged if it incriminated the witness.

7. Swan, Ch. J., in United States v. Field, 190 F.2d 554, 555 (C.A. 2, 1951) holding Field in contempt for refusal to answer fully about the books of the Bail Fund of the Civil Rights Congress. The quoted statement, however, may not have been intended to go beyond the holdings as to corporations and associations, as Wilson v. United States and United States v. White, supra, were the only cases cited.

8. Johnson v. United States, 228 U.S. 457, 33 S.Ct. 572, 57 L.Ed. 919 (1913) (books of bankrupt transferred to trustee under Act properly used as evidence to convict him); Ex parte Fuller, 262 U.S. 91, 43 S.Ct. 496, 67 L.Ed. 881 (1923) (similar).

9. Uniform Rules of Evidence, Rule 25(d).

1. 8 Wigmore, Evidence, §§ 2263–2266; Inbau, Self-Incrimination: What Can an Accused Person be Compelled to Do? (C. C. Thomas, Springfield, Ill., 1950); Notes, Martin, Intoxication Tests and Other Bodily Examinations, 19 Tex.L.Rev. 463 (1941); Methods of Scientific Crime Detection as Infringements of Personal Rights, 44 Harv.L.Rev. 842 (1931); Compulsory Action or Exhibition as Violating the Privilege, 17 Minn.L.Rev. 187 (1933); Shaw,

Admissibility of Non-testimonial Evidence Extracted from the Accused before and at the Trial, 5 N.C. L.R. 333, 1927; Compulsory Bodily Action or Exhibition as Violating the Privilege against Self-crimination, 17 Minn.L.R. 187, 1933; Thomas, Self-incrimination Protection against Physical Disclosures, 1 Vand.L.Rev. 243 (1948); Use of Evidence Obtained by Examination or Test as Violation of Constitutional Rights, 164 A.L.R. 967; Dec.Dig.Crim. Law, ☞393.

2. See § 120 herein, and the following incisive sumary: "The ecclesiastical courts, when examining causes over which they had jurisdiction, and especially when interrogating heretics, administered to the accused the 'oath ex officio.' The judges could then put the accused to answer any questions whether relevant to the inquiry or not, and a refusal to answer was tantamount to an admission of guilt. The first popular antagonism toward these courts was spurred because of the manner of calling any accused without a formal presentment. This feeling came to embrace the oath ex officio as an odious procedure also. Later when the Court of Star Chamber and the Court of High Commission for Ecclesiastical Causes had assumed most of the functions of the ecclesiastical courts, the feeling against the oath reached a pitch. The common law courts were vying with these courts for authority and helped bring about their downfall. In 1641 when the Court of Star Chamber and the Court of High Commission were abolished the oath ex officio went with them. The antagonism against the oath then spread to its use in the common law courts. The reaction enlarged the rule so that it came to be doubted that any person should be bound to incriminate himself on any charge before any court. Many cases at this time quote the maxim 'nemo tenetur prodere seipsum.' "It is seen then that the purpose of the rule was to prohibit the court from extracting an admission of guilt from the lips of the accused." Note, 13 Md.L. Rev. 31, 32 (1953).

which a witness would, by the traditional judicial processes [3] be required to do. These were only (1) to give oral testimony as evidence of the facts stated, and (2) to produce, in court, under judicial order, documents and other objects.[4] As expounded by Wigmore [5] and widely accepted in recent opinions,[6] only these forms of coerced conduct constitute that "testimonial compulsion" against which the privilege protects. No other compelled conduct or its products, however unlawful or inadmissible on other grounds,[7] is within the protection of this privilege.[8] In jurisdictions following this view, the accused without breach of this privilege may be fingerprinted [9] and photographed,[10] deprived of his papers and other objects in his possession,[11] may be physically examined,[12] may have his blood and other bodily fluids taken for tests without his consent,[13] may be re-

3. Especially the subpoena ad testificandum and the subpoena duces tecum.

4. Orders for production of incriminating documents held violations: Temple v. State, 15 Okl.Cr. 146, 175 Pac. 555, syl. 1 (1918); State v. George, 93 N.H. 408, 43 A.2d 256, syl. 14 (1945); Boyle v. Smithman, 145 Pa. 255, 23 Atl. 397, syl. 1 (1892) (penal action); and cases cited 8 Wigmore, Evidence, § 2264, n. 1; Dec.Dig.Crim.Law, ⚿393(1)c.

5. 8 Evidence, § 2263.

6. See, e. g., People v. Trujillo, 32 Cal.2d 105, 194 P. 2d 681, 685, syl. 5 (1948) (use in evidence of clothing taken from accused); Block v. People, 125 Colo. 36, 240 P.2d 512, syl. 7 (1951) (blood for intoxication test taken when accused was unconscious); State v. Robinson, 221 La. 19, 58 So.2d 408, syl. 4, 5 (1952) (accused after arrest on instruction of officer rolled up his sleeve and disclosed hypodermic scars); State v. Sturtevant, 96 N.H. 99, 70 A.2d 909, syl. 1, 2 (1950) (reckless driving causing death: blood sample taken from accused when he was not shown capable of consent); State v. Alexander, 7 N.J. 585, 83 A.2d 441, 443, syl. 1 (1951) (blood of accused taken for venereal testing used to ascertain type for identification), noted 4 Wash.U.L.Q. 583; State v. Cram, 176 Ore. 577, 160 P.2d 283, 284, 164 A.L.R. 952 (1945) (blood of accused taken while unconscious and used for intoxication test); State v. Gatton, 60 Oh.App. 192, 20 N.E.2d 265 (1938), noted 24 Minn.L.Rev. 444 (drunk driving: refusal to submit to examination, admissible); Comm. v. Stratti, 166 Pa.Super. 577, 73 A.2d 688, syl. 4–7 (1950) (blood taken without consent for identification); Barrett v. State, 190 Tenn. 366, 229 S.W.2d 516, syl. 4 (1950) (accused required by officers in jail to put on hat to aid witness to identify him); Owens v. Comm., 186 Va. 689, 43 S.E.2d 895, 899, syl. 4, 5 (1947) (silence under accusation). Most of these opinions rely upon the holding in Holt v. United States, 218 U.S. 245, 252, 31 S.Ct. 2, 6, 54 L. Ed. 1021 (1910), wherein Holmes, J., said: "Another objection is based upon an extravagant extension of the Fifth Amendment. A question arose as to whether a blouse belonged to the prisoner. A witness testified that the prisoner put it on and it fitted him. It is objected that he did this under the same duress that made his statements inadmissible, and that it should be excluded for the same reasons. But the prohibition of compelling a man in a criminal court to be witness against himself is a prohibition of the use of physical or moral compulsion to extort communications from him, not an exclusion of his body as evidence when it may be material."

7. See ch. 14, herein.

8. See Uniform Rules of Evidence, R. 23(3) ("An accused in a criminal action has no privilege to refuse, when ordered by the judge, to submit his body to examination or to do any act in the presence of the judge or the trier of the fact, except to refuse to testify."), and R. 25(b) (c) (" . . . no person has the privilege to refuse to submit to examination for the purpose of discovering or recording his corporal features and other identifying characteristics, or his physical or mental condition; and no person has the privilege to refuse to furnish or permit the taking of samples of body fluids or substances for analysis. . . . ").

9. Bartletta v. McFeeley, 107 N.J.Eq. 141, 152 Atl. 17, syl. 1 (1930); People v. Sallow, 100 Misc. 447, 165 N.Y.S. 915, syl. 2 (Gen.Sess.1917); Inbau, op. cit. 32; Notes, 63 A.L.R. 1325, 16 A.L.R. 371; Seder, 37 J. Crim.Law 511 (1947).

10. Shaffer v. United States, 24 App.D.C. 417, 426, syl. 2 (1904); Inbau, op. cit. 38.

11. McIntire v. State, 190 Ga. 872, 11 S.E.2d 5, syl. 5, 134 A.L.R. 813 (1940); People v. Richter's Jewelers, 291 N.Y. 161, 51 N.E.2d 690, syl. 2, 150 A.L.R. 560 (1943); Dec.Dig.Crim.Law, ⚿393(2).

12. O'Brien v. State, 125 Ind. 38, 25 N.E. 137, syl. 3 (1890) (forcible examination of body for scars); Green Lake County v. Domes, 247 Wis. 90, 18 N.W. 2d 348, 159 A.L.R. 204 (1945) (examination of accused for drunkenness by doctor, with neurological but not blood-tests); Inbau, op. cit. 13.

13. Block v. People, State v. Sturtevant, State v. Alexander, and State v. Cram, cited and described note 6, supra; Notes, 39 Va.L.Rev. 215 (1953); 164 A.L.R. 967, 25 A.L.R.2d 1407; Inbau, op. cit. ch. 12.

quired to give a specimen of his handwriting,[14] may be compelled to assume positions taken by the perpetrator of the crime,[15] and may be forced to participate in a police "line up," [16] to stand up for identification,[17] put on articles of clothing,[18] or display a scar [19] or a limp.[20] The list is illustrative, not exhaustive. This view most nearly achieves the aim of holding the privilege within limits which will enable law enforcement officers to perform their tasks without unreasonable obstruction.

Under a second view, the line is drawn between enforced *passivity* on the part of the accused and enforced *activity* on his part.[21] Submission may be compelled but not active cooperation, for then he is made "to be a witness" or "to give evidence." This is a distinction which is aesthetically attractive but which seems to have no basis in history, practicality or justice. Under this view, the prisoner could, for example, be required to submit to finger-printing [22] and the extraction of blood.[23] He could not be required to

Other constitutional questions arise, particularly of unreasonable searches and seizures, and of due process. These are discussed in the above authorities and in ch. 14, herein.

14. Beltran v. Sampson and José, 53 Phil.Is. 570 (1929), described in Inbau, op. cit. 45.

15. State v. Neville, 175 N.C. 731, 95 S.E. 55, syl. 1 (1918) (rape: accused placed at window of victim's home where she first saw him); Inbau, op. cit. 30.

16. Meriwether v. State, 63 Ga.App. 667, 11 S.E.2d 816, syl. 7 (1940) (by a court adopting the second view, later described in text).

17. People v. Clark, 18 Cal.2d 449, 116 P.2d 56, syl. 6 (1941) (ordered to stand during trial and remove visor); People v. Gardner, 144 N.Y. 119, 38 N.E. 1003, syl. 2 (1894). Contra: Smith v. State, 247 Ala. 354, 24 So.2d 546, syl. 12 (1946). See Inbau, op. cit. 27; Dec.Dig.Crim.Law, ☞193(3).

18. Barrett v. State, described in note 6, supra, and cases cited in Note, Pretrial Requirement that Suspect Try on Particular Apparel, 18 A.L.R.2d 796. A holding to the contrary as to requiring accused who had taken the stand to try on a hat, in Allen v. State, 183 Md. 603, 39 A.2d 820 (1944), seems difficult to justify, see excellent note, 13 Md.L.Rev. 31. Even if the privilege be considered to extend so far, it should have been held to be waived by taking the stand, see § 131, herein.

19. See the illuminating opinion of Hawley, J., in State v. Ah Chuey, 14 Nev. 79, 1879, 33 Am.Rep. 530, sustaining the ruling of the trial judge in compelling the accused to exhibit his arm so as to reveal tattoo marks. "The truth," he said, at page 88, "forces itself upon my mind that no evidence of physical facts can . . . be held to come within the letter or spirit of the Constitution."

20. Requiring the accused to walk in presence of identifying witness before trial was seemingly approved in Funderburgh v. State, 144 Tex.Cr. 35, 160 S.W.2d 942, syl. 1 (1942). Requiring the accused to

stand and walk over by the prosecuting witness was sanctioned in State v. Clark, 156 Wash. 543, 287 Pac. 18, 19 (1930).

21. Cooper v. State, 86 Ala. 610, 6 So. 110 (1889) (error to admit evidence that accused declined, on request made to him while under arrest for burglary, to walk in his stocking feet across the hallway of the burglarized house); Davis v. State, 131 Ala. 10, 31 So. 569, 571, syl. 6, 7 (1902) (error to admit evidence that defendant refused to allow his shoes to be taken, to compare with tracks; "the accused . . . cannot be compelled to do an affirmative act, or to affirmatively say anything which may tend to criminate him," distinguishing the case of silence by the prisoner when statements are made in his presence, which may be an admission; query, if the shoes had been taken forcibly and compared with the tracks, would evidence of this be admitted under this test?); Allen v. State, 183 Md. 603, 39 A.2d 820, 822 (1944) (error to require accused at trial to put on hat; ". . . privilege is directed not merely to the giving of oral testimony but embraces as well the involuntary furnishing of evidence by the accused by some affirmative act in open court which might aid in establishing his guilt."); State v. Griffin, 129 S.C. 200, 124 S.E. 81, syl. 2, 6, 35 A.L.R. 1227 (1924) (sheriff's testimony that he forced defendant to remove her shoe, and he then compared shoe with track, not violative of the privilege; but his testimony that he compelled her to put her foot in track and that she would not do it in the right way is violative: the "line of cleavage," as the court calls it, is hard to trace in these facts). See also Apodaca v. State, 140 Tex.Cr. 593, 146 S.W.2d 381, syl. 2 (1940) (examination of accused by policemen for drunkenness, by causing him to walk a line, make sudden turns, place finger on nose, and furnish urine for analysis, is violation of privilege); Note, Martin, 19 Tex.L.Rev. 470.

22. See note 9, supra.

23. See note 13, supra.

aid in re-enacting the crime [24] or to give a specimen of his handwriting.[25] He could only be compelled in court to do such simple things as standing when required, which might be justified as within the traditional exercise of the judge's power to regulate the conduct of the trial.[26]

A third view, for which only scattering support can be found, is that any evidence secured by compulsion from the prisoner, whether by requiring him to act or by his mere passive submission, is within the privilege.[27] Presumably no court today would carry out such a notion consistently, as to do so would prevent such established practices as compulsory finger-printing and requiring the accused at the trial to stand up for identification.

There are borderline cases, as to which it may be debated whether the compelled conduct is communication used as evidence of its truth, which alone would be privileged under the first test. Among these may be mentioned (1) requiring a specimen of the voice of the suspect; (2) requiring the suspect to submit to a lie-detector test; (3) a compulsory psychiatric examination; and (4) compulsory narco-analysis, or subjection to the so-called "truth serum," followed by questioning as to guilt. The first would seem not intended to be a communication, or to be used as such, but only as a bodily demonstration.[28] As to the second, the answer is the same.[29] The questions of the examiner are usually followed by answers but in the main it is not the answers that are used for their truth but the blood-pressure and respiration reactions which are the crucial part of the test.[30] Similarly, in the sanity examination, the questions are not designed to elicit admissions of guilt as evidence of their truth, but rather to test the coherence and rationality of the subject. They are not used testimonially but as symptoms of abnormality or the reverse.[31] On

---

24. Aiken v. State, 16 Ga.App. 848, 86 S.E. 1076, syl. 2 (1915). See note 15, supra.

25. See People v. Sturman, 209 Mich. 284, 289, 176 N.W. 397, 399 (1920) ("Quite likely it would have been error to compel the witness, against objection, to make the signatures" but here no objection). See note 14, supra.

26. The opinion concedes this in Allen v. State, supra n. 21, and see the exhaustive Note, Required Exhibitions and Acts of Accused during Trial, 171 A.L.R. 1144.

27. See, e. g., State v. Height, 117 Iowa 650, 91 N. W. 935, syl. 3 (1902) (rape: compulsory examination by doctor for venereal disease, violation of self-crimination privilege included in due process provision of Iowa constitution); State v. Newcomb, 220 Mo. 54, 119 S.W. 405, syl. 6 (1909) (similar).

28. Accordingly the courts adopting the first view would presumably hold it not privileged. Johnson v. Comm., 115 Pa. 369, 9 Atl. 78, 81, syl. 3 (1887) (no objection, dictum, not privileged); and see Inbau, op. cit., ch. IX. Two states, seemingly following the second view, have held it privileged (at least where particular words spoken at the time of the crime are required to be repeated, though this seems not to be an adequate ground of distinction) as compelled activity. State v. Taylor, 213 S.C. 330, 49 S.E.2d 289, syl. 2–5, 16 A.L.R.2d 1317 (1948),

annotated, noted by Fuller, 27 N.C.L.Rev. 262; 24 Ind. L.J. 587; Beachem v. State, 144 Tex.Cr. 272, 162 S.W.2d 706, syl. 3, 4 (1942), noted by Levy, 21 Tex.L.Rev. 816. A voice comparison is, however, an unreliable means of identification. See McGehee, The Reliability of the Identification of the Human Voice (1937) 17 J.Gen.Psy. 249, abstracted in (1943) 33 J.Crim.L. 487.

29. Note, 44 Harv.L.Rev. 842, 845 (1931); McCormick, Deception Tests, 15 Calif.L.Rev. 484, 502 (1927). Inbau, op. cit. 67, seems to approve this analysis but thinks many courts would decline to accept it.

30. For description of the tests, and of the reasoning of the courts in declining to admit evidence of their results, see § 174, herein.

31. The courts on this ground fairly uniformly hold that an order for mental examination of the accused does not violate the privilege. See cases cited below, and other decisions collected in Dec.Dig.Crim. Law ⬅393(1) f. But they often condition the holding by the requirement that the accused should not be forced to answer questions. Comm. v. Musto, 348 Pa. 300, 35 A.2d 307, syl. 12–14 (1907) (here accused declined to answer questions and "no worthwhile examination could be made"). Or hold that answers indicating guilt shall not be put in evidence. State v. Meyers, 220 S.C. 309, 67 S.E.2d 506, syl. 1, 2, 4 (1951). Sometimes the result is based partly on the ground that an absence of objection to

the other hand, the fourth class of cases, those of drug-induced statements, where the drug is administered without consent, the statements are used testimonially to prove the facts stated and seem to fall within the privilege.[32]

Another recurrent question in these cases is the question of consent,[33] for of course if there is consent there is no compulsion. If a suspected prisoner is directed by a policeman to do certain acts or to submit to a test, and he complies without objection, has he consented?[34] Perhaps most people even though unwilling would not object under these circumstances,[35] but it seems that on the claim of privilege the question of consent would be one of fact for the court,[36] and the want of objection would be some evidence of consent. Probably the courts adopting the wider doctrines of privilege tend to right the balance with a wider application of the doctrine of consent. Thus, when the argument is made against the admission of the results of blood-tests for intoxication that the accused was too drunk to consent, some courts have said that even though he was too much under the influence of liquor to drive safely he may yet have been sober enough to give a valid consent to a test.[37] Here again, a preliminary question of fact for the judge.[38]

127. Sanctions for the Enforcement of the Privilege.

The common law view that the illegality of the obtaining of evidence is no ground for exclusion [1] has not been applied to testimony or objects wrongly secured from a witness, in spite of his claim of the privilege against self-incrimination. Consequently, such evidence will be excluded at his instance when offered against him in a subsequent proceeding.[2] Moreover, in the instant case, if his

---

the order spells consent. Hunt v. State, 248 Ala. 217, 27 So.2d 186, syl. 9, 16–18 (1946); Clements v. State, 213 Ark. 460, 210 S.W.2d 912 (1948).

32. Inbau, op. cit. 69. Such statements if they admit the crime would likewise be banned as involuntary confessions. Despres, Legal Aspects of Drug-Induced Statements, 14 U.Chi.L.Rev. 601, 605 (1947).

33. See discussion and citations in Notes, 39 Va.L. Rev. 215, 219 (1953); 164 A.L.R. 976, 25 A.L.R.2d 1413.

34. Some courts seem to presume compulsion even where the state proves that no resistance or objection was made. People v. Corder, 244 Mich. 274, 221 N.W. 309, syl. 2 (1928); State v. Matsinger, 180 S.W. 856, syl. 3 (Mo.1915). Others place the burden on the defendant to show that he protested. Touchston v. State, 154 Fla. 547, 18 So.2d 752, syl. 2 (1944); State v. Miller, 71 N.J.L. 527, 534, 60 Atl. 202 (1905).

35. Both because of fear of authority and moral suasion. Note, 44 Harv.L.Rev. 842, 846 (1931).

If the prisoner refuses to comply, when he is not privileged to refuse, such refusal may be proved against him at the trial. State v. Nutt, 78 Oh.App. 336, 65 N.E.2d 675, syl. 1 (1946) (submission to urinalysis); Inbau, op. cit. 77.

36. See § 53, herein.

37. Bowden v. State, 246 P.2d 427, 431, syl. 3, 4 (Okl. Cr.1952); Halloway v. State, 146 Tex.Cr. 353, 175 S.W.2d 258, syl. 3 (1943).

38. State v. Duguid, 50 Ariz. 276, 72 P.2d 435, syl. 4 (1937).

1. See § 137, herein.

2. State v. Drew, 110 Minn. 247, 124 N.W. 1091, syl. 2 (1910) (schedules filed by accused in involuntary bankruptcy proceedings, seemingly without objection, erroneously received here where accused then objected to their admission on ground of privilege); State v. Allison, 116 Mont. 352, 153 P.2d 141, syl. 3 (1944) (testimony given by accused at coroner's inquest, without knowledge of his rights and without aid of counsel and under belief that he had to answer questions put to him, was inadmissible in subsequent prosecution for murder as compelling accused to testify against himself); Apodaca v. State, 140 Tex.Cr. 593, 146 S.W.2d 381, syl. 2 (1941) (evidence as to results of compulsory intoxication tests); State v. Lloyd, 152 Wis. 24, 139 N.W. 514, 517 (1913) ("The constitutional rights of the citizen against being compelled to incriminate himself are amply protected by upholding him in his refusal to give such evidence, and by rejecting the incriminating evidence which he is ordered or compelled to give notwithstanding his refusal, when this evidence is offered against him."); 58 Am.Jur. Witnesses, § 55; Dec.Dig.Crim.Law, ⊂═◦393(1) e. g. See also Uniform Rules of Evidence, Rule 38. "Evidence of a statement or other disclosure is inadmissible against the holder of the privilege if the judge finds that he had and claimed a privilege to refuse to make the

claim of privilege is wrongly overruled he may under prevailing practice refuse to answer and if committed for contempt, secure release by habeas corpus.[3] Or if he is a party he may answer and if judgment goes against him assign as error on appeal the overruling of his claim of privilege.[4]

128. The Danger against which the Privilege Protects: Incrimination, Penalties and Forfeitures, Disgrace, Civil Liability.

The characteristic feature of the privilege of the ordinary witness is the protection against being compelled to give answers or furnish documents which will create the danger of his conviction for crime.[1] Shortly after this privilege was recognized equity courts were found denying discovery of facts which would subject the party to a forfeiture,[2] and this ground of protection has continued,[3] though it should probably be regarded as independent of the classic and constitutional privilege against self-incrimination. Similarly, a privilege protecting against answers which would subject the witness to a penalty,[4] enforced by civil action, grew up on the analogy of protection against danger of conviction of crime. On the other hand, there is no privilege against being compelled to give answers which will subject the witness to ordinary civil liability not amounting to a penalty or forfeiture.[5]

disclosure but was nevertheless required to make it."

3. Ex parte Irvine, 74 Fed. 954, 959, 960 (Circ.Ct.S.D. Ohio 1896, Taft, Circ.J.); Ex parte Arvin, 232 Mo. App. 796, 112 S.W.2d 113, syl. 3 (1937); Ex parte Martin, 141 Oh.St. 87, 47 N.E.2d 388, syl. 10 (1943). The remedy was granted without discussion of its propriety in Counselman v. Hitchcock, 142 U.S. 547, 12 S.Ct. 195, 35 L.Ed. 110 (1892). See 39 C.J.S., Habeas Corpus, § 37; Dec.Dig.Hab.Corp. ⊂⇒22(2).

4. This seems to be generally assumed as obvious. See People v. Brown, 72 N.Y. 571, 573 (1878) (error of court in denying privilege against self-disgrace to witness enures to his benefit as a party). But see 8 Wigmore, Evidence, § 2270(2).
If the claim of privilege of a non-party witness is wrongly overruled the losing party cannot complain. See § 73, herein.

1. Is a witness required to disclose facts which would subject him only to juvenile proceedings, which are not punitive but reformative? The majority in In re Sadlier, 97 Utah 291, 85 P.2d 810, syl. 2 (1938) held that the self-crimination privilege applied, but it is believed that the contrary argument of the dissenters is stronger. See the discriminating note, Kraus, 13 So.Calif.L.Rev. 157, but compare Dendy v. Wilson, 142 Tex. 460, 179 S.W.2d 269, syl. 10, 11, 151 A.L.R. 1217 (1944).

2. Probably the result is a mere implementation of the substantive rule that equity will not lend its aid to a forfeiture. 8 Wigmore, Evidence, § 2250, pp. 296, 297.

3. Seddon v. Commercial Salt Co., L.R. [1925] Ch.D. 187 (discovery denied in suit to declare lease forfeited); 8 Wigmore, Evidence, § 2256; 70 C.J., Witnesses, §§ 892, 893; Dec.Dig., Witnesses, ⊂⇒295.

4. United States v. Saline Bank, 1 Pet. 100, 7 L.Ed. 69 (1828) (suit to charge bank and stockholders for deposits by the government and for discovery; discovery denied because it would subject defendants to penalty under laws of Virginia prohibiting unincorporated banks); Robson v. Doyle, 191 Ill. 566, 61 N.E. 435, syl. 4 (1901) (discovery sought in aid of actions for penalty for gambling, brought by informer, denied); 8 Wigmore, Evidence, § 2257; 70 C.J. Witnesses, §§ 892, 893; Dec.Dig., Witnesses, ⊂⇒295. By what seems the better view, disbarment is not a "penalty" or "forfeiture." In re Rouss, 221 N.Y. 81, 116 N.E. 782, syl. 5 (1917) (immunity statute protecting a witness against "penalty or forfeiture" for matter disclosed, does not exempt him from disbarment: opinion by Cardozo, J.). A contrary holding in Florida State Board of Architecture v. Seymour, 62 So.2d 1 (Fla.1952) is criticized in Note, 7 Miami L.Q. 592, but supported in Note, 51 Mich. L. Rev. 1081 as necessary to implement the purpose of the immunity statute, that of eliciting testimony.

5. In re Coburn, 165 Cal. 202, 131 Pac. 352, syl. 14, 15 (1913) (proceeding to declare respondent incompetent: he cannot object to being called on ground he might be asked for testimony injurious to his interest); Boston & M. Ry. Co. v. State, 75 N.H. 513, 77 Atl. 996, syl. 4 (1910) (no privilege to refuse answers which may expose him to a civil suit or pecuniary loss); 8 Wigmore, Evidence, § 2254.
Where the civil liability though in some aspect punitive is predominantly remedial, the privilege is inapplicable. Crary v. Porter, 157 F.2d 410, syl. 4 (C.C.A. 8, 1946) (treble damages for overcharge under Emergency Price Control Act); Southern Ry. Co. v. Bush, 122 Ala. 470, 26 So. 168, 173, syl. 7 (1899) (death action, discovery allowed; though under former decisions action is punitive, it is remedial not penal, "for the redress of private and not public

In the early 1700s a privilege was recognized against compelling answers, as to matters not material to the issues, which would disgrace or degrade, though not incriminate, the witness.[6] This privilege has become obsolete in England [7] and in most of our states,[8] except where statutes have preserved the relic.[9] The policy behind this former privilege is now more appropriately served by rules restricting cross-examination as to collateral misconduct of a witness to impeach him,[10] or permitting the judge in his discretion to restrict it,[11] and the rule forbidding extrinsic proof of such misconduct.[12]

129. How Near Must the Question Come to the Facts of a Crime? Who Decides Whether the Answer Called for Would be Incriminating? [1]

The problem of reconciling the interest of the government in ascertaining facts necessary for law enforcement, and the interest of the witness in protection against compulsion to disclose his own crimes is one of the most perplexing dilemmas in judicial administration.[2] If the balance of skepticism is swung too far against the claim of the witness the privilege will cease to have much protective value except against compelled direct admissions of crime; if too far in his favor, the power of the government to elicit facts from unwilling witnesses, except where immunity is given, will practically cease.

The difficulty centers around the inquiry, when does a question, which is innocent on its face, call for a fact which is "incriminatory"? Common examples of such questions [3] are, "Do you know Mr. X? " [4], "What is your business? " [5], and "Were you in

wrongs"). A like result would clearly follow as to liability for exemplary damages, according to Mr. Wigmore. 8 Evidence, § 2257.

But, of course, a witness in a civil action may claim privilege as to incriminating facts though they would be material to the issue of civil liability. Board of Com'rs v. Maretti, 93 N.J.Eq. 513, 117 Atl. 483, 486, 487 (1922) (suit for accounting for fraud: defendant need not answer as to facts showing crimes). A party, however, by bringing a suit or tendering a defense may invite the issue and waive the privilege. See § 130, herein.

6. 3 Wigmore, Evidence, § 986.

7. 3 Wigmore, Evidence, § 986.

8. In re Vince, 2 N.J. 443, 67 A.2d 141, 145 (1949) (Burling, J. surveys in enlightening fashion the history and policy of the question); Lanove v. State, 97 Tenn. 101, 36 S.W. 711, syl. 2 (1896); Carroll v. State, 32 Tex.Cr. 431, 24 S.W. 100 (1893); decisions are collected in 3 Wigmore, Evidence, § 987; 70 C.J., Witnesses, §§ 894, 895; Dec.Dig., Witnesses, ⇔296. The constitutional protection against self-incrimination does not extend to protection against self-disgrace. Brown v. Walker, 161 U.S. 591, 605, 16 S.Ct. 644, 40 L.Ed. 819, 824 (1896).

9. See, e. g., Calif.Code Civ.Proc. § 2065 (". . . nor need [a witness] give an answer which will have a direct tendency to degrade his character, unless it be to the very fact in issue or to a fact from which the fact in issue would be presumed. . . .").

10. See § 42, herein.

11. See § 42, herein.

12. See § 42, herein.

1. 8 Wigmore, Evidence, §§ 2260, 2261, 2271; In re Jennings, 154 Ore. 482, 59 P.2d 702 (1936) (comprehensive review of the cases and doctrines by Rossman, J.); Falknor, Self-Crimination Privilege: "Links in the Chain," 5 Vand.L.Rev. 479 (1952) (able critical review of the federal decisions); Rapacs, Allowance of the Privilege against Self-Incrimination, 19 Minn.L.Rev. 426 (1935); Dec.Dig.. Witnesses, ⇔297, 308.

2. "When two principles come in conflict with each other, the court must give them both a reasonable construction, so as to preserve them both to a reasonable extent. The principle which entitles the United States to the testimony of every citizen, and the principle by which every witness is privileged not to accuse himself, can neither of them be entirely disregarded." Marshall, C. J. in United States v. Burr, 25 Fed.Cas. 38, 39 (1807).

3. These and other types of "innocent" questions are discussed and their implications acutely analyzed in Falknor, op.cit., preceding note.

4. E. g., United States v. Flegenheimer, 82 F.2d 751, syl. 2 (C.C.A.2, 1936) (not incriminatory); Alexander v. United States, 181 F.2d 480, syl. 2 (C.A. 9, 1950) (incriminatory to ask if witness knew man identified as officer of Communist Party).

5. See, e. g., United States v. Weinberg, 65 F.2d 394, 395 (C.C.A.2, 1933) cert. den. 290 U.S. 675, 54 S.Ct. 93 (claimed danger of prosecution under income

Detroit on October 3? " [6]

When the witness claims privilege not to answer such a question, there are certain doctrines about the judicial process in passing on the claim that are fairly well agreed upon. First, the statement of the witness that the answer will incriminate, though it must be given weight because it is under oath, and because only the witness knows what his answer will be,[7] is not conclusive.[8] The judge decides. Second, the judge in passing on the probable danger to the witness,

looks to the immediate setting of other testimony in the case, the background of testimony in other cognate proceedings, to indictments [9] and other official charges against the witness, and even, it seems in appraising the likelihood of prosecution, to newspaper statements about the plans of the prosecutor.[10] Third, in measuring the probability of incrimination the trial judge has the best opportunity for a perceptive "sizing up" of the situation,[11] and on this account his decision should not be disturbed on review unless clearly wrong.[12]

---

tax law, held, not incriminatory); Hoffman v. United States, 341 U.S. 479, 71 S.Ct. 814, syl. 9, 95 L.Ed. 1118 (1951) (witness, a racketeer who had served a sentence under a narcotics charge, privileged to refuse to answer).

6. Ex parte Bommarito, 270 Mich. 455, 259 N.W. 310, syl. 4 (1935) (as had appeared in another trial, witness was in company of H at night club in Detroit on night when H was shot; held, asking witness if he was in Detroit that night not incriminating; he "objected too soon").

7. In re Jennings, 154 Ore. 482, 59 P.2d 702, syl. 7 (1936).

8. People v. Kynette, 15 Cal.2d 731, 104 P.2d 794, syl. 7 (1940); People v. Kert, 304 Mich. 148, 7 N.W.2d 251, syl. 3 (1943). The classic statement on the question is that of Marshall, C. J. in United States v. Burr, 25 Fed.Cas. 38, 40 (1807), as follows: "It is the province of the court to judge whether any direct answer to the question which may be proposed will furnish evidence against the witness. If such answer may disclose a fact which forms a necessary and essential link in the chain of testimony which would be sufficient to convict him of any crime, he is not bound to answer it, so as to furnish matter for that conviction. In such a case, the witness must himself judge what his answer will be, and if he say, on oath, that he cannot answer without accusing himself, he cannot be compelled to answer." This is susceptible of an interpretation giving too wide a power to the witness, since almost any question "may" conceivably in theoretical possibility call for an answer which will be part of the circumstantial proof of a crime. It must be qualified by the condition that under all the facts the judge must find a substantial probability of danger. See the later discussion in this section. And Marshall's actual holding that a question to a witness as to his present knowledge of the meaning of a letter in cipher (charged to be treasonable) was not privileged, because present knowledge is

not sufficient to prove prior knowledge at the time of the plot, is consistent with that qualification.

9. United States v. Weisman, 111 F.2d 260, syl. 5 (C.C.A.2, 1940).

10. United States v. Weisman, 111 F.2d 260, 262 (C.C.A.2, 1940) (newspaper article stating prosecutor would soon indict owner of big advertising agency, which could have pointed to witness); Hoffman v. United States, 341 U.S. 479, 71 S.Ct. 814, syl. 10, 95 L.Ed. 1118 (1951) (contemnor's supplemental record on appeal, including newspaper article showing witness photographed with federal narcotics officer who was pictured in an accusing pose). The courts have not made clear how these are competent. If offered to show the prosecutor's intentions they are hearsay, but perhaps the court may be justified in dispensing with the hearsay rule in passing on this preliminary question of fact, see § 53, herein. If offered to show the witness' apprehension they would not be hearsay (see § 228, herein) but it is not easy to see their relevance. The state of fear of the witness seems irrelevant. It is the judge's appraisal of the danger that is significant.

11. The trial judge in assessing the claim "must be governed as much by his personal perception of the peculiarities of the case as by the facts actually in evidence." Taft, J., in Ex parte Irvine, C.C.S.D. Ohio, 1896, 74 F. 954, 960.

12. Mason v. United States, 244 U.S. 362, 366, 37 S.Ct. 621, 61 L.Ed. 1198 (1917) ("Ordinarily, he is in much better position to appreciate the essential facts than an appellate court can hold and he must be permitted to exercise some discretion, fructified by common sense, when dealing with this necessarily difficult subject. Unless there has been a distinct denial of a right guaranteed, we ought not to interfere."); Russell v. United States, 12 F.2d 683, 693, syl. 12, 14 (C.C.A.6, 1926); State v. Beery, 198 Minn. 550, 270 N.W. 600, syl. 2 (1936). These opinions speak of the judge's decision as discretionary but doubtless this is not intended to suggest that the

A classic statement of the test is that "the Court must see, from the circumstances of the case, and the nature of the evidence which the witness is called to give, that there is reasonable ground to apprehend danger to the witness from his being compelled to answer."[13] It seems that to meet this test the court must find (1) that there is substantial probability that the witness has committed a crime under the law of the forum, and (2) that the fact called for is an essential part of the crime,[14] or is a fact which taken with other facts already proved, or which may probably be proved, would make out a circumstantial case of guilt.[15]

Under these tests, a danger which the judge considers "imaginary or unsubstantial"[16] will not suffice. Manifestly, the danger that the answer may incriminate a third person is no ground of privilege.[17] Moreover, the privilege may not be asserted to a non-incriminating question on the ground that the witness anticipates that a later question will be incriminatory.[18] Again it seems that a question which may elicit information which will enable the prosecution to secure evidence of the witness' guilt from other sources, should not be regarded as incriminatory.[19] To stimulate such exploration for other evidence has been thought to be the main purpose of the privilege.[20]

granting of the privilege is matter of grace, but only that the superior position of the judge in appraising the situation should be given weight on appeal.

13. Cockburn, C. J., in The Queen v. Boyes, 1 B. & S. 311, 330, 121 Eng.Rep. 730, 738 (Q.B.1861), approved in Ex parte Reynolds, 20 Ch.Div. 294 (Ct.App. 1882) and in Mason v. United States, 244 U.S. 362, 365, 37 S.Ct. 621, 61 L.Ed. 498 (1917).

14. E. g., Alston v. State, 1896, 109 Ala. 51, 20 So. 81 (witness asked "if he did not shoot Dean Edwards"); People v. Spain, 1923, 307 Ill. 283, 138 N.E. 614 (witness in bribery-conspiracy investigation asked whether he gave money to member of legislature).

15. See the definition of incrimination in Model Code of Evidence, Rule 202: "A matter will incriminate a person within the meaning of these Rules if it constitutes, or forms an essential part of, or, taken in connection with other matters already disclosed, is a basis for a reasonable inference of, such a violation of the laws of this State as to subject him to liability to punishment therefor . . .", and see L. Hand, Circ.J., in United States v. Weisman, 111 F.2d 260, 262 (C.C.A.2, 1940): "All crimes are composed of definite elements, and nobody supposes that the privilege is confined to answers which directly admit one of these; it covers also such as logically, though mediately, lead to any of them; such as are rungs of the rational ladder by which they may be reached. A witness would, for example, be privileged from answering whether he left his home with a burglar's jimmy in his pocket, though that is no part of the crime of burglary."

16. The Queen v. Boyes, at page cited note 13, supra.

17. Rogers v. United States, 340 U.S. 367, 371, 71 S.Ct. 438, syl. 3, 95 L.Ed. 344 (1951); People v.

Schultz, 380 Ill. 539, 44 N.E.2d 601, syl. 1, 5, 6 (1942).

18. Ex parte Bommarito, 270 Mich. 455, 259 N.W. 310, syl. 4 (1935) (described in note 6, supra); In re Jennings, 154 Ore. 482, 59 P.2d 702, 717 (1936) ("The witness is not permitted to surmise that further questions will follow which will tend to convict him of some wrongdoing. To permit a witness otherwise innocent of wrongful conduct to refuse to answer whether he was present when the alleged crime was committed, merely because the state might turn upon him next, would produce an intolerable condition. . . . Eyewitness testimony would then be available only as a favor, and justice would be at the sufferance of those who were willing to testify."

19. This was seemingly once the established view. Ward v. State, 2 Mo. 120, 122 (1829) (witness compellable to answer question, "Who bet at the game of faro, not naming yourself?" over objection that answer may disclose names of those who may be used as witnesses against himself); La Fontaine v. Southern Underwriters, 83 N.C. 133, 141 (1880) (approving Ward v. State, supra); 8 Wigmore, Evidence, § 2261. This view, regrettably, is clouded by the fact that in Counselman v. Hitchcock, 142 U.S. 547, 564, 12 S.Ct. 195, 35 L.Ed. 1110 (1892) the court held that immunity from the use of incriminating evidence against the witness was not sufficient protection of the witness to support a law compelling him to testify, because it would not prevent "the use of his testimony to search out other testimony to be used in evidence against him." This unfortunate holding is discussed in § 135, herein, dealing with immunity statutes.

20. See 8 Wigmore, § 2251, and § 136, herein on the policy of the privilege.

The foregoing discussion has attempted to outline what has been the prevailing attitude in the English courts and the American courts, state and federal, as to the approach to this problem of judicial administration. It is an attitude which gives substantial weight to the government's need in law enforcement for reasonably free access to information which witnesses possess. Some recent expressions and holdings of our highest court, however, are indicative of a change of view in the direction of recognizing the privilege when there is a mere possibility of danger, and yielding to the claim unless it is *"perfectly clear . . .* that the witness is mistaken and that the answer *cannot possibly"* have a tendency to incriminate.[21] One is reminded of Wigmore's comment, that "A stranger from another legal sphere might imagine . . . that the guilty criminal was the fond object of the Court's doting tenderness, guiding him at every step in the path of unrectitude, and lifting up his feet lest he fall into the pits digged for him by justice and by his own offences." [22] Fortunately, state courts which regard this change of view as unwise are free to adhere to the earlier and, it is submitted, more balanced and expedient attitude.

130. Waiver by Partial Disclosure by Ordinary Witness.[1]

It is accepted generally in this country that an ordinary witness may by entering upon the story of a crime waive his privilege against disclosure of other facts which are part of the same story.[2] When does this

---

21. The quoted phrases, italicized as above, taken from Temple v. Comm., 75 Va. 892, 898 (1880) appear in Hoffman v. United States, 341 U.S. 479, 488, 71 S.Ct. 814, 95 L.Ed. 1118 (1951). In this latter case, the witness called before a federal grand jury investigating violations of various laws including those relating to liquor, narcotics, and the white slave traffic, was asked (a) what his occupation was, and (b) whether he knew and had recently seen and talked to one Weisberg, against whom a subpena to appear before the grand jury had been issued and who had failed to appear. He declined to answer and was committed for contempt. The Court of Appeals affirmed, considering that there was no showing that there was any probability that (a), a routine question would call for an incriminating answer, or that the answer to (b) would differentiate the witness "from a considerable number of blameless people." The Supreme Court reversed, holding as to (a) that the court should have considered evidence (see note 10, supra) tendered after the commitment that the witness had previously been convicted of a narcotics offense, and was pictured with a narcotics officer during the hearing in a newspaper article, and that in this setting it was not "clear" that the answers would not incriminate, and as to (b) made a like holding. Obviously, as to both sets of questions there is room for reasonable difference of opinion, even under the "substantial probability" test of the earlier cases. It is the extreme language, quoted in the text above, requiring that the answers "cannot possibly" have a tendency to incriminate, that arouses doubts. The difficulties of applying this latter standard are pointed out by some of the judges in United States v. Coffey, 198 F.2d 438

(C.A.3, 1952, opinion by Hastie, Circ.J.) and Kiewel v. United States, 204 F.2d 1, 7, 8 (C.A.8, 1953, concurring opinion by Sanborn, Circ.J.) and in a Note, Recent Extensions of the Privilege against Self-Incrimination, 53 Col.L.Rev. 275 (1953). An enthusiastically extreme application of the formula is seen in Marcello v. United States, 196 F.2d 437, syl. 5–10 (C.A.5, 1952).

22. 8 Wigmore, Evidence, p. 317.

1. 8 Wigmore, Evidence, § 2276(b) (1); 58 Am.Jur., Witnesses, §§ 95–99; Notes, Sherbow, Self-Incrimination and Waiver, 10 Md.L.Rev. 158 (1949), Disclosure as Waiver, 147 A.L.R. 255, Same, Federal cases, 95 L.Ed. 354, 360; Dec.Dig., Witnesses, ☞ 305(1).

2. See, e.g., Rogers v. United States, 340 U.S. 367, 371, 71 S.Ct. 438, 95 L.Ed. 344 (1951) (witness having testified she was treasurer and had books of Communist Party could not decline to name person to whom she had delivered books; three judges dissenting); United States v. St. Pierre, 132 F.2d 837, syl. 3, 4 (C.C.A. 2, 1942) (witness before grand jury having testified to embezzlement, cannot withhold name of person to whom he delivered embezzled money; acute opinion by L. Hand, Circ. J.; Frank, Circ. J., dissents elaborately); Ex parte Senior, 37 Fla. 1, 19 So. 652, syl. 7 (1896) (witness in election contest having testified that he voted is bound on cross-examination to answer questions as to his residence, despite claim of privilege).
In England, however, a witness who has entered, without invoking his privilege, on a story of his crime, may halt midstream and claim privilege against further disclosure. Reg. v. Garbett, 2 C. & K. 474,

waiver occur? First, it seems clear that there is no waiver on this theory until the witness discloses a fact that "incriminates" him,[3] i. e., one that he would have been privileged to refuse to answer.

We have seen that he is so privileged when the question calls for a fact that is an essential part of a crime, or is a link in a chain of circumstantial proof of a crime, and in the light of the entire setting the judge believes that there is a substantial probability that the answer would endanger a witness.[4] This is a vague and elusive standard which a judge is far better qualified to apply than is a witness. But waiver presupposes that the person waiving knows of the existence of the right which he relinquishes.[5] A witness would doubtless be held responsible for knowing generally of the existence of the privilege.[6] An ordinary lay witness would often not realize the incriminating quality of

some essential fact of the crime, as of the fact of kinship in the crime of incest. Still more often would he fail to understand the incriminating quality of a fact constituting a link in a circumstantial chain. It is believed, then, that a second rule may be stated, that the answer will not be a waiver as to further disclosure, unless the witness knew that he was charging himself with criminal conduct, or if the fact were less obviously connected with culpability, that he was privileged because of the probability of danger.[7] That he had the advice of counsel, or was a lawyer himself, or was warned of his rights by the judge, would be circumstances tending to show such knowledge.

As to the extent of the waiver, it is said that the witness having testified to the incriminating fact, waives his privilege as to all further facts relevant to the same transaction.[8] This likewise is a vague criterion,

---

495, 175 Eng.Rep. 196 (C.C.R., 1847). And the English lead is followed in a Maryland case. Chesapeake Club v. State, 63 Md. 446, 455, 462 (1885).

3. McCarthy v. Arndstein, 262 U.S. 355, 359, syl. 1, 2, 43 S.Ct. 562, 67 L.Ed. 1023 (1923) ("where the previous disclosure . . . is not an actual admission of guilt or incriminating facts, he is not deprived of the privilege of stopping short . . . whenever it may fairly tend to incriminate him"); United States v. Toner, 173 F.2d 141, syl. 11 (C.A. 3, 1949); Foster v. People, 18 Mich. 266, 274 (1869). See also United States v. Costello, 198 F.2d 200, 203, 204, syl. 4 (C.A. 2, 1952) (witness' voluntary statement that he always upheld constitution and laws did not open door to specific questions that might incriminate).

4. See next preceding section, herein.

5. "There can be no waiver if the defendants do not know their rights." Rutledge, J. in Wood v. United States, 128 F.2d 265, 277 (Ct.App.D.C. 1942).

6. See United States v. Thomas, 49 F.Supp. 547, 551 (W.D.Ky. 1943), pointing out that earlier cases requiring that the witness be informed of the privilege have not been followed. But see State v. Allison, 116 Mont. 352, 153 P.2d 141, syl. 6 (1944) (unwarned witness at inquest did not waive privilege by testifying; but question was as to admissibility of earlier testimony at a later trial).

7. Judges frequently mention this condition in their statements of the rule of waiver. See, e.g., Ex parte

Senior, 37 Fla. 1, 19 So. 652, 656 (1896) ("with full knowledge of his rights"); Georgia R. & Bkg. Co. v. Lybrend, 99 Ga. 621, 27 S.E. 794, 800 (1896) ("being fully aware of his right to maintain silence").

8. People v. Freshour, 55 Cal. 375 (1880) (after testifying to a cattle theft in which he took part, cannot claim privilege as to "general plan" between him and defendant; disclosing part of a transaction, "must disclose the whole"); Duckworth v. District Court, 220 Iowa 1350, 264 N.W. 715, 718, syl. 3 (1936) (after relating a part, may be compelled "to give the entire transaction"); State v. Wentworth, 65 Me. 234, 246 (1875) (a witness, "consenting to testify to a matter incriminating himself must testify in all respects relating to that matter," so far as material; but here witness was an accused). In the following cases the questions were held to be beyond the scope of the waiver. State v. Doran, 215 La. 151, 39 So.2d 894, syl. 5 (1949) (in suit for custody of child father testified child was not within state three days before proceedings started: held, not a waiver as to questions designed to show that he had kidnapped the child; sed quaere); Evans v. O'Connor, 174 Mass. 287, 54 N. E. 557, syl. 1 (1899) (action by husband for seduction of his wife; wife called for defendant wished to testify to her relations with defendant in 1893 only, but trial judge ruled that if she did, she could be cross-examined as to relations in 1894 and 1895; held, error, would not waive "as to other unlawful

analogous to the standard by which some states limit the cross-examination to the matters opened in the direct,[9] with which rule the present one is sometimes assimilated.[10] On account of this vagueness a reasonable lee-way in application should be accorded the trial judge.

A mechanical limitation has been placed upon the application of this doctrine of waiver. This limitation is calculated to encourage culprits to bribe and intimidate witnesses against them to change their testimony. This is the restriction that the waiver by disclosure of incriminating facts is strictly confined in effect to the very proceedings in which the first testimony is given.[11] Consequently, a witness of a murder who freely testifies before the grand jury to the facts of the killing by another and his own complicity, when called as a witness at the trial of the other killer, may claim privilege.[12] Similarly one who has signed an affidavit as to another's guilt of conducting a gambling establishment and has thus initiated the prosecution, may refuse to give evidence of the gambling at the trial.[13] The rule, like the rule denying admission to such former statements as substantive evidence,[14] protects chiefly the person accused of crime, and gives very little protection to the witness. If he has already given material evidence of his own guilt, such evidence, in the form of a transcript of his testimony, or of a signed affidavit, can readily be proved against him if he is tried for the crime. The present testimony will not add to his hazard except as additional facts or details are brought out. It is submitted that the rule proposed in the Uniform Rules,[15] that any holder of a privilege who on any occasion has freely "made disclosure of any part of the matter" has waived the privilege as to that matter, represents the wiser view. However, in respect to the present privilege the rule of waiver might well be limited to prior disclosures in writing or in the form of sworn testimony.

131. Waiver by an Accused Who Takes the Stand.[1]

An ordinary witness has no privilege to decline altogether to testify, and by taking the stand he waives nothing. He has a choice only when he is asked an incriminat-

---

acts, wholly unconnected with the act of which [she] has spoken"; result seems questionable); People v. Forbes, 143 N.Y. 219, 230, 38 N.E. 303, syl. 2, 3 (1894) (grand jury investigation of death due to release of gas in college freshman dining hall; sophomore student who testified that he had no connection with the transaction on the evening of the banquet, was held entitled to claim privilege as to questions about who placed the gas-containers beneath the dining hall; had he testified to any "incriminating" facts?).

9. See § 21, herein.

10. See, e.g., Graul v. United States, 47 App.D.C. 543, 549, 550 (1918); and People v. Freshour and State v. Wentworth, in note 8, above.

11. Overend v. Superior Court, 131 Cal. 280, 63 Pac. 372, syl. 2 (1900) (testimony at preliminary hearing no waiver for trial); Ex parte Sales, 134 Cal.App. 54, 24 P.2d 916, syl. 4 (1933) (testimony before grand jury); Samuel v. People, 164 Ill. 379, 45 N. E. 728, syl. 1 (1896) (affidavit indorsed on information); Duckworth v. District Court, 220 Iowa 1350, 264 N.W. 715, syl. 8 (1936) (grand jury testimony),

noted critically in 32 Ill.L.Rev. 117; Apodaca v. Viramontes, 53 N.M. 513, 212 P.2d 425, syl. 3 (1949) (testimony before grand jury); Temple v. Comm., 75 Va. 892, 896 (1881) (same); 8 Wigmore, Evidence, § 2276(4); 58 Am.Jur., Witnesses, § 99.

12. As in Ex parte Sales, note 11, above.

13. As in Samuel v. People, note 11, above.

14. See § 39, herein.

15. Uniform Rules of Evidence, Rule 37: "A person who would otherwise have a privilege to refuse to disclose or to prevent another from disclosing a specified matter has no such privilege with respect to that matter if the judge finds that he or any other person while the holder of the privilege has (a) contracted with anyone not to claim the privilege or, (b) without coercion and with knowledge of his privilege, made disclosure of any part of the matter or consented to such a disclosure made by any one."

1. 8 Wigmore, Evidence, § 2276(2); 58 Am.Jur., Witnesses, §§ 96–99; 70 C.J., Witnesses, §§ 888, 889; Dec. Dig., Witnesses, ⊕⇒305(2).

ing question. The accused is in a vastly different position. He has an option to stay off the stand altogether, or to testify. As his privilege is wider, so correspondingly his waiver is wider, than that of the ordinary witness who answers an incriminating question. By volunteering to become a witness he volunteers to answer all relevant inquiries about the charge against him which is on trial.[2]

The crucial question here is whether and to what extent he retains a privilege for questions about other crimes not now on trial. There are two views. First, that the accused by taking the stand "throws away his shield" and thus may be examined about other crimes, whether they be relevant to the issue, or relevant merely upon credibility.[3] Of course, the accused can claim the benefit of the rules, other than privilege,

which curtail this sort of impeachment by collateral crimes.[4] The second is the most widely prevailing, and perhaps the more reasonable view. This would limit the waiver to other crimes relevant to the issue on trial,[5] thus maintaining the privilege in respect to crimes relevant only upon credibility.[6]

It is generally and wisely held—though there is some dissent—that by volunteering to become a witness, he makes himself amenable to give relevant evidence in all the ways that an ordinary witness may be called on to furnish it.[7] Accordingly, he has surrendered his privilege against self-incrimination in respect to furnishing demonstrative evidence by producing objects[8] or documents[9], by bodily exhibitions,[10] or by pronouncing words,[11] or by giving specimens of handwriting.[12] The same result should fol-

---

2. Johnson v. United States, 318 U.S. 189, 195, 63 S.Ct. 549, syl. 1, 87 L.Ed 704 (1943). In addition to the question of the scope of the waiver, the allowability of questions by the prosecution to the accused is much affected by the rules about the scope of cross-examination. In states having the "wide-open" rule of cross-examination, there is no restriction. But in those which limit the cross-examination to the scope of the direct, there are obvious dangers in allowing the accused by limiting the scope of the direct to limit the inquiries of the prosecution. These dangers may be mitigated in those states which recognize the right of the prosecutor to recall the accused, who has testified on his own behalf, as a state's witness. Fitzgerald v. Comm., 269 Ky. 844, 108 S.W.2d 1040, syl. 10 (1937); Hamit v. State, 42 Okl.Cr. 168, 275 Pac. 361, syl. 5 (1929). The problem is discussed in § 26, herein.

3. People v. Casey, 72 N.Y. 393, 398, 399 (1878) (assault; cross-examination as to other assaults to affect credibility proper).
Questions about *convictions* of crime to affect credibility do not raise the present problem since such questions are not incriminating, see § 128, herein.

4. People v. Redmond, 265 App.D. 307, 38 N.Y.S.2d 727, syl. 1, 2 (1942). See as to such rules, §§ 42, 47, herein.

5. Johnson v. United States, 318 U.S. 189, 63 S.Ct. 549, syl. 3, 87 L.Ed. 704 (1943); Lacy v. State, 137 Tex.Cr. 362, 128 S.W.2d 1165, syl. 5 (1939) (murder: shooting another person shortly after fatal shoot-

ing, as bearing on defense of duress and showing malice).

6. State v. Pancoast, 5 N.D. 516, 67 N.W. 1052, syl. 14 (1896).

7. See Note, Requiring Accused to Exhibit Self or Perform Acts during Trial, 171 A.L.R. 1144, 1181.

8. State v. Schopmeyer, 207 Ind. 538, 194 N.E. 144, syl. 3 (1935) (teacher charged with assault by beating pupil with hose may properly be requested to produce hose).

9. Powell v. Comm., 167 Va. 558, 189 S.E. 433, 441, 110 A.L.R. 90 (1937) (if defendant had taken stand, "he might then have been questioned as to the whereabouts of these notes, and since he had them, he might have been told to produce them").

10. Neely v. United States, 2 F.2d 849, syl. 5 (C.C.A.4, 1924) (rolling up sleeve to exhibit scar); Williams v. State, 98 Ala. 52, 13 So. 333, syl. 4 (1893) (to stand up so that jury might judge her age). Contra: State v. Allen, 183 Md. 603, 39 A.2d 820, syl. 8, 10, 171 A.L.R. 1138 (1944) (requiring accused to try on a hat). See Sherbow, Note, 10 Md.L.Rev. 159, 162.

11. State v. Jones, 188 Wash. 275, 62 P.2d 44, syl. 2 (1936) (to show whether he had impediment in speech).

12. State v. Vroman, 45 S.D. 465, 188 N.W. 746, syl. 2 (1922); Long v. State, 120 Tex.Cr. 373, 48 S.W.2d 632, syl. 2 (1932) (one judge dissenting).

low as regards orders to furnish samples of blood for tests, or submission to psychiatric examinations or to lie-detector tests.[13] The self-incrimination privilege should be regarded as waived. Other objections, such as those based upon due process, the privilege of bodily integrity or lack of scientific acceptance, so far as they may be persuasive, would still be open.[14]

The surrender by the accused of his privilege, to constitute a waiver, must be voluntary. Thus, a defendant who took the stand, under pressure of a suggestion by a juror at the close of the evidence, could complain that his right to remain silent was violated.[15]

If the accused takes the stand for the sole purpose of testifying upon a preliminary question of fact upon which the admission of other evidence depends, should this be taken as a complete waiver? The question has arisen only as to testimony disputing the voluntariness of a confession. As to this the testimony of the accused is essential to present his contention, and it would be unfortunate to penalize his testifying on this dispute, and most of the cases limit the waiver to the particular issue.[16]

By taking the stand at a preliminary hearing or before the grand jury, or at a previous trial, the accused does not—though as an original question there could be a strong con-

trary argument—waive his right to remain silent at the present trial.[17] His testimony, however, voluntarily given at the previous hearing may be used against him at the later trial.[18]

132. Comment on the Failure of the Accused to Testify.[1]

Under the classic common law practice the accused as an interested party was entirely incompetent as a witness. Not only could he not be called by the government; he could not even testify in his own behalf. When this latter disability was swept away in this country in the Civil War era, by statutes permitting but not requiring the accused to testify,[2] a new problem arose. The accused now has an option—to testify or remain silent—which he never had before. Shall the usual inference from failure to answer an accusation or from failure to produce evidence under one's control be available here? The legislatures generally concluded that the usual inference and argument, if applied here, would unduly discourage the exercise of the new privilege and in nearly all the states adopted enactments, in various forms, which operate to forbid comment by the court or by counsel for the state on the failure of the defendant to take the stand.[3] A few states, in accord with the pol-

---

13. See § 126, as to whether these acts are within the privilege at all, irrespective of waiver.

14. See chs. 14 and 20, herein.

15. Blair v. Comm., 166 Va. 715, 185 S.E. 900, syl. 2 (1936).

16. State v. Thomas, 208 La. 548, 23 So.2d 212, syl. 1–3 (1945); Hawkins v. State, 193 Miss. 586, 10 So. 2d 678, syl. 5 (1942); Enoch v. Comm., 141 Va. 411, 126 S.E. 222, syl. 7 (1925). Contra: People v. Trybus, 219 N.Y. 18, 113 N.E. 538, syl. 6 (1916).

17. 8 Wigmore, Evidence, § 2276, pp. 450, 451, supports the text and conforms to general tradition. The cases he cites, however, are all cases involving the question how far an ordinary witness testifying at one hearing waives his privilege at a later proceeding—a question discussed in the next preceding section herein.

18. People v. Arnold, 43 Mich. 303, 5 N.W. 385 (1880); 58 Am.Jur., Witnesses, § 100.

1. 8 Wigmore, Evidence, §§ 2272–2273; 23 C.J.S., Crim.Law, §§ 1098, 1099; Dec.Dig., Crim.Law, ☞721, 721½.

2. The first state allowing the accused to testify was Maine in 1864. See Reeder, Comment on Failure of Accused to Testify, 31 Mich.L.Rev. 40 (1932); Hutchinson, Comment, 46 id. 372, 378 (1948).

3. The statutes are set out in 2 Wigmore, Evidence, § 488, from which these references are taken. The United States Code Annotated, Title 18, § 3481 provides ". . . His failure to make such request shall not create any presumption against him." This is the commonest form, see, e. g., Mass.G.L.(Ter.Ed.) c. 233, § 20, subd. 3; New York, Code Cr.Proc. § 393; North Carolina, G.S. § 8–54. There are many variants: Illinois, S.H.A. ch. 38, § 734: ". . . and

icy-views of most of the writers,[4] permit the comment either by constitutional provision,[5] by statute,[6] or by judicial decision.[7]

In general, of course, the prosecution may comment in argument upon the adverse party's failure to produce witnesses or documents under his control,[8] and manifestly the prosecution may likewise argue that the state's evidence or some part of it is uncontradicted or undisputed. Whether this latter stock argument may be employed when the proof shows that the accused is the only person who could have contradicted it is in conflict.[9] Probably the better view is that such an argument is not a violation of the statute unless in the particular case the argument seems to have been specifically planned by counsel and probably understood by the jury as a comment on the silence of the accused.

If the state were to call the accused as a witness and thus force him before the jury to claim his privilege this would probably be held equivalent to an implied comment.[10] It is likewise held that a demand by the state in the jury's presence that the accused produce a document in his possession is improper.[11] This is often placed on the ground that it is "compulsion" to produce and hence a violation of the privilege against self-incrimination.[12] That this is the kind of compulsion that the constitution-makers meant seems most improbable.[13] Nor can the ruling easily be sustained on the ground that the demand is an implied comment upon his failure to testify. A comment upon a failure to produce evidence in his power is generally sanctioned.[14]

If counsel for accused undertakes to explain his client's failure to take the stand, the

---

his neglect to testify shall not create any presumption against him, nor shall the Court permit any reference or comment to be made to or upon such neglect"; Texas, Vernon's Ann.C.C.P. art. 710: " . . . but the failure of any defendant to so testify shall not be taken as a circumstance against him, nor shall the same be alluded to or commented on by counsel in the cause." The most sedulous attempt to shackle the reasoning faculty is seen in Indiana, Burns' Ann.St. § 9–1603: "But if the defendant do not testify, his failure to do so shall not be commented upon or referred to in the argument of the cause, nor commented upon, referred to, or in any manner considered by the jury trying the same; and it shall be the duty of the Court, in such case, in its charge, to instruct the jury as to their duty under the provisions of this section."

4. See the concluding paragraphs of this section.

5. Calif., Const.Amendment Nov. 6, 1934 (adding to Art. I, § 13, after "due process of law," the clause: "but in any criminal case, whether the defendant testifies or not, his failure to explain or to deny by his testimony any evidence or facts in the case against him may be commented upon by the Court and by counsel, and may be considered by the Court or the jury"; Ohio, Const.Amendment to Sect. 10, Art. I ("No person shall be compelled, in any criminal case, to be a witness against himself; but his failure to testify may be considered by the Court and jury and may be made the subject of comment by counsel."

6. Iowa, I.C.A. § 781.12. Its validity was upheld in State v. Ferguson, 226 Iowa 361, 283 N.W. 917, syl. 2–4 (1939); Vermont, Acts of 1935, No. 52, validity sustained in State v. Baker, 115 Vt. 94, 53 A.2d 53, syl. 6–8 (1947).

7. Parker v. State, 61 N.J.L. 308, 39 Atl. 651, syl. 3 (1898). See also State v. Heno, 119 Conn. 29, 174 Atl. 181, syl. 5 (1934), holding that statute prohibiting comment "to the court or jury" does not forbid comment by judge, which is proper.

8. State v. Harding, 205 Iowa 853, 216 N.W. 756, 758 (1927) (failure to produce witnesses); Note, 68 A.L. R. 1108, 1139; Dec.Dig., Crim.Law, ⊂⇒721(6). See § 249, herein, as to the use of this argument in general. As to documents see 8 Wigmore, § 2273(2).

9. Allowable. People v. Novak, 370 Ill. 220, 18 N.E. 2d 235, syl. 3 (1938); People v. Earl, 299 Mich. 579, 300 N.W. 890, syl. 5, 6 (1941). Contra: Boone v. State, 90 Tex.Cr. 374, 235 S.W. 580, 582 (1921) (dictum). See 23 C.J.S., Crim.L., § 1098, notes 6, 21.

10. But see 8 Wigmore, Evidence, § 2268(2) (a).

11. See cases collected in Note, 110 A.L.R. 101. See for a contrary view, 8 Wigmore, Evidence, § 2268 (2) (b).

12. See, e. g., Powell v. Comm., 167 Va. 558, 189 S.E. 433, syl. 8, 110 A.L.R. 90 (1937).

13. See the discussion of the question whether comment is compulsion in the next to last paragraph of this section.

14. See note 8, supra.

prosecutor may of course answer this argument.[15]

A few states make a fetish of the prohibition by punishing any infraction by automatic reversal [16] but most courts will consider whether objection was adequately made, whether the judge has effectively instructed the jury so as to cure the error, and whether guilt was so clearly established as to render the error immaterial.[17]

Under the practice most widely prevailing the court may properly instruct the jury on his own motion that the defendant's failure to testify shall not be taken against him,[18] and upon request the defendant is entitled to have the jury so instructed.[19]

Analogous problems about comment and inferences from silence may arise when the accused does take the stand. If he fails to deny or explain facts proved against him and presumably within his knowledge comment on this failure is allowed.[20] We have seen that defendant's privilege is waived by taking the stand only as to matters relevant to the crime on trial. If he properly asserts it for matter beyond this limit presumably no adverse comment would be permitted. How if he erroneously claims privilege for matter within the scope of the waiver, and the answer is not insisted on? It seems that the refusal should be subject to inference on the theory discussed above, if the refusal is a failure to deny or explain adverse facts.[21] But if the trial judge, even though erroneously, sustains the claim of privilege, adverse comment has been regarded as unfair.[22] The courts are divided on the question of the propriety of comment, when the accused testifies at the present trial, upon his failure to testify at a previous trial of the same charge, or his refusal to appear as a witness before the grand jury or at the examining trial.[23]

15. United States v. Feinberg, 140 F.2d 592, syl. 5 (C.C.A.2, 1944); People v. Schultz, 210 Mich. 297, 178 N.W. 89, 91 (1920). Contra but unsound: People v. Young, 316 Ill. 508, 147 N.E. 425, syl. 3 (1925).

16. Rice v. State, 185 Okl.Cr. 400, 92 P.2d 857, syl. 1, 2 (1939) (under Okl.Sts. 1931, sec. 3068, which provides ". . . if commented on by counsel it shall be ground for a new trial"); Elliott v. Comm., 172 Va. 595, 1 S.E.2d 273, syl. 4, 5 (1939) (harmless error doctrine inapplicable because comment deprives accused of fair trial: three judges dissenting), see excellent note, 30 J.Crim.L. 434.

17. Milton v. United States, 110 F.2d 556, syl. 2, 3 (Ct.App.D.C. 1940); Comm. v. Richmond, 207 Mass. 240, 93 N.E. 816, syl. 13, 14 (1911); People v. Hoch, 150 N.Y. 291, 44 N.E. 976, 981, syl. 9 (1896) (two judges dissenting); Note, 84 A.L.R. 784; Dec.Dig., Crim.Law, ⇨1171(5).

18. Becher v. United States, 5 F.2d 45, 49, syl. 10 (C.C.A.2, 1924) ("It is no doubt better if the defendant requests no charge upon the subject, for the trial judge to say nothing about it; but to say that when he does, it is error, carries the doctrine of self-incrimination to an absurdity"); Eubank v. State, 104 Tex.Cr. 628, 286 S.W. 234, syl. 1 (1926); State v. Comer, 176 Wash. 257, 28 P.2d 1027, syl. 20 (1934).

19. Bruno v. United States, 308 U.S. 287, 60 S.Ct. 198, 84 L.Ed. 257 (1939) (the court also holds that

such a refusal to instruct is not a "technical error" which may be disregarded; this seems questionable), and see instructive note, Kent, 38 Mich.L.Rev. 1322; People v. Greeben, 352 Ill. 582, 186 N.E. 162, syl. 10 (1933); 23 C.J.S., Crim.Law, § 1266.

20. Caminetti v. United States, 242 U.S. 470, 492, 37 S.Ct. 192, 61 L.Ed. 442, 456 (1917) (comment by court); Blanda v. People, 67 Colo. 541, 189 Pac. 249, syl. 1 (1920); 8 Wigmore, Evidence, § 2273(4).

21. Johnson v. United States, 318 U.S. 189, 196, 63 S. Ct. 549, 553, 87 L.Ed. 704 (1943) (dictum); State v. Ober, 52 N.H. 459, 464 (1873).

22. Johnson v. United States, next preceding note.

23. Allowing the comment: Raffel v. United States, 271 U.S. 494, 46 S.Ct. 566, 70 L.Ed. 1054 (1926) (questions by judge eliciting fact of previous silence, approved, interesting opinion by Stone, J.); People v. McCrea, 303 Mich. 213, 6 N.W.2d 489, 517, syl. 34 (1942) (proper to cross-examine accused about his silence before grand jury). Contra: State v. Youngquist, 176 Minn. 562, 223 N.W. 917, syl. 4 (1929) (cross-examination as to defendant's claim of privilege in separate trial of co-defendant, improper); Hays v. State, 101 Tex.Cr. 162, 274 S.W. 579 (1925) (cross-examination as to silence at examining trial, improper); 8 Wigmore, Evidence, § 2273, note 8. As to inference in a civil trial from the party's claim of privilege in a criminal trial, see Note, 2 A.L.R.2d 1297. When a witness other than the accused

Its pertinence to credibility is apparent—you now tell an exculpatory story, why did you not tell it when you had an opportunity before? But the argument that taking the stand now is a waiver of the right to be free from comment on a prior exercise of privilege,[24] is a weak one, and allowing the comment tends somewhat to discourage the accused from testifying at the present time, which seems inexpedient.[25]

In the jurisdictions where comment by court or counsel is permitted,[26] it is usually held that the court should explain to the jury that the prosecution has the burden of adducing evidence of guilt, independent of the inference from silence,[27] and that where the defense witnesses assert that the defendant was not in a position to know, then if these assertions are believed, the defendant's failure to deny or explain shall not be taken against him.[28] An instruction that the jury should give the defendant's silence such importance as they saw fit has been disapprov-

ed as empowering the jury to treat it as a confession.[29]

In 1931 and 1934 the American Bar Association, and in 1938 its Committee on the Administration of Justice adopted resolutions recommending the abrogation of the statutes prohibiting comment.[30] A law to that effect in South Dakota, however, in 1936 was declared invalid as contravening the constitutional privilege against compulsion to testify,[31] and this was followed by a like holding in Massachusetts followed in 1938.[32] Allowance of comment was "moral compulsion," which was thought to be prohibited equally with physical coercion. In 1947, however, in Vermont the tide of decision turned and a statute permitting comment to the jury was sustained.[33] This conclusion, it is believed, is sound both historically and in point of expediency.

The adoption into English law of the maxim that no man shall be compelled to accuse himself was a reaction against judicial compulsion enforced by imprisonment, and oc-

---

claims his privilege, no inference therefrom prejudicial to the accused is allowable. Billeci v. United States, 184 F.2d 394, syl. 4 (C.A.D.C. 1950), Note, 24 A.L.R.2d 895.

24.   Raffel v. United States, next preceding note.

25.   Note, 36 Harv.L.Rev. 207 (1922).

26.   See notes 4–7, supra.

27.   Waugh v. The King [1950] App.Cas. 203, 212 (P. C.); People v. Adamson, 27 Cal.2d 478, 165 P.2d 3, 11, syl. 26 (1946) (but refusal not here prejudicial).

28.   People v. Albertson, 23 Cal.2d 550, 584, 145 P.2d 7, 25 (1944) (by Traynor, J., concurring); People v. Sanchez, 35 Cal.2d 522, 219 P.2d 9, 14, syl. 11 (1950) (where defendant relied on partial defense of intoxication sufficient to destroy volition and memory, and counsel for state commented on failure to testify, court should have instructed jury as to limitation upon inference); Parker v. State, 61 N.J.L. 308, 39 Atl. 651, 654 (1898). See notes, Goodfellow, Limits on Right to Comment, 34 Calif.L.Rev. 764 (1946); Way, Comment on Failure to Testify, 65 N. J.L.J. 97, 101–3 (Feb. 26, 1942) (an excellent study of New Jersey decisions and experience).

29.   State v. Kisik, 99 N.J.L. 385, 125 Atl. 239 (Ct. Errors & App. 1924), criticised 8 Wigmore, Evidence, p. 415, note.

30.   See references in the learned opinion of Sherburne, J., in State v. Baker, 115 Vt. 94, 53 A.2d 53, 56 (1947); 8 Wigmore, Evidence, pp. 425, 426; Vanderbilt, Minimum Standards of Judicial Administration, 381, 579–581 (1949).

31.   State v. Wolfe, 64 S.D. 178, 266 N.W. 116, syl. 7, 104 A.L.R. 464 (1936) (able dissents by Rudolph, J., and Bakewell, Circ. J.). See Comments, 50 Harv.L. Rev. 356, 1936, 22 Corn.L.Q. 392, 1937.

32.   In re Opinion of the Justices, 300 Mass. 620, 15 N.E.2d 662, 1938 (but with a cogent dissenting opinion by Lummus, J.). See the acute and comprehensive Comment on this case by Swope, 37 Mich.L. Rev. 777, 1939, and shorter Notes, 25 Va.L.Rev. 90, 1938; 87 U.Pa.L.Rev. 122, 1938. Compare State v. Ferguson, 226 Iowa 361, 283 N.W. 917, syl. 2, 1939, holding in a state where the privilege against self-incrimination is only statutory, not constitutional, that the statute giving the accused the privilege not to testify does not forbid comment on his silence.

33.   State v. Baker, 115 Vt. 94, 53 A.2d 53, syl. 6–8 (1947) (comprehensive opinion by Sherburne, J.; two judges dissenting), discussed in an instructive note, 57 Yale L.J. 145.

casionally by torture.[34] And certainly when in the late 1700s the earliest American constitutional embodiments of the privilege were adopted,[35] comment on silence was not contemplated as an evil to be guarded against. It was more than half a century later that the first statute permitting the accused to testify was passed.[36] Moreover, the compulsive effect of allowing comment must be slight, since even when comment is not allowed, the defendant and his counsel know that the jury without being told will observe his failure to speak and will look on his defence with skepticism. The number of defendants who fail to testify and who yet are acquitted must be almost negligible.[37] Allowing the comment will not encourage the prosecutor to abate his diligence in collecting evidence. He does not know whether the accused will testify or remain silent, and in any event he must make out a prima facie case of guilt, before the defendant will be called on to make the choice. Moreover, allowing the comment will avoid the numerous appeals and reversals necessary to hold the line between proper argument and forbidden comment.[38] Furthermore, if a greater number of defendants are encouraged to testify this would tend to make for more truth and justice in criminal trials.[39] Finally, a survey of the experience of the judges in the five states where comment is allowed reveals that an overwhelming majority of these judges believe that the allowance of comment has promoted a juster enforcement of law.[40]

Will an innocent man ever choose to remain silent rather than tell his story? Fanciful motives are sometimes suggested, such as a desire to shield someone else; or a fear that due to his shyness or stupidity he will break down under cross-examination, and create a worse impression than he would by remaining silent. But a more substantial motive is created by the rule [41] which permits the prosecutor to cross-examine the accused upon his past convictions of crime.[42] Here the accused may well tremble before he takes the stand. Of course, he should acknowledge his criminal record on direct examination, rather than have it extorted on cross.[43] But even so (and particularly when the past crimes are of like nature with the present charge) the jury will be heavily prejudiced against the man who is thus re-

---

34. See the scholarly account of the conditions which the privilege was intended to remedy in the dissenting opinion of Lummus, J., in In re Opinion of the Justices, 300 Mass. 620, 15 N.E.2d 662, 665, 666 (1938), and § 120, herein.

35. See § 120, above.

36. Maine, Laws, 1864, c. 280, p. 214.

37. See Arthur Train, The Prisoner at the Bar, 209–212 (1923 ed.) (out of 300 defendants tried, 23 failed to take the stand, and in this group 21 were convicted, 1 was acquitted, and 1 secured a disagreement; results in the other group not given).

38. The plethora of decisions will appear upon examination of Dec.Dig., Crim.Law, ☞721, 721½.

39. Note, 57 Yale L.J. 145, 149 (1947).

40. "178 judges answered the questionnaire. . . . The replies of the Judges show that 93.65 per cent regard comment as an important and proper aid in the administration of justice, while only 2.65 per cent consider it definitely unfair to the accused (the others listing it as relatively unimportant). Over 85 per cent say that it seldom if ever causes the prosecuting attorney to be less diligent in his search for evidence of guilt.

"The answers of the Judges are most important, partly because of the lack of any prejudice in their point of view and partly because many of them have had experience both as prosecuting officers and as defense counsel before being elevated to the Bench." Report of Section on Judicial Administration, Am. Bar Asso. (1938), quoted in 8 Wigmore, Evidence, p. 426, and in Vanderbilt, Minimum Standards of Judicial Administration, p. 581 (1949).

41. See § 43, herein.

42. The importance of this motive is demonstrated in Way, op. cit. note 28, supra.

43. "Even in the case of a respondent with mental or language deficiencies, or with a prior criminal record which may affect his credibility as a witness, if his counsel will bare these in his direct examination, rather than wait to have them shown upon cross-examination, the jury will give him fair consideration if his testimony rings true." Sherburne, J., in State v. Baker, 115 Vt. 94, 53 A.2d 53, 59 (1947).

vealed as a jail-bird. Accordingly, the proposals of the Uniform Rules which allow the comment [44] but forbid the cross-examiner to question the accused as to past convictions or otherwise prove them,[45] seem humane and just. Another modification deserving of consideration is that of confining the function of commenting on the defendant's silence to the judge, as in England [46] and in Connecticut.[47] The judge can be held responsible for a moderate and logical explanation of the inferences, whereas the prosecutor's comments on this shadowy but often overwhelming inference from silence are likely to be unduly emotional. It may be wholesome to restrict his argument to the other facts and inferences in the case.

133. The Privilege of the Witness Is Personal.[1]

Neither the party,[2] where he is distinct from the witness, nor the party's attorney,[3]

nor even the witness's attorney,[4] may claim the privilege. Only the witness may make the claim.[5] Of course, if the privilege is granted without adequate basis, and thus relevant testimony is excluded, the aggrieved party may complain.[6] If, however, the privilege is erroneously denied and the witness thus forced to testify then, unless the witness and party are one, the party is held to have no ground of grievance.[7]

134. Public Records: Required Records and Reports.[1]

A document, entry or writing which is part of the state's official records (whether open to the public or not) is of course subject to be produced upon judicial order without regard to any claim of privilege against self-incrimination of the person who has custody.[2] The state's interest in its records has

44. Rule 23(4): "If an accused in a criminal action does not testify, the judge and counsel may comment upon accused's failure to testify, and the trier of fact may draw all reasonable inferences therefrom."

45. Rule 21: ". . . If the witness be the accused in a criminal proceeding, no evidence of his conviction of a crime shall be admissible for the sole purpose of impairing his credibility unless he has first introduced evidence admissible solely for the purpose of supporting his credibility."

46. Reg. v. Rhodes [1899] 1 Q.B. 77, 83, interpreting statute which provided that the silence of the accused "shall not be made the subject of any comment by the prosecution."

47. State v. Heno, 119 Conn. 29, 174 Atl. 181, syl. 5 (1934).

1. 8 Wigmore, Evidence, § 2270; Note, Persons Entitled to Waive or Claim Privilege, 30 Col.L.Rev. 686 (1930); 70 C.J., Witnesses, §§ 902–906; Dec.Dig., Witnesses, ⊙⊐306, 307.

2. State v. Hamilton, 304 Mo. 19, 263 S.W. 127, syl. 4 (1924) (statutory rape: accused cannot complain of court's failure to advise prosecutrix of her privilege); Phleps v. Phleps, 133 N.J.Eq. 392, 32 A.2d 81, syl. 4 (1943) (in proceeding by defendant to take deposition of third person complainant could not object to questions proposed on ground that they might incriminate such third person).

3. O'Chiato v. People 73 Colo. 192, 214 Pac. 404, syl. 3 (1923) (error to sustain objection of state's attorney to question of defendant to witness); State v. Andrews, 82 Vt. 314, 73 Atl. 586 (1909) (same).

4. In re O'Shea, 166 Fed. 180, syl. 7 (D.N.J.1908); Ward v. Martin, 175 N.C. 287, 95 S.E. 621, syl. 2 (1918) (party-witness, not his attorney, must claim).

5. The party has no right to demand that the judge warn the witness of his privilege not to answer. State v. Mungeon, 20 S.D. 612, 108 N.W. 552, 553 (1906) (citing numerous authorities).

6. See cases cited n. 3, supra.

7. See § 73, note 8, herein.

1. 8 Wigmore, Evidence, §§ 2259c, 2259d; Meltzer, Required Records, the McCarran Act and the Privilege against Self-Incrimination, 18 Univ. of Chi.L. Rev. 687 (1951), also as Univ. of Chicago Reprint and Pamphlet Series, No. 10; Morgan, Self-Incrimination, 34 Minn.L.Rev. 1, 34–38 (1949); Note, Quasi Public Records and Self-Incrimination, 47 Col.L. Rev. 838 (1947); Model Code of Evidence, Rule 207; Uniform Rules of Evidence, Rule 25(e).

2. Bradshaw v. Murphy, 7 C. & P. 612, 173 Eng.Rep. 269 (Nisi Prius, 1836) (vestryman ordered to produce vestry-book required by statute to be kept, despite claim of privilege); People v. Coombs, 158 N. Y. 532, 53 N.E. 527, syl. 5 (1899) (false vouchers prepared by coroner's clerk and found in coroner's office properly required to be produced under sub-

precedence over the private claims of the person in possession.

More recent, and more expansible, than the public records escape from the privilege is a doctrine of required private records which has emerged with the developement of the nineteenth century system of regulation of business enterprise. Under this doctrine the state or the federal government, in their respective spheres, may in certain circumstances validly impose on one who engages in a particular business, profession, calling or activity an obligation to make records and reports of his operations and activities. Furthermore, when this duty is thus validly imposed, the records kept and reports made are not within the protection of the self-incrimination privilege but are subject to compulsory production by the person affected with the duty.[3]

This exemption of records and reports from the privilege has sometimes been justified on the ground that the legislature could have excluded the person from the activity and since the greater power includes the less, it could impose as a condition the waiver of the privilege by submitting to the requirement of records and reports. As to activities which could be prohibited entirely such as the sale of liquor or narcotics, this theory seems persuasive, but the recent cases have applied the required-records-exemption from

pena; "it cannot be said that a public officer is privileged to retain in a public office a fraudulent record . . .". See also Wilson v. United States, 221 U.S. 361, 380, 31 S.Ct. 538, 544, 55 L.Ed. 771 (1911); Davis v. United States, 328 U.S. 582, 66 S.Ct. 1256, syl. 3, 90 L.Ed. 1453 (1946) (gasoline ration coupons, being property of government, may be required to be produced by dealer, suspected of violation of rationing laws, without infringing privilege).

3. Shapiro v. United States, 335 U.S. 1, 32, 68 S.Ct. 1375, 92 L.Ed. 1787 (1948) (prosecution for violation of Emergency Price Control Act, 50 U.S.C.A.Appendix, § 901 et seq., by defendant, a wholesaler of fruit and produce: defendant produced under subpena in administrative hearing certain sales records, for which he claimed privilege, and contended at his trial that such compelled production of privileged documents entitled him to immunity from prosecution—under the provisions of the Price Control Act; held, being records validly required by the Act and regulations thereunder to be kept subject to inspection by the Administrator, they were not privileged and the claim of immunity was properly denied; four judges dissenting), noted 47 Mich.L. Rev. 271, 22 So.Calif.L.Rev. 303; People v. Henwood, 123 Mich. 317, 320, 82 N.W. 70 (1900) (prosecution of druggist for failure to file with prosecuting attorney reports of liquor sold as required by Local Option Law; held, the requirement does not offend search and seizure and self-incrimination privileges, but is valid police regulation, "for the prevention of intemperance, pauperism and crime"); City of St. Joseph v. Levin, 128 Mo. 588, 31 S.W. 101, syl. 1, 2 (1895) (conviction for violation of ordinance requiring pawnbrokers to keep records of property received and to submit them to police for inspection on demand; held, ordinance is a valid

police regulation and in absence of showing of criminal conduct by defendant, there is no infringement of his privilege; but the court said, obiter, that in a criminal proceeding the defendant could not be required to produce the record). But see State v. Pence, 173 Ind. 99, 89 N.E. 488 (1909) (conviction of druggist for illegal sale of whiskey; statute required that druggists shall retain all prescriptions upon which whiskey sold; held, in absence of provision subjecting prescriptions to official inspection, which could have been validly provided, a judicial order here to produce prescriptions was violation of defendant's self-incrimination privilege). Cases are collected in 8 Wigmore, § 2259d, note 2. Frankfurter, J., reviews many of them, and explains them on the public records principle in his dissent in Shapiro v. United States, supra, at page 59 of the official report. A case not precisely in point but looking in the same general direction is United States v. Kahriger, 345 U.S. 22, 73 S.Ct. 510, 515, 97 L.Ed. 754 (1953). There the court sustained the validity of the requirement of the Gamblers' Occupational Tax Act, 26 U.S.C.A. §§ 3285, 3290, 3291, that persons engaged in the business of accepting wagers pay certain excise taxes and register their names and residences with the federal collector. As to the privilege question the court said in part: "Assuming that respondent can raise the self-incrimination issue, that privilege has relation only to past acts, not to future acts that may or may not be committed. 8 Wigmore (3d ed., 1940) § 2259(c). If respondent wishes to take wagers subject to excise taxes under § 3285, supra, he must pay an occupational tax and register. Under the registration provisions of the wagering tax, appellee is not compelled to confess to acts already committed, he is merely informed by the statute that in order to engage in the business of wagering in the future he must fulfill certain conditions."

the privilege to ordinary businesses not of the bannable kind.[4]

What are the limits of the power to require records and reports and of the consequent curtailment of the privilege? We feel sure that the power does not extend to a requirement that "each citizen . . . keep a diary that would show where he was at all times, with whom he was, and what he was up to."[5] Doubtless the records and reports requirement must be directed toward some class of acts and activities that would normally be lawful rather than criminal.[6] A requirement that every person who kills another with firearms should report the fact to the sheriff would presumably fall afoul of the privilege. It seems also that the power to require records and reports and to exempt them from privilege could only be exerted as a means of carrying out some other distinct governmental power,[7] such as the power to tax,[8] the power to regulate prices in an emergency,[9] or the state's police power to regulate activities dangerous to the health, safety, and morals of the community.[10] To make easier the investigation and punishment of crime generally, or of a particular kind of crime, would not suffice as the only footing of the power. Where the independent regulatory power under the constitution and the privilege against self-incrimination come in conflict each must yield to some extent, so that a viable accommodation may be found. Perhaps in the present state of the law, the limits can be no more definitely stated than to say with Vinson, C. J., that the bounds have not been over-stepped "when there is a sufficient relation between the activity sought to be regulated and the public concern so that the Government can constitutionally regulate or forbid the basic activity concerned, and can constitutionally require the keeping of particular records, subject to inspection by the Administrator."[11]

These principles are tested and applied in the decisions holding valid the report provisions of the "hit and run" statutes. These statutes require that a person operating a motor vehicle which is involved in a collision causing damage to person or property shall report his name and residence and other information to the person injured and to the police. These have sometimes been sustained on the ground that since the legislature could exclude such vehicles altogether from the highways they can attach as a condition to the privilege of operation the waiver of the self-crimination privilege in respect to such reports.[12] But today the constitutional power to exclude such vehicles altogether seems a doubtful and unrealistic premise. Other courts have argued that such a requirement does not compel self-incrimination because the collision may well be accidental and not criminal. When, however, the circumstances indicate reckless or wanton conduct by the person compelled to report, the required statement identifying himself as a person involved clearly meets the accepted test of incrimination, that is, the existence of substantial danger that the required statement will furnish evidence of an essential element of a crime.[13] There remains what seems the

---

4. See, e. g., Shapiro v. United States, 335 U.S. 1, 68 S.Ct. 1375, 92 L.Ed. 1787 (1948) (wholesale fruit and produce); Hagen v. Porter, 156 F.2d 362 (C.C. A.9, 1946) (dairy products); Rodgers v. United States, 138 F.2d 992, 996 (C.C.A.6, 1943) (cotton production); Davis, Administrative Law, § 35.

5. See Jackson, J., dissenting, in Shapiro v. United States, supra, at page 71 of the official report.

6. See 8 Wigmore, § 2259c.

7. See Meltzer, op. cit., 18 U.Chi.L.Rev. at 715.

8. As to which see Sullivan v. United States, 274 U.S. 259, 47 S.Ct. 607, 71 L.Ed. 1037 (1927) and the acute discussion in Meltzer, op. cit., 18 Uni.Chi.L. Rev. 715–719.

9. As in Shapiro v. United States, supra, note 3.

10. On the scope of this power see Rottschaefer, Constitutional Law, § 234 (1939).

11. In Shapiro v. United States, 335 U.S. 1, 32, 68 S.Ct. 1375, 92 L.Ed. 1787 (1948).

12. As in People v. Rosenheimer, 209 N.Y. 115, 102 N.E. 530, 532 (1913) and in State v. Sterrin, 78 N. H. 220, 98 Atl. 482, 483 (1916).

13. See §§ 128, 129, above.

most rational ground for upholding the statute, namely, that the regulation requiring reports is a "reasonable exercise of the police power," [14] and that the privilege against self-incrimination yields to the extent necessary to make effective this power of protecting safety on the highways. [15]

Finally, it seems that the exemption (within the limits indicated above) of required records and reports is consistent with the history of the privilege. Such advance requirements for providing information in aid of regulatory controls were not a part of the pattern of oppression which the privilege was devised to prevent. [16]

135. Termination of Liability to Punishment: Immunity Statutes. [1]

If at the time of the claim of privilege, the liability of the witness to be convicted of the offense inquired about has been terminated,

the danger against which the privilege is directed does not exist, and the claim of privilege fails. This is so when the witness has already been convicted [2] or acquitted [3] of the offense, when he has been pardoned, [4] or when prosecution has been barred by the statute of limitations. [5]

Moreover, the device of making a witness compellable to talk by giving him a grant of immunity has in recent decades been more and more frequently resorted to. This could probably be most justly and conveniently managed if power were recognized in the prosecuting attorney to apply to the trial judge for such a grant of immunity to a witness protected by the privilege, and authority of the judge to make such an order were conceded. This power and authority are accorded in Texas, [6] but the other states in the absence of enabling statute [7] have held otherwise. [8] Consequently, it has been neces-

---

14. Ex parte Kneedler, 243 Mo. 632, 147 S.W. 983, 984 (1912). See also People v. Thompson, 259 Mich. 109, 242 N.W. 857, 859 (1932) where the argument based on police power is similarly stressed. But both opinions rely likewise upon the theory of waiver by acceptance of license. See Notes, Validity of hit-and-run statutes, 101 A.L.R. 918, 66 A.L.R. 1234.

15. See the able exposition of this view in Mamet, Constitutionality of Compulsory Chemical Tests, 36 J.Crim.L. 132, 144 (1945).

16. See Morgan, op.cit., 34 Minn.L.Rev. at 37, 38, Meltzer, op.cit., 18 U.Chi.L.Rev. at 713, and § 120, herein.

1. 8 Wigmore, Evidence, §§ 2279–2284; 70 C.J., Witnesses, §§ 883–886; 58 Am.Jur., Witnesses, §§ 84–93; Dec.Dig., Witnesses, ⬅ 303, 304. Brownell, Immunity from Prosecution versus Privilege against Self-Incrimination, 28 Tul.L.Rev. 1 (1953); Dixon, The Fifth Amendment and Federal Immunity Statutes, 22 Geo.Wash.L.Rev. 447, 554 (1954); Brown, Immunity for Witnesses in Congressional Hearings, 1 U.C.L.A.L.Rev. 183 (1954).

2. 8 Wigmore, Evidence, § 2279(a).

3. Holt v. State, 39 Tex.Cr. 282, 45 S.W. 1016, syl. 5 (1898) (semble).

4. 8 Wigmore, Evidence, § 2280a. But the efficacy of this, as an escape for the prosecutor from the wit-

ness' refusal to testify is much diminished by the holding, seemingly unsound, in Burdick v. United States, 236 U.S. 79, 35 S.Ct. 267, 59 L.Ed. 476 (1915) that a witness who declines to accept a pardon, may still stand on his privilege.

5. Moore v. Backus, 78 F.2d 571, syl. 9 (C.C.A. 7, 1935) (but burden is on the one who contests the privilege to show that no prosecution was pending when the statute ran); Hale v. Henkel, 201 U.S. 43, 66, 67, 26 S.Ct. 370, 50 L.Ed. 652, 662 (1906) (dictum).

6. Ex parte Muncy, 72 Tex.Cr. 541, 163 S.W. 29, syl. 3, 8, 9 (1914) (one judge dissenting); Ex parte Copeland, 91 Tex.Cr. 549, 240 S.W. 314, 317 (1922).

7. Statutes sometimes confer the power on prosecutor and judge in particular situations, see, e.g., Mich.Comp. Laws 1948, § 767.6 quoted and construed in People v. Woodson, 309 Mich. 391, 15 N.W.2d 679, 680 (1944) (immunity may be granted to witness before one-man grand jury); Ill.Rev.St. 1874, c. 38, sec. 35, applied in People v. Rockola, 346 Ill. 27, 178 N.E. 384 (1931) (judge may enter order for immunity in investigation or trial of bribery offense).

8. The decisions are reviewed in Apodaca v. Viramontes, 53 N.M. 514, 212 P.2d 425 (1949) (able opinion by Sadler, J.) and in the annotation, Power of prosecuting attorney to extend immunity, 13 A.L.R.2d 1439.

sary in the federal jurisdiction and in the states to provide by statute for such immunity.[9] These statutes are usually limited to witnesses in prosecutions for particular offenses, such as gambling, bribery, prostitution, and violations of the anti-trust laws.

It is clear that the failure of such immunity statutes to protect against the disgracing effect of the incriminating answers does not affect their validity.[10] It is plain also that the immunity granted does not include immunity from punishment for perjury committed in the course of the compelled testimony itself.[11] The cases thus far, moreover, have favored the view that the fact that witness is not protected against prosecution in another jurisdiction for the transactions disclosed, does not entitle him to refuse to answer.[12]

To be effective as depriving the witness of privilege, is it sufficient that the immunity statute merely protect the witness from the use against him in a criminal prosecution of the testimony compelled? The historical purpose of the privilege was to protect the witness against being compelled to convict himself by words from his own mouth.[13] Statutes granting immunity merely against the use of the testimony satisfy this historical purpose, give a reasonable degree of protection and were generally upheld in state and federal courts [14] down to 1892. In that year, in Counselman v. Hitchcock [15] the highest court passed on the constitutional sufficiency of a federal immunity statute which provided only that the compelled testimony should not be "given in evidence or in any manner used against him" in any criminal proceeding.[16] The court held it insufficient because it did not "prevent the use of his testimony to search out other testimony to be used in evidence against him" [17] and further held that "no statute which leaves the party or witness subject to prosecution after he answers the criminating questions put to him can have the effect of supplanting the privilege conferred by the Constitution of the United States." [18]

Surely this was a wrong turning at a critical point. Perhaps few decisions in history have resulted in freeing more rascals from punishment. Its soundness may be disputed on several grounds. First, the theory that furnishing a clue to other evidence which will incriminate, is itself incriminatory, goes beyond the traditional scope of "giving evidence against oneself," [19] and is a far-fetched and impolitic extension. One of the strongest policy-arguments for the privilege is that it encourages prosecutors to prepare their proofs more thoroughly rather than relying upon compelling disclosures of guilt from the accused,[20] but this holding discourages that very search for other confirming evidence. Second, even conceding that the witness was entitled to this protection against disclosing sources of other evidence of guilt, then the reasonable construction of the statute, sup-

---

9. See the immunity statutes collected and summarized in 8 Wigmore, Evidence, § 2281, note 11.

10. Brown v. Walker, 161 U.S. 591, 605, 16 S.Ct. 644, 40 L.Ed. 819 (1896).

11. Glickstein v. United States, 222 U.S. 139, 142, 32 S.Ct. 71, 56 L.Ed. 128 (1911) (immunity statute should not be construed to confer license to give false testimony); People v. Kramer, 257 App.D. 598, 14 N.Y.S.2d 161, syl. 2 (1939); 8 Wigmore, Evidence, § 2282(c).

12. See § 124, above.

13. See § 120, above.

14. United States v. McCarthy, 18 F. 87 89 (Circ. Ct., Brown, J., 1883); People v. Kelly, 24 N.Y. 74, 82 (1861) (masterly discussion by Denio, J.); La Fontaine v. Southern Underwriters' Ass'n, 83 N. C. 132, 141 (1880). Contra: Comm. v. Emery, 107 Mass. 171, 182 (1871).

15. 142 U.S. 547, 12 S.Ct. 195, 35 L.Ed. 1110.

16. See 35 L.Ed. 1113, where the statute is quoted.

17. 35 L.Ed. 1114.

18. 35 L.Ed. 1122.

19. See § 129, above, at note 19; 8 Wigmore, Evidence, § 2261.

20. See § 136, herein.

porting its validity, was that in providing that the testimony should not be "in any manner used against him" it enacted that no other evidence procured by the use of the first testimony would be used against him. Surely such protection is all that could reasonably be demanded, and the insistence upon complete immunity for punishment is an unjust and unnecessary obstruction to law enforcement. While the state courts in interpreting their own constitutional provisions have generally followed the Counselman doctrine requiring complete immunity,[21] they are not bound to do so,[22] and it is to be hoped that they may some day revert to the earlier and more reasonable tradition.

Immunity statutes have as their purpose not a gift of amnesty but the securing of testimony which because of privilege could not otherwise be procured.[23] If the witness is willing to give the evidence voluntarily, there is no reason for buying it with immunity. But the traditional language of early immunity statutes did not make clear the conditions of exchange. They merely provided that in certain proceedings the privilege did not exist, but the witness had an immunity.[24] This vagueness has provoked disputes. Must the witness have been compelled by subpena to appear? Not unless the immunity statute so provides,[25] but the subpena is some evidence that the testimony was compulsory. Must the witness claim his privilege not to answer? Many modern statutes explicitly so provide,[26] but in the absence of such provision, there is conflict. The highest court holds such claim is not required,[27] on the ground that to deny the immunity, when the literal words of the law confer it, makes the statute a trap for the witness. The dissenting view,[28] for which there is strong support in state holdings,[29] is that the witness in the absence of the immunity statute would be required to claim the privilege or lose it, and there is no reason to believe that the statute was intended to change this. This being so, why endow with immunity one who has waived the privilege to be silent? Moreover, the requirement of a claim, and consequent ruling, lessens the danger that immunity will be con-

---

21. See, e. g., Ex parte Carter, 166 Mo. 604, 66 S.W. 540 (1902); People v. O'Brien, 176 N.Y. 253, 68 N.E. 353 (1903); In re Beer, 17 N.D. 184, 115 N.W. 672 (1908). Contra: Duff v. Salyers, 220 Ky. 546, 295 S.W. 871, syl. 6 (1927). Decisions are collected in Note, Adequacy of Immunity, 118 A.L.R. 602.

22. See § 121, above.

23. Heike v. United States, 227 U.S. 131, 142, 33 S.Ct. 226, 228, 57 L.Ed 450 (1913).

24. See the statutes listed and summarized in 8 Wigmore, Evidence, § 2281, note 10.

25. Atkinson v. State, 190 Ind. 1, 128 N.E. 433, syl. 1 (1920) (witness notified by prosecuting attorney to appear before grand jury is "required" to testify under terms of immunity act); 8 Wigmore, Evidence, § 2282, p. 508. But the statutes frequently do limit the immunity to witnesses appearing under subpena, see, e. g., Federal Compulsory Testimony Act of Feb. 11, 1893, 49 U.S.C.A. § 46, relating to investigations of the Interstate Commerce Commission. See also Note, 25 Calif.L.Rev. 622 (1937).

26. See, e. g., the federal statutes which confer immunity when a person testifies under compulsion, "after having claimed his privilege against self-in-

crimination," listed by Frankfurter, J., dissenting in United States v. Monia, 317 U.S. 424, 442, 63 S.Ct. 409, 417, 87 L.Ed. 376 (1943).

27. United States v. Monia, 317 U.S. 424, 63 S.Ct. 409, 87 L.Ed. 376 (1943) (opinion by Roberts, J.).

28. See the extensive opinion by Frankfurter, J., United States v. Monia, supra.

29. State v. Backstrom, 117 Kan. 111, 230 Pac. 306 (1924); Ross v. Crane, 291 Mass. 28, 195 N.E. 884, syl. 4 (1935); State v. Luquire, 191 N.C. 479, 132 S.E. 162, syl. 2 (1926); Comm. v. Richardson, 229 Pa. 609, 79 Atl. 222, syl. 5 (1911); State v. Davidson, 242 Wis. 406, 8 N.W.2d 275, syl. 4, 145 A.L.R. 1411 (1943). In all of these cases, except the last, the court mentioned that the witness had not appeared under compulsion of subpena.

Contra: People v. Fryer, 175 Cal. 785, 167 Pac. 382 (1917) (three judges dissenting); People v. Sharp, 107 N.Y. 427, 445 (1887) (the witness could not be required, in order to gain the indemnity . . . to go through the formality of an objection . . . which . . . would be useless"). See 8 Wigmore, Evidence, § 2282, note 8; Note, 145 A.L.R. 1416.

ferred by inadvertence of government counsel, unaware that his question touches upon a criminal transaction of the witness.

Under this, which seems the more expedient view, the counsel for the government, would have the opportunity to yield to the privilege, or to insist upon the question and invoke the judge's ruling requiring the witness to answer, in return for the immunity. If the evidence given is not within the scope of the privilege, as where required records are called for,[30] there is no basis for granting the compensatory immunity. Similarly, even though the witness claims the privilege, if his testimony does not disclose any facts which could by reasonable possibility constitute evidence of crime, there is no *quid pro quo* of incriminating evidence to exchange for immunity.[31]

Many of the difficulties and miscarriages in the application of the immunity statutes would disappear if Congress and the several state legislatures would displace the present scattered and piecemeal enactments by a well-planned and comprehensive Immunity Act. The major objectives of the Model State Witness Immunity Act [32] have been described as follows:

"(1) Adaptation of the scope of immunity to satisfy but not exceed the minimum required under the constitution of the state. . . .

"(2) Extension of immunity provisions to make them operative in proceedings or investigations relating to any criminal offense, or, at least, to those criminal offenses most frequently associated with organized crime.
. . .

"(3) Requirement that no immunity be granted except in exchange for evidence protected by the privilege against self-incrimination. Where no privilege exists, no immunity need be given in order to compel evidence. . .

"(4) Requirement that grants of immunity be preceded by (a) claim of privilege, (b) order to give evidence and (c) compliance with that order.

---

30. Shapiro v. United States, 335 U.S. 1, 68 S.Ct. 1375, syl. 1–5, 92 L.Ed. 1787 (1948). As to non-privileged character of required records, see 134, above.

31. State v. Carchidi, 187 Wis. 438, 204 N.W. 473, syl. 4 (1925). In that case the defendant was prosecuted for obtaining money for a mortgage by false pretenses. He pleaded immunity by reason of testimony given by him about the transaction, at a grand jury hearing.

The court (Owen, J.) held the immunity statute inapplicable, saying ". . . we have no doubt that these statutes were passed for the express purpose of placing at the disposal of public prosecutors evidence which the constitutional provision denied, and that, in order to entitle a witness to the immunity granted by these statutes, the evidence given by him must have been of a character which he was privileged to withhold under the constitutional provision." For similar expressions as to the effect of statements professing innocence, see Ex parte Copeland, 91 Tex.Cr. 549, 240 S.W. 314, 317, syl. 4 (1922).

32. This Act, omitting formal parts, reads: Section 1. *Compelling Evidence in Criminal Proceedings; Immunity.* In any criminal proceeding before a court or grand jury, [or examining Magistrate] if a person refuses to answer a question or produce evidence of any other kind on the ground that he may be incriminated thereby, and if the prosecuting attorney, in writing [and with the approval of the Attorney General,]** requests the court to order that person to answer the question or produce the evidence the court after notice to the witness and hearing shall so order [, unless it finds that to do so would be clearly contrary to the public interest,] *** and that person shall comply with the order. After complying, and if, but for this section, he would have been privileged to withhold the answer given or the evidence produced by him, that person shall not be prosecuted or subjected to penalty or forfeiture for or on account of any transaction, matter or thing concerning which, in accordance with the order, he gave answer or produced evidence. But he may nevertheless be prosecuted or subjected to penalty or forfeiture for any perjury, false swearing or contempt committed in answering, or failing to answer, or in producing, or failing to produce, evidence in accordance with the order.

** Alternative I.: Under this alternative, the model act includes this first bracketed provision and excludes the second.

*** Alternative II.: Under this alternative, the model act includes this second bracketed provision and excludes the first."

1952 Handbook, Nat.Conf.Com'rs Unif.St.Laws, 256, 257. The Act was approved in 1952 by the Uniform Laws Conference and by the American Bar Association. 77 Rep.Am.B.Asso. 126. In the Handbook the Act is followed by a valuable detailed commentary.

"(5) Requirement that no immunity be granted except (a) on request of the prosecuting attorney and (b) with the approval of the Attorney General where the latter serves as central coordinator for the state's enforcement of its criminal laws, or with the court's approval (mandatory unless a grant is 'clearly contrary to the public interest') where the Attorney General does not so serve." [33]

136.　The Policy of the Privilege.[1]

It is of the greatest importance that lawyers and judges should study and appraise the expediency of the self-crimination privilege. Whether a judge considers that the privilege is an obstructive anachronism or an immutable principle of justice will and should [2] influence his interpretation of the constitutional provision, and thus determine whether the privilege will be extended to new fields or withdrawn from areas of present application. The starting-point in the consideration of any privilege is the realization that its universal and immediate effect upon the search for truth is to close off one avenue of information about the facts.[3] The policy-issue, then, is whether the resulting benefits justify this sacrifice of the interest of truth. Some of the points in favor of the privilege, with some answering qualifications, are given below.

1.　It protects the privacy of the individual by shielding him from judicial inquisition, just as the privilege against unreasonable searches and seizures protects the privacy of his home. It must be recalled, however, that the protection of privacy afforded by the privilege is limited. It is only when a person is formally accused, or officially suspected of crime that he may not be examined as a witness at all.[4] In all other situations the witness must answer non-incriminating questions and must suffer the humiliation of claiming his privilege when the question is incriminating. Not much is left of his privacy then. Moreover, the analogy to searches and seizures is seriously mislead-

ing. It is only "unreasonable" searches and seizures that are forbidden. When reasonable grounds are shown a search-warrant will issue. Accordingly, if the citizen were required to answer about his crimes, but only under judicial supervision, at a trial where the inquiries are relevant to the issue or at a judicial investigation where there are reasonable grounds for calling him as a witness, the interest of privacy as to forced disclosures would be protected as much as the privacy of the home is now protected.

2.　If the door were opened to judicial inquiries about incriminating matter, before trial, of witnesses not yet formally charged with crime, this would promote tyrannical conduct by the judge, and create danger of blackmail and oppression.[5] Certainly any civilized system would provide safeguards for such inquiries. Under our tradition the examination would normally be conducted by the prosecuting attorney in public and under supervision of the magistrate, and a right to counsel should perhaps be accorded the witness. It is forcibly argued likewise that the obstacles which the present privilege sets up to effective pre-trial judicial investigations, actually contribute to causing enforcement officers to resort to the "third degree" methods in questioning pris-

---

33. 1952 Handbook, 252, 253.

1. 8 Wigmore, Evidence, § 2251; 5 Bentham, Rationale of Judicial Evidence, 207 et seq. (1827); Meltzer, Required Records, 18 Uni.Chi.L.Rev. 687–701 (1951) (a subtle and penetrating discussion); Judge John C. Knox, Self-incrimination, 74 U.Pa.L.Rev. 139, N.Y. City Bar Asso., 7 Lectures on Legal Topics, 47 (1925-6) and list of references in Note, 61 Yale L.J. 110, note 25 (1952). A strong argument supporting the privilege is Griswold, The Fifth Amendment: An Old and Good Friend, 40 A.B.A.J. 502 (1954).

2. But see the contrary views of Frank, Circ. J., dissenting in United States v. St. Pierre, 132 F.2d 837, 847 (C.C.A. 2, 1942).

3. See § 72, herein.

4. See § 122.

5. 8 Wigmore, Evidence, p. 307(b).

oners privately.[6] Excessive restrictions on public judicial examination may lead to abuses in examinations behind closed doors.

3. The inability of the prosecutor to call the accused as a witness stimulates him to investigate the facts more thoroughly from other sources, whereas if the accused were callable, the practice of questioning would lead to bullying and abuse.[7] The first point seems more applicable to pre-trial hearings than to the trial. A prosecutor, it is believed, would seldom slack investigation in reliance on a hope of convicting the accused out of his own mouth. As to pre-trial hearings he might sometimes be content with statements of guilt by the accused, without further search for witnesses, but the danger to justice from such reliance seems small. The second point, that bullying and abuse would be promoted if questioning were permitted has force. The evil exists under the present system when the accused "voluntarily" takes the stand, and subjects himself to cross-examination. This may often be savage in tone and unduly prejudicial in matter. Ethical restraints and judicial control of the examination should be relied on to curb such abuses.[8]

4. As to ordinary witnesses, not the accused, if they were subject to answer incriminating questions, their present reluctance to testify would be increased, thus adding to the difficulties of proof.[9] Nevertheless, the value of the privilege as an inducement to the witness (who has a choice) to appear and testify is heavily discounted by the limitations on the privilege [10] and the embarrassment of asserting it. It seems highly probable that the assertion of the privilege suppresses more testimony than the enticement of the privilege produces.[11]

5. Requiring a man to testify about his alleged crimes creates an undue pressure and temptation for him to commit perjury. This danger always exists when a man is required to make a choice between good and

evil. It seems to be outweighed by the need for the disclosure of facts in the administration of justice.

6. If the accused were compelled to be a witness, this would place the nervous, timid or ill-favored witness at an unfair disadvantage. It is true that he would be at a disadvantage, but the privilege does little to lessen this. He cannot afford to exercise his privilege to be silent, because his silence will turn the jury against him far more than his handicap will. As Arthur Train says, "A man accused of crime sooner or later has to tell what he knows—or take his medicine." [12]

7. If a duty to give incriminating evidence were recognized it would be very difficult to enforce. Certainly this would be true in many cases. In some cases, where the penalty for the crime is greater than that for refusing to answer, enforcement would be impossible. Sometimes the recalcitrance of the witness would out-last the time-limits of the trial. Nevertheless, in many situations there would be little difficulty. At least the door to truth, though not wide open, would be open wider than it is now. In pretrial hearings or the taking of depositions the lee-way of time for enforcement would be greater than at the trial. Experience would indicate when to use (a) mere comment by court and counsel on the silence, (b) punishment for contempt in re-

---

6. See Pound, Legal Interrogation of Persons Accused or Suspected of Crime (1934) 24 J.Crim.L. and Criminology 1014 (1934). See also 3 Wigmore, Evidence § 851, p. 320; Kauper, Judicial Examination of the Accused—A Remedy for the Third Degree (1932) 30 Mich.L.Rev. 1224.

7. 8 Wigmore, Evidence, p. 309.

8. See §§ 42 and 43, herein.

9. 8 Wigmore, Evidence, p. 307(a).

10. Meltzer, op. cit., 699.

11. Ibid.

12. Courts, Criminals, and the Camorra, 19 (1912), quoted in 8 Wigmore, Evidence, p. 314.

fusing to answer, and (c) commitment of the witness to jail until he answers.

Some independent arguments against the privilege may be noted.

1. The privilege is an institution which is built on sentimental association, rather than on its value in protecting substantial human interests. We associate the process of judicial inquisition with the practice of torture because historically some of the courts that used the one, practiced the other also.[13] The guilt inherent in one casts its sinister gleam upon the other. Again the self-incrimination privilege, though never embodied in the great English charters, found its way (partly because of this association with torture) [14] into the American bills of rights. There it is now found in the company of religious freedom, freedom of speech and the press, and protection of the privacy of the home. Despite its arbitrary and irrational character, it has acquired a borrowed radiance from its close connection with these other rights which are genuine essentials of ordered liberty.[15] It has gained a sort of sanctity by association.

2. The privilege operates principally in aid of the guilty: the innocent have no need of it. Probably its purpose and effect from the time of its origin was the obstruction of the enforcement of criminal laws which a part of the community conceived to be unrighteous.[16]

3. It runs counter to common-sense practices of investigation in the ordinary affairs of life. No one would think it unfair for an employer, when an employee is charged with taking cash from the till, to call on the employee to give his side of the story, or suffer dismissal. This discrepancy brings law in disrepute.

4. This same contradiction between the privilege and the felt need for access to this primary source of information—the accused party himself—places a strain upon the courts in administering the privilege. Juries are ordered to disregard the silence of the accused—a manifest impossibility. Inroads, exceptions and escapes are carved out, with uncertain boundaries. The consequence is a great volume of disputed questions on the application of the privilege. This unreality and uncertainty add to the burden of the incubus, the very essence of which is obstruction to the ascertainment of facts.

---

13. See Bentham, op. cit., quoted in 8 Wigmore, Evidence, p. 305.

14. See Pittman, The Constitutional and Colonial History of the Privilege, 21 Va.L.Rev. 763, 779, 783 (1935); Meltzer, op. cit. 694.

15. See the famous statement of Cardozo, J., in Palko v. Connecticut, 302 U.S. 319, 325, 326, 58 S.Ct. 149, 152, 82 L.Ed. 288 (1937): "What is true of jury trials and indictments is true also, as the cases show, of the immunity from compulsory self-incrimination. . . . This too might be lost, and justice still be done. Indeed, today as in the past there are students of our penal system who look upon the immunity as a mischief rather than a benefit, and who would limit its scope, or destroy it altogether. No doubt there would remain the need to give protection against torture, physical or mental. . . . Justice, however, would not perish if the accused were subject to a duty to respond to orderly inquiry."

16. 1 Stephen, Hist.Crim. Law 342 (1883) (quoted 8 Wigmore, Evidence, pp. 311, 312): "In the old Ecclesiastical Courts and in the Star Chamber [the 'ex officio' oath] was understood to be and was used as an oath to speak the truth on the matters objected against the defendant—an oath, in short, to accuse oneself. It was vehemently contended by those who found themselves pressed by this oath that it was against the law of God, and the law of nature and that the maxim 'nemo tenetur prodere seipsum' was agreeable to the law of God, and part of the law of nature. In this, I think, as in most other discussions of the kind, the real truth was that those who dislike the oath had usually done the things of which they were accused, and which they regarded as meritorious actions, though their judges regarded them as crimes. People always protest with passionate eagerness against being deprived of technical defences against what they regard as bad law, and such complaints often give a spurious value to technicalities when the cruelty of the laws against which they have afforded protection has come to be commonly admitted. . ."

CHAPTER 14

EVIDENCE ILLEGALLY OBTAINED

137. The Traditional Common Law Doctrine: The Illegal Obtaining of Evidence Is Not a Ground of Exclusion.[1]

Until after the beginning of the present century it was almost universally accepted that the illegality of the means by which evidence was procured is no ground of objection to its admission. Accordingly, the fact that a paper or other object was acquired by trespass,[2] breach of trust,[3] or other wrongful conduct[4] is, under this view, not a reason for excluding. The problem now most often arises in connection with the offer of evidence which has been secured by officers through a search of a vehicle or premises which the objector claims was conducted in violation of the applicable constitutional provision forbidding unreasonable searches and seizures. In a majority of the states the common law doctrine is still applied, even in respect to evidence obtained in violation of such constitutional prohibitions, to deny that such invasion furnishes a ground for exclusion.[5] The person wronged has his remedy against the trespasser, but this is no reason, so the classical argument went, to exclude the evidence when relevant, nor would the courts halt the present trial to consider the "collateral" issue of the lawfulness of the means by which the evidence was obtained.[6] There were, however, at least two kinds of illegally secured evidence,

---

1. 8 Wigmore, Evidence, §§ 2183–2184b; Note, 150 A.L.R. 560, 134 A.L.R. 819, and earlier notes cited therein; 20 Am.Jur., Evidence, §§ 393–402; 22 C.J. S., Crim.Law, § 657, 31 C.J.S., Evidence, § 187; Dec.Dig., Crim.Law, ⊙394, 395.

2. State v. Griswold, 67 Conn. 290, 34 Atl. 1046, 1047 (1896).

3. Stockfleth v. De Tastet, 4 Camp. 11, 171 Eng.Rep. 4 (N.P.1814).

4. Stevison v. Earnest, 80 Ill. 513, 517 (1875) (illegal removing of records).

5. See authorities collected in the references cited in note 1, supra. In Wolf v. Colorado, 328 U.S. 25, 38, 69 Sup.Ct. 1359, 1367, 93 L.Ed. 1782 (1949) the following thirty states are listed as adhering to this view: Ala., Ariz., Ark., Calif., Colo., Conn., Del., Ga., Kans., La., Me., Md., Mass., Minn., Neb., Nev., N.H., N.J., N.M., N.Y., N.C., N.D., Ohio, Ore., Pa., S.C., Texas, Utah, Vt., Va. Since that time, however, Delaware has reversed its stand, and gone over to the Federal (see § 139 below) view. Rickards v. State, 6 Terry. 573, 77 A.2d 199, syl. 19, 20 (Sup.Ct.1950, two justices dissenting).

6. "If the search warrant were illegal, or if the officer serving the warrant exceeded his authority, the party on whose complaint the warrant issued, or the officer, would be responsible for the wrong done; but this is no good reason for excluding the papers seized as evidence if they were pertinent to the issue, as they unquestionably were. When papers are offered in evidence the court can take no notice how they were obtained, whether lawfully or unlawfully; nor would they form a collateral issue to determine that question." Wilde, J. in Comm. v. Dana, 2 Metc. (Mass.) 329 (1841), quoted in Adams v. New York, 192 U.S. 585, 24 Sup.Ct. 372, 374, 48 L.Ed. 575 (1904).

namely, involuntary confessions [7] and testimony secured in violation of the self-incrimination privilege,[8] as to which this approach has never been observed.

138. The Policy Considerations.[1]

When evidence has been secured in violation of constitutional or statutory guaranties of civil rights, and is offered as proof of crime, judges are responsible for resolving a conflict of supremely important interests. Among judicial statements supporting the traditional resolution of this policy issue, the following are significant examples:

Cardozo, J.: "No doubt the protection of the statute would be greater from the point of view of the individual whose privacy had been invaded if the government were required to ignore what it had learned through the invasion. The question is whether protection for the individual would not be gained at a disproportionate loss of protection for society. On the one side is the social need that crime shall be repressed. On the other, the social need that law shall not be flouted by the insolence of office. There are dangers in any choice. The rule of [admissibility] strikes a balance between opposing interests. We must hold it to be the law until those organs of government by which a change of public policy is normally effected shall give notice to the courts that the change has come to pass." [2]

Wheeler, J.: "When evidence tending to prove guilt is before a court, the public interest requires that it be admitted. It ought not to be excluded upon the theory that individual rights under these constitutional guaranties are above the right of the community to protection from crime. The complexities and conveniences of modern life make increasingly difficult the detection of crime. The burden ought not be added to by giving to our constitutional guaranties a construction at variance with that which has prevailed for over a century at least. The cases in which in recent years some of the courts have either excluded this class of evidence or ordered articles taken from the accused returned to him have been in prosecutions for violations of the laws against policy, gambling, fraud, and intoxicating liquors. The next case may be one of murder, and the prosecutor be compelled by the ruling of the court to return to the accused the certain evidence of his guilt and the accused go free—his constitutional rights against search protected above the right of society against his crime. . . . If the question recurs, Where is the accused's remedy? the answer must be by a civil action, the only form of remedy known for the protection of the individual against a trespass. It may be that the officer would be guilty of a contempt. If violations of these constitutional rights shall multiply, undoubtedly the General Assembly can provide for a penalty for subsequent violations. A penalty upon an officer for an illegal search made without reasonable ground would furnish adequate protection against such a public wrong." [3]

---

7. See § 111, herein. It may be noted, however, that one of the reasons for excluding forced confessions is their unreliability, whereas unlawfulness in the acquisition of evidence does not ordinarily detract at all from its reliability. See Atkinson, Evidence Obtained through Unreasonable Searches and Seizures, 25 Col.L.Rev. 11 (1925).

8. See § 127, herein. The same rule of exclusion is applied to evidence obtained in violation of any privilege, where duly claimed, by Uniform Rule 38 ("Evidence of a statement or other disclosure is inadmissible against the holder of the privilege if the judge finds that he had and claimed a privilege to refuse to make the disclosure but was nevertheless required to make it.").

1. 8 Wigmore, Evidence, § 2184 (strongly espousing the traditional rule of admissibility); Atkinson, op. cit., 25 Col.L.Rev. 11 (1925) (a realistic argument for exclusion); Chafee, The Progress of the Law, Evidence, 1919–1922, 35 Harv.L.Rev. 673, 695 (1922) (favoring exclusion).

2. People v. Defore, 242 N.Y. 13, 150 N.E. 585, 589 (1926).

3. State v. Reynolds, 101 Conn. 224, 125 Atl. 636, 639, 640 (1924).

The countervailing considerations which have actuated those courts favoring a rule of exclusion are well expressed in these statements:

L. Hand, Circ. J.: "As we understand it, the reason for the exclusion of evidence competent as such, which has been unlawfully acquired, is that exclusion is the only practical way of enforcing the constitutional privilege. In earlier times the action of trespass against the offending official may have been protection enough; but that is true no longer. Only in case the prosecution which itself controls the seizing officials, knows that it cannot profit by their wrong, will that wrong be repressed." [4]

Vinson, J.: "The rights given by the IVth Amendment are something quite distinct from the determination of whether the defendant was driving under the influence of liquor. The two problems must be considered together, however, in effectuating either the protection of the Constitution, or the punishment of the guilty. When two interests conflict, one must prevail. To us the interest of privacy safeguarded by the Amendment is more important than the interest of punishing all those guilty of misdemeanors. Happy would be the result if both interests could be completely protected. If this declaration is admissible and justice meted out on the issue of drunken driving, where is the defendant's remedy for the inexcusable entry into his home? The casuist answers— a civil action against the officers. That remedy has been found wanting.[5] Such remedy scarcely satisfies the non-belligerent, non-legal mind of a person whose security has already been violated and who stands convicted. To follow that procedure means delay, expense, unwanted publicity; it asks the individual to stake too much, and to take too great a chance, in the hope of compensating the interference to his privacy. A criminal remedy is also possible, but it is likely to be too strict or too lax. If criminal actions are brought consistently against the enforcing officers, before long their diligence will be enervated. If no prosecutions are brought, which appears to be the case,[6] it cannot be said that statutory criminal provisions afford any deterrent to the infringement of the IVth Amendment. Even if the criminal and civil remedies worked, the protection would not be complete. The Amendment does not outline the method by which the protection shall be afforded, but some effective method must be administered; the protection granted by constitutional provisions must not be dealt with as abstractions. A simple, effective way to assist in the realization of the security guaranteed by the IVth Amendment, in this type of case, is to dissolve the evidence that

4. United States v. Pugliese, 153 F.2d 497, 499 (C.C. A. 2, 1945).

5. "Snyder v. United States, 4 Cir., 285 F. 1, 3. We have been able to find among the reported federal cases only one action for damages against an officer for an alleged unreasonable search. Hunt v. Evans, 56 App.D.C. 97, 10 F.2d 892. There was no recovery since the court held that the search warrant was good on its face and the plaintiff invited the search. The number of cases in which the courts have said that there was an unreasonable search and seizure negatives any contention that actions for damages are not brought because the IVth Amendment is never infringed." [Footnote, here renumbered, from original report.]

6. "On November 23, 1921, the following provision became law: "That any officer . . . who shall search any private dwelling as defined in [Title 27] the National Prohibition Act . . . without a warrant directing such search . . . shall be guilty of a misdemeanor . . . ." 42 Stat. 223, 18 U.S.C.A. § 53. While the effect of this provision has been judicially recognized (Poulos v. United States, 6 Cir., 8 F.2d 120, 121, there is not one reported case where an officer has been tried for violation. This provision was repealed on August 27, 1935 (49 Stat. 872), but at the same time there was enacted a similar statute applying to the "enforcement of any law of the United States." 49 Stat. 877, 18 U.S.C.A. § 53a. Likewise, to date, there is not one reported case of an officer tried for violation of this provision." [Footnote from report.]

the officers obtained after entering and remaining illegally in the defendant's home." [7]

139. The Development in the Federal Courts and in Many States of a Rule of Privilege or Exclusion.[1]

While there had been an earlier excursion [2] from the traditional view, the present practice in the Federal courts in respect to evidence secured by illegal search stems from the Weeks case decided in 1914.[3] In that case the highest court held that it was prejudicial error to admit against the accused in a Federal court papers seized in his home by a Federal officer without a warrant in violation of the Fourth Amendment. The court

[7]. Nueslein v. District of Columbia, 115 F.2d 690, 695 (C.A., D.C.1940). A still more recent and extensive appraisal of the ineffectiveness of the civil remedy against offending officers, in contrast with practical workings of the Federal sanction of excluding the fruits, appears in the dissenting opinion of Murphy, J., in Wolf v. Colorado, 338 U.S. 25, 42–46, 69 Sup.Ct. 1359, 93 L.Ed. 1782 (1949). See also the searching and realistic discussions in Note, Judicial Control of Illegal Search, 58 Yale L.J. 144 (1948); Hall, Police and Law in a Democratic Society, 28 Ind.L.J. 133 (1953); Note, Search and Seizure in Illinois, 47 N.W.U.L.Rev. 493 (1952); Allen, Due Process and State Criminal Procedures: Another Look, 48 N.W.U.L.Rev. 16, 26 (1953); Paulsen, The Fourteenth Amendment and the Third Degree, 6 Stan.L.Rev. 411, 413 (1954).

[1]. Attention is centered in this discussion upon the evidential aspects. As to what searches and seizures are within the constitutional prohibition, see Fraenkel, Concerning Searches and Seizures, 34 Harv.L.Rev. 361 (1921); Recent Developments, 13 Minn.L.Rev. 1 (1928); Wood, The Scope of the Constitutional Immunity against Searches and Seizures, 34 W.Va.L.Rev. 1 (1927); Willis, Constitutional Law, 531–542 (1936); Grant, The Constitutional Basis of the Rule Forbidding the Use of Illegally Seized Evidence, 15 So.Calif.L.Rev. 60 (1941); Circumventing the Fourth Amendment, 14 So.Calif. L.Rev. 359 (1941); Fraenkel, Recent Developments in the Federal Law of Searches and Seizures, 33 Iowa L.Rev. 473 (1948); Trimble, Search and Seizure under the Fourth Amendment as Interpreted by the Supreme Court, 41 Ky.L.J. 196 (1953); Notes, Judicial Control of Illegal Search, 58 Yale L.J. 144 (1948) (practical effect of exclusionary rule and of the limitations upon it); Protection against Illegal Search, 9 Wash. & Lee L.Rev. 192 (1952). Among the important doctrines are the following:

(a) that which limits the restraint to Federal officers or those acting for them; see, e. g., Lowrey v. United States, 128 F.2d 477, C.C.A.Ark., 1942; Note, 91 U.Pa.L.Rev. 359 (1941) (evidence obtained by state officers); Note, Admissibility in Federal Courts of Evidence Obtained Illegally by State Authorities, 51 Col.L.Rev. 128 (1951).

(b) the limitation to searches for "implements" and "fruits" of crime, forbidding a search for "evidence," see People v. Defore, 242 N.Y. 13, 150 N.E.

585, syl. 3 (1926); United States v. Lefkowitz, 285 U.S. 452, 463–7, 52 S.Ct. 420, 76 L.Ed. 877, 82 A.L. R. 775 (1932); LaRue v. State, 149 Tex.Cr.App. 598, 197 S.W.2d 570, (1946) (a striking fact-case); Handler, The Constitutionality of Investigations by the Federal Trade Commission, 28 Col.L.Rev. 905, 910, 4 Sel.Essays Const.Law 621, 627 (1928) (citing the literature); Note, Limitations on Seizure of "Evidentiary" Objects: a Rule in Search of a Reason, 20 U.Chi.L.Rev. 319 (1953) (acute, extensive);

(c) the doctrine which empowers an officer making a lawful arrest to search as incidental thereto the immediate premises where the arrest is made, see United States v. Rabinowitz, 339 U.S. 56, 70 Sup.Ct. 430, 94 L.Ed. 653 (1950); and

(d) the holdings to the effect that a vehicle on the highway may be searched without a warrant when probable cause for the search exists, see Brinegar v. United States, 338 U.S. 160, 69 Sup.Ct. 1302, 93 L.Ed. 1879 (1949); Note, Search of Motor Vehicles, 30 N.C.L.Rev. 421 (1952).

[2]. In Boyd v. United States, 116 U.S. 616, 618, 6 Sup. Ct. 524, 29 L.Ed. 746 (1885), it was held that an order to produce an incriminating document amounted to an unlawful search—a most questionable holding—and that being secured in violation of the Fourth Amendment (as well as the Fifth) it was inadmissible. So far as it held that the product of an illegal search was inadmissible, it was impliedly discredited by the opinion in Adams v. New York, 192 U.S. 585, 24 Sup.Ct. 372, 48 L.Ed. 574 (1904), which, though distinguishable as a review of state action, gave wholesale approval to the traditional doctrine of the admissibility of illegally obtained evidence.

[3]. Weeks v. United States, 232 U.S. 383, 34 Sup.Ct. 341, 58 L.Ed. 652 (1914).

Another leading case in the same line of succession is Silverthorne Lumber Co. v. United States, 251 U.S. 385, 40 Sup.Ct. 182, 64 L.Ed. 319 (1920), which went beyond the mere exclusion of the immediate fruits of the search. There the premises of the defendant company were unlawfully searched and papers taken and photographed. Thereafter the originals were returned under order of court. On the basis of the knowledge so secured the District Attorney secured a new indictment and an order for production of some of the papers formerly seized.

did not, however, reject entirely the traditional approach. They seized upon the statements in the earlier decisions that the courts would not turn aside to consider the "collateral issue" of illegal acquisition, and impliedly limited their present holding of inadmissibility to cases wherein the accused, as in the present case, had made a timely motion before trial to suppress or return the evidence. This leading decision has established in the Federal courts a rule of exclusion which, with two qualifications, abrogates in that jurisdiction the classical rule that illegal acquisition is no ground of objection. The qualifications are that the rule of exclusion was held applicable only (1) when *constitutional* safeguards have been violated in securing the evidence [4] and (2) when a timely pretrial motion has been presented.

The requirement of a pre-trial motion to suppress has, however, been much relaxed in later pronouncements. It has been held that when the accused for want of knowledge of the wrongful seizure or for other reasons has had no opportunity to make such a motion, or when the illegality of the seizure appears from the government's own proof, the objection may be made for the first time at the trial.[5] And now the Federal Rules of Criminal Procedure open the door still wider by providing that "The motion to suppress evidence * * * shall be made before trial or hearing unless opportunity therefor did not exist or the defendant was not aware of the grounds for the motion, but the court in its discretion may entertain the motion at the trial or hearing." [6]

More than two-fifths of the states have ranged themselves in general agreement with the Federal doctrine excluding evidence secured in violation of constitutional guaranties against unreasonable searches and seizures.[7] The tide seems to be flowing in that direction. In several states the traditional doctrine of admissibility has been abrogated or modified by statute.[8] Of the states adher-

---

On appeal from a contempt conviction for violating this order, the judgment was reversed and Holmes, J., in language often quoted, said, "The essence of a provision forbidding the acquisition of evidence in a certain way is that not merely evidence so acquired shall not be used before the Court but that it shall not be used at all. Of course this does not mean that the facts thus obtained become sacred and inaccessible. If knowledge of them is gained from an independent source they may be proved like any others, but the knowledge gained by the Government's own wrong cannot be used by it in the way proposed."

4. Accordingly it is held that papers taken by trespass or theft by a private person, without participation by the government, may be used in evidence in the prosecution of crime, and the government will not be required to return them before trial. Burdeau v. McDowell, 256 U.S. 465, 41 Sup.Ct. 574, 65 L.Ed. 1048 (1921).

5. Agnello v. United States, 269 U.S. 20, 46 Sup.Ct. 4, syl. 6, 70 L.Ed. 145, 51 A.L.R. 409 (1925) (objection at trial sufficient, where illegality of seizure uncontroverted and accused "maintained" he never had the article seized—but what he "maintained" seems not the test, but what the judge finds as to the fact of his knowledge).
Examples of holdings that the objection at the trial came too late: Segurola v. United States, 275 U.S.

106, 48 Sup.Ct. 77, syl. 5, 6, 72 L.Ed. 186 (1927); United States v. Weinecke, 138 F.2d 561, syl. 3–5 (C.C.A. 7, 1943, opinion by Minton, J.).

6. The quoted provision is the last sentence of Rule 41(e). The rules became effective March 21, 1946. The holding in United States v. Asendio, 171 F.2d 122, syl. 6 (C.A. 3, 1948) that the judge was required to grant a new trial for the admission of evidence which was the fruit of an illegal search, though not objected to, seems insupportable. See Notes, 28 Neb.L.Rev. 631, 28 Tex.L.Rev. 273.

7. The following seventeen states are listed for this view in Wolf v. Colorado, 338 U.S. 25, 38, 69 Sup. Ct. 1359, 1367, 93 L.Ed. 1782 (1949): Fla., Idaho, Ill., Ind., Iowa, Ky., Mich., Miss., Mo., Mont., Okla., S. D., Tenn., Wash., W. Va., Wis., Wyo. The decisions are collected in an appendix to the opinion in that case. To these should be added Delaware, which has since adopted the Federal view by decision (Rickards v. State (1950) 6 Terry. 573, 77 A.2d 199, 205), and North Carolina and Texas which have passed laws to like effect. See note 8, below.

8. Maryland, St.1947, Apr. 25, c. 752, p. 1849 (evidence secured by illegal search or seizure inadmissible in misdemeanor cases); North Carolina, St. 1951, Apr. 9, c. 644, § 1 (evidence of facts discovered, or evidence obtained, by illegal search inadmissible); Texas, Vernon's Ann. C.C.P. art. 727a, amend-

ing generally to the Federal rule of exclusion, most have specifically accepted the requirement when feasible of a pre-trial motion to suppress,[9] others have rejected it,[10] and in others the point seems undecided.

We have suggested, in the discussion of the distinction between rules of exclusion and rules of privilege, that the right to object to evidence obtained by unreasonable search is properly classed as a privilege.[11] The ground of objection is not at all that the evidence is unreliable or misleading, but that the interest of privacy of a particular person or persons has been wrongfully invaded. Accordingly it seems that the right of objection should attach, not to any party against whom the evidence is offered, but only to those individuals, if they happen to be parties, whose interest of security in "their persons, houses, papers and effects" has been invaded. This

has been the predominant view in the state and Federal courts,[12] and though some doubt has been cast upon it by a recent decision of the highest court,[13] the broader implications of the holding were not discussed, and it seems questionable that the court intended to repudiate generally in this field the privilege theory that only the one whose ox is gored can complain.

140. Is the Federal Rule of Exclusion Imposed on the States as a Requirement of Due Process?

This question was presented in Wolf v. Colorado.[1] The court said: "The security of one's privacy against arbitrary intrusion by the police—which is at the core of the Fourth Amendment—is basic to a free society. It is therefore implicit in 'the concept of ordered liberty' and as such enforceable against the States through the Due

---

ed Acts 1953, 53d Leg., p. 669, ch. 253, § 1 ("No evidence obtained by an officer or other person in violation of any provision of the constitution or laws of the United States or of this state shall be admitted in evidence against the accused on the trial of any criminal case").

9. State v. Robinson, 71 Idaho 290, 230 P.2d 693, syl. 5 (1951); People v. Dalpe, 361 Ill. 607, 21 N.E.2d 756, syl. 4 (1939); People v. Heibel, 305 Mich. 710, 9 N.W.2d 826 (1943); State v. Jackson, 336 Mo. 1069, 83 S.W.2d 87, syl. 3, 103 A.L.R. 339 (1935) and cases collected in Dec.Dig., Crim.Law, ☞394(t); 31 C.J.S., Crim.Law, § 1062, note 46.

10. Youman v. Comm., 189 Ky. 152, 224 S.W. 860, syl. 6 (1920); State v. Bass, 153 Tenn. 162, 281 S.W. 936, syl. 7 (1926); 31 C.J.S., Crim.Law, § 1062, note 62.

11. See § 74, herein.

12. See § 74, herein. See also Agnello v. United States, 269 U.S. 20, 35, 46 Sup.Ct. 4, 7, 70 L.Ed. 145, 51 A.L.R. 409 (1925), where the court held that a can of narcotics was illegally seized in a room occupied by Agnello and was erroneously received against him, but said: "But the judgment against the other defendants may stand. The introduction of the evidence of the search and seizure did not transgress their constitutional rights." This evidence, however, had not been received against the other defendants. But compare McDonald v. United States, 335 U.S. 451, 69 Sup.Ct. 191, 93 L.Ed.

451 (1948), where evidence secured by wrongful search of a lodger's room was admitted, despite the lodger's motion to suppress, against the lodger and against a guest temporarily in the room, and the convictions of both were reversed on this ground. The case is critically noted in 62 Harv. L.Rev. 1229. This "personal interest" limitation, however, is criticised as inequitable and as calculated to weaken the deterrent effect of the rule of exclusion, in Note, 58 Yale L.J. 144, 154–158 (1948).

13. United States v. Jeffers, 342 U.S. 48, 72 Sup.Ct. 93, 96 L.Ed. 59 (1951). In that case the defendant had permission to enter the room in a hotel rented to and occupied by his aunts. Without their knowledge he deposited in a closet of the room twenty bottles of narcotics. Federal officers wrongfully entered the room without a warrant and seized the narcotics. Federal law declares the narcotics contraband and provides that "no property rights shall exist" therein. 26 U.S.C.A. § 3116. The seized narcotics were admitted over defendant's objection and he appeals his conviction. Against the government's contention that the defendant had no standing to question the seizure, the court said, "It being his property, for purposes of the exclusionary rule, he was entitled on motion to have it suppressed as evidence on his trial." See Notes, 50 Mich.L.Rev. 931, 31 Neb.L.Rev. 618, 25 So.Cal. L.Rev. 364.

1. 338 U.S. 25, 69 Sup.Ct. 1359, 93 L.Ed. 1782 (1949), extensively noted in 38 Calif.L.Rev. 498, 50 Col.L. Rev. 364, 45 Ill.L.Rev. 1.

Process Clause. . . . Accordingly, we we have no hesitation in saying that were a State affirmatively to sanction such police incursion into privacy it would run counter to the guaranty of the Fourteenth Amendment. But the ways of enforcing such a basic right raise questions of a different order." [2] The court then called attention to the fact that thirty of the states and ten jurisdictions of the British Commonwealth of Nations that evidence unlawfully secured should nevertheless be received, and concluded: "We cannot brush aside the experience of States which deem the incidence of such conduct by the police too slight to call for a deterrent remedy not by way of disciplinary measures but by overriding the relevant rules of evidence. There are, moreover, reasons for excluding evidence unreasonably obtained by the federal police which are less compelling in the case of police under State or local authority. The public opinion of a community can far more effectively be exerted against oppressive conduct on the part of police directly responsible to the community itself than can local opinion, sporadically aroused, be brought to bear upon remote authority pervasively exerted throughout the country.

"We hold, therefore, that in a prosecution in a State court for a State crime the Fourteenth Amendment does not forbid the admission of evidence obtained by an unreasonable search and seizure." [3] Three justices

dissented and two filed extensive and vigorous dissenting opinions. The prevailing opinion observed that two questions remain open, whether Congress could abrogate for the Federal courts the rule of exclusion, or conversely, could impose such rule by legislation upon the states.

141. A Conviction Based on Evidence Secured through Shockingly Brutal Methods by State Officers may be a Denial of Due Process.[1]

We have seen that a state conviction based on a forced confession violates due process, while one based on evidence obtained by an unreasonable search and seizure does not. In Rochin v. California [2] the highest court was faced with a state conviction for possessing narcotics based upon evidence obtained by a series of illegal acts. State officers unlawfully entered Rochin's home and forced their way into his bedroom, where they found two capsules on a stand by the bed. When they asked whose they were, Rochin put them in his mouth. The officers then assaulted him in an attempt to take them from his mouth, without avail, then handcuffed him and took him to a hospital. There they caused a doctor to force an emetic through a tube into Rochin's stomach. This brought up the capsules, which contained morphine, and were the chief evidence for his conviction. The highest court reversed the conviction as a denial of due process. Frankfurter, J., for the

---

2. Pp. 27, 28, official report.

3. Pp. 31, 32, 33. See also Stefanelli v. Minard, 342 U.S. 117, 72 Sup.Ct. 118, 96 L.Ed. 138 (1951). There the plaintiff was being prosecuted in a New Jersey state court and alleged that the prosecution would use as evidence against him the fruits of an unlawful seizure, which if committed by Federal officers would have been a violation of the Fourteenth Amendment. Plaintiff sought in a Federal Court an injunction against the use against him of this evidence, relying on the Civil Rights Act, 42 U.S.C.A. § 1983, which gives redress for "deprivation of any rights, privileges, or immunities secured by the Constitution and laws." The Supreme Court affirmed the denial of the injunction. The court declined to decide whether a case was stated

under the Civil Rights Act, but justified the result as a proper exercise of the discretion of Federal equity courts to refrain from interfering by injunction with state criminal prosecutions and trials. See the acute analysis of the case in Falknor, Evidence, 1951 Annual Survey Am.L. 835, 843.

1. See the masterly discussion of the problems presented by the Rochin case in Allen, Due Process and State Criminal Procedures: Another Look, 48 N.W.U.L.Rev. 16 (1953).

2. 342 U.S. 165, 72 Sup.Ct. 205, 96 L.Ed. 183, 25 A.L.R.2d 1396 (1952). See Note, Examination and tests of suspects as violating Federal Constitution, 96 L.Ed. 194, and extensive notes in 40 Calif.L.Rev. 311, 66 Harv.L.Rev. 122, 50 Mich.L.Rev. 1367.

majority, relied on the analogy of convictions based on forced confessions. He said: "This is conduct that shocks the conscience. Illegally breaking into the privacy of the petitioner, the struggle to open his mouth and remove what was there, the forcible extraction of his stomach's contents—this course of proceeding by agents of government to obtain evidence is bound to offend even hardened sensibilities. They are methods too close to the rack and the screw to permit of constitutional differentiation." [3]

In order to avoid, however, the implication that the court was condemning the humane administration of such scientific methods as blood-tests for intoxication or for paternity, he continued: "In deciding this case we do not heedlessly bring into question decisions in many States dealing with essentially different, even if related, problems. We therefore put to one side cases which have arisen in the State courts through use of modern methods and devices for discovering wrongdoers and bringing them to book. It

does not fairly represent these decisions to suggest that they legalize force so brutal and so offensive to human dignity in securing evidence from a suspect as is revealed by this record." [4]

Two concurring justices [5] deploring the vagueness of the "civilized standards" measure of due process, and espousing the view that the Fourteenth Amendment imposes on the States the restrictions of the Federal Bill of Rights, [6] would have based the result here upon the conclusion that the evidence was secured in violation of the self-incrimination privilege. [7]

It is a severe disciplining of the state judicial processes to pronounce a sentence of nullity upon a conviction based upon evidence which has no taint of unreliability, though secured by violent and brutal methods. The implications of the decision are as indefinite as the standard of "conduct that shocks the conscience." [8] Nevertheless, it commands approval as a wholesome admonition to law enforcement officers and as a

---

3. P. 172, official report.

4. P. 174.

5. Black and Douglas.

6. The view urged by the same justices, and rejected by the majority, in Adamson v. California, 332 U.S. 46, 67 Sup.Ct. 1672, 91 L.Ed. 1903, 171 A.L.R. 1223 (1947).

7. A position of questionable soundness, see § 126, herein.

8. Both the indefiniteness and the disciplinary influence of the Rochin doctrine have been lessened by the decision in Irvine v. California, 347 U.S. 128, 74 Sup.Ct. 381, 98 L.Ed. —— (1954). Here the state conviction for bookmaking rested upon evidence obtained by state officers through methods described as "obnoxious" and "almost incredible." "The police strongly suspected petitioner of illegal bookmaking but were without proof of it. On December 1, 1951, while Irvine and his wife were absent from their home, an officer arranged to have a locksmith go there and make a door key. Two days later, again in the absence of occupants, officers and a technician made entry into the home by the use of this key and installed a concealed microphone in the hall. A hole was bored in the roof of the house and wires were

strung to transmit to a neighboring garage whatever sounds the microphone might pick up. Officers were posted in the garage to listen. On December 8, police again made surreptitious entry and moved the microphone, this time hiding it in the bedroom. Twenty days later, they again entered and placed the microphone in a closet, where the device remained until its purpose of enabling the officers to overhear incriminating statements was accomplished." By a five-to-four decision, the attack on the judgment on due process grounds failed. The Wolf case (see next preceding section) rather than Rochin was held controlling. As Jackson, J., for four of the five prevailing justices, said, "However obnoxious are the facts in the case before us, they do not involve coercion, violence or brutality to the person, but rather a trespass to property, plus eavesdropping." This retreat from the broader implications of the Rochin case is disappointing to one who feels that the court's control of lawless enforcement by state officers has been a civilizing influence. In the persuasive words of Frankfurter, J.'s dissent: "The effort to imprison due process within tidy categories misconceives its nature and is a futile endeavor to save the judicial function from the pains of judicial judgment."

dramatization of the need for nationwide support of decent standards of humanity in criminal law administration.

142. Evidence Obtained by Wire-Tapping.[1]

In 1928 it was contended before the highest court that evidence procured by Federal officers through tapping telephone wires, which was forbidden by the local state statute, was wrongfully received. By a five to four decision, however, the court held that the tapping was not a search or seizure, there being no entry upon premises of the defendants, and that, if the statute could validly be applied to Federal officers, the illegal procurement of the evidence (in the absence of violation of constitutional rights) was no ground of exclusion.[2] In an eloquent and exhaustive dissenting opinion Brandeis, J., urged that wire-tapping by government officers violates the Fourth Amendment, as well as the Fifth, and Holmes, J., expressed the view that "apart from the Constitution the government ought not to use evidence obtained and only obtainable by a criminal act."

Thereafter in 1934 Congress enacted the Communications Act regulating communications by wire or radio and providing in section 605 that "no person not being authorized by the sender shall intercept any communication and divulge or publish the existence, contents, substance, purport, effect, or meaning of such intercepted communication

to any person."[3] Being moved, doubtless, by its consciousness of the increasing prevalence and abuses of wire-tapping the court in 1937 in the first Nardone case[4] held that this provision applied to Federal officers and that the prohibition of "divulgence" forbade divulgence by giving evidence of the intercepted communications in a Federal court.

This revolutionary decision was soon followed by holdings which greatly extended the scope of the prohibition. The second Nardone case[5] held that, in case of unlawful wire-tapping, not only are the communications themselves excluded but likewise the information gained by the government as a result of the wire-tap is inadmissible,[6] and consequently it was error to refuse to permit the accused to examine the prosecution as to the uses to which it had put such information. Again, in the Weiss case[7] the court determined that intra-state messages, intercepted by wire-tapping, are protected from disclosure equally with interstate communications. The same case held, moreover, that consent of one of the conversers secured by confronting him with recordings of the conversation and by promises of leniency is not "authorization by the sender" under Section 605.

These extensions have been followed by some significant restrictions on the prohibition.

First, the use by Federal officers of a device such as the detectaphone to overhear

---

1. 8 Wigmore, Evidence, § 2184b. Among the more important articles in the flood of periodical material (see Index to Legal Periodicals, Criminal Law, subtitle Evidence) are these: Bernstein, The Fruit of the Poisonous Tree, 37 Ill.L.Rev. 99 (1942); Rosenzweig, The Law of Wire-Tapping, 32 Corn. L.Q. 514, 33 id. 73 (1947); Westin, The Wire-Tapping Problem, 52 Col.L.Rev. 165 (1952). See also 20 Am.Jur., Evidence, § 399; Dec.Dig., Crim.Law, ☞394(d).

2. Olmstead v. United States, 277 U.S. 438, 48 Sup. Ct. 564, 72 L.Ed. 944, 66 A.L.R. 376 (1928).

3. 47 U.S.C.A. § 605.

4. Nardone v. United States, 302 U.S. 379, 58 Sup. Ct. 275, 82 L.Ed. 314 (1937).

5. Nardone v. United States, 308 U.S. 338, 60 Sup. Ct. 266, 84 L.Ed. 307 (1939).

6. The most acute and extensive discussion of the implications of this holding is Bernstein, The Fruit of the Poisonous Tree, 37 Ill.L.Rev. 99 (1942). Some limitations upon the effectiveness of this doctrine are suggested in Note, Exclusion of Evidence Obtained by Wire-Tapping: An Illusory Safeguard, 61 Yale L.J. 1221 (1952).

7. Weiss v. United States, 308 U.S. 321, 60 Sup.Ct. 269, 84 L.Ed. 298 (1939).

the words of one party to the telephone conversation is not an "interception" and, if accomplished without a trespass is not a search or seizure.[8]

Second, the right to object to the use of intercepted conversations is limited to those persons whose interest of privacy has been infringed, namely, the participants in the conversation.[9] This is in keeping with the tradition followed in respect to privileges generally, that is, those grounds of exclusion which are based not on the unreliable or prejudicial character of the evidence, but on the policy of protecting some interest other than the ascertainment of truth.[10] The result, however, has been criticized as furnishing too great an incentive for the continuance of the practice of wire-tapping.[11]

Third, the Communications Act has been construed, in the absence of any specific expression of an intent to do so, as not requiring the exclusion of wire-tap evidence in the state courts.[12] The court did not intimate that the power of Congress would not extend so far, in carrying out its function of regulating the national system of communications, if there were a clear manifestation of intent to do. This holding, obviously, was a drastic limitation of the potential effectiveness of Section 605 in curbing the evil of wire-tapping.

Despite the great number of state statutes regulating or forbidding wire-tapping,[13] and

---

8. Goldman v. United States, 316 U.S. 129, 62 Sup. Ct. 993, 86 L.Ed. 1322 (1942).

As to the "interception" question, the holding leaves open the important and practical question of the admissibility of testimony or recordings based on the "monitoring" (overhearing) over an extension-telephone of a conversation between a "stool-pigeon" or police-agent and a suspect. The police-agent of course knows and consents to the monitoring. The recordings in such a case were held inadmissible in United States v. Polakoff, 112 F. 2d 888, syl. 2, 134 A.L.R. 607 (C.C.A.2, 1940). It was held in an opinion by Learned Hand, J., first, that this was an "interception," and second, that the consent of the stool-pigeon was not the authorization of "the sender" since both parties to the conversation must consent. Clark, J., dissented vigorously from both holdings. Certiorari was denied, 311 U.S. 653, 61 Sup.Ct. 41, 85 L.Ed. 418. A contrary view is expressed in United States v. Lewis, 87 F.Supp. 970 (D.D.C.1950), noted 45 N.W. U.L.Rev. 689. The same problem was presented in Reitmeister v. Reitmeister, 162 F.2d 691, 697, C.C.A.N.Y., 1947, but one of the judges expressed the view that the Polakoff holdings were overruled by the Goldman case. The question is acutely discussed in Bernstein, The Fruit of the Poisonous Tree, 37 Ill.L.Rev. 99, 108–113 (1942).

In the picturesque case of On Lee v. United States, 343 U.S. 747, 72 Sup.Ct. 967, 96 L.Ed. 1270 (1952), a friend of the defendant entered the customers' room of defendant's laundry and defendant there made damaging admissions to him. This friend was a secret government agent and had a small microphone in his inside pocket. Another government agent was stationed outside with a receiving set which picked up the conversation transmitted through the microphone, and this agent testified to the admissions of defendant thus overheard. The court held, with four justices dissenting, that the evidence was not the fruit of an unlawful search, there being no trespass, nor was its use a violation of Section 605. "There was no interference with any communications facility which he possessed or was entitled to use. He was not sending messages to anybody or using a system of communications within the Act." See notes, 40 Calif. L.Rev. 429, 66 Harv.L.Rev. 127, 21 U.Cin.L.Rev. 484.

9. Goldstein v. United States, 316 U.S. 114, 62 Sup. Ct. 1000, syl. 1, 5–8, 86 L.Ed. 1312 (1942) (testimony of co-conspirators induced by divulging contents of wire-taps was admitted: held, accused not being a party to intercepted conversations could not complain); Notes, 16 Temple U.L.Q. 436 (excellent), 55 Harv.L.Rev. 141, 30 Corn.L.Q. 111 (interpreting this and the Goldman case as a swing back from the advanced position of the Nardone cases).

10. See §§ 72, 73, herein and see the discussion of the similar problem in respect to searches and seizures in §§ 74, 139, above.

11. Westin, op. cit., 52 Col.L.Rev. 165, 178.

12. Schwartz v. Texas, 344 U.S. 199, 73 Sup.Ct. 232, 97 L.Ed. 231 (1952). After this decision Texas amended its statute so as to make inadmissible evidence obtained in violation of the laws of the United States. Laws of 1953, amending Vernon's Ann.C.C.P. art. 727a.

13. These are cited and classified in Rozenzweig, op. cit., 33 Corn.L.Q. 73–75, Westin, op. cit., 52 Col.L. Rev. 165, 181, 182, Bernstein, op. cit., 37 Ill.L.Rev. 99, 108.

the interpretation by the highest court of Section 605 as a prohibition of the practice, there is abundant evidence that the practice is widespread by Federal officers,[14] by state enforcement officials,[15] and by private individuals.[16] There are warnings on the one hand that the abuse of this method of spying upon private speech is undermining our feeling of freedom and casting upon our government the odium of a police state.[17] There is strong insistence, on the other hand, that wire-tapping when used as a means of detecting conspiracies against national security or plots against human life is an essential and justifiable method of defending the community against those who endanger it.[18]

The best hope of improvement lies in the acceptance of responsibility by Congress for a comprehensive legislative regulation of the entire area of wire-tapping.[19] One proposal,[20] supported by a thoroughgoing study of the factual and legal background, would forbid wire-tapping, under criminal and civil penalties, except in the investigation of crimes against national security and those directly affecting the safety of human life. As to the former, authority for wire-tapping could be given only by the Attorney General or an agency designated by the Secretary of Defence. As to crimes against human safety *ex parte* orders permitting wire-tapping would be issuable upon a proper showing by a Federal district court to Federal officers, and by a state criminal court to state officers.

14. See the data collected in Westin, op. cit., 52 Col.L.Rev. 167–172, and particularly the reports of the trials and appeals of Judith Coplon, where the wire-tapping was authorized by the Attorney General and was continued, in the first case cited, to include the conversations of the accused with her counsel during the trial. United States v. Coplon, 91 F.Supp. 867 (D.D.C.), rev'd, 191 F.2d 749 (D.C.Cir.1951), cert. denied, 342 U.S. 926 (1952); United States v. Coplon, 88 F.Supp. 921 (S.D.N.Y.), rev'd, 185 F.2d 629 (2d Cir.1950), cert. denied, 342 U.S. 920 (1952).

Several attorney-generals have interpreted Sec. 605 as not prohibiting wire-tapping alone, but only when it is followed by "divulgence." Statement of Attorney General McGrath, N. Y. Times, Jan. 9, 1950, p. 15, col. 5; 86 Cong.Rec.App. 1471 (1940) (statement of Attorney General Jackson), cited in Westin, op. cit., 52 Col.L.Rev. 168, note 16.

15. Westin, op. cit., 52 Col.L.Rev. 165, 166, 195, 196 (New York).

16. Westin, op. cit., 52 Col.L.Rev. 167, 168.

17. See the remarks of Brandeis, J., dissenting in Olmstead v. United States, 277 U.S. 438, 475, 48 Sup.Ct. 564, 571, 72 L.Ed. 944 (1928); "The evil incident to invasion of the privacy of the telephone is far greater than that involved in tampering with the mails. Whenever a telephone line is tapped, the privacy of the persons at both ends of the line is invaded, and all conversations between them upon any subject, and although proper, confidential, and privileged, may be overheard. Moreover, the tapping of one man's telephone line involves the tapping of the telephone of every other person whom he may call, or who may call him. As a means of espionage, writs of assistance and general warrants are but puny instruments of tyranny and oppression when compared with wire tapping."

18. See 8 Wigmore, Evidence, § 2184b, and the statements and letters appearing in the evidence at hearings of Congressional Committees, referred to in Westin, op. cit., 52 Col.L.Rev. 186, 187, notes. Arguments on both sides are summarized in Notes, 2 Stan.L.Rev. 744, 751 (1950), 53 Harv.L.Rev. 863, 869.

19. The Attorney General's proposals currently pending in Congress are discussed in Brownell, Public Security and Wire-Tapping, 39 Corn.L.Q. 195 (1954). See also Pogue, Wire-Tapping and the Congress, 52 Mich.L.Rev. 430 (1954), and in the valuable symposium, Rogers, The Case for Wire Tapping, 63 Yale L.J. 792 (1954) and Donnelly, Comments and Caveats, id. 799.

20. Westin, op. cit., 52 Col.L.Rev. 200–208.

CHAPTER 15

PRIVILEGES FOR GOVERNMENTAL SECRETS

143. Other Principles Distinguished.

In discussing the evidential privileges and rules of exclusion in respect to the production and admission of writings and information in the possession of government officers, it is well to mark off at the outset some other principles which may hinder the litigant seeking facts from the government, but which are beyond our present inquiry. Among them are these: (a) questions of substantive privilege of government officers from liability for their acts and words,[1] (b) questions as to the general exemption of the chief executive and other high officers from judicial process to enforce their appearance or attendance or to compel them to give evidence,[2] and (c) questions as to the irremovability of official records.[3]

144. The Common Law Privileges for Military or Diplomatic Secrets and Other Facts the Disclosure of Which Would be Contrary to the Public Interest.[1]

In the last half-century in this country and in England, where the activities of government have so multiplied in number and widened in scope, the need of litigants for the disclosure and proof of documents and other information in the possession of government officials has correspondingly increased. When such needs are asserted and opposed, the resultant questions require a delicate and judicious balancing of the public interest in the secrecy of "classified" official information against the public interest in the protection of the claim of the individual

[1] See, e. g., Spalding v. Vilas, 161 U.S. 483, 16 S.Ct. 631, syl. 3, 40 L.Ed. 780 (1896) (exemption of Postmaster General from civil liability for official statement); Prosser, Torts, § 94(3); 8 Wigmore, Evidence, § 2368.

[2] See 8 Wigmore, Evidence, §§ 2369–2371.

[3] See, e. g., Dunham v. Chicago, 55 Ill. 357 (1870) (court will not order removal where certified copies will serve as well); 8 Wigmore, Evidence, § 2373.

[1] 8 Wigmore, Evidence, §§ 2378, 2378a, 2379; Phipson, Evidence, 196, 197 (9th ed., 1952); Sanford, Evidentiary Privileges against the Production of Data within the Control of Executive Departments, 3 Vand.L.Rev. 73 (1949) (an able and comprehensive discussion); Berger and Krash, 59 Yale L.J. 1451 (1950) (an acute argument against immunity); Note, Three Non-Personal Privileges, 29 N.Y.U.L.Rev. 194 (1954); 58 Am.Jur., Witnesses, §§ 533, 535; 70 C.J., Witnesses, § 616; Dec.Dig., Witnesses, ⬅ 216.

to due process of law in the redress of grievances.[2]

It is generally conceded that a privilege and a rule of exclusion should apply in the case of writings and information constituting military or diplomatic secrets of state.[3] Wigmore seems to regard it as doubtful whether the denial of disclosure should go further than this,[4] but statutes in this country have often stated the privilege in broader terms,[5] and the English decisions seem to have accepted the wide generalization that official documents and facts will be privileged whenever their disclosure would be injurious to the public interest.[6] Probably this wider principle would likewise generally be accepted by the courts of this country as a matter

---

2. "Besides, the public good is in nothing more essentially interested, than in the protection of every individual's private rights, as modelled by the municipal law." 1 Blackstone, Commentaries *139 (1765), referred to in Pound, Administrative Discretion and Civil Liberties in England, 56 Harv.L. Rev. 806, 814 (1943).

3. 8 Wigmore, Evidence, § 2378(5). Examples of decisions in which the existence of a privilege for military or diplomatic secrets was affirmed or assumed: Aaron Burr's Trial, Robertson's Rep. I, 121, 127, 186, 255, II, 536 (1807) described and quoted from in 8 Wigmore, Evidence, § 2379, p. 799 (subpena duces tecum issued by Marshall, C. J., to President Jefferson to produce correspondence with General Wilkinson, over objection of government that it involved relations with France and Spain; C. J. Marshall: "There is certainly nothing before the Court which shows that the letter in question contains any matter the disclosure of which would endanger the public safety; . . . if it does contain any matter which it would be imprudent to disclose, which it is not the wish of the Executive to disclose, such matter, if it be not immediately and essentially applicable to the point, will of course be suppressed. . . ." 8 Wig. p. 799); Totten v. United States, 92 U.S. 105, 23 L.Ed. 605 (1875) (action by former spy, after Civil War, for services during war under contract with President; held, action denied since its maintenance will endanger secrecy of such employments); Firth Sterling Steel Co. v. Bethlehem Steel Co., 199 Fed. 353, syl. 2 (E.D.Pa.1912) (copies of drawings of armor-piercing projectiles made by Navy and classed as secret, excluded by court on objection, though witness did not claim privilege, recognizing "rule of public policy forbidding the disclosure of military secrets.") In United States v. Reynolds, 345 U.S. 1, 73 S.Ct. 528, 531, 532, 97 L.Ed. 727 (1953), Vinson, C. J., for the court, after referring to "the privilege against revealing military secrets, a privilege which is well established in the law of evidence," said: "Judicial experience with the privilege which protects military and state secrets has been limited in this country. English experience has been more extensive, but still relatively slight compared with

other evidentiary privileges. Nevertheless, the principles which control the application of the privilege emerge quite clearly from the available precedents. The privilege belongs to the Government and must be asserted by it; it can neither be claimed nor waived by a private party. It is not to be lightly invoked. There must be a formal claim of privilege, lodged by the head of the department which has control over the matter, after actual personal consideration by that officer."

Rule 33 of the Uniform Rules of Evidence (following Rule 227 of the Model Code) provides: "(1) As used in this Rule, 'secret of state' means information not open or theretofore officially disclosed to the public involving the public security or concerning the military or naval organization or plans of the United States, or a State or Territory, or concerning international relations.

"(2) A witness has a privilege to refuse to disclose a matter on the ground that it is a secret of state, and evidence of the matter is inadmissible, unless the judge finds that (a) the matter is not a secret of state, or (b) the chief officer of the department of government administering the subject matter which the secret concerns has consented that it be disclosed in the action."

4. See 8 Wigmore, Evidence, §§ 2378, 2378a, 2379.

5. See Calif.C.C.P. § 1881, par. 5: "A public officer shall not be examined as to communications made to him in official confidence, when the public interests would suffer by the disclosure." This has been substantially copied in Colorado (adds "in the judgment of the court"), Idaho, Iowa, Minnesota, Montana, Nebraska, Nevada, North Dakota, Oregon, South Dakota, Utah and Washington. A Georgia statute is broader still. Code 1933, §§ 38–1102, 38–1711 ("official persons" cannot be required "to disclose any State matters of which the policy of State and the interest of the community require concealment"). All these provisions are cited in 8 Wigmore, Evidence, § 2378, p. 786, note 7. See also Dec.Dig., Witnesses, ☞216.

6. The opinion of Viscount Simon, L.Ch., for the House of Lords in Duncan v. Cammell, Laird & Co., [1942] App.C. 624 accepts this principle and reviews the supporting precedents.

of common law,[7] and doubtless it is justified in point of policy. The obvious danger of oppressive administration from such a broad principle of immunity must be sought in a widened conception of the judge's controlling responsibility for the balancing of the public and the private interests involved.[8]

145. Privileges against Disclosure Created by Federal Statute and Departmental Regulations.[1]

Congress has enacted that "The head of each department is authorized to prescribe regulations, not inconsistent with law, for the government of his department, the conduct of its officers and clerks, the distribution and performance of its business, and the custody, use, and preservation of the records, papers, and property appertaining to it."[2] The phrase relating to the "custody, use and preservation of the records, papers," etc., was early assumed by administrators to authorize regulations requiring the subordinate

officers, who are actually in possession of most of such papers and records, to decline to produce them when served with a subpena issued by a court. Examples of such regulations are cited below.[3] Usually they provide that upon an application to the head of the department or a rule served upon him by the court, he may grant or refuse the request for production.

In so far as such regulations purport to empower the subordinate officer having custody of the paper to refuse to produce it in court upon subpena, or to testify to its contents, the highest court has consistently upheld their validity.[4] The consequent inability of litigants to secure Federal official papers or evidence of their contents when such papers are relevant to the issues in private suits is a serious and recurrent obstacle to the presentation of proof. It is true that the litigant may apply for production to the head of the department, but this recourse will often fail, and the resort to legal process

---

7. The Uniform Rules of Evidence, Rule 34 (following the Model Code, R. 228) provides:

"(1) As used in this Rule, 'official information' means information not open or theretofore officially disclosed to the public relating to internal affairs of this State or of the United States acquired by a public official of this State or the United States in the course of his duty, or transmitted from one such official to another in the course of duty.

"(2) A witness has a privilege to refuse to disclose a matter on the ground that it is official information, and evidence of the matter is inadmissible, if the judge finds that the matter is official information, and (a) disclosure is forbidden by an Act of the Congress of the United States or a statute of this State, or (b) disclosure of the information in the action will be harmful to the interests of the government of which the witness is an officer in a governmental capacity."

8. See the discussion in § 147, below.

1. Sanford, op.cit., 3 Vand.L.Rev. 73, 86; Berger and Krash, op. cit., 59 Yale L.J. 1450, 1460; Notes, Governmental Privilege to Withhold Documents in Private Litigation, 47 N.W.U.L.Rev. 519 (1952); Discovery of Documents under the Federal Rules, 18 U.Chi.L.Rev. 122 (1950); Governmental Privilege against Disclosure—Federal Cases, 95 L.Ed. 425, Statutes or Regulations relating to Divulgence of

Information Acquired by Public Officers, 165 A.L.R. 1302; Dec.Dig., Federal Civil Procedure, ⊂⇒1593.

2. 5 U.S.C.A. § 22, R.S. § 161.

3. See, e. g., the regulations of the Attorney General set out in United States v. Ragen, 340 U.S. 462, 71 S.Ct. 416, 95 L.Ed. 417 (1951), those of the Treasury summarized in Fowkes v. Dravo Corp., 5 F.R.D. 51 (E.D.Pa.1945), and those of the Department of Labor set out in Walling v. Richmond Screw Anchor Co., 4 F.R.D. 265, 268 (E.D.N.Y.1943).

4. Boske v. Comingore, 177 U.S. 459, 20 S.Ct. 701, syl. 1, 3, 44 L.Ed. 846 (1900) (statute conferring rule-making power on heads of departments valid under the "necessary and proper" clause and Treasury regulation prohibiting production of records by collector of internal revenue valid; collector punished for contempt by state court for non-production discharged on habeas corpus); United States v. Ragen, 340 U.S. 462, 71 S.Ct. 416, 95 L.Ed. 417 (1951) (similar regulations of Attorney General approved, following above decision in its application to subordinate officers; "When one considers the variety of information contained in the files of any government department and the possibilities of harm from unrestricted disclosure in court, the usefulness, indeed the necessity, of centralizing determination as to whether subpoenas duces tecum will be willingly obeyed or challenge is obvious.").

against the head will be hedged with practical difficulties such as the territorial limits upon the service of subpena, and the probable assertion of privilege upon the taking of his deposition.[5]

The result of this general authorizing Act, implemented by restrictive regulations of the departments to the general effect that all papers are to be withheld from the courts unless the head otherwise determines, seems unfortunate and one-sided. The starting-point should be that all official papers are available to the courts when relevant in litigation, except where for special reasons of policy they should be withheld. Congress could best reconcile the interests of the government and the individual citizen by enacting a general rule of availability together with principles and standards for the guidance of the departments in classifying records and information which would be protected from disclosure.[6]

When the issue as to production by the Secretary is finally drawn, and the standard by which the claim of privilege is to be measur-ed is ascertained, who shall determine whether the standard has been satisfied, the executive or the judge? We shall discuss this question in a later section.[7]

146. Effect of the Presence of the Government as a Litigant.[1]

As appears from the preceding section, in suits between parties other than the Government, the heads of department are free to require their subordinates to decline to produce documents and information, and the parties are remitted to a not very hopeful attempt to persuade or to compel the head of the department to make the disclosure. When the Government itself is a party and resists disclosure, the picture changes. The argument that the privilege conferred by the statute and regulations described in the last section is waived when the Government itself invokes the court's aid by bringing suit is generally accepted.[2] The court may grant an order of discovery but if called on for enforcement it may give the Government the choice of making the disclosure or suffering a dismissal of the action.[3] The discovery

---

5. See Note, 47 N.W.U.L.Rev. 519, 523.

6. Perhaps the beginnings of such an approach may be glimpsed in the following provisions of the Atomic Energy Act, 42 U.S.C.A. § 1810:

"(a) It shall be the policy of the Commission to control the dissemination of restricted data in such a manner as to assure the common defense and security. . . .

"(b) (1) The term 'restricted data' as used in this section means all data concerning the manufacture or utilization of atomic weapons, the production of fissionable material, or the use of fissionable material in the production of power, but shall not include any data which the Commission from time to time determines may be published without adversely affecting the common defense and security."

See Haydock, Some Evidentiary Problems and Atomic Energy, 61 Harv.L.Rev. 468, 469 (1948).

7. See § 147, below.

1. Note, 95 L.Ed. 425, 445; Berger and Krash, op.cit., 59 Yale L.J. 1451, 1453; Note, The Executive Evidential Privilege in Suits against the Government, 47 N.W.U.L.Rev. 258 (1952).

2. United States v. Andolschek, 142 F.2d 503, 506 (C.C.A.2d 1944) (in prosecution of inspectors of

Alcohol Tax Unit for illegal dealings with permittees, error to sustain government's claim of privilege for reports of inspectors to their superiors as to these dealings; L. Hand, J.: "While we must accept it as lawful for a department of the government to suppress documents, even when they will help determine controversies between third persons, we cannot agree that this should include their suppression in a criminal prosecution, founded upon those very dealings to which the documents relate, and whose criminality they will, or may, tend to exculpate."); United States v. Grayson, 166 F.2d 863, 870, syl. 18, 19 (C.C.A.2d 1948) (prosecution for fraudulent use of mails and violation of Securities Act, held error to exclude as confidential pertinent documents in possession of Securities and Exchange Commission); United States v. General Motors Corp., 2 F.R.D. 528, syl. 6 (N.D.Ill.1942) (objection that Government not required to answer interrogatories overruled).

3. "The government must choose; either it must leave the transactions in the obscurity from which a trial may draw them, or it must expose them." United States v. Andolschek, 142 F.2d 503, 506 (C.C.A.2d 1944). In United States v. Cotton Valley Operators Committee, 9 F.R.D. 719 (W.D.La.1949),

provisions of the Rules of Civil Procedure have no exception for the Government and are held to authorize orders for discovery against it.[4]

The same results have generally been reached in actions against the Government. The Federal Tort Claims Act recites that "The United States shall be liable . . . *in the same manner* and to the same extent as a private individual . . ." [5] (emphasis supplied). This has been held to constitute a waiver of the Government's privilege, under the general statute and regulations, of non-disclosure of routine records and information.[6] Doubtless, however, no court would construe the waiver to extend to the common law privileges for military or diplomatic secrets and for confidential matters the disclosure of which would be seriously

harmful to the national interest.[7] And even as to the routine or "house-keeping" records where the interest of secrecy is a minor one, the courts have been inclined in these suits against the Government not to incur the friction and embarrassment incident to contempt process against officials but to use the power given by the Rules [8] when discovery is refused to make an order that the matters regarding which the questions were asked shall be taken as established against the Government.[9]

147. The Scope of the Judge's Function in Determining the Validity of the Claim of Privilege.[1]

When the head of department has made a claim of privilege for documents or information under his control as being military or diplomatic secrets or other matters the dis-

---

a civil anti-trust action, the Government failed to comply with the order to produce certain reports and correspondence and the action was dismissed. The judgment was affirmed by an equally divided court in 339 U.S. 940, 94 L.Ed. 1356, 70 S.Ct. 793.

It is persuasively urged that no mechanical rule of waiver should control but that the respective interests should be weighed, with discrimination between the government's role as proprietor and its function as law-enforcer. Note, 18 U.Chi.L.Rev. 122, 128 (1950).

4. United States v. General Motors Corp., 2 F.R.D. 528, syl. 6 (N.D.Ill.1942). The Rules apply generally in actions to which the United States is a party. Sherwood v. United States, 112 F.2d 587, 590, syl. 2 (C.C.A.2d 1940).

5. 28 U.S.C.A. § 2674.

6. Wunderly v. United States, 8 F.R.D. 356 (E.D. Pa.1948); Cresmer v. United States, 9 F.R.D. 203 (E.D.N.Y.1949); Branner v. United States, 10 F.R.D. 468, syl. 6 (E.D.Pa.1950) reversed in United States v. Reynolds, 345 U.S. 1, 73 S.Ct. 528, 531, 97 L.Ed. 727 (1953), but the question of waiver was left undecided. See also similar holdings under the Suits in Admiralty Act, 46 U.S.C.A. § 743, which provides that such suits "shall proceed . . . according to the rules of practice obtaining in like cases between private parties." O'Neill v. United States, 79 F.Supp. 827, syl. 3 (E.D.Pa.1948), vacated on other grounds, 174 F.2d 931 (C.A.3, 1949); Bank Line, Ltd. v. United States, 76 F.Supp. 801, syl. 1 (S.D.N.Y.1948).

7. See expressions to that effect in the opinions in O'Neill v. United States and Bank Line, Ltd. v. United States, in next preceding note. Moreover, the Supreme Court in Reynolds v. United States, 345 U.S. 1, 73 S.Ct. 528, 531, 97 L.Ed. 727 (1953), where the court found that there was a valid claim that the information sought was a military secret, said that this was "privileged" matter under Fed. Rules Civ.Proc. rule 34 relating to discovery and hence the Government's amenability to the Rules did not make the matter discoverable.

8. Fed.Rules Civ.Proc. Rule 37(b) (2).

9. See lower court's order described in United States v. Reynolds, 345 U.S. 1, 73 S.Ct. 528, 530, 97 L.Ed. 727 (1953). For similar orders see Bank Line, Ltd. v. United States, 76 F.Supp. 801, 805, syl. 3 (S.D. N.Y.1948); O'Neill v. United States, 79 F.Supp. 827, 830, syl. 6 (E.D.Pa.1948).

1. 8 Wigmore, Evidence, §§ 2378a, 2379; Sanford, op. cit., Haydock, op.cit., 61 Harv.L.Rev. 468, 472–478; 3 Vand.L.Rev. 73, 93–96; Notes, 18 U.Chi.L.Rev. 122 (1950), McAllister, 41 J.Crim.L. 330 (1950); 47 N.W. U.L.Rev. 259, 268 (1952), 47 N.W.U.L.Rev. 519, 527 (1952); 29 N.Y.U.L.Rev. 194 (1954).

The discussions of the subject which impressed me as the ablest are those of Wigmore cited above and the opinion of Morris, J., in Reynolds v. United States, 192 F.2d 987, 996–998 (C.C.A.3, 1952). Though the decision was reversed in the highest court (345 U.S. 1, 73 Sup.Ct. 528, 97 L.Ed. 727), this opinion was adopted by three justices as expressing substantially their views.

closure of which would be dangerous to the public interest, is this claim conclusive upon the judge? Is he entitled to ascertain the content of the information withheld, and to apply for himself the standard of danger to the public interest? A decision of the House of Lords in 1942 limits the judge's function to ascertaining whether the claim is made by the proper officer in proper form. If he decides that it is, the claim is conclusive.[2] An earlier decision of the Privy Council had held that when the executive claim was made, the judge might nevertheless have the power to inspect the papers withheld and to decide whether disclosure would be injurious to the public.[3] The cases may be distinguished, in that the first-mentioned was between private suitors and involved secret naval plans and the other was an action against the state and related to reports about wheat in a public warehouse, but the underlying question as to the scope of power remains.

When the privilege relates to official papers and information sought by the citizen as a means of proof in the assertion of his claims, and the disclosure is opposed as harmful to general security or welfare, the question is one of balancing conflicting policies. The head of an executive department can appraise the public interest of secrecy as well (or perhaps in some cases better [4]) than the judge, but his official habit and leaning tend to sway him toward a minimizing of the interest of the individual. Under the normal administrative routine the question will come to him with recommendations from cautious subordinates against disclosure and in the press of business the chief is likely to approve the recommendation about such a seemingly minor matter without much independent consideration.[5] The determination of questions of fact and the applications of legal standards thereto in passing upon the admissibility of evidence and the validity of claims of evidential privilege are traditionally the responsibility of the judge.[6] As a public functionary he has respect for the executive's scruples against disclosure and at the same time his duties require him constantly to appraise private interests and to reconcile them with conflicting public policies. He seems better qualified than the executive to weigh both interests understandingly and to strike a wise balance.[7]

[2.] Duncan v. Cammel, Laird & Co., [1942] App.C. 624. The holding is vigorously criticized in a Note, 69 L.Q.Rev. 449 (1953).

[3.] Robinson v. State of South Australia, [1931] App.C. 704.

[4.] Haydock, op.cit., 61 Harv.L.Rev. 468, 474, instances the possibility that the court may be called on to determine whether certain data concern the production of fissionable material, and he comments that the court's lack of expertness would be apparent, as contrasted with the knowledge of the executive.

[5.] See the graphic comments of Wigmore to like effect. 8 Evidence, p. 793.

In speaking of the grounds which should influence the executive, Simons, L. Ch., said in Duncan v. Cammel Laird & Co., [1942] App.C. 624, 642: "It would not be a good ground that, if they were produced, the consequences might involve the department or the government in parliamentary discussion or in public criticism, or might necessitate the attendance as witnesses or otherwise of officials who have pressing duties elsewhere. Neither would it be a good ground that production might tend to expose a want of efficiency in the administration or tend to lay the department open to claims for compensation. In a word, it is not enough that the minister of the department does not want to have the documents produced. The minister, in deciding whether it is his duty to object, should bear these considerations in mind, for he ought not to take the responsibility of withholding production except in cases where the public interest would otherwise be damnified, for example, where disclosure would be injurious to national defence, or to good diplomatic relations, or where the practice of keeping a class of documents secret is necessary for the proper functioning of the public service." And in Robinson v. State of South Australia, [1931] App.C. 704, 715, the court declared that "the fact that production of the documents might in the particular litigation prejudice the Crown's own case" is not a legitimate reason for claiming privilege.

[6.] See § 53, herein.

[7.] A good analysis of this balancing process and an instructive example of its exercise appears in the

What of the danger that the judge by inquiring into the contents of the papers or the facts, in passing upon the validity of the claim of privilege, may effect a disclosure which even if the privilege is ultimately sustained will destroy the secrecy sought to be protected? Even where the general responsibility for inquiry is recognized, there is room for flexibility. In war-time the statement by the defence department of a military need for secrecy would seldom be questioned.[8] In some circumstances, as where the Navy's plans for construction of a submarine are sought,[9] the information "on its face" could be found to be a secret of state without further inquiry. In other cases,

judges have directed that the information, or so much as is necessary, be disclosed privately to the judge alone, as a basis for his determining the claim of privilege.[10] The judge as a responsible public official can be trusted with such an official secret, and the objection to the private one-sided hearing has little force when the alternative is no hearing at all.

The preponderance of view among the lower federal courts [11] and among the writers [12] seems to support the judge's power and responsibility for inquiry as opposed to the conclusiveness of the claim of privilege by the executive. A recent decision by the highest court,[13] though in that case the order design-

opinion of Mathis, D. J., in United States v. Schneiderman, 106 F.Supp. 731, 735–738 (S.D. Calif.1952).

8. Compare the comments of C. E. Clark, J., in Bank Line, Ltd. v. United States, 163 F.2d 133, 139 (C.C.A.2, 1947).

9. As in Duncan v. Cammel, Laird & Co., [1942] App.C. 624.

10. As in Evans v. United States, 10 F.R.D. 255, 257, 258 (W.D.La.1950) ("It is not the exclusive right of any such agency of the Government to decide for itself the privileged nature of any such documents, but the Court is the one to judge of this when such contention is made. This can be done by presenting to the Judge, without disclosure in the first instance to the other side, whatever is claimed to have that status."), and in the lower court as described and approved in Reynolds v. United States, 192 F.2d 987, 997 (C.A.3, 1951). While the lower courts' disposition of the particular case was reversed in the Supreme Court of the United States, see note 13, infra, yet the power to require disclosure *in camera* in an appropriate case seemingly was not denied.

11. United States v. Doheny and Fall, reported by excerpts from stenographic record in Morgan and Maguire, Cases on Evidence, 3d ed. 1951 (Sup.Ct. D.C.1926) (Admiral Robison required by court to tell in general terms of an interview of witness with Secretary of Navy as to the necessity of establishing the security of Pacific Coast against a "foreign power," despite witness's statement of objections by the Secretary); Walling v. Richmond Screw Anchor Co., 4 F.R.D. 265, 269, syl. 6 (E.D. N.Y.1943); United States v. Schine Chain Theatres, 4 F.R.D. 108, syl. 2 (W.D.N.Y.1944); Zimmerman v. Poindexter, 74 F.Supp. 933, syl. 3, 4 (D.Hawaii,

1947); United States v. Cotton Valley Operators Committee, 9 F.R.D. 719 (W.D.La.1949), affirmed by an equally divided court in 339 U.S. 940, 70 Sup.Ct. 793, 94 L.Ed. 1356; and the decisions cited in the next preceding note.

A contrary practice, however, is enjoined by 28 U.S. C.A. § 2507, which provides that the Court of Claims may call on any department or agency for information or papers, but that the head "may refuse to comply when, in his opinion, compliance will be injurious to the public interest." The section was applied and interpreted in Pollen v. United States, 85 Ct.Cl. 673 (1937) and in Pollen v. Ford Instrument Co., 26 F.Supp. 583, syl. 2 (E.D.N.Y.1939).

12. Thus, of the writers cited in note 1, above, all adopt this view except Haydock and the writer of the last-listed note.

13. United States v. Reynolds, 345 U.S. 1, 73 Sup.Ct. 528, 97 L.Ed. 727 (1953). This was an action under the Federal Tort Claims Act, 28 U.S.C.A. § 2671 et seq., by the widows of three civilians killed in the crash of an air force plane. The plaintiffs sought discovery of the report of the Air Force's official investigation of the accident and the statements of the surviving crew members taken therein. The Secretary of the Air Force claimed privilege in the interest of security, mentioning that the plane was on a "highly secret mission" (it appeared later, a mission to test new electronic equipment) but offering to produce the three surviving crew members, without cost, for examination by the plaintiffs, and to allow them to refresh their memories from their statements. The District Court ordered the Government to produce the documents so that it might determine whether they contained privileged matter. The Government declined, and the court then ordered that, under Rule 37, the issue of negligence be taken as established for the plaintiffs.

ed to implement the direction for disclosure was reversed, seems to look in the same direction.[14] This principle, it is believed, should govern in suits between private persons as well as in those wherein the government is a party. There are opportunities in the latter for indirect enforcement which avoids a test of the power to compel, which do not exist in the private suits. But even in the private suits, if an order on the Government for disclosure is pronounced, and physical enforcement were not deemed constitutional or practicable,[15] the order would at least have the force of a declaratory judgment that production should be made. It

would usually be complied with, and if not the courts would have done what they could to see that due regard is given to the individual's right as part of the general good.

148. The Privilege against the Disclosure of the Identity of an Informer.[1]

Informers are shy and timorous folk, and if their names were subject to be readily revealed, this source of information would be almost cut off. On this ground of policy, a privilege and a rule of inadmissibility are recognized in respect to disclosure of the identity of such an informer,[2] who has given

---

After affirmance in the Court of Appeals (192 F.2d 987) the Supreme Court reversed. It held that in view of the Government's offer to make available the evidence of the surviving crewmen, and of the showing of the secret military character of the information sought, the plaintiffs' necessity did not outweigh the Government's need for secrecy.

14. See the following passages of the opinion of Vinson, C. J., for the court: "The court itself must determine whether the circumstances are appropriate for the claim of privilege, and yet do so without forcing a disclosure of the very thing the privilege is designed to protect. . . . Regardless of how it is articulated, some like formula of compromise must be applied here. Judicial control over the evidence in a case cannot be abdicated to the caprice of executive officers. Yet we will not go so far to say that the court may automatically require a complete disclosure to the judge before the claim of privilege will be accepted in any case. It may be possible to satisfy the court, from all the circumstances of the case, that there is a reasonable danger that compulsion of the evidence will expose military matters which, in the interest of national security, should not be divulged. When this is the case, the occasion for the privilege is appropriate, and the court should not jeopardize the security which the privilege is meant to protect by insisting upon an examination of the evidence, even by the judge alone, in chambers. . . . In each case, the showing of necessity which is made will determine how far the court should probe in satisfying itself that the occasion for invoking the privilege is appropriate." 345 U.S. 1, 73 Sup.Ct. 528, 533, 97 L.Ed. 727.

15. See 8 Wigmore, Evidence, §§ 2369-2371.

1. 8 Wigmore, Evidence, § 2374; 56 Am.Jur., Witnesses, § 534; 70 C.J., Witnesses, § 616, p. 454;

Dec.Dig., Witnesses, ☞216. See also Comments, An Informer's Tale: Its Use in Judicial and Administrative Proceedings, 63 Yale L.J. 206 (1953) (a valuable critique); Three Non-Personal Privileges, 29 N.Y.U.L.Rev. 194, 200 (1954). The policy of the privilege seems drawn in question by the vigorous language of Mr. Justice Douglas's dissent in United States v. Nugent, 346 U.S. 1, 13, 73 Sup.Ct. 991, 97 L.Ed. 417 (1953) where the court held that one who claimed draft exemption was not entitled, in an advisory hearing in the Department of Justice, to see the F.B.I. reports containing information received from informers.

2. Marks v. Beyfus, 25 Q.D.Div. 494 (Ct.App.1890) (action for malicious prosecution; plaintiff sought to elicit from Director of Public Prosecutions, the name and statement of informers—who were presumably the present defendants—but the witness declined unless the judge was of opinion that he should disclose, but the judge declined to order him to answer; on plaintiff's appeal, held, no error— not a matter of discretion, but judge should exclude under the rule of policy, except where the evidence is needed to establish the innocence of an accused); Worthington v. Scribner, 109 Mass. 487, 12 Am.Rep. 736 (1872) (action for false charges made to U. S. Treasury that plaintiff was an imposter; interrogatories to the defendant as to his giving this information; held defendant privileged not to answer); Dellastatious v. Boyce, 152 Va. 368, 147 S.E. 267, syl. 9 (1929) (action for damages for trespass on premises and false arrest against prohibition inspector and special deputies in execution of warrant; error in requiring officer to disclose from whom he secured information on which warrant was issued).

Uniform Rules of Evidence, Rule 36: "A witness has a privilege to refuse to disclose the identity of a person who has furnished information purporting to disclose a violation of a provision of the laws of

information about supposed crimes to a prosecuting or investigating officer or to someone for the purpose of its being relayed to such officer.[3] The privilege seemingly runs to the government or state, and may be invoked by its officers who as witnesses or otherwise are called on for the information,[4] and runs also, it seems, to one charged with being such informer,[5] and when neither the government nor the informer is represented at the trial, doubtless the judge as in other cases of privilege [6] may invoke it for the absent holder.[7] It is disputed whether the privilege is confined to disclosure of identity[8] or extends also to the contents of the communication.[9] Seldom will the contents of the statement be competent if the name is

undisclosed, but it is believed that the policy of the privilege does not apply to shielding the purport of the communication from disclosure. Of course, if revealing the contents will in the circumstances probably reveal the identity of the informer, the privilege should attach.

The privilege has two important qualifications, one obvious and the other not so obvious but just. The first is that when the identity has already become known to those who would have cause to resent the communication, the privilege ceases.[10] The second is that when the privilege is asserted by the state in a criminal prosecution, and the evidence of the identity of the informer becomes important to the establishment of

---

this State or of the United States to a representative of the State or the United States or a governmental division thereof, charged with the duty of enforcing that provision, and evidence thereof is inadmissible, unless the judge finds that (a) the identity of the person furnishing the information has already been otherwise disclosed or (b) disclosure of his identity is essential to assure a fair determination of the issues."

3. See Hardy's Trial, 24 How.St.Tr. 99 (1794), quoted 8 Wigmore, p. 751 (Erle, L.C.J.: "I cannot satisfy myself that there is any substantial difference between the case of this man's going to a justice of the peace . . . or to some other person who communicated with a justice. . . .").

4. This is probably the most frequent source of objection, see, e. g., Marks v. Beyfus, note 2, above; Wilson v. United States, 59 F.2d 390 (C.C.A.3, 1932) (on petition to suppress evidence secured on liquor raid; deputy prohibition commissioner refused to answer question as to source of information on raid and was committed for contempt; held, the court should have sustained his claim of privilege).

5. See, e. g., cases wherein the claim of privilege was successfully made by the alleged informer or on his behalf; Worthington v. Scribner, note 2, above; Wells v. Toogood, 165 Mich. 677, 131 N.W. 124, syl. 1 (1911) (action for slander against alleged informer; when officer was asked as to complaint of theft made to him by defendant, defendant's counsel objected).

6. See § 73, herein.

7. See the statement of Bowen, L. J., in Marks v. Beyfus, described note 2, above: ". . . the

privilege does not depend upon the witness claiming it when asked the question; but the judge should refuse to allow the question as soon as it is asked." (p. 500). The Uniform Rule (note 1, above) describes the doctrine as a rule of inadmissibility as well as privilege, but since no element of unreliability or prejudice is involved (see § 72, herein) it may be preferable to class it as a privilege throughout.

8. This is the view of Wigmore (§ 2374, p. 753) and the form in which the doctrine is stated in many of the leading opinions, see, e. g., Marks v. Beyfus, Worthington v. Scribner, both cited in note 2, above, and Scher v. United States, 305 U.S. 251, 254, 59 Sup.Ct. 174, 83 L.Ed. 151 (1938) (". . . public policy forbids disclosure of an informer's identity"). See also Bowman Dairy Co. v. United States, 341 U.S. 214, 221, 71 Sup.Ct. 675, 95 L.Ed. 879 (1951), where in an anti-trust prosecution it was held that the government could be required to produce complaints and statements received from third persons, but that the court must be "solicitous to protect against disclosures of the identity of informants. . . ."

9. Numerous opinions state the doctrine as including the contents of the statement but usually in situations where the wider coverage is not material. See, e. g., Michael v. Matson, 81 Kan. 360, 105 Pac. 537, syl. 4 (1909) and Wells v. Toogood, note 5, above.

10. "It [the privilege] does not apply when the informer is known or when the communication has been divulged." Comm. v. Congdon, 265 Mass. 166, 165 N.E. 467, 470 (1928).

the defence, the court will require the disclosure,[11] and if it is still withheld, that the prosecution be dismissed.[12]

149. Statutory Privileges for Certain Reports of Individuals to Government Agencies: Accident Reports, Tax Returns, etc.[1]

A policy faintly similar to that which has prompted the common law privilege for the identity of informers may be thought to have some application to all reports required by law to be made by individuals to government agencies giving information needed in the administration of their public functions. If the statements may be used against the reporters, they may in some degree be discouraged from making full and true reports. On the other hand, such reports often deal with facts highly material in private litigation, and an early report to government may be reliable and pressingly needed for ascertainment of the facts. The latter interest has prevailed with the courts, and in the absence of a statutory provision creating the privilege there is no privilege for these reports.[2] Nevertheless, in legislative halls

11. Regina v. Richardson, 3 Fost. & F. 693, 176 Eng. Rep. 318 (N.P.1863) (murder by poison, policeman who testified to finding poison in defendant's premises in consequence of information received required, over his objection, to give names of informants as being "material to ends of justice"); Wilson v. United States, 59 F.2d 390, syl. 2–5 (C.C.A.3, 1932) (motion to suppress evidence seized in club: seizure justified in testimony of officer that admittance had been secured by use of key given by member: officer required to give name of member; "If what is asked is useful evidence to vindicate the innocence of the accused or lessen the risk of false testimony or is essential to the proper disposition of the case, disclosure will be compelled."). This escape from the privilege is often invoked where the question arises as to the existence of probable cause for an arrest or seizure without a warrant. When a sufficient showing of cause is afforded by what the arresting officers saw and heard at the scene, the information received from informants is of no importance and disclosure of their identity will not be required. Scher v. United States, 305 U.S. 251, 254, 59 Sup.Ct. 174, 83 L.Ed. 151 (1938). But when a part of the grounds of probable cause relied on is the report or complaint by an informant, the courts divide as to whether the name must be revealed. Requiring disclosure: United States v. Keown, 19 F.Supp. 639, syl. 5 (W.D.Ky.1937) (able opinion by Hamilton, D. J., reviewing authorities; accused entitled to know whether informants were worthy of belief); United States v. Blich, 45 F.2d 627, syl. 4 (D.Wyo.1930). Contra: United States v. Li Fat Tong, 152 F.2d 650, syl. 3, 4 (C.C.A.2, 1945) (officers testified that they received information that accused was coming in on plane with narcotics in baggage; they met him on landing, and while they were talking to him he dropped bottle containing narcotics, and admitted having purchased narcotics; he was then arrested and his baggage seized; held, court properly refused to require disclosure of informants' identities; "We cannot see that the proof at the trial would have tended to establish innocence if the names of the informers had been given for it is not disputed that the defendant was carrying narcotics") and cases cited in Note, 59 A.L.R. 1555, 1559. The question is one of balancing the public interest in law enforcement against the policy of discouraging unreasonable searches and seizures.

12. "It is a sound rule to keep secret information furnished to the state of violations of its laws, but this commendable public policy must yield to a higher, or at least an equal, right accorded to an accused to have a court investigate the facts material to his offense in a criminal prosecution, and sometimes the departments of government will be put to a choice of either foregoing a criminal prosecution or disclosing the source of material information necessary to the conduct of orderly judicial procedure." United States v. Keown, 19 F.Supp. 639, 646 (W.D.Ky.1937). A like choice is put to the state in respect to neighboring privileges. Centoamore v. State, 105 Neb. 452, 181 N.W. 182 (1920) (asserted privilege—see 8 Wigmore, Evidence, § 2375—for confidential communications to public prosecutor; where necessary to defence, must be disclosed); United States v. Krulewitch, 145 F.2d 76, syl. 3, 4 (C.C.A.2, 1944) (same as last); United States v. Andolschek, 142 F.2d 503, 506, syl. 6 (C.C.A.2, 1944) (privilege for government documents may not be insisted on if government chooses to prosecute for transaction to which those documents relate).

1. 8 Wigmore, Evidence, § 2377; Note, Statutes Relating to Divulgence of Information Acquired by Public Officers, 165 A.L.R. 1302; 58 Am.Jur., Witnesses, §§ 533, 536; Dec.Dig., Witnesses, ⊂⇒216.

2. Peden v. Peden's Adm'r, 121 Va. 147, 92 S.E. 984, 2 A.L.R. 1414 (1917) (report of property for taxation) and see Panik v. Didra, 370 Pa. 488, 88 A.2d 730, syl. 1, 6 (1952) (report of accident required by city ordinance not privileged in absence of provision for privilege). Compare, however, Gerry v.

when bills requiring such reports are proposed the need for encouraging frank and full reports looms large to the proponents, but the judges and lawyers who would urge the need for truth in litigation are not alerted to oppose the privilege. Accordingly, there has been incorporated in a very large

number of statutes requiring various kinds of reports a privilege for the reporter against their use in court. Probably the most frequent of such statutory privileges are those for reports of accidents on the highways [3] and industrial accidents [4] and for returns of property [5] and income [6] for taxation.

Worcester Consol. St. Ry. Co., described in note 4, below.

3. An extensive opinion discussing some of the problems arising under the statutory privilege for highway accident reports, quoting from the statutes and citing cases from various states, is that of Knutson, J., in Rockwood v. Pierce, 235 Minn. 519, 51 N.W.2d 670 (1952) (oral admissions made by defendant to highway patrolman as basis for latter's official report, which would be privileged under M.S.A. § 169.09, subd. 13, are not privileged). The case is noted in 36 Minn.L.Rev. 540. The statutes and cases are collected in Note, 165 A.L.R. 1302, 1315, and in 8 Wigmore, Evidence, § 1377, note 3.

4. Louisville & N. Ry. Co. v. Stephens, 298 Ky. 328, 182 S.W.2d 447, syl. 25 (1944) (action for death: error to admit reports made by Railway to Interstate Commerce Commission, which are privileged under provisions of Boiler Inspection Act, 45 U.S. C.A. §§ 33, 41; Gerry v. Worcester Consol. St. Ry. Co., 248 Mass. 559, 143 N.E. 694, 697, syl. 10 (1924) (death injury: report of injury erroneously received as admission in view of St.1913, c. 746, providing that reports to Industrial Accident Board "shall be kept available by the said Board, and shall be furnished in request to the State Board of Labor and Industries for its own use": "In giving this information to the Industrial Accident Board, the defendant's report was in the nature of a privileged communication; and although not expressly privileged by the words of the statute, it was not intended that these reports should be availed of in an action at law arising out of the subject-matter of the suit."); Winningham v. Travelers' Ins. Co., 93 F.2d 520, syl. 3 (C.C.A.Tex.1937) (physician's report of injury made for employer to Industrial Accident Board inadmissible against employer under Tex.Vernon's Ann.Civ.St. art. 8309, § 5).

5. Brackett v. Comm., 223 Mass. 119, 111 N.E. 1036, syl. 12 (1916) (corporation tax return); Williams v. Brown, 137 Mich. 569, 100 N.W. 786, syl. 2 (error to permit discrediting plaintiff, who had testified as to value of property, by producing his statements while listing property for taxes, in view of statute limiting use of such statements); Re Manufacturers Trust Co., 269 App.Div. 108, 53 N.Y.S.2d 923 (1945) (corporation's franchise tax return; interpreting statute forbidding divulging of tax information).

6. Provisions for secrecy of state income tax returns are construed in In re Valecia Condensed Milk Co., 240 Fed. 310 (C.C.A.7, 1917) (St.Wis.1915, § 1087 m

24 forbidding divulgence by state officer validly requires him to refuse production though ordered by subpena of Federal court) and in Oklahoma Tax Comm. v. Clendinning, 193 Okl. 271, 143 P.2d 143, 151 A.L.R. 1035 (1943), annotated on this topic (construing sec. 1454, Uniform State Tax Procedure Act, 68 O.S. 1951).

The Internal Revenue Code of 1954 provides, in Sec. 6103: "(1) Returns made with respect to taxes imposed by chapters 1, 2, 3, and 6 upon which the tax has been determined by the Secretary or his delegate shall constitute public records; but, except as hereinafter provided in this section, they shall be open to inspection only upon order of the President and under rules and regulations prescribed by the Secretary or his delegate and approved by the President.

". . . (3) Whenever a return is open to the inspection of any person, a certified copy thereof shall, upon request, be furnished to such person under rules and regulations prescribed by the Secretary or his delegate. The Secretary or his delegate may prescribe a reasonable fee for furnishing such copy." See also Sec. 7213(a) as to unauthorized disclosure.

Other subsections of Sec. 6103 provide for inspection by state officers, inspection of corporate returns by shareholders, and inspection by Committees of Congress. The regulations relating to inspection of returns appear in Code of Fed.Regs., Title 26, secs. 458.1–458.315. Sec. 458.52 provides that the return of an individual may be inspected by him, his attorney in fact, or his personal representatives, heirs, etc. Sec. 458.204 deals with the furnishing of the original returns or copies for use in litigation. Sec. 458.205 provides that a copy of a return may be furnished to any person who is entitled to inspect it.

The greater number of decisions favor the view that in private civil litigation a party may be required to produce copies of his Federal income tax returns. Connecticut Importing Co. v. Continental Distilling Corp., 1 F.R.D. 190, syl. 1–9 (D.Conn.1940) (leading opinion by Hincks, J.) (plaintiff's retained copies ordered to be produced for inspection); The Sultana, 77 F.Supp. 287, syl. 2 (W.D.N.Y.1948) (personal injury; on issue of plaintiff's earning power he was ordered to procure certified copies to be produced for inspection); Reeves v. Pennsylvania R. Co., 80 F.Supp. 107, syl. 1–3 (D.Del.1948) (same as last, movant required to reimburse expense of obtaining certified copies); Paramount Film Distributing

150. **The Secrecy of Grand Jury Proceedings: (a) The Privilege for the Votes and Expressions of Grand Jurors: (b) The Privilege for Communications of Witnesses to the Grand Jury.**

To guard the independence of action of the accusatory body, to protect the reputations of those investigated but not indicted, and to prevent the forewarning and flight of those accused before publication of the indictment, the taking of evidence by the grand jurors and their deliberations have traditionally been shrouded in secrecy.[1] The ancient oath administered to the jurors bound them to keep secret "the King's counsel, your fellows' and your own." Two privileges are incident to this system. First, the grand jurors have a privilege against the disclosure by any one of their communications to each other during their deliberations and of their individual votes.[2]

Second, the communications of complainants and other witnesses in their testimony before the grand jury are privileged against disclosure by anyone, but this privilege is temporary only.[3] When the grand jury has published its action in the matter under investigation the need for secrecy is much diminished and the privilege ceases.[4] The purport of the former testimony may then be disclosed in any proceeding in which it is relevant, as for example, to discredit a witness by proving his prior inconsistent testimony,[5] to refresh his memory,[6] or to prove a criminal charge of perjury.[7]

Corp. v. Ram, 91 F.Supp. 778, syl. 3–6 (E.D.S.C.1950) (conspiracy by motion picture exhibitors for false reporting of film rentals); June v. George C. Peterson Co., 155 F.2d 963, syl. 10 (C.C.A.7, 1946) (no discussion). See also Ex Parte Frye, 155 Oh.St. 345, 98 N.E.2d 798 (1951) (Federal statute prohibiting publication of income tax returns, does not prohibit discovery in hands of accountant of work sheets from which client's income tax returns were prepared). Contra: Peterson v. Peterson, 70 S.D. 385, 17 N.W.2d 920, syl. 2 (1946) (divorce; order requiring husband to procure and produce certified copies of returns reversed; Federal statute prohibiting publication of returns gives husband privilege which only he can waive); O'Connell v. Olsen & Ugelstadt, 10 F.R.D. 142 (N.D.Oh.1949) (motion for production of returns denied: privileged under statute and regulations); Maddox v. Wright, 103 F. Supp. 400 (D.C., 1952) (same as last).

1. 8 Wigmore, Evidence, § 2360. See Goodman v. United States, 108 F.2d 516, 127 A.L.R. 265 (C.C.A.9, 1939) upholding right of court to require oath of secrecy from witnesses before grand jury, and Note, Duty of Secrecy of Members, Witnesses and Other Persons in Proceedings before Grand Jury, 127 A.L.R. 272; 38 C.J.S., Grand Juries, § 43; 24 Am.Jur., Grand Jury, §§ 47, 48; Dec.Dig., Grand Jury, ⊂⊃41; Federal Rules of Criminal Procedure, Rule 6(e), Secrecy of Proceedings and Disclosure.

2. Wm. J. Burns Internat. Detective Agency v. Holt, 138 Minn. 165, 164 N.W. 590, syl. 2 (1917) (conversations among members, during deliberations, about employing detectives, excluded); Opinion of the Justices, 96 N.H. 530, 73 A.2d 433, syl. 4, 8 (1950) (power of legislative investigating committee does not extend to inquiring into grand jurors' votes and opinions); 8 Wigmore, Evidence, § 2361. But the privilege does not extend to deliberations in the course of preparing a report which was outside the lawful functions of the grand jury. Bennett v. Stockwell, 197 Mich. 50, 163 N.W. 482, syl. 4 (1917).

3. United States v. Socony-Vacuum Oil Co., 310 U.S. 150, 233, 60 Sup.Ct. 811, 849, syl. 37, 84 L.Ed. 1129 (1940) (grand jury testimony is ordinarily confidential, but when jury's function ended, disclosure proper where ends of justice require it); 8 Wigmore, Evidence, §§ 2362, 2363; Uniform Rules of Evidence, Rule 3: "A witness has a privilege to refuse to disclose a communication made to a grand jury by a complainant or witness, and evidence thereof is inadmissible, unless the judge finds (a) the matter which the communication concerned was not within the function of the grand jury to investigate, or (b) the grand jury has finished its investigation, if any, of the matter, and its finding, if any, has lawfully been made public by filing it in court or otherwise, or (c) disclosure should be made in the interests of justice."

4. Atwell v. United States, 162 Fed. 97, syl. 2 (C.C.A. 4, 1908); Ex parte Montgomery, 244 Ala. 91, 12 So. 2d 314, syl. 6 (1943).

5. State v. Bovino, 89 N.J.L. 586, 99 Atl. 313, syl. 2 (1916); Comm. v. Carr, 137 Pa.Super. 546, 10 A.2d 133, 138, syl. 11, 12 (1939).

6. United States v. Socony-Vacuum Oil Co., 310 U.S. 150, 233, 60 Sup.Ct. 811, 849, 84 L.Ed. 1129 (1940).

7. Izer v. State, 77 Md. 110, 26 Atl. 282, syl. 1 (1893) (on charge of perjury in testimony before grand jury, grand jurors are not rendered incompetent by their oath of secrecy to testify as to what accused swore to before them).

TITLE 6

RELEVANCY AND ITS COUNTERWEIGHTS: TIME, PREJUDICE, CONFUSION AND SURPRISE

CHAPTER 16

RELEVANCY

Sec.
151. Relevance as the Presupposition of Admissibility
152. The Meaning of Relevancy

151. Relevance as the Presupposition of Admissibility.

Relevance, as we shall see, is <u>probative worth,</u> and common sense would suggest that if there is to be any practice of excluding evidence which is offered, the first ground of exclusion should be the want of probative value. Correspondingly, in the search for the truth of the issue, reason would suggest that if evidence is <u>logically probative</u> it should be received unless there is some distinct ground for refusing to hear it. Thayer, by recognizing and announcing these simple truths, placed the Anglo-American system of evidence rules in a new and just perspective. He said:

"Observe, at this point, one or two fundamental conceptions. There is a principle—not so much a rule of evidence as a presupposition involved in the very conception of a rational system of evidence, as contrasted with the old formal and mechanical systems—which forbids receiving anything irrelevant, not logically probative.
. . .

"There is another precept which should be laid down as preliminary, in stating the law of evidence; namely, that unless excluded by some rule or principle of law, all that is logically probative is admissible. This general admissibility, however, of what is logically probative is not, like the former

principle, a necessary presupposition in a rational system of evidence; there are many exceptions to it. . . .

"In stating thus our two large, fundamental conceptions, we must not fall into the error of supposing that relevancy, logical connection, real or supposed, is the only test of admissibility; for so we should drop out of sight the chief part of the law of evidence. When we have said (1) that, without any exception, nothing which is not, or is not supposed to be, logically relevant is admissible; and (2) that, subject to many exceptions and qualifications, whatever is logically relevant is admissible; it is obvious that, in reality, there are tests of admissibility other than logical relevancy. Some things are rejected as being of too slight a significance, or as having too conjectural and remote a connection; others, as being dangerous, in their effect on the jury, and likely to be misused or overestimated by that body; others, as being impolitic, or unsafe on public grounds; others, on the bare ground of precedent. It is this sort of thing, as I said before,—the rejection on one or another practical ground, of what is really probative,—which is the characteristic thing in the law of evidence; stamping it as the child of the jury system."[1]

1. Thayer, Preliminary Treatise on Evidence, 264–266 (1898). For opinions adopting this approach

314

152. The Meaning of Relevancy.[1]

In the courtroom the terms relevancy and materiality are often used interchangeably, but materiality in its more precise meaning looks to the relation between the propositions for which the evidence is offered and the issues in the case. If the evidence is offered to prove a proposition which is not a matter in issue nor probative of a matter in issue, the evidence is properly said to be immaterial. As to what is "in issue", that is, within the range of the litigated controversy, we look mainly to the pleadings, read in the light of the rules of pleading and controlled by the substantive law. Thus, in an action on a bond where the only plea is a denial of execution, evidence offered by the defendant of a release would be immaterial,[2] and in a suit for workmen's compensation, evidence of contributory negligence would be immaterial, whether pleaded or not, since the statute abrogates it as a defense. But matters in the range of dispute may extend somewhat beyond the issues defined in the

pleadings. Thus, under flexible modern systems of procedure issues not raised by the pleadings may be tried by express or implied consent of the parties.[3] In addition, the parties may draw in dispute the credibility of the witnesses and, within limits, produce evidence assailing and supporting such credibility.[4] Moreover, we must recognize that a considerable lee-way is allowed even on direct examination for proof of facts which are not really offered as bearing on the dispute, however defined, but merely as details which fill in the background of the narrative and give it interest, color and life-likeness.

We start, then, with the notion of materiality, the inclusion of certain questions or propositions within the range of allowable controversy in the lawsuit. Relevancy, in legal usage, embraces this test and something more. Relevancy in logic is the tendency of evidence to establish a proposition which it is offered to prove.[5] Relevancy, as employed by judges and lawyers, is the tendency of the evidence to establish a material

---

see Hadley v. Baltimore & Ohio R. Co., 120 F.2d 993, 995 (C.C.A.Pa.1941); Godsy v. Thompson, 352 Mo. 681, 691, 179 S.W.2d 44 (1944). See also 1 Wigmore, Evidence, §§ 9, 10.

1. A most illuminating discussion, to which I am much indebted, is G. F. James, Relevancy, Probability and the Law, 29 Calif.L.Rev. 689 (1941). Also valuable is Trautman, Logical or Legal Relevancy— a Conflict in Theory, 5 Vand.L.Rev. 385 (1952). The major contributions in this country are Thayer, Preliminary Treatise on Evidence, 263–276, 515–518 (1898) and 1 Wigmore, Evidence, § 12 (Distinctions between Relevancy and Admissibility); §§ 25, 26 (Circumstantial and Testimonial Evidence); §§ 27–29a (General Considerations Affecting Relevancy); §§ 31, 32 (Required Degree of Probability of Proposed Inference); §§ 38–42 (General Theory of Circumstantial Evidence). See also Phipson, Evidence, Ch. V (8th ed. 1942); Decennial Digests, Criminal Law, ☞338, Evidence, ☞99, 100, 114–117, 143–147.

2. See James, op. cit., 29 Calif.L.Rev. 689, 690, 691. See also 1 Wigmore, Evidence, § 2; Model Code of Evidence, Rule 1(8) (" 'Material matter' means a matter the existence or non-existence of which is provable in the action."), and comment.

3. See, e.g., Federal Rules of Civil Procedure, Rule 15(b) ("When issues not raised by the pleadings are tried by express or implied consent of the parties, they shall be treated in all respects as if they had been raised in the pleadings. Such amendment of the pleadings as may be necessary to cause them to conform to the evidence and to raise these issues may be made upon motion of any party at any time, even after judgment; but failure so to amend does not affect the result of the trial of these issues. . . .").

4. See ch. 5, Impeachment, herein.

5. Text-writers and judges occasionally use the term in this sense. "The guiding principle is well stated in Stephen's Digest of the Law of Evidence (Chap. 1, p. 36), in these words: 'The word "relevant" means that any two facts to which it is applied are so related to each other, that according to the common course of events one either taken by itself or in connection with other facts proves or renders probable the past, present, or future existence or non-existence of the other.' " Baldwin, J., in Plumb v. Curtis, 66 Conn. 154, 166, 33 Atl. 998, 1000 (1895). See also Texas & P. Ry. Co. v. Coutourie, 135 Fed. 465, 469 (C.C.A.N.Y.1904).

proposition.[6] Thus, as James points out, "evidence may be excluded as 'irrelevant' for either of these two quite distinct reasons: because it is not probative of the proposition at which it is directed, or because that proposition is not provable in the case."[7] Our discussion, however, will henceforth leave materiality aside as mainly a matter of substantive law and of pleading rules, and center on the other aspect, the test of the probative quality of the evidence.

The characterization of evidence as "direct" or "circumstantial"[8] points to the kind of inference which is sought to be drawn from the evidence to the truth of the proposition for which it is offered. If a witness testifies that he saw A stab B with a knife, and this testimony is offered to prove the stabbing, the inference sought is merely from the fact that the witness made the statement, and the assumption that witnesses are worthy of belief, to the truth of the asserted fact. This is direct evidence.[9] When, however, the evidence is offered also for some further proposition based upon some inference other than merely the inference from assertion to the truth of the fact asserted, then the evidence is circumstantial evidence of this further fact-to-be-inferred.

Thus in the case mentioned if the stabbing were proved and the culprit in doubt, testimony that A fled from the scene, offered to show his probable guilt, would be direct evidence of the flight but circumstantial evidence of his murderous act.[10] Similarly, testimony of a witness that he recognized A as one present on the scene would be direct evidence of the facts asserted, but testimony that he saw someone who was disguised and masked, but had a voice and a limp like A's, would be circumstantial evidence that the person seen was A.[11] Evidence offered for the "direct" inference merely, the truth of the fact asserted, has its own questions of probative value, but these are approached by the common law in terms of the qualification of witnesses, not in terms of relevancy.[12] In our usage questions of relevancy arise only in respect to circumstantial evidence.

Under our system, molded by the tradition of jury-trial and of predominantly oral proof, a party offers his evidence not in mass, but item by item. The problem of relevancy may arise as to each fact proposed to be elicited by successive questions of counsel, or by successive offers of writings or other objects. Such items are normally offered and admitted or rejected as units,[13] though

---

6. " 'Relevancy is that which conduces to the proof of a pertinent hypothesis. Hence it is relevant to put in evidence any circumstances which tend to make the proposition at issue more or less improbable.' Whar.Ev. §§ 20, 21." State v. Witham, 72 Me. 531, 537 (1881). See also Stewart v. State, 138 Tex.Cr. 286, 135 S.W.2d 103, 104 (1940); Words and Phrases, titles Relevancy and Relevant; Uniform Rules of Evidence, R. 1(2): " 'Relevant evidence' means evidence having any tendency in reason to prove any material fact."

7. Op.cit., 29 Calif.L.Rev. at 691.

8. For discussion of the meaning of these terms, see 1 Wigmore, Evidence, § 25 (preferring "testimonial," instead of "direct"); 1 Chamberlayne, Modern Law of Evidence, § 15 (1911). Judicial definitions are collected in 7 Words and Phrases 225 et seq. (1952).

9. It also embraces objects or documents offered in evidence to show their existence, characteristics or contents, or a view of some scene by the court.

Here again the proof by perception depends upon the truthfulness of the identifying testimony of the authenticating witness.

10. ". . . Circumstantial evidence is direct evidence as to the facts deposed to but indirect as to the factum probandum." Brown v. State, 126 Tex.Cr. 449, 72 S.W.2d 269, 270 (1934).

11. Compare Welch v. State, 143 Tex.Cr. 529, 154 S.W.2d 248, syl. 1 (1941). For other situations illustrating the distinction, and judicial discussions, see State v. Riggs, 61 Mont. 25, 201 Pac. 272, 281 (1921); People v. Bretagna, 298 N.Y. 323, 83 N.E. 2d 537 (1949); Texas & N. O. R. Co. v. Warden, 125 Tex. 193, 197, 78 S.W.2d 164, 166 (1935). As to the relative probative values of these two kinds of evidence, see 1 Wigmore, Evidence, § 26.

12. This is pointed out in 2 Wigmore, Evidence, § 475.

13. And consequently "an offer of proof cannot be denied as remote or speculative because it does not

of course the judge will consider any proof already made by the proponent as indicating the bearing of the item offered, and may in his discretion ask the proponent what additional circumstances he expects to prove. But when it is offered and judged singly and in isolation, as it frequently is, it cannot be expected by itself to furnish conclusive proof of the ultimate fact to be inferred.[14] Thus the common argument of the objector that the inference for which the fact is offered "does not necessarily follow" is untenable, as it supposes a standard of conclusiveness which probably no aggregation of circumstantial evidence, and certainly no single item thereof, could ever meet. This same practice of determining the admissibility of items of evidence singly as they are offered leads to another distinction, often stressed in judicial opinions. This is the distinction between relevancy and sufficiency. The test of

relevancy, which is to be applied by the trial judge in determining whether a particular item or group of items of evidence is to be admitted is a different and less stringent one than the standard used at a later stage in deciding whether all the evidence of the party on an issue is sufficient to permit the issue to go to the jury.[15] A brick is not a wall.

What is the standard of relevance or probative quality which evidence must meet if it is to be admitted? We have said that it must "tend to establish" the inference for which it is offered.[16] How strong must this tendency be? Some courts have announced tests, variously phrased, which seem to require that the evidence offered must render the inference for which it is offered more probable than the other possible inferences or hypotheses,[17] that is, the chances must

---

14. Thus, in a prosecution for possessing unstamped distilled spirits, the court in considering the relevancy of evidence that the defendant had previously had such unstamped spirits in the same place, said: "Its relevancy did not, and indeed could not, demand that it be conclusive; most convictions result from the cumulation of bits of proof which, taken singly, would not be enough in the mind of a fair minded person. All that is necessary, and all that is possible, is that each bit may have enough rational connection with the issue to be considered a factor contributing to an answer. Wigmore § 12." Learned Hand, Circ. J., in United States v. Pugliese, 153 F.2d 497, 500 (C.C.A.2d, 1946). To like effect are Riss & Co. v. Galloway, 108 Colo. 93, 114 P.2d 550, 552 (1941); Mobley v. State, 41 Fla. 621, 26 So. 732, 1899; White v. State, 59 Fla. 53, 52 So. 805, 1910; and Tyrrell v. Prudential Ins. Co., 109 Vt. 6, 192 Atl. 184, 188, syl. 8, 115 A.L.R. 392, 1937.

cover every fact necessary to prove the issue. If it be an appropriate link in the chain of proof, that is enough." McCandless v. United States, 298 U. S. 342, 347, 56 S.Ct. 764, 766, 80 L.Ed. 1205, 1936 (proceedings for condemnation of ranch; as bearing on value as potential sugar-plantation, owner offered evidence that water was available at a distance; held, exclusion not sustainable on theory that proponent did not also offer to show the probable cost of bringing the water to the land and the amount of probable enhancement); 31 C.J.S., Evidence, § 160.

15. Ensley Holding Co. v. Kelley, 229 Ala. 650, 158 So. 896, syl. 9 (1934); People v. Graves, 137 Cal.App. 1, 29 P.2d 807, 811, 30 P.2d 508 (1934) (an interesting case of circumstantial proof of bribery); McDonald v. Kansas City Gas Co., 332 Mo. 356, 59 S.W.2d 37, 43 (1932); 31 C.J.S. Evidence, § 160; 1 Wigmore, Evidence, § 29.

16. The inference is from the known to the unknown and is based on human experience that when a particular set of circumstances is present, certain other circumstances are usually present also. Redomsky v. United States, 180 F.2d 781, 783 (C.A.9, 1950).

17. See, e.g., Engel v. United Traction Co., 203 N.Y. 321, 323, 96 N.E. 731 (1911) (injury to plaintiff in collision with electric car; admission of evidence that motorman was later discharged for "a piece of foolishness," ground for reversal. "A fact is admissible as the basis of an inference only when the desired inference is a probable or natural explanation of the fact and a more probable and natural one than the other explanations, if any."). See also State ex rel. District Attorney v. Ingram, 179 Miss. 485, 491, 176 So. 392, 394 (1937) ("Circumstantial evidence is admissible in civil cases where consistent with the theory sought to be established, and inconsistent with any other theory, and where it amounts to a high degree of probability. Jones on Evidence (3 Ed.), section 899."); People v. Nitzberg, 287 N.Y. 183, 187, 38 N.E.2d 490, 138 A.L.R. 1253 (1941) (". . . a fact is

appear to preponderate that the inference claimed is the true one. It is believed, however, that while this might be a reasonable standard by which to judge the sufficiency of all of a party's proof to enable him to get to the jury on the issue, it makes too heavy a demand upon a given item of proof at the admissibility stage, when we are gathering our bits of information piece by piece. And, in fact, much circumstantial evidence is commonly received which does not meet so stringent a test. Thus, when a violent death is shown and A is charged with the homicide, evidence that A as beneficiary in a policy on the life of the victim had a motive for the slaying will be admitted.[18] Yet if we state our reasoning in deductive form,[19] one of the assumptions which would be necessary to support admission under this test would be the proposition that when a homicide is proved, and a person is shown to have had a motive for the killing, it is more probable than not that this person was the killer. Few would contend that human experience

would support this proposition. Similarly with evidence that A had an opportunity to commit the killing,[20] or that he expressed an intention to do so shortly before the death.[21] Though motive, opportunity and design may well be thought when aggregated to make A's guilt more probable than not, singly they each manifestly fall short of establishing so high a probability. It is believed that a more modest standard would better reflect the actual practice of the courts, and that the most acceptable test of relevancy is the question, does the evidence offered render the desired inference *more probable than it would be without the evidence?*[22] There are other formulas of relevancy found in the opinions which though expressed in more general terms seem consistent with the test suggested.[23] It may be asked, how does the judge know whether the evidence does make more probable the truth of the fact to be inferred? Is an attempt at suicide by a prisoner charged with murder relevant to show

relevant to another fact when the existence of the one renders the existence of the other highly probable, according to the common course of events").

18. See, generally as to relevance of facts showing motive as evidence of an act, 2 Wigmore, Evidence, §§ 385, 390, 391.

19. The value of testing arguments on the relevancy of particular items of circumstantial evidence by stating them in deductive syllogistic form is shown, with enlightening illustrations, in James, op.cit., 29 Calif.L.Rev. 694–700.

20. 1 Wigmore, Evidence, § 131.

21. 1 Wigmore, Evidence, §§ 102, 103.

22. Thus, in the leading case of Mutual Life Insurance Co. v. Hillmon, 145 U.S. 285, 295, 12 S.Ct. 909, 36 L.Ed. 706 (1892), the court in discussing the admissibility of certain letters of one Walters expressing an intention of going with Hillmon on a trip to Kansas, said: "The letters in question were competent, not as narratives of facts communicated to the writer by others, nor yet as proof that he actually went away from Wichita, but as evidence that, shortly before the time when other evidence tended to show that he went away, he had the intention of going, and of going with Hillmon, which made it more probable both that he did go

and that he went with Hillmon than if there had been no proof of such intention." This test is ably advocated in James, op. cit., 29 Calif.L.Rev. at 699 et seq.

23. "Ordinarily any fact which makes probable the existence of another fact in dispute is relevant to prove the disputed fact." Riss & Co. v. Galloway, 108 Colo. 93, 97, 114 P.2d 550, 135 A.L.R. 878 (1941).

". . . The tendency of the courts is to permit the introduction of any testimony which will tend to throw light on the merits, and aid in the correct solution of the issues . . . ." Ames v. MacPhail, 289 Mich. 185, 192, 286 N.W. 206 (1939).

"The criterion of relevancy is whether or not the evidence adduced tends to cast any light on the subject of inquiry.' Wharton's Criminal Evidence (11th ed.) vol. 1, par. 224, p. 268." State v. Page, 215 N.C. 333, 334, 1 S.E.2d 887 (1939).

"But yet the competency of a collateral fact to be used as the basis of legitimate argument, is not to be determined by the conclusiveness of the inferences it may afford in reference to the litigated fact. It is enough if these may tend, even in a slight degree, to elucidate the inquiry, or to assist, though remotely, to a determination probably founded in truth." Stevenson v. Stewart, 11 Pa. 307, 308 (1849).

consciousness of guilt?[24] There are no statistics for attempts at suicides by those conscious of guilt and those not so conscious which will shed light on the probability of the inference. The answer must filter through the judge's experience, his judgment, and his knowledge of human conduct and motivation. He must ask himself, could a reasonable jury believe that the attempt makes it more probable that he was conscious of guilt, and if the answer is yes, the evidence is relevant.

Relevant evidence, then, is evidence that in some degree advances the inquiry, and thus has probative value, and is prima facie admissible. But relevance is not always enough. There may remain the question, is its value worth what it costs? There are several counterbalancing factors which may move the court to exclude relevant circumstantial evidence if they outweigh its probative value.[25] In order of their importance, they are these. First, the danger that the facts offered may unduly arouse the jury's emotions of prejudice, hostility or sympathy.[26] Second, the probability that the proof and the answering evidence that it provokes may create a side-issue that will unduly distract the jury from the main issues.[27] Third, the likelihood that the evidence offered and the counter-proof will consume an undue amount of time.[28] Fourth, the danger

---

[24]. See State v. Lawrence, 196 N.C. 562, 577, 146 S. E. 395, syl. 6 (1929) (admissible) and an excellent Note by J. B. Fordham, 7 N.C.L.Rev. 290 (arguing for exclusion).

[25]. Uniform Rules of Evidence, R. 45: "Except as in these rules otherwise provided, the judge may in his discretion exclude evidence if he finds that its probative value is substantially outweighed by the risk that its admission will (a) necessitate undue consumption of time, or (b) create substantial danger of undue prejudice or of confusing the issues or of misleading the jury, or (c) unfairly and harmfully surprise a party who has not had reasonable opportunity to anticipate that such evidence would be offered."
This formula is paraphrased in State v. Haney, 219 Minn. 518, 18 N.W.2d 315, syl. 3 (1945) (in trial for carnal knowledge of girl it was error to permit questioning of accused as to similar offences with other girls), and the corresponding Model Code Rule 303 is quoted approvingly in Utah State Farm Bureau Fed. v. National Farmers' Union Serv. Corp., 198 F.2d 20, 24, syl. 8 (C.A.Utah, 1952). For a similar statement of these countervailing factors see Kurn v. Radencic, 193 Okl. 126, 141 P.2d 580, 581, 582 (1943). The factors of confusion, surprise and prejudice are discussed in 1 Wigmore, Evidence, § 29a. Though The Uniform Rule, supra, appears to extend the discretionary balancing process to direct evidence, seemingly at common law it is limited to circumstantial evidence. Bunten v. Davis, 82 N.H. 304, 133 Atl. 16, 45 A.L.R. 1409, 1416 (1926).
In appraising the probative worth of the offered evidence, before determining whether it is outweighed by the countervailing dangers, the distance in time of the happenings or facts offered will often cause the court to discount its value. This factor is often termed "remoteness." See, e. g., Bankers

Trust Co. v. International Trust Co., 108 Colo. 15, 113 P.2d 656, syl. 5 (1941), and cases cited Dec. Dig., Evidence, ⊂⊃145. The term, however, is often used to describe a lack of probative weight due to other reasons. Bishop v. Copp, 96 Conn. 571, 114 Atl. 682, syl. 12 (1921); Sherburne v. Meade, 303 Mass. 356, 21 N.E.2d 946, syl. 4 (1939).

[26]. Rogers v. Rogers, 80 N.H. 96, 97, 114 Atl. 270 (1921) ("The test therefore to determine the admissibility of relevant facts capable of exciting prejudice is to inquire whether the prejudice they will excite will be so great as to overbalance any assistance they may be to the trier."); 31 C.J.S. 869, note 21.

[27]. Veer v. Hagemann, 334 Ill. 23, 28, 165 N.E. 175 (1929) ("Where the confusion of issues will not be compensated by the assistance of useful evidence it is proper to exclude the evidence offered. Whether such offered evidence should be admitted where its admission will tend to confuse the issues is left to the sound discretion of the trial court."); McCaffrey v. Schwartz, 285 Pa. 561, 576, 132 Atl. 810 (1926) (personal injury: mortality tables may under particular facts be excluded in judge's discretion when would tend to confuse or mislead the jury); 31 C.J.S. 869, note 18.

[28]. ". . . so far as the introduction of collateral issues goes, that objection is a purely practical one —a concession to the shortness of life." Holmes, J., in Reeve v. Dennett, 145 Mass. 23, 11 N.E. 938, 943 (1887). See also McDonald v. Kansas City Gas. Co., 332 Mo. 356, 59 S.W.2d 37, 43 (1932). This danger of undue consumption of time is usually mentioned in company with other dangers, as in Thompson v. American Steel & Wire Co., 317 Pa. 7, 175 Atl. 541 (1934). That was an action for injury to plaintiff's farm by fumes from defendant's

of unfair surprise to the opponent when, having no reasonable ground to anticipate this developement of the proof, he would be unprepared to meet it.[29] Often, of course, several of these dangers such as distraction and time-consumption, or prejudice and surprise, emerge from a particular offer of evidence. This balancing of intangibles—probative values against probative dangers—is so much a matter where wise judges in particular situations may differ that a lee-way of discretion is generally recognized.[30] In some areas, such as the proof of character, the situations have been so constantly repeated that the lee-way of discretion has hardened

into rules; these are discussed in the next chapter.[31] Some others where the element of discretion remains prominent are developed in a later chapter.[32]

Judges and text-writers have sometimes described the process of excluding evidence having probative value, by reason of these counter-factors of prejudice, confusion, time-consumption and surprise, as the application of a standard of "legal relevancy."[33] This same term, "legal relevancy," is used to describe the aggregate of rules which have been produced, as indicated above, by the use as precedents of discretionary rulings on the balance of value against dangers.[34]

---

plant, and the trial judge excluded defendant's evidence about another farm which sustained similar damage though out of range of the fumes. This was sustained as within his discretion. The court said: "He [the judge] must, therefore, determine in the first instance whether evidence which, though logically relevant on the ultimate issue, may nevertheless be excluded because its general effect on the trial will be to confuse the issue by distracting the attention of the jury from the primary to collateral issues, or by unduly prolonging the trial, or perhaps by unfairly surprising the other side."

29. This is usually coupled with the danger of prejudice and confusion of issues. Thompson v. American Steel & Wire Co., next previous note; Kurn v. Radencic, 193 Okl. 126, 141 P.2d 580, 581, 582 (1943). This ground of objection can be avoided by giving reasonable notice to the adversary of intention to offer the evidence.

A pre-trial conference would be an appropriate time to give this notice and to invoke the judge's tentative ruling as to whether the probative value of the "collateral" evidence will outweigh its dangers. See James, op. cit., 29 Calif.L.Rev. 703.

30. Duvall v. Birden, 124 Conn. 43, 51, 198 Atl. 255 (1938) (exclusion for remoteness sustained as in judge's discretion); Gerry v. Neugebauer, 83 N.H. 23, 26, 136 Atl. 751 (1927) (whether unduly prejudicial for judge's discretion); Thompson v. American Steel & Wire Co., 317 Pa. 7, 11, 175 Atl. 541 (1934) ("He is constantly faced with questions on evidence in their special relation to the issue to be tried He must deal with such questions in the light of the purposes of the ultimate inquiry and does so in the exercise of what is known as judicial discretion. He should see that nothing relevant is excluded, so long as its admission will not unduly distract the attention of the jury from the

main inquiry, by first requiring the ascertainment of an unnecessary quantity of subordinate facts from which the main inferences would ultimately be made. His conclusion or decision on such points will not be interfered with on appeal save for manifest abuse of power."); Iverson v. Prudential Ins. Co., 126 N.J.L. 280, 283, 19 A.2d 214 (1940) (remoteness); Hutteball v. Montgomery, 187 Wash. 516, 518, 60 P.2d 679 (1936) (collision: defendant's speed earlier, several miles from scene of accident, excluded: judge's ruling approved: discretionary and "should not be disturbed unless clearly wrong."); 31 C.J.S. 868, 869. For discriminating discussions of the scope of discretion and the need for such lee-way, see Judge Russell McElroy, Some Observations Concerning the Discretions Reposed in Trial Judges, Model Code of Evidence, 356 (1942); James, op. cit., 29 Calif.L.Rev. 704; Trautman, Logical or Legal Relevancy, 5 Vand.L.Rev. 385, 392–394 (1952).

31. Ch. 17.

32. Ch. 18.

33. "All evidence must be logically relevant. . . . The fact, however, that it is logically relevant, does not insure admissibility. It must also be legally relevant. A fact which, in connection with other facts, renders probable the existence of a fact in issue, may still be rejected, if in the opinion of the judge and under the circumstances of the case it is considered essentially misleading or too remote." Hoag v. Wright, 34 App.Div. 260, 54 N.Y.S. 658, 662 (1898).

34. Thus, in State v. LaPage, 57 N.H. 245, 288 (1876) in holding inadmissible evidence of another crime relevant only as showing a propensity to that kind of crime, the court said: " . . . although undoubtedly the relevancy of testimony is originally a matter of logic and common-sense, still there are

Again, "legal relevancy" has been taken as a standard requiring a "plus value"—more than a bare minimum of probative worth[35]—a standard which is doubtless implicit in the balancing process. It seems better to discard the term "legal relevancy" altogether.[36] Its use tends to emphasize conformity to precedent in an area where the need for discretionary responsibility for weighing of value against dangers in the particular case should be stressed. Moreover, to maintain a single standard of "relevancy," by the application of the test suggested herein, will make for clearer thinking in an area where confusion and uncertainty have been rife.

many instances in which the evidence of particular facts as bearing upon particular issues has been so often the subject of discussion in courts of law, and so often ruled upon, that the united logic of a great many judges and lawyers may be said to furnish evidence of the sense common to a great many individuals, and, therefore, the best evidence of what may be properly called commonsense, and thus to acquire the authority of law. It is for this reason that the subject of relevancy of testimony has become, to so great an extent, matter of precedent and authority, and that we may with

McCormick Evidence HB—21

entire propriety speak of its legal relevancy." See also 1 Wigmore, Evidence, § 12.

35. Hebert v. Boston & M. R. R., 90 N.H. 324, 326, 8 A.2d 744, 746 (1939) (a questionable holding that relevant direct evidence should have been rejected because unworthy of belief) relying on 1 Wigmore, Evidence, § 28.

36. This seems to have been Thayer's view. Preliminary Treatise on Evidence, 265 (1898) ("The law furnishes no test of relevance"). See the persuasive argument for abjuring "legal relevancy" in James, op. cit., 29 Calif.L.Rev. 693, 694, 702-704.

CHAPTER 17

CHARACTER AND HABIT

153. Character: In General.[1]

A conspicuous instance in which rules of admissibility have been molded by the effort to balance probative values against countervailing dangers of prejudice, distraction, etc., is the area of rules about the admissibility of evidence of character. The result is a complex of interwoven doctrines and distinctions which are not always easy to keep steadily in sight in the process of planning the proofs and putting on the evidence. It should be noticed at the outset that two considerations are paramount in the analysis and decision of problems of proof in this field.

The first is the *purpose* for which the evidence of character is offered: The two usual alternative purposes are these: (a) to prove the character of a person where the question of what that character is or was, is one of the ultimate issues in the case,[2] and (b) to prove the character of a man as circumstantial evidence of what his acts (and some-times his accompanying state of mind) probably were.[3] In the one case the search for character is crucial and essential. In the other it represents only one of the types of proof usually available to prove conduct, and a type which is of somewhat inferior persuasive force. This consideration, then, of the purpose of the character-proof bears upon the probative weight of the evidence and on the need for its use.

The second consideration is the distinction between different types of proof which may be offered as evidence of character. These

---

1. 1 Wigmore, Evidence, §§ 52–80; Ladd, Techniques and Theory of Character Testimony, 24 Iowa L.Rev. 498 (1939) (excellent); Hale, Character Evidence, 22 So.Calif.L.Rev. 341 (1949) (brief, helpful); Udall, Character Proof, 18 U.Cin.L.Rev. 283 (1949) (good survey); Note, Evidence of Character in Pennsylvania, 13 Temp. U.L.Q. 109, 1938; Decennial Digests, Evidence, ⊂⊃106, 152, 155(2), Criminal Law, ⊂⊃369–381.

2. 1 Wigmore, Evidence, §§ 70–81.

3. 1 Wigmore, Evidence, §§ 55–69.

types are (a) testimony as to the conduct of the person in question as reflecting his character,[4] and (b) testimony of a witness as to his opinion of the person's character based on observation,[5] and (c) testimony as to his reputation.[6] These are listed in the order of their pungency and persuasiveness. In the same order, they differ in their tendency to arouse undue prejudice, to confuse and distract, to engender time-consuming side-issues and to create a risk of unfair surprise. Modern common law doctrine makes the neutral and unexciting reputation-evidence the preferred type, which will usually be accepted where character-evidence can come in at all, whereas the other two, when they are received at all, are received only in limited and defined situations.

154. Character in Issue.[1]

A person's possession of a particular character trait may be an operative fact which under the substantive law determines the legal rights and liabilities of the parties.

When this is so, and when such character-trait has been put in issue by the pleadings, the fact of character must of course be open to proof, and the courts have usually held that it may be proved by evidence of specific acts.[2] While this is the method most likely to create prejudice and hostility, it is also the most decisive revelation of character, which is here the center of inquiry. We are willing to incur a hazard of prejudice here, and even surprise, which we are not when character is sought to be shown by specific acts on other occasions, only for a remoter and often doubtful inference as to the person's *acts* which are the subject of suit.

Moreover, in some of these situations wherein character for care or competence is at issue, the courts have reversed the usual preference for reputation as the vehicle of proof of character and have held that reputation is not even admissible as evidence of character, and that specific acts must be adduced if character is to be shown, though reputation may then come in as evidence

---

4. 1 Wigmore, Evidence, §§ 191–213.

5. 7 Wigmore, Evidence, §§ 1980–1986.

6. 5 Wigmore, Evidence, §§ 1608–1621.

1. 1 Wigmore, Evidence, §§ 70, 81, 202–213.

2. Thus, in defamation when the slander charged bad character, and the defendant pleads truth, character is in issue and specific instances may be shown, subject usually to the proviso that notice of them is given in the plea. See Moore v. Davis, 27 S.W.2d 153, syl. 3 (Tex.Comm.App. 1930) (libel charging plaintiff with unfitness as judge: evidence of subsequent acts showing unfitness proper); Talmadge v. Baker, 22 Wis. 65 (1868) (slander: "he is in the habit of picking up things"; evidence of particular thefts wrongly excluded); 1 Wigmore, Evidence, § 207. To be distinguished is the situation where reputation itself (not character) comes into issue, when defendant seeks to show that plaintiff's reputation was bad, in mitigation of damages. This in most jurisdictions is allowed. See 1 Wigmore, Evidence, §§ 70–74.

So in a prosecution for seduction when the statute requires that the victim must have been "of previous chaste character," her previous acts of intercourse with others are received. Burrow v. State, 166 Ark. 138, 265 S.W. 642, syl. 2 (1924). But the issue may be regarded as one merely of physical virginity, not of chaste disposition. People v. Kehoe, 123 Calif. 224, 55 Pac. 911, syl. 3 (1898) (unchastity must be shown by acts of intercourse not mere indecencies); 1 Wigmore, Evidence, § 205.

When an employer's liability to a servant hinged upon negligent failure to select a competent fellow-servant, character was in issue and acts showing incompetence were received. Morrow v. St. Paul City Ry. Co., 74 Minn. 480, 77 N.W. 303, syl. 3 (1898). Contra: Hatt v. Nay, 144 Mass. 186, 10 N.E. 807, syl. 1 (1887). But a single instance might not be sufficient. Holland v. Southern Pac. Co., 100 Calif. 240, 34 Pac. 666 (1893). Cases are collected in 1 Wigmore, Evidence, § 208.

More important today are the situations where the owner of a motor vehicle or any dangerous object is charged with liability for the acts of a person using it on grounds of negligent entrustment of the vehicle or object to an incompetent or unfit person. Here again the character of the custodian is in issue and his acts come in to show it. Clark v. Stewart, 126 Oh.St. 263, 185 N.E. 71, syl. 2 (1933) (acts of recklessness of defendant's son received, though defendant admitted that his son, the driver, was acting as agent in the course of father's business); Guedon v. Rooney, 160 Ore. 621, 87 P.2d 209, syl. 9, 120 A.L.R. 1298 (1939), annotated on this point.

that such character was known to the defendant.[3]

Similarly, in these cases where character is part of the ultimate issue, and where as we have seen it may be proven by the person's acts, the argument is strong for the allowability of opinion-evidence as to character from one who has observed the man and his conduct. It is surely a proper case for opinion, since an impression from facts too detailed to recite may be valuable to the trier of fact. The fact that specific acts may be enquired into upon cross-examination, and thus the trier's attention be unduly distracted, is hardly an objection since the door has already been opened to specific acts as evidence of character in issue. This argument for opinion-evidence has prevailed with many courts when the character involved is for care, competence, skill, or sanity—the non-moral traits.[4] As to traits of *moral* character, peacefulness, honesty and the like, presumably most courts would frown on opinion-evidence, even when character is in issue, in view of the current tradition against opinions where the character of a witness [5] or of an accused is in question.[6]

The Uniform Rule goes further and in keeping with its purpose of liberalizing and simplifying the rules in this area it would admit all three types of evidence to show character when character is in issue.[7]

155. Character as Circumstantial Evidence of Conduct and State of Mind:[1] (a) General Rule of Exclusion.

It will always be relevant, if we have the task of proving that A committed a certain act, and possibly of proving also his guilty or innocent state of mind, to show that A is the kind of man (in his disposition, tendencies, character) who is likely to act in that fashion with the intent charged. A thief will often steal but a man who is looked up to usually will not. And the law in two important instances at least, namely in its permission to an accused to prove his good character [2] and in its practice of witness-impeachment,[3] sanctions this use of character. But in what are probably the greater number of cases when character could be offered for this purpose, the law sets its face against it. So while what we have called the exceptions could be stated as the rule,[4] it is believed that it is more accurate and illuminating to

---

3. Young v. Fresno Flume & Irrigation Co., 24 Cal. App. 286, 141 Pac. 29, 32 syl. 7 (1914) (employer's liability to servant based on unfitness of fellow servant); Guedon v. Rooney, 160 Ore. 621, 87 P.2d 209, 217, syl. 8–10, 120 A.L.R. 1298 (1939), annotated on this question (negligent entrustment of automobile to unfit driver).

4. Lewis v. Emery, 108 Mich. 641, 66 N.W. 569, syl. 1 (1896) (competency of fellow servant; citing prior cases). Contra: Purkey v. Southern Coal & Transportation Co., 57 W.Va. 595, 50 S.E. 755, syl. 2 (1905) (competency of fellow servant). Cases are collected in 7 Wigmore, Evidence, § 1984.

5. See §§ 41, 44.

6. See § 158.

7. Uniform Rules of Evidence, R. 46: "When a person's character or a trait of his character is in issue, it may be proved by testimony in the form of opinion, evidence of reputation, or evidence of specific instances of the person's conduct, subject, however, to the limitations of Rules 47 [see § 155, note 4, herein] and 48 [see § 156, note 1, herein]."

1. See 1 Wigmore, Evidence, §§ 54–68; Dec.Dig., Evidence, ⊆106, 32 C.J.S., Evidence, §§ 423–432.

2. See § 158, herein.

3. See §§ 41, 44, 49, herein.

4. It is so stated in Uniform Rules of Evidence, R. 47: "Subject to Rule 48, [see § 156, note 1, here′n] when a trait of a person's character is relevant as tending to prove his conduct on a specified occasion, such trait may be proved in the same manner as provided by Rule 46, except that (a) evidence of specific instances of conduct other than evidence of conviction of a crime which tends to prove the trait to be bad shall be inadmissible, and (b) in a criminal action evidence of a trait of an accused's character as tending to prove his guilt or innocence of the offense charged, (i) may not be excluded by the judge under Rule 45 if offered by the accused to prove his innocence, and (ii) if offered by the prosecution to prove his guilt, may be admitted only after the accused has introduced evidence of his good character."

say that the approach in this area is that evidence of character in any form, whether reputation, opinion from observation, or specific acts, will not generally be received to prove that the person whose character is sought to be shown, engaged in certain conduct, or did so with a given intent, on a particular occasion.[5] To this rule, as we have said, there are important exceptions which will be developed in later sections. The reason for the general rule is that character when used for this purpose is not essential as it is when character is the issue, and generally it comes with too much dangerous baggage of prejudice, distraction from the issues, time-consumption and hazard of surprise.[6]

156. Character to Evidence Conduct—(b) Application of Rule of Exclusion to Evidence of Character for Care: Previous Accidents: "Accident Proneness."

The rule excluding character as evidence of acts has long been applied with relative consistency in negligence cases. Where a negligent act by the defendant or his servant

is in issue most courts will reject proof of the actor's reputation for care or negligence [1] or opinion testimony from observation of his character in this respect.[2] A minority of courts, however, have admitted such proof for this purpose, when there are no eye-witnesses available who saw the happening.[3] If these courts go so far in rejecting the policy of exclusion—and this policy is obviously open to reasonable debate—it is arguable that they should go further still and admit the evidence of character when there are eye-witnesses but their evidence is conflicting. There is almost as much need for evidence of character in such case, it seems, as when eye-witnesses are wanting.

The rule of exclusion is even more uniformly applied, as would be expected, when evidence of negligent conduct of the party or his agent on other occasions is sought to be proved and its only substantial relevance is as showing a propensity for negligent acts and thus enhancing the probability of negligence on the occasion in suit.[4] This is the most pungent way of showing a negli-

---

5. This generalization in the texts is usually stated as the rule for civil cases. See 1 Wigmore, Evidence, § 64; Jones, Evidence in Civil Cases, §§ 148, (4th ed. 1938). I have preferred to state the doctrine more broadly, since even in criminal cases the permission to the accused to use character as evidence of innocence seems better understood as an exception rather than the rule.

6. See § 152, above.

1. Denbigh v. Oregon-Washington R. & Navigation Co., 23 Idaho 663, 132 Pac. 112, syl. 1 (1913) (judge rightly excluded evidence that engineer "was known as a prudent and careful engineer"); Phinney v. Detroit United Ry. Co., 232 Mich. 399, 205 N.W. 124, syl. 5 (1925) (testimony of conductor that motorman had a reputation for recklessness inadmissible); Baltimore & O. R. Co. v. Colvin, 118 Pa.St. 230, 12 Atl. 337, syl. 3 (1888) (error to receive evidence of reputation of flagman for carelessness); 1 Wigmore, Evidence, § 65; Uniform Rules of Evidence, R. 48: "Evidence of a trait of a person's character with respect to care or skill is inadmissible as tending to prove the quality of his conduct on a specified occasion."

2. Harriman v. Pullman Palace-Car Co., 85 Fed. 553, syl. 1 (C.C.A.Mo.1898) (action for negligent act of

porter, injuring plaintiff: error to admit evidence for defendant that porter "was usually careful, competent, courteous and attentive"); Louisville & N. R. Co. v. Adams' Adm'r, 205 Ky. 203, 265 S.W. 623, syl. 8 (1924) (death at a crossing: error to receive testimony that decedent was careful driver); 1 Wigmore, Evidence, § 65. But a history of being careful about a particular danger may come in as being nearer to habit than to character. Hussey v. Boston & M. R. Co., 82 N.H. 236, 133 Atl. 9, syl. 7 (1926) (death of a lineman; no witnesses; evidence of his "habitual care in the presence of charged wires" proper). As to evidence of habit, see § 162, below.

3. Linde v. Emmick, 16 Cal.App.2d 676, 61 P.2d 338, syl. 23 (1936) (evidence of plaintiff's witnesses that he was a careful driver inadmissible because here the plaintiff himself testified to his actual operation of the car); Toledo, St. L. & K. C. Ry. Co. v. Bailey, 145 Ill. 159, 162, 33 N.E. 1089, syl. 3 (1893) (evidence that engineer, killed in boiler explosion, was competent and careful proper when no eye-witnesses).

4. Nesbit v. Cumberland Contracting Co., 196 Md. 36, 75 A.2d 339, syl. 1, 2 (1950) (plaintiff sues for injuries sustained when he drove his car into a pile

gent dispostion but its probative force has traditionally been thought too slight, where conduct is the issue, to overbear the dangers of prejudice, distraction by side-issues, and unfair surprise.[5]

An article [6] calls attention to the theory developed in recent scientific studies of accidents that a limited group of persons have a special pre-disposition for accidents. They are "accident prone." In the case of drivers, inadequate training, defective vision, and certain mental attitudes and emotional traits may be identified as characteristic of the members of this group.[7] The writers of the article suggest that the findings in respect to "accident proneness" invite a reconsideration of the rule forbidding the use of character for negligence and history of accidents as evidence of negligent acts on the occasior. in suit.[8] They would advocate, apparently, that on the issue of negligence, proof of accident proneness by expert opinion, based on clinical tests and interviews and on the past accident record, be received. However, they also point out that these

studies have not yet disclosed any connection between accident proneness and fault or carelessness [9] and thus they have seemingly not yet gone far enough to persuade the courts to abandon the present evidentiary rule. Nevertheless, the policy-basis of the prohibitory rule, both as applied to character-evidence based on reputation or individual opinion, and even as applied to proof of past accidents where they are not isolated but repeated, is so doubtful that the courts may profitably be alert to the future developments of these scientific studies, in appraising the desirability of maintaining the legal barriers.

157. Character to Evidence Conduct—(c) Application of Rule of Exclusion to Forbid the Prosecution to Introduce Evidence Initially of Bad Character of Accused: Other Crimes.

The disfavor for receiving proof of the character of a person as evidence that on a particular occasion he acted in keeping with his disposition is strongly felt when the state seeks to show that the accused is a bad man and thus more likely to have committed the

---

of dirt and rocks left on highway by defendant; on cross-examination plaintiff was asked if he considered himself a good driver and he answered "Yes"; then, over objection, he was asked about and admitted convictions for driving without license and reckless driver, held, error, convictions for traffic offenses not admissible to impeach—compare § 43, herein—and it was calculated to be used to show reckless character to show negligence on this occasion, an inadmissible inference); Brownhill v. Kivlin, 317 Mass. 168, 57 N.E.2d 539, syl. 3 (1944) (action for negligent burning of garage brought against administratrix of deceased, who was burned to death in same fire; plaintiff charged that deceased, whose body was in rear part of car, had caused fire by careless smoking; held proper to exclude evidence that on three previous occasions deceased had caused fires by going to sleep while smoking; but is not the propensity here so specific as to amount to a habit? See § 162, infra); Ryan v. International Harvester Co., 204 Minn. 177, 283 N.W. 129, syl. 2 (1938) (collision: defendant's question to his driver seeking to show that he had never previously had a collision, properly excluded); Grenadier v. Surface Transportation Co., 271 App.Div. 130, 66 N.Y.S.2d 130, syl. 1, 2 (1946) (injury from bus-accident, error

to permit plaintiff to cross-examine driver about prior accidents); 1 Wigmore, Evidence, § 199.
But the previous accident or negligent act may have some other and weightier relevancy than merely showing character or disposition, and thus escape the present objection. Dallas Ry. & Term. Co. v. Farnsworth, 148 Tex. 584, 227 S.W.2d 1017, syl. 2, 3 (1950) (action for injury alleged to be due to abrupt starting of street car when plaintiff alighted; held, plaintiff's testimony that previously on same trip motorman started car abruptly admissible as tending to show that motorman was nervous and in a hurry).

5. See 1 Wigmore, Evidence, § 199.

6. James and Dickinson, Accident Proneness and Accident Law, 63 Yale L.J. 769 (1950). Among the sources which they cite are N. Maier, Psychology in Industry 350 (1946); Rawson, Accident Proneness, 6 Psychosomatic Med. 88 (1944); Bristol, Medical Aspects of Accident Control, 107 A.M.A.J. 653, 654 (1936); Blain, The Automobile Accident—A Medical Problem, 3 J.Crim.Psychopathology 37 (1941).

7. Op. cit., 63 Yale L.J. 772–775.

8. Op. cit., 63 Yale L.J. 793.

9. Op. cit., 63 Yale L.J. 775.

crime. The long-established rule, according-ly, forbids the prosecution, unless and until the accused gives evidence of his good char-acter, to introduce initially evidence of the bad character of the accused.[1] It is not ir-relevant, but in the setting of jury-trial the danger of prejudice outweighs the proba-tive value.

This danger is at its highest when char-acter is shown by other criminal acts, and the rule about the proof of other crimes is but an application of the wider prohibition against the initial introduction by the prose-cution of evidence of bad character. The

rule is that the prosecution may not intro-duce evidence of other criminal acts of the accused unless the evidence is substantially relevant for some other purpose than to show a probability that he committed the crime on trial because he is a man of criminal charac-ter.[2] There are numerous other purposes for which evidence of other criminal acts may be offered, and when so offered the rule of ex-clusion is simply inapplicable. Some of these purposes are listed below but warning must be given that the list is not complete, for the range of relevancy outside the ban is almost infinite; and further that the purposes are

[1]. Martin v. People, 114 Colo. 120, 162 P.2d 597, syl. 1 (1945) (reputation); State v. Willard, 346 Mo. 773, 142 S.W.2d 1046, syl. 4 (1940) (same); Jones v. La-Crosse, 180 Va. 406, 23 S.E.2d 142, syl. 1 (1942) (character for drunkenness); 1 Wigmore, Evidence, §§ 55, 57; Dec.Dig.Crim.Law, ⬤376.

[2]. For a similar formulation see Model Code of Evi-dence, Rule 311: ". . . evidence that a person committed a crime or civil wrong on a specified occasion is inadmissible as tending to prove that he committed a crime or civil wrong on another occa-sion if, but only if, the evidence is relevant solely as tending to prove his disposition to commit such a crime or civil wrong or to commit crimes or civil wrongs generally.", approved in Swann v. United States, 195 F.2d 689, 690 (C.C.A.4, 1952) (excellent discussion by Soper, J.), and in State v. Scott, 111 Utah 9, 175 P.2d 1016, 1022 (1947) (illuminating dis-cussion by Wolfe, J.). See also Lovely v. United States, 169 F.2d 386, 388, 389 (C.C.A.4, 1948) (fine opinion by Parker, J.).

See also Uniform Rules of Evidence, R. 55: "Subject to Rule 47 [see § 155, note 4] evidence that a per-son committed a crime or civil wrong on a specified occasion, is inadmissible to prove his disposition to commit crime or civil wrong as the basis for an in-ference that he committed another crime or civil wrong on another specified occasion but, subject to Rules 45 [see § 152, note 25] and 48 [see § 156, note 1], such evidence is admissible when relevant to prove some other material fact including absence of mistake or accident, motive, opportunity, intent, preparation, plan, knowledge or identity."

A frequent form of statement is a general rule that evidence of other crimes is inadmissible except when offered for certain particular named purposes. See, e. g., People v. Molineux, 168 N.Y. 264, 61 N.E. 286, 293, 294 (1901): "The general rule of evidence applicable to criminal trials is that the state cannot prove against a defendant any crime not alleged in

the indictment, either as a foundation for a sepa-rate punishment, or as aiding the proofs that he is guilty of the crime charged. . . . The excep-tions to the rule cannot be stated with categorical precision. Generally speaking, evidence of other crimes is competent to prove the specific crime charged when it tends to establish (1) motive; (2) intent; (3) the absence of mistake or accident; (4) a common scheme or plan embracing the commis-sion of two or more crimes so related to each other that proof of one tends to establish the others; (5) the identity of the person charged with the commis-sion of the crime on trial." In that case, a prosecu-tion for murder by poisoning, the evidence was held not to fit any of these exceptions.

A somewhat similar form of statement of the rule has sometimes been embodied in statutes. See, e. g., Mich.Comp.Laws 1948, § 768.27; Ohio, R.C. § 2945.59, discussed in 5 Oh.St.L.J. 232 (1939). It has, however, been criticized as a departure from earlier common law doctrine and as leading to inexpedient results, in J. Stone, Exclusion of Sim-ilar Fact Evidence: England, 46 Harv.L.Rev. 954 (1933), America, 51 Harv.L.Rev. 988 (1938). For general discussions, see 1 Wigmore, Evidence, §§ 192–194, 1 Wharton, Criminal Evidence, §§ 343–368. More localized treatments: C. J. Morgan, Other Offences, 3 Vand.L.Rev. 779 (1950); Notes, 18 Brooklyn L.Rev. 80 (1951), 35 Calif.L.Rev. 131 (1947); 28 N.C.L.Rev. 124 (1949); 54 W.Va.L.Q. 142 (1952). Cases, as the sands of the sea, are collected in Dec.Dig.Criminal Law, ⬤365, 369–374; 22 C.J. S., Criminal Law, §§ 663–665, 682–691. See Note, Other Crimes in Minnesota, 37 Minn.L.Rev. 608 (1953).

The spirit of the rule condemns not only evidence of other crimes not independently relevant, but also questions which, though negatively answered, carry with them the insinuation that the accused commit-ted the other crimes. State v. Haney, 219 Minn. 518, 18 N.W.2d 315, syl. 8 (1945).

not mutually exclusive, for a particular line of proof may fall within several of them. Neither are they strictly co-ordinate. Some are phrased in terms of the immediate inferences sought to be drawn, such as plan or motive, others in terms of the ultimate fact, such as knowledge, intent, or identity which the prosecution seeks to establish.[3] The list follows.

(1) To complete the story of the crime on trial by proving its immediate context of happenings near in time and place.[4] This is often characterized as proving a part of the "same transaction" or the "res gestae."

(2) To prove the existence of a larger continuing plan, scheme, or conspiracy, of which the present crime on trial is a part.[5] This will be relevant as showing motive, and hence the doing of the criminal act, the identity of the actor, and his intention, where any of these is in dispute.

(3) To prove other like crimes by the accused so nearly identical in method as to ear-mark them as the handiwork of the accused.[6] Here much more is demanded than the mere repeated commission of crimes of the same class, such as repeated burglaries or thefts. The device used must be so unusual and distinctive as to be like a signature.[7]

(4) To show a passion or propensity for illicit sexual relations with the particular

---

3. "Motive, intent, absence of mistake, plan, and identity are not really all on the same plane. Intent, absence of mistake, and identity are facts in issue —*facta probanda.* Motive, plan, or scheme are *facta probantia,* and may tend to show any *facta probanda.*" Stone, op. cit., 51 Harv.L.Rev. 988, 1026n.

4. People v. De Pompeis, 410 Ill. 587, 102 N.E.2d 813, syl. 9 (1952) (armed robbery: sex offense committed on victim in course of hold-up admissible to show force and intimidation); Marshall v. State, 227 Ind. 1, 83 N.E.2d 763, syl. 18–20 (1949) (kidnapping: other crimes committed against victim admissible as res gestae); State v. Ward, 337 Mo. 425, 85 S.W.2d 1, 1935 (rape; evidence of other attacks by accused upon prosecutrix and her sister on same occasion).

5. Makin v. Attorney General of New South Wales, [1894] App.C. 57 (Privy Council) (murder of an infant left with defendants for their care, with an inadequate premium; evidence that the bodies of ten other babies were found buried in the gardens of three houses formerly occupied by the accused, properly received, on question whether adoption bona fide and deaths accidental); State v. Long, 195 Ore. 81, 244 P.2d 1033, syl. 20 (1952) (that defendant after killing owner of truck, for which he is now on trial, in use of truck next day for robbery shot F.B.I. man while leaving scene of robbery properly proved as part of planned course of action); Haley v. State, 84 Tex.Cr. 629, 209 S.W. 675, syl. 7, 8 (1919) (murder: that defendant desiring to continue illicit relations with wife of deceased, formed a plan to kill his own wife and deceased, provable but state's evidence here of his poisoning his wife not sufficiently cogent to be received).

6. R. v. George Joseph Smith, (1915) reported in Notable British Trials, (1922), and described in Mar-

joribanks, For the Defence: The Life of Edward Marshall Hall, 321 (1937) (the famous "brides of the bath" case; defendant accused of murdering his wife, who left her property to him by will, by drowning her in the bathtub: defendant leaves their boarding-house on a pretended errand, and then on his return purports to discover his wife drowned in the tub and so reports to the land-lady; held proper to show that he had previously married several wives, who left him their property and were discovered by him drowned in the bath); People v. Peete, 28 Cal.2d 306, 169 P.2d 924, syl. 7 (1946) (where defendant had been previously convicted of killing another who was killed by means of a bullet from behind, severing the spinal cord at the neck, and deceased in present prosecution was shot from behind at close range in an attempt to sever the spinal cord, evidence of the prior homicide was admissible as tending to identify defendant as the murderer.); and see Note, 35 Col.L.Rev. 131, which at p. 136 examines the distinction between this and purpose (2), above; Whiteman v. State, 119 Ohio St. 285, 164 N.E. 51, 63 A.L.R. 595, 1928 (robbery; evidence of other robberies committed by defendants according to same peculiar plan, as used in the robbery now on trial, that is, by using uniforms, impersonating officers, and stopping cars, thus "earmarking" the crimes as committed by the same persons).

7. See, e. g., State v. Sauter, 125 Mont. 109, 232 P.2d 731, 732, syl. 1–4 (1951) (forcible rape by defendant and S in automobile after picking victim up in barroom; held, error to admit evidence of rapes accomplished after similar pick-ups of other victims; "too common . . . to have much evidentiary value in showing a systematic scheme or plan"; two judges dissenting).

person concerned in the crime on trial.[8] Other like sexual crimes with other persons do not qualify for this purpose.[9] It is arguable that certain unnatural sex crimes are in themselves so unusual and distinctive that previous such acts by the accused with anyone are strongly probative of like acts upon the occasion involved in the charge,[10] but the danger of prejudice is likewise enhanced here, and most courts do not admit such acts with other persons for this purpose.[11]

(5) To show, by similar acts or incidents, that the act on trial was not inadvertent, accidental, unintentional [12] or without guilty knowledge.[13]

8. State v. Terry, 199 Iowa 1221, 203 N.W. 232 (1925) (incest); Sykes v. State, 112 Tenn. 572, 82 S.W. 185 (1903) (statutory rape: previous acts show the relation and tend to make probable the commission of the crime); Gephart v. State, 249 S.W.2d 612, syl. 11 (Tex.Cr.1952) (similar to last). See an extensive Note, Evidence of other sex offences, 167 A.L.R. 565. Other notes: 2 Ala.L.Rev. 108 (1949); 96 U.Pa.L. Rev. 872 (1948); 98 id. 116 (1949), 23 Temp.L.Q. 133 (1949), 25 Tex.L.Rev. 421 (1947), 9 Wash. & Lee L. Rev. 86 (1952).

9. Landon v. State, 77 Okl.Cr. 190, 140 P.2d 242, syl. 7 (1943) (statutory rape on daughter: other offenses with another daughter on other occasions excluded); State v. Williams, 36 Utah 273, 103 Pac. 250, syl. 1-3 (1909) (statutory rape). But though not receivable to show propensity such evidence may come in on other theories. Landon v. State, supra (res gestae); Comm. v. Ransom, 169 Pa.Super. 306, 82 A.2d 547, syl. 1-5 (1951), affirmed on lower court's opinion, 369 Pa. 153, 85 A.2d 125 (1952) (charge of robbery and rape; other attempts at forcing intercourse on others during previous two days and up to two hours before offense admitted to show design or intent).

10. A few decisions have admitted the evidence seemingly on the theory, in part at least, of showing a special propensity. See, e. g., State v. Edwards, 224 N.C. 527, 31 S.E.2d 516, syl. 4 (1944) (incest); State v. Jackson, 82 Oh.App. 318, 81 N.E.2d 546, syl. 5 (1948) (incest). See also Comm. v. Kline, 361 Pa. 434, 65 A.2d 348, syl. 5 (1949) (statutory rape on daughter: State allowed to prove that defendant indecently exposed himself to a neighbor woman, as showing he was an exhibitionist and thus had a moral trait consistent with the crime on trial).

11. See, e. g., State v. Searle, 125 Mont. 467, 239 P. 2d 995, syl. 1, 3 (1952) (sodomy); State v. Start, 65 Ore. 178, 132 Pac. 512, syl. 4 (1913), and cases cited in Note, 167 A.L.R. 565, 611, 615.

12. People v. Williams, 6 Cal.2d 500, 58 P.2d 917, 1936 (larceny of coin-purse; state's theory and evidence were that defendant posing as customer standing near owner of bag, took purse from bag while owner was shopping; defendant claimed to have picked the purse from the floor, thinking it lost; held, evidence of detectives that they had seen defendant take another purse from another woman's bag in same manner, admissible); State v. Lapage, 57 N.H. 245, 294 (1876) (Cushing, C. J.; "Another class of cases consists of those in which it becomes necessary to show that the act for which the prisoner was indicted was not accidental,— e. g., where the prisoner had shot the same person twice within a short time, or where the same person had fired a rick of grain twice, or where several deaths by poison had taken place in the same family, or where the children of the same mother had mysteriously died. In such cases it might well happen that a man should shoot another accidentally, but that he should do it twice within a short time would be very unlikely. So, it might easily happen that a man using a gun might fire a rick of barley once by accident, but that he should do it several times in succession would be very improbable. So, a person might die of accidental poisoning, but that several persons should so die in the same family at different times would be very unlikely."); 2 Wigmore, Evidence, § 302. The similarity of the other acts need not be as great as under purpose (3) in the text above, nor is a connection by common plan as in purpose (2) demanded. The trial judge has a range of discretion in determining whether the probative value justifies admission. United States v. Feldman, 136 F.2d 394, syl. 9 (C.C.A.2, 1943). Subsequent as well as prior acts have been held admissible for this purpose. Schmeller v. United States, 143 F.2d 544, syl. 19 (C.C.A.6, 1944). However, when the act charged is not equivocal, but the criminal intent is a necessary conclusion from the act, this theory of other acts as showing intent may not be availed of. People v. Lonsdale, 122 Mich. 388, 81 N.W. 277, syl. 2 (1899) (abortion where there was no room for inference of accident or that operation was performed to save life); State v. Barker, 249 S.W. 75, 77 (Mo.1923) (automobile theft); 1 Wharton, Criminal Evidence, § 350 (11th ed. 1935).

13. United States v. Brand, 79 F.2d 605, C.C.A.N.Y., 1935 (knowingly transporting stolen car in interstate commerce; evidence of previous sale of a stolen car); People v. Marino, 271 N.Y. 317, 3 N.E. 2d 439, 105 A.L.R. 1283, 1936 (similar); 2 Wigmore, Evidence, §§ 301, 310, 324; Dec.Dig., Crim.Law, ⊙370. In prosecutions for knowingly receiving stolen property, there should, it seems, be no hard and fast requirement that it be proved that the de-

(6) To establish motive.[14] This in turn may be evidence of the identity of the doer of the crime on charge, or of deliberateness, malice, or a specific intent constituting an element of the crime.

(7) To show, by immediate inference, malice, deliberation, ill-will or the specific intent required for a particular crime.[15]

(8) To prove identity. This is accepted as one of the ultimate purposes for which evidence of other criminal conduct will be received.[16] It is believed, however, that a need for proving identity is not ordinarily of itself a ticket of admission, but that the evidence will usually follow, as an intermediate channel, some one or more of the other theories here listed. Probably the second (larger plan), the third (distinctive device) and the sixth (motive) are most often resorted to for this purpose.[17]

(9) Evidence of criminal acts of accused, constituting admissions by conduct, intended to obstruct justice or avoid punishment for the present crime.[18]

---

fendant knew that the other property was stolen. United States v. Brand, supra, but cf. Edwards v. United States, 18 F.2d 402 (C.C.A.8, 1927) and see McKusick, Other Crimes to Show Guilty Knowledge and Intent, 24 Iowa L.Rev. 471 (1939). Seemingly receiving by defendant of other like stolen goods after the occasion on trial would not be admitted to show knowledge earlier. Witters v. United States, 106 F.2d 837, syl. 5, 6, 125 A.L.R. 1031 (C.A. D.C.1939). Unless it is shown to be part of a common scheme, as in State v. Haddad, 221 La. 337, 59 So.2d 411, syl. 3 (1952) (gang used defendant as a fence); and compare State v. Kuhnley, 74 Ariz. 10, 242 P.2d 843.

14. State v. Simborski, 120 Conn. 624, 182 Atl. 221, syl. 9–17 (1936) (murder of an officer who was seeking to arrest defendant; fact that defendant had committed two burglaries a short time previously on the same morning admissible to show motive, and as res gestae); State v. Long, 195 Ore. 81, 244 P.2d 1033, syl. 12 (1952) (murder of owner of truck: that defendant a short time afterward used the truck to commit robbery admitted); Comm. v. Heller, 269 Pa. 467, 87 A.2d 287, syl. 4, 5 (1952) (murder of wife: evidence of illicit relations with sister-in-law and attempt to procure her to get divorce admissible); State v. Gaines, 144 Wash. 446, 258 Pac. 508 (syl. 2, 3), 1927 (murder of daughter; evidence of incestuous relations between defendant and deceased and that daughter was threatening to end the relation). See also comment, 14 Wash.L.Rev. 147, 1939; 2 Wigmore, § 390, especially note 2; Dec.Dig.Crim.Law, ⊂⇒371(12).

15. Copeland v. United States, 152 F.2d 769, syl. 1 (C.A.D.C.1945) (murder in first degree; that defendant after shooting deceased pursued and shot sister of deceased, proper to show first act done, not accidentally or in self-defense but with deliberate intent to kill); Dunson v. State, 202 Ga. 515, 43 S.E. 2d 504. 508 (1947) (wife-murder: previous acts of violence to wife, to show malice); Clark v. State, 151 Tex.Cr. 383, 208 S.W.2d 637, syl. 6 (1948) (murder, by beating, of five year old stepson: previous whippings, to show malice); 2 Wigmore, Evidence, §§ 363–365; 1 Wharton, Criminal Evidence, § 353 (11th ed. 1935); Dec.Dig.Crim.Law, ⊂⇒371.

16. People v. McMonigle, 29 Cal.2d 730, 177 P.2d 745, syl. 3, 5 (1947) (murder of girl enticed by accused into his automobile; evidence that a naval T shirt, similar to that worn by murderer, was stolen by accused some weeks before, properly received to show plan to entice, and identity); State v. King, 111 Kan. 140, 206 Pac. 883, syl. 2, 4, 22 A.L.R. 1006 (1922) (murder: victim, an employee of defendant, disappeared, after which accused was in possession of his effects; ten years later victim's body found burned in defendant's premises; held, finding of other bodies on same premises of persons who had disappeared and whose effects were in defendant's possession, admissible to identify accused as murderer); Helton v. Comm., 244 S.W.2d 762, syl. 4, 5 (Ky.1951) (assault committed as member of mob of miners; accused denied being present; "other incidents" on same morning presumably involving accused, admissible to show larger plan, motive and identity); State v. Bock, 229 Minn. 449, 39 N.W.2d 887, syl. 1–5 (1949) (attempt to pass forged check, by making small purchase and getting cash for balance; evidence of similar subsequent passing of other checks at other stores, under similar plan, admissible in discretion to identify person who attempted to pass check in question here; but error to exclude evidence of accused that some other person passed these other checks) and cases collected 1 Wharton, Criminal Evidence, § 348 (11th ed. 1935), 22 C.J.S., Criminal Law, § 684.

17. See decisions cited under these headings, above, and cases in next preceding note.

18. People v. Spaulding, 309 Ill. 292, 141 N.E. 196 (1923) is a striking instance. That was a prosecution for murder of A and it was held proper for the state to prove that the accused had later killed the only eye-witness of the murder and buried his body.

(10) To impeach the accused when he takes the stand as a witness, by proof of his convictions of crime or by eliciting on the cross-examination of the accused (as permitted in most but not all jurisdictions) his admissions as to crimes or other misconduct reflecting on his credibility, whether or not they have been the subject of conviction.[19]

Some general observations may be added. In the first place, it is clear that the other crime, when it is found to be independently relevant and admissible, need not be established beyond a reasonable doubt, either as to its commission or as to defendant's connection therewith,[20] but for the jury to be entitled to consider it there must of course be substantial evidence of these facts,[21] and some courts have used the formula that it must be "clear and convincing." [22] And it is believed that before the evidence shall be admitted at all, this factor of the substantial or unconvincing quality of the proof should be weighed in the balance.

Two considerations, one substantive and the other procedural, affect the ease or difficulty of securing admission of proof of other crimes. The first is that the courts are stricter in applying their standards of relevancy when the ultimate purpose of the state is to prove identity, or the doing by the accused of the criminal act charged than they are when the evidence is offered on the ultimate issue of knowledge, intent or other state of mind.[23] The second is that when the crime charged involves the element of knowledge, intent, or the like, the state will often be permitted to show other crimes in rebuttal, after the issue has been sharpened by the defendant's giving evidence of accident or mistake, more readily than it would as part of its case in chief at a time when the court may be in doubt that any real dispute will appear on the issue.[24]

19. See §§ 42, 43, herein.

20. People v. Lisenba, 14 Cal.2d 403, 429, 94 P.2d 569, 583, syl. 8 (1939); Note, 13 So.Calif.L.Rev. 511; Scott v. State, 107 Oh.St. 475, 141 N.E. 19, 26 (1914); 1 Wharton, Criminal Evidence, § 366 (11th ed. 1935).

21. People v. Albertson, 23 Cal.2d 550, 557–581, 596–599, 145 P.2d 7, 22, syl. 2 (1944) (citing cases) and authorities cited in the next preceding note.

22. Wrather v. State, 179 Tenn. 666, 678, 169 S.W.2d 854, 858 (1943). See also State v. Porter, 229 Iowa 282, 294 N.W. 898, syl. 7 (must be clearly shown).

23. Jones v. Comm., 303 Ky. 666, 198 S.W.2d 969, 970, 971 (1947) ("The application of the rule of admissibility is more liberal in the matter of establishing guilty knowledge or intent where intent is a material ingredient of the offense charged, for a series of similar offenses tends to show the party knew or intended to do what he was doing on the particular occasion. Where the purpose is to identify the defendant, the circumstances may govern the degree of liberality or strictness. . . . where it is a question of the particular individual committing the particular offense, as it was here, the latitude is much smaller."); and see People v. Molineux, 168 N.Y. 264, 313, 61 N.E. 286, 302 (1901) ("As to identity: Another exception to the general rule is that, when the evidence of an extraneous crime tends to identify the person who committed it as the same person who committed the crime charged in the indictment, it is admissible. There are not many reported cases in which this exception seems to have been affirmatively applied. A far larger number of cases, while distinctly recognizing its existence, have held it inapplicable to the particular facts then before the court.").

24. See, e. g., People v. Knight, 92 Calif.App. 143, 216 Pac. 96 (lewd acts with children; defendant testifies that he committed the acts but with no lewd intent; held no error to receive evidence of similar acts with other children: "defendant opened the door"); State v. Gilligan, 92 Conn. 526, 103 Atl. 649, syl. 5 (1918) (murder by keeper of old folks' home of one of the inmates: receiving evidence of other poisonings where state's evidence did not suggest possibility of accident, held error, "without prejudice to its possible admission in rebuttal"); The remarks of Lord Sumner in Thompson v. The King, [1918] App.C. 221, 232 are pertinent: "Before an issue can be said to be raised, which would permit the introduction of such evidence so obviously prejudicial to the accused, it must have been raised in substance if not in so many words, and the issue so raised must be one to which the prejudicial evidence is relevant. The mere theory that a plea of not guilty puts everything material in issue is not enough for this purpose. The prosecution cannot credit the accused with fancy defences in order to rebut them at the outset with some damning piece of prejudice."

There is an important consideration in the practice as to the admission of evidence of other crimes which is little discussed in the opinions. This is the question of rule versus discretion. Most of the opinions ignore the problem and proceed on the assumption that the decision turns solely upon the ascertainment and application of a rule. If the situation fits one of the classes wherein the evidence has been recognized as having independent relevancy, then the evidence is received, otherwise not. This mechanical way of handling such questions has the advantage of calling on the judge for a minimum of personal judgment. But problems of lessening the dangers of prejudice without too much sacrifice of relevant evidence can seldom if ever be satisfactorily solved by mechanical rules. And so here there is danger that if the judges, trial and appellate, content themselves with merely determining whether the particular evidence of other crimes does or does not fit in one of the approved classes, they may lose sight of the underlying policy of protecting the accused against unfair prejudice. The policy may evaporate through the interstices of the classification.

Accordingly, some of the opinions recognize that the problem is not merely one of pigeon-holing, but one of balancing,[25] on the one side, the actual need for the other-crimes-evidence in the light of the issues and the other evidence available to the prosecution,[26] the convincingness of the evidence that the other crimes were committed and that the accused was the actor, and the strength or weakness of the other-crimes evidence in supporting the issue, and on the other, the degree to which the jury will probably be roused by the evidence to overmastering hostility.

Such a balancing calls for a large measure of individual judgment about the relative gravity of imponderables. Accordingly, some opinions stress the element of discretion.[27] It should be recognized, however, that this is not a discretion to depart from the principle that evidence of other crimes, having no substantial relevancy except to ground the inference that accused is a bad man and hence probably committed this crime, must be excluded. The lee-way of discretion lies rather in the opposite direction, empowering the judge to exclude the

Compare the situation where the defendant or his lawyer for him imprudently makes claim to an unblemished character or record. Holding that this opens the door to evidence of other crimes: People v. Westek, 31 Cal.2d 469, 190 P.2d 9, 13, 18 (1948); Molton v. People, 118 Colo. 147, 193 P.2d 271, 272 (1948); but see Keene v. Comm., 307 Ky. 308, 210 S.W.2d 926 (1908); Morgan and Maguire, Cases on Evidence, 173 (3d ed. 1951).

25. See, e. g., Quarles v. Comm., 245 S.W.2d 947, 948 (Ky.1951) (". . . evidence of an independent offense is inadmissible even though it may have some tendency to prove the commission of the crime charged, because the probative value of the evidence is greatly outweighed by its prejudicial effect. This is especially so where the evidence is of an isolated, wholly disconnected offense. But the balance of scales is believed to be the other way where there is a close relationship to the offense charged.").

26. The importance of this is clearly pointed out by Beach, J., in State v. Gilligan, 92 Conn. 526, 103 Atl. 649, 652, 653, syl. 4 (1918). See also the remarks of Olney, J., in Adkins v. Brett, 184 Cal. 252,

193 Pac. 251, 254 (1920). In discussing a question of the admission of a declaration, competent for one purpose, incompetent for another, he said: "The matter is largely one of discretion on the part of the trial judge. If the point to prove which the evidence is competent can just as well be proven by other evidence, or if it is of but slight weight or importance upon that point, the trial judge might well be justified in excluding it entirely, because of its prejudicial and dangerous character as to other points."

27. See, e. g., Neff v. United States, 105 F.2d 688, 692, syl. 9 (C.C.A. 8, 1939) (admissibility of other crimes in discretion of court, stated as ground for affirming judge's ruling admitting such evidence); King v. United States, 144 F.2d 729, syl. 9 (C.C.A. 8, 1944) (similarity of other offense determined on appeal from record, but remoteness in time is in judge's discretion); State v. Bock, 229 Minn. 449, 39 N.W.2d 887, syl. 2 (1949) (whether separate offenses are so closely connected with crime on trial as to show general scheme, in judge's discretion); State v. Gavle, 234 Minn. 186, 48 N.W.2d 44, 56, syl. 14 (1951) (like Neff case, above).

other crimes evidence, even when it has substantial independent relevancy, when in his judgment its probative value for this purpose is outweighed by the danger that it will stir such passion in the jury as to sweep them beyond a rational consideration of guilt or innocence of the crime on trial.[28] Discretion implies not only lee-way but responsibility. A decision clearly wrong on this question of balancing probative value against danger of prejudice will be corrected on appeal as an abuse of discretion.[29]

158. Character to Evidence Conduct—(d) The Exception to the General Rule of Exclusion Permitting the Accused to Produce Evidence of his Good Character:[1] Cross-Examination and Rebuttal by State.

The prosecution, as we have seen in the preceding section, is forbidden to initiate evidence of the bad character of the defendant when offered merely to show that he is a bad man and hence more likely to commit a crime. The objection is not that the evidence is not relevant for this purpose, but that its value is overbalanced by the danger of undue prejudice which the evidence would arouse. When the table is turned, and the accused himself offers evidence of his good character to show that he was unlikely to have committed the crime, the relevancy remains. The basic premise is the one by which we order our daily lives, that people generally act in keeping with their character. But the danger of prejudice now is almost wholly lacking.[2] So it is generally agreed that the accused in all criminal cases[3] may produce evidence of his good character as substantive evidence of his innocence. In

[28] State v. Goebel, 36 Wash.2d 367, 218 P.2d 300, 306, syl. 5 (1950) (Hill, J.: ". . . this class of evidence, where not essential to the establishment of the state's case, should not be admitted, even though falling within the generally recognized exceptions to the rule of exclusion, when the trial court is convinced that its effect would be to generate heat instead of diffusing light, or, as is said in one of the law review articles above referred to, where the minute peg of relevancy will be entirely obscured by the dirty linen hung upon it. This is a situation where the policy of protecting a defendant from undue prejudice conflicts with the rule of logical relevance, and a proper determination as to which should prevail rests in the sound discretion of the trial court, and not merely on whether the evidence comes within certain categories which constitute exceptions to the rule of exclusion.").

[29] See, e. g., Noor Mohamed v. The King, [1949] App. C. 182, 192, 193 (Privy Council) (murder by poisoning wife; death by poison of previous wife admitted; held, while judge had discretion to balance relevancy against prejudice, here erroneously exercised), critically noted, 12 Mod.L.Rev. 232; State v. Gilligan, 92 Conn. 526, 103 Atl. 649, 653 (1918) (murder by poisoning: other deaths by poisoning admitted and conviction reversed on this ground; "Courts are not infrequently required in criminal cases to pass upon preliminary questions of fact in order to determine the admissibility of evidence, and no doubt courts are vested with considerable discretionary powers in passing upon such preliminary questions . . . we think it would be an abuse of discretion to permit proof of similar

but unconnected poisonings in a case where the state's evidence had already gone so far toward eliminating accident or mistake as to leave no reasonable doubt, in the absence of rebutting evidence, that the poison, if administered by the accused, must have been knowingly administered."); State v. Goebel, next preceding note.

[1] See 1 Wigmore, Evidence, §§ 55–60, 3 id. § 925; 1 Wharton, Criminal Evidence, §§ 330–338 (11th ed. 1935); Udall, Character Proof in the Law of Evidence, 18 Univ.Cin.L.Rev. 283, 299 (1949); 22 C.J.S., Criminal Law, §§ 676–679; Dec.Dig.Criminal Law, ☞377–381.

[2] There may be some danger that the jury will be induced by the evidence of good character to out-step their function by pardoning a man whom they believe to be guilty, but this kind of equitable dispensing power is one that the community while it does not explicitly sanction, probably does not disapprove.

[3] It is said that the practice of permitting evidence of good character was introduced in the reign of Charles II, and was then confined to capital cases. Reddick v. State, 25 Fla. 112, 433, 5 So. 704 (1889). And later the evidence was limited to cases where under the other testimony guilt was in doubt. Daniels v. State, 2 Pen.(Del.) 586, 48 Atl. 196 (1901). But these limitations are now abandoned, and the character evidence itself may be relied on by the accused to engender the doubt. See the above cases and 1 Wharton, Criminal Evidence, § 330 (11th ed. 1935).

courtroom parlance this is often termed "placing his character in issue," but the phrase is misleading. Character is almost never one of the ultimate issues or operative facts determining guilt or innocence. It is merely circumstantial evidence bearing on the probability that the accused did or did not commit the act charged with the required guilty intent.[4] What the accused does, then, and what he has the exclusive power to do, is to initiate, and thus open the door to, circumstantial evidence of character.

Character for what? A few courts permit proof of "general good character"[5] but the prevailing and more practical view limits the inquiry to the trait or traits involved in the crime on trial[6]—honesty in theft cases, peaceableness in murder, and the like.[7]

By a rule of relatively recent origin and doubtful expediency,[8] the only way in which character for this purpose can be proved is by evidence of reputation.[9] This excludes evidence of specific acts or blameless life and rules out opinion-evidence as to the character of the accused for the trait in question based on the witness' knowledge and observation. Reputation-evidence, though muted and colorless, is thought to have the advan-

4. See, e. g., Comm. v. Beal, 314 Mass. 210, 50 N.E. 2d 14, syl. 23 (1943) (defendant may prove good character for purpose of establishing the improbability of his having done the wrong imputed to him).

5. Thus in North Carolina the inquiry seems to be limited to "general character." State v. Sentelle, 212 N.C. 386, 193 S.E. 405, syl. 3, 4 (1937) (driving while intoxicated: inquiry as to reputation for sobriety improper: must ask as to general character, but witness may then volunteer as to respect in which character good or bad!). See also United States v. Latin, 139 F.2d 569, syl. 3 (C.C.A. 2, 1943) (setting up unregistered still: defendant entitled to prove good reputation as to "moral character"); State v. Quinn, 344 Mo. 1072, 130 S.W.2d 511, syl. 7 (1939) (when offense is only malum prohibitum, proper to prove trait of law-abiding citizenship).

6. Hawley v. United States, 133 F.2d 966, syl. 4 (C.C.A.1943); State v. Howland, 157 Kan. 11, 138 P.2d 424, syl. 1, 2 (1943) (rape: defendant not entitled to prove good reputation for veracity); People v. Van Gaasbeck, 189 N.Y. 408, 82 N.E. 718, syl. 1 (1907); 1 Wigmore, Evidence, § 59; Dec.Dig. Criminal Law, ⊗377; 22 C.J.S., Criminal Law, § 677e.

7. It is easy to confound the situation when the character is "put in issue" by proof of good reputation as evidence of innocence, and the distinct situation, with different rules, of the taking the stand by the accused as a witness. In the latter case, the prosecution may impeach his credibility by evidence of the bad reputation of the accused. Then the trait involved is veracity, and it is veracity-character at the time he testifies that we are interested in. Moreover, the accused cannot support his veracity-character as a witness until the prosecution has first attacked it. State v. Howland, 157 Kan. 11, 138 P.2d 424, syl. 1, 2 (1943) (prosecution for statutory rape, defendant offered evidence of good reputation for veracity: held properly excluded, (1) as substantive evidence because not the trait involved in the crime, (2) as supporting credibility because state had not attacked his veracity-character); People v. Trahos, 251 Mich. 592, 232 N.W. 357, syl. 1, 2 (1930) (receiving stolen goods: defendant's evidence of good reputation for veracity can only be considered on his credibility not as evidence of innocence); State v. Colson, 193 N.C. 236, 136 S.E. 730, syl. 3 (1927) (defendant testified but did not give evidence of good character: the state produced evidence of his bad character, held, this evidence could only be considered on his credibility, not as evidence of guilt). See 3 Wigmore, Evidence, § 925.

8. See 6 Wigmore, Evidence, § 1686, for a discussion of the history and policy of the rule.

9. Blakely v. State, 30 Ala.App. 397, 6 So.2d 603, syl. 2 (1942); Berger v. State, 179 Md. 410, 20 A.2d 146, syl. 1 (1941); State v. Dancer, 116 N.J.Law 487, 184 Atl. 800, syl. 4 (1936); People v. Van Gaasbeck, 189 N.Y. 408, 82 N.E. 718, syl. 2 (1907). Dec.Dig.Criminal Law, ⊗379; 22 C.J.S., Criminal Law, § 678. A witness who testifies that he lives in the community where the accused resides, but that he has never heard the defendant's character in respect to the particular trait discussed is qualified to testify to his good reputation in that respect. People v. Van Gaasbeck, supra; Note, Negative Proof of Good Character, 67 A.L.R. 1210.

A few states cling to the earlier tradition and permit the accused to produce not only reputation-evidence, but testimony of those who know his good character from observation of his conduct. State v. Ferguson, 222 Iowa 1148, 270 N.W. 874, syl. 7, 15 (1937); State v. Hartung, 239 Iowa 414, 30 N.W.2d 491, syl. 7 (1948); Sabo v. State, 119 Ohio St. 231, 163 N.E. 28 31, syl. 2 (1928). It would be permitted under Model Code of Evidence, Rule 306(2) (a) and under Uniform Rules of Evidence, Rules 46, 47.

tage of avoiding distracting side-issues as to particular acts and incidents in the past life of the accused.[10]

It is character at the time of the alleged crime that bears most nearly on the inference of innocence or guilt, and the reputation evidence must be confined to reputation at that time or a reasonable time before.[11] The reputation is usually said to be limited to that which obtained in the community where the accused lived,[12] but this should be extended to embrace any considerable group with whom he constantly associated in his business, work, or other continued activity, and who might reasonably be thought to have a collective opinion about him.[13]

It is a merciful dispensation to the accused of hitherto blameless life to allow him to open this door of character. To those with spotted records, however, it is a far more dangerous move to open this door than might at first glance be assumed. In the first place, the witness who has testified to the good reputation of the accused for the particular trait, may be cross-examined as to his means of knowledge of community-opinion, not only generally, but specifically as to whether he "has heard" that the defendant has committed particular criminal acts inconsistent with the reputation vouched for on direct.[14] Logically, but surprisingly, the courts hold that the witness may not be asked "if he knows" that the accused has committed such other crimes.[15] As to indictments or other official charges, convictions, or repeated arrests, or crimes

---

10. "If a witness is to be permitted to testify to the character of an accused person, basing his testimony solely on his own knowledge and observation, he cannot logically be prohibited from stating the particular incidents affecting the defendant and the particular actions of the defendant which have led him to his favorable conclusion. In most instances it would be utterly impossible for the prosecution to ascertain whether occurrences narrated by the witness as constituting the foundation of his conclusion were or were not true. They might be utterly false, and yet incapable of disproof at the time of trial. Furthermore, even if evidence were accessible to controvert the specific statements of the witness in this respect, its admission would lead to the introduction into the case of innumerable collateral issues which could not be tried out without introducing the utmost complication and confusion into the trial, tending to distract the minds of the jurymen and befog the chief issue in litigation." Willard Bartlett, J., in People v. Van Gaasbeck, 189 N.Y. 408, 82 N.E. 718, 721 (1907).

11. People v. Willy, 301 Ill. 307, 133 N.E. 859, 864, syl. 2, 3, 6 (1922); Comm. v. White, 271 Pa. 584, 115 Atl. 870, syl. 2, 3 (1922) (remoteness of earlier reputation in judge's discretion); 22 C.J.S., Criminal Law, § 677b.

12. See, e. g., Baugh v. State, 218 Ala. 87, 117 So. 426, syl. 8 (1928).

13. Hamilton v. State, 129 Fla. 219, 176 So. 89, syl. 15, 112 A.L.R. 1013 (1937) (admitting reputation in locality where accused worked as a hotel employee). The Annotation, 112 A.L.R. 1020 reviews the cases pro and con. See also 22 C.J.S., Criminal Law, § 677c.

14. Vinson v. State, 247 Ala. 22, 22 So.2d 344, syl. 1 (1945); Carnley v. State, 143 Fla. 756, 197 So. 441, syl. 5 (1940); Comm. v. Becker, 326 Pa. 105, 191 Atl. 351, syl. 18 (1937); Garza v. State, 129 Tex.Cr. 443, 88 S.W.2d 113, syl. 3, 4 (1936) and cases cited 3 Wigmore, Evidence, § 988, Dec.Dig.Witnesses, ☞274, Note, 71 A.L.R. 1504, 1505, et seq. Of course, the inquiry must relate to crimes or misconduct relevant to the trait vouched for on direct. Albertson v. Comm., 312 Ky. 68, 226 S.W.2d 523, syl. 5 (1950) (peace and quiet: cross-examination as to illegal liquor traffic excluded); Kennedy v. State, 150 Tex.Cr. 215, 200 S.W.2d 400, syl. 2 (1947) (peace, quiet, law-abidingness, veracity; illicit relations with woman excluded).

But there are indications in at least three states of a practice forbidding inquiry altogether as to particular acts or rumors thereof. See Viliborghi v. State, 45 Ariz. 275, 285, 43 P.2d 210, 215, syl. 10, 11 (1935) (". . . the questions must not be in such form as to imply specific acts of misconduct of the party, but should be confined to the source of his knowledge of the reputation and what he has heard from such sources."); People v. Page, 365 Ill. 524, 6 N.E.2d 845 (1937), and comment 25 Ill.Bar J. 335; compare People v. Hannon, 381 Ill. 206, 44 N.E.2d 923, syl. 3–5 (1942); State v. Robinson, 226 N.C. 95, 36 S.E.2d 655, syl. 4, 5 (1946).

15. Stewart v. United States, 104 F.2d 234, 235 (Ct. App.D.C.1939) (". . . the witness on cross-examination should be asked only—'Have you heard?'—not—'Do you know?'"); Comm. v. Thomas, 282 Pa. 20, 127 Atl. 427, syl. 1, 2 (1925); Couch v. State, 135 Tex.Cr. 479, 121 S.W.2d 367, syl. 4 (1938); Note, 71 A.L.R. 1504, 1543. Nevertheless,

committed in public, or the fact of imprisonment, all of which would usually be known to the community and thus affect reputation, it would seem allowable to ask the witness if he "knows" of these,[16] but some decisions require the "have you heard" form of inquiry as to these matters also.[17]

The rule permitting the cross-examiner to ask the character witness whether he "has heard" of other particular crimes of accused involving the same trait is pregnant with possibilities of destructive prejudice.[18] The mere asking by a respected official of such a question, however, answered, may well suggest to the jury that the imputation is true. The courts agree that propounding such a question in bad faith may be ground of reversal.[19] But establishing such bad faith may be a hopeless task.[20] It has been persuasively suggested that this danger of false suggestion and the hazard that the consideration of the case on trial will be overwhelmed by the importation of other misdoings of the accused, should be avoided by limiting the cross-examination to a general one on opportunities for knowledge of reputation excluding altogether any inquiries about other crimes or rumors thereof.[21]

testimony of good reputation by a witness who knows of criminal acts has a whited sepulchre quality, and a few courts permit him to be asked, "Do you know?" State v. Shull, 151 Ore. 224, 282 Pac. 237, 71 A.L.R. 1598, 1500 (1929); State v. Cyr, 40 Wash.2d 840, 246 P.2d 480, syl. 9 (1952).

16. State v. Jacobs, 195 La. 281, 196 So. 347, syl. 7 (1940) (arrest); State v. Carroll, 188 S.W.2d 22, syl. 1 (Mo., 1945) (arrests or accusations); Lyons v. State, 76 Okl.Cr. 41, 133 P.2d 898, syl. 4 (1943) (charges).

17. Wright v. State, 247 Ala. 180, 23 So.2d 519, syl. 2 (1945) (served time in penitentiary for assault to murder); McNaulty v. State, 138 Tex.Cr. 317, 135 S.W.2d 987, syl. 2 (1940) (that defendant had been charged with aggravated assault).

18. The considerations of fairness and policy which make for and against the prevailing practice were ably marshaled and evaluated in the opinions of Jackson, J., for the court and Rutledge, J., dissenting, in Michelson v. United States, 335 U.S. 469, 69 Sup.Ct. 213, 93 L.Ed. 168 (1948), noted in 34 Iowa L. Rev. 700, 40 J.Crim.L. 58, 47 Mich.L.Rev. 843, 22 So. Cal.L.Rev. 489, and other reviews. The trial, held in 1947, was for bribery of a revenue agent. The accused, on direct examination, acknowledged a conviction for a trade mark violation in 1927. He produced witnesses of his good reputation for honesty, truthfulness and veracity, some of whom testified that they had known him for thirty years. On cross-examination they were asked, "Did you ever hear that on Oct. 11, 1920, the defendant . . . was arrested for receiving stolen goods?" They answered, no. The prosecutor assured the court, in private, of the truth of the fact of such arrest, which was not questioned, and the judge explained to the jury the limited purpose of the question. The court affirmed. Jackson, J., for the court concludes: "We concur in the general opinion of courts, textwriters and the profession that much of this law is archaic, paradoxical and full of compromises and compensations by which an irrational advantage to one side is offset by a poorly reasoned counter-privilege to the other. But somehow it has proved a workable even if clumsy system when moderated by discretionary controls in the hands of a wise and strong trial court. To pull one misshapen stone out of the grotesque structure is more likely simply to upset its present balance between adverse interests than to establish a rational edifice."

19. See expressions to this effect in People v. Young, 25 Cal.App.2d 148, 77 P.2d 271, syl. 10 (1938); State v. Dixon, 190 S.W. 290, 293, syl. 4 (Mo.Sup.1916), and cases cited 71 A.L.R. 1541–1543. But actual reversals on this ground are exceedingly rare.

20. In the absence of a showing to the contrary, it will be presumed that the prosecutor acted in good faith. People v. Burke, 18 Cal.App. 72, 122 Pac. 435, syl. 8 (1912). Trial judges sometimes assume that they are helpless when defendant objects on the ground of bad faith. See State v. McDonald, 231 S.W. 927, 930 (Mo.1921). But as Wigmore points out in criticizing the holding, the judge could have questioned the prosecutor, in the absence of the jury, as to whether he had credible grounds for asking the question. Evidence, § 988, note 1.

21. See the dissenting opinion of Rutledge, J., in Michelson v. United States, 335 U.S. 469, 496, 69 Sup.Ct. 213, 228, 93 L.Ed. 168 (1948), where he says: "My own preference and, I think, the only fair rule would be to foreclose the entire line of inquiry concerning specific incidents in the defendant's past, both on cross-examination and on new evidence in rebuttal. This would leave room for proper rebuttal without turning the defendant's trial for a specific offense into one for all his previous misconduct, criminal or other, and would put the prosecution on the same plane with the defendant in rela-

Such a rule, it seems, would tend to give too free a license to the parade of false or biassed character-witness. Yet the asserted dangers of the prevailing practice are real and a curb is needed. The trial judge, it is believed, should be required by rule, before permitting the prosecuting counsel to cross-examine the character-witness on rumors of misconduct of the accused, or upon arrests, charges or convictions, to request the prosecutor to give his professional statement to the judge (in the absence of the jury) that he has reasonable ground to believe, and does believe, that the crimes or misconduct, which are imputed by the rumors, or which are the subject of the arrests or charges, were actually committed by the accused, and that the judgments of conviction inquired about were actually pronounced. Reasonable grounds would require, it is suggested, that the prosecutor's assurance be based on the statements of witnesses, believed to be credible, who purport to have first-hand knowledge.

The other available counterthrust of the prosecution to the defendant's proof of good reputation is not so deadly. This is the power of the state to produce witnesses in rebuttal who will swear to his bad reputation,[22] limited of course to the trait or traits opened by the defendant [23] and to the period before the offense and not too remote.[24] Just as in the case of the reputation-witnesses of the accused, the witnesses for the prosecution are limited on direct to assertions about the reputation and may not testify to particular acts [25] or rumors thereof.[26] Should the state be allowed to prove at this stage, in rebuttal of good reputation, judgments of conviction for crimes involving the same trait in or near the community where the accused lived, and within a reasonable time before the commission of the crime on trial? The cases are few and divided,[27] but such convictions would bear strongly on reputation, are provable with entire certainty, and while they carry a danger of prejudice, it is avoidable by the accused, who need not inject the issue of reputation. The argument here against the use of convictions is far less strong than against the use of convictions to impeach the accused when he

---

tion to the use of character evidence. This, it seems to me, is the only fair way to handle the matter."

22. See cases collected in 3 Wigmore, Evidence, § 988, 22 C.J.S., Criminal Law, §§ 677, 678; Dec.Dig., Criminal Law, ☜378–380.

23. Mimbs v. State, 189 Ga. 189, 5 S.E.2d 770, syl. 3 (1939) (dictum).

24. State v. Van Osten, 68 R.I. 175, 26 A.2d 858, syl. 8 (1942).

25. Helms v. State, 254 Ala. 14, 47 So.2d 276, syl. 11, 12 (1950) (wife-murder, error to allow state in rebuttal of good reputation, to prove that accused had been placed under peace-bond; but isn't this, in a rural community as here, a matter likely to affect reputation?); Mimbs v. State, 189 Ga. 189, 5 S.E.2d 770, syl. 3 (murder; error to prove a previous fight); State v. Miller, 60 Idaho 79, 88 P.2d 526, syl. 5 (1939) (drunken driving; previous intoxication); Dec.Dig., Criminal Law, ☜380.

26. Of course, the accused might cross-examine the state's bad-reputation witnesses as to whether they "have heard" comment on praiseworthy actions of the accused, but manifestly the browsing here is not as rich as in the prosecution's "have you heard" cross-examination.

27. See, e. g., Eley v. United States, 117 F.2d 526, 529, syl. 6 (C.C.A. 6, 1941) (tax and liquor violations; accused produced witnesses to his character; held, error to allow prosecution to prove previous convictions for similar offences and specific acts after the offence on trial, on issue of reputation; "There was no proof that the prior convictions and the subsequent unlawful acts of the appellant were known to the community, or that they in any wise impaired the reputation of the appellant as a man of honesty and integrity."); Giles v. State, 71 Ga. App. 736, 32 S.E.2d 111, syl. 7, 8 (1944) (convictions admissible, but here arrests offered, and they are inadmissible); Comm. v. Harvie, 345 Pa. 516, 28 A.2d 926, syl. 1, 2 (1942) (conviction admissible, but here record equivocal); 32 C.J.S. 1078, 1079. See also Roach v. State, 127 Tex.Cr.R. 37, 74 S.W.2d 656, syl. 5 (Tex.Crim.1934) (felony indictment provable whether has resulted in conviction or acquittal); Locke v. Comm., 149 Va. 447, 141 S.E. 118, syl. 3 (1928) (prosecution of 18 year old boy for assault to rape young girl; mother testified he had never been in serious trouble; held, this opened

takes the stand as a witness.[28] If he stays off the stand, the jury despite instructions will usually assume his guilt, but no such assumption is likely to be made from his failure to open the door of reputation.

159. Character to Evidence Conduct—(e) Exception to General Rule of Exclusion, under Minority View, for Proof of Party's Character in Civil Cases Where Crime Is in Issue.[1]

The common law relaxed its ban upon evidence of character to show conduct to the extent of permitting the accused to open the door by producing evidence of his good reputation.[2] This was a special dispensation to criminal defendants whose life or liberty were at hazard. Should the same dispensation be accorded to the party in a civil action who has been charged by his adversary's pleading or proof with a criminal offence involving moral turpitude? The peril of judgment here is less, and most courts have declined to pay the price in consumption of time and distraction from the issue which the concession entails.[3] A growing minority, however, have been impressed with the serious consequences to the party's standing, reputation, and relationships which such a charge, even in a civil action, may bring in its train,[4] and have followed the appealing criminal analogy, by permitting the party to introduce evidence of his good reputation for the trait involved in the charge.[5] The

---

door for state to prove that he been charged with offences in juvenile court).

28. See § 43, herein.

1. 1 Wigmore, Evidence, § 64; Note, Evidence of character on issue of fraud in civil action, 78 A. L.R. 643, Note, 13 Tex.L.Rev. 531, 1935; Note, Character in civil action for assault, 154 A.L.R. 121; 32 C.J.S., Evidence, § 426; Dec.Dig., Evidence, ⊜106.

2. See § 158.

3. Calif. Code Civ.Proc. § 2053 ("evidence of the good character of a party is not admissible in a civil action . . . unless the issue involves his character"); Bosworth v. Bosworth, 131 Conn. 389, 40 A.2d 186, syl. 2, 3 (1944) (error in wife's action of divorce for cruelty to permit her to prove defendant had been divorced by former wife for cruelty); Johnson v. Richards, 50 Idaho 150, 294 Pac. 507, syl. 30, (1930) (suit against defendant for alienation of affection, and adultery alleged in aggravation of damages, defendant denies adultery and seeks to prove reputation for chastity); Koontz v. Farmers' Mut. Ins. Assn., 235 Iowa 87, 16 N.W.2d 20, syl. 7, 8 (1944) (suit on fire policy; defendant charges plaintiff with setting fire; held, plaintiff's evidence of good reputation rightly excluded); Kornec v. Mike Horse Mining, etc. Co., 120 Mont. 1, 180 P.2d 252, syl. 17 (1947) (action for assault; defendant's good reputation for peacefulness excluded); Baker v. First National Bank of Santa Rosa, 176 Okl. 70, 54 P.2d 355, (1936) (replevin: issue, whether defendants took stolen bonds with knowledge or in good faith).

4. See, e.g., Start, J., in Hein v. Holdridge, 78 Minn. 468, 81 N.W. 522, 523 (1900), admitting evidence of good reputation in an action for seduction: ". . .

such evidence ought to be received in a civil action when it is of a character to bring it within all of the reasons for admitting such evidence in criminal cases. Civil actions for an indecent assault, for seduction, and kindred cases, are of this character; for such cases are not infrequently mere speculative and blackmailing schemes. The consequences to the defendant of a verdict against him in such a case are most serious, for the issue as to him involves his fortune, his honor, his family. From the very nature of the charge, it often happens that an innocent man can only meet the issue by a denial of the charge, and proof of his previous good character."

5. Nickolay v. Orr, 142 Minn. 346, 172 N.W. 222 (1919) (recognizing rule as stated in text, and citing Minnesota decisions, but held here inapplicable to an action for indecent assault where plaintiff sought to show defendant's bad reputation and other similar acts); Waggoman v. Ft. Worth Well Machinery & Supply Co., 124 Tex. 325, 76 S.W.2d 1005, 1006 (1934) (plaintiff sued for false imprisonment and to cancel a note for duress; counterclaim charging plaintiff with embezzlement; held plaintiff properly permitted to introduce evidence of his good character for honesty and veracity; holding seemingly is erroneous as to latter trait); Hess v. Marinari, 81 W.Va. 500, 94 S.E. 968, syl. 2, 3 (1918) (assault; with claim for punitive damages; such claim requires finding of criminal intent, and defendant entitled as in criminal case entitled to show his good character for peace). Compare, however, Skidmore v. Star Ins. Co., 126 W.Va. 307, 27 S.E.2d 845, syl. 10, 11 (1943), which approves the majority rule rejecting evidence of character to show conduct in civil cases, and distinguishes the Hess case on the inadequate ground that criminal intent was there

balance of expediency is a close one, and since this is so, the minority view which favors the admission of evidence concededly relevant, is probably the wiser one.

Civil actions for assault and battery seem often to be treated as in a class by themselves.[6] When the issue is merely whether the defendant committed the act charged, then the courts would presumably admit or exclude defendant's evidence of good reputation according to their alignment with the majority or minority view on the general question, as discussed above. But when the defendant pleads self defence, he may show the plaintiff's reputation for turbulence if he proves it was known to him, on the issue of reasonable apprehension.[7] Similarly, when on a plea of self defence or otherwise there is an issue as to who committed the first act of aggression, most courts (regardless of their alignment on the general question) seem to admit evidence of the good or bad reputation of both plaintiff and defendant for peacefulness as shedding light on their probable acts.[8] This cannot be justified, as is sometimes attempted, on the ground that character is here "in issue"—the issue is clearly one of conduct—but probably there is in these cases a special need even beyond that in most cases of charges of crime in civil actions, for knowing the dispositions of the parties.

160. Character to Evidence Conduct—(f) Exception to General Rule of Exclusion Admitting Evidence as to Character of Deceased in Homicide on Issue of Aggression in Self-Defence.[1]

When the accused has produced evidence that the deceased attacked him, thus grounding a claim of self-defence, this when met by counter-evidence raises an issue of conduct: was the deceased or the accused the first aggressor? It is almost universally held that when such evidence has been produced the accused may introduce testimony of the reputation of the deceased for turbulence and violence.[2] It is equally well settled of course that the prosecution may meet this by re-

---

6. See the extensive collection of decisions in Note, 154 A.L.R. 121.

material. See also as to West Virginia law, Mourikas v. Vardianos, 169 F.2d 53, syl, 9–12 (C.C.A.W. Va.1948), noted 22 So.Cal.L.Rev. 486, 51 W.Va.L. Rev. 273. Some courts have extended this principle to include charges of fraud, regardless of criminality. Rogers v. Atlantic Life Ins. Co., 135 S.C. 89, 133 S.E. 215, syl. 8 (1926) (whether deceased made false and fraudulent statements in application for life insurance; his good reputation for honesty provable by beneficiary); Continental Nat. Bank v. First Nat. Bank, 108 Tenn. 374, 68 S.W. 497, syl. 8 (1902) (suit charging that defendant bank induced plaintiff bank to lend money on certain paper by false representations pursuant to a fraudulent conspiracy in which one Duncan, a nonparty to the suit, was involved; held, proper to admit testimony as to the good character of Duncan for honor and integrity, since his honor was assailed though he was not a party to the suit). Contra: Grant v. Pendley, 39 S.W.2d 596, 78 A.L.R. 638 (Tex.Comm.App.1931) (pleading charging party with procuring deed by fraud not ground for permitting party to introduce evidence of his good reputation for honesty and veracity).

7. Dingle v. Hickman, 32 Del. 49, 119 Atl. 311 (1922); Glahn v. Mastin, 115 Kan. 557, 224 Pac. 68, syl.1 (semble) (1924); Note, 154 A.L.R. 129.

8. Cain v. Skillin, 219 Ala. 228, 121 So. 521, syl. 7, 64 A.L.R. 1022 (1919) (defendant entitled to show plaintiff's character for turbulence though defendant did not know of it); Neimeyer v. McCarty, 221 Ind. 688, 51 N.E.2d 365, syl. 7, 11, 154 A.L.R. 115 (1943) (court, though adhering to majority view on general question of proof of reputation in civil cases, holds that reputation of both parties is "in issue," when dispute as to who was first aggressor); Brown v. Simpson, 293 Ky. 755, 170 S.W.2d 345, syl. 1 (1943) (similar to last).

1. 1 Wigmore, Evidence, § 63, 1 Wharton, Criminal Evidence, § 339, 40 C.J.S., Homicide, § 272, 26 Am. Jur., §§ 343–349, Dec.Dig., Homicide, ⚖188, Note, 64 A.L.R. 1029.

2. State v. Wilson, 235 Iowa 538, 17 N.W.2d 138, syl. 17 (1945); Kinder v. Comm., 263 Ky. 145, 92 S.W.2d 8, syl. 6 (1936); People v. Cellura, 288 Mich. 54, 284 N.W. 643, syl. 4, 5 (1939); Meeks v. State, 135 Tex.Cr. 170, 117 S.W.2d 454, syl. 6 (1938).

There is another use of testimony of the reputation for violence of the deceased, which does not transgress the policy against evidence of character to show conduct. This is the use of the reputation

butting testimony of his good reputation for peacefulness.[3] It is generally agreed also that the prosecution may not enter such proof as part of its main case.[4] The conflict arises as to the condition under which the state may offer such proof in rebuttal. By one view, it is allowed only when the accused directly opens the character-door by adducing evidence of bad character or reputation for violence.[5] This has the advantage of permitting the accused to give evidence of self-defence and still keep out altogether this "collateral" evidence of character, in keeping with the general tradition against using evidence of character to show conduct. It restricts the opportunity for the appeal to pity and vengeance implicit in the praise of the character of the deceased. It has, moreover, an attractive consonance with the rule as to the exclusive privilege of the accused to put his own character "in issue." On the other hand, when the crucial question as to who was the first attacker, on which the just decision of the murder charge may depend, is in doubt, the character of the dead man for peace or violence has a revealing significance which may well be thought to outweigh the possibility of prejudice, here so

much less than in the case of an attack on the character of the accused. Accordingly, Wigmore and a growing group of courts have favored the view that whenever the accused claims self-defence and offers evidence that the deceased was the first aggressor, the state in rebuttal may produce evidence of the peaceful reputation of the deceased.[6] To the present writer this seems the wiser solution.

161. Character to Evidence Conduct—(g) Exception to General Rule of Exclusion, in the Practice of Admitting Evidence of Character to Impeach a Witness.

The familiar practice of allowing proof of bad character of a witness for veracity, by the testimony of reputation-witnesses and by evidence of conviction of crime seems to constitute another exception to the traditional policy against using evidence of character to show conduct, here to show that the witness may have testified to an untruth. The scope of this exception is discussed in the chapter on impeachment.[1]

162. Habit and Custom as Evidence of Conduct on a Particular Occasion.[1]

Character and habit are close akin. Character is a generalized description of one's dis-

---

of deceased for violence, when such reputation is proved to be known to the accused, as evidence of the defendant's reasonable apprehension of immediate danger. People v. Allen, 378 Ill. 164, 37 N.E. 2d 854, syl. 7 (1941); 2 Wigmore, Evidence, § 246; Dec.Dig., Homicide, ⇙188(2).

3. Henry v. State, 87 Tex.Cr. 148, 220 S.W. 1108, 1110, syl. 7 (1920) (arguendo).

4. People v. Dunn, 233 Mich. 185, 206 N.W. 568, syl. 2 (1925) (arguendo); Miller v. State, 63 Okl.Cr. 64, 72 P.2d 520, syl. 3 (1937); 40 C.J.S. 1226, note 83.

5. Richardson v. State, 123 Miss. 232, 85 So. 186, syl. 1 (1920); Miller v. State, 63 Okl.Cr. 64, 72 P.2d 520, syl. 4 (1937); (dictum); Lee v. Comm., 188 Va. 360, 49 S.E.2d 608, syl. 3–5 (1948) (but here the state's own witnesses testified that the deceased was the first aggressor), noted 3 Ark. L.Rev. 464, 6 W. & L.L.Rev. 224.

6. Sweazy v. State, 210 Ind. 674, 5 N.E.2d 511 (1937); Butler v. State, 131 Tex.Cr. 543, 100 S.W.2d 707, syl. 8 (1937); 3 Wigmore, Evidence, § 63, note 2. Some decisions reach like results by holding that

in the particular case the threats or acts of aggression of deceased proved by accused were such as to constitute an attack on his character for peacefulness. State v. Rutledge, 243 Iowa 179, 47 N.W.2d 251, syl. 23, 24 (1951); State v. Brock, 56 N.M. 338, 244 P.2d 131 (1952). But to draw a line between those acts of aggression sufficient to raise the issue of self-defence which are and those which are not attacks on character, seems unrealistic.

1. See §§ 41–44.

1. 1 Wigmore, Evidence, §§ 92–97, 20 Am.Jur., Evidence, §§ 332, 333; Notes, Habit and Custom to Show Negligence or Care, 14 Univ.Detroit L.J. 32 (1951), Habit Evidence of Negligence, 25 Boston U.L.Rev. 64 (1945), Falknor, "Customary" Negligence, 12 Wash.L.Rev. 35 (1937); Habit or Reputation as to Care, 15 A.L.R. 125, 18 A.L.R. 1109; Dec.Dig., Evidence, ⇙138, 139.

Model Code of Evidence, Rule 307: "(1) Habit means a course of behavior of a person regularly repeated in like circumstances. Custom means a course of

position, or of one's disposition in respect to a general trait, such as honesty, temperance, or peacefulness.[2] "Habit," in modern usage, both lay and psychological, is more specific.[3] It describes one's regular response to a repeated specific situation. If we speak of character for care, we think of the person's tendency to act prudently in all the varying situations of life, in business, family life, in handling automobiles and in walking across the street. A habit, on the other hand, is the person's regular practice of meeting a particular kind of situation with a specific type of conduct, such as the habit of going down a particular stairway two stairs at a time, or of giving the hand-signal for a left turn, or of alighting from railway cars while they are moving. The doing of the habitual acts may become semi-automatic.

Character may be thought of as the sum of one's habits though doubtless it is more than this. But unquestionably the uni-

formity of one's response to habit is far greater than the consistency with which one's conduct conforms to character or disposition. Even though character comes in only exceptionally as evidence of an act,[4] surely any sensible man in investigating whether X did a particular act would be greatly helped in his inquiry by evidence as to whether he was in the habit of doing it. We are shocked, then, to read such judicial pronouncements as the following: "For the purpose of proving that one has or has not done a particular act, it is not competent to show that he has or has not been in the habit of doing other similar acts."[5] But surely, if "habit" is used in the sense we have suggested above, expediency and sound reason would lead to the opposite approach, namely that evidence that an act was habitually done by X under like circumstances will be received as evidence that it was done by X on the particular occasion.[6] Nevertheless, the

behavior of a group of persons regularly repeated in like circumstances.
"(2) Evidence of a habit of a person is admissible as tending to prove that his behavior on a specified occasion conformed to the habit. Evidence of a custom of a group of persons is admissible as tending to prove that their behavior on a specified occasion conformed to the custom.
"(3) As tending to prove habit or custom under Paragraph (2).
"(a) a witness may state his opinion under Rule 401, and
"(b) evidence of specific instances of behavior of the person or the group of persons is admissible if the proponent offers admissible evidence of a sufficient number of such instances to warrant a finding of the habit or custom."
See also Uniform Rules of Evidence, R. 50: "Testimony in the form of opinion is admissible on the issue of habit or custom. Evidence of specific instances of behavior is admissible to prove habit or custom if the evidence is of a sufficient number of such instances to warrant a finding of such habit or custom."
2. See § 153, above.
3. "A settled disposition or tendency to act in a certain way, esp. one acquired by frequent repetition of the same act; a settled practice, custom, usage; a customary manner of acting." 1 Shorter Oxford Eng.Dict. 850 (1933).

"Habit is a product of acquisition. In this respect it differs from instinct, with which otherwise it has much in common. We say we do a thing from habit, e. g., nod back when a person not recognized nods to us, when as a consequence of long practice and frequent repetition the action has become in a measure organized, and thus shorn of some of its original appanage of full consciousness or attention. The characteristic note of habit is mechanicality. . . . The oft-repeated action becomes habitual and so automatic because the nervous centers engaged have taken on special modifications, have, according to the customary physiological figure, become "seamed" by special lines of discharge." James Sully, The Human Mind, vol. II, p. 224 (1892), excerpts from quotations in Wigmore, Science of Judicial Proof, 127, 128 (3d ed., 1937). See also William James, The Principles of Psychology, ch. 4 (1890).

4. See §§ 155–161, above.
5. Knowlton, J., in Comm. v. Nagle, 157 Mass. 554, 32 N.E. 861 (1893).
6. Wallis v. Southern Pac. Co., 184 Cal. 662, 195 Pac. 408, syl. 1, 15 A.L.R. 117 (1921) (habit of deceased, killed at crossing, of stopping his team at this and other crossings, and going ahead to track to look for trains; held admissible, leaving open the question whether limited to situation where there are no eye-witnesses); Hodges v. Hill, 175

judge should possess the discretion usual in this field of circumstantial evidence to exclude if the habit is not sufficiently regular and uniform, or the circumstances sufficiently similar, to outweigh the danger, if any, of prejudice or confusion.[7]

The reluctance of some courts to accept this view of the general admissibility of habit

to show an act,[8] and the doctrine of other courts that evidence of habit will be received only when there are no eye-witnesses,[9] are probably due to a failure to draw a clear line between character and habit. This is contributed to by the popular custom of describing character in terms of "habits," such as "habits of care"[10] or "habits of intemperance."[11] In consequence these courts mis-

---

Mo.App. 441, 161 S.W. 633, syl. 3 (1913) (In an action for damages for the killing of plaintiff's mare by collision with defendant's horse and buggy on the highway, evidence that plaintiff's son, who rode the mare at the time of the accident, was in the habit of riding her along the highway at the place of the accident at a high speed, was admissible.); Smith v. Boston & M. R. Co., 70 N.H. 53, 47 Atl. 290, 291, syl. 1 (1900) ("Cate's uniform habit of slackening the speed of his horse to a walk at the Waukewan crossing, and looking and listening for the approach of a train before attempting to pass the crossing, tended to show that he did so on his fatal trip."); Model Code of Evidence, Rule 307(1), and Uniform Rules of Evidence, R. 50, both quoted note 1, supra.

7. See § 152, above.

8. See, e. g., Comm. v. Nagle, supra note 5; Zucker v. Whitridge, 205 N.Y. 62, syl. 2, 98 N.E. 209 (1912) (fatal crossing accident, with several eyewitnesses; on issue of contributory negligence plaintiff introduced testimony that deceased when about to cross railway tracks "usually looked to right and left of him and put a restraining hand on my arm before crossing"; held, reversible error, probative value does not outweigh danger of "collateral issues," expenditure of time and confusion; "we are not now called upon to decide whether [such] evidence . . . is competent when there is no eye-witness. . . .").

9. In a substantial number of states, including California and Illinois, an exception to the rule excluding character evidence on the issue of particular negligent conduct, is made where there are no eye-witnesses. See Young v. Patrick, 323 Ill. 200, 153 N.E. 623, 1926; Linde v. Emmick, 16 Cal.App.2d 676, 61 P.2d 338, syl. 23, 1936. And the California court has, unwisely it would seem, limited evidence of specific habit to cases where there are no eye-witnesses. Boone v. Bank of America Ass'n, 220 Cal. 93, 29 P.2d 409, syl. 3, 1934 (habit of speeding on motorcycle on particular road). Compare Notes, 20 Calif.L.Rev. 208, 1931, and 1952 U.C. L.A. Intramural L.Rev. 1.

10. The use of such expressions has served to obscure the distinction between character and specific

habit, so that judges of distinction have occasionally treated evidence of a particular habit to show a particular act in accord, as if it had no greater relevance than general character for care. See, e. g., Louisville & N. R. Co. v. McClish, 115 F. 268, syl. 5, C.C.A.Tenn., 1902 (habit of jumping on moving trains at a particular place); Missouri, Kansas & Texas R. Co. v. Johnson, 92 Tex. 380, 48 S.W. 568, 1898 (engineer's habit of going to sleep while running his engine). A case on the border between habit and isolated acts of carelessness is Brownhill v. Kivlin, 317 Mass. 168, 57 N.E.2d 539, 1944 (Negligent burning of garage, defendant's previous acts of carelessness in smoking excluded), Note, 25 Boston U.L.Rev. 64, 1945.

11. The phrase may denote a general disposition for excessive drinking, or may amount to a specific habit of drinking a certain number of glasses of whiskey every day on going home from work, and according to medical beliefs such addiction may amount to a specific abnormality or disease. The probative force of such "habits" to prove drunkenness on a particular occasion depends on the degree of regularity of the practice and its coincidence with the occasion. On the other hand, "habits" of sobriety may well point to unvarying temperance or abstention and would seem to be highly probative on the question of sobriety on the particular occasion. Contra: Chesapeake & Ohio R. Co. v. Riddle, 24 Ky.L.Rep. 1687, 72 S.W. 22, syl. 4 (1903). Evidence of a habit of drinking may be probative enough to be admissible, when there is other evidence, but not sufficient standing alone to show a drunken condition at a particular time. See Lewis v. Houston Elec. Co., 39 Tex.Civ.App. 625, 112 S.W. 593 (1905) ("Such evidence would certainly have a material effect upon ordinary minds in determining the issue of intoxication on the particular occasion, and should be allowed to go to the jury. If there is no evidence raising the issue of intoxication on the particular occasion under consideration, evidence as to the habits of the person in this regard would be immaterial and therefore inadmissible."). Conflicting cases are collected in 1 Wigmore, Evidence, § 96.

takenly apply to evidence of specific habit, the restrictions developed for the far less probative and more prejudicial evidence of character.

On the other hand evidence of the "custom" of a business organization or establishment, if reasonably regular and uniform, is usually received much more willingly by the courts,[12] perhaps because there is here no temptation to confuse this with evidence of character. Thus, it is usually held that when a letter has been written and signed in the course of business and placed in the regular place for mailing, evidence of the custom of the establishment as to the mailing of such letters is receivable as evidence that it was duly mailed.[13]

Proof of the existence of the person's habit or of the custom of the business may be made by testimony of a witness to his conclusion that there was such a habit or practice.[14] It also may be made by evidence of specific instances,[15] though these latter would be subject to the judge's discretion to require that the instances be not too few or too many, and that the time be near and the circumstances be sufficiently similar.

---

12. Moffitt v. Connecticut Co., 86 Conn. 527, 86 Atl. 16, syl. 3 (1913) (practice under rule of company to stop cars at particular corner admitted as evidence that car did not stop at place asserted by plaintiff); Comm. v. Torrealba, 316 Mass. 24, 54 N.E.2d 939, syl. 12 (1944) (custom of store to give sales slip with each purchase received as evidence that goods found in defendant's possession, with no record of sale, were stolen); Lundquist v. Jennison, 66 Mont. 516, 214 Pac. 67, syl. 5 (1923) (breach of warranty of seed wheat; defendant denied selling seed wheat; proof that defendant was engaged in business of selling seed wheat generally received as evidence of sale to plaintiff); Buxton v. Langan, 90 N.H. 13, 3 A.2d 647, syl. 2 (1939) (rule or practice of defendant's shop for employees to test brakes before renting out car); and cases cited 1 Wigmore, Evidence, § 93, note; Dec.Dig., Evidence, ⊂⊃139.

13. This is assumed in the cases and the issue centers upon whether such evidence is sufficient. Some courts, possibly the majority, say that it is not, and that the employee who did the mailing must be produced, though he can only rely, for his testimony that it was mailed, upon the custom. Lieb v. Webster, 30 Wash.2d 43, 190 P.2d 701, syl. 1 (1948); Frank v. Metropolitan Life Ins. Co., 227 Wis. 613, 277 N.W. 643, syl. 1 (1938); Notes, 47 Mich.L.Rev. 420, 25 A.L.R. 9, 13; 86 A.L.R. 541, 544. But probably the more reasonable view is that the evidence is sufficient. Myers v. Moore-

Kile Co., 279 Fed. 233 (C.C.A.Tex.1922); Prudential Trust Co. v. Hayes, 247 Mass. 311, 142 N.E. 73, syl. 1 (1924).

14. This is the method usually employed. See, e. g., Security Mut. Life Ins. Co. v. Klentsch, 169 Fed. 104 (C.C.A.8, 1909) (custom of insured as to payment by cash or check); Fourth Nat. Bank v. Wilson, 168 N.C. 557, syl. 2 (1915) (custom of bank as to sending notices); Smith v. F. W. Heitman Co., 44 Tex.Civ.App. 358, 98 S.W. 1074, syl. 3 (1906) (custom of business as to mailing letters); 1 Wigmore, Evidence, § 93, 2 id. § 375; Model Code of Evidence, Rule 307(3) (a), see note 1, supra.

15. Whittemore v. Lockheed Aircraft Corp., 65 Cal. App.2d 737, 151 P.2d 670, syl. 12 (1944) (evidence that on all four occasions when W flew plane he occupied left hand seat admissible as evidence of his probable conduct on particular occasion); Reagan v. Manchester St. Ry. Co., 72 N.H. 298, 56 Atl. 314, syl. 1 (1903) (testimony of defendant's motorman that he had gone through place of collision "a good many times" at 20 miles an hour competent as tending to show that defendant habitually ran its cars at high speed). 2 Wigmore, Evidence, §§ 375, 376, Model Code of Evidence, Rule 307(3) (b), supra n. 1.

But the line is close between particular instances to show habit or custom, and particular instances to show character for negligence which on an issue of conduct would not be allowed. See § 156, supra.

CHAPTER 18

SIMILAR HAPPENINGS AND TRANSACTIONS

163. Similar Previous Claims, Suits or Defences of a Present Party, Offered against Him.[1]

In this area the need for the exposure of fraudulent claims comes in conflict with the need for the protection of innocent litigants from unfair prejudice. At two extremes the practice is fairly well agreed on. Thus, when it is sought to be shown merely that the plaintiff is a chronic litigant, or a chronic personal injury litigant, the courts consider that the slight probative value is overborne by the danger of prejudice, and they exclude the evidence.[2] At the other extreme, if it is proved not merely that the party has made previous claims or brought suits but that such former claims were similar to the present claim and were false and fraudulent, then the strong relevance of these facts to evidence the falsity of the present claim is apparent and most courts admit them.[3]

The intermediate situation is the difficult one. The evidence offered is that the present party, now suing for a loss claimed to be accidental, such as a loss of property by fire, or personal injury in a collision, has made repeated previous claims of similar losses. Here the relevance is substantial, based on the premise that under the doctrine of chances repeated injuries of the same kind are unlikely to happen to one person by accident.[4] On the other hand such evidence is prejudice-arousing and standing alone

---

1. 3 Wigmore, Evidence, § 963.

2. Dent v. Monarch Life Ins. Co., 231 Mo.App. 283, 98 S.W.2d 123, syl. 5 (1936) (In action on accident policy, permitting cross-examination relating to suits insured had previously brought and claims she had presented to other parties, which suits and claims were not related to case in issue, held abuse of discretion); Palmeri v. Manhattan Ry. Co., 133 N.Y. 261, 30 N.E. 1001, syl. 2 (1892) (action for slander and false imprisonment; judge properly excluded evidence that she was "an habitual litigant"); L. B. Price Mercantile Co. v. Moore, 263 S.W. 657, syl. 7 (Tex.Civ.App.1924) (evidence of other actions by plaintiff and members of her family for personal injuries, having no connection with or bearing on issue involved, to show they were chronic litigants, held properly excluded). Compare Monaghan, The Liability Claim Racket, 3 Law & Cont.Prob. 491 (1936).

3. Sessner v. Comm., 268 Ky. 127, 103 S.W.2d 647, syl. 5 (1937) (disbarment for asserting fictitious claims, evidence of other unfounded claims allowed to show system and plan); People v. Evans, 72

Mich. 367, 377, 40 N.W. 473, 478, syl. 1 (1888) (rape: similar false charges by prosecuting witness against other men, allowed though she denied them on cross-examination; tends to show hallucinations and is not "collateral"); Fairfield Packing Co. v. Southern Mut. F. Ins. Co., 193 Pa. 184, 44 Atl. 317, syl. 1 (1899) (action on fire policy; evidence that employee of and witness for plaintiff made intentional false statement in another proof of loss for same fire, allowed). Contra: Rau v. State, 133 Md. 613, 105 Atl. 867, syl. 3 (1919) (statutory rape; question on cross-examination of prosecutrix, whether she made similar charge falsely against another man, excluded); Comm. v. Regan, 105 Mass. 593 (1870) (similar to last). Cases are collected in 3 Wigmore, Evidence, § 863, note 2. Compare Glueck, Litigious Paranoia, 5 J.Am.Inst. Crim.Law 371 (1915).

4. In Mintz v. Premier Cab Ass'n, 127 F.2d 744 (C.A.D.C.1942), where plaintiff sued for injury in a taxicab collision, it was held proper to allow cross-examination of plaintiff about two claims for personal injury within two years before this one, and to allow counsel to argue that this showed

344

would seldom be sufficient to support a finding of fraud. It seems that the judge, balancing in his discretion probative value against prejudice, should admit the evidence only when the proponent has produced or will produce other evidence of fraud.[5]

We have been discussing the problem in terms of the discrediting by circumstantial evidence of the verity of a party's claim or defence. Similar facts and inferences may be used in attacking the veracity of witnesses.[6] Moreover, it should be noticed that, in keeping with the customary relaxation of the standard of relevancy on cross-examination,[7] it is generally easier to secure the courts' approval of this sort of evidence when sought to be elicited on cross-examination of a party, than when offered by the proponent through the testimony of his own witnesses.

164. Other Misrepresentations and Fraudulent Devices.[1]

The policy against proving other misconduct of a party for the sole purpose of evidencing his character or disposition as raising the inference that he was probably guilty of the misconduct charged in the suit,[2] finds expression in civil as well as in criminal cases. Where redress for fraud or misrepresentation is sought, three alternative theories may be available to support the admission of evidence of other misrepresentations or fraudulent conduct by the party.

1. When under the applicable substantive law, knowledge or intent by such party is an essential ingredient for liability, then if it be proved that the party has made other misrepresentations, of similar purport, and false in fact, this tends to show that the representations in suit were made with *knowledge* of their falsity and with *intent* to deceive.[3] This inference does not require that the other representations should have been identical in purport nor made under precisely like circumstances. Only a reasonable approximation in purport, time and circum-

she was "claim-minded." The court said: "Fortuitous events of a given sort are less likely to happen repeatedly than once. . . . Negligent injury is not unusual, but it is unusual for one person, not engaged in hazardous activities, to suffer it repeatedly within a short period and at the hands of different persons. The court's rulings were therefore right. That all three of appellant's stories may have been true affects the weight of the evidence, not its admissibility. It was for the jury to decide from all the evidence, and from its observation of appellant on the stand, whether she was merely unlucky or was 'claim-minded.'"

In San Antonio Traction Co. v. Cox, 184 S.W. 722, syl. 1 (Tex.Civ.App.1916) the court conceded the force of the argument from probabilities, but held the evidence inadmissible. There the plaintiff sued for injury due to the sudden start of the car from which he was alighting. The defendant offered evidence that 17 claims for similar injuries in alighting from cars had been made by other members of the plaintiff's family! The court held that this was rightly rejected and said: "The evidence fails to connect plaintiff with the other claims, except in one instance in which he was with a cousin when he had his fall, and also witnessed the release executed by him to the company. We fail to find in the testimony given or excluded that evidence of concerted action such as is required to constitute a conspiracy. It is just as probable, if not more so, that each incident stood alone as that a conspiracy existed, and it is mere guesswork to say that any of the parties conspired together."

5. See Concordia Fire Ins. Co. v. Wise, 114 Okl. 254, 246 Pac. 595, syl. 3, 46 A.L.R. 456 (1926) (action on fire-policy, frequent previous fires and collection of insurance, excluded especially since it did not appear that any of the properties were over-insured); Keiter v. Miller, 111 Pa.Super. 594, 170 Atl. 364, syl. 1 (1934) (in action on alleged contract to pay for board and lodging furnished defendant's minor son, where defense was that boy was to be cared for in return for his companionship, permitting cross-examination of defendant as to whether he raised same defense respecting other children cared for by strangers held error).

6. See cases and references cited in note 3, above.

7. See § 29, supra.

1. 2 Wigmore, Evidence, §§ 301–304, 321, Dec.Dig., Evidence, ⚷135.

2. See §§ 155, 157, above.

3. Shea v. United States, 236 Fed. 97, syl. 2–6 (C.C.A. 6, 1916) (use of mails to defraud, by bogus betting on pretended turf exchange; other similar fraud by de-

stance is needed to ground the inference of knowledge or intent.

2. If the actual making of the misrepresentations charged in the suit is at issue, then to show the party's *conduct* in making the representations or committing the other acts of fraud as alleged, it is competent to prove other representations closely similar in purport or other fraudulent acts, when they may be found to be parts of a larger or continuing *plan* or *design*, of which the acts or misrepresentations in suit may also be found to be an intended part or object.[4] Similarly, it would seem that if the identity of the perpetrator of the fraud in suit were in doubt, then other fraudulent acts of the party so like the conduct in suit as to earmark them as the product of the same mind and hand, would be received to show that he was the perpetrator.[5]

3. The courts have not generally gone so far, but it is believed that the admission of

evidence of previous similar misrepresentations to show the making of the present representations should, in civil cases at least, be extended to cover the situation where there is testimony asserting the making of the misrepresentation at issue, and testimony denying it. Here it seems that evidence in reply of other like misrepresentations by the party (whether or not part of a plan or scheme) will be of much value to the trier upon the disputed question and that this need outweighs the danger of prejudice. While such evidence standing alone would not of course be sufficient to establish the issue, it can be of great value in resolving the conflict.

165.   Other Contracts.[1]

Evidence of other contractual transactions between the same parties is readily received when relevant to show the probable meaning they attached to the terms of the contract

---

fendants at another fake turf exchange admissible to show knowledge and intent, but not an unrelated fraud by defendants involving stock transactions); People v. Sceri, 407 Ill. 90, 95 N.E.2d 80, syl. 1, 2 (1950) (confidence game by passing bogus express money orders, evidence that by same devices passed other such orders on same day admissible to show guilty knowledge); Stubly v. Beachboard, 68 Mich. 401, 422, 36 N.W. 192, syl. 2 (1888) (defrauding of plaintiff into making advances by misrepresenting value and title to land; evidence that defendants had defrauded others by similar representations proper to show knowledge and intent); 2 Wigmore, Evidence, § 321, note.

But the evidence cannot come in on this theory if liability attaches from mere misrepresentation without regard to knowledge and intent. Johnson v. Gulick, 46 Neb. 817, 65 N.W. 883, syl. 2, 3 (1896); Stowe v. Wooten, 62 S.W.2d 67, syl. 2 (1933); Standard Mfg. Co. v. Slot, 121 Wis. 14, 98 N.W. 923, syl. 1 (1904). The other representations must be shown to be false. Boyer v. United States, 132 F. 2d 12, 13 (C.A.D.C.1942). Seemingly, if intent rather than knowledge is sought to be shown, acts subsequent as well as before the conduct in suit, may be considered. Johnson v. State, 75 Ark. 427, 88 S.W. 905, syl. 5 (1905); 2 Wigmore, § 316.

4. Mudsill Mining Co. Ltd. v. Watrous, 61 Fed. 163, 179 (C.C.A.Mich.1894) (rescission for fraud in sale of silver mine through device of "salting" ore with

powdered silver; salting of ore by defendant to secure favorable reports in course of previous negotiations for sale of mine to others admissible to show that it was defendant who did the salting on this occasion); Anderson v. State, 218 Ind. 299, 32 N.E. 2d 705, syl. 7 (1941) (Dictum: "From the design so shown it may be inferred that the act carrying out that design was committed by the one who conceived the plan. But here the similar transactions may not be anonymous but must be connected by independent evidence with the person accused. Then they may be used to prove that he did the act carrying out the plan so conceived."); Albrecht v. Rathai, 150 Minn. 256, 185 N.W. 259, 261 (1921) (". . . the other similar frauds shown may be of such a character as to show a series of connected fraudulent doings, a general scheme to defraud, broad enough to include that under consideration, and of which it is a part, so as to make them competent as substantive proof of it."); 2 Wigmore, Evidence, § 304.

Courts often seem to overlook the availability of this theory of admissibility and by their strictness in limiting admissibility to the purpose of showing knowledge and intent seem unduly to hamper the investigation of fraud. See the forceful comment of S. T. Morris, 24 Tex.L.Rev. 351 (1946).

5. See § 157.

1. 2 Wigmore, Evidence, § 377; Dec.Dig., Evidence, ☞129(6).

in litigation.[2] Likewise, when the authority of an agent is in question, other similar transactions carried on by him in behalf of the alleged principal are freely admitted.[3]

However, when evidence of other contracts is offered as evidence on the issue of the terms or making of the contract in suit, the courts have shown a surprisingly stiff attitude, beguiled perhaps by the mystical influence of the *res inter alios acta* phrase or misled by a confusion of the requirements of sufficiency and relevancy.[4] When the evidence offered is of other contracts between the same parties, they have been willing to acknowledge that other similar contracts showing a custom, habit or continuing course of dealing between the same parties may be received as evidence of the terms of the present bargain.[5] Many courts, however,

draw a line here and hold that a party's other contracts with third persons offered as evidence of the terms of the disputed contract are inadmissible.[6]

This is too inflexible and bars out information valuable to the trier. Contracts of a party with third persons may show the party's customary practice and course of dealing and thus be highly probative as bearing on the terms of his present agreement.[7] Even short of such extensive acts, when a business man has once adopted a particular mode of handling a bargaining topic, such as warranty, discount or the like, in a certain kind of transactions, it is often easier for him to follow the same solution in respect to the same feature of a new contract, than it is to work out a new one.

2. See, e. g., Bourne v. Gatliff, 11 C. & F. 45, 49, 70, 8 Eng.Rep. 1019 (H.L.1844) (to ascertain meaning of bill of lading provision as to delivery of goods to owner, previous transactions may be looked to).

3. Lytle v. Bank of Dothan, 121 Ala. 215, 26 So. 6, syl. 2 (1899) (authority to execute notes for defendant, other notes executed for him and recognized, admitted); Texas Land and Loan Co. v. Watson, 3 Tex.Civ.App. 233, 22 S.W. 873, syl. 1 (1893).

4. See § 152, above.

5. Wood v. Finson, 91 Me. 280, 39 Atl. 1007, syl. 2 (1898) (whether seller of oil agreed to insure it; previous sales between parties where seller insured, admissible; " . . . while the fact of whether there had been insurance effected on previous sales, or not, might not be conclusive as to what was done in this particular instance, it was admissible on the question of probability or improbability of the contract being as claimed by plaintiff."); Winakur v. Sapourn, 156 Md. 662, 145 Atl. 342, syl. 1 (1929) (previous practice between parties, as evidence that bill of sale was taken for security). But an isolated previous instance, unaccompanied by any offer to prove additional instances going to show a continued course of dealing would presumably be rejected. See Roney v. Clearfield County Grange Mut. Fire Ins. Co., 332 Pa. 447, 3 A.2d 365, syl. 1, 2 (1939).

6. Roberts v. Dixon, 50 Kan. 436, 31 Pac. 1083, syl. 2 (1893) (plaintiff sues for amount of loan; defence, not a loan but a deposit of money to invest in cattle at depositor's risk; held, error to permit defendant to prove that he had made similar cattle-investment contracts with third persons); Stuart v.

Kohlberg, 53 S.W. 596 (Tex.Civ.App.1899) (where plaintiff claims that he signed the bond under an agreement with defendant that the latter should hold him harmless against loss by reason thereof, evidence that defendant, at the time he was endeavoring to procure the bond, solicited another to act as surety, under an agreement to save him harmless, is inadmissible).

7. Woodward v. Buchanan, [1870] 5 Q.B. 285 (dispute whether defendant as owner and principal had ordered work to be done on houses; held, evidence that defendant had ordered other work on same houses from third persons, properly received); Moody v. Peirano, 4 Cal.App. 411, 88 Pac. 380, syl. 7 (1907) (suit for breach of warranty of wheat, sold as "White Australian"; defendant denies warranty; held, proper for judge in discretion to permit plaintiff to prove that defendant had sold other wheat from same shipment to third persons as "White Australian"); Murphy v. Backer, 67 Minn. 510, 70 N.W. 799, syl. 1, 2 (1897) (claim that note was usurious: court allowed defendant to be cross-examined about other usurious loans to other persons, held proper in discretion); Ogden Commission Co. v. Campbell, 66 Utah 563, 244 Pac. 1029, 1030 (1926) (conceding the principle but held inapplicable). See Chandler v. People's National Bank, 140 S.C. 433, 138 S.E. 888, syl. 4 (1927) (where party testified this contract was like others, others admissible), and Maloney Tank Mfg. Co. v. Mid-Continent Petroleum Corp., 49 F.2d 146, syl. 13, C.C.A. Okl., 1931 (other contracts may show a "uniform course of dealing").

No strict rules or limits of admissibility are appropriate. There is no danger of unfair prejudice here. Seemingly, the courts should admit the evidence of other contracts in all cases where the testimony as to the terms of the present bargain is conflicting, and where the judge in his discretion finds that the probative value of the other transactions outweighs the risk of waste of time and confusion of issues.[8]

166. Other Sales of Similar Property as Evidence of Value.[1]

In case of ordinary personal property, where market value is sought, of course the most obvious resort is to evidence of what other similar property, whether wheat, shoes, horses, or what not, currently sold for on the market at that place. Not only may evidence of witnesses who know of such sales at first hand be received for this purpose,[2] but price lists and market reports contained in newspapers, though they would be hearsay if offered to show the actual sales recited,[3] and would be excluded by some courts on that ground, should be admitted as circumstantial evidence of what traders would have paid for such property, where such lists and reports are identified by witnesses as the lists and reports which were actually relied upon by traders in buying and selling of such commodity.[4]

Where the property, such as a pedigreed bull or a Rembrandt etching, is not of a standardized sort, one encounters difficulties as to whether any other like article sold is sufficiently similar for its price to be indicative.

Any tract of land is considered unique, and consequently it is in cases of land valuation, and especially in condemnation cases, that the question of admissibility of evidence of prices paid on other sales is most frequently discussed. A few states have been unwilling to admit such evidence save in exceptional circumstances.[5] This seems to put too heavy a strain on opinion evidence and the general

---

8. In Moody v. Peirano, described in the next preceding note, the court said: "The number and frequency of the sales in which the warranty had been made, and their proximity in time to the sale made to the plaintiff, would be circumstances addressed to the discretion of the court in determining the relevancy of the testimony; and, unless it should clearly appear therefrom that the court had abused its discretion, its action in admitting the evidence could not be regarded as error. These circumstances would also be addressed to the jury in determining the inference to be drawn from the testimony, or the strength of the probability in support of which it was introduced. The weight or conclusiveness to be given by the jury is entirely distinct from the question of the relevancy of the testimony." See also Wilkinson v. Dilenbeck, 184 Iowa 81, 168 N.W. 115, 116 (1918) where the trial judge's action in excluding testimony as to defendant's promises to other persons was sustained and the court said: "There is some force in the suggestion that such testimony had a tendency to corroborate the claims of the various plaintiffs, and that some latitude along that line could have been permitted. Some discretion, however, must be permitted to the trial court as to how far it will permit a digression from the main issue to collateral ones which bear only on the question of corroboration."

1. 2 Wigmore, Evidence, §§ 463, 464; McCormick, Damages 177–179 (1935); 20 Am.Jur., Evidence, §§ 375–381; Dec.Dig., Evidence, ☞142, 32 C.J.S. 444–450; Notes, 36 Corn.L.Q. 137 (1950); 118 A.L.R. 870, 174 A.L.R. 386.

2. See Goralnik Hat Co. v. Delohery Hat Co., 98 Conn. 560, 120 Atl. 283 (1923).

3. Doherty v. Harris, 230 Mass. 341, 119 N.E. 863 (1918). Even though hearsay, if they are shown to be regularly kept and generally relied on, they will be admitted in many jurisdictions under a special exception to the rule excluding hearsay. Sisson v. Cleveland & T. R. Co., 14 Mich. 489, 496, 90 Am.Dec. 252 (1866).

4. Fairley v. Smith, 87 N.C. 367, 42 Am.Rep. 522 (1882); Marden, Orth & Hastings Corporation v. Trans-Pacific Corporation, 109 Wash. 296, 186 Pac. 884 (1920); Rice v. Eisner, 16 F.2d 358 (C.C.A.N.Y. 1926) ("bid" and "asked" quotations on stocks from financial journal).

5. City of Los Angeles v. Hughes, 202 Cal. 731, 262 Pac. 737 (1928); Board of Education of City of Minneapolis v. Heywood Mfg. Co., 154 Minn. 486, 192 N.W. 102 (1923) (inadmissible except where other evidence unobtainable); Commission of Conservation of Department of Conservation v. Hane, 248 Mich. 473, 227 N.W. 718 (1929), commented on

knowledge of the jurors, and the view of the majority of courts which admits such evidence,[6] within safeguarding limits,[7] seems preferable. These safeguards are the following: The sales of the other tracts must have been sufficiently near in time, and the other land must be located sufficiently near the land to be valued, and must be sufficiently alike in respect to character, situation, usability, and improvements, to make it clear that the two tracts are comparable in value and that the price realized for the other land may fairly be considered as shedding light on the value of the land in question.[8] Manifestly, the trial judge in applying so vague a standard must be granted a wide discretion.[9]

Since the market value sought is the estimate of what a willing buyer would have paid a willing seller, prices on other sales of a forced character are inadmissible.[10] This excludes awards in condemnation of other land,[11] and many courts would automatically exclude evidence offered by the condemner of prices paid to other owners, on the theory that the threat, express or implied, of condemnation makes the sale too compulsive to be a fair indication of value.[12] On the other hand this compulsion is not like a forced sale under execution. The owner here may have his land taken but he knows that he will be entitled to a judicial award of its market value. So, under what seems the better view, the evidence of the price paid should come in if the condemner can satisfy the judge that the price paid was sufficiently voluntary to be a reasonable index of value.[13] In any event, the sale must be genuine, and the price must be actually paid or substantially secured.[14]

For prices on other lands to be admitted, they must be sale prices, and not mere offers.[15] These would often be of great sig-

---

in 14 Minn.L.Rev. 689; Broomall v. Pennsylvania R. Co., 296 Pa. 132, 145 Atl. 703 (1929).

6. See, e. g., United States v. Ham, 187 F.2d 265, syl. 3, 4 (C.C.A. 8, 1951); Rhodes v. Davis, 374 Ill. 65, 28 N.E.2d 113, syl. 2 (1940); Lawrence v. O'Neill, 317 Mass. 393, 58 N.E.2d 140, syl. 9 (1944); Langdon v. Loup River Pub. Power Dist., 142 Neb. 859, 8 N.W.2d 201, syl. 14 (1943) (qualifying earlier holdings); Village of Lawrence v. Greenwood, 300 N.Y. 231, 90 N.E.2d 53, syl. 3, 4 (1949), noted 36 Corn.L.Q. 137 (overruling earlier holdings); and see cases cited in Notes, 118 A.L.R. 870, 174 A.L.R. 387.

7. See cases under note 8, infra.

8. U. S. v. Nickerson, 2 F.2d 502 (C.C.A.Mass.1924); Campbell v. City of New Haven, 101 Conn. 173, 125 Atl. 650 (1924); Wassenich v. City and County of Denver, 67 Colo. 456, 186 Pac. 533 (1920); East Side Levee and San Dist. v. Jerome, 306 Ill. 577, 138 N.E. 192 (1923) (excluded; too dissimilar); Condemnation of Land in West Park District under Kansas City Ordinance No. 37008 v. Boruff, 295 Mo. 28, 243 S.W. 167 (1922); In re Condemnation of Lands (In re State Road and Bridge Commission), 180 Wis. 45, 192 N.W. 380 (1923). The burden is on the proponent of the evidence of other sales, to prove as preliminary that the property and conditions were similar. City of Chicago v. Harbecke, 409 Ill. 425, 100 N.E.2d 616, syl. 5 (1951).

9. Forest Preserve District of Cook County v. Barchard, 293 Ill. 556, 127 N.E. 878 (1920); Tucker v.

Town of Hampton, 96 N.H. 28, 69 A.2d 695, syl. 2 (1949); Hervey v. City of Providence, 47 R.I. 378, 133 Atl. 618 (1926); Charleston & W. C. R. Co. v. Spartanburg Bonded Warehouse, 151 S.C. 542, 149 S.E. 236 (1929).

10. Finch v. Grays Harbor County, 121 Wash. 486, 209 Pac. 833, 835, 24 A.L.R. 644 (1922); State Highway Comm. v. Lally (N.J.Sup.), 147 Atl. 487 (1929); Monongahela West Penn Public Service Co. v. Monongahela Development Co., 101 W.Va. 165, 132 S.E. 380, 382 (1926).

11. Shoemaker Co. v. Munsey, 37 App.D.C. 95 (1911); City of Chicago v. Lehmann, 262 Ill. 468, 104 N.E. 829, 831 (1914); City of Springfield v. Schmook, 68 Mo. 394 (1878).

12. Lynn v. City of Omaha, 153 Neb. 193, 43 N.W.2d 527, syl. 1 (1950), and cases cited in Note, 174 A.L.R. 395.

13. Amory v. Comm., 321 Mass. 240, 72 N.E.2d 549, 559, syl. 25, 26, 174 A.L.R. 370, 384 (1947); Chesapeake & Ohio Ry. Co. v. Johnson, 134 W.Va. 619, 60 S.E.2d 203, syl. 8 (1950), and cases cited in Note, 174 A.L.R. 396.

14. See Muccino v. Baltimore & O. R. Co., 33 Ohio App. 102, 168 N.E. 752 (1929), and comment 39 Yale L.J. 748.

15. The following include cases of evidence of offers to buy or sell the land in question, as well as offers on similar land: Thornton v. City of Birmingham,

nificance, but the effort to determine their genuineness would lead to collateral disputes and waste of time at the trial. However, if one of the parties to the present action has himself offered to buy or sell the land in question, or other similar neighboring land, evidence of this offer may be offered against (not for) him as an admission.[16]

167. Other Accidents and Injuries in Negligence Cases.[1]

Proof of other similar accidents and injuries, offered for various purposes in negligence cases, is another kind of evidence which may present for consideration the counter-pulls of the probative value of and need for the evidence on the one hand, and on the other the danger of surprise, prejudice, undue consumption of time and distraction of

the jury's attention from the issues.[2] A few courts, influenced by an early Massachusetts decision,[3] have adopted a more or less inflexible rule of exclusion.[4] Most courts, however, wisely confide in the trial judge's discretion,[5] reviewable only for abuse, the responsibility for determining the balance of advantage and of admitting or excluding the evidence. Even in these liberal jurisdictions, most trial judges will scrutinize cautiously offers of evidence of other accidents, and counsel for proponent must be prepared to overcome opposition and to convince the judge of the preponderant value and need for such proof. The prospects for success will be much affected by the purpose for which the proof is offered, which in turn determines whether, and how strictly, the requirement of proof of similarity of conditions will be ap-

---

250 Ala. 661, 35 So.2d 545, syl. 11, 7 A.L.R.2d 773 (1948); Peagler v. Davis, 143 Ga. 11, 84 S.E. 59, Ann.Cas.1917A, 232 (1915) (price at which property listed and advertised); Music v. Big Sandy & K. R. R. Co., 163 Ky. 628, 174 S.W. 44, Ann.Cas.1916E, 689 (1915) (offer by witness on stand); Stanley v. Sumrell, 163 S.W. 697, 700 (Tex.Civ.App.1914); Atkinson v. Chicago & N. W. Ry. Co., 93 Wis. 362, 67 N.W. 703, 705 (1896); Sharp v. U. S., 191 U.S. 341, 24 S.Ct. 114, 48 L.Ed. 211 (1903) (offers by third person to buy land in question). Contra: City of Chicago v. Lehmann, 262 Ill. 468, 104 N.E. 829 (1914); Royal Auto Sales Co. v. Bush, 47 R.I. 29, 129 Atl. 594 (1925) (offer to prove rental value). See exhaustive Note, Offer as Evidence of Value, 7 A.L.R.2d 781.

16. Offers by owner to sell, admissible against him, Springer v. City of Chicago, 135 Ill. 552, 26 N.E. 514, 12 L.R.A. 609, 613 (1891); Kaufman v. Pittsburg, C. & W. R. Co., 210 Pa. 440, 60 A. 2 (1904); Phelps v. Root, 78 Vt. 493, 63 Atl. 941, 944 (1906); City of Grand Rapids v. Luce, 92 Mich. 92, 52 N.W. 635 (1892); unless too remote in time to be relevant, Lewisburg & N. R. Co. v. Hinds, 134 Tenn. 293, 183 S.W. 985, L.R.A.1916E, 420 (1916).

1. 2 Wigmore, Evidence, §§ 252, 458; C. Morris, Proof of Safety History in Negligence Cases, 61 Harv.L.Rev. 205 (1948) (a penetrating and practical discussion on which the present treatment is based); 65 C.J.S., Negligence, § 234; 38 Am.Jur., Negligence, §§ 314, 315; Dec.Dig., Negligence, ⊖ 125; Notes, 2 U.Chi.L.Rev. 647 (1935), 20 Iowa L. Rev. 846, (1935), 28 Tex.L.Rev. 76 (1950) (crossing accidents), 128 A.L.R. 595 (comprehensive).

2. See § 152, supra.

3. Collins v. Dorchester, 6 Cush. (Mass.) 396 (1850).

4. See, e. g., Fox Tucson Theaters Corp. v. Lindsay, 47 Ariz. 388, 56 P.2d 183, syl. 7 (1936); Diamond Rubber Co. v. Harryman, 41 Colo. 415, 92 Pac. 922, 924, syl. 2, 3 (1907); Hudson v. Chicago & N. W. Ry. Co., 59 Iowa 581, 13 N.W. 735, syl. 2 (1882); Bremner v. Newcastle, 83 Me. 415, 22 Atl. 382, (1891). But this influence is on the wane. See, e. g., O'Mara v. Newton & N. W. Ry. Co., 140 Iowa 190, 118 N.W. 377, syl. 1, 2 (1908); Robitaille v. Netoco Community Theatres, 305 Mass. 265, 25 N. E.2d 749, 128 A.L.R. 592, 594 (1949).

5. Cogswell v. C. C. Anderson Stores Co., 68 Idaho 205, 192 P.2d 383, syl. 10, 11 (1948); Robitaille v. Netoco Community Theatres, next preceding note; Benner v. Term. R.R., 348 Mo. 928, 156 S.W.2d 657, syl. 13 (1941); Lee v. Meier & Frank Co., 166 Ore. 600, 114 P.2d 136, syl. 9 (1941); 2 Wigmore, Evidence, § 344. Some leading decisions, however, favoring admissibility do not mention the element of discretion. See, e. g., District of Columbia v. Armes, 107 U.S. 519, 524, 2 Sup.Ct. 840, 27 L.Ed. 618 (1882). The court in Taylor v. Northern States Power Co., 192 Minn. 415, 256 N.W. 674, 675, syl. 2 (1934), seems to cast doubt on the proposition that admission is discretionary, and reversed for the judge's action in excluding the evidence. The case was one, however, where the ruling might well have been considered an abuse of discretion. See Henderson v. Bjork Monument Co., 222 Minn. 241, 24 N.W.2d 42, syl. 8 (1946), where the role of discretion is reaffirmed.

plied. Among the purposes for which the evidence may be tendered are the following:

1. To prove the existence of a particular physical condition, situation or defect. A fireman injured by coal falling from the tender, alleged that this was due to the fact that a bolt was missing from a hinge on the tender gate. To show this fact, he was allowed to prove a later collapse of the gate and the replacement of the bolt.[6] But this is a sensational way of proving it, and unless the fact is substantially disputed, the judge might not find sufficient need for the evidence.

2. To show that the plaintiff's injury was caused by the alleged defective or dangerous condition or situation.[7] For this purpose the other accidents may have occurred after, as well as before, the injury sued for.[8] Ordinarily the need is plainer here than in the next previous situation, since the issue of cause is usually in genuine dispute and the inference of causation is an elusive one as to

which circumstantial evidence is appropriate. It must appear that conditions of the other accident and of the present one were similar.[9]

The next two theories are the ones most frequently invoked.

3. To show that the situation as of the time of the accident sued for was dangerous.[10] This points to a quality of the objective situation, namely, its capacity to produce or cause harm. This is the chief battleground over the admissibility of other accidents. If it is material to establish that the situation was hazardous, the fact that it has produced harm on other occasions is a natural and convincing way of showing it. Other methods such as expert testimony as to danger, which is likely to evoke an objection as being an opinion on the issue,[11] or reliance on a description of the situation plus the jury's general knowledge of its dangerous quality,[12] may be inadequate in particular

---

6. Gulf, C. & S. F. Ry. Co. v. Brooks, 73 S.W. 571, syl. 4 (Tex.Civ.App.1903). See also Hebenheimer v. St. Louis, 269 Mo. 92, 189 S.W. 1180, 1183, syl. 9 (1916) (that coal hole cover had slipped previously when passers-by stepped on it properly received to show it was in condition in which it would tilt when stepped on).

7. Gorman v. County of Sacramento, 92 Cal.App. 656, 268 Pac. 1083, syl. 8 (1928) (prior accidents to show boy rode bicycle off bridge by reason of absence of guard rails); Carter v. Yardley & Co., 319 Mass. 92, 64 N.E.2d 693, syl. 2, 164 A.L.R. 559 (1946) (In action to recover for a burn sustained as result of using perfume manufactured by defendant, testimony of other witnesses that same perfume irritated their skins was competent to show probability that injury to plaintiff was caused by some harmful ingredient in perfume other than by her own peculiar susceptibility and to authorize inference that skin of plaintiff and the witnesses was normal.); Wight v. H. G. Christman Co., 244 Mich. 208, 221 N.W. 314, syl. 15 (1928) (previous fires set by steam shovel to show that fire burning plaintiff's house came from that source). The other accident may also help to show notice. Young v. Bank of America, 95 Cal.App.2d 725, 214 P.2d 106, syl. 6, 16 A.L.R.2d 1155 (1950) (injury to infant from defect in check on swinging door). And danger. Ringelheim v. Fidelity Trust Co.,

330 Pa. 69, 198 Atl. 628, syl. 1 (1938) (fall on floor due to excess of floor polish, other falls show cause and dangerous character of place).

8. Ringelhiem v. Fidelity Trust Co., supra.

9. Ringelheim v. Fidelity Trust Co., supra.

10. Henwood v. Chaney, 156 F.2d 392, syl. 8, 9 (C C.A. 8th 1946, cert. den. 329 U.S. 760, 67 S.Ct. 113) (fall in slippery railroad yard; other falls admitted); City of Birmingham v. Levens, 241 Ala. 47, 200 So. 888, syl. 1 (1941) (fall from stumbling over iron stake in sidewalk); City and County of Denver v. Brubaker, 97 Colo. 501, 51 P.2d 352, syl. 2 (1935) (falls on icy sidewalk); Lindquist v. Des Moines Union Ry. Co., 239 Iowa 356, 30 N.W.2d 120, syl. 8 (1948) (automobile ran into side of boxcar blocking crossing: similar accidents to show hazard and notice; repudiating exclusionary rule of earlier decisions); 39 C.J.S., Negligence, § 234 (4).

Other accidents after, as well as before, may be relevant for this purpose. Taylor v. Northern States Power Co., 192 Minn. 415, 256 N.W. 674, syl. 1 (1934) (fall on wet, slippery linoleum floor).

11. See § 12, supra.

12. The situation may so clearly speak for itself that evidence of other accidents is unnecessary and inadmissible. City of Birmingham v. McKinnon, 200

cases. The requirement of similarity of conditions is probably at its strictest here.[13]

4. To prove that the defendant knew of the danger, or ought in the exercise of reasonable care to have learned of it.[14] If the defendant's duty to maintain a safe place were absolute this theory would not be available. Usually, however, his liability is restricted to a duty merely to use reasonable care to maintain safe conditions including the duty to inspect when due care so requires. An injury occurring from a newly arising peril before the owner has learned of, or had a reasonable opportunity to appreciate, the danger would not be actionable. This restriction on liability widens the scope of evidence by offering an additional theory for receiving proof of other accidents and injuries.

Here, of course, is one instance where the other happening must have occurred before the injury sued for. When possible the proponent will prove directly that the defendant had knowledge of the other accident, but often the nature, frequency,[15] or notoriety [16] of the happenings will afford circumstantial evidence that the defendant was apprised of them, or that the danger had existed so long that the defendant by due inspection should have learned of it. Since all that is required here is that the previous injury should be such as to attract the defendant's attention to the dangerous situation which resulted in the litigated accident, the strictness of the requirement of similarity of conditions imposed when the purpose is to show causation or danger is here much relaxed.[17] The warning

Ala. 11, 75 So. 487, 489, syl. 5 (1917) (where stake and wire were about two feet above sidewalk situation certainly and obviously dangerous).

13. Illustrative cases wherein the requirement was held not satisfied: Wilkins v. G. Fox & Co., 125 Conn. 738, 7 A.2d 434, syl. 3 (1939) (injury while getting on an escalator, other injuries, in getting off, not similar); Robitaille v. Netoco Community Theatres, 305 Mass. 265, 25 N.E.2d 749, 128 A.L. R. 592, 595 (1940) (injury from fall on loose carpet, error to receive evidence other girls fell at same spot, in absence of evidence condition of carpet same at that time); Foreman v. Chicago, R. I. & P. Ry. Co., 181 Okl. 259, 74 P.2d 350, syl. 6 (1937) (crossing accident: no error to exclude other accidents in absence of showing of identity of conditions); Note, 128 A.L.R. 601–603.

14. See, e. g., Hecht Co. v. Jacobsen, 180 F.2d 13, syl. 6 (C.A.D.C.1950) (accident to child on escalator; accident to another child seven years before on a similar model escalator but on a different floor, received); Lynch v. L. B. Sprague, Inc., 95 N.H. 485, 66 A.2d 697, syl. 11 (1949) (action by guest against hotel for injury sustained when ladder for entering upper bunk fell; evidence hooks pulled out of other ladders received); and cases cited in 2 Wigmore, Evidence, § 252, and in Note, 128 A.L.R. 596.

15. Moore v. Bloomington D. & C. Ry. Co., 295 Ill. 63, 67, 128 N.E. 721, 722 (1920).

16. Lombar v. East Tawas, 86 Mich. 14, 20, 48 N. W. 947, 948, syl. 2 (1891).

17. McCormick v. Great Western Power Co., 214 Cal. 658, 8 P.2d 145, syl. 6, 7 (1932) (plaintiffs

sued for shocks received from defendant's high tension wires while installing iron work on fifth floor of building under construction; evidence that other workmen had been injured by defendant's wires during construction of a nearby building received); Taylor v. Stafford, 196 Ill. 288, 63 N.E. 624, syl. 1 (1902) (the plaintiff claimed injuries from stumbling on a stake protruding between the planks of a side-walk; the court held that evidence that there were other stakes protruding along the same block was held properly received, "not to prove negligence," but to show a general unsafe condition of the side-walk "from which notice may fairly be inferred"). See also cases holding that proof of other defects may be received to show notice, e. g., Shaw v. Sun Prairie, 74 Wis. 105, 42 N.W. 271, syl. 1 (1889) (suit for fall on defective side-walk; evidence of condition of side-walk for 50 or 60 feet each way from the place of fall, and its generally defective condition, properly admitted to show constructive notice to city). The distinction, however, is occasionally overlooked. See Thompson v. Buffums, Inc., 17 Cal.App.2d 401, 62 P.2d 171, syl. 1, 2 (1936). In that case the plaintiff was injured while walking down the stairs at defendant's store. She caught her shoe in a defective safety-tread on the tenth step. Plaintiff, cross-examining the defendant's superintendent asked him, "Have any other women fallen on these particular stairs." Excluded. This ruling was sustained on appeal, on the ground that the inquiry was not limited to the tenth step. See also Moore v. Bloomington D. & Co. R. Co., 295 Ill. 63, 128 N.E. 721, syl. 5 (1920) (evidence of accidents on north side of railway crossing not competent to show either notice or dangerous condition in suit for ac-

radius of the happening is wider than its relevance for these other purposes.

5. When the defendant by pleading, opening statement, or by the testimony of his witnesses has asserted that the injury sued for could not have been caused by the defendant's conduct as alleged, then the plaintiff may show other similar happenings to rebut the claim of impossibility.[18]

Absence of other accidents or injuries.[19] It would seem that if other accidents and injuries are admisssible where circumstances are similar, in the judge's discretion, to show such matters as the existence of a particular defect or condition, or that the injury sued for was caused in a certain way, or that a situation is dangerous, or that defendant knew or should have known of the danger, then logically it would follow that proof of the absence of such accidents during a period of similar exposure and experience, would generally be receivable to show the non-existence of these facts.

It is true that frequently the proof of absence of accidents does not have as much persuasive force, to show a safe situation, as the proof of another accident may in establishing danger, but that, it seems, is a matter of weight merely. Particular decisions excluding evidence of this kind of "safety-history" may sometimes be justified on the ground that the persons passing in safety do not appear to have been exposed to the same test and use as occurred at the time of the injury sued for.[20] However, specific proof to that effect should not be required when the experience sought to be proved is so extensive as to justify the inference that it included an adequate number of situations like the one in suit.[21]

There are nevertheless a considerable number of decisions laying down a general rule against proof of absence of other accidents. A few of these are by courts aligned with the minority group denying admission generally to proof of other accidents.[22] But some are

---

cident which occurred on south side of same crossing).

18. Texas & N. O. Ry. Co. v. Glass, 107 S.W.2d 924, syl. 3–5 (Tex.Civ.App.1937) (suit for destruction of barn by sparks from locomotive; testimony by defendant's experts that defendant's oil-burning locomotives are so constructed as not to emit sparks; held, plaintiff may rebut by evidence as to other fires set by such locomotives). An analogous problem is presented in such cases as Auzene v. Gulf Public Service Co., 188 So. 512, La.App., 1939. The plaintiff sued for injury from the explosion of a Coca-Cola bottle. The defendant's witnesses testified that its method of bottling was such that explosions could not occur. The plaintiff offered evidence of other instances of explosions, and it was held that the evidence was competent. A similar result was reached in Perry v. Kelford Coca-Cola Bottling Co., 196 N.C. 175, 690, 145 S.E. 14, 146 S.E. 805, 1928. Contra: Parsonnet v. Keil's Newark Bakery, Inc., 119 N.J.Law 301, 196 Atl. 661, 1938. Cases are collected in Decennial Digests, Negligence, ⬤125, Food, ⬤25(i).

19. 65 C.J.S., Negligence, § 234b; 38 Am.Jur., Negligence, § 315; Note, 128 A.L.R. 595, 606; Dec. Dig., Negligence, ⬤125.

20. See, e. g., Taylor v. Town of Monroe, 43 Conn. 36 (1875) (action for injury to plaintiff, who was

McCormick Evidence HB—23

driving buggy, when horse ran away, and overturned buggy, at bridge; plaintiff charged that highway was unduly raised and the railing was defective; held, no error to exclude evidence that in ordinary use of this highway there had been no accidents: absence of accidents would be relevant only if similar experience with runaway horses had been shown); Wray v. Fairfield Amusements Co., 126 Conn. 221, 10 A.2d 600, syl. 8, 9 (1940) (suit for accident to passenger in roller-coaster, held, where injury alleged to be due to defective strap on seat, error to admit evidence generally of absence of accidents to other passengers; should have been limited to experience of passengers riding in the particular seat of the particular car).

21. Erickson v. Walgreen Drug Co., 232 P.2d 210, syl. 4–7 (Utah 1951) (suit for injury from fall on terrazzo floor in entrance-way, rendered slippery by rain; error to exclude evidence that no complaint or report about anyone slipping had been received during 15 years though 4000 to 5000 persons entered the store every day).
As to the hearsay question see § 229.

22. See, e. g., Sanitary Grocery Co., Inc. v. Steinbrecher, 183 Va. 495, 32 S.E.2d 685, syl. 4, 5 (1945) (action by customer for injury from sharp corner of shelving; evidence that 1000 customers had used

by courts which by rule or discretion would admit proof of other accidents.[23] This paradoxical position has sometimes been defended as being justified on grounds of auxiliary policy.[24] It is believed, however, that this justification cannot be sustained. There is here no danger of arousing the prejudice of the jury, as the proof of another accident may do. Moreover, the danger of spending undue time and incurring confusion by raising "collateral issues," conjured up in some of the opinions,[25] seems not at all borne out by experience in jurisdictions where the evidence is allowed. The defendant will seldom open this door if there is any practical possibility that the plaintiff may dispute the fact. The trend of recent decision seems to favor admissibility, and it is believed that evidence of absence of other accidents may be relevant to show, (1) the non-existence of the defect or condition alleged,[26] (2) that the injury was not caused by the defect or condition charged,[27] (3) that the situation was not dangerous,[28] or (4) want of knowledge of, or of ground to realize, the danger.[29]

store daily for eleven months without injury irrelevant).

23. See, e. g., Blackwell v. J. J. Newberry Co., 156 S.W.2d 14, syl. 9–11 (Mo.App.1941) (injury to customer from small concealed step-ladder in aisle).

24. See the interesting opinion of Anderson, J., in Blackwell v. J. J. Newberry Co., supra.

25. See Temperance Hall Association v. Giles, 33 N. J.L. 260, 265 (1869) ("The offer was to show that ten thousand persons passed these premises in each year since the hall was erected, without accident. The admission of this evidence would carry with it the right to cross examine as to the circumstances under which each individual of the multitude passed, and the degree of caution and circumspection used by each; and, also, the right to introduce evidence of the dangers encountered, and by the exercise of superior vigilance, avoided by each one of these individuals, together with evidence that some one or more of them had met with accidents at the place; in turn opening the way for evidence as to the degree of care exercised by such as had not been so fortunate as to escape. . . .").

26. Birmingham Union Ry. Co. v. Alexander, 93 Ala. 133, 9 So. 525 527, syl. 5 (1891) (action against street-railway for injury due to insufficient surfacing and ballasting of its track; "It would therefore have been competent for the plaintiff to prove that other similar casualties had happened at that crossing as tending to show a defective condition of the track. On like considerations the defendant should be allowed the benefit of proof that the track, as it was at the time, was constantly crossed by other persons, under similar conditions, without inconvenience, hindrance, or peril, as evidence tending to show the absence of the alleged defect, or that it was not the cause to which the injury complained of be imputed. The negative proof in the one case, equally with the affirmative proof in the other, serves to furnish the means of applying to the matter the practical test of common experience."); Menard v. Cashman, 93 N.H. 273, 41 A.2d 222, syl. 2 (1945) (In action against owner of building for personal injuries sustained in fall on stairway, evidence that other persons had descended stairs without falling was admissible, as tending to show that stairway was in suitable condition.). The contrary holding in Johnson v. Kansas City Pub. Service Co., 360 Mo. 429, 228 S.W.2d 796, syl. 6 (1950) seems hard to sustain in justice or common sense. There a passenger in a streetcar sued for injury said to be due to tripping over loose metal strip in vestibule. Defendant's witnesses swore that there was no such loose strip. The court held that evidence that over 750 passengers had used the vestibule in the 24-hour period without tripping was properly rejected.

27. Birmingham Union Ry. Co. v. Alexander, supra.

28. Nubbe v. Hardy Continental Hotel System, 225 Minn. 496, 31 N.W.2d 332, syl. 8 (1948) (action for injury due to fall on stairs; error to exclude evidence of defendant's manager that he had not had any reports of other accidents; admissible to show not dangerous, and that defendant was not chargeable with knowledge).

29. Nubbe v. Hardy Continental Hotel System, supra.

CHAPTER 19

INSURANCE AGAINST LIABILITY

168. Insurance against Liability.[1]

This is one of the controversial corners of evidence law. The practice bears the marks of the pressures and counter-pressures of opposing special interests, and the present evidential rule may eventually disappear as the common law principles of negligence liability are displaced by new legislative systems of apportionment of risk for highway accidents.[2]

The starting-point is the accepted doctrine that the fact that defendant is protected by a policy of insurance against liability up to a given amount is not relevant as evidence of negligence.[3] The financial protection may somewhat diminish the normal incentive to be careful, but this is of slight effect since the motive of regard for personal safety is usually present and is a much stronger in-

centive, and in any event it is overborne by the counter-argument that the fact of insurance marks the defendant as one of the insured class, who may be assumed to be the more prudent and careful group as compared to the uninsured class.

Upon this principle of irrelevancy to show negligence—a rather inadequate foundation—has been built a general rule that evidence of the fact of such insurance is inadmissible[4] unless it falls within some one of a group of exceptional situations.[5] In these situations presumably the trial judge's discretionary power to exclude could still be invoked if he should consider that the need for and value of the evidence were outweighed by its likelihood of misuse by the jury.[6] What are these exceptions?

1. 2 Wigmore, Evidence, § 282a; 20 Am.Jur. Evidence, §§ 388–392; Notes, 56 A.L.R. 1418, 74 A.L.R. 849, 95 A.L.R. 388, 105 A.L.R. 1319, 4 A.L.R.2d 761; Black, Admissibility of Evidence that Defendant Has or Has Not Liability Insurance, 38 W.Va. L.Q. 362, 1932; Allen, Why Do Courts Coddle Automobile Indemnity Companies, 61 Am.L.Rev. 77, 1927; Gusmano, Admissibility in New York of Evidence That Defendant Is Insured, 14 St. John's L.Rev. 319, 1940; Roach, Evidence of Liability Insurance in Texas, 29 Tex.L.Rev. 949 (1951); Wilson, Evidence of Liability Insurance in Texas, 2 Baylor L. Rev. 25 (1949).

Analogous problems arise as to disclosure of insurance held by plaintiffs. See McDonald v. Alamo Motor Lines, 22 S.W.2d 1023 (Tex.Civ.App.1949), Note, 2 Baylor L.Rev. 462.

2. See, e.g., Green, The Individual's Protection under Negligence Law: Risk Sharing, 47 Northwestern Univ.L.Rev. 751 (1953); Philbrick, Loss Apportionment in Negligence Cases, 99 U. of Pa.L.Rev. 572 (1951); Malone, Damage Suits and the Contagious Principle of Workmen's Compensation (Tort Liability: Absolute Liability Challenges Moral Fault), 12 La.L.Rev. 231, 9 N.A.C.C.A. L.J. 20 (1952);

Ehrenzweig, Negligence without Fault: Trends Toward an Enterprise Liability for Insurable Loss (1951).

3. See, e.g., Sutton v. Bell, 79 N.J. Law 507, 77 Atl. 42, syl. 1 (1910); Barrett v. Bonham Oil & Cotton Co., 57 S.W. 602 (Tex.Civ.App. 1900). Uniform Rules of Evidence, R. 54: "Evidence that a person was, at the time a harm was suffered by another, insured wholly or partially against loss arising from liability for that harm is inadmissible as tending to prove negligence or other wrongdoing."

4. Instances of reversals for admission of the evidence: James Stewart & Co. v. Newby, 266 Fed. 287, 296, syl. 6 (C.C.A. Va. 1920); Watson v. Adams, 187 Ala. 490, 65 So. 528, syl. 1 (1914); Roche v. Llewellyn Ironworks Co., 140 Cal. 563, 74 Pac. 147, syl. 9 (1903).

5. For a listing and discussion of these situations, see Rapoport, Proper Disclosure during Trial that Defendant Is Insured, 26 Corn.L.Q. 137 (1940). See also Note, 4 A.L.R.2d 761, 775–786.

6. Gerry v. Neugebauer, 83 N.H. 23, 136 Atl. 751, syl. 7 (1927) (plaintiff in cross-examining defendant's witness, having brought out that he was interviewed by defendant's counsel, sought to elicit

First, the fact of insurance may be relevant upon some other issue, such as agency [7] or ownership [8] or control [9] of the vehicle or instrumentality involved.

Second, the fact of insurance may be relevant as bearing upon the credibility of a witness.[10]

Third, the admission of a party bearing on negligence or damages may include a reference to the fact of insurance which cannot be severed without substantially lessening the evidential value of the admission.[11]

Fourth, the fact of insurance may be elicited unintentionally by examining counsel, when the witness makes an unexpected or unresponsive reference to insurance.[12] The witness often is unaware of the conspiracy of silence about insurance and makes with utmost naturalness a reference to this all-pervading fact. The reference will be stricken on request but is usually not a ground for mistrial or reversal.

There is a fifth situation which though not an exception to the rule excluding evidence of insurance actually results in bringing before the jurors at the outset a strong intimation that the defendant is actually insured. This is the practice which obtains in most of the states of permitting the plaintiff's counsel in examining the prospective jurors upon their qualifications where it ap-

---

that witness had also been interviewed by insurance adjuster; held, while proper to impeach, yet defendant was entitled to trial judge's discretionary ruling as to whether the answer would do more harm than good; excellent discussion by Snow, J.); see § 152.

7. Biggins v. Wagner, 60 S.D. 581, 245 N.W. 385, syl. 1, 85 A.L.R. 385 (1932) (whether truck-driver-owner was employee or independent contractor).

8. Layton v. Cregan v. Mallory Co., 263 Mich. 30, 248 N.W. 539, syl. 1, 4 (1933) (where ownership of colliding automobile denied, plaintiff entitled to discovery of policy, which would be admissible on this issue).

9. Perkins v. Rice, 187 Mass. 28, 72 N.E. 323, syl. 1 (1904) (defendant admitted ownership of premises but denied that he had control of elevator).

10. Vindicator Consol. Gold Min. Co. v. Firstbrook, 36 Colo. 498, 86 Pac. 313, syl. 2 (1906) (witness who testified to execution of release allowed to be cross-examined about his relation with insurance company and fact that it would have to pay judgment); Dempsey v. Goldstein Bros. Amusement Co., 231 Mass. 461, 121 N.E. 429, syl. 2, 3 (1919) (physician who examined plaintiff properly required to testify that he was employed to do so by insurance company); Aguilera v. Reynolds Well Service, 234 S.W. 2d 282, syl. 1–3 (Tex.Civ.App.1950, error refused), Note, Langley, 29 Tex.L.Rev. 845 (held error for judge to refuse to allow cross-examination of apparent disinterested witness to skid-marks at collision, to show that he was local agent of company which wrote defendant's liability policy). But the judge has a lee-way of discretion. Gibson v. Grey Motor Co., 147 Minn. 134, 179 N.W. 729, 730 (1920); Gerry v. Neugebauer, note 6, supra; Demp-

sey v. Goldstein Bros. Amusement Co., supra (as to extent).

When a witness for plaintiff is impeached by a prior inconsistent written statement, may the plaintiff show that the statement was prepared for the witness to sign by an adjuster for the insurance company? Texas Co. v. Betterton, 126 Tex. 359, 88 S.W.2d 1039, syl. 1, 1936 (no); Smith v. Pacific Truck Express, 164 Or. 318, 100 P.2d 474, syl. 13, 1940 (yes).

11. Schlenker v. Egloff, 133 Cal.App. 393, 24 P.2d 224, 1933 (where reference to insurance company is severable from rest of statement, prejudicial error to prove that part); McCurdy v. Flibotte, 83 N.H. 143, 139 Atl. 367, 1927 (plaintiff points out the tracks showing he was on right side of road; defendant replies "I should worry; I have got insurance"); Hutchinson v. Knowles, 108 Vt. 195, 184 Atl. 705 (1936) (some months after injury defendant told plaintiff "Don't worry, my insurance company said they would settle for your injuries"); Reid v. Owens, 98 Utah 50, 93 P.2d 680, 684, 685, 126 A.L.R. 55, 1939, ("My boy was careless. . . . We have taken out insurance to protect him"; properly received. The reference to insurance was itself freighted with admission"). Compare Herschensohn v. Weisman, 80 N.H. 557, 119 Atl. 705, 28 A.L.R. 514 (1923) where plaintiff, a passenger in defendant's automobile, warned the defendant to be careful or he would kill somebody, and the defendant said: "Don't worry, I carry insurance for that." This was held admissible. Cases are collected in Note, 4 A.L.R.2d 761, 781, 782.

12. Pillsbury Flour Mills v. Miller, 121 F.2d 297, syl. 6 (C.C.A.Mo.1941); Williams v. Consumers' Co., 352 Ill. 51, 185 N.E. 217, 219, syl. 4 (1933); Cain v. Kohlman, 344 Pa. 63, 22 A.2d 667, syl. 9 (1941); Note, 4 A.L.R.2d 761, 784–786.

pears that the defendant is protected by insurance,[13] to question them about their possible interest in or employment by a liability insurance company.[14]

Under the pressure of the enactment of more and more stringent financial responsibility laws, the practice of securing insurance protection against liability is rapidly becoming almost universal. In 1950 in seven states and the District of Columbia 90% or more of the vehicles were insured. In the same year throughout the country 73% were insured.[15] When the rule against the disclosure of insurance originated doubtless the existence of such protection for defendants was exceptional and a "hush, hush" policy could be effective. But when we consider the ways in which the fact of insurance may be properly disclosed in evidence or suggested at the beginning of the trial upon the examination of jurors, and the fact that insurance has become usual rather than

exceptional, it seems likely today that in nearly all cases the jury will either be informed of the fact of insurance or will consciously assume that the defendant is so protected.[16] The rule against the introduction of evidence of insurance thus becomes a hollow shell, except as it incidentally protects the defendant against improper argument that the jury should be influenced in their finding of liability or damages by the fact of insurance.

May the defendant give evidence that he is not protected by insurance? In view of the premise on which the rule prohibiting evidence of insurance is based that there is danger that the fact will be used prejudicially by the jury, and in view of the inevitable assumption by jurors today that a defendant is probably insured, fairness seems to demand that a defendant be permitted to avoid the danger by showing that he is not insured. The courts, however, have consid-

---

13. In some states it is customary before asking the question of the jurors for counsel to consult the court privately and request permission to do so. See Moore v. Edmunds, 384 Ill. 545, 52 N.E.2d 216, 218 (1943); Carter v. Rock Island Bus Lines, 345 Mo. 1170, 139 S.W.2d 458, 459 (1940); Lynch v. Alderton, 124 W.Va. 446, 20 S.E.2d 657, 660 (1942) (error to ask question before privately consulting the court). At such consultation out of the jury's presence it is proper for the judge to require the defendant's attorney to give the name of any liability insurer he represents. White v. Teague, 353 Mo. 247, 182 S.W.2d 288, syl. 4 (1944).

14. Examples of opinions approving the practice: Moniz v. Bettencourt, 24 Cal.App.2d 718, 76 P.2d 535, syl. 2 (1938) (whether interested in named company or any other); Montanick v. McMillin, 225 Iowa 442, 280 N.W. 608, syl. 4 (1938) (particular company); Lidfors v. Pflaum, 115 Ore. 148, 236 Pac. 1059, syl. 4–6 (1925) (interrogation proper if done in good faith); Lunn v. Ealy, 176 Tenn. 374, 141 S.W.2d 893, syl. 5–8 (1940) (whether interested in any liability insurance company doing business in state, properly allowed in judge's discretion). It has been suggested that the general question as to interest in any such company should first be asked, and only if answered yes, should inquiry be made as to a particular company. Dowd-Feder, Inc. v. Truesdell, 130 Oh.St. 530, 200 N.E. 762, syl. 3 (1936); Santee v. Haggart Const. Co., 202 Minn. 361, 278

N.W. 520, 521 (1938); Low, Note, 28 Dicta 150, 155 (1951).

In Texas, however, the practice of interrogating jurors about insurance has been frowned on by the intermediate appellate courts. Green v. Ligon, 190 S.W.2d 742, 747, syl. 10 (Tex.Civ.App. 1945), and cases cited therein. And in Illinois the right to inquire seems to be hedged in by impractical restrictions. Wheeler v. Rudek, 397 Ill. 438, 74 N.E.2d 601, 4 A.L.R.2d 748 (1947); Notes, 15 U.Chi. L.Rev. 986, 43 Ill.L.Rev. 650.

It has been suggested that this information could be gained without prejudice by examining the entire venire at the time they are first assembled before drawing a panel for any particular case. Comment, 52 Harv.L.Rev. 166 (1938). Or by the use of a questionnaire. Boos, Note, 43 Mich.L.Rev. 621 (1944).

15. Marryott, Automobile Accidents and Financial Responsibility, 287 The Annals 83 (1953).

16. With increasing frequency the judges assert the jurors assume that the defendant is insured. See Learned Hand J., in Brown v. Walter, 62 F.2d 798, 800, C.C.A.Vt., 1933; Collins, J., in Takoma Park Bank v. Abbott, 179 Md. 249, 19 A.2d 169, 176, 1941; Holt, J., in Odegard v. Connolly, 211 Minn. 342, 1 N.W.2d 137, 139, 1941; Bliss, C. J., in Connelly v. Nolte, 237 Iowa 114, 21 N.W.2d 311, 320 (1946) ("He [the juror] doesn't require a brick house to fall on him to give him an idea.").

ered that the balance lies the other way, and have excluded the evidence, as "a form of the inadmissible plea of poverty," [17] except in cases where the plaintiff has injected the suggestion that the defendant is insured.[18]

A re-examination of the soundness and expediency of the general rule forbidding disclosure of the fact of insurance seems desirable. That such fact is irrelevant to show negligence is as we have suggested hardly a sufficient foundation for the rule. The conspiracy of silence is hard to maintain. The truth will out, and the results are extensive arguments on appeal upon elusive questions of prejudice and good faith, and a considerable number of reversals and retrials. The heart of the policy of non-disclosure is really surrendered when the jurors are allowed to be examined upon their connection with insurance companies.

The courts have recently shown some tendency to relax their former stiffness in enforcing the rule by reversals.[19] It is submitted that they might well go further and consider whether evidence of the fact of insurance, though irrelevant on negligence, should not come in pursuant to another long-established policy. This is the principle that every litigant is entitled to know the identity of the party with whom he is contesting [20] and the court is entitled to know the parties that are using its officers and facilities. The company which under its policy is given the exclusive right to employ counsel, defend the suit and control the decision as to settling or contesting the action, is surely a party in all but name. The jury as a part of the tribunal are entitled to the knowledge of the existence of this masked but controlling party.[21] They will then make some assumptions as to the capacity of the insurance company to pay. These are no different from similar assumptions as to the capacity to pay of other corporations who may be parties of record before them. The corrective is not a futile effort at concealment, but an open assumption by the court of its function of explaining to the jury its duty of deciding according to the facts and the substantive law, rather than upon sympathy and ability to pay. The legislatures of Louisiana and Wisconsin have implemented the same policy by statutes which permit the insurance company to be named as a party defendant.[22]

---

17. Piechuck v. Maguziak, 82 N.H. 429, 135 Atl. 534 (1926). Accord: Rojas v. Buocolo, 142 Tex. 152, 177 S.W.2d 962 (1944) (question by juror to one of several defendants). See cases cited in Notes, 4 A.L.R.2d 761, 773, 5 Stanford L.Rev. 143 (1952).

18. Whitman v. Carver, 337 Mo. 1247, 88 S.W.2d 885, syl. 1 (1935) (when plaintiff testified that defendant had stated he had insurance, proper for defendant to testify that he had not so stated, and did not know whether a certain policy covered him). When plaintiff mistakenly questions the jurors on their interest in insurance companies, the defendant may prove that he is not insured. Stehonwer v. Lewis, 249 Mich. 76, 227 N.W. 759, syl. 4, 74 A.L.R. 844 (1939); Vick v. Moe, 74 S.D. 144, 49 N.W.2d 463, syl. 1 (1951). And where some defendants are insured and some not, and the jurors are questioned about insurance, it seems that those not insured should be allowed to show this fact, but the court held to the contrary in

Clayton v. Wells, 324 Mo. 1176, 26 S.W.2d 969, syl. 1 (1930).

19. See statement in Note, 4 A.L.R.2d 761, 764.

20. 8 Wigmore, Evidence, § 2313, and see § 94, herein.

21. See the similar reasoning of Eberly, J., in Jessup v. Davis, 115 Neb. 1, 211 N.W. 190, 56 A.L.R. 1403 (1926) which sustained the right of plaintiff to elicit from the defendant on cross-examination the fact of insurance. Three judges dissented, however, and the holding was later overruled in Fielding v. Publix Cars, Inc., 130 Neb. 576, 265 N.W. 726, 105 A.L.R. 1306 (1936). See Beghtol, Present Rule as to Disclosure of Insurance, 15 Neb.L.B. 327, (1937).

22. La. L.S.A.–R.S. 22:655; Wis.St.1953, §§ 85.93, 260.11. These statutes are set out in part in Note, 4 A.L.R.2d 761, 767. See also Notes, Statutes Permitting Joinder of Insurance Companies, 20 Corn.L.Q. 110, 113 (1934), Joinder under Compulsory Insurance Laws, 39 Ill.L.Rev. 81 (1944).

CHAPTER 20

EXPERIMENTAL AND SCIENTIFIC EVIDENCE

169. Experimental Evidence.[1]

Testing the truth of hypotheses by the use of controlled experiments is one of the key-techniques of modern scientific method.[2] The courts in their task of investigating facts make extensive use of this technique, but under conditions which prevent them from exploiting the process to the full limits of its usefulness. The doctrines relating to experimental evidence are simple and the principal task of the lawyer is to recognize the opportunities for their use, to seize such opportunities boldly, and when experiments are employed to plan them inventively,[3] so that the results derived will be convincing to judge and jury. We are dealing here with experiments carried out before trial and presented at the trial through descriptions given by witnesses of the experiment and its results. Experiments conducted in the court-room itself during the trial are discussed in the chapter on Demonstrative Evidence.[4]

The opportunities are of limitless variety. Some of the types of experiments most frequently encountered are these: testing firearms to show the patterns of powder and shot made upon the object at different distances;[5] experiments by human beings in the holding

[1] Wigmore, Evidence, §§ 445–460; 20 Am.Jur., Evidence, §§ 755–762; Decennial Digests, Evidence ⚖︎150, Criminal Law ⚖︎388; Note, Experimental Evidence, 34 Ill.L.Rev. 206, 1939; Notes, 9 N.C.L. Rev. 453 (1935); 8 A.L.R. 18, 72 A.L.R. 863, 85 A.L.R. 479.

[2] See Conant, On Understanding Science, 104 (1946); Cohen, Reason and Nature, 82 (1931).

[3] Examples of such inventiveness are seen in such cases as People v. Freeman, 107 Cal.App.2d 44, 236 P.2d 396, syl. 9 (1951) (prosecution for burning woods by throwing lighted matches from moving car; state showed moving pictures depicting experiment in which wooden matches were tossed to side of road from jeep with fires resulting); Torgeson v. Missouri-Kansas-Texas R. Co., 124 Kan. 798, 262 P. 564, syl. 2, 55 A.L.R. 1335, 1928 (witnesses described tests they had made as to the safest way of approaching a particular crossing in an automobile, comparing these

methods: (1) merely stopping to look; (2) stopping and going to the track to look; (3) stopping and going to the point whence one could see farthest down the track.); Coca-Cola Bottling Co. v. Breckenridge, 196 Ark. 1177, 114 S.W.2d 7 (1938) (action for injury sustained in drinking coca-cola with spider in bottle; doctor-witness testified that he drank coca-cola with spider in it; also that he made culture from spider kept in coca-cola and injected in rabbits without toxic effect). See also a case described in Note, 34 Ill. L.Rev. 206, 210 (1939) where the services of a "magician" were ingeniously and effectively employed.

[4] See § 182.

[5] State v. Criger, 151 Kan. 176, 98 P.2d 133, syl. 5, 6 (1940) (shot-pattern); Cooper v. State, 61 Okl. Cr. 318, 67 P.2d 981, syl. 3–5 (1937) (powder-burns); Williams v. State, 147 Tex.Cr. 178, 179 S.W.2d 297, syl. 5 (1944) (shot-pattern).

of firearms to determine whether a given gun-shot wound could have been self-inflicted;[6] tests of the visibility of objects or persons at a given distance;[7] and tests of the speed of locomotives and motor vehicles and of the effectiveness of their brakes and headlights.[8] Some specialized tests and experiments of recent origin, such as lie-detector tests, blood-tests for paternity and intoxication, and firearms identification are briefly discussed later in the present chapter.[9]

Here again, as in the problems presented in the preceding sections of this chapter, the question is one of weighing the probative value of the evidence of experiments against the dangers of misleading the jury (who may attach exaggerated significance to the tests), unfair surprise, and, occasionally, undue consumption of time.[10] The danger of arousing

hostility or prejudice is seldom present in respect to this type of evidence. Usually the best gauge of the probative value of experiments is the extent to which the conditions of the experiment were identical with or similar to those obtaining in respect to the litigated happening.[11] Accordingly, counsel in planning experiments must seek to make the conditions as nearly identical as may be, and in presenting the evidence he must be prepared to lay the foundation by preliminary proof of similarity of conditions.[12] Though the similarity formula is sometimes over-rigidly applied, most courts will recognize that the requirement is a relative one,[13] so that where a high degree of similarity is not attainable, the court might still conclude that the results of the experiment are of substantial enlightening value to the jury and

---

6. Downing v. Metropolitan Life Ins. Co., 314 Ill. App. 222, 41 N.E.2d 297, syl. 5–7 (1942) (admitted); Epperson v. Comm., 227 Ky. 404, 13 S.W.2d 247, syl. 7 (1929) (excluded because tests made with body of deceased do not show what she could have done when living).

7. Carpenter v. Kurn, 348 Mo. 1132, 157 S.W.2d 213, syl. 3, 4 (1941) (tests for ascertaining distance one standing on tracks could tell that a person sitting and dressed like deceased was human being). In a similar case, the court held that the fact that the persons making the tests knew beforehand that the object was a human being, whereas the engineer running the train did not, weakened the value of test, but did not require its exclusion. Norfolk & W. Ry. Co. v. Henderson, 132 Va. 297, 111 S.E. 277, syl. 10 (1922). But this is a weakness which in the interest of justice should be avoided in the planning of such visibility tests.

8. People v. Crawford, 41 Cal.App.2d 198, 106 P.2d 219, syl. 8–10, 1940 (facts closely resemble those in James M. Cain's novel, The Postman Always Rings Twice); Stevens v. People, 97 Colo. 559, 51 P.2d 1022, syl. 5 (1935) (experiment to show whether headlight would illuminate oncoming car when passing at particular place); Crecelius v. Gamble-Skogmo, 144 Neb. 394, 13 N.W.2d 627, syl. 5–7 (1944) (test of distance in which truck could be stopped). See Note, 72 A.L.R. 863.

9. See §§ 173–178.

10. 2 Wigmore, Evidence, § 443.

11. The requirement of similarity is constantly repeated. See, e. g., Navajo Freight Lines v. Mahaffy, 174 F.2d 305, syl. 6–8 (C.A.N.Mex.1949) (collision; evidence of experiment with automobile to see whether there was sufficient downgrade so that it would roll down road-way, held properly rejected for want of showing of similarity as to vehicle and wind conditions); Harper v. Blasi, 112 Colo. 518, 151 P.2d 760, syl. 6 (1944) ("A certain witness for the defendant was permitted to detail an experiment conducted with a mask, an artificial eye and rimless glasses, ostensibly to determine whether a blow struck as plaintiff had testified could have resulted in the alleged injury. His conclusion was that 'an ordinary man taking a swing with the right hand at the right eye would have to be a regular prize fighter to do the damage.' We think the experiment and its description improper. There was no similarity of conditions, no way of establishing equality of strength or skill. . . ."); 32 C.J.S., Evidence, § 590.

12. See Navajo Freight Lines v. Mahaffy, supra. The burden is on the proponent. McGough v. Hendrickson, 58 Cal.App.2d 60, 136 P.2d 110, syl. 12, 13 (1943) (experiment to show visibility of pedestrian on highway; burden to show similarity as to time of day and season of year not satisfied); Enghlin v. Pittsburgh County Ry. Co., 169 Okl. 106, 36 P.2d 32, 37, syl. 4, 94 A.L.R. 1180 (1934) (experiment with same street-car, same place to show maximum speed, burden satisfied).

13. Lever Bros. Co. v. Atlas Assur. Co., 131 F.2d 770, 777, syl. 11 (C.C.A.Ind.1942).

admit the evidence.[14] Manifestly, if the trial judge is to be given responsibility for exercising such an indefinable value-judgment he must be accorded a reasonable leeway of discretion reviewable only for abuse.[15]

Moreover, the experiment may be offered, exceptionally, for a purpose that does not depend for its persuasiveness upon identity or similarity of conditions. Thus if one party contends that it is impossible *under any conditions* for a given result to follow certain acts or omissions, the other party may prove by experiment that on a particular occasion the consequence has actually occurred. Of course he is not hampered by a "similar-

conditions" requirement.[16] He has only to meet the terms of the challenge. Similarly, the proponent may offer to prove that the agency for which he is responsible was not the cause of the injurious result. An experiment showing that the same result has happened *under different conditions,* and in the absence of that agency, has some logical value to increase the probability of the proponent's contention.[17] It seems also that experiments designed to show the general traits and capacities of materials involved in the controversy might often reasonably be admitted in evidence without confining such experiments to the conditions surrounding the litigated situation.[18]

14. Downing v. Metropolitan Life Ins. Co., 314 Ill. App. 222, 41 N.E.2d 297, syl. 5–7 (1942) (experiment by other men to determine whether deceased could have shot himself); Pool v. Day, 143 Kan. 226, 53 P.2d 912, syl. 4 (1936) (distance in which automobile could stop at different speeds, using automobile of different make and greater braking surface); Erickson's Dairy Products Co. v. Northwest Baker Ice Mach. Co., 165 Ore. 553, 109 P.2d 53, syl. 6, 7 (1941) (action for causing fire in building by failing to protect wall during welding operations; experiment by welding near a piece of wallboard, properly received over objection board different from wall itself; "After all, we must assume that the jury was composed of men and women of ordinary sense and intelligence who would take into consideration the dissimilarity of which plaintiff complains."). Compare Lincoln Taxi Co. v. Rice, 251 S.W.2d 867, syl. 2, 3 (Ky.1952), where the court announced a similar liberal criterion, but held that the experiment in question did not meet it.

15. State v. Keller, 246 P.2d 817, syl. 4, 5 (Mont. 1952); Randall v. State, 73 Ga.App. 354, 36 S.E.2d 450, 462, syl. 20 (1946) (citing cases); Franks v. Jirdon, 146 Neb. 585, 20 N.W.2d 507, syl. 9 (1945); Mintz v. Atlantic Coast Line R. Co., 236 N.C. 109, 72 S.E.2d 38, syl. 9, 10 (1952).

16. Chambers v. Silver, 103 Cal.App.2d 633, 230 P. 2d 146, syl. 1 (1951) (Where collision occurred when defendant's automobile veered onto wrong side of road and his sole defense, in suit for injuries to plaintiffs, was that main leaf in spring at front wheel had broken when wheel crossed two-inch deposit of soil on road and vehicle had thereby been rendered impossible to control, and mechanic testified for defendant that it was physically impossible to drive automobile with this type suspension in such condition, it was prejudicial error to refuse

plaintiffs' rebuttal evidence as to an experiment in which automobile with same suspension system was driven without loss of control over 2 x 4 boards at a speed of 45 to 50 miles per hour.); Horn v. Elgin Warehouse Co., 96 Ore. 403, 190 Pac. 151, syl. 3, 4 (1920) (plaintiff sued seller of wheat for breach of his warranty that it was Red Chaff wheat, plaintiff alleging it was not Red Chaff wheat; defendant allowed to prove that witnesses had planted same wheat and it produced Red Chaff wheat, without any showing of similarity of conditions.) Of course, if the conditions prevailing at the time of the experiment are more unfavorable to the proponent than the conditions of the crucial happening this satisfies the requirement. People v. Spencer, 58 Cal.App. 197, 208 Pac. 380, 393 (1922).

17. Lincoln v. Taunton Copper Mfg. Co., 91 Mass. 181, 191 (1864) (action for injury to plaintiff's land by contamination with copper from defendant's mill; plaintiff's expert having testified that he has obtained copper from grasses on plaintiff's land, defendants may introduce similar testimony that copper exists and has been obtained in grasses not exposed to contamination from defendant's mill).

18. Guinan v. Famous Player-Lasky Corp., 267 Mass. 501, 167 N.E. 235, 245, syl. 32–34 (1929) (Action for injury due to ignition and explosion of a quantity of motion picture film in a street car. Experiments to show inflammable and explosive character of such film were admitted. These consisted of subjecting pieces of film to various degrees of heat, contact with electric sparks, burning, and pulverizing film, inserting it in cartridge and firing from revolver. Held, since impracticable to duplicate conditions, and since the properties of film are important in this case, judge properly admitted).

It seems that in respect to certain types of cases and issues, the use of experimental evidence has far greater possibilities for aiding the court in the true determination of facts than have as yet been realized. This seems to be due to the failure of courts and lawyers to recognize that the adversary system of party-presentation of evidence must continually be modified, to keep it in step with the march of justice. It needs to be modified here by a rule of court providing first, that no experiment shall be used in evidence unless reasonable *notice* shall have been given the adversary, with an opportunity to makes suggestions as to planning and to be present at the test;[19] and second, empowering the court, in discretion, on application of either party, to appoint an *impartial* person to conduct or supervise an experiment.[20] If the parties can agree on such a person the judge would be required to appoint him. A test thus conducted would in many cases be so conclusive a settlement of the controlling issue that a trial, being a foregone conclusion, would be avoided. In any case evidence of the results of such a test would give to the tribunal the benefit of the scientific method of controlled experiment far more completely than does our present system of secret one-sided experiments.

170. Some Problems in the Use of Scientific Techniques and Devices as Sources of Proof:[1] In General.

In a work of this scope we cannot cover the vast and growing body of experience in

---

19. Under present practice, absence of notice and opportunity to be present are not a ground of rejection, but may be argued on the weight. Burg v. Chicago, R. I. & P. Ry. Co., 90 Iowa 106, 57 N.W. 680, 683, syl. 5 (1894) (evidence of tests made by defendant railway using locomotive and train, of visibility of person on track, and of stopping power of brakes); Sinclair Oil & Gas Co. v. Albright, 161 Okl. 272, 18 P.2d 540, 543, syl. 3–5 (1933) (experiment as to effect of horse's drinking polluted water). But see Byers v. Nashville C. & St. L. Ry. Co., 94 Tenn. 345, 29 S.W. 128, syl. 4 (1895) (error to reject experiment like that in the Burg case, supra, for lack of notice).

Under the proposed practice, a pre-trial hearing or conference such as is provided for under Rule 16 of the Federal Rules of Civil Procedure would be an appropriate occasion for giving notice of a proposed experiment and for negotiation about its planning.

20. Compare Rules of the Supreme Court (England), Order 37a, sec. 1 and sec. 5: "1. In any case which is to be tried without a jury involving any question for an expert witness the Court or a Judge may in his discretion at any time on the application of any party appoint an independent expert (to be called 'the Court expert') to inquire and report upon any question of fact or of opinion not involving questions of law or construction (hereinafter called 'the issue for the expert').

"5. If the court expert is of opinion that any experiment or test of any kind is necessary to enable him to report in a satisfactory manner (other than any experiment or test of a trifling character), he shall communicate the fact to the parties or their solicitors and shall endeavour to arrange

with them as to the expenses involved and as to the persons to attend and other similar matters. Failing agreement between the parties all such matters shall be determined by the Court or Judge." Annual Practice, 1953 pp. 673, 674.

See also §§ 8, 17, as to common-law powers and statutory provisions for appointment of expert witnesses by the court, in this country.

1. The genius of Wigmore created at Northwestern University Law School a Crime Detection Laboratory where creative pioneer work was done. His Science of Judicial Proof (3d ed., 1937) is a storehouse of data about many techniques of scientific proof. Among other leaders is Professor Inbau, of Northwestern Law School, formerly director of the Laboratory. His "Index of Police Science materials," compiling the contributions of the Laboratory, is to be found in the Wigmore volume, supra, p. 1004, and in 27 J.Crim.Law & Criminology 263 (1936). A most interesting account of these techniques and their results in specific cases is Baker and Inbau, "The Scientific Detection of Crime," 17 Minn.L.Rev. 602 (1933). See also Perkins, Elements of Police Science, Part One (1942), and Turner, Forensic Science and Laboratory Technics (1949), both with excellent photographs. For discriminating discussions see Notes, "Scientific Gadgets in the Law of Evidence," 53 Harv.L.Rev. 285 (1939), and Rowell, Evidence Obtained by Scientific Devices and Analyses, 6 Ark.L.Rev. 181 (1952), 5 Univ. of Fla.L.Rev. 5 (1952).

Extraordinary work in inspiring doctors and lawyers to pool and publish their knowledge about scientific proof has been done by Professor Hubert Winston Smith, Director of the Law-Science Institute, Uni-

the various fields of scientific proof. The topic alone of medical science as a source of legal evidence is the subject of many comprehensive text-books and of an extensive body of articles. Moreover, the rushing stream of new scientific devices, such as the recently developed method of recording the waves or currents given off by the cerebral tissue, by tracings known as electro-encephalograms,[2] the employment of wire and tape recordings as media of proof[3] and the even more recent device for measuring the speed of motor vehicles, known as the radar speedmeter,[4] soon renders obsolete any attempt at comprehensive description. Only a very limited sampling of a few of the areas, which have been the subject of wide discussion by the judges and commentators, will here be attempted.

We face at the outset the question, to what extent must the device, technique or theory be shown to have won scientific acceptance before the results or conclusions based thereon can be used in evidence? The court which first faced the question of the admissibility of the results of a "lie-detector" examination announced as the test whether the supporting theory had gained "general acceptance" among "physiological and psychological authorities."[5] The court held that this test was not met and rejected the evidence, and this particular kind of evidence has been rejected with like reasoning by other courts ever since. By contrast, another court quite recently, considering the admissibility of the results of the use of the Harger breath test for measuring intoxication seemingly rejected this criterion of general scientific acceptance, and said: "Dr. Beerstecher [a biochemist] testified that the instrument in question is accurate and he gave his reasons for it. He admitted that there are others who disagree with its accuracy. The objection to his testimony, therefore, goes to its weight and not to its admissibility."[6]

It seems that the practice approved in the second case is the one followed in respect to expert testimony and scientific evidence generally. "General scientific acceptance" is a proper condition upon the court's taking judicial notice of scientific facts, but not a criterion for the admissibility of scientific evidence. Any relevant conclusions which are supported by a qualified expert witness should be received unless there are other reasons for exclusion. Particularly, its probative value may be overborne by the familiar dangers of prejudicing or misleading the jury, unfair surprise and undue consumption

---

versity of Texas. He is both a lawyer and a physician and was the organizer of a symposium consisting of 110 articles in different law and medical reviews about legal and medical problems of scientific proof in particular fields of litigation, civil and criminal. See Scientific Proof and Relations of Law and Medicine: Index to First and Second Symposium Series (Pamphlet, Univ. Ill., Urbana, 1946), Table of Contents, Second Series, 32 Va.L.Rev. 904 (1946), and earlier Indexes, 10 U.Chi.L.Rev. 369 (1943), 16 So.Calif.L.Rev. 213 (1943). See also the valuable general article, Smith, "Scientific Proof," 52 Yale L.J. 586, 10 U.Chi.L.Rev. 243, 21 Can.Bar Rev. 707, 16 So.Calif.L.Rev. 120 (1943). This series constitutes a unique repository of the contributions of the two professions in this area. Highly useful compilations published in this series are Dr. Smith's masterly bibliographies, "Books Dealing with Problems of Joint Interest to the Legal and Medical Professions," 24 N.C.L.Rev. 201; "Articles on Medicine and Law in the United States, 1941–1944," 24 N.C.L.Rev. 221 (1946).

2. See Smith, Scientific Proof, 10 U.Chi.L.Rev. 243, 259 (1943).

3. See the valuable article, Conrad, Magnetic Recordings in the Courts, 40 Va.L.Rev. 23 (1954).

4. Lee, Note, Use of Radar Speedmeter, 30 N.C.L.Rev. 385 (1952).

5. Frye v. United States, 293 Fed. 1013, 1014 (C.A. D.C. 1923), wherein the court said: "Just when a scientific principle or discovery crosses the line between the experimental and demonstrable stages is difficult to define. Somewhere in this twilight zone the evidential force of the principle must be recognized, and while courts will go a long way in admitting expert testimony deduced from a well-recognized scientific principle or discovery, the thing from which the deduction is made must be sufficiently established to have gained general acceptance in the particular field in which it belongs."

6. Beauchamp, J., in McKay v. State, 155 Tex.Cr. 416, 235 S.W.2d 173, 175 (1950).

of time.[7] On this footing the novelty and want of acceptance at that time of the lie-detector lessened the probative value of the test and probably heightened the danger of misleading the jury. If the courts had used this approach, instead of repeating a supposed requirement of "general acceptance" not elsewhere imposed, they might have arrived at some practical way of utilizing a technique of investigation which has proved so fertile as a means of ascertaining truth.

Among the weaknesses of our judicial process in the area of scientific proof are (1) the selection of experts by the parties, so that the experts chosen are often biased and are sometimes not highly qualified, as where a general practitioner is called upon a question of sanity, and (2) the inadequacy of the jury to decide between disputing experts.

Many of the devices described herein, such as the lie-detector, the truth-serum and the blood-tests, when administered without consent, raise questions of the privilege against self-incrimination, which have been discussed in the chapter relating to that privilege.[8]

171. The Theory of Probabilities as Applied to Questions of Identification.

Scientific proof has as one of its chief areas of operation the field of identification. This includes the identification of persons, through fingerprints, photographs and measurements, or by testimony describing a highwayman, whose identity is disputed. It likewise includes the search for the authorship of a document by means of identifying the handwriting of the writer or identifying the characteristics of the typewriter used from the peculiarities of the typescript. Similarly, a revolver used in a murder may be identified by tracing the marks found on the fatal bullet or the empty cartridge left at the scene of the killing. These and many other techniques of identification have been developed and refined by scientists and technicians in university and police laboratories and by independent scientific specialists, particularly during the last half century. Probably the extent of their accomplishments in making it possible to furnish evidence of identification to a high degree of certainty has not been appreciated by most people who have not studied the results of their work, or learned of it through the perusal of detective fiction.

A dramatic way of expressing this high degree of attainable certainty is through the formula of probabilities.[1] A person, A, is suspected of a crime. The eye-witnesses,

---

7. See § 152, supra. See also the illuminating discussion of these balancing considerations of auxiliary policy and of probative value, as applied to "lie-detector" evidence, in Trautman, Logical or Legal Relevancy, 5 Vand.L.Rev. 385, 395 (1952).

8. See § 126, herein.

1. See Wigmore, Principles of Judicial Proof, § 154 (3d ed., 1937); Osborn, Questioned Documents, 225–236, 596–599 (2d ed. 1929); Note, 28 Harv.L.Rev. 693 (1915).

People v. Risley, 214 N.Y. 75, 108 N.E. 200 (1915) was a prosecution for offering in evidence a typewritten document, knowing that it had been fraudulently altered by the insertion of two words. At the trial the state offered as an expert witness a professor of mathematics, who testified about the probability against the appearance of seven particular identifying traits which appeared in the typing of the inserted words, all of which corresponded to defects in a typewriter possessed by the accused. He likewise testified that multiplying these separate odds, "the

probability of these defects being reproduced by the work of a typewriter other than the machine of defendant, was one in four thousand million." The conviction was reversed for the admission of this evidence. The holding may be justified on the ground of the lack of qualification of the witness to testify to the underlying facts as to the odds against the appearance of each particular defect, but the following remarks of Seabury, J., dissenting, seem more persuasive: "Common sense at once recognizes how remote is the probability that all of these defects should recur in these six identical letters in any other typewriter. Indeed, if the district attorney, basing his argument upon matters of common knowledge and the general perception of all men, had pointed out that there was not one chance in four thousand millions that these identical defects would be found in these identical six letters of another typewriter, he would, I think, have been within his rights. Substantially the same statement did not become prejudicial because it is made by one learned in the higher mathematics."

who did not recognize the criminal, were able to report certain facts about him, as to which we may estimate the probabilities that any unknown person would possess that particular mark. He was of medium height (one out of two), red-haired (one out of five), had a noticeable paunch (one out of three), and walked with a slight limp (one out of ten). The person suspected, A, has all of these characteristics. None of these traits is rare or unusual, and it may be argued as to each one separately that it is a mere ordinary coincidence that A and the unknown criminal both happen to be red-haired, and so on through the list. But the theory of probabilities brings this argument up short. Under that theory, in calculating the chances that A and the unknown are different persons, you do not merely add together the odds against the appearance of each of the several traits, but rather you multiply them. Accordingly, the odds against A's not being the criminal would not be twenty to one but three hundred (2 x 5 x 3 x 10) to one. Scientific techniques of identification consist largely of isolating the traits of difference (e. g., the whorls of the fingerprint and the lines of the bullet) and devising means for discovering, measuring and displaying those differences, as with the chemical tests for ink and paper, the enlarged photograph, and the comparison-microscope. Thus the identifying traits of a particular fingerprint or manuscript become so numerous that the resulting odds in favor of a correct conclusion may be counted

in astronomical figures which amount in practice to a certainty.

172. Questioned Documents.[1]

The process of identifying by witnesses the authorship of a letter, deed or other writing may be carried through at various levels. At one level the proponent has the simple task of prima facie authentication of the writing as the writing of X, to secure its admission. Here all you need is someone who has enough knowledge of the general character of X's manner of writing to be able to say, "This looks like X's handwriting." If he has seen X write, or has corresponded with him and claims to know his writing, that is enough.[2]

The second stage is the situation where there is a real dispute as to the genuineness of the writing, but the parties either because the amount involved is small or because they are ignorant of the power and resources of professional document examiners of the highest class, content themselves with secondary experts, such as a bank cashier,[3] or a long-time principal of a business college and teacher of handwriting.[4] It has been said that these may qualify by study without practice or by practice without study.[5] The side-line or part-time expert is of course much superior to the layman who has only a general acquaintance with the person's style of writing. The secondary expert by comparing the questioned writing with samples of

---

1. 7 Wigmore, Evidence, §§ 1991–2028; Wigmore, The Science of Judicial Proof, §§ 44–46, 159–163 (3d ed. 1937); Albert S. Osborn, Questioned Documents (2d. ed. 1929); Albert S. and Albert D. Osborn, Questioned Document Problems (1944); Scott, Recent Questioned Document Law, 16 U.Kan.City 68 (1948); Dec.Dig. Criminal Law, ⟐452(4), 458, 478(2), 491, 494, Evidence, ⟐474(14), 480, 511, 561–567, 568(3).

2. See § 189. The unreliability of this kind of testimony in distinguishing genuine from simulated handwriting is interestingly demonstrated in these articles: Inbau, Lay Witness Identification of Handwriting (An Experiment), 34 Ill.L.Rev. 433;

Hilton, The Detection of Forgery, 30 J.Crim.L. & Criminology 568 (1939).

3. State v. Wickett, 230 Iowa 1182, 300 N.W. 268, syl. 9 (1941).

4. First Galesburg Nat. Bank v. Federal Reserve Bank, 295 Ill.App. 524, 15 N.E.2d 337, syl. 4, 5 (1938).

5. Fenias v. Reichenstein, 124 N.J.L. 196, 11 A.2d 10, syl. 3–5 (1940) (commissioner of registration and his assistants who were shown to have compared thousands of signatures each year and to have had experience in comparing voters' signatures were competent to testify concerning genuineness of signatures on petition).

genuine writings [6] before the jury may give substantial assistance in reaching a just result. Nevertheless the gulf between the "second best" handwriting expert and the professional document examiner of good standing [7] is so wide that when the client's purse and the amount at stake will justify it, the conscientious and well-informed lawyer will insist on submitting the facts to such an examiner for his opinion, before accepting responsibility for trying the issue.

At this third level where one of the parties has the benefit of the testimony of a full-time accredited examiner of documents, the scientific method, in the investigation of the facts, in the preparation of the exhibits for analysis and comparison, and in the explanation of the reasons for the conclusion, is seen at its best. Osborn's Questioned Documents,[8] an invaluable and authoritative treatise, dis-

cusses, with illustrations, the following traits in writing: [9] flow or movement, line quality, alignment, pen position, pen pressure, and shading; arrangement, size, proportions, spacing and slant; systems of writing, such as Spencerian; characteristics of copied or traced writings; and characteristics of writing done with particular kinds of pens or pencils. Analysis of ink, paper and subject matter may show the age of the document and help to identify fraudulent erasures and alterations.

Similar, and often more easily and certainly demonstrable, is the identification of the authorship of typewritten documents.[10] The make and age of the machine, the kind of paper, ribbon and ink used, may usually be readily identified. Then the particular machine used will be searched for, then the person who operated it. As to the former,

---

6. The use of specimens of genuine handwriting for comparison with the disputed document is, of course, almost essential for the formation and explanation of an opinion as to genuineness. To avoid "collateral issues" the earlier practice required that the specimens be limited to writings already in the case (e. g., signatures to pleadings or bonds) or those admitted by the adversary to be genuine. The use of specimens of genuine handwriting for comparison with the disputed document is, of course, almost essential for the formation and explanation of an opinion as to genuineness. To avoid "collateral issues" the earlier practice required that the specimens be limited to writings already in the case (e. g., signatures to pleadings or bonds) or those admitted by the adversary to be genuine. This has been liberalized in England and most states, by statute or decision, to permit the use of specimens proved to the judge's satisfaction to be genuine. People v. Parmelee, 309 Mich. 431, 15 N.W.2d 696, syl. 1 (1944); 7 Wigmore, Evidence, §§ 2015, 2016; Dec.Dig. Crim.Law ⬤=491, Evidence, ⬤=197, 564.

7. A Kentucky judge marks the difference when in describing the experts called by one party, he said, ". . . one has made the study of handwriting his vocation while to the others it is but an avocation, to one it is his work to the others it is a diversion, one makes it his business the others make it a sideline." Drury, C., in Polley v. Cline's Exec'r, 263 Ky. 659, 93 S.W.2d 363, 368 (1936).

The professional organization of accredited experts is the American Society of Questioned Document Examiners. The society and its work are described in Cooper, Foiling Forgers is Their Business, 28 Science Digest, no. 6, p. 56 (Dec.1950).

8. 2d ed. 1929.

9. See Osborn, op. cit., chs. 8–19.

10. See Osborn, op. cit., ch. 32, and Osborn, Fraudulent Typewriting, 20 A.B.A.J. 708 (1934); Osborn and Osborn, Questioned Document Problems, chs. 18, 19 (1944).

Recent cases of questioned typewritten documents: Harlan v. Blume, 190 S.W.2d 273, syl. 5, 6 (Mo.App. 1945) (trial judge ordered photographs of disputed letters to be made, and apparently called a typewriter salesman and repairman to testify as to differences); In re Bundy's Estate, 153 Ore. 234, 56 P. 2d 313, 106 A.L.R. 714 (1936) (will-contest; typewritten will, which daughter contended was typed in office of testator's lawyer was shown by expert to have been typed on daughter's own machine: good discussion by Rossman, J.); In re Cravens' Estate, 206 Okl. 174, 242 P.2d 135 (1952) (will-contest; expert document examiner convinced court, contrary to testimony of attesters, that alterations were typed by different person than one who typed original will; court stresses need for expert in disputes over typewritten documents, and the feasibility of identifying writer of such document) and see cases in Note, Opinion Evidence as to Typewritten Documents and Typewriting Machines, 106 A.L.R. 721.

among the factors of individuality are the relation of each letter to the neighboring letters, its position in relation to the line of writing, the comparative weight of impression of the different sides of the letter, and finally defects or scars in the various letters. Due to the wear and imperfections of machine tools, no two machine products, such as a rifle-barrel, a bolt or a pin will be precisely alike under the microscope, and accordingly, no two type-faces of different typewriters are exactly alike even when new. Wear and tear in use produce further marks of individuality in each type-face. As to the writer himself, he may be known by his habits of touch, spacing, speed, arrangement, punctuation and by vagaries in spelling and the like, as shown by comparison with samples of his writing.

The chief instruments of investigation are the microscope and the camera,[11] though these may be supplemented by chemical and fluoroscopic tests. In reaching his conclusions the examiner will prepare photographs, photo-micrographs, or enlarged photographs of the disputed document and of the genuine writings used for comparison. For more graphic comparison, the corresponding parts of the disputed or genuine writings may be cut out and placed alongside each other in a detailed exhibit of comparative features.

Such exhibits may be displayed by the expert witness to the court and jury as illustrative of his testimony.[12] They are usually essential to a convincing demonstration.

The professional examiner possessed of genuine qualifications will not claim more power than he has, i. e., if given adequate standards and adequate time and facilities for comparing these with the disputed writing, he can tell the false from the true. The secondary expert, whether honest or dishonest, may claim to be able to distinguish them on momentary inspection. It seems that any one who claims to be an expert should be subject to a testing of his claim on cross-examination by presenting him with true and fabricated writings and asking him to distinguish.[13] Since in fairness he may properly request time for examination and testing, the judge should have a discretion to say whether under the circumstances the test is worth the time it will take.

"When the half-gods go, the gods arrive." With the growing realization by lawyers of the scientific advances in the process of document-identification, the courts are coming to give freer play to qualified examiners to give fully their reasons for their conclusions,[14] and to recognize that such reasoning in a particular case may amount to a demonstration so certain and convincing that it may

---

11. Osborn, Questioned Documents, chs. 5, 6 (2d ed. 1929) and see Scott, Photographic Evidence, Ch. 12 (Disputed Documents) (1942), an invaluable treatise, graphically illustrated, written by a lawyer who is also a document examiner.

12. Rowell v. Fuller's Estate, 59 Vt. 688, 10 Atl. 853, 861, syl. 2 (1887); Adams v. Ristine, 138 Va. 273, 122 S.E. 126, syl. 16–18, 31 A.L.R. 1413 (1924) (including display of enlarged and "side by side" comparison photographs); Fenelon v. State, 195 Wis. 416, 217 N.W. 711, syl. 4 (1928).

13. Browning v. Gosnell, 91 Iowa 448, 59 N.W. 340, syl. 7 (1894); Hoag v. Wright, 174 N.Y. 36, 66 N.E. 579, syl. 3 (1903); 7 Wigmore, Evidence, § 2015. Contra: Nordyke v. State, 213 Ind. 243, 11 N.E.2d 165, syl. 8 (1937); Fourth National Bank v. Mc-

Arthur, 168 N.C. 48, 84 S.E. 39, syl. 2 (1915). See Note, 128 A.L.R. 1315, 1340–1349.

14. In re Varney, 22 F.2d 231, 236, 237, 1927; Venuto v. Lizzo, 148 App.Div. 164, 132 N.Y.S. 1066, 1911; State v. Young, 210 N.C. 452, 187 S.E. 561 (1936) (conviction reversed for judge's refusal to allow expert to give his reasons completely). The expert's opinion is valuable only as it is based upon satisfactory reasons. Greenstreet v. Greenstreet, 65 Idaho 36, 139 P.2d 239, 243 (1943); Brien v. Davidson, 225 Iowa 595, 281 N.W. 150, 153, rehearing den. 282 N.W. 480 (1938). In re Barrie, 393 Ill. 111, 65 N.E. 2d 433, syl. 6–9 (1946) is a case where the court considered minutely the reasons given by the expert in the light of its inspection of the writing and declared them unfounded.

overcome direct testimony of purported eye-witnesses to the contrary.[15]

173. Miscellaneous Tests and Techniques Employed in Criminal Investigation.[1]

Many of the methods of identification and investigation employed in police laboratories have become widely known, such as finger-printing,[2] examination of questioned writings,[3] identification of firearms by micro-scopic study of bullets and cartridges,[4] and chemical analysis of poisons and narcotics.[5] Others less familiar may be important re-sources of the police in the search for the criminal or the proof of his guilt, such as tests of the skin of the hand of a suspect for powder residue to determine whether he has shot a fire-arm (dermal nitrate tests[6]); microscopic[7] and spectrographic[8] analysis of hair,[9] fibers,[10] seminal stains,[11] minute fragments of glass,[12] dust, dirt, and scrapings,[13] fragments of paper, wood and metal[14] (especially in bomb-explosions). The possi-bilities of detection and proof which may be achieved by the expert and imaginative use of these scientific techniques are revealed by many reported cases.[15]

---

15. Cases emphasizing the possibility that expert tes-timony to forgery may outweigh direct testimony of genuineness: Boyd v. Gosser, 78 Fla. 64, 82 So. 758, 6 A.L.R. 500 (1918), annotated (a striking fact case); Preston v. Peck, 271 Mass. 159, 171 N.E. 54 (1930); In re Reuter's Estate, 148 Neb. 776, 29 N.W. 2d 466 (1947); In re Young's Estate, 347 Pa. 457, 32 A.2d 901, 154 A.L.R. 643 (1943); Adams v. Ris-tine, 138 Va. 273, 122 S.E. 126, 31 A.L.R. 1413 (1924). With these contrast cases where the eye-witness testimony prevailed, such as Jones v. Jones, 406 Ill. 448, 94 N.E.2d 314 (1950); Wright's Exec'r v. Simp-son, 232 Ky. 148, 22 S.W.2d 583 (1929). Courts and legislatures, unwisely it seems, sometimes lay down general rules of priority, see, e. g., Jones v. Jones, supra (expert cannot prevail over disinterested and unimpeached eye-witnesses); Tex.Vernon's Ann.C.C. P. art. 731 (". . . Proof by comparison only shall not be sufficient to establish the handwriting of a witness who denies his signature under oath"). See Note, Testimony of Handwriting Experts Opposed to That of Attesting Witnesses, 154 A.L.R. 649.

1. One of the best recent descriptions of these tech-niques is Turner, Forensic Science and Laboratory Technics (Charles C. Thomas, publisher, Springfield, Ill., 1949). Many are also discussed in Wigmore, Science of Judicial Proof (3d ed. 1937), which also reprints at p. 1004 Inbau's excellent bibliography, An Index of Police Science Materials.

2. See Wigmore, op. cit. § 155; Turner, op. cit., ch. 4.

3. See preceding paragraphs, this section.

4. See Wigmore, § 157, Turner, ch. 5.

5. See Turner, ch. 8.

6. See Turner, sec. 62.

7. O'Neill, Police Microanalysis, 25 J.Crim.L. 674, 835 (1934–35).

8. Wilson, Spectographic Analysis, 25 J.Crim.L. 160 (1934).

9. Kirk et al., Casting of Hairs, 40 J.Crim.L. 236 (1949); Turner, ch. 6.

10. Turner, ch. 7; Burd and Kirk, Clothing Fibers as Evidence, 32 J.Crim.L. 353 (1941); Lourdermilk, The Identification of Cloth Ash, 24 J.Crim.L. 503 (1933); Keeler, Identification of Adhesive Tape, 28 J.Crim.L. 904 (1938).

11. Turner, sec. 134.

12. Turner, secs. 121–130; Roche and Kirk, Micro-chemical Techniques: Differentiation of Similar Glass Fragments, 38 J.Crim.L. 168.

13. Turner, sec. 131.

14. Pirk, Metallurgical Examinations in Criminal Cases, 30 J.Crim.L. 900 (1940); Wilson, Comparison and Identification of Wire in a Coal Mine Bombing Case, 28 J.Crim.L. 873 (1938).

15. See, e. g., People v. Wallage, 353 Ill. 95, 186 N.E. 540 (1933) (identification of hit-and-run driver by dent of button and print of fiber on car, from cloth-ing of victim); Territory v. Young, 32 Hawaii 628 (1933) (analysis of dirt on criminal's shoe); State v. Johnson, 37 N.M. 280, 21 P.2d 813 (1933) (particles of strangled victim's lipstick found on hands of murderer); Ferrell v. Comm., 177 Va. 861, 14 S.E. 2d 293 (1941) (murderer identified and convicted up-on testimony of F. B. I. operative who compared plaster cast of heel-print with defendant's rubber-heel, and testified to the methods used in identify-ing a shot-gun shell found at the scene as having been fired from defendant's gun); State v. Clark, 156 Wash. 543, 287 Pac. 18 (1930) (assault on child by person who lay in wait under the shelter of a blind made of fir branches cut from surrounding trees; the cut sections of branches were examined under microscope and knife-markings on them cor-responded identically with those made on similar wood cut by the knife found on accused); Magnu-son v. State, 187 Wis. 122, 203 N.W. 749, (1925) (mur-der by time-bomb sent in package by mail at Christ-

174. Detection of Deception: The Lie Detector.[1]

The appliance now commonly in use is called a polygraph.[2] It is attached to the person of the man who is being questioned and makes a record, on a moving chart, of the questions and of the subject's changes in blood-pressure and rate of breathing as each question is asked. Some machines, in addition, measure pulse changes and changes in the resistance of the skin to a minute electrical current, due to sweat-gland activity. The interrogation will first allow time for allowing the subject to quiet down, and for recording his individual general level of bodily activity. Then key-questions relating to the crime or other happening (Did you rob the supermarket?) will be interspersed with neutral or irrelevant questions (How often have you smoked today?), so that the bodily reactions accompanying the two kinds of questions, and their answers, may be compared.

In most persons, as has always been popularly believed, lying and consciousness of guilt are accompanied by emotion or excitement that expresses itself in bodily changes, —the blush, the gasp, the quickened heartbeat, the clenched hand, the sweaty palm, the dry mouth. The skilled cross-examiner may face the witness with his lies and involve him in a knot of new ones, so that these visible signs of lying become apparent to the jury. This is part of the demeanor of the witness that the jury is told they may observe and consider upon credibility.[3] The polygraph is able to record accurately some of these bodily changes alongside the very questions that produced them, and thus enables the skilled interpreter to make an analysis of truth or falsehood on a scientific basis, comparable to the doctor's diagnosis of health or disease.

True, the interpreter, like the diagnostician, must possess the "feel" or intuition, which comes from experience, in order to reach accurate results, but it seems that his technique has much to contribute to the difficult process of judicial fact-finding. It has been widely and successfully employed in criminal investigation and in business.[4] We

---

mas-time; investigation and proof covered handwriting and spelling peculiarities of inscription on wrapper, analysis of glue, ink, wood and metal fragments by specialists to whom the materials were submitted by prosecutor; the case is a model of scientific investigation, and as the court says: ". . . it discloses what may be done by a diligent prosecuting officer who has an intelligent comprehension of the things that are necessary to establish guilt in a case of this importance."). See also Wigmore, Science of Judicial Proof, § 158 (3d ed. 1937); Baker and Inbau, The Scientific Detection of Crime, 17 Minn.L.Rev. 602 (1933); Koehler, Tracing the Lindbergh Kidnapping Ladder, 27 J. Crim.L. 712 (1937); C. W. Muehlberger, The Investigation of Bombs and Explosions, 28 J.Crim.L. 406, 581 (1937).

1. The most practical and complete treatment is Inbau, Lie Detection and Criminal Investigation (2d ed. 1948). A recent symposium, The Polygraphic Truth Test, with articles by Wicker, Cureton, and Trovillo, and comments thereon, appears in 22 Tenn.L.Rev. 711–774 (1953) and was issued by the Review as a separate pamphlet. It is an invaluable compendium of recent opinion and progress in the field. See also two lively and informative

discussions: Smallwood, Lie-Detectors: Discussions and Proposals, 29 Corn. L.Q. 534 (1944), and Streeter and Belli, The Fourth Degree, 5 Vand. L.Rev. 549 (1952); 3 Wigmore, Evidence, § 999; Note, 23 A.L.R.2d 1306; Dec.Dig., Crim.Law, ☞388, Evidence, ☞150.

2. For descriptions of the machine and its use, see Inbau op. cit. 5–17; Trovillo, op. cit., 22 Tenn.L. Rev. 748–757.

3. See, e. g., State v. McLaughlin, 126 Conn. 257, 10 A.2d 758, syl. 7 (1940); 3 Wigmore, Evidence, § 946, Dec.Dig., Witnesses, ☞315.

4. "Some 200,000 persons in the United States have taken polygraph tests of deception in the last 20 years. Three hundred specialists have qualified, or are becoming qualified as experts in the giving and interpreting of polygraph tests. Literally the murders of thousands of men, women, and children whose violent and ignominious deaths remained mysterious, have been solved through the review by experts of polygraph charts.

"The state of Illinois has 45 such examiners; California 32; New York, 26; Indiana, 16; District of Columbia, 14; Texas, 13; Ohio, 13; and Michigan, Georgia, and Tennessee, 8 each. In addition to

cannot in our hearts be so confident of the reliability of the present system of resolving conflicts in testimony by impeachment, cross-examination and inferences from demeanor, that we can afford to reject scientific aid in the task.

No one could reasonably contend, at this stage of development, that the lie-detector test should be conducted in the court-room at the trial.[5] The conditions are too exciting, and the judge and jury are not competent to interpret the results. The issue is, shall the examiner who conducted the test be permitted to give his testimony presenting the chart and explaining his conclusion as to whether the subject believed he was telling the truth or was consciously lying in his answers to the crucial questions?

What is the attitude of the courts? The question arises in different ways. (1) When the state and the accused stipulate for the administering of the test, and for its admission in evidence, the trial judges have generally admitted the expert's evidence giving the results.[6]

(2) When the results of a test, as above, taken under stipulation between the state and the accused, has been offered at the trial, and the judge's ruling thereon has been appealed, the appellate decisions are in conflict. One court approved the judge's ruling admitting the evidence.[7] Another sustained his ruling rejecting it.[8] The former result seems the just and expedient one.

(3) When the accused selects his own examiner and without any agreement with the

approximately 100 police departments using the tests, there are 55 personal consultants who employ them in connection with investigative and personnel examinations." Trovillo, op. cit., 22 Tenn.L.Rev. 743. See also McEvoy, The Lie Detector Goes into Business, 38 Reader's Digest, no. 226, p. 69 (Feb.1941).

5. In State v. Cole, 354 Mo. 181, 188 S.W.2d 43, syl. 12, 13 (1945) the accused requested the trial judge that a lie-detector might be used in examining the witnesses in court including the accused himself. In sustaining the denial of the request the court said, "Such dramatics before the jury would distract them and impede the trial."

6. In Smallwood, op. cit., 29 Corn.L.Q. 540, n. 49, twelve cases in widely scattered trial courts are cited, Trovillo, op. cit., 22 Tenn.L.Rev. 33, reports that "55 experts have gone into court with their polygrams and testified as to the indications in the charts before judges and juries in municipal district and superior courts." But in the strange case of Le Fevre v. State, 242 Wis. 416, 8 N.W.2d 288, syl. 1 (1943), the judge, when the defendant offered the report and findings of the examiner, admitted the report but excluded the findings at the instance of the state. The district attorney testified that the test was made by an examiner chosen by the state under a stipulation that either the state or the defendant could introduce the finding, and that the result was actually favorable to the defendant. The upper court approved the ruling, but reversed the conviction for insufficiency of the evidence. Perhaps the result can be sustained on the ground that from the district attorney's evidence that the tests were favorable to the accused he got all the

benefit that he would have secured if the findings had been admitted. Three judges dissented. See Note, 1943 Wis.L.Rev. 430.

7. People v. Houser, 85 Cal.App.2d 686, 193 P.2d 937, syl. 6, 7 (1948) (offered by state over objection of accused though he had stipulated that expert was qualified and that results should be admitted).

8. Boeche v. State, 151 Neb. 368, 37 N.W.2d 593, syl. 3 (1949). In that case it was held that, where the defendant on trial for forgery offered in evidence the results of a test by a polygraph operator of the state crime laboratory with eight months' experience. Defendant had voluntarily submitted to the test, and claimed it supported his innocence. The judge on the state's objection rejected the evidence, and the majority held that this ruling was right as the test "has not yet received general scientific acceptance." The case is notable for the fact that three judges, in an able opinion written by Chappell, J., rejected this reasoning, and held that if an adequate showing of the qualification of the expert had been made, and if an adequate foundation of proof of the scientific soundness of the tests had been furnished, the evidence would have been admissible. This dissenting opinion may have broken ground for a new advance.

Compare also Peterson v. State, 157 Tex.Cr.R. 255, 247 S.W.2d 110, syl. 1, 2 (1952) where the accused, having voluntarily taken a test by an operator of the state, offered the operator to testify to the result, but this was excluded. The ruling was affirmed on the grounds (1) that the bill of exceptions failed to disclose what the excluded testimony would have shown, and (2) the results being inadmissible for the state are so also for the accused. Another case

state, submits to the test, and offers the result in evidence, the trial courts have usually excluded the evidence [9] and the upper courts have uniformly sustained them.[10]

(4) Occasionally, a reference to the taking of a lie-detector test, or the refusal to take such a test is sought to be introduced in the testimony. These cases are collected and described in the note.[11]

The foregoing rulings embrace the greater number of the actual reported holdings. The courts have not been confronted with the situation which is a strategic one for the future of the technique. That is the case where the accused voluntarily but without any agreement as to the use of the results in evidence submits to the test and the expert's conclusions adverse to the accused are offered in evidence by the state. Though nearly all of the reported decisions deal with the

third situation above, where the defendant whose interest is to select any expert or charlatan who will find in his favor offers his own ex parte test-results to prove his innocence, the opinions do not limit themselves to the particular situation presented, but declare the inadmissibility of lie-detector results generally.

One reason usually given for these general pronouncements is that the tests have not yet won sufficient scientific acceptance of their validity. Frequently the opinions seem to demand a universality of scientific approval, which as pointed out above,[12] has no basis in the standard applied to other kinds of expert testimony in scientific matters. If we thus deflate the requirement to the normal standard which simply demands that the theory or device be accepted by a substantial body of scientific opinion, there can be little

---

where an accused voluntarily submitted to a test by a state operative, but where his offer of the results was rejected at the trial and on appeal is Henderson v. State, 94 Okl.Cr. 45, 230 P.2d 495, 502, syl. 7, 8 (1951). The court in an extensive discussion contended that there was want of acceptance and of reliability. Its reasoning on the latter point is somewhat vitiated by a failure, in appraising the factor of error, to distinguish clearly between cases where the results are inconclusive and those where the conclusions are incorrect. See Wicker, op. cit., 22 Tenn.L.Rev. 719.

9. In one notable case, however, the trial judge received such evidence, and his judgment overruling the state's objection is the only reported opinion upholding the admissibility of lie-detector tests. People v. Kenny, 167 Misc. 51, 3 N.Y.S.2d 348 (Co.Ct.1938). The opinion reflects a strong foundation laid by testimony vouching for the scientific basis and reliability of the test, given by Professor Summers of Fordham University.

10. Frye v. United States, 293 Fed. 1013 (Ct.App.D.C. 1923) (discussed above, § 170, n. 5; People v. Becker, 300 Mich. 562, 2 N.W.2d 503, syl. 4, 5, 139 A.L.R. 1171 (1942) ("There was no testimony offered which would indicate that there is at this time a general scientific recognition of the tests"); State v. Pusch, 77 N.D. 860, 46 N.W.2d 508, syl. 4 (1950); State v. Bohner, 210 Wis. 651, 246 N.W. 314, syl. 6 (1933).

11. Testimony that an officer pointed out to the accused the parts of his test-chart where he was

lying, doubtless offered on the theory that his failure to deny was an implied admission, was held inadmissible. Leeks v. State, 245 P.2d 764, syl. 15 (Okl.Cr.1952). In People v. Wochnick, 96 Cal. App.2d 124, 219 P.2d 70, syl. 3 (1950), noted 35 Minn. L.Rev. 310, an officer testified that defendant had been told that he had been placed on the lie detector for a test and that there was a violent reaction when he was shown a certain exhibit; and that when he was asked for an explanation of such reaction he stated that he could not explain it. Though the judge instructed the jury not to consider this as evidence of the result of the test, the upper court held that the evidence was wrongly received. Similarly, it was held in State v. Kolander, 236 Minn. 209, 52 N.W.2d 458, syl. 7 (1952) that evidence introduced by the state that the accused, when requested to do so by the sheriff, declined to submit to a test, was erroneously received. Less strict than those holdings is Tyler v. United States, 193 F.2d 24 syl. 12 (Ct.App.D.C.1951, cert.den.). There the accused confessed after taking a polygraph test. An officer was allowed to testify that he stated to the defendant that the machine indicated that he was lying. The defendant claimed that his confession was involuntary, and the judge held that the officer's statement was receivable not to show the accused was lying, but as bearing on voluntariness as showing the circumstances leading to the confession. The upper court approved this ruling.

12. See § 170.

doubt that the lie-detector technique meets this requirement. An inquiry made in 1952 among polygraph examiners and psychologists seems to substantiate the foregoing statement.[13]

Another reason, cognate with the foregoing, is that the tests have not been shown to possess that degree of reliability in actual practice to entitle them to consideration by judge and jury. Of course, no demand for infallibility in results could be supported, nor do our present methods of evaluating testimony have any very high degree of reliability. Obviously the lie-detector tests have substantial probative worth. The issue properly is, does their reliability-value outweigh the dangers of prejudicing or misleading the jury or of undue consumption of time? Studies which have been made of the reports of practicing examiners seem to indicate that "with highly trained and experienced examiners, we can expect correct judgments in about 80 per cent of the cases, inability of the examiner to make a confident judgment in about 17 per cent, and incorrect judgments in about three per cent." [14] Seemingly this degree of accuracy is sufficient to outweigh the dangers mentioned. The danger of prej-

udice or misleading is appreciable, but not overwhelming. It must be remembered that the jury would not witness the giving of the test but would hear only a description and interpretation of its results by the examiner. His interpretation may be tested on cross-examination and when debatable could be contested by the testimony of another expert. Such a contest, however, would rarely be profitable and consequently the consumption of time would seldom be extensive.

In the light of these findings, it is believed that the courts' wholesale exclusion of lie-detector test-results, for want of scientific acceptance and proved reliability, is not supported by the facts. Many courts can easily recede from this position, in a case where the foregoing facts as to acceptance and reliability are adequately proven by the expert himself as a foundation for his testimony giving the test-results.[15] In most of the cases where the results were held inadmissible no such foundation was laid,[16] and the decisions may be explained on that ground, since the scientific facts were not so indisputable and readily verifiable as to enable the court to take judicial notice of them.[17] The day for

13. Dr. Cureton summarizes the results of the survey as follows:

"(1) Of the 199 Examiners, 83 per cent believe the polygraph is highly valid for recording physiological reactions, 47 per cent recommend court testimony by competent examiners, and 83 per cent recommend periodic examination of certain personnel in business and industry.

"(2) Of the 230 psychologists who have conducted polygraphic tests of deception in experimental situations or observed or conducted such tests on criminal suspects, employed personnel, or applicants, 63 per cent consider the polygraph highly valid for recording physiological reactions, 51 per cent recommend court testimony, and 28 per cent recommend use in business and industry.

"(3) Of the small group of 35 psychologists who are also Examiners, 63 per cent think the polygraph is highly valid for recording physiological reactions, 60 per cent recommend court testimony, and 51 per cent recommend use in business and industry.

"4. No appreciable proportion of any group considers the polygraph invalid and useless when in

competent hands." A Consensus as to the Validity of Polygraph Procedures, 22 Tenn.L.Rev. 728, 740 (1953).

14. Cureton, op.cit., 22 Tenn.L.Rev. 729. The quotation continues: "To attain this record the examiner, after training, requires *several years* of experience. Even trained examiners, with less experience, make incorrect judgments in at least 10 per cent of the cases, and report ambiguous records in more than 20 per cent." The statement is based on a report of Dr. Dael Wolfle on the lie detector for the armed services in 1941, when he was a member of the Emergency Committee in Psychology of the National Research Council.

15. As in People v. Kenny, supra n. 9.

16. As is pointed out in the opinions in People v. Becker, cited in note 10, supra, and in Boeche v. State (dissenting opinion), cited in n. 8, supra.

17. In People v. Forte, 279 N.Y. 204, 18 N.E.2d 31, 32, syl. 2, 3 (1938), the defendant at the end of his trial for first-degree murder, moved to reopen the

judicial notice will dawn after another decade of such explanations by expert witnesses.

The simple doctrine of wholesale exclusion seems, accordingly, an inadequate solution based upon estimates of acceptance and reliability which are no longer valid. When the courts turn from the answer "never" to the answer "yes, when expedient" the real difficulty becomes apparent. This is the difficulty of limiting admissibility to the only tests which are sufficiently reliable, namely, those administered and interpreted by "highly trained and experienced examiners." [18] So far, professional organizations of examiners [19] are in their infancy, and they have adopted no standards of training, but their officers can doubtless be called upon to furnish information as to qualified experts.

It is believed that the courts should meet the need for this new resource for fact-finding and minimize the dangers, by substituting for the rule of exclusion a standard of discretion, and by holding accordingly that the judge may in his discretion admit expert testimony giving the results of a test of an accused or other witness, offered by the state or the accused or by a civil party when the judge finds (a) that the expert is highly trained and experienced, and (b) that the probative value outweighs the danger of prejudice, confusion and waste of time.

In addition, by rule of court or by decisional recognition of powers traditional to the common-law judge,[20] it should be declared that on application of either party on notice a reasonable time before trial, or on the judge's own motion,[21] a test of a party or a witness may be provided for, with the results to be admissible in evidence if the expert can reach a conclusion satisfactory to himself as to truth or deception. If the person to be tested refuses to undergo the test, there is an end of the matter [22] except that if he is a party, his refusal may be proved against him.[23]

175. Statements Made While under the Influence of Drugs or Hypnosis.

Another possible method by which the truthfulness of the story of a witness may be tested is the inducing of a mental state in which his normal power of "censorship" is removed, and in which it becomes difficult or impossible for him to suppress his thoughts or devise a falsehood.[1] That alcohol has an

---

case so that he could be given a lie-detector test. The motion was refused, and this was assigned as error after his conviction. The court of appeals affirmed and said: "We cannot take judicial notice that this instrument is or is not effective for the purpose of determining the truth. . . . Evidence relating to handwriting, finger printing and ballistics is recognized by experts as possessing such value that reasonable certainty can follow from tests. Until such a fact, if it be a fact, is demonstrated by qualified experts in respect to the 'lie detector,' we cannot hold as matter of law that error was committed in refusing to allow defendant to experiment with it."

[18]. See note 14, supra.

[19]. They are the International Society for the Detection of Deception, C. B. Hanscom, Secretary, School of Business, University of Minnesota, and the American Academy of Forensic Sciences, Prof. Ralph Turner, Secretary, School of Police Science and Administration, Michigan State College, East Lansing, Michigan. See Trovillo, op. cit., 22 Tenn.L.Rev. 764.

[20]. See §§ 8, 17.

[21]. Trial judges, feeling the need of more light upon difficult problems of veracity, suggested lie-detector tests, and admitted the results of the tests, in State v. Lowry, 163 Kan. 622, 185 P.2d 147 (1947) and in Stone v. Earp, 331 Mich. 606, 50 N.W.2d 172 (1951). In each instance these hopeful expedients were discouraged by appellate holdings that it was error to admit the evidence.

[22]. Apparently, in the present state of the art, it is impossible to make a reliable test upon a person who is unwilling but is physically compelled to submit. See Wicker, op. cit., 22 Tenn.L.Rev. 718, Trovillo, id. 744.

[23]. In the case of an accused this would raise questions of self-incrimination, which are considered in §§ 80, 132, herein.

[1]. See the illuminating article, Despres, Legal Aspects of Drug-Induced Statements, 14 U.Chi.L.Rev. 600 (1947). See also Kleinfeld, The Detection of Deception—A Resumé, 8 Fed.Bar A.J. 153, 167

influence in this direction is attested by the old maxim, *in vino veritas*. A physician administering the "twilight sleep" drug, scopolamine, to a woman in childbirth discovered that at a certain stage of anaesthesia the subject answered questions with child-like honesty.[2] Similar effects are produced by the injection of barbiturates, such as sodium amytal and sodium pentothal, which were widely used in World War II in the treatment of mental strains and neuroses produced by combat conditions. All of these drugs have been extensively employed in the investigation of crime and in the securing of confessions, and in attempts to test the guilt or innocence of convicts. If the drug were administered without the consent of the subject, it seems clear that a confession so induced would be excluded as "involuntary."[3] If the subject consented to the use of the drug then the admissibility of the confession, it seems, would depend upon whether the judge found that he had a reasonable capacity to understand and speak the truth when he confessed.[4]

It has been suggested that the best field of usefulness for the examination under narcosis is the clearing of innocent suspects.[5] Defendants so far have offered such drug-induced statements without avail.[6] Since this technique is even more clearly in the experimental stage than the lie-detector method, judicial notice of its validity could not be accorded. If, however, a foundation should be laid by evidence of experts as to the validity of the method and as to its correct application in the particular instance so that in the opinion of the experts the power of conscious contriving was removed and the statements were not actuated by fantasy or suggestion[7] —ever present dangers here—such statements under voluntary narcosis could reasonably be admitted. Even when offered by the party on his own behalf, the "hearsay" or "self-serving" objection need not prevail. If the offering party has testified, the statement may be offered, not to prove the facts stated therein, but as a prior consistent statement to support his credibility, escaping the rule against such form of support by reason of the foundation showing the unique trustworthiness of this type of prior statement. Or if the party has not testified, and the statement must come in as evidence of its truth, an exception to the hearsay rule on the ground of special trustworthiness could well be argued for. The further validation by experiment and practice, of the scientific theory of the trustworthiness of drug-induced statements, and the further development of the skill of

---

(1947); 3 Wigmore, Evidence, § 998; Wigmore, Principles of Judicial Proof, § 311 (3d ed. 1947); Muehlberger, Criminal Confessions under Narcosis, 26 J.Crim.L. 449 (1935).

2. See the article by Dr. R. H. House, the original experimenter in this field, The Use of Scopolamine in Criminology, 18 Tex.St.Med.J. 259, 261 (1927), quoted in Despres, op. cit., 14 U.Chi.L.Rev. 602.

3. See the forcible argument to this effect in Despres op. cit., 14 U.Chi.L.Rev. 605–610. See also Note, 44 Harv.L.Rev. 842, 845 (1931). Compare the holdings that a confession designedly procured by making the declarant drunk is inadmissible. McNutt v. State, 68 Neb. 207, 94 N.W. 143, syl. 4 (1903); 2 Wigmore, Evidence, § 499, note 6.

4. Bell v. United States, 47 F.2d 438, 74 A.L.R. 1098, 1101 (App.D.C.1931) ("sufficient mental capacity to know what he was saying").

5. See Muehlberger, op. cit., 26 J.Crim.L. 450, Despres, 14 U.Chi.L.Rev. 603, 610.

6. People v. McNichol, 100 Cal.App.2d 554, 224 P.2d 21, syl. 2, 5 (1950) (check-passing: defense, that accused was too drunk to know what he was doing: statement of accused under sodium pentothal to psychologist excluded because proponent's theories for admissibility untenable); State v. Hudson, 314 Mo. 599, 289 S.W. 920, syl. 2 (1926) (statement under "truth telling serum" properly rejected. "We are not told from what well this serum is drawn, or in what alembic its alleged truth-compelling powers are distilled.").

7. "The authorities agree that the subject pours out both fact and fancy. Dr. Lorenz observes: 'Much care must be exercised by the experimenter to evaluate the results. He must discriminate, *if possible*, what is the product of fantasy and what of fact.'" Despres, op. cit., 14 U. of Chi.L.Rev. 605.

technicians in administering the method, will presumably be followed by the development of appropriate legal doctrines permitting the uses of such statements in evidence.

There seems to be less scientific support for the reliability of declarations made under hypnotic influences than in the case of drug-induced statements.[8] The hypnotic subject is, of course, ultra-suggestible, and this fact manifestly endangers the reliability of statements made under hypnosis. Thus far, the courts have rejected confessions induced by hypnosis,[9] and statements made under hypnosis by the accused offered in his own behalf.[10]

176. Chemical Tests for Drunkenness.[1]

This is a field where the courts, despite formidable conflicts in expert opinion, have been persuaded rather quickly to use the results of scientific experimentation.

The present discussion will be limited to the questions of the admissibility of the various chemical tests as dependent upon their reliability, on the assumption that the tests are administered without objection, and leaving

for separate treatment the questions of privilege which arise when the tests are administered involuntarily.[2] Presumably, it is the amount of alcohol in the brain that determines the extent of intoxication. However, since (except in case of autopsy after death) the brain tissue cannot be taken for analysis, resort must be had to other substances. Of these, the blood undoubtedly affords upon analysis the most satisfactory and reliable results, and the admission of blood-tests when supported by adequate preliminary proof has been generally approved.[3] Resort has also been had, with the sanction of some decisions and statutes,[4] to tests also of the urine [5] and of the breath.[6]

Dissenting scientists have objected to all these tests upon the ground, among others, of the existence of wide individual variations in sensitivity or tolerance to alcohol.[7] But the weight of medical and scientific opinion seems to favor the view that experience has demonstrated that the results of the tests are of great practical value in determining whether the persons tested are under the in-

---

8. Despres, op. cit., 14 Uni. of Chi.L.Rev. 607; Burtt, Legal Psychology, 133–138 (1931).

9. Rex v. Booher, [1928] 4 Dom.L.Rep. 795 (nisi prius: judge, not satisfied that confession not secured by hypnotism or mental suggestion, excludes it), noted in 42 Harv.L.Rev. 704.

10. People v. McNichol, 100 Cal.App.2d 554, 224 P.2d 21, syl. 6 (1950) (sodium pentathol); State v. Hudson, 289 S.W. 920, syl. 2 (Mo.1926) ("truth serum," not defined); State v. Lindemuth, 56 N.M. 257, 243 P.2d 325, syl. 9 (1952) (sodium pentothal); Henderson v. State, 230 P.2d 495, syl. 8, 23 A.L.R. 2d 1292 (Okl.Cr.1951) ("truth serum"); Orange v. Comm., 191 Va. 423, 61 S.E.2d 267, syl. 6 (1950) ("truth serum").

1. Donigan, Chemical Test Case Law (pamphlet pub. by Traffic Institute, Northwestern Univ., Evanston, Ill., 1950) (best single source); Ladd and Gibson, The Medico-Legal Aspects of the Blood Test for Intoxication, 24 Iowa L.Rev. 191 (1939) (excellent); Ladd and Gibson, Legal Medical Aspects of Blood Tests, 29 Va.L.Rev. 749 (1943); H. W. Newman, M. D., Proof of Alcoholic Intoxication, 34 Ky.L.J. 250 (1946) (clear, moderate statement of the scien-

tific basis and value of the tests); Notes, Wilson and Edman, 51 Mich.L.Rev. 72 (1952); Rowell, 5 Univ.Fla.L.Rev. 5, 11 (1952), 127 A.L.R. 1513, 159 A.L.R. 209; Dec.Dig. Crim.Law, ☜388.

2. See §§ 126, 137, 139, 141, herein.

3. E. g., State v. Koenig, 240 Iowa 592, 36 N.W.2d 765, syl. 4 (1949); State v. Sturtevant, 96 N.H. 99, 70 A.2d 909, syl. 3 (1950) (in judge's discretion); Sandel v. State, 253 S.W.2d 283, syl. 4 (Tex.Cr. 1952); Kuroske v. Aetna Life Ins. Co., 234 Wis. 394, 291 N.W. 384, syl. 4, 5, 127 A.L.R. 1505 (1940) (but not here conclusive).

4. See New York statute quoted later in this section.

5. Toms v. State, 239 P.2d 812, syl. 9 (Okl.Cr.1952).

6. See notes 13–16, below.

7. Rabinowitch, Medico-Legal Aspects of Chemical Tests, 39 J.Crim.L. 225 (1948) (able and extensive canvassing of the numerous scientific factors of error); Gardner, Breath Tests for Alcohol, 31 Tex. L.Rev. 289 (1953) (an acute lawyer's study of the scientific literature). Both of these are required reading for counsel preparing to cross-examine experts supporting the tests.

fluence of alcohol.[8] Following the recommendation of committees of the National Safety Council and of the American Medical Association,[9] thirteen states have adopted statutory standards of proof [10] which are thought to embody the general conclusions warranted by the most careful and extensive experimentation in the field. The New York statute is typical. In actions involving the operation of a motor vehicle by a person in an intoxicated condition, it provides that evidence of the alcohol content of the blood, as shown by an analysis of his breath, blood, urine, or saliva, made within two hours after arrest, may be admitted. It further provides that "(a) evidence that there was, at the time, five-hundredths of one per centum, or less, by weight of alcohol in his blood, is prima facie evidence that the defendant was not in an intoxicated condition; (b) evidence that there was, at the time, more than five-hundredths of one per centum and less than fifteen-hundredths of one per centum by weight of alcohol in his blood is relevant evidence, but it is not to be given prima facie effect in indicating whether or not the defendant was in an intoxicated condition; (c) evidence that there was, at the time, fifteen-hundredths of one per centum, or more by weight of alcohol in his blood, may be admitted as prima facie evidence that the defendant was in an intoxicated condition." In

the absence of such a statute, it is customary for the expert witness interpreting the test-results to give evidence explaining the effect of the particular finding as to alcohol content of the blood, in accordance with the scale upon which the New York statute is based.[11]

There is usually some delay in making the test after the collision or other crucial happening, but as the average rate of metabolism of alcohol in the body of persons generally is known and furnishes a fairly reliable guide, the amount of alcohol concentration at the time of the earlier happening can usually be estimated with reasonable accuracy.[12]

The breath-test has the advantage of convenience. It does not require a physician or medical technician to extract a sample, as does the blood-test. It may be administered by a trained policeman. Moreover, it is least likely to arouse objection, and thus to raise doubtful questions of privilege. Its reliability as an index of the alcoholic content of the blood, however, is clouded by the fact that the formula generally used for conversion from alcohol in the breath to that in the blood is to multiply the former by 2000. Consequently any error in the original analysis and computation of the amount in the breath would be magnified 2000-fold in the report of alcohol in the blood.[13] On the other

8. See authorities cited in n. 1, above, and particularly these answers to Rabinowitch, supra: Harger, 39 J.Crim.L. 402 (1948) and Muehlberger, id. 411. See also Harger, "Debunking" the Drunkometer, 40 J.Crim.L. 497 (1949) (answering other critics).

9. See Donigan, Chemical Test Law, 7 (1950); Muehlberger, op. cit., 39 J.Crim.L. 411, 412 (1948).

10. Ariz.Laws 1950, 1st Sp. Sess. c. 3, § 54; Ind. Burns' Ann.St. § 47–2003; Me.R.S.1944, c. 19, § 121; Neb.R.S.1951 Supp. § 39–727.01; N.H.Laws 1949, c. 204; N.Y. Vehicle & Traffic Law, McKinney's Consol.Laws, c. 71 § 70, subd. 5; N.D.R.C.1949 Supp. § 39–0801; Ore. ORS 483.630; S.C.Act June 7, 1949, 46 Stat. at Large, p. 466, § 57; S.D. Laws 1949, c. 42; U.C.A.1943, 57–7–111; Wash. R.C.W. 46.56.010; Wis.St.1953, § 85.13; this list appears in Note, 51 Mich.L.Rev. 71, 77 (1952).

11. See, e. g., State v. Haner, 231 Iowa 348, 1 N.W. 2d 91, 92 (1941); Toms v. State, 239 P.2d 812, 818 (Okl.Cr.1952).

12. See Newman, op. cit., 34 Ky.L.J. 250, 257–8; but compare Gardner, op. cit., 31 Tex.L.Rev. 289, 297. See also Toms v. State, 239 P.2d 812, 820, syl. 10 (Okl.Cr.1952) (urine and breath tests taken 1½ hours after collision held not too remote; expert testified that a human body will burn about "⅓ of an ounce of alcohol an hour, or about .015% of blood alcohol per hour").

13. Gardner, op. cit., 31 Tex.L.Rev. 289, 292. For other factors of error, see Newman, op. cit., 34 Ky. L.J. 250, 265 (1946); Rabinowitch, op. cit., 39 J. Crim.L. 225, 242–244.

hand, there is substantial scientific support for the reasonable reliability of such tests,[14] and statutes in some of the states, as in New York,[15] expressly sanction the use of the breath-test. The decisions on the admissibility of breath-tests reflect the division in scientific opinion, with a slight preponderance favoring admission.[16] Until scientific knowledge and continued experience enable the courts to take judicial knowledge that this test is, or is not, reasonably reliable, the trial judge should in passing on admissibility weigh the probative value of the offered test-results in the particular case, in the light of the accompanying expert testimony, pro and con, against the danger that the jury may be misled or unduly prejudiced by their admission.

The party offering the results of any of these chemical tests must first lay a foundation by producing expert witnesses who will explain the way in which the test is conducted, attest its scientific reliability, and vouch for its correct administration in the particular case.[17]

It is important to remember that none of these tests is conclusive, that it is always open to the opponent to adduce countervailing evidence of his sobriety. It is important also that the police in making arrests for drunken driving follow a carefully established procedure designed to secure and record all the relevant information as to the drunkenness or sobriety of the suspect obtainable from observation and questioning, so that the chemical tests may be supplemented by all available data needed for a rounded and reliable judgment on the issue of intoxication.[18]

177. Identification of Blood in Criminal Investigation.

In the investigation of crime it is often important to know whether a particular stain is blood or not, and if it is, whether it is human blood. Laboratory techniques are available by which these questions can usually be answered.[1] When the substance is found to be human blood, then the search for the person from whom the blood came may be carried a step further by employing the methods

14. Ladd and Gibson, op. cit., 24 Iowa L.Rev. 191, 199, 200; articles by Muehlberger and Harger, cited note 8, supra.

15. See note 10, supra.

16. Admissible: People v. Bobczck, 343 Ill.App. 544, 99 N.E.2d 567, syl. 2 (1951); Toms v. State, 239 P.2d 812, syl. 11, 12 (Okl.Cr.1952); McKay v. State, 155 Tex.Cr. 416, 235 S.W.2d 173, syl. 1–3 (1951) (conflict in scientific opinions goes only to the weight of the evidence). Contra: People v. Morse, 325 Mich. 270, 38 N.W.2d 322, syl. 1 (1949) (one doctor and two policemen with brief training in the use of the test gave evidence in support; five doctors testified that they are not reliable, one saying "You have got a continuous series of errors, some for and some against so that the thing works like a slot-machine"; held, error to admit the test-results, which have not yet gained general scientific recognition).

17. Illustrative cases as to the foundation requirements: Nichols v. McCoy, 38 Cal.2d 447, 240 P.2d 569, syl. 2 (1952) (proof held sufficient to identify the blood received for testing by state toxicologist as decedent's blood: two judges dissenting); Ab-

rego v. State, 157 Tex.Cr.R. 264, 248 S.W.2d 490, syl. 1 (1952) (identification of blood sufficient); Hill v. State, 256 S.W.2d 93, syl. 6 (Tex.Cr.1953) (testimony of police officer as to result of breath alcohol test was improper where there was no proof that chemicals used in machine used for test were compounded to proper percentage or that officer and machine were under periodic supervision of one who understood scientific theory of machine).

Suggestions as to the examination of witnesses for the purpose of laying the foundation and presenting the evidence of test-results may be found in Ladd and Gibson, op. cit., 24 Iowa L.Rev. 191, 263–267, Ladd and Gibson, op. cit., 29 Va.L.Rev. 749, 755–758, and Donigan, Chemical Test Case Law, 71–80 (1950).

18. See Muehlberger, op. cit., 39 J.Crim.L. 411, 412, 413. Ideally these observations should be in the form of a clinical examination by a physician, but as a regular routine this is not feasible. Id., 415.

1. Turner, Forensic Science and Laboratory Technics, ch. 9 (C. C. Thomas, Springfield, Ill., 1949) (describing precipitin and other tests); Boyd, Forensic Immunology, 36 J.Crim.L. 455 (1946).

of the rapidly developing technique of blood group testing. Under the first of the standard classifications, the following groups were recognized:

> "Group O, in which you will find approximately 45% of the population;
> "Group A, in which you will find approximately 42% of the population; and
> "Group B, in which you will find approximately 10% of the population, and
> "Group AB, in which you will find the remaining 3%." [2]

In a recent leading case, the accused was charged with rape, and evidence was received to the effect that blood found on the coat of accused was of type O, and that the blood of the alleged victim was of the same type. As stated above, 45% of the population have blood of this type. The court overruled an objection to this evidence on the ground of remoteness and said: "The objection of remoteness goes to the weight of the evidence rather than to its admissibility. To exclude evidence merely because it tends to establish a possibility, rather than a probability, would produce curious results not heretofore thought of. In this case the fact that the accused was somewhere near the scene of the crime would not, in itself, establish a probability that he was guilty, but only a possibility, yet such evidence is clearly admissible as a link in the chain." [3]

178. Blood-Tests to Determine Paternity.[1]

The classification of blood-types mentioned in the preceding paragraph was the outgrowth of the pioneer work of Landsteiner in 1900 in the recognition of blood groups, for which he was awarded the Nobel Prize, and the later demonstration by other workers that these blood-characteristics are inheritable. Landsteiner discovered that when the red corpuscles from one person's blood were mixed with the serum from the blood of others the red corpuscles would sometimes gather into clumps, or agglutinate. Experimenting with the mixing of sera from the blood of various people, with the red corpuscles in the blood of others, and the consequent agglutination or failure to agglutinate, it was possible to differentiate the blood-types according to the presence or not of certain agglutinogens. These are acted upon by correspondingly classified substances (anti-A and anti-B) in the sera to produce this clumping of corpuscles. Thus if a person's blood possesses only the agglutinogen A, he is classed in group A; if only B, in that group; if both A and B, in group AB; and if it possesses neither then in group O. From the studies of scores of thousands of tests of the blood of parents and children, the two following laws were derived: (1) group A or B does not and cannot appear in the blood of a child unless it appears in the blood of one or both parents, and (2) a parent of group AB cannot have offspring of group O,

---

2. Quoted from the testimony of Dr. Freimuth in the opinion in Shanks v. State, 185 Md. 437, 45 A. 2d 85, 163 A.L.R. 931, 934 (1945).

3. Shanks v. State, 185 Md. 437, 45 A.2d 85, 163 A. L.R. 931, 937 (1945). A case of similar facts and like holding is Comm. v. Stratti, 166 Pa.Super. 577, 73 A.2d 688, syl. 7 (1950).

1. 1 Wigmore, Evidence, § 165a; Wigmore, The Science of Judicial Proof, §§ 88–90; Schatkin, Disputed Paternity Proceedings (3d ed. 1953). The topic has captivated the interest of law review writers, and the following list is a selection from a rich array: Williams, The Use of Blood Grouping Tests in Parentage Proceedings—a Scientific

Basis, 50 Mich.L.Rev. 582 (1952); Yantis, Blood Test Exclusions as Decisive Evidence, 24 Rocky Mt.L.Rev. 237 (1952); Fedder, Justice through Science: the Blood Grouping Test, 3 So.Car.L.Q. 325 (1951); Greene, "Blood Will Tell," 1 Mercer L.Rev. 266 (1950); Dr. Ronald L. Denton, Blood Groups and Disputed Parentage, 27 Can.Bar Rev. 537 (1949); Keeffe and Bailey, "A Trial of Bastardy Is a Trial of the Blood," 34 Corn.L.Q. 72 (1948); Maguire, Survey of Blood Group Decisions and Legislation, 16 So.Cal.L.Rev. 161 (1943); Dr. William C. Boyd, Protecting the Evidentiary Value of Blood Group Determinations, 16 So.Cal.L.Rev. 193 (1943). See also Note, Blood Grouping Tests, 163 A.L.R. 939 (1946).

and a group O parent cannot have a child of group AB.[2]

The practical workings of these laws may be represented by the following table:[3]

Child	Known Parent	Unknown Parent Must Be	Unknown Parent Cannot Be
O	O	O, A, B	AB
	A	O, A, B	AB
	B	O, A, B	AB
	AB	Impossible for parent to be AB when child is in O	
A	O	A, AB	B, O
	A	O, AB, A, B	Exclusion impossible
	B	A, AB	B, O
	AB	O, AB, A, B	Exclusion impossible
B	O	B, AB	A, O
	A	B, AB	A, O
	B	O, AB, A, B	Exclusion impossible
	AB	O, AB, A, B	Exclusion impossible
AB	O	Impossible for parent to be O when child is in AB	
	A	B, AB	A, O
	B	A, AB	B, O
	AB	A, AB, B	O

It was computed that under the ABO classification the chances were about one in six[4] that a test of the blood of one falsely charged with the parenthood of a child would show his innocence rather than merely proving inconclusive.

In 1927 two additional inheritable qualities of the red blood cells were discovered by Landsteiner and Levine. These characteristics were termed M and N, and their recognition enables the analyst to classify blood as M, N, or MN. Every human being must belong to one of these types. Upward of 35,000 mother-child tests have established these conclusions:[5]

"(1) Factor M or factor N cannot appear in a child unless present in one or both parents;

"(2) a parent of group M cannot give rise to a child of group N, nor a parent of group N to a child of group M.

"We have therefore the following 'possible' and 'not possible' types of offspring of the various MN matings:

Parental Groups	Children POSSIBLE	Children NOT POSSIBLE
M × N	MN	M, N
M × M	M	N, MN
N × N	N	M, MN
M × MN	M, MN	N
N × MN	N, MN	M
MN × MN	M, N, MN	All possible

The MN series is independent of the ABO groupings, and the addition of the new classification raised the chances of the falsely accused father of demonstrating his exclusion to one in three.[6]

Pursuing the onward march, in 1940 Weiner, a student of Landsteiner, announced the discovery of the rhesus blood factor, which provides a new and additional basis for classification of inherited qualities of the blood.[7] The discovery was made by immunizing rabbits and guinea-pigs with blood from the rhesus monkey and mixing the antiserums thus procured with the human blood to be tested. The anti-rhesus serum from

2. Denton, op. cit., 27 Can.Bar Rev. 542.

3. Copied by permission from Greene, op. cit., 1 Mercer L.Rev. 268.

4. Denton, op. cit., 27 Can.Bar Rev. 545.

5. Denton, op. cit., 27 Can.Bar Rev. 544.

6. Denton, op. cit., 27 Can.Bar Rev. 545.

7. Williams, op. cit., 50 Mich.L.Rev. 588–595, Keeffe and Bailey, op. cit., 34 Corn.L.Q. 73–75, Yantis, op. cit., 24 Rocky Mt.L.Rev. 240. A judge in New York accepted as conclusive the result of the use of this test by its developer, Dr. Wiener. Saks v. Saks, 189 Misc. 667, 71 N.Y.S.2d 797, syl. 5 (Dom.Rel.Ct.N.Y. City, Panken, J., 1947).

animals enables the analyst to classify all human blood as Rh positive and Rh negative, and by further experimentation with anti-sera prepared by immunizing human volunteers, twelve types in all of agglutinogens based on the rhesus factor have been identified. Again, laws of exclusion, based on the genetic principles applied in the ABO and MN series, have been formulated and verified by extensive experimentation. It is estimated that the discovery of this new series of blood-characteristics increases the chances of the alleged father falsely accused of proving his exclusion to better than even odds, i. e., he can do so in about 55% of the cases.[8]

These three systems which we have described do not exhaust the story. In 1949 a scientist in this field stated that three additional unrelated systems or series of heritable blood characteristics were known, but not then sufficiently explored and verified to be used as a basis for unqualified conclusions.[9] Doubtless further investigation will add new analytical tools which will further increase the chances of reaching certainty about the hidden facts in paternity cases.

How far are these contributions to scientific proof available to the courts and how effectively have they been used?

Frequently the parties will agree to the taking of the tests, and thus the test-results will be available. Often, however, one party will refuse consent and an application will be made by the other for an order for the administration of the tests. A substantial number of states have statutes empowering the court to make such an order [10] and others have held that it is within the "inherent" power,[11] on the analogy to the similar power to order an examination of the plaintiff in an action for personal injury.[12] In view of the trifling nature of the invasion involved and the magnitude of the interests at stake, it has properly been held not to violate common-law or constitutional privileges of bodily privacy under due process clauses,[13] nor under the sounder view should it be thought within the purview of the self-incrimination privilege.[14] The statute may be mandatory [15] or discretionary,[16] but if discretionary, surely the range of reasons for refusal should be narrowly limited.[17]

---

8.   Keeffe and Bailey, op. cit., 34 Corn.L.Q. 75.

9.   Denton, op. cit., 27 Can.Bar Rev. 540.

10.   The following are listed in Yantis, op. cit., 24 Rocky Mt.L.Rev. 243: Maine, R.S.1944, c. 153, § 34; New York, Civil Practice Act, § 306-a, Domestic Relations Law, McKinney's Consol.Laws, c. 14, § 126-a, Code Cr.Proc. § 68-a, Domestic Relations Court Act of the City of New York, § 34; New Jersey, N.J.S.A. 2A:83-2, 3; Maryland, Code 1951, art. 12, § 17, Ohio, R.C. §§ 2317-47, 3111-16; Wisconsin, St.1953, §§ 52.36, 325.23; North Carolina, G.S. § 49-7; South Dakota, S.D.C. 36.0602, Sup.Ct.Rule 540.

11.   State v. Damm, 64 S.D. 309, 266 N.W. 667, syl. 3, 104 A.L.R. 441 (1936), a celebrated case of conversion on rehearing, and see other holdings pro and con cited in Note, 163 A.L.R. 944, 945.

12.   See, e. g., Depfer v. Walker, 123 Fla. 862, 169 So. 660, syl. 7 (1936); Carnine v. Tibbetts, 158 Ore. 21, 74 P.2d 974, syl. 1-3 (1938); contra: Austin & N. W. Ry. Co. v. Cluck, 97 Tex. 172, 77 S.W. 403, syl. 1 (1903). Cases are collected in Notes, 51 A.L.R. 183, 108 A.L.R. 143, Dec.Dig. Damages, ⟨key⟩206(1).
In Beach v. Beach, 72 App.D.C. 318, 114 F.2d 479, syl. 2-4, 131 A.L.R. 804 (1940) it was held that Rule 35

(a) of the Federal Rules of Civil Procedure providing for ordering a physical or mental examination of a party is broad enough to authorize an order for blood tests of wife, child and husband in an action by the wife for maintenance.

13.   Cortese v. Cortese, 10 N.J.Super. 152, 76 Atl.2d 717, 719, syl. 11 (1950) (cogent opinion by Brennan, J.A.D.) disapproving Bednarik v. Bednarik, 18 N.J. Misc. 633, 16 A.2d 80 (Ch.1940). For Notes on Cortese, see 63 Harv.L.Rev. 1271, 35 Iowa L.Rev. 714, 7 W. and L.L.Rev. 208.

14.   See § 126, herein.

15.   E. g., Maine, R.S.1944, c. 153, § 34 (. . . "the court . . . shall order . . ."); New York, Civil Practice Act, § 306-a (similar), and the Ohio statutes quoted in State v. Morris, 156 Oh.St. 333, 102 N.E.2d 450, 451 (1951). See also State v. Snyder, 157 Oh.St. 15, 104 N.E.2d 169, syl. 6 (1952).

16.   As in New Jersey, N.J.S.A. 2A:83-3 (". . . the court . . . may direct").

17.   Thus, in Cortese v. Cortese, 10 N.J.Super. 152, 76 A.2d 717, 720, syl. 5-9 (1950) the court, recognizing a discretion, held that the refusal in that case was

When an adequate foundation of expert testimony, vouching the reliability of the technique and the correctness of its application in the particular case, has been laid, evidence of the results of the tests when they are interpreted by the experts as excluding the possibility that the person charged is the father, would now be generally received.[18] When the child is born of a married mother during wedlock, results of the blood-tests may be offered to show that the husband was not the father. In many jurisdictions the rule has been that the presumption of legitimacy can be rebutted only by showing certain particular facts, such as that the husband had no opportunity of access, or that he was impotent, or that the child was of another race.[19] Shall the new source of uniquely reliable scientific proof be availed of to rebut the presumption? Should the social policy of fastening upon the husband the responsibility for children born during the marriage prevail at this point over the policy that a man shall not be answerable for a child that is clearly not his? To hold that the presumption is so far conclusive that rebuttal by blood-tests is not allowable[20] would often give an escape from responsibility to the true father, and the cases admitting the tests in rebuttal[21] reflect the more expedient view.

When the scientists unanimously report that the tests have been accurately administered and adequately checked, and that they show that the man charged could not have been the father, should this be accepted as true? When a lady in California a few years ago claimed that Charles Chaplin was the father of her little girl, blood-tests were made by physicians, chosen one by the child's guardian, one by the defendant, and a third by the other two. These three physicians reported the results: Charles Chaplin, Group O, the mother, Group A, the child, Group B. He *could not* have been the father. But the lady testified (over Chaplin's denial) to intercourse with him at the appropriate season. The court said this made a conflict, which was properly submitted to the jury, and the jury having found for the lady, the verdict stands.[22] It seems, however, that if the scientific evaluation of this test is accepted, the situation is one where the courts might

---

unfounded, and said that in the absence of substantial reasons to the contrary, "we think the demonstrated utility of this tool of evidence should move trial courts in civil actions to employ it freely." Probably this decision more nearly indicates the modern trend than the holdings in Dale v. Buckingham, 241 Iowa 40, 40 N.W.2d 45, syl. 1 (1949) and State v. Damm, 64 S.D. 309, 266 N.W. 667, syl. 5, 104 A.L.R. 441 (1936), sustaining, on debatable grounds, the judge's exercise of discretion to deny the order.

18. See the statutes cited in note 10 supra; see also Beach v. Beach, 72 App.D.C. 318, 114 F.2d 479, 480, 481, 131 A.L.R. 804 (1940) and State v. Damm, 64 S.D. 309, 266 N.W. 667, 104 A.L.R. 441 (1936) in both of which the power of the court to order the tests was affirmed, and the admissibility of the evidence was discussed. Cases are collected in Note, 163 A.L.R. 950–958.

19. See 9 Wigmore, Evidence, § 2527; 7 Am.Jur. Bastards, §§ 43–50.

20. As in Hill v. Johnson, 102 Cal.App.2d 94, 226 P.2d 655, syl. 1–3, 5 (1951) (suit by minor, born in wedlock, against third person as his father: held, error to admit tests to show husband could not have been the father).

21. Schulze v. Schulze, 35 N.Y.S.2d 218 (S.Ct.1942) (husband's action for divorce and declaration of non-paternity: evidence as to access in conflict: held test-results admissible and with other evidence sufficient to rebut presumption); C. v. C. (described, note 25, infra); Cortese v. Cortese, 10 N.J.Super. 152, 76 A.2d 717, 721, syl. 12, 13 (1950) (in wife's suit against husband for support of child, error to deny order for blood-tests, nor does presumption of legitimacy justify such refusal); State v. Clark, 144 Oh.St. 305, 58 N.E.2d 773, syl. 4–6 (1944) (bastardy proceeding brought by woman whose child was conceived during prior marital relation).

22. Berry v. Chaplin, 74 Cal.App.2d 652, 169 P.2d 442, syl. 22–28 (1946, hearing den'd). Other cases holding the tests are not conclusive: Arais v. Kalensnikoff, 10 Cal.2d 428, 74 P.2d 1043, syl. 2, 12, 115 A.L.R. 163 (1937); Harding v. Harding, 22 N.Y.S.2d 810, syl. 8–11 (Dom.Rel.Ct., 1940); State v. Clark, 144 Oh.St. 305, 58 N.E.2d 773, syl. 6 (1944) (dictum); State v. Holod, 63 Oh.App. 16, 24 N.E.2d 962, syl. 1 (1939).

well apply the familiar doctrine that "where the testimony of a witness is contradicted by incontrovertible physical facts the testimony of such witness cannot be accepted, it being either mistaken or false, and a verdict based on it will not be sustained." [23] A recent case [24] in Maine blazed the trail for this view. In a bastardy proceeding the defendant admitted intercourse and the plaintiff girl, when asked if she had accused anyone else, said, "There is no other one to accuse." The court ordered a blood test by three physicians, one being the principal expert in that region. Eleven tests produced identical results. They excluded the possibility that defendant was the father. The jury, as usual, found the defendant *was* the father, probably on the doctrine of assumption of risk. The Supreme Judicial Court set aside the verdict, saying: "The skill and accuracy with which the blood grouping tests were here conducted were clearly and convincingly demonstrated by the testimony of disinterested witnesses. . . . The statement by the complainant, 'There is no other one to accuse,' even if interpreted as a denial of intercourse with any man other than the respondent, is not sufficient to overcome the overwhelming effect of this positive testimony by disinterested witnesses." [25] It seems that the certain reliability of blood-tests, carefully and expertly performed and adequately checked, to show nonpaternity is now so universally accepted by scientists that the courts are entitled to take judicial notice thereof [26] and could wisely accord them conclusive effect.[27]

The statutes usually provide that the results of the test when they *exclude* paternity of the person charged shall be received.[28] The decisions, with or without the aid of statute, have denied admission when the tests show that the person charged *could* have been the father and they are offered as evidence of his paternity.[29] Such decisions are

23. Lamp v. Pennsylvania R. R., 305 Pa. 520, 158 Atl. 269, 84 A.L.R. 1217 (1931), where the court also quoted the following from an earlier decision: "It is vain for a man to say his auto was struck in the back when the only injury thereto is at the side near the front wheel, or to insist the collision was at one place when the broken glass and other unmistakable evidences thereof are at another. A court cannot accept as true that which the indisputable evidence demonstrates is false." Id. at 524, 158 Atl. at 271, 84 A.L.R. at 1219.

24. Jordan v. Mace, 144 Me. 351, 69 A.2d 670, (1949).

25. Other cases where the court has set aside verdicts which were contrary to the test-results: State v. Wright, 59 Oh.App. 192, 17 N.E.2d 428 (1938) (reversed on other grounds 135 Oh.St. 187, 20 N.E.2d 229); Comm. v. Zammarelli, 17 Pa.D. & C. 229 (1931); Euclide v. State, 231 Wis. 616, 286 N.W. 3, (1939). An even stronger holding for conclusiveness is C. v. C., 200 Misc. 631, 109 N.Y.S.2d 276, 278 (S. Ct.Sp.Term, 1951). There the husband sued for divorce on grounds of adultery and for a determination that he was not the father of her last born child. There was strong evidence of the husband's access, but the blood-tests, performed and thrice repeated, showed that plaintiff could not be the father (mother, group A, child, group B, plaintiff group A). Murphy, J., despite the evidence of access, the mother's denial of adultery, and the presumption of legitimacy found for the plaintiff and

said ". . . the blood grouping test is, in my opinion, conclusive. . . ." The case is noted approvingly in 38 Corn.L.Q. 75. A like decision is Ross v. Marx, 21 N.J.Super. 95, 90 A.2d 545, 546, syl. 2, 3 (Co.Ct.1952), where the court said, "For a court to declare that these tests are not conclusive would be as unrealistic as it would be for a court to declare that the world is flat." The Uniform Act on Blood Tests to Determine Paternity, sec. 4 gives conclusiveness to the tests excluding paternity, when the experts agree. 1952 Handbook, Nat.Conf. Com'rs on Unif.St.Laws, 445.

26. In Cortese v. Cortese, 10 N.J.Super. 152, 76 A.2d 717, 720 (1950), the court said, "It is plain we should hold, as we do, that this unanimity of respected authorities justifies our taking judicial notice of the general recognition of the accuracy and value of the tests when properly performed by persons skilled in giving them." For other judicial expressions, mostly accord, see Note, 163 A.L.R. 949, 950.

27. See authorities cited Note 25, supra.

28. See statutes cited in note 10, supra.

29. State v. Morris, 156 Oh.St. 333, 102 N.E.2d 450, syl. 1-3 (statute permitting results of tests to be received "in cases where exclusion is established" requires that tests which merely show a possibility be excluded). And see Flippen v. Meinhold, 156 Misc. 451, 282 N.Y.S. 444 (City Ct.1935) (application

understandable as manifestations of a desire to move slowly in the judicial use of these new tests, and particularly to avoid such use of the tests in evidence as might lead juries to give them exaggerated weight in establishing paternity. Nevertheless, it may be doubted whether the wholesale exclusion of the tests when they show that the person charged belongs to one of the groups to which the father must have belonged, is a wise practice. The question is one of identity. Every identifying mark of the father, however common the trait, such as height, weight, color of hair, is relevant, and it is from the multiplying significance of such accumulation of identifying traits that circumstantial proof of identity gains its persuasive power.[30] The tests may show that the unknown father must have belonged to groups O, A, B, which make up 97% of the population.[31] To prove that the person charged belongs to one of these groups certainly has only a minimum of identifying value, which in a jury case would be outweighed by the danger of misleading. On the other hand, the tests may reveal that the father must have belonged to groups B or AB, which together make up only 13% of the population. To prove then that the person accused belongs to this small minority class, has high identifying significance which would be substantially corroborative of other evidence that he was the father. This probative value is clearly recognized in the closely analogous cases where the blood found at the scene of a crime, or on the clothes of the accused or his victim, is classified as to bloodgroups and used as evidence of identity.[32] Accordingly, the Uniform Act embodies a compromise, as follows: "If the court finds that the conclusions of all the experts, as disclosed by the evidence based upon the tests, are that the alleged father is not the father of the child, the question of paternity shall be resolved accordingly. If the experts disagree in their findings or conclusions, the question shall be submitted upon all the evidence. If the experts conclude that the blood tests show the possibility of the alleged father's paternity, admission of this evidence is within the discretion of the court, depending upon the infrequency of the blood type."[33] In view of the probability that the development of new, additional tests may further narrow the groups in which the potential father must fall, the practice suggested in the Uniform Act seems an expedient solution.

---

by woman suing for support of child for order for blood-tests denied because results of test could not be used to establish paternity).

30. See the illuminating opinion of Marbury, C. J. in Shanks v. State, 185 Md. 437, 45 A.2d 85, 163 A.L.R. 931, 936–939 (1945).

31. See chart p. 379, supra, and list of percentages of population in each group, p. 378, supra.

32. See § 177, supra.

33. 1952 Handbook, Nat. Conf. Com'rs on Unif.St. Laws, 445.

TITLE 7

DEMONSTRATIVE EVIDENCE

CHAPTER 21

DEMONSTRATIVE EVIDENCE

Sec.
179. Demonstrative Evidence in General
180. Maps, Models, etc.
181. Photographs
182. Bodily Demonstrations and Other Experiments in Court
183. Views
184. Exhibits in the Jury Room

179. Demonstrative Evidence in General.[1]

There is a kind of evidence which is called, variously, real, demonstrative, objective or autoptic evidence. It consists of tangible things, such as bullets, knives, diamond rings and lug-wrenches, submitted for inspection, which enable the judge or jury by the direct use of their senses to perceive facts about these things in evidence. Documents also, except when they are statements offered to prove their truth, such as business records, are the commonest kind of demonstrative evidence, but they have developed their own rules and will mostly be treated in other chapters.[2] Demonstrative evidence stands in contrast with testimonial evidence, where the trier is asked to believe that certain facts are true only because the witness (or the hearsay declarant) states them to be so.

Nevertheless, it is true that demonstrative evidence also rests in part upon testimonial evidence. Objects or things offered in evidence do not generally identify themselves. Accordingly the demonstrative evidence must first be authenticated by testimony of a witness who testifies to facts showing that the object has some connection with the case which makes it relevant.[3] But when

---

1. See 4 Wigmore, Evidence, §§ 1150–1169; 32 C.J.S., Evidence, §§ 601–622; Decennial Digests, Evidence, ☞188–195; Criminal Law, ☞404(1–4); Trial, ☞28 and 375.

2. See, e. g., Ch. 22 (authentication) and Ch. 23 (documentary originals).

3. This is usually called "identifying" the object. Burris v. American Chicle Co., 120 F.2d 218, 222, syl. 2 (1941) ("[The rope] was positively identified by the plaintiff as the one which broke and caused his injuries. Such an identification was prima facie sufficient and the judge correctly admitted it; leaving the ultimate fact of its identification to the jury."); Lestico v. Kuehner, 204 Minn. 125, 283 N.W. 122, syl. 8, 9 (1938) (guest sues for injury in an overturn; defence, due to sudden deflation of tire; defendant offered punctured casing, and "identified" it; excluded on ground proponent did not by calling all persons who had been in possession of it, show it

had not been tampered with; held, error, there is no such "chain of possession" requirement). It is sometimes said that the proponent must prove that the object is in substantially the same condition as at the time of the occurrence in question. Gutman v. Industrial Commission, 71 Oh.App. 383, 50 N.E.2d 187, syl. 2 (1942) (automobile steering wheel); Allen v. Porter, 19 Wash.2d 503, 143 P.2d 328, syl. 10, 11 (1943) (motorcycle headlight). Such proof is customary and desirable where the fact is so, but even when the condition has changed substantially the object may still be relevant and admissible, if the change is not such as to make the evidence unduly misleading. Pilot Life Ins. Co. v. Wise, 61 F.2d 481, syl. 2 (C.C.A.5, 1932) (bottle; showing insufficient); United States v. S. B. Penick & Co., 136 F.2d 413, syl. 3 (C.C.A.2, 1943) (sample bottles of drugs, sufficient); Chicago R. I. & P. Co. v. Murphy, 184 Okl. 240, 86 P.2d 630, syl. 5 (1939) (no error to admit wheel rim, salvaged from fire, where plaintiff tes-

384

this requisite is complied with the judge or jury ascertains the facts about the object by inspection and the use of their senses.

The demonstrative evidence may be direct [4] evidence, as when it is offered to prove the facts about the object as an end in itself, as where the race or nationality of a person is in issue and the person is offered for inspection [5] on that issue, or where a scar or crippled member is displayed to show the extent of injury.[6] On the other hand, it may be circumstantial, when the facts about the object offered are proved as the basis of an inference that other facts are true. Examples are the offering of a child in a filiation suit to show his resemblance and hence kinship with the putative father,[7] or the coat which the accused wore when arrested when offered to show his identity with the culprit who has been described as wearing a dark coat.

We may likewise classify demonstrative evidence into that which is *original,* in that it had some connection with the transaction in suit at the time it occurred, and that which is *prepared,* such as sketches, models and plaster casts,[8] or *selected,* such as writings used as standards for comparison,[9] or samples of materials similar to the ones in issue.[10]

Demonstrative evidence of the *direct* kind is always relevant, since it bears immediately on the facts in issue. Ordinarily, inspection of the object itself is the most satisfying and persuasive means of ascertaining its qualities, and when these qualities are in issue, such inspection will always be permitted unless there is in the particular situation some overriding contrary consideration of prejudice or of physical difficulty.[11] When the demonstrative evidence, on the other hand, is circumstantial or inferential in its bearing,

tified rim in same condition except for being smoked, as at time of accident), and see 2 Wigmore, Evidence, § 437(11); 32 C.J.S., Evidence, § 607; Dec. Dig., Evidence, ⟹194.

4. For the distinction between direct and circumstantial evidence, see § 152, herein.

5. See, e. g., United States v. Hang Chung, 134 Fed. 19, syl. 2–4 (C.C.A.6, 1904) (appearance to be considered in determining whether of Chinese descent).

6. See, e. g., Moore v. Tremelling, 100 F.2d 39, syl. 11 (C.C.A.Idaho, 1938) (malpractice; exhibition of plaintiff's hip proper to show condition at time of trial); Dec.Dig., Evidence, ⟹188, 192.

7. The trend of decision seems to follow the view of Wigmore (Vol. 1, § 166) that the exhibition of the child is allowable provided the judge finds he is old enough to possess "settled features or other corporal indications." State v. Danforth, 73 N.H. 215, 60 Atl. 839, 842, syl. 4 (1905) (dictum); Lohsen v. Lawson, 106 Vt. 481, 174 Atl. 861, 95 A.L.R. 309 (1934) (judge properly refused to require production of child of less than six months); Notes, 40 A.L.R. 111, 11 Corn.L.Q. 380 (1926).

In Berry v. Chaplin, 74 Cal.App.2d 652, 169 P.2d 442, syl. 29 (1946), the trial judge's order requiring the defendant to stand beside the mother with the child in her arms before the jury for comparison was approved over the objection that it was an appeal to emotion. In the same case, the court held that a jury verdict finding paternity could stand, although blood-tests demonstrated with certainty, under accepted scientific theory, that the defendant could not be the father. See § 178, herein.

8. See cases collected in Dec.Dig., Evidence, ⟹194.

9. See note 6, § 172, supra.

10. E. K. Hardison Seed Co. v. Jones, 149 F.2d 252, syl. 1 (C.C.A.6, 1945) (samples of seeds from shipments made by defendant received to show quality of the whole); Sellew v. Middletown, 121 Conn. 331, 185 Atl. 67, syl. 1, 2 (1936) (action for injury in fall on stones; court in discretion properly admitted pan of stones, testified by plaintiff to be similar to those on walk; "It is only where it appears that it can be of real assistance and is not likely to be given undue weight by them, that the trial court may in its discretion admit it.")

11. Helmick v. Rankin, 166 Pa.Super. 189, 70 A.2d 362, syl. 2, 3 (1950) (where issue was whether books properly kept, error to exclude books); 4 Wigmore, Evidence, § 1051. See Barrows v. Mutual Life Ins. Co., 48 N.M. 206, 147 P.2d 362, syl. 3 (1944) (when physical condition of party is material he has a right when testifying to exhibit condition to jury). See also Smith v. State, 248 Ala. 363, 27 So.2d 495, syl. 3 (1946) (rape; clothing of victim properly admitted, where shows facts material to issue, though cumulative and having some tendency to inflame jury) and see cases on admission of gruesome demonstrative evidence in criminal cases, collected in 4 Wigmore, Evidence, § 1157, note 3, Dec.Dig., Crim.

then (as in other cases of circumstantial evidence) the trial judge, in determining admissibility, has a wider power of balancing the probative value of the evidence against its dangers of undue prejudice, distraction of the jury from the issues, and waste of time.[12] Here again, however, when the balance wavers the court should lean toward admission.

180. Maps, Models, etc.[1]

The appeal to the visual impression to add vividness to verbal narrative and description is increasingly recognized as one of the effective skills of courtroom persuasion. Among these visual aids, constantly resorted to, are maps, sketches, diagrams, models, duplicates, and casts. While occasionally they may be allowed to be used informally for illustration as points of reference by the

witness, as if he were pointing to a window in the courtroom to illustrate a statement of distance, they are by standard practice required to be identified by the witness, verified by him as correct,[2] and formally introduced in evidence as part of his testimony, in which they are incorporated by reference.[3] As such, they are demonstrative evidence[4] of the prepared as distinguished from the original sort.[5] These aids are so useful in giving clarity and interest to spoken statements[6] that it may be argued that no special control over their admission is needed, beyond the requirement for all testimony that it be relevant.[7] The traditional form of statement, however, still prevails that these kinds of auxiliary evidence are admissible in the trial judge's discretion.[8] And in view of the extreme lengths to which some current practice has gone in the use of visual mate-

Law, ⊂⇒404. There are many such cases wherein photographs of the body of the victim are offered. When materiality appears, the courts have been disinclined to hold that their probative value is outweighed by the danger of prejudice. See Hawkins v. State, 219 Ind. 116, 37 N.E.2d 79, syl. 11–22 (1941); Turrell v. State, 221 Ind. 662, 51 N.E.2d 359, syl. 12 (1943); Rex v. Cartman [1940] N.Z.L.R. 725, Notes, 18 Can.Bar Rev. 813; 159 A.L.R. 1413; 14 La.L.Rev. 421 (1954).

12. See § 152, herein.

1. 3 Wigmore, Evidence, §§ 790, 791; Dec.Dig., Evidence, ⊂⇒194 (duplicates, models and casts), 358 (maps, plats, and diagrams); 32 C.J.S., Evidence, §§ 604–606 (duplicates, models, and casts).

2. This requirement is stated in Cincinnati, N. O. & T. P. Ry. Co. v. Duvall, 263 Ky. 387, 92 S.W.2d 363, 366 (1936) (error to exclude model of car step which was proved to be exact duplicate). See Hadrian v. Milwaukee Elec. Ry. & Transport Co., 241 Wis. 122, 1 N.W.2d 755, syl. 4 (1942) (error to admit model which grossly distorted proportions of original).

3. "A photograph or model is used only as a 'nonverbal mode of expressing a witness' testimony' (Wigmore on Evidence, § 790), and as a testimonial aid it may often help the jury to understand the evidence 'more clearly than they could from the words of any witness.' Bernard v. Pittsburg Coal Co., 137 Mich. 279, 100 N.W. 396, 398. The proposed aid must be sponsored by a witness who uses it to relate his personal knowledge or scientific skill

and understanding." Butzel, J., in Finch v. W. R. Roach Co., 295 Mich. 589, 295 N.W. 324, 326 (1940).

4. Cincinnati, N. O. & T. P. Ry. Co. v. Duvall, 263 Ky. 387, 92 S.W.2d 363, 366 (1936) ("a species of real evidence").

5. See next previous section, herein.

6. ". . . the practice of admitting photographs and models in evidence in all proper cases should be encouraged. Such evidence usually clarifies some issue, and gives the jury and the court a clearer comprehension of the physical facts than can be obtained from the testimony of witnesses." Gose, J., in Kelly v. Spokane, 83 Wash. 55, 145 Pac. 57, 58 (1914).

7. The holding in Cincinnati, N. O. & T. P. Ry. Co. v. Duvall, described in note 2, above, seems to support this view.

8. New York Life Ins. Co. v. Gamer, 106 F.2d 375, syl. 6 (C.C.A., Mont., 1939, cert. den.); San Mateo County v. Christen, 26 Cal.App.2d 375, 71 P.2d 88, syl. 1, 2 (1937, hearing den.) (eminent domain: engineer's model of tract excluded; "while models may frequently be of great assistance . . . even when constructed to scale they may frequently, because of the great disparity in size . . . also be very misleading, and trial courts must be allowed wide discretion . . ."); Finch v. W. R. Roach Co., 295 Mich. 589, 295 N.W. 324, syl. 5 (1940) (was in court's discretion to admit model of ladder though measurements not exact as to one dimension); 32 C.J.S., Evidence, § 606, note 47.

rials in dramatizing and emotionalizing the presentation of cases, the existence of discretionary control may be needed to prevent abuse of a technique which used with due restraint is a valuable aid to the administration of justice.[9]

181. Photographs.[1]

As with demonstrative evidence generally, the prime condition on admissibility is that the photograph be identified by a witness as a portrayal of certain facts relevant to the issue, and verified by such a witness on personal knowledge as a correct representation of these facts.[2] The witness who thus lays the foundation need not be the photographer nor need the witness know anything of the time or conditions of the taking.[3] It is the facts represented, the scene or the object, that he must know about, and when this knowledge is shown, he can say whether the photograph correctly portrays these facts. When the photograph is thus verified it comes in as demonstrative evidence [4] which

9. For enlightening discussions from the plaintiff's viewpoint, see Belli, Demonstrative Evidence and the Adequate Award, 22 Miss.L.J. 284 (1951); Dooley, Demonstrative Evidence—Nothing New, 42 Ill.B.J. 136 (1953); from defendant's viewpoint, Sedgwick, Demonstrative Evidence, 20 Ins. Counsel J. 218 (1953) (highly informative); from both points of view, Hinshaw, Use and Abuse of Demonstrative Evidence, 40 A.B.A.J. 479; Garment, Real Evidence: Use and Abuse, 14 Brooklyn L.J. 261 (1948). See also Young, Proof of Danger and Safety by Real Evidence and Experiments, 26 Tex.L.Rev. 188 (1947).

1. 3 Wigmore, Evidence, §§ 790–798a; Scott, Photographic Evidence (1942), the standard work; 32 C.J.S., Evidence, §§ 709–716; Dec.Dig., Evidence, ☜359, 380. As to the admissibility of gruesome photographs, see § 179, note 11.

2. Edelson v. Higgins, 43 Cal.App.2d 759, 111 P.2d 668, syl. 5 (1941) (testimony that photographs correctly represented conditions at time of accident is sufficient verification); Gwynn Oak Park v. Becker, 177 Md. 528, 10 A.2d 625, syl. 7 (1940) (similar to last); Oklahoma City v. Lycan, 193 Okl. 170, 141 P.2d 1013, syl. 4 (1943) (must be shown by extrinsic evidence to be faithful representation); Dec.Dig., Evidence, ☜380. Though the photograph was taken a considerable time later, it comes in if it is shown to be an accurate picture of the conditions at the crucial time. Tulsa Yellow Cab, etc. Co. v. Solomon, 181 Okl. 519, 75 P.2d 197, syl. 6 (1938); Empire Gas & Fuel Co. v. Muegge, 135 Tex. 520, 143 S.W.2d 763, syl. 8 (1940). And even if the scene as photographed has changed since the time in question, the photograph may still come in, with an explanation by the witness of the changes, when the picture of the changed scene will be helpful to the jury in understanding the conditions at the time in controversy. Dallas Ry. Co. v. Durkee, 193 S.W.2d 222, syl. 11–14 (Tex.Civ.App.1946).
The foundational proof for X-ray photographs presents a special problem, since the verifying witness will usually not have seen the object pictured (ordi-

narily a concealed bone) and thus cannot say that the picture faithfully portrays what he saw. Accordingly, the witness must furnish a guaranty of correctness by identifying the picture as that of a given person's bodily member in question, describing the experience of the photographer, vouching for the accuracy and condition of the machine, describing the manner of taking the particular picture, and showing that this method followed standard practice. Instances of sufficient verification. Bauer v. Reavell, 219 Iowa 1212, 260 N.W. 39 (1935); Federal Underwriter Exchange v. Cost, 132 Tex. 290, 123 S.W.2d 332, syl. 8 (1932). Inadequate. Ligon v. Allen, 157 Ky. 101, 162 S.W. 536 (1914); Gulf Research Development Co. v. Linder, 177 Miss. 123, 170 So. 646, syl. 4 (1936). See also 3 Wigmore, Evidence, § 795; Scott, X-Ray Pictures as Evidence, 44 Mich.L.Rev. 773, 791 (1946). As to the function of such evidence, see Donaldson, Medical facts that can and can not be proved by X-ray, 41 Mich.L.Rev. 875 (1943).
In general, the standard of faithfulness of the photographic representation is a relative one. "When it is offered as a general representation of physical objects as to which testimony is adduced for the mere convenience of witnesses in explaining their statements, very slight proof of accuracy may be sufficient; but when it is offered as representing handwriting which is to be subjected to minute and detailed examination, or any object where slight differences of height, breadth, or length are of vital importance, much more convincing proof should be required." Hamersley, J., in Cunningham v. Fair Haven & W. R. Co., 72 Conn. 244, 43 Atl. 1047, 1049 (1899).

3. Kortz v. Guardian Life Ins. Co., 144 F.2d 676, syl. 11, 12 (C.C.A.Colo.1944) (by the photographer or any other qualified person); Adamcsuk v. Holloway, 338 Pa. 263, 13 A.2d 2, syl. 2–4 (1940).

4. "In this case the photograph was evidently offered as demonstrative evidence. As such they are competent whenever it is important that the locus in quo, or any object, person, or thing, be described

is part of the testimony of the witness,[5] and incorporated in it by reference. The adjective "illustrative" aptly describes the role of the picture thus incorporated in the testimony, but it is sometimes used as contrasted with "substantive" evidence.[6] It is believed that this distinction is groundless, and that the photograph, as part of the descriptive testimony, is just as much substantive evidence as the testimony of a witness describing the features of a scene or object without a photograph would be.[7] It may be correctly described as both "illustrative" and "substantive." [8]

The interest and vividness of photographs may be heightened by the creative ingenuity of counsel in planning for the photographing of posed, or artificially reconstructed scenes. People, automobiles, and other objects are placed on the scene to conform to the de-

scriptions of the original crime or collision given by the witnesses. When the posed photographs go no further than to portray the positions of the persons and objects as reflected in the undisputed testimony, their admission is generally approved.[9] When the photographs portray the reconstructed scene as testified to by the proponent's witnesses, but the adversary's testimony is or will be substantially conflicting as to the features and positions pictured, then there is danger that one party's version will be unduly emphasized,[10] and the judge should have a discretion to exclude the posed photograph,[11] unless opportunity can be afforded to the opponent to prepare a similar pictured reconstruction of the scene as portrayed by his witnesses.[12]

In respect to the admission of moving pictures,[13] with or without sound, the element

---

to the jury. In such cases they serve to explain or illustrate and apply the testimony, and are aids to the court or jury in comprehending the questions in dispute, as affected by the evidence." Mitchell, J., in Stewart v. St. Paul City Ry. Co., 78 Minn. 110, 80 N.W. 855 (1899).

5. Finch v. W. R. Roach Co., 295 Mich. 324, 295 N.W. 324, 326, syl. 3 (1940).

6. Queen City Coach Co. v. Lee, 218 N.C. 320, 11 S.E.2d 341, syl. 10 (1940); Morrison v. Cottonwood Developement Co., 38 Wyo. 190, 266 Pac. 117, 120, syl. 3, 4 (1928) and authorities there cited. The practical consequence of accepting it is that the adverse party may be entitled to an instruction that an "illustrative" photograph is "not substantive evidence." See Honeycutt v. Cherokee Brick Co., 196 N.C. 556, 146 S.E. 227 (1929). Or may be entitled to demand that the photograph or other exhibit be not taken with them by the jury in their deliberations. Most courts simply ignore any such distinction. See cases cited 3 Wigmore, Evidence, § 792, note 1; Dec.Dig., Evidence, ☞359.

7. See Anderson, The Admissibility of Photographs as Evidence, 7 N.C.L.Rev. 443 (1929); Gardner, The Camera Goes to Court, 24 N.C.L.Rev. 233 (1946) (a lively and sensible article, with illustrations); 2 Wigmore, Evidence, § 791, n. 2.

8. See Baustian v. Young, 152 Mo. 317, 53 S.W. 921, 922 (1899).

9. See, e. g., Reed v. Davidson Co., 97 Colo. 462, 50 P.2d 532, syl. 3 (1935) (reconstructed scene of colli-

sion); Cincinnati, N. O. & T. P. Ry. Co. v. Duvall, 263 Ky. 387, 92 S.W.2d 363, syl. 2 (1936) (injury from stepping from platform to steps of car; error to exclude picture of another woman stepping from platform to car-step); Pollack v. State, 215 Wis. 200, 253 N.W. 560, syl. 31 (1934) (murder; photographs of defendants in positions they indicated they occupied at time of shooting). See 6 Wigmore, Evidence, § 798; Notes, Posed Photographs, 27 A.L.R. 913, 19 A.L.R.2d 877; 37 C.J.S. 264.

10. Thus, in speaking of pictures of a reconstructed murder scene, the court said, "Their effect, if not their purpose, . . . was to bring out in striking captivating fashion the version of the difficulty as given the jury in this witness's evidence." Fore v. State, 75 Miss. 727, 23 So. 710, 712 (1898).

11. Examples of cases admitting such evidence. State v. Ebelsheiser, 242 Iowa 49, 43 N.W.2d 706, 19 A.L.R.2d 865, 873 (1950) (murder-scene); Hughes v. State, 126 Tenn. 40, 148 S.W. 543, syl. 2–5 (1912) (same). Properly excluded, in discretion. Lynch v. Missouri-Kansas-Texas R. Co., 333 Mo. 89, 61 S.W.2d 918, syl. 5 (1933) (crossing collision); Fabbio v. Diesel, 1 Wash.2d 234, 95 P.2d 788, syl. 4 (1939) (child killed by truck).

12. Compare 8 Wigmore, Evidence, p. 202.

13. 3 Wigmore, Evidence, § 798a; Notes, 83 A.L.R. 1315, 129 A.L.R. 361; 32 C.J.S. 625; Dec.Dig., Evidence, ☞359(6).

of discretion is more often emphasized in the opinions,[14] than in cases involving still pictures. Perhaps the principal reason for this is administrative. While the principles applied to still pictures are generally applicable here [15] the still picture entails only a minimum expenditure of time and little distraction of attention. But to show the movie in court, a good deal of time must be spent in installing the projector and screen, darkening and arranging the courtroom, and in the showing of the film, and may involve likewise a good deal of diversion of attention from the issues and interruption of the march of the trial. Moreover, there are great possibilities of distortion and falsification due to the choice of light, angle, speed and position of the camera, but these are different in degree only from the possibilities of perversion of still pictures.

These considerations loomed as larger obstacles to the judges when this kind of evidence was first offered than they do today when the use of them in court has lost the shock of novelty. Undoubtedly the discretion has always been more favorably exercised in the admission of moving-pictures of what we have called the original (non-posed) sort, such as pictures of personal injury claimants [16] climbing trees or playing baseball, than in the case of pictures of artificial or reconstructed activities.[17] but even these latter have recently been allowed to be shown [18] when their value seemed to outweigh their danger. Although it is desirable to have the operator present to testify to the fact that the machine was operated normally as to lighting, speed, angle and position,[19] it may be sufficient, unless the judge in his discretion requires further verification, for any person who witnessed the scene pictured to testify that the picture faithfully represented the objects and activities as he saw them.[20] Undoubtedly this process of reproducing movement, background, color and sound will more and more be recognized by lawyers and judges as a valuable resource for adding vividness, accuracy and entertainment to the presentation of facts.[21]

14. See, e. g., Morris v. E. I. Dupont, etc. Co., 346 Mo. 126, 139 S.W.2d 984, 129 A.L.R. 352, 358 (1940); Denison v. Omaha & C. B. St. Ry. Co., 135 Neb. 307, 280 N.W. 905, syl. 1 (1938).

15. Morris v. E. I. Dupont, etc. Co., supra, loc. cit.; Housewright v. State, 154 Tex.Cr. 101, 225 S.W.2d 417, syl. 1 (1950).

16. Admitted. Kortz v. Guardian Life Ins. Co., 144 F.2d 676, syl. 11 (C.C.A.Colo.1944); Heiman v. Market St. R. Co., 21 Cal.App.2d 311, 69 P.2d 178, syl. 4 (1937); McGoorty v. Benhart, 27 N.E.2d 289, syl. 7–9 (Ill.App.1940); Boyarsky v. G. A. Zimmerman Corp., 240 App.Div. 361, 270 N.Y.S. 134, syl. 3–8 (1934) (error to exclude). Trial judge's discretion upheld in excluding. Massachusetts Bonding & Ins. Co. v. Worthy, 9 S.W.2d 388, syl. 6 (Tex. Civ.App.1928).
Compare Rogers v. City of Detroit, 209 Mich. 86, 286 N.W. 167, syl. 4 (1939); where the tables were turned, and where the plaintiff was unable to appear in court, moving pictures taken in her home of the pulsation of her throat were admitted.

17. The judge's discretion in excluding was upheld in State v. United Railways & Elec. Co.. 162 Md. 404, 159 Atl. 916, syl. 11, 12, 83 A.L.R. 1307 (1932) (pictures of other street-cars going around curve, to show swaying); Sprinkle v. Davis, 111 F.2d 925, syl. 10, 11 (C.C.A.Va.1940) (movie offered to show how far from point on highway approaching automobile could be seen).

18. People v. Dabb, 32 Cal.2d 491, 197 P.2d 1, syl. 6–8 (1948) (sound motion picture of re-enactment by defendants, as part of their confession, of "hold-up" and murder); Richardson v. Missouri-Kansas-Texas Ry. Co., 205 S.W.2d 819 (Tex.Civ.App.1947) (technicolor motion picture of operation of planing machine, with foreman as actor, showing how the plaintiff might have had his hand injured, under defendant's theory).

19. As in Richardson v. Missouri-K-T Ry. Co., 205 S.W.2d 819, 824, syl. 7 (Tex.Civ.App.1947).

20. Kortz v. Guardian Life Ins. Co., 144 F.2d 676, 679, syl. 11–13 (C.C.A.Colo.1944); Richardson v. Missouri-K-T Ry. Co., supra, syl. 8.

21. Resourcefulness in the use of motion pictures in criminal cases seems especially notable. See People v. Dabb, next preceding note; Comm. v. Roller, 100 Pa.Super. 125 (1930) (talking motion picture of defendant's confession received); Jones v. State, 151 Tex.Cr. 519, 209 S.W.2d 613, syl. 19 (1948) (bribery of sheriff; movie of defendant's entering

182. Bodily Demonstrations and Other Experiments in Court.

Ordinarily, the mere exhibition of the injured part of the body of the plaintiff in a personal injury action is allowable as being the best and most direct evidence of a material fact.[1] But where, beyond mere displaying of the injured parts, the plaintiff is called on in court to move the injured member, or submit to manipulation by a doctor, there is more doubt. Two dangers are then apparent, the resultant outcries or other manifestation of pain may unduly arouse the sympathy of a jury, and the opportunity for false, pretended expressions of pain is obvious. Nevertheless, such demonstrations are generally considered to be under the discretionary control of the judge,[2] and are

often approved,[3] but occasional cases in which it has been ruled an abuse of discretion,[4] make the procedure somewhat hazardous for the plaintiff.

The general requirement of similarity of conditions applied to experimental evidence generally applies with equal force to experiments in court.[5] Manifestly, the trial judge can best determine whether the confusion and delay incident to the court-room experiment outweigh its value, and his wide discretionary power to permit or exclude the experiment is constantly emphasized.[6]

Simple demonstrations by a witness are usually permitted, and may be strikingly effective in adding vividness to the spoken word.[7] Other cases in which courtroom ex-

sheriff's home at time of alleged crime, admitted); Housewright v. State, 154 Tex.Cr. 101, 225 S.W.2d 417, syl. 1, 2 (1950) (pictures of accused being booked at jail on charge of driving while drunk).

The Supreme Court of Florida has prescribed, in cases where it is appropriate, a practice which has great possibilities for using motion pictures in the service of impartial truth, i. e., their taking under the direction of a court-commissioner, upon notice to opposing counsel. See Gulf Life Ins. Co. v. Stossel, 131 Fla. 127, 179 So. 163 (1938). This would be especially adapted to pictures of experiments or reproductions of crimes and accidents.

2. Calumet Paving Co. v. Butkus, 113 Ind.App. 232, 47 N.E.2d 829, syl. 4 (1943); Yellow Cab Co. v. Henderson, 183 Md. 546, 39 A.2d 546, syl. 10, 175 A.L.R. 267 (1944); 4 Wigmore, Evidence, § 1158; 32 C.J.S., Evidence, § 610; Dec.Dig., Evidence, ⊂⊃ 192. In Shell Petroleum Co. v. Perrin, 179 Okl. 142, 64 P.2d 309, syl. 5 (1936), the court held there was no error in permitting the mother of a little girl suing for injury to an eye, to remove the girl's glass eye before the jury, distinguishing cases where a severed limb has been preserved and displayed to the jury. In Zeller v. Mayson, 168 Md. 663, 179 Atl. 179, syl. 1–3 (1935), it was held that the trial judge in his discretion could properly permit the plaintiff, a dancer, suing for personal injury, to exhibit her scarred knees to the jury. Dietz v. Aronson, 244 App.Div. 746, 279 N.Y.S. 66 (1935), holds in a malpractice action that the trial judge erred, to the plaintiff's detriment, in refusing to permit the jury to examine the infant plaintiff's throat to ascertain the results of a tonsil operation, by comparison with a diagram of a normal throat.

2. See Notes, Permitting demonstration to show effect of injury, 103 A.L.R. 1355; Demonstrations before the Jury, 34 Ky.L.J. 309 (1946).

3. See, e. g., Florida Motor Lines v. Bradley, 121 Fla. 591, 164 So. 360, syl. 4, 5 (1936) (showing extent to which plaintiff could bend leg, causing cry of pain); Happy v. Walz, 244 S.W.2d 380, syl. 1–3 (Mo. App. 1951) (manipulation of feet and legs by doctor, no pain or outcry; good discussion by Dew, J.); Wilson & Co. v. Campbell, 195 Okl. 323, 157 P.2d 465, syl. 6 (1945) (plaintiff demonstrated numbness of leg by sticking pin in it).

4. See, e. g., Landro v. Gt. Northern Ry. Co., 117 Minn. 306, 135 N.W. 991, syl. 2 (1912) (manipulation of sacroiliac joint, to show pain, criticised but not here prejudicial); Meyer v. Johnson, 224 Mo.App. 565, 30 S.W.2d 641, syl. 1 (1930) (manipulation of spine with outcries); Lampa v. Hakola, 152 Ore. 626, 55 P.2d 13 (1936) (injury to back, demonstrated by bending and outcries).

5. See § 169, herein.

6. See, e. g., Green v. State, 223 Ind. 614, 63 N.E.2d 292, syl. 1–3 (1945) (in trial for robbery defendant's counsel presented five masked men to witness and asked him to identify defendant in thirty seconds; held, judge in discretion properly refused to permit experiment for want of similarity of conditions).

7. Thus, in Backstrom v. New York Life Ins. Co., 194 Minn. 67, 259 N.W. 681, syl. 3 (1935), where the issue was suicide or accidental shooting, the witness who found the body was allowed to demonstrate the position of the body and the gun, by lying on the floor. And in Ham v. State, 102 Tex.Cr.R. 124,

periments have been sanctioned are described below.[8] Far more numerous are the cases where it has been held that the trial judge properly exercised his discretion to exclude such experiments.[9] Nevertheless, the persuasive possibilities of this type of evidence, when discreetly used, present an opportunity and a challenge to the resourcefulness of the advocate.

183. Views.[1]

There is a common law [2] power in the trial judge upon due notice to the parties to order a view by the jury, or in a judge-tried case, to take a view himself,[3] of premises [4] or objects [5] when their appearance or condition is relevant to the issue. The power extends to criminal [6] as well as civil cases. The details of the proceeding are regulated in nearly all jurisdictions by statute or rule of court [7] and differ from state to state. This method of presenting facts to the tribunal is often time-consuming and disruptive to the pace and movement of the trial. Accordingly, the judge who has the responsibility for expeditious progress in dispatch of the calendar, is vested with a wide lee-way of discretion in granting or refusing a view.[8] Among the

277 S.W. 653 (1925), it was held proper for the state's witness in a liquor prosecution to pour out some of the liquor, to light it with a match, and to taste it and testify to its intoxicating quality.

8. Leonard v. Southern Pacific Co., 21 Or. 555, 28 Pac. 887, 15 L.R.A. 221 (1892) (railway accident which defendant claimed was due to loosening of rail by some evil-disposed person; defendant produced rail with scar on flange, due as witness claimed, to engine striking rail; plaintiff allowed to bring wheel in court and run it against rail to prove that it could not cause such scar); Chicago Telephone Supply Co. v. Marne & E. Tel. Co., 134 Iowa 252, 111 N.W. 935 (1907) (tests in court of telephone apparatus alleged to be defective).

9. See Rex v. Duncan, [1944] 1 K.B. 713, Ct.Crim. App. (accused, a spiritualist medium, prosecuted under old statute for pretended witchcraft offered to give a demonstration before the jury of calling departed spirits); Coca Cola Co. v. Langston, 198 Ark. 59, 127 S.W.2d 263, syl. 3 (1939) (witness offered to swallow teaspoon of ground glass); Spires v. State, 50 Fla. 121, 39 So. 181, 7 Ann.Cas. 214 (1905) (rape; prosecutrix testified that she identified assailant by flash of pistol: refusal to permit experiment to determine whether jury could recognize person in dark from flash of pistol). See Dec. Dig., Trial, ☞27.

1. 4 Wigmore, Evidence, §§ 1162–1169; 64 C.J., Trial, § 90, § 1005; 53 Am.Jur., Trial, §§ 441–451, § 1128; Dec.Dig., Trial, ☞28.

2. Springer v. City of Chicago, 135 Ill. 552, 26 N.E. 514, 517, syl. 3, 4 (1891); State v. Perry, 121 N.C. 533, 27 S.E. 997 (1897).

3. Some courts consider it mandatory on the judge to notify the parties and give them an opportunity to be present, if he takes a view. Denver Omnibus & Cab Co. v. J. R. Ward Auction Co., 47 Colo. 446, 107 Pac. 1073 (1910); Elston v. McLaughlin, 79 Wash. 355, 140 Pac. 396, syl. 1, 2 (1914). Others

consider that such notice should ordinarily be given but is a discretionary matter. Adalex Const. Co. v. Atkins, 214 Ala. 53, 106 So. 338, syl. 8 (1925); Carter v. Parsons, 136 Neb. 515, 286 N.W. 696, syl. 2, 3 (1939). As to whether he may treat the facts observed as evidence, see Note, 97 A.L.R. 335, and notes 14, 15, below.

4. Yeary v. Holbrook, 171 Va. 266, 198 S.E. 441 (1938) (scene of collision); Doman v. Baltimore & O. Ry. Co., 125 W.Va. 8, 22 S.E.2d 703 (1942) (land alleged to be damaged by overflow caused by defendant's bridge).

5. American Glycerin Co. v. Eason Oil Co., 98 F.2d 479, syl. 11 (C.C.A.Okl.1938) (stating general rule); Denison v. Omaha & C. B. St. Ry. Co., 135 Neb. 307, 280 N.W. 905, syl. 2 (1938) (jury properly allowed to view closing mechanism of street-car door). The view may, in the judge's discretion, include the performance of experiments. Richardson v. Northwestern Ry., 124 S.C. 314, 117 S.E. 511, syl. 2 (1923) (running engine and train over crossing); 4 Wigmore, Evidence, § 1164, note 3.

6. Schoenfeld v. United States, 277 Fed. 934, syl. 8 (C.C.A.2, 1921); Comm. v. Chance, 174 Mass. 245, 54 N.E. 551, syl. 1 (1899) (under statute, granting or denying view of scene of murder was in judge's discretion); Note, Motion for View in Criminal Case, 124 A.L.R. 841.

7. See the rules and statutes in England, Canada, and the United States compiled in 4 Wigmore, Evidence, § 1163, notes 7, 8.

8. Nearly every opinion stresses this, see, e. g., Hodge v. United States, 126 F.2d 849, syl. 4 (C.A.D.C., 1942) (denial upheld); Nunnelly v. Edgar Hotel, 36 Cal.2d 493, 225 P.2d 497, syl. 10, 11 (1950) (order for view sustained, no abuse of discretion); Dec.Dig., Trial, ☞28(2). The judge in his discretion may deny a view though both parties request it. Floyd v. Williams, 198 Miss. 350, 22 So.2d 365 syl. 4 (1945).

factors which he will consider are the degree of importance to the issue of the information to be gained by a view, the extent to which this has been or could be adequately secured from photographs, maps, diagrams, and the like,[9] and the extent to which the premises or object have changed in appearance or condition since the controversy arose.[10] The judge's own presence at the jury-view, though desirable, is usually not regarded as mandatory,[11] but the jury is conducted by a court-officer and the judge appoints one or more "showers," to show the jury the features of the scene which have been referred to in the testimony.[12] Usually the parties and their counsel are allowed to be present.[13]

The impression on the senses of the jury or judge from a view of a building, a dam, or a wrecked automobile, is information of the most direct and convincing kind about the relevant facts. It is exactly the same process of proof as obtains when objects are exhibited to the jury in the court-room as demonstrative evidence. Some courts, however, troubled by the fact that the impressions gained from the view may not be embodied in the record on appeal in the same way that the testimony of witnesses is transmitted, have put the cart before the horse and have said that since such information cannot be reflected in the record it cannot be evidence. They have said that the purpose of the view is solely to aid the jury to understand and evaluate the testimony of the witnesses.[14] It runs counter to common sense, however, to suppose that jurors, no matter how they may be instructed, will disregard the evidence of their own senses, as to the location of a building or a dam, or as to the condition of a wrecked car, when it comes in conflict with contrary testimony of all the witnesses. It seems that the more realistic conclusion is the one reached by a substantial number of other courts, namely, that the knowledge de-

9. Floyd v. Williams, supra.

10. Rodgers v. Okl. Wheat Pool Term. Corp., 186 Okl. 171, 96 P.2d 1040, syl. 2 (1940).

11. Snyder v. Mass., 291 U.S. 97, 114, 54 Sup.Ct. 330, 78 L.Ed. 674, 90 A.L.R. 575 (1934); Morris v. Corona Coal Co., 215 Ala. 47, 109 So. 278, syl. 6 (1926).

12. State v. Perry, 121 N.C. 533, 27 S.E. 997 (1897). In some jurisdictions the convenient practice is followed of appointing counsel for both parties as showers. Snyder v. Mass., 291 U.S. 97, 113, 54 S.Ct. 330, 78 L.Ed. 674, 90 A.L.R. 575 (1934). It is error for the jury to be given information by bystanders or witnesses, other than the showers. State v. Perry, supra; Yeary v. Holbrook, 171 Va. 266, 198 S.E. 441, syl. 10 (1938).

13. Recognizing the need for the presence of counsel, or a representation of the party. City of Chicago v. Baker, 98 Fed. 830, syl. 1 (C.C.A.Ill.1900) (better to allow representative to be present but discretionary); Shahan v. American Tel. & Tel. Co., 72 Ga.App. 749, 35 S.E.2d 5, syl. 9 (1945) (counsel); Alesko v. Union Pac. R. Co., 62 Idaho 235, 109 P.2d 874, syl. 8 (1941) (counsel but not parties, who here talked to jury). In fairness, it seems that the parties' right to be present so that they may make suggestions to their counsel about the view, should be recognized. In criminal cases some jurisdictions accord the accused this right. See, e. g., Noell v.

Comm., 135 Va. 600, 115 S.E. 679, syl. 3, 30 A.L.R. 1345 (1923), with note. Other states, adopting the position that the view is not the taking of testimony, and not historically part of the "trial," hold that allowing the accused to be present is a matter for the judge's discretion. Comm. v. Belenski, 276 Mass. 35, 176 N.E. 501, syl. 3 (1931). And the highest court has determined that refusal to grant the defendant's request to be present, where his counsel was present, and where there was no showing of resulting injustice, was not a denial of due process under the Fourteenth Amendment. Snyder v. Mass., 291 U.S. 97, 54 S.Ct. 330, 78 L.Ed. 674, 90 A.L.R. 575 (1934) (four justices dissenting). The prevailing opinion of Cardozo, J., and the dissent of Roberts, J., give fully the arguments of history and policy. Cases are collected in Notes, Presence of Accused during View, 30 A.L.R. 1358, 90 id. 597; 14 Am.Jur., Crim.Law, §§ 196, 201, 202.

14. Dempsey-Vanderbilt Hotel v. Hutsman, 153 Fla. 800, 15 So.2d 903, syl. 10 (1944); Huyink v. Hart Publications, 212 Minn. 87, 2 N.W.2d 552, syl. 5 (1942); Portland-Seattle Auto Freight v. Jones, 15 Wash.2d 603, 131 P.2d 736, syl. 5 (1942); Dec.Dig., Trial, ⊂⇒28(1). For an extreme application, see Chambers v. Murphy, [1953] 2 Dom.L.R. 705 (judge erred in using information gained from view as basis for disbelieving driver's testimony that his vision was obstructed), noted 31 Can.Bar Rev. 305.

rived from a view is evidence which the jury may use as a basis for finding the facts so disclosed.[15]

184. Exhibits in the Jury Room.[1]

Under modern American law demonstrative evidence, such as writings,[2] maps,[3] models,[4] photographs,[5] X-ray photographs,[6] and articles such as weapons or pieces of clothing,[7] may be taken by the jury in their retirement. Depositions[8] and transcripts of former testimony[9] are not within the rule.

They are not exhibits but are simply one form of the testimony of witnesses, which should not in this manner be unduly emphasized. But should documents, articles and other exhibits be given this special prominence by their presence with the jury in its deliberations? Important documents, such as contracts or ledger-sheets, and maps, models, photographs and the like, where they reflect the undisputed physical facts, would frequently be of vital help to the jury, whereas writings or exhibits of minor relevance[10]

15. Neel v. Mannings, Inc., 19 Cal.2d 647, 122 P.2d 576, 580, syl. 4 (1942) (sustaining jury's verdict as to dangerous stairs; ". . . the jury made an inspection of the defendant's premises and observed . . . the stairway . . . The knowledge acquired by this visit to the scene of the accident, supplementing the information embodied in the above-mentioned exhibits relative to the dimensional facts as to the construction of the stairway, was independent evidence in the case, and undoubtedly it had much to do with the jury's determination of this issue in accord with the plaintiff's claim."); In re State Highway, 129 Neb. 822, 263 N.W. 148, 149 (1935); Comm. v. Descalakis, 246 Mass. 12, 140 N.E. 470, 478 (1923) (murder: accused not entitled to be present at views; "Inevitably that which the jury see on a view will be utilized in reaching a verdict. In that sense that which is disclosed on a view is evidence. It is rightly described as such. . . . In another more strict and narrow sense a view may be thought not to be evidence. Plainly it is not testimony. It is not given by witnesses. It is not offered in the presence of the judge presiding at the trial."); 4 Wigmore, Evidence, § 1168. Some of these courts, however, hold that the verdict or finding must be supported by testimony apart from the view. In re State Highway, supra. As to the effect of the view upon the judge's power to direct a verdict, or grant a new trial, for insufficiency of the evidence see the discussion in Keeney v. Ciborowski, 304 Mass. 371, 24 N.E.2d 17, 18 (1940). See the able article, Hardman, Evidentiary Effect of a View, 53 W.Va.L.Rev. 103 (1951) (analyzing local decisions).

1. 6 Wigmore, Evidence, § 1913; Abbott's Civil Jury Trials, § 385, 5th ed. 1935 by Viesselman; 53 Am. Jur., Trial, §§ 921–935; 64 C.J., Trial, §§ 816–827; Dec.Dig., Trial, ☞ 307.

2. Tubbs v. Dwelling House Ins. Co., 84 Mich. 646, 48 N.W. 296, (1891) (writing sued on); Houston etc. Ry. Co. v. Wilson, 37 Tex.Civ.App. 405, 84 S.W. 274, syl. 4 (1904) (verified statement of claim).

The English common law rule at the time of the Revolution limited the writings which could be taken to those under seal. For interesting explanations of this now obsolete limitation see Henshaw, J., in Higgins v. Los Angeles Gas & Elec. Co., 159 Cal. 651, 115 Pac. 313, 315 (1911) and Young, J., in Wilson v. People, 103 Colo. 150, 84 P.2d 463, 467 (1938).

3. Chitwood v. Philadelphia & R. Ry. Co., 266 Pa. 435, 109 Atl. 645, syl. 2–4 (1920) (plan and photographs of scene of accident, error not to send where no question of their accuracy).

4. Blazinski v. Perkins, 77 Wis. 9, 45 N.W. 947, syl. 3 (1890).

5. Younger Bros. v. Ross, 151 S.W.2d 621, syl. 7 (Tex.Civ.App.1939) (photograph of scene of accident is "written evidence" within statute).

6. Texas Employers' Ins. Co. v. Crow, 148 Tex. 113, 221 S.W.2d 235 (1949) (excellent discussion by Harvey, J.), noted 48 Mich.L.Rev. 721. So also X-ray plates. Becker v. Prudential Ins. Co., 124 Pa.Super. 138, 188 Atl. 400, syl. 3 (1937). And X-ray films. Cooney v. Hughes, 310 Ill.App. 371, 34 N.E.2d 566, syl. 5 (1941).

7. Fowler v. Fowler, 63 Colo. 451, 168 Pac. 648, syl. 2 (1917) (pistol used by wife and coat worn by husband).

8. Gray v. Pennsylvania R. Co., 139 Atl. 66, syl. 6 (Del.Super.1927); Butler v. Abilene Mut.L.Ins.Co., 108 S.W.2d 972, syl. 5 (Tex.Civ.App.1937); O'Mara v. Kroetch, 170 Wash. 440, 16 P.2d 818, syl. 2 (1933). But occasionally it has been held discretionary to permit them to be taken. Stites v. McKibben, 2 Oh.St. 588, 592 (1853).

9. State v. Solomon, 96 Utah 500, 87 P.2d 807, syl. 7–10 (1939).

10. Thus a contradictory statement taken from a witness containing only minor discrepancies with his testimony was properly withheld in the judge's discretion. Durdella v. Trenton-Philadelphia Coach Co., 349 Pa. 482, 37 A.2d 481, syl. 2 (1944).

would if sent to the jury room often be stressed beyond their intrinsic value. There is thus a need for discretion and discrimination. Accordingly most jurisdictions allow the judge in his discretion to determine whether a given document or exhibit shall be sent with the jury.[11] Some other courts, however, have construed statutes or rules which provide that "the jury may take" writings and exhibits as being mandatory upon request of a party.[12]

It is only when the writing or exhibit has been introduced in evidence that it is allowed to be taken. It seems, however, that this re-

quirement should be applied according to the substance rather than the form, and accordingly if the writing or article has been read or exhibited to the jury in connection with the testimony even though not formally offered it should be treated for this purpose as in evidence.[13]

As to the use to which the jury may put the writings and exhibits, it seems that they may test the validity of the inferences for which such items of evidence are offered, by examining them,[14] and by such reasonable manipulation or experimentation [15] as is appropriate for the purpose.

---

11. See, e. g., Murray v. United States, 130 F.2d 442, syl. 7 (C.A.D.C.1942); Routh v. Williams, 141 Fla. 334, 193 So. 71, syl. 8 (1940); Hermitage Land & Timber Co. v. Scott's Ex'rs, 93 S.W.2d 1, syl. 7 (Ky. 1936); Rich v. Daily Creamery Co., 303 Mich. 344, 6 N.W.2d 539, syl. 6 (1942).

12. See, e. g., Texas Employers' Ins. Ass'n v. Applegate, 205 S.W.2d 412, syl. 1 (Tex.Civ.App.1947).

13. Hilker v. Agricultural Bond & Credit Corp., 96 S.W.2d 544, syl. 10 (Tex.Civ.App., 1936); Blazinski v. Perkins, 77 Wis. 9, 45 N.W. 947, syl. 3 (1890).

14. Thus the judge in his discretion may permit a questioned document, together with specimens of handwriting for comparison, to go with the jury. Goins v. United States, 99 F.2d 147, syl. 6-8 (C.C.A. 4, 1938). Contra: People v. White, 365 Ill. 499, 6 N.E.2d 1015, syl. 10, 11 (1937). And the jurors in their retirement may use a magnifying glass. In re Thomas' Estate, 155 Cal. 488, 101 Pac. 798, syl. 6 (1909) (dictum). And see State v. Everson, 166 Wash. 534, 7 P.2d 603, 80 A.L.R. 106 (1932) (that jury examined walking stick of pedestrian killed by car, with magnifying glass not introduced in evidence, for indications that it had been dragged, not ground for new trial: not new evidence but merely a more critical examination of an exhibit). But compare State v. Burke, 124 Wash. 632, 215 Pac. 31, syl. 7-9 (1923) where it was held that for the jury to secretly secure a microscope from the bailiff and to use it to discover from the exhibits new facts

not known to the parties was "misconduct." One gets the impression that the parties should themselves have used the jury's scientific methods.

15. Higgins v. Los Angeles Gas & Elec. Co., 159 Cal. 651, 115 Pac. 313, syl. 3 (1911) (good statement by Henshaw, J., of the general rule, not clear whether particular experiment approved); Saunders v. State, 4 Okl.Cr. 264, 111 Pac. 965, syl. 15 (1910) (murder: not improper for some of jury to put on coat of deceased to see the location of bullet holes); Hoover v. State, 107 Tex.Cr. 600, 298 S.W. 438, syl. 8 (1927) (jurors, one holding pistol reenact the murder, not improper); Taylor v. Comm., 90 Va. 109, 17 S.E. 812, syl. 12 (1893) (murder from ambush: state put in evidence cartridges found at the scene; defendant then put in evidence cartridges fired just before trial from his Winchester rifle, showing that the mark of the plunger was different; no misconduct for jury to take the rifle apart in the jury room discovering that the plunger had been recently tampered with). Compare Wilson v. United States, 116 Fed. 484 (C.C.A.9, 1902) (smuggling of opium "prepared for smoking": whether so prepared was required to be proved by prosecution and could be left to be ascertained by jury on retirement by experimenting with the opium to see if it would burn). See Note, Experiments in the Jury Room, 80 A.L.R. 108. As to whether liquor may be taken as an exhibit, and whether the jury may taste or smell it, see 30 Am.Jur. 494; Note, 80 A.L.R. 111.

TITLE 8

WRITINGS

CHAPTER 22

AUTHENTICATION[1]

185. General Theory: No Assumption of Authenticity.

One who seeks to introduce evidence of a particular fact, or item of proof, must generally give evidence (or offer assurance that he will do so) of those circumstances which make this fact or item relevant to some issue in the case. In respect to writings one of the commonest and most obvious of these circumstances on which relevancy may depend is the *authorship* of the writing. By whom was it written, signed, or adopted? Certainly any intelligible system of procedure must require that if the legal significance of the writing depends upon its authorship by a particular person, some showing must be made that he was the author, if the writing is to be accepted for consideration. The question is, what showing? In the everyday affairs of business and social life, the practice is to look first to the writing itself and if it bears the purported signature of X, or recites that it was made by him, we assume if no question of authenticity is raised that the writing is what it purports to be, that is, the writing of X.

It is just here that the common law trial procedure departs sharply from men's customs in ordinary affairs, and adopts the opposite attitude, namely, that the purported signature or the recitation of authorship on the face of the writing will not be accepted as sufficient preliminary proof of authenticity to secure the admission of the writing in evidence.[2] While this negative attitude fur-

1. 7 Wigmore, Evidence, §§ 2128–2169; 4 Jones, Evidence, §§ 1661–1682 (2d ed., 1926); Tracy, The Introduction of Documentary Evidence, 24 Iowa L. Rev. 436, 1939; Decennial Digests, Evidence, ☜ 369–382; Criminal Law, ☜444, 445; 32 C.J.S., Evidence, §§ 733–752; Uniform Rules of Evidence, Rules 67–69, 71.

2. McGowan v. Armour, 248 F. 676, syl. 2 (C.C.A.8th 1918) (letter bearing purported writer's signature, found in addressee's pocket, excluded); Burgess v. Simmons, 207 Ga. 291, 61 S.E.2d 410, syl. 1 (1950) (letter); State v. Golden, 67 Idaho 497, 186 P.2d 485, syl. 11 (1947) (letter); Beltran v. State, 144 Tex. Cr. 338, 163 S.W.2d 211, syl. 1 (1942) (written confession purporting to be signed by accused); 7 Wigmore, Evidence, § 2130, note 1; Dec.Dig., Evidence, ☜370(1).

This attitude of judicial skepticism seems to be carried to questionable extremes in cases of advertisements in the name of a party. See, for example, Mancari v. Frank P. Smith, Inc., 114 F.2d 834, 72 App.D.C. 398, 131 A.L.R. 301, annotated, 1940, noted

nishes a slight obstacle to the fraudulent or mistaken presentation of forged writings, it may be questioned whether this benefit is not outweighed by the time and expense of proving the authenticity of innumerable genuine writings which correctly show their origin on their face.

This negative attitude extends also to the authority of agents. Thus if an instrument recites that it is signed by A as agent for P, not only must additional proof be given that it was signed by A, but also of the fact that he was P's agent and authorized to sign.[3]

The term authentication is here used in the limited sense of proof of authorship. It is sometimes employed in a wider meaning, embracing all proof which may be required as a preliminary to the admission of a writing, chattel, photograph or the like. Thus in the case of business records not only is proof of authorship required for admission, but at common law various other facts such as that they were made in the course of the business must also be proved as part of the "foundation."[4] Similarly the identity of a bullet offered in a murder case as the fatal bullet,[5] or the correctness of a photograph[6] would be part of the necessary foundation-proof for admission. These requirements, distinct as they are from authenticity, are more conveniently treated in other chapters.[7]

186. Escapes from the Requirement of Producing Evidence of Authenticity.

The task of authenticating a writing by formal proof even when there seems to be no substantial doubt of genuineness may be troublesome. The writings may be numerous and executed by different persons. The need for authentication may be overlooked until the moment for introduction and the authenticating witness may not then be at hand. Fortunately by careful planning the party may often avoid the burden.

Notice to Admit. Under the practice in the Federal courts as provided by Rules 36 and 37(c) and under similar rules and statutes in other jurisdictions,[1] he may serve upon the adversary a written request for the admission of the genuineness of any relevant document, tendering a copy, and if the adversary unreasonably fails within a specified time to make such admission, he may secure an order of court charging him with the expense incurred in making the authenticating proof.

Securing Admission at Pre-Trial Conference. Under Rule 16 in the Federal courts and under analogous rules and statutes in

---

26 Iowa L.Rev. 134, 15 So.Calif.L.Rev. 115. The plaintiff sued because his name was mentioned in a widely distributed printed circular which purported to be issued by a manufacturer of shoes and by defendant, a local retailer. Held, by two judges to one, that the terms of the circular did not make a prima facie case of defendant's authorship and that the trial judge properly directed a verdict for defendant. To similar effect is Lochner v. Silver Sales Service, 232 N.C. 70, 59 S.E.2d 218, syl. 9 (1950). Cases are collected in 7 Wigmore, Evidence, § 2150 and the law review notes cited above.

Where, in addition to the purport of the writing, fortifying circumstances are offered to show authenticity, it has been said that if sufficiency is doubtful, the question is one for the judge's discretion. Cook-O'Brien Const. Co. v. Crawford, 26 F.2d 574, syl. 4 (C.C.A.Ariz.1928); Lundgren v. Union Indemnity Co., 121 Minn. 122, 213 N.W. 553, syl. 2 (1927).

3. Lee v. Melvin, 40 So.2d 837, syl. 1, 2 (Fla.1949); Bass v. African Methodist Episcopal Church, 155 Ga. 57, 116 S.E. 816, syl. 11 (1923); Wiseth v. Traill County Telephone Co., 70 N.D. 44, 291 N.W. 689, syl. 2 (1940); Dec.Dig., Evidence, ⇐370(5); 32 C.J.S. Evidence, § 734. Proof of later ratification by P meets the requirement. In re Johnson's Estate, 210 Iowa 891, 232 N.W. 282, syl. 4 (1930).

4. See §§ 284–288, herein.

5. See § 179, herein.

6. See § 181, herein.

7. See cross-references in notes 4–6, supra.

1. England, The Annual Practice 1946–1947, O. 32, rr. 2, 4; Ill.S.H.A. ch. 110, § 259.18; Mass.G.L.(Ter.Ed.) ch. 231, § 69; Mich. Court Rules, rule No. 42; N.J. R.S. 2:27–161; New York, Laws 1941, ch. 254, added to Civil Practice Act as § 322; Wis.St.1953, § 327.-22.

many states,[2] it is provided that a pre-trial conference of the attorneys may be called by the court to consider among other things, "the possibility of obtaining admissions of fact and of documents which will avoid unnecessary proof."[3] Of course, similar stipulations often are secured in informal negotiation between counsel, but a skilful judge may create at a pre-trial conference an atmosphere of mutual concession unusually favorable for such admissions. This objective of the pre-trial practice has been considered one of its most successful features.[4]

Statutes and Rules Requiring Special or Sworn Denial of Genuineness of Writing. A common provision of Practice Acts and Rules of Procedure requires that when an action is brought upon a written instrument, such as a note or contract, copied in the complaint, the genuineness of the writing will be deemed admitted unless a sworn denial be included in the answer.[5] A useful and somewhat analogous provision is contained in the Illinois Practice Rules, enabling a party who seeks to put in evidence a public record to serve a copy on the opposing party and thus to secure its admission in evidence unless the adversary denies its accuracy by affidavit filed and served within ten days.[6]

Writings Which "Prove Themselves": Acknowledged Documents, Certified Copies, and Law Books Which Purport to be Printed by Authority. There are certain kinds of writings which are said to "prove themselves" or to be "self-identifying." In consequence one of these may be tendered to the court and, even without the shepherding angel of an authenticating witness, will be accepted in evidence for what it purports to be. This convenient result is reached in two stages. First, by statutes which often provide that certain classes of writings, usually in some manner purporting to be vouched for by an official, shall be received in evidence "without further proof." This helpful attribute is most commonly given by these statutes to (1) deeds, conveyances or other instruments, which have been acknowledged by the signers before a notary public,[7] (2) certified copies of public records,[8] and (3) books of statutes which purport to be printed by public authority.[9]

---

2. Nims, Pre-Trial, 13–58 (1950) which gives an account of the practice in various states and districts.

3. Rule 16(3), Federal Rules of Civil Procedure (Rev. Ed.1952).

4. See articles by United States judges, Delehant, 28 Neb.L.R. 1, 21 (1948); Kloeb, 9 Oh.St.L.J. 203, 206 (1948); and see Nims, Pre-Trial, 116 (1950).

5. See, e. g., Calif.Code Civ.Proc. § 447; Texas Rules of Civil Procedure, rule 169.

6. Ill. Supreme Court Rules, rule 18(3), S.H.A. ch. 110, § 259.18(3).

7. See, e. g., Calif.Code Civ.Proc. §§ 1948, 1951 ("Every private writing except last wills and testaments may be acknowledged or proved and certified" like conveyances and certificate is evidence of execution); applied in Fares v. Morrison, 54 Cal. App.2d 773, 129 P.2d 735, syl. 2 (1942); Illinois, S.H.A., ch. 30, § 34 (conveyances duly acknowledged may be read without further proof, applied in Carter Oil Co. v. McQuigg, 27 F.Supp. 182, 187, syl. 13 (E.D.Ill., 1939)) New York, Civil Practice Act, §§ 384, 386 (similar to California, supra). These statutes are compiled in 5 Wigmore, Evidence, §

1676, and are discussed in Tracy, Introduction of Documentary Evidence, 24 Iowa L.Rev. 436, 439 (1939). Decisions are collected in Dec.Dig., Evidence, ☞370(4).

8. See, e. g., State v. Nagel, 75 N.D. 495, 28 N.W.2d 665, syl. 15, 16 (1947) (certified copy of birth-certificate admissible, and court will take judicial notice of genuineness of signature of certifying official). The doctrine and statutes are discussed in 5 Wigmore, Evidence, § 1677. Dec.Dig., Evidence, ☞ 338–349 collects the cases.

9. See the Uniform Proof of Statutes Act, adopted or adapted in 23 states and territories, which provides that "Printed books or pamphlets purporting on their face to be the session or other statutes of any of the United States, or the territories thereof, or of any foreign jurisdiction, and to have been printed and published by the authority of any such state, territory or foreign jurisdiction or proved to be commonly recognized in its courts shall be received in the courts of this state as prima facie evidence of such statutes." This and other like Acts are compiled in 5 Wigmore, Evidence, § 1684. Their most frequent and useful employment is in

But in the first two of these classes of writings, which can qualify only when the acknowledgment is certified by a notary or the copy certified by the official who has custody of the record, how is the court to know without proof that the signature or seal appearing on the writing is actually that of the official whose name and title are recited?

This second step is supplied by the traditional doctrines which recognize the seal or signature of certain types of officers, including the keeper of the seal of state, judicial officers, and notaries public, as being of themselves sufficient evidence of the genuineness of the certificate.[10] Moreover in many state codes particular provisions supplement or clarify tradition by specifying that the seals or signatures of certain classes of officialdom shall have this self-authenticating effect.[11]

187. Authentication by Direct Proof—(a) In General.

The simplest form of direct testimony authenticating a writing as that of X, is the production of a witness who swears that he saw X sign the offered writing.[1] Other examples would be the testimony of X himself, the signer, acknowledging execution, or the admission of authenticity by an adverse party in the present action, either made out of court and reported by another witness or shown by the party's own letter or other writing, or in the form of the party's testimony on the stand.[2] It is generally held that business records may be authenticated[3] by the evidence of one familiar with the books of the concern, such as a custodian or supervisor, who has not made the record or seen it made, that the offered writing is actually part of the records of the business.[4]

188. Authentication by Direct Proof—(b) Requirement of Production of Attesting Witnesses.[1]

Our rules about the production of subscribing witnesses are survivals of archaic law. They have their origins in Germanic practice earlier than jury trial, when pre-appointed transaction-witnesses were the only kind of witnesses that could be summoned or heard in court. When jury trial came in the attesting witnesses at first were summoned along with the jurors themselves, and this practice seems to have lingered until the middle fifteen hundreds.[2] The rule in its modern

the proof of statutes of sister states and of foreign countries, see § 326.

10. The history and theory of the subject are reviewed and the decisions and statutes collected in 7 Wigmore, Evidence, §§ 2161–2168.

11. See 7 Wigmore, Evidence, §§ 2162, 2167, where the statutes are compiled.

1. Manifestly this is a sufficient authentication. Matthews v. J. B. Colt Co., 145 Md. 667, 125 A. 840, syl. 1 (1924); Cottingham v. Doyle, 122 Mont. 301, 202 P.2d 533 (1949); Lancaster v. Marshall, 69 R.I. 422, 34 A.2d 718, syl. 2 (1943).

2. See Ch. 27, herein.

3. Merely supplying the requirement that the books be identified as such, though other foundation-proof may be required before the records will be accepted as evidence of the facts recorded under the hearsay exception for Business Records. See §§ 284–288, herein.

4. Hood v. Commonwealth Trust and Savings Bank, 376 Ill. 413, 34 N.E.2d 414, syl. 13 (1941) (cashier could "identify" bank's books, though some entries made before he was employed); Mitchell v. City of Mobile, 244 Ala. 442, 13 So.2d 664, syl. 12 (1943) (chief clerk, city's ledgers); Bohlke v. Wright, 200 Wash. 374, 93 P.2d 321, syl. 4 (1939) (divisional manager of telephone company: slips made by operators showing time of calls and parties thereto). To be contrasted is the holding that the testimony of an assistant rent attorney purporting to identify the pamphlet of rent regulations of the O.P.A., and an order and endorsement of the rent director was insufficient. Powell v. Anderson, 147 Neb. 872, 25 N.W.2d 401, syl. 1–7 (1946), criticized in Note, 14 U.Chi.L.Rev. 675 (1947).

1. 4 Wigmore, Evidence, §§ 1287–1321; 4 Jones, Commentaries, §§ 1663–1676; Dec.Dig. Evidence, ⊂⊃ 374; 32 C.J.S. Evidence, § 739; 20 Am.Jur. Evidence § 923–929; Note, 35 L.R.A. 321.

2. Thayer, Preliminary Treatise on Evidence, 502 (1898), quoted in 4 Wigmore, Evidence, § 1287.

common law form requires when a document signed by subscribing witnesses is sought to be authenticated by witnesses, that an attesting witness must first be called,[3] or all attesters must be shown to be unavailable,[4] before other witnesses can be called to authenticate it.[5]

The requirement has no application where the foundation for introducing the document is the opponent's judicial admission[6] of its genuineness,[7] either by stipulation of the parties in writing or in open court, or under modern rules and statutes by the opponent's failure to deny the genuineness of the writing.[8] Proof of an informal written admission of genuineness or the opponent's admission of genuineness while on the witness stand are of equivalent reliability and should have the same effect of dispensing with the production of an attester, but the American decisions seem to deny generally that any extra-judicial admission will dispense with the attester.[9]

The requirement is that the attesting witnesses be called before other authenticating witnesses are heard, but it is not required that the attesters give favorable testimony establishing the writing. So even if they profess want of memory[10] or even deny that they attested,[11] the writing may be established by other proof, and conversely if they support the writing, other proof may establish that it is not authentic.[12] Moreover, since the party calling the attester is required by law to do so, the prohibition upon impeaching one's own witness is held inapplicable.[13]

This requirement of calling particular persons, or accounting for them, to authenticate the writing is often inconvenient, and of doubtful expediency, and various exceptions have been carved out by the courts, as for ancient documents,[14] writings only "collaterally" involved in the suit,[15] and for certified copies of recorded conveyances, where the

---

3. If there are several attesters only one need be called. Sowell v. Bank of Brewton, 119 Ala. 92, 24 So. 585, syl. 1 (1898) (note); Shirley v. Fearne, 33 Miss. 353, syl. 2, 69 Am.Dec. 375 (deed, where two attesters, though only one required by law). But the Chancery rule in England required the calling or accounting for all attesters, and the provisions of American statutes in will cases vary. 4 Wigmore, Evidence, § 1304.

4. Howard v. Russell, 104 Ga. 230, 30 S.E. 802, syl. 2 (1898) (semble: deed); But seemingly if there are more attesters than the law requires only the number required must be accounted for. Snider v. Burks, 84 Ala. 57, 4 So. 225, 226 (1888) (three witnesses to a will, only two accounted for, sufficient).

5. For a summary statement of the rule, see 4 Wigmore, Evidence, § 1289.

6. As to meaning, see § 242.

7. Jones v. Henry, 84 N.C. 320, 323 (1881) (stipulation of record, "defendants admit execution of bond" dispenses with producing attester); 4 Wigmore, Evidence § 1296.

8. See § 186, supra.

9. See, e. g., Richmond & D. Ry. Co. v. Jones, 92 Ala. 226, 9 So. 276, syl. 5, 6 (1891) (error to allow adversary on stand to be asked if it is his signature to

a writing, which is attested) and discussion and citations, 4 Wigmore, Evidence, § 1300).

10. Gillis v. Gillis, 96 Ga. 1, 23 S.E. 107, syl. 2 (1895).

11. Newell v. White, 29 R.I. 343, 73 A. 798, syl. 1–3 (1908).

12. In re O'Connor's Estate, 105 Neb. 88, 179 N.W. 401, syl. 5, 12 A.L.R. 199 (1920).

13. In re Warren's Estate, 138 Ore. 283, 4 P.2d 635, syl. 6, 79 A.L.R. 389 (1931).

14. Smythe v. Inhabitants of New Providence Township, 263 F. 481, 484 (C.C.A.N.J.1920) ("the subscribing witnesses are presumed to be dead"); 20 Am.Jur. Evidence, § 932.

15. Steiner v. Tranum, 98 Ala. 315, 13 So. 365, syl. 1 (1893) (trover for horse: note given by plaintiff as evidence of his purchase, held "collateral"); Lugosch v. Public Service Ry. Co., 96 N.J.Eq. 472, 126 A. 170 (Ch.1924) (writing offered to impeach, "collateral"). Compare Snead v. Stephens, 242 Ala. 76, 5 So.2d 740, syl. 3 (1941) where it was held that in a suit for destruction of plaintiff's mortgage lien on cotton by defendant's resale of the cotton, the mortgage itself was not collateral. The reversal of the judgment for plaintiff because of his failure to produce the subscribing witness to a writing the genuineness of which was not actually in doubt, illustrates the profitless aridity of the requirement.

original is not required to be produced.[16] A more sweeping reform has been adopted by statutes in many states which provide that it shall no longer be essential to call attesting witnesses, except as to writings required by law to be attested.[17] Usually the only writings required to be attested are wills, and commonly there are detailed probate statutes in the states regulating the procedure of making proof of a will, and the calling of attesting witnesses.[18]

189. Authentication by Direct Proof—(c) Proof of Handwriting.

A witness is placed on the stand. "Will you state whether you are acquainted with the handwriting of X." "I am." "Will you look at this letter (or at the signature) and tell me whether it is in the handwriting of X." "It is." This is part of the familiar routine of authenticating writings.[1] Perhaps the most distinctive rules about this method of authentication are the practical working rules, which have accumulated in centuries of judicial experience, as to what is a sufficient qualification, if the adversary, as he may do, questions the witness's profession of knowledge by cross-examining him on his qualifications at the outset.[2] The standard is far from pedantic. Thus one who can read[3] may be qualified if he has seen the person write even though only once[4] and long ago.[5] Or he may qualify if he has seen writings *purporting* to be those of the person in question under circumstances vouching their genuineness, as where he has had an exchange of correspondence with the person,[6] or has seen writings which the person has admitted to be his own,[7] or has become familiar with his writings by acting as clerk or custodian in an office where such writings are and in the course of business would naturally be kept.[8] Similarly, specimens of the handwriting of the person, themselves authenticated as genuine, may be produced for comparison with the writing sought to be proven,

---

16. Powers v. Russell, 13 Pick.(Mass.) 69, 75 (1832); 4 Wigmore, Evidence, § 1318. Seemingly some courts would admit the original recorded deed, without calling subscribers under statutes providing that they "prove themselves." See Foxworth v. Brown, 120 Ala. 59, 24 So. 1, 4 (1898) and § 186, supra.

17. See, e. g., New York, Civil Practice Act, § 331; Texas, Vernon's Ann.Civ.St. (as amended 1933), art. 3734a. In England (Evidence Act 1938, ch. 28, sec. 3) and Massachusetts, G.L.(Ter.Ed.) c. 233, § 68, the requirement is specifically limited to wills. The statutes are compiled in 4 Wigmore, Evidence, § 1290 note 4. The Uniform Rules of Evidence, R. 71 provides: "When the execution of an attested writing is in issue, whether or not attestation is a statutory requisite of its effective execution, no attester is a necessary witness even though all attesters are available unless the statute requiring attestation specifically provides otherwise."

18. See statutes collected in 4 Wigmore, Evidence, § 1304, note 6.

1. See Tracy, Documentary Evidence, 24 Iowa L.Rev. 436, 442-5 (1939); 4 Jones, Evidence, § 1662 (2d ed. 1926); Dec.Dig. Evidence, ⊜378(4).

2. For detailed treatment see 3 Wigmore, Evidence, §§ 694-708; Hershberger v. Hershberger, 345 Pa. 439, 29 A.2d 95, syl. 8-13 (1942).

3. People v. Corey, 148 N.Y. 476, 42 N.E. 1066, syl. 1 (1895).

4. State v. Bond, 12 Idaho 424, 86 P. 43, 47 (1906); State v. Freshwater, 30 Utah 442, 85 P. 447, syl. 2 (1906).

5. In re Diggins' Estate, 68 Vt. 198, 34 A. 696, syl. 6 (1896) (once, 20 years before, seemingly thought sufficient).

6. W. T. Rawleigh Co. v. Overstreet, 71 Ga.App. 873, 32 S.E.2d 574, syl. 15 (1944); Poole v. Beller, 104 W.Va. 547, 140 S.E. 534, syl. 2 (1927) (correspondence between members of family).

7. Hershberger v. Hershberger, 345 Pa. 439, 29 A.2d 95, syl. 13 (1942) (witnesses had charged account of person with checks purporting to have been drawn by him, and he had not questioned them).

8. Hamilton v. Smith, 74 Conn. 374, 50 A. 884, syl. 5 (1902) (surveyor who used and copied maps of former town surveyor may testify to their genuineness); and see State v. Meyers, 36 Idaho 396, 211 P. 440, syl. 5 (1922) (president of dental board who corresponded with secretary of board qualified to identify latter's handwriting).

and submitted to the jury for their inference that the offered writing is genuine.[9]

It will be objected, however, that these methods of proving genuineness are too crude and unreliable. If a writing is questioned no person not trained in the science and art of document examination is competent to distinguish a skilled forgery from a genuine writing.[10] Even less conceivable is it that an unskilled layman who saw the person write once a decade ago could make such a differentiation. It must be remembered, however, that these liberal standards of qualification were worked out for the process of authentication, that is, such prima facie identification as merely suffices to secure the admission of the document in evidence. Not one in a hundred of documents so authenticated is questioned, and if such authentication-requirement beyond the writing's own purport is needed, which is doubtful, this simple layman's assertion, made on a minimum basis of knowledge, that this looks like his handwriting, is sufficient for this limited purpose of authentication. As we shall see, if there develops an actual controversy over genuineness, then the issue should be resolved mainly upon the testimony of handwriting experts and both the legal qualifications and the requirements of good advocacy demand a much more scientific approach.[11]

190. Authentication by Circumstantial Evidence—(a) Ancient Documents.[1]

When a generation has passed since a document was written, the maker, those who witnessed the making and even those who know the handwriting of the party will often be dead or inaccessible. The need for resorting to circumstantial evidence is clear. Supporting circumstances such as fair appearance, proper custody, prompt recording, and in case of deed or will, possession taken under the instrument, suggest themselves as indications of genuineness. Age itself, moreover, gives some inference of verity, in that it is unlikely that a writing would be forged for fruition after the lapse of a generation. These considerations have led the courts to develop a definite rule-of-thumb practice for circumstantial authentication of old writings.[2] Under this practice a writing is sufficiently authenticated as an "ancient document" if the party who offers it proves to the judge's satisfaction that it is thirty years old,[3] if the judge finds that it is unsuspicious in appearance,[4] and if the party further

---

9. Flickema v. Henry Kraker Co., 252 Mich. 406, 233 N.W. 362, syl. 2, 3 (1930); Poole v. Beller, 104 W.Va. 547, 140 S.E. 534, syl. 2 (1927).

10. See the interesting article, Inbau, Lay Witness Identification of Handwriting (An Experiment), 34 Ill.L.Rev. 433; Hilton, The Detection of Forgery, 30 J.Crim.L. & Criminology, 568, 1939.

11. See § 172.

1. 7 Wigmore, Evidence, §§ 2137–2146; 4 Jones, Evidence, §§ 1679–1682 (2d ed. 1926); Dec.Dig., Evidence, ⟨key⟩372; 32 C.J.S., Evidence, §§ 743–752.

2. See Uniform Rules of Evidence, R. 67: "Authentication of a writing is required before it may be received in evidence. Authentication may be by evidence sufficient to sustain a finding of its authenticity or by any other means provided by law. If the judge finds that a writing (a) is at least thirty years old at the time it is offered, and (b) is in such condition as to create no suspicion concerning its authenticity, and (c) at the time of its discovery was in a place in which such a document, if authentic, would be likely to be found, it is sufficiently authenticated.

thentic, would be likely to be found, it is sufficiently authenticated.

3. The time is figured from the execution of the writing (not when it goes into effect, as in case of a will) to the time of offering (not the time of bringing suit). Reuter v. Stuckart, 181 Ill. 529, 54 N.E. 1014, syl. 1 (1899). Age may be proved circumstantially by appearance and contents. Comm. v. Ball, 277 Pa. 301, 121 A. 191, syl. 2, 29 A.L.R. 626 (1923) (121 year old minute book of turnpike corporation). While doubtless the purported date is some evidence of age, it is not sufficient alone to prove it. Rio Bravo Oil Co. v. Staley Oil Co., 138 Tex. 198, 158 S.W.2d 293, 295, syl. 2 (1942).

4. Campbell v. Bates, 143 Ala. 338, 39 So. 144, syl. 1 (1905) (interlineation not suspicious under the circumstances); Elkhorn Coal Corp. v. Bradley, 216 Ky. 599, 288 S.W. 326, syl. 2, 3 (1926) (claim that ink appeared new not sustained, where genuineness verified by testimony); Roberts v. Waddell, 94 S.W.2d 211, syl. 2 (Tex.Civ.App.1936) (purported

proves that the writing is produced from a place of custody natural for such a writing,[5] and under the condition obtaining in some jurisdictions, that if the writing is a dispositive one like a will or a deed, possession has been taken under it.[6] The doctrine of authentication by age, however, is not limited to such dispositive instruments, but extends to writings generally, and has been applied, for example, to contracts,[7] letters,[8] maps,[9] books of account,[10] and public [11] and church [12] records.

In the case of a writing which purports to be executed by an agent, executor or other person acting under a power or authority for another, proof of the facts which authenticate the writing as an ancient document, gives rise to the presumption that the person signing was duly authorized.[13]

Satisfaction of the ancient document requirements will serve to authenticate an ancient copy of an original writing,[14] and a fresh certified copy of an instrument of record for thirty years will prove the ancient

---

deed rejected because mutilated and on other grounds).

5. In re Buttrick, 185 Mass. 107, 69 N.E. 1044, syl. 2 (1904) (possession by heir of grantee, meets the test); Wright v. Hull, 83 Oh. 385, 94 N.E. 813, syl. 1 (1911) (inadmissible as ancient document where no proof of proper custody, and where there were suspicious circumstances); Rio Bravo Oil Co. v. Staley Co., 138 Tex. 198, 158 S.W.2d 293, syl. 1, 2 (1942) (want of proof of age and proper custody).

6. In a few states, older decisions holding that possession is indispensable, may still be law. See, e. g., Davison v. Morrison, 86 Ky. 397, 5 S.W. 871, syl. 1 (1887) (not admissible against one in possession holding under adverse title of record); Homer v. Cilley, 14 N.H. 85, 98 (1843) (possession for thirty years, or at least for twenty, required). But the trend is toward the view that either possession or other additional confirmatory circumstances, such as payment of taxes by the grantee, or recording, will suffice. Gaston v. Guthrie, 162 Ga. 103, 132 S.E. 764, syl. 2 (1926); Clark v. Owens, 18 N. Y. 434, 438 (1858). And some courts reject altogether any requirement of proof of possession or other corroborative facts. Appeal of Jarboe, 91 Conn. 265, 99 A. 563, 565 (1917) (semble); Ammons v. Dwyer, 78 Tex. 639, 649, 15 S.W. 1049, syl. 4 (1890). Decisions are collected in 7 Wigmore, Evidence, § 2141, 22 C.J., Evidence, § 1181; Dec. Dig., Evidence, ☞372(5).

7. Blandy-Jenkins v. Dunraven, [1899] 2 Ch. 121 (contract of settlement of suit).

8. Bell v. Brewster, 44 Oh.St. 690, 694, 10 N.E. 679, syl. 3 (1887); Smith v. Lynn, 152 S.W.2d 838, syl. 9 (Tex.Civ.App.1941) (used as admission of predecessor in title).

9. Plattsmouth Bridge Co. v. Globe Oil & Refining Co., 232 Iowa 1118, 7 N.W.2d 409, syl. 2 (1943) (county surveyor's plat).

10. Cole v. Lea, 35 App.D.C. 355, syl. 1 (1910).

11. McGuire v. Blount, 199 U.S. 142, 26 S.Ct. 1, syl. 4, 50 L.Ed. 125, (1905) (protocol showing probate of will); Enfield v. Ellington, 67 Conn. 459, 34 A. 818, syl. 2, 3 (1896) (town clerk's list of electors). And a new certified copy of an ancient deed (where the original deed is unavailable) comes in as would the original, as evidence of its genuineness. Emory v. Bailey, 111 Tex. 337, 234 S.W. 660, syl. 4, 18 A.L.R. 901 (1921).

12. Bergman v. Carson, 226 Iowa 449, 284 N.W. 442, syl. 2 (1939); Sinkora v. Wlach, 239 Iowa 1392, 35 N.W.2d 40, syl. 5–11 (1948) (both cases involved copies of foreign church records of birth, etc.; in the second case, the copy was held to be insufficiently proved).

13. Wilson v. Snow, 228 U.S. 217, 33 S.Ct. 487, syl. 1, 57 L.Ed. 807 (1913) (deed of executrix; ". . . the ancient deed proves itself, whether it purports to have been signed by the grantor in his own right, as agent under power of attorney or—the original records having been lost—by an administrator under a power of sale given by order of court, not produced but recited in the deed itself"); Baumgarten v. Frost, 143 Tex. 533, 186 S.W.2d 982, syl. 1, 159 A.L.R. 428 (1945) (presumption recognized, but here receiver's assignment could not be presumed authorized where court's records intact and failed to show confirmation).

14. And hence to show the terms and execution of the original. See Schell v. City of Jefferson, 357 Mo. 1020, 212 S.W.2d 430, syl. 4 (1948) (ancient copy of city plat, original not available, held wrongly excluded, one judge dissenting); and see 7 Wigmore, Evidence, § 2143; 32 C.J.S. Evidence, § 746c. But there is a contrary view, that the ancient document doctrine does not apply to copies. McCreery v. Lewis, 104 Me. 33, 70 A. 540, syl. 2, 19 L.R.A.N.S. 438 (1908), criticised Wigmore, ubi supra, p. 598.

writing,[15] but in addition before the copy can come in, the original documents rule must be satisfied by showing that the original is unavailable.[16] Admission of a writing as an ancient document does, however, as we have seen, dispense with the production of attesting witnesses.[17]

In addition to the effect of the age of the instrument as authenticating it, there is a distinct doctrine that recitals in ancient instruments may be received as evidence of the facts recited. This latter doctrine constitutes one of the exceptions to the rule against hearsay and is discussed at another place.[18]

191. Authentication by Circumstantial Evidence—(b) Custody.[1]

If a writing purports to be an official report or record and is proved to have come from the proper public office where such official papers are kept, it is generally agreed that this authenticates the offered document as genuine.[2] This result is founded on the probability that the officers in custody of such records will carry out their public duty to receive or record only genuine official papers and reports. Similarly, where a public office is the depository for private papers, such as wills, conveyances, or income tax returns, the proof that such a purporting deed, bill of sale, tax return or the like has come from the proper custody is usually accepted as sufficient authentication.[3] This again can be sustained on the same principle if it appears that the official custodian had a public duty to verify the genuineness of the papers offered for record or deposit and to accept only the genuine.

Should not the practice of accepting as prima facie genuine a document which comes from a natural custody be extended beyond the field of public duty, and be recognized for writings found in private custody? It seems that it should,[4] but that here the practice should be discretionary, and that if the judge finds that the purport of the writing and the fact that it was found in a place and custody natural for such a paper, and the other attending circumstances, make its genuineness substantially probable, it should come in. The strictness of some of the decisions [5] at this point seems misguided when we remember that these facts are offered

---

15. Hodge v. Palms, 54 C.C.A. 570, 117 F. 396, 398 (Mich.1902); Fielder v. Pemberton, 136 Tenn. 440, 189 S.W. 873, syl. 2, Ann.C.1918E, 905.

16. Sudduth v. Central of Ga. Ry. Co., 77 So. 350, syl. 7 (Ala.1917); Woods v. Bonner, 89 Tenn. 411, 18 S.W. 67, syl. 4 (1890); Emory v. Bailey, 111 Tex. 337, 234 S.W. 660, 662 (1921) ("on filing proper affidavit of loss," under statute).

17. See § 188, above.

18. See § 298, herein.

1. 7 Wigmore, Evidence, §§ 2158–2160; Dec.Dig. Evidence, ☞366, Criminal Law, ☞444.

2. United States v. Ward, 173 F.2d 628, syl. 3 (C.A.2d, 1949) (records taken from files of Office of Selective Service, and identified by custodian); City of Columbus v. Ogletree, 102 Ga. 293, 29 S.E. 749, syl. 7 (1897) (city council minutes); McLeod v. Crosby, 128 Mich. 641, 87 N.W. 883, syl. 2 (1901) (file-papers in a criminal case).

3. Morgan v. United States, 149 F.2d 185, syl. 4 (C. C.A.5th, 1945) (price list of corporation taken from file of rationing board); Wausau Sulphate Fibre

Co. v. Commissioner, 61 F.2d 879, syl. 1 (C.C.A.7th, 1932) (waiver bearing purported signature of taxpayer, from Bureau's files); Lewis v. United States, 38 F.2d 406, syl. 4 (C.C.A.9th, 1930) (copy, certified by custodian of company's income tax return, in Internal Revenue Department's file).

4. See, e. g., Johnson v. United States, 89 F.2d 913, syl. 2, 3 (1937) (ledger sheets of brokerage firm proved not by person who made the entries but by supervising custodian, sufficiently authenticated); People v. Ramsey, 83 Cal.App.2d 707, 189 P.2d 802, syl. 14 (1948) (in abortion prosecution, looseleaf notebook found in defendant's cupboard beside telephone containing hour of appointment with full name and address and telephone number of prosecuting witness was properly admitted notwithstanding absence of proof as to how long book had been in cupboard, who placed it there or who wrote notations in it).

5. Cohen v. New York Life Ins. Co., 21 F.2d 278, syl. 2 (C.C.A.Pa.1927) (secondary evidence of terms of note found in pocket of coat of deceased, implying an intent to commit suicide, excluded);

only as a prima facie showing of genuineness, freely open to counter-proof.

192. Authentication by Circumstantial Evidence—(c) Knowledge: Reply Letters and Telegrams.[1]

When a letter, signed with the purported signature of X, is received "out of the blue," with no previous correspondence, the traditional "show me" skepticism of the common law trial practice [2] prevails, and the purported signature is not accepted as authentication,[3] unless authenticity is confirmed by additional facts.[4]

One circumstance recognized as sufficient is the fact that the letter discloses knowledge that only the purported signer would be likely to have.[5] Moreover, a convenient practice recognizes that if a letter has been writ-

ten to X, and the letter now offered in evidence purports to be written by X and purports to be a reply to the first letter (that is either refers to it, or is responsive to its terms) and has been received without unusual delay, these facts authenticate it as a reply-letter.[6] This result may be rested upon the knowledge-principle, mentioned above. In view of the regularity of the mails the first letter would almost invariably come exclusively into the hands of X, or those authorized to act for him, who would alone know of the terms of the letter. It is supported also by the fact that in common experience we know that reply-letters do come from the person addressed in the first letter.

These same arguments apply to reply-telegrams, but with a reduced degree of certain-

---

People v. Manganaro, 218 N.Y. 9, 112 N.E. 436, syl. 2, 3 (1916) (murder: writing bearing purported signature of accused found on the dresser in his bedroom the day after the homicide, improperly admitted); State v. Manos, 149 Wash. 60, 270 P. 132, syl. 2–4 (1928) (prosecution for being a common gambler; accused was lessee of second floor of building; in one room was his office and the other room was used for gambling; held, error to admit telegram purporting to be signed by accused to supplier of gambling equipment, and purported reply telegram, found in desk, in office of accused).

1. 7 Wigmore, Evidence, §§ 2148, 2153–2154; 22 C.J. Evidence, § 1111; 32 C.J.S. Evidence, § 706b; Dec.Dig. Evidence, ⊂⊃378, Criminal Law, ⊂⊃444.

2. See § 185, above.

3. McClendon v. State, 243 Ala. 218, 8 So.2d 883, syl. 3, 4 (1942); State v. Golden, 67 Idaho 497, 186 P. 2d 485, syl. 9–11 (1947); Morrison v. Southern States Finance Co., 197 N.C. 322, syl. 1 (1929); 32 C.J.S. 606, note 39.

4. See, e. g., Greenbaum v. United States, 80 F.2d 113, 125, syl. 17 (C.C.A.9th, 1935) where a letter purporting to be signed for a corporation by an agent was held to be authenticated when it was shown that the person was an agent and that the city of posting was the place of business of the company. See also Taylor-Wharton Iron & Steel Co. v. Earnshaw, 259 Mass. 554, 157 N.E. 855, syl. 1, 4 (1927) (authenticity confirmed by fact that check, enclosed in letter, was paid).

5. Chaplin v. Sullivan, 67 Cal.App.2d 728, 155 P.2d 368, 372, syl. 7 (1945) ("letter states facts which

could only be known to purported writer"); Irving v. Goodimate Co., 320 Mass. 454, 70 N.E.2d 414, syl. 6 (1946) (fact that letter referred to previous conversations between plaintiff and officer of defendant is confirmatory circumstance); People v. Adams, 162 Mich. 371, 127 N.W. 354, 360, syl. 6 (reference to conversations); People v. Dunbar, 215 N.Y. 416, 109 N.E. 554, 556 (same); State v. Woodmansee, 156 Ore. 607, 69 P.2d 298, syl. 1–4 (1937) (series of letters showing intimate knowledge of details of life of alleged writer); Comm. v. Nolly, 290 Pa. 271, 138 A. 836, syl. 3 (1927) (letter referred to matters known only to witness and alleged writer); Note, Proof of Authenticity, 9 A.L.R. 984. It seems that a statement after a letter is written about its contents may identify the declarant as the writer. See Deadrick v. Deadrick, 182 Ga. 96, 185 S.E. 89, syl. 2 (1936).

6. Marcotte's Estate v. Clay, 170 Kan. 189, 224 P.2d 998, syl. 1 (1950) (fact that letter is reply authenticates, especially where reply written on purported signer's business stationery); Gulf Refining Co. v. Bagby, 200 La. 258, 7 So.2d 903, syl. 10, 11 (1942); Whelton v. Daly, 93 N.H. 150, 37 A.2d 1, syl. 6 (1944) (Page, J.: "It is a fair inference, considering the habitual accuracy of the mails, that the letter addressed to B reached the real B, and that an answer referring to the tenor of A's letter and coming back in due course of mail, leaves only a negligible chance that any other than B has become acquainted with the contents of A's letter so as to forge a reply."); Lewis v. Couch, 179 Okl. 418, 65 P.2d 988, syl. 3 (1937); Connor v. Zanuzoski, 36 Wash.2d 458, 218 P.2d 879, syl. 6, 7 (1950).

ty. Some of the employees of the telegraph company, as well as the addressee, know the contents of the first telegram. Moreover, the instances of mis-delivery of telegrams may be more numerous relatively than mis-deliveries of letters. These considerations have led some courts to reject for reply-telegrams this theory of authentication.[7] The contrary view, that the inference of authenticity of the reply-telegram is substantial and sufficient,[8] seems more reasonable and expedient.

When the reply-letter purports to be signed by an agent or other representative of X, the addressee of the first letter, the authority of the signing representative is presumed.[9]

The first step in authentication of the reply-letter is to prove that the first letter giving its date was duly mailed at a given time and place addressed to X.[10] Seemingly oral testimony to these facts should suffice as to the first letter if the reply-letter refers to it by date.[11] If, however, the reply-letter only refers to it by reciting or responding to

its terms, then since the terms of the first letter become important,[12] probably it would be necessary to satisfy the Documentary Originals Rule. If X, as usually would be the case, is the party-opponent, and has the first letter in his hands, it would be necessary to give him notice to produce it, before a copy could be used to prove its terms.[13]

193. Authentication by Circumstantial Evidence—(d) Knowledge: Reply Telephone Message.[1]

If a witness testifies that he received a telephone call "out of the blue," and that the voice at the other end declared, "This is X calling," followed by a message from the purported X, this is not a sufficient authentication of the message as coming from X.[2] The needed link, however, will be supplied if the witness testifies that he recognized X's voice,[3] or if the message reveals that the speaker had knowledge of facts that only X would be likely to know,[4] or if other confirm-

7. Smith v. Easton, 54 Md. 138, 146, 39 Am.St.Rep. 355 (1880); Howley v. Whipple, 48 N.H. 487, 488 (1869).

8. Peterman v. Vermont Savings Bank, 181 La. 403, 159 So. 598, 602 (1935); Morneault v. Cohen, 122 Me. 543, 120 A. 915, syl. 3 (1923); People v. Hammond, 132 Mich. 422, 93 N.W. 1084, syl. 4 (1903); Western Twine Co. v. Wright, 11 S.D. 521, 78 N. W. 942, syl. 3 (1899); Note, Proving Authorship of Telegram, 52 A.L.R. 583.

9. Reliance Life Ins. Co. v. Russell, 208 Ala. 559, 94 So. 748, syl. 11 (1922) (to rebut presumption of genuineness of reply letter not sufficient to show that purported sender did not sign it but must show that he did not authorize another to sign for him); Capitol City Supply Co. v. Beury, 69 W.Va. 612, 72 S.E. 657, syl. 4 (1911) (similar to last); Anstine v. McWilliams, 24 Wash.2d 230, 163 P.2d 816, syl. 1–4 (1945) (authority of purported agent, signing for principal presumed: full discussion and citations); Dec.Dig. Evidence, ⊂⊃378(3).

10. Consolidated Grocery Co. v. Hammond, 99 C.C.A. 195, 175 F. 641, syl. 1 (Fla.1910) (statement in purported reply letter referring to previous letter does not suffice); Kvale v. Keane, 39 N.D. 560, 168 N.W. 74, syl. 3, 4 (1918) (must make preliminary proof that first letter was duly addressed, stamped and posted).

11. See § 198, herein.

12. See § 198, herein.

13. See § 203, herein.

1. 7 Wigmore, Evidence, § 2155; Notes, Anglin, 11 N.C.L.Rev. 344 (1933), 26 Wash.U.L.Q. 433 (1941), 71 A.L.R. 5, 105 A.L.R. 326; Dec.Dig. Evidence. ⊂⊃148; 20 Am.Jur. §§ 365–370; 31 C.J.S. Evidence, § 188, 22 C.J. Evidence, § 160.

2. Meyer Milling Co. v. Strohfeld, 224 Mo.App. 508, 20 S.W.2d 963, syl. 5 (1929), certiorari quashed and holding approved, 325 Mo. 901, 30 S.W.2d 462, syl. 2 (1930).

3. United States v. Easterday, 57 F.2d 165, syl. 5 (C. C.A.2d 1932); Comm. v. Del Giorno, 303 Pa. 509, 154 A. 786, syl. 1 (1931); Note, 105 A.L.R. 334. See Note, The Reliability of the Identification of the Human Voice, 33 J.Crim.L. 487 (1943).

4. National Aid Life Ass'n v. Murphy, 78 S.W.2d 223, syl. 7, 8 Tex.Civ.App., 1935; Morriss v. Finkelstein, 145 S.W.2d 439, syl. 13, Mo.App., 1940, Note, 26 Wash.U.L.Q. 433 and see remarks of Learned Hand, Circ. J., in Van Riper v. United States, 13 F.2d 961, 968. C.C.A.N.Y., 1926. Compare Smithers v. Light, 305 Pa. 141, 157 A. 489, 1931, where one purporting to be customer X calls up a broker's office and orders the sale of designated stocks

ing circumstances make it probable that X was the speaker.[5]

The case stands differently, however, when the witness testifies that he himself put in a call to the number listed in the telephone directory as the number of X, and that a voice answered, "This is X speaking," followed by a conversation. It is generally considered in such a situation that the accuracy of the telephone transmission system and the probable want of motive to falsify or of opportunity for premeditated fraud gives special reliability to the answering speaker's identification of himself and that the authentication is sufficient.[6] Moreover, it is likewise usually held that when the witness calls the number of a business establishment and asks

for a particular kind of employee, as "a salesman" or "the manager" and is connected with some one who identifies himself as such, this is evidence that he holds this position,[7] and generally that whoever holds himself out in the telephone conversation as qualified to transact business within the scope of the ordinary affairs of the concern, is presumed to be authorized to speak for the employer.[8]

194. Function of Judge and Jury in Authentication.[1]

If direct testimony of the authorship of a writing or of an oral statement is given, this is sufficient authentication and the judge has no problem on that score.[2] The writing or statement comes in, if relevant and not otherwise objectionable. When the authenticat-

---

in the broker's hands owned by X. Here the authentication was held insufficient without adverting to the knowledge-factor.

5. Andrews v. United States, 78 F.2d 274, 105 A.L.R. 322, 325 (C.C.A.10, 1935) (record of telephone company that long distance call came from accused to witness, and subsequent correspondence between the parties to the call relating to the subject of the conversation); International Harvester Co. v. Caldwell, 198 N.C. 751, 153 S.E. 325, syl. 1 (1930) (witness called office of plaintiff company and asked for information; answering person said she did not know, but would have book-keeper call, and later a person called who described himself as book-keeper and gave the information); State v. Silverman, 148 Ore. 296, 36 P.2d 342, syl. 1–3 (1934) (whether call to witness, asking him to come and fix car, came from someone acting at defendant's request held sufficiently shown by purport of call, defendant's admissions and facts about car); Colbert v. Dallas Joint Stock Land Bank, 136 Tex. 268, 150 S.W.2d 771, syl. 7, 8 (1941) (purport of conversation showing knowledge and subsequent confirmatory acts).

6. Smith v. Hollander, 257 P. 577, syl. 11 (Cal.App. 1927) (call for individual at her telephone number); Epperson v. Rostatter, 90 Ind.App. 8, 168 N.E. 126, syl. 1 (1929) (similar); Bradley v. Illinois Cent. R. Co., 291 Ky. 25, 163 S.W.2d 26, syl. 1 (1942) (call to business office, person answering did not give his name); Rice v. Fidelity & Casualty Co., 250 Mich. 398, 230 N.W. 181, syl. 2 (1930) (call for particular officer at insurance office, answerer gave relevant information). See, however, the dictum to the contrary in Colbert v. Dallas Joint Stock Land Bank, 136 Tex. 268, 150 S.W.2d 771, syl. 7

(1941). And compare Holland v. O'Shea, 342 Ill. App. 515, 95 N.E.2d 515 (1950), noted 1951 U. Ill.L.F. 483, which denies application of the rule to the situation where one calls the business number of a firm or corporation and asks to speak to one who works there about a matter of private concern to that person. When the responding voice purports to be that of the person called, this was held not to authenticate, distinguishing the case where the call was for an employee or officer about company matters. But the reliability of the inference of authenticity in the type-situation actually presented is so great that the decision goes against common sense.

7. Irving Tanning Co. v. Shir, 295 Mass. 380, 3 N.E.2d 841, syl. 1 (1936) (book-keeper); Connally v. Davis, Agent, 114 Neb. 556, 208 N.W. 626 (yardmaster).

8. John Alt Furn. Co. v. Maryland Casualty Co., 88 F.2d 36, syl. 7 (C.C.A.Mo.1937); Potomac Ins. Co. v. Armstrong, 206 Ky. 434, 267 S.W 188, 189, syl. 1 (1924) (installation of business telephone is invitation to do business with those who answer); Zurich Gen. Accident & Liability Ins. Co. v. Baum, 159 Va. 404, 165 S.E. 518, 520, 521, syl. 3 (1932). But it was held that where the caller asked for information about a past happening, instead of negotiating about some present transaction, the presumed authority did not extend to the answering admission. Shelton v. Wolf Cheese Co., 338 Mo. 1129, 93 S.W.2d 947, syl. 8 (1936).

1. Dec.Dig., Evidence, ⊂⇒282, 32 C.J.S. Evidence, §§ 624, 625; 22 C.J. Evidence, §§ 1203, 1204.

2. See §§ 187–189, above.

ing evidence is circumstantial, however, the question whether reasonable men could find its authorship as claimed by the proponent, may be a delicate and balanced one, as to which the judge must be accorded some latitude of judgment.[3] Accordingly, it is often said to be a matter of discretion.[4] It must be noticed, however, that authenticity is not to be classed as one of those preliminary questions of fact conditioning admissibility under technical evidentiary rules of competency or privilege. As to these latter, the trial judge will permit the adversary to introduce controverting proof on the prelim-

inary issue in support of his objection, and the judge will decide this issue, without submission to the jury, as a basis for his ruling on admissibility.[5] On the other hand, the authenticity of a writing or statement is not a question of the application of a technical rule of evidence. It goes to genuineness and relevance, as the jury can readily understand, and if a prima facie showing is made, the writing or statement comes in, with no opportunity then for evidence in denial.[6] If evidence disputing genuineness is later given, the issue is for the jury.[7]

3. See §§ 190–193, above.

4. Lundgren v. Union Indemnity Co., 171 Minn. 122, 213 N.W. 553, syl. 2, 52 A.L.R. 580 (1927) (telegrams, sought to be authenticated by knowledge disclosed in them; exclusion, where more convincing evidence available, not abuse of discretion); People v. Dunbar Contracting Co., 215 N.Y. 416, 109 N.E. 554, syl. 2 (1915) (telephone call); State v. Woodmansee, 156 Ore. 607, 69 P.2d 298, syl. 2 (1938) (letter, authentication by contents).

5. See § 53, herein.

6. Verzan v. McGregor, 23 Cal. 339, 341 (1863); Flournoy v. Warden, 17 Mo. 435, 441 (1853); 7 Wigmore, Evidence, § 2135, note 2.

7. Barham v. Bank of Delight, 94 Ark. 158, 126 S.W. 394, syl. 3, 4 (1910) (reply-letter, disputed); Coleman v. McIntosh, 184 Ky. 370, 211 S.W. 872, syl. 3 (1919) (letter containing admission); West v. Houston Oil Co., 56 Tex.Civ.App. 341, 120 S.W. 228, syl. 6, 7 (1909) (ancient deed).

CHAPTER 23

THE REQUIREMENT OF THE PRODUCTION OF THE ORIGINAL WRITING AS THE "BEST EVIDENCE"

195. The "Best Evidence" Rule.

Thayer [1] tells us that the first appearance of the "best evidence" phrase, is a statement in 1700 by Holt, C. J. (in a case in which he admitted evidence questioned as secondary) to the effect that "the best proof that the nature of the thing will afford is only required." [2] This statement given as a reason for receiving evidence, that it is the best which can be had—a highly liberalizing principle—naturally gives birth to a converse and narrowing doctrine that a man must produce the best evidence that is available—second-best will not do. And so before 1726 we find Baron Gilbert in one of the earliest treatises on Evidence saying, "the first and most signal rule in relation to evidence is this, that a man must have the utmost evidence the nature of the fact is capable of . . ." [3] Blackstone continues the same broad generalizing and combines both the positive and negative aspects of the "best evidence" idea when he says, " . . . the best evidence the nature of the case will admit of shall always be required, if possible to be had; but if not possible then the best evidence that can be had shall be allowed." [4] Greenleaf in this country in 1842 was still repeating these wide abstractions. [5]

Thayer, however, writing in 1898, points out that these broad principles, though they had some influence in shaping specific evidence rules in the 1700s, were never received

1. Preliminary Treatise on Evidence at the Common Law, 489 (1898).

2. Ford v. Hopkins, 1 Salk. 283, 91 Eng.Rep. 250.

3. Gilbert, Evidence, 2d ed. 4, 15–17, quoted Thayer, op. cit. 490.

4. 3 Blackstone, Commentaries, 368, quoted Thayer op. cit. 491.

5. 1 Greenleaf, Part 2, ch. 4, secs. 82–97, quoted and analyzed in Thayer, op. cit., 484–487.

as adequate or accurate statements of governing rules, and that actually "the chief illustration of the Best Evidence principle, the doctrine that if you would prove the contents of a writing, you must produce the writing itself" is an ancient rule far older than any notion about the "best" evidence.[6] While some modern opinions still refer to the "best evidence" notion as if it were today a general governing legal principle [7] most would adopt the view of modern textwriters [8] that there is no such general rule.[9] The only actual rule that the "best evidence"

phrase denotes today is the rule requiring the production of the original writing.[10]

196. Original Document Rule.[1]

The specific tenor of this requirement needs to be definitely stated and its limits clearly understood. The rule is this: in proving the terms of a writing, where such terms are material, the original writing must be produced, unless it is shown to be unavailable for some reason other than the serious fault of the proponent. The discussion in the sections which follow will serve to add content to this framework.

---

6. Thayer, op. cit. 497–506.

7. See, e. g., Gay v. United States, 118 F.2d 160, syl. 8 (C.C.A. 7th 1941) (error to admit doctor's interpretation of X-ray without producing plate, not "best evidence"); Roddy v. State, 65 Idaho 137, 139 P.2d 1005, syl. 12–14, (1943) (report made up from records properly excluded); Pettit v. Campbell, 149 S.W.2d 633, syl. 3–11 (Tex.Civ.App.1941) (error to admit oral testimony as to purport of testimony of another witness embodied in deposition); and see other cases cited Dec.Dig., Evidence, ☞157.

8. See 4 Wigmore, Evidence, § 1174, Thayer, Preliminary Treatise on Evidence, 489 (1898), 2 Jones, Evidence, § 757 (2d ed., 1926). See also The Best Evidence Rule—A Criticism, 3 Newark L.R. 200 (1938).

9. See, e. g., Herzig v. Swift & Co., 146 F.2d 444, syl. 1 (C.C.A.N.Y.1945); Catlin v. Justice, 288 Ky. 270, 156 S.W.2d 107, syl. 11 (1941) (best evidence principle in modern practice generally confined to writings); Michigan Bankers' Ass'n v. Ocean Accident and Guarantee Corp., 274 Mich. 470, 264 N.W. 868, 872, syl. 4 (1936) (best evidence rule confined to proof of contents of documents); Federal Underwriters Exchange v. Ener, 126 S.W.2d 769, syl. 8 (1939) (doctor who took X-ray picture may testify to what it showed without producing it).

10. As a moral argument, however, which may be marshaled on many evidence questions, the idea still has appeal. ". . . The fact that any given way of proof is all that a man has must be a strong argument for receiving it if it be in a fair degree probative; and the fact that a man does not produce the best evidence in his power must always afford strong ground of suspicion." Thayer, op. cit. 507. The "best evidence" notion has sometimes been given as a reason for admitting hearsay evidence when it is the most reliable which can be procured. See, e. g., Edwards v. Swilley, 196 Ark. 633, 118 S.W.2d 584, syl. 1 (1938). Contra: Fordson Coal

Co. v. Vanover, 291 Ky. 447, 164 S.W.2d 966, syl. 1 (1942).

1. 4 Wigmore, Evidence, §§ 1177–1282, 2 Jones, Evidence, §§ 752–862 (2d ed. 1926); Dec.Dig., Crim.Law, ☞398–403, Evidence, ☞157–187; 32 C.J.S. Evidence, §§ 776–850; 20 Am.Jur., Evidence, §§ 403–449. See also Model Code of Evidence, Rule 602, and the comments thereon in Rogers, The Best Evidence Rule, 1945 Wis.L.Rev. 278. The Uniform Rules of Evidence, R. 70, is as follows: "(1) As tending to prove the content of a writing, no evidence other than the writing itself is admissible, except as otherwise provided in these rules, unless the judge finds (a) that the writing is lost or has been destroyed without fraudulent intent on the part of the proponent, or (b) that the writing is outside the reach of the court's process and not procurable by the proponent, or (c) that the opponent, at a time when the writing was under his control has been notified, expressly or by implication from the pleadings, that it would be needed at the hearing, and on request at the hearing has failed to produce it, or (d) that the writing is not closely related to the controlling issues and it would be inexpedient to require its production, or (e) that the writing is an official record, or is a writing affecting property authorized to be recorded and actually recorded in the public records as described in Rule 63, exception (19).

"(2) If the judge makes one of the findings specified in the preceding paragraph, secondary evidence of the content of the writing is admissible. Evidence offered by the opponent tending to prove (a) that the asserted writing never existed, or (b) that a writing produced at the trial is the asserted writing, or (c) that the secondary evidence does not correctly reflect the content of the asserted writings, is irrelevant and inadmissible upon the question of admissibility of the secondary evidence but is relevant and admissible upon the issues of the existence and content of the asserted writing to be determined by the trier of fact."

197. The Reason for the Rule.

The policy-justification for the rule preferring the original writing lies in the facts (1) that precision in presenting to the court the exact words of the writing is of more than average importance, particularly as respects operative or dispositive instruments, such as deeds, wills and contracts, since a slight variation in words may mean a great difference in rights, (2) that there is a substantial hazard of inaccuracy in the human process of making a copy by handwriting or typewriting, and (3) as respects oral testimony purporting to give from memory the terms of a writing, there is a special risk of error, greater than in the case of attempts at describing other situations generally. In the light of these dangers of mis-transmission, accompanying the use of written copies or of recollection, largely avoided through proving the terms by presenting the writing itself, the preference for the original writing is justified.

198. Proving the Terms.

It is apparent that this danger of mistransmission of the contents of the writing, which is the reason for the rule, is only important when evidence other than the writing itself is offered for the purpose of proving its terms. Consequently, evidence that a certain document is in existence [1] or as to its execution [2] or delivery [3] is not within the rule and may be given without producing the document.[4]

Furthermore, it should be noted that many facts are recorded or recited in written memorials such as books or memoranda, which memorials are not made by the law the sole repository of the transaction. In other words the transactions described are not regarded by the law as essentially *written* transactions, as are written contracts, deeds, and judgments. Where this is so, testimony descriptive of such oral transactions is not within the scope of the present rule, and it may be given without the use or production of the written memorandum. Thus evidence that a payment has been made may be given without producing the receipt,[5] or of a marriage, without the marriage certificate.[6] And, under familiar practice, oral evidence of a man's former testimony is receivable, though it has been taken down and embodied in a written transcript.[7] Likewise, the recording of certain facts or transactions in books of account or memoranda or sound recordings does not preclude the proof of the facts independently of the books or records,[8]

1. Firestone Service Stores v. Wynn, 131 Fla. 94, 179 So. 175, syl. 9, 10 (1938) (suit by insurance company as subrogee of insured, for damage to automobile: existence of policy provable without production).

2. Singer v. Alexander City Bank, 223 Ala. 677, 138 So. 263, syl. 1 (1931) (question whether witness had conveyed the attached property and to whom, allowed).

3. Pecos & N. T. R. Co. v. Cox, 150 S.W. 265, syl. 7 (Tex.Civ.App.1912).

4. See Dec.Dig. Evidence, ⊂⇒159, 161(1) This sort of evidence will require the witness to describe the writing generally, but such a general description is not usually considered as equivalent to "proving its terms." See, e. g., Chambless v. State, 231 P.2d 711, syl. 1 (Okl.Crim.1951) (officers could testify there was a Federal retail liquor license in defendant's place, but could not give its "contents"). And see the cases in § 200, below.

5. Catlin v. Justice, 288 Ky. 270, 156 S.W.2d 107, syl. 14 (1941) (payment of taxes).

6. Lopez v. Missouri K. & T. Ry. Co. of Texas (1920, San Antonio), 222 S.W. 695 (foreign marriage).

7. Meyers v. United States, 171 F.2d 700, syl. 18, 11 A.L.R.2d 30 (C.A.D.C.1948), noted 23 So.Cal.L.Rev. 113.

8. Herzig v. Swift & Co., 146 F.2d 444, syl. 2 (C.C.A. N.Y.1945) (amount of earnings without producing books); People v. Kulwin, 102 Cal.App.2d 104, 226 P.2d 672, syl. 3, 4 (1951) (policeman who overheard conversation between defendants can testify to it without producing sound-recording); State v. Walso, 196 Minn. 525, 265 N.W. 345, syl. 2 (1936) (rental income); Mars v. Meadville Telephone Co., 344 Pa. 29, 23 A.2d 856, syl. 7, 8 (1942) (earnings); State v. Braica, 78 R.I. 32, 78 A.2d 374, syl. 3 (1951) (oral statement of defendant provable though reduced to writing and signed); Callen v. Collins, 135 S.W. 651, syl. 1 (Tex.Civ.App., 1911) (witness could testify

though of course if the proof of the facts is sought to be made by showing the contents of the books and records, the present rule applies, and the original books or records themselves must be produced or accounted for.[9] If the books or other records are produced or tendered, but are complicated or voluminous, an expert who has examined them may testify as to his calculations, summaries and conclusions to aid the court or jury to understand them.[10]

The question sometimes arises whether it is competent, without producing the books or records, to give evidence that the books or records do *not* contain any entry of a particular character. Such negative evidence is ordinarily deemed not to be testifying to the contents of the records and not to require their production.[11] But it is apparent that it might go to such extremes as actually to amount to a description of the entries that are in the books, by stating what they are not, and would then come within the rule requiring production.[12]

199. What are Writings? Application to Objects Inscribed and Uninscribed.

A rule which permitted the judge to insist that all evidence must pass his scrutiny as being the "best" or most reliable means of proving the fact would be a sore incumbrance upon the parties, who in our system have the responsibility of proof. In fact, as we have seen no such general scrutiny is sanctioned, but only as to "writings" is a demand for the "best," the original, made.[1] Accordingly, as to objects bearing no writing, the judge (unless in some exceptional cases when the exact features of the object have become as essential to the issue, as the precise words of a writing usually are [2] may not exclude oral testimony describing the object and demand that the object itself be produced.[3] The need for precise accuracy of portrayal is not usually so great as in the case of a writing. If, however, the object, such as a policeman's badge, a revolver, an engagement ring, or a tomb-stone, bears a number or inscription the terms of which are relevant, we face the

---

to amount of timber scaled from personal knowledge without producing his memorandum made at the time).

9. Berry v. Joiner (1907) 45 Tex.Civ.App. 461, 101 S.W. 289 (syl. 4) (statement of condition of a depositor's account inadmissible without the books).

10. Augustine v. Bowles, 149 F.2d 93, syl. 4 (C.C.A. Cal.1945); Hooven v. First Nat. Bank, 134 Okl. 217, 273 P. 257, 66 A.L.R. 1203 (1928).

11. Scott v. Mayor of Mt. Airy, 64 Ga.App. 828, 14 S.E.2d 127, syl. 2 (1941) (that there was no ordinance levying the tax for which execution issued); Cohen v. Boston Edison Co., 322 Mass. 239, 76 N.E. 2d 766, syl. 3 (1948) (bank clerk allowed to testify that there was no ledger sheet showing account with plaintiff); 4 Wigmore, Evidence, § 1244(5).

12. Compare Williams & Guyon v. Davis, 56 Tex. 250, syl. 2, 3 (1882) where oral evidence that the probate records of certain counties did not disclose that a certain estate was closed, held equivalent to evidence that the case was pending and to require production of the records.

1. See § 195, above.

2. The classic instance is Chenie v. Watson, Peake Add.Cas. 123, 170 Eng.Rep. 217 (Nisi Pr. 1797) where

the question was whether plaintiff's bushel measure matched the public measure, which was in court, and Lord Kenyon refused to permit a witness to testify that he had compared them, for "the best evidence . . . was a production of both measures, and a comparison of them before the jury."

3. Hocking v. Ahlquist, [1944] K.B.D. 120 (prosecution for manufacturing clothing in violation of war-time restrictions as to number of pockets, etc.: held error for judge to dismiss the prosecution for failure to produce the offending articles; instructive opinion by Lord Caldecote, C. J.); Feeney v. Young, 191 App. Div. 501, 181 N.Y.S. 481 (1920) (error to exclude description of motion picture alleged to represent the plaintiff). The holdings are usually in form of approval of the judge's refusal to exclude description and require production: Korol v. United States, 82 A.2d 129, syl. 5–7 (Mun.Ct.App.D.C. 1951) (containers of eggs alleged to be adulterated and misbranded); Lamble v. State, 96 N.J.L. 231, 114 A. 346, syl. 4 (1921) (door of an automobile bearing defendant's fingerprints); Williams v. State, 179 Tenn. 247, 165 S.W.2d 377 (1942) (whiskey); State v. Campbell, 116 Utah 74, 208 P.2d 530, syl. 1, 2 (1949) (stolen articles).

question, shall we treat it as a chattel or as a "writing"? Probably most modern cases would support the view advocated by Wigmore,[4] that the judge shall have a discretion,[5] to follow the one analogy or the other in the light of such factors as the need for precise information as to the exact inscription, the ease or difficulty of production, and the simplicity or complexity of the inscription.

200. Writings Involved Only Collaterally.

At nearly every turn in human affairs some writing—a letter, a bill of sale, a newspaper, a deed—plays a part. Consequently any narration by a witness is likely to include many references to transactions consisting partly of written communications or other writings. A witness to a confession, for example, identifies the date as being the day after the crime because he read of the crime in the newspaper that day, or a witness may state that he was unable to procure a certain article because it was patented. It is apparent that it is impracticable to forbid such references except upon condition that the writings (e. g. the newspaper, and the patent) be produced in court. Consequently, it is clear that where the effect of a writing is summarily or generally stated by the witness, without purporting to give its contents in detail, and the terms of the writing are unlikely to be disputed, or are not the subject of any important issue in the case, then such writing is regarded as a "collateral" one, and the witness' statement of its effect without producing the writing itself, is permissible.[1]

---

4. 4 Wigmore, Evidence, § 1182.

5. See, e. g., State v. Lewark, 106 Kan. 184, 186 P. 1002, syl. 3 (1920) (receiving stolen automobile: judge in discretion properly permitted testimony that engine number appeared to be altered, without requiring production of automobile; Quillen v. Comm., 284 Ky. 792, 145 S.W.2d 1048, syl. 2 (1940) (theft of automobile, testimony as to license-number properly allowed without producing plate, where number not disputed); Mattson v. Minn. & N. W. R. Co., 98 Minn. 296, 108 N.W. 517, syl. 1 (1906) (wrappers on dynamite, not shown to be detachable; proper exercise of discretion to allow description without production).

It seems that mechanical recordings of oral words should be subject to a similar rule of discretion, when it is sought to prove the content of the recording. See Kilpatrick v. Kilpatrick, 123 Conn. 218, 193 A. 765, syl. 13 (1937) (court in discretion properly permitted contents of record, made available to adversary, to be proved by transcript rather than by playing in court). Compare, however, People v. King, 101 Cal.App.2d 500, 225 P.2d 950, syl. 1 (1950) (error for judge to admit disc recordings of original tape recordings of defendants' conversations in jail, where police according to routine had erased original tapes for re-use), noted critically, 64 Harv.L.Rev. 1369. The Uniform Rules of Evidence, R. 1, subsec. 13, have widened the definition of "writing" as follows: " 'Writing' means handwriting, typewriting, printing, photostating, photographing and every other means of recording upon any tangible thing any form of communication or representation, including letters, words, pictures, sounds, or symbols, or combinations thereof." Since the documentary originals rule (R. 70, subsec. 1) is phrased in terms of "writings" the result, unfortunately, may be to encourage a more inflexible rather than a discretionary practice about the use of reproductions of wire and tape recordings, motion pictures, and other new forms of "writings."

1. Reed v. State, 234 Ala. 306, 174 So. 498, syl. 6 (1937) (that relator was a registered voter, in election mandamus suit, could be proved orally since it bore only on qualification to sue, and hence was collateral); Hale v. Hale, 199 Ga. 150, 33 S.E.2d 441, syl. 1, 2 (1945) (that ancestor had made contribution to church fund for buying cemetery land in dispute, held "collateral," but probably best explainable as not a written transaction, see § 198, above); Coonrod v. Madden, 126 Ind. 197, 25 N.E. 1102 (1890) (under plea of payment in suit on note, defendant introduced a check which he testified was given in part payment; held, testimony of plaintiff that check was received in payment of another note, described but not produced, proper, as collateral); Louisiana Ry. & Nav. Co. v. Morere, 116 La. 997, 41 So. 236, syl. 8 (1906) (oral evidence of sale of another tract receivable where sale bears only on value of property here in dispute); Wilson Transportation Co. v. Owens-Illinois Glass Co., 125 N.J.L. 636, 17 A.2d 581, syl. 3 (1941) (where plaintiff sought to show damages due to defendant's breach of contract, by showing plaintiff sold its trucks acquired to haul defendant's goods, documentary proof of ownership not required); Van Valkenberg v. Venters, 200 Okl. 504, 197 P.2d 284, syl. 2 (1948) (oral evidence of ownership by plaintiff allowable in forcible detainer proceedings, since title is not in issue); Smith v. Olson, 50 S.D. 81, 208 N.W. 585, syl. 5 (1926) (superintendent's finding of insolvency of bank admissible as qualifying him to sue to

This exception is a necessary concession to the need for expedition of trials and clearness of narration, which outweighs, in the case of such merely incidental references to documents, the need for perfect exactitude in the presentation to the court of the contents of the document.

It is manifest, however, that this test of "collateralness" is an exceedingly vague one, not dependent upon a technical analysis of the formal issues made on the pleadings, but rather upon the probability of substantial room for controversy as to the very terms of the writing. If no such dispute seems probable, then the trial judge should have power to relax the rule requiring the document to be produced and allow its net effect to be summarily stated. Here as elsewhere in the application of this purely administrative rule, the trial judge's discretion should be reviewed only for grave abuse.[2]

201. Excuses for Non-production of the Original Writing—(a) Loss or Destruction.[1]

The professed purpose of the production of documents rule being to secure, not the writing at all hazards, but the best *obtainable*

evidence of its contents, if the document cannot as a practical matter be produced, because of its loss [2] or destruction,[3] the production of the original is excused and other evidence of its contents is received. Otherwise, the enforcement of a right would often depend solely upon the availability of a document.

Loss or destruction may sometimes be provable by direct evidence but more often the only available method is circumstantial, usually by proof of search for the document and inability to secure it. It would seem that to show inability to locate the document by the search, offered as circumstantial evidence of loss or destruction, evidence of the declarations of a former custodian of the document of whom inquiry was made that it had been lost or destroyed would be admissible,[4] but if offered as direct evidence of the fact of loss or destruction itself, it would be incompetent as hearsay.[5]

Where loss or destruction is sought to be shown circumstantially by proof of unsuccessful search, it is obvious that upon the thoroughness and appropriateness of the

enforce stockholders liability, but not as evidence on the merits); Burnett v. Amicable Life Ins. Co., 195 S.W.2d 237, syl. 5 (Tex.Civ.App. 1946) (in suit on life policy where claim asserted by assignee, may be shown by oral evidence that insured owed note to assignee, as evidence of latter's insurable interest as creditor); Cochran v. William M. Rice Institute, 123 S.W.2d 359, syl. 5 (Tex.Civ.App. 1938) (photostatic copy of affidavit received as prior inconsistent statement; not basis of suit but collateral); State v. Clark, 64 W.Va. 625, 63 S.E. 402, syl. 13 (1908) (oral testimony that murder victim was constable, allowable, "the official character of the officer was only incidentally and collaterally involved"). Other decisions are collected in 4 Wigmore, Evidence, § 1254, 2 Jones, Evidence, §§ 769–773 (2d ed. rev. 1926); Dec.Dig., Evidence, ⊙171, Crim.Law, ⊙401, 32 C.J.S., Evidence, § 781, 22 C.J. Evidence, § 1224. See also Note, Secondary Evidence of Collateral Writing, 11 N.C.L.Rev. 342 (1933).

2. Compare 4 Wigmore, Evidence, § 1253.

1. 4 Wigmore, Evidence, §§ 1193–1198, 2 Jones, Evidence, §§ 812–832 (2d ed. rev. 1926), Dec.Dig. Evi-

dence, ⊙178, 32 C.J.S., Evidence, §§ 823, 824, 22 C.J., Evidence, §§ 1315–1322.

2. Nu Car Carriers v. Traynor, 75 App.D.C. 174, 125 F.2d 47, syl. 1 (1942); Cotton v. Courtright, 215 Ala. 474, 111 So. 7, syl. 11 (1927).

3. Haskell v. Merrill, 242 S.W. 331, syl. 8 (Tex.Civ.App.1922).

4. Massie v. Hutcheson, 296 S.W. 939, syl. 19 (Tex. Civ.App., 1927), error refused (testimony that deceased grantee said: "Ashes tell no story" when questioned concerning deed, held admissible over objection that it was hearsay). See Interstate Investment Co. v. Bailey (Ky.1906) 93 S.W. 578, 580 ("What Elijah Davis learned that Stidham said about the loss of the paper may not have been evidence of its loss . . . yet it was evidence of his good faith in not prosecuting the inquiry further.") 4 Wigmore, Evidence, § 1196(3).

5. Moore v. State, 179 Miss. 268, 175 So. 183, syl. 1 (1937) (testimony that addressee of letter said she had destroyed it properly excluded as hearsay, but error to admit secondary evidence of letter's contents).

search will depend the convincing character of the proof. It was laid down in an early decision[6] that when the writing is last known to have been in a particular place or in the hands of a particular person, that place must be searched or the person produced, and in a later case, it is said that the last custodian must be produced or his absence accounted for.[7] It is believed, however, that these statements were not designed as rules but rather as general guides or cautions. Clearly, the decision of the question as to whether it is feasible to produce the original document is wholly reposed both as it involves law and fact, in the first instance in the trial judge as a preliminary question,[8] addressed to his discretion reviewable only for abuse.[9] Furthermore, the character of search required to show probability of loss or destruction will, as a practical matter, depend upon the circumstances of each case. The apparent importance or triviality of the document, and the lapse of time since it was last seen, for example, bear upon the extent of search required before loss or destruction may be inferred.[10] The only requirement should be that all reasonable avenues of search should be explored to the extent that reasonable diligence under the circumstances would dictate.

If the original document has been destroyed by the person who offers evidence of its contents, the evidence is not admissible unless such person, by showing that such destruction was accidental or was done in good faith, without intention to prevent its use as evidence, rebuts to the satisfaction of the trial judge, any inference of fraud.[11]

202. Excuses for Non-production of the Original Writing—(b) Possession by a Third Person.[1]

When the writing is in the hands of a third person who is within the geographical limits of the trial court's *subpena* power, the safest course is have a writ of *subpena duces tecum* served on the possessor summoning him to bring the writing to court at the trial,[2]

---

[6]. Cook v. Hunt, 24 Ill. 535, 550 (1860).

[7]. Vandergriff v. Piercy (1883), 59 Tex. 371.

[8]. Comm. v. Steadman, 156 Pa.Super. 312, 40 A.2d 96, syl. 1–4 (1944) (trial judge must satisfy himself that letter allegedly destroyed was actually written and delivered and that it was destroyed); McDonald v. Hanks, 52 Tex.Civ.App. 140, 113 S.W. 604, 609, syl. 5 (1908).

[9]. Barraco v. Kostens, 189 Md. 94, 54 A.2d 326, syl. 5 (1947) (specific performance: sufficiency of search for lost deed for judge, reviewable only for abuse of discretion); Jarrett v. St. Francois County Fin. Co., 185 S.W.2d 855, 861, syl. 8 (Mo.App.1945); Holley v. Mucher, 165 S.W.2d 1015, 1018, syl. 3, 4 (Tex. Civ.App.1942).

[10]. Gathercole v. Miall, 15 M. & W. 319, 329, 335, 153 Eng.Rep. 872, 876, 879 (Exch.1846, by Barons Pollock and Alderson); St. Louis S. W. Ry. Co. v. Turner, 225 S.W. 383, 387 (Tex.Civ.App.1920).

[11]. Reynolds v. Denver & Rio Grande W. Ry. Co., 174 F.2d 673, syl. 1 (C.A. 10, 1949) (secondary evidence admissible, if no "fraud or bad faith" in the destruction); McDonald v. United States, 89 F.2d 128, 136, syl. 16–24 (C.C.A. 8, 1937) (conviction for kidnaping: Held, government not precluded from giving evidence of the numbers on the ransom bills by

fact that subordinate official had called in the bills and improvidently had them destroyed: acute discussion by Faris, Circ. J.); Crosby v. Little River Sand, etc. Co., 212 La. 1, 31 So.2d 226, syl. 1, 2 (1947) (job sheets made up from job cards admissible, where cards had been destroyed according to usual practice of party); Shrimpton v. Netzorg, 104 Mich. 225, 62 N.W. 343, syl. 4 (1895) (secondary evidence allowed where party to whom letter addressed testified he was not in habit of keeping letters, and had looked for this in wastebasket but too late). Accordingly, the condition laid down in some opinions (e. g., Booher v. Brown, (1944) 173 Ore. 464, 146 P.2d 71, 75, syl. 6) that the party must be "without neglect or default" seems overstrict.

[1]. 4 Wigmore, Evidence §§ 1211–1213; Dec.Dig. Evidence, ☞179(3); 32 C.J.S. Evidence, §§ 830, 831, 22 C.J. Evidence, §§ 1325–1331.

[2]. Many decisions require this. See, e. g., Security Trust Co. v. Robb, 142 Fed. 78, 80 (C.C.A.N.J.1906); Schall v. Northland Motor Car Co., 123 Minn. 214, 216, 143 N.W. 357, syl. 4 (1913) (in possession of trustee in bankruptcy; "he is subject to subpena the same as other citizens"); Menasha Woodenware Co. v. Harmon, 128 Wis. 177, 181, 107 N.W. 299 (1906). If the possessor disobeys the summons, the party's production of the original is of course excused.

though some decisions will excuse resort to subpena if the possessor is privileged not to produce it,[3] and others suggest that proof of a hostile or unwilling attitude on his part will be a sufficient excuse.[4]

If the writing is in the possession of a third person out of the state or out of the reach of the court's process, this fact according to the view of many courts is of itself a sufficient excuse for non-production.[5] This practise has merit as a rule of thumb, easy to apply, but the policy of the original document requirement, and probably the weight of reason, supports the view of those courts equally numerous who demand a further showing. They require that before secondary evidence

is used, the proponent must show either that he has made reasonable efforts without avail to secure the original from its possessor,[6] or circumstances which persuade the court that such efforts would have been fruitless.[7]

203. Excuses for Non-production of the Original Writing—(c) Failure of Adversary Having Possession to Produce after Notice.[1]

A frequently-used method of showing that it is impracticable for the proponent to produce the original writing is to prove, first, that the original is in the hands of his adversary or under his control,[2] and second, that the proponent has notified him to produce it at the trial and he has failed to do so.

---

[3]. See, e. g., People v. Powell, 71 Cal.App. 500, 236 P. 311, syl. 8 (1925) (letters tending to incriminate possessors).

[4]. See. e. g., Mahanay v. Lynde, 48 Cal.App.2d 79, 119 P.2d 430, syl. 1 (1941) (adversary's mother got possession of paper and refused to give it back); Ragley-McWilliams Lumber Co. v. Hare, 130 S.W. 864, 868 (Tex.Civ.App.1910) (family Bible of third person, which plaintiffs tried to and were unable to obtain).

[5]. E. g., Hartzell v. United States, 72 F.2d 569, 578, syl. 22 (C.C.A.8, 1934); Hoyle v. Mann, 144 Ala. 516, 41 So. 835, syl. 12 (1906); Moss v. State, 208 Ark. 137, 185 S.W.2d 92, syl. 3 (1945); Miller v. McKinnon, 103 Ga. 553, 29 S.E. 467, syl. 1 (1897); Blaty v. Gray, 217 Mich. 531, 187 N.W. 360, syl. 3 (1922); Haire v. State, 118 Tex.Cr. 16, 39 S.W.2d 70, syl. 6 (1931); Bourn v. Dobbins, 92 W.Va. 263, 115 S.E. 424, syl. 1 (1922) (approving rule though here reasonable efforts to obtain were shown).

[6]. E. g., Londoner v. Stewart, 3 Colo. 47, 50 (1876); McDonald v. Erbes, 231 Ill. 295, 83 N.E. 162 (1907); Sherman v. Sherman, 290 Ky. 237, 160 S.W.2d 637, syl. 1–4 (1942); Summons v. State, 156 Md. 390, 144 A. 501, syl. 10–13 (1929); Gasser v. Great Northern Ins. Co., 145 Minn. 205, 176 N.W. 484, syl. 6 (1920) (sufficiency of efforts a matter for judge's discretion); Mahoney-Jones Co. v. Osborne, 189 N.C. 445, 127 S.E. 533, syl. 6 (1925); Pringey v. Guss, 16 Okl. 82, 83, 86 P. 292, syl. 1, 8 Ann.C. 412 (1906); Bruger v. Princeton & S. etc. Ins. Co., 129 Wis. 281, 109 N.W. 95, syl. 5 (1906).
In the McDonald, Sherman, Summons and Bruger cases, supra, it is suggested that in some circumstances due diligence may require the proponent to take the deposition of the out-of-state possessor of the writing, but since this entails expense and inconvenience

and will usually result in securing only a copy of the writing, it should seemingly not usually be required when the proponent produces a reliably authenticated copy.

[7]. Missouri, K. & T. Ry. Co. v. Dilworth, 95 Tex. 327, 67 S.W. 88, 89, syl. 3 (1902) (way-bill in hands of carrier outside the state, which they probably would not part with); Bruger v. Princeton & S., etc., Ins. Co., 129 Wis. 281, 109 N.W. 95, 97 (1906) ("unless it is clear that they would have been fruitless").
On this ground, efforts to secure public records in another state or country, which are not allowed to be removed under their law or practice, would not be required to be shown before using a copy. Sansoni v. Selvaggi, 121 N.J.L. 274, 2 A.2d 355, syl. 2 (1938) (postal savings pass-book impounded by post-office in Italy); De la Garza v. McManus, 44 S.W. 704, syl. 2 (Tex.Civ.App.1898) (deed in archives in Mexico, presumably not removable, provable by examined copy). As to domestic public records, see § 204, herein.

[1]. 4 Wigmore, Evidence, §§ 1202–1210; 2 Jones, Evidence, §§ 833–855; Dec.Dig., Evidence, ☞184, 185 (1–12), Crim.Law, ☞402(2); 32 C.J.S., Evidence, §§ 832–834; 22 C.J. Evidence, §§ 1332–1340; 20 Am. Jur. Evidence, §§ 440–448.

[2]. Main v. Aukam, 4 App.D.C. 51, 55 (1894) (where placed by party notified in the hands of a co-defendant subject to call). And it may still be in his control though out of the jurisdiction. Missouri, K. & T. R. Co. v. Elliott, 102 Fed. 96, syl. 3 (C.C.A.Ind. Terr.1900); Cutter-Tower Co. v. Clements, 5 Ga. App. 291, 63 S.E. 58, syl. 3 (1908). The possession is sufficiently proved when the proponent shows that he has mailed the writing to the party charged with possession. Rosenthal v. Walker, 111 U.S. 185, 193, 4 Sup.Ct. 382, 28 L.Ed. 395 (1883).

Observe that the notice is a mere request, without compulsive force,[3] and is designed merely to account for non-production of the writing by the proponent, and thus to enable him to use secondary evidence of the writing's terms. If the proponent actually needs the production of the original itself he will resort to *subpena duces tecum* or under modern rules the motion for an order to produce. But when the notice is offered as an excuse for resorting to secondary evidence the adversary cannot fairly complain that he was only requested, not compelled, to make the writing available.

An oral notice may be sufficient,[4] but the safest and almost universal practice is to give written notice beforehand to the party or his attorney, describing the particular documents desired, and then to call upon the adversary orally at the trial for the writings requested.[5] It is held that the nature of the complaint or of the defense may constitute a sufficient implied notice that the pleader is charging the adversary with possession of the original and that he considers its produc-

tion essential.[6] As to the time of serving notice it is sufficient if it allows the adversary a fair opportunity under the existing circumstances to produce the writing at the trial.[7] Accordingly, if it appears at the trial itself that the adversary has the original paper in the court-room, an immediate notice then and there is timely.[8]

Some exceptions, under which notice is unnecessary before using secondary evidence of a writing in the adversary's possession, have been recognized. The first is well-sustained in reason. It dispenses with the need for notice when the adversary has wrongfully obtained or fraudulently suppressed the writing.[9] The others seem more questionable. There is a traditional exception that no notice is required to produce a writing which is itself a notice.[10] This is understandable in respect to giving notice to produce a notice to produce, which would lead to an endless succession of notices, but there seems little justification for extending the exception, as the cases do, to notices generally. Finally an exception is made by the majority view

---

3. Bova v. Roanoke Oil Co., 180 Va. 332, 23 S.E.2d 347, syl. 2, 144 A.L.R. 364 (1942). The failure to produce, however, might have another tactical consequence, namely, that of giving rise to an inference adverse to the party so failing. Missouri K. & T. R. Co. v. Elliott, 102 Fed. 96, 102, syl. 4 (C.C.A.Ind. Terr.1900).

4. Especially when given in open court during the trial. Kerr v. McGuire, 28 N.Y. 446, 453 (1863).

5. For details of the practice, see 2 Jones, Evidence, §§ 840–843 (2d ed. rev. 1926); 4 Wigmore, Evidence, § 1208.

6. How v. Hall, 14 East 274, 104 Eng.Rep. 606 (K.B. 1811) (trover for a bond); Reliance Lumber Co. v. Western U. Tel. Co., 58 Tex. 394, 399, 44 Am.Rep. 620 (1883) (action against telegraph company for failure to deliver messages); State v. Rowen, 104 Ore. 1, 200 Pac. 901, 905, syl. 7 (1921) (forgery of a deed). And so where a defensive pleading charges the plaintiff with possession of a document necessary to the proof of the defense. J. L. Owens Co. v. Bemis, 22 N.D. 159, 133 N.W. 59, syl. 1, 37 L.R.A., N.S., 232, 1911.

7. Beard v. Southern R. Co., 143 N.C. 136, 55 S.E. 505, syl. 5 (1906) (notice during trial not timely when ad-

versary would have to go to his home in another town to get the writing). See also Waddell v. Trowbridge, 94 W.Va. 482, 119 S.E. 290, syl. 1, 4, 1923 (notice to produce given at the trial timely as to one document, not as to another).

8. Dwyer v. Collins, 7 Exch. 639, 155 Eng.Rep. 1104 (1852); Leonard v. Taylor, 315 Mass. 580, 53 N.E.2d 705, syl. 4 (1944) (arguendo); 4 Wigmore, Evidence, § 1204.

9. Calif.Code Civ.Proc. § 1938 ("where it has been wrongfully obtained or withheld by the adverse party"); Nealley v. Greenough, 25 N.H. 325, 330 (1852) (obtaining by fraud, principle recognized, not here proven); Cheatham v. Riddle, 8 Tex. 162, 166 (1852) (party's principal "had gotten possession of the bill of sale and fled the country with it"): 2 Jones, Evidence, § 848 (2d ed.rev.1926); 4 Wigmore, Evidence, § 1207.

10. Colling v. Treweek, 6 B. & C. 394, 108 Eng.Rep. 497 (1827); Calif.Code Civ.Proc. § 1938 (notice unnecessary "where the writing is itself a notice"); 4 Wigmore, Evidence, § 1206; 2 Jones, Evidence, § 849 (Rev.Ed.1926).

for writings in the hands of the accused in a criminal prosecution.[11] It seems to have been supposed that the notice would be a form of compulsion to produce evidence against himself. It is true that requesting the accused before the jury to produce the writing may be claimed to put undue pressure upon him to produce,[12] but it is perfectly unnecessary to give the notice before the jury,[13] and if given in writing in advance of the trial, and if compliance is requested out of the jury's presence, these acts cannot have the slightest compulsive effect.[14] Accordingly, the minority view, that unless the indictment itself gives sufficient notice, the prosecution must give notice to the accused to produce documents in his hands before secondary evidence can be used,[15] seems much the fairer and more reasonable stand.

204. Excuses for Non-production of the Original Writing—(d) Public Records.[1]

If the contents of the judgment of a court or of an executive proclamation are to be proved, shall the proponent be required to produce the original writing? The accepted view is that, in general, public and judicial records and public documents are required by law to be retained by the official custodian in the public office designated for their custody, and courts will not require them to be removed.[2] To require removal would be inconvenient for the public who might desire to consult the records and would entail a risk of loss of or damage to the official documents. Accordingly, statutes and rules have

---

11. Under this view, secondary evidence is received without notice to accused to produce. See, e. g., Lisansky v. United States, 31 F.2d 846, 67 A.L.R. 67, syl. 1 (C.C.A. 4, 1929); Dean v. State, 240 Ala. 8, 197 So. 53, syl. 5 (1940); Moore v. State, 130 Ga. 322, 60 S.E. 544, syl. 4 (1908); People v. Gibson, 218 N.Y. 70, 112 N.E. 730, syl. 7 (1916) (a considered dictum); and cases cited in Dec.Dig., Crim.Law, ☞402(2); 16 C.J., p. 617, § 1219; 22 C.J.S., Criminal Law, p. 1196, § 706; Note, 67 A.L.R. 78.

12. And many courts hold that it is a violation of the self crimination privilege. See, e. g., McKnight v. United States, 54 C.C.A. 358, 115 Fed. 972, syl. 2 (1902); Comm. v. Valeroso, 273 Pa. 213, 116 Atl. 828, syl. 1 (1922); Powell v. Comm., 167 Va. 558, 189 S.E. 433, 110 A.L.R. 90, syl. 1 (1937); Note, 110 A.L.R. 101. For criticisms of this view, see 8 Wigmore, Evidence, § 2268.

13. The propriety of notice away from the jury's presence is suggested in Sprague v. State, 203 Ind. 581, 181 N.E. 507, 511 (1932); Harris v. State, 150 Tex.Cr.R. 137, 199 S.W.2d 522, syl. 4 (1947).

14. "The object of the notice is not to compel the party to produce the paper, for no such power is assumed, either directly or indirectly, by placing him under a disadvantage if he does not produce it. Its object is to enable the prisoner to protect himself against the falsity of the secondary evidence." State v. Kimbrough, 13 N.C. (2 Dev.L.) 431 (1830).

15. See, e. g., Rex v. Ellicombe, 5 Car. & P. 522, 172 Eng.Rep. 1081 (1933); State v. Martin, 229 Mo. 620, 129 S.W. 881, syl. 2 (1910) and cases collected in Note, 67 A.L.R. 84.

1. 4 Wigmore, Evidence, §§ 1215–1222; 2 Jones, Evidence, § 785 (2d ed. rev. 1926); 1 Greenleaf, Evidence, § 91 (13th ed. 1876); 20 Am.Jur., Evidence, § 430.

2. Doe v. Roberts, 13 M. & W. 520, 530, 153 Eng.Rep. 217 (Exch.1844, per Pollock, C. B.) ("When directed to be kept in any particular custody, and so deposited they are provable by examined copies . . . on the ground of the great inconvenience of removing them"); Ridgway v. Farmers' Bank, 12 Serg. & R. 255, 262 (Pa.1825) ("Tilghman, C. J. It is a rule of law, that where an original is of a *public* nature, and admissible in evidence, an examined copy is evidence. This rule is necessary, for the preservation of public papers, and for the public convenience, because those papers should always be in a known place, to which access may be had by all.").

See also the widely copied provision of the Calif. Code of Civ.Proc., § 1855: "There can be no evidence of the contents of a writing, other than the writing itself, except in the following cases: . . . 4. When the original has been recorded, and a certified copy of the record is made evidence by this code or other statute."

If, however, the original record of which proof is to be made is a record of the very court which is trying the present case, then it seems, since the original writing can be produced without violating the rule and policy against removal, production should be required, if formal proof is to be made. Roby v Title Guarantee & Trust Co., 166 Ill. 336, 46 N.E. 1110, syl. 8 (1896); 4 Wigmore, Evidence, § 1215(b). But judicial notice would be simpler, see § 327.

provided for the issuance of certified copies and for their admission in evidence in lieu of the original.[3] In addition, examined copies, authenticated by a witness who has compared it with the original record, are usually receivable.[4]

205. Which is the "Writing Itself" That Must be Produced?[1] Telegrams,[2] Counterparts.[3]

We have said that the rule dealt with in this chapter requires that when the contents of a writing is sought to be proved, the *writing itself* must be produced if practicable.[4]

Let us assume two writings, X and Y. Y was written after X and is a reproduction of it. For illustration, X may be a telegram written by the sender and handed to the company for transmission, Y the message delivered to the addressee; or X may be a libelous handwritten letter given to a stenographer for copying and sending, X may be the letter received by the person to whom addressed; or X may be the ledger sheet in the creditor's books and Y may be the account rendered made up therefrom and sent to the debtor.

Let us suppose now that a party in court offers document Y, in any of the forms above, in evidence. How do we tell whether the document offered is the "writing itself" the contents of which are sought to be proved, or whether it is merely a "copy" tendered as evidence of the terms of some other writing? The answer, it seems clear, can only be derived from the purport of the proponent's offer. He is the master of what he is seeking to prove.

If he says that he is offering Y as evidence of the contents of X, then the original documents requirement is surely applicable, unless some excuse or exception appears. If he says, however, that he is offering Y as evidence of its own terms only, then the original documents rule is clearly inapplicable. The "writing itself" is produced. The fact that it happens to be a copy of another writing the terms of which are not sought to be proved is immaterial.[5] The question then of the admissibility of Y will usually not be one of evidence law. It will rather be one of the substantive law of contracts, defamation, property or the like. The problem usually is this: Is Y itself significant as being a writing which has been so dealt with by the parties as to affect, in some way material to the is-

---

1. See, e. g., Fed.Rules Civ.Proc. rule 44(a) ("An official record or an entry therein, when admissible for any purpose, may be evidenced by an official publication thereof or by a copy attested by the officer having the legal custody of the record, or by his deputy, and accompanied with a certificate that such officer has the custody. . . ."); Vernon's Ann.Civ.St.Tex. art. 3731a, sec. 4 ("Such writings [official statements, etc.] may be evidenced by an official publication thereof or by a copy attested by the officer having the legal custody of the record or his deputy. . . ."); Wis.St.1951, § 327.18(2) ("*Copies as Evidence.* A certified copy of any written or printed matter preserved pursuant to law in any public office or with any public officer in this state, or of the United States, is admissible in evidence whenever and wherever the original is admissible, and with like effect.").

4. See cases quoted in note 2, above. Nor are certified copies preferred to examined copies. Smithers

v. Lowrance, 100 Tex. 77, 93 S.W. 1064, syl. 3 (1906); 4 Wigmore, Evidence, § 1273(1).

1. 4 Wigmore, Evidence, § 1232.

2. 4 Wigmore, Evidence, § 1236; 2 Jones, Evidence, §§ 801–806 (2d ed. rev. 1926); Dec.Dig., Evidence, ⊂⇒168, 183(14); 22 C.J., Evidence, §§ 1238, 1306; 32 C.J.S., Evidence, §§ 792, 814.

3. 4 Wigmore, Evidence, § 1233, 2 Jones, Evidence, § 797; Dec.Dig Evidence, ⊂⇒186(6); 32 C.J.S. Evidence § 821, 22 C.J. Evidence, § 1313.

4. See § 196, above.

5. Compare McDonald v. Hanks, 52 Tex.Civ.App. 140, 113 S.W. 604, 607 (1908), where the court said: "If a writer desiring to preserve a copy of a letter, writes at the same time two copies exactly alike, one of which he proposes to send and the other to keep, it is a matter of indifference which copy he sends, but the one sent becomes the original and the other a copy, no matter by what force of evidence it is shown to be an absolutely accurate copy."

sues, their substantive rights? Illustrative holdings are cited below.[6]

A written transaction, such as a contract, lease, deed or the like may be evidenced by several counterparts, or identical copies of the written terms, all of them being signed, or at any rate, designed to be considered as of equal force as embodying the transaction. They are frequently termed "duplicate (or triplicate, quadruplicate, etc.) originals." Each of these counterparts is admissible as an "original" without producing or accounting for the others,[7] but before resorting to secondary evidence, all of the counterparts must be shown to be unavailable.[8]

206. Mechanical Reproductions: Letter-Press Copies; Carbons; Photostats; Printed and Multigraph Copies.[1]

The old-fashioned method of taking copies of letters and records was by the use of a letter-press. The original was written or typed in copying ink or with copying pencil. On this were placed a sheet of tissue paper and a damp cloth and all three were pressed together in the letter press. The resulting impression on the tissue-paper was generally a highly reliable reproduction, but it was less so when blurred by over-dampness of the cloth or when varied by wrinkling of the tissue. Influenced presumably by these latter possibilities, the courts decline to treat letter-press copies as equivalent to the originals.[2]

This system of retaining copies of correspondence and records has been largely superseded by the use of carbons. Here the copy is made by the same stroke of the pen or pencil as the original, and there is an analogy to the practice of signing counterparts where each copy was intended to be an

---

6. Telegrams. Conyers v. Postal Tel. Co., 92 Ga. 619, 622, 19 S.E. 253, syl. 3 (1893) (action for penalty for delay in delivery: message received admissible when offered by plaintiff: message delivered to telegraph company seemingly assumed to be the "original," but it "cannot deny" that message given to plaintiff is the same); Anheuser-Busch Brewing Co. v. Hutmacher, 127 Ill. 652, 657, 21 N.E. 626, syl. 2 (1889) (action on contract for services by plaintiff: contract properly shown by telegraph messages received by plaintiff: when sender, defendant here, has initiated the telegraphic correspondence, messages delivered to addressee are "originals"); Wilson v. Minneapolis & N.W.R. Co., 31 Minn. 481, 18 N.W. 291 (1884) (similar to last: contract of hiring may be proved by message received, when employer initiated use of telegraph: facts raise question whether if telegraph company telephones message to addressee, the message is still to be regarded as a writing, and whether in so telephoning it is acting as representative of the sender or of the addressee); Durkee v. Vermont Cent. R. Co., 29 Vt. 127, 140 (1856) (suit on contract made by exchange of telegrams; when sender first employs telegraph, message received is original, when sendee employed message given by sender to the company is original. As to when the telegraphic acceptance of an offer becomes effective upon delivery to the telegraph company, see Restatement, Contracts, Secs. 64, 67; 1 Williston, Contracts, §§ 82, 83, 94 (Rev.Ed.1936).

Account stated. Missouri Pac. R. Co. v. Palmer, 55 Neb. 559, 76 N.W. 169, syl. 8 (1898) (personal injury: bill rendered to plaintiff for medical service objected to as being copy of account in doctor's books; held, properly admitted, since bills received and not objected to made plaintiff liable for them).

Copy of a prior letter attached to and incorporated by reference in a later contract, is part of the contract, and provable without accounting for the letter. Comer v. Comer, 120 Ill. 420, 430, 11 N.E. 848, syl. 5 (1887).

7. Hayes v. Wagner, 220 Ill. 256, 77 N.E. 211, 212 (1906) ("In order to introduce an original duplicate, it is not necessary that the other should also be produced. . . ."); Quinn v. Standard Oil Co., 249 Mass. 194, 144 N.E. 53, syl. 3, 5 (1924) (doctrine applied to duplicate original of a bilateral contract but not to purported duplicate of a unilateral covenant not to sue—no reason given why doctrine of counterparts should not apply to unilateral instruments); Sarasohn v. Kamaiky, 193 N.Y. 203, 86 N.E. 20, syl. 3 (1908) (each counterpart is an original).

8. Norris v. Billingsley, 48 Fla. 102, 37 So. 564, syl. 3 (1904); Peaks v. Cobb, 192 Mass. 196, 77 N.E. 881 (1906); Bryson & Hartgrove v. Boyce, 41 Tex.Civ. App. 415, 92 S.W. 820, syl. 1 (1906).

1. 4 Wigmore, Evidence, § 1234; 2 Jones, Evidence, § 798; Dec.Dig., Evidence, ☞174(1), 186(6); 32 C.J.S., Evidence, §§ 815, 816, 821; 22 C.J., Evidence, §§ 1307, 1308, 1313, 1314; 20 Am.Jur., §§ 427, 428; Notes, 51 A.L.R. 1498 (carbons), 142 A.L.R. 1270 (photographic copies).

2. Spottiswood v. Weir, 66 Cal. 525, 6 Pac. 381, syl. 2 (1885) (press-copy is secondary); Westinghouse Co.

equal embodiment of the contract or other transaction. Indeed, today counterparts usually consist of an original and one or more carbons, all duly signed in multiplicate. What makes them counterparts is the signing with intent to make them equal. Consequently, the doctrine of counterparts can hardly apply to the retained carbon-copy of a letter—the writer does not intend the copy to be a communication at all.[3] But the fact that many counterparts today are made by the use of carbons and the notion that writings made by the same stroke are like counterparts has caused a growing number of courts to treat all carbons, when authenticated as true reproductions, as if they were duplicate originals, i. e., as admissible without accounting for the original.[4]

Another method of reproduction, that of photography, is rapidly growing in vogue in business and government offices. This method may be followed by taking full-size photographs or photostats, or more often today in the making of copies of correspondence, records and books by taking the pictures on rolls of micro-film which later is read through a magnifying reader, or a particular part may be reproduced by a photographic enlargement. A Federal appeals court in a celebrated case held that "recordak" photographs of checks which had been paid, preserved by the bank as part of its regular records were admissible as originals under the Federal Business Records Act. Mr. Justice Sutherland, speaking for the court, said:

> ". . . the best evidence rule should not be pushed beyond the reason upon which it rests. It should be 'so applied,' as the Supreme Court held in an early case, 'as to promote the ends of justice, and guard against fraud or imposition.' Renner v. Bank of Columbia, 9 Wheat. 581, 597, 6 L.Ed. 166. . . . The rule is not based upon the view that the so-called secondary evidence is not competent, since, if the best evidence is shown to be unobtainable, secondary evidence at once becomes admissible. And if it appear, as it does here, that what is called the secondary evidence is clearly equal in probative value to what is called the primary proof, and that fraud or imposition, reasonably, is not to be feared, the reason upon which the best evidence rule rests ceases, with the consequence that in that situation, the rule itself must cease to be applicable, in consonance with the well established maxim—cessante ratione legis, cessat ipsa lex."[5]

Since that time a Uniform Act[6] making photographic copies, regularly kept, of busi-

---

v. Tilden, 56 Neb. 129, 76 N.W. 416, syl. 4 (1898), and cases cited 22 C.J. 1021, note 39. For a more liberal attitude, see McAuley v. Siscoe, 110 Kan. 804, 205 Pac. 346, 347 (1922).

3. Lockwood v. L. & L. Freight Lines, 126 Fla. 474, 171 So. 236, syl. 1, 2 (1936).

4. Oberlin v. Pyle, 114 Ind.App. 21, 49 N.E.2d 970, syl. 3, 4 (1943) (carbon of report, signed, of physician, retained as office copy); Liberty Nat. Bank & Trust Co. v. Louisville Trust Co., 295 Ky. 825, 175 S.W.2d 524, syl. 4 (1943) (carbon of letter); International Harv. Co. v. Elfstrom, 101 Minn. 263, 112 N.W. 252 (1907) (duplicate order-sheet sued on as contract); Carter v. Carl Merveldt & Son, 183 Okl. 152, 80 P.2d 254 (1938); Note, 51 A.L.R. 1498; 32 C.J.S. 750, note 57. Contra: Lockwood v. L. & L. Freight Lines, 126 Fla. 474, 171 So. 236, syl. 1 (1936) (carbon is duplicate original only when intended to stand equal); Mauritz v. Schwind, 101 S.W.2d 1085,

syl. 30 (Tex.Civ.App.1937) (carbon of letter) noted in 24 Tex.L.Rev. 105.

5. United States v. Manton, 107 F.2d 834, 845 (C.C.A. 2d 1938).

6. The Uniform Photographic Copies of Business and Public Records as Evidence Act was approved in 1949. 9 Unif.Laws Ann. 417 (1951). See also Uniform Rules of Evidence, R. 72: "The content of any admissible writing made in the regular course of "a business" as defined by Rule 62 or in the regular course of duty of any "public official" as defined by said rule, may be proved by a photostatic, microfilm, microcard, miniature photographic or other photographic copy or reproduction or by an enlargement thereof, when duly authenticated, if it was in the regular course of such business or official activity to make and preserve such copies or reproductions as a part of the records of such business or office. The introduction of such copy, reproduc-

ness and public records admissible without accounting for the original records has been approved, adopted in a number of states,[7] and incorporated in substance as an amendment to the Federal Business Records Act.[8] In the cases, however, in which photographs of writings have been offered to show the terms of the original, without the aid of specific statutes, they have been almost uniformly treated as secondary evidence inadmissible unless the original is accounted for.[9]

There is warrant for believing that the courts would accept as primary evidence of the contents of a given book or a given issue of a newspaper any other book or newspaper printed from the same sets of fixed type, or the same plates or mats.[10] A like result should be reached as to all copies run off from the same mat by the multigraph, lithoprint or other duplicating process.

From this brief survey of the treatment of the different kinds of mechanically produced copies, favorable to carbons, but unfavorable to photostats which are generally more accurate, one gets the impression that the practice is bred by mysticism out of unthinking habit. If, like Mr. Justice Sutherland, we remind ourselves that the sole policy of the

original documents requirement is to secure accurate information about the contents of material writings, free of the infirmities of memory and the mistakes of hand-copying, we may well conclude that each of these forms of mechanical copying is sufficient to fulfill the policy. Insistence upon the original, or accounting for it, places costs, burdens of planning and hazards of mistake upon the litigants. These may be worth imposing where the alternative is accepting memory or hand-copies. They are probably not worth imposing when risks of inaccuracy are reduced to a minimum by the offer of a mechanically produced copy. The courts, it is submitted, might well bring common law into harmony with common sense by accepting all mechanically produced copies, authenticated as accurate reproductions and appearing to be such,[11] to evidence the terms of the original, but recognizing a discretion in the judge to require production of the original also, if it can be conveniently secured without unduly delaying the trial.

207. Preferences among Copies and between Copies and Oral Testimony.[1]

The policy of the original document requirement is that of specially safeguarding

---

tion or enlargement does not preclude admission of the original writing if it is still in existence."

7. Georgia, Laws 1950 p. 73; South Dakota, Sup.Ct. Order No. 1, 1950, SDC 36.1003; Virginia, Code 1950, §§ 8–279.1, 8–279.2; Washington, RCW 40.20.-010, 40.20.020. See also the Acts cited in the informative Note, Photographic Copies of Business and Public Records, 34 Ia.L.Rev. 83, 86 (1948).

8. 28 U.S.C.A. § 1733(b), added by Act Aug. 28, 1951, c. 351 §§ 1, 3, 65 Stat. 206.

9. Hosey v. Southport Petroleum Co., 244 Ala. 45, 12 So.2d 93, syl. 6 (1943); Olson v. New York Life Ins. Co., 229 Iowa 1073, 295 N.W. 833, syl. 4 (1941); People v. Wells, 380 Ill. 347, 44 N.E.2d 32, syl. 11, 142 A.L.R. 1262 (1942) (forgery; to show other forgeries as part of same plan state offered recordaks of other checks so forged, held, secondary, distinguishing United States v. Manton, supra n. 5, on ground that it rested on a statute rendering business records admissible), and cases cited in Note, 142 A.L.R. 1270.

10. See Rex v. Watson, 2 Stark. 116, 129, 171 Eng. Rep. 591, 598 (N.P.1817) (to prove contents of printed placards which had been posted, other placards from same printing admitted); People ex rel. Thompson v. Chicago R. I. & P. Ry. Co., 329 Ill. 467, 160 N.E. 841, syl. 4 (1928) (contest of bond election: as evidence of contents of ballots used in election, other ballots produced by same setting of type admitted as "duplicate originals," but here used ballots had been destroyed); 4 Wigmore, Evidence, § 1234(3).

11. An example of such scrutiny is Long v. Long, 361 Pa. 598, 65 A.2d 683, syl. 2 (1949), where the court declined to receive as an "original" a carbon copy of a purported declaration of trust of one deceased, where the purported signature appeared to be an impression from a carbon of different color from that used in the body.

1. 4 Wigmore, Evidence, §§ 1265–1280; 2 Jones, Evidence, §§ 859–862 (2d ed. rev. 1926); Note, Klein, Degrees of Secondary Evidence, 38 Mich.L.Rev. 864 (1940); Dec.Dig., Evidence, ☜186; 32 C.J.S., Evi-

the accuracy of the presentation in court of the terms of a writing. If the original is unavailable does the same policy require a preference among the secondary methods of proving the terms? Some means of proof are clearly more reliable than others. In order of reliability the list might go something like this: (1) a mechanically produced copy, such as a photograph, a carbon, a letter-press copy, etc.,[2] (2) a first-hand copy by one who was looking at the original while he copied (immediate copy, sworn copy), (3) a copy, however made, which has been compared by a witness with the original and found correct (examined copy), (4) a second-hand or mediate copy, i. e., a copy of a first-hand copy, (5) oral testimony as to the terms of the writing, with memory aided by a previously made memorandum, and (6) oral testimony from unaided memory. There are many additional variations.

There is one rule of preference that is reasonable and is generally agreed on by the courts, namely, that for judicial and other public records, a certified, sworn or examined copy is preferred,[3] and other evidence of the terms of the record cannot be resorted to unless the proponent has no such copy available, and the original record has been lost or destroyed so that a copy cannot now be made.[4]

Apart from this there are two general approaches to the problem. First, the view fathered by some of the English decisions and espoused by a minority of the American cases, to the effect that there is no preference —that there are "no degrees of secondary evidence." [5] This has the merit of simplicity and ease of administration, but it seems to abandon too easily (when the original is unavailable) the policy of special safeguards of accuracy in presenting the contents of a writing. A man who has at home a photostatic copy of a material letter will be allowed to recite its terms on the stand from memory, with no pressure upon him to give the court the benefit of the accurate copy except the hazard—fairly dangerous, it is true—of adverse inference from his failure to produce the copy.

The second approach is the more expedient. This is the practice obtaining in the majority of states that have passed on the question, which discriminates between types of secondary evidence,[6] and prefers a copy to oral

---

dence, § 784; 22 C.J., Evidence, § 1379; 20 Am.Jur., Evidence, § 404.

2. See § 206, above.

3. Jones v. Melindy, 62 Ark. 203, 208, 36 S.W. 22, syl. 2 (1881) (proof of record of mortgage not provable by testimony of custodian; use of examined or certified copy required); Inhabitants of Rumford v. Inhabitants of Upton, 113 Me. 543, 95 Atl. 226, syl. 11 (1915); 4 Wigmore, Evidence, §§ 1269, 1273. This requirement has been relaxed in most states, by statute or decision, to permit a witness to be asked on cross-examination about his conviction of crime, for impeachment. Hall v. Gordon, 70 App.D.C. 33, 128 F.2d 461, syl. 4 (1942) (applying D.C.Code 1951, § 14–305); State v. English, 132 Conn. 573, 46 A.2d 121, syl. 6 (1946); Clemens v. Conrad, 19 Mich. 170, 175 (1869) (Cooley, C. J.: "The danger that he will falsely testify to a conviction that never took place or that he may be mistaken about it, is so slight, that it may almost be looked upon as purely imaginary. . . ."). Contra: People v. Grizzle, 381 Ill. 278, 44 N.E.2d 917, syl. 13 (1942). See 4

Wigmore, Evidence, § 1270, Dec.Dig. Witnesses, ☞ 350, 359.

4. People v. Cotton, 250 Ill. 338, 95 N.E. 283, syl. 2 (1911).

5. Doe d. Gilbert v. Ross, 7 M. & W. 102, 151 Eng. Rep. 696, 698 (Exch.1840) (shorthand notes of counsel's statement at a former trial of the contents of a settlement allowed, though attested copy, requiring but not bearing a stamp was in existence); Goodrich v. Weston, 102 Mass. 362 (1869) (copy of a letter-press copy allowed, though latter available); Magie v. Herman, 50 Minn. 424, 52 N.W. 909 (1892) (oral testimony to contents of telegram held admissible though apparently a copy was in existence). It has been said that England, Massachusetts, Minnesota, Texas and Tennessee are committed to this view, and Connecticut, Nebraska, Maine and Mississippi have had one or two decisions favoring this approach. Klein, Note, 38 Mich. L.Rev. 864, 865 (1940).

6. The law review writer mentioned in the preceding note finds that eight jurisdictions are committed to

testimony,[7] and may, under conditions varying from state to state, prefer an immediate copy to a more remote one.[8] In formulating this general approach of discrimination among types of secondary evidence, these courts seek to avoid a position which would require the proponent to produce or account for all possible copies that may have existed. A reasonable standard is that suggested by an early New York judge who said,

"I do not mean to contend that there are any arbitrary or inflexible degrees of secondary evidence, rendering it necessary for a party, who is driven to that description of proof, to show affirmatively, in every instance, that there is no higher degree within his power, than the one he offers; but I think it may be safely said, that where it appears in the very offer, or from the nature of the case itself, or from the circumstances attending the offer, that the party has better and more reliable evidence at hand, and equally within his power, he shall not be permitted to resort to the inferior degree first." [9]

Even simpler and equally just it seems would be a rule that a proponent before using recollection-testimony should be required to show that he does not have a copy under his control and conveniently available, and similarly before using a remote copy he should show that he does not have a first-hand copy available.[10]

208. Adversary's Admission as to the Terms of a Writing.[1]

In the leading English case of Slatterie v. Pooley,[2] decided in 1840, the question was whether the plaintiff could prove the terms of a material writing by testimony of a witness that he heard the defendant orally admit that the writing named a certain person in a list of debtors. The writing was in court and doubtless clearly disclosed the same fact, but it was excluded because unstamped. Baron Parke in holding the testimony of the oral admission receivable, said "what a party himself admits to be true, may reasonably be presumed to be so."

---

this view, namely, the Federal Courts, Alabama, Arkansas, Georgia (by statute), Illinois, Iowa, Missouri, and Pennsylvania; and that five have shown a leaning to this view, i. e., Maryland, New Jersey, Vermont, Virginia and Wisconsin. Klein, Note, 38 Mich.L.Rev. 864, 865 (1940).

7. Riggs v. Tayloe, 9 Wheat. 483, 486, 6 L.Ed. 140 (1824) (original contract destroyed, oral testimony permitted; "the party [after accounting for original] may read a counterpart or if there is no counterpart, an examined copy, or if there should not be an examined copy, he may give parol evidence of its contents."); Robinson v. Singerly Paper, etc. Co., 110 Md. 382, 72 Atl. 828, syl. 4 (1909) (where no presumption that better secondary evidence exists party may use any competent evidence unless adversary shows that proponent could have produced better); Cleveland v. Burnham, 64 Wis. 347, 357, 359, 25 N.W. 407, 410, 411 (1885) (corporation's list of shareholders "higher evidence" as to transfer of stock than recollection-testimony about entry of transfer on books).

8. When the original is a public record and hence not producible, a certified or examined copy may be obtained at any time, and a copy of a copy would everywhere be excluded. Lasater v. Van Hook, 77

Tex. 650, 655, 14 S.W. 270, syl. 4 (1890) (deed-record; examined copy of a certified copy excluded). When the original is unavailable and there is no copy of record, then under the majority view the proponent would be required to produce an immediate copy, if available, before using a copy of a copy. Schley v. Lyon, 6 Ga. 530, 538 (1949); State v. Cohen, 108 Iowa 208, 78 N.W. 857, syl. 5 (1899). Contra, under the minority, "no degrees" doctrine: Goodrich v. Weston, 102 Mass. 362 (1869) (described note 5, supra).
The various situations are distinguished and the decisions collected in 4 Wigmore, Evidence, § 1275.

9. Slossen, J. in Healy v. Gilman, 1 Bosw. (14 N.Y. Super.) 235 at 242 (1857), quoted in Note, 38 Mich. L.Rev. 864, 874 (1940).

10. This is an adaptation of views expressed in 4 Wigmore, Evidence, § 1268, and in Tracy, Book Review, 39 Mich.L.Rev. 267, 271, 272 (1940).

1. 4 Wigmore, Evidence, §§ 1255–1257; 2 Jones, Evidence, §§ 789–793; Dec.Dig., Evidence, ☞172; 32 C.J.S., Evidence, § 788; 22 C.J. Evidence, §§ 1301, 1302; 20 Am.Jur., Evidence, § 425; Note, 17 Tex.L. Rev. 371 (1939).

2. 6 M. & W. 665, 151 Eng.Rep. 579 (Exch.1840).

At first blush, this plausible suggestion seems to sustain the conclusion, and fairly to satisfy the purpose of the original documents requirement, namely that of safeguarding the accuracy of the proof of the terms of writings. If the party made the admission favorable to his opponent, it is reasonably sure to be true, and many American courts leap the ditch with Baron Parke to the conclusion.[3] But the real danger, unmentioned by Baron Parke, lies in the hazard of inaccuracy or untruth in the reporting of the oral admission by the witness. This is the sort of hazard that the original documents rule is designed to minimize.

Accordingly some other American decisions have rejected oral admissions of the terms of a writing.[4] A written admission stands on a different footing. Writings can be forged but forgery today is pretty surely detectable, and hence more hazardous than perjury and far less prevalent than the slips of memory of oral testimony.

The desirable solution, toward which, it is believed, the decisions may be drifting, is to receive the party's admissions to evidence the document's terms, when the circumstances are such as would usually make us reasonably sure that he actually made the admissions, namely, (1) when the admission is in writing and is produced in evidence,[5] or (2) when the party himself, on the stand in this or some other trial or hearing, makes the admission about the contents of the writing [6] or concedes on the stand that he made such an admission on a former occasion. Oral testimony by another witness, that he heard the party's admission as to the terms of a writing, though sanctioned by Slatterie v. Pooley, should be excluded.

209. Review of Rulings Admitting Secondary Evidence.

It will be seen from the earlier sections of this chapter that the requirement of the production of original writings, with the several excuses for non-production and the exceptions to the requirement itself, make up a fairly complex set of regulations for administration by the trial judge. Mistakes in the application of these rules are, understandably, not infrequent. The purpose of this system of rules, on the other hand, is simple and practical. That purpose is to secure the most reliable information as to the contents of

---

3. In the following cases testimony of a third person as to a party's oral admission was received: Dunbar v. United States, 156 U.S. 185, 196, 15 Sup.Ct. 325, 39 L.Ed. 390 (1895) (oral admission that telegram received by witness was identical with one sent by party); Metropolitan Life Ins. Co. v. Hogan, 63 F.2d 654, syl. 6, 7, C.C.A. Ill., 1933 (oral admission by insurance company's agent that paper received from beneficiary was a "death-claim"); Morey v. Hoyt, 62 Conn. 542, 556, 26 Atl. 127, 131, syl. 4 (1893) (approving Slatterie v. Pooley); Purinton v. Purinton, 101 Me. 250, 63 Atl. 925, 115 Am.St.Rep. 309, 8 Ann.Cas. 205, syl. 1, 2, 1906 (divorce sought by wife; testimony of witness for husband that witness had heard wife read aloud from letters she had written to another man; held admissible, as "primary" evidence).

4. E. g., Grimes v. Fall, 15 Cal. 63, 65 (1860) (oral testimony that party admitted that he was assignee under what the court assumed to be a written assignment, held, inadmissible); Bellamy v. Hawkins, 17 Fla. 750, 758, syl. 6, 7 (1880) (admission by executor as to amount allowed him by court's order, excluded), and see 4 Wigmore, Evidence, § 1256, n. 4.

5. Written admissions were held receivable in Clarke v. Warwick C. M. Co., 174 Mass. 434, 54 N.E. 887, syl. 1 (1899); Swing v. Cloquet Lumber Co., 121 Minn. 221, 141 N.W. 117, L.R.A. 1918C, 660, syl. 1, 1913 (suit against policyholder in mutual company to recover assessment; written admission by defendant in letter describing his policy admissible for plaintiff; "The rule is sound in principle, at least when the admissions are in writing"); Cumberland Mut. F. Ins. Co. v. Giltinan, 48 N.J.L. 495, 7 Atl. 424, syl. 2 (1886) (statement by insured in proof of loss); Taylor v. Peck, 21 Grat., Va., 11, 19, 1871 (forcible detainer, by landlord against tenant; defendant allowed to introduce plaintiff's receipt for rent, reciting time for which rent paid, to show his possession rightful, though lease in writing).

6. Instances where admissions on the witness-stand were received, though without distinguishing them from other oral admissions: Barnett v. Wilson, 132 Ala. 375, 31 So. 521, syl. 3 (1902); Gardner v. City of Columbia Police Dep't, 216 S.C. 219, 57 S.E.2d 308, syl. 8–10 (1950).

documents, when those terms are disputed. A mystical ideal of seeking "the best evidence" or the "original document," as an end in itself is no longer the goal. Consequently when an attack is made, on motion for new trial or on appeal, upon the judge's admission of secondary evidence, it seems that the reviewing tribunal, should ordinarily make inquiry of the complaining counsel, "Does the party whom you represent actually dispute the accuracy of the evidence received as to the material terms of the writing?" If the counsel cannot assure the court that such a good faith dispute exists, it seems clear that any departure from the regulations in respect to secondary evidence must be classed as harmless error.[1]

1. Compare, however, National Fire Ins. Co. v. Evertson, 153 Neb. 854, 46 N.W.2d 489, syl. 6–8 (1951), where the possibility of this approach was overlooked. There a judgment was reversed, partly on the ground that a material written settlement was proved only by a carbon copy. On the motion for new trial the winning plaintiff produced the original writing which corresponded with the carbon, but the court on appeal said that the judgment could not be "propped up" in that way.

CHAPTER 24

THE PAROL EVIDENCE RULE[1]

---

1. Comprehensive treatments: 9 Wigmore, Evidence, §§ 2400–2478; 3 Williston, Contracts, §§ 629–647 (1936); Corbin, Contracts, §§ 573–596 (1951); 32 C.J.S., Evidence, §§ 851–1015; 20 Am.Jur., Evidence, §§ 1091–1176; Dec.Dig., Evidence, ⊙⊶384–469. See also Am.L.Inst. Restatement of Contracts, §§ 228, 229, 237–244; Uniform Commercial Code—Sales, Sec. 2–202 (Official Draft, 1952).

General discussions in the periodicals: Strahorn, The Unity of the Parol Evidence Rule, 14 Minn.L.Rev. 20 (1929); McCormick, The Parol Evidence Rule as a Procedural Device for Control of the Jury, 41 Yale L.J. 365 (1932); Comment, The Parol Evidence Rule: A Conservative View, 19 U.Chi.L.Rev. 348 (1952).

Discussions of the decisions in particular states: Brunson, Scope and Operation of Parol Evidence Rule in Arkansas, 4 Ark.L.Rev. 168 (1950); Loth and Jennings, The Parol Evidence Rule in Iowa, 20 Ia.L.Rev. 713 (1935); Wilson, The Parol Evidence Rule in Nebraska, 4 Neb. L. Bulletin 115 (1925); Chadbourn and McCormick, The Parol Evidence Rule in North Carolina, 9 N.C.L.Rev. 151 (1931); Stansbury, North Carolina Evidence, Ch. 15 (1946);

TOPIC 1

THE PROCEDURAL ASPECT OF THE RULE OF INTEGRATION [2]

210. The Problems Incident to the Determination of Defences or Claims Based upon Alleged Oral Agreements Preceding or Accompanying Writings: Differing Attitudes of Judge and Jury.

In a Minnesota case,[3] the action was upon a written contract whereby the defendant guaranteed the payment of "any and all sums of money" to be furnished by the plaintiff until further notice to a flour mill corporation. The defendant contended that it was orally agreed that the guaranty should apply only to sums furnished for the purchase of grain by the milling company locally, at the small town where its mill and elevator were situated, whereas the sums sued for were advanced for purchases of grain in the Minneapolis market, to be shipped to the mill. At the trial the jury accepted this contention and judgment went for the defendant. To the appellate court, however, the defense was unacceptable, because of the "rule which prevents the destruction of the obligation of a written contract by evidence of preceding or contemporaneous oral agreements." Significantly, the court added: "Without that rule there would be no assurance of the enforceability of a written contract. If such assurance were removed today from our law, general disaster would result, because of the consequent destruction of confidence, for the tremendous but closely adjusted machinery of modern business cannot function at all without confidence in the enforceability of contracts."

The court assumes as self-evident that without some special assurance of the enforcement of contracts *as written*, as against claims of inconsistent oral agreements, business men generally will be seriously handicapped in the prosecution of commercial enterprise. Like most of the law's basic assumptions, this one has never been tested by any survey of the actual effects in business of the presence or absence of such assurance. But there can be little doubt that a belief in the soundness of this apprehension has been one of the chief motives of judges in the development and preservation of the nexus of doctrines called by the name of the Parol Evidence Rule. Despite the probable importance to the business world of some reliable guaranties of the integrity of written transactions, the difficulties in extending such protection are apparent in a country where, by law and common habit, nearly all kinds of agreements may be oral, and where disputed fact-claims are ordinarily left to the arbitrament of a group of twelve men, not selected for any special competence for the task of judging.

When an issue arises involving choice between a writing and an alleged oral agreement, usually the one who sets up the spoken against the written word is economically the under-dog. He may be a person who has signed a note at the bank for himself or his

---

Hale, The Parol Evidence Rule [in Oregon], 4 Ore.L. Rev. 91 (1925); Harrison, Pennsylvania Rule as to Introducing Promises to Affect Written Instruments, 74 U.Pa.L.Rev. 235 (1926); supplementing an article by Folz, 52 Am.L.Reg. 601 (1904), H.S.R., A Decade of Gianni v. Russel, The Modern Pennsylvania Parol Evidence Rule, 83 U.Pa.L.Rev. 500 (1935); Note, Bressler and Taylor, A Critique of the Parol Evidence Rule in Pennsylvania, 100 U.Pa.Rev. 703 (1952) (an acute discussion of the justice factor); McCormick and Ray, Texas Law of Evidence, ch. 30 (1937); Moreland, Parol Evidence Rule in Virginia, 3 Wash. and Lee L.Rev. 185 (1942); Wunschel,

Parol Evidence Rule in West Virginia—When Is a Writing Complete?, 41 W.Va.L.Q. 273 (1935); Grassy, Parol Evidence Rule in Wisconsin, 1940 Wis.L. Rev. 427.

2. Am.L.Inst.Restatement, Contracts, sec. 228: "What Is Integration. An agreement is integrated where the parties thereto adopt a writing or writings as the final and complete expression of the agreement. An integration is the writing or writings so adopted." See also 9 Wigmore, § 2425 (Integration of Jural Acts).

3. Cargill Commission Co. v. Swartwood, 159 Minn. 1, 7, 198 N.W. 536, 538 (1924).

neighbor and who asserts that it was agreed that the note or endorsement should not be enforced until certain funds should be realized by the debtor, or he may be a farmer who has purchased a tractor on credit and who resists collection on the ground that the agent of the tractor company orally warranted the power-rating of the tractor in a way not specified in the written sales agreement. The types of transaction wherein is involved this kind of competition between claims based upon writings and those based upon alleged oral agreements dealing with the same affair, are infinitely various, but usually if there is a difference between the two parties in economic status, the one who relies upon the writing is likely to be among the "haves," and the one who seeks escape through the oral word will probably be ranged among the "have nots," in Sancho Panza's classification. The average jury will, other things being equal, lean strongly in favor of the side which is threatened with possible injustice and certain hardship by the enforcement of the writing.

"The written word remains," a genuine and veracious memorial, so far as it goes, of what was actually agreed to. On the other hand, the narrative by a witness of the purported substance of words, spoken many months or even years before, is subject to a very high probability of error,[4] even when recounted by a disinterested person. It is doubtful whether a jury is likely to take sufficient account of this factor of unreliability. Moreover, the witness who recounts the oral bargaining seldom is, in fact, disinterested. He is usually the party himself, who is struggling, honestly or dishonestly, to escape the hardship of the terms nominated in the bond.[5] The struggle is all too often, consciously or unconsciously, the father of the recollected conversation. From all these sources springs grave danger that honest expectations, based upon carefully considered written transactions, may be defeated through the sympathetic, if not credulous, acceptance by juries of fabricated or wish-born oral agreements.[6] Likewise, some peril to justice and to the stability of business transactions lies in the possibility that earlier and tentative oral agreements which were a part of the preliminary parleying, but were actually understood by both parties to be abandoned when omitted in the final written agreement, will be stoutly asserted by one party at the trial as having been intended to stand alongside the writing. When a genuine, but superseded, oral agreement is thus set up, it will be even harder for the jury to reject the claim based on such agreement than if it were fabricated from the whole cloth.

The danger of undermining confidence in written bargains generally is one which can be appreciated by a trial judge, who looks

---

4. Coke reports Popham, C.J., as saying, in the Countess of Rutland's case: "Also it would be inconvenient that matters in writing made by advice and on consideration, and which finally import the certain truth of the agreement of the parties, should be controlled by averment of the parties, to be proved by the uncertain testimony of slippery memory." 3 Co. 51 (1604).

5. It is possible that the protection which it afforded to writings may have served to lengthen the life of the archaic and irrational rule which disqualified parties from testifying.

6. To recognize these dangers is not to overlook the corresponding dangers on the other tack. When a written contract has, after lengthy negotiations, been prepared for signing, and a term orally agreed upon has been omitted or distorted by the scrivener, an oral assurance that "it will be all right" may often serve to gloss the matter over to a signature, especially where the contingency provided for in the oral understanding seems remote. The party may hesitate to delay matters by insisting on having the writing amended. Especially is this true today, when many transactions are consummated by standardized printed contracts. These are tendered by agents who are often instructed by their principals not to permit the written forms to be altered, even when, as so often happens, they do not fit exactly the individual requirements of the customer. Cf. Llewellyn, What Price Contract?, 40 Yale L.J. 704, 747 (1931).

back on many similar cases and is trained to take a long view. Moreover, he is likely, during his practice, to have imbibed some understanding from his clients of the needs of business, and to know from extended observation how to discount testimony for the warping of self-interest. The jury, on the other hand, is likely to pass over these considerations in its urge of sympathy for a party whom the shoe of the written contract pinches. This sympathy may occasionally deflect even the decision of the trial judge who sees, and often personally knows, the harassed party. The appellate judge, remote from local acquaintance and local political interest, is free to adopt a still closer approach to the Jovian detachment of the "long view."

The continental legal system, with no civil jury, and with most contracts required to be entirely in writing, has little trouble in guarding written bargains from oral encroachment. This danger to written transactions is peculiarly inherent in the common-law methods of trial.

211. Evolution of Doctrines Giving Special Control to the Judge: Rule against Varying the Writing: Completeness of Writing: Exception for "Collateral" Agreements.

How did the common-law judges make pro-vision against this danger, which, as we have seen, flows chiefly from the peculiar institution of the untrained jury, a body numerous enough to invite emotional organ-playing by counsel, and usually unguided in this country by any specific advice from the trial judge? The danger from allowing juries to do their worst with written transactions was doubtless sensed intuitively by the judges,[1] but this was prevented from emerging into consciousness and expression by the prevailing idolatry of the jury as a symbol of political liberty.[2] Otherwise, they might frankly have reserved for the judge's decision (as one of the exceptions to the general practice) the question of fact as to whether an alleged oral agreement set up in competition with a writing, was actually made, and, if so, whether it was intended to be abandoned or to survive, when the writing was signed. Forbidden this straight path by their own preconceptions, by a zig-zag route they came out near the same goal. The approach was made through doctrinal devices[3] which gave no hint of any departure from the usual division of functions between judge and jury, but which were subtly convenient for jury control in cases where written transactions were

---

1. That the parol evidence rule chiefly stems from an anxiety to protect written bargains from re-writing by juries, is confirmed by the comparative freedom which was allowed in chancery in respect to reformation, and in regard to oral variations asserted as a ground for denying specific performance. Of the latter, a recent example is John T. Stanley Co., Inc. v. Lagomarsino, 49 F.2d 702 (C.C.A.2d, 1931). It is true that other doors for jury intervention in support of oral variations have not been closed, as in the case of oral agreements that the writing shall not go into effect until the happening of a condition, and likewise oral agreements modifying the written terms *after* the execution of the document. Each of these escapes from the writing presents difficulties to the one who attempts it, and, in any event, the fact that protection in some situations has not been perfect, does not disprove the desire to furnish it generally.

2. Mr. Justice Blackstone, for example, in his Commentaries (3 Bl.Comm. 294, *379), begins his eulogy thus: "Upon these accounts the trial by jury ever has been, and I trust ever will be, looked upon as the glory of the English law. . . . It is the most transcendent privilege which any subject can enjoy, or wish for, that he cannot be affected either in his property, his liberty, or his person, but by the unanimous consent of twelve of his neighbours and equals. A constitution, that I may venture to affirm has, under Providence, secured the just liberties of this nation for a long succession of ages. And therefore a celebrated French writer (Montesq. Sp.L. xi. 6), who concludes, that because Rome, Sparta, and Carthage have lost their liberties, therefore those of England in time must perish, should have recollected that Rome, Sparta, and Carthage, at the time when their liberties were lost, were strangers to the trial by jury."

3. See Note, Tests for Determining whether Entire Agreement is Embodied in the Writing, 70 A.L.R. 752.

threatened by claims of agreed oral variations not credited by the judge.[4]

In the first place, they said, "Parol evidence is inadmissible to vary, contradict, or add to the terms of a written instrument." The phrase becomes a shibboleth, repeated in ten thousand cases. It obviously enables the judge to head off the difficulty at its source, not by professing to decide any question as to the credibility of the asserted oral variation, but by professing to exclude the evidence from the jury altogether because forbidden by a mysterious legal ban. An alternative device to the same end was the use of the formula that when a writing (variously qualified) is executed, it is "conclusively presumed" to embody the whole agreement. If conclusively presumed, then, of course, no evidence of additional oral agreements can be heard. This all-inclusive prohibition by rule of law against any competition of oral agreements with written was effective enough as a jury-excluding formula, but as an actual standard of decision for judges it was wholly illusory.

Thus, for example, some writings are obviously mere skeleton memoranda, not intended to cover all the terms agreed on, and where this is so, the oral terms must be provable, if elementary justice is to be done. But in revising the original formula against "varying, altering, or contradicting" by recognizing an exception for mere partial memoranda, or incomplete instruments, care had to be taken not to open the door to jury-determination as to whether the exception was applicable. The exception was sought to be stated in terms of the "completeness" of the writing. The writing is the "sole criterion" of its own completeness, they said, and the judge, traditionally literate and hence trained to interpret writings by inspection, ascertains whether it is "complete on its face."[5] Thus far the reins are still tightly held by the judges. But the doctrine of exclusive resort to the writing (even as mitigated by the exception for obviously skeleton memoranda), while useful in aiding the judges to retain command, is much too narrow to meet the actual need. This need is for recognition of reasonable and genuine oral agreements dealing with matters related to those covered by the written document, but not intended by the parties to be superseded by the writing, even where the writing, so far as appearance goes, is seemingly a formal and completed one. Two devices were used to meet this need, without opening the door to blundering by the jury in the china-shop.

First, the language devised for the obviously sketchy memoranda, to the effect that the incompleteness was to be measured by the instrument "on its face" and hence, though this was seldom mentioned explicitly, was for the judge to determine himself by inspection, was repeated. "The only criterion of the completeness of the written contract . . . is the writing itself."[6] It soon became evident, however, that while the face of the writing would usually show whether it was intended as a mere memorandum, and not as a plenary instrument at all, yet a mere inspection could never show whether a writing, full and deliberate in form, did or did not cover all the agreements entered into by the parties about the subject-matter. Conse-

---

4. It is not intended to suggest that these doctrinal devices were newly invented by the judges, consciously, to meet this need, in modern times. Thayer and Wigmore have traced too clearly the origin of the parol evidence formula against "varying the writing," to a primitive formalism which attached a mystical and ceremonial effectiveness to the *carta* and the seal. (9 Wigmore, Evidence, § 2426). The writer merely ventures to submit that this formalism, abandoned elsewhere in so many areas of modern law, had here a special survival value—the escape from the jury—which led the judges to retain for writings the conception that they had a sort of magical effect of erasing all prior oral agreements.

5. Brautigam v. Dean, 85 N.J.L. 549, 556, 89 Atl. 760, 763 (1914); Thompson v. Lobby, 34 Minn. 374, 26 N.W. 1 (1885).

6. Ibid. 377, 26 N.W. at 2.

quently, in these latter cases the door had to be opened wider if any thing at all was to come in. So the formula was revised: The writing is still the sole criterion by which to determine whether it is "complete," but it is the writing considered in the light of all the surrounding circumstances. All, that is, except one. You may consider the entire situation leading up to the signing of the writing except the most crucial of all data, i. e., the purport of the alleged agreement which has been left out of the writing.[7] Of course, no trial judge has ever actually followed any such practice of barring the door to an alleged oral agreement without first asking the mysterious stranger to identify himself. Counsel will always be asked to detail the nature of the oral agreement desired to be proved, or the evidence of its terms will be admitted *de bene* until a final ruling on its admissibility is made.[8] The artificiality of the elaborations of this doctrine of what we might call "facial completeness," and its falsity as a picture of what the trial judge actually does, result from the clumsiness of "completeness" as a doctrinal vehicle. It

carries very well the relatively easy cases dealing with skeleton memoranda and with contracts or conveyances where some essential or almost universally customary term is omitted from the writing.[9] It collapses when the courts burden it with the heavy freightage of cases where the writing shows no such obvious deficiency and where the underlying doubts are whether the alleged oral agreement really was made and, if so, whether the writing was intended to displace it.

A more practical and workable expedient for the admission of oral agreements considered by the judge as probably genuine and probably intended to remain in effect alongside the writing was the importation here of the term "collateral." The word, through long usage in other connections, had acquired a rich patina of technical legalism. Consequently, it would not occur to any one to suggest the submission to a jury of the question whether an alleged oral warranty by a landlord (at the time of making a written lease) that the drains of the house were in good order, was "collateral" to the lease.[10] Appar-

---

7. Wheaton Roller-Mill Co. v. John T. Noye Mfg. Co., 66 Minn. 156, 160, 68 N.W. 854 (1896).

8. Other courts, in revulsion from this narrow formula, that the "completeness" of the writing is to be determined from the face of the writing itself, have proceeded to the opposite extreme. They say that if it appears in evidence that oral agreements were made, and not included in the writing, it then follows that the writing is "incomplete," and if incomplete, then the parol evidence rule does not apply. See Exum v. Lynch, 188 N.C. 392, 125 S.E. 15 (1924). Though this reasoning has been justly criticized (4 Page, Contracts (1920) § 2153, n. 8), it seems a more logical application of the "completeness" standard than the doctrine which would require "completeness" to be ascertained without examining the alleged oral agreement, by the omission of which the writing is claimed to have been left incomplete. The difficulty lies in the inadequacy of "completeness" as a standard.

9. See, e. g., O'Keefe v. Bassett, 132 Conn. 659, 46 A.2d 847, syl. 4 (1946) (writing which failed to cover duties of one of the parties was incomplete and could be supplemented by oral agreement as to such duties).

10. See De LaSalle v. Guildford, L.R. 2 K.B. 215 (1901). Examples of American decisions recognizing the "collateral agreement" classification are Sickelco v. Union P. Ry. Co., 111 F.2d 746, syl. 6 (C.C.A.Cal.1940); Bundy v. Liberty Ins. Co., 150 Kan. 658, 95 P.2d 550, syl. 3 (1939); Kikas v. County Com'rs, 200 Md. 360, 89 A.2d 625, syl. 8 (1952); Taylor v. More, 195 Minn. 448, 263 N.W. 537, syl. 5 (1935); Mitchell v. Lath, 247 N.Y. 377, 160 N.E. 646, syl. 4, 68 A.L.R. 239 (1928); Dec. Dig., Evidence, ☞441. See 3 Corbin, Contracts, § 594; Am.L.Inst. Restatement, Contracts, Sec. 240(1) ("An oral agreement is not superseded . . . by a subsequent . . . integration . . . if the agreement is not inconsistent with the integrated contract, and (a) is made for separate consideration, or (b) is such an agreement as might naturally be made as a separate agreement by parties situated as were the parties to the written contract." Instances of "collateral" agreements held enforcible: Higgins v. Belson, 66 Idaho 736, 168 P.2d 813, syl. 1, 2 (1946) (written contract for sale of crop of potatoes, oral agreement by buyer to segregate seed-potatoes and hold for seller); Levin v. Cook, 47 A.2d 505, syl. 5 (Md.1946) (writ-

ently, the idea of allowable collateral agreements has enabled judges to follow their common sense and instinct for justice by furnishing them an escape from the formula against "varying, contradicting, or adding to" the writing, when a litigant seeks to establish an oral agreement which might reasonably have been intended to stand after the writing was signed.[11]

212. The Escape from the Writing by the Formula Relating to Contracts Partly Oral, Partly Written.

The older techniques thus far described have served several purposes fairly well. The "rule of evidence" against "varying" the writing by "parol" enabled the judge to cut out at the outset—by excluding evidence—mischievous claims of dubious oral agreements. He could thus protect investments founded on written bargains. The "exception" for "incomplete" writings, for "collateral" oral agreements, or the even wider escape-valve used by some courts of "contracts partly oral and partly written," permitted the genuine supplementary oral bargains to be recognized and enforced. The rough-and-ready phrases about "varying the writing" of

the seventeenth century English judges are elaborated in the appellate opinions of the American courts of the last hundred years, and these same formulas thus come to serve as the handles by which the appellate courts may revise the results reached both by judge and jury below.[1] A judge who finds a line of opinions which repeat the formula that "a writing may not be varied by parol" and also another equally respectable parallel line of opinions repeating the refrain that "when a writing is partly written and partly oral, the oral part may be shown,"[2] is in the situation, happy for the probable interests of justice in that individual case, where he can decide either way and for either decision can justify himself to counsel and parties by invoking an unimpeachable rule.[3] Nevertheless, the doctrines of the cases, thus mutually inconsistent and "paired," have furnished him little guidance for decision except to provide a choice of formulas for deciding for either side.

The apparent wide-open door to the enforcement of oral agreements, as part of the bargain represented by the writing, which is offered by the "partly oral and partly written" formula has been acceptably narrowed

---

ten sale of building, oral warranty that heating plant was in good condition).

11. In 1876, Sir James Fitz-James Stephen, after having stated in traditional terms the rule against varying the writing, thus rationalizes the doctrine of "collateral" oral agreements: "The party may prove the existence of any separate oral agreement as to any matter on which a document is silent, and which is not inconsistent with its terms, if from the circumstances of the case, the court infers that the parties did not intend the document to be a complete and final statement of the whole of the transaction between them. . . ." Stephen, Digest of the Law of Evidence (5th ed. 1901) art. 90.

1. See Green, Judge and Jury (1930) c. 14.

2. Greenleaf apparently first made this lion and lamb lie down together. As appears from the following passage, courts gladly repeated the miracle: "The rule is unquestioned that parol evidence is inadmissible to contradict or vary the terms of a valid written instrument: 1 Greenleaf, Evidence

(16th ed. 1899) § 275. But it is equally well settled that the rule does not apply 'in cases where the original contract was verbal and entire, and a part only of it was reduced to writing.' Ibid. § 284, a; 2 Parsons on Contracts (5th ed. 1866) 553, note." Cobb v. Wallace, 5 Coldwell 539, 544 (Tenn.1868). A similar pairing of opposites is strikingly disclosed in the opinion of the court in Exum v. Lynch, supra note 8. The contradiction was bared in the following judicial comment: "If we may go outside of the instrument to prove that there was a stipulation not contained in it, and so that only part of the contract was put in writing, and then, because of that fact, enforce the oral stipulation, there will be little value left in the rule itself." Eighmie v. Taylor, 98 N.Y. 288, 294 (1885).

3. This availability on occasion of two categorically opposite rules has been often noticed. Pound, The Call for a Realist Jurisprudence (1931) 44 Harv.L. Rev. 697, 704; Llewellyn, Some Realism about Realism, ibid. 1222; W. W. Cook, The Utility of Jurisprudence in the Solution of Legal Problems (1928) 5 Lectures on Legal Topics (N.Y.B.A.) 335.

by a newer concept. This is the formula of "partial integration." [4] This is the notion that the writing may be effective "as a final expression of [the parties'] agreement with respect to such terms as are included therein" and as to these terms may not be varied by earlier or contemporaneous expressions, but will not preclude "evidence of consistent additional terms unless the court finds the writing to have been intended also as a complete and exclusive statement" of the entire agreement.[5] This is an understandable middle ground between the one extreme view that no writing can be varied by parol, and the other that all writings can be supplemented by any oral parts of the same transaction.

213. The Substantive Aspect of the Parol Evidence Rule.

The greatest task of the new theory-builder is to tear away the shaky walls of the old structure. James Bradley Thayer, the great pioneer in the rationalization of the rules of evidence, struck his axe in deep at this point. Though he saw clearly enough "that the older law and the older decisions . . . were often mainly concerned in keeping matters out of the hands of juries," [1] he was offended at the device of treating the protective rule as an "evidence rule." This ran counter to the central theme around which Thayer arranged all his teaching about the subject of evidence—the dogma that a rule of evidence is not one which defines obligations but which operates to exclude *relevant* evidence. Doubtless this classification usually makes for clear thinking. It serves to segregate for unified treatment the rules of exclusion which are built around the weaknesses of juries from the mass of substantive rules which incidentally result in excluding evidence of transactions that they render ineffective.[2] Doubtless, also, the parol evi-

---

4. 9 Wigmore, Evidence, § 2430.

5. The quotations are from Uniform Commercial Code, § 2–202 (Official Draft, 1952).

1. Thayer, Preliminary Treatise on Evidence at the Common Law (1898) 409.

2. The principal practical consequence of the now accepted theory that the parol evidence rule is a rule of substantive law, rather than a rule of evidence, is that a failure to object to evidence of an oral agreement is not a waiver, as a failure to assert an objection upon mere exclusionary rule of evidence would be (see § 52, herein). Watkins Salt Co. v. Mulkey, 225 Fed. 739, syl. 1 (C.C.A.N.Y. 1915) (where party did not object to the evidence of the oral agreement, but moved for non-suit on the ground of the parol evidence rule, he sufficiently asserted his position); Higgs v. De Maziroff, 263 N.Y. 473, 189 N.E. 555, syl. 4, 92 A.L.R. 807 (1934) (similar to last). A few courts seem to permit the parol evidence rule to be invoked for the first time on appeal. See Ritson v. Atlas Assur. Co., 272 Mass. 73, 171 N.E. 448, syl. 6 (1930); South Texas Implement & Machine Co. v. Anahuac Canal Co., 280 S.W. 521, syl. 5 (Tex.Comm.App.1926). But the preponderant, and it is believed the fairer, view is that the party must have raised the question in some fashion at the trial, as by motion for judgment on this ground or by request for instructions, as a condition to his raising it on appeal. Cohn v. Chapman, 150 Ark. 258, 234 S.W. 42, syl.

3 (1921); Higgs v. De Maziroff, supra; Note, 92 A.L.R. 810, 811, and see 3 Am.Jur., Appeal and Error, § 253. It is believed that the point should not be allowed to be raised for the first time on motion for new trial, but the only case found is to the contrary. Nagel v. Modern Investment Corp., 132 Conn. 698, 46 A.2d 605 (1946).

It is often stated and as often challenged, that the parol evidence rule does not apply against or in favor of one who is a stranger to the written transaction. Thus an insurance company, defending under a clause in its policy by which the insured warrants that he is the sole and unconditional owner of property insured, may seek to show that when the property was conveyed to the owner it was orally agreed that a lesser interest than that mentioned in the deed should pass. Compare Ex parte St. Paul Fire & Marine Insurance Co., 236 Ala. 543, 184 So. 267, syl. 2 (1938). Or a taxpayer may assert that written contracts made with its employees for the purchase of stock by the latter were really understood to be gifts. See Indianapolis Glove Co. v. United States, 96 F.2d 816, syl. 2–4, C.C.A.Ind., 1938. It seems that the rule of integration does apply to such controversies when the real issue is: What was the effect of the transaction upon the rights of the original parties? See Harris, Does the Parol Evidence Rule Apply When One of the Parties to the Controversy Is a Stranger to the Contract? 22 Ill.L.Rev. 274 (1927); Willis-

dence doctrine fails to fit into this category of rules of evidence with any comfort. Nevertheless, though excluded from the family fold of rules of evidence, it can claim common ancestry in distrust of the jury.

Thayer was not content with charging that the parol evidence rule was misbranded when called a rule of evidence. He tells us that it is a rule of the substantive law defining contracts, deeds, judgments, or the like. Doubtless, in a sense, this is true. What is the rule of substantive law which, as between prior oral expression and later written deed or contract, selects the effective part of the transaction? Wigmore, in one of the most brilliant chapters of his great treatise, shows the relation between the process which he calls "integration" and the whole body of doctrine relating to the creation of jural transactions generally.[3] So far as any widely applicable modern principle may be stated, it is that the terms of the transaction (contract, deed, or the like) are to be obtained from the intention of the parties as revealed by their conduct and language. Among several expressions from which such an agreement or other jural act is sought to be derived, an earlier tentative expression will be rejected in favor of a later expression intended as final. This would be true obviously if both the earlier and the later expression were oral.[4] It is but a simple application of this rationale, to say that where an earlier tentative oral expression is followed by a later writing, then *if the writing was intended* to supersede the earlier expression, the law gives it that effect. This, in effect, is the theory of "integration." It is simple and rational and sets up no special rule for writings different from that applicable to transactions wholly oral. Is it possible that to this clear residuum may be reduced the formidable parol evidence rule, of which Thayer said, "Few things are darker than this, or fuller of subtle difficulties"?

214. The Procedural Aspect of the Parol Evidence Rule: The Judge's Special Control of the Jury: Treatment of This Aspect by the Text-Writers.

The writer takes leave to suggest that while this generalization that the later writing will supersede the earlier oral expression, if the parties so intended, is accurate enough, and is doubtless best classified as a rule of substantive law and not as a rule of evidence, yet it is not the most significant phase of the obscure and complicated technique for protecting writings which has traditionally gone by the name of the parol evidence rule. Indeed, the formula would, of itself, extend no special protection to writings at all. As before suggested, a later *oral* expression, *if so intended,* would as completely supersede all prior negotiations as an "integrating" writing would. So far as this formula suggests, the question of whether the writing was intended to supplant earlier expressions would be assumed to go, in case of dispute, unreservedly to the jury in the normal course. Such a picture of the parol evidence doctrine, it is submitted, throws the high-light upon its family resemblance to the substantive rules for the creation of jural acts, but leaves in the shadow the rugged features distinctive to and characteristic of this phase of judicial administration at the common law. This throwing of light on the family relationship was a notable achievement, which res-

---

ton, Contracts, § 647; 3 Corbin, Contracts, § 596; Note, 54 W.Va.L.Rev. 85 (1951).

3. 9 Wigmore, Evidence, ch. LXXXVIII; cf. Strahorn, The Unity of the Parol Evidence Rule (1929) 14 Minn.L.Rev. 20.

4. Compare the following passage from the judgment in Kain v. Old, 2 B. & C. 627 (1824): "Where the whole matter passes in parol, all that passes

may sometimes be taken together as forming parcel of the contract, though not always, because matter talked of at the commencement of a bargain may be excluded by the language used at its termination. But if the contract be in the end reduced into writing, nothing which is not found in the writing can be considered as a part of the contract."

cued the parol evidence doctrine from the dark avenues of mystery. There is danger that the peculiar, and probably valuable, function which it performs in giving a special protection to writings may be under-emphasized and neglected, and thus become atrophied and finally lost.

That function, of course, is *procedural*. It is the reservation in the trial judge of a special and added authority over the question: Was this writing intended by the parties to displace this asserted oral term or agreement, if there was any such oral expression? Thayer was entirely aware that the parol evidence doctrine had been used by the judges to serve this purpose,[1] but his main preoccupation was with the pioneer job of driving the parol evidence rule out of the "evidence" fold. Wigmore explicitly recognizes this special allocation of authority to the trial judge,[2] but he cites no decisions to the point and apparently treats it as a minor and incidental feature of the subject. Williston, in his lucid and realistic treatment of the matter, follows, in the main, the lines laid down by Thayer and Wigmore. Like them, he touches but casually this question of "Who decides whether the document was intended to supersede that alleged oral agreement?" —a question which will be decisive of the result in most actual cases of competition between an alleged oral agreement and a written document. By couching his discussion of "collateral" oral agreements in terms of "admissibility," [3] however, he reverts to the earlier "rule-of-evidence" phraseology. He implies that the "court" passes on the question of whether the parties intended the signed document to displace the alleged oral agreement by the mechanism of determining, at the outset, whether he will permit the evidence of the alleged oral agreement to be considered by the jury at all.

Wigmore, after stating that this question of intent is for the judge—a proposition which in its frank and naked delegation of the decision of a fact-issue to the judge might cause uneasiness to traditional-minded courts—suggests, in tentative presumption-form, a formula which tends somewhat to narrow the fact-inquiry. He says:

> "In deciding upon this intent, the chief and most satisfactory index for the judge is found in the circumstance whether or not the particular element of the alleged extrinsic negotiation is dealt with at all in the writing. If it is mentioned, covered or dealt with in the writing, then presumably the writing was meant to represent all of the transaction on that element; if it is not, then probably the writing was not intended to embody that element of the negotiation." [4]

---

1. Thayer, Preliminary Treatise on Evidence at the Common Law 401, 409 (1898).

2. 9 Wigmore, Evidence, § 2430, at p. 98: "Whether a particular subject of negotiation is embodied by the writing *depends wholly upon the intent of the parties* thereto. . . . This intent must be sought where always intent must be sought (ante, §§ 42, 1714, 1790), namely in the *conduct and language* of the parties and the *surrounding circumstances.* . . . There is a preliminary question for the judge to decide as to the intent of the parties, and upon this he hears evidence on both sides; his decision here, *pro or con,* concerns merely this question preliminary to the ruling of law. If he decides that the transaction was covered by the writing, he does not decide that the excluded negotiations did not take place, but merely that *if* they did take place they are nevertheless legally immaterial. If he decides that the transaction was not intended to be covered by the writing, he does not decide that the negotiations did take place, but merely that *if* they did, they are legally effective, and he then leaves to the jury the determination of fact whether they did take place." Instances of cases approving this practice: Delzell v. Cent. Pub. Utility Corp., 56 F.Supp. 25, syl. 1, 2 (D.Del.1943); Mitchell v. David, 51 A.2d 375, syl. 3, 4 (Mun.App.D.C.1947) (action on lease, defence, oral agreement to repair).

3. 2 Williston, Contracts (1920) §§ 638, 639.

4. 9 Wigmore, Evidence, § 2430, pp. 98, 99. This formula, though it may seem unduly favorable to the claim under the oral agreement, has been approved in many cases. See, e. g., Senters v. Elkhorn & Jellico Coal Co., 284 Ky. 667, 145 S.W.2d 848, 850 (1940); Arman v. Structiform Eng. Co., 147

Williston makes an extremely significant contribution by formulating a still more flexible and usable rubric, as follows:

"The test of admissibility is much affected by the inherent probability of parties who contract under the circumstances in question, simultaneously making the agreement in writing which is before the court and also the alleged parol agreement. The point is not merely whether the court is convinced that the parties before it did in fact do this, but whether parties so situated generally would or might do so." [5]

This, as will be observed, is given as a test of admissibility, that is, of action by the judge. This formula is paraphrased in the Contracts Restatement, which provides that the writing does not displace the oral agreement if the latter is not inconsistent with the writing and is such "as might naturally be made as a separate agreement by parties situated as were the parties to the written contract." [6]

Corbin [7] recognizes that the question whether the parties have assented to the writing as an integration is a question of fact, but he considers that the judge may either decide it himself, or may invoke "the aid of a jury's verdict." Such flexibility may be convenient, but most courts, it is believed, will want a guide for their feet.

215. The Judge's Control—Treatment of This Aspect in the Decisions.

The anaesthetic qualities of the language-technique about "contradicting," "admissibility," and "completeness" which the courts have inherited, and the pre-occupation of the great text-writers, Thayer, Wigmore, and Williston, with the substantive aspect of the parol evidence doctrine, have contributed to the almost complete absence in the reported appellate opinions of any real discussion of the practical administrative problem of division of power between judge and jury. Doubtless the traditional practice of handling the matter at the trial as one of admissibility, without any jury-intervention, has become so completely second nature to judges and lawyers that it would rarely raise a query. Certainly, the appellate opinions almost universally assume that there is no fact problem but solely a legal point as to admissibility of evidence under a technical rule. In the rare instances of attempts by counsel to invoke a jury hearing on some issue relating to the oral agreement, or of claims on appeal that the trial judge has improperly checked resort to the jury, the appellate

---

Neb. 658, 24 N.W.2d 723, 728, syl. 8 (1946); Danielson v. Bank of Scandinavia, 201 Wis. 392, 230 N.W. 83, 85, 70 A.L.R. 746 (1930).

5. 3 Williston, Contracts, § 638 (rev. ed. Williston and Thompson, 1936). Instances of judicial use of this formula: Magee v. Robinson, 218 Ark. 54, 234 S. W.2d 27, syl. 2 (1950); Kikas v. County Com'rs, 200 Md. 360, 89 A.2d 625, syl. 8 (1952); Taylor v. More, 195 Minn. 448, 263 N.W. 537, syl. 5 (1935); Mitchell v. Lath, 247 N.Y. 377, 160 N.E. 646, 647, syl. 4 (1928) (the oral agreement "must be one that parties would not ordinarily be expected to embody in the writing"; leading case with able majority and dissenting opinions); Gianni v. R. Russel & Co., 281 Pa. 320, 126 Atl. 791, 792 (1924) ("whether parties, situated as were the ones to the contract, would naturally and normally include" the oral agreement in the writing: but the opinion arrays all the conflicting tests as if they were equivalents). Other

recent cases with careful discussions of the problem of integration: In re Simplot's Estate, 215 Iowa 578, 246 N.W. 396 (1933); Markoff v. Kreiner, 180 Md. 150, 23 A.2d 19, syl. 9–19 (1941); Bjornstad v. Northern States Power Co., 195 Minn. 439, 263 N.W. 289 (1935); Warren v. Pulley, 193 Okl. 88, 141 P.2d 288, syl. 1–4 (1943); Central Trust Co. v. Virginia Trust Co., 120 W.Va. 23, 197 S.E. 12 (1938). See the comprehensive annotation, Tests for determining whether entire agreement is embodied in the writing, 70 A.L.R. 752. See also Note, 33 Va.L.Rev. 778 (1947).

6. Am.L.Inst.Restatement Contracts, sec. 240(1) (b) (1932). A Pennsylvania case, Gianni v. R. Russel & Company, 281 Pa. 320, 126 A. 791, 792 (1924), was one of the first in which court, in dealing with this problem made extensive use of the ideas of this modern group of law writers.

7. 3 Corbin, Contracts, § 595 (1951).

courts have, in perhaps a majority of cases, said that the question of whether the writing "expressed the whole agreement," or was "complete," [1] is for the trial judge.

An early and unequivocal pronouncement is that of the New Jersey court in Naumberg v. Young.[2] In that case a tenant of a factory building sued the landlord for breach of an oral guaranty that the engine and boiler in the leased building were in repair and were adequate for the tenant's business. The trial court heard this evidence, but, it appearing that there was a written lease which was silent on the subject, the plaintiff was nonsuited. In affirming this result, the upper court, in reference to the parol evidence doctrine, said:

"Undoubtedly this rule of evidence presupposes that the parties intended to have the terms of their agreement embraced in the written contract. If it was designed that the written contract should contain only a portion of the terms mutually agreed upon, and that the rest should remain in parol, the parties have not put themselves under the protection of the rule. But in what manner shall it be ascertained whether the parties intended to express the whole of their agreement in the written contract? *The question is one for the court, for it relates to the admission or rejection of evidence.*" [3] [Italics mine.]

The Supreme Court of the United States plumped decisively on the same side,[4] and *dicta* or decisions upholding the power of the trial judge to determine whether the writing is "complete," "contains the entire agreement," or was intended to supersede the oral negotiation, have come from California,[5]

---

1. Of course, these are alluringly simplified ways of saying that the parties have intended to supersede the oral agreement, if made, with the document.

2. 44 N.J.L. 331 (1882).

3. Ibid. 338.

4. Seitz v. Brewers' Refrig. Co., 141 U.S. 510, 517, 12 Sup.Ct. 46, 48 (1891) (Oral warranty of machinery asserted against written contract of sale, which contained no warranty. The trial court directed a verdict against the claim of warranty. Affirmed. "Whether the written contract fully expressed the terms of the agreement was a question for the court. . . ."). The court did not mention an interesting decision of the previous year (Bank of British North America v. Cooper, 137 U.S. 473, 11 Sup.Ct. 160), in which the question arose at the trial whether certain cable transfer-bills given by a bank to a customer were decisive as to the terms of the agreement. On appeal, the court said: "Such bills may or may not be the contract. They may be nothing more, and intended to be nothing more, than memoranda or receipts. Whether they are the entire contract or simply in the nature of receipts is not a question of law for the court, but one of fact for the jury." Watkins Salt Co. v. Mulkey, 225 Fed. 739 (C.C.A.2d 1915), follows the Seitz case. Of similar effect is South Florida Lumber Mills v. Breuchaud, 51 F.2d 490, 493 (C.C.A.5th 1931), wherein it was held that the trial judge correctly declined to submit to the jury the question whether earlier oral agreements were superseded by the writing. The interesting opinion, by Hutcheson, circuit judge, adopts the "intention" test on the authority of the Wigmore treatise, and says that its application is "primarily" for the trial court. An unusually clear statement by a trial judge of his duty to determine the preliminary question of fact appears in McDonnell v. General News Bureau, Inc., 93 F.2d 898, 900, C.C.A.Pa.1937.

5. Harrison v. McCormick, 89 Cal. 327, 26 Pac. 830 (1891) (Written contract for sale of "Montana lump" coal, with no mention of sample. Defendant, when sued for price, seeks to show that it was orally agreed that the coal would equal coal previously furnished. Admitted. Judgment for defendant. Held, error: "The question whether a writing is upon its face a complete expression of the agreement of the parties is one of law for the court. . . ."); Thoroman v. David, 199 Cal. 386, 249 Pac. 513 (1926) (A contract to sell house and land was in the form of written escrow instructions to a title guaranty company. There was no reference in the writing to the furniture in the house. Plaintiff, the purchaser, sued for the furniture. The trial judge admitted plaintiff's testimony that the furniture was orally agreed as included. Defendant's witnesses testified in denial. At the trial, apparently without a jury, the court found that the furniture was included. Held, on appeal, that the evidence of the oral agreement was inadmissible, and that the finding was unsupported. The court quotes the above excerpt from the Harrison opinion); Stephan v. Lagerqvest, 52 Cal.App. 519, 199 Pac. 52 (1921) ("Whether writings which pass between parties contain the complete contract which they have made is a question of law, and is to be determined from the face of the instruments.

Connecticut,[6] Minnesota[7] and Pennsylvania.[8] Other cases are not classifiable with entire certainty but seem to lend countenance to this view.[9]

The earliest expression to the contrary comes from Tennessee. In Cobb v. Wallace,[10] an action was brought for conversion by the wrongful detention of a coal barge. The barge belonged to the plaintiff, who loaded it with coal and sold the coal to the defendants. Defendants gave a brief receipt for the coal and barge, which contained a promise that the defendants would pay $3 per day "until the barge is returned." The evidence showed that it had been orally agreed that the barge should be returned as soon as the coal was unloaded at destination. Instead, the defendants kept the barge and hired it out to others. The trial judge charged the jury that the oral contract "could not be looked to," and that under the terms of the writing "the contract for the use of the barge would not be terminated until the defendant so elected." On appeal, the court, in the course of an extended opinion, in which several errors were pointed out, said: "The plaintiffs had the right to have

the question, whether the parol contract had been made as alleged, *and whether the writing introduced embraced all the terms of such previous parol contract,* [italics mine] submitted to the jury; and it was error in the court to withdraw this question of fact from the jury, and to decide it itself." The receipt was apparently intended as a mere partial memorandum, so that, in any view, it seems that the trial judge erred in instructing the jury to disregard the alleged oral agreement. Of course, if the evidence of the oral agreement was competent, but the making of the oral agreement was disputed, it was for the jury to determine that dispute. But the italicized phrase is the first suggestion (so far as the writer has discovered) that the jury is to decide, free from preliminary intervention by the trial judge, whether the writing was intended to supplant all prior negotiations.[11] How far the court meant to go in this decision is questionable. It gave only a sideglance at this minor point, unnecessary as it was to the disposition of the case.

As is customary, the idea is uncritically adopted by the encyclopedias,[12] and from them in a sprinkling of judicial opinions.[13]

. . .."). Seemingly contra, is the language of the opinion in Luitweiler Co. v. Ukiah Co., 16 Cal. App. 198, 207, 116 Pac. 707, 711 (1911), affirmed by the Supreme Court, without adopting the opinion, 16 Cal.App. 198, 116 Pac. 712 (1911).

6. Brosty v. Thompson, 79 Conn. 133, 136, 64 Atl. 1, 2 (1906) ("For the trial court," but it does not appear whether there was a jury); Pyskoty v. Sobusiak, 109 Conn. 593, 145 Atl. 58 (1929).

7. Taylor v. More, 195 Minn. 448, 263 N.W. 537, syl. 6 (1935).

8. Gianni v. R. Russel & Co., 281 Pa. 320, 126 Atl. 791, syl. 4 (1924); Walker v. Saricks, 360 Pa. 594, 63 A.2d 9, syl. 2 (1949).

9. Offutt v. Doyle, 135 Ky. 296, 122 S.W. 156(4) (1909); Ft. Worth & D. C. Ry. v. Wright, 30 Tex. Civ.App. 234, 70 S.W. 335 (1902); Standard Scale & Supply Co. v. Baltimore Enamel and Novelty Co., 136 Md. 278, 110 Atl. 486 (1920). See also McNeeley v. McWilliams, 13 Ont.App.Rep. 324, 330 (1886), and the discussion of this and other Canadian cases, by Professor McRae, in 4 Canadian Encyclopedic Digest (Ont. ed. 1928) 803.

10. 5 Coldwell 539 (Tenn.1868).

11. The same confused assumption that the jury must determine both whether the writing was exclusive, and, if not, whether the alleged oral agreement actually was made, appears in a later Tennessee case. Hines v. Willcox, 96 Tenn. 148, 159, 33 S.W. 914, 916 (1896) ("The question as to whether the entire contract was reduced to writing, or an independent collateral agreement was made, was a question of fact, and where there was any evidence to sustain the contention, it was a matter for the jury to determine, and not for the court.").

12. e. g., 6 R.C.L. 55; 22 C.J. 1291.

13. Gordon v. Curtis Bros., 119 Ore. 55, 248 Pac. 158 (1926). In Hirsch v. Salem Mills Co., 40 Ore. 601, 604, 67 Pac. 949, 68 Pac. 733 (1902), the question of whether the oral contract survived the writing was held to be one of "fact" not determinable on the pleadings, but only "by a trial and upon testimony," but this does not quite mean that the jury must decide it. Two interesting Massachusetts cases may be thought to indicate a tendency toward

Conceivably, all that some of the opinion writers who place this question in the jury's hands mean to suggest is that after the judge has approved the oral agreement as one which might normally stand with the writing, he should still leave to the jury to say whether these parties actually did intend to supersede the oral agreement. If so, they are unobjectionable. Always, however, the treatment is casual, the traditional and seemingly contrary view is ignored, and the extent to which the courts mean to go in turning the question over to the jury is beclouded by the language that the jury must say whether the writing "contains the entire agreement." This may mean, whether the writing was intended to supersede the oral agreement or, less probably, it may mean, whether there was in fact any oral agreement at all outside the writing.

In this comparison, the balance of clear-cut judicial opinion would seem to incline toward the traditional practice, approved by the Federal Supreme Court.

216. The Judge's Control—Expediency of the Various Solutions.

Recent opinions signalize a new judicial willingness to search for a sound engineering technique in dividing the load between judge and jury in law-suits where alleged spoken words are set up in rivalry with written words.[1] They challenge us to an examination of the feasibility of some of the available expedients.

First, the crude, older method of choice by the trial judge between the rule against "varying, altering, or adding to, a writing," and the formulas for "incomplete writings" and "collateral contracts," with the real motives for the choice left almost inarticulate, while it furnished the needed protection to writings, is specious and outworn. It falsely couches in terms of a technical rule of exclusion a device for giving special power to the judge to determine at the threshold fact-questions (Was the oral agreement made? Was it abandoned?) upon which the genuineness of the alleged oral terms, as part of the final bargain, depends.[2]

Second, we may advocate the plan of resolving the whole matter into one of the application of the standard of expressed intent, with no special treatment for written transactions, except this, that the trial judge shall determine as a preliminary fact-question whether a given alleged oral agreement was intended by the parties to be abandoned when the writing was signed. This solution has the merit of comparative simplicity, welcome after a century of obscurantism about "contradicting" writings. It has behind it

---

the enlarged view of the jury's function, but in Thomas v. Barnes, 156 Mass. 581, 31 N.E. 683 (1892), the writing was not signed by the party who asserted the oral contract, and in Corey v. Woodin, 195 Mass. 464, 81 N.E. 260 (1907), the question of intention to supersede the oral contract with the writing, which was treated as a jury-question, related to a novation rather than an "integration." See also MacDonald v. Kavanaugh, 259 Mass. 439, 156 N.E. 740, syl. 4 (1927).

1. See, e. g., Gianni v. Russel, 281 Pa. 320, 126 Atl. 791, 792 (1924) (Schaffer, J.: "When does the oral agreement come within the field embraced by the written one? This can be answered by comparing the two, and determining whether parties, situated as were the ones to the contract, would naturally and normally include the one in the other if it were made. If they relate to the same subject-matter, and are so interrelated that both would be executed

at the same time and in the same contract, the scope of the subsidiary agreement must be taken to be covered by the writing. This question must be determined by the court. . . ." A clear recognition by a trial judge of his duty to determine the preliminary question of fact appears in McDonnell v. General News Bureau, Inc., 93 F.2d 898, 900, (C.C.A.Pa.1937).

2. Compare the rule that when the genuineness of the writing itself is challenged all that the trial judge requires, before admitting the writing, is only a *prima facie* showing. If the adversary's evidence raises a dispute, the issue is for the jury. Hamsher v. Kline, 57 Pa. 397 (1868); Flournoy v. Warden, 17 Mo. 435 (1853). For discussion of the functions of judge and jury in dealing with fact-questions which condition the admissibility of evidence under technical rules of exclusion, see § 53, herein.

the great authority of the Wigmore treatise. It presents these difficulties, however. In the first place, judges are reluctant to avow an assumption of control over the ascertainment of intent, so traditionally associated with jury-responsibility in the fields of crime, tort and contract. It is significant that even the enlightened opinion in the *Gianni* case, though quoting approvingly from the section of the Wigmore treatise which contains the statement that the question is one of intent, and is for the judge to decide, does not quote that statement, but prefers rather to place the question in the judge's hands in terms of what would normally have been done by parties in these circumstances. A further, and overriding, objection is this: the intention formula leaves out of account the principal need for a special hand-on-the-rein by the judge. This need is that of striking down at the outset claims of oral variants on the writing, variants which in fact the judge believes never were entered into but are fabrications, designed or unconscious. As already suggested the real service of the parol evidence doctrine is here. Seldom from the cases does one gain the impression that the dispute is really over whether an admitted oral agreement was intended to be superseded by the writing. Where the adversary's position is to be gleaned from the report, which is surprisingly seldom, it appears most often that he denies that any such oral counter-agreement was ever entered into. Where the judge's real doubts are on this score, little help is derived from a formula which directs attention solely to whether—assuming it to have been made—the oral agreement was intended by the parties to be superseded. It is comparable to the situation where a judge is called on to consider whether a certain copy of a document meets the requirements of the best evidence rule, when the real issue is whether the original document from which it was copied is not itself a forgery.

But a third course naturally presents itself. Why set up any special safeguards here? Treat the question of the genuineness of the alleged oral agreement and that of the parties' intention to supplant it by the document, as other fact-questions are treated. Let the trial judge use the same machinery for control of the jury which he always has available. If, in his opinion, reasonable minds could reach but one conclusion from the evidence, he is empowered to withdraw that question from the jury. Perhaps if judges were called upon habitually to use this device in the speech-versus-document situation, it would lend itself readily enough to the adequate protection of written transactions from the vagaries of juries. As such situations offer themselves to the trial judge, however, one party testifies that an agreement outside the writing was made, and that it was understood that this outside agreement was to be binding, together with the writing. Naturally, a trial judge—especially a timid, elective one—would shrink from a ruling that reasonable men could not believe this direct assertion on the stand. We are here in the realm of the vaguest opinion, where every conclusion is overweighted with the individual experiences and preconceptions of its advocate. With due realization of this, the writer believes that the usual formula for jury-control is inadequate here, and that the traditional reservation of a special and added power in the judge is desirable.

Dean Hale suggests a fourth solution: "The basic evils of the rule in its present form are, first, that it is a pretense, and second, that the collateral inquiries which arise whenever it confronts the court are artificial, capricious, and arbitrary. The cure. Let the parol evidence rule be phrased and operate as a rule of presumption. When the terms of an agreement have been reduced to writing by the parties, let it be presumed that the writing contains with exactness and completeness all those terms, but allow this presumption to be overcome by clear and convincing proof to the contrary." [3] This proposal could mean that the evidence must be "clear and convincing" to the judge before he shall admit the evidence of outside oral expressions for the jury's consideration, or it could mean that he shall admit it without scrutiny simply instructing them not to act on it unless "clear and convincing" to them. If the former, the control is firm and the proposal would be a desirable solution; if the latter, the control would, it is believed, be almost ineffectual.

There remains a fifth expedient. As foreshadowed in the above discussion, the writer urges its claims as the most acceptably fashioned for use by our present judges with our present juries. The expedient suggested is this: Let the trial judge, after hearing the testimony as to the alleged oral agreement, including the evidence of substantiating circumstances, compare it with the terms of the writing, and if he considers that it is one which parties situated as these were would "naturally and normally" have recited in the writing itself, had they made it and intended it to stand, then he will reject the evidence thus tentatively heard. On the other hand, if (in the terms of the Restatement) he concludes that the alleged oral pact is "such an agreement as might normally be made as a separate agreement by parties situated as were the parties to the written contract," then he will allow the evidence to go to the jury.[4] In this way, the argument on the objection or motion to exclude will be aimed at abstract impersonal probabilities, and the ruling will not brand any witness as a liar. He will still, if he admits the evidence and the proof is conflicting, submit to the jury the issues: was the oral agreement made as claimed, and, if so, was it intended to be displaced by the written terms?

If the parol evidence doctrine is to be administered chiefly by juries and not by judges, its special protection for written transactions dwindles and fades. Perhaps such special protection is no longer needed. The telephone, and the urgent call for high speed in certain types of important transactions, such as security trading, have accustomed business men to rely upon word-of-mouth, and to dispense with the safeguard of writing.[5] And conceivably, jurors, in this day of

---

3. Hale, The Parol Evidence Rule, 4 Ore.L.Rev. 91 (1925). A similar solution is urged in the excellent note by Bressler and Taylor, A Critique of the Parol Evidence Rule in Pennsylvania, 100 U.Pa.L.Rev. 703, 721 (1952).

4. Of course, by familiar process, in transactions of standardized pattern and frequent recurrence in litigation, the judges narrow the range of judgment by seeking to treat the cases of each type uniformly. Thus, in a given jurisdiction, we find numerous such rules as that oral agreements to treat a deed as a mortgage may be shown, or that oral agreements that an indorser is to be treated as a co-maker may not. A similar crystallizing process, accompanied by a counter-process in which, from time to time, some of the crystals are dissolving again into fluid, is characteristic of the administration of justice under wide general concepts, such as "reasonable care," "fraud," "judicial power" and *id omne genus.*

5. This is suggested in a letter from Professor Nathan Isaacs, from which I take the liberty of quoting: "In the first place, the business man of today relies and must rely less and less on writing than he did even fifty years ago. The telephone has something to do with this change, but a more important factor is the speed required in modern business. It is true that our facilities for rapid writing have increased, but our need for rapidity in transactions has increased much more rapidly. The result is that the business man is accustomed to seeing millions of dollars worth of securities change hands on the stock exchange without the scratch of a pen. But this is not the whole or even the most important part of the story. Even where writing is resorted to two forces have conspired to prevent the writing from containing or even purporting to contain the "whole" contract. One of these is the growing complexity of transactions, and the other is a phase of the speed already mentioned, which shows itself in the brevity of business letters and other memoranda.

"To fill the gaps which necessarily result in the modern business contract, we resort more and more to the standardizing elements (customs, statutes, rules of trade associations, chambers of commerce, exchanges), but a great many blanks still remain to

universal education, are more able and willing to sift critically and intelligently testimony about oral negotiations preceding a writing. Perhaps, on the contrary, it might be thought that the jury, even assuming a personnel more intelligent than that of fifty years ago, is less adequate than ever, in view of the increased demands of present-day litigation.

Around considerations such as these should center the discussion which will shape the future evolution of the parol evidence doctrine. The protection afforded by that doctrine will wax or wane as the judge or the jury takes the upper hand in its administration.

TOPIC 2

INTERPRETATION [1]

217. The Parol Evidence Rule Inapplicable to Evidence Offered in Aid of Interpretation.

The rule of Integration makes the written instrument the sole repository of the legal transaction, in the sense that the transaction (contract, transfer, release or the like) must be derived from the written terms alone. But written instruments are not self-sufficient and automatic mandates which the courts can always enforce merely by inspecting the instrument, and stamping it with a judicial fiat. Written words can be translated into appropriate action by the court only

through the process of ascertaining what the words stand for in the way of particular conduct or particular tangible objects. This process of interpretation is one which every human expression is subjected to wherever it is sought later to be used by human beings as a measure of conduct. The party who seeks to perform his contract, or claim his rights under a deed, the lawyer who advises about the rights created by the writing, the judge who decrees its enforcement, and the party who undertakes to obey the decree— each of these must interpret a writing. This process is often unnoticed and frequently simple, but often again the meaning of the writing is a contested question between the parties, and evidence is adduced to solve the issue. The distinction between such interpretative evidence even where it consists of expressions of the parties to the instrument, and evidence of such expressions when offered to be used as a part of the contract, deed or other transaction, and hence prohibited by the Parol Evidence Rule, is clear. The one type of evidence concedes the supremacy of the writing and merely seeks to illuminate its meaning. The other seeks to displace, or annex itself to, the writing. Evidence of the prior statements, negotiations, and agreements of the parties, offered strictly for the purpose of interpretation, may be excluded under restrictions upon interpretative sources discussed in the following sec-

be filled in by oral understanding. The real danger therefore to the business man that comes from a strict enforcement of the parol evidence rule, is that as contracts are made today essential parts are in danger of being excluded. In other words, I mean to suggest that however fitting the parol evidence rule may have been when it grew up, it is not in strict accord with the needs of business today."

1. A comprehensive treatment of the entire subject of interpretation, with its numerous rules, often varying in respect to contracts, conveyances, wills, and statutes, is impracticable in a brief treatise on Evidence. Nevertheless, its relationship to the Parol Evidence Rule is so intimate that it is essential in treating the former to show how far the

restrictions of the rule of integration are relaxed to let in for another purpose the prior and contemporary agreements which if offered professedly as additional parts of the transaction embodied in the writing would be excluded. Consequently, the emphasis in this treatment is upon that small area of the law of interpretation where it neighbors the Parol Evidence Rule, namely, the admissibility of evidence of prior and contemporaneous statements and negotiations of the parties to aid in interpreting a writing. As to this, see 9 Wigmore, Evidence, §§ 2460–2467; 3 Williston, Contracts (Rev.Ed.1936), §§ 629, 630; 3 Corbin, Contracts, §§ 538–543 (1951); 32 C.J.S., Evidence, §§ 959–962; 20 Am.Jur., Evidence, §§ 1141–1162; Dec.Dig., Evidence, ☞448–463.

tions, but such evidence is not within the prohibition of the Parol Evidence Rule.[2]

218. By Whose Standard Is the Meaning to Be Tested?

A writing provides that "one ton" of sugar shall be delivered at a certain time and place. A ton may mean 2000 or 2200 pounds. The weight given, again, may mean net weight after deduction for the weight of the container, or it may mean the gross weight. Let us assume that the writing is a contract between A and B, and that to the community generally the ordinary meaning of the quoted words is 2000 pounds net. But locally, in the sugar trade the words mean 2000 pounds gross. To both A and B, however, the words meant 2200 pounds net. Again, to vary the facts we may suppose that A attributed one meaning to the words (different from the others) and B still another or fourth meaning. Wigmore distinguishes these as follows:[1] ". . . the possible standards fall roughly into four classes,—the standard of the community or *popular* standard, meaning the common and normal sense of words; the *local* standard, including the special usages of a religious sect, a body of traders, an alien population, or a local dialect; the *mutual* standard, covering those meanings which are peculiar to both or all the parties to a transaction, but shared in common by them; and the *individual* standard of one party to an act, as different from that of the other party or parties, if any."

In the process of fixing a meaning upon the writing so that it may be the basis for concrete action at the hands of the court— the process of interpretation—which of these standards of meaning will the court be guided by? The choice may lead to different results.

It seems clear, first, that the general guide in interpretation is to give effect to the expectations of the party, or all the parties, to the instrument, so far as this can be done with due regard to the security of written transactions generally. Normally, the court can, unless information is given to the contrary, assume that the party or parties used the words in the *popular* or normal acceptation, and would apply that standard.

But if it appeared that at the time and place of the writing's execution, persons in the situation of the party or parties attached a "local" or special provincial or trade meaning to the words, it would seem *prima facie* more probable that this local, rather than the general popular signification was the one

---

2. Rotberg v. Dodwell & Co., 152 F.2d 100, syl. **3, 4** (C.C.A.N.Y.1945) (oral statement of party's attorney that he would require release of future claims admissible to show general release was meant to include such claims) ; Arbuckle v. Lumbermen's Mut. Casualty Co., 129 F.2d 791, syl. 2 (C.C.A.N.Y. 1942) (where policy ambiguous as to where car was to be stored, insured's statements at time policy issued admissible) ; Cohn v. Kramer, 124 F.2d 791, syl. 5 (C.C.A.Mich.1942) (oral promise by lessee to get films as good as those at Senate Theater admitted to show what was meant by written promise to get product and adopt policy which would insure successful operation of theater leased) ; Stoops v. Smith, 100 Mass. 63, 1 Am.Rep. 85, 97 Am.Dec. 76 (1868) (action on written contract to publish plaintiff's card in advertising chart ; evidence of defendant's statement as to what kind of chart would be published and at what places, wrongly excluded) ; Weston v. Ball, 80 N.H. 275, 116 Atl. 99, syl. 2–4 (1922) (illuminating opinion by Peaslee,

J.) ; Hammond v. Capitol City Mut. Fire Ins. Co., 151 Wis. 62, 138 N.W. 92, Ann.C.1914C, 57 (policy covering property of "Hammond Bros." evidence of oral agreement with agent that it should cover individual property of partner, as well as partnership property) ; 3 Corbin, Contracts, § 543 (1951). But compare Armstrong Paint and Varnish Works v. Continental Can Co., 301 Ill. 102, 133 N.E. 711 (1921), where the court draws a distinction between evidence of "surrounding circumstances" and "conversations and parol agreements" holding the former admissible as interpretative evidence and the latter inadmissible. So also Remington Rand Inc. v. Sugarland Industries, 137 Tex. 409, 153 S.W.2d 477, 484 (1941), and see 3 Williston, Contracts, § 630 (Rev.Ed.1936). Contra: Laclede Const. Co. v. T. J. Moss Tie Co., 185 Mo. 25, 84 S.W. 76, 88 (1894).

1. 9 Wigmore, Evidence, § 2460. See also Am.L.Inst. Restatement, Contracts, § 227, comment.

adopted, and the court would apply that meaning.[2]

A more difficult problem arises where the sole party (as the testator in a will, or donor in a gift) has, or the parties (as in case of a contract) have, adopted a meaning different from the "popular" meaning and from the "local" meaning if there is one. Wigmore contends that here the special meaning attached by the party or parties should again prevail,[3] and Corbin seems to agree.[4] Applied with caution,[5] this approach seems best calculated to attain justice in the greatest number of cases. Against this view must be opposed that of Williston,[6] and of the weight of authority,[7] which for reasons of policy accepts the risks of injustice in a particular case rather than to permit written transactions generally to be put to the hazard of too wide a possible range of individual interpretations,

which might be thought to facilitate fabricated claims. On the other hand, if the words have several possible "ordinary" or "local or trade" meanings, then the "mutual" standard (or individual standard in a unilateral transaction) if it coincides with one of these, may with comparative safety (since it conforms to a meaning more widely accepted than merely by the parties) be accepted.[8]

Thus far the two types of transaction, unilateral or one-party transactions such as wills or gifts, and bilateral transactions participated in by two or more parties such as contracts, have been treated without distinction, for they are alike when in the bilateral transaction all the parties agree on the same meaning. But in a bilateral transaction, it is clear that no one of the parties is entitled to have his private, unexpressed meaning

---

2. Eustis Packing Co. v. Martin, 122 F.2d 648, syl. 1, 2 (C.C.A.Fla.1941) (evidence of local trade meaning of term in written contract, "good and merchantable citrus fruit"); Ermolieff v. RKO Radio Pictures, 19 Cal.2d 543, 122 P.2d 3, syl. 3–5 (1942) (in interpreting a film distribution contract, evidence that in the moving picture trade "United Kingdom" includes Eire, admissible); Kelly v. Robb, 58 Tex. 377, syl. 1 (1883) (evidence that locally in the lumber trade "saw timber" means pine suitable for manufacture of lumber); 9 Wigmore, Evidence, §§ 2463, 2464; Dec.Dig., Evidence, ☞457.

3. 9 Wigmore, Evidence, § 2462. But he concedes that the proof that the parties did agree upon a private meaning should be required to be convincing and that when it is evidenced by antecedent oral agreements these should not be used to evade the parol evidence policy against substituting oral terms for the written. Id., § 2463. It must be remembered that both the parol evidence rule and the restrictions on evidence of the parties' expressions are partly motivated by the courts' unwillingness to trust the protection of writings to juries. 9 Wigmore, Evidence, § 2461, p. 188. It is believed that the formula developed by Williston for use in integration cases (see § 214, supra) could be adapted for use here, when an oral agreement is offered as evidence of the intended meaning of the writing, by stating as the test, If the parties had intended to attach to the written word the meaning indicated by this oral agreement, would they

have been expected naturally and normally to add a written explanation to that effect?

4. 3 Corbin, Contracts, § 539.

5. See note 3, supra.

6. 3 Williston, Contracts, § 611 (Rev.Ed.1936).

7. Rowe v. Chesapeake Mineral Co., 156 F.2d 752, syl. 5 (C.C.A.6th 1946) ("coal and mineral" in deed, unambiguous); Trumbull Elec. Mfg. Co. v. John Cooke Co., 130 Conn. 12, 31 A.2d 393, syl. 5 (1943) (good discussion by Ells, J.); Insley v. Myers, 192 Md. 292, 64 A.2d 126, syl. 5 (1949); and cases cited 9 Wigmore, Evidence, § 2463, note 6. See also the cases in note 2, next section.

It seems, however, that this doctrine would be relaxed to permit a showing of a private meaning of the parties embodied in a code agreed on, this being so verifiable as to create little danger of imposture. 9 Wigmore, Evidence, § 2463, but see 3 Williston, Contracts, § 612. So also, it seems, to permit a showing of the property intended to be covered by an erroneous description. See Sands v. Sands, 122 W. Va. 697, 12 S.E.2d 918 (1941) and comment by Dean Hardman, 47 W.Va. L.Q. 319.

8. Walsh v. Walsh, 18 Cal.2d 439, 116 P.2d 62, syl. 8 (1941) (where language employed in contract fairly susceptible of either of two constructions, without doing violence to its usual and ordinary import, conversations and declarations of the parties may be proved to show their intent).

prevail as against the others,[9] but the court must here, as even Wigmore agrees, apply the ordinary meaning, or if there is one, the local meaning.[10] The same principle protects the purchaser without notice, against any claim that a meaning not known to him and peculiar to a previous party or parties should be enforced against him.[11] Finally, it must be borne in mind that the process of interpretation which seeks to pronounce, as near as may be, the actual or probable meaning of the parties, must have some *expression* upon which to act, for an unexpressed meaning or intention can be given no effect as part of a written transaction.[12]

219. Ambiguity as Prerequisite to the Admissibility of Evidence to Aid in Interpretation.

Two propositions, one the converse of the other, are commonly announced in the deci-sions on this subject. These are, first, that where the writing is ambiguous extrinsic evidence will be received to explain its mean-ing, and, second, that if the writing is not ambiguous, such evidence will not be re-ceived. As to the first proposition, there can be no dissent, and all courts and writers agree as to the soundness of admitting evidence to resolve doubts in the meaning of the writ-ing.[1]

The second branch of the rule, to the ef-fect that if the writing is clear and unam-biguous, extrinsic evidence to explain its meaning will not be received, likewise finds frequent expression in the decisions.[2] Never-theless, it requires qualifications for the rule as usually announced is so broad as to be misleading. In the first place, no writing which is to be the basis of judicial action can be considered only in the abstract.[3] Evi-

---

9. Pettee v. Omega Chapter, 86 N.H. 496, 170 Atl. 1, 3, syl. 2 (1934) (thoughts or acts of one party before the contract, not known to other not usable to ex-plain meaning); Marx v. Luling Co-Operative Ass'n (1897), 17 Tex.Civ.App. 408, 43 S.W. 596, syl. 2 (A guaranty to a corporation's creditor was signed by its directors. The terms were such as would normal-ly create individual liability on the signers, but they added after their names "As Board of Directors." Held, evidence inadmissible that they intended by this added expression to negative individual liability where this purpose was unknown to the creditor.); 3 Corbin, Contracts, § 538, p. 45 (1951); Atlantic Northern Airlines v. Schwimmer, 12 N.J. 293, 96 A. 2d 652, syl. 6 (1953). See also Eustis Mining Co. v. Beer, Sondheimer & Co., 239 Fed. 976, 984, D.C.1917; Smart v. Huckins, 82 N.H. 342, 134 Atl. 520, syl. 8, 10 (1926) (declaration by grantor, at a time subse-quent to the deed, as to land intended to be conveyed, inadmissible).

10. Jefferson Fire Ins. Co. v. Greenwood (Tex.Civ. App.1911), 141 S.W. 319, syl. 2 (applicant returned fire policy with letter to effect that it was not drawn up as desired, and that the agent should "let it alone until I see you before you make another policy"; held, evidence that he meant for policy to remain in force, inadmissible).
To be compared with the Marx Case, in the next pre-ceding note is Southern Bade Co. v. Smith (Tex.Civ. App.1911) 141 S.W. 185, syl. 2, where a written prom-ise, "We agree" to pay, was signed "S., President of the Southern Cotton Association," and evidence was admitted to show that it was agreed *by all parties* that S. should not be individually liable.

11. Axelrad and Langacre, Parol Evidence and the Bona Fide Purchaser, 5 U. Chi.L.Rev. 656 (1938), 9 Wigmore, Evidence, § 2463, p. 207.

12. Meader v. Allen, 110 Iowa 588, 81 N.W. 799, syl. 2, 3 (1900) (in well-drilling contract landowner was to furnish "casing"; held, can prove parties under-stood "casing" was 5 inch casing, but cannot give evidence that it was understood that owner would furnish pump and tubing, not mentioned in con-tract); 3 Williston, Contracts, § 610 (Rev.Ed.1936).

1. Union Paving Co. v. United States, 150 F.2d 390, syl. 3 (C.C.A.Calif.1945); Leslie v. Minneapolis Teachers Retirement Fund Ass'n, 218 Minn. 369, 16 N.W.2d 313, syl. 1–3 (1944); 32 C.J.S., Evidence, § 959, note 50; Dec.Dig., Evidence, ⊕448(b)(c).

2. See, e. g., Hines v. Ward Baking Co., 155 F.2d 257, 260 (C.C.A.Ill.1946) ("Illinois recognizes the ele-mentary principle that, where no doubt exists as to the meaning of words used in a writing, extrinsic evidence is not admissible to show the intention of the parties in using those words or the circum-stances surrounding the execution of the agree-ment."); Tupper v. Hancock, 319 Mass. 105, 64 N.E.2d 441, syl. 3 (1946) (general release cannot be shown to have been conditional); Kleih v. Van Schoyk, 250 Wis. 413, 27 N.W.2d 490, syl. 2, 4 (1947) (conveyance of "right of way" could not be read as giving fee simple); 32 C.J.S., Evidence, § 959, note 70; Dec.Dig., Evidence, ⊕448(d).

3. Compare Adams v. Maris, 213 S.W. 622, 624 (Tex. Com.App.1919), where the court said, "In fact, it is

dence of the surrounding circumstances must be resorted to, in order to identify the sub-ject-matter [4] and the persons referred to in the writing [5] and to reveal the relations of the parties and the situation from which the transaction arose.[6] Secondly, a writing may when read by the judge, who in the absence of evidence as to local or technical meanings, will apply the ordinary sense to the words, have a certain clear meaning, but notwith-standing this apparent clarity, evidence should be admitted to show that the words were used by both parties in a special, local, or trade sense variant from the ordinary meaning.[7] If so used, this special meaning should prevail, though a meaning peculiar to the parties and not backed by local or trade usage would not. If these views are cor-rect, then, the rule could be more accurately stated as follows: if a writing, when con-sidered in the light of all relevant evidence as to the character of its subject-matter and the facts (other than the parties' views and expressions) surrounding its execution, has a clear and sensible meaning, when the words are read in their ordinary sense or in any local or technical sense which the evi-dence shows to have been appropriate, it is not competent to vary that meaning by proof that the party or parties attached a different, individual meaning to the writing. It is believed that the cases in which the more sweeping rule is announced will be found on their facts to require no broader statement than the foregoing. Moreover, even as thus qualified, it is doubtful whether the search for the mutual or individual mean-ing should be restricted by rule. The wiser and juster approach is that of Bowen, L.J., who thought that the "plain meaning rule" should be regarded "not so much as a canon of construction as a counsel of caution, to warn you . . . not to give way to guesses or mere speculation as to the prob-abilities of an intention, but to act only on such evidence as can lead a reasonable man to a distinct conclusion." [8]

220. Evidence Receivable to Aid in Inter-pretation:[1] Facts Constituting the Background: Negotiations and Agreements between the Par-ties: Practical Construction: Declarations of Intention.

Whenever a writing is found to require interpretation, the relevant background facts,

---

well nigh impossible to consider in the abstract words expressive of an intention."

4. Rockford Trust Co. v. Moon, 370 Ill. 250, 18 N.E.2d 447, syl. 3 (1938) (parol evidence will be received to apply deed to subject-matter but not to change legal effect); Maxwell-Davis, Inc. v. Hooper, 317 Mass. 149, 57 N.E.2d 537, syl. 1 (1944); Murphy v. Dilworth, 137 Tex. 32, 151 S.W.2d 1004, syl. 2 (1941) (even though contract unambiguous on its face, parol evi-dence admissible to apply it to subject with which it deals); Fuller v. Virginia Trust Co., 183 Va. 704, 33 S.E.2d 201, syl. 7 (1945); Dec.Dig., Evidence, ⊕⥺458, 460.

5. Hamlyn v. Hamlyn, 103 Ind.App. 333, 7 N.E.2d 644, syl. 2 (1937) (to show whether "children or grandchildren" was intended to include adoptive children); In re Soper's Estate, 196 Minn. 60, 264 N.W. 427, syl. 2 (1935) (to show that "my wife" in trust instrument was intended by donor to mean not his lawful wife whom he had deserted, but the per-son with whom he was living and who was thought by the community to be his wife); Dec.Dig., Evi-dence, ⊕⥺459. Similarly parol evidence may be used to show whether a party contracted in an individual or representative capacity. Lincoln Nat. Life Ins. Co. v. Harwick, 115 F.2d 892, syl. 3–5 (C.C.A.Ill. 1941); Dec.Dig., Evidence, ⊕⥺459(2).

6. Reilly Tar & Chem. Corp. v. Lewis, 301 Ill.App. 459, 23 N.E.2d 243, syl. 5 (1939); First Nat. Bank v. Rush, 210 S.W. 521, syl. 2 (Tex.Comm.App.1919) (though writing unambiguous on its face); Kleuter v. Joseph Schlitz Brewing Co., 143 Wis. 347, 128 N.W. 43, 32 L.R.A.,N.S., 383 (1910) (able opinion by Marshall, J.).

7. See authorities cited in § 218, note 2, supra.

8. In re Jodell, 44 Ch.D. 590 (1890). Other able crit-ical comments: 9 Wigmore, Evidence, §§ 2461, 2462; 3 Corbin, Contracts, § 542 (1951); 3 Williston, Con-tracts, § 609 (Rev.Ed.1936); McBaine, Rule against Disturbing Plain Meanings, 31 Calif.L.Rev. 145 (1943).

1. 9 Wigmore, Evidence, §§ 2463–2467, 4 Jones, Com-mentaries on Evidence, § 1541 (2d ed. 1946); Phip-son, Evidence, Ch. 47 (9th Ed. 1952); 20 Am.Jur., Evidence, §§ 1159–1162; 32 C.J.S., Evidence, § 960; Dec.Dig., Contracts, ⊕⥺175(2), Evidence, ⊕⥺448c.

such as those bearing on the nature and condition of the property involved, the relations of the parties, and the surrounding circumstances generally, may be freely shown so that the court, in ascertaining their intentions, may place itself in the shoes of the parties.[2]

We have seen that opinions of courts and text-writers differ as to when in the case of multiple-party writings it is allowable to apply the "mutual" standard of the intention of the parties as the guide to interpretation, but that all agree that this should be done when in the normal or popular sense the words admit of several meanings, or where there is doubt whether the normal or some local or trade meaning is intended.[3] When a search for the mutual meaning is allowable,

then the negotiations of the parties, conversations, declarations of one made in the other's presence, and oral agreements leading up to the transaction are receivable to show the sense in which they understood the words in the writing.[4] But in construing a writing which embodies such a multi-lateral transaction, one party cannot offer his own declarations as to what he understood by the words, not heard or assented to by the other party.[5] Nor can he offer his testimony as to what he intended by the words.[6] In such transactions the individual standard is clearly inapplicable.[7] It seems, however, that to show the "mutual" meaning one party's declarations as to his meaning should be usable as admissions by his adversary to show that

---

[2]. See, e. g., In re Tidewater Coal Exchange, 292 Fed. 225, 232, syl. 3 (C.C.A.2, 1923, by Learned Hand, D.J.); Sarnia Steamships, Ltd. v. Continental Grain Co., 125 F.2d 362, syl. 1, 2 (C.C.A.7, 1942); In re Landwehr's Estate, 286 Mich. 698, 282 N.W. 873, syl. 3 (1938); Atlantic Northern Air Lines v. Schwimmer, 12 N.J. 293, 96 A.2d 652, syl. 3, 11 (1953) (able opinion by Heher, J.); 9 Wigmore, Evidence, § 2470; 32 C.J.S. 911. Previous contracts or dealings between the parties may be a relevant and admissible part of the background. Ingram-Day Lumber Co. v. Schultz, 45 F.2d 359, syl. 4 (C.C.A.Ill.1930) (to ascertain the subject-matter and the sense in which terms were used); 32 C.J.S. 906, 907.

[3]. See §§ 218, 219, above.

[4]. Air Conditioning Corp. v. Honaker, 296 Ill.App. 221, 16 N.E.2d 153, syl. 4 (1938) (statements of seller's agent to buyer received as evidence of meaning of "Air Conditioner" in sale contract); Stoops v. Smith, 100 Mass. 63, 1 Am.Rep. 85, 97 Am.D. 76 (1868) (defendant's statements to plaintiff as to kind of chart he would publish received as evidence of meaning of "advertising chart" in contract); Smith v. Vose & Sons Piano Co., 194 Mass. 193, 80 N.E. 527, 9 L.R.A.,N.S., 966, 120 Am.St.Rep. 539 (1907) (contract to procure "water" by drilling, held, proper to show understanding of parties that fresh water, not salt, was meant); Atlantic Northern Air Lines v. Schwimmer, 12 N.J. 293, 96 A.2d 652, syl. 11 (1953) (antecedent negotiations and attendant circumstances, to show intended scope of release of all claims); Weston v. Ball, 80 N.H. 275, 116 Atl. 99, syl. 2 (1922) (plaintiff's statements, in negotiations, as to his qualifications admissible to show meaning of "superintendent" in contract of hire);

Streppone v. Lennon, 143 N.Y. 626, 37 N.E. 638 (1894) (oral agreement to show that written contract to do brickwork on building was not intended to require contractor to furnish the brick); Scott v. Walden, 140 Tex. 31, 165 S.W.2d 449, syl. 2, 154 A. L.R. 1 (Tex.Comm.App.1942) (oral negotiations to show duration of right of way granted in deed, over grantor's retained land, where deed indicated that perpetual easement was not intended); Ethredge v. Diamond Drill Contracting Co., 196 Wash. 483, 83 P.2d 364, syl. 2, 3 (1938) (conversations held admissible to show that "drilling" in a particular clause of an oil well contract meant "drilling on the bottom of the hole"); Hammond v. Capitol City Mut. Fire Ins. Co., 151 Wis. 62, 138 N.W. 92, Ann.C.1914C, 57 (what was said by parties at time of negotiating fire insurance contract, in determining whether policy to "Hammond Bros." covered individual property of partners); 3 Williston, Contracts, § 630 (Rev.Ed.1936); 9 Wigmore, Evidence, §§ 2465, 2466.

[5]. Carson v. McCaskill, 111 S.C. 516, 99 S.E. 108, syl. 4 (1919) (declarations of grantor to show meaning intended by words describing property granted, excluded).

[6]. Southwestern Milling Co. v. Niemeyer, 76 Ind.App. 278, 131 N.E. 831, syl. 2 (1921).

[7]. Eustis Mining Co. v. Beer, Sondheimer & Co., 239 Fed. 976, 984 (D.C.1917) (Learned Hand, D.J.: "It makes not the least difference whether a promisor actually intends that meaning which the law will impose upon his words. The whole House of Bishops might satisfy us that he had intended something else, and it would make not a particle of difference in his obligations.").

the declarant's understanding was the same as the proponent's.[8]

The words and acts of the parties in performance of the writing are received as a "practical construction" of its terms, according to their mutual understanding of its meaning.[9]

Where the transaction embodied in the writing is a unilateral one, as a will or a deed of gift, then the donor's individual meaning may govern, when there is doubt whether one of several normal meanings, or whether the normal or a local meaning was intended by him.[10] Here evidence of surrounding circumstances may come in,[11] and evidence of the donor's other expressions may be received to show the sense in which he habitually employed the term used in the writing.[12] There is, however, an ancient doctrine, largely confined in application to will cases, that excludes direct declarations by the donor as to his intention or meaning in using the par-

ticular terms employed in the very writing under interpretation.[13] The wisdom and justice of this rule as applied to declarations offered not to supply omitted provisions but to resolve a substantial doubt raised by the circumstances as to the meaning of the written word, is surely questionable. Under this doctrine, his instructions given for the drafting of the instrument, which would seem highly relevant and helpful in ascertaining his meaning, have been excluded.[14] The traditional view is that such declarations should be rejected because they would be likely to be used not merely for the legitimate purpose of ascertaining the meaning of the final writing, but rather would be used in substitution for the writing. Thus to supersede the writing by the outside expressions would violate the spirit of the Parol Evidence Rule,[15] and would offend the policy of the statutes requiring wills and conveyances to be in writing.[16] To the rule that such declarations of

---

8. See n. 9, infra. The holding in Eustis Mining Co. v. Beer, Sondheimer & Co., next preceding note, is however to the contrary.

9. Floyd v. Ring Const. Co., 165 F.2d 125, syl. 2 (C.C. A.Minn.1948); Lutterloh v. Patterson, 211 Ark. 814, 202 S.W.2d 767, syl. 4 (1947); Burton v. Douglass, 141 Wis. 631, 123 N.W. 611, syl. 1 (1909) (meaning of "vicinity" in agreement not to compete); 32 C.J. S. 908, note 14. But the rule against disturbing a "plain meaning" (see § 219, supra) has been applied here. Koshland v. American Woolen Co., 289 Mass. 308, 194 N.E. 102, syl. 3, 97 A.L.R. 938 (1938); 32 C.J.S. 909, note 15. One party's acts relevant only to show the meaning he individually placed on the writing, offered on his own behalf, should not be received when the standard is the mutual meaning. See Hayday v. Hammermill Paper Co., 184 Minn. 8, 237 N.W. 600, 604 (1931). But the other party should be allowed to offer the adversary's acts, as admissions, to show he accepted the meaning contended for by the proponent. See Green v. Travelers Ins. Co., 286 N.Y. 358, 36 N.E.2d 620, syl. 4 (1941).

10. See §§ 218, 219, above.

11. Ladd v. Ladd, 74 N.H. 380, 382, 68 Atl. 462, 463 (1907) 9 Wigmore, Evidence, § 2470.

12. Ackerman v. Crouter, 68 N.J.E. 49, 59 Atl. 574, syl. 2 (1905) (that testator habitually called certain

tracts the "W. farm"); 9 Wigmore, Evidence, § 2467, n. 2.

13. Appleton v. Rea, 389 Ill. 222, 58 N.E.2d 854, syl. 5 (1945); Jones v. Bennett, 78 N.H. 224, 99 Atl. 18, syl. 7 (1916) (declarations of testatrix at time of execution that she intended by "heirs" to describe nieces and nephews, excluded); Peet v. Commerce & E. S. Ry. Co., 70 Tex. 522, 523, 8 S.W. 203, syl. 2 (1888) ("The court should have excluded the evidence of declaration made by Mrs. Keller about the time the will was written as to the persons she intended to take under it."); 9 Wigmore, Evidence, § 2471, note 6.

14. Watts' Estate, 186 Cal. 102, 198 Pac. 1036, syl. 1 (1921) (statements of testatrix to draftsmen that by "my heirs" she meant her relatives, not her husband's); Fersinger v. Martin, 183 Md. 135, 36 A.2d 716, syl. 3 (1944); Hanley v. Fernell, 54 R.I. 84, 170 Atl. 88, syl. 1 (1934).

15. See statements to this effect in Jones v. Bennett, 78 N.H. 224, 99 Atl. 18, 21, syl. 10 (1916) and in Richardson v. McCloskey, 261 S.W. 801, 815, syl. 17 (Tex.Civ.App.1924).

16. To this effect, see Hanley v. Fernell, 54 R.I. 84, 170 Atl. 88, 89, syl. 1 (1934) and Heidenheimer v. Bauman, 84 Tex. 174, 182, 19 S.W. 382, syl. 1, 31 Am.St.Rep. 29 (1892).

intention are inadmissible, Wigmore lists certain exceptions, namely (1) cases of "equivocation" [17] or "double-meaning," i.e., expressions fitting two objects equally *well*, and similarly, (2) misdescriptions [18] which fit two objects equally *ill* (e.g., bequest to X son of Y, Y having two sons but neither named X), and (3) cases where the evidence is offered to rebut some artificial prima facie presumption [19] as to the intention of the person in question, e.g., the presumption that an advancement is intended as payment of a prior bequest. As some recent decisions indicate,[20] these exceptions when applied with understanding liberality will usually furnish an adequate escape from the danger of injustice inherent in the rule excluding declarations of intention.

---

[17] An alternative expression is "latent ambiguity."
9 Wigmore, Evidence, § 2472.

[18] 9 Wigmore, Evidence, § 2474.

[19] 9 Wigmore, Evidence, § 2475.

[20] See, e.g., Aultman v. Meyers, 239 Iowa 940, 33 N.W.2d 400, syl. 8 (1948) (donor's declarations of intention held admissible to aid in interpreting trust instrument which was ambiguous as to whether the estate after donor's death should be distributed by trustee or by donor's executor); Shoemaker's Executor v. Consorti, 305 Ky. 866, 205 S.W.2d 697, syl. 1 (1947) (on question whether legatees were to get the sums above their names, or those below their names in the will, testator's declarations that he intended to leave enough to particular legatee to enable him to go in business, admissible).

[1] See § 213, herein.

[2] 9 Wigmore, Evidence, §§ 2404–2423; 3 Williston, Contracts, § 634 (Rev.Ed.1936); 3 Corbin, Contracts, § 580 (1951); Am.L.Inst., Restatement, Contracts, §§ 238, 241; Dec.Dig., Evidence, ⊂⟩428–437.

[3] This is clear, where no legal transaction is intended and the writing is executed for a morally justifiable purpose. McCartney v. McCartney, 93 Tex. 359, 55 S.W. 310, syl. 1, 2 (1900) (deed displayed to deranged wife to quiet her fears of destitution); 9 Wigmore, Evidence, § 2406, but compare § 2435. See also Tracy, Admissibility of Parol Evidence that Writing Is a Sham, 33 Mich.L.Rev. 410 (1935).

TOPIC 3

VOID OR VOIDABLE WRITINGS

221. The Rule Inapplicable to Proof of Facts Rendering the Instrument Inoperative, Void, or Voidable: Mistake, Fraud, Illegality, etc.

The Parol Evidence Rule operates to define the written transaction and limit it to the written terms.[1] It denies effectiveness as part of the transaction to expressions outside the writing, but it has no bearing at all upon the question whether the transaction embodied in the writing is valid or legally effective.[2] Consequently it is settled that the Parol Evidence Rule does not apply to evidence of agreements and expressions of the parties outside the instrument, whether contract, deed, release, or other writing, when such evidence is offered to show that the writing was never intended to be operative at all,[3] or that it was only intended to be ef-

---

And by the preponderant view the writing may be shown to be a mere mask where the purpose of the pretence was to deceive third persons. New York Trust Co. v. Island Oil & Transport Corp., 34 F.2d 655, 656, syl. 3 (C.C.A.N.Y.1929) (claim denied on account of apparent sales of oil, fabricated to deceive Mexican government; L. Hand, J.: "As compensation this would be fruitless; as punishment it would be capricious; as law, it would create an obligation ex turpi causa"); P. A. Smith Co. v. Muller, 201 Cal. 219, 256 Pac. 411 (1927) (defendant claimed written contract to purchase glass was a sham to enable plaintiff, a dealer, to secure glass from manufacturers); Bernstein v. Kritzer, 253 N.Y. 410, 171 N.E. 690 (1930) (contract of sale of stock, and guaranty by defendant of payment of price, claimed to be a pretence to foil creditors; "The jury has decided that the story . . . is true, and however incredible this may appear to us, we cannot disturb the finding."), and cases cited 3 Corbin, Contracts, 237–239 (1951). Contra: Graham v. Savage, 110 Minn. 510, 126 N.W. 394, syl. 3–6, 136 Am. St.Rep. 527, 19 Ann.Cas. 1022 (1910) (writing fixing agent's commission lower than orally agreed, to deceive other agents); Kinnear & Gager Mfg. Co. v. Miner, 88 Vt. 324, 92 Atl. 459 (1914) (facts like those in P. A. Smith Co. v. Muller, supra, two judges dissenting). The problem was involved in Zell v. American Seating Co., 138 F.2d 641, syl. 8, 9, C.C.A. N.Y., 1943 (plaintiff employed by written contract to secure government contracts for war materials fixing flat salary, seeks to enforce oral agreement for commissions, on ground writing was merely

fective for any purpose upon the happening of a condition precedent,[4] (except that the old doctrine lingers in some states as to deeds alone, that a delivery to the grantee himself

signed to avoid public criticism of commission agreements; interesting opinion by Frank, J., holds plaintiff's claim not foreclosed by integration rule) reversed in inconclusive memorandum opinion by subdivided court, 322 U.S. 709, 64 Sup.Ct. 1053, 88 L.Ed. 1552 (1944). Notes, Burlingame, 29 Corn.L.Q. 545, 43 Mich.L.Rev. 217; Pressley, 22 Tex.L.Rev. 509.

It is sometimes held that when there is a conceded and actual oral contract between the parties of different tenor than the purported written agreement, the defence of "sham" is precluded. Buser v. Everly, 115 Kan. 674, 224 Pac. 66 (1924). But probably most courts would not accede to this. See, e. g., Southern St. Ry. Advertising Co. v. Metropole Shoe Mfg. Co., 91 Md. 61, 46 Atl. 513 (1900) (defendant allowed to show that writing was a sham to deceive others and that actual oral agreement was for a different rate and duration); Grierson v. Mason, 60 N.Y. 394 (1875) (similar).

4. Pym v. Campbell, 6 El. & Bl. 370, 119 Eng.Rep. 903 (K.B., 1856) (written contract, orally agreed not to be effective until approved by A, and he did not approve); Ware v. Allen, 128 U.S. 590, 9 Sup.Ct. 174, 32 L.Ed. 563 (1888) (similar to last); Severance v. Knight-Counihan Co., 29 Cal.2d 561, 177 P.2d 4, 172 A.L.R. 1107, 1109 (1947) (oral condition effective if nothing in writing inconsistent); Smith v. Dotterweich, 200 N.Y. 299, 93 N.E. 985, 33 L.R.A.,N.S., 892 (1911) (contract for issuance of life insurance policy, with oral understanding not to be issued unless loan could be secured for policyholder); Jefferson Standard Life Ins. Co. v. Morehead, 209 N.C. 174, syl. 3–5 (1936) (note for financing of fraternity house: could be shown that note was not to be effective until 25 endorsers obtained); Kryl v. Mechalson, 259 Wis. 204, 47 N.W.2d 899, syl. 1, 2 (1951) (contract for concert, not to be binding if local union objected); 9 Wigmore, Evidence, § 2408; 3 Williston, Contracts, § 634 (Rev.Ed.1936); 3 Corbin, Contracts, § 589 (1951); Dec.Dig., Evidence, ☞444.

But it is not always easy to distinguish the cases, as above, of condition precedent to delivery of the instrument, and those cases of another type where the writing is finally executed and intended as an effective instrument, but there is sought to be asserted an outside oral agreement that some one of its provisions should be subject to a certain condition. An oral condition of this latter type is subject to the Parol Evidence Rule and may be excluded by it. Skelton v. Grimm, 156 Minn. 419, 195 N.W. 139 (1923) (written contract for sale of land, orally agreed not to be enforcible against buyer except as person to whom buyer re-sold should perform);

may not be shown to be conditional)[5] or that a written contract lacks consideration,[6] or that it is voidable, or subject to reformation by reason of mistake,[7] or vitiated by fraud,[8]

Lake Harriet State Bank v. Miller, 138 Minn. 481, 164 N.W. 989 (1917) (suit against indorser of note who sought to prove oral agreement by indorsee that he would stamp over the indorsement the words "without recourse"); Hoover v. Hoover, 228 Iowa 981, 291 N.W. 154, syl. 5–7 (1940) (agreement that note should only be payable out of the profits of certain land). But in the following cases it was held that the jury could find conditional delivery: S. F. Bowser & Co. v. Fountain, 128 Minn. 198, 150 N.W. 795, L.R.A.1916B, 1036, (agreement that written order for gas station pump should not be effective unless salesman learned that it could be shipped to buyer within two weeks); Minar Rodelius Co. v. Lysen, 202 Minn. 149, 277 N.W. 523 (1938) (replevin for automobile: title claimed under defendant's written contract for exchange of cars; defense, that when writing delivered it was agreed that there was to be no deal if the defendant by the next day decided not to go through with it).

5. E. g., Wipfler v. Wipfler, 153 Mich. 18, 116 N.W. 545, syl. 1 (1908) (deed effective despite oral condition where delivered to grantee with no express agreement for recall); Holt v. Gordon, 107 Tex. 137, 174 S.W. 1097 (1915). Contra: Chillemi v. Chillemi, 197 Md. 257, 78 A.2d 750, syl. 4 (1950) (illuminating opinion by Delaplaine, J.). Decisions are collected in 9 Wigmore, Evidence, § 2408, notes 8–13.

6. McFarland v. Shaw, 45 S.W.2d 193, syl. 2, 3 (Tex. Comm.App.1932) (that note payable to bank was signed for bank's accommodation).

7. As to what types of mistake will be ground for relief, the principles involved are outside the scope of this work. For some of the limitations see 9 Wigmore, Evidence, §§ 2413–2418; 3 Corbin, Contracts, Chs. 27, 28, 29 (1951). But it is clear that whether or not other rules may prevent relief, the Parol Evidence Rule is no obstacle to such relief where the instrument is attacked for mistake. Gross v. Stone, 173 Md. 653, 197 Atl. 137, syl. 6, 7 (1938) (deed rescinded for unilateral mistake of grantor as to meaning of "in fee" contributed to by unconscionable conduct of other party); Wells v. Niagara Land & Timber Co., 243 Mich. 550, 220 N.W. 667, syl. 1 (1928) (mistake as to acreage causing mistake in agreed price); Badger Savings B. & L. Ass'n v. Mutual B. & S. Ass'n, 230 Wis. 145, 283 N.W. 466, syl. 5 (1939) (reformation for mistaken description); Dec.Dig. Evidence, ☞433.

8. Globe Steel Abrasive Co. v. National Metal Abrasive Co., 101 F.2d 489, syl. 7 (C.C.A.Ohio, 1939) (oral promise made without intention to perform may be shown as grounding attack for fraud with-

duress[9] or undue influence,[10] or that it is invalidated by illegality.[11]

TOPIC 4

MERGER OR INTEGRATION CLAUSES

222. **Merger Clauses:[1] Effect upon Claims of Oral Promises, Warranties, Fraud, Conditions and Interpretative Evidence.**

In certain types of relatively standardized transactions, particularly in the sale to consumers of appliances such an automobiles, air-conditioners, tractors, and television sets, it is customary for the standard printed form of contract or order-blank to include a clause, frequently in fine print, providing that there are no promises, warranties, conditions or representations not appearing in the writing.[2] Seldom are these provisions actually read by the purchaser and even less often would he understand their effect upon the statements and promises made by the salesman. What are the consequences of such a clause?

Oral promises and warranties. As against a claim by the party, when sued on the writing, of a collateral oral promise or warranty, the merger clause has generally been accepted as a practically automatic and conclusive answer to such a claim.[3] The view is usually taken that it demonstrates that the writing was intended to be the complete embodiment of the transaction. In this area the merger-clause has most successfully fulfilled the aim of the draftsman. The ques-

out infringing parol evidence rule); Harris v. Delco Products, 305 Mass. 362, 25 N.E.2d 740, syl. 1, 2 (1940) (representation that well would strike good water provable despite parol evidence rule, but not actionable, being matter of opinion); Samuel and Nathan Goldstein v. Gilman, 93 N.H. 106, 36 A.2d 268, syl. 2, 3 (1944); 9 Wigmore, Evidence, § 2439; Dec.Dig., Evidence, ☞434.

9. Berg v. Hoffman, 275 N.Y. 132, 9 N.E.2d 806, syl. 4 (1937) (pressure of fear of loss exerted by trusted adviser); Dec.Dig., Evidence, ☞435.

10. In re Kellogg, 41 Cal.App.2d 833, 107 P.2d 964, syl. 9 (1941) (dictum); Dec.Dig., Evidence, ☞436.

11. Comm. v. Weinfeld's, Inc., 305 Mass. 108, 25 N.E.2d 198, syl. 1–3 (1940) (written agreement for lease of building attacked as mask for oral agreement of employment, as device to escape statute limiting hours of work; Sanger v. Miller, 26 Tex.Civ.App. 111, 62 S.W. 425, syl. 1 (1901) (suit on written contract of sale of cotton; defendant allowed to show oral agreement for purchase of futures and for margins constituting the sale a gambling transaction; 9 Wigmore, Evidence, § 2439; Dec.Dig., Evidence, ☞437.

1. 3 Corbin, Contracts, § 578 (1951); 3 Williston, Contracts, § 811A; Comments, Hartsfield, The Merger Clause and the Parol Evidence Rule, 27 Tex.L.Rev. 361 (1949), Hewins, Special Provisions in Contracts to Exclude Contentions Based upon Parol Evidence, 32 Ill.L.Rev. 938 (1938); Maddever, Effect of Merger Clauses, 20 Corn.L.Q. 91 (1934). See also a comprehensive Note, Warranties, Disclaimers and the Parol Evidence Rule, 53 Col.L.Rev. 858 (1953), which includes a discussion of the effect of the Uniform Commercial Code, especially §§ 2–202 and 2–316.

2. Examples of carefully drafted merger clauses appear in Southwest Packing Co. v. Cincinnati Butcher's Supply Co., 139 F.2d 201 (C.C.A.5th 1943); Miami Lime & Chemical Co. v. York Ice Machine Corp., 104 F.2d 312 (C.C.A.5th 1939); Stapely Co. v. Newby, 57 Ariz. 24, 110 P.2d 547 (1941); Ross Seed Co. v. Sturgis Co., 297 Ky. 776, 181 S.W.2d 426 (1944); Alford v. Rowell, 44 N.M. 392, 103 P.2d 119 (1940); Primrose Petroleum v. Allen, 219 N.C. 461, 14 S.E.2d 402 (1941). See also the illuminating comment on drafting such clauses in Llewellyn, Counselling and Advocacy, 46 Col.L.Rev. 167, 172–3, 1946.

3. See, e. g., Upper Mississippi Towing Corp. v. Calmes, 162 F.2d 177, syl. 1 (C.C.A.La.1947) (oral warranty); Southwestern Packing Co. v. Cincinnati Butchers' S. Co., 139 F.2d 201, syl. 2 (C.C.A.Tex.1944) (same); Hall v. Remp, 73 Cal.App.2d 377, 166 P.2d 372, syl. 7 (1946); Willson v. Riddle, 128 Conn. 100, 20 A.2d 402, syl. 1 (1941) (warranty); Ross Seed Co. v. Sturgis Implement Co., 297 Ky. 776, 181 S.W.2d 426, syl. 2 (1944); Silberman v. Crane, 158 Pa.Super. 186, 44 A.2d 598, syl. 2–4 (1945) (alleged oral agreement that contract terminable by defendant at will: excluded, though defendant did not read contract and swears that plaintiff misrepresented its contents: seems questionable); Valley Refrigeration Co. v. Lange Co., 242 Wis. 466, 8 N.W.2d 294, syl. 5, 8, 9 (1943) (oral warranty).

Under the better view, the merger-clause does not preclude reliance on implied warranties, obligations which the courts consider fairly incident to the sale, unless the clause expressly excludes them. Hartsfield, op. cit., 27 Tex.L.Rev. 365, Hewins, op. cit., 32 Ill.L.Rev. 949.

tion is whether the courts have not gone too far in this direction. When the contract is drafted to fit the particular transaction, and both parties are at an equality in choosing the language, there can be little objection to applying here the doctrine that one who assents to a writing without reading it is bound by its terms.[4] But when we have a "contract of adhesion," a standard form which the customer understands is offered on a "take-it or-leave-it" basis[5] and the form contains a merger clause in fine print,[6] not actually read by or explained to the customer, the situation is quite different. These are circumstances in which the judge should be free to find that a party such as the customer might "naturally and normally" sign the writing and still reasonably believe that the oral promises or warranties of the salesman were intended by the seller to be effective.[7] Or under the Wigmore test the judge should be free to find that these parties, the salesman and the customer, did not in signing the writing intend to supersede the oral promises.[8] Moreover, if it is argued that the writing by implication from the merger-clause, or specifically as is frequently the case, notifies the customer of the salesman's lack of authority, the counter-arguments should be considered that the customer who has not read has not received knowledge, and that the salesman has apparent authority to make reasonable oral agreements and statements which the seller knows are in practice necessary to induce sales. A few decisions look in this more liberal direction.[9]

Fraud. Here the effectiveness of the merger-clause is at lowest ebb. The attack on the validity of the contract for misrepresentation, whether innocent or dishonest, is simply not within the prohibition of the parol evidence rule.[10] Nor can a merger clause, if that is added, protect against an attack by one party for conscious misrepresentation by the other.[11] Public policy forbids the en-

---

4. Am.L.Inst.Restatement, Contracts, sec 70: "One who makes a written offer which is accepted, or who manifests acceptance of the terms of a writing which he should reasonably understand to be an offer or proposed contract, is bound by the contract, though ignorant of the terms of the writing or of its proper interpretation."

5. For a persuasive argument that such contracts require the application of different doctrines from those evolved for "arms length" contracts based upon the policy of encouraging freedom of contract, see Kessler, Contracts of Adhesion—Some Thoughts about Freedom of Contract, 43 Col.L.Rev. 628 (1943).

6. There is occasional legislative recognition of the concealing and deceptive effect of fine print merger clauses in "contracts of adhesion." Thus, a Virginia statute has the effect that when a sales contract on a printed form furnished by the seller contains a merger clause in type smaller than pica, it shall not preclude the buyer from relying on a collateral agreement. Va.Code 1950, § 11–4, and see other analogous legislation described in the wide-ranging and informative Note, Contract Clauses in Fine Print, 63 Harv.L.Rev. 494, 497 (1950).

7. See Am.L.Inst.Restatement, sec. 240(1) (b) provides that the collateral agreement is not superseded by the writing if it "is such an agreement as might naturally be made as a separate agreement by parties situated as were the parties to the written contract." See §§ 214, 216, supra.

8. See § 214, supra.

9. Thus, in one case "business compulsion" was held to avoid the effect of the merger clause. Champlin v. Transport Motor Co., 177 Wash. 659, 33 P.2d 82 (1934), noted 10 Wash.L.Rev. 59 (critical), 44 Yale L.J. 156 (approving). Other judges have cut the Gordian knot of the merger clause simply by branding it a "false declaration" when there were in fact oral agreements intended to survive. Straceuer v. Nunnally Bros. Co., 11 La.App. 541, 121 So. 617, rehearing denied, 123 So. 911 (1929), and see Air Conditioning Corp. v. Honaker, 296 Ill.App. 221, 16 N.E.2d 153, 155 (1938) ("A merger clause reciting as true matters which are not true and which a defendant shows to be false might easily prove an efficient means of fraud"); Johns Manville Corp. v. Heckart, 129 Ore. 505, 277 P.2d 821 (1929) (merger clause not controlling against oral warranty, where undisputed testimony shows writing not complete and hence statement "no promises, etc." is not true).

10. See § 221, note 8, supra.

11. Gloeser v. Moore, 283 Mich. 425, 278 N.W. 72, syl. 1, 2 (1938) (stock subscription); Bowersock v. Barker, 186 Okl. 48, 96 P.2d 18, 127 A.L.R. 130 (1939) (sale of automobile); Morse Chain Co. v. T. W. Meiklejohn, Inc., 237 Wis. 383, 296 N.W. 106, syl. 1

forcement of an agreement relieving from the legal consequences of fraud.[12] A few courts have limited this rule as to the inefficacy of the merger clause to cases of fraud in the "execution" of the writing and have declined to apply it to cases of fraud in the "inducement" of the bargain [13] but this view seems to be losing favor.[14] When the representations are innocently made, or when the principal is innocent of complicity in the conscious misstatements of the agent, the better view seems to be that a "no representations" clause will protect the principal against liability for damages in deceit for loss of the value of the bargain.[15] The other party, however, is entitled to defend against liability on the contract so induced,[16] and to be restored to his former position by rescission and restitution.[17] The same result, it seems, should follow even where the customer should have realized the agent's want of authority.[18] The principal knows that the agent must ordinarily make statements to procure the contract, and despite the merger clause, should not be allowed to make a profit from the bargain if the procuring statements were false. Doubtless the signing by the party of a writing containing a provision that no representations have been made would be receivable against him as an evidentiary admission that no representations were made, and presumably also as an admission that, if made, they were not relied on. If the party, however, gives evidence that he did not read, or did not understand, the provision and this were believed by the trier of fact, the virus of the admissions would be completely extracted.

Other attacks upon the validity or effectiveness of the writing.[19] The traditional approach to the solution of problems of the effect of a merger clause upon challenges to the validity or effectiveness of the writing is that such clause does not preclude the attack, since if the writing falls the merger clause as a part of it falls also. This view has been taken in cases wherein the writing is claimed to be a sham,[20] or to have been delivered

---

(1941) (dealership contract); Notes, 75 A.L.R. 1032, 127 A.L.R. 132, 133 A.L.R. 1360; Dec.Dig., Evidence, ☞434.

12. Callahan v. Jursek, 100 Conn. 490, 124 Atl. 31, syl. 8 (1924); Bridger v. Goldsmith, 143 N.Y. 424, 38 N.E. 458, 459 (1894).

13. J. I. Case Threshing Machine Co. v. Broach, 137 Ga. 602, 73 S.E. 1063, syl. 2 (1912); Eastern Adv. Co. v. Shapiro, 263 Mass. 228, 161 N.E. 240, syl. 1 (1928); Distributors Inv. Co. v. Patton, 130 Tex. 449, 110 S.W.2d 46, syl. 3 (1937).

14. Good opinions rejecting the limitation are Bates v. Southgate, 308 Mass. 170, 31 N.E.2d 551, 133 A.L.R. 1349 (1941) and Angerosa v. White Co., 290 N.Y.S. 204 (4th Dept. 1936), affirmed without opinion, 275 N.Y. 524, 11 N.E.2d 325 (1937). The limitation is disapproved in 3 Williston, Contracts, § 811A and see 9 Wigmore, Evidence, § 2439. See also Texas & Pacific Ry. Co. v. Presley, 137 Tex. 232, 152 S.W. 2d 1105, syl. 2 (1941) (setting aside release for fraud in inducement, despite merger clause which was read by releasor).

15. Speck v. Wylie, 1 Cal.2d 625, 36 P.2d 618, 95 A. L.R. 760 (dictum); Am.L.Inst.Restatement, Agency, §§ 259, 260. But the greater number of decisions may be to the contrary. National Equipment Corp.

v. Volden, 190 Minn. 596, 601, 252 N.W. 444, 835 (1934) and see cases cited 127 A.L.R. 143–145.

16. J. I. Case Threshing Mach. Co. v. McKay, 161 N.C. 584, 77 S.E. 848, syl. 3 (1913).

17. Speck v. Wylie, 1 Cal.2d 625, 36 P.2d 618, 95 A.L. R. 760 (1934), with note on this point; Gower v. Weiser, 269 Mich. 6, 256 N.W. 603, syl. 2, 3 (1934); Roseberry v. Hart-Parr Co., 145 Minn. 142, 176 N.W. 175, syl. 2 (1920); Am.L.Inst.Restatement, Agency, § 260(2). Cases pro and con are assembled in Note, 95 A.L.R. 763.

18. This is the implication of the cases cited in the next previous note. See also cases collected in Note, 95 A.L.R. 766, 767, and the comments under § 259(b) and § 260(2), Am.L.Inst.Restatement, Agency. But in a case wherein the purchaser read in the written order the statement that "the company makes no representations" regarding previous sales in the territory, the purchaser could not rescind for the agent's statement about previous sales, since he could not have relied upon it. Ernst Iron Works v. Duralith, 270 N.Y. 165, 200 N.E. 283, syl. 2–5 (1936).

19. See § 221, supra.

20. Southern St. Ry. Adv. Co. v. Metropole Shoe Mfg. Co., 91 Md. 61, 46 Atl. 513, 516 (1900).

with the understanding that it should not take effect until the happening of some event that did not occur.[21] Other decisions, however, in the latter situation, sometimes by the same courts, have held that a merger clause providing that there are no oral conditions or even one reciting that there are no oral agreements, will preclude the showing of an oral condition on delivery.[22] The section of the Restatement of Contracts giving effect to oral conditions on delivery "if there is nothing in the writing inconsistent therewith"[23] has been interpreted as justifying this result,[24] but most of the cases applying this provision have involved an asserted inconsistency with substantive terms of the written agreement.[25] Here again, a writing which provides that there are no outside conditions or agreements, when signed by a party claiming an oral condition would be an evidentiary admission, of more or less persuasive effect according to the circumstances.

Interpretative Evidence. As we have seen,[26] evidence of agreements or expressions of the parties, offered not to add to the writing but to explain its meaning are not within the ban of the Parol Evidence Rule, though subject to other limitations. Similarly, merger clauses providing that the writing is the entire agreement, or that there are no other agreements, have been held not to be intended to preclude proof of prior oral agreements or negotiations when offered in aid of interpretation.[27]

---

21. Kryl v. Mechalson, 259 Wis. 204, 47 S.W.2d 899 (1951), noted 37 Iowa L.Rev. 434; White Showers, Inc. v. Fischer, 278 Mich. 32, 270 N.W. 205, 207, syl. 2 (1936); Walter Pratt & Co. v. G. W. Chaffin & Co., 136 N.C. 350, 48 S.E. 768 (1904); Rule v. Connealy, 61 N.D. 57, 237 N.W. 197, 200 (1931). This result is supported by Hewins, op. cit., 32 Ill.L.Rev. 938, 948, and by Hartsfield, op. cit., 27 Tex.L.Rev. 361, 371, who collects Texas decisions pro and con. See also 3 Williston, Contracts, § 634 (Rev.ed.1936).

22. Hanrahan-Wilcox Corp. v. Jenison Machinery Co., 23 Cal.App.2d 642, 73 P.2d 1241, syl. 6 (1937) (oral condition held to contradict merger clause providing that writing constituted the entire contract, and also to be inconsistent with other substantive terms); New Prague Flouring Mill Co. v. Hewett Grain & Provision Co., 226 Mich. 35, 196 N.W. 890, syl. 1 (1924) (merger clause recited there were no "collateral agreements": "it is neither consistent or reasonable for a party to stipulate . . . that what is true is not true, and then appeal to a court to relieve it of its folly"); White v. Fisheries Products Co., 183 N.C. 228, 111 S.E. 182, syl. 2 (1922); Edward T. Kelly Co. v. Von Zakobiel, 168 Wis. 579, 171 N.W. 75, syl. 2 (1919) (merger clause, "no conditions").

23. Sec. 241.

24. Hanrahan-Wilcox Corp. v. Jenison, note 22, supra.

25. See, e. g., Fadex Foreign Trading Corp. v. Crown Steel Corp., 272 App.Div. 273, 70 N.Y.S.2d 892, 894, syl. 2 (1947) (alleged oral condition on effectiveness of writing held inconsistent with provisions in writing as to time of delivery of goods and as to time of payment) and numerous decisions cited in the opinion.

26. See § 217, supra.

27. Wood v. Phoenix Ins. Co., 199 Ga. 461, 34 S.E.2d 688, 692, syl. 5 (1945) (provision in sales contract as to "purchase price" could be explained by evidence of oral understanding that it included insurance, carrying charges and interest despite "no agreements" clause; "if a contract is in fact ambiguous . . . such a stipulation would not prevent explanation in the usual manner"); Air Conditioning Corp. v. Honaker, 296 Ill.App. 221, 16 N.E.2d 153, syl. 4 (1938) (evidence of negotiations properly received to show that "Air Conditioner" in writing meant apparatus that would purify and heat the air in purchaser's restaurant, notwithstanding "no agreement" clause).

TITLE 9

THE HEARSAY RULE AND ITS EXCEPTIONS

CHAPTER 25

THE HEARSAY RULE

223. The History of the Rule against Hearsay.[1]

Ask the man on the street what he knows about the law of evidence. Usually the only doctrine he will be able to mention is the one called by the old English word hearsay. In an oft-quoted passage, Wigmore calls it "that most characteristic rule of the Anglo-American law of Evidence—a rule which may be esteemed, next to jury trial, the greatest contribution of that eminently practical legal system to the world's methods of procedure."[2] How did this rule come about?

It will be remembered that the jury in its earlier forms was in the nature of a committee or special commission of qualified persons in the neighborhood to report on facts or issues in dispute. So far as necessary its members conducted its investigations informally among those who had special knowledge of the facts. Attesting witnesses to writings were summoned with the jurors and apparently participated in their deliberations,[3] but the practice of calling witnesses to appear in court and testify publicly about the facts to the jury, is a late development in jury trial. Though something like the jury existed at least as early as the 1100's,[4] this practice of hearing witnesses in court does not become

frequent until the later 1400's. The change-over to the present conception that the normal source of proof is not the private knowledge or investigation of the jurors, but the testimony of witnesses in open court is a matter of gradual evolution thereafter. Finally, in the early 1500's it has become, though not yet the exclusive source of proof, the normal and principal one.[5]

It is not until this period of the gradual emergence of the witness testifying publicly in court that the consciousness of need for exclusionary rules of evidence begins to appear.

---

1. The fullest and best account is in 5 Wigmore, Evidence, § 1364 (3d ed. 1940), and the brief discussion here is based upon that. Following Wigmore's account, but with a slightly variant interpretation of the facts is 9 Holdsworth's History of English Law, 214–219 (1926). The story of the development of jury trial and of the emergence of the practice of producing witnesses in court to testify before the jury is recounted in Thayer, Preliminary Treatise on Evidence, chs. 2–4, esp.ch. 3 (1898). See also Plucknett, A Concise History of the Common Law, 122–127 (4th ed. 1948).

2. 5 Wigmore, Evidence, p. 27 (3d ed. 1940).

3. Thayer, Preliminary Treatise on Evidence, 97 (1898).

4. Thayer, op.cit. at pp. 53–65.

5. 5 Wigmore, Evidence, p. 12 (3d ed. 1940).

It had indeed been required even of the early witnesses to writings that they could speak only of "what they saw and heard" [6] and this requirement would naturally be applied to the new class of testifying witnesses. But when the witness has heard at first hand the statement of X out of court that he has seen and heard a blow with a sword, or witnessed a trespass on land, as evidence of the blow or the trespass, a new question is presented. Certainly it would seem that the earlier requirement of knowledge must have predisposed the judges to skepticism about the value of hearsay.[7]

Accordingly, it is the value of hearsay, its sufficiency as proof, that is the subject of discussion in this gestation period. In Continental Europe there had already developed a system of evaluating witnesses and their proofs quantitatively, based on a requirement of two witnesses, or their fractional equivalents, as "full proof." [8] In this system, Wigmore says, at this period there were rules "declaring (for example) one witness upon personal knowledge to be equal to two or three going upon hearsay." [9] And so through the reigns of the Tudors and the Stuarts there is a gradually increasing drumfire of criticism and objections by parties and counsel against evidence of oral hearsay declarations. While the evidence was constantly admitted, the confidence in its reliability was increasingly undermined.[10] It was derided as "a tale of a tale" [11] or "a story out of another man's mouth." [12] Parallel with this increasingly discredited use of casual oral hearsay was a similar development in respect to transcribed statements made under oath before a judge or judicial officer, not subject to cross-examination by the party against whom it is offered.[13] In criminal cases in the 1500's and down to the middle 1600's the main reliance of the prosecution was the use of such "depositions" to make out its case.[14] As oral hearsay was becoming discredited, uneasiness about the use of "depositions" began to take shape, first in the form of a limitation that they could only be used when the witness could not be produced at the trial.[15] It will be noted that the want of oath and the unreliability of the report of the oral statement cannot be urged against such evidence but only the want of cross-examination and observation of demeanor.

It was in the first decade after the Restoration that the century or so of criticism of hearsay had its final effect in decisions rejecting its use, first as to oral hearsay and then as to depositions. Wigmore finds that the period between 1675 and 1690 is the time of crystallization of the rule against hearsay.[16] For a time the rule was qualified by the notion that hearsay while not independently admissible, could come in as confirmatory of other evidence, and this qualification survived down to the end of the 1700's in the limited form of admitting a witness's prior consistent statements out of court to cor-

---

6. Thayer, op.cit. at pp. 101, 519; 9 Holdsworth, History of English Law, 211 (1926).

7. See Thayer, op.cit. at pp. 518, 519; 9 Holdsworth, History of English Law, p. 215 (1926).

8. See the highly interesting description of this system and its origins in canon law theories built on Biblical texts, and its rejection in the common law courts, in 7 Wigmore, Evidence, § 2032 (3d ed. 1940). See also 9 Holdsworth, op.cit. at pp. 203–211, and 5 Ency.Soc.Sc. title Evidence, 638 (1931).

9. 5 Wigmore, op.cit. at p. 14, n. 25.

10. 5 Wigmore, op.cit., pp. 15, 16.

11. Colledge's Trial, 8 How.St.Tr. 549, 663 (1681) (counsel for prosecution warning his own witness), cited by Wigmore, op.cit., at p. 17.

12. Gascoigne's Trial, 7 How.St.Tr. 959, 1019 (1680) (warning by judge, but evidence finally admitted) cited Wigmore, op.cit. at p. 16.

13. Wigmore, op.cit., pp. 19–26.

14. 9 Holdsworth, History of English Law, p. 218 (1926).

15. Wigmore, op.cit., p. 21.

16. Wigmore, op.cit., p. 16.

roborate his testimony.[17] But we may conclude that the rule against hearsay taking form at the end of the seventeenth century is not a matter of "immemorial usage" nor an inheritance from Magna Charta but, in the long view of English legal history, is a late child of the common law.

224. The Reasons for the Exclusion of Hearsay.[1]

Holdsworth thinks that the immediate influences leading to the crystallization of the rule against hearsay, at the particular time in the late 1600's when this occurred, were first, a strong dictum by Coke in his Third Institute denouncing "the strange conceit that one may be an accuser by hearsay,"[2] and second, the rejection of the attempt to naturalize in English law the requirement of two witnesses[3] and the consequent urge to provide some compensating safeguard.[4] However, as we have seen in the next preceding section, a century of increasing protests against the use of hearsay had preceded the establishment of the rule, but most of the specific weaknesses of hearsay, which were the underlying reasons for the adoption of the rule, and which have explained its survival, were not clearly pointed out until after the beginning of the 1700's when the newly established rule came to be rationalized by the judges and the text writers.

Among the earliest of these criticisms, and one often repeated in judicial opinions down to the present, is the objection that the declarant who made the hearsay statement commonly speaks or writes without the solemnity of the oath administered to witnesses in a court of law.[5] The oath may be important in two aspects. As a ceremonial and religious symbol it may induce in the witness a feeling of special obligation to speak the truth, and also it may impress upon the witness the danger of criminal punishment for perjury, to which the judicial oath or an equivalent solemn affirmation would be a prerequisite condition. Wigmore considers that the objection for want of an oath is incidental and not essential, and suggests that this is demonstrated by the fact that a hearsay statement, even if under oath, is still rejected.[6] But the fact that the oath is not the only requirement, as we shall see that it is not, to satisfy the rule against hearsay surely does not prove that it is not an essential or important one.

Another objection early asserted and repeated of late is the want of opportunity, in respect to the out-of-court declarant, for

---

17. Wigmore, op.cit., pp. 17, 18.

1. See 5 Wigmore, Evidence, s 1362 (3d ed. 1940); Morgan and Maguire, Cases on Evidence. pp. 599–602 (2d ed. 1942); Morgan, Hearsay, 25 Miss.L.J.I. (1953); Morgan, Hearsay Dangers and the Application of the Hearsay Concept, 62 Harv.L.Rev. 177 (1948).

A wider question as to the background influences which have produced our system of exclusionary rules, and among them the hearsay rule and its exceptions, is the question whether jury trial or the adversary system has been the more pervasive formative influence. See Thayer, Preliminary Treatise on Evidence, 2–4, 47, 180 (1898); Morgan, The Jury and the Exclusionary Rules of Evidence, 4 Univ.Chi.L.Rev. 247, 258 (1937).

2. Coke thus condemned the holding in Thomas's case, Dyer 99b (1553) to the effect that under a statute of Edward VI requiring two witnesses in treason if one accuser speaks from his own knowl-edge, "and he relate it to another, the other may well be an accuser." Coke, Third Inst. 25 (1641).

3. See next preceding section, note 9.

4. 9 Holdsworth, History of English Law, pp. 217, 218 (1926).

5. The want of oath is usually coupled with lack of cross-examination in stating the objection. Hawkins, Pleas of the Crown, b. II, c. 46, § 44 (1716), quoted 5 Wigmore, Evidence, p. 4 (3d ed. 1940); Gilbert, Evidence, p. 4 (1760 edition); Chapman v. Chapman, 2 Conn. 348, 7 Am.Dec. 277 (1817); Chiordi v. Jernigan, 46 N.Mex. 396, 129 P.2d 640, 644 (1942) ("The basis for its exclusion is that it is not subject to the tests which ordinarily can be applied to ascertain its truthfulness by cross-examination of the declarant; and because not given under the sanctity of an oath, and because the declarant is not subject to the penalties of perjury.").

6. 5 Wigmore, op.cit., p. 7.

observation of his demeanor, with the light that this may shed on his credibility, that would be afforded if he were a witness on the stand.[7]

A third reason urged against the admission of hearsay is the danger in the case of an oral reporting of an out-of-court statement that the witness reporting the statement may do so inaccurately. It seems probable that the reporting of words spoken is subject to special dangers of inaccuracy beyond the fallibility common to all reproduction from memory of matters of observation,[8] and this has seemed to the courts and seems to the writer, a substantial danger in the admission of hearsay. It is true as Wigmore points out[9] that not all hearsay is subject to this danger. Written statements can be produced in court and can be tested with reasonable accuracy for genuineness and freedom from alteration. Moreover, as Morgan has urged, the reporting in court of oral words for non-hearsay purposes, as in proving the making of an oral contract or the utterance of a slander,[10] is subject to this same risk of misreporting. Neither argument seems conclusive. If one has a general rule against all hearsay, this danger attaching to most but not all hearsay, surely gives some support to the existing rule, even if we think that a rule treating written hearsay differently from oral would be preferable. As to "operative" words, oral contracts, slanders and the like,

it is true that the danger is similar to that in oral hearsay but the need for the proof is manifestly greater, and hence it might well be thought that the risk in proving words for this purpose must be borne but not for the other.

It would be generally agreed today that a fourth factor is the main justification for the exclusion of hearsay. This is the lack of any opportunity for the adversary to cross-examine the absent declarant whose out-of-court statement is reported by the witness. Thus as early as 1668 we find a court rejecting hearsay because "the other party could not cross-examine the party sworn."[11] Recent judicial expressions stress this as the principal reason for the hearsay rule.[12] Cross-examination, as Bentham pointed out,[13] was a distinctive feature of the English trial system, and the one which most contributed to the prestige of the institution of jury trial. He called it "a security for the correctness and completeness of testimony." The nature of this safeguard which hearsay lacks is indicated by Chancellor Kent: "Hearsay testimony is from the very nature of it attended with . . . doubts and difficulties and it cannot clear them up. 'A person who relates a hearsay is not obliged to enter into any particulars, to answer any questions, to solve any difficulties, to reconcile any contradictions, to explain any obscurities, to remove any ambiguities; he entrenches him-

---

7. This objection is commonly bracketed with those of want of oath and opportunity to cross-examine. See, e.g., People v. Bob, 29 Cal.2d 321, 175 P.2d 12, syl. 5 (1946) (not available for jury to judge his credibility); Appalachian Stave Co. v. Pickard, 266 Ky. 565, 99 S.W.2d 472, syl. 4 (deportment not subject to observation); State v. Opie, 179 Ore. 187, 170 P.2d 736, syl. 12 (1946) (deprives party of right to confront the declarant as a witness).

8. Compare Gardner, The Perception and Memory of Witnesses, 18 Corn.L.Q. 391, 393, 405, f.n. 107 (1933).

9. 5 Wigmore, Evidence, § 1363 (1) (3d ed. 1940).

10. Where the utterance of the words is an "operative fact," see Morgan, A Suggested Classification of Utterances Admissible as Res Gestae, 31 Yale L.J. 229 (1922). This article is a pathbreaking guide in the analysis of hearsay.

11. 2 Rolle's Abr. 679, pl. 9 (1668), cited by Morgan, Jury Trials and the Exclusionary Rules of Evidence, 4 U.Chi.L.Rev. 247, 253 (1937).

12. Novicki v. Department of Finance, 373 Ill. 342, 26 N.E.2d 130, syl. 2 (1940); Sconce v. Jones, 343 Mo. 362, 121 S.W.2d 777, syl. 2 (1938).

13. Rationale of Judicial Evidence, b. II, ch. IX, and b. III, ch. XX, (1827) quoted 5 Wigmore, Evidence, § 1367 (3d ed. 1940).

self in the simple assertion that he was told so, and leaves the burden entirely on his dead or absent author.' . . . The plaintiff by means of this species of evidence would be taken by surprise and be precluded from the benefit of a cross-examination of S. as to all those material points which have been suggested as necessary to throw full light on his information." [14] Similarly, a Georgia judge has said that cross-examination "is the most efficacious test which the law has devised for the discovery of truth." [15] Morgan has recently analyzed the protective function of cross-examination and concludes (1) that while the fear of exposure of falsehoods on cross-examination is a stimulus to truth-telling by the witness, actual exposure of wilful falsehood is rarely accomplished in actual practice and (2) that the most important service of cross-examination in present-day conditions is in affording the opportunity to expose faults in the perception and memory of the witness.[16] These conclusions seem well-sustained.

It is easy, however, to overplay the unreliability of hearsay. Eminent judges have spoken of its "intrinsic weakness." [17] If this were meant to imply that all hearsay of its very nature is unworthy of reliance in a court of law, of course the implication is quite insupportable. The contrary is proved by the fact that courts are constantly receiving, as we shall see, hearsay evidence of various kinds under the numerous exceptions to the hearsay rule,[18] and by the doctrine established in most jurisdictions that when hearsay evidence which would have been excluded if objected to, is let in without objection, such evidence may be used, if it appears to be reliable in the particular case, as sufficient to sustain a verdict or finding of the fact thus proved.[19] The truth, of course, is that hearsay evidence, ranging as it does from mere third-hand rumors to sworn affidavits of credible observers, has as wide a scale of reliability, from the highest to the lowest, as we find in testimonial or circumstantial evidence generally, depending as they all do upon the frailties of perception, memory, and veracity of men and women. Indeed, it is the failure of the courts to adjust the rules of admissibility more flexibly and realistically to these variations in the reliability of hearsay that as we shall see constitutes one of the pressing needs for liberalization of evidence law.[20]

225. A Definition of Hearsay.[1]

Too much should not be expected of a definition. It cannot furnish answers to all the complex problems of an extensive field (such as hearsay) in a sentence. The most it can accomplish is to furnish a helpful starting-point for discussion of the problems, and a memory-aid in recalling some of the solu-

14. Quoted from Coleman v. Southwick, 9 John. 50 (N.Y.1812), in 5 Wigmore, op. cit. § 1362.

15. Nisbet, J. in McCleskey v. Leadbetter, 1 Ga. 551, 555 (1846).

16. Hearsay Dangers and the Application of the Hearsay Concept, 62 Harv.L.Rev. 177, 186, 188 (1948).

17. Marshall, C. J. in Mima Queen v. Hepburn, 7 Cranch 295 (1813) and Story, J. in Ellicott v. Pearl, 10 Pet. 412, 436, 9 L.Ed. 475 (1836), both cited 5 Wigmore, Evidence, § 1363 (3d ed. 1940).

18. See Chs. 26–34, infra. See Ladd, The Hearsay We Admit, 5 Okla.L.Rev. 271 (1952).

19. See Note, 104 A.L.R. 1130, and § 54, supra, where the matter is developed.

20. See § 300, infra.

1. For valuable discussions, see 5 Wigmore, Evidence, § 1361, 6 id. § 1766 (3d ed. 1940); Morgan, The Hearsay Rule, 12 Wash.L.Rev. 1 (1937); A Suggested Classification of Utterances Admissible as Res Gestae, 31 Yale L.J. 229 (1922); Some Suggestions for Defining and Classifying Hearsay, 86 U.Pa.L.Rev. 258 (1938); Hearsay Dangers and the Application of the Hearsay Concept, 62 Harv.L.Rev. 177 (1948); Leflar, Theory of Evidential Admissibility—Statements Made Out of Court, 2 Ark.L.Rev. 26 (1947).

For cases discussing and illustrating the nature of hearsay, see Morgan, Evidence 1941–1945, 59 Harv. L.Rev. 481, 541 (1946); Decennial Digests, Crim. Law, ☞419, Evidence, ☞314–324.

tions. But if the definition is to remain brief and understandable, it will necessarily distort some parts of the picture. Simplification is falsification.

With these warnings the following definition is proposed. Hearsay evidence is testimony in court or written evidence, of a statement made out of court, such statement being offered as an assertion to show the truth of matters asserted therein, and thus resting for its value upon the credibility of the out-of-court asserter.[2]

What strikes one's attention at once about this definition is that it fixes a stringent condition on the popular notion of hearsay as being merely what a witness says he heard someone else say. In truth, that popular notion is quite inadequate as a definition of what is excluded by the hearsay rule. This employment of a popular term in a non-popular usage is unfortunate, and is responsible for some confusion in handling hearsay problems in class-room and court, but the introduction of a new technical term for prohibited hearsay would add as many difficulties as it would remove.

Why must the complicated and confusing condition be added, that the out-of-court statement is only hearsay when offered for the truth of the matter asserted? The answer is clear when we revert to the principal reasons for the exclusion of hearsay, namely the want of the normal safeguards of oath, confrontation and cross-examination for the

credibility of the out-of-court declarant.[3] W, a witness, reports on the stand that D, a declarant, has stated that X was driving a stolen car 60 miles an hour at a given time and place. If the proponent is trying with this evidence to prove those facts about X's conduct we are vitally interested in the credibility of D, his opportunity and capacity to observe, his powers of memory, and his tendency to lie or tell the truth. Then the want of oath, confrontation and opportunity to cross-examine D may greatly diminish the value of his testimony. But the same evidence of D's declaration may be offered for quite different purposes, as for example, to show that D at the time he spoke, was conscious, or was able to speak English, or as evidence of the utterance by D of defamatory statements in an action for slander brought by X. Where offered for these purposes, the evidence would still be evidence of an out-of-court statement by D, but its value would not at all hinge upon D's credibility. Hence, when the declarations are offered for these purposes, the want of safeguards for his credibility is of no consequence. We are interested only in the question, did D speak these words, and for that we have the testimony of W, on the stand, fully supported by all the safeguards.

In the light of our discussion, then, we can say that the suggested definition, which is supported by many recent judicial expressions,[4] seeks to limit the term "hearsay" to

2. Two problems dealt with in later discussion are left ambiguous in the definition, first, the problem of whether acts evincing belief are to be treated as hearsay when offered to prove the fact believed (see sec. 229, infra) and second, the question whether depositions and former testimony are to be admitted (when the rules do admit them) under an exception to the hearsay rule, or as satisfying the standards safeguarded by the hearsay rule (§ 230, infra).
Compare the following provisions of the Uniform Rules of Evidence:
R. 62(1): "'Statement' means not only an oral or written expression but also nonverbal conduct of

a person intended by him as a substitute for words in expressing the matter stated."
R. 63: "Evidence of a statement which is made other than by a witness while testifying at the hearing offered to prove the truth of the matter stated is hearsay evidence and inadmissible except: [then follow 31 subsections defining the exceptions]."

3. See the next preceding section.

4. These opinions approve one or more elements of the definition. Hooper-Holmes Bureau v. Bunn, 161 F.2d 102, syl. 8 (C.C.A.Fla.1947); United States v. Campanaro, 63 F.Supp. 811, syl. 1, 2 (E.D.Pa.1945); People v. Kynette, 15 Cal.2d 731, 104 P.2d 794, syl.

situations where the out-of-court assertion is offered as equivalent to testimony to the facts so asserted by a witness on the stand. Only then does the want of such safeguards as cross-examination become material.

When the witness reports on the stand that one declarant stated to him that another declarant made a given statement, this may be termed "double hearsay," if both statements are offered to prove the facts asserted. "Multiple hearsay" would include double hearsay and instances where the chain of repeated statements is longer still, as where the witness reports that A told him that B said that C had stated a given fact. Multiple hearsay is, of course, even more vulnerable to all the objections which attach to simple hearsay, and it seems that if it is to come in at all, each of the out-of-court statements must satisfy the requirements of some exception to the hearsay rule.[5]

The requirement in the definition of hearsay is that the statement be offered to prove the truth of the matter asserted. What if the immediate purpose is to prove the fact asserted but the ultimate purpose is to draw a circumstantial inference of another fact, not asserted in the statement? Suppose the witness reports that D told him, a week before D's body was found in the bay, that he was planning to go fishing the next day with X in the latter's boat. If offered to show D's intent it is plainly hearsay, and it seems at

least equally subject to the hearsay weaknesses if a further inference is to be built upon the inference that D's intent was what he said it was. Accordingly we find the courts treating the statement as hearsay wherever the *first* purpose is to prove the fact asserted in it, even though other secondary inferences are sought to be built upon the first.[6]

226. Distinction between Hearsay Rule and Rule Requiring First-Hand Knowledge.

There is a rule, more ancient than the hearsay rule, and having some kinship in policy, which is to be distinguished from it. This is rule that a witness is qualified to testify to a fact susceptible of observation, only if it appears that he had a reasonable opportunity to observe the fact.[1] Thus, if a witness testifies that on a certain day the westbound train came in to the station at X on time, and from his other evidence it appears that he was not in X at the time in question, and hence could only have spoken from conjecture or report, the proper objection is not hearsay but want of personal knowledge. Conversely, if the witness testifies that his brother told him that he came in on the train and it arrived on time, the objection for want of knowledge of when the train arrived is inappropriate, because the witness purports to speak from his own knowledge only of what his brother said, and as to this he presumably had knowledge. If the testimony in this lat-

---

24 (1940); People v. Radley, 68 Cal.App.2d 607, 157 P.2d 426, syl. 4 (1945); Stone v. Union Fire Ins. Co., 106 Colo. 522, 107 P.2d 241, syl. 1 (1940); Griffith v. Thrall, 109 Ind.App. 141, 29 N.E.2d 345, syl. 16 (1940); State v. Barnes, 164 Kan. 424, 190 P.2d 193, syl. 5 (1948); Davis v. Bennett's Adm'r, 279 Ky. 799, 132 S.W.2d 334, syl. 3 (1939); In re Thomasson's Estate, 347 Mo. 748, 148 S.W.2d 757, syl. 10, 11 (1941); Hamilton v. Huebner, 146 Neb. 320, 19 N.W.2d 552, syl. 4 (1945); Teague v. Wilson, 220 N.C. 241, 17 S.E.2d 9, syl. 2 (1941); Grand Forks Bldg. & Dev. Co. v. Implement Dealers Mut. Fire Ins. Co., 75 N.D. 618, 31 N.W.2d 495, syl. 1 (1948); In re Ryman, 139 Pa.Super. 212, 11 A.2d 677, syl. 15

(1940); Moen v. Chestnut, 9 Wash.2d 93, 113 P.2d 1030, syl. 11 (1941).

5. See Uniform Rules of Evidence, R. 66: "*Multiple Hearsay.* A statement within the scope of an exception to Rule 63 shall not be inadmissible on the ground that it includes a statement made by another declarant and is offered to prove the truth of the included statement if such included statement itself meets the requirements of an exception."

6. This reasoning is implicit in the cases which discuss the admissibility of declarations of state of mind to prove an act, as a question of the scope of an exception to the hearsay rule. See § 270, infra.

1. See § 10, supra.

ter case was offered to show the time of the train's arrival, the appropriate objection is hearsay.[2] The distinction is one of the form of the testimony, whether the witness purports to give the facts directly upon his own credit (though it may appear later that he was speaking only on the faith of reports from others) or whether he purports to give an account of what another has told him and this is offered to evidence the truth of the other's report. Judicial opinions frequently describe as hearsay evidence which on more accurate analysis would indicate that want of the knowledge-qualification is the appropriate objection.[3]

227. Instances of the Application of the Hearsay Rule.

A few recent and typical examples of the rejection of evidence under the general hearsay rule excluding extra-judicial assertions offered to prove the facts asserted will indicate the scope of its operation. Evidence of the following oral statements has been excluded: to show a written acknowledgment of the plaintiff by G as his son, the illiterate mother's testimony that H read to her a writing to that effect signed by G;[1] in a prosecution for procuring R to burn his house, testimony of a state insurance commissioner that the sheriff told him that M said that R told him that he set the house on fire;[2] testimony of members of a family that their deceased father told them after coming home from work that he had been injured while working on a motor, to show the cause of his death;[3] testimony by a witness who came up after a highway accident that the driver told him that the automobile belonged to defendant;[4] testimony in a criminal case offered by the accused that a third person has confessed to the crime;[5] testi-

2. For discussion of the distinction, see 2 Wigmore, Evidence, § 657 (3d ed. 1940), 5 id. §§ 1361, 1363(3).

3. See, e. g. Fotie v. United States, 137 F.2d 831, syl. 12 (C.C.A.8th, 1943) (conclusions of immigration inspectors based upon reports of testimony, as to person's citizenship, termed "hearsay"); State v. Vinzant, 200 La. 301, 7 So.2d 917, syl. 17 (1942) (coroner's evidence as to who was driving car in accident based only on investigation made two hours after accident); State v. Conway, 351 Mo. 126, 171 S.W.2d 677, syl. 10 (1943) (testimony of officer as to money in possession of accused when arrested, apparently based on reports of others); People v. Capola, 263 App.Div. 57, 31 N.Y.S. 590, syl. 3 (1941) (officer's testimony of facts derived from his investigation in neighborhood); Robertson v. Coca Cola Bottling Co. of Walla Walla, Wash., 195 Or. 668, 247 P.2d 217, syl. 5 (1952) (testimony of bottling plant manager as to strength and thickness of glass in bottle based upon measurements made by third parties); State v. Turcotte, 68 R.I. 119, 26 A.2d 625, syl. 5 (1942) (similar to last). When a hearsay statement is offered as coming within an exception to the hearsay rule, it is usually required that the declarant must meet the knowledge-qualification, see § 10, supra. This is sometimes confused with the hearsay objection. See, e. g. Snyder v. Portland Traction Co., 182 Ore. 344, 185 P.2d 563, syl. 5 (1947) (written report of accident by policeman offered under Uniform Business Records as Evidence Act, based on what he was told, said to be "pure hearsay"); Haas v. Kasnot, 371 Pa. 580, 92 A.2d

171, syl. 7 (1952) (written report compiled by several officers who followed witness to scene of accident, inadmissible under Uniform Business Records as Evidence Act).

1. Teague v. Wilson, 220 N.C. 241, 17 S.E.2d 19, syl. 1 (1941).

2. State v. Kluttz, 206 N.C. 726, 175 S.E. 81, syl. 2 (1934).

3. Hamilton v. Huebner, 146 Neb. 320, 19 N.W.2d 552, syl. 10 (1945). The case is debatable on the question whether the declarations were admissible under the exception for excited utterances, see § 272, infra. A similar holding as to decedent's statements to physician that he had sustained a fall is Krug v. Mutual Ben. etc. Ass'n, 120 F.2d 296, syl. 1 (C.C.A.Mo.1941). Contra: State v. Lamance, 348 Mo. 484, 154 S.W.2d 110, syl. 7 (1941). See also American Gen. Ins. Co. v. Jones, 255 S.W.2d 502, syl. 4 (Tex.1953) (statements of deceased prior to accident as to his duties inadmissible to prove scope of employment).

4. Davis v. Bennett's Adm'r, 279 Ky. 799, 132 S.W.2d 334, syl. 7 (1939).

5. Goldsmith v. State, 232 Ala. 436, 168 So. 547, syl. 1 (1936); Donnelly v. United States, 228 U.S. 243, 33 S.Ct. 449, syl. 12, 57 L.Ed. 820 (1913). Compare the discussion in § 255, infra, as to whether such confessions should come in as declarations against interest.

mony of a witness to what an interpreter told her was said by a third person in a language she did not understand; where the interpreter was not acting as an agent of the third person.[6] In criminal cases, the arresting or investigating officer will often explain his going to the scene of the crime or his interview with the defendant, or a search or seizure, by stating that he did so "upon information received" and this of course will not be objectionable as hearsay,[7] but if he becomes more specific by repeating definite complaints of a particular crime by the accused, this is so likely to be misused by the jury as evidence of the fact asserted that it will be excluded as hearsay.[8]

Instances of exclusion of written statements as hearsay when offered in court as evidence of their truth are likewise frequent. Thus, the following have been determined to be hearsay: in a suit by a nurse against a decedent's estate for services, the decedent's written directions to his executor stating that he owed no debts;[9] in a prosecution for a crime in Maryland, evidence offered by the defense to prove alibi in the form of a receipt written across the face of a salesslip for oil sold at a filling station in South Carolina on the date of the crime;[10] to show the whereabouts of a note and mortgage sued on, letters from the foreign administrator of the deceased holder and letters from the American consul in the foreign country;[11] in an action on a fire policy, a letter offered by defendant from its deceased agent stating that insured had failed to notify him of a mortgage on the property;[12] in an action on a fire policy, the written report of an expert employed by the insurer, reciting his findings as to the extent of the damage to the property;[13] in a divorce suit, the report of an investigator, acting at the request of the court pursuant to statute, of interviews with the parties and other persons as to the facts in issue.[14]

228. Out-of-Court Utterances to Which the Hearsay Rule Is Inapplicable.[1]

The hearsay rule forbids evidence of assertions to prove the facts asserted in them. Manifestly, proof of utterances and writings may be made with an almost infinite variety of other purposes, not resting for their value upon the veracity of the out-of-court declarant and hence falling outside the hearsay classification. A few of the types of non-hearsay utterances are these.

Writings and utterances proved as operative facts.[2] When a suit is brought for

---

6. Gulf, C. & S. F. Ry. Co. v. Ginn, 131 Tex. 548, 116 S.W.2d 693, syl. 3, 116 A.L.R. 795 (1938), with note on this point. The objection may be on the ground of hearsay, or for want of personal knowledge, depending upon the form of the testimony, see the next preceding section.

7. Lufkin v. State, 144 Tex.Cr. 501, 164 S.W.2d 709, syl. 5 (1942) and see cases in next note.

8. Smith v. United States, 105 F.2d 778, syl. 1 (Ct. App.D.C.1939); State v. Kimble, 214 La. 58, 36 So. 2d 637, syl. 1, 2 (1948); Commander v. State, 140 Tex.Cr. 38, 139 S.W.2d 806, syl. 1, 2 (1940). Contra: Amos v. State, 209 Ark. 55, 189 S.W.2d 611, syl. 12 (1945).

9. Heil v. Zahn, 187 Md. 603, 51 A.2d 174, syl. 8 (1947).

10. Morrow v. State, 190 Md. 559, 59 A.2d 325, syl. 1 (1948). But the sales slip itself was held to be admissible for the non-hearsay purpose of corroborating a witness who testified he saw the sale made and the slip delivered.

11. Boehmer v. Heinen, 143 Neb. 200, 9 N.W.2d 216, syl. 3, 5 (1943).

12. Stone v. Union Fire Ins. Co., 106 Colo. 522, 107 P.2d 241, syl. 2 (1940).

13. Grand Forks Bldg. & Dev. Co. v. Implement Dealers Mut. F. Ins. Co., 75 N.D. 618, 31 N.W.2d 495, syl. 3, 4 (1948) (excluded though expert was a witness as to most of the facts in the report).

14. Dier v. Dier, 141 Neb. 685, 4 N.W.2d 731, syl. 12 (1942) (held error for the court to use the report as evidence, although he had offered to produce for cross-examination the investigator and the persons interviewed).

1. See 6 Wigmore, Evidence, § 1770 (3d ed. 1940).

2. See Morgan, A Suggested Classification of Utterances Admissible as Res Gestae, 31 Yale L.J. 229 (1922).

breach of a written contract, it would not occur to anyone, when a writing is offered as evidence of the contract sued on, to suggest that it is hearsay. Similarly proof of oral utterances by the parties in a contract suit constituting the offer and acceptance which brought the contract into being, are not evidence of assertions offered testimonially but rather of utterances—verbal conduct—to which the law attaches duties and liabilities. Other obvious instances are evidence of the utterance by the defendant of words relied on as constituting a slander or deceit for which damages are sought. In an action for damages for the conversion of a quantity of corn, claimed by the plaintiff as landlord as his share of the crop, under an oral partition with the tenant, evidence was offered by the plaintiff that the tenant pointed out to him the pile of corn in question and said, "Here is your share, this belongs to you." The court said: "There is no question but that plaintiff owned some corn. It was necessary to identify it. The division made his share definite. This division and identity was made by the acts of tenant in husking the corn and putting it in separate cribs and then his telling Hanson which was his share, and the latter's acquiescence therein." [3] Other cases illustrating the principle are described in the note.[4]

Utterances and writings offered to show effect on hearer or reader.[5] When it is proved that D made a statement to X, with the purpose of showing, circumstantially, the probable state of mind of X, such as notice, knowledge,[6] or motive,[7] or to show the information which X had as bearing on the reasonableness [8] or good faith [9] of the subsequent con-

---

3. Hanson v. Johnson, 161 Minn. 229, 201 N.W. 322 (1924).

4. State v. Sweeney, 180 Minn. 450, 231 N.W. 225, 73 A.L.R. 380, syl. 8, 9, 1930 (defendant prosecuted for accepting bribes as an alderman, in confederation with Maurer, another alderman; held, evidence of conversations of Maurer and third persons in which bribes were arranged for, admissible as "utterances within the issue" and "verbal acts"); Commonwealth v. Wiswesser, 134 Pa.Super. 488, 3 A.2d 983, syl. 6, 1939 (prosecution for corrupt solicitation of a juror; conversations of defendant's agent with juror held admissible and not hearsay); Patterson-Stocking, Inc. v. Dunn Bros. Storage Warehouses, Inc., 201 Minn. 308, 276 N.W. 737, syl. 1, 1937 (evidence of instructions given by owner to driver admissible to show whether driver was acting with owner's consent at time of accident; owner's words and conduct were part of fact in issue); Glassman v. Barron, 277 Mass. 376, 178 N.E. 628, syl. 8, 1931 (in broker's action for commission for procuring exchange of defendant's property for that of C. and H. held, evidence of conversations of plaintiffs with C. and H. in furtherance of the projected trade admissible to show that plaintiffs' activities were the efficient cause of the trade).

5. See 6 Wigmore, Evidence, § 1790 (3d ed. 1940).

6. People v. Jones, 293 Mich. 409, 292 N.W. 350, syl. 2 (1940) (prosecution of detectives for assault on X: proof that letter accusing defendants of extortion written by X was shown to defendants before the assault, held proper. "The letter in the instant case is not objectionable as hearsay because it was not offered to establish the substantive truth of its contents, but to show that defendants knew that Roberson made the accusations. From this the jury were asked to infer a motive of retaliation."

7. People v. Jones, in preceding note; State v. Morgan, 211 La. 572, 30 So.2d 434, syl. 1 (1947); Commonwealth v. Ricci, 332 Pa. 540, 3 A.2d 404, syl. 7, 1939 (witness, who had identified defendant as person who had committed murder in her presence, allowed to state, over hearsay objection, that the reason for her hesitation was that she had been told by police that defendant was in jail at the time of the murder).

8. Crespin v. Albuquerque Gas & Elec. Co., 39 N.M. 473, 50 P.2d 259, syl. 9 (1935) (action against electric power company for injury from shock when plaintiff picked up live wire; plaintiff's evidence that fellow employee told him that current was off, held not hearsay and proper); McAfee v. Travis Gas Corp., 137 Tex. 314, 153 S.W.2d 442, syl. 18–21, 1941 (plaintiff sues for injury due to gas explosion, when man to whom plaintiff was pointing out leaks in pipeline struck match: on issue of contributory negligence plaintiff's evidence that the man told him he was an employee of the pipe-line company, admissible to show information on which plaintiff acted); Moen v. Chestnut, 9 Wash.2d 93, 113 P.2d 1030, syl. 10–12 (1941) (as bearing on reasonableness of actions of driver of car involved in collision, evidence on her behalf that her companion before action warned her that intersection they were approaching was dangerous, proper and not hearsay).

9. Dolson v. Central Business Men's Ass'n, 235 Mich. 80, 209 N.W. 95, syl. 2 (1926) (plaintiff sued on policy

duct of X, the evidence is not subject to attack as hearsay. The same rationale applies to proof by the defendant in cases of assault or homicide of communicated threats made to him by the person whom he is alleged to have killed or assaulted. If offered to show his reasonable apprehension of danger it is not offered for a hearsay purpose.[10] Its value for these purposes does not depend on the truth of the statement.

Declarations offered to show circumstantially the feelings or state of mind of the declarant. The substantive rules often make rights and duties depend on the existence of particular states of mind or feeling. The intent to steal or to kill, to have a certain paper take effect as a deed or a will, or the maintenance or transfer of the affections of a wife, are examples of states of mind or emotion which may come into issue in litigation. Moreover, such mental or emotional states may become relevant as circumstantial evidence of other facts, as for example when evidence of a plan or design in a man's mind is received as evidence that he later carried it out by suitable actions.

When in one of these ways an inquiry is afoot into the thoughts, desires, hopes or fears of the person in question, an obvious resort is to evidence of such of his actions as would shed light on the inquiry. His significant conduct, however, will manifestly consist not only of what he did but what he said. His non-verbal conduct offered to show his state of mind or feelings presents no hearsay difficulty. It must merely meet the usual requirement of relevancy. But when we seek to show his mind or feeling by what he said, we are met with the question: is it hearsay?

Applying the definition earlier suggested [11] we would say that if the utterance would reasonably be understood as an assertion of the declarant of the existence of his state of mind or feelings which it is offered to prove, it would be hearsay. As such, we shall see that it would still be admitted under an exception to the hearsay rule, if it met certain requirements of spontaneity and apparent sincerity.[12] But, actually, such direct declarations of thoughts and feelings are much less frequently offered in evidence, than are declarations which only impliedly, indirectly, or inferentially indicate the existence of the mental or emotional state they are tendered to prove. Declarants offered for this purpose are not hearsay.[13] Some examples may illustrate the types of evidence discussed. In a contested will case the proponent might seek to support the validity of testator's be-

---

and attacked release for fraud; defendant allowed to prove information on which it acted in procuring release, to show good faith); Trainor v. Buchanan Coal Co., 154 Minn. 204, 191 N.W. 431, 1923 (action by buyer against sellers for failure to ship goods, which sellers were entitled to withhold under the contract if "in their judgment buyer's credit becomes impaired," held, sellers may prove that they received Bradstreet report that buyer's credit was poor); Texas Employers' Ins. Ass'n v. McDonald, 238 S.W.2d 817, syl. 5 (Tex.Civ.App.1951) (testimony as to conversation with adjusters, admissible on question of good cause for failure to file claim for workmen's compensation within prescribed time).

10. Many courts, however, require that overt acts of hostility by the threatener must be shown in order to let in proof of communicated threats. See, e. g. State v. Albright, 144 Mo. 638, 46 S.W. 620, syl. 7 (1898); 2 Wigmore, Evidence, § 647; Decennial Digests, Homicide, ☞190(8).

McCormick Evidence HB—30

11. See § 225, supra.

12. See § 268, infra.

13. Hooper-Holmes Bureau, Inc. v. Bunn, 161 F.2d 102, syl. 8 (C.C.A.Fla.1947) (slander action against corporation issuing mercantile reports: declaration of one C. defendant's agent that he would fix it so that plaintiff would not be able to get a job in Miami, held admissible to show malice and for this purpose not hearsay). See In re Thomasson's Estate, 347 Mo. 748, 148 S.W.2d 757, syl. 10, 11 (1941) (petition filed in former suit with present party's connivance offered to show present party's design to defraud and participation in conspiracy, not hearsay). See also Callen v. Gill, 7 N.J. 312, 81 A.2d 495, syl. 3–4 (1951) (testimony as to observation of child including remarks made by the child, admissible as non-hearsay evidence of child's state of mind in custody case).

quest to his son Harold against the charge of undue influence by showing that long before the time when the alleged influence was exerted, the testator had shown a special fondness for Harold. For this purpose evidence might be offered (a) that the testator had paid the expenses of Harold, and for none other of his children, in completing a college course, (b) that the testator said, "Harold is the finest of my sons," and (c) that he said, "I care more for Harold than for any of my other children." When offered to show the testator's feelings toward his son, item (a) would present no hearsay question, while under the rationalization suggested by Wigmore,[14] item (b) would be considered a non-hearsay declaration raising a circumstantial inference as to the testator's feelings,[15] and (c) a direct statement offered to prove the fact stated, and hence dependent for its value upon the veracity of the declarant, would be considered hearsay, but would be admitted, if made under circumstances of apparent sincerity, by the exception to the hearsay rule admitting declarations of a present state of mind or feelings.

Knowledge.[16] This circumstantial non-assertive use of utterances to show state of mind is perhaps most clearly applicable to declarations evincing knowledge, notice, consciousness, or awareness of some fact, which latter fact is established by other evidence in the case.

Thus if evidence is given that the operator of a machine stated before the accident sued on, that the brakes were defective, this would be admissible as evidence tending to show circumstantially that he knew of the defective condition, if it was defective.[17] To show the latter fact, other evidence is relied on. The notion is that proof that one talks about a matter raises an inference, apart from veracity, that he was conscious or aware of it.

Here it seems that even though the statement of knowledge is explicit, "I know the brakes are bad," and it is offered to show he did know it, it can rest on the non-hearsay ground that (bad brakes having been otherwise shown) his remark tends to show that if the brakes were bad he was aware of it. The coincidence between the evidence of bad brakes and his mention of it is significant, apart from any reliance on his veracity. Of course, this theory is only available where the *immediate* inference sought to be drawn is the declarant's knowledge at the very time of the declaration. Thus if the declarant, a week after the accident stated that he knew of the bad brakes before the accident, and this is offered to show his pre-

---

14. 6 Wigmore, Evidence, § 1790 (3d ed. 1940).

15. See, e. g., Loetsch v. New York City Omnibus Corp., 291 N.Y. 308, 52 N.E.2d 448, syl. 4, 5 (1943), a suit by a husband for the death of his wife. On the issue of damages, which was measured by the pecuniary value to the husband of his wife's continuance of life, the defendant offered in evidence the will of the wife, containing this statement: "Whereas I have been a faithful, dutiful, and loving wife to my husband, Dean Yankovich, and whereas he reciprocated my tender affections for him with acts of cruelty and indifference, and whereas he has failed to support and maintain me in that station of life which would have been possible and proper for him, I hereby limit my bequest to him to one dollar." On appeal, the exclusion of this statement was held erroneous, and the court (Thacher, J.) said, "Such declarations are evidence of the decedent's state of mind and are probative of a disposition on the part of the declarant which has a very vital bearing upon the reasonable expectancy, or lack of it, of future assistance or support if life continues. . . . No testimonial effect need be given to the declaration, but the fact that such a declaration was made by the decedent, whether true or false, is compelling evidence of her feelings toward, and relations to, her husband. As such it is not excluded under the hearsay rule but is admissible as a verbal act."

16. See 2 Wigmore, op. cit., § 266; 22 C.J.Evidence, § 302; 31 C.J.S.Evidence, § 257.

17. Borderland Coal Co. v. Kerns, 165 Ky. 487, 177 S.W. 266, syl. 1 (1915) (declarations by foreman before accident as to incompetence of fellow servant received to show foreman's and company's knowledge); McCall's Ferry Power Co. v. Price, 108 Md. 96, 69 A. 832, syl. 12 (1908) (similar to last) and cases cited in Note, 141 A.L.R. 704, 713.

vious knowledge, it seems that this is hearsay and can come in only under some exception to the hearsay rule, such as for admissions of parties and their agents.[18]

In a recent Wisconsin case [19] evidence was received in a trial for mistreatment of a little girl, that the girl in reporting the incident gave a description of the house and its surroundings and of the room and its furnishings, where the mistreatment occurred. Other evidence showed that this description fitted exactly the house and room where the defendant lived. Morgan suggests that this evidence depended for its value upon "the observation, memory and veracity" of the girl and thus shares the hazards of hearsay.[20] It seems, however, that the testimony has value apart from her veracity. Other witnesses have described the physical situation in the house. Her testimony is not relied on for that, but to show her knowledge as a "trace," as it were, on her mind of her visit at the time of the crime, which the undisputed proof showed was the only occasion when she could have acquired such knowledge.

Insanity. One of the main sources of proof of mental competency or incompetency is the conduct of the person in question, showing his normal or abnormal response to the circumstances of his environment. By this test, every act of the subject's life, within reasonable limits of time, would be relevant to the inquiry.[21] As to non-verbal conduct no problem of hearsay is considered to be involved, though since abnormal conduct can be simulated the significance of such acts may in some degree be dependent upon the want of deceptive intent. The same approach is adopted in receiving evidence of verbal conduct, as for example, statements tending to show the existence of hallucinations or insane delusions, which are characteristic symptoms of most forms of mental disorder.[22] Such expressions are treated as evidence of irrational conduct, rather than as hearsay statements of belief offered to show that the declarant does entertain the belief which he asserts.[23] Even if the declaration were in the

---

18. Kutchera v. Minneapolis St. P. & S. S. M. Ry. Co., 54 N.D. 897, 212 N.W. 51, syl. 2 (1927) (statement of agent of railway made after accident that he knew machine was dangerous held improperly admitted: extensive discussion); Note, 141 A.L.R. 704.
The agent's declaration showing his then knowledge is of course evidence of his knowledge at a later time. Fox v. Manchester, 183 N.Y. 141, 75 N.E. 1116, 2 L.R.A.,N.S., 474, 1905 (dictum). A few decisions, admitting "post rem" declarations, suggest by their facts that as to declarations after the crucial event, the circumstances may well show that the knowledge must have been acquired before the happening sued on. Wainwright v. Westborough Country Club, 45 S.W.2d 86, Mo.App., 1932; Fenner v. American Surety Co. of N. Y., 97 S.W.2d 741, syl. 5, Tex.Civ.App., 1936. These and other cases are discussed in Note, 141 A.L.R. 704.
The distinction between the use of statements to show knowledge as of the time of the statement and assertions as to past mental state seems to have been ignored in Garford Trucking Corp. v. Mann, 163 F. 2d 71, syl. 3 (C.C.A.Mass.1947) cert. den. 332 U.S. 810, 68 S.Ct. 112, and see the discriminating Note, 27 Neb.L.Rev. 450. There the issue was the motive for deviation by a truck driver from the instructed route, and evidence was held admissible of the

driver's declarations ten days after the accident that he took the deviating route because in his opinion he could make better time on that route. Possibly the result can be supported as a declaration of his belief at the later time as to the desirability in the master's interest of the deviating route used as evidence that at the earlier time when the accident occurred he entertained the same belief, from which a then intent to serve the master's interest could be inferred.

19. Bridges v. State, 247 Wis. 350, 19 N.W.2d 529, syl. 4, 5 (1945). See Note, 44 Mich.L.Rev. 480.

20. Morgan, Evidence 1941–1945, 59 Harv.L.Rev. 481, 544 (1946).

21. 2 Wigmore, Evidence, § 228 (3d ed. 1940); Green, Proof of Mental Incompetency and the Unexpressed Major Premise, 53 Yale L.J. 271, 276 (1944); Decennial Digests, Insane Persons, ☞20.

22. See Green, op. cit., next previous note, at pp. 272, 273.

23. United States v. Roberts, 62 F.2d 594, syl. 4 (C.C. A.Colo.1932) (Action on war risk insurance policy claiming total disability from tuberculosis and dementia praecox; evidence received of his statement

form of an express assertion of belief, "I believe that I am King Henry the Eighth," it seems clear that the courts would admit it on the non-hearsay theory of verbal conduct offered circumstantially,[24] though possibly the proponent might also succeed on an alternative theory of the use of the statement as hearsay coming in under the exception for declarations of present mental state, namely, belief. But there is obvious common sense in the judicial tendency to treat alike all irrational expressions, regardless of form, offered to show mental incompetence, and to admit them all under the simpler formula of non-hearsay conduct.

The foregoing discussion has given only some of the more frequently occurring instances of the admission of evidence of out-of-court declarations as circumstantial evidence rather than as assertions used testimonially. Morgan has demonstrated by examples and analysis that some of the types of evidence so classified do involve substantial risks of inaccuracy in language, faults of observation and memory, and conscious decep-

tion on the part of the out-of-court declarant —risks which the hearsay rule was intended to protect against by its insistence upon the opportunity for cross-examination.[25] Nevertheless, the strict administration of the hearsay rule and the narrowness and rigidity of its numerous exceptions, have perverted its sound purpose to obstructive results.[26] A more flexible and discretionary standard for the admission of evidence of out-of-court declarations is presently needed. It is believed therefore that the current tendency toward freedom in the use of the theory of verbal conduct as circumstantial evidence is a wholesome trend.

Indirect versions of hearsay statements: results of inquiries: reputation. If the apparent purpose of offered testimony is to use an out-of-court statement to evidence the truth of facts stated therein, the hearsay objection cannot be obviated by eliciting the purport of the statements in indirect form. Thus evidence as to the purport of "information received" by the witness,[27] or a statement of the results of investigation made by

---

showing he was under hallucination that doctors were in a conspiracy against him, held proper. "If a man comes into the office of a doctor or a lawyer, and makes utterly irrational statements, the fact that he makes the statements is some proof of a mental disease. Such statements are not admitted as proof of the facts stated; their evidentiary value lies in the fact that they were made. The question is not whether the statements are true, but whether they were made. They are not within the hearsay rule." In re Ryman, 139 Pa.Super. 212, 11 A.2d 677, syl. 15, 16 (1940) (will-contest, statements of deceased received that his wife was unfaithful, that he was not father of her children, and they were trying to poison him, held proper, not hearsay; extensive discussion); Peareson v. McNabb, 190 S.W. 2d 402, syl. 5 (1945) (will-contest, evidence of testatrix's statements showing many delusions held not hearsay and properly received); 2 Wigmore, Evidence, s 228, 6 id. § 1790 (3d ed. 1940); Decennial Digests, Insane Persons, ☜20.

24. Compare, however, Hinton, States of Mind and the Hearsay Rule, 1 Univ.Chi.L.Rev. 394, 397, 398 (1934) where the learned author says: "It has sometimes been argued by judges and writers that,

where the issue is the sanity of the testator, and some absurd statement by him is proved, e. g., "I am the Emperor Napoleon," no hearsay use is involved because we are not seeking to prove that he really was Napoleon, and hence that we are making a purely circumstantial use of his words to prove his irrational belief. The difficulty is that this view ignores the implied assertion of belief. If the statement had taken the form, "I believe that I am Napoleon," and were offered to prove that the testator so believed, it would be generally conceded that the statement was hearsay, and receivable only because of an exception to the rule. The former assertion is simply a short method of stating the speaker's opinion or belief. Implied assertions seem to fall within the hearsay category as well as express assertions."

25. Hearsay Dangers and the Application of the Hearsay Concept, 62 Harv.L.Rev. 177 (1948).

26. See § 300, herein.

27. Hobart v. Hobart Estate Co., 26 Cal.2d 412, 159 P.2d 958, syl. 35 (1945) (dictum); Dougherty v. City of New York, 267 App.Div. 828, 45 N.Y.S.2d 808, syl. 1 (1944), and see the cases in § 227, notes 7 and 8.

other persons,[28] or a doctor's statement that after an examination of the plaintiff conducted by himself and other physicians, "we decided that [his condition] was the result of an injury," [29] all offered as evidence of the facts asserted out of court, have been held to be hearsay.

Analogous questions arise in respect to evidence by a witness that he has made inquiries among the residents of a given place where a certain person is alleged to live, and that he has been unable to find anyone who knows him or has any information about him. Upon an issue as to whether due diligence has been shown in attempting to locate a missing witness or other person, it is clear that testimony as to results of similar inquiries is not hearsay, but is merely a narration of the acts and efforts claimed to constitute such diligence.[30] However, the inquiries and the inability to secure information, may be offered as evidence of the non-existence of the person sought to be located, or of the fact that no such person lives at the place in question. Then it can be argued that this is merely an indirect way of placing in evidence the statements of those of whom inquiry was made for the purpose of proving the truth of the fact stated, namely their want of knowledge of such a person. Such evidence has occasionally been excluded on this ground.[31] It is true that the residents of whom inquiry was made could be brought in to testify to their want of knowledge of the person,[32] but it would usually be more convenient and equally just to permit the evidence of fruitless inquiries, as most of the cases do,[33] and leave the adversary to bring in direct proof of the existence or residence of the person, which if his claim is true he will most often be easily able to do. An escape from the hearsay objection is furnished by the theory that fruitless inquiries are evidence of inability of the inquirer to find after diligent search and this in turn is circumstantial evidence of the non-existence or non-residence of the person in question.[34] Where as here a choice of reasonable theories is presented, the expediency of the result may properly sway the choice.

Reputation. In the earlier stages of jury-trial, when the jurors were expected to seek out the facts by neighborhood inquiries (instead of having the witnesses bring the facts through their testimony in court) community reputation was a frequent source of information for the jurors. When in the late 1600's the general doctrine excluding hearsay began to take form [35] the use of reputation either directly by the jurors or through the testimony of the witnesses, in certain areas of proof, was so well established that exceptions to the hearsay rule for reputation in

---

28. Greenland Development Corp. v. Allied Heating Products Co., 184 Va. 588, 35 S.E.2d 801, syl. 13, 164 A.L.R. 1312 (1945) (trial court excluded on grounds of want of knowledge and of hearsay and ruling held correct; as to which rule was applicable, the form of the testimony, not clearly disclosed, would determine, see § 226, supra).

29. Village of Ponca v. Crawford, 18 Neb. 551, 26 N. W. 365, syl. 4 (1886).

30. New York Central Ry. Co. v. Pinnell, 112 Ind.App. 116, 40 N.E.2d 988, syl. 4 (1942); 5 Wigmore, Evidence, § 1414.

31. See, e. g., State v. Rosenthal, 123 Wis. 442, 102 N.W. 49, syl. 2 (1905).

32. See State v. Rosenthal, next previous note, and a case in which this form of proof was used, Dunn v. State, 15 Okl.Cr. 245, 176 P. 86, 90 (1918).

33. People v. Sanders, 114 Cal. 216, 46 P. 153, syl. 6 (1884) (inquiries at many places where the person was claimed to have been, exemplifying the inconvenience of requiring production of residents); People v. Sharp, 53 Mich. 523, 19 N.W. 168 (1884); State v. Wentworth, 37 N.H. 196, 200, 217 (1858); Thomas v. State, 54 Okl.Cr. 97, 14 P.2d 953 (1932).

34. See Note, 46 Harv.L.Rev. 715 (1933); 5 Wigmore, Evidence, § 1414(2). The result could also be rationalized as the recognition of a special exception to the hearsay rule. Jendresak v. Chicago & N. W. R. Co., 330 Ill.App. 157, 70 N.E.2d 863, syl. 8 (1946) (dictum).

35. See § 223, supra.

these ancient uses soon came to be recognized.[36]

Reputation is a composite description of what the people in a community have said and are saying about a matter. A witness who testifies to reputation testifies to his generalized memory of a series of out-of-court statements. Whether reputation is hearsay depends on the same tests we have applied to evidence of particular out-of-court statements.[37] Accordingly proof of reputation will often not be hearsay at all. Thus, in an action for defamation, where an element of damages is injury to the plaintiff's reputation, and the defendant offers on the issue of damages, evidence that the plaintiff's reputation was bad before the slander,[38] the evidence is not hearsay. Another example is proof of reputation in the community offered as evidence that some person in the community had knowledge of the reputed facts.[39]

Applying again the general definition we may conclude that evidence of reputation is hearsay only when offered to prove the truth of the fact reputed and hence depending for its value on the veracity of the collective asserters.[40] There are exceptions to the rule against hearsay, for reputation of particular facts, often restricted to certain uses and issues.[41]

Evidence of reputation, not falling within the established exceptions, when offered to prove the fact reputed, is constantly being excluded as hearsay,[42] as for example, when reputation is offered to prove ownership,[43] sanity,[44] or the existence of a partnership.[45]

229. Conduct as Hearsay.

Statement of the problem. One intriguing question which stands at the hearsay threshold is whether the hearsay stigma attaches only to evidence of what someone has previously said or written, or whether it may also include evidence of what he has *done.* We have seen that the hearsay rule applies only to evidence of out-of-court statements offered for the purpose of proving that the facts are as asserted in the statement.[1] Evidence of such statements made for any other purpose, e. g., to prove the making of a declaration as evidence of the publication of a slander, or to show that the one who uttered or heard it had notice of the facts asserted, is, of course, not hearsay. It is only where the statement is offered as the basis for the inferences, first, that the declarant *believed* it, and, second, that the facts were in accordance with his belief, that the evidence is hearsay. These inferences are believed to be too unreliable to permit the evidence to be thus used by a jury. The declarant, in the first place, may be consciously lying and hence not have believed what he says, and second, even though he believed it, he may, due to faulty information or observation, have been mistaken. All this is the

---

36. 5 Wigmore, Evidence, § 1580.

37. See § 225, supra.

38. As to the restrictions upon, and the allowability of such evidence in the various states, see 1 Wigmore, Evidence, §§ 70–76.

39. Brennan v. Mayo, Sheriff, 105 Mont. 276, 72 P.2d 463, syl. 1 (1937); 2 Wigmore, Evidence, § 254; 20 Am.Jur.Evidence, § 462.

40. Brown v. Brown, 242 Ala. 630, 7 So.2d 557, syl. 3 (1942); 5 Wigmore, Evidence, §§ 1580, 1609; 20 Am.Jur.Evidence, § 461, and see § 299, herein.

41. See § 299, herein.

42. See cases collected in Decennial Digests, Evidence, ⊜322, 324; 20 Am.Jur., Evidence, § 461.

43. Brown v. Brown, 242 Ala. 630, 7 So.2d 557, syl. 3, 4 (1942); Louisville & N. Terminal Co. v. Jacobs, 109 Tenn. 727, 72 S.W. 954, syl. 4 (1903); 5 Wigmore, Evidence, § 1626(a). As to whether solvency or financial standing may be thus proved, the decisions are divided, see 5 Wigmore, Evidence, § 1623; 20 Am.Jur.Evidence, § 465.

44. In re Nelson's Will, 210 N.C. 398, 186 S.E. 480, 105 A.L.R. 1441 (1936) with annotation on this point; 5 Wigmore, Evidence, § 1621(a).

45. Greep v. Bruns, 160 Kan. 48, 159 P.2d 803, 811 (1945); 5 Wigmore, Evidence, § 1624.

1. See § 225, supra.

well-worn everyday logic leading to the exclusion of hearsay statements. Does it apply to anything other than statements? More particularly does it apply to evidence of *conduct*? For example, if the sanity of X is in question, is it hearsay to prove that Y, who has been shown to have known X well all his life, agreed to marry him, when such evidence is offered to support the inference that Y believed him sane, and hence that he *was* sane? If the issue is as to which member of a group insulted S, is evidence that B, her brother, who heard the insult, and thereupon attacked D, one of the crowd, hearsay when offered to show that D was the insulter? Other examples, gleaned from the opinions of the judges in the leading case on the subject[2] are: (1) proof that the underwriters have paid the amount of the policy, as evidence of the loss of a ship; (2) proof of payment of a wager, as evidence of the happening of the event which was the subject of the bet; (3) precautions of the family, to show the person involved was a lunatic; (4) as evidence of sanity, the election of the person in question to high office; (5) "the conduct of a physician who permitted a will to be executed by a sick testator; " (6) "the conduct of a deceased captain on a question of seaworthiness, who, after examining every part of the vessel embarked in it with his family."

These instances bring out in clear relief the problem: does apparent belief translated into *action* stand in any better case as respects the hearsay rule than apparent belief translated into *statements*?

By way of prelude, it must be observed that the line of cleavage between action and statements is one that must be drawn in the light of substance, rather than form. No one would contend, if, in response to a question "who did it?", one of the auditors held up his hand, that this gesture could be treated as different from an oral or written statement, in the application of the hearsay rule, any more than could the sign-speech of the dumb. So also a gesture may accompany and give meaning to speech, as where A "identifies" B as a sought-for criminal,[3] or where an eye-witness "points out" the scene of an accident.[4] Obviously, though described in terms of conduct, the actions are as much a part of the speaker's effort at expression as his words are, and of course in all such cases where the gesture or other act is done, so far as appears, solely for the purpose of expression it is on a parity for all present purposes with any purely verbal statement.

On the other hand, it seems equally clear that since hearsay is limited to assertions offered for their truth, *conduct* may properly include *words* used for other purposes than assertion, e. g., words of imprecation, words of discharge to a servant, words used in voting for a candidate for office, words of gift or conveyance, and our identical problem would arise where these words are used to prove the belief of the declarant regarding a certain fact, for the purpose of showing the truth of the belief—the same problem in another form as arises when the actor's nonverbal conduct is offered for similar purposes.

---

2. See quotations from Wright v. Tatham, 5 Cl. & F. 670, 739 (1838); and same case below, 7 Ad. & El. 313, 386 (1837), in Wigmore, Evidence, § 267.

3. McBride v. State, 20 Ala.App. 434, 102 So. 728 (1925); Ramos v. State, 141 Tex.Cr. 126, 147 S.W. 2d 809, syl. 1 (1941) (rape-prosecutrix's identification for officer of accused as attacker, held hearsay). But compare Commonwealth v. Powers, 294 Mass. 59, 200 N.E. 562, syl. 1 (1936) (in prosecution for taking automobile prosecutor allowed to testify that he identified defendant at police line-up with defendant's knowledge, and defendant denied guilt, held admissible and not hearsay).

4. Jackson v. Vaughn, 204 Ala. 543, 86 So. 469 (1920); Byrd v. State, 89 Tex.Cr.Rep. 371, 231 S.W. 399 (1921). See also Elliott v. Commonwealth, 45 F. Supp. 902, syl. 17 (D.Ky.1942) (in murder trial while jury viewing scene a deputy jailer pointed out bullet holes which he indicated were caused by fatal shooting; held, hearsay but objection waived); Ellis v. United States, 138 F.2d 612, syl. 8 (C.C.A. 8th, 1943) (in prosecution for transporting girls for immoral purpose, evidence that during investigation girls "identified" cabin where they stayed with accused, hearsay and incompetent).

Of this last type was the evidence offered in the leading case above referred to,[5] i. e., evidence that a <u>letter was written to the decedent consulting him seriously</u> in matters of business was <u>offered to show that the writer believed him sane</u>, as proof of his sanity. Of similar type would be evidence of an official's revocation in another state of a driver's license to show the driver's unfitness for employment,[6] or evidence of the decision of the Superintendent of Banks to close a bank as evidence of the bank's insolvency,[7] or evidence of an offer of a position as a choir-singer as evidence that the offeree was a skilled musician.[8] The distinction may be illustrated by supposing that, on an issue (in a suit between third parties) of whether at a certain time A was indebted in a certain sum to B, evidence is offered, (a) that A wrote to B *admitting* the debt, (b) that A *paid* the amount of the alleged debt to B, and (c) that A *requested* C to pay the amount of the claimed debt to B. The evidence under (a) is typical hearsay, and our problem here is whether the non-verbal conduct (b), and the verbal, but not assertive, conduct (c), is also hearsay.

State of the authorities: Affirmative acts. Strangely enough, though the problem seems one which, theoretically at least, brings into question the whole scope of the hearsay rule, it has only once received any adequate discussion in any decided case, so far as the writer is aware. It was a celebrated and hard-fought cause, which wound its way from the common law courts to chancery and back again, and was argued and reargued, and elicited numerous opinions, in the King's Bench, the Exchequer Chamber, and the House of Lords, which fill literally hundreds of pages in the reports. One John Marsden was a country gentleman, seized of certain rich manors in Lancashire, who died at a ripe old age, leaving his estate by will to one Wright, who had risen from a menial station to the position of steward and general man of

business for Marsden. Marsden's heir at law, Admiral Tatham, in 1830 instituted litigation, including an action of ejectment for the real estate, to oust the menial intruder from these manors, on the ground, *inter alia,* of Marsden's mental incompetency to make a will. So great was the prejudice supposed to prevail in Lancashire, that one of the branches of the litigation was tried in the York assizes. At the ejectment trial, the ex-steward Wright, the defendant, supporting the will, offered in evidence several letters all written to the deceased by persons no longer living. Among them was one from a relative in America, giving news and expressing affection, and of a tenor such as would be written to one of ordinary understanding, and there were likewise three others which related to matters of business which presumably would only be written to one who was believed by the writers to be able to comprehend and act intelligently upon practical affairs.[9] All these letters were admitted by the trial judge as evidence of the testator's competency, and the jury returned a verdict for the defendant sustaining the will, after hearing a mass of other evidence which fills two volumes in the verbatim report.[10] Sir Frederick Pollock the

5. Wright v. Tatham, supra note 2.

6. Cf. McCurdy v. Flibotte, 83 N.H. 91, 139 Atl. 367 (1927).

7. Cf. Smith v. Olson, 50 S.D. 81, 208 N.W. 585 (1926).

8. Cf. Carpenter v. Asheville Power and Light Co., 191 N.C. 130, 131 S.E. 400 (1926).

9. The letters are set out in full in 112 Eng.Rep. Repr. 490–494 (1837). One of the letters, from the Vicar of the Parish, strongly urges the testator to have his attorney meet with the attorney of the Parish, for the purpose of agreeing upon a statement of facts about some dispute between the testator and the Parish to be laid before counsel to whose opinions both sides should submit. Another is from a curate appointed by the testator, written on his resignation and expressing his gratitude and respect. Two others invite the testator to come, in company with the steward, to certain meetings to be held apparently for purposes connected with local public business or politics.

10. 112 Eng.Rep. Repr. 492, note (a) (1837).

elder, on behalf of the victorious ex-steward, argued strongly that the letters were properly admitted, as showing "treatment" of the testator as a sane man by those who knew him, but the King's Bench held against him, and the case went down for a new trial, the letters were then excluded, and this time the heir, Admiral Tatham, secured a verdict against the will, and the question of the admissibility of the letters again started up the rounds of the judicial ladder. The case was twice acutely argued in the Exchequer Chamber, and all of the judges who considered the point seemed to have agreed in holding that the letters, in the absence of evidence that Marsden, the addressee, acted upon or at least read them, were inadmissible as being equivalent to hearsay evidence of the opinions of the writers. The holding was perhaps most pithily put by Baron Parke in these words:

> "The conclusion at which I have arrived is, that proof of a particular fact which is not of itself a matter in issue, but which is relevant only as implying a statement or opinion of a third person on the matter in issue, is inadmissible in all cases where such a statement or opinion not on oath would be of itself inadmissible; and, therefore, in this case the letters which are offered only to prove the competence of the testator, that is the truth of the implied statements therein contained, were properly rejected, as the mere statement or opinion of the writer would certainly have been inadmissible."

This opinion prevailed with all the other judges who alluded to this question, both in the Exchequer Chamber and on the further appeal to the House of Lords, though the judges of the former court were equally divided upon the question whether the proof sufficiently showed that the testator had read and acted on the letters so as to render them admissible on that ground. Finally in 1838, the House of Lords ended eight years of strenuous litigation by holding the letters inadmissible.

In no subsequent case has the problem been brought out so clearly—no Pollock and Parke have again crossed swords upon it—but there are a few distinct judicial rulings in America which announce the governing principle in the same fashion as did the English judge in Wright v. Tatham.

Thus, in Thompson v. Manhattan Ry.,[11] where the issue was whether the plaintiff had actually suffered an injury to the spine, as she claimed, the court rejected evidence that her physician treated her for spinal injuries, and said:

> "We think such proof was in the nature of hearsay. The treatment of the plaintiff for a particular disease was no more than a declaration of the physician that she was suffering from such a disease. As the declaration would not be competent, we think proof of the treatment would not be competent."

A similar question arises when one charged with crime claims that the crime was committed by another, and offers evidence that such other person took refuge in flight after the crime was committed. Of course, evidence that this third person had *confessed* the crime would clearly be a hearsay statement, and as such would be excluded by most courts,[12] and the question whether evidence of flight would also be hearsay raises our problem directly. The courts have called the flight-evidence "hearsay" and have held it must be excluded,[13] except where it comes within some indefinable range of proximity to

---

11. 11 App.Div. 182, 42 N.Y.Supp. 896 (2d Dep't 1896).

12. Donnelly v. United States, 228 U.S. 243, 33 Sup. Ct. 449 (1913).
But a few courts admit the evidence as a declaration against interest. Hines v. Commonwealth, 136 Va. 728, 117 S.E. 843 (1923); see § 255, herein and Wigmore, op. cit. §§ 1476–1477. See also People v. Lettrich, 413 Ill. 172, 108 N.E.2d 488, syl. 8, 9 (1952) (evidence of the confession of another admitted, where "justice demands a departure from the rule").

13. State v. White, 68 N.C. 158 (1872); Levison v. State, 54 Ala. 520 (1875); State v. Piernot, 167 Iowa 853, 149 N.W. 446 (1914).

the crime, in time and space, and hence is admitted, though hearsay, as part of the *res gestae*.[14] There is a sprinkling of other cases which more or less directly support the view that "hearsay" includes conduct.[15] Some are

dicta and some are explainable on other grounds.

On the other hand, there are other cases whose implications at least would favor the view that evidence of conduct is outside the

14. Terry v. State, 13 Ala.App. 115, 69 So. 370 (1915); People v. Mendez, 193 Cal. 39, 223 Pac. 65 (1924). The former case seems to require strictly that the evidence to be part of the *res gestae* must show the flight as following immediately and hence "instinctively" upon the crime. The latter would seemingly be satisfied if there were any facts which would fairly indicate a casual connection between the crime and the flight.

15. Gresham v. Manning, 1 Ir.R.C.L. 125 (1867) (Action by hotel owner for obstruction of light by neighboring land-owner. On the issue of whether the light was actually obstructed, evidence that certain guests refused to take the rooms alleged to be darkened, and that they gave as their reason that they were too dark, was held hearsay and inadmissible.) Hanson v. State, 160 Ark. 329, 254 S.W. 691 (1923) (On an issue of whether a bank was in a failing condition at a certain time, evidence that at that time other banks followed the unusual practice of demanding payment from this bank in cash of collections made through it was held inadmissible as hearsay. But the lack of testimonial knowledge would seem to be a clearer objection.) Gill v. State, 194 Ark. 521, 108 S.W.2d 785, syl. 2, 1937 (in prosecution for stealing cattle evidence for the state, on question of ownership of cattle, that purchasers of hides from stolen cattle returned them to alleged owners because of their convincing identification, held, erroneously admitted). In re Louck's Estate, 160 Cal. 551, 558, 117 Pac. 673, 676 (1911). (Question of survivorship as between two persons killed in the same train wreck. The witness was asked if he knew why L, one of the decedents, was placed on a stretcher and the other decedent not. Ruling out the question was held no error. "The only purpose of such a question would be to elicit a statement from the witness that those placing the body on the stretcher believed Mr. Loucks was alive. Their belief was not pertinent but only a statement of the physical facts supporting such belief was admissible in evidence." Other objections to the question are obvious.) In re De Laveaga's Estate, 165 Cal. 607, 133 Pac. 307 (1913). (On the issue of the sanity of a testatrix, the court said that the fact that relatives of the testatrix by their conduct treated the testatrix as incompetent, and managed her affairs without consulting her, would be inadmissible if standing alone, but admissible where the circumstances indicate acquiescence by the testatrix in this treatment where a sane person would not acquiesce. The case in this respect is somewhat similar to Wright v. Tatham, supra note 2, which

would have admitted the letters had it been proved that the testator had read the letters.) In re Hine, 68 Conn. 551, 37 Atl. 384 (1897) (On issue of capacity in a will case, evidence that boys in the street made fun of the testatrix was excluded as "hearsay.") Similar evidence was admitted by the trial court in Wright v. Tatham, supra note 2; see 112 Eng.Rep. Repr. 492. Compare Griffith v. Thrall, 109 Ind.App. 141, 29 N.E.2d 345, syl. 16, 17 (1940) (in will-contest for mental incapacity evidence that witness had heard people call testatrix "Poor Carrie," hearsay but not prejudicial). Pitner v. Shugart Bros., 150 Ga. 340, 103 S.E. 791 (1920) (Action for nuisance in operating a cotton gin near a dwelling. Evidence that fire insurance rates were raised because of the operation of the gin was held, in the head note, not elaborated in the opinion, to be "hearsay." The issue upon which the evidence was offered was not stated.) People v. Bush, 300 Ill. 532, 133 N.E. 201 (1921) (evidence that a certain inmate of an institution was not put in the venereal ward, offered to show that she did not have a venereal disease, excluded as "hearsay"); Caruthers v. Balsley, 89 Ill. App. 559 (1899) (where the issue was as to the disposition of a certain horse, evidence that a veterinarian had refused to treat him on the ground that he was a man-eating horse held inadmissible as hearsay); Daly v. Publix Cars, 128 Neb. 403, 259 N.W. 163, syl. 4, 1935 (in suit by passenger against operator of taxicab for injury incurred when another automobile collided with taxicab; evidence offered by taxicab operator that driver of other automobile paid damages to taxicab, excluded as hearsay as to passenger); Stallings v. State, 29 Tex. App. 220, 63 S.W. 127 (1901) (to show certain debts not paid, evidence that creditor thereafter preserved bill for same, held hearsay); Wells v. State, 43 Tex. Cr.Rep. 451, 67 S.W. 1020 (1902) (evidence that husband of rape victim assaulted accused inadmissible when offered to show husband believed defendant was the assailant); Brittain v. State, 52 Tex.Cr.Rep. 169, 105 S.W. 817 (1907) (evidence that third person picked out marked money which had been stolen from a large lot held hearsay); Ray v. State, 88 Tex.Cr.Rep. 196, 225 S.W. 523 (1920) (witness having stated he had been indicted for theft at instance of express company was asked if the express company had not made a compromise of his claim for malicious prosecution; held, hearsay); Murray v. State, 56 Tex.Cr.Rep. 438, 120 S.W. 437 (1909) (evidence in prosecution for liquor-selling that certain ladies asked the accused to quit selling "Frosty" held hearsay); Gillespie v. State, 73

pale of hearsay. Thus on questions of family relationship, the fact that the person in question was treated as a relative by members of the family is admitted.[16] Similarly, the fact that the neighbors have treated a couple as man and wife is evidence of the marriage,[17] as is of course the evidence of their cohabitation as such,[18] and evidence that parents have treated a child as legitimate is admissible to show legitimacy.[19] Perhaps the familiar doctrine that *acts* of ownership, control, or possession are admissible (even on behalf of the actor) as evidence of ownership [20] has a similar implication. So also, the fact that one purports to carry out the official duties of an office is admissible as evidence that he is the incumbent.[21]

It is observable, however that all of these instances are of the admission of what is usually presented as evidence of conduct of a *generalized* sort. It is either conduct of a given person extending over a substantial period of time, or the united similar actions of the members of a group such as a family or neighborhood. It is different from evidence of an isolated act of an individual.

The cases do offer examples of the admission of somewhat more individualized conduct, however. Thus in Martin v. John-

ston,[22] the court held admissible, on the issue of whether a person, then in an asylum, was competent at the time to make his will, evidence as to whether he was then actually held under restraint. The case of Meserve v. Folsom [23] must be counted on the same side. There the plaintiff claimed to be domiciled in Sutton, and the defendant contested this. The defendant was allowed by the trial court to ask the plaintiff whether he was allowed to vote in Sutton, to which the plaintiff objected as hearsay, but was forced to answer that he was not. On appeal the court approved this ruling, and in response to the plaintiff's argument that the evidence that he was not allowed to vote was but hearsay evidence of the belief of the board of civil authority as to his residence, said:

> "But the question was not admitted for the purpose of proving what the board said or did respecting the plaintiff's residence in Sutton. It was admitted to show a *fact*—to show that one of the characteristics of residence was lacking."

To be similarly classified are cases where to prove the existence of a contract, or its terms, evidence that one of the parties has acted in a way consistent only with such a contract, or such terms, is received.[24] Final-

---

Tex.Cr.Rep. 585, 166 S.W. 135 (1914) (Seduction: on issue of chaste character of prosecutrix, accused seeks to ask whether witness who had gone riding at night with her, before the crime, had not requested one *E*, who had seen them riding, not to tell anybody. Held, hearsay); Powell v. State, 88 Tex.Cr. Rep. 367, 227 S.W. 188 (1921) (The defendant, charged with theft for selling his grandmother's cow in her absence, claimed to have acted under belief that she had authorized the sale. Evidence for the state that the grandmother on her return demanded the cow and not the money was held hearsay); Fitch v. Benis, 107 Vt. 165, 177 A. 193, syl. 1–3, 1935 (action for damages arising from automobile collision; evidence that a police officer arrested the plaintiff, immediately after the accident for driving while intoxicated, held inadmissible).

16.   Greaves v. Greenwood, 2 Ex.D. 289 (1877).

17.   Fleming v. Fleming, 4 Bing. 266 (1827); Re Thompson; Langham v. Thompson, 91 L.T. (n. s.) 680 (1904).

18.   Wigmore, op. cit., § 268.

19.   Woodward v. Blue, 107 N.C. 407, 12 S.E. 453 (1890), and other cases cited in Wigmore, op. cit. § 269.

20.   Jones v. Williams, 2 M. & W. 326 (1837).

21.   Commonwealth v. John McCue, 16 Gray 226 (Mass.1860).

22.   1 F. & F. 122, 123 (1858).

23.   62 Vt. 504, 20 Atl. 926 (1890). See also United States v. Sessin, 84 F.2d 667, syl. 3 (1936) (veteran claiming tuberculosis disability properly allowed to testify that when he arrived at hospital he was taken to tuberculosis ward; held not hearsay).

24.   Wigmore, op. cit. § 272, citing Reg. v. Fordingbridge (Inhabitants), E.B. & E. 678 (1858), 4 Jur. (n. s.) 951 (1858) (the fact that J D worked as apprentice admitted to show that an apprenticeship indenture had been executed); and Wrigley v. Cornelius, 162 Ill. 92, 44 N.E. 406 (1896) (to show that a

ly, cases may be found in which testimony is admitted that police officers, after seizing an alleged gaming house, heard on the telephone there incoming calls of customers seeking to place bets, as evidence of the character of the place.[25]

Silence as hearsay. In addition to the miscellaneous instances of positive conduct, discussed above, there are perhaps even more numerous situations where a failure to act

or speak has been offered for a similar purpose. Probably most of these cases fall in the following classes: (a) on an issue as to defects in goods, or unwholesomeness of food served, evidence is offered by the seller that goods or food of the same quality have been sold or served to other customers and that there has been no complaint by the other customers,[26] (b) on the question of the existence of an injury or injurious situation, or the

---

contract was as he claimed, plaintiff was allowed to show that he acted under it, in a way consistent only with a belief that its terms were as claimed).

25. Billeci v. United States, 184 F.2d 394, syl. 3 (C.A. D.C.1950); People v. Radley, 68 Cal.App.2d 607, 157 P.2d 426, syl. 2–4 (1945); State v. Tolisano, 136 Conn. 210, 70 A.2d 118, syl. 1, 13 A.L.R.2d 1405 (1949); Commonwealth v. Jensky, 318 Mass. 350, 61 N.E.2d 532, syl. 2 (1945). Contra: Bloss v. State, 127 Tex.Cr. 216, 75 S.W.2d 694, syl. 6 (1934).

26. *Admissible*: Steil v. Holland, 3 F.2d 776, syl. 7 (C.C.A.9th, 1925) (no other complaints from purchasers of similar woolen goods); Baer Grocer Co. v. Barber Milling Co., 223 Fed. 969, syl. 1 (C.C.A.4th, 1915) (no complaints on flour to prove no deterioration in quality); Katz v. Delohey Hat Co., 97 Conn. 665, 118 Atl. 88, syl. 11 (1922) (no complaints on fur from same lot as plaintiff's to show good quality); Mears v. N. Y., N.H. & H.R.R., 75 Conn. 171, 52 Atl. 610, syl. 9 (1902) (express company agent receiving box from railroad made no complaint, offered to show that box was then in good condition); Ogden v. Rosedale Inn, 189 So. 162, syl. 5 (La.App. 1939) (no other complaints about shrimp salad held "of great value . . . in determining genuineness of plaintiff's claim"); MacLehan v. Loft Candy Stores, 172 So. 367, syl. 1 (La.App.1937) (no other complaints from 300 mince pies sold); Schuler v. Union News Co., 295 Mass. 350, 4 N.E.2d 465, syl. 1 (1936) (no other complaints from 300 turkey sandwiches sold on particular day or from any sandwiches sold during year); Monahan v. Economy Grocery Stores Corp., 282 Mass. 548, 185 N.E. 34 (1938) (no complaints received on any other of 72,000 cans of corn sold by defendant); Landfield v. Albiani Lunch Co., 268 Mass. 528, 168 N.E. 160, syl. 1, 3 (1929) (absence of complaints about food held "competent evidence that it was not unwholesome"); Gracey v. Waldorf System, 251 Mass. 76, 146 N.E. 232 (1925) (no complaints on food); Kinston Cotton Mills v. Rocky Mount Hosiery Co., 154 N.C. 462, 70 S.E. 910, syl. 2, 3 (1911) (correspondence showing complaints and evidence of no complaints on yarn both admitted); St. Louis S. W. Ry. v. Arkansas & T. Grain Co., 42 Tex.Civ.App. 125, 95 S.W. 656, syl.

6, 7 (Tex.Civ.App.1906) (failure of other purchasers of corn to complain admitted over hearsay objection; compare with later Texas cases below).

Inadmissible: United States v. 11¼ Dozen Packages, Etc., 40 F.Supp. 208, syl. 5 (W.D.N.Y.1941) (no complaints received on drug over ten-year period held incompetent as "clearly hearsay"); Winter-Loeb Grocery Co. v. Boykin, 203 Ala. 187, 82 So. 437, syl. 9, 10 (1919) (sale of seeds); Siegel, King & Co. v. Penny & Baldwin, 176 Ark. 336, 2 S.W.2d 1082, syl. 6 (1928) (no complaints on other pipe sold inadmissible because circumstances may have been different and purchasers may have been damaged without complaining); Hutchinson Lumber Co. v. Dickerson, 127 Ga. 328, 56 S.E. 491, syl. 2 (1907) (others' acceptance of lumber irrelevant on issue of breach of warranty on defendant's lumber); Van Lill Co. v. Frederick City Packing Co., 155 Md. 303, 141 Atl. 898, syl. 4, 5 (1928) (absence of complaints from purchasers of rejected corn too remote to have probative force); Webster v. Moore & Son, 108 Md. 572, 71 Atl. 466, syl. 7 (1908) (that other tomatoes were sold as No. 3 standard and accepted as such without complaint irrelevant on issue of quality of tomatoes sold defendant); Osborne & Co. v. Bell, 62 Mich. 214, 28 N.W. 841, syl. 1 (1886) (no complaints on other machines sold, irrelevant as to workability of this machine); Bloom's Son Co. v. Haas, 130 Mo. App. 122, 108 S.W. 1078, syl. 3 (1908) (shipments of rice to others without complaint held wholly irrelevant and highly prejudicial to defendant); James K. Thomson Co. v. International Compositions Co., 191 App.Div. 553, 181 N.Y.Supp. 637, syl. 4 (1920) (evidence that rejected goods were sold to others without complaint inadmissible as hearsay); Altkrug v. William Whitman Co., 185 App.Div. 744, 173 N.Y.Supp. 669, syl. 4 (1919) (no complaints from sale of rejected goods declared "hearsay evidence as to opinions of other customers"); Shaw Cotton Mills v. Acme Hosiery Mills, 181 N.C. 33, 106 S.E. 24, syl. 4 (1921) (statements in letters that rejected goods had been resold without complaint were "at most . . . self-serving, and tended only to prove a negative"; their exclusion by trial court was not reversible error); Reed Grocery Co. v. Miller, 36 Okla. 134, 128 Pac. 271, syl. 1 (1912) (no

happening of an injurious event, evidence is offered of the absence of complaint by other persons affected,[27] and (c) on the issue of the happening of some event affecting a member of the family, or a claim to or disposition of property by such member, evidence is offered from other members of the family that he never mentioned such matter.[28] Taking

complaints from other sales of hominy "wholly irrelevant"); Goldsmith v. Ohio Truss Co., 283 S.W. 299, syl. 3 (Tex.Civ.App.1926) (on issue of whether plaintiff shipped more goods than defendant ordered, evidence that no others complained of receiving too many goods excluded); Elmberg Co. v. Dunlap Hdw. Co., 267 S.W. 258, syl. 4 (Tex.Comm.App. 1924) (no complaints from other machines held irrelevant); George W. Saunders Live Stk. Comm. Co. v. Kincaid, 168 S.W. 977, syl. 3 (Tex.Civ.App.1914) (failure of other packers to complain of disease in hogs inadmissible as hearsay). I am indebted for citations and descriptions of many of the cases in this footnote and the two following footnotes to the excellent Note by Wallace C. Murchison, 24 N.C.L. Rev. 274, 278 et seq. (1946).

27. *Admissible:* Louisville & N. R. R. v. Varner, 129 Ga. 844, 60 S.E. 162, syl. 1 (1908) (failure to complain of injury admitted); West Chicago St. Ry. v. Kennelly, 170 Ill. 508, 48 N.E. 996, syl. 2 (1897) (daily visitor had not heard plaintiff complain before accident, admissible on issue of whether prior accident caused plaintiff's injury); Sullivan v. Minn. St. Ry., 161 Minn. 45, 200 N.W. 922, syl. 3 (1924) (evidence in personal injury action that no other claim was made on defendant arising out of same accident admissible in discretion of trial court); Atlantic Coast Line R. R. v. Searson, 137 S.C. 468, 135 S.E. 567, syl. 16 (1926) (evidence that neither defendant nor predecessors made any complaint as to railroad right of way admitted); Fogg v. Oregon Short Line R. R., 78 Utah 105, 1 P.2d 954, syl. 6 (1931) (in action for injury to knee during employment wife permitted to testify that husband did not complain of pain in knee after prior auto accident); Lincoln v. Hemenway, 80 Vt. 530, 69 Atl. 153, syl. 4 (1908) (neighbor did not hear of plaintiff's injury until end of August, admissible to corroborate plaintiff's statement that injury occurred in August and not in April).
Inadmissible: Menard v. Cashman, 94 N.H. 428, 55 A.2d 156, syl. 15 (1947) (in action for fall on stairway in store, evidence that no complaint of any defect in stairs had been to tenant of store by customers, held, if not hearsay it was "at most only evidence of inconclusive silence and properly excluded in the exercise of the court's discretion"); Southern Ry. v. Mayer, 159 S.C. 332, 157 S.E. 6, syl. 5 (1931) (testimony of owner of other land on railroad's right of way that railway company had not complained of encroachment, excluded).

28. *Admissible:* Latham v. Houston Land & Trust Co., 62 S.W.2d 519, syl. 3 (Tex.Civ.App.1933) (testimony that widow and attorney had never heard alleged settlor mention trust fund held not hearsay and admissible on issue of existence of fund); Sloan v. Sloan, 32 S.W.2d 513, syl. 6 (Tex.Civ.App. 1930) (deceased did not state at dinner party that he and plaintiff were married, admitted on issue of marriage); Donovan v. Selinas, 85 Vt. 80, 81 Atl. 235, syl. 1 (1911) (fact that member of household never heard husband claim ownership of property relevant to show wife's ownership). See also State v. Childers, 196 La. 554, 199 So. 640, syl. 15 (1940) (on trial for forging wills where one defendant claimed form for will drawn by certain lawyer, since deceased, evidence of clerk in such lawyer's office that lawyer never mentioned having drawn alleged will, held, not hearsay; relevant to refute defendant's claim).

Inadmissible: Planters' Chemical & Oil Co. v. Stearnes, 189 Ala. 503, 66 So. 699, syl. 4 (1914) (testimony that signers never heard any of other signers say they signed notes individually inadmissible except as it tends to contradict plaintiff's evidence that they signed as individuals); Gilbert v. Gilbert, 22 Ala. 529, syl. 7 (1853) (relatives and neighbors of decedent had not heard of will before his death); Segars v. City of Cornelia, 60 Ga.App. 457, 4 S.E.2d 60, syl. 5 (1939) (that wife said nothing to husband about signing easement, though they consulted each other about all business transactions, excluded; wife's denial of signing would be hearsay); Sherling v. Continental Trust Co., 175 Ga. 672, 165 S.E. 560, syl. 3 (1932) (testator never said anything to witnesses about alleged oral contract of testator, to prove no contract existed; held irrelevant, immaterial and in nature of hearsay); Treschman v. Treschman, 28 Ind.App. 206, 61 N.E. 961, syl. 9 (1901) (testimony that defendant's son never heard anything said in family about defendant having trouble with her stepdaughter, and never heard stepdaughter mention that defendant injured her); Hinson v. Morgan, 225 N.C. 740, syl. 1 (1945) (in action to set aside tax foreclosure sale, where commissioner made conveyance to Mrs. L, since deceased, and she reconveyed, testimony of Mrs. L's husband, that he knew that she did not pay anything for deed or receive payment for reconveyance, because he had never heard her mention such payments, held clearly hearsay); Lake Drainage Commissioners v. Spencer, 174 N.C. 36, 93 S.E. 435, syl. 1 (1917) (fact that mother, now dead, said nothing to her children about having been served with summons, inadmissible as hearsay when offered to show that it was not served on her); Karlen v. Trebble, 45 S.D. 570, 189 N. W. 519, syl. 3 (1922) (witness living with plaintiff

these silence cases as a whole, there is probably a greater proportion of instances where the evidence is admitted, than in the cases of affirmative conduct, but the preponderance in number of cases is again with those which exclude the evidence. The instances where the hearsay problem is recognized or mentioned are even more infrequent than in the cases of positive conduct.

Views of text-writers and commentators. Wigmore [29] suggests that the theory of circumstantial evidence is broad enough to admit evidence of conduct or utterances as evidencing belief of a past fact to show the truth of the fact, but that the objection to it is "that the pretended double inference is equivalent to giving credit to a testimonial assertion and involves therefore a danger of evasion of the Hearsay Rule." Without expressing any decided opinion as to the proper solution of the problem, he thus summarizes the result of the common law decisions: "It followed that instinct of compromise which has affected so many British institutions; it conceded something to both principles."

A succession of writers in the law reviews have pointed out the extent to which conduct, including silence, shares the dangers of hearsay, and the extent to which it is free from those dangers.[30] They have criticised the apparent assumption by most of the courts that wherever conduct (including silence) is offered to show belief, to show the truth of the fact believed, it is to be excluded as hearsay. This excludes too much evidence that is valuable and significant. They have accordingly advocated a more flexible and discriminating handling of the problem.

Conclusions. Based in part upon the discussion of these commentators, and upon a selection from their occasionally divergent views, the suggestions which follow are submitted.

The existing practice, it seems, should be modified in one of two ways. If according to present orthodoxy, we are to continue to classify as hearsay, acts to show the actor's belief to show the truth of the fact believed, then an exception to the hearsay rule should be recognized for such evidence, under reasonable safeguards for its reliability.[31]

---

had not heard plaintiff's mother or father or anyone else claim ownership of auto, held incompetent for any purpose).

29. Wigmore, op. cit. § 267; see also ibid. §§ 268–273. In § 459 he seems to confine the hearsay rule to "utterances" but doubtless this is done *alio intuitu*.

30. Seligman, An Exception to the Hearsay Rule, 26 Harv.L.Rev. 146, 148, 149 (1912); McCormick, The Borderland of Hearsay, 39 Yale L.J. 489 (1930); Morgan, Hearsay and Non-Hearsay, 48 Harv.L.Rev. 1138 (1935), The Hearsay Rule, 12 Wash.L.Rev. 1, 7 (1937), Some Suggestions for Defining and Classifying Hearsay, 86 U.Pa.L.Rev. 258, 262 (1938), Hearsay Dangers and the Application of the Hearsay Concept, 62 Harv.L.Rev. 177, 190, 197 (1948); Falknor, Silence as Hearsay, 89 U.Pa.L.Rev. 192 (1940); Murchison, Silence as Hearsay, 24 N.C.L. Rev. 274 (1946).

31. Among the most practical proposals for such safeguards are the following by Dean Falknor: ". . . The suggestion, then, is that while hearsay should be defined so as to include not only utterances but also non-assertive conduct, where relevancy depends upon inferences from the con-

duct to the belief of the actor to the fact believed, evidence of such non-assertive conduct should be exceptionally admitted if, but only if, the trial judge first finds that (a) the actor had personal knowledge of the fact (i. e., the occurrence of the event or the existence of the condition) to the proof of which the evidence is offered; more precisely, that it fairly appears that the actor observed or had the opportunity to observe such event or condition and that nothing appears to cast substantial doubt upon the quality of his recollection at the time of the conduct; and (b) that the conduct was important or significant to the actor in his affairs and so vouched his belief "as to give reasonable assurance of trustworthiness", and (c) in the case of negative conduct (i. e., inaction) or silence, that such negative conduct or silence was a detriment to the actor." Silence as Hearsay, 89 U.Pa.L.Rev. 192, 216 (1940).

It is to be noted that even under the presently "orthodox" theory of conduct as hearsay, the court should apply to conduct the recognized exceptions that would admit verbal statements despite the hearsay rule. Conduct, it seems, would often qualify as the equivalent of an admission of a party, a declaration against interest, or a statement of bod-

The taboo of hearsay is strong, however, and securing recognition for a new exception in this ill-explored area, would be an uphill task. The present writer believes, accordingly that much the more viable path to improvement is the alternative theory which would limit hearsay to assertions, namely to statements, oral or written, or acts intended to be communicative, such as signals and the sign-language, when offered to prove the truth of the facts asserted. Other acts and conduct, including silence, when offered to show belief to prove the fact believed, would be classed (as many decisions have classed it) as circumstantial evidence.[32] The debate, then, upon the admission of any particular item of conduct-evidence offered for this purpose, would be upon the question whether it meets the standard of relevancy by which all circumstantial evidence is tested. This standard, applied by the trial judge, is whether the probative value of the evidence, upon the inference for which it is offered, is sufficiently substantial to justify the time involved in receiving it, and to outweigh any dangers of confusion and prejudice.[33]

The application of this general standard to conduct-evidence offered for this purpose should, it seems, require the trial judge to consider these preliminary questions: Does it appear that the person whose conduct is in question had an opportunity to observe the facts sought to be inferred from his conduct? Were his acts, or his inaction, so related to his important interests that it is substantially unlikely that he would thus have acted, or failed to act, unless he believed that the inferred facts were true? Is the person in question available as a witness, and if so are the circumstances such as to make it more expedient to call him rather than to consider inferences from his conduct? It seems that a negative answer to any of these questions should require the exclusion of the evidence. With such an approach, however, it is submitted that a great deal of evidence, which common sense tells us is highly valuable and significant, and which is excluded under the traditional method of handling the problem, would be admitted. Moreover, the necessity of a responsible judgment by the trial judge, rather than of a merely mechanical response, would be clarified and emphasized.[34]

---

ily condition. See Morgan, The Hearsay Rule, **12** Wash.L.Rev. **1,** 10 (1937).

32. This approach is adopted by the decisions, forming a numerous though a minority group, which decline to treat conduct as hearsay, see notes, 16–25, supra. It is persuasively advocated by Murchison, 24 N.C.L.Rev. 274, 282 (1946). This seems also to be the view adopted in Uniform Rule 62(1), which includes in the definition of statement "non verbal conduct . . . intended . . . as a substitute for words in expressing the matter stat-

ed," and Rule 63, which limits "hearsay" to "statements."

33. See § 152, herein, **1** Wigmore, Evidence, §§ 38, 39, and James, Relevancy, Probability and the Law, 29 Calif.L.Rev. 689, 701 (1941).

34. The breadth of the trial judge's discretion on passing on the admissibility of the absence of complaints is stressed in Sullivan v. Minneapolis St. Ry. Co., 161 Minn. 45, 200 N.W. 922, syl. 3 (1924) and in Menard v. Cashman, 94 N.H. 428, 55 A.2d 156, syl. 15 (1947).

CHAPTER 26

TESTIMONY TAKEN AT A FORMER HEARING OR IN ANOTHER ACTION [1]

230. Introductory: Is It Hearsay? Scope of Statutes.

Under requirements which are designed to guarantee an adequate opportunity of cross-examination, evidence may be received in the pending case, in the form of a written transcript or an oral report, of a witness's previous testimony. This testimony may have been given by deposition or at a trial, either in a separate case or proceeding, or in a former hearing of the present pending case.[2] This is frequently called former testimony. Such evidence may be classified, depending upon the precise formulation of the rule against hearsay, as an exception to the hearsay prohibition on the one hand, or as a class of evidence where the requirements of the hearsay rule are complied with, on the other. The former view is accepted generally by the courts [3] and textwriters; [4] the latter is espoused by Wigmore.[5] The present writer has followed the former classification by adopting a definition of hearsay which would include all testimony given by deposition or at a previous trial or hearing, in the present or another litigation, provided it is now offered as evidence of the facts testified to.[6] Only testimony given orally at the present trial or hearing, and subject to cross-examination, would when offered to prove the facts recited escape the name of hearsay. The reasons for this choice are, first, it follows the usage

---

1. See Wigmore, Student Text, §§ 235, 245, 246, 313, Evidence, §§ 1370, 1371, 1386–1389 (Requirements of Adequate Opportunity to Cross-Examine); §§ 1402–1415 (Unavailability of Witness); §§ 1660–1669 (Proof by Official Notes, Records, Reports, Etc.); §§ 2098, 2099, 2103 (Must Entire Testimony be Proved?); Hinton, Changes in Hearsay Exceptions, 29 Ill.L.Rev. 422, 427, 1934. See also Hale, The Missouri Law of Former Testimony, 14 St. Louis Law Rev. 375, 1929, an excellent statement for general purposes despite its local slant.
See also Decennial Digests, Evidence, ☞ 575–583, Criminal Law, ☞540–548; 22 C.J., Evidence, §§ 510–534; 31 C.J.S., Evidence, §§ 384–402.

2. For decisions stating the rule, see, e. g., State v. Carr, 67 S.D. 481, 294 N.W. 174, syl. 1 (1940); State v. Ortego, 22 Wash.2d 552, 157 P.2d 320, syl. 4 (1945).

3. George v. Davie, 201 Ark. 470, 145 S.W.2d 729, syl. 3 (1941); Walker v. Walker, 14 Ga. 242, 249 (1853); Lone Star Gas Co. v. State, 137 Tex. 279, 153 S.W.2d 681, syl. 14 (1941).

4. See, e. g., 1 Greenleaf, Evidence, § 163 (3rd ed. 1846); 3 Jones, Commentaries on Evidence, § 1177 (2d ed. 1926); McKelvey, Evidence, § 227 (5th ed. 1944).

5. 5 Wigmore, Evidence, § 1370. This view has occasionally been approved by the courts, see, e. g., Habig v. Bastian, 117 Fla. 864, 158 So. 508, 510 (1935), and has been adopted by other text-writers, e. g. Chamberlayne, Trial Evidence, § 729 (2d ed. by Tompkins, 1936); 1 Elliott, § 496 (1904).

6. See § 225, supra.

most familiar to the profession, and second, it probably facilitates the wider admission of former testimony, which is generally of a relatively high degree of trustworthiness, under a liberalized exception. An insistence upon the equivalent of a present opportunity to cross-examine disregards the other elements of special reliability in former testimony such as the oath, the solemnity of the occasion, and in the case of transcribed testimony, the accuracy of reproduction of the words spoken.[7]

Many of the exceptions to the hearsay rule have been developed almost solely through the judicial process, others have been widely regulated by statute, and the present exception is of the latter class. It will be impossible, however, in this brief work to describe the variations in the statutes of the different states. The usual approach, however, is that these statutes on former testimony are "declaratory" of the common law, so far as they go, and not the exclusive test of admissibility. Accordingly, if the evidence meets the common law requirements, it will usually come in even though the permissive provisions of the statute do not mention the particular common law doctrine which the evidence satisfies,[8] and correspondingly when the common law imposes a restriction not mentioned in the statute, the restriction will govern, unless the circumstances show a legislative intention to abrogate it.[9]

It is important to notice at the outset that evidence of former testimony may often be given without meeting the requirements discussed in this chapter such as identity of parties and issues and unavailability of the witness. These requirements are applicable only when the evidence is offered for the hearsay purpose of proving the facts recited in the former testimony and its admission is sought under this particular exception. When the proof of the former testimony is relevant for some non-hearsay purpose,[10] as to show the commission of the act of perjury,[11] or to show that the witness by testifying adversely to the accused furnished the motive for the murder of the witness,[12] or to refresh recollection, or impeach a witness at the present trial by proving that he testified differently on a former occasion,[13] the restrictions of the hearsay exception do not apply. Likewise, if offered for a hearsay purpose but under some other exception, e. g., as the ad-

---

7. The restrictions upon the use of former testimony are attributed to the dominance in Anglo-American trials of the adversary or contentious theory of procedure rather than to a consideration of the capacities of the jury to evaluate such evidence. Morgan, The Jury and the Exclusionary Rules of Evidence, 4 U.Chi.L.Rev. 247, 256 (1937).

8. State v. Moore, 40 N.M. 344, 59 P.2d 902, syl. 9 (1936) (witness whose testimony was given at preliminary hearing, was absent from state; held, reported testimony admissible though statute mentioned only death of witness as ground of admission); State v. Ham, 224 N.C. 128, 29 S.E.2d 449, syl. 10 (1944) (statute making testimony on preliminary hearing admissible when subscribed and certified does not limit admission under common law practice where stenographer swears report accurate, though not subscribed or certified).

9. Illinois Steel Co. v. Muza, 164 Wis. 247, 159 N.W. 908 (1916) (Wis.St. 1951, § 325.31 providing for admission of former testimony "where the party against whom it is offered shall have had an opportunity to cross-examine" is declaratory of common law and hence is qualified by condition that the opportunity to cross-examine must be on substantially the same issues), cited approvingly in In re Sweeney's Estate, 248 Wis. 607, 22 N.W.2d 657 (1946).

10. See 5 Wigmore, Evidence, § 1387, notes 5–7.

11. See State v. Wykert, 198 Iowa 1219, 199 N.W. 331, syl. 2 (1924) where admissibility for this purpose is assumed, and where proof of former testimony of other witnesses to show the materiality of the perjured testimony is also sanctioned.

12. Suggested by the facts in Nordan v. State, 143 Ala. 13, 39 So. 406, syl. 15 (1905) though the opinion does not quite reach this point.

13. People v. Ferraro, 293 N.Y. 51, 55 N.E.2d 861, syl. 3 (1944). See also People v. Hawley, 111 Calif. 78, 43 P. 404, syl. 5 (1896) (testimony of accused at preliminary hearing admissible to impeach: it seems that it would have been as readily receivable as an admission).

McCormick Evidence HB—31

mission of a party-opponent,[14] only the requirements of the exception under which it is offered, and not those of the present exception need be satisfied.

231. The Requirement of Oath and Opportunity for Cross-Examination: The Rule of Confrontation.

The former testimony, to be admitted under this exception to the hearsay rule, must have been given under the sanction of the oath[1] or such form of affirmation as is accepted as legally sufficient. More important, because more often drawn in question, is the requirement that the party against whom the

former testimony is now offered, or a party in like interest, must have had a reasonable opportunity to cross-examine.[2] Such reasonable opportunity requires that he, or his counsel, must have been present at the former hearing,[3] or must have had adequate notice and opportunity to appear. Actual cross-examination, of course, is not essential, if the opportunity was afforded and waived.[4] The question has been raised in criminal cases whether if the accused is not represented by counsel at the preliminary hearing but is allowed to question the witnesses himself, sufficient opportunity for cross-examination is afforded.[5] Only in cases where the accused

---

14. Bogie v. Nolan, 96 Mo. 85, 9 S.W. 14, syl. 1 (1888); Tuttle v. Wyman, 146 Neb. 146, 18 N.W.2d 744, syl. 7 (1945). See 5 Wigmore, Evidence, § 1416(1).

1. The opinions speak of oath and cross-examination as the requirements. See, e. g., Smythe v. Inhabitants, 263 F. 481, 487 (C.C.A. N.J. 1920); Habig v. Bastian, 117 Fla. 864, 158 So. 508, 511 (1935). A case has not been found, naturally, where oath was lacking but opportunity for cross-examination was afforded, but it has been held that predicate for admission of former testimony is not laid without a showing that the witness was sworn. Monahan v. Clemons, 212 Ky. 504, 508, 279 S.W. 974 (1926).

2. Fender v. Ramsey, 131 Ga. 440, 62 S.E. 527, syl. 1 (1908) (ex parte affidavit used in former trial inadmissible); Kostlan v. Mowery, 208 Iowa 623, 226 N.W. 32, syl. 2 (1929) (rule stated); Edgerley v. Appleyard, 110 Me. 337, 86 A. 244, syl. 4, Ann.Cas. 1914D, 474 (testimony taken at coroner's inquest inadmissible for want of opportunity to cross-examine); School Dist. v. Sachse, 274 Mich. 345, 264 N.W. 396, syl. 1 (1936) (rule stated); Citizens' Bank and Trust Co. v. Reid Motor Co., 216 N.C. 432, 5 S.E.2d 318, syl. 5 (1939) (direct examination taken before Workmen's Compensation Commissioner where witness refused to submit to cross-examination not receivable in evidence in judicial proceeding for compensation); and cases cited 22 C. J. Evidence, § 516; 31 C.J.S., Evidence, § 390; Decennial Digests, Evidence, ⊂⇒578.

3. But where testimony taken at a coroner's inquest was offered, and it appeared that counsel for the present party was present at the inquest, it was held inadmissible absent a showing that he was accorded as opportunity to cross-examine in behalf of the party against whom it is now offered. Jackson v. Chilly, 16 Colo. 103, 26 P. 331, syl. 2 (1891).

4. State v. Logan, 344 Mo. 351, 126 S.W.2d 256, syl. 8, 9, 122 A.L.R. 417 (1939) (murder: witness at former trial not cross-examined by counsel for accused); Bradley v. Mirick, 91 N.Y. 293 (1883) (on previous trial, defendant's counsel not appearing trial proceeded as on default, and plaintiff's testimony taken: held admissible on a second trial: opportunity for cross-examination waived); State v. Swiden, 62 S.D. 208, 252 N.W. 628, syl. 2 (1934) (where defendant, one of several persons charged, waived examining trial, testimony taken at examining trial of other defendants, admissible at defendant's final trial; this application of the principle seems debatable); 5 Wigmore, Evidence, § 1371; 3 Jones, Commentaries on Evidence, § 1182 (2d ed. 1926).

5. Held adequate: People v. Hunley, 313 Mich. 688, 21 N.W.2d 923, syl. 4 (1946) (defendant had cross-examined); Hill v. State, 58 Nev. 28, 68 P.2d 569, syl. 2 (1937) (The defendant, a man of seventy, was charged with murdering another old man by cutting him with a knife, in a fight, and the defendant claimed self-defense. At the preliminary hearing before a magistrate, the defendant seemingly was not represented by counsel. The State examined at this hearing one Mix, a crucial witness, and the defendant seemingly did not cross-examine. At the final trial, Mix could not be found and the State offered his testimony at the previous hearing. The defendant objected and called the magistrate who testified that the defendant appeared to be unfamiliar with judicial proceedings, and that he did not "believe he could examine or cross-examine very well." The court overruled the objection and on appeal this ruling was sustained, the court relying on the fact that the defendant's testimony at the final trial indicated that he then "understood very well what evidence would tend to help him as well as what would tend to prejudice his case.") It hardly seems practical to apply the same rigorous

was shown to be mentally unbalanced,[6] or has not been apprised of his right to cross-question the witness[7] or where he has been denied adequate opportunity to secure counsel[8] has the objection prevailed. An improper curtailment of the right to cross-examine to elicit former convictions of crime for impeachment purposes has been held to be a denial of an adequate opportunity to cross-examine,[9] but restrictions by the judge upon cross-examination where they fall within the range of the judge's discretionary control would surely not be such a denial.

Is the opportunity for direct and redirect examination the equivalent of the opportunity for cross-examination? If party A (or his predecessor in interest) calls and examines a witness in the first hearing, and this testimony is offered against A in a second trial, may it come in against the objection of want of opportunity to cross-examine? The decisions sensibly hold that it may.[10]

Confrontation.[11] The Sixth Amendment to the Federal Constitution adopted in 1787 re-

quires "that in all criminal prosecutions, the accused shall enjoy the right . . . to be confronted with the witnesses against him." [12] The Massachusetts Declaration of Rights of 1780 provides that "every subject shall have a right . . . to meet the witnesses against him face to face." Nearly every state constitution has a like provision.[13] If literally applied they would prevent altogether the use for the prosecution in criminal cases of former testimony or of dying declarations, public records or other evidence coming in under the traditional exceptions to the hearsay rule. They have not been literally applied.

In the late 1700's when these provisions were first included in American bills of rights the general rule against hearsay had been accepted in England for 100 years,[14] but it was equally well established that former testimony taken in the presence of the accused and subject to cross-examination was received against him if the witness was dead or unavailable.[15] There lingered, however, the

standard to this collateral question of admissibility, as would be applied in determining whether the original trial without counsel was a denial of due process.
In Poe v. State, 95 Ark. 172, 129 S.W. 292, syl. 7 (1910) it was held that the fact that the accused was not represented by counsel was not a ground for exclusion. It did not appear whether the accused, a negro youth, cross-examined, or was accorded an opportunity to do so, or was capable of cross-examining. The holding seems questionable.

6. Combs v. State, 52 Okl.Cr. 99, 2 P.2d 1037 (1931).

7. Commonwealth v. Lenousky, 206 Pa. 277, 55 A. 977, syl. 2 (1903).

8. People v. Sperduto, 221 App.Div. 577, 224 N.Y.S. 529, 531 (1927).

9. Gill v. State, 148 Tex.Cr. 513, 188 S.W.2d 584, syl. 6 (1945) and see the original opinion in the same case, 147 Tex.Cr. 392, 181 S.W.2d 276, syl. 1–3 (1944).

10. Louisville & N. Ry. Co. v. Scott, 232 Ala. 84, 167 So. 572, syl. 10 (1936); Roberts v. Gerber, 187 Wis. 282, 202 N.W. 701, syl. 3 (1925) (deposition); 5 Wigmore, Evidence, § 1389. Under certain circumstances the testimony might also be admissible as the admission of a party, see § 246, Notes 10–13, herein.

11. See generally 5 Wigmore, Evidence, §§ 1365, 1395–1400; Decennial Digests, Criminal Law, ☞662; 23 C.J.S., Criminal Law § 999; Notes, Use in criminal case of former testimony, 15 A.L.R. 495, 79 id. 1392, 122 id. 425, 159 id. 1240.

12. This provision, of course, is not binding directly upon the state courts. West v. Louisiana, 194 U.S. 258, 263, 24 S.Ct. 650, 652 (1904) (use of testimony taken at preliminary examination, the accused present and his counsel cross-examining, against accused at final trial not deprivation of any Federal right under Sixth or Fourteenth Amendment). Whether the "fundamental justice" standard of the Fourteenth Amendment (see, e. g., Palko v. Connecticut, (1937), 302 U.S. 319, 325, 58 S.Ct. 149, 151, 152; Adamson v. California, (1947) 332 U.S. 46, 53, 67 S.Ct. 1672, 1676) may in any degree limit the use of hearsay by the prosecution in state courts, seems yet undecided.

13. They are collected and quoted in 5 Wigmore, Evidence, § 1397.

14. See § 223, supra.

15. Rex v. Vipont, 2 Burr. 1163, 97 Eng.Repr. 767 (1761) (semble); Rex v. Radbourne, 1 Leach C. L. 457 (1787); Rex v. Jolliffe, 4 Term R. 285, 100 Eng. Repr. 1022 (1791), all cited 15 A.L.R. 498, 500.

traditional practice, thought to be sanctioned by an old statute of Philip and Mary,[16] of admitting in criminal trials the testimony of witnesses taken before coroners or before committing magistrates in the absence of the accused, upon a showing that the witness was dead or insane or kept away by the accused.[17] It seems probable that the purpose of the American provisions for confrontation was to guarantee the maintenance in criminal cases of the hard-won principle of the hearsay rule, without abandoning the accepted practice of using former testimony, given subject to cross-examination by a witness now unavailable, which had not been questioned as to fairness, but forbidding here the practice of using depositions taken in the absence of the accused. This last had been much complained of,[18] and was later abandoned by the English judges [19] and forbidden by statute.[20] The interpretation has, in the main, been consonant with this purpose.

The production of the prosecution's witnesses at the final trial is important to the accused in three ways.[21] First, in the light of the common law tradition, it affords an opportunity for cross-examination. Second, it enables the accused to look the prisoner in the eye, which was once supposed to, and perhaps does, make a false accusation more difficult. Third, the judge or jury will see the demeanor of the witness on the stand and thus be enabled better to weigh his credibility. When testimony has been taken at a former hearing, with an opportunity for the accused to cross-examine, it furnishes the first two incidents as completely as testimony at the trial. So the question comes down to whether the third is indispensable. The cases today all accept the conclusion that it is not. It may be dispensed with, but it is nevertheless valuable and worth according, if we can. But when we cannot, when the witnesses are not available for production at the trial, the courts now agree that the former testimony, taken with opportunity to cross-examine, may be received against the accused without infringing the confrontation provisions.[22] The confrontation provisions raise other questions not appropriate for discussion here, but as applied to the admission of former testimony, and the application of the hearsay rule, the main problems are these:

What causes of unavailability are sufficient to justify dispensing with demeanor evidence? The following have been held sufficient, besides death: [23] absence from the

---

16. 1 and 2 Philip and Mary, ch. 13 (1553).

17. See e. g. Rex v. Baker, 2 Strange 1240, 93 Eng. Repr. 1156 (1746) (semble), cited 15 A.L.R. 498; 5 Wigmore, Evidence, § 1364(8).

18. "I do not think any part of the old procedure operated more harshly upon prisoners than the summary and secret way in which justices of the peace, acting frequently the part of detective officers, took their examinations and committed them for trial. It was a constant and most natural and reasonable topic of complaint by the prisoners who were tried for the Popish Plot that they had been taken without warning, kept close prisoners from the time of their arrest, and kept in ignorance of the evidence against them till the very moment when they were brought into court to be tried." 1 Stephen, Hist.Crim. Law of England, 225 (1883).

19. 5 Wigmore, Evidence, § 1364 (8); 9 Holdsworth, Hist.Eng. Law 219 (1926).

20. 11 and 12 Vict. ch. 42 (1848), known as Sir John Jervis's Act; see 1 Stephen, Hist.Crim. Law of England, 220 (1883).

21. See 5 Wigmore, Evidence, §§ 1395, 1396.

22. State v. Gaetano, 96 Conn. 306, 114 A. 82, 15 A.L.R. 458 (1921); Comm. v. Gallo, 275 Mass. 320, 175 N.E. 718, 79 A.L.R. 1380 (1931); People v. Moore, 306 Mich. 29, 10 N.W.2d 296, syl. 2, 3 (1943); State v. McO'Blenis, 24 Mo. 402, 69 Am.Dec. 435 (1857); State v. Logan, 344 Mo. 351, 126 S.W.2d 256 (1939); McMurrey v. State, 145 Tex.Crim. 439, 168 S.W.2d 858, syl. 7 (1943); State v. Ortego, 22 Wash.2d 552, 157 P.2d 320, syl. 3–5, 159 A.L.R. 1232, annotation at p. 1242 (1946).

It is perhaps worth noting that the confrontation provisions never explicitly require confrontation *at the final trial.*

23. Mattox v. United States, 156 U.S. 237, 15 S.Ct. 337 (1895); Note, 15 A.L.R. 515, 516.

state,[24] illness,[25] insanity,[26] and the effective claim by the witness of a privilege not to testify.[27] The confrontation provisions influenced the courts in the earlier decisions toward stricter requirements in this regard than in applying the standard of availability in civil cases [28] in administering the other exceptions to the hearsay rule, but the present trend here as in the civil cases is toward the acceptance of any genuine showing of unavailability whatever the cause.[29]

May depositions (with opportunity for cross-examination) be taken by the prosecution and used against the accused, the witness being unavailable? Provided the proper provisions are made to enable indigent defendants to be represented at the taking,

there seems just reason to permit the state, as the accused is usually permitted, to take and use the depositions of witnesses who cannot be produced. The shadow of the confrontation provisions was enough to deter the early legislatures, in making provision for depositions, to omit provision for their taking in criminal cases by the state.[30] The courts having permitted the use for the state of testimony at a preliminary hearing or at a former trial, there could be no principle which could ban the taking and use by the state of a deposition.[31] But the doubt-provoked omission remains a sufficient obstacle in most of the states—there is no enabling statute. The need for such statutes to prevent the flouting of justice has been pointed

24. Smith v. State, 147 Ga. 689, 95 S.E. 281, 15 A.L.R. 490 (1918) (witness moved her residence to another state and refuses to attend trial). If shown that the witness will be out of the state indefinitely, this suffices. Norton v. State, 148 Tex.Crim. 294, 186 S.W.2d 347, syl. 3, 4 (1945). But a temporary absence has been held insufficient. State v. Anderson, 219 Wis. 623, 263 N.W. 587 (1935) (witness for state, a deputy district attorney away on two weeks vacation). But should not the witness be deemed unavailable for the present trial, so as to admit the former testimony unless the trial judge considers his production so important as to warrant an adjournment or continuance if the defendant so requests?

Of course, absence of the witness by procurement of, or connivance with, the accused is an ample showing of unavailability. State v. Brown, 285 S.W. 995 (Mo.1926); Note, 15 A.L.R. 524.

Moreover, if the state proves that the whereabouts of the witness is unknown and that after diligent search he cannot be located, this is enough. State v. Ortego, 22 Wash.2d 552, 157 P.2d 320, 326, 159 A.L.R. 1232 (1945).

25. It has been frequently said that the illness must be permanent or indefinite. See State v. Wheat, 111 La. 860, 35 So. 955 (1904); Note, 15 A.L.R. 522, 523. But the later trend seems toward making ability to attend the present trial the test. See People v. Droste, 160 Mich. 66, 125 N.W. 87, syl. 3 (1910); Note, 159 A.L.R. 1247. Compare next previous note.

26. Marler v. State, 67 Ala. 55, 42 Am.Rep. 95 (1880); Note, 15 A.L.R. 522.

27. McCoy v. State, 221 Ala. 446, 129 So. 21, syl. 4 (1930) (privilege of wife not to testify against husband); Note, 79 A.L.R. 430.

28. See, as reflecting this earlier attitude, Spencer v. State, 132 Wis. 509, 112 N.W. 462, 464 (1907) (calling attention to stricter attitude in criminal cases). Contrast the liberal statement of grounds in Langham v. State, 12 Ala.App. 46, 68 So. 504, 509 (1915).

29. "In Ibanez v. Winston, 222 Mass. 129, at page 130, 109 N.E. 814, it was said that the rule touching the reproduction at a second trial of testimony given at a former trial of the same case by a witness since deceased or insane 'in both civil and criminal cases is the same. The reason for the admission of such testimony is founded upon necessity and has for its end the attainment of substantial justice.'" Commonwealth v. Gallo, 275 Mass. 320, 175 N.E. 718, 723, 79 A.L.R. 1380, 1387 (1931).

30. See 5 Wigmore, Evidence, § 1398.

31. In upholding a statute empowering the prosecution to take and use depositions, the court (per Fritz, J.) said: " . . . the rule as to confrontation by witnesses is sufficiently complied with under the Constitution, as well as at common law, if the accused met the witnesses face to face, at the time that they were testifying, and if he then had the opportunity of cross-examining them. That is the primary purpose, and, when complied with, fully satisfies the rule as to confrontation. The personal appearance of the witnesses before the judge and the jury, on the trial, is of advantage also. However, that is but a secondary purpose, and that is not a right secured to an accused at common law, or under the Constitution." State v. Shaugnessy, 212 Wis. 322, 249 N.W. 522, 525 (1933).

out by the American Law Institute,[32] and in 1944 an eminent advisory group reported to the Supreme Court of the United States that seventeen states have by statute conferred at least a partial right upon the prosecution to use depositions.[33] They recommended that a similar provision be included in the Federal Rules of Criminal Procedure.[34] The court, without statement of reasons, denied the recommendation and limited the taking of depositions to the defendant.[35] It seems that it would have been difficult to state adequate reasons. Thus, in the Federal Courts and in two-thirds of the states, the prosecution remains without this needed resource for proof of its case.

Do the confrontation provisions in state and Federal constitutions limit the use for the prosecution of hearsay declarations fall-

ing within the exceptions to the hearsay rule? This was once a matter of doubt but it has now been established for a hundred years that those exceptions which were accepted when these provisions were included in the earliest American constitutions were not intended to be abrogated.[36] Most if not all of the common-law exceptions were so accepted by the 1780's. Accordingly the prosecution's use of dying declarations,[37] official written statements,[38] and regular entries[39] in the course of business is frequent and approved. There seems no reason to doubt that the other traditional exceptions as developed and liberalized by judicial decisions should be similarly treated. New statutory liberalizations of the hearsay exceptions should likewise, it seems, meet with no obstacle from these provisions,[40] so long as

---

32. American Law Institute, Model Code of Criminal Procedure, § 58 (1930) and Note in Tentative Draft No. 1, p. 239 (1928).

33. "See Ala.Code 1940, Tit. 15, § 299; Cal.Const. art. 1, § 13; Cal.Pen. Code (Deering, 1941) §§ 1335–1345, Colo.Stat.Ann. (Michie, 1935) c. 48, §§ 470–473; Idaho Code Ann. (1932) § 19–724; Ind.Stat. Ann. (Burns, 1933) § 9–1610; La. Code Crim.Proc. Ann. (Dart, 1932) arts. 157–159; Me.Rev.Stat. (1930) c. 146, § 19; Mass.Gen. Laws (1932) c. 277, §§ 76–77; Mont.Rev. Codes Ann. (Anderson & McFarland, 1935) §§ 12187–12197; Nev.Comp. Laws (Hillyer, 1929) § 10654; N.Y. Code Crim.Proc. § 219; Ohio Const. art. 1, § 10; Ohio Gen.Code Ann. (Page, 1939) §§ 13444–10–13444–11; S.C. Code (1942) § 1016; Vt.Pub.Laws (1933) § 2385; Wash.Rev.Stat. Ann. (Remington, 1932) tit. 14, § 2306; Wis.Stat. (1939) § 326.06; Wyo.Rev.Stat.Ann. (Courtright, 1931) §§ 33–806–33–811." Fed. Rules of Crim.Proc., Second Prelim. Draft, 93 (1944). See also 5 Wigmore, Evidence, § 1398, n. 6.

34. Proposed Rule 17, Advisory Committee's Final Report of Proposed Rules, June, 1944, pp. 17–20. Clause (c) was as follows: "*Defendant's Counsel and Payment of Expenses.* If a defendant is without counsel the court shall advise him of his right and assign counsel to represent him unless the defendant elects to proceed without counsel or is able to obtain counsel. If it appears that a defendant at whose instance a deposition is to be taken cannot bear the expense thereof, the court may direct that the expenses of travel and subsistence of the defendant's attorney for attendance at the examination shall be paid by the government. In

that event the marshal shall make payment accordingly."

35. Federal Rules of Crim.Proc., Rule 15 (1946).

36. Campbell v. State, 11 Ga. 374 (1852); Lambeth v. State, 22 Miss. 352, 357 (1852); State v. McO'-Blenis, 24 Mo. 416, 435 (1857).

37. Mattox v. United States, 156 U.S. 237, 243 (1895); Campbell v. State, next preceding note, Lambeth v. State, next preceding note.

38. State v. Torello, 103 Conn. 511, 131 A. 429, (certified copy of report of analysis of liquor by state chemist); Comm. v. Slavski, 245 Mass. 405, 140 N.E. 465, syl. 4, 5 (1923) (similar to last); People v. Nisonoff, 293 N.Y. 597, 59 N.E.2d 420, (1944) (assistant medical examiner's report of autopsy; excellent opinion by Conway, J.).

39. United States v. Leathers, 135 F.2d 507, syl. 3 (C.C.A.2d 1943) (air mail stamp affixed by bank in regular course of business); State v. Guaraneri, 59 R.I. 173, 194 A. 589, syl. 10, 11 (1937) (hospital records).

40. "The appellant Thomas argues that the records in question would not be admissible under the early common law rules and that the recent judicial and statutory changes we have referred to are in contravention of the Sixth Amendment. But statements by relatives as to pedigree, declarations against interest, and most important of all in criminal trials, dying declarations, have long been recognized as admissible. It is not necessary to say what limits the Sixth Amendment may set to the extention of exceptions to the rule against

the traditional bases for the hearsay exceptions, namely that hearsay may be admitted when it is (a) specially needed and (b) specially trustworthy, are preserved in the statutory extensions.[41]

Wigmore's exposition of confrontation has brought light into the dark corners of the subject, and has greatly contributed to the present liberal interpretation of the constitutional provisions. Consequently, strict and literal interpretations from the pre-Wigmore era must be read with caution.

232. "Identity of Parties" as a Supposed Requirement.[1]

The haste and pressure of trials compel lawyers and judges to speak in catch-words or shorthand phrases in talking about evidence rules. Thus "identity of parties" is often spoken of as a requirement for the admission of former testimony.[2] It is a convenient phrase to indicate a situation where the underlying requirement of adequacy of the present opponent's opportunity of cross-examination would usually be satisfied. But a *requirement* of identity of parties—and so we shall see of "identity of issues" [3]—is hardly a useful generalization, because it obscures the end in view, and because it must be hedged with qualifications too many and too wide for the rule to be helpful. Some of these follow.

It is clear, for example, that if the two present adversary parties, proponent of the evidence and his opponent, were parties in the former proceedings in which the testimony was taken, it is immaterial that there are additional parties in either or both proceedings not common to the two suits.[4]

Again, whether we have regard to the present party offering the former testimony, or only to the present party against whom it is offered (which we shall see is the better view) it is sufficient that the present party, though not the same, is a successor in interest to the corresponding party in the former suit.[5] This notion, to which the courtroom

---

hearsay. Probably the permissible extension is a question of degree. We think that business records kept as a matter of ordinary routine are often likely to be more reliable than dying declarations. It cannot be reasonably argued that the extension of the common law book entry rule which we discussed in Massachusetts Bonding & Ins. Co. v. Norwich Pharmacal Co., supra, or the statute cited above [The Federal Business Records Act, 28 U.S.C.A. § 1732], involve any violation of the Sixth Amendment." A. N. Hand, J., for the court in United States v. Leathers, 135 F.2d 507, 511 (C.C.A.2d 1943).

41. The Massachusetts Hearsay Act (G.L. [Ter.Ed.] c. 233, § 65) for example, might probably be held to satisfy these requirements, but an Act patterned on Rule 503 of the Model Code of Evidence supposedly would not.

1. See generally 5 Wigmore, Evidence, § 1386; 3 Jones, Commentaries on Evidence, §§ 1178, 1179 (2d ed. 1926); 1 Elliott, Evidence, § 508 (1904); 20 Am.Jur., Evidence, § 690; 31 C.J.S. Evidence §§ 387, 388; Dec.Dig. Evidence, ☞580; Note, Former testimony—identity of parties, 142 A.L.R. 673; Hale, Missouri Law on Use of Former Testimony, 14 St. Louis L.Rev. 375, 385 (1929).

2. Unfortunately some statutes are phrased in this way, see e. g. Calif.Code of Civ.Proc. § 1870, sub-

sec. 8: ". . . evidence may be given upon a trial of the following facts: . . . 8. The testimony of a witness deceased, or out of the jurisdiction, or unable to testify, given in a former action between the same parties, relating to the same matter; . . .." But the court has said that it "should receive a liberal construction." Smith v. Schwartz, 35 Cal.App.2d 659, 96 P.2d 816, 819 (1940).

3. See the next section.

4. Philadelphia, W. & B. R. Co. v. Howard, 13 How. 307, 14 L.Ed. 157 (1851) (additional co-plaintiff in former suit); Allen v. Chouteau, 102 Mo. 309, 14 S.W. 869, 871 (1890) (additional parties in former suit); Note, 142 A.L.R. 689.

5. See Bryan v. Malloy, 90 N.C. 508, 511 (1883) where the court said "Privity in the sense here used is a privity to the former action. To make one a privy to an action, he must be one who has acquired an interest in the subject-matter of the action, either by inheritance, succession, or purchase from a party to the action subsequent to its institution." The opportunity for cross-examination of the predecessor in interest is sufficient as a practical protection to the successor. Briggs v. Briggs, 80 Calif. 253, 22 P. 334, 335 (1889). See the compilations of statutes, 5 Wigmore, Evidence, § 1387, n. 4, and of cases construing the statutes, Note, 142 A.L.R. 716.

attaches the slogan "privity" is again sometimes spoken of as a requirement, rather than merely as a situation which satisfies the aim of adequate protection of the party-opponent. As a requirement it is indefensibly strict.[6]

Even more important is another inroad upon "identity." This is the recognition, under Wigmore's guidance,[7] by modern judges who place substance before form, that it is only the party *against* whom the former testimony is now offered, whose presence as a party in the previous suit is significant.[8] The older decisions which insisted on "reciprocity" or "mutuality," that is, that the party *offering* the former testimony in the present suit must also have been a party in the prior proceeding,[9] seem without any supporting basis in fairness or expediency. It is said by the sponsors of the older view that if the party against whom the testimony is offered were seeking to use the same testimony against the offering party he could not do so, because the present proponent was not a party to the former suit. This is true, if identity or privity is insisted on, but the result in that imaginary situation seems to have little bearing on the question of what is fair in respect to the actual situation where former testimony is offered against a party who did have adequate opportunity to cross-examine. The "reciprocity" doctrine can best be explained as proceeding from a mere uneasiness over the extension of the admission of former testimony to the entire area in which the justifying grounds are applicable.[10]

6. There is no magic for this purpose in the fact of succession. The question is whether the former party had substantially the same motive to cross-examine about the same matters as the present party would have. So the better later cases look to "identity of interest" rather than to succession, see note 13, infra.

7. Evidence, vol. 5, § 1388, p. 103.

8. Insul-Wool Insulation Corp. v. Home Insulation, 176 F.2d 502, syl. 1 (C.A. 10, 1949) (depositions taken in prior action for infringement admissible against plaintiff in subsequent action against other defendants for infringement of same patent); Wade v. King, 19 Ill. 300 (1857) ("It is sufficient, if the same matter were in issue in both cases, and those against whom the depositions are offered, or those under whom they claim the estate or right in question, had opportunity of cross-examining the witnesses and testing the truth of their testimony."); North River Ins. Co. v. Walker, 161 Ky. 368, 170 S.W. 983, syl. 1 (1914) (suit on fire insurance policy, defense, arson by plaintiff and her deceased husband, held testimony of deceased witness taken at examining trial of plaintiff and husband admissible against plaintiff); Young v. Reed, 192 So. 780, syl. 11 (La.App.1939); Harrell v. Quincy, O. & K. R. Co., 186 S.W. 677, syl. 5, 6 (Mo.1916) (quoting Wigmore); School District v. Sachse, 274 Mich. 345, 264 N.W. 396, syl. 1, 2 (1936) (evidence taken in criminal trial for fraud admitted against same defendant when sued civilly for restitution).

9. Morgan v. Nicholl, L.R. 2 C.P. 117 (1866) (action in ejectment by father; plaintiff seeks to use testimony of deceased witness taken in former action for the same land brought by son who supposed that his father was dead; excluded on ground that testimony could not have been used by defendants against present plaintiff for want of privity or identity of parties); Metropolitan St. Ry. Co. v. Gumby, 99 F. 192, 198 (C.C.A.N.Y.1900) (suit by infant's mother claiming damages for loss of services due to injury, held, testimony of deceased witness taken in former suit brought in infant's behalf against the same defendant for the same injury could not be used by plaintiff, no privity or reciprocity); McInturff v. Insurance Co. of North America, 248 Ill. 92, 93 N.E. 369, syl. 4, 140 Am. St.Rep. 153, 21 Ann.Cas. 176 (1910) (M. was tried on criminal charge for arson; after trial he kills T., witness for state; M. then sues on fire insurance policy; held, insurance company cannot use testimony of T. given at the criminal trial; surely this is a flagrant sacrifice of justice on the altar of technicalism); Concordia Fire Ins. Co. v. Wise, 114 Okl. 254, 246 P. 595, syl. 5, 46 A.L.R. 456 (1926) (suit on fire policy; former testimony in trial of present plaintiff for arson, not admissible against him in present action); Note, 142 A.L.R. 687, citing additional cases. Referring to some of these cases, the North Carolina court said: "These authorities, in our opinion, sacrifice substance to form, and exclude material evidence which has been subjected to the tests of truth, and in favor of a party who has had an opportunity to cross-examine." Hartis v. Charlotte Elec. Ry. Co., 162 N.C. 236, 237, 78 S.E. 164 (1913).

10. See the court's remarks in the McInturff case in the next preceding note: "If the rule contended for by plaintiff in error were good law, then in an action against a carrier by a passenger for a personal

Moreover, under what seems the practical and expedient view, if the party against whom the former testimony is now offered though not a party to the former suit, nor in "privity" as a successor in interest of any party therein, yet actually cross-examined the witness (personally or by counsel) about the matters which he would now want to cross-examine about, or was actually accorded a fair opportunity for such cross-examination and had a like motive for such examination, then the former testimony may be received.[11] Finally, the natural next step is to recognize, as progressive courts have done, that neither identity of parties nor privity between parties is essential. These are merely means to an end. Consequently, if it appears that in the former suit a party having a like motive to cross-examine about the same matters as the present party would have, was accorded an adequate opportunity for such examination, the testimony may be received against the present party.[12] Identity of interest, in the sense of motive, rather than technical identity of cause of action or title, is the test. Thus in a recent leading Missouri case, testimony taken in a previous suit by the husband for loss of services of the wife resulting from an injury, was admitted against the wife who sued in a separate action for her own injury from the same accident. Since the two causes of action are independent there was no "privity" or succession of rights between husband and wife, the plaintiffs in the two suits, but the court said that there was nevertheless "a complete iden-

---

injury the testimony of a witness since deceased would be admissible against the same carrier for an injury sustained in the same accident by another passenger, an employé, a licensee, or a trespasser, simply because the carrier against whom the testimony was offered had on the former trial an opportunity to cross-examine the witness. This rule would carry us too far afield for proof, and we cannot sanction it." (93 N.E. at p. 371).

11. In re Durant, 80 Conn. 140, 67 A. 497, syl. 10, 10 Ann.Cas. 539 (1907) (disbarment proceedings charging that defendant conspired to procure perjured testimony of Mrs. D in a divorce suit; testimony of Mrs. D in that divorce suit now offered against defendant, who had cross-examined as attorney for the wife: held admissible. "The requirement of an identity of parties is only a means to an end. This end was attained when the defendant availed himself of the unrestricted opportunity to cross-examine Mrs. Delkescamp."); Kreuger v. Sylvester, 100 Iowa 647, 69 N.W. 1059, syl. 5 (1897) (civil action for assault; testimony, "cross-examined by counsel," taken in previous criminal prosecution for assault, admitted; "admissibility . . . seems to turn on the right to cross-examine, rather than on the precise identity of the parties"); Brownlee v. Bunnell, 31 Ky.L. 669, 103 S.W. 284, syl. 1 (1907) (former testimony received against defendants in present suit on ground that though not parties to former suit they employed lawyers who defended the action at their instance); Charlesworth v. Tinker, 18 Wis. 633, 635 (1864) (facts similar to Kreuger v. Sylvester, same holding, relying on statute giving power to complain-

ant to control prosecution for assault; ". . . the true test . . . is, did the party who is to be affected by it have the power of cross-examining the witness, or at least have an opportunity of doing so?"). Compare Rumford Chemical Works v. Hygienic Chemical Co., 215 U.S. 156, 30 S.Ct. 45, syl. 2, 54 L.Ed. 137 (1909) (testimony in a former suit inadmissible against one who contributed to expense of defending former suit, but had no "right to intermeddle").

Seemingly requirements of identity or privity of parties or of identity of issues, like other procedural rules, have been relaxed in disbarment proceedings. Werner v. State Bar, 24 Cal.2d 611, 150 P.2d 892, syl. 3, 1944; Note, 161 A.L.R. 898.

12. This view has been applied to admit testimony taken in an action for personal injuries, in a later death action following the death of the original plaintiff. Lyon v. Rhode Island Co., 38 R.I. 252, 94 A. 893, syl. 1, 2, L.R.A.1916A 983; Hartis v. Charlotte Elec. Ry. Co., 162 N.C. 236, 78 S.E. 164, Ann.Cas.1915A 811; St. Louis Southwestern R. Co. v. Hengst, 81 S.W. 832, syl. 1, 3 (Tex.Civ.App.1904). Cases pro and con on the particular question are cited in Cook, Admissibility in Death Action of Deposition in Prior Personal Injury Action, 5 So. Calif.L.Rev. 209 (1932), Note, 142 A.L.R. 707.

See also Cox v. Selover, 171 Minn. 216, 213 N.W. 902, syl. 1 (1927) (testimony taken in former trial against guarantor admissible in later trial against the principal maker of note, who intervened after the first trial; "their interests are substantially the same") and see cases collected in Note, 142 A.L.R. 685, 696.

tity of interest." [13] Morgan calls this decision "a sensible extension of the established rule" and observes: "When the trustworthiness of testimony given in open court, under oath and subject to cross-examination, is compared with that of numerous utterances receivable as exceptions to the hearsay rule, the restrictions enforced as to its admissibility seem little short of ridiculous. Were the same strictness applied to all hearsay, evidence of reported testimony would constitute the only exception to the hearsay rule." [14]

233. Identity of Issues.[1]

Questions as to identity of the issues, or of the facts, involved in the former and present proceedings often arise in association with questions about identity or privity of parties. This is to be expected because any supposed requirement of identity of issues, is like the rule about parties,[2] merely a means of fulfilling the policy of securing an adequate

opportunity of cross-examination by the party against whom testimony is now offered or by someone in like interest. It is often said that the issue in the two suits must be the same.[3] But certainly the policy mentioned does not require that all the issues (any more than all the parties) in the two proceedings must be the same, but at most that the issue on which the testimony was offered in the first suit must be the same as the issue upon which it is offered in the second. Additional issues in either proceeding are of no consequence.[4] Moreover, insistence upon precise identity of issues, which might have some appropriateness if the question were one of res judicata or estoppel by judgment, are out of place here where the question is not of binding anyone, but merely of the salvaging, for what it may be worth, of the testimony of a witness not now available in person. Accordingly, modern opinions qualify the requirement by demanding only "substantial" identity of issues.[5]

---

13. Bartlett v. Kansas City Public Service Co., 349 Mo. 13, 160 S.W.2d 740, 745, syl. 7–9, 142 A.L.R. 666 (1942).

14. The Law of Evidence, 1941–1945, 59 Harv.L.Rev. 481, 551 (1946).

2. See 5 Wigmore, Evidence, §§ 1386, 1387; 3 Jones, Commentaries on Evidence, § 1180 (2d ed. 1926); 31 C.J.S., Evidence, § 389; 20 Am.Jur., Evidence, § 691; Decennial and Current Digests, Evidence ⊂⇒579, Crim.Law, ⊂⇒545; Hale, Missouri Law on Former Testimony, 14 St. Louis L.Rev. 375, 383 (1929).

2. See the next preceding section.

3. Statutes occasionally so provide, e. g., New Mexico, 1941 Comp. § 19–101(43) par. (a) (1) ("in any subsequent trial or hearing of the same issue between the same parties"); Pennsylvania, 19 P.S. § 582 ("of the same criminal issue").

4. Bartlett v. Kansas City Pub. Service Co., 349 Mo. 13, 160 S.W.2d 740, 743, 142 A.L.R. 666 (1942) (Testimony taken in suit by husband for loss of wife's services admitted against wife in suit by her for personal injuries in the same accident; "It is true that in the former proceeding there was an additional issue as to the loss of services by the husband. In other words, the question of substantive liability in the two cases was the same but the measure of damages was different. However, nei-

ther of these witnesses testified to anything having a bearing upon the question of damages. Their evidence concerned only the issue of primary negligence of the defendant."); Hartis v. Charlotte Elec. Ry. Co., 162 N.C. 236, 240, 78 S.E. 164, Ann. Cas.1915A 811 (Testimony given by plaintiff in action for personal injuries received in action brought for her death in same accident; "The cross-examination in the two cases would be practically the same, as the two facts to be investigated in each would be negligence, and the extent of the injuries, unless it would be broader and more extended in the first, due to the fact that in an action for personal injury recovery may be had for expenses, pain, loss of time, impaired capacity to make a living, etc., while in an action for wrongful death the injury as to damages is confined to the single question of the present value of net earnings, based on life expectancy."); Walkerton v. Erdman, 23 Can.S.Ct. 352, 367 (1894) (similar to last, two judges dissenting). Earlier Court of Appeals decisions in Missouri to the contrary are seemingly disapproved in the Bartlett case, supra, and are acutely criticised in Hale, op. cit., 14 St. Louis L.Rev. 375, 383, 384.

5. State v. Brinkley, 354 Mo. 337, 189 S.W.2d 314, 329, syl. 29 (1945); State v. Brown, 331 Mo. 556, 56 S.W.2d 405, 409, syl. 1 (1932); Proulx v. Parrow, 115 Vt. 232, 56 A.2d 623, 628, syl. 6 (1948). See

Must the form of the proceeding, the theory of the case, or the nature of the relief sought be same? Though there have been occasional holdings imposing such requirements,[6] it is manifest that they have no pertinence to the policy of adequacy of opportunity for cross-examination, and the more convincing opinions reject them.[7] Thus, in criminal cases where the first indictment charges one offense, e. g., robbery, and the second, another distinct offense, such as murder of the person robbed, it is usually considered sufficient that the two indictments arise from the same transaction.[8] Moreover, it seems reasonable to hold, as does an Oregon case, that where the fact testified to in the first case, namely, a polygamous marriage, was there material only as part of the defendant's scheme to commit larceny, the crime there charged, of the jewels of the supposed wife, such testimony may nevertheless be received upon a later indictment of the defendant for polygamy.[9] The motive to cross-examine the witnesses upon the fact of the polygamous marriage was sufficiently strong in the first case, even though conceivably not as compelling as it would have been in the second, to warrant its admission. It seems, then, that the requirement should be restated, not as one of identity or even of substantial identity of issues, but merely as a requirement that the issues in the first proceeding and hence the purpose for which the testimony was there offered, must have been such that the present opponent (or some person in like interest) had an adequate motive for testing on cross-examination the credibility of the testimony now offered.

234. Unavailability of the Witness.[1]

One of principal limitations upon the use of former testimony is the requirement that

McDougald v. Imler, 153 Fla. 619, 15 So.2d 418, syl. 1 (1943) (former trial, issue, simple negligence, present issue, gross negligence; sufficiently identical). Some statutes likewise adopt "substantial" identity of issues as the test. Georgia, Code, § 38–314; Wisconsin, St.1951, § 325.31.

6. Tom Reed Gold Mines Co. v. Moore, 40 Ariz. 174, 11 P.2d 347, syl. 4 (1932) (under statute limiting use to "the same action" testimony taken in personal injury action cannot be used in later death action); Hooper v. Southern Ry. Co., 112 Ga. 96, 37 S.E. 165, 168, syl. 1(b), (1900) (testimony taken in suit for personal injuries to minor brought by father as next friend not admissible in suit by father for his own loss of the child's services, there being different defenses available in the two suits—not substantially the same issue); Seward v. Schmidt, 49 N.E.2d 696, syl. 1 (Oh.App.1942) (similar to last case).

7. See, e. g., Hartis v. Charlotte Elec. Ry. Co., 162 N.C. 236, 237, 78 S.E. 164, Ann.Cas.1915A ("[The authorities which require identity of causes of action] sacrifice substance to form") and other cases cited in note 4 supra; Rhode Island Hospital Trust Co. v. Sherman, 56 R.I. 355, 185 A. 601, syl. 4, 5 (1936) (testimony taken in suit by administrator of husband, admissible in suit by administrator of wife, where an issue in both suits was validity of alleged gift of wife to son).

8. Fox v. State, 102 Ark. 393, 144 S.W. 516, syl. 3 (1912) (first trial of defendant for being accessory to murder, second, for being accessory to robbery, on same occasion); State v. Boyd, 140 Kan. 623, 38 P.2d 665, syl. 10 (1934) (embezzlement, misappropriation by custodian of public funds); State v. Brown, 331 Mo. 556, 56 S.W.2d 405, syl. 1 (1932); State v. Brinkley, 354 Mo. 337, 189 S.W.2d 314, syl. 29, 30 (1945) (first trial manslaughter prosecution against officers who arrested present defendant and his companion, who died after the arrest; second trial, prosecution of defendant for perjury in testifying before grand jury that he and his companion were beaten by officers at time of first arrest); State v. Swiden, 62 S.D. 208, 252 N.W. 628, syl. 2 (1934) (robbery, murder); State v. Dawson, 129 W. Va. 279, 40 S.E.2d 306, syl. 2 (1946) (testimony of victim, at hearing for robbery, admissible, when he later succumbs, at trial of robber for murder); Cases are collected in Note, 122 A.L.R. 430, 431, and earlier notes there referred to.

9. State v. Von Klein, 71 Ore. 159, 142 P. 549, syl. 5 (1914), and see State v. Brinkley, next preceding note. But compare Williams v. State, 2 Okl.Crim. 399, 276 P. 515, syl. 2 (1929) (defendant, a young woman and her companion, Barnett were tried for robbery of Mrs. H, while in an automobile with defendant; evidence taken at former trial of present defendants, for robbery of K., also in defendant's automobile, to show "scheme or plan"; excluded, disapproving Von Klein case, supra).

1. See 5 Wigmore, Evidence, §§ 1401–1414; 3 Jones, Commentaries on Evidence, §§ 1183–1189 (2d ed.

the witness be proven to be unavailable for production in person at the present trial.[2] This is a requirement common to many of the exceptions to the hearsay rule[3] and the determination as to what constitutes a sufficient showing of unavailability should probably be worked out uniformly for all such exceptions. The tendency of the courts, however, has been to limit the holding to the particular exception, rather than to discuss it as a general question.

This sort of separatism is especially marked in the case of former testimony. This is due to the influence of constitutional provisions requiring "confrontation" in criminal cases, and to the custom of enacting separate statutes to regulate the use of former testimony generally in civil cases, and the use of depositions taken in the present suit. Accordingly, unavailability as applied to former testimony in criminal cases has already been discussed as a part of the subject of confron-

tation.[4] Emphasis here will be upon the requirement as applied to former testimony in civil cases, with only incidental illustration from the criminal cases, and with a final mention of the deposition situation.

The following grounds are generally accepted.

(1) *Death,* of course.

(2) *Absence.* Permanent or indefinite residence without the state should always suffice.[5] Residence within the state but beyond the limits in which the trial court's subpena runs would seem sufficient.[6] Some courts, however, would require in both cases an additional showing that the witness's deposition could not have been taken.[7] In view of the greater hazards of forgetting and of pressures, the later statement, the deposition, can hardly be justifiably preferred to the earlier testimony, and this requirement, therefore, seems misconceived.[8] *Temporary*

1926); **1** Elliott, Evidence, §§ 498–503 (1904); **31** C.J.S., Evidence, §§ 391–396; 22 C.J. §§ 517–523; 20 Am.Jur., Evidence, §§ 700–709; Dec.Dig., Evidence, ⬤576, 577, Criminal Law, ⬤542, 543.

2. For general statements of the rule, see, e. g., Burns v. Leath, 236 Ala. 615, 184 So. 176, syl. **1** (1938); Nelson v. Lee, 249 Ala. 549, 32 So.2d 22, syl. **6** (1947); Clark v. Boston & Maine R. Co., 87 N.H. 434, 182 A. 175, syl. 2 (1936); Schofield v. Rideout, 233 Wis. 550, 290 N.W. 155, syl. **3**, 133 A.L.R. 834 (1940).

Iowa, however, has a more liberal and seemingly (see § 238, infra) more sensible practice. See LaSell v. Tri-States Theater Corp., 235 Ia. 492, 17 N.W.2d 89, syl. 1 (1945) (former testimony usable if witness not in court, without any showing that he is unavailable.)

And this like other requirements is relaxed in disbarment cases. Werner v. State Bar, 24 Cal.2d 611, 150 P.2d 892 (1944); In re Santosuosso, 318 Mass. 489, 62 N.E.2d 105 (1945); State v. Gudmundsen, 145 Neb. 324, 16 N.W.2d 474 (1944); Morgan, Evidence 1941–5, 59 Harv.L.Rev. 481, 552 (1946).

3. E. g., declarations against interest (§ 257, herein), regular entries in the course of business (§ 288), dying declarations (§ 259) and declarations as to matters of family history (§ 297).

4. See § 231, supra.

5. Wolski v. National Life and Accident Ins. Co., 135 Neb. 643, 283 N.W. 381, syl. 10, 11 (1939) (per-

manent); Norton v. State, 148 Tex.Cr.R. 294, 186 S.W.2d 347, syl. 4 (Tex.Cr.1945) (time of return indefinite).

6. Gaty v. United Rys. Co., 261 S.W. 61, syl. 6–8 (Mo., 1923) (former testimony admissible, under statute, where witness resides in another county or 40 miles from the place of trial); and see Toledo Traction Co. v. Cameron, 137 F. 48, 57, syl. 8, **9** (C.C.A.Ohio, 1905) (former testimony admitted under common law rule, where witness resides out of the district and more than 100 miles from place of trial, and hence beyond reach of process; extensive discussion by Severens, Circ.J.).

Nor, by what seems the better view, need the proponent show that he has endeavored to secure the voluntary attendance of the witness. Giberson v. Mills Co., 187 Pa. 513, 41 A. 525, syl. 2 (1898) (witness out of state); McGovern v. Hayes, 75 Vt. 104, 53 A. 326, syl. 3 (1902) (same).

7. Stephens v. Hoffman, 275 Ill. 497, 114 N.E. 142, syl. 2 (1916); A. T. Stearns Lumber Co. v. Howlett, 239 Mass. 59, 131 N.E. 217, syl. 2 (1921); Morris v. Davis, 292 S.W. 574, syl. 1 (Tex.Civ.App. 1927), and cases cited pro and con, 22 C.J. 435, 31 C.J.S. 1201.

8. Toledo Traction Co. v. Cameron, 137 F. 48, 62 (C.C.A.Ohio, 1905) (admitting former testimony of witness out of reach of process; "True, his deposition might have been taken. But that would not

absence beyond the state or beyond reach of process, would of course be enough if shown to be by the opponent's procurement,[9] and would without this feature be held an adequate showing by most courts.[10] Exceptionally, the testimony of the witness in person might be so essential as to justify a postponement of the trial until the witness's return, but the burden should be upon the opponent of moving such postponement before trial, if he knows the witness's former testimony will be offered, or if not, when it is offered. Inaccessibility of the witness is likewise established if the proponent shows that

he has made diligent search and has been unable to learn of his whereabouts.[11]

(3) *Physical disability* to attend the trial, or to testify, is a recognized ground. As in the case of absence, it seems that incapacity to testify at the particular trial should be the test, without regard to the permanency of the condition.[12] If the disability is temporary the opponent it seems would be sufficiently protected, where the evidence is of substantial importance, by his right to seek a postponement of the trial, in the judge's discretion, until the witness can be produced.[13] Some courts, however, announce the rule that the disability must be perma-

be his testimony in open court. There would be no confrontation of the jury with the witness."); Ross-Lewin v. Germania Life Ins. Co., 20 Colo. App. 262, 265, 78 P. 305, syl. 1 (1904) (testimony at former trial is evidence of as high an order as deposition given before an officer outside of court).

9. Reynolds v. United States, 98 U.S. 145, 160, syl. 4, 25 L.Ed. 244 (1878); and see cases collected 22 C.J. 436, note 25; 31 C.J.S., Evidence, 1202, note 6.

10. Apparently this is the prevailing view in civil cases. Great Northern R. Co. v. Ennis, 236 F. 17, syl. 6 (C.C.A.Mont., 1916); Mechanics' Bank v. Woodward, 74 Conn. 689, 51 A. 1084, syl. 7 (1902); Minneapolis Mill Co. v. Minneapolis, etc. R. Co., 51 Minn. 304, 53 N.W. 639, syl. 4 (1892), and cases cited 22 C.J. 435, 436. Other courts have said that temporary absence will not suffice, unless an effort has been made to place the witness under subpena. See, e. g., Liverpool, etc. Ins. Co. v. Dickenson, 244 Ala. 381, syl. 6, 7, 13 So.2d 570 (1943). And in criminal cases a stricter view prevails. See note 24, § 231, supra.

11. Pine Bluff Co. v. Bobbitt, 174 Ark. 41, 294 S.W. 1002, syl. 1, 2 (1927); Comm. v. Gallo, 275 Mass. 320, 175 N.E. 718, syl. 7, 8 (1931); State v. Ortego, 22 Wash.2d 552, 157 P.2d 320 (1945); 5 Wigmore, Evidence, § 1405.

12. Chase v. Springvale Mills, 75 Me. 156, syl. 3 (1883); People v. Droste, 160 Mich. 66, 125 N.W. 87, syl. 3 (1910) (". . . we are unable to appreciate any good reason why the people or respondent should have the benefit of such evidence, in cases where the witness is dead or permanently ill, and be denied that benefit when the witness is only temporarily ill. In all three cases, the important fact is identical—the witness cannot be produced

in person, to testify before the jury."); People v. Hawthorne, 293 Mich. 15, 291 N.W. 205, syl. 2 (1940) (semble); 5 Wigmore, Evidence, § 1406; 20 Am.Jur.Evidence, § 704.

13. Williams v. State, 156 Ark. 205, 210, 246 S.W. 503, 505, syl. 5 (1922) (conviction of rape; admission of written statement of victim's mother, taken at preliminary hearing, approved, upon showing that she was sick. "The court knew the length of the term of the court, the relationship of the absent witness to the prosecuting witness, the importance of her testimony, and all of the attendant circumstances. In cases of this sort much must be left to the discretion of the trial court in order to prevent the trial of cases from being unnecessarily delayed. Where the testimony of the absent witness is of such a character that the rights of the accused can be better protected by the presence of the absent witness, the court should continue the case until the next term. This course would depend upon the particular circumstances of each case. No such showing was made here."); Chase v. Springvale Mills Co., 75 Me. 156, 162 (1883). But in McCrorey v. Garrett, 109 Va. 645, 64 S.E. 978, 980, syl. 4, 24 L.R.A.,N.S., 139 (1909) the court in affirming the judge's exclusion of the former testimony of a witness, ill with typhoid, places the burden on the proponent. "If the evidence of this witness was material, the defendant should, when the case was called, have moved for a continuance in order that he might secure the presence of the witness at some subsequent time, and not have waited until the trial was in progress to substitute for the living witness the stenographer's notes of his evidence at a former trial." Why should such a burden be placed upon one who seeks to use this the most reliable of all the classes of evidence falling within the hearsay exceptions?

nent,[14] and this stricter view prevails generally in criminal cases.[15]

(4) *Mental Incapacity.* The decisions, in general terms, recognize insanity as a ground of unavailability.[16] They do not discuss the question whether the derangement must be such that it disqualifies the person from testifying about the matter in question. Of course, not all insanity renders the witness so incompetent. Competency to testify requires only a minimum degree of ability to observe, remember and recount.[17] If the person is proved to have become insane since the former testimony was given, it seems that the admission of the earlier testimony should depend not on whether the subsequent insanity has rendered the witness incompetent, but whether having in mind the witness's later loss of mental powers the previous testimony is probably substantially more reliable than the present testimony of the insane person would be, a question upon which some discretion must be conceded to the trial court.[18]

Failure of Memory. If the witness has lost his memory of the relevant matters, because of the failure of his faculties due to disease or senility, this is a good ground of unavailability.[19] If the gap in the recollection or fading of memory is due merely to the lapse of time, the effect is the same, namely the inability of the witness to give to the court his former first-hand knowledge of the facts. In common sense it seems that the legal consequence, that is, the use of the former testimony, should likewise be the same. Some courts, however, have jibbed at this point, on the ground that this would open the door to a perjured claim of forgetfulness by a witness who learns that the adversary has discovered facts which give a new handle for cross-examination.[20] The danger of the success of such an attempt, which would expose the witness to cross-examination on his motives and his memory, seems greatly outweighed by the need for the use of the former testimony when the assertion of forgetfulness is true. Forgetfulness by a disinterested witness of facts of no personal moment to him, in the course of a delayed law-suit, is frequent and familiar enough. The inconvenience of this narrow view, that forgetfulness is not a ground of unavailability, it seems, should be avoided by treating lapse of

---

14. Smith v. United States, 106 F.2d 726, syl. 8 (C.C. A.4th, 1939); Markowitz v. Milwaukee Elec. Ry. and Light Co., 230 Wis. 312, 284 N.W. 31, syl. 2 (1939) (but the circumstances were special as it was the plaintiff's counsel who was seeking to use, on a third trial, the plaintiff's own former testimony).

15. See § 231.

16. Marler v. State, 67 Ala. 55, 65, 42 Am.Rep. 95 (1880) ("There is no real or practical difference between the death of the mind and the death of the body." But there is. One is total, the other may be partial, and not disqualifying.); Atwood v. Atwood, 86 Conn. 579, 89 A. 29, syl. 5, Ann.C. 1914B 281; Whitaker v. Marsh, 62 N.H. 477 (1883) ("mental condition was such he was incapacitated to testify"); Security Realty & Developement Co. v. Bunch, 143 S.W.2d 687, syl. 4 (Tex.Civ.App.1940).

17. See § 62.

18. See People v. Crandall, 43 Cal.App.2d 238, 110 P.2d 682, syl. 2–5 (1941) where a somewhat comparable problem was presented. See also Tift v. Jones, 74 Ga. 469 (1885) where it was held that the deposition of a witness taken when he was well and strong would be admitted, though the witness testified at the trial, where the latter testimony was hesitating and uncertain due to illness and weakening of memory.

19. State v. New Orleans Waterworks Co., 107 La. 1, 38, 31 So. 395 (1901); Rothrock v. Gallaher, 91 Pa. 108, 112 (1879); 5 Wigmore, Evidence, § 1408; Note, 129 A.L.R. 843, 845.

20. Rio Grande Southern Ry. Co. v. Campbell, 55 Colo. 493, 136 P. 68, syl. 2, Ann.C.1914C 573; A. T. Stearns Lumber Co. v. Howlett, 239 Mass. 59, 61, 131 N.E. 217, syl. 3 (1921). See also, to similar effect in rejecting this as a ground of unavailability, Stein v. Swenson, 46 Minn. 360, 49 N.W. 55, syl. 7, 24 Am.St.Rep. 234 (1891); Turner v. Missouri-Kansas-Texas Ry. Co., 346 Mo. 28, 142 S.W. 2d 455, syl. 18–20, 129 A.L.R. 829 (1940); Velott v. Lewis, 102 Pa. 326, 333 (1883); 22 C.J., Evidence, § 522, n. 35; 31 C.J.S., Evidence, § 395, n. 14; 20 Am.Jur. § 703. Contra (sustaining forgetfulness as a ground): Anderson v. Gaither, 120 Fla. 263, 162 So. 877, syl. 3 (1935) and see 5 Wigmore, Evidence, § 1408, note 6.

memory if complete as a ground of unavailability, of if partial as a ground for admitting both the former, and the present testimony of the witness.[21] Perhaps a liberalization for former testimony of the requirements for memoranda of past recollection recorded, especially the requirement as to the time of making the memorandum, might be a convenient basis for this extension of the use of former testimony.[22]

Supervening Disqualification or Exercise of Privilege.[23] If the witness was competent at the time the former testimony was taken, but later becomes incompetent, as by the death of the adverse party, under the Dead Man's Statutes,[24] or by becoming so insane as to disqualify him to testify,[25] the requirement of unavailability is satisfied. Similarly, if the witness exercises a privilege not to testify at all, such as the privilege of the accused in a criminal case,[26] or the privilege of one spouse not to testify against the other,[27]

the witness is properly regarded as unavailable.

Depositions. Depositions taken in the cause in which they are offered might be thought to stand in a better position than depositions or testimony taken in another suit, since in most instances there is no problem of identity of issues and parties. But the statutes and rules of court which regulate depositions almost universally impose this requirement of unavailability (with great variations among the states as to the particular grounds) both upon the permission to take the deposition and upon its actual use in evidence in criminal trials and civil actions at law.[28] In a few jurisdictions the old practice in equity suits whereby the case was normally tried upon deposition evidence alone [29] seems to survive, but probably most states,[30] like the Federal jurisdiction,[31] have adopted for what formerly would have been equity cases the same practice as for law

---

21. See Anderson v. Gaither, 120 Fla. 263, 162 So. 877, 879, syl. 3 (1935) ("The admission in evidence of Stuart's deposition taken in 1929, although Stuart was personally in court and called as a witness at the last trial held in 1933, was (at least) within the sound discretion of the court, when it appeared from the circumstances that witness's memory at time of giving the earlier deposition was obviously clearer as to details than his personal testimony given from the witness stand four years later. Both versions together constituted appropriate evidence to be received and considered in connection with each other."—citing authorities).

22. See the discussion of the requirements of that theory, § 277, herein. These include the requirements that the witness must guarantee that the former statement was true, and in most states that the witness cannot speak from present memory. Instances of cases of the admission of former testimony where it seems that the court may have been influenced by this analogy: People v. McFarlane, 138 Cal. 481, 487, 488, 71 P. 568 (1903); State v. New Orleans Waterworks Co., 107 La. 1, 38, 31 So. 395 (1901).

23. See Wigmore, Evidence, §§ 1409, 1410.

24. Habig v. Bastian, 117 Fla. 864, 158 So. 508, syl. 5 (1935).

25. See § 62, supra.

26. Woodward v. State, 21 Ala.App. 417, 109 So. 119, syl. 4, 5 (1926); State v. Reidie, 142 Kan. 290, 46 P.2d 601, syl. 1 (1935).

27. McCoy v. State, 221 Ala. 466, 129 So. 21, syl. 4 (1930).

28. See statutes and rules collected in 5 Wigmore, Evidence, § 1411, and see Decennial Digests, Depositions, ☞10–14 (taking), 89–91 (admissibility); 26 C.J.S., Depositions, §§ 9–11, 92.

29. "The rule was universal to try all equity cases on depositions." Dickerson v. Askew, 82 Miss. 436, 440, 34 So. 15 (1903); 30 C.J.S., Equity §§ 451, 489.

30. See 21 C.J. 555, n. 11; 30 C.J.S., Equity, § 853, n. 89.

31. Federal Rules of Civil Procedure, Rule 26(d) (3) ". . . the deposition of a witness, whether or not a party, may be used by any party for any purpose if the court finds: 1, that the witness is dead; or 2, that the witness is at a greater distance than 100 miles from the place of trial or hearing, or is out of the United States, unless it appears that the absence of the witness was procured by the party offering the deposition; or 3, that the witness is unable to attend or testify because of age, sickness, infirmity, or imprisonment; or 4, that the party offering the deposition has been unable to procure the attendance of the witness by subpoena; or 5, upon application and notice, that such exceptional circumstances exist as to make it desirable, in the interest of justice and with due regard to the importance of presenting the testimony of witnesses orally in open court, to allow the deposition to be used".

actions, namely, that of using viva voce testimony except where the unavailability of the witness creates a necessity for resort to depositions. There are some departures from this restriction upon the use of depositions taken in the cause. At least one state, Texas,[32] has abandoned it, and a substantial number of courts have recognized a discretion to permit the use of a deposition though the witness is available [33] or even present in court, if the interests of justice so require.[34]

235. The Character of the Tribunal and of the Proceedings in Which the Former Testimony Was Taken.

If the accepted requirements of the administration of the oath, adequate opportunity to cross-examine on substantially the same issue, and present unavailability of the witness, are satisfied then the character of the tribunal whether judicial, legislative, or administrative, and the form of the proceedings are immaterial, and the former testimony should be received.[1] Accordingly, when these conditions are met, testimony taken before arbitrators,[2] or before a committing magistrate at a preliminary hearing,[3] or in a sworn examination before the Comptroller by the Corporation Counsel of a person asserting a claim against a city,[4] has been held admissible. For lack in the particular proceeding of some of these requisites, testimony given in the course of a coroner's inquest,[5] of a Senate Committee hearing on a presidential nomination,[6] and of a general ex-

---

32. The former requirement was held to have been repealed. Schmick v. Noel, 64 Tex. 406, 408 (1885); Cook v. Denike, 216 S.W. 437, syl. 2 (Tex.Civ.App., 1919). But apparently if the deponent is present at the trial, the judge has a discretion to require that he be examined. See note 33, infra. In Georgia it appears that, in the judge's discretion, a deposition may be read though the witness is present. Darden v. Mayor, 35 Ga.App. 777, 134 S.E. 813, syl. 6 (1926).

33. See the collection of Court Rules of the various Canadian provinces on the subject, compiled in 5 Wigmore, Evidence, § 1411, note 1, most of which seem to give a discretion to the judge as to the use of depositions.

34. Candler v. Smith, 50 Ga.App. 667, 179 S.E. 395, syl. 18 (1935); O'Connor v. Andrews, 81 Tex. 28, 37, 16 S.W. 628 (1891); 18 C.J.Depositions, § 350, note 91; 26 C.J.S., Depositions, § 92, note 39; Decennial Digests, Depositions, ⚷90. See also LaSell v. Tri-States Theater Corp., 235 Ia. 492, 17 N.W.2d 89, syl. 4, 5 (1945) (transcript of testimony properly received, though witness appeared in court before the reading of the transcript was completed; court said same result would follow if Civil Procedure Rule 144(d), relating to depositions were controlling, such rule permitting depositions to be used if witness unavailable, or "under exceptional circumstances making it desirable in the interests of justice, having due regard for the importance of witnesses testifying in open court").

1. See 6 Wigmore, Evidence, §§ 1373–1376; 22 C. J., Evidence, §§ 511, 512; 31 C.J.S., Evidence, §§ 385, 386.

2. Bailey v. Woods, 17 N.H. 365, 372 (1845) ("It does not seem to be an objection to the competency of the evidence of the deceased witness, that it was given at a hearing before arbitrators. We do not understand that the admissibility of such evidence depends so much upon the particular character of the tribunal, as upon other matters. If the testimony be given under oath in a judicial proceeding, in which the adverse litigant was a party, and where he had the power to cross-examine, and was legally called upon to do so, the great and ordinary tests of truth being no longer wanting, the testimony so given is admitted in any subsequent suit between the parties. Greenl.Ev. 1. It seems to depend rather upon the right to cross-examine, than upon the precise nominal identity of the parties. Id. An arbitration is a judicial proceeding, and the principle of the rule seems to apply as well to cases of this character as to technical suits at law."). The principle was reaffirmed in Orr v. Hadley, 36 N.H. 575, 580 (1858) but the testimony was excluded because of want of opportunity for cross-examination by the present opponent or one in like interest.

3. Jackson v. State, 133 Neb. 786, 277 N.W. 92, syl. 5 (1938); Dec.Dig.Crim.Law, ⚷539–545, and see § 231, supra.

4. Boschi v. City of New York, 187 Misc. 875, 65 N.Y.S.2d 425, syl. 4 (S.Ct., 1946, good opinion by Pecora, J.); Rothman v. City of New York, 273 App.Div. 780, 75 N.Y.S.2d 151 (1947).

5. Edgerley v. Appleyard, 110 Me. 337, 86 A. 244, syl. 4 (1913) (for want of opportunity of cross-examination—a leading case); 6 Wigmore, Evidence, § 1374. Occasionally it is made competent by statute. Los Angeles County v. Industrial Accident Commission, 123 Cal.App. 12, 11 P.2d 434, syl. 3 (1932) (in workmen's compensation proceedings).

6. Newman v. United States ex rel. Frizzel, 43 App. D.C. 53, syl. 1 (1914) (here said to be incompetent

amination before the referee under the Bankruptcy Act,[7] has been excluded.

It has been held that if the court in the former proceeding lacked jurisdiction of the subject-matter, the former testimony is inadmissible,[8] but it was determined in a Colorado case,[9] that the fact that it may ultimately be held that the court is without power to grant the relief sought, does not deprive the court of power to compel attendance of witnesses and to administer oaths, and accordingly the former testimony was held admissible.[10] The question it seems is not one of regularity but of reliability. A glaring usurpation of judicial power would call for a different ruling, but where the first court has substantial grounds for believing that it has authority to entertain the proceeding, and the party called upon to cross-examine should consider that the existence of jurisdiction is reasonably arguable, it seems that the guaranties of reliability are present. The question it seems should be viewed, not as one of limits of jurisdiction, but of whether the sworn statements of a witness, now dead or unavailable, about the facts of which he had knowledge, were made under such circumstances of opportunity and motive for cross-examination as to make them suffi-

ciently trustworthy to be used in the effort to ascertain the truth.

236. Objections and Their Determination.

May objections to the former testimony, or parts thereof, which could have been asserted when it was first given in evidence, be made for the first time when offered at the present trial? There are sweeping statements in some opinions that this may always be done,[1] and in others that it is never allowable.[2] The more widely approved view, however, is that objections which go merely to the form of the testimony, as on the ground of leading questions, unresponsiveness, or opinion, must be made at the original hearing, when they can be corrected,[3] but objections which go to the relevancy or the competency of the evidence may be asserted for the first time when the former testimony is offered at the present trial.[4]

Whether the former testimony meets the requirements of the present exception to the hearsay rule, may depend upon a question of fact, namely, whether the witness was in fact dead, incapacitated, absent or otherwise unavailable. This question, like other questions of fact upon which depends the admission of evidence under some technical rule,[5] is to be

---

and irrelevant) reversed on other grounds, 238 U.S. 537, 35 S.Ct. 881 (1915).

7. In re National Boat and Engine Co., 216 F. 208, syl. 3 (D.Me.1914) (for want of a defined issue); Todd v. Bradley, 99 Conn. 307, 122 A. 68, syl. 13 (1923) (here the testimony of third person; use of bankrupt's testimony as admission distinguished).

8. In re Colbert's Estate, 51 Mont. 455, 153 P. 1022, syl. 2 (1915); Deering v. Schreyer, 88 App.Div. 457, 85 N.Y.S. 275 (1903), noted 17 Harv.L.Rev. 422. The court in McAdams' Executors v. Stilwell, 13 Pa.St. 90 (1850) assumes that jurisdiction is essential.

9. Jerome v. Bohn, 21 Colo. 322, 40 P. 570, syl. 3 (1895).

10. The result would, of course, be even more clearly called for if the testimony were taken in the course of an inquiry by the first court into the question of jurisdiction, as the Colorado court suggests. Compare United States v. United Mine Workers, 330 U.S. 258, 289–295, 67 S.Ct. 677, 693–697, 91 L.Ed. 884 (1947).

1. See, e. g., Calley v. Boston & Maine R. R., 93 N.H. 359, 42 A.2d 329, syl. 6, 7, 159 A.L.R. 115 (1915) (open to all proper objections, here on ground that question on cross-examination assumed facts not in evidence).

2. Leach v. Nelson, 50 N.D. 538, 196 N.W. 755, syl. 2 (1924) (objections not taken at the first trial may not be interposed at the second—nature of objection not disclosed), critically noted 8 Minn.L.Rev. 629.

3. Sherman Gas & Elec. Co. v. Belden, 103 Tex. 59, 123 S.W. 119, syl. 4, 27 L.R.A.,N.S., 237 (1909) (unresponsiveness). Supporting this distinction are 3 Jones, Commentaries on Evidence, 2156 (2d ed. 1926) and Notes, 159 A.L.R. 119 and 8 Minn.L.Rev. 629 (1924). The same distinction is widely taken in respect to objections to evidence taken by deposition. See 26 C.J.S., Depositions, § 101.

4. Aetna Ins. Co. v. Koonce, 233 Ala. 265, 171 So. 269, syl. 6 (1936) (dictum).

5. See, generally, § 53, herein, and 9 Wigmore, Evidence, § 2550.

determined by the trial judge, not by the jury.[6] The decision is said to lie in his discretion,[7] in the sense that it will not be reversed if reasonably supported by the evidence but only where it can be said to be an abuse of discretion.[8] It would be desirable and convenient for the trial judge to be allowed to consider on this preliminary question any evidence which he deems reliable,[9] and statutes sometimes permit affidavits [10] and doctor's certificates[11] to be used, but in their absence, it is usually held that the trial judge can only consider evidence that meets the demands of the jury-trial rules.[12]

237. Method and Scope of Proof.[1]

In proving the former testimony at least four theories of admissibility may be employed.

(1) Any *first-hand* observer of the giving of the former testimony may testify to its purport from his unaided memory.[2] This and the next method were formerly used much more frequently than in the present era of court stenographers. The witness, to qualify, need not profess to be able to give the exact words of the former witness,[3] but he must, if the evidence is to come in under the present exception, satisfy the court that he is able to give the substance of all that the witness has said, both on direct and cross-examination,[4] about the subject-matter relevant to the present suit.[5] By the more convenient practice the proponent need not prove all of the former testimony relevant to the present case, but only such as he de-

---

6. State v. Maynard, 184 N.C. 653, 113 S.E. 682, syl. 3 (1922) (court should determine whether witness absent by defendant's procurement; no error to refuse to submit question to jury); Dec.Dig. Crim.Law, ☞736(1).

7. Smith v. United States, 106 F.2d 726, syl. 10 (C. C.A.4th, 1939) (sufficiency of showing of unavailability, where witness temporarily ill); People v. Centers, 56 Cal.App.2d 631, 133 P.2d 29, syl. 1 (1943) (sufficiency of showing of diligence in search for absent witness); New York Central R. Co. v. Pinnell, 112 Ind.App. 113, 40 N.E.2d 988, syl. 2 (1942) (similar to last case); See Ben Realty Co. v. Gothberg, 56 Wyo. 294, 109 P.2d 455, 462 (1941) (whether showing should be made that out-of-county witness was requested to attend trial).

8. Smith v. United States, 106 F.2d 726, syl. 8 (C.C. A.4th, 1939); People v. Cavazos, 25 Cal.2d 198, 153 P.2d 177, syl. 2, 3 (1944); New York Central R. Co. v. Pinnell, 112 Ind.App. 113, 40 N.E.2d 988, syl. 3 (1942); State v. Maynard, 184 N.C. 653, 113 S.E. 682, syl. 4 (1922).

9. See 1 Wigmore, Evidence, § 4, 5 id. § 1385(1).

10. See, e. g., Nowak v. Joseph, 283 Ky. 735, 142 S.W.2d 970, syl. 2 (1940) (affidavit as to absence of witness authorized by statute, but here insufficient).

11. Such a certificate was accepted in Lyons v. State, 76 Okl.Crim. 41, 133 P.2d 898, syl. 3 (1943), but whether by statute or by consent does not appear.

12. People v. Plyer, 126 Cal. 379, 58 P. 904, syl. 2 (1899) (affidavit incompetent); Valenzuela v. State, 30 Ariz. 458, 248 P. 36, syl. 1 (1926) (similar). The cases are ably discussed in Maguire and Epstein,

Evidence in Preliminary Controversies, 36 Yale L.J. 1100 (1927). See also Note, 79 A.L.R. 1392, 1415. Cino v. Driscoll, 130 N.J.L. 535, 34 A.2d 6, syl. 6 (1943) applies this rule (with debatable soundness) to an administrative hearing.

1. See 4 Wigmore, Evidence, § 1330, 5 id. §§ 1666–1669, 7 id. §§ 2098, 2099, 2103; Dec.Dig.Crim.Law, ☞582, Evidence, ☞547; 22 C.J.Evidence, §§ 524–532; 31 C.J.S. §§ 397–401.

2. Maxwell v. Wilmington City Ry. Co., 40 A. 945, syl. 2, (Del.Super.1893) (coroner's juror); McRorie v. Monroe, 203 N.Y. 426, 96 N.E. 724, syl. 1 (1911) (observer's evidence as to former testimony used to impeach, competent, no requirement that court stenographer be called); State v. Bixby, 27 Wash.2d 144, 177 P.2d 689, syl. 12 (1947) (judge at former trial competent, though stenographer's transcript also in evidence); 4 Wigmore, Evidence, § 1330.

3. Ruch v. Rock Island, 97 U.S. 693, syl. 1, 24 L. Ed. 1101 (1878) (precise language not necessary; "if a witness from mere memory, professes to give the exact language, it is a reason for doubting his good faith and veracity"); Scoville v. Hannibal & St. J. R. Co., 94 Mo. 84, 87, 6 S.W. 654 (1888) (substance sufficient, but requirement not satisfied); 7 Wigmore, Evidence, § 2098, note 4.

4. Tibbets v. Flanders, 18 N.H. 284, 292 (1846); Monahan v. Clemons, 212 Ky. 504, syl. 1, 276 S.W. 924 (1926).

5. Bennett v. State, 32 Tex.Cr. 216, 22 S.W. 684, syl. 1 (1893) ("If a witness can testify to the substance of all that is said on direct and cross examination upon one subject, it will be admissi-

sires to use, leaving to the adversary to elicit such of the remaining part as he wishes.[6]

(2) A first-hand observer may testify to the purport of the former testimony by using a memorandum, such as the judge's, counsel's, or the stenographer's notes, or the stenographer's transcript, to *refresh the present memory* of the witness.[7]

(3) In most of the states the magistrate's report of the testimony at a preliminary criminal hearing,[8] and the official stenographer's transcribed notes of the testimony [9] at the trial of a case, civil or criminal, are admitted, when properly authenticated, as evidence of the fact and purport of the former testimony under the hearsay exception for *official written statements*.[10] There is no rule of preference for these reports, however, and any observer, including the stenographer himself, may be called to prove the former testimony without producing the official report or transcript.[11]

(4) A witness who has made written notes or memoranda of the testimony at the time of the former trial, or while the facts were fresh in his recollection, and who will testify that he knows that they are correct may use such notes as memoranda of *past recollection recorded*.[12]

238. The Need for Improvement in Existing Practice.

The intricate restrictions upon the admission of evidence of former testimony are un-

---

ble, though there may be other portions of said testimony, as to other matters, not remembered by the witness."); Foley v. State, 11 Wyo. 464, 72 P. 627, syl. 9 (1903) (must state "the whole of what was said on the particular subject which he is called to prove"); 7 Wigmore, Evidence, §§ 2098, note 4, 2099(4). But the sensible qualification, that it suffices if the proponent is able to fill the gaps by the testimony of other witnesses has been made in a case where the former testimony was proved, not under the present exception, but to support a charge of perjury. Commonwealth v. Shooshanian, 210 Mass. 123, 96 N.E. 70, syl. 1 (1911).

6. Waller v. State, 102 Ga. 684, 28 S.E. 284, syl. **2** (1897); City of Boulder v. Stewardson, 67 Colo. 582, 189 P. 1, syl. 5 (1920); Randall v. Peerless Motor Car Co., 212 Mass. 352, 99 N.E. 221, syl. 33 (1912).

7. Ruch v. Rock Island, 97 U.S. 693, syl. 1, 24 L.Ed. 1101 (1878) (counsel's notes); Carpenter v. Tucker, 98 N.C. 316, 3 S.E. 831, syl. 2 (1887) (same); North River Ins. Co. v. Walker, 161 Ky. 368, 170 S.W. 983, syl. 2 (1914). As to the requirements generally in respect to refreshing memory, see sec. herein.

8. Haines v. State, 109 Ga. 526, 35 S.E. 141, syl. **1** (1900); 5 Wigmore, Evidence, § 1667 (citing cases pro and con).

9. See, e. g., Snyder v. Cearfoss, 190 Md. 151, 57 A.2d 786, syl. 5–7 (1948); Blalock v. Whisnant, 216 N.C. 417, 5 S.E.2d 130, syl. 1, 2 (1939) (transcript contained in case on appeal); Proulx v. Parrow, 115 Vt. 232, 56 A.2d 623, syl. 6, 7 (1948) (certified copy of transcript). Statutes to this effect in about thirty states, and the Federal Rules of Civil Proc.R. 80 are cited and summarized in 5

Wigmore, Evidence, § 1669, note 2. See also cases (and statutes cited therein) in Dec.Dig.Evidence, ⊂==582(3).

10. For the requirements of this exception see Ch. 33, herein.

11. Napier v. Commonwealth, 306 Ky. 75, 206 S.W.2d 53, syl. 4–6 (1947) (county attorney's evidence as to testimony before grand jury); Terry v. State, 132 Tex.Cr. 283, 103 S.W.2d 766, syl. 6 (1937) (stenographer can testify from recollection); **4** Wigmore, Evidence, § 1330(2).

Nevertheless, it seems that it would be a more just and convenient practice to require that the proponent before resorting to recollection-testimony should produce for inspection by the adversary and the court (and their use in evidence if desired) the stenographer's notes or transcript of the testimony, or should show that he has no such notes or transcript under his control. See the forthright declaration of Lumpkin, J.: "Can it be doubted that the proof taken down in writing and agreed on *as true*, under the eye and sanction of the Court, is better than the recollection of any body as to what the deceased witness did swear? So far from excluding this testimony, we should seriously doubt whether the Court would not have erred, had it admitted the other, which is inferior, while the higher proof was in existence, and in the power of the party to produce." Walker v. Walker, 14 Ga. 242, 249 (1853). See also the dissenting opinion of Prettyman, J., in Meyers v. United States, 171 F.2d 800, 814 (C.A.D.C.1948, cert. den.) and the able note, Brown, 23 So.Calif.L.Rev. 113.

12. See, e. g., State v. Maynard, 184 N.C. 653, 113 S.E. 682, syl. 2 (1922) (proper for stenographer to read his notes of preliminary examination, where he testifies to their correctness, though not subscribed or certified as required for official record);

derstandable as the reflections of an earlier era when there were no court reporters,[1] and as logical deductions from the premise that cross-examination is the only substantial safeguard for the reliability of such evidence. But when we view them in comparison with doctrines admitting other types of oral declarations as exceptions to the hearsay rule, such as admissions, declarations against interest, declarations of present bodily or mental state, and excited or spontaneous utterances, which seem far less reliable, the restrictions upon declarations in the form of sworn testimony in open court or official hearing, seem fantastically strict. As Morgan says, "Were the same strictness applied to all hearsay, evidence of reported testimony would constitute the only exception to the hearsay rule." [2]

In the light of this broader view, therefore, it seems that the most immediate improvement would come from the wider acceptance among the courts of the attitude that the present scheme of admissibility of former testimony should be applied with a reasonable liberality favoring in case of doubt the admission of this type of evidence.[3] Particularly is a liberal attitude needed in the definition and administration of the standards of unavailability of the witness,[4] and in a flexible and realistic approach to the question of when the interest of the present party-opponent was sufficiently represented in the former proceeding so that it may be said that some one in like interest had a fair opportunity to cross-examine.[5]

Beyond this, however, it is clear that the present scheme itself closes the door far too narrowly to this relatively highly valuable and useful class of evidence. It seems that the practice should be broadened in two main directions.

First, it appears that in civil cases, where the present vouchers of trustworthiness, namely the oath and sufficient likeness of parties and issues to guarantee an adequate opportunity for cross-examination are satisfied, the further requirement that the witness be proven unavailable should be abandoned. A discretionary power should be reserved in the trial judge to require that the witness be produced for cross-examination if he is available and need appears. Other hearsay declarations most frequently received, such as admissions, declarations of bodily and mental condition, and excited utterances,

---

Newton v. State, 150 Tex.Cr. 500, 202 S.W.2d 921, syl. 3 (1947) (stenographer may read from notes, if he swears correct); 3 Wigmore, Evidence, § 737(1).

For the requirements of this theory of admissibility, see §§ 276–278 herein.

1. "Since an official stenographic report of former testimony, given in the same cause with full privilege of cross examination, is now available in courts of record, the caution sometimes expressed where parol testimony is relied upon to prove the former testimony of the witness is not so essential." Bouldin, J. in Aetna Ins. Co., v. Koonce, 233 Ala. 265, 171 So. 269, 271 (1936).

2. The Law of Evidence, 1941–1945, 59 Harv.L.Rev. 481, 552 (1946).

3. Conspicuous instances of this attitude are to be found in the holdings of Prentice, J. in In re Durant, 80 Conn. 140, 67 A. 497, 10 Ann.C. 539 (1907); Traynor, J. in Werner v. State Bar, 24 Cal.2d 611, 150 P.2d 894, 161 A.L.R. 198 (1944); Butzel, J. in 274 Mich. 345, 264 N.W. 396 (1936);

Hays, J. in Bartlett v. Kansas City Pub. Service Co., 349 Mo. 13, 160 S.W.2d 740, 142 A.L.R. 666 (1942); Ellison, J. in State v. Brinkley, 354 Mo. 337, 189 S.W.2d 314 (1945); and Parkhurst, J. in Lyon v. Rhode Island Co., 38 R.I. 252, 94 A. 893 (1915).

4. See §§ 231, 234, supra.

5. See §§ 232, 233, supra.

As appears in In re Durant and Werner v. State Bar, cited in note 3, supra, the requirements of identity of parties and of issues, and the requirement of unavailability are relaxed in disbarment cases. As Morgan well says, "Why should any stricter requirement be enforced in ordinary litigation?" Article cited, note 1, supra, at p. 552. Consider in contrast such a case as McLean v. Scheiber, 212 N.C. 544, 193 S.E. 708 (1937) where the court, with perfect orthodoxy, held that in a mother's suit for loss of her son's services from an injury, the defendant could not introduce a transcript of the son's testimony in his own suit for the same injury!

require no showing that the declarant is unavailable. Proof of unavailability, and the tripping intricacies of its varying requirements are the constant stumbling block to the use of former testimony. Moreover, the prohibition against the use of the former testimony when the witness is available more often than not hinders the full ascertainment of the truth. The constant factor favoring the reliability of the former testimony as against the present testimony of the witness, is that of nearness of time and recency of memory. Obviously, where the fact is material and disputed, the practice should permit the production of *both* the former testimony and the witness on the stand. In criminal cases, however, the present requirement of unavailability is embodied in the constitutional guaranty of confrontation, and a change in the constitutional provisions or their interpretation could hardly be expected unless and until favorable experience in civil cases should convince the profession that the change could fairly be applied in the trial of crimes.

Second, I suggest that if the witness *is* unavailable, then the need for the sworn, transcribed former testimony in the ascertainment of truth is so great, and its reliability so far superior to most, if not all the other types of oral hearsay coming in under the other exceptions,[6] that the requirements of identity of parties and issues be dispensed with. This dispenses with the opportunity for cross-examination, that great characteristic weapon of our adversary system. But the other types of admissible oral hearsay, admissions, declarations against interest, statements about bodily symptoms, likewise dispense with cross-examination, for declarations having far less trustworthiness than the sworn testimony in open court, and with a far greater hazard of fabrication or mistake in the reporting of the declaration by the witness. Probably here again, for similar reasons, the change should at first be confined to civil cases.

These proposals for amending the practice are substantially those embodied in the provisions of the Model Code of Evidence.[7] A much more modest liberalization is provided for in the Uniform Rules of Evidence.[8]

---

6. The failure of existing rules admitting these other types of hearsay declarations to furnish guaranties of trustworthiness comparable to the test of cross-examination is demonstrated in detail in Morgan, Foreword, Model Code of Evidence, pp. 36–49 (1942).

7. See Rule 503: "Evidence of a hearsay declaration is admissible if the judge finds that the declarant

"(a) is unavailable as a witness, or

"(b) is present and subject to cross-examination."

Rule 511: "Evidence of a hearsay statement which consists of testimony given by the declarant as a witness in an action or in a deposition taken according to law for use in an action is admissible for any purpose for which the testimony was admissible in the action in which the testimony was given or for use in which the deposition was taken, unless the judge finds that the declarant is available as a witness and in his discretion rejects the evidence."

See also the Comment appended to Rule 511 explaining the effect of the two rules.

8. Rule 63, subsec. (3) admits as an exception to the rule against hearsay, "Subject to the same limitations and objections as though the declarant were testifying in person, (a) testimony in the form of a deposition taken in compliance with the law of this state for use as testimony in the trial of the action in which offered, or (b) if the judge finds that the declarant is unavailable as a witness at the hearing, testimony given as a witness in another action or in a deposition taken in compliance with law for use as testimony in the trial of another action, when (i) the testimony is offered against a party who offered it in his own behalf on the former occasion, or against the successor in interest of such party, or (ii) the issue is such that the adverse party on the former occasion had the right and opportunity for cross examination with an interest and motive similar to that which the adverse party has in the action in which the testimony is offered."

CHAPTER 27

ADMISSIONS OF A PARTY–OPPONENT[1]

239. Nature and Effect.

Admissions are the words or acts of a party-opponent, or of his predecessor or representative, offered as evidence against him. As indicated, they may be classified as *express* admissions, which are statements of the opposing party, or of some person such as an agent or a predecessor in interest, for whose words he may be held responsible, and admissions by *conduct* of the party-opponent or of those representing him. Among the many theories on which the probativeness and admissibility of admissions have been explained and supported, the following seem most helpful.

Morgan's view[2] is that admissions come in as an exception to the hearsay rule,[3] since they are (at least in the case of express admissions) declarations made out of court, not subject to cross-examination, and received as evidence of the truth of the matter declared. Usually such exceptions are justified on the ground that the evidence meeting the requirements of the exception possesses special reliability (greater than hearsay generally) and is especially needed, because of the unavailability of the declarant by reason of his death, absence or the like. But no objective guaranty of trustworthiness is furnished by the admissions-rule. The party is not even required to have had first-hand knowledge of the matter declared, and the declaration may have been self-serving when it was made. As to reliability, he says "the party whose declarations are offered against him is in no position to object on the score of lack of confrontation or of lack of opportunity for cross-examination. It seems quite as clear that he ought not to be heard to com-

1. General references: 4 Wigmore, Evidence, §§ 10-48–1087; Phipson, Evidence, ch. 18 (9th ed. 1952); Morris, Admissions and the Negligence Issue, 29 Tex.L.Rev. 407 (1951); Dec.Dig., Evidence, ⟨=200-265, Crim.Law, ⟨=405-415; 31 C.J.S., Evidence, §§ 270–283; Uniform Rules of Evidence, Rules 63(7), 63(8), 63(9) (1953).

2. E. M. Morgan, Admissions as an Exception to the Hearsay Rule, 30 Yale L.J. 355 (1921). See also his later discussions, Admissions, 12 Wash.L.Rev. 181 (1937), The Law of Evidence, 1941–1945, 59 Harv. L.Rev. 481, 556 (1946); Admissions, 1 U.C.L.A.L. Rev. 18 (1953).

3. See Kamanosuke v. United States, 127 F.2d 683, syl. 12 (C.C.A. Calif. 1942).

plain that he was not under oath." [4] Similarly, as to need, he answers that as in case of other exceptions where unavailability is not required, the declarations out of court may well be more trustworthy than the party's testimony would be, and further, "the admission is always offered against the declarant and he cannot object to its being received as prima facie trustworthy, particularly when he is given every opportunity to qualify and explain it." [5] This notion that it does not lie in the opponent's mouth to question the trustworthiness of his own declarations is an expression of feeling rather than logic but it is an emotion so universal that it may stand for a reason. The feeling that one is entitled to use the opponent's words is heightened by our contentious or adversary system of litigation.

Wigmore, after pointing out that the party's declaration has generally the probative value of any other person's assertion, says that it has in addition a special value when offered *against* him, in that he is discredited (like a witness impeached by contradictory statements) by his statements inconsistent with his present claim asserted in his pleadings and in the testimony on which he relies. And it passes the gauntlet of the hearsay rule, which requires that extra-judicial assertions be excluded if there was no opportunity for the opponent to cross-examine, because it is the opponent's own declaration and "he does not need to cross-examine himself." He then adds that "the Hearsay Rule is satisfied" since the party "now as opponent has the full opportunity to put himself on the stand and explain his former assertion." [6]

Strahorn, in a valuable article, suggests an alternative theory which classes all admissions of a party offered against him, whether words or acts, as being *conduct* offered as circumstantial evidence rather than for its assertive, testimonial value. Its circumstantial value is that which Wigmore pointed out, namely, the quality of inconsistency with the party's present claim. "The hearsay rule applies to those statements for which the only justification is their narrative content. It is inapplicable to those which are conduct, i.e., for which the trustworthiness of the utterance is a matter of indifference. So it is with admissions. The writer feels that inasmuch as all admissions, express and otherwise, can be rationalized as the relevant conduct of the speaker, it is unnecessary to predicate their admissibility on the basis of a possible narrative effect not possessed by all of them." [7]

The present writer finds Morgan's classification of admissions as an exception to the hearsay rule, and his explanation therefor, most convincing as to express admissions and Strahorn's theory of admissions as circumstantial evidence most satisfactory as to admissions by conduct.

Despite the analogy drawn in Wigmore's and Strahorn's discussions to the proof of a witness's prior contradictory statements to impeach, it is clear today that admissions of a party come in as substantive evidence of the facts admitted, [8] and that no foundation

---

[4] 30 Yale L.J. 361.

[5] 30 Yale L.J. 361.

[6] 4 Wigmore, Evidence, pp. 2–5 (3d ed. 1940), approved in Milton v. U. S., 71 App.D.C. 394, 110 F.2d 556 (1940).

[7] John S. Strahorn, Jr., The Hearsay Rule and Admissions, 85 U.Pa.L.Rev. 484, 564 at 573, 576 (1937). For a similar judicial discussion of the rationale, see Schloss v. Traunstine, 135 N.J.L. 11, 49 A.2d 677, syl. 4–6 (1946).

[8] Olson v. Hodges, 236 Ia. 612, 19 N.W.2d 676, syl. 7 (1945) (error to instruct the jury that an admission merely as discrediting the party's testimony); Lambros v. Coolahan, 185 Md. 463, 45 A.2d 96, syl. 2, 3 (1945) (report by witness of party's oral admission, though denied by party, sufficient to take the issue to jury); Litman v. Peper, 214 Minn. 127, 7 N.W.2d 334, syl. 2 (1943) (admission, though making of it denied by party, sufficient to take case to jury on issue of negligence); Peterson v. Richards, 73 Utah 59, 272 P. 229, syl. 5, 6 (1928) (suffi-

or predicate, by examining the party himself, such as may be required for impeaching evidence,[9] is prerequisite for proof of admissions.[10]

When we speak of admissions, without qualifying adjective, we customarily mean evidential admissions, that is, words oral or written, or conduct of a party or his representative offered in evidence against him. These *evidential* admissions are to be distinguished from *judicial* admissions. Judicial admissions are not evidence at all, but are formal admissions in the pleadings, or stipulations, oral or written, by a party or his counsel which have the effect of withdrawing a fact from issue and dispensing wholly with the need for proof of the fact.[11] Thus the judicial admission, unless it should be allowed by the court to be withdrawn, is conclusive, whereas the evidential admission is not conclusive (unless the adversary should fail to meet it with contrary evidence) but is always subject to be contradicted or explained.[12]

Confessions of crime are, of course, but one kind of admissions, but in technical as in pop-

ular parlance a confession signifies a sweeping acknowledgment of guilt, whence it comes that in criminal cases the term "admissions" has been used as meaning acknowledgments of incriminating facts not constituting a complete confession. This distinction is elaborated, and the question how far the restrictive rules about confessions apply to these incomplete "admissions" is discussed, in the chapter on Confessions.[13]

A type of evidence with which admissions may be confused is evidence of Declarations against Interest. Such declarations, coming in under a separate exception to the hearsay rule, to be admissible must have been against the declarant's interest when made.[14] No such requirement applies to admissions. If a party states that a note or deed is forged, and then later buys the note or the land, and sues upon the note or for the land, obviously the previous statement will come in against him as an admission, though he had no interest when he made the statement. Of course, most admissions are actually against interest when made, but there is no such requirement.[15] Hence the common phrase in judi-

---

cient to support finding of fact); Decennial Digests, Evidence, ☞200, 217, 222(1), 265(1); 4 Wigmore, Evidence, §§ 1055, 1056. But particular testimony attesting to an oral admission may be so inherently incredible that reasonable men could not believe it, and hence insufficient to support a finding. Other circumstances such as the want of knowledge of the admitter may deprive it of substantial weight in a particular case. Binewicz v. Haglin, 103 Minn. 297, 115 N.W. 271 (1908). Washington courts seem to have crystallized a rule that evidence of a verbal admission, denied by the party, and uncorroborated by other facts, is insufficient to sustain a finding. See Kennett v. Federici, 200 Wash. 156, 93 P.2d 333, syl. 1 (1939). To fetter judgment by such a rule seems unwise.

9. See § 37, herein.

10. Howe v. Messimer, 84 Mont. 304, 275 P. 281, syl. 1 (1929); 4 Wigmore, Evidence, § 1051(1).

11. Polk v. Missouri-Kansas-Texas R. Co., 341 Mo. 1213, 111 S.W.2d 138, syl. 4, 114 A.L.R. 873 (1937); Dec.Dig. Evidence, ☞265(7); Wigmore, Evidence, §§ 1058, 2588–2595.

12. Cooper v. Brown, 126 F.2d 874, syl. 19 (C.C.A.3d 1942); Pierce v. Gruben, 237 Ia. 329, 21 N.W.2d 881, syl. 4 (1946) (contradiction allowed); Aide v. Taylor, 214 Minn. 212, 7 N.W.2d 757, 759 (1943) ("Plaintiff's testimony cannot be rejected simply because at the hospital he gave the statement containing a contrary version"); Rosenblatt v. Percy, 313 Mass. 757, 49 N.E.2d 114, syl. —— (1943) (wrongful death; plaintiffs introduced evidence that defendant in criminal proceeding had pleaded guilty to negligent driving; evidence that defendant did this to save time and expense admitted); 4 Wigmore, Evidence, §§ 1058, 1059.

13. See § 113, herein.

14. See § 253, herein.

15. One of the clearest expressions to this effect is in State v. Anderson, 10 Ore. 448, 452 (1882). On a charge of murdering his brother, the state gave in evidence defendant's admissions that he had no means before his brother's death. In holding these admissible over the objection that they were not against interest, the court said: "But the admissibility of a party's own previous statements or declarations in respect to the subject in contro-

cial opinions, "admissions against interest," [16] is an invitation to confuse two separate exceptions to the hearsay rule. Other apparent distinctions are that the admissions must be the statements of a party to the lawsuit (or his predecessor or representative) and must be offered, not for, but against him, whereas the Declaration against Interest need not be and usually is not made by a party or his predecessor or representative, but by some third person.[17] Finally, the Declaration against Interest exception admits the declaration only when the declarant, by death or otherwise, has become unavailable as a witness, whereas obviously no such requirement is applied to admissions of a party.[18]

If there are several parties on one side of the litigation, whether plaintiffs or defendants, the admission of one of these co-parties (unless he happens to have been the agent or representative of the others),[19] is admissible only against himself and not against the other parties with whom he is aligned.[20]

240. Testimonial Qualifications: Mental Competency: Personal Knowledge [1]

The application of the standards of competency of witnesses to declarants whose statements are offered in evidence under the various hearsay exceptions has never been worked out comprehensively by the courts, but is usually treated as an isolated problem with respect to the particular exception under consideration. In so far as outmoded testimonial restrictions still survive, such as disqualification for conviction of crime, marital disqualification, and the test of ability to understand the obligation of an oath as applied to small children,[2] it seems that these requirements should not in general be extended to hearsay declarants nor in particular to admissions. But as to the qualification of mental capacity as applied to young children and insane persons, in its modern form of a mere requirement that the witness must only possess such minimum capacity to observe, remember and narrate the facts as will enable him to give some aid to the trier,[3] it would seem sensible to apply that standard to the out-of-court declarant and the party making admissions.[4] If it does not appear

---

versy, as evidence against him, does not in any manner depend upon the question whether they were for or against his interest at the time they were made, or afterwards. The opposite party has a right to introduce them if relevant and voluntarily made, no matter how they may stand or have stood in relation to the interest of the party making them." For similar expressions, see Caswell v. Maplewood Garage, 84 N.H. 241, 149 A. 746, syl. 4 (1930). On the same principle rest the cases admitting the party's previous offers to buy or sell, or valuation for tax-purposes at a different value than he now contends for. Erceg v. Fairbanks Exploration Co., 95 F.2d 850, syl. 6 (C.C.A. 9th, 1938) (offer to buy); Manning v. Lowell, 173 Mass. 100, 53 N.E. 160, syl. 3 (1899) (valuation to secure tax reduction). See 4 Wigmore, Evidence, § 1048, notes 3 and 4.

16.   E.g., in Kellner v. Whaley, 148 Neb. 259, 27 N.W.2d 183, 189 (1947).

17.   Downs v. McCampbell, 203 S.W.2d 302, syl. 12 (Tex.Civ.App.1947).

18.   The distinctions are fully expounded in Elliotte v. Lavier, 299 Mich. 353, 300 N.W. 116, syl. 6, 7

(1941) and McComb v. Vaughn, 358 Mo. 951, 218 S.W.2d 548, syl. 1–5 (1949); and see 4 Wigmore, Evidence, §§ 1048, 1049.

19.   See §§ 244, infra.

20.   Bristol v. Moser, 55 Ariz. 185, 99 P.2d 706, 709 (1940) ("when the interest or the liability of the co-parties is several, the admission of one is not competent against the others"); People v. Leary, 28 Cal.2d 727, 172 P.2d 34, syl. 6 (1946) (criminal defendant's admissions receivable against him, though tried jointly with others, provided they are properly limited to the defendant who made them); 4 Wigmore, Evidence, § 1076; Decennial Digests, Evidence, ☞222(10); Criminal Law, ☞406(1).

1.   See 4 Wigmore, Evidence. § 1053.

2.   See Ch. 7, herein.

3.   See § 62.

4.   In Ammundson v. Tinholt, 228 Minn. 115, 36 N.W.2d 521, 524, syl. 1, 2 (1949), declarations of plaintiff after an accident were held properly excluded because the evidence showed undisputedly that he was suffering from shock so as to be "incapable of

that this minimum capacity was wanting, then the immaturity or insanity of the declarant would only affect the credibility of the admission [5] or other declaration. And so of intoxication, hysteria and similar temporary derangements. If the party making the admission, or other declarant, was not shown to be incapable of making any rational statement, his intoxication or other derangement would be considered only as affecting the credibility of the statement.[6]

The requirement that a witness speak from first-hand knowledge would seem to be applicable to hearsay declarations generally [7] and it has sometimes been applied to admissions,[8] but the traditional view and the greater number of decisions hold that it is not.[9]

telling how the collision happened," and the court said: "Utterances of a party incapable of recollecting and narrating the facts to which his utterances relate are inadmissible as admissions. If the lack of such ability conclusively appears, the utterances should be excluded entirely; but, if the evidence raises a fact issue as to whether it is lacking, the utterances should be received as admissions and their weight should be determined by the jury under an appropriate instruction. Aide v. Taylor, 214 Minn. 212, 7 N.W.2d 757, 145 A.L.R. 530. Lack of ability to narrate what the witness has observed amounts to what Wigmore well calls a lack of testimonial capacity. 2 Wigmore, Evidence (3 ed.) §§ 478, 479, 506. In Jacobson v. Carlson, 302 Mich. 448, 4 N.W.2d 721, utterances of plaintiff while dazed and *unable to answer* were held to be inadmissible as admissions. In analogous cases, the rule is well settled that where a party is so incapacitated mentally, whether by disease, intoxication, or otherwise, as to be incapable of recollecting and narrating what occurred, his utterances are inadmissible as admissions. Cannady v. Lynch, 27 Minn. 435, 8 N.W. 164, discussion of rule; Martinez v. People, 55 Colo. 51, 132 P. 64, Ann.Cas.1914C, 559, and note, words spoken while declarant was asleep; Hartford v. Palmer, 16 John., N.Y. 143, witness unable to narrate because of his intoxication; People v. Carlin, 194 N.Y. 448, 87 N.E. 805, declarant unable to recollect facts narrated."

It is submitted, however, that in case of doubt the question of the existence of a qualifying minimum of capacity should be decided by the judge as a preliminary question, see § 70, herein.

5. McAffee v. United States, 111 F.2d 199, syl. 3 (App.D.C.1940) (confession, insanity); Atchison, T. & S. F. R. Co. v. Potter, 60 Kan. 808, 58 P. 471, syl. 1 (1899) (action for personal injuries to boy less than seven years old at time of trial; trial court found him incompetent as a witness because of inability to understand an oath, and excluded evidence of his statements just after the accident, offered by defendant; held, latter ruling was error; "his declarations are to be cautiously received, on account of his age, but the value and force of the same are . . . for . . . the jury"; court intimated that judge in applying the oath-test,

should have permitted the boy to testify but added, "As declarations against interest [sic] are not made under oath, that test is not applicable; and where as in this case, the infant appears to be able to relate facts, his declarations should be received . . . "). A Note, Infant's admissions as evidence in civil cases, 89 A.L.R. 708, collects the cases, nearly all of which involve declarations of minors of relatively mature years.

6. Bell v. United States, 47 F.2d 438, syl. 4, 74 A.L. R. 1098 (App.D.C.1931) (intoxication, short of mania, does not exclude confession); Note, 74 A.L.R. 1102; Aide v. Taylor, 214 Minn. 212, 7 N.W.2d 757, syl. 5 (1943) (statement made by injured plaintiff in hospital while affected by pain and drugs admissible but not conclusive; weight is for jury, unless party incapacitated from making rational admission, as where he is in coma); Friedman v. United Railways Co., 293 Mo. 235, 238 S.W. 1074, syl. 7 (1922) (party in hysterical state after accident); Middle Tennessee R. Co. v. McMillan, 134 Tenn. 490, 184 S.W. 20, syl. 12 (1915) (injured party semi-conscious after accident).

7. See e.g. §§ 262, 277, and 286, herein.

8. Coca-Cola Bottling Co. v. Munn, 99 F.2d 190, 197, syl. 17, 18, C.C.A.N.C., 1938 (previous admission by plaintiff, now suing for injury due to lye in bottled drink, that it would be impossible for a bottle to have any lye in it after going through defendant's plant, held properly excluded); Paschall v. Gulf, C. & S. F. Ry. Co., 100 S.W.2d 183, 192, 193, syl. 13, Tex.Civ.App., 1936 (action for death of husband in collision, letter of wife, who was not present, that family was not holding defendant, a friend of deceased, responsible, written before investigating facts, held improperly admitted—a very appealing result on the facts).

9. Smedra v. Stanek, 187 F.2d 892, syl. 3, 4 (C.A. Colo. 1951) (defendant surgeon said he had been delayed because sponge-count, conducted by nurses, did not come out correctly); London Guarantee & Accident Co. v. Woelfle, 83 F.2d 325, 336, syl. 15, C.C.A. Mo., 1936 (acts of insurance company's agents in paying disability instalments on accident policies, received as admission that insured sustained an accidental fall, though agents had no first-hand

These latter argue that when a man speaks against his own interest it is to be supposed that he has made an adequate investigation. While this self-disserving feature might attach to most admissions, we have seen that admissions are competent evidence though not against interest when made. As to these the argument does not apply, and it seems sufficient to justify the general dispensing with the knowledge qualification to say that admissions which become relevant in litigation usually concern some matter of substantial importance to the declarant upon which he would probably have informed himself so that they possess, even when not based on first-hand observation, greater reliability than the general run of hearsay.

241. Admissions in Opinion-Form: Conclusions of Law.

If the want of knowledge of the party does not exclude his admissions, as indicated in the preceding section, it would seem clear that the opinion-rule should not. As we have seen, that rule has as its object the regulation of the interrogation of a witness on the stand, so as to elicit his answers in the more concrete form rather than in terms of inference. In its modern form it is a rule of preference for the more concrete answers, if the witness can give them, rather than a rule of exclusion.[1] In any view, this rule designed to promote the concreteness of answers on the stand, is grotesquely misapplied to out-of-court statements, such as admissions, where the declarant's statements are made without thought of the form of courtroom testimony and where it can only be applied by excluding the statement, whereas in the courtroom if the opinion objection is sustained, counsel may reframe his question in the preferred form. Accordingly, the prevailing view is that admissions in the form of opinions are competent.[2] Most often the

knowledge, but merely formed opinion from investigation); Janus v. Akstin, 91 N.H. 373, 20 A.2d 552, syl. 2 (1941) (action for attack by defendant's dog, defendant's statement that dog jumped on the decedent held admissible though defendant not present); Reed v. McCord, 160 N.Y. 330, 341, 54 N.E. 737, syl. 3 (1899) (statement by defendant, employer, as to how injury happened, though he was not present); Salvitti v. Throp, 343 Pa. 642, 23 A. 2d 445, syl. 4, 5 (1942) (automobile collision; evidence that owner of truck acknowledged that his driver was at fault admitted, though owner not present). See also Wigmore, Evidence, § 1053; and Note, Defendant's admissions regarding accident occurring in his absence, 138 A.L.R. 845.

This question is often joined with the problem whether repetition of another's statement is an adoptive admission, see Reed v. McCord, supra, and § 246, infra.

1. See § 18, herein.

2. Pekelis v. Transcontinental & Western Air, 187 F.2d 122, syl. 4 (C.A. 2, 1951) (report by airline investigating board as to cause of accident); Strickland v. Davis, 221 Ala. 247, 128 So. 233, syl. 3–5 (1930) (defendant after accident said it was his fault; held admissible, rejecting the application to admissions of requirements for testimony on the stand, and the objection that the statement expressed a conclusion of law); Hege v. Tompkins, 69 Ind.App. 273, 121 N.E. 677, 680, syl. 10 (1919)

(statement by defendant in accident report that deceased had been injured in course of employment, admissible; "Admitting, without deciding, that such statement is a conclusion of law, still we know of no rule that requires an admission to be disregarded because made in the form of a conclusion of law rather than a statement of fact"); Swain v. Oregon Motor Lines, 160 Ore. 1, 82 P.2d 1084, syl. 3, 118 A.L.R. 1225 (1938) (plaintiff, bus passenger suing for injury in collision with automobile, stated in accident report that driver of automobile to blame, admissible; extensive discussion); Wells v. Burton Lines, 228 N.C. 422, 45 S.E.2d 569, syl. 4, 5 (1947) (plaintiff after collision said it was his fault); Grodsky v. Consolidated Bag Co., 324 Mo. 1067, 26 S.W.2d 618, syl. 2 (1930) ("Plaintiff's statement that it was her 'opinion the truck driver was entirely responsible for the accident' was inconsistent with her subsequent action in attempting to place the blame upon other parties. The trial court did not err in admitting the statement."; extensive discussion, but see Wright v. Quattrochi, below); Woods v. Townsend, 144 Tex. 594, 192 S. W.2d 884, syl. 6 (1946) (will-contest for undue influence; admission of proponent, "we got the papers fixed . . . but the old man didn't know what he was doing"); Southern Passenger Motor Lines v. Burke, 187 Va. 53, 46 S.E.2d 26, syl. 13 (1948) (plaintiff's statement that collision not due to fault or negligence of defendant's driver); 4 Wig-

question arises in connection with statements of a participant in an accident that it was his fault, or not the fault of the other participant. Against these and like statements, the additional objection is often urged that they are conclusions of law. But this should be no objection either. While conceivably a party might give an opinion on an abstract question of law,[3] such are not the statements actually offered in evidence. These always include in them an application of a standard to the facts; thus they suggest what the declarant thinks the facts are to which he is applying the standard of "fault," or other legal or moral standard involved in his statement. The factual bearing is not to be ignored merely because the statement may also indicate the party's assumptions as to the law.[4]

242. Admissions in Pleadings:[1] Withdrawn Plea of Guilty.

The final pleadings upon which the case is tried state the contentions of each party as to the facts, and by admitting or denying the opponent's pleading, they define the fact-

issues which are to be tried by the process of proof. Thus, the court must look to the pleadings as part of the record in passing on the relevancy of evidence, and in ascertaining the issues to be submitted to the jury. For these purposes it is not necessary to offer the pleadings in evidence.[2] They are used as judicial and not as evidential admissions, and for these purposes, until withdrawn or amended, are conclusive.[3] But suppose a party desires to use an averment or admission in his adversary's final pleading, as a basis in his argument for the existence of some subordinate fact or as the foundation for some adverse inference. The greater number of states permit the party to do this by quoting or reading the pleading as part of the record,[4] but a substantial minority require that the party, in order to make this use of it, must first have introduced the relevant passage from the opponent's pleading as part of his own evidence during the course of the trial.[5] Such requirement affords an opportunity to the pleader to give explanatory evidence, such as that the allegation was made through inadvertence or mistake,[6] so

---

more, Evidence, § 1053(3); Note, Opinions about Accident as Admissions, 118 A.L.R. 1230.

Contra: Wright v. Quattrochi, 330 Mo. 174, 49 S.W.2d 3, syl. 2, 3 (1932) (defendant said he had talked to driver and it was driver's fault, held incompetent as conclusion of law, distinguishing Grodsky case, supra, because admitter was witness in that case, and not in this); Kellner v. Whaley, 148 Neb. 259, 27 N.W.2d 183, syl. 10 (1947) (dictum that admission to be admissible must not be opinion or conclusion of law); 31 C.J.S. Evidence, § 272(b).

3. Compare City of Okmulgee v. Wall, 196 Okl. 536, 167 P.2d 44, syl. 3, 4 (1946) where counsel's argument that his client's petition did not allege permanent damage was held not receivable as an admission that the land was not permanently injured.

4. See decisions cited in note 2, supra.

1. 4 Wigmore, Evidence, §§ 1064–1067; 3 Jones, Commentaries on Evidence, §§ 993–1006 (2d ed. 1926); Decennial Digests, Evidence, ⊙208, 265(8) (11); 31 C.J.S., Evidence, §§ 300–306; Notes, 14 A.L.R. 22, 90 A.L.R. 1393.

2. Hildreth v. Hudloe, 282 S.W. 747, 748 (Mo.App. 1926).

3. Carver v. Carver, 199 Ga. 352, 34 S.E. 509, 510 ("the plaintiff was bound by the solemn and unstricken allegation contained in her petition"); Johnson & Wright, Inc. v. Rickard, 115 Vt. 118, 52 A.2d 786, 788 (1947) ("Such an admission is, in general, conclusive and irrevocable, but when it is clearly shown that it was made improvidently and by mistake, the court, in its discretion, may relieve the party of the consequences of his error").

4. Grand Trunk Western Ry. Co. v. Lovejoy, 304 Mich. 35, 7 N.W.2d 212, syl. 1 (1942); Hildreth v. Hudloe, 282 S.W. 747, syl. 4 (Mo.App.1926); Gibson v. Koutsky-Brennan-Vana Co., 143 Neb. 326, 9 N.W.2d 298, syl. 5 (1943); and cases cited in 4 Wigmore, Evidence, § 1064, note 1.

5. Louisville & N. R. Co. v. Hull, 113 Ky. 561, 68 S.W. 433, syl. 3 (1902); Gossler v. Wood, 120 N.C. 69, 27 S.E. 33, (1897); Mullen v. Union Cent. L. Ins. Co., 182 Pa. 150, 37 A. 988, syl. 3 (1897) (affidavit of defense).

6. This reason is given in Smith v. Nimocks, 94 N.C. 243, (1886).

far as this may be allowable, and avoids the possibility of a surprise inference from the pleading in closing argument. It may be that these considerations justify the departure from consistency.

Moreover, under the traditional systems of pleading at common law and in chancery, there were certain limitations upon the use of the pleadings against the pleader whether sought to be used as judicial admissions, or offered in evidence as admissions, as the local practice might dictate. These were based upon the artificial and often fictitious forms of statement customary under those systems. For example the practice of pleading inconsistent counts and inconsistent defences,[7] each unqualified in form, necessitated the rule that as to each separate issue only the pleadings leading up to that particular issue could be considered against the pleader, and not the other counts or defenses on which other issues were raised.[8] Moreover, the traditional bill in chancery included

by ancient custom fictitious assertions [9] such as the charge of confederacy [10] and consequently, in other actions in the law courts at least, the bill could not be used against the pleader as an admission,[11] but the answer, which was originally required to be under oath, was intended to be taken as true, and was usable against the answering party.[12]

Under the modernized systems of pleading which now obtain in England, in most of the states, and in the Federal courts, the fictions which had encrusted the older system have largely been stripped away. In some states, pleadings are required to be verified by the party under oath,[13] and in all the modernized systems, the party is required to plead the facts plainly and according to what he believes is the truth of the matter.[14] Consequently, the general approach today is that any pleading may be used against the pleader as an admission of the facts stated therein.[15] The retention, in a modern system, of

---

7. "Records containing from ten to fifteen special counts or pleas are by no means rare. . . .
Of these, the greater proportion and frequently the whole relate to the same substantial cause of action or defence. They are merely different expositions of the same case, and expositions of it often inconsistent with each other." Report of Common Law Procedure Commission, Parlt. Papers 1830, quoted in 9 Holdsworth, Hist.Eng.Law 305, 306 (3d ed. 1944).

8. Fifer v. Clearfield & Cambria Coal & Coke Co., 103 Md. 1, 62 A. 1122, syl. 2 (1906) (stating rule and citing English cases under common law system; here a plea of fraud in an action on contract, excluded as an implied admission of execution of contract as evidence on issue of authority of purported agent who signed contract for defendant); Morris v. Henderson, 37 Miss. 492, 508 (1859) (action for recovery of land, held defendant's plea of improvement in good faith not receivable as evidence of his possession, where that is denied by another plea). Wigmore, rightly it seems, terms the rule "a purely artificial one, an exception to principle, and is rendered necessary solely by the peculiar theory of common law pleading" (that issues were to be tried independently). § 1064.

9. "Under the name of a *bill*, a volume of notorious lies . . ." Bentham, Rationale of Evi-

dence, Works [ed. Bowring] vi, 43, quoted 9 Holdsworth, Hist.Eng.Law, 339 (3d ed. 1944).

10. For the description of this and other fictions, and specimen bills, see Holdsworth, op. cit. 379, 380, 394.

11. Though earlier admitted, it had become settled otherwise in the late 1700s. Doe v. Syburn, 7 T.R. 2, 101 Eng.Rep. 823 (1797); 4 Wigmore, Evidence, § 1065, note 7.

12. Lady Dartmouth v. Roberts, 16 East 334, 339, 104 Eng.Rep. 1116 (1812).

13. Clark, Code Pleading, § 36 (2d ed. 1947).

14. Clark, op. cit. § 41. He points out that the professed theory of the common law system also, as of any intelligible system, was that the truth should be pleaded, but as we have seen the actual practice came to be that of tolerating constant pleading of matter known to be untrue.

15. Stolte v. Larkin, 110 F.2d 226, syl. 10 (C.C.A. Minn.1940); Burch v. Grace St. Corp., 168 Va. 329, 191 S.E. 672, 677, syl. 9 (1937) ("We no longer treat pleadings as mere fiction. They are treated as the solemn statements of fact, upon the faith of which the rights of the parties are to be adjudged. Not only is the evidence required to follow the pleadings, but if a prior inconsistent pleading sets out

ancient fictions, such as the pleading of inconsistent counts or of separate contradictory pleas, may require the ancient limitations upon the use of such counts or pleas as admissions.[16] It is submitted, however, that permission to plead in the alternative, or hypothetically, as allowed under many modern codes,[17] is not intended to allow fictitious assertions, but to meet a practical need of the pleader who is justifiably uncertain as to what he can prove.[18] Thus it would be inappropriate to apply to such pleadings any rule prohibiting their use as admissions on a separate issue [19] by resorting by analogy to the common law restriction, yet it seems that the trial judge should have the duty to prevent the adversary from prejudicially distorting an alternative pleading into a straight-out admission of one of the alternative statements, or converting a contingent assertion into an unconditional one.[20]

In a civil case a pleading, or allegation therein, when amended, withdrawn, or superseded by a substitute pleading, ceases to be usable as a conclusive judicial admission,[21] but is admissible in evidence in the case in which filed at the instance of the adversary as an evidentiary admission.[22]

The question whether a plea of guilty, formerly tendered, in a criminal case shall come in evidence as an admission where the accused is later allowed to plead not guilty and is tried on the charge, presents balanced considerations of policy. On the one hand, a plea of guilty if freely and understandingly made is so likely to be true that to withhold it from the jury seems to ask them to do justice without knowledge of one of the most significant of the relevant facts. Similar admissions would be received in civil cases without hesitation, leaving it to the adver-

P. 505

---

a different state of facts, such prior pleading may be used to discredit the present claim of the party."); Decennial Digests, Evidence, ☞208(1) (2).

16. See, e. g. Biscayne Beach Theater v. Hill, 151 Fla. 1, 9 So.2d 109, syl. 3 (1942) (under statute allowing contradictory pleas, where defendant pleads general denial and also assumption of risk in confession and avoidance, confession in latter plea not usable by plaintiff as admission of negligence denied under the general denial).

17. See, e. g., Federal Rules of Civil Procedure, Rule 8(e) (2) ("A party may set forth two or more statements of a claim or defense alternatively or hypothetically, either in one count or defense or in separate counts or defenses . . .") and statutes, rules and decisions listed in Clark, Code Pleading, § 42 notes 141, 142 (2d ed. 1947).

18. Clark, op. cit. 255. While the Federal rule cited in the preceding note further provides that "a party may also state as many separate claims and defenses as he has regardless of consistency" such statements are to be made subject to Rule 11 which provides that an attorney's signature to a pleading is a certificate that he believes "there is good ground to support it." It has been argued, however, that a rule entitling a party to plead in the alternative and inconsistently should bring into play the common law restriction (see note 7, supra) upon using pleadings upon a separate issue as admissions. Denman, Note, 17 Tex.L.Rev. 191 (1939).

19. But see, e. g., Pullin v. First Nat. Bank, 86 Ind. App. 473, 158 N.E. 579, syl. 4 (1927) (action by customer against bank for damages for failure of cashier to credit checks to plaintiff's account; held, alleged admissions in bank's plea of estoppel not admissible as evidence of facts on which issue joined by general denial).

20. For instances of recognition of court's duty to protect pleader against unjustifiable use of his pleadings by adversary, see Hardwick v. Kansas City Gas Co., 355 Mo. 100, 195 S.W.2d 504, syl. 8 (1946) (where pleading offered to show inconsistency and asserted inconsistency did not exist); Dallas Ry. and Terminal Co. v. Hendricks, 139 Tex. 467, 166 S.W.2d 116, syl. 1 (1942) (former pleading offered "to show he has changed his pleading" held calculated to prejudice pleader's defenses).

21. Taliaferro v. Reirdon, 197 Okl. 55, 168 P.2d 292, syl. 1, 2 (1946); Kirk v. Head, 137 Tex. 44, 152 S. W.2d 726, syl. 9 (1941).

22. Cramer v. Kolodney & Meyers, 129 Conn. 468, 29 A.2d 579, syl. 9 (1943); Carver v. Carver, 199 Ga. 352, 34 S.E.2d 509, syl. 5 (1945); Hesse v. Diehl, 279 Mich. 168, 271 N.W. 721, syl. 3 (1937) (amount of damages claimed before amendment); Morgan v. Kroger Grocery & Baking Co., 348 Mo. 542, 154 S.W.2d 44, syl. 13 (1941); Polakoff v. Hill, 261 App. Div. 777, 27 N.Y.S.2d 142, syl. 1 (1941) (defamation by radio, original answer admitting use of defamatory words held admissible, though use of words

sary to rebut or explain.[23] But here, liberty or life is at stake, and there are strong possibilities that the plea may have been induced by pressure or mistake, yet the formal acknowledgment of guilt may nevertheless be given crucial weight by the jury. It seems, then, that in the case of pleas of guilty given at the preliminary hearing to determine whether the accused shall be held to await the action of the grand jury, since such pleas do not form the issue at the trial, and consequently no court has passed on the question whether they have been freely and voluntarily made, they should be treated on the analogy to confessions. Accordingly, if such a plea is offered as evidence at the trial the court should determine as a preliminary question whether it was freely and understandingly made, or extorted by undue pressure or by promise of leniency or induced by material mistake of fact or law. On the other hand if the former plea of guilty was given at the arraignment and so would have formed the basis for judgment, unless allowed to be withdrawn by the court and a new plea substituted, it seems that the admissibility of the plea at the trial should first depend on the basis for the action of the judge in allow-

ing withdrawal. If the local practice requires him before granting such withdrawal[24] to be satisfied that the first plea was induced by undue pressure, promise of leniency or material mistake, or was pleaded by counsel without authority or was entered by the clerk by inadvertence when no such plea was made, then the order allowing withdrawal is a finding of sufficient cause to deny admission to the plea as evidence. If, however, the statute allows a withdrawal as of right without cause,[25] or the practice permits the judge to allow withdrawal in his discretion as a matter of grace, then it seems again that the judge before whom the evidence is offered should decide as a preliminary question of fact, if the evidence is objected to, whether the plea was freely and understandingly made, or was induced by any of the disabling causes just recited, and determine admissibility accordingly. It is stated generally that the greater number of decisions admit in evidence the plea of guilty given at the preliminary hearing[26] and exclude such a former plea when given at arraignment and later permitted to be withdrawn,[27] but it is believed that some of the divergences in the results of cases admitting

---

denied in amended answer); Decennial Digests, ⇒ 208(6).

[23]. See, e. g., Morrissey v. Powell, 304 Mass. 268, 23 N.E.2d 411, syl. 14, 17 (1939) (in action for personal injuries defendant's plea of guilty to criminal charge of driving while drunk, though the plea was later withdrawn and upon a trial he was acquitted, held competent), Notes, 124 A.L.R. 1527, 40 Col.L. Rev. 915, 8 Duke B.A.J. 134, 26 Va.L.Rev. 514.

[24]. As to the rules obtaining in the different jurisdictions in respect to the conditions upon withdrawal see Dec.Dig. Criminal Law, ⇒274, 22 C.J.S., Criminal Law § 421.

[25]. See, e. g., the statute cited in People v. Ryan, 82 Calif. 617, 23 P. 121 (1890) and in Clark v. State, 72 Ga.App. 603, 34 S.E.2d 608 (1945), both permitting the accused as of right to withdraw his plea at any time before judgment.

[26]. Note, 141 A.L.R. 1335; United States v. Adelman, 107 F.2d 497, syl. 4 (C.C.A.2d 1939); Barnhardt v. State, 169 Ark. 567, 275 S.W. 909, syl. 6 (1925); People v. Sanderson, 129 Cal.App. 531, 18 P.2d 982,

syl. 2 (1933); State v. Briggs, 68 Iowa 416, 27 N.W. 358, syl. 8 (1886); People v. Gould, 70 Mich. 240, 38 N.W. 232, 234 (1888); Adams v. State, 138 Neb. 613, 294 N.W. 396, syl. 9 (1940); State v. Ingram, 204 N.C. 557, 168 S.E. 837, syl. 2 (1933).

Contra: Wood v. United States, 128 F.2d 265, 141 A.L.R. 1318 (C.A.D.C.1942) (Rutledge, J. in extensive opinion argues that to admit in evidence plea of guilty taken either before commissioner, as here, or before court on arraignment, where prisoner is asked how he pleads, is a violation of the privilege against self-incrimination).

[27]. 20 Am.Jur., Evidence, § 481, n. 17; and see cases collected in Dec.Digests, Crim.Law, ⇒406(4), 22 C.J.S. Crim.Law, § 733, notes 21, 22. Among the cases denying admissibility are Kercheval v. United States, 274 U.S. 220, 224, 47 S.Ct. 582, 583, 71 L.Ed. 1009 (1927) ("The effect of the court's order permitting the withdrawal was to adjudge that the plea of guilty be held for naught. Its subsequent use as evidence against petitioner was in direct conflict with that determination."); People v. Ryan, 82 Cal. 617, 23 P. 121 (1889); State v. Meyers,

and those excluding the evidence may be explained upon a consideration of whether under the practice of the particular jurisdiction the court by refusing to accept or by permitting the withdrawal of the plea has or has not already determined that circumstances existed which would make it unfair to receive it as an admission.[28]

The use of pleadings as evidentiary admissions is by no means confined to the situations discussed above of their employment in the very case in which the pleading was filed.

A party's pleading in one case, whether a final one, or one later withdrawn, amended or superseded, is freely usable against him as an evidentiary admission in any other litigation,[29] unless excluded under the limitations described above [30] based on the prevalence of fictitious or hypothetical allegations in the traditional systems.[31] Especially frequent is the use of a plea of guilty to a criminal charge offered as an admission in a later civil suit arising from the same transaction.[32] There is no requirement that the

99 Mo. 117, 12 S.W. 516 (1889); Heath v. State, 23 Okl.Cr. 382, 214 P. 1091 (1923). Upholding admissibility: State v. Carta, 90 Conn. 79, 96 A. 411, syl. 6 (1916) (two judges dissenting, extensive opinions pro and con); People v. Steinmetz, 240 N.Y. 411, 148 N.E. 597, syl. 4 (1925) (careful discussion in majority and dissenting opinion). 4 Wigmore, Evidence, § 1067 marshals opposing views and decisions without taking sides. For notes on recent decisions see 3 Ark.L.Rev. 471 (1949); 28 N.Y.U.L.Rev. 1186 (1953).

28. Thus in State v. Carta, 90 Conn. 79, 96 A. 411 1916), cited in the next preceding note, where the withdrawn plea was held admissible the prevailing opinion emphasized the notion that the judge was presumed to have ascertained that the plea was understandingly made before accepting it, and the view that permission to withdraw it is a matter of discretion, whereas the minority considered that this discretion would only be exercised when "the plea was not entered voluntarily, or resulted from ignorance, inadvertence, unfairness or deceit." The Federal rules relating to accepting and withdrawing pleas of guilty are Rules of Criminal Procedure (1946), Rule 11 (". . . The court may refuse to accept a plea of guilty, and shall not accept the plea without first determining that the plea is made voluntarily with understanding of the nature of the charge. . . ."); Rule 32(d) ("A motion to withdraw a plea of guilty or of *nolo contendere* may be made only before sentence is imposed or imposition of sentence is suspended; but to correct manifest injustice the court after sentence may set aside the judgment of conviction and permit the defendant to withdraw his plea.").

The distinction between the preliminary plea and the plea-at-arraignment situations suggested in the text is borne out by the following passage from the opinion of Swan, Circuit Judge in United States v. Adelman, 107 F.2d 497, 499 (C.C.A.2d 1939): "When a court allows a defendant to withdraw a plea of 'guilty' it is because the court finds that circumstances exist which make it unfair to hold him to

it. Such circumstances make it equally unfair to use it against him as an admission. The Kercheval case deals only with a plea withdrawn with leave to substitute a plea of not guilty. When a defendant pleads guilty before a commissioner who has no power to do more than hold him for bail, he does not have to withdraw this plea in order to plead not guilty to the indictment. The plea before the commissioner had not been held to have been obtained by unfair practice and we see no reason why it might not be received in evidence as freely as any extra-judicial admission of guilt."

29. Rogers v. Edward L. Burton Co., 137 F.2d 284, syl. 3 (C.C.A.Utah, 1943); Missouri Pacific R. Co. v. Zolliecoffer, 209 Ark. 559, 191 S.W.2d 587, syl. 5 (1946); Bartalotta v. Calvo, 112 Conn. 385, 152 A. 306, syl. 16 (1930) (superseded pleading); Himelson v. Galusz, 309 Mich. 512, 15 N.W.2d 727, syl. 3 (1944); Decennial Digests, Evidence, ☜208(2); 31 C.J.S., Evidence, § 433.

30. See notes 7, 10, supra, this section.

31. See, e. g., Brickley v. Atlantic Coast Line R. Co., 153 Fla. 1, 6, 13 So.2d 300, syl. 3 (1943) (applying general rule that common law pleadings in other causes are excluded, quoting 4 Wigmore, Evidence, 3d ed. § 1066).

32. Vaughan v. Jonas, 31 Cal.2d 586, 191 P.2d 432, syl. 2 (1948) (plea of guilty to misdemeanor assault admissible in civil action for wounding, despite fact that judgment of conviction on plea was suspended and later vacated upon defendant's fulfilling conditions of probation); Piechota v. Rapp, 148 Neb. 442, 27 N.W.2d 682, syl. 10, 11 (1947) (death action, defendant's plea of guilty to reckless driving admissible but not the complaint for higher offense); Decennial Digests, Evidence, ☜207(4). The defendant, however, may give evidence explaining his reasons for the plea. Moulin v. Bergeron, 135 Conn. 443, 65 A.2d 478, syl. 2 (1949); Race v. Chappell, 304 Ky. 788, 202 S.W.2d 626, syl. 2, 3 (1947), Decennial Digest, Evidence, ☜263(4), compare Motley v. Page, 250 Ala. 265, 34 So.2d 201,

present offeror of the evidence should have been a party to the proceeding in which the pleading was filed.[33]

How far is it necessary to connect the pleading with the party against whom it is sought to be used in evidence as an admission? Certainly if it be shown to have been sworn to,[34] or signed by the party himself that would be sufficient.[35] More often, however, the pleading is prepared and signed by counsel, and the older view, originating under the common law and equity systems of pleading, with their tolerance of fictions,[36] holds that it is not sufficient to show that the pleading was filed or signed by the party's attorney of record, and that the statements therein will be presumed to be merely "suggestions of counsel" unless other evidence is produced that they were actually sanctioned by the client.[37] In jurisdictions having a modernized system of fact-pleading, this view seems inconvenient and unrealistic. A substantial number of courts in these states have adopted the sensible view that plead-

ings shown to have been prepared or filed by counsel employed by the party, are prima facie regarded as authorized by him and are entitled to be received as his admissions.[38] It is open to the party to give evidence that the pleading was filed upon incorrect information and without his actual knowledge but such a showing goes only to the weight, not the admissibility of the pleading.[39]

243. Testimony by the Party against Himself.[1]

It happens not infrequently that a party while testifying on the stand or on pre-trial examination may admit some fact which if true is fatal, or at least adverse, to his cause of action or defense. If at the end of the trial the party's admission stands uncontradicted, then like uncontradicted testimony generally it is conclusive against him. Frequently this situation is what the courts are referring to when they say that a party is "bound" by his own testimony.[2] But the

---

syl. 7 (1948) (can explain but not contradict record by testifying he understood he was pleading guilty to lesser offense). Similarly the plea of guilty on preliminary hearing in a former case, when relevant, comes in as an admission in a later criminal case. Comm. v. Crecorian, 264 Mass. 94, 162 N.E. 7, syl. 7 (1928).

However, a plea of nolo contendere or non vult, where allowed, is regarded by tradition as a mere statement of unwillingness to contest, and no more, and is not receivable in another proceeding as an admission of guilt. Federal Deposit Ins. Corp. v. Cloonan, 165 Kan. 68, 193 P.2d 656, syl. 1–4 (1948); State v. LaRose, 71 N.H. 435, 52 A. 943, syl. 3 (1902); 4 Wigmore, Evidence, § 1066, note 4.

33. Dolinar v. Pedone, 63 Cal.App.2d 169, 146 P.2d 237, syl. 9 (1944); Note, 14 A.L.R. 56.

34. Hall v. Guthrie, 10 Mo. 621 (1847) (sworn bill in chancery); Johnson v. Butte, 41 Mont. 158, 108 P. 1057, syl. 2 (1910) (admission in sworn answer); Note, 14 A.L.R. 33; Decennial Digests, Evidence, ☞208(4).

35. Radclyffe v. Barton, 161 Mass. 327, 37 N.E. 373, syl. 2 (1894); Note, 14 A.L.R. 26.

36. See discussion earlier in this section.

37. Fidelity & Deposit Co. v. Redfield, 7 F.2d 800, syl. 5 (C.C.A.Idaho, 1925); Reichert v. Jerome H. Sheip, Inc., 206 Ala. 648, 91 So. 618, syl. 6 (1921); 31 C.J.S. Evidence, § 301, notes 33, 34.

38. Kunglig Jarnvagsstyrelson v. Dexter & Carpenter, 32 F.2d 195, syl. 2, 3 (C.C.A.N.Y.1929) (superseded pleading); Carlson v. Fredsall, 228 Minn. 461, 37 N.W.2d 744, syl. 5–8 (1949) (overruling earlier case which held doctrine inapplicable to a superseded pleading); Houston E. & W. T. Ry. Co. v. DeWalt, 96 Tex. 121, 70 S.W. 531, syl. 2 (1902) (superseded pleading); 20 Am.Jur. Evidence, § 630, note 4.

39. Cases cited in next preceding note, and see Anderson v. Tway, 143 F.2d 95, syl. 6 (C.C.A.Ky.1944).

1. See 9 Wigmore, Evidence, § 2594a, Notes, 50 A.L.R. 979, 80 A.L.R. 624, 169 A.L.R. 798, 22 Va.L.Rev. 365 (1936), 36 Mich.L.Rev. 688 (1938); Decennial Digests, Evidence, ☞265(10); 31 C.J.S. Evidence, § 381(d).

2. See, e. g., Bell v. Johnson, 142 Kan. 360, 46 P.2d 886 (1935); Goodwin v. E. B. Nelson Grocery Company, 239 Mass. 232, 132 N.E. 51 (1921); Fulghum v. Atlantic Coast Line Railroad Company, 158 N.C. 555, 74 S.E. 584, 39 L.R.A.,N.S., 558 (1912); Thompson v. Purcell Construction Company, 160 N.C. 390,

controversial question is whether he is bound in the sense that he will not be allowed to contradict his own statement by other testimony, or if contradictory testimony has been received the judge and jury are required to disregard it and to accept as true the party's self-disserving testimony, as a judicial admission.

Three main approaches are reflected in the decisions. First, the view that a party's testimony in this respect is like the testimony of any other witness called by the party, that is, the party is free (as far as any rule of law is concerned) to elicit contradictory testimony from the witness himself or to call other witnesses to contradict him.[3] Obviously, however, the problem of persuasion may be a difficult one when the party seeks to explain or contradict his own words, and

equally obviously the trial judge would often be empowered to say, on motion for directed verdict, that reasonable minds in the particular state of the proof could only believe that the party's testimony against his interest was true.

Second, the view that the party's testimony is not conclusive against contradiction except when he testifies unequivocally to matters in his peculiar knowledge,—either subjective facts, such as his own motivation, and what he himself knew or felt, or objective facts of observation where he could not have been mistaken.[4]

Third, the doctrine widely espoused in the recent decisions, that a party's testimony adverse to himself is in general to be treated as a judicial admission, conclusive against him,[5] so that he may not bring other witnesses to

---

76 S.E. 266 (1912); Thalhimer Bros., Inc., v. Casci, 160 Va. 439, 168 S.E. 433 (1933); Virginia Electric & Power Co. v. Vellines, 162 Va. 671, 175 S.E. 35 (1934); Frazier v. Stout, 165 Va. 68, 181 S.E. 377 (1935).

3. Alamo v. Del Rosario, 69 App.D.C. 47, 98 F.2d 328, syl. 5–9 (1938) (personal injury from automobile collision; plaintiff testified that defendant, his host, the driver, stopped the car, whereas negligence alleged was that he made an untimely left turn; held, jury entitled to believe other witnesses; masterly exposition of the policy of the doctrine, by Edgerton, J.); Pullman Co. v. Teutschmann, 169 F.2d 979, syl. 1 (C.A., Ore.1948) (following Oregon decision, cited infra, this note); Frost v. Los Angeles Ry. Co., 165 Cal. 365, 132 P. 442, syl. 9 (1913) (instruction that statements by plaintiff against his interest must be accepted as true, held erroneous); Kanopka v. Kanopka, 113 Conn. 30, 154 A. 144, syl. 4, 5, 80 A.L.R. 619 (1931) (collision; plaintiff, foreigner speaking through interpreter, excited at time of accident and trial, not concluded by her testimony; general rule that party's testimony, unless intended as unequivocal concession, not conclusive); Cox v. Jones, 138 Ore. 327, 5 P.2d 102, syl. 3 (1931) (automobile collision at intersection, plaintiff's testimony as to her own speed and as to seeing approaching truck not conclusive); Wiley v. Rutland Ry. Co., 86 Vt. 504, 86 A. 808, syl. 1 (1913) (injury to pedestrian run over by backing train; plaintiff's testimony as to when she looked at track, not a judicial admission).

4. Harlow v. Laclair, 82 N.H. 506, 136 A. 128, syl. 3, 50 A.L.R. 973 (1927) (plaintiff, a man, sues de-

fendant, a woman, for money advanced to buy a car; he testified that part of the consideration was her agreement to be his mistress; she denied the agreement; held, he was properly non-suited because the illicit agreement was peculiarly in his knowledge); Feuerstein v. Grady, 86 N.H. 406, 169 A. 622, syl. 3, 4 (1933) (testimony of plaintiff, a foreigner, as to circumstances of accident, not conclusive under preceding case); Sarkise v. Boston & Maine R. Co., 88 N.H. 178, 186 A. 332, syl. 4 (1936) (plaintiff, injured by train while playing baseball on tracks, bound by his unequivocal account of what he saw and did); Cote v. Stafford, 94 N.H. 251, 51 A.2d 144, syl. 1 (1947) (not bound by testimony as to objective fact where jury can reasonably say that witness was honestly mistaken).

5. Stearns v. Chicago R. I. and P. R. Co., 166 Iowa 566, 578, 148 N.W. 128, syl. 7 (1914) (plaintiff's testimony that he did not stop his train as he should have, though contradicted, conclusive on contributory negligence); Feary v. Metropolitan St. R. Co., 162 Mo. 75, 62 S.W. 452, syl. 15 (1901) (approving instruction that plaintiff's statements on stand conclusive against him); Miller v. Stevens, 63 S.D. 10, 256 N.W. 152, syl. 3 (1934) (girl riding in car sues driver; her testimony, though contradicting testimony was given by defendant, held conclusive against her); Kimmell v Tipton, 142 S.W.2d 421, syl. 2, 3 (Tex.Civ.App.1940); Massie v. Firmstone, 134 Va. 450, 114 S.E. 652, syl. 4 (1922) (plaintiff real estate broker suing for commission testified that his commission was conditional on sale going through and that it had not; despite contradictory testimony, plaintiff bound by his own evidence).

contradict it, and if he or his adversary does elicit such conflicting testimony it will be disregarded. Obviously, this general rule demands many qualifications and exceptions. Among these are the following: (1) The party is free to contradict, and thus correct, his own testimony; only when his own testimony taken as a whole unequivocally affirms the statement does the rule of conclusiveness apply.[6] The rule is inapplicable, moreover, when the party's testimony (2) may be attributable to inadvertence[7] or to a foreigner's mistake as to meaning,[8] or (3) is merely negative in effect,[9] or (4) is avowedly uncertain, or is an estimate or opinion [10] rather than an assertion of concrete fact, or (5) relates to a matter as to which the party could easily have been mistaken, such as the swiftly moving events just preceding a collision in which the party was injured.[11]

Of these three approaches the first, which rejects any restrictive rule and leaves to the judgment of the jurors, the judge, and the appellate court, to evaluate the party's testimony and the conflicting evidence, in the circumstances of the particular case, with only the standard of reason to guide them, seems preferable in policy and most in accord with the tradition of jury trial.

The second theory, binding the party as to facts within his peculiar knowledge, is based on the assumption that as to such facts the possibility that he may be mistaken substantially disappears. This assumption is unfounded. "If he is human it does not disappear. Knowledge may be 'special' without being correct. Often we little note nor long remember our 'motives, purposes, or knowledge.' There are few if any subjects on which plaintiffs are infallible." [12]

The third theory, now perhaps most in vogue with the courts, is of doubtful expediency. In the first place the party's testimony, uttered by a layman in the stress of examination, cannot with justice be given the conclusiveness of the traditional judicial admission in a pleading or stipulation,[13] deliberately drafted by counsel for the express purpose of limiting and defining the facts in issue.[14] Again, a general rule of conclusiveness necessitates an elaboration of qualifications and exceptions which represent a transfer to the appellate court of some of the traditional control of the jury by the trial judge, or in a non-jury case of the judge's fact-finding function. These duties call for an exercise of judgment by the judge who has heard and seen the witnesses. The su-

---

6. Chaplain v. Dugas, 323 Mass. 91, 80 N.E.2d 9, syl. 4, 5 (1948).

7. Security National Bank v. Johnson, 195 Okl. 107, 155 P.2d 249, syl. 5, 169 A.L.R. 790 (1944) (where doubtful whether statement of party was a slip of the tongue, and was inconsistent with other parts of his testimony, question is for jury).

8. Krikorian v. Dailey, 171 Va. 16, 197 S.E. 442, syl. 9 (1938).

9. Waller v. Waller, 187 Va. 25, 46 S.E.2d 42, 45 (1948).

10. Diel v. St. Louis Public Service Co., 238 Mo.App. 1046, 192 S.W.2d 608, 611, syl. 3 (1946) (plaintiff's testimony as to distance the car was away when he stopped, a mere estimate and not conclusive); Burris v. Kansas City Public Service Co., 226 S.W.2d 743, syl. 4, 5 (Mo.App.1950) (similar; good discussion by Bour, C.); Petit v. Klinke, 254 S.W.2d 769, syl. 2, 3 (Tex.1953) (party not necessarily bound by his opinion-testimony).

11. Crew v. Nelson, 188 Va. 108, 49 S.E.2d 326, syl. 9 (1948).

12. Edgerton, Circ. J., in Alamo v. Del Rosario, 69 App.D.C. 47, 98 F.2d 328, 332 (1938).

13. As to judicial admissions see § 239, supra, and 9 Wigmore, Evidence, §§ 2588–2594.

14. This much, however, should be conceded, even under the liberal view contended for that a party is not generally concluded by his testimony. That is, if a party testifies deliberately to a fact fatal to his case, the judge if his counsel, on inquiry, indicates no intention to seek to elicit contradictory testimony, may give a non-suit or directed verdict. Under these circumstances, the party and his counsel advisedly manifest an intention to be bound. See Kanopka v. Kanopka, 113 Conn. 30, 154 A. 144, 147 (1931), Edgecomb v. Callahan, 132 Cal.App. 248, 22 P.2d 521 (1933) and the annotator's discussion, 169 A.L.R. 801. Compare Oscanyan v. Arms Co., 103 U.S. 261, 263, 26 L.Ed. 539 (1880) holding it proper to direct a verdict on counsel's opening statement.

pervision by appellate judges of this trial process can best be exercised under a flexible standard, rather than a rule of conclusiveness.

Moreover, this rule leads to mechanical solutions, unrelated to the needs of justice, in certain special situations. One is the situation where the opponent by adroit cross-examination has maneuvered the party into an improvident concession.[15] One is the case of the defendant who is protected by liability insurance and who testifies to facts which will help the plaintiff to win.[16] Another is the situation where both parties testify against their respective interests.[17] Here the rule of conclusiveness may be thought to decide the issue against the party who has the burden of proof.[18]

Finally, the moral emphasis is wrong. Early cases where the rule of conclusiveness was first used may have been cases where the judges were outraged by seeming attempts by parties to play fast and loose with the court. But an examination of numerous recent decisions convinces the writer that this is far from being the typical situation of the party testifying to self-disserving facts. Instead of the unscrupulous party, it is the one who can be pushed into an admission by the ingenuity or persistence of adverse counsel,[19] or it is the unusually candid or conscientious party willing to speak the truth to his own hurt, who is penalized by the rule of conclusiveness.[20] It is to be hoped that the courts may revert to the older, simpler, and more flexible practice.

15. See, e. g., Driscoll v. Virginia Elec. & Power Co., 166 Va. 538, 181 S.E. 402 (1935).

16. In Vondrashek v. Dignan, 200 Minn. 530, 274 N.W. 609, syl. 3 (1937), the plaintiff, a lady who was a guest in the defendant's automobile, sued for severe personal injuries sustained when the defendant drove the car into the center pier of a railway viaduct which crossed a boulevard. Shortly before the accident they visited a night club and the defendant had several drinks. The defense was conducted in the defendant's name by counsel employed by a liability insurance company. At the trial the defendant's negligence was conceded, but counsel contended that the plaintiff was guilty of contributory negligence in riding with a driver whom she knew to be affected by liquor. The defendant, in his own behalf, testified, "I was not strictly sober but nobody could tell that I was under the influence of liquor." Thereafter, defendant's counsel sought to introduce evidence of tests for intoxication made upon defendant after the accident for the purpose of showing that he must have been visibly affected. Excluded on the ground that the defendant could not dispute his own testimony. Verdict and judgment for plaintiff. On appeal, the judgment was affirmed, and the court held, within the rule of the New Hampshire cases cited in note 4, supra, that this was a matter peculiarly within the plaintiff's knowledge and he was bound by his testimony. Surely this application of the "peculiar knowledge" exception is highly questionable, and the disregarding of the distinct interest of the insurance company seems unjust. See Note, 36 Mich.L.Rev. 688 (1938). Other decisions seem preferable, which deny conclusiveness to the defendant's testimony, though uncontradicted, when

an insurance company is interested (Christi v. Eager, (1942) 129 Conn. 62, 26 A.2d 352, syl. 4, 5) or permit the insurance company counsel to produce evidence contradicting the defendant. King v. Spencer, 115 Conn. 201, 161 A. 103, syl. 1 (1932), Note, 32 Col.L. Rev. 1243. Compare Horneman v. Brown, 286 Mass. 65, 190 N.E. 735 (1935) (permitting counsel defending under liability insurance policy to impeach defendant by prior inconsistent statement).

17. See, e. g., Sutherland v. Davis, 286 Ky. 743, 151 S.W.2d 1021, syl. 5–9 (1941) (suit by woman, guest, who had been picked up by defendant, driver of car; plaintiff testified that she knew that defendant was too drunk to drive and that she could have alighted after she knew this; defendant testified that though he had had some drinks, he was sober; held, the admissions by plaintiff precluded recovery, and she was barred from producing any evidence to the contrary).

18. See Chakales v. Djiovanides, 161 Va. 48, 170 S.E. 848, syl. 12 (1933) and Note, 169 A.L.R. at 815.

19. See, e. g., Gilbert v. Bostona Mines Co., 121 Mont. 397, 195 P.2d 376, syl. 7 (1948); Kipf v. Bitner, 150 Neb. 155, 33 N.W.2d 518, syl. 5–9 (1948) (admission extracted from plaintiff on taking of deposition, not conclusive).

20. "Since his testimony was adverse to his interests, he is more likely to have been mistaken than lying. The proposed rule actually punishes him for two things, his honesty and his error." Edgerton, J. in Alamo v. Del Rosario, 69 App.D.C. 47, 98 F.2d 328, 331 (1938), and see Burruss v. Suddith, 187 Va. 473, 47 S.E. 546, syl. 3 (1948).

244. Representative Admissions.[1]

When a party to the suit <u>has expressly authorized another person</u> to <u>speak on his behalf</u>, it is an obvious and accepted extension of the admission rule, to admit against the party the statements of such person.[2] In the absence of express authority, how far will the statements of an agent be received as the principal's admission by virtue of the employment relationship? The early texts and cases used as analogies the doctrine of the master's substantive responsibility for the acts of the agent, and the notion then prevalent in evidence law that words accompany-

ing a relevant act are admissible as part of the *res gestae*. Thus they formulated the theory that the agent's statements could be received against the principal only when made at the time of, and in relation to, some act then being performed in the scope of the agent's duty.[3] This rather clumsy[4] theory finds reflection in some current opinions, where the fashion lingers of testing the admissibility of the agent's statements by the test of "res gestae."[5] A simpler theory seems to have gained wider currency in the later writings[6] and opinions.[7] This is the view that the evidential admissibility of the

---

1. Uniform Rules of Evidence, R. 63(9) admits as an exception to the hearsay rule the following: *"Vicarious Admissions*. As against a party, a statement which would be admissible if made by the declarant at the hearing if (a) the statement concerned a matter within the scope of an agency or employment of the declarant for the party and was made before the termination of such relationship, or (b) the party and the declarant were participating in a plan to commit a crime or a civil wrong and the statement was relevant to the plan or its subject matter and was made while the plan was in existence and before its complete execution or other termination, or (c) one of the issues between the party and the proponent of the evidence of the statement is a legal liability of the declarant, and the statement tends to establish that liability".

2. Nuttall v. Holman, 110 Utah 375, 173 P.2d 1015, syl. 3 (1946).

3. "The acts of an agent, within the scope of the authority delegated to him, are deemed the acts of the principal. . . . 'But it must be remembered,' says Greenleaf, 'that the admission of the agent cannot always be assimilated to the admission of the principal. The party's own admission, whenever made may be given in evidence against him; but the admission or declaration of his agent binds him only when it is made during the continuance of the agency in regard to a transaction then depending, *et dum fervet opus*. It is because it is a verbal act and part of the *res gestae* that it is admissible at all; and, therefore, it is not necessary to call the agent to prove it; but wherever what he did is admissible in evidence, there it is competent to prove what he said about the act *while he was doing it*.' 1 Greenleaf, § 113." Harlan, J. in Vicksburg & Meridian Railroad v. O'Brien, 119 U.S. 99, 104, 30 L.Ed 299 (1886). For similar expressions, see Fairlie v. Hastings, 10 Ves.Jr. 123, 127, 32 Eng.Rep. 792 (Ch., 1804), 2 Jones, Evidence, § 944 (2d ed.1926).

4. The *res gestae* term had been applied (a) to words of the agent used not for a hearsay purpose but as fixing substantive liability upon the principal as constituting, for example, a deceit or an acceptance of an offer, or (b) to spontaneous exclamations following an exciting event. See §§ 272, 274, herein, and Morgan, A Suggested Classification of Utterances Admissible as Res Gestae, 31 Yale L.J. 229 (1922). In likening the hearsay use of the agent's admissions to these earlier situations by employing the same term, *res gestae*, the courts were obscuring the simpler notion of representation, and were inviting the application of requirements imposed on the other types of evidence and inappropriate here.

5. See, e. g., Muntz v. Travelers Mutual Casualty Co., 229 Iowa 1015, 295 N.W. 837, 840, 841 (1941), Note, 41 Col.L.Rev. 922 (excluding statement of insurance solicitor on day after application and after fatal accident to insured, that it was a blessing that agent had covered insured with policy the day before); Brown v. Montgomery Ward Co., 217 N.C. 368, 8 S.E. 2d 199, syl. 3 (1940) (statement shortly after plaintiff was injured by fall in store, by salesman standing nearby, that the washing machine was leaking grease "again," rejected, not part of res gestae).

6. See 4 Wigmore, Evidence, § 1078; Morgan, Admissions, 12 Washington L.Rev. 181, 193 (1937); Notes, 3 Baylor L.Rev. 594 (1951), 43 Harv.L.Rev. 936 (1930); Comment, 4 Tex.L.Rev. 506, (1926); Restatement, Agency, §§ 284–291, especially § 286: "Statements of an agent to a third person are admissible in evidence to prove the truth of facts asserted in them as though made by the principal, if the agent was authorized to make the statement or was authorized to make, on the principal's behalf, true statements concerning the subject matter," and § 288: "(1) Authority to do an act or conduct a transaction does not of itself include authority to make statements concerning the act or transaction.

7. See Note 7 on following Page.

agent's statements as admissions of the principal is measured by precisely the same tests as the principal's substantive responsibility for the acts and conduct of the agent, that is, the words of the agent will be received in evidence as the admissions of the principal, if they were spoken or written within the scope of the authority of the agent to speak or write for the employer. This formula makes it plain that the statements of an agent employed to give information may be received as the employer's admissions, regardless of want of authority to act, and conversely that authority to act, e. g., the authority of a chauffeur to drive a car, would not carry with it automatically the authority to make statements to others describing what he was doing or had done. Examples of cases applying one or the other of these two tests are given below.[8]

Probably the most frequent employment of both of these tests is in the exclusion of statements made by employees after an accident, to the injured party, to a police officer, or to some by-stander, about the accident not made in furtherance of the employer's interest, but as a "mere narrative." [9] This is the logical application of these tests,

(2) Authority to make statements of fact does not of itself include authority to make statements admitting liability because of such facts."

7. McNicholas v. New England Tel. & Tel. Co., 196 Mass. 138, 81 N.E. 889, 891 (1907) ("Declarations of an agent are not admissible against the principal, unless they are made within the scope and course of his employment."); Decker v. Consolidated Feed Coal & Lumber Co., 137 N.J.L. 154, 59 A.2d 15, 16 (1948) (". . . the statement must be made in the course of the business entrusted to the one making and within the scope of his authority.")

8. Admissions of agent received against principal: Adams Express Co. v. Berry & Whitmore Co., 35 App.D.C. 208, 31 L.R.A.,N.S., 309, syl. 1 (1910) (express company agent calls on shipper in answer to inquiry about jewelry shipped and admits that it was stolen by employee); Attalla Compress & Storage Co. v. Adams, 16 Ala.App. 624, 80 So. 628 (1918) (manager of warehouse responding to owner's inquiry as to disposition of property stored); Home Insurance Co. of N. Y. v. Hall, 192 Ark. 283, 91 S.W. 2d 609, syl. 3, 4, 1936 (admission of insurance adjuster seeking to settle claim, that policy had not been canceled); Arenson v. Skouras Theatres Corp., 131 N.J.L. 303, 36 A.2d 761, syl. 4, 5 (1944) (report of theater employee to manager as to condition causing injury, in presence of plaintiff, admissible); Standefer v. Aultman & Taylor Co., 34 Tex.Civ.App. 160, 78 S.W. 552, syl. 1 (1904) (state manager of implement company calling upon purchaser of machine who had made complaint, admits that machine was worthless and not as ordered).

Statements of agent excluded: Muntz v. Travelers Mutual Casualty Co., supra, note 4; Friedman v. Forest City, 239 Iowa 112, 30 N.W.2d 752, 760, syl. 20 (1948) (admissions of engineer sent by city to plaintiff's home to investigate complaints by plaintiff of vibration from electric plant, excluded. "Apparently Jennings was employed to work for the city,

not to talk for it."); Parsons v. Dwight State Co., 301 Mass. 324, 17 N.E.2d 197, 198, syl. 5, 118 A.L.R. 1099 (1938) (injury to plaintiff by defective shower bath; conversation between manager and repair man as to condition of plumbing, excluded); State ex rel. S. S. Kresge Co. v. Shain, 340 Mo. 145, 152, 101 S.W.2d 14 (1936) (written statements made by manager of store and by fellow-employee—to whom, not disclosed—about cause of an accident to employee three months before); Shelton v. Wolf Cheese Co., 338 Mo. 1129, 93 S.W.2d 947, 952 (1936) (plaintiff's attorney testifies to alleged admission made to him over the telephone by one who said he was defendant's manager); Lakeside Hospital v. Kovar, 131 Ohio St. 333, 2 N.E.2d 857, syl. 3 (1936) (husband's suit against hospital for negligent administration by nurse of blood-infusion from wrong bottle, causing death of wife; held, statement of managing director made to plaintiff's attorney who called at hospital, inadmissible).

It is important to distinguish situations where the declaration of the agent comes in on other theories. Thus, if the agent and the principal are both parties to the suit, the agent's admission is of course received against him, though it may not be admissible against the master. Square Deal Cartage Co. v. Smith's Admr., 307 Ky. 135, 210 S.W.2d 340, syl. 6 (1948). Again, the agent's declaration often comes in as a spontaneous exclamation made under stress of excitement (see § 272, herein). MacDonald v. Appleyard, 94 N.H. 362, 53 A.2d 434, syl. 13 (1947) (statement of truck-driver immediately after collision that he was trying to fix his lights admissible against employer, not as admission, but as spontaneous declaration); Levandowski v. Studey, 249 Wis. 421, 25 N.W.2d 59, syl. 1 (1946) (similar).

9. Northwestern Union Packet Co., 87 U.S. 528, 22 L. Ed. 406, syl. 4 (1874) (statement by captain of boat on which injury occurred, respecting the accident, made to plaintiff two days later); Beaule v. Weeks, 95

but the assumption that the test for the master's responsibility for the agent's *acts* should be the test for using the agent's statements as *evidence* against the master is a shaky one. The evidence should be tested by its trustworthiness. The rejection of such post-accident statements coupled with the admission of the employee's testimony on the stand is to prefer the weaker to the stronger evidence. The agent is well informed about acts in the course of the business, his statements offered against the employer are normally against the employer's interest, and while the employment continues, the employee is not likely to make such statements unless they are true. Accordingly, the commentators have advocated a widening of the common law tests,[10] such as is embodied in the Model Code provision which lets in the

agent's statement, if "the declaration concerned a matter within the scope" of the declarant's employment", and was made before the termination of the agency or employment." [11] Some of the recent cases, in result if not in theory, support this wider test.[12] Its acceptance by courts generally seems expedient.

Under any of these views, the party offering evidence of the alleged agent's admission must first prove the fact and scope of the agency of the declarant for the adverse party.[13] This he may of course do by the testimony of the asserted agent himself, or by anyone who knows, or by circumstantial evidence. Evidence of the purported agent's past declarations asserting the agency, are inadmissible hearsay when offered to show the relation.[14] If this preliminary fact of the

N.H. 453, 66 A.2d 148, syl. 5 (1949) (statement of truck driver to policeman, half hour after accident, that he had not stopped at the stop sign); Raffetto v. Warner Bros. Theatres, 121 N.J.L. 333, 2 A.2d 595, syl. 2 (1938) (action for injury to wife from fall on theater stairs, statement of manager to husband after the accident that he thought the defect in stair had been attended to).

10. Model Code of Evidence, Comment on Rule 508 (a), p. 251 (1942); Comment, 47 Col.L.Rev. 1227 (1947). See also Morgan, The Rationale of Vicarious Admissions, 42 Harv.L.Rev. 461 (1929).

11. Model Code of Evidence, Rule 508(a). This is now embodied in Uniform Rules of Evidence, R. 63(9) (a), set out in note 1, above.

12. Slifka v. Johnson, 161 F.2d 467, syl. 2, C.C.A.N.Y., 1947, Notes, 47 Col.L.Rev. 1227, 60 Harv.L.Rev. 976 (broker, authorized to arrange for change of insurance policies, in letter of instructions to insurance company, states, "The above change . . . is for purpose of avoiding payment of tax."; held admissible. "It would be strange to have a rule of agency binding a principal to unauthorized acts of an agent, when done within the apparent scope of his authority, and yet to adopt a rule of evidence which would exclude statements naturally made in the course of the agency. Such a rigid view does not accord with the current broadening of the rules of evidence or with the spirit of contemporary remedial statutes."); Myrick v. Lloyd, 27 So.2d 615, syl. 2, 3, Fla. 1946 (suit against father for injury occurring while son driving father on business trip; father sends son with injured person to hospital; on way to hospital

son says he was to blame; held, admissible); Whitaker v. Keough, 144 Neb. 790, 14 N.W.2d 596, syl. 12, 13, 1944 (defendant's chauffeur immediately after collision said, "Lady, I am sorry. I just saw you the instant I collided with you"; held, receivable as admission of employer).

13. Labor Hall Ass'n v. Danielsen, 24 Wash.2d 75, 163 P.2d 167, syl. 9, 161 A.L.R. 1079 (1945); 4 Wigmore, Evidence, § 1078; Decennial Digests, Evidence, ☞ 258(1); 20 Am.Jur. Evidence, § 597.

14. Neither the fact nor the extent of the agency can be so proved. Standard Mutual Ben. Corp. v. State, 197 Ark. 333, 122 S.W.2d 459, syl. 2 (1938); Home Owners' Loan Corp. v. Thornburgh, 187 Okl. 699, 106 P.2d 511, syl. 4 (1940), and see Comment, Evidence of Statements by Alleged Agent after Accident to Establish Agency, 36 Ky.L.J. 471 (1948). But the purported agent's declarations if offered to show that the other party dealt with him as an agent would not be hearsay, and would be admitted. Friend Lumber Co. v. Armstrong Bldg. Finish Co., 276 Mass. 361, 177 N.E. 794, syl. 1, 80 A.L.R. 599 (1931), with note on this point. And the asserted agent's declarations may come in to show his intention to act for the principal rather than for himself, either under the hearsay exception for declarations of mental state (see § 268, herein) or as circumstantial evidence of the intention. Mattan v. Hoover, 350 Mo. 506, 166 S.W.2d 557, syl. 10–14 (1942) (declaration of vacuum cleaner salesman after accident that he was on his way to make a demonstration).

declarant's agency is disputed, the question is for the judge.[15]

Attorneys.[16] Borrowing a popular term, how far is a lawyer the "mouthpiece" of the client? If an attorney is employed to manage a party's conduct of a lawsuit he has *prima facie* authority to make relevant judicial admissions by pleadings, by oral or written stipulations, or by formal opening statement, which unless allowed to be withdrawn are conclusive.[17] Such formal and conclusive admissions should be, and are, framed with care and circumspection, and in a leading English case, such admissions are contrasted with an attorney's oral out-of-court statement, and the latter characterized as "merely a loose conversation,"[18] and it is often said that the client is not "bound" by the "casual" statements of his attorney out of court.[19] The use of the word "bound" is obviously misleading. The issue is not whether the client is "bound," as he is by a judicial admission, but whether the attorney's extra-judicial statement is admissible against the client as a mere evidential admission made by an agent on his behalf. The older cases manifest a natural if unconscious tendency to protect the client against the hazard of evidence of statements by his attorneys more strictly than in respect to statements by other types of agents.[20] The later cases, properly it seems, measure the authority of the attorney to make out-of-court admissions by the same tests of express or implied authority as would be applied to other agents,[21] and when they meet these tests admit as evidentiary admissions the statements of attorneys in letters or oral conversations made in the course of efforts for the collection or resistance of claims, or negotiations for the settlement of suits or controversies, or the management of any other business in behalf of the client.[22]

Partners.[23] A partner is an agent of the partnership for the conduct of the firm business.[24] Accordingly, when the existence and

---

15. See § 53, herein.

16. 4 Wigmore, Evidence, § 1063; 2 Jones, Evidence, §§ 955–959 (2d ed. 1926); Morgan, Admissions, 12 Wash.L.Rev. 181, 188 (1937); Decennial Digests, Evidence, ☞246; 20 Am.Jur. Evidence, § 592.

17. See the discussion of judicial admissions, supra, § 242.

18. Petch v. Lyon, 9 Q.B. 147, 153, 115 Eng.Rep. 1231, 1233 (1846).

19. A recent expression of this traditional view is found in Jackson v. Schine Lexington Corp., 305 Ky. 823, 205 S.W.2d 1013, 1014, syl. 1–4 (1947) (copy of intended pleading, never filed, sent to plaintiff's attorney by defendant's, containing admission, held inadmissible. "The general rule is that an attorney has no power to prejudice his client by admissions of fact made out of court. Though he may be the agent of his client, such agency does not carry the implication of authority to make binding admissions other than in the actual management of the litigation.")

20. See, e.g., Wagstaff v. Wilson, 4 Barn. & Ad. 339, 110 Eng.Rep. 483 (1832) (trespass for taking a horse; letter offered from defendant's attorney of record stating that defendant had distrained the horse, written in reply to letter from plaintiff's attorney to defendant, excluded for want of proof that it was written with defendant's sanction); Saunders v. McCarthy, 90 Mass. 42, 45 (1864) (oral statements by attorney of relevant facts during conversation with adverse party before suit for the purpose of settling the controversy, held, "mere matters of conversation").

21. "If the admission is clearly within the scope of his agency, express or implied, he has the same authority to bind his client as any other agent." Offutt, J. in Brown v. Hebb, 167 Md. 535, 175 A. 602, 607, 97 A.L.R. 366 (1934).

22. Suntken v. Suntken, 223 Iowa 347, 272 N.W. 132, syl. 2–6 (1937) (distinct admissions of fact in attorney's letter written in course of negotiations for compromise); Brown v. Hebb, 167 Md. 535, 175 A. 602, syl. 5–7, 97 A.L.R. 366 (1937) (doctor sends bill for $1500, patient's lawyer replies by letter offering $300 "for the services rendered" held admissible as an acknowledgement of a debt for services, tolling limitations); McGarity v. New York Life Ins. Co., 359 Pa. 308, 59 A.2d 47, syl. 6 (1948) (statement by counsel for executor as ground for rejecting claim against deceased, admissible against executors).

23. 4 Wigmore, Evidence, § 1078, p. 126; Decennial Digests, Evidence, ☞249; Note, Admissions of Partner as Evidence, 73 A.L.R. 447.

24. As to the scope of the partner's agency, see Crane, Partnership, § 49 (1938).

scope of the partnership has been proved,[25] the statement of a partner made in the conduct of the business of the firm comes in evidence as the admission of the partnership.[26] What of statements of a former partner made after dissolution? The cases are divided,[27] but it seems that since a continuing power is recognized in each former partner to do such acts as are reasonably necessary to wind up and settle the affairs of the firm,[28] he should likewise be regarded as having authority to speak for the former partners in making such statements of fact as are reasonably incident to collecting the claims and property and paying the debts of the firm.[29] Beyond this, it seems that his admissions should be competent only against himself.

Co-conspirators.[30] Analogous to partnerships are conspiracies to commit a crime or an unlawful or tortious act. If A and B are engaged in such a conspiracy the acts and declarations of B occurring while the conspiracy is actually in progress and in furtherance of the design are proveable against A, because they are acts for which he is criminally or civilly responsible, as a matter of

---

25. This, of course, must be established by evidence other than the out-of-court declarations of the purported partner. Caswell v. Maplewood Garage, 84 N.H. 241, 149 A. 746, syl. 11, 73 A.L.R. 433 (1930) (partner not authorized to admit out of court that a previous automobile collision occurred when car was driven on firm business; but doesn't the authority to admit this for the firm depend on whether the statement was made—as it might be—as part of the conduct of firm business?); Belt v. McGehee, 9 S.W.2d 407, syl. 7 (Tex.Civ.App.1928) (partner's admissions come in when existence of partnership proved by other evidence). See note 13, supra, for like holdings as to agents' admissions.

26. Uniform Partnership Act, sec. 11: "An admission made by any partner concerning partnership affairs within the scope of his authority as conferred by this act is evidence against the partnership."; English Partnership Act: "An admission or representation made by any partner concerning the partnership affairs, and in the ordinary course of its business, is evidence against the firm."; Wieder v. Lorenz, 164 Ore. 10, 99 P.2d 38, syl. 2 (1940) (failure by one member of firm to answer letter to him on firm business, admitted against partnership); King v. Wesner, 198 S.C. 289, 16 S.E.2d 289, syl. 6 (1941) statement of partner about accident of employee, made to representative of Industrial Commission who was investigating accident was in course of firm business and admissible against firm); Note, 73 A.L.R. 454.

Sometimes the courts in stating the rule ignore the limitation that the statement must be in the course of the firm business, see Adair v. Kansas City Term. Ry. Co., 282 Mo. 133, 153, 220 S.W. 920 (1920). And sometimes, on the other hand, courts which recognize the limitation assume too easily that statements, particularly those made after accidents to the victim by a member of the firm, are not made in furtherance of affairs of the partnership. Looney v. Bingham Dairy, 75 Utah 53, 282 P. 1030, 73 A.L.R. 427 (1929) (statement by dairy partner made to parents of boy who had been injured at dairy, that horse that had kicked boy was mean, inadmissible as not made in pursuit of partnership business; query).

Morgan, Admissions, 12 Wash.L.Rev. 181, 194 (1937) points out the failure of the courts to apply as consistently to statements by partners as in case of admissions by agents, the test of authority to speak. He says: "[In a tort case] a partner admits the existence of a defect in the instrumentality involved. Is this receivable against the other partners? Theoretically no, unless the speaker was authorized to talk about it. And such is the holding in about half of the pertinent cases. In the others, it seems to be assumed that the partner has such authority, for the evidence is received. And in contract actions, the holdings are almost unanimous to that effect. In this respect the language of many of the decisions makes no distinction between the situation where the words would be operative to create legal relations and the situation where they can have no operative effect and are merely narrative and evidential. If they are to be harmonized with the agency cases, it must be on the ground that each partner has authority to talk about any partnership transaction."

27. They are collected in Note, 73 A.L.R. 459-473.

28. Crane, Partnership, § 80 (1939).

29. Feigler v. Whitaker, 22 Ohio St. 606, 10 Am.Rep. 778 (1872); and other decisions cited in Crane, Partnership, 357, 358 (1939). Contra: Miller v. Neimerick, 19 Ill. 172 (1857).

30. 4 Wigmore, Evidence. § 1079, Jones, Commentaries on Evidence, § 943 (1926); Decennial Digests, Criminal Law, ☞423-427, Evidence, ☞253; Morgan, Admissions, 12 Wash.L.Rev. 181, 194 (1937).

substantive law.[31] But B's declarations may also be proved against A as representative admissions, to prove the truth of the matter declared, and only then are they within our present topic. The courts seldom discriminate between declarations offered as conduct constituting part of the conspiracy and declarations offered as a vicarious admission of the facts declared,[32] and even when offered for the latter purpose, generally impose the same test, namely that the declaration must have been made while the conspiracy was continuing,[33] and must have constituted a step in furtherance of the venture.[34] This seems fairly consistent with the test of implied authority to speak as applied to agent's statements, since damaging admissions of

fact by one conspirator, unless made to further the common unlawful design, could seldom or never be thought to have been authorized by the fellow-conspirator, since it would only be calculated to frustrate the plot. On the other hand if we subject the evidence to the more realistic test of trustworthiness, there is strong argument for abandoning the limitation of "furtherance" or "implied authority." What one of the conspirators admits while the plot is afoot about the plan or the happenings in its execution, is said by one who has special knowledge and generally is against the declarant's interest. Accordingly with the support of some of the cases and statutes,[35] the Model Code has widened the scope of conspirators' declarations by

---

Rationale of Vicarious Admissions, 42 Harv.L.Rev. 461, 464 (1929).

31. 4 Wigmore, Evidence, § 1079.

32. See, e. g., Schine Chain Theatres v. United States, 334 U.S. 110, 117, 68 S.Ct. 947, 951, 92 L.Ed. 1245 (1948) (where in a suit for injunction against antitrust law violations the court said: "It is sufficient at this point to say that since a conspiracy between Schine and each of the named distributors was established by independent evidence, these inter-office letters and memoranda were admissible against all conspirators as declarations of some of the associates so far as they were in furtherance of the unlawful project.")

33. Lutwak v. United States, 344 U.S. 604, 617, 73 Sup.Ct. 481, syl. 14, 97 L.Ed. 593 (1953); Rimmer v. United States, 172 F.2d 954, syl. 10 (C.A., 5th, 1949) (statements made by conspirator by way of confession after arrest, held inadmissible); People v. Davis, 56 N.Y. 95, 102 (1874) (prosecution of doctor for procuring abortion; declarations of woman after she had returned home as to what was done at doctor's office, held inadmissible as declaration of fellow conspirator, because the object of the conspiracy had been effected).
The existence of the conspiracy must be proved independently to justify the admission of the declaration. State v. Fields, 234 Mo. 615, 623, 138 S.W. 518, syl. 4 (1911); 4 Wigmore, Evidence, § 1079(a). But in his discretion, the court may vary the order of proof, and admit the declaration contingent upon the later production of the preliminary proof. Wigmore, loc. cit.; United States v. Pugliese, 153 F.2d 497, syl. 10 (C.C.A.2d 1945); State v. Hayes, 127 Conn. 543, 18 A.2d 895, 920, syl. 58–61 (1941).

By the better view, when the declaration is offered not as an act but as an evidentiary admission against a fellow-conspirator, the question of the existence of the conspiracy is for the decision of the trial judge as a preliminary question of fact. Runnels v. Lowell Sun Co., 318 Mass. 466, 62 N.E. 2d 121, syl. 8 (1945). Contra, that the proponent need only offer prima facie proof of conspiracy, and the question is for the jury. People v. Talbott, 65 Cal.App. 654, 151 P.2d 317, syl. 10 (1944); Page v. Pilot Life Ins. Co., 192 S.C. 59, 5 S.E.2d 454, syl. 4 (1940).

34. United States v. Goodman, 129 F.2d 1009, 1013, syl. 4, 5 (C.C.A., 2d, 1942) (conspiracy to violate the Bankruptcy Act; declarations of one conspirator that defendant had been his partner in the bankrupt's business held inadmissible. "We are unable to imagine any way in which they could have furthered the objects of a conspiracy to conceal assets, transfer assets or falsify books").

35. See, e. g., International Indemnity Co. v. Lehman, 28 F.2d 1, 4, syl. 4 (C.C.A., 7th, 1928) (counterclaim for conspiracy to defraud; held, declaration of conspirator as to plaintiff's act in putting fraudulent appraisement on land to be exchanged for other land, admissible though the declaration was not "in furtherance," sufficient that act described was "in furtherance"); and also Sec. 1870, Calif. Code Civ.Proc. quoted in part as follows in People v. Talbott, 65 Cal.App. 654, 151 P.2d 317, 321 (1944): "In conformity with the preceding provisions, evidence may be given upon a trial of the following facts: . . . 6. After proof of a conspiracy, the act or declaration of a conspirator against his co-conspirator, and relating to the conspiracy".

providing: "Evidence of a hearsay declaration is admissible against a party to the action if the judge finds that . . . the party and the declarant were participants in a plan to commit a crime or civil wrong and the hearsay declaration was relevant to the plan or its subject-matter and was made while the plan was in existence and before its execution was complete. . . ."[36] This seems a wise extension.

Declarations of principal offered against surety. It is asserted that wherever two parties are jointly liable as obligors, the declarations of one are receivable as an admission against the other.[37] The element of authorization to speak in furtherance of the common enterprise, as in the case of agency, partnership or conspiracy, can hardly be spelled out from the mere relation of joint obligors, and admissibility of declarations on this broad basis of joint obligations has been criticised.[38] In fact, almost all the modern cases adduced in support are cases involving the special situation of declarations of a principal offered as admissions against a surety, guarantor, indemnitor or other person secondarily liable.[39] Such declarations are usually held admissible,[40] and the practice is sanctioned by a provision in the California Code of Civil Procedure,[41] substantially embodied in the Model Code of Evidence, Rule 508, subs. (c) as follows: "Evidence of a hearsay declaration is admissible against a party to the action if the judge finds that . . . one of the issues between the party and the proponent of the evidence is a legal liability of the declarant, and the matter declared tends to establish that liability."[42] The facts that the matters admitted are likely to be in the special knowledge of the declarant, and that the admissions will nearly always be against the declarant's interest, again support the trustworthiness of such evidence.

245. Declarations by "Privies in Estate": Joint Tenants and Predecessors in Interest.[1]

The notion that "privity," or identity of interest, as between the declarant and the party against whom the declaration is of-

---

36. Rule 508(b). This is now embodied in Uniform Rule 63(9) (b), note 1, above.

37. 4 Wigmore, Evidence, § 1077.

38. Morgan, Admissions, 12 Wash.L.Rev. 181, 195 (1937).

39. See 4 Wigmore, Evidence, § 1077, cases cited note 3.

40. See, e. g., Scovill Mfg. Co. v. Cassidy, 275 Ill. 462, 114 N.E. 181, 185, syl. 8, 9 (1916) (statement of president of corporation, whose account was guaranteed by defendant, made to plaintiff, to whom guaranty was made, admissible since made as part of the operations of the business which was the subject of the guaranty, citing authorities); Linnell v. London & Lancashire Indemnity Co., 74 N. D. 379, 22 N.W.2d 203, syl. 1, 2 (1946) (suit on fidelity bond of manager of business; books kept by manager or under his supervision with respect to business covered by bond, admissible against surety); United American Fire Ins. Co. v. American Bonding Co., 146 Wis. 573, 131 N.W. 994, syl. 1 (1911) (suit on surety bond of agent of insurance company; agent's statement to secretary of insurance company as to amount collected, made after he had resigned but while he was under

duty to account, admissible as "res gestae"). Contra: Atlas Shoes Co. v. Bloom, 209 Mass. 563, 95 N.E. 952, syl. 8 (1911) (admissions of one, whose account was guaranteed by defendant, that he had received goods described in account presented to him, inadmissible against defendant).

41. Sec. 1851: "And where the question in dispute between the parties is the obligation or duty of a third person, whatever would be the evidence for or against such person is prima facie evidence between the parties." This is quoted and applied to the declarations of a defaulting employee in a suit on his fidelity bond, in Nye and Nissen v. Central Surety and Ins. Corp., 71 Cal.App.2d 570, 163 P.2d 100, syl. 5 (1945).

42. This is now incorporated in Uniform Rule 63 (9) (c), see note 1, above.

1. 4 Wigmore, Evidence, §§ 1080–1087; Morgan, Rationale of Vicarious Admissions, 42 Harv.L.Rev. 462, 470 (1929), Admissions, 12 Wash.L.Rev. 181, 197 (1937); Model Code of Evidence, Comment on Rule 508 (1942); Dec.Digests, Evidence, ☞226, 229–236; 31 C.J.S., Evidence, §§ 322–341; 20 Am.Jur., Evidence, §§ 604–607.

fered, justifies its introduction against the party as an admission is generally accepted by the courts. Thus the declaration of one joint tenant or joint owner against another is received,[2] but not that of a tenant in common,[3] a co-legatee or co-devisee,[4] or a co-trustee,[5]—so strictly is the distinction derived from the law of property applied in this context. The more frequent and important application of this property-analogy is the use of declarations of a predecessor in title to land or personalty or causes in action, against his successor. The successor has been thought of as acquiring his interest burdened with the same liability of having the declarations used against him that his prede-

cessor was subject to.[6] The declarations presumably must relate to the declarant's interest in the property or to his transactions and intentions in reference thereto, and they must have been made while he was the owner of the interest now claimed by the successor-party, not before the declarant acquired, or after he parted with such interest.[7] Under this theory are received the declarations of grantors, transferors, donors, and mortgagors of land and personalty against the transferees and mortgagees;[8] of decedents against their representatives, heirs and next of kin;[9] by a prior possessor against one who claims prescriptive title relying on such prior possession;[10] and of former holders of notes

2. 4 Wigmore, Evidence, § 1081, p. 147; La Furia v. New Jersey Ins. Co., 131 Pa.Super. 413, 200 A. 167, syl. 7–9 (1938) (in suit against fire insurance company by husband and wife, where property held by entireties, husband's admission receivable against wife).

3. Dan v. Brown, 4 Cow. (N.Y.) 483, 492 (1825). See Pope v. Hogan, 92 Vt. 250, 102 A. 937, syl. 7 (1918) (admission of tenant by entireties, excluded).

4. Shailer v. Bumstead, 99 Mass. 112, 127 (1868). And most courts go to the extreme of saying that since it is not admissible against the others, it is not even admissible against the co-legatee himself who made the declaration, since there can only be a judgment for or against the will as a whole. See, e. g., McMillan v. McDill, 110 Ill. 47 (1884); Look v. French, 346 Mo. 972, 144 S.W.2d 128, 131, syl. 3, 4 (1940) (rule held here inapplicable).

5. Davies v. Ridge, 3 Esp. 101, 170 Eng.R.R. 553 (N.P.1800).

6. See the expressions of judges and writers quoted in 4 Wigmore, 135, 136 (3d ed. 1940).

7. Thus a mortgagor's statements are receivable as admissions against the mortgagee, when made before, but not when made after the mortgage was delivered. Howard v. Franklin Ins. Co., 226 S.W. 447, syl. 1 (Tex.Civ.App.1920); Johnson v. Tuttle, 108 Vt. 291, 187 A. 515, syl. 3–5, 106 A.L.R. 1291 (1936). For cases supporting the principle generally, see 4 Wigmore, Evidence, § 1085; Dec.Dig.Evidence, ⊂⊃230(3); 31 C.J.S., Evidence, § 605; 20 Am. Jur. Evidence, § 605.

8. Liberty Nat'l Bank & Trust Co. v. Merchants' and Manufacturers' Paint Co., 307 Ky. 184, syl. 5 (1948) (statement of predecessor about party-wall); Greiner v. Comm., 334 Pa. 299, 6 A.2d 67, syl. 8 (1939)

(principle applied against Commonwealth); 4 Wigmore, Evidence, § 1082; Dec.Dig. Evidence, 231–233.

9. Ferrell v. Wight, 187 Ga. 360, 200 S.E. 271, syl. 2 (1938) (under Code 1933, § 38–403); Mannix v. Baumgardner, 184 Md. 600, 42 A.2d 124, syl. 6 (1945); International Shoe Co. v. Hawkinson, 72 N. D. 622, 10 N.W.2d 590, syl. 3 (1943); Dec.Dig. Evidence, ⊂⊃236.

But where the representative sues under the Death Injury Acts, many courts by a hypertechnical insistence upon "privity" have said that since the statute gives a new cause of action at death, the administrator's claim is not derivative, and the declarations of the deceased are not receivable against him as admissions. See, e. g., Eldredge v. Barton, 232 Mass. 183, 122 N.E. 272, syl. 4 (1919) (decedent's statements come in against the administrator as admissions on the count for conscious suffering under the Survival Act, but not on the count under the Death Act); McComb v. Vaughn, 358 Mo. 951, 218 S.W.2d 548, syl. 1–5 (1949) (in action by widow for death of truck-driver in collision with motorcycle, statements made by deceased before collision that he had been driving without lights, not receivable against widow as admission for want of "privity" nor as declaration against interest because adverseness to interest probably not apparent to deceased when made). This result, criticised in 4 Wigmore, Evidence, § 1081, note 3, has been rejected by many courts who now either find the necessary "privity" or admit the statements as declarations against interest. See Kwiatkowski v. John Lowry, Inc., 276 N.Y. 126, 11 N.E.2d 563 (1937); Notes, 114 A.L.R. 921, 22 Minn.L.Rev. 734.

10. Pitts v. Pitts, 213 Ark. 379, 210 S.W.2d 502. syl. 1, 2 (1948); Atlantic Coast Line Ry. Co. v. Gunn, 185 Ga. 108, 194 S.E. 365, syl. 8, 9 (1938).

and other choses in action against their assignees.[11]

The importation into the evidence field of the niceties of property doctrines of identity of interest and privity of estate has been criticized by Morgan. "The dogma," he says, "of vicarious admissions, as soon as it passes beyond recognized principles of representation, baffles the understanding. Joint ownership, joint obligation, privity of title, each and all furnish no criterion of credibility, no aid in the evaluation of testimony." Wigmore counters, more persuasively, that "the Hearsay rule stands in dire need, not of stopping its violation, but of a vast deal of (let us say) elastic relaxation. And this is one of the places where that relaxation can best be granted, in view of the commonly useful service of this class of evidence. After the heat of a controversy has brought it into court, testimony on the stand is often much less trustworthy than the original statements of the same persons made before controversy." Following Morgan's view, the Model Code omits any provision for admitting these declarations, and this omission is doubtless justified by the fact that the declarations would nearly always come in under the Code's liberal rules admitting declarations against interest, without any showing that the declarant is unavailable to be produced as a witness.[12]

246. Admissions by Conduct—(a) Adoptive Admissions.[1]

One may expressly adopt another's statement as his own. That is an explicit admission like any other and is to be classed as an express admission. In this text the term adoptive admission is applied to evidence of affirmative acts of a party which manifest circumstantially the party's assent to the truth of a statement made by another person.[2]

The mere fact that the party declares that he has heard that another person has made a given statement is not standing alone sufficient to justify a finding that the party has adopted the third person's statement.[3] The circumstances surrounding the party's declaration must be looked to in order to de-

---

11. Smith v. Goethe, 159 Calif. 628, 115 P. 223, syl. 7 (1911) (statements by former holders of notes receivable against subsequent holders, who took after maturity); Frick v. Reynolds, 6 Okl. 638, 52 P. 391, syl. 5 (1898) (former holder's declaration as to unsoundness of horse for which note given, admissible against later holders unless they took for value in good faith). But if the note passes to a holder in due course who takes free of most defenses, and admissions of a prior holder tending to show such defenses would be inadmissible. See 4 Wigmore, Evidence, § 1084; Dec.Dig. ☞234, 235.

In a suit on a life-insurance policy by the beneficiary may the declarations of the insured in his lifetime be offered by the defendant insurance company against the beneficiary, as the admissions of a predecessor in interest? The answer has been made to turn upon the technical distinction between policies wherein the insured reserves the power to change the beneficiary and those where no such power is reserved. See Rosman v. Travelers' Insurance Co., 127 Md. 689, 96 A. 875, Ann. Cas.1918C, 1047, syl. 2, 1916; Wigmore, Evidence, § 1081, n. 6; Note, 86 A.L.R. 146.

12. See Model Code of Evidence, Rules 502, 503, 509. So also The Uniform Rules of Evidence, Rules 63 (7–10).

1. 4 Wigmore, Evidence, §§ 1069–1075; Model Code of Evidence, Rule 507, and commentary; Uniform Rule 63(8). Each of them would include admissions by silence in the class of adoptive admissions. I have classified them separately, see the next section herein.

2. See Uniform Rule 63(8), which recognizes as an exception to the hearsay rule: "*Authorized and Adoptive Admissions.* As against a party, a statement (a) by a person authorized by the party to make a statement or statements for him concerning the subject of the statement, or (b) of which the party with knowledge of the content thereof has, by words or other conduct, manifested his adoption or his belief in its truth". This is an adaptation of Model Code of Evidence, R. 507.

3. Stephens v. Vroman, 16 N.Y. 381 (1857) (stresses the hearsay nature of the statements, without discussing whether repetition is adoption); Reed v. McCord, 160 N.Y. 330, 54 N.E. 737, 740 (1899) (em-

termine whether the repetition did indicate an approval of the statement.[4]

The question of adoption often arises in life and accident insurance cases when the insurance company offers against the beneficiary the statements which the beneficiary has attached to the proof of death or disability, such as the certificate of the attending physician, or the coroner's report. The fact that the beneficiary has thus tendered it as an exhibit accompanying a formal statement or "proof" presented for the purpose of having the company act upon it by paying the claim, should certainly be enough, standing alone, to secure the admission of the accompanying statements.[5] In actual life, however, the surrounding circumstances often show that an inference of adoption would be most unrealistic. This is clear when the beneficiary expressly disavows the accompanying statement,[6] and it seems that exclusion of the attached statement should likewise follow when the statements of the beneficiary in the proofs are clearly contrary to those in the exhibits.[7] Moreover, if the company's agent prepared the proof for signature and procured the accompanying documents, as he frequently does as a helpful service to the beneficiary, it seems reasonable to hold that the inference of adoption of statements in the exhibits should not be drawn, if the agent has failed to call the beneficiary's attention to inconsistencies between the proof and the exhibits.[8] Again the argument seems strong that if accompanying statements, such as the certificate of the attending physician as to particular facts called for, are required to be furnished under the terms of the policy, such statements are not then attached by the choice or will of the beneficiary, and the sponsorship inferable from a voluntary tendering of another's statement cannot here be inferred.[9] Most courts would agree upon the prima facie inference of adoption of exhibits, but there is wide variation of view as to the various qualifications suggested above.

Does the introduction of evidence by a party constitute an adoption of the statements therein, so that they may be used against him as admissions [10] in a subsequent lawsuit? When a party offers in evidence a deposition

---

ployer's statement as to facts of accident, though he was without personal knowledge, admissible, but distinguishing a statement that "he had heard" that such was the fact, which would be inadmissible).

4. Circumstances show adoption. In re Gaines' Estate, 15 Cal.2d 255, 100 P.2d 1055, syl. 4–6 (1940) (statement by nephew to bank officers, as to what uncle said was his purpose in placing deposit box and bank account in joint tenancy with nephew). Insufficient to show adoption. Cowan v. Allamakee County Benevolent Soc., 232 Ia. 1387, 8 N.W.2d 433, syl. 7, 8 (1943) (insurance beneficiary's statement that the doctors told him that insured had died of cancer).

5. Cases admitting the statements on this theory are numerous, see e. g., Russo v. Metropolitan Life Ins. Co., 125 Conn. 132, 3 A.2d 844, syl. 3, 4 (1939) (but court stressed there was no contractual obligation here to furnish the doctor's certificate filed with the proof); Rudolph v. John Hancock Mut. Life Ins. Co., 251 N.Y. 208, 167 N.E. 223, syl. 1, 2 (1929) (statement in doctor's certificate an adoptive admission, though contrary to beneficiary's own statement in the proof of death, and though attending doc-

tor's statement required by policy; three judges dissenting); Thornell v. Missouri State Life Ins. Co., 249 S.W. 203, syl. 2 (Tex.Com.App.1923) (rule applied though proofs prepared by agents of company). Decisions are collected in 4 Wigmore, Evidence, § 1073, note 10; Dec.Dig. Evidence, ⊂⊃215 (1), Note, 96 A.L.R. 335, and earlier notes cited therein.

6. Goldschmidt v. Mutual Life Ins. Co., 102 N.Y. 486, 7 N.E. 408 (1886).

7. See the dissenting opinion in the Rudolph case, supra n. 5.

8. New York Life Ins. Co. v. Taylor, 147 F.2d 297, syl. 5 (C.A.D.C.1945).

9. This view is supported by the decision in Bebbington v. Calif. Western Life Ins. Co., 15 Cal.2d 255, 100 P.2d 1055, syl. 5 (1947), Note, 61 Harv.L.Rev. 535. The Rudolph case, note 5, supra, is opposed.

10. Thus escaping the requirements which would be imposed if it were offered under the hearsay exception for Former Testimony (see ch. 26, herein) such as identity of parties and issues, and unavailability of the witness.

or an affidavit to prove the matters stated therein, he knows or should know the contents of the writing so offered, and presumably he desires that all of the contents be considered on his behalf, since he is at liberty to offer only part, if he desires. Accordingly, it is clear that the writing so introduced may in another suit be used against him as an adoptive admission.[11] In respect to oral testimony, however, the inference of sponsorship of the statements is not always so clear, but there is authority for the statement that when the proponent has placed the witness on the stand to prove a particular fact, and the witness so testifies, this is an adoptive admission of such fact in a later suit.[12] But how is the party offering the testimony in the later suit to show that a given statement of the witness at the former trial was intended to be elicited by the proponent who put him on the stand, or was contrary to or outside that intention? The form of the proponent's question would usually, but not always, give the clue. In view of the prevailing custom of interviewing one's witness before putting him on the stand, it would seem that a practical working rule would admit against the proponent the direct testimony of his own witness as presumptively elicited to prove the facts stated, in the absence of counter-proof that the testimony came as a surprise to the interrogator, or was repudiated in the course of argument. Testimony elicited on cross-examination may be drawn out to reveal the witness's mendacity and should not be assumed to have been relied on by the examiner as evidence of the facts stated,[13] but such reliance must affirmatively appear.

In conformity with the views expressed in the general discussion herein of the judge's function in determining preliminary questions of fact, it is believed that the question of fact whether the party's conduct manifested his assent to the statement of the other person is a preliminary question for the judge. Unless he so finds, the statement is excluded.[14]

Similar to adoptive admissions are the instances where the party has referred an inquirer to another person whose anticipated statements he approves in advance.[15] These admissions by reference to a third person seem classifiable as representative or vicarious admissions, rather than adoptive.

11. Richards v. Morgan, 10 Jurist N.S. 559, 122 Eng. Rep. 600 (Q.B.1864) (depositions); Hallett v. O'Brien, 1 Ala. 585, 589 (1840) (affidavit or deposition said to be adopted if used in evidence, but not here where merely filed); 4 Wigmore, Evidence, § 1075, note 2.

12. Bageard v. Consol. Traction Co., 64 N.J.L. 316, 45 A. 620, 621 (1900) (dictum); Keyser Canning Co. v. Klots Throwing Co., 98 W.Va. 487, 496, 128 S.E. 280, syl. 5 (1925) ("Of course a party is not bound by everything his witness may say on the stand, as an admission on his part, particularly where he does not know beforehand what the witness is going to say; but if he puts a witness on the stand, as defendant did in this case, to prove a particular fact in issue, he is bound thereby as an admission on a subsequent trial."), and see the dictum of Cockburn, L.C.J., in Richards v. Morgan, cited in next preceding note, quoted 4 Wigmore, Evidence, 3d ed. pp. 110–112. Contra: British Thomson-Houston Co. v. British, etc., Cables, Ltd. [1924] 2 Ch. 160 (the prevailing opinions seem most unpersuasive but the dissenting opinion of Sargant, J., is convincingly cogent).

13. In O'Connor v. Bonney, 57 S.D. 134, 231 N.W. 521 (1930) questions and answers on cross-examination by the present defendant of expert witnesses at a previous trial of the present malpractice action, were held inadmissible against the defendant.

14. Model Code of Evidence, Rule 507 and commentary thereon, adopt this view. I have encountered no cases on the point.

15. See, e. g., General Finance Co. v. Stratford, 109 F.2d 843, syl. 1–3 (C.A.D.C.1940) (plaintiff in garnishment directed by garnishee's agent to go over records with bookkeeper; bookkeeper's statements admissible against garnishee); 4 Wigmore, Evidence, § 1070. Some of the cases there collected seem to hold that a mere mention of a third person as a reliable source of information might be enough, but it seems that either clear approval in advance of what the third person shall say should be required, or an authorization to the third person to speak in the party's behalf, in which case you have a representative admission by an agent.

247. Admissions by Conduct—(b) Silence.[1]

If a statement is made by another person in the presence of a party to the action, containing assertions of facts which, if untrue, the party would under all the circumstances naturally be expected to deny, his failure to speak is circumstantial evidence that he believes the statements to be true and his conduct is thus receivable against him as an admission of such belief.[2] The justification for receiving such evidence is not based upon the assumption that the party has intended to express his assent and thus has adopted the statement as his own, nor upon the theory that a duty or obligation to speak has been cast upon him, but rather upon the probable state of belief to be inferred from his conduct.[3] Since it is the failure to deny that is significant, an equivocal or evasive response may similarly be used against him on this theory,[4] but if his total response adds up to a clear-cut denial, this theory of implied admission is not properly available.[5]

Likewise, the circumstances of the situation may be such that a failure to deny is more naturally explainable on some other inference than that of belief in the truth of the statement,[6] and the evidence is then excluded. Such situations are presented, for example, when the statement is made by a witness in court, and an immediate denial by the party would be a breach of decorum;[7] when the statement is made after an accident

---

[1.] See 4 Wigmore, Evidence, §§ 1071–1073; Morgan, Admissions, 12 Wash.L.Rev. 181, 187 (1937); Maguire, Adoptive Admissions in Massachusetts, 14 Mass.L.Q., May, 1929, p. 62 (an original and penetrating discussion); Dec.Dig., Evidence, ☞220, Crim.Law, ☞407; 31 C.J.S., Evidence, §§ 294–298; 20 Am.Jur., Evidence, §§ 567–577.

The Model Code of Evidence, R. 507 provides: "Evidence of a hearsay statement is admissible against a party to the action if the judge finds that . . . (b) the party with knowledge of the content of the statement by words or other conduct manifested his adoption or approval of the statement or his belief in its truth." To like effect is Uniform Rule 63 (8).

[2.] See e. g., Comm. v. Kenney, 12 Met. 235 (Mass. 1847), a leading case, and Ruth v. Rhodes, 66 Ariz. 129, 185 P.2d 304, syl. 2–4 (1947); and Owens v. Comm., 186 Va. 689, 43 S.E.2d 895, syl. 2–6 (1947) (discussing the question whether taking silence as tacit admission violates self-crimination theory) for judicial expositions.

[3.] See the commentary, Model Code, R. 507.

[4.] People v. Wilson, 61 Cal.App. 611, 215 P. 565, syl. 6, 1923 (prisoner under arrest accused of murder, replies, "I have got an attorney that will do my talking for me"); Comm. v. Hebert, 264 Mass. 571, 163 N.E. 189, syl. 6, 7 (1928) (Defendant charged with procuring abortion. In his presence and hearing, Mrs. Lyman accused him of performing the operation. The defendant was then asked if he knew this woman, and he answered, "I have no recollection of ever seeing this woman." He was then asked, "What do you say as to what she has just accused you of?" and he replied, "I have nothing to say."); Commonwealth v. Graham, 279 Mass. 466, 181 N.E. 506, 1932 (defendant brought to bedside of injured woman is accused of cutting her during drunken spree and replies "I must have been crazy if I did it"); Cobb v. State, 27 Ga. 648, 672, 697, 1859 (defendant, when letter of convicted confederate read to him in prison, adjuring him to confess and save his soul, said "I won't confess"). Excluded: People v. Hanley, 317 Ill. 39, 147 N.E. 400, 1925 (when asked by police whether confederate's confession was true, accused answered "It will take twelve men to try me").

But if the party both denies and admits, his blowing hot and cold will be received. Commonwealth v. Grieco, 323 Mass. 629, 83 N.E.2d 873, syl. 1 (1949).

[5.] Commonwealth v. Twombly, 319 Mass. 464, 66 N.E.2d 362, syl. 1 (1946); People v. Wysocki, 267 Mich. 52, 255 N.W. 160, syl. 2 (1934).

[6.] "That silence or an equivocal reply is not always indicative of a consciousness of guilt cannot be gainsaid, for the Scriptures bear witness that when Jesus stood under accusation before Pontius Pilate, the governor, and was asked, 'Art thou the King of the Jews?' he replied, 'Thou sayest,' and 'when he was accused of the chief priests and elders, he answered nothing. Then said Pilate unto him, 'Hearest thou not how many things they witness against thee?' And he answered him to never a word; insomuch that the governor marvelled greatly. Matt. chap. 27, v. 11–14; 4 Wigmore on Evidence § 1072, pp. 84–85." People v. Simmons, 28 Cal.2d 699, 712, 172 P.2d 18, 26 (1946).

[7.] Jones v. State, 184 Tenn. 128, 196 S.W.2d 491, syl. 2, 4 (1946) (accusatory testimony at preliminary hearing). But if the party has a later opportunity to testify in rebuttal, his failure to do so may (except in the case of an accused who fails to take

or collision, and the party is suffering from shock or injury or is occupied in helping other victims; [8] and again when it appears that the party's failure to deny the statement is prompted by his lawyer's advice to remain silent.[9]

Obviously, proof of the party's conduct requires proof of the statement itself to which he has thus reacted. The statement technically avoids the hearsay objection, since it is not offered as evidence of the truth of its assertions,[10] but merely as giving meaning to the defendant's silence or evasive response. Nevertheless, there is a danger that the jury may give independent credit to the statement itself, and this is a danger that needs to be taken in account.

It is especially serious in the case of persons suspected of crime who are sometimes confronted with detailed statements of others who have confessed implicating such suspects as accomplices.[11] Moreover, an inexperienced person arrested or detained by the police for questioning may well be uncertain, even if innocent, whether to get implicated in a word-battle with accusers and police. The courts in a substantial number of states have sought to guard against these dangers by a hard-and-fast rule that the silence of a person when faced with an accusatory statement while under arrest, is inadmissible.[12] An equal or greater number of courts have the more flexible practice of merely considering arrest as one of the factors bearing on the interpretation of the party's silence.[13]

Probably the most effective protection against the hearsay danger and against the

---

the stand at all) create an inference against him, see, e. g., Curry v. Stewart, 301 Ky. 645, 192 S.W.2d 739, syl. 1 (1946); Miller v. Dyess, 137 Tex. 135, 151 S.W.2d 186, 137 A.L.R. 578, 583 (1941). Compare Friedman v. Forest City, 239 Iowa 112, 30 N.W.2d 752, syl. 23 (1948) (silence of member of City Council at hearing where plaintiff's attorney made complaint, not proveable to impeach).

8. Gerulis v. Viens, 130 Me. 378, 156 A. 378, syl. 2, 76 A.L.R. 1387 (1931); Lichtenstein v. Cascio, 274 App.Div. 309, 83 N.Y.S.2d 195 (1948); Beck v. Dye, 200 Wash. 1, 92 P.2d 1113, syl. 6, 9, 127 A.L.R. 1022 (1939). Compare the questionable holding in Doherty v. Edwards, 227 Iowa 1264, 290 N.W. 672, syl. 7, 8, 1940 (evidence that dying man, who was occupant of car, after accident said to defendant, the driver, "We were going too fast," and that defendant said nothing, admissible). See Note, Silence when statement is made regarding circumstances of an accident, 76 A.L.R. 1391.

9. People v. McGee, 31 Cal.2d 229, 187 P.2d 706, syl. 14 (1947) ("The officer told defendant that he 'was accused of the murder of Arthur Rypdahl' and 'asked him if he cared to affirm or deny that accusation. . . .' He answered, 'I am not going to answer that question. My attorney told me not to unless he was present.'" Held, error to charge on silence as admission).

10. See § 225, herein.

11. Such practice by police officers is referred to as requiring caution on the part of the courts, in People v. Simmons, 28 Cal.2d 699, 172 P.2d 18,

28 (1946) and in People v. Spencer, 78 Cal.App.2d 652, 178 P.2d 520, 523 (1947).

12. State v. Bates, 140 Conn. 326, 99 A.2d 133, syl. 2, 3 (1953) (rule applied where accused at liberty on bail), critically noted 15 U.Pitt.L.Rev. 376; Commonwealth v. Anderson, 245 Mass. 177, 139 N.E. 436, syl. 17 (1923); People v. Abel, 298 N.Y. 333, 83 N.E.2d 542, syl. 1 (1949); Crabb v. State, 86 Okl. Cr. 323, 192 P.2d 1018, syl. 1 (1948); Moree v. State, 147 Tex.Cr. 564, 183 S.W.2d 166, syl. 6, 7 (1944); 4 Wigmore, Evidence, § 1072, n. 10; 46 Harv.L.Rev. 1162 (1933); 47 Mich.L.Rev. 715 (1949).

13. Scott v. State, 249 Ala. 304, 30 So.2d 689, syl. 7 (1947); People v. Simmons, 28 Cal.2d 699, 172 P.2d 18, syl. 12, 13 (1946) (but reversed because conduct of accused did not show implied admission); Camper v. State, 187 Tenn. 511, 216 S.W.2d 18, syl. 2 (1948) (semble). Cases pro and con are listed in Notes, 80 A.L.R. 1259, 1262, 115 A.L.R. 1517; Dec. Dig.Crim.Law, ☞407(2). The justice of any rule which permits the silence of one accused of crime to be taken as an admission is acutely criticised by Barrett, Note, 35 Calif.L.R. 128 (1947). He suggests that accused persons who are guilty are as likely, if not more likely to deny the accusation, than if they are innocent, hence the silence is not relevant to show guilt. It is believed, however, that silence under accusation, while it tends to show inexperience, tends also to show guilt. See Maguire, Adoptive Admissions, cited Note 1, supra, at p. 78. See also Note, pursuing the same inquiry, 31 C.J. Crim. Law 461 (1940).

misinterpretation of the bewildered silence of the inexperienced prisoner would be afforded by a more responsible assumption by the trial judge of his function of deciding preliminary questions of fact determining the admissibility of evidence.[14] To entitle the jury to consider evidence of silence or evasive response as an admission, these facts must be found:[15] first, that the alleged statement was actually made; second, that the party's reaction of silence or evasion took place as claimed; third, that the party heard and understood the statement—if proponent gives evidence that it was made in his presence this makes a prima facie showing;[16] and fourth, that under all the circumstances appearing, the party's conduct makes it probable that he believed the statement to be true. The first of these areas of fact seems obviously for the jury to decide under the traditional division of functions, if the judge determines that the evidence is admissible. There is no danger that the jury will misuse the statement-evidence if they find that no such statement was actually made. As to the second, third, and fourth areas of fact, there is a danger that the jury if it is left solely to them may disregard these questions and give credence to the third party's statement merely because it was made. Certainly the trial judge has at least the duty of determining as a preliminary question whether a reasonable jury *could* find these facts and inferences in favor of proponent,[17] and it would seem that his control should go further, and unless he finds to his own satisfaction the truth of such facts and inferences, he should exclude the evidence.[18] If he is so satisfied and admits the statement and the accompanying conduct of the party, the jury has the right to consider for themselves the same testimony as to these prelim-

---

14. See § 53, herein.

15. See the statement of Shaw, C. J. in Comm. v. Kenney, 12 Metc. (53 Mass.) 235, 237 (1847): "In some cases, where a similar declaration is made in one's hearing, and he makes no reply, it may be a tacit admission of the facts. But this depends on two facts; first, whether he hears and understands the statement, and comprehends its bearing; and secondly, whether the truth of the facts embraced in the statement is within his own knowledge, or not; whether he is in such a situation that he is at liberty to make any reply; and whether the statement is made under such circumstances, and by such persons, as naturally to call for a reply, if he did not intend to admit it." See also Maguire, op.cit. at pp. 63, 66.

16. This is the common-sense practice, ordinarily followed by trial courts, see 4 Wigmore, Evidence, § 1071, p. 74, but a stricter rule, that the proponent must go further and show that the party did hear or must have necessarily heard has sometimes been stated, see 31 C.J.S., Evidence, § 295(b); Ruth v. Rhodes, 66 Ariz. 129, 185 P.2d 304, syl. 4 (1947).

17. People v. Simmons, 28 Cal.2d 699, 172 P.2d 18, 25 syl. 10 (1946); McCarty v. Bishop, 102 S.W.2d 126, syl. 7 (Mo.App.1937); Johnson v. Underwood, 102 Ore. 680, syl. 11 (1922); 31 C.J.S., Evidence, § 296.

18. The opinions have seldom isolated the problem or adequately discussed it. The following cases seem to support the view that the judge if not satisfied of the preliminary facts should exclude. Pulver v. Union Investment Co., 279 F. 699, syl. 10 (C.C.A. Minn. 1922) (whether circumstances called for a reply); Weightnovel v. State, 46 Fla. 1, 35 So. 856, syl. 5 (1903) (whether statement made in the hearing of the defendant); Friedman v. Forest City, 239 Iowa 112, 30 N.W.2d 752, syl. 26 (1948) (whether reply was called for under the circumstances); see also Model Code of Evidence, R. 507, quoted n. 1, supra. Compare Gila Valley Ry. Co. v. Hall, 232 U.S. 94, 103, 34 S.Ct. 229, 232 (1914) where the question arose whether the plaintiff received notice of a defective wheel, and hence assumed risk of a subsequent injury. Notice depended on whether he heard a conversation which occurred within twenty yards of him. Held, the trial court properly excluded evidence of the conversation on the ground that he was not satisfied that the plaintiff heard it.

For the jury: Byrd v. State, 78 Ga.App. 824, 52 S.E.2d 330, syl. 2 (1949) (whether defendant heard the statement and whether circumstances called for a reply) and see cases collected in Note, 80 A.L.R. 1277. But even if the judge is to exclude, if he fails to find the preliminary facts, the jury could consider the same questions in passing on the weight of the testimony. Probably it is this function that many of these opinions are affirming, rather than denying (or considering) the judge's power to exclude the evidence if he finds the necessary preliminary facts to be lacking.

inary facts in determining the weight to be given, and the inferences to be drawn from, the party's conduct.[19]

Failure to reply to a letter or other written communication.[20] If a written statement is handed to a party and read by him, in the presence of others, his failure to deny assertions contained therein, when under the circumstances it would be natural for him to deny them if he did not acquiesce, may be received as an admission, as in case of similar failure to deny an oral statement.[21] Moreover, if a party receives a letter containing several statements, which he would naturally deny if untrue, and he states his position as to some of the statements, but fails to comment on the others, this failure will usually be received as evidence of an admission.[22] More debatable is the question whether the failure to reply at all to a letter or other written communication shall come in as an admission by silence. Certainly such failure to reply will often be less convincing than silence in the face of an oral charge.[23] And

it is often announced as a "general rule," subject to exceptions, that failure to answer a letter is not receivable as an admission.[24] This negative form of statement seems undesirable as tending toward over-strict rulings excluding evidence of material value.[25] It is believed that the more acceptable view is that the failure to reply to a letter, containing statements which it would be natural under all the circumstances for the addressee to deny if he believed them untrue, is receivable as evidence of an admission by silence.[26] Two factors particularly tend to show that a denial would be naturally forthcoming, first, where the letter was written as part of a mutual correspondence between the parties,[27] and second, where the proof shows that the parties were engaged together in some business or other relationship or transaction which would make it improbable that an untrue communication from one to the other about the transaction or relationship would be ignored.[28] The most common in-

---

19. See § 53.

20. See 4 Wigmore, Evidence, § 1073, notes 3 and 4; Decennial Digests, Evidence, ⊙≈220 (8); 31 C.J.S., Evidence, § 297 (b); Notes, 8 A.L.R. 1163, 34 A.L.R. 560, 55 A.L.R. 460.

21. See Grier v. Deputy, 40 A. 716 (Del.1894) (item in newspaper read to party); 31 C.J.S. 1064, citing cases.

22. See, e. g., Wieder v. Lorenz, 164 Ore. 10, 99 P.2d 38, syl. 6, 7 (1940).

23. "Men use the tongue much more readily than the pen. Almost all men will reply to and deny or correct a false statement verbally made to them. It is done on the spot and from the first impulse. But when a letter is received making the same statement, the feeling which readily prompts the verbal denial not unfrequently cools before the time and opportunity arrive for writing a letter. Other matters intervene. A want of facility in writing, or an aversion to correspondence, or habits of dilatoriness may be the real causes of the silence. As the omission to reply to letters may be explained by so many causes not applicable to silence when the parties are in personal conversation, we do not think the same weight should be attached to it as evidence." Aldis, J. in Fenno v. Watson, 31 Vt. 345, 352 (1858).

24. See, e. g., Fidelity & Casualty Co. v. Beeland Bros. Merc. Co., 242 Ala. 591, 7 So.2d 265, 267 (1942); Note, 8 A.L.R. 1163, 31 C.J.S., p. 1065.

25. See cases described in the second paragraph of note 28, infra, this section.

26. For comparatively liberal formulations see opinions of C. E. Clark, Circ. J. in Boerner v. U. S., 117 F.2d 387, 390, 391, syl. 6, 7, (C.C.A.2d 1941), of the court in Simpson v. Bergmann, 125 Cal.App. 1, 13 P.2d 531, 534, syl. 8 (1932) and of Jones, J. in Mahoney v. Kennedy, 188 Wis. 30, 205 N.W. 407, 411, syl. 1 (1925).

27. The significance of this is always conceded, see, e. g., Boerner v. U. S., 117 F.2d 387, 391 (C.C.A.2d 1941); Wieder v. Lorenz, 164 Ore. 10, 99 P.2d 38, 44, 45, (1940); 22 C. J., p. 326, note 8 (b); 31 C.J.S., Evidence, p. 1064, note 35; Note, 8 A.L.R. 1163.

28. Willard Helburn, Inc. v. Spiewak, 180 F.2d 480, 482 (C.A.N.Y.1950) (letter stating terms of previous oral transaction between caller and callee, held, circumstances such as to make an answer natural); Simpson v. Bergmann, 125 Cal.App. 1, 13 P.2d 531, 534, syl. 8–11 (Cal.App. 1932) (failure of corporation, which was furnishing lumber for dwelling, to reply to letter wherein owner asserted

stance of this latter situation is the transmission by one party to such a business relationship to the other of a statement of account or bill rendered. A failure to question such a bill or statement is uniformly received as evidence of an admission of its correctness.[29] On the other hand, if the negotiations have been broken off by one party's taking a final stand, thus indicating his view that further communication would be fruit-

less,[30] or if the letter was written after litigation was instituted, these circumstances tend to show that failure to answer is not to be received as an admission.[31]

248. Admissions by Conduct—(c) Flight and Similar Acts.[1]

"The wicked flee when no man pursueth." Many acts of a defendant after the crime seeking to escape the toils of the law are received as admissions by conduct, constituting

---

that company was contractor's surety, *held* admissible on question of existence of suretyship contract. "In the present case, while there was no previous correspondence or contract directly between the company and the owner, we have the circumstance that the lumber company was furnishing the lumber to be used in constructing the dwelling, which it knew was being erected by Allison as contractor; and when during the course of construction a claim was made by the owner that the company was surety for performance by Allison, and that the latter was failing to comply with his contract, the letter reasonably called for some reply."); Ross v. Reynolds, 112 Me. 223, 91 A. 952, syl. 8 (1914) (failure of seller to reply to letter from buyer, complaining that automobile sold had been misrepresented by seller); Keeling-Easter Co. v. R. B. Dunning, 113 Me. 34, 92 A. 929, syl. 3 (1915) (similar to last); Trainer v. Fort, 310 Pa. 570, 578, 165 A. 232 (1933) (action by real estate broker for commission under oral contract made over the telephone with defendant; letter written by defendant to plaintiff immediately after conversation reciting terms of agreement differently, and unanswered by plaintiff, admissible).

But this factor is often disregarded, and a letter from one with whom the addressee is engaged in business transactions is treated as if it no more called for a reply than would a letter from a stranger, "a bolt from the blue." See, e. g., A. B. Leach & Co. v. Peirson, 275 U.S. 120, 48 S.Ct. 57, 72 L.Ed. 194, 55 A.L.R. 457 (1927) (suit by one who had purchased bonds from defendant investment concern upon alleged oral agreement by defendant's agent, that defendant would repurchase bonds at same price on demand. Held, defendant's failure to answer plaintiff's letter asserting such contract, inadmissible. Holmes, J.: "A man cannot make evidence for himself by writing a letter containing the statements that he wishes to prove. He does not make the letter evidence by sending it to the party against whom he wishes to prove the facts. He no more can impose a duty to answer a charge than he can impose a duty to pay by sending goods." But isn't it "natural" to answer such a letter from

a customer who has bought bonds? Of course, it is the silence, not the letter alone, that is significant, and the question is one not of duty but of probability); Fidelity & Casualty Co. v. Beeland Bros. Merc. Co., 242 Ala. 591, 7 So.2d 265, syl. 2, 3 (1942) (claim by assisting attorneys in suit defended by liability insurance company for attorney's fees against insurance company, which defended on ground plaintiffs were employed by insured; letter written by plaintiffs to defendants, after original suit concluded, setting out their version of the arrangement for their services, and unanswered, excluded. Wouldn't a wider practice of admissibility tend to prolong negotiations and promote settlement of disputes?) This restrictive attitude is especially marked in the seduction, breach of promise, and bastardy cases, where the defendant fails to answer an accusatory letter from the alleged victim. See e. g., Snead v. Commonwealth, 138 Va. 787, 121 S.E. 82, syl. 3, 4, 34 A.L.R. 550 (1924) (opinion collects and discusses the cases). See also the statement of Kay, L. J. in Wiedeman v. Walpole, 24 Q.B.D. 537 (1890), a breach of promise case where the woman's letters claiming the promise went unanswered, "It is clearly a letter which nine out of ten men would refuse to answer. . ." But does not the naturalness of a reply depend on the nature and extent of the actual relationship of the parties?

29. Milliken v. Warwick, 306 Mass. 192, 28 N.E.2d 224, syl. 5, 7 (1940); Bradley v. McDonald, 218 N.Y. 351, 113 N.E. 340, syl. 3 (1916).

30. Whorley v. Patton-Kjose Co., 90 Mont. 461, 5 P.2d 210, 217 (1931) (dictum); 22 C.J. Evidence, § 363, n. 5, 31 C.J.S., Evidence, § 297, n. 34.

31. Canadian Bank of Commerce v. Coumbe, 47 Mich. 358, 11 N.W. 196, 199 (1882).

1. See, for general statements, State v. Torphy, 217 Ind. 383, 28 N.E.2d 70, 72 (1940); State v. Barry, 93 N.H. 10, 34 A.2d 661 (1943); State v. Henderson, 182 Ore. 147, 184 P.2d 392, 413, syl. 20 (1947). See also 2 Wigmore, Evidence, § 276; Decennial Digests, Criminal Law, ☜351.

circumstantial evidence of consciousness of guilt and hence of the fact of guilt itself. In this class are flight from the locality after the crime,[2] assuming a false name,[3] resisting arrest,[4] attempting to bribe arresting officers,[5] forfeiture of bond by failure to appear,[6] escapes or attempted escapes from confinement,[7] and attempts of the accused to take his own life.[8] It is characteristic of circumstantial evidence that any one such circumstance is not conclusive, but is subject to varying interpretations, but the accepted technique is for the judge to receive the evidence, and permit the defendant to bring in evidence in denial or explanation.[9] This method is probably the most practical one

available for all these types of conduct mentioned above except attempted suicide. As to this the interpretation is so unusually ambiguous and the danger of prejudice so great that it is arguable that the trial judge should be required to exclude it if he finds the act was the product of mental abnormality or that it should be rejected generally.[10]

249. Admissions by Conduct—(d) Failure to Call Witnesses or Produce Evidence:[1] Refusal to Submit to a Physical Examination.[2]

When it would be natural under the circumstances for a party to call a particular witness,[3] or to take the stand himself as a witness,[4] or voluntarily to produce documents or other objects in his possession as

---

2. State v. Ford, 109 Conn. 490, 146 A. 828, syl. 3 (1929) (hit and run driver) and see decisions cited n. 1, supra.

3. People v. Waller, 14 Cal.2d 693, 96 P.2d 344, syl. 6 (1939).

4. People v. Flannelly, 128 Calif. 83, 60 P. 670, syl. 4 (1900) (homicide; flight and resistance admissible though no denial of killing and resistance was another crime); Lassiter v. State, 135 Tex.Cr. 352, 120 S.W.2d 262, syl. 2 (1938).

5. Cortes v. State, 135 Fla. 589, 185 So. 323, 327, syl. 7, 8 (1938).

6. Affronti v. U. S., 145 F.2d 3, syl. 4 (C.C.A., 8th 1944) (government could show defendant by failing to appear forfeited bonds in other cases pending against him, as well as this one); Williams v. State, 148 Tex.Cr. 427, 187 S.W.2d 667, syl. 6 (1945).

7. People v. Arnold, 199 Calif. 471, 250 P. 168, syl. 26 (1926) (attempt to escape from jail by sawing bars); Anderson v. Commonwealth, 100 Va. 860, 42 S.E. 865, syl. 2 (1902).

8. People v. Duncan, 261 Ill. 339, 103 N.E. 1043, syl. 8 (1914); Commonwealth v. Goldenberg, 315 Mass. 26, 51 N.E.2d 762, syl. 5 (1943); State v. Painter, 329 Mo. 314, 44 S.W.2d 79, syl. 5 (1931); State v. Lawrence, 196 N.C. 562, 146 S.E. 395, syl. 6 (1929) (but Brogden, J. dissented on this point); Commonwealth v. Giacobbe, 341 Pa. 187, 19 A.2d 71, syl. 3 (1941). In State v. Coudotte, 7 N.D. 109, 72 N.W. 913 (1897) the court's opinion criticises the use of the evidence, but the actual holding was not on admissibility, but to the effect that the evidence of attempted suicide was not sufficient to constitute

the required corroboration of an accomplice's testimony.

9. See, e. g., Goforth v. State, 183 Ala. 66, 63 So. 8 (1913) (postcards mailed by accused to indicate nonconcealment); State v. Desmond, 109 Ia. 72, 80 N.W. 214, syl. 3 (1899) (fear of mob-violence). See 4 Wigmore, Evidence, § 276(e) and Hutchins and Slesinger, Consciousness of Guilt, 77 U.Pa.L.Rev. 725, 740 (1929) ("It is important . . . that when consciousness of guilt is relied on by the prosecution, careful attention be paid to the alternative explanations of his conduct advanced by the accused, including such data as may appear through a psychiatric examination.")

10. See the penetrating discussion of the problem in Fordham, Note, 7 N.C.L.Rev. 290 (1929).

1. See 2 Wigmore, Evidence, §§ 285–291; Decennial Digests, Evidence, ☞77, Crim. Law, ☞317; 31 C.J.S. Evidence, § 156; 20 Am.Jur. Evidence, §§ 187–193.

2. 8 Wigmore, Evidence, § 2220, note 19; Decennial Digests, Damages, ☞206(8).

3. Ross v. Koenig, 129 Conn. 403, 28 A.2d 875, syl. 9 (1942).

4. United States v. Fields, 102 F.2d 535, 537, syl. 5, 6 (1939).

A similar inference is available if a party takes the stand but fails to give evidence as to relevant matters within his knowledge. Caminetti v. United States, 242 U.S. 470, 492–495, 37 S.Ct. 192, 197–198, 61 L.Ed. 442 (1917) (accused as witness: comment by judge); State v. Feinberg, 105 Conn. 115, 134 A. 228, syl. 2 (1926) (similar).

evidence,[5] and he fails to do so, his adversary may use this failure as the basis for invoking an adverse inference. An analogous inference may be drawn if a party unreasonably declines to submit, upon request, to a physical examination.[6]

Most of the controversy arises in respect to the failure to call a witness. It is generally agreed that when a potential witness is available, and appears to have special information relevant to the case, so that his testimony would not merely be cumulative,[7] and where his relationship with one of the parties is such that the witness would ordinarily be expected to favor him,[8] then if such party does not produce his testimony, the inference arises that it would have been unfavorable.

It is often said that if the witness is "equally accessible" to both parties, no inference springs from the failure of either to call him.[9]

This can hardly be accurate, as the inference is frequently allowed when the witness could easily be called or subpenaed by either party. What is probably meant is that when so far as appears the witness would be as likely to be favorable to one party as the other, there will be no inference.[10] But even here, it seems that equality of favor is nearly always debatable, and that though the judge thinks the witness would be as likely to favor one party as the other, he should permit either party to argue the inference against the adversary.[11] At least, it would appear in this supposed case of "equal favor," if the witness's knowledge is directed toward a particular issue, that then the argument should be available against the party who has the burden of persuasion on that issue.

A party may be at liberty to call a witness, but may have a privilege against the witness's being called by the adversary, as when under the local statute an accused in a

---

5. Hamburg-Am. S. P. Co. v. U. S., 250 F. 747, 767, syl. 19 (1918); Gray v. Callahan, 143 Fla. 673, 197 So. 396, 400, syl. 11 (1940).

6. Texas & N. O. Ry. Co. v. Rooks, 292 S.W. 536, syl. 3, 4 (Tex.Com.App.1927) (but request addressed to attorneys insufficient); see note 2 supra. See also Welsh v. Gibbons, 211 S.C. 516, 46 S.E.2d 147, syl. 3, 4 (1948) (refusal of plaintiff, suing for injury from contents of soft-drink bottle, to permit chemical analysis of contents, proveable as admission of weakness of his case).

7. Pacific-Atlantic S. S. Co. v. U. S., 81 F.Supp. 777, syl. 9 (E.D. Va. 1948); Note, Larkin, 34 Corn.L.Q. 637; Wright v. Safeway Stores, 7 Wash.2d 341, 109 P.2d 542, 135 A.L.R. 1367, 1372 (1941) and annotation at 1376.

8. For example, if the potential witness is the family doctor of the party. American Employers' Ins. Co. v. Kellum, 185 S.W.2d 113, syl. 2 (Tex.Civ.App. 1944). Or an employee. Chicago & N. W. Ry. Co. v. Kelly, 84 F.2d 569, syl. 6 (1936); Patton v. Oakman, 298 Mich. 672, 299 N.W. 761, syl. 7 (1941). Husband. Penn. Fire Ins. Co. v. Thomason, 293 Ky. 142, 168 S.W.2d 547, syl. 2 (1943).

9. Ellerman v. Skelly Oil Co., 227 Minn. 65, 34 N.W. 2d 251, syl. 2 (1948) (defendant not subject to inference for failure to call employee involved in injury sued for, where employee had been discharged four years before trial—"equally accessible");

Note, 33 Minn.L.Rev. 423; cases cited 2 Wigmore, Evidence, § 288, n. 1, 31 C.J.S., p. 858, n. 27.

10. See Deaver v. St. Louis Pub. Service Co., 199 S. W.2d 83, 85 (Mo.App.1947) "However the availability of a witness is not to be determined from his mere physical presence at the trial or his accessibility for the service of a subpoena upon him. On the contrary, his availability may well depend, among other things, upon his relationship to one or the other of the parties, and the nature of the testimony that he might be expected to give in the light of his previous statements or declarations about the facts of the case"); United States v. Beekman, 155 F.2d 580, syl. 6 (C.C.A.2d 1946) (employees of defendant not called by him; government comment allowed: when likelihood of bias, not "equally available").

11. Wigmore urges this view. Evidence, § 288. It is approved in United States v. Beekman, 155 F.2d 580, syl. 8 (C.C.A.2d 1946) (Frank, J.); State v. Johnson, 151 La. 625, 92 So. 139, 141 (1922) (Thompson, J.); Baker v. Salvation Army, Inc., 91 N.H. 1, 12 A.2d 514, syl. 8 (Page, J.). A good instance of this common sense approach is Dawson v. Davis, 125 Conn. 330, 5 A.2d 703, syl. 8, 9 (1939) where the absent potential witness was the plaintiff's nephew but the defendant claimed under a transaction with him and it was held that an inference against defendant was warranted.

criminal case may call his wife, but the state may not. Again, it may be clear that all the information that the witness has is subject to a privilege which the party may exert, as in the case where by statute the party is privileged against disclosure by his physician of information learned in consultation or examination. In these situations probably the majority of courts would forbid an adverse inference from a failure to call.[12] Of course, an inference from the failure of the accused himself in a criminal case to take the stand is forbidden by statute in most states.[13] The policy considerations in respect to the allowability of comment upon the exercise of evidential privileges are discussed in another chapter.[14]

The specific procedural effect of the inference from failure to call a witness is seldom discussed, doubtless because local usage is so familiar that other possibilities are not considered.

Some courts say that the party's failure to call the witness or produce the evidence creates a "presumption"[15] that the testimony would have been unfavorable. It is usually phrased in terms, however, of "may" rather than "must" and seemingly could at most be only a permissive, not a mandatory presumption.[16] Moreover, unlike the usual presumption, it is not directed to any specific presumed fact or facts which are required or permitted to be found. One who has the burden of producing evidence of a fact in issue, cannot supply the lack of proof by relying on this "presumption."[17] "The extent of a party's right to invoke his opponent's failure to call an available witness, when such right exists, is to impair the value of the latter's proofs, and to give greater credence to the positive evidence of the former, upon any issue upon which it is shown that such witness might have knowledge."[18]

A possible practical effect of calling it a presumption is that it might incline some courts adopting this usage to regard its inclusion in the instructions as a matter of right. Most courts customarily speak of the party's conduct as creating an "inference."[19] Doubtless some of these courts would consider that the party has a right to have such inference explained in the instructions, on proper request. Others no doubt would say that the instruction is proper but not re-

---

12. Party's failure to call physician. Merrill v. St. Paul City Ry. Co., 170 Minn. 332, 212 N.W. 533, syl. 3 (1927). Contra: Killings v. Metropolitan Life Ins. Co., 187 Miss. 265, 192 So. 577, syl. 3, 131 A.L.R. 684 (1940) (approving instruction allowing the inference: two judges dissenting). Failure to call spouse. Knowles v. People, 15 Mich. 408 (1867). Contra: Comm. v. Spencer, 212 Mass. 438, 99 N.E. 266 (1912) (semble). See Note, Instructions on inference from failure to call privileged witness, 131 A.L.R. 693.

13. See § 132, herein.

14. See § 80, herein.

15. See, e. g., Stephenson v. Golden, 279 Mich. 710, 276 N.W. 849, syl. 44 (1938); Robinson v. Haydel, 177 Miss. 233, 171 So. 7 (1937); Wolfe v. Wolfe, 120 W.Va. 389, 198 S.E. 209, syl. 2 (1938).

16. See discussion of these terms in § 308, herein.

17. Stimpson v. Hunter, 234 Mass. 61, 125 N.E. 155, syl. 5 (1919) (plaintiff dentist suing father for serv- ices to son, could not invoke their failure to testify though in court, to supply lacking proof of authority or ratification); Hucheson v. Savings Bank, 129 Va. 281, 105 S.E. 677, syl. 8 (1921) ("There is no presumption against a defendant for failure to call witnesses when the plaintiff carrying the burden of proof has not made a prima facie case"). This result is a logical application of our system of allocating to the respective parties the burden of producing evidence as to particular issues, but as Wigmore points out the contrary view might be more promotive of justice. Evidence, § 290, note 12.

18. Snow, J. in Stocker v. Boston & M. R. Co., 84 N.H. 377, 151 A. 457, 70 A.L.R. 1320, 1323, (1930). See Note, Inference from failure to produce witness as substantive proof, 70 A.L.R. 1326.

19. See, e. g., Gross v. Williams, 149 F.2d 84, syl. 2 (C. C.A. Ark.1945); National Life Co. v. Brennecke, 195 Ark. 1088, 115 S.W.2d 855, syl. 7 (1938); Dawson v. Davis, 125 Conn. 330, 5 A.2d 703, syl. 9 (1939).

quired.[20] Still others would condemn it as a comment on the evidence.[21]

Of course, all courts permit counsel to argue the inference where the inference is an allowable one. Most of the courts, moreover, whether or not they customarily include in their instructions a charge on the "presumption" or "inference," assume that they are required to keep a firm rein upon arguments on this inference. In these jurisdictions reversals for arguments thought to be unjustified by the rules as to when the inference is allowable, are fairly frequent.[22]

In jurisdictions where the judge retains his common law power to comment on the evidence, certainly a fair comment on failure to produce witnesses or evidence is traditionally allowable. In other jurisdictions, there is no harm if local practice sanctions a discretion in the judge to include such an instruction. It is submitted, however, that a practice which gives a party a right to such instruction is undesirable.[23] If made a matter of

right it is hard to escape the development of elaborate rules of law defining the circumstances when the right exists. To make it a matter of right has the advantage, it is true, of focussing past experience on the problem presented at the trial, but the cost here of complex rules far outweighs the gain.

A similar effect, of spinning a web of rules, flows from the practice of tight control of the argument on the inference. It is wiser to hold that if an argument on failure to produce proof is fallacious, the remedy is the usual one, namely the answering argument and the jury's good sense.[24] Thus the judge would be called on to intervene only when the argument can be said, under the general standard, to be not merely weak or unfounded, but unfair and prejudicial.[25]

250. Admissions by Conduct—(e) Misconduct Constituting Obstruction of Justice.[1]

A party's failure to produce evidence when he is free to produce or withhold, may as we

---

20. See Knott v. Hawley, 163 Minn. 239, 202 N.W. 785 (1925), and see 64 C.J., Trials, § 464.

21. Hartman v. Hartman, 314 Mo. 305, 284 S.W. 488, syl. 2 (1926).

22. See, e. g., Ellerman v. Skelly Oil Co., 227 Minn. 65, 34 N.W.2d 251 (1948) (described in n. 9, supra); Neale v. Nassau Elec. Ry. Co., 161 App.Div. 95, 146 N.Y.S. 263 (1914). Cases passing on the propriety of arguments on this inference are collected in 64 C.J. Trials, § 290.

23. "If it commends itself to reason, born of common judgment and experience, the jury will apply it without hint or argument from the Court. The practice of placing this mere argument in instructions violates the plain provisions of Section 1530 of the 1942 Code. Those cases are sound which deny to the inference any quality other than mere argument. Here again a safe and logical test is: if counsel is free to argue it, the Court is not." Chief Justice Julian P. Alexander, Presumptions: Their Use and Abuse, 17 Miss. L.J. 1, 14 (1945).

24. In United States v. Cotter, 60 F.2d 689, 692, syl. 4 (C.C.A.2d 1932) the court (L. Hand, J.) in rejecting defendant's complaint of the judge's refusal to instruct the jury to disregard the prosecution's argument based on defendant's failure to call witnesses, said, "A judge is not required to intervene here any

more than in any other issue of fact. He must indeed, as he always must, keep the prosecution in a criminal case within bounds; . . . just as he must keep passion out of the debate and hold the parties to the issues. But he is not charged with correcting their non sequiturs; the jury are to find these for themselves. So the judge in the case at bar was not required to correct the argument, that the failure of the defendants to call the four witnesses was a ground for supposing that they would swear against them. He might have done so, but he need not; so far as we know, Sears v. Duling, 79 Vt. 334, 65 A. 990, is the only decision to the contrary and it does not persuade us." See also Alabama Power Co. v. Goodwin, 210 Ala. 657, 99 So. 158, syl. 5, 6 (1924) (trial judge must not pass upon the logical propriety of arguments); 64 C.J. Trial, § 268.

25. In passing on this the trial judge has a substantial measure of discretion. Lebas v. Patriotic Assur. Co., 106 Conn. 119, 137 A. 241, syl. 2, 4 (1927); 64 C.J., Trials, §§ 248, 307.

1. 2 Wigmore, Evidence, §§ 278, 291; 1 Jones, Evidence, §§ 105, 106 (2d ed., 1926); Maguire and Vincent, Admissions Implied from Spoliation, 45 Yale L.J. 226 (1935); Decennial Digests, Crim.Law, ☞ 351(8), 351(10), 408, Evidence, ☞78, 79, 110, 219(2); 31 C.J.S. Evidence, §§ 151–155, 293.

have seen in the preceding section be treated as an admission. As might be expected, wrongdoing by the party in connection with his case, amounting to an obstruction of justice may likewise be proven against him as an admission by conduct. By resorting to wrongful devices he gives ground for believing that he thinks his case is weak and not to be won by fair means. Accordingly, a party's false statement about the matter in litigation, whether before suit [2] or on the stand,[3] his fabrication of false documents,[4] his undue pressure, by bribery [5] or intimidation [6] or other means, to influence a witness to testify for him or to avoid testifying, his destruction of relevant documents,[7] his attempt to corrupt the jury,[8] his hiding [9] or transferring [10] property in anticipation of judgment—all these are instances of this type of admissions by conduct. Of course, it is not enough to show that a third person did the acts, such as bribing a witness, charged as obstructive. They must be fastened to the party himself, or in the case of a corporation to one of its superior officers, by showing that he did the act or authorized it by words or other conduct.[11] Moreover, the circumstances of the act must manifest bad

---

2. People v. Roche, 49 Cal.App.2d 459, 121 P.2d 865, syl. 5 (1942) (prosecution for failure to stop after accident, statements of accused denying and then admitting she was driving the automobile); Commonwealth v. Lettrich, 346 Pa. 497, 31 A.2d 155, syl. 2, 7 (1943) (child-murder by custodian, false statements as to child's whereabouts to avert inquiry and suspicion).

3. Sheehan v. Goriansky, 317 Mass. 10, 56 N.E.2d 883, syl. 4 (1944) (defendant's testimony which from other evidence jury could find to be false); Hall v. Merrimack Mut. Fire Ins. Co., 91 N.H. 6, 13 A.2d 157, syl. 5 (1940) (deliberately false testimony at first trial, acknowledged to be false at the second).

4. Western States Grocery Co. v. Mirt, 190 Okl. 299, 123 P.2d 266, syl. 5 (1942) (falsified witness-statement placed in evidence).

5. People v. Gambony, 402 Ill. 74, 83 N.E.2d 321, syl. 4 (1949) (indecent liberties with a child: attempts to "buy off" the prosecuting witnesses); Davis v. Commonwealth, 204 Ky. 601, 265 S.W. 10, syl. 2, 3 (1924) (letter offering bribe for favorable testimony); Login v. Waisman, 82 N.H. 500, 136 A. 134, syl. 7 (1927).

6. People v. Bloom, 370 Ill. 144, 18 N.E.2d 197, syl. 3 (1939).

7. Welborn v. Rigdon, 231 S.W.2d 127, syl. 13 (Mo. 1950) (suit by plaintiff for money advanced to improve defendant's property; defendant's conduct in wilfully destroying plaintiff's receipts held "an admission of plaintiff's claim").

8. People v. Marion, 29 Mich. 31, 39 (1874); McHugh v. McHugh, 186 Pa. 197, 40 A. 410 (1898).

9. State v. Bruce, 24 Me. 71 (1844) (procuring property by threats; evidence of concealment).

10. Burdett v. Hipp, 252 Ala. 37, 39 So.2d 389, syl. 5 (1949) (defendant's conveyance of his property to kin after suit filed).

11. People v. Moore, 70 Cal.App.2d 158, 160 P.2d 857, syl. 4–9 (1945) (cousin of accused paid money to prosecuting witness to "ease up" on the case; requirement satisfied by showing that accused was seen talking to persons involved during trial and that he passed money to cousin); Morgan v. Commonwealth, 283 Ky. 588, 142 S.W.2d 123, syl. 1 (1940) (attempted bribery of witness, error to admit because no showing of defendant's connection with the act); Ware v. State, 204 Miss. 107, 37 So.2d 18, syl. 1 (1948) (evidence that witness for accused had offered to "buy off" the prosecution, held error to admit, but court overlooked its competency for impeachment); Meacham v. Gjarde, 194 Wash. 526, 76 P.2d 605, syl. 5, 6 (1938) (misconduct of counsel not admissible without proof of authorization by party—a clear holding that implied or general authority is not enough).

The suggestion in the text as to corporations is taken from Maguire and Vincent, Spoliation, 45 Yale L.J. 226, 251 (1935). Compare City of Austin v. Howard, 158 S.W.2d 556, syl. 18, 19 (Tex.Civ.App.1942) (attempts by Mayor and City Manager to prevent witness from testifying in suit against City, held admissible though assent of Council not shown. "Manifestly they were actively interested and participating on behalf of the City in the conduct of the trial as they had a right to do, and their conduct should be deemed, under such circumstances, to be within the general scope of their authority."). But in Nowack v. Metropolitan Street Ry. Co., 166 N.Y. 433, 439, 60 N.E. 32, 34 (1901) evidence of attempted bribery by defendant's mere claim agent was held receivable, not only as the representative admission of defendant corporation, but because it cast doubt upon the other witnesses secured by him.

faith. Mere negligence is not enough,[12] for it does not sustain the inference of consciousness of a weak case.

What is the probative reach of these various kinds of "spoliation" admissions, beyond their great tactical value in darkening the atmosphere of the party's case? [13] They should, it seems, entitle the proponent to an instruction that the adversary's conduct may be considered as tending to corroborate the proponent's case generally, and as tending to discredit the adversary's case generally.[14] This is worth while in itself and as carrying with it the corresponding right of the proponent's counsel to argue these inferences. But a crucial and perplexing question remains, namely, does the adverse inference from the party's obstructive conduct supply the want of any evidence of a fact essential to the other party's case? Certainly the primitive impulse is strong, and an analogy has been suggested to the practice under statutes and rules permitting the court to enter a default against a party who refuses to answer an interrogatory.[15] Certainly also when the conduct points toward an inference about a particular specific fact, as in the case of bribery of an attesting witness to absent himself from the probate hearing, or the destruction of a particular deed or letter, there is likely to be a greater willingness to allow an inference as to the fact,[16] though your only other information is the proponent's claim about it in his pleading. Where the conduct is not directed toward suppression of any particular fact, as in at-

---

12. Berthold-Jennings Lumber Co., 80 F.2d 32, syl. 12–15 (C.C.A.Mo.1935) (action for overcharge: waybills covering shipments had been destroyed by defendant, held, doctrine of spoliation inapplicable; only applies to conduct indicating fraud, whereas destruction here was routine, with no desire to suppress evidence); Gallup v. St. Louis I. M. and S. Ry. Co., 140 Ark. 347, 215 S.W. 586, syl. 1 (1919) (similar to last).

13. For an illuminating discussion, see Maguire and Vincent, Admissions Implied from Spoliation, 45 Yale L.J. 226, 235–249 (1935).

14. See Maguire and Vincent, op. cit. at 243–249, and see Prudential Insurance Co. v. Lawnsdail, 235 Ia. 125, 15 N.W.2d 880, syl. 1 (1944) (destruction of record "authorizes an inference which tends to corroborate the evidence" on the other side); Hay v. Peterson, 6 Wyo. 419, 45 P. 1073, 1076–9, syl. 4 (1896) (destruction of records of deceased by plaintiff, defendant entitled to instruction on presumption but one requested by him not properly qualified).

The courts often speak of a "presumption" against the spoliator. Long v. Earle, 277 Mich. 505, 269 N.W. 577, syl. 2 (1936); Dec.Dig. Evidence, ☞78, 79. Most presumptions may stand in lieu of proof of specific facts, see §§ 308, 310, but this "presumption" against the spoliator is usually given only a general persuasive effect, rather than a probative one. Walker v. Herke, 20 Wash.2d 239, 147 P.2d 255, syl. 5 (1944), as to which see n. 17, infra.

15. As in Rule 37(b) (2) (iii), Federal Rules of Civil Procedure, and compare Feingold v. Walworth Bros. Inc., 238 N.Y. 446, 454, 144 N.E. 675, 678 (1924) applying a statute of similar purport, discussed in Maguire and Vincent, op. cit. at 235. See also Crook v. Schumann, 292 Ky. 750, 167 S.W.2d 836, syl. 12, 13 (1943) (defendant's disobedience to order to produce records on which proof of plaintiff's case depends; court had discretion to enter decree pro confesso but should have given defendant notice before doing so).

16. See 2 Wigmore, Evidence, § 291, wherein the author contends that the failure or refusal to produce, or the destruction of a document, sufficiently identified by the proof, is evidence from which alone its contents can be inferred to be unfavorable to the one chargeable with the obstructive conduct. For an excellent opinion supporting this view see McCleery v. McCleery, 200 Ala. 4, 75 So. 316, syl. 2–5 (1917, by McClellan, J.).

Compare also the famous case of Armory v. Delamirie, 1 Stra. 505, 93 Eng.Rep. 664 (K.B.1722) where the chimney sweeper's boy found a mounted jewel and took it to a goldsmith's shop to be valued. But the goldsmith's apprentice kept the stone, and gave back only the socket. The boy sued the goldsmith for the conversion of the jewel. After evidence had been given of what a jewel of the finest water that would fit the socket would be worth, the Chief Justice instructed the jury, "that unless the defendant did produce the jewel, and shew it not to be of the finest water, they should presume the strongest against him, and make the value of the best jewels the measure of their damages." It will be noted that in this picturesque landmark case, the limits of the inference were marked out by the evidence of the size of the socket, and of the value of the finest jewel that would fit it.

tempts to "buy off" the prosecution, to sub-orn the jury, or to defeat recovery by con-veyance of property, an inference as to the existence of a particular fact not proved seems to be more strained. Without advert-ing to this distinction most of the decisions have supported the general doctrine that the inference from obstructive conduct by the adversary will not supply a want of proof of a particular fact essential to the proponent's case.[17]

251. Admissions by Conduct—(f) Offers to Compromise Disputed Claim, Excluded as Privi-leged.[1]

In general. If a claimant's offer to com-promise a disputed claim for a given sum, or his adversary's offer to pay a sum in compromise, is tendered in evidence in a suit on the claim against the offering party, it seems clearly relevant as showing the value he placed on the claim. It is sometimes said to be irrelevant as showing only a willingness to buy peace, or as being only hypothetical,

---

17. Gage v. Parmelee, 87 Ill. 329, 343, syl. 7 (1877) (Bill to set aside for fraud a partnership settle-ment agreement; proof showed that on being shown a copy of the bill, defendant burned all the bills and papers of the firm. "This culpable act of the destruction of the books justly prejudices the case of the appellee, and we have the inclina-tion to give to it the full legitimate effect against him that may be warranted. But we do not see how, under the proofs in the case, it can be made avail of here, to the advantage of appellant, un-less there be allowed to it the effect of supplying proof. This, we do not think, can rightly be done. Proof must be made of the allegations of the bill. The destruction of the books does not make such proof. The presumption of law does not go to that extent.

In the weighing of conflicting testimony, there might be scope for the operation of this presumption against the appellee; or, in the denial to him of any benefit of secondary evidence."); Login v. Waisman, 82 N.H. 500, 136 A. 134, syl. 6–8 (1927) (evidence, though probably not competent, that de-fendant had bribed an eye-witness to leave the state; held, such evidence will not take plaintiff's case to jury, without other evidence of essential facts of agency and negligence); Jakel v. Brock-elman Bros., 91 N.H. 453, 21 A.2d 155, syl. 3 (1941) (plaintiff, patron who fell on floor of shop, testified that attendant swept up substance where she fell, but not as to what the substance was, held, not to supply necessary proof that there was danger-ous substance on the floor); Patch v. Protection Lodge, 77 Vt. 294, 329, 60 A. 74, syl. 15 (1905); (presumption for spoliation does not relieve other party of burden from producing evidence to prove his case so far as he has burden); Walker v. Herke, 20 Wash.2d 239, 147 P.2d 255, syl. 5–10 (1944) (extensive discussion, citing cases). 31 C.J.S., Evi-dence, § 153.

Supporting the contrary view, that evidence of spoli-ation does supply proof of facts alleged by the proponent, are statements in the following opin-ions, though the holdings may not reach so far:

Middleton v. Middleton, 188 Ark. 1022, 68 S.W.2d 1003, 1006, syl. 2, 3 (1934) (son destroyed father's will leaving part of his property to daughters; in suit by daughters to establish as lost will, son cannot rely on statute requiring proof of contents by disinterested witnesses, only proof possible be-ing that of interested witnesses, which was fur-nished); Pomeroy v. Benton, 77 Mo. 64, 85 (1882) (suit by partner after dissolution agreement to set aside agreement and hold the other partner to ac-count as fraudulent trustee: defendant destroyed records necessary for ascertaining amount of prof-its made on goods for which he was required to account; held, because of spoliation, amount claimed in plaintiff's complaint, $200,000, would be taken as measure; but on rehearing, some evi-dence relevant to amount was found in the record, and by reference thereto, recovery was much re-duced); Gough v. Gough, 321 Mo. 414, 11 S.W.2d 729, syl. 10 (1928) (similar to last); and see In re Lambie's Estate, 97 Mich. 49, 56 N.W. 223, 225, syl. 3 (1893) (where proponent of earlier will is shown to have destroyed later revoking will, latter is presumed to have been legally executed and its terms may be proved by declarations of testatrix). A sprinkling of decisions has even gone further and has ascribed to spoliation the effect of a con-clusive presumption, that the despoiler cannot dis-pute. Middleton v. Middleton, supra ("where the instrument destroyed is of such nature as to de-stroy all evidence, there follows a conclusive pre-sumption that if produced it would have estab-lished the claim of the adversary"). Or hold that the despoiler cannot dispute the presumption by his own unsupported testimony. Downing v. Plate, 90 Ill. 268, 273 (1878). But recent cases reject the conclusive presumption theory. Hall v. Mer-rimack Mut. Fire Ins. Co., 91 N.H. 6, 13 A.2d 157, 159 (1940); Walker v. Herke, 20 Wash.2d 239, 147 P.2d 255, 261 (1944).

1. 4 Wigmore, Evidence, §§ 1061, 1062; Jones, Evi-dence, §§ 1052–7 (2d ed.1926); Dec.Digests, Evidence, ☞213, 214, 219(3), Crim.Law, ☞408; 31 C.J.S., Evidence, §§ 285–290; 22 C.J., Evidence, §§ 347–352.

which is no more than to say it is an offer and as such conditioned on acceptance. I have given reasons in another chapter for concluding that the only substantial ground for excluding offers of compromise is not that they are irrelevant, but the reason of policy that their admission would discourage what the law wants to encourage, the settlement of disputes.[2] On this basis, the rule should be classified as a rule of privilege, rather than a rule of competency. One has the privilege if he has made the offer in question, and is a party to the suit in which the evidence is offered.[3]

To call into play the policy, there must be an actual dispute,[4] or at least an apparent difference of view between the parties as to the validity or amount of the claim.[5] An offer to pay an admitted claim is not privileged.[6] There is no policy of encouraging compromises of undisputed claims. They should be paid in full. If the validity of the claim and the amount due are undisputed, an offer to pay a lesser sum in settlement would accordingly be admissible.[7] If the validity of the claim is conceded, but the amount is unliquidated, doubtful or disputed, it seems that an offer to pay or accept a certain sum should be privileged.

What is excluded? The offer of course,[8] and any suggestions or overtures of settlement.[9] How far do any accompanying statements of fact made by either party during negotiations or correspondence looking to settlement share the privilege? It is sometimes loosely said that the privilege covers also statements and admissions made as part of the effort to compromise and with that end in view.[10] But the generally accepted doctrine is that an admission of fact in the

---

2. See § 76, herein.

3. See § 76, herein.

4. Wartell v. Novograd, 49 R.I. 191, 141 A. 461, syl. 11 (1928) (action for money had and received; offer to pay a lesser amount comes in as an admission that party had that much of plaintiff's funds; the amount due being admitted, there was nothing to compromise); West v. Cashin, 83 S.W. 2d 1001, syl. 9 (Tex.Civ.App.1935).

5. ". . . a controversy exists within the meaning of the rule whenever anything has transpired within the knowledge of the parties which has made the interests of the parties hostile. Even though no one has ever intimated that he claims a cause of action against the other, yet, if anything has happened which is calculated to produce litigation, the fact that one person offered to pay for a release of that possible cause of action and that the other refused to grant the release on such terms characterizes the transaction as an offer of compromise of an existing controversy, without proof of any previous claims or negotiations." Starnes v. St. Joseph Ry. etc. Co., 22 S.W.2d 73, 79 (Mo.App.1929), affirmed 331 Mo. 44, 52 S.W.2d 852, syl. 5 (1932).

6. Firestone Tire & Rubber Co., 65 A.2d 338, syl. 7 (Mun.Ct.App.D.C.1949) (claim for damage to car asserted by bailor against parking station; defendant's agent offered to pay in full less salvage value); McComas v. Clements, 137 Kan. 681, 21 P.2d 895, syl. 1 (1933) (car collision, defendant at scene of accident said he would take care of bills).

7. Person v. Bowe, 79 Minn. 238, 82 N.W. 480 (1900) (plaintiff sued for wages claimed to be due him as a farm laborer, and offered evidence that when he demanded his pay the defendant said that he could not pay then, but would let the plaintiff have $20, and would pay the rest about the middle of November, and if the plaintiff "would throw off five dollars" he would at once pay the claim); Vigeant v. Fidelity Nat. Bank & Trust Co., 239 Mo.App. 36, 188 S.W.2d 533, syl. 4, 5 (1945) (claim for commission of $4250 for sale of realty for bank, president of bank "arbitrarily" refused to pay more than $2100—"that is all the bank can afford to pay").

An offer made before any dispute has arisen is not privileged. West v. Cashin, 83 S.W.2d 1001, syl. 9, Tex.Civ.App., 1935.

8. Outlook Hotel Co. v. St. John, 287 F. 115, syl. 3, 4 (C.C.A.N.J.1923) (letter offering settlement privileged though not expressly without prejudice).

9. Wood v. Morrisey, 31 F.Supp. 449, syl. 3 (D.C.La. 1940) ("we might discuss compromise, if you care to submit an offer"); Armstrong v. Kline, 64 Cal. App.2d 704, 149 P.2d 445, syl. 11, 12 (1944) ("she asked me what I thought about settling"); North River Ins. Co. v. Walker, 161 Ky. 368, 170 S.W. 983, syl. 3, 4 (1914) ("if you will come to Paducah we will try to make a compromise settlement.").

10. 31 C.J.S. p. 285, n. 17, and compare cases cited, e. g. Boyes v. Evans, 14 Cal.App.2d 472, 58 P.2d 922, 926 (1936); Schmitt v. Eagle Roller Mill Co., 199 Minn. 382, 272 N.W. 277, 285 (1937).

course of negotiations is not privileged [11] unless it is hypothetical [12]—"we admit for the sake of the discussion only"—or unless it is expressly stated to be "without prejudice," [13] or unless it is inseparably connected with the offer,[14] so that it cannot be correctly understood without reading the two together.[15] As to the first exception it must be said that admissions of fact by negotiators are seldom made in hypothetical form, and the burden would be on the objector to establish that such an admission was so intended.[16] In fact, it is believed that admissions in the course of settlement negotiations are usually made with more than average wariness and deliberation.[17] As to the second, the practice of using the term "without prejudice" or the equivalent is an English custom which has not been fully naturalized here, and it is not certain how far our courts today would give deference to the party's advance claim of privilege in this form. As to the admission

forming an integral part of the offer, it seems that in a judge-tried case, such admission should be received since the judge can be trusted to consider it only in its aspect as an admission of a distinct fact.[18]

Evidence of present party's compromise with third persons. In an action between P and D it seems clear that a compromise-offer or a completed compromise by D with T, a third person, having a claim similar to P's arising from the same transaction may be relevant as showing D's belief in the weakness of his defense in P's present action. Nevertheless, the same consideration of policy which actuates the courts to exclude an offer of compromise made by D to P, namely the danger of discouraging compromises, applies here with almost equal force. Accordingly the prevailing view is that the compromise-offer or payment made by the present defendant is privileged when offered as an implied admission of liability.[19] But,

11. Calvin Hosmer, Stolte Co. v. Paramount Cone Co., 285 Mass. 278, 189 N.E. 192, syl. 4 (1934); Sanderson v. Barkman, 272 Mich. 179, 261 N.W. 291, syl. 2 (1935) (statement about circumstances of accident during negotiations about compromise); Lewis v. Lewis, 192 N.C. 267, 134 S.E. 486, syl. 3 (1926) ("distinct admission of an independent fact"); Cole v. Harvey, 200 Okl. 564, 198 P.2d 199, syl. 4, 5 (1948) (suit for work done; no error in receiving evidence of statements of amount due, during negotiations for compromise); Dunning v. Northwestern Elec. Co., 186 Ore. 379, 199 P.2d 648, syl. 4 (1948) (reference in letter to injuries sustained "when you ran into fallen pole"). See Note, Admissions made during discussion of compromise, 80 A.L.R. 919.

12. Jones v. Jernigan, 29 N.M. 399, 223 P. 100, syl. 2 (1924).

13. White v. Old Dominion S. S. Co., 102 N.Y. 660, 6 N.E. 289 (1886) and cases cited, Note 80 A.L.R. 924, 925; 31 C.J.S., Evidence, § 288.

14. Boylan v. McMillan, 137 Ia. 142, 114 N.W. 630, syl. 3 (1908) (recitals in letter of compromise, held inseparable from offer); Brown v. Hebb, 167 Md. 535, 175 A. 602, 97 A.L.R. 366, 374 (1934) (lawyer's letter for patient to doctor, offering compromise amount for disputed doctor's bill, adding "he informs me that his information is that the offer is a very liberal one for the services rendered," held, quoted phrase not "inseparable," but admissi-

ble to show an acknowledgment of the services and debt, removing the bar of the statute of limitations). To like effect is Stanley v. Beaty, 148 Kan. 492, 83 P.2d 637, syl. 2 (1938) ("I . . . will gladly pay you for your services, but could we not come to an agreeable and reasonable settlement," admissible in trial before judge as acknowledgment that she owed a bill for services).

15. Home Ins. Co. v. Baltimore Warehouse Co., 93 U.S. 527, 548, 23 L.Ed. 868, 871 (1876); Sanford v. John Finnegan Co., 169 S.W. 624, syl. 5 (Tex. Civ.App.1914).

16. "Admissions made expressly for the purpose of effecting a compromise of a matter under controversy, if not accepted, cannot be proved against the party making them; but, where it does not appear that such admissions were made in confidence of a compromise, they will be admissible in evidence." City of Anadarko v. Argo, 35 Okl. 115, 128 P. 500, 501 (1912).

17. Consequently the writer would question the soundness in fact of Wigmore's reference to "the general hypothetical nature of discussions attending a compromise-negotiation." Wigmore, Evidence, § 1062.

18. Stanley v. Beaty, 148 Kan. 492, 83 P.2d 637, 638 (1938).

19. Hawthorne v. Eckerson Co., 77 F.2d 844, syl. 6 (C.C.A.2d, 1935); Brown v. Pacific Elec. Ry. Co.,

though inadmissible for this purpose, it may well come in for another purpose. A defendant for example places on the stand in a personal injury case a witness who was injured in the same collision. Here it seems clear that if the witness has made a claim on his own account against the defendant, inconsistent with his present favorable testimony, this may be proved to impeach the witness. And it further seems reasonable that if the witness has been paid or promised money in compromise of his claim, this may likewise be shown in impeachment, as evidence of bias.[20] The need for evaluating the credibility of the witness may be as insistent as the policy of encouraging compromise. If, however, the witness sought to be impeached by showing the compromise with a third person, is one of the present parties, the question is more debatable. The danger that the evidence will be used substantively as an admission is greater, and as the party's interest is apparent the need for additional evidence on credibility is less. Such impeachment of party-witnesses, however, has occasionally been sanctioned.[21]

Compromise-evidence in criminal cases.[22] An offer by the accused to pay money to "buy off" the prosecuting witness and stifle prosecution, though sometimes mistakenly theorized as an offer of compromise and held inadmissible,[23] is not within the policy of encouraging compromises, and hence is not usually regarded as privileged.[24] Indeed, we have seen that it is classed as an implied admission and received in evidence as such.[25]

---

79 Cal.App.2d 613, 180 P.2d 424, syl. 1–5 (1947) (collecting decisions) noted 21 So.Calif.L.Rev. 414; Whitney v. Louisville & N. R. Co., 296 Ky. 381, 177 S.W.2d 139, 140 (1942); Carpenter v. Boston & M. R. Co., 295 Mass. 103, 3 N.E.2d 184, syl. 6 (1936); Note, Evidence that defendant has paid third persons, 20 A.L.R.2d 304, 306, 308. Contra: McEntire v. Baygent, 229 S.W.2d 866, syl. 1, 2 (Tex.Civ.App., 1950), but the Texas decisions are conflicting, see Note, 21 Tex.L.Rev. 298 (1943); Allcorn, Compromise Settlements in Evidence, 1 Baylor L.Rev. 160 (1948).

A settlement which is wholly between third parties, arising out of the transaction in suit, is not within the privilege since the evidence will not harm the parties to the compromise. But when offered to show an acknowledgment of liability by the payor, as evidence that he was liable, it would be an offer of conduct as hearsay and excluded as such by most courts. See, e. g., Daly v. Publix Cabs, 128 Neb. 403, 259 N.W. 163, syl. 4, 1935 (in suit by passenger against operator of taxicab for injury incurred when another automobile collided with taxicab; evidence offered by taxicab operator that driver of other automobile paid damages to taxicab, excluded as hearsay as to passenger). See § 229, herein.

20. Joice v. Missouri-Kansas-Texas R. Co., 354 Mo. 439, 189 S.W.2d 568, 161 A.L.R. 383, syl. 16–19 (1945); Rynar v. Lincoln Transit Co., 129 N.J.L. 525, 30 A.2d 406, syl. 1–10 (1945) (Case, J., discusses balance of need for impeachment and danger of improper use; here admissible in judge's discretion); Note, 161 A.L.R. 395. Of course, the opponent would be entitled to an instruction lim-

iting the use of the evidence to the question of credibility. But one court seems to overlook the bearing on bias and to insist that the proponent present evidence that the settlement was a cover for bribery. See Bratt v. Western Air Lines, 169 F.2d 214, syl. 5 (C.C.A.Utah, 1948). Compare Kaplan v. Loev, 327 Pa. 465, 194 A. 653 (1937) where impeachment of this kind was (it seems erroneously) held improper because it might disclose the existence of insurance against liability.

A similar problem arises as to the proof of a compromise-settlement in support of the witness, to explain the signing by the witness of a statement inconsistent with his testimony. See Johnson v. Minnihan, 355 Mo. 1208, 200 S.W.2d 334, syl. 1–6 (1947) (after being cross-examined about written statement secured from him by defendant, but which he denied he read, witness allowed to testify on redirect that he signed statement in order to secure a settlement of his own claim against defendant).

21. Luis v. Cavin, 88 Cal.App.2d 107, 198 P.2d 563, syl. 10 (1948); Burke v. Commercial Standard Ins. Co., 38 So.2d 644, syl. 5 (La.App.1949).

22. See Dec.Dig. Crim.Law, ☞408.

23. See, e. g., Richardson v. State, 28 Ala.App. 432, 186 So. 574, syl. 13, 14 (1939).

24. Grace v. Comm., 302 Ky. 796, 196 S.W.2d 417, syl. 3, 4 (1946); State v. Givens, 87 S.C. 525, 70 S.E. 162, syl. 3 (1911); Carter v. State, 161 Tenn. 698, 34 S.W.2d 208, syl. 2–4 (1931); 4 Wigmore, Evidence, § 1061(d) (8).

25. See § 250, supra.

On the other hand, offers by the accused to the state's attorney to plead guilty in return for leniency seem to be within the policy. Effective criminal law administration in many localities would hardly be possible if a large proportion of the charges were not disposed of by such compromises. Accordingly most courts seem to recognize such offers as privileged.[26] If the transaction on which the prosecution is based gives rise also to a civil right of action, a compromise or offer of compromise of the civil claim if no agreement to stifle the criminal prosecution is involved should seemingly be privileged when offered at the criminal trial.[27]

Effect of acceptance of offer of compromise. If an offer of compromise is accepted and a contract is thus created, the party aggrieved may sue on the contract and obviously may prove the offer and acceptance.[28] Moreover, if after such a contract is made and the offering party repudiates it, the other may elect to sue on the original cause of action and here again it seems the repudiating party may not claim privilege against proof of the compromise.[29] The shield of the privilege does not extend to the protection of those who repudiate the agreements the making of which the privilege is designed to encourage.

252. Admissions by Conduct—(g) Safety Measures after an Accident.[1]

After an accident causing injury, the owner of the premises or of the enterprise will often take remedial measures by repairing a defect, installing a safety device, changing safety rules, or discharging the employee apparently at fault. Are these new safety measures, which might have prevented the injury, admissible as evidence of negligence, of an implied acknowledgement by conduct that due care required that these measures should have been taken before the injury? It seems that in many instances such evidence, particularly when the remedial measures follow immediately the happening of the injury, may be very persuasive of the actor's belief as to the precautions required by due care before the accident. Nevertheless, the courts often broadly assert that such evidence offered for this purpose is irrelevant.[2] While, like all circumstantial evidence, it admits of varying explanations,[3] some of them consistent with due care, it seems that for this purpose it would often meet the usual standards of relevancy.[4] The predominant reason for excluding such evidence, it seems, is not lack of probative significance but the very urgent policy against discouraging the taking of safety measures.[5] At all events

26. Bennett v. Comm., 234 Ky. 333, 28 S.W.2d 24, syl. 3, 4 (1930); State v. McGunn, 208 Minn. 349, 294 N.W. 208, syl. 2 (1940); State v. Abel, 320 Mo. 445, 8 S.W.2d 55 (1928); Stafford v. State, 125 Tex. Cr. 174, 67 S.W.2d 285, syl. 3 (1934); Note, 12 Tex. L. Rev. 510 (1934) (suggesting distinction adopted in text.

27. Ecklund v. United States, 159 F.2d 81 (C.C.A. 6th, 1947) (prosecution for selling automobile above ceiling price).

28. Union Trust Co. v. Resisto Mfg. Co., 169 Md. 381, 181 A. 726, syl. 2 (1935); 31 C.J.S., Evidence, § 290.

29. Reese v. McVittie, 119 Colo. 91, 200 P.2d 390, syl. 3, 4 (1948).

1. 2 Wigmore, Evidence, § 283; 3 Jones, Evidence, §§ 1041–1043 (2d ed. 1926); Decennial Digest, Negligence, ☞131; Note, Repairs after an accident, 170 A.L.R. 7–111.

Uniform Rules of Evidence, Rule 51: *"Subsequent Remedial Conduct.* When after the occurrence of

an event remedial or precautionary measures are taken, which, if taken previously would have tended to make the event less likely to occur, evidence of such subsequent measures is not admissible to prove negligence or culpable conduct in connection with the event." Model Code of Evidence R. 308 is similar.

2. See, e. g., Columbia and P. S. R. Co. v. Hawthorne, 144 U.S. 202, 12 S.Ct. 591, 36 L.Ed. 405 (1892); Terre Haute & I. R. Co. v. Clem, 123 Ind. 15, 23 N.E. 965, 966 (1890); Morse v. Minneapolis & St. Louis R. Co., 30 Minn. 465, 16 N.W. 358, 359 (1883).

3. See § 152.

4. See § 152.

5. See § 77. Compare the court's statement in Ashland Supply Co. v. Webb, 206 Ky. 184, 266 S.W. 1086, 1925: "There are two reasons why evidence of subsequent repair should not be admitted. One is that, while it may be necessary to subsequently

the courts do exclude, when offered as admissions of negligence or fault, evidence of remedial safety measures taken after an injury,[6] such as repairs,[7] changes in construction,[8] installation of new safety devices[9] such as lights, gates, or guards, changes in rules and regulations,[10] changes in the practice of the business,[11] or the discharge of an employee charged with causing the injury.[12]

It is said that where the evidence of repairs or the like is relevant for other purposes it will be received.[13] Thus evidence of subsequent repairs or changes has been admitted as evidence of the defendant's ownership or control[14] of the premises or his duty to repair[15] where these are disputed; as evidence, where defendant incautiously puts in issue the possibility or feasibility of preventive measures, to show such possibility or practicability;[16] as evidence, where the jury has taken a view, or where the defendant has introduced a photograph of the scene,

repair the appliance, it does not follow from that that the appliance was defective at the time of the accident. The other reason is that, if such evidence were admitted, it would have a tendency to cause employers to omit making needed repairs for fear that the precaution thus taken by them could be used as evidence against them."

6. An analogous doctrine is applied when a person concerned in an accident gives or offers aid to the victim. "The defendant, not knowing whether it was liable or not, had the humanity to take plaintiff, who was struck by its engine, to a hospital in Danville, and employed Dr. Miller to attend him. It was an act of mercy which no court should hold in any respect was an implied admission or circumstance tending to admit liability. If a court should so hold, it would tend to stop, instead of encourage, one injuring another from giving aid to the sufferer." Barber v. Southern Ry. Co., 193 N. C. 691, 138 S.E. 17, 19, (1927). See cases collected in 2 Wigmore, Evidence, § 283a, n. 1, and in Note, Evidence of payment or offer of payment of medical and hospital expense, 20 A.L.R.2d 291.

7. Kentucky & W. Va. Power Co. v. Stacy, 291 Ky. 325, 164 S.W.2d 537, 170 A.L.R. 1, syl. 1 (1942); Potter v. Dr. W. H. Groves etc. Hospital, 99 Utah 71, 103 P.2d 280, syl. 4 (1940).

8. Limbeck v. Interstate Power Co., 69 F.2d 249, syl. 4 (C.C.A. 8th 1934).

9. Erickson's Dairy Products Co. v. Northwest etc. Co., 165 Ore. 553, 109 P.2d 53, syl. 3. 4 (1941) (use of asbestos to protect wall against fire).

10. Ware v. Boston & M. R. Co., 92 N.H. 373, 31 A.2d 58, syl. 5 (1943).

11. Hatfield v. Levy Bros., 18 Cal.App.2d 798, 112 P.2d 277, syl. 1, 2 (1941) (evidence that defendant company stopped waxing floor after accident), reversed on other grounds, 18 Cal.2d 798, 117 P.2d 841 (1941).

12. Armour & Co. v. Skene, 153 F. 241, syl. 4 (C.C.A. Mass.1907) (discharge of driver one year after accident erroneously admitted but not prejudicial);

Turner v. Hearst, 115 Cal. 394, 47 P. 129, syl. 4 (1896) (libel; error to permit plaintiff to prove discharge of reporter, "similar to proof of precaution taken after an accident").

13. See, e. g., Norwood Clinic Inc. v. Spann, 240 Ala. 427, 199 So. 840, 843 (1941) ("if such evidence has a tendency to prove some other disputed issue," admissible.

14. Dubonowski v. Howard Savings Institution, 124 N.J.L. 368, 12 A.2d 384, syl. 1 (1941) (control by landlord of stairs); Scudero v. Campbell, 288 N.Y. 328, 43 N.E.2d 66, syl. 1 (1942) (similar).

15. Carleton v. Rockland, T. & C. St. Ry., 110 Me. 397, 86 A. 334, syl. 1, Ann.C.1915A 1209 (repairs by street railway of steps leading from platform).

16. Reynolds v. Maine Mfg. Co., 81 N.H. 421, 128 A. 329, syl. 7 (1925) (proof of use of chain on wagon after accident allowable to contradict a witness of defendant who testified that a chain could not be used); Jefferson v. City of Raleigh, 194 N.C. 479, 140 S.E. 76, syl. 3 (1927) (plaintiff's eye injured by flying sliver of iron, proof allowed that defendant furnished goggles on similar work after accident, to answer testimony that use of goggles was impracticable). But if the defendant does not inject the issue of feasibility, such proof should not ordinarily be allowed for this purpose. Conry v. Boston & M. R. Co., 227 Mass. 411, 116 N.E. 733, syl. 2 (1917); Kansas City M. & O. Ry. Co. v. Meakin, 146 S.W. 1057, syl. 3 (Tex.Civ.App.1912). Unless perhaps the nature of the accident as proven by plaintiff might raise a doubt whether preventive measures were practicable. See, e. g., Indianapolis, etc., R. R. Co. v. Horst, 93 U.S. 291, 295, 296, 23 L.Ed. 898 (1876). Or unless the plaintiff relies on a statute which is construed to make proof of feasibility a part of plaintiff's case. See Thompson v. Issaquah Shingle Co., 43 Wash. 253, 86 P. 588, syl. 5 (1906) (statute requiring guards on saws "that can be guarded advantageously"). But even in these latter cases, the plaintiff might be limited to other types of evidence, such as opinion or customary practices of such businesses, where these are available and sufficient

to explain that the situation at the time of the accident was different;[17] as evidence of what was done later to show that the earlier condition as of the time of the accident was as plaintiff claims, if the defendant disputes this;[18] as evidence that the faulty condition, later remedied, was the cause of the injury by showing that after the change the injurious effect disappeared;[19] and as evidence contradicting facts testified to by the adversary's witness and thus impeaching credibility.[20]

As suggested above, the extrinsic policy of encouraging remedial safety measures is the predominant reason for holding evidence of such measures to be privileged. It is apparent that the free admission of such evidence for purposes other than as admissions of negligence is likely to defeat this paramount policy. It is submitted that before admitting the evidence for any of these other purposes, the court should be satisfied that the issue on which it is offered is of substantial importance and is actually, and not merely formally in dispute, that the plaintiff cannot establish the fact to be inferred conveniently by other proof,[21] and consequently that the need for the evidence outweighs the danger of its misuse.[22] The defendant of course, upon request, will be entitled to an instruction limiting its use to the issue upon which it is admitted.[23]

See Miniea v. St. Louis Cooperage Co., 175 Mo.App. 91, 157 S.W. 1006, 1012, syl. 16 (1913); Blais v. Flanders Hardware Co., 93 N.H. 370, 42 A.2d 332, 335, syl. 3–6 (1945) ("descriptive testimony could readily be given").

17. Lunde v. National Citizens' Bank, 213 Minn. 278, 6 N.W.2d 809, syl. 6 (1942) (view); Achey v. Marion, 126 Iowa 47, 101 N.W. 435, syl. 2 (1904) (to explain photograph introduced by defendant). But the plaintiff may not introduce a photograph of the altered scene merely for the purpose of showing the repairs in the guise of explanation. Gignoux v. St. Louis Pub. Service Co., 180 S.W.2d 784, syl. 1–5 (Mo.App.1944); Hadges v. New York Rapid Transit Corp., 259 App.Div. 154, 18 N.Y.S.2d 304, syl. 2 (1940).

18. Chicago v. Dalle, 115 Ill. 386, 5 N.E. 578, syl. 1 (1885) (injury due to alleged loose plank in sidewalk, evidence that sidewalk repaired at this place to show previous condition); Chicago, B. & Q. R. Co. v. Krayenbuhl, 65 Neb. 889, 91 N.W. 880, 885, 59 L.R.A. 920 (1902) (agent's locking of turntable to show it was unlocked at time of injury to child); Eargle v. Sumpter Lighting Co., 110 S.C. 560, 96 S. E. 909, syl. 10 (1918) (defect in electrical appliances proveable, where necessary, by evidence of later repairs). But it is obvious that this doctrine, unless limited to cases where the condition is disputed and the proof by repairs is essential, can serve to rob the principal rule of practical effect. See e. g. City of Montgomery v. Quinn, 246 Ala. 154, 19 So. 2d 529, syl. 2, 3 (1944) (action for death caused by falling of rotten limb of tree; act of city in immediately removing other dead limbs admitted to show condition); Williams v. Milner Hotels Co., 130 Conn. 507, 36 A.2d 20, syl. 3–5 (1944) (suit by guest for injury by being bitten by rat while in bed in his room; apparently existence of rat

holes was formally denied in pleadings but not actually in dispute; plaintiff allowed to introduce photographs showing holes covered with tin, as evidence of previous condition). See critical note on the last case, 92 U.Pa.L.Rev. 456.

19. Kentucky Utilities Co. v. White Star Coal Co., 244 Ky. 759, 52 S.W.2d 705, syl. 5, 6 (1932) (proof that everything went well following a second fire, when a defective transformer was removed, admissible to show cause); Texas & N. O. R. Co. v. Anderson, 61 S.W. 424, syl. 1, 2 (Tex.Civ.App.1901) (evidence of removal of obstruction in ditch and that thereafter flood water ran off plaintiff's land, admitted to show obstruction cause of flooding).

20. Koskoff v. Goldman, 86 Conn. 415, 85 A. 588, syl. 4, 5 (1912); Lombardi v. Yulinsky, 98 N.J.L. 332, 119 A. 873, syl. 2 (1923) (where defendant testified that he always put up danger lights at night on pile of bricks on highway, and evidence showed accident resulted from lack of light, proper to ask on cross-examination if he put up light after accident, as bearing on credibility).

21. Schuman v. Bader & Co., 227 Ill.App. 28 (1922) (repairs not admissible to prove prior condition where plaintiff had proved such condition by other witnesses); Mineia v. St. Louis Cooperage Co., see note 16, supra; Blais v. Flanders Hardware Co., note 16, supra.

22. Smith v. Twin State Gas & Elec. Co., 83 N.H. 439, 144 A. 57, 63, syl. 12, 61 A.L.R. 1015 (1928) ("Evidence of subsequent repairs not being competent to show negligence, it should not be used for other purposes incidentally in issue unless the reasons therefor are counterbalancing").

23. Lunde v. National Citizens' Bank, 213 Minn. 278, 6 N.W.2d 809, syl. 7 (1942); Lombardi v. Yulinsky, 98 N.J.L. 332, 119 A. 873, syl. 2 (1923).

CHAPTER 28

DECLARATIONS AGAINST INTEREST

253. General Requirements: Distinction between Declarations against Interest and Parties' Admissions.[1]

To satisfy this exception to the hearsay rule, two main requirements must be met: first, the declaration must state facts which are against the pecuniary or proprietary interest of the declarant or the making of the declaration itself must create evidence which would endanger his pocket-book if the statement were not true;[2] second, the declarant must be unavailable at the time of trial.[3] These two requirements, when satisfied, fur-

nish respectively the safeguard of special trustworthiness and the requisite of special need for the use of hearsay, which are the justifying elements of most of the exceptions to the hearsay rule. Minor qualifications may be added. The interest involved must not be too indirect or remote.[4] The declarant, as in the case of hearsay exceptions generally,[5] must, so far as appears, have had the opportunity to observe the facts,[6] as witnesses must have.[7]

Judicial opinions and some texts[8] fail to distinguish this exception from the one for

---

1. 5 Wigmore, Evidence, §§ 1455–1477; see the able and extensive discussions in Jefferson, 58 Harv.L. Rev. 1 (1944) and Morgan, 5 Vanderbilt L.Rev. 451 (1952); briefer discussions, Mabry, 20 Rocky Mt. L.Rev. 97 (1947), Putnam, 1945 Wis.L.Rev. 439, Coombs, Montana L.Rev. 97 (Spring, 1941), Morgan, Declarations against Interest in Texas, 10 Tex.L. Rev. 399 (1932); Dec.Dig., Evidence, ☞272–284, Crim.Law, 417(15); 31 C.J.S., Evidence, §§ 217–224.

2. See §§ 254–256, below.

3. See § 257, below.

4. See, e. g., Smith v. Blakey, L.R.[1916] 2 Q.B. 326 (letter of clerk advising employer of arrival of "three huge cases" in his charge and stating terms of contract with consignor, held not admissible, "the possibility that this statement might make him liable in case of their being lost is an interest of too remote a nature") and Tennison v. St. Louis-San Francisco Ry. Co., 228 S.W.2d 718, syl. 1 (Mo. 1950) (action for wrongful discharge of brakeman for intoxication: statement of another brakeman that plaintiff was not intoxicated not admissible as against interest on theory that discharge would aid declarant's advancement). This com-

mon-sense requirement is sometimes strained, see In re Forsythe's Estate, 221 Minn. 303, 22 N.W. 2d 19, syl. 16 (1946) (declarations of legatee casting doubt on sanity of testatrix before her death admissible as a declaration against interest, without discussion of contingent nature of the interest).

5. See, e. g., §§ 262, 277, 286.

6. The requirement is often more stringently stated as demanding that the facts must have been "within the declarant's peculiar knowledge." See, e. g., Gleadow v. Atkins, 1 C. and M. 410, 149 Eng.Rep. 459 (Exch.1833); Price v. Humble Oil & Ref. Co., 152 S.W.2d 804, 813, syl. 16 (Tex.Civ.App.1941). But doubtless nothing more than the usual knowledge qualification is intended to, or can reasonably, be required. See Aetna Life Ins. Co. v. Strauch, 179 Okl. 617, 67 P.2d 452, 454, syl. 3 (1937) ("must have concerned a fact personally cognizable by declarant"); Windorski v. Doyle, 219 Minn. 402, 18 N.W.2d 142, 146, syl. 9 (1945) ("a matter of which he was personally cognizant"); 9 Wigmore, Evidence, § 1471(a); 31 C.J.S. 965, § 220.

7. See § 10.

8. See, e. g., 3 Jones, Evidence, ch. 10, Admissions and Declarations (2d ed. rev. 1926).

parties' admissions.[9] It is probably desirable to accept the traditional distinctions, adopted by Wigmore,[10] and to draw the line clear between the two exceptions.[11] Under this view, the admissions of a party-opponent come in without satisfying any of the requirements for declarations against interest. The admissions need not have been against interest when made,[12] though it will usually happen that they were. The admitting party need not be, and seldom is, unavailable.[13] Nor does the party need to have had personal knowledge of the fact admitted.[14] Accordingly, when the admission of a party, or a party's predecessor in interest, is sought to be introduced, it should be offered as, and tested by the requirements for parties' admissions, not those for declarations against interest. On the other hand, when the statements were those of a non-party declarant, now dead or unavailable and the position of the declarant is found not to meet the requirements of "privity" necessary to class him as a party's predecessor, then the theory of declarations against interest may be a case-saving ticket of admission.[15]

254. Declarations against Pecuniary or Proprietary Interest;[1] Declarations Affecting Claim or Liability for Damages.

The traditional field for this exception is that of declarations against proprietary or pecuniary interest. Common instances of the former are acknowledgments that the declarant does not own certain land or personal property,[2] or that he has conveyed or transferred it.[3] Moreover, a statement by one in possession that he holds an interest less than complete ownership has traditionally been regarded as a declaration against interest,[4] though it is obviously ambivalent, and in England has even been received when offered to establish the existence of the interest claimed by the declarant.[5] Similarly, declarations of an owner in possession as to his boundary line have been classed as declarations against interest, though this seems questionable unless

---

9. See ch. 27, herein.

10. 5 Wigmore, Evidence, § 1475: see also 2 Chamberlayne, Evidence, § 1235 (1911) ; 31 C.J.S. 959, 960.

11. Among opinions emphasizing the distinction are Elliotte v. Lavier, 299 Mich. 353, 300 N.W. 116, syl. 6, 7 (1941) (Butzel, J.) and Roe v. Journegan, 175 N.C. 261, 95 S.E. 495, syl. 4, 5 (1918) (Allen, J.).

12. See § 254, herein.

13. See Ch. 27, herein.

14. See § 240, herein.

15. See, e. g., Kwiatowski v. John Lowry, Inc., 276 N.Y. 126, 11 N.E.2d 563, 114 A.L.R. 921 (1937), annotated (in death action, statements against interest by decedent come in as declarations against interest); Aetna Life Ins. Co. v. Strauch, 179 Okl. 617, 67 P.2d 452 (1937) (suit by administrator of wife against insurance company on policy on her life; confession of husband, since electrocuted, of plot to secure policy and kill her, admitted as declaration against interest) and see 31 C.J.S., Evidence, § 219d.

1. 5 Wigmore, Evidence, §§ 1458–1460; 31 C.J.S. Evidence, § 219.

2. In re Thompson, 205 Fed. 556, 560, syl. 5 (D. Ct.N.J.1913) (statement of bankrupt, in possession of dredge, that another, not himself, was the owner).

3. Dean v. Wilkerson, 126 Ind. 338, 26 N.E. 55 (1890) (declarations of father, offered by the son after father's death, that he had given notes to son); Smith v. Moore, 142 N.C. 277, 55 S.E. 275, syl. 2 (1906) (declaration by deceased life tenant that she had made a deed to her son-in-law and the reason for making the deed); First Nat. Bank v. Holland, 99 Va. 495, 39 S.E. 126, 128 (1890) (husband's declaration of gift to wife).

4. McLeod v. Swain, 87 Ga. 156, 13 S.E. 315 (1891) (plaintiff in ejectment offers her former tenant's declarations that they held land as her tenants); Lamar v. Pearre, 90 Ga. 377, 17 S.E. 92, syl. 6 (1892) (possessor's declarations that land had been bought with trust funds); Dooley v. Baynes, 86 Va. 644, 10 S.E. 974, syl. 1 (1890) (possessor's declarations that he held only a life estate).

5. In Regina v. Overseers of Birmingham, 1 B. & S. 763, 121 Eng.Rep. 897 (K.B.1861) and in Regina v. Governors and Guardians of Exeter, L.R. 4 Q.B. 341 (1869) declarant's assertions of tenancy were admitted, not to prove that he did not have a fee simple, but that he had a tenancy at the stated rental. Morgan and Maguire, Cases on Evidence, 599 (3d ed. 1951). This use is disapproved in 5 Wigmore, Evidence, § 1458.

he had previously made a wider claim, but the cases present situations where the declarations could have come in without question as admissions of a party's predecessor.[6]

In respect to declarations against pecuniary interest, the clearest example is the acknowledgment that the declarant is indebted.[7] Here the fact acknowledged, standing alone, is against interest, and the statement would ordinarily be so likewise, as evidence which could be used against him to prove the debt. Less obviously an acknowledgment of receipt of money in payment of a debt owing to the declarant is also traditionally classed as against interest.[8] Here the fact of payment, looked on at the time it is received and assuming it is then undisputed, is advantageous to the receiver. But looking at the

declaration retrospectively as the courts do, they say it is against interest because it is evidence of the reduction or extinguishment of the debt.[9] Of course, a receipt for money which the receiver is to hold for another is an acknowledgment of a debt.[10] Similarly, a statement that one holds money in trust is against interest.[11]

We have seen that an acknowledgment of indebtedness by the declarant is recognized as against interest. The English cases seem to have been narrowly channeled in the areas of debt and property, but the American cases have properly extended the field of declarations against interest to include acknowledgment of facts which would give rise to a liability for unliquidated damages for tort [12] or

---

6. Carr v. Bizzell, 192 N.C. 212, 134 S.E. 462, syl. 1 (1926); Barlow v. Greer, 222 S.W. 301, syl. 3 (Tex. Civ.App.1920).

7. German Ins. Co. v. Bartlett, 188 Ill. 165, 58 N.E. 1075, syl. 1 (1900) (in suit of deceased husband's creditors against wife to whom he had conveyed property, she was allowed to prove his declarations that he was indebted to her); Truelsch v. Northwestern Mut. Life Ins. Co., 186 Wis. 239, 202 N.W. 352, syl. 1, 2 (1925) (suit by wife on life policy on husband; husband's employer claims lien on policy for money embezzled and used to pay premiums; husband's letter to wife before his suicide acknowledging defalcations admitted as declaration against interest: good opinion by Burr W. Jones, J.)

8. Palter Cap Co. v. Great Western Life Assur. Co., [1936] 2 D.L.R. 304 (physician's entry in cash book of money received from patient, to show date of consultation); Mentzer v. Burlingame, 85 Kan. 641, 118 Pac. 698, syl. 1 (1911) (declaration of holder that notes were paid).

9. See, e. g., Coffin v. Bucknam, 12 Me. 471, 473 (1835) (entry of part payment on note by deceased former holder admitted for administrator suing on note, to avoid statute of limitations; "the indorsement was then clearly against his interest, furnishing proof that he had received part of the contents of the note"; Chenango Bridge Co. v. Paige, 83 N.Y. 178 (1880) (treasurer's books showing amount of tolls received admitted "as they charged him with the amount of such tolls"). Cases supporting this theory are cited and analyzed in Jefferson, op. cit., 58 Harv.L.Rev. at 8–17, and Morgan, op. cit., 5 Vand.L.Rev. 454–456. Wigmore,

however, without adequate discussion, rejects it. § 1462.

10. Manning v. Lechmere, 1 Atk. 453, 26 Eng.Rep. 288 (Ch.1737) (L.Ch. Hardwicke: "Where there are old rentals, and bailiffs have admitted money received by them, these rentals are evidence of the payment because no other can be had"); Barry v. Bebbington, 4 Term R. 514, 100 Eng.Rep. 1149 (1792) (steward's receipts); Keesling v. Powell, 149 Ind. 372, 49 N.E. 265 (1898) (statement by tax officer that taxes had been paid in).

11. Gleadow v. Atkin, 1 Cr. & M. 410, 149 Eng.Rep. 459 (Ex., 1833).

12. Pennsylvania R. Co. v. Rochinski, 158 F.2d 325 (C.A.D.C.1946) (acknowledgment by passenger that he had dropped suit-case while trying to place it in rack, which injured fellow-passenger), noted 15 Geo.Wash.L.Rev. 486; Weber v. Chicago, R. I. & P. Ry. Co., 175 Iowa 358, 151 N.W. 852, 864, syl. 13, 14 (1915) (action by passenger for injury in derailment: declaration of K., who later became insane, that he had unbolted the rails, admitted as against interest as constituting "basis of an action against him for damages"); Halvorsen v. Moon & Kerr Lbr. Co., 87 Minn. 18, 91 N.W. 28 (1902) (plaintiff sues defendant for destruction of his shop from fire on defendant's premises; held, defendant entitled to prove declarations of S., plaintiff's employee, since deceased, that plaintiff's fire due to boiling over of lard kettle, of which S. was in charge, while S. had gone out of the room; the facts furnish the basis of a "pecuniary claim" for negligence); Windorski v. Doyle, 219 Minn. 402, 18 N.W.2d 142, syl. 9, 10 (1945) (action against tavern owner for death of patron struck by another pa-

seemingly for breach of contract.[13] A corresponding extension to embrace statements of facts which would constitute a defense to a claim for damages which the declarant would otherwise have, has been recognized in this country.[14]

255. Penal Interest:[1] Interest of Prestige or Self-Esteem.

In 1844 in the Sussex Peerage Case[2] the House of Lords, ignoring precedents, determined that a declaration confessing a crime committed by declarant is not receivable as a declaration against interest. This decision, perhaps more than any other, has been influential in confining the development of this exception to the hearsay rule within narrow materialistic limits. It has been generally followed in this country in criminal cases.[3]

In civil cases, the courts, while not repudiating the limitation, have sometimes been able to justify the admission of the third person's confession of crime upon the somewhat artificial theory that the particular crime was also a tort and thus the fact declared was against material interest in subjecting the declarant to liability for damages.[4]

Can the practice of excluding such confessions in criminal cases be justified? Certainly not on the ground that an acknowledgment of facts rendering one liable to criminal punishment is less trustworthy than an acknowledgment of a debt. The motivation for the exclusion is probably a different one, namely, the fear of opening a door to a flood of perjured witnesses falsely testifying to con-

---

tron; declarations of bartender, since dead, that assault was unprovoked, and that he had warned offending patron against threats, held receivable for plaintiff as declaration against interest; the facts "may reasonably furnish a basis of a pecuniary claim against him as he was in sole charge of the bar-room;" in this case, consciousness of speaking against interest seems unlikely and the real source of reliability seems rather the absence of motive to falsify). But compare Aetna Life Ins. Co. v. Strauch, 179 Okl. 617, 67 P.2d 452, syl. 3, 4 (1937) where the confession of a husband who had insured his wife's life for his own benefit and then murdered her, was received as a declaration against interest, but the court derided the theory that it was against interest as admitting a tort liability and relied on the theory that the facts confessed deprived him of the right to collect the policy.

13. Jefferson, op. cit., 58 Harv.L.Rev. at 30, n. 62, but the cases cited are explainable under the theory of admissions of a party's predecessor.

14. Georgia Railroad & Banking Co. v. Fitzgerald, 108 Ga. 507, 509, 34 S.E. 316, syl. 1 (1899) (action for death of brakeman, in coupling cars; declaration of deceased that injury was caused by his foot striking an obstacle on tracks, held admissible against widow who claimed death due to "flying switch," first because she is "in privity" with deceased, and hence an admission, and second, declaration against interest, but query as to latter, whether he was probably conscious that the fact was against interest); Walker v. Brautner, 59 Kan. 117, 121, 124, 52 Pac. 80 (1898) (action for death of engineer: his declarations after the collision that he had not kept a lookout received as

against interest); Kwiatowski v. John Lowry Inc., 276 N.Y. 126, 11 N.E.2d 563, 114 A.L.R. 916 (1937) (death action; statements by deceased showing no liability admissible both as admissions and as declarations against interest); Jewell v. El Paso Elec. Co., 47 S.W.2d 328, syl. 4 (Tex.Civ. App., 1932) (death action; statement of deceased that it was his own fault, admitted as against interest); Note, Admissibility of statements by deceased against interest in death actions, 114 A.L.R. 921. But compare Tucker v. Oldbury Urban Dist. Council, [1921] 2 K.B. 317 (Ct.App.) where in death action for alleged injury causing blood poison, declarations of deceased after time of alleged injury that he left work because of a whitlow," were held properly rejected because he then had made no claim and was not conscious that the statement was against interest.

1. 5 Wigmore, Evidence, §§ 1476, 1477, Notes, 21 Minn. L.Rev. 181 (1937), 162 A.L.R. 446; 22 C.J.S., Criminal Law, § 749; Dec.Dig., Criminal Law, ☞417 (15).

2. 11 Cl. & F. 85, 8 Eng.Rep. 1034.

3. Donnelly v. United States, 228 U.S. 243, 272, 33 Sup.Ct. 449, 57 L.Ed. 820 (1913) (Holmes, Lurton, and Hughes, J.J., dissenting); Bryant v. State, 197 Ga. 641, 30 S.E.2d 259, syl. 16, 17 (1944); Rushing v. State, 88 Okl.Cr. 82, 199 P.2d 614, syl. 9, 10 (1948); Comm. v. Antonini, 165 Pa.Super. 501, 69 A.2d 436, syl. 10, 11 (1949) (offered against the accused), and numerous cases cited in sources in note 1, supra.

4. See, e. g., Weber v. Chicago, R. I. & P. Ry. Co., 175 Iowa 358, 151 N.W. 852, 864, syl. 13, 14 (1915) (confession that declarant had unbolted rail, causing derailment of train).

fessions that were never made. This fear seems reflected in the Texas decisions which while receiving such confessions, have hedged their admission with restrictions seeking to limit their use to situations where they are most needed and most reliable.[5]

Wigmore, however, is probably right in believing that the argument of the danger of perjury is a dubious one since the danger is one that attends all human testimony, and in concluding that "any rule which hampers an honest man in exonerating himself is a bad rule, even if it also hampers a villain in falsely passing for an innocent."[6] Under this banner, saluted also by Holmes, J.,[7] in a famous dissent, a few progressive courts have relaxed the rule of exclusion of declarations against penal interest in particular situations.[8] Moreover, one divisional court in a civil case, has espoused the general principle that declarations against penal interest should stand on a parity with those against pecuniary and proprietary interest,[9] only to find another division of the same court refusing, in a later criminal case, to depart from the rule of exclusion.[10]

5. Cameron v. State, 153 Tex.Cr. 374, 217 S.W.2d 23, syl. 4, 5 (1949) (admissible when the state is relying solely upon circumstantial evidence, when guilt of declarant is inconsistent with guilt of accused and when facts show that declarant was so situated that he might have committed crime.)

6. 5 Wigmore, Evidence, § 1477.

7. "The confession of Joe Dick, since deceased, that he committed the murder for which the plaintiff in error was tried, coupled with circumstances pointing to its truth, would have a very strong tendency to make anyone outside of a court of justice believe that Donnelly did not commit the crime. I say this, of course, on the supposition that it should be proved that the confession really was made, and that there was no ground for connecting Donnelly with Dick. The rules of evidence in the main are based on experience, logic, and common sense, less hampered by history than some parts of the substantive law. There is no decision by this court against the admissibility of such a confession; the English cases since the separation of the two countries do not bind us; the exception to the hearsay rule in the case of declarations against interest is well known; no other statement is so much against interest as a confession of murder; it is far more calculated to convince than dying declarations, which would be let in to hang a man (Mattox v. United States, 146 U.S. 140, 36 L.Ed. 917, 13 Sup. Ct.Rep. 50); and when we surround the accused with so many safeguards, some of which seem to me excessive; I think we ought to give him the benefit of a fact that, if proved, commonly would have such weight. The history of the law and the arguments against the English doctrine are so well and fully stated by Mr. Wigmore that there is no need to set them forth at greater length. 2 Wigmore, Ev. §§ 1476, 1477." Holmes, J., dissenting in Donnelly v. United States, 228 U.S. 243, 277, 33 Sup.Ct. 449, 57 L.Ed. 820 (1913).

8. See, e. g., People v. Lettrich, 413 Ill. 172, 108 N.E. 2d 488, syl. 8, 9 (1952), noted 6 Vand.L.Rev. 924; Brennan v State, 151 Md. 265, 135 Atl. 148, syl. 10, 11, 48 A.L.R. 342 (1926) (bastardy; declarations of third person, who associated with prosecutrix, and committed suicide on day child born, admitting he was father and letter stating suicide prompted by responsibility for pregnancy, admissible—two judges dissenting); Thomas v. State, 186 Md. 446, 47 A.2d 43, syl. 4, 167 A.L.R. 390 (1946) (where witness for state has himself confessed to crime for which accused is tried, accused entitled to show that confession and circumstances under which it was made, as bearing upon the reliability of his own confession which he claims was made under mistake: the witness of course was not unavailable, but the court supported its holding under present principle); Hines v. Comm., 136 Va. 728, 117 S.E. 843, syl. 8, 9, 35 A.L.R. 431 (1923) (murder, with circumstantial evidence pointing both to accused and to third person, since deceased; held, accused entitled to prove third person's confession; persuasive opinion by Kelly, P.); Newberry v. Comm., 191 Va. 318, 61 S.E.2d 318, syl. 10, 11 (1950) (defendant charged with murder of his wife; circumstances indicated his brother as possible killer; brother refused to testify on ground of immunity as joint indictee; held, "under facts and circumstances of this case," accused was entitled to introduce brother's confession).

9. Sutter v. Easterly, 354 Mo. 282, 189 S.W.2d 284, syl. 5–7, 162 A.L.R. 437 (1945) (suit to set aside a judgment for fraud; affidavit of witness on whose testimony judgment secured confessing perjury at party's behest, admissible as declaration against interest, witness now claiming privilege; "This statement subjected him not only to the possibility of indictment and imprisonment, but to the prospect of being held up to public shame in his community. It is completely unrealistic to say that a statement of such character is not 'against one's interest' and 'unlikely to be either deliberately false or heedlessly incorrect.'"; masterly opinion by Douglas, J.).

10. State v. Gorden, 356 Mo. 1010, 204 S.W.2d 713, syl. 3 (1947) (prosecution of father for incest with

Moreover, the restriction to material interests, ignoring as it does other motives just as influential upon the minds and hearts of men, should be more widely relaxed. Declarations against social interests, such as acknowledgments of facts which would subject the declarant to ridicule or disgrace,[11] or facts calculated to arouse in the declarant a sense of shame or remorse,[12] seem adequately buttressed in trustworthiness and should be received under the present principle.[13]

256. Balancing the Interests.[1]

(a) *The English Tradition.* The determination, in cases of conflicting interests, of what declarations were receivable as against interest, was discussed in the English decisions of the 1700s and early 1800s with what seems to us a rather arid casuistry.

It was, however, a casuistry mainly directed toward widening rather than contracting admissibility, by expanding the old, narrow categories such as bailiffs' and receivers' entries, and declarations of possessors claiming a limited interest, under a new principle of declarations against interest. The tendency was to look only to the prima facie aspect of the declaration and if that were disserving to admit it, though offered to prove a fact that was obviously self-serving.[2] This tendency finds reflection also in some later English and American holdings,[3] but the courts today may probably be expected when new types of declarations are offered to scrutinize more often the purpose for which the evidence is offered, and limit the use of the declaration only to show facts against the declarant's interest.[4] Similarly, the earlier cases adopted

daughter; daughter claims privilege against self-incrimination; held, daughter's confession inadmissible as declaration against interest; would violate right of accused to confront the witness; "civil authorities" not controlling).

11. See State v. Alcorn, 7 Idaho 599, 64 Pac. 1014, 1017 (1901) (homicide by abortion of unmarried girl: victim's declaration that she was pregnant admissible here as res gestae; "the declaration was against the interest of deceased").

12. See Uniform Rules of Evidence, R. 63, subs. (10), which admits under an exception to the hearsay rule "a statement which the judge finds was at the time of the assertion so far contrary to the declarant's pecuniary or propriety interest or so far subjected him to civil or criminal liability or so far rendered invalid a claim by him against another or created such risk of making him an object of hatred, ridicule or social disapproval in the community that a reasonable man in his position would not have made the statement unless he believed it to be true."

13. See quotation from Sutter v. Easterly, supra note 9. Probably some cases admitting declarations made before death, that the declarant has shot himself with intent to commit suicide, may best be justified on this ground. See, e. g., Commonwealth Life Ins. Co. v. Clarke, 276 Ky. 151, 123 S.W.2d 811, syl. 4 (1938).

1. 5 Wigmore, Evidence, §§ 1463, 1464; Jefferson, op. cit., 58 Harv.L.Rev. 43–63; Morgan, op. cit., 5 Vand.L.Rev. 470–473.

2. See, e. g., Warren v. Greenfield, 2 Strange 1129, 93 Eng.Rep. 1079 (K.B.1740) (to show surrender of a widow's interest in 1699, attorney's book containing a charge for drawing the surrender, and entry of payment therefor, admitted to fortify the presumption from lapse of time); Peaceable d. Uncle v. Watson, 4 Taunt. 16, 128 Eng.Rep. 232 (C.P.1811) (declaration of tenant that he was tenant of X, to show he was such tenant and hence that X was seized); Higham v. Ridgway, 10 East 109, 103 Eng. Rep. 717 (K.B.1808) (to prove date of birth, midwife's entry showing attendance on birth and charge therefor, coupled with entry of payment of charges six months later, admitted since entry of payment "was in prejudice of the party making it").

3. See, e. g., Queen v. Governors and Guardians of Exeter, L.R. 4 Q.B. 341 (1869) (entry by occupier of house that he was tenant at certain rent, and had paid it, admissible as against interest, to show both facts of tenancy and payment); Taylor v. Witham, 3 Ch.D. 605 (1875) (Taylor paid Witham £2000 and after Taylor's death his executor contends this was a loan and Witham asserts it was a gift; entry in Taylor's books of three month's interest, £20 paid by Witham, admitted for the executor to show a loan since "the natural meaning of the entry standing alone" was against interest); Knapp v. St. Louis Trust Co., 199 Mo. 640, 98 S.W. 70, syl. 3 (1906) (on issue of testamentary capacity, doctor's entry of charge for attendance for "hyperaemia of brain" and entry of payment on same day admitted, relying on Higham v. Ridgway, supra).

4. See, e. g., Allen v. Dillard, 15 Wash.2d 35, 129 P.2d 813, syl. 16 (1942). That was a suit to enforce an alleged contract by J. to leave part of her estate

the practice, when a declaration against interest was shown, to admit other declarations which formed part of the same statement, even though these latter declarations were neutral as to the declarant's interest or even self-serving.[5] A certain latitude as to contextual statements, neutral as to interest, giving meaning to the declaration against interest seems defensible, but bringing in self-serving statements contextually seems questionable.

(b) *Disserving Quality Dependent on Outside Facts.* It may often happen that a declaration acknowledging some act, or some relationship, of the declarant may be for his interest or against his interest dependent upon outside facts not disclosed in the declaration. Admissibility then should hinge on these external facts. Thus admissibility of a statement that declarant is a member of a certain partnership should depend upon whether the firm is clearly solvent, or is on the other hand of doubtful solvency or insolvent.[6] A declaration that one has a contract to purchase a given amount of wheat at a certain price is against, or for interest, depending upon the market value of wheat when the declaration was made.

(c) *Disserving Quality Dependent upon Purpose for Which Declaration Is Offered: The Relativity of Interest.* Most quantitative statements except the "all" or "nothing" kind, have a double aspect. One who declares, "I hold a ten-year lease on the X building" is declaring, first, that his leasehold is for not less than ten years, and second, that it is for not more than ten years. The like is obviously true of declarations about the amount of a debt owed to or by the declarant, or of the acreage or boundary of his farm. Thus it seems that if the claim of the ten year lease is offered to show that declarant had a tenancy of that duration, as against an adverse contention that the tenancy was for only five years, it should be obviously rejected as in favor of interest. If, on the other hand, it were offered to rebut a claim by the adversary that the tenancy was for fifteen years it should be received as against interest. Moreover, it is believed that when so offered it is immaterial that the declaration was *made* by the declarant with the self-assertive purpose of claiming as much as he could. He would still have been conscious that if his lease were actually longer it would be against his interest to claim less. This type of dec-

---

to plaintiff. Plaintiff offered a declaration of T., that he and J. had agreed to leave their property to each other or the other's heirs. The court held in a discriminating opinion by Beals, J., that while the declaration may have been against interest in reciting T's obligation under the contract, it was not so in reciting J.'s promise and could not be received to prove such promise.

5. The leading case for admitting contextual statements is Higham v. Ridgway, described supra n. 2, where the entry of payment made six months after the entry of charge for the services was held to bring in the latter. "By the reference to the ledger, the entry there is virtually incorporated in the other entry [of payment], of which it is explanatory." See also Smith v. Moore, 142 N.C. 277, 286, 55 S.E. 275, 278 (1906) ("The declaration is admissible as an entirety, including statements therein which were not in themselves against interest, but which are integral or substantial parts of the declaration, the reason why this is so being that the portion which is trustworthy, because against interest, imparts credit to the whole declaration.")

Cases to like effect are cited in 5 Wigmore, Evidence, § 1465, and in Jefferson, op. cit., 58 Harv. L.Rev. 57–63, where he criticises the doctrine. See also the Model Code of Evidence, R. 509(2) (". . . a declaration against interest and such additional parts thereof, including matter incorporated by reference, as the judge finds to be so closely connected with the declaration against interest as to be equally trustworthy.").

6. Compare Humes v. O'Bryan, 74 Ala. 64, 78, syl. 4, 5, 1883. This was a suit against Humes upon an alleged partnership debt contracted by Glover in the operation of a plantation. The court held that a declaration by Glover, made when the plantation business was insolvent, that Humes was not a partner, was a declaration against interest, but otherwise if the business had not been insolvent. See also Flood v. Russell, L.R., Ireland [1891] 29 Ch. 91, 96, involving a wife's declaration that her husband had made his will leaving her a half-interest in his property, where it appeared that under the terms of a family settlement and under the law of survivorship she would have taken a larger interest if he had died intestate.

larations should be judged self-serving or disserving depending upon whether they are offered to show that the amount is not less than, or not more than, the amount asserted by the declarant.[7]

(d) *Declarations Containing Self-Serving and Disserving Facts.* When a declaration contains statements of facts in favor of interest, and in addition statements of facts against interest, three methods of handling the evidence under this exception have been advocated. First, admit the entire declaration because part is disserving [8] and hence by a kind of contagion of truthfulness, all will be trustworthy. Second, compare the strength of the self-serving interest and the disserving interest in making the statement as a whole, and admit it all if the disserving interest preponderates, and exclude it all if the self-serving interest is greater.[9] Third, admit the disserving parts of the declaration, and exclude the self-serving parts.[10] The third solution seems the most realistic method of adjusting admissibility to trustworthiness, where the serving and disserving parts can be severed.

In determining whether a particular statement is against interest, where the declarant had both self-serving and disserving motives, the balancing of one against the other is of course appropriate.[11] The classic instance is the acknowledgment of receipt of part payment on a note. If the payment is acknowledged as made before the statute of limitations has run, the statement is preponderantly against interest and comes in under the exception.[12] If the payment is acknowledged to be made after the running of the statute, in a jurisdiction where such a payment revives the note, it is considered preponderantly in favor of interest.[13]

(e) *Motive to Falsify.*[14] It has traditionally been stated as a requisite to admissibility under this exception that there must have been no motive to falsify the facts.[15] This is too sweeping, and the limitation can probably best be understood merely as a qualification that even though a declaration be against interest in one respect, if it appears that the declarant had some other motive whether of self-interest or otherwise, which was likely to lead him to misrepresent the facts, the declaration will be excluded.[16]

---

7. This is the view of the commentators. The only case presenting the question held to the contrary. Veach's Adm'r v. Louisville & I. Ry. Co., 190 Ky. 678, 238 S.W. 35, syl. 2, 3 (1921) (death action: to show that decedent earned *at least* so much, decedent's income tax return showing an income of $4000 for the year, held inadmissible as "self-serving," whereas it seems that if her income were less she would have been conscious that it was against her interest to report so much), criticised in Note, 30 Yale L.J. 854, 5 Wigmore, Evidence, § 1464, n. 2, Morgan, op. cit., 5 Vand.L.Rev. 471.

8. Higham v. Ridgway, and other authorities cited in note 5, supra.

9. Massee-Felton Lbr. Co. v. Sirmans, 122 Ga. 297, 50 S.E. 92, syl. 2 (1905) (sheriff's entry showing tax execution, levy on land, sale and charging himself with price paid by bidder and discharging himself by stating that he applied the money to the tax, held, admitted as a whole because, on balance against interest).

10. Allen v. Dillard, 15 Wash.2d 35, 129 P.2d 813, syl. 13 (1942), described note 4, supra; Jefferson, op.

cit., 58 Harv.L.Rev. 50; and see Morgan, op. cit., 5 Vand.L.Rev. 470–473.

11. Demasi v. Whitney Trust & Savings Bank, 176 So. 703, 711, syl. 17–19 (La.App., 1937) (affidavit by depositor signed in order to get remaining funds in disputed account, stating that challenged withdrawals were with her consent, rejected as a whole because self-interest in getting cash preponderated); 5 Wigmore, Evidence, § 1464, note 2.

12. Addams v. Seitzinger, 1 W. & S. 243 (Pa.1841); 5 Wigmore, Evidence § 1466.

13. Small v. Rose, 97 Me. 286, 54 Atl. 726, syl. 2 (1903).

14. 5 Wigmore, Evidence, § 1464; Jefferson, op. cit., 58 Harv.L.Rev. 52–57; 31 C.J.S. Evidence, § 221.

15. See, e. g., German Ins. Co. v. Bartlett, 188 Ill. 165, 58 N.E. 1075, 1077 (1900); Halvorsen v. Moon & Kerr Lumber Co., 87 Minn. 18, 91 N.W. 28, 29 (1902).

16. Demasi v. Whitney Trust & Savings Bank, 176 So. 703, syl. 17–19 (La.App.1937) (affidavit of de-

257. Unavailability of the Declarant.[1]

There is strong argument for dispensing with any requirement that the declarant be unavailable as a witness as a prerequisite for receiving his declarations under this exception to the hearsay rule. The reasoning which admits the admissions of a party [2] and spontaneous declarations (such as excited utterances or declarations of present mental or bodily state),[3] without regard to the availability of the party or the declarant—namely that the admission, or the spontaneous declaration, is just as credible as his present testimony would be—seems equally applicable to the declaration against interest.[4] However, the early English cases limited the scope of the exception to decedents' declarations [5] and the only question has been whether other grounds of unavailability would be accepted. Only in recent decades has insanity been recognized as a ground.[6] Any reason why the declarant cannot be brought in at the trial should suffice, such as physical incapacity,[7] absence of the witness from the jurisdiction [8] or inability of the party to find him,[9] his supervening disqualification as a witness,[10] or his successful claim of privilege.[11] But the holdings are checkered.

positor that previous withdrawals had been with her consent, excluded because it appeared that affidavit was presented by bank for her signature as prerequisite to her withdrawing balance of account); Roe v. Journegan, 175 N.C. 261, 95 S.W. 495, syl. 5 (1918) (issue as to delivery of deed of 1881 from father to son; son's declaration thereafter that he had no land and that his father had offered him some but he would not accept it, excluded, because son "evidently thought the deed of 1881, conveying to him a life estate was injurious to him" and apparently believed he would get the land in fee by deed or inheritance). But occasionally this kind of counter-motive seems to be treated as a mere matter of credibility. See Johnson v. Peterson, 101 Neb. 504, 163 N.W. 869, 871, syl. 3 (1917).

1. 5 Wigmore, § 1456, Jefferson, op. cit., 58 Harv. L. Rev. 6–8, Morgan, op. cit., 5 Vand.L.Rev. 475; 31 C.J.S., Evidence, § 218.

2. See ch. 27, and especially § 239.

3. See Ch. 30, and especially §§ 265, 268, 272, 273.

4. Accordingly, the Uniform Rules of Evidence, R. 63, subs. 10 dispenses with the requirement of unavailability.

5. Harrison v. Blades, 3 Camp. 457, 170 Eng.Rep. 1444 (N.P.1813) (Illness insufficient; "if such a relaxation . . . were permitted there would be very sudden indispositions and recovery"); Stephen v. Gwenap, 1 M. & Rob. 120, 174 Eng.Rep. 41 (Ex. 1831) (absence of witness in America insufficient).

6. Weber v. Chicago, R. I. & P. Ry. Co., 175 Iowa 358, 151 N.W. 852, 861, syl. 14 (1915); Jones v. Henry, 84 N.C. 320, 324 (1881) (dictum); New Amsterdam Cas. Co. v. First Nat. Bank, 134 S.W.2d 470, syl. 1 (Tex.Civ.App.1939).

7. See Griffith v. Sauls, 77 Tex. 630, 14 S.W. 230, syl. 1 (1890) (declarations of bystander as to running of boundary-line, which court assumed would be competent if declarant shown unavailable, held, fact that declarant was old and had lost power of speech sufficient; "In what would he be better than a dead man, in so far as the production of his testimony is concerned?"). Compare Harrison v. Blades, note 5, supra.

8. Sufficient. Walnut Ridge Merc. Co. v. Cohn, 79 Ark. 338, 96 S.W. 413, 416, syl. 7 (1906) (receipt inadmissible because writer not shown to be "dead or beyond the jurisdiction of the court"); Shearman v. Atkins, 21 Mass. 283, 293, syl. 3 (1826). Contra: Stephen v. Gwenap, supra, note 5.

9. Pennsylvania R. Co. v. Rochinski, 158 F.2d 325 (1946) (defendant's claim agent unable to find declarant at address he gave; sufficient to show unavailability) noted 15 Geo.Wash.L.Rev. 486.

10. Disqualification for interest, sufficient. Dwight, v. Brown, 9 Conn. 83, 93 (1831); Harriman v. Brown, 35 Va. (8 Leigh) 697, 713 (1837). Contra: Tom Love Grocery Co. v. Maryland Casualty Co., 166 Tenn. 275, 61 S.W.2d 672, syl. 4 (1933) (declarant disqualified by conviction for burglary: "The exception should not be extended to include infamy along with insanity and death as another ground of unavailability").

11. Sutter v. Easterly, 354 Mo. 282, 189 S.W.2d 284, syl. 5, 162 A.L.R. 437 (1945) (suit to set aside judgment secured by perjured testimony: affidavit of witness who participated in conspiracy to secure the judgment received as declaration against interest, ground of unavailability the fact that the affiant refused in present suit to testify about the conspiracy claiming self-crimination privilege) noted 24 Tex.L.Rev. 217, but see State v. Gordon, 356 Mo. 1010, 204 S.W.2d 713, syl. 3 (1947) where this ground of unavailability is held insufficient to let in a declaration against the accused in a criminal case, as being inconsistent with right of confrontation.

CHAPTER 29

DYING DECLARATIONS

258. Introductory.[*]

Of the doctrines which authorize the admission of special classes of out-of-court statements as exceptions to the hearsay rule, that relating to dying declarations is the most mystical in its theory and the most arbitrary in its limitations. The notion of the special likelihood of truthfulness of deathbed statements was widespread, of course, long before the recognition, in the early seventeen hundreds, of a general rule against hearsay. It is natural enough, then, that about as soon as we find a hearsay rule we find also a recognized exception for dying declarations.[†]

259. Requirements that Declarant Must Have Been Conscious of Impending Death and that Death Actually Ensue.

The central notions on which rests the popular reverence for deathbed statements are embodied in the first two limiting rules. Unlike the more recent limitations, which will be mentioned later, these two rules are rational enough, though possibly they have drawn too sharply the lines of restriction.

The first is—and this is the commonest battle-ground of admissibility—that the declarant must at the time he made his statement have been conscious that death was near and certain.[1] He must have lost all hope of recovery.[2] It is quite arguable that a belief in the probability of impending death would make most men strongly disposed to tell the truth and hence guarantee the needed special reliability. But belief in certainty, not mere likelihood, is the formula insisted on and rigorously applied. Usually this belief is proven by evidence of the declarant's own statements of such belief at the time, his expression of his "settled hopeless expecta-

---

[*] See 5 Wigmore, Evidence, §§ 1430–1452; Decennial Digests, Homicide, ⊛200–221, Evidence, 275½; Howard L. Smith, Dying Declarations, 3 Wis.L.Rev. 193 (1925) (criticising the narrowness of the common law rules of admissibility); Ryan, Dying Declarations in Colorado, 21 Rocky Mt.L.Rev. 106 (1948); Notes, Townsend, Dying Declarations in North Carolina, 14 N.C.L.Rev. 380 (1936), Warp, Dying Declarations in Ohio, 12 U.Cin.L.Rev. 570 (1938); Klugman, Admissibility of Dying Declarations, 39 J.Crim.L. 646 (1949); 40 C.J.S. 1249–1287; 26 Am.Jur. 425–452.

[†] See the early cases listed in 5 Wigmore, Evidence, § 1430, note.

[1] For statements of the formula, see, e. g., People v. Tilley, 406 Ill. 398, 94 N.E.2d 328, 331, syl. 3 (1950); State v. Bright, 215 N.C. 537, 2 S.E.2d 541, syl. 1 (1939); Thomas v. Comm., 183 Va. 501, 32 S.E.2d 711, syl. 9 (1945).

[2] Shepard v. United States, 290 U.S. 96, 54 Sup.Ct. 22, syl. 2, 5, 78 L.Ed. 196 (1933) (leading opinion by Cardozo, J.); Tillman v. State, 44 So.2d 644, syl. 3 (Fla.1950); People v. Allen, 300 N.Y. 322, 90 N.E.2d 48, syl. 6 (1949). But if made under consciousness of doom a later revival of hope will not be ground of exclusion. State v. Reed, 53 Kan. 767, 37 Pac. 174, syl. 4 (1894); Crum v. Comm., 242 Ky. 568, 46 S.W. 2d 1093, syl. 2 (1932).

tion." [3] That the deceased should have made such a statement is not required,[4] however, and his belief may be shown circumstantially by the apparent fatal quality of the wound,[5] by the statements made to the declarant by the doctor or by others that his condition is hopeless,[6] and by other circumstances.[7]

What if the preliminary evidence that declarant was conscious of impending death is ambiguous or is disputed by contrary evidence? Who decides this preliminary question? Under the traditional practice all such questions of fact are for the trial judge, and most courts would follow that practice here.[8] Other courts, however, as in the case of confessions,[9] have adopted a practice of admitting the dying declarations if reasonable men could differ as to whether the declarant was conscious that death was at hand.[10] They seek to enforce the safeguard contemplated by the rule by instructing the jury to disregard the supposed dying declaration altogether, unless they find it was made when the decedent believed he was about to die. Juries are interested in guilt or innocence, not in the exclusion of relevant evidence, and it cannot be supposed that such an admonition will be obeyed when the circumstances of the declaration persuade the jury of its truth.

The second rational limitation is the obvious one that the declarant must be dead, when the evidence is offered.[11] It is not required that the death must have followed at any very short interval after the declaration. Periods even extending into months have been held not too long. The test is the declarant's belief in the nearness of death when he made the statement, not the actual swiftness with which death ensued.[12]

---

3. See, e. g., Long v. Comm., 262 Ky. 619, 90 S.W.2d 1007, syl. 4 (1936).

4. State v. Mitchell, 209 N.C. 1, 182 S.E. 695, syl. 1 (1935); Comm. v. Knable, 369 Pa. 171, 85 A.2d 114, syl. 2 (1952), and see Shepard v. United States, 290 U.S. 96, 100, 54 Sup.Ct. 22, 98 L.Ed. 196 (1933) ("There is no unyielding ritual of words to be spoken by the dying"); Note, 12 Oh.St.L.J. 130 (1951).

5. Bland v. State, 210 Ga. 100, 73 S.E.2d 51, syl. 12 (1953). But the mere fact that the wound was mortal would not alone show consciousness of doom unless its nature were such as to reveal to the declarant its fatal character. Fulton v. State, 209 Miss. 565, 47 So.2d 883, syl. 5 (1950).

6. Sisk v. State, 182 Ga. 448, 185 S.E. 777, syl. 5 (1936) (doctor); State v. Peters, 90 N.H. 438, 10 A.2d 242, syl. 3, 4 (1939) (nurse).

7. See cases collected in 5 Wigmore, Evidence, § 1442; Dec.Dig., Homicide, ☞203–205.

8. E. g., Comer v. State, 212 Ark. 66, 204 S.W.2d 875, syl. 7 (1947); Tillman v. State, 44 So.2d 644, syl. 3, 4 (Fla.1950); People v. Hubbs, 401 Ill. 613, 83 N.E.2d 289, 297, syl. 16 (1949) (admissibility for court, weight for jury); State v. Rich, 231 N.C. 696, 58 S.E.2d 720, syl. 4 (1950). Cases pro and con are collected in 5 Wigmore, Evidence, § 1451, and in Dec.Dig., Homicide, ☞218. But if the judge admits the declaration the jury in appraising its weight may consider, among other factors of credibility, whether they believe that the declaration was made under a sense of impending death. Comm. v. Kna-

ble, 369 Pa. 171, 85 A.2d 114, syl. 4 (1952) (semble); and see State v. Custer, 336 Mo. 514, 80 S.W.2d 176, syl. 4–6 (1935) (jury not concluded by judge's ruling admitting dying declaration from considering on credibility whether made under sense of impending death). Hence they are entitled to hear the evidence as to the circumstances of the making of the declaration. Conway v. State, 177 Miss. 461, 171 So. 16, syl. 2 (1936); State v. Dotson, 96 W.Va. 596, 123 S.E. 463, 464 (1924).

9. See § 112, herein.

10. Emmett v. State, 195 Ga. 517, 25 S.E.2d 9, 19, syl. 5 (1943); People v. Denton, 312 Mich. 32, 19 N.W.2d 476, syl. 1 (1945); Berry v. State, 143 Tex. Cr. 67, 157 S.W.2d 650, syl. 5 (1942). Some states seem to follow the somewhat inconsistent practice of delegating to the judge the preliminary question of fact as to consciousness of impending death, but require him if he decides to admit the declaration, to direct the jury to disregard it if they find there was no such consciousness. See People v. Rulia Singh, 182 Cal. 457, 476, 188 Pac. 987, 995, syl. 2 (1920); State v. Garver, 190 Ore. 291, 225 P.2d 777, 780, syl. 14 (1950).

11. State v. Carden, 209 N.C. 404, 183 S.E. 898, syl. 7 (1936); 5 Wigmore, Evidence, § 1431.

12. See, e. g., Emmett v. State, 195 Ga. 517, 25 S.E.2d 9, syl. 6, 7 (1943) (survived 3½ months, admitted); People v. Denton, 312 Mich. 32, 19 N.W.2d 476 (1945) (survived 11 days); 5 Wigmore, Evidence, § 1441; Dec.Dig., Homicide, ☞204.

260. Limitation to Use in Prosecutions for Homicide, and Other Arbitrary Limitations.

If the courts in their creation of rules about dying declarations had stopped here, we should have had a narrow, perhaps, but rational and understandable practice. The requirement of consciousness of impending death guarantees a substantial degree of special reliability, and the requirement that declarant be dead and thus unavailable as a witness is an ample showing of the necessity for the use of hearsay. This simple rationale of dying declarations sufficed the courts up to the beginning of the eighteen hundreds, and such declarations were admitted in civil and criminal cases without distinction [1] and seemingly without untoward results. The subsequent history of the rule is an object-lesson in the dangers of the use by the judges of our system of precedents to preserve and fossilize the judicial mistakes of an earlier generation.

A mistake this development seems to have been. Sergeant East in 1803 in his widely used treatise, Pleas of the Crown, wrote: "Besides the usual evidence of guilt in general cases of felony, there is one kind of evidence more peculiar to the case of homicide, which is the declaration of the deceased, after the mortal blow, as to the fact itself, and the party by whom it is committed. Evidence of this sort is admissible in this case on the fullest necessity; for it often happens that there is no third person present to be an eye-witness to the fact; and the usual witness on occasion of other felonies, namely, the party injured himself, is gotten rid of." [2] This was seized upon for what it was obviously not intended to be, namely, an announcement that the sole justification of the admission of dying declarations is the necessity of punishing murderers, who might otherwise escape for lack of the testimony of the victim. This need is an urgent one, admittedly, but the proposition that the use of dying declarations should be limited to instances where it exists surely does not follow from the existence of the need. Nevertheless this proposition has been elaborated into a series of what may well be classed as arbitrary limiting rules, as contrasted with the two rational limitations already mentioned.

The first of these is the rule that the use of dying declarations is limited to criminal prosecutions for homicide.[3] Although the English courts in the seventeen hundreds had not hesitated to do so,[4] the courts building upon the new theory of necessity now refuse to admit dying declarations in civil cases,[5] whether death actions or other civil cases, or in criminal cases other than those charging homicide as an essential part of the offense. Thus in prosecutions for abortion [6] and rape,[7] though death of the woman may have ensued, the declarations are held inadmissible. Probably this restriction proceeds from an ob-

---

1. See Wright v. Littler, 3 Burr. 1244, 1247, 1255, 97 Eng.Rep. 812 (K.B. 1761) (in ejectment, death-bed statement that declarant had forged a will, received) and other cases cited 5 Wigmore, Evidence, § 1431, note 1.

2. East, 1 Pleas of the Crown, 353, 1803, quoted 5 Wigmore, Evidence, § 1431.

3. People v. Stison, 140 Mich. 216, 103 N.W. 542, syl. 1 (incest, excluded); Taylor v. Comm., 122 Va. 886, 94 S.E. 795, 797 (1918) (assault); Dec.Dig., Homicide, ☞211.

4. See note 1, above.

5. Prudential Ins. Co. v. Keeling's Adm'x, 271 Ky. 558, 112 S.W.2d 994, syl. 1, 2 (1938) (claim for double indemnity for fatal accident, in suit on life policy); Ross v. Cooper, 38 N.D. 173, 164 Pac. 679, syl. 3–5 (1917) (death injury); Blair v. Rogers, 185 Okl. 63, 89 P.2d 928 (1939) (death injury); Dec.Dig., Evidence, ☞275½. For statutes relaxing this restriction, see § 264, herein.

6. Winfrey v. State, 174 Ark. 729, 296 S.W. 82, syl. 2 (1927); State v. Meyer, 64 N.J.L. 382 (1900) (death not an essential element of the crime, but only affected the punishment). But where the crime charged is homicide by abortion, the declaration is admissible. State v. Yochelman, 107 Conn. 148, 139 Atl. 632, syl. 6 (1927) (manslaughter); Piercy v. State, 138 Neb. 301, 293 N.W. 99, syl. 4 (1940).

7. Frogge v. Comm., 296 Ky. 726, 178 S.W.2d 405, syl. 1 (1944).

scure feeling on the part of the judges that dying declarations, despite their supposed guaranty of trustworthiness, are a dangerous kind of testimony, which a jury is likely to handle too emotionally. But is their emotion likely to be less in a murder prosecution than in a civil action for death or in a prosecution for abortion?

Our concept of necessity limited to protection of the state against the slayer who might go free because of the death of his victim, spins out into another consequence. This is the further limitation that not only must the charge be homicide, but in order that the dying declaration may come in, the defendant in the present trial must be charged with the death of the declarant.[8] In a case [9] where a marauder shot a man and his wife at the same time, and the defendant was put on trial for the murder of the husband only, the dying declaration of the wife identifying the defendant as the assailant was offered by the State. It was excluded under this doctrine. Wigmore's comment is, "Could one's imagination devise a more senseless rule of exclusion, if he had not found it in our law?" [10]

Somewhat less arbitrary, but a source of profitless controversy, is the third of these corollary limitations, i. e., that the declarations are admissible only insofar as they relate to the circumstances of the killing and to the events more or less nearly preceding it in time and leading up to it.[11] Under this rule declarations about previous quarrels between the accused and his victim would be excluded, while transactions between them leading up to and shortly before the present attack would be received.[12] The vagueness of the criterion invites reversals.

261. Admissible on Behalf of Accused as Well as for Prosecution.

One might have anticipated that the strict application of this concept of necessity would have lead the courts to restrict the use of dying declarations to introduction by the prosecution, but the unfairness of such a result was too apparent, and it is well settled that they will be received on behalf of the defendant.[13]

262. Application of Other Evidentiary Rules: Personal Knowledge: Opinion: Rules about Writings.

Other principles of evidence law present recurrent problems in their application to dying declarations. If it appears that the declarant did not have adequate opportunity to observe the facts recounted, the declaration will be rejected for want of the knowledge-qualification.[1] This requirement is sometimes confused with the opinion-rule, and this confusion leads the courts often to declare that opinions in dying declarations will be ex-

---

8. People v. Cox, 340 Ill. 111, 172 N.E. 64, syl. 6, 7, 69 A.L.R. 1215 (1930) (annotated); State v. Puett, 210 N.C. 633, 188 S.E. 75, syl. 5 (1936); Dec. Dig., Homicide, ☞211.

9. Westberry v. State, 175 Ga. 115, 164 S.E. 905 (1932).

10. 5 Wigmore, Evidence, § 1433, note 1.

11. Lucas v. Comm., 153 Ky. 424, 155 S.W. 721, syl. 3 (1913); Walthall v. State, 144 Tex.Cr. 585, 165 S.W.2d 184, syl. 3 (1942); 5 Wigmore, Evidence, § 1344; Dec.Dig., Homicide, ☞214(2).

12. Smith v. Comm., 236 Ky. 736, 33 S.W.2d 688, syl. 6 (1930) (that defendant had fired on deceased at previous times); Jones v. State, 236 P.2d 102, syl. 16 (Okl.Cr.1951) (that defendant had threatened to kill deceased the day before the killing); Webb v.

State, 133 Tex.Cr. 32, 106 S.W.2d 683, syl. 5 (1937) (describing previous quarrel, on same afternoon, which had subsided, excluded).

13. Mattox v. United States, 146 U.S. 140, 151, 13 Sup.Ct. 50, 53, 36 L.Ed. 917 (1892); State v. Puett, 210 N.C. 633, 188 S.E. 75, syl. 4 (1936).

1. Jones v. State, 52 Ark. 347, 12 S.W. 704, syl. 2 (1889) (where declarant could not see who shot him, declaration that H. shot him properly excluded); Strickland v. State, 167 Ga. 452, 145 S.E. 879, 881, syl. 3 (1928) (requirement satisfied); 5 Wigmore, Evidence, § 1445(2). When there is room for doubt as to whether the statement is based on knowledge, the question is for the jury. Bland v. State, 210 Ga. 100, 78 S.E.2d 51, syl. 11 (1953).

cluded.[2] Of course the opinion rule, designed as a regulation of the manner of questioning of witnesses in court, is entirely inappropriate as a restriction upon out-of-court declarations.[3] Accordingly, most courts including some that have professed to apply the opinion rule here, admit declarations such as "He shot me down like a dog," [4] "He shot me without cause," [5] and "He done it a-purpose" [6] and the like,[7] which would ordinarily be excluded as opinions, if spoken by a witness on the stand.

Another such problem is the application of the Documentary Originals (Best Evidence) Rule.[8] Oftentimes the dying victim, perhaps as different people visit him, will make several oral statements about the facts of the crime, and in addition, he may make a written statement by his own hand, or the person hearing the statement may write it down and procure the declarant to sign it. When is the writing required to be produced or its absence accounted for? As to the separate oral statement, it is clear that this is provable without producing a later writing.[9] It is equally clear, of course, that the terms of a written dying statement cannot be proved as such without producing the writing.[10] What

if the witness who heard the oral statement, which was taken down and signed, offers to testify to what he heard? Wigmore argues that the execution of the writing does not call into play the rule of Integration (the Parole Evidence rule) since that is limited to contracts and other "legal acts," [11] but to a limited extent the courts have held otherwise. They have not excluded evidence of other oral statements on the same occasion, not embraced in the writing,[12] but as to oral declarations taken down and embodied in a writing signed or adopted by the deceased, these cannot be proved by one who heard them, but only by producing the written statement itself if available.[13] Even though it represents a departure from the usual practice of freedom in proving oral statements, and an extension of the doctrine of integration into a new field, the result seems well justified by the crucial need here for accuracy in transmitting to the tribunal the exact terms of the declarant's statement.

263. Instructions as to the Weight to be Given to Dying Declarations.[1]

There has been much theorizing in texts and opinions as to the weight to be given to

---

2. E.g., Roberts v. Comm., 301 Ky. 294, 191 S.W.2d 242, syl. 2 (1946) (but declarations here held admissible); State v. Wilks, 278 Mo. 481, 213 S.W. 118, syl. 2 (1919); Hollywood v. State, 19 Wyo. 493, 120 Pac. 471, syl. 11 (1912).

3. See Comm. v. Plubell, 367 Pa. 452, 80 A.2d 825, syl. 4 (1951), and Pendleton v. Comm., 131 Va. 676, 109 S.E. 201, 209, syl. 13 (1921), following 5 Wigmore, Evidence, § 1447. See § 18, herein.

4. State v. Saunders, 14 Ore. 305, 12 Pac. 441, syl. 3 (1886). See Finley v. State, 92 Tex.Cr. 543, 244 S. W. 527, syl. 1 (1922) ("He shot me in cold blood.").

5. State v. Williams, 168 N.C. 191, 83 S.E. 714, syl. 1 (1914).

6. Pippin v. Comm., 117 Va. 919, 86 S.E. 152, syl. 4 (1915).

7. Decisions are collected in 5 Wigmore, Evidence, § 1447; Notes, Dying Declarations Involving Opinions, 25 A.L.R. 1370, 63 A.L.R. 567; 40 C.J.S., Homicide, § 299; Dec.Dig., Homicide, ☞215(4).

8. See Ch. 23, herein.

9. Gray v. State, 185 Ark. 515, 48 S.W.2d 224, syl. 1, 2 (1932); Dunn v. People, 172 Ill. 582, 50 N.E. 137, syl. 1 (1898); State v. Sweeney, 203 Iowa 1305, 214 N.W. 735, syl. 6 (1927).

10. See § 209, herein.

11. 5 Wigmore, Evidence, § 1450(b).

12. Comm. v. Haney, 127 Mass. 455 (1879) (oral declarations of consciousness of impending death on same occasion as the written statement, allowed to be proved).

13. Rex v. Gay, 7 C. & P. 230, 173 Eng.Rep. 101 (N.P. 1835); Williams v. State, 26 Ala.App. 531, 163 So. 333, syl. 9, 10 (1935) (rule stated but here not shown to be signed); People v. Glenn, 10 Calif. 32, 37 (1858) (prosecution bound to produce writing but having done so can prove similar oral declarations made at other times); Couch v. State, 93 Tex.Cr. 27, 245 S.W. 692, syl. 4 (1922) (similar to Williams v. State, above). Contra: State v. Whitson, 111 N.C. 695, 16 S.E. 332, syl. 4 (1892) (dictum).

1. Cases are collected in Notes, 32 Neb.L.Rev. 461 (1953), 167 A.L.R. 147; 40 C.J.S., Homicide, § 304.

dying declarations, abstractly or in comparison with the testimony of a witness. In consequence the practice has grown up in some states of requiring [2] or permitting [3] the judge to instruct the jury that such declarations are to be received with caution. In other states such instructions are held to be improper.[4] Again one court requires that the jury be told that a dying declaration is not to be regarded as having the same value and weight as sworn testimony.[5] Others consider it proper to direct the jury that they should give the dying declaration the same weight as the testimony of a witness.[6] While there may be merit in a standardized practice of giving cautionary instructions, the direction to give the declaration equal weight with sworn testimony seems of questionable wisdom. The weight of particular dying declarations depends upon so many factors varying from case to case that no standardized instruction will fit all situations. Certainly in jurisdictions where the judge retains his common law power to comment on the weight of the evidence, the dying declaration is a most appropriate subject for such individualized comment. But where he is shorn (as in most American jurisdictions) of this power, it seems wiser to leave the weight of the declaration to the argument of counsel, the arbitrament of the jury, and the consideration of the judge on motion for new trial.

264. Decisional and Statutory Extensions of Common Law Admissibility.

One court, that of Kansas, has had the statesmanship to break the shackles of those restrictions on the use of dying declarations which we have termed the arbitrary and irrational ones. "We are confronted," the court said, "with a restrictive rule of evidence commendable only for its age, its respectability resting solely upon a habit of judicial recognition, formed without reason, and continued without justification." [1] The court concluded that in an action by the executor of the seller to recover upon a land sale contract the dying statement of the seller of "the truth about the sale" should be admitted. Two states have taken a short step forward by enacting statutes which admit dying declarations in civil actions for death injuries [2] Colorado has carried the reform to broader ground by a statute which admits dying declarations "in all civil and criminal trials and other proceedings before Courts, Commissions and other tribunals." [3] To similar effect is the Uniform Rule which without any limitation upon the type of action in which the evidence is offered, admits "a statement by a person unavailable as a witness because of his death if the judge finds that it was made voluntarily and in good faith and while the declarant was conscious of his impending death and believed that there was no hope of his recovery."[4]

2. Humphreys v. State, 166 Tenn. 523, 64 S.W.2d 5, syl. 6 (1933); State v. Mayo, 42 Wash. 540, 85 Pac. 251, syl. 9, 7 Ann.C. 881 (1906).

3. Dowdell v. State, 194 Ga. 578, 22 S.E.2d 310, syl. 4 (1942); Comm. v. Meleskie, 278 Pa. 383, 123 Atl. 310, syl. 2 (1924).

4. People v. Dallen, 21 Cal.App. 770, 132 Pac. 1064, syl. 10 (1913); Shenkenberger v. State, 154 Ind. 630, 57 N.E. 519, syl. 8 (1900).

5. People v. Mleczko, 298 N.Y. 153, 81 N.E.2d 65, syl. 8 (1948); People v. Bartelini, 285 N.Y. 433, 35 N.E.2d 29, 167 A.L.R. 139, 146 (1941). See also approving such a charge, Mitchell v. Comm., 178 Va. 407, 17 S.E.2d 370, syl. 5 (1941).

6. State v. Johns, 152 Iowa 383, 132 N.W. 832, syl. 9 (1911). See also Hubbard v. State, 208 Ga. 472, 67 S.E.2d 562, syl. 8 (1951) holding it not erroneous to instruct that dying declarations "stand upon the same plane of solemnity as statements made under oath."

1. Thurston v. Fritz, 91 Kan. 468, 475, 138 Pac. 625, 50 L.R.A.,N.S., 1167, Ann.Cas.1915D, 212 (1914).

2. Ark.Stats. § 28–712; North Carolina, G.S. § 28–173.

3. Colo., '35 C.S.A. c. 63, § 21.

4. Uniform Rules of Evidence, R. 63, sub. 5.

CHAPTER 30

SPONTANEOUS DECLARATIONS

TOPIC 1. DECLARATIONS OF BODILY CONDITION

TOPIC 1

DECLARATIONS OF BODILY CONDITION

265. Declarations as to Declarant's Bodily Feelings, Symptoms and Condition.[1]

Declarations of the declarant's present bodily condition and symptoms, including pain and other feelings, are admissible to evidence the facts declared, as an exception to the Hearsay Rule.[2] The special reliability is said to be furnished by the spontaneous quality of the declarations, supposedly assured by the fact that the declarations must purport to describe a condition presently existing at

---

[1.] 6 Wigmore, Evidence, §§ 1718–1723; 3 Jones, Evidence, §§ 1212–1217 (2d ed. rev. 1926); McBaine, Admissibility in California of Declarations of Physical or Mental Condition, 19 Calif.L.Rev. 231 (1931); Note, Strause, 51 Mich.L.Rev. 902 (1953); Note, Kuykendall, 13 N.C.L.Rev. 228 (1935); Note, 64 A.L.R. 557; Dec.Dig. Evidence, ☞127, 128, 268; 31 C.J.S. Evidence, §§ 242–246.

[2.] For statements of the rule, see Northern Pac. R. Co. v. Urlin, 158 U.S. 271, 274, 15 S.Ct. 840, 39 L. Ed. 977 (1895); Yellow Cab Co. v. Henderson, 183 Md. 546, 39 A.2d 546, 550 (1944); Munden v. Met-

ropolitan Life Ins. Co., 213 N.C. 504, 196 S.E. 872, 874 (1938). The Uniform Rules of Evidence, R. 63 (12) admits as an exception to the hearsay rule: "Unless the judge finds it was made in bad faith, a statement of the declarant's (a) then existing state of mind, motion or physical sensation, including statements of intent, plan, motive, design, mental feeling, pain and bodily health, but not including memory or belief to prove the fact remembered or believed, when such a mental or physical condition is in issue or is relevant to prove or explain acts or conduct of the declarant, or (b) pre-

the time of the declaration.[3] It must be acknowledged, however, that this assurance of reliability is not absolute but only relative, since some of such statements purporting to describe present symptoms or the like are not spontaneous but are calculated mis-statements. But a reasonable assumption is that most of them are sincere and spontaneous. This assumption likewise gives the basis for finding a special need for this kind of hearsay declarations, even though the declarant is available as a witness,[4] namely that being probably spontaneous, they will be of greater probative value than his present testimony, subject to the distortions of calculation, would be.[5]

Under the traditional and most widely prevailing view, this kind of declaration is not required to be made to a doctor but is likewise received when made to members of the family, friends or other persons.[6] The limitation to statements of present condition excludes descriptions of past pain or symptoms[7] and rules out likewise accounts of past happenings furnishing the cause of the condition.[8]

While most of the opinions and texts prescribe that the declarations to be received under this head must be "natural and spontaneous" expressions of the bodily condition,[9] it is not always clear whether this requires some further showing for admissibility beyond the fact that the declaration purports to describe a then existing condition of the declarant. Probably, however, the trial judge has the duty to consider the circumstances under which the declarations were made and to determine (largely in his discretion) whether they were uttered spontaneously or designedly with a view to making evidence.[10]

---

vious symptoms, pain or physical sensation, made to a physician consulted for treatment or for diagnosis with a view to treatment, and relevant to an issue of declarant's bodily condition."

3. See 6 Wigmore, Evidence, § 1714.

4. In this as in the other classes of spontaneous declarations treated in this chapter no requirement is made that the declarant be unavailable at the time of the trial. 6 Wigmore, Evidence, § 1714.

5. See 6 Wigmore, Evidence, § 1714.

6. DeWitt v. Johnson, 170 Okl. 625, 41 P.2d 476, 478 (1935) (parent); Frangos v. Edmunds, 179 Ore. 557, 173 P.2d 596, 603, syl. 13 (1946) (wife); Bagley v. Mason, 69 Vt. 175, 37 Atl. 287, 288, syl. 4 (1896) (attendant); and cases cited 6 Wigmore, Evidence, § 1719, note 9; Note, 64 A.L.R. 557, 31 C.J.S. 994, note 6.
In New York, however, and a substantial minority of states following her lead, the limitation has been adopted that the declaration must have been made to a physician, unless made immediately after the injury or consisting of inarticulate screams, gestures, or the like. Kennedy v. Rochester City & B. R. Co., 130 N.Y. 654, 29 N.E. 141, syl. 1 (1891); Springfield C. R. Co. v. Hoeffner, 175 Ill. 634, 51 N.E. 884, 887 (1898); 6 Wigmore, Evidence, § 1719; Note, 64 A.L.R. 565.

7. Lowery v. Jones, 219 Ala. 201, 121 So. 704, syl. 2, 64 A.L.R. 553 (1929); Martin v. P. H. Hanes Knitting Co., 189 N.C. 644, 127 S.E. 688, syl. 3 (1925).

Sometimes, however, courts seem to classify as declarations of "present" symptoms, descriptions which include the past, see Hartford Accident & Indemnity Co. v. Baugh, 87 F.2d 240 (C.C.A.Tex. 1937) ("He came to the office and told me that his sputum was stained with blood," held, admissible), Note, 36 Mich.L.Rev. 142; Bloomberg v. Laventhal, 179 Cal. 616, 178 Pac. 496, syl. 2 (1919) (statements by plaintiff that he had pains in the head and could not sleep).

8. Roth v. Travelers' Protective Ass'n of America (1909) 102 Tex. 241, 248, 115 S.W. 31, syl. 7, 132 Am. St.Rep. 831, 20 Ann.Cas. 97 (declarant described to a friend a fall on the ice, and complained of headache; former excluded, latter admitted). Declarations as to cause may, however, qualify as excited utterances, see § 272, herein.

9. See, e. g., 3 Jones, Evidence, § 1213, p. 2226 (2d ed. rev. 1926) ("Where the bodily or mental feelings of a person are to be proved, the usual and natural exclamations of such person, which are the spontaneous manifestations of pain and naturally flow from the pain being suffered by him at the time, are competent and original evidence"); Rogers v. City of Detroit, 289 Mich. 86, 286 N.W. 167, 169 (1939) ("The controlling test of the admissibility of exclamations of pain is 'spontaneity'"); 31 C.J.S. 991, note, 67.

10. Hewitt v. Eisenbart, 36 Neb. 794, 55 N.W. 252, syl. 3 (1893) (declarant's statement to employer in response to question, that he couldn't use spade because of the condition of his leg, not improperly re-

266. Declarations of Bodily Condition Made to Physicians Consulted for Treatment.[1]

Statements of a presently existing condition made by a patient to a doctor consulted for treatment are universally admitted as evidence of the facts stated,[2] and some states will admit only statements made under these circumstances.[3] Such statements are likely to be less spontaneous than those made to friends and relatives, being usually given in answer to questions, but they have the added factor of reliability that the patient knows that the kind of treatment he receives, and its value and helpfulness, may largely depend on the accuracy of the information which he gives to the doctor. There is no inclination here, as in the case of statements to doctors employed only to testify, to exclude statements of "subjective" symptoms.

The argument of special reliability of the patient's statements made in consultation for treatment is a strong one and has induced some courts to extend the scope of the hearsay exception to include statements of the patient as to *past* symptoms, when made to a doctor for treatment.[4] Certainly such decla-

---

ceived; "The trial court must be permitted to exercise its discretion very largely in determining whether the declarations were made under such circumstances as to permit the inference that they were genuine expressions, and the jury must be left to determine whether or not such inference shall be drawn."). And see St. Louis & S. F. Ry. Co. v. Chaney, 77 Kan. 276, 94 Pac. 126, 128, syl. 1, 2 (1908) (proof of statements of present pain without any showing that they were not made with deliberation; held, improperly admitted; "When such evidence is offered, it should, at least, appear fair upon its face to the court before being submitted to the consideration of the jury, which, as before said, is the final arbiter as to its value."). This discretion should not be fettered with hard and fast rules. Thus the fact that the statement was made in answer to a question should not automatically exclude it. Hewitt v. Eisenhart, supra; Texas & Pac. R. Co. v. Barron, 78 Tex. 421, 423, 14 S.W. 698 (1890) (evidence that plaintiff said in answer to question as to whether he was hurt, "I do not know," and then put his hand on his stomach and said, "I feel very strange; I do not feel right in here; I am afraid I am hurt." The evidence was held admissible.) Contra: Ready v. Hafeman, 239 Wis. 1, 300 N.W. 480, syl. 10 (1941). Nor should the fact that the declaration was made after the claim or controversy arose be always controlling. Kansas City, Ft. S. & M. R. Co. v. Stoner, 51 Fed. 649, 657, syl. 4 (C.C.A.Ark.1892); Fleming v. City of Springfield, 154 Mass. 520, 28 N.E. 910, syl. 2 (1891); Bagley v. Mason, 69 Vt. 175, 37 Atl. 287, syl. 5 (1896). But compare the modern doctrine which excludes statements made by declarant to his physician employed only to testify, see § 267, herein.

1. 6 Wigmore, Evidence, §§ 1719, 1720; 3 Jones, Evidence, § 1217; 31 C.J.S. Evidence, § 246; Dec.Dig. Evidence, ☞128; Notes, 67 A.L.R. 10, 80 A.L.R. 1527, 130 A.L.R. 977.

2. Northern Pac. R. Co. v. Urlin, 158 U.S. 271, 15 Sup. Ct. 840, syl. 5, 39 L.Ed. 977 (1895); People v. Fogel-

song, 116 Mich. 556, 74 N.W. 730, syl. 6 (1898) (but not declarations of past symptoms); McDuffie v. Root, 300 Mich. 286, 1 N.W.2d 544, syl. 6 (1942); Cuneo Press Co. v. Industrial Comm., 341 Ill. 569, 173 N.E. 470, syl. 3 (1930) (includes statements made to an examining physician, when examination not made in contemplation of suit).

3. See note 6, next previous section.

4. Meaney v. United States, 112 F.2d 538, 540, 130 A.L.R. 975 (C.C.A.2d 1940) (patient's statement of past history improperly excluded; masterly opinion of L. Hand, J., acutely appraising elements of trustworthiness); Roosa v. Boston Loan Co., 132 Mass. 439, 440 (1882) ("While a witness, not an expert, can testify only to such exclamations and complaints as indicate present existing pain and suffering, a physician may testify to a statement or narrative given by his patient in relation to his condition, symptoms, sensations, and feelings, both past and present. In both cases these declarations are admitted from necessity, because in this way only can the bodily condition of the party, who is the subject of the injury, and who seeks to obtain damages, be ascertained. But the necessity does not extend to declarations by the party as to the cause of the injury, which is the principal subject matter of inquiry, and which may be proved by other evidence.); Kennedy v. Upshaw, 66 Tex. 442, 450, 1 S.W. 308, syl. 3 (1886) (statement of patient, since deceased, to physician as to past physical condition, given with a view to treatment held admissible in will contest); Missouri, K. & T. R. Co. of Texas v. Dalton, 56 Tex.Civ.App. 82, 120 S.W. 240, 244, syl. 6 (1909) (evidence of doctor: " . . . he said his headaches had previously been more severe," admitted). Other cases holding that the doctor may testify that his opinion is partly based on the patient's "history" of past symptoms look in the same direction. See, e. g., People v. Wilson, 25 Cal.2d 341, 153 Pac. 720, syl. 12, 13 (1944); State v. Blydenberg, 135 Iowa 264, 112 N.W. 634, syl. 7 (1907). But they

rations are necessary for diagnosis, and when the circumstances are consistent with good faith, they are highly reliable and a wider acceptance of this extension may well be expected.[5]

It would seem, moreover, that the same practical guaranty of trustworthiness would attach to those parts of the "history" given by the patient to the doctor for treatment which describe the general character of the cause or external source of the condition to be treated, so far as this description is pertinent to the purpose of treatment. The professional standards for the regulation of hospitals require the gathering of this information from the patient [6] and the person treated will be fully conscious that his treatment may

well be affected by his report as to the cause, whether a fall, a crushing by a heavy object, or a collision. Other features of the incident, such as the place where it occurred or who was at fault, seem unrelated to treatment. Some courts have accepted the view that these statements as to external cause when relevant to treatment and made to a doctor employed for that purpose are admitted as evidence of the fact stated.[7] This conclusion, particularly in actions for death where there were no eye-witnesses other than the victim, seems the view most consonant with the demands of justice. The greater number of courts, however have thus far declined to permit such declarations as to cause, even when made to a doctor for treatment, to be used as substantive evidence.[8]

---

are distinguishable, since this use of the declarations is not "substantive." Chicago R. I. & R. Ry. Co. v. Jackson, 63 Okl. 32, 162 Pac. 822, syl. 4 (1917) (able opinion by Sharp, J., collecting the decisions).

5. See, e. g., Moore v. Summers Drug Co., 206 N.C. 711, 175 S.E. 96, syl. 1 (1934), noted, 13 N.C.L.Rev. 228, where the court received, in a claim for death, the decedent's declaration to a doctor, as to when his pain had first arisen, without adverting to any distinction between past and present symptoms. Statements of the duration of an illness, are received though they include an element of the past. 5 Wigmore, Evidence, § 1722(b). And the line between past and present symptoms can hardly be sharply drawn, see § 265 supra, note 7.

6. See § 290.

7. Stewart v. Baltimore & Ohio Ry. Co., 137 F.2d 527, syl. 6 (C.C.A.2d 1943) (action for death of railway hostler, allegedly due to exertion while throwing switch; decedent's declarations to doctor as to nature and extent of his exertions admissible but not his statement that the switch was out of order); Lathem v. Hartford Acc. & Ind. Co., 60 Ga.App. 523, 3 S.E.2d 916, syl. 1 (1939) (review of workmen's compensation award for unwitnessed injury; declaration of decedent to doctor that his pain was due to lifting heavy box held competent as being descriptive of present pain and necessary to prevent miscarriage of justice: able opinion by MacIntyre, J.); Hillman v. Utah Power & Light Co., 56 Idaho 67, syl. 1, 51 P.2d 703 (1935) (workmen's compensation; statement to doctor as to how accident occurred, by hitting head on regulator panel, competent); Valentine v. Weaver, 191 Ky. 37, 228 S.W. 1036, syl. 7

(1921) (workmen's compensation: award denied because no proof injury occurred in employment; affirmed, declaration of deceased that he stuck splinter in hand, and the time when, competent but not the place where—a fine line, my masters); Baker v. Industrial Comm., 44 Oh.App. 539, 186 N.E. 10, syl. 4 (1933) (declaration, while seeking treatment for strangulated hernia, that condition caused by fall, competent in workmen's compensation proceeding). Other cases let in similar declarations as part of the doctor-witness's explanation of the grounds of his opinion, but they are distinguishable. See, e. g., Comm. v. Colangelo, 256 Mass. 165, 152 N.E. 241, syl. 4 (1926) (statutory rape: girl's statement as to time of intercourse); Walker v. Great Atlantic & Pac. Tea Co., 131 Tex. 57, 112 S.W.2d 170, syl. 3 (1938) (statement of patient, violently ill, as to what he had eaten for dinner).

8. Walker v. Prudential Ins. Co., 127 F.2d 938, syl. 4 (C.C.A.Fla., 1942) (declaration as to circumstances attending wound from shooting); Comm. v. Dawn, 302 Mass. 255, 19 N.E.2d 315, 318 (1939) (abortion: statement to physician as to cause of condition, inadmissible); Beck v. Whittlesberger, 181 Mich. 463, 148 N.W. 247, 249, syl. 3 (1914) (statement of declarant as to how he hurt his hand); Goetz v. J. D. Carson Co., 357 Mo. 125, 206 S.W.2d 530, syl. 2 (1947) (workmen's compensation, declarations as to how declarant sprained his ankle properly excluded) and numerous cases cited 6 Wigmore, Evidence, § 1722 (a), note 1. But such statement if made shortly after the injury may come in under the theory of excited utterances. London Guarantee & Acc. Co. v. Woelfle, 83 F.2d 325, syl. 11 (C.C.A.Mo.1936) (dictum), see § 272, herein.

267. Physicians Employed only to Testify: Restrictions on Admission of Statements to, and Testimony by Such Experts.[1]

Many courts draw a sharp line, evidentially, between physicians consulted for treatment and those employed solely as prospective expert witnesses. As to the latter, they have been inclined to impose special restrictions which are set out below.

1. It has been held, probably by the majority of courts that have passed on the question, that descriptive statements of present pain or symptoms when made to a doctor employed only to testify[2] do not qualify for admission as substantive evidence under the present exception to the hearsay rule for statements of bodily condition.[3]

2. The rule prevails generally that expert witnesses may testify to the information upon which they have relied in reaching their conclusions,[4] and in respect to medical witnesses this practice would permit the doctor to give a general account not only of facts observed, but of the "history" including the patient's statements as to injury, past symptoms, and present feelings as of the time of the examination.[5] When presented for this purpose, the statements are not evidence of the matters stated, and hence not hearsay, but are merely explanatory of the opinion, enabling the jury to weigh it in the light of its basis. Most courts make no distinction, in respect to using the "history" as grounds of opinion between doctors who attended for treatment and those who examined the patient only to prepare themselves to testify.[6] A few courts, however, have held or intimated that these latter experts may not recount what the patient has told them, even for the non-hearsay purpose of explaining the grounds of opinion.[7]

---

1. See Hudspeth, Note, Statements to Physicians, 24 Tex.L.Rev. 387 (1946).

2. A doctor who is consulted for treatment but with the expectation that he will also testify is held not to be within the restriction. Chicago Rys. Co. v. Kramer, 234 Fed. 245, syl. 7 (C.C.A.Ill. 1916); Judd v. Caledonia, 150 Mich. 480, 114 N.W. 346, syl. 2 (1907) (semble); El Paso & S. W. Ry. Co. v. Polk, 49 Tex.Civ.App. 269, 108 S.W. 761, syl. 4 (1908).

3. United States v. Nickle, 60 F.2d 372, syl. 2 (C.C.A.8, 1932); Pierce v. Heusinkveld, 234 Iowa 1348, 14 N.W.2d 275, syl. 15 (1944); Sund v. Chicago R. I. & P. Ry. Co., 164 Minn. 24, 204 N.W. 628, syl. 1 (1925); Brotherhood of L. F. & E. v. Raney, 101 S.W.2d 863, syl. 6 (Tex.Civ.App., 1937) ("statements as to subjective symptoms"); Stewart v. Everts, 76 Wis. 35, 42, 44 N.W. 1092, syl. 4 (1890) and cases cited 6 Wigmore, Evidence, § 1721; 31 C.J.S., p. 997, note 27; Note, 130 A.L.R. at 978. This restriction has been held not to apply to irrational statements reported by a doctor examining for mental disease. United States v. Roberts, 62 F.2d 594, syl. 4 (C.C.A.10, 1932). Nor, under what seems the wiser view, to inarticulate expressions or like bodily responses, though these, of course, could sometimes be simulated. Missouri, K. & T. Ry. Co. v. Johnson, 95 Tex. 409, 411, 67 S.W. 768, syl. 1 (1902) ("exclamations, shrinkings, and other expressions which appear to be the instinctive or spontaneous betrayal of pain are ad-

missible"). Contra: Greinke v. Chicago City Ry. Co., 234 Ill. 564, 85 N.E. 327, syl. 6 (1908) (strength of hands and use of limbs); Comstock v. Georgetown, 137 Mich. 541, 100 N.W. 788, syl. 3 (1904) (flinching).

4. Commercial Standard Ins. Co. v. Robinson, 137 Tex. 184, 151 S.W.2d 795, syl. 3 (1941) (reasons and grounds for conclusions) and cases cited Dec.Dig. Evidence, ☞555(c).

5. See Wigmore, Evidence, §§ 655, 1720(1); Notes, 67 A.L.R. at 18, 80 A.L.R. at 1528, 130 A.L.R. at 979; Lowery v. Jones, 219 Ala. 201, 121 So. 704, 64 A.L.R. 553, syl. 4 (1929); Curfman v. Monongahela, etc. Co., 113 W.Va. 85, 166 S.E. 848, syl. 3, 4 (1932).

6. Groat v. Walkup Drayage & Whse. Co., 14 Cal.App. 2d 350, 58 P.2d 200, syl. 9 (1936); Johnson v. Bangor R. & E. Co., 125 Me. 88, 94, 131 Atl. 1, (1925); Cronin v. Fitchburg & L. St. Ry. Co., 181 Mass. 202, 63 N.E. 335 (1902); Estes v. Babcock, 119 Wash. 270, 205 Pac. 12, syl. 4 (1922).

7. In the following cases it is said that such experts may not recite the "history," but the distinction between using it as substantive evidence and as grounds of opinion was not mentioned. Kabai v. Majestic Collieries Co., 293 Ky. 783, 170 S.W.2d 357, syl. 2 (1943) (but here allowed where examination conducted at defendant's request); Cruce v. Gulf, Mobile, & Ohio R. Co., 361 Mo. 1138, 238 S.W.2d 674, syl. 10 (1951) (may recite patient's statements only as to present

3. The minority group of courts which adopt this last restriction limit correspondingly the admissibility of the opinions of the expert who has been employed only to examine and testify. Such experts, they hold, are confined to giving opinions based solely upon the objective facts observed by them (or upon a hypothetical question), and are barred from giving an opinion based even in part upon "subjective" facts, that is, upon what the patient has said about the history of his injury or his sufferings and symptoms.[8] This runs counter to the practice of medical consultants in considering such histories in forming their professional conclusions upon which they act decisively every day, and counter also to the general rule as to medical testimony which admits conclusions so formed.[9]

There seems to be no serious objection in fairness or policy to the restriction in paragraph 1, above, upon the admission of the descriptive statements of the party when examined by a doctor employed to testify. All that can be charged is that it adds a troublesome complication on rather insubstantial grounds. But the limitations in paragraphs 2 and 3 are of doubtful wisdom. They seem designed to hamper a proper practice of personal injury claimants in preparing their cases for trial, that of securing eminent physicians or surgeons to make an examination for the purpose of later aiding the court and jury in understanding the claimant's physical state. That such professional men of wide reputation may be more effective as witnesses than the perhaps differently qualified doctors who have treated the patient is no argument against their evidence. It might serve the interests of fairness for the court to have the discretionary power to exclude such evidence offered for the claimant if the claimant refused to permit a similar examination by reputable physicians of the defendant's choosing. If the physician's expert opinion should be allowed in evidence though based partly on what was told him when he was called in solely to prepare him to testify, as it seems it should, he should be allowed in accordance with the general rule as to experts, to recount as part of the explanation of the basis of his opinion, the statements made to him by the patient, i. e., the "history" of the case. Such an explanation is to some extent a necessary measure by which to assess the value of the opinion, and the weight which the jury would give to the statements made under those circumstances may be easily exaggerated. However, the opponent certainly is entitled to have the evidence limited by the court to purposes of elucidation, and the jury instructed not to consider the "history" as evidence of the facts recounted. Furthermore, if the evidence of the "history" given to the witness by the patient were apparently being elaborated for the purpose of giving an independent force to these statements, the court could, in its discretion, confine the witness to a general statement of the "history."

symptoms); Slacke v. Yellow Taxi Corp., 260 App. Div. 1046, 24 N.Y.S.2d 490, syl. 3, (1940); Brotherhood of L. F. & E. v. Raney, 101 S.W.2d 863, syl. 6 (Tex.Civ.App.1937).

8. Nashville, C. & St. L. Ry. Co. v. York, 127 F.2d 606, 611, syl. 9 (C.C.A.6, 1942); Lehigh Stone Co. v. Industrial Comm., 315 Ill. 413, 146 N.E. 533, syl. 4 (1925); Preveden v. Metropolitan Life Ins. Co., 200 Minn. 523, 274 N.W. 685, syl. 1 (1937); Texas Employers' Ins. Co. v. Morgan, 187 S.W.2d 603, syl. 4 (Tex.Civ.App. 1945), and cases cited in Note, 65 A.L.R. 1217, 1219; Dec.Dig. Evidence, ⊂⊃555(k). As to escape from the restriction by resort to hypothetical questions, see

Lee v. Minneapolis St. Ry. Co., 230 Minn. 315, 41 N.W.2d 433, syl. 2, 3 (1950).

9. Kaufman v. Kaufman, 164 F.2d 519, syl. 2 (C.A.D.C. 1947) (annulment for impotency, psychiatrist's opinion resting largely on history and symptoms given by husband, received); State v. Blydenburg, 135 Iowa 264, 112 N.W. 634, syl. 7 (1907); People v. Wilson, 25 Cal.2d 341, 153 P.2d 720, syl. 13, 14 (1944); Yellow Cab. Co. v. Henderson, 183 Md. 546, 39 A.2d 546, syl. 6, 7 (1944) (doctor's opinion based partly on history given by mother of injured child, received); Danner v. Chandler, 205 Okl. 185, 236 P.2d 503, syl. 1 (1951) (rejecting restriction upon doctors employed only to testify); 3 **Wigmore, Evidence,** § 688(1).

TOPIC 2

DECLARATIONS OF MENTAL STATE

268. Declaration of Declarant's Present Mental or Emotional State, Condition or Attitude.[1]

As a later outgrowth of the exception for declarations of bodily pain or feeling, there evolved the present exception to the hearsay rule admitting statements or declarations of a presently existing mental state, attitude, feeling or emotion of the declarant.[2] Among the statements commonly received are those declaring intention, purpose, design, motive, assent, knowledge or belief. Among the emotions so expressed are affection, desire, ill-will, fear and submission. The special reliability of such hearsay declarations lies again in their spontaneity and probable sincerity assured by the requirements that they must purport to relate to a then existing condition of mind or emotion, as of the time of the statement, and must have been made under circumstances indicating apparent sincerity.[3] The special need for the use of the declarations does not rest in the unavailability of the declarant—this is not required—but has been supported on the ground that if the declarant were called, "his own memory of his state of mind at a former time is no more likely to be clear and true than a bystander's recollection of what he then said."[4] Like most of our arguments of policy in the evidence field, this ground rests upon an unproveable assumption, but the exception itself which makes available to the court in difficult controversies a type of evidence which is probably helpful, seems a useful one.

A distinction has been mentioned in the general chapter on hearsay[5] which may be recalled here. That is the difference between direct statements of mental or emotional state, such as "I plan to spend the rest of my life here in New York" or "I have lost my affection for my husband" (which when offered to show the plan or the loss of affection are hearsay, but come in under the exception) and statements which prove mental state or emotion circumstantially. Of this latter sort would be a statement "I have been happier in New York than in any other place," to show intent to remain there, or a declaration, "My husband is a detestable wretch" to show want of affection. Despite this difference which is pointed out by the writers,[6] the courts tend to treat the two kinds of expressions interchangeably, and to treat the latter type as if they were hearsay declarations coming in under the present exception, instead of justifying their admission on the ground that they are not hearsay but are simply circumstantial evidence to which the hearsay objection does not apply. Per-

---

1. 6 Wigmore, Evidence, §§ 1714, 1715, 1725–1740; Hinton, States of Mind and the Hearsay Rule, 1 U. Chi.L.Rev. 394 (1934) (learned, wise, witty); McBaine, Admissibility in California of Declarations of Physical and Mental Condition, 19 Calif.L.Rev. 231, 367 (1931); Morgan, Evidence 1941–1945, 59 Harv.L.Rev. 481, 570 (1946); Comment, Statements Evidencing Mental Condition, 3 Ark.L.Rev. 189 (1949); Dec.Dig. Evidence, ☞268, 269, 271(6), Crim.Law, ☞415(1) (3) (5); 31 C.J.S. Evidence, §§ 254–259; Model Code of Evidence R. 513, and commentary. For a scholarly discussion of the rule, and collection of authorities, see the opinion of Mallery, J., in Raborn v. Hayton, 34 Wash.2d 105, 208 P.2d 133 (1949).

2. See the statement of the rule in Uniform Rules of Evidence, R. 63(12), set out in § 265, note 2, above.

3. Elmer v. Fessenden, 151 Mass. 359, 24 N.E. 208 (1889) ("made with no apparent motive for misstatement"); 6 Wigmore, Evidence, § 1714 ("without any obvious motive to misrepresent"). But compare Smith v. Smith, 364 Pa. 1, 70 A.2d 530, syl. 11 (1950) where the court treats the fact that the declarations of intent were "self-serving" as going only to the weight.

4. Mutual Life Ins. Co. v. Hillmon, 145 U.S. 285, 295 12 Sup.Ct. 909, 912, 36 L.Ed. 706 (1892) by Gray, J.

5. See §§ 225, 228, supra.

6. 6 Wigmore, Evidence, § 1715, Hinton, op. cit., 1 Univ.Chi.L.Rev. 394, 397, 398.

haps this treatment gives a needed safeguard. These expressions used circumstantially to evidence state of mind or emotion can be analyzed as non-hearsay, since they are not literally used to prove the matter asserted. While their value does not depend on the veracity, it does depend on the sincerity of the declarant.[7] Hence it may well be appropriate to impose upon the expressions used circumstantially to show state of mind or emotion the same requirement applied to the hearsay declarations, namely, that they must have been made under circumstances indicating apparent sincerity.

One limitation upon the present exception to the hearsay rule is necessary if the exception is not to swallow up the rule. This limitation is that the courts will not extend the present exception to admit a declaration that the declarant *remembers* or *believes* a certain matter as evidence that the matter so remembered or believed is true.[8]

269. Declarations Offered to Show State of Mind or Emotion in Issue.

The substantive law often makes legal rights and liabilities hinge upon the existence of a state of mind or emotion in a person involved in the transaction in question. When this is so, and a legal proceeding arises from the transaction, the pleadings may put in issue such mental state. To ascertain it becomes an ultimate object of search. The intent or ill-will or the like is not sought to be proved as circumstantial evidence of the person's earlier or later conduct but as an operative fact upon which a cause of action or defense depends. Ascertainment of the state of mind is an end in itself. In this class of cases the justification in the next previous section, in terms of special need and special reliability, for the use of hearsay declarations is at its strongest. Accordingly, although this classification is not often specifically mentioned in the opinions, it is in this group of cases that such declarations are most readily and liberally received.[1] Doubts and difficulties on the score of relevancy and probative value which are often present when mental state is sought to be proved as circumstantial evidence of declarant's conduct or of other facts, are absent here.

Common instances of statements used for this purpose are declarations of intention to make a certain place one's home offered as evidence of domicil,[2] declarations expressive of mental suffering offered to prove that element of damages,[3] a statement of willingness to allow one the use of declarant's automobile as evidence that the car was used with the owner's consent under the terms of an insurance policy,[4] declarations accompanying a transfer of property showing an intent, or a lack of intent, to defraud credi-

---

7. Hinton, op.cit. at p. 400.

8. "Declarations of intention casting light upon the future, have been sharply distinguished from declarations of memory, pointing backwards to the past. There would be an end, or nearly that, to the rule against hearsay if the distinction were ignored." Cardozo, J., in Shepard v. United States, 290 U.S. 96, 106, 54 Sup.Ct. 22, 78 L.Ed. 196 (1933), and see Uniform Rules of Evidence, Rule 63(12).

1. See Hinton, op.cit., 1 U.Chi.L.Rev. 394 at 403, Hutchins and Slesinger, State of Mind in Issue, 29 Col.L.Rev. 147 (1929).

2. Matter of Newcomb, 192 N.Y. 238, 84 N.E. 950, syl. 8 (1908) (testatrix on advice of lawyer before making will wrote to friends announcing her intention

to make New Orleans her permanent home, held, admissible, and good faith was for the judge in judge-tried case); Smith v. Smith, 364 Pa. 1, 70 A.2d 630, syl. 11, 12 (1950) (statements of intent to live in Florida admissible though self-serving); Note, Evidentiary Factors in the Determination of Domicil, 61 Harv.L.Rev. 1232, 1237 (1948); 6 Wigmore, Evidence, §§ 1727, 1784.

3. Missouri, K. & T. R. Co. v. Linton, 141 S.W. 129, syl. 1 (Tex.Civ.App.1911) (action for damages for mental anguish for defendant's breach of contract to carry corpse of plaintiff's son; plaintiff's declaration that "She felt like her heart would burst and that she could not live," admitted).

4. American Employers Ins. Co. v. Wentworth, 90 N.H. 112, 5 A.2d 265, syl. 4, 5 (1939).

tors,[5] and declarations of ill-will to show malice, or expressions of a required specific intent, in criminal cases.[6]

The requirement is as we have seen[7] that the declaration must describe a then-existing state of mind or feeling, but this doctrine is not as restrictive in its effect as might be supposed. Another principle widens the reach of the evidence. This is the notion of the continuity in time of states of mind.[8] If a declarant on Tuesday tells of his then intention to go on a business trip the next day for his employer, this will be evidence not only of his intention at the time of speaking but of a similar purpose the next day when he is on the road.[9] And so of other states of mind.[10]

Moreover, the theory of continuity looks backward too.[11] Thus, when there is evidence that a will has been mutilated by the maker his subsequent declarations of a purpose inconsistent with the will are received to show his intent to revoke at the time he mutilated it.[12] Accordingly, we find the courts saying that whether a payment of money or a conveyance was intended by the

5. Sanger Brothers v. Colbert, 84 Tex. 668, syl. 3, 19 S.W. 863, syl. 2 (1892) (declaration by transferor when receiving price that he intended to pay his debts, "admissible as a part of the res gestae"). As to a husband's declarations offered to show intent to defraud wife of her interest in his property, see Ibey v. Ibey, 93 N.H. 434, 43 A.2d 157, syl. 8–11, 1945, 55 A.2d 872, syl. 2, 1947.

6. See, e. g., Hall v. State, 31 Tex.Cr.R. 565, 21 S.W. 368, syl. 1 (1893) (assault with intent to murder: defense, drunkenness preventing entertaining the specific intent; evidence of previous threats against the life of the victim admitted); Note, Crystal, Admissibility of General Threats to Show Malice, 20 Tex.L.Rev. 487 (1942); 6 Wigmore, Evidence, § 1732. These declarations of an accused offered against him are admissible also as admissions, see ch. 27, herein.

7. See the next preceding section.

8. Compare Prof. Chafee's picturesque statement, "The stream of consciousness has enough continuity so that we may expect to find the same characteristics for some distance up or down the current. But there is a point beyond which such evidence becomes irrelevant. Hudson River water at West Twenty-third St. Ferry is no proof of its quality above Fort Edward." Progress of the Law—Evidence, 1919–1922, 35 Harv.L.Rev. at 444, 1922.

9. Lewis v. Lowe & Campbell Athletic Goods Co., 247 S.W.2d 800, syl. 2, 3 (Mo.1952). As to the admissibility generally of the employee's declarations to show that he was on a mission for the master, see, e. g., Prater v. Traders & General Ins. Co., 83 S.W.2d 1038, syl. 3, Tex.Civ.App.1935. Mattan v. Hoover Co., 350 Mo. 506, 166 S.W.2d 557, syl. 14, 1942; Ervin v. Myrtle Grove Plantation, 206 S.C. 41, 32 S.E.2d 877, syl. 3, 4, 1945, and see Doke v. United Pac. Ins. Co., 15 Wash.2d 536, 131 P.2d 436, syl. 2, 3, 1942. But contrast the narrower holding of some cases, that the declaration must immediately accompany some significant act. See Boyer Chem.

Lab. Co. v. Industrial Commission, 366 Ill. 635, 10 N.E.2d 389, 113 A.L.R. 264, 1937 and Notes, 113 A.L.R. 268, 32 Ill.L.Rev. 740, 5 U.Chi.L.Rev. 303, 26 Ill.B.J. 250.

10. Ickes v. Ickes, 237 Pa. 582, 85 Atl. 885, syl. 4 (1912) (alienation of affection; husband's declaration of motive for leaving wife day before departure admissible as evidence that same attitude prevailed when he left); Re Goldsberry, 95 Utah 379, 81 P.2d 1106, syl. 6, 117 A.L.R. 1444 (1938) (undue influence: declarations of testatrix day before will executed admissible to show her "influenced state of mind"; Raborn v. Hayton, 34 Wash.2d 105, 208 P.2d 133, 137, syl. 10 (1949) (action against husband who murdered wife to set aside deed procured by him from her: attorney's testimony, presumably based on her declarations, that she did not intend to deliver the deed without agreed payment from husband, declared six days before her death, admitted; "This supports the inference that since there was no intervening payment, she had the same intent until her death").

11. See Mattan v. Hoover, 350 Mo. 506, 166 S.W.2d 557, syl. 14 (1942) (statement of agent after collision as to his intention admissible as evidence on question whether he was on mission for master at time of collision); Garford Trucking Corp. v. Mann, 163 F.2d 71, syl. 3, 4 (C.C.A.Mass.1947, cert. den.) (issue whether truck driver who had collision while taking a circuitous route to his destination had merely deviated or had departed entirely from his mission; declarations of driver in hospital ten days later that he took route because in his opinion he could make better time on it though it was longer properly admitted as bearing on his purpose at time of collision; criticised in Note, 27 Neb.L.Rev. 450 as admitting a declaration of a past state of mind, but probably sustainable as a declaration of present belief to show a previous belief and purpose).

12. Crampton v. Osborn, 356 Mo. 125, 201 S.W.2d 336, 342, syl. 11, 12 (1947); 6 Wigmore, Evidence, § 1737.

donor as a gift may be shown by his declarations made before, at the time of, or after the act of transfer.[13]

However, the duration of states of mind or emotion varies with the particular attitudes or feelings in question, and with the nature of the exciting cause. Therefore, the declaration must mirror a mental state which in the light of all the circumstances including proximity in time, has some probability of being the same condition which obtained at the material time. As in all instances where the inadmissible shades into the admissible according to relative degrees of probative force, the line between the admissible and the too remote being one that

no two men would draw at exactly the same place, the admission of the evidence where there is room for doubt on this score should be left to the discretion of the trial judge.

The issue as to state of mind may not be merely whether a given mental or emotional state existed but whether the defendant's acts caused the state of mind or feeling.[14] In such cases the declarations will frequently describe inseparably the acts and their effect on the declarant's mind or emotion. When this is so, the normal practice is to admit the declaration and direct the jury to consider it only in proof of the declarant's mental state or feeling, and to disregard it as evidence of the offending conduct.[15] This is

13. Casey v. Casey, 97 Cal.App.2d 875, 218 P.2d 842, syl. 3 (1950) (declarations of decedent made before and after conveyance to show whether she intended the grant as a gift or in trust); O'Neal v. O'Neal, 9 N.J.Super. 36, 74 A.2d 614, syl. 3 (1950) (oral declarations of brother paying price of land conveyed to sister, of intent to make gift, to rebut resulting trust). See also Whitlow v. Durst, 20 Cal.2d 523, 127 P.2d 530, 531 (1942) where the issue was whether a property settlement between husband and wife had been avoided by a reconciliation, and declarations of the husband made after the alleged reconciliation, stating that they were still separated and would never be reconciled, were held properly received. In Williams v. Kidd, 170 Calif. 631, 151 Pac. 1, syl. 10, (1915), declarations of a father some time after he had handed to daughter's husband a deed of gift to her, that he did not want it to take effect until his death, were held admissible. To the objection that a grantor's subsequent declarations will not be heard in disparagement of the gift, the court answered that this objection will not be applied where as here the very question is whether there was an effective gift by delivery and this depends on intent. As to this "disparagement" doctrine, see Note, Subsequent Declarations by Donor, 105 A.L.R. 399, 402, 410. But certain cases hold that if the donor's intention to convey is shown by unequivocal words at the time of manual delivery, contrary declarations of intent before or after will not be received. Shaver v. Canfield, 21 Cal.App.2d 734, 70 P.2d 507, syl. 6, 7 (1937); Wilbur v. Grover, 140 Mich. 187, 103 N.W. 583, syl. 1, 4 (1905). These holdings seem questionable in their implication that as a matter of substantive law the effectiveness of a gift is not dependent on internal intent but is tested by the "objective" standard proper to contracts. See Note, 26 Calif.L.Rev. 631 (1938).

14. Instances of declarations showing the effect on declarant's mind and the motive for his acts: Ickes v. Ickes, 237 Pa. 582, 85 Atl. 885, 44 L.R.A.,N.S., 1118, syl. 5, 1912 (daughter-in-law sues father-in-law for alienation; latter offers evidence that son said he was leaving wife because she was with child by another man); Williamson v. Williamson, 183 Wash. 71, 48 P.2d 588, syl. 3, 4, 1935 (similar to last); Carpenters' Union v. Citizens' Committee, 333 Ill. 225, 164 N.E. 393, 63 A.L.R. 157, 177, 1928 (evidence of reasons given by employer for discharge of union employees, offered by plaintiff union, in suit against third persons to enjoin interference.) See 6 Wigmore, Evidence, § 1729.

15. Greater New York Live Poultry Chamber of Commerce v. United States, 47 F.2d 156, syl. 3–5 (C.C.A. 2d 1931) (conspiracy in restraint of interstate trade in poultry: declarations of receivers as to why they refused to sell to recalcitrant market men admissible to show state of mind of declarants but not to show external facts declared as reasons, and defendants would have been entitled to instruction to that effect if it had been requested); Adkins v. Brett, 194 Cal. 252, 193 Pac. 251, syl. 9, 10 (1920) (alienation: wife's statements about relations with defendant admissible to show her feelings but defendant entitled to instruction that they are not competent to prove the acts and conduct of defendant described in the statements; leading opinion by Olney, J.). See also Johnson v. Richards, 50 Idaho 150, 294 Pac. 507, syl. 19 (1930) (husband's declarations concerning wife, when admissible in wife's suit for alienation of affections, are competent only to indicate husband's state of mind.); Elmer v. Fessendren, 151 Mass. 359, 24 N.E. 208, syl. 1 (1889) (In an action for a slander by reason of which plaintiff's workmen left his employment, it is error to exclude the declarations of the workmen as to their

mental gymnastics which is probably beyond the jury's ability and more certainly beyond their willingness to attempt. In the ordinary case this practice of admitting with limiting instructions is mere symbolism that does little harm, but in a case where the mental state is proveable by other available evidence not subject to objection, and the danger of harm from the illicit use by the jury of the offered declarations is substantial, the judge's discretion to exclude the latter has been recognized.[16]

270. Declarations of Intention to Show Subsequent Acts of Declarant.

In the cases discussed in the last section the declarant's mental state, e. g., malice or intent to defraud, was in issue, and the declarations evincing such mental state bore directly upon this ultimate issue, or if indirectly, only to the extent of asking for an inference that the same mental state existed shortly before or after the declarations. In the cases now to be considered, an additional step is added. By the declaration a mental state is proved not as an end in itself, but as a basis for the further inference that the mental state found outlet in conduct. The general principle is clear that evidence of design is relevant and admissible to show conduct.[1] Is there any reason why the exception letting in the hearsay declarations of the declarant's present state of mind should not be extended to include statements of intention to show later acts? Here the special reliability of the declarations, judged in the light of the ultimate purpose of showing external acts, is much less, since for many reasons the cup of intention and the lip of action may never meet. Conceding the correct transmission of the declarations by the witness, the declaration of X that he is going to kill Y, is far more valuable as ground for the conclusion that X then bore malice against Y, than it is as a basis for the conclusion that X actually did later kill Y. Moreover, the special need for the use of hearsay is less, since we are not searching for a state of mind which only one man can know, but for acts that may have been seen by many witnesses. Accordingly, it has been ably urged that the use of statements of in-

reasons for leaving, made at the time, where there is independent testimony in the case that defendant repeated the alleged slander to them.); Scott v. Townsend, 106 Tex. 322, 166 S.W. 1138, 1144 (1914) (undue influence; testatrix's declarations admissible to show effect on her mind but not the acts of influence). See Notes, Declarations on Issue of Undue Influence, 79 A.L.R. 1447, 148 A.L.R. 1225.

[16]. "But it is not difficult to imagine cases where it [a limiting instruction] would not suffice, and the opponent could justly ask for more. The matter is largely one of discretion on the part of the trial judge. If the point to prove which the evidence is competent can just as well be proven by other evidence, or if it is of but slight weight or importance upon that point, the trial judge might well be justified in excluding it entirely, because of its prejudicial and dangerous character as to other points. A number of the authorities cited by defendant's counsel are distinguishable from the present case upon this ground. This would emphatically be true where there is good reason for believing that the real object for which the evidence is offered is not to prove the point for which it is ostensibly offered and is competent, but is to get before the jury declarations as to other points, to prove which the evidence is incompetent. The same thing would be true as to the introduction of repeated declarations, when once the point for which they are competent has been amply shown. It may also be that the portions of the declaration which there is danger may be misused by the jury are not so interwoven with the balance of the declaration but that they can be disassociated from it without impairing the meaning or effect of the declaration for the purpose for which it is admissible. In such a case evidence of such portions of the declaration may be excluded on proper objection, when offered, if there is opportunity for such objection, or, if there is not, may be stricken out on motion subsequently. The point of the matter is that the opponent of such evidence, so likely to be misused against him, is entitled to such protection against its misuse as can reasonably be given him without impairing the ability of the other party to prove his case, or depriving him of the use of competent evidence reasonably necessary for that purpose." Olney, J. in Adkins v. Brett, 184 Cal. 252, 193 Pac. 251, 254 (1920). See also § 59, herein.

[1]. 1 Wigmore, Evidence, §§ 102–113, and decisions later cited and discussed in this section.

tention to show conduct be limited to cases where the declarant is unavailable as a witness.[2] In fact the declarant has been unavailable in most of the cases where the statements have been received, but the courts have not noticed the suggestion that this requirement be imposed.

Counsel and courts have not until recent decades recognized as widely the probative value and the theory of admissibility of these declarations of intention and design to show conduct, as in the case of the well established practice of receiving similar declarations to show intent or some other mental state which is itself in issue. Nevertheless, the modern cases and texts leave no room to doubt the statement that the accepted principle today is that evidence of declarations of a plan, design or intention presently entertained by the declarant is, subject to the usual limitations as to remoteness in time and apparent sincerity common to all declarations of mental state, admissible when offered as evidence that the design was carried out by acts or omissions of the declarant.[3]

The leading case is Mutual Life Insurance Co. v. Hillmon.[4] In that case the defense to an action on a policy on the life of Hillmon was that Hillmon was not dead, and that the body claimed to be his was that of one Walters. On this issue, it was held that letters of Walters to his family announcing his intention of going as an employee with Hillmon to the locality where the body was later actually found, were admissible. This was a strong case, for it permitted the inference that the declarant went with Hillmon, though that involved not only the carrying out of the intention by acts of the declarant, but also the co-operation of another person.

Acceptance of this theory of admissibility and recognition of occasions for its application have come slowly as to some types of declarations. Thus while most authoritative recent opinions have admitted under this theory declarations of intention to commit suicide offered by the accused in homicide cases as evidence that the victim took his own life,[5] or in insurance cases to show suicide as a defense,[6] yet many of the older

---

2. Hutchins and Slesinger, State of Mind to Prove an Act, 38 Yale L.J. 283 1929), and 13 Minn.L. Rev. 674, approved in McBaine, Declarations of Physical or Mental Condition in California, 19 Calif.L.Rev. 231, 367, at 371 (1931), but disapproved by Judge Hinton, States of Mind and the Hearsay Rule, 1 U.Chi.L.Rev. 394, 416 (1934).

3. 6 Wigmore, Evidence, §§ 1725, 1726, and cases cited and discussed later in this section. For a recent exposition of the theory of admissibility, see opinion of Heber, J., in Schloss v. Trounstine, 135 N.J.L. 11, 49 A.2d 677, syl. 2 (S.Ct.1946).

4. 145 U.S. 285, 12 Sup.Ct. 909, 36 L.Ed. 706 (1891). Of the innumerable comments provoked by this celebrated case, the following are noteworthy, E. W. Hinton, States of Mind and the Hearsay Rule, 1 U.Chi.L.Rev. 394, 403-423, 1934 (reviewing previous discussions); Eustace Seligman, An Exception to the Hearsay Rule, 26 Harv.L.Rev. 146, 1912; Hutchins and Slesinger, State of Mind to Prove an Act, 38 Yale L. J. 283, 1929, and 13 Minn.L.Rev. 674; J. M. Maguire, The Hillmon Case—Thirty-three Years After, 38 Harv.L.Rev. 709, 1925. For the stormy political history of the

case, see Wigmore, Principles of Judicial Proof, 970, 971, 3d ed. 1937.

5. Bowie v. State, 185 Ark. 834, 49 S.W.2d 1049, syl. 6 (1932); Comm. v. Trefethen, 157 Mass. 180, 188, 31 N.E. 961, syl. 2 (1892) (leading opinion by Field, C. J., overruling previous holding); State v. Ilgenfritz, 215 Mo. 615, 632, 173 S.W. 1041, syl. 4 (1915) (overruling earlier decisions); People v. Conklin, 175 N.Y. 333, 343, 67 N.E. 624, 627, syl. 7 (1903) (declarations three years before death erroneously excluded but not here prejudicial); Comm. v. Santos, 275 Pa. 515, 119 Atl. 596, syl. 3–6 (1923) (declarations shortly before, and two or three weeks before death properly admitted; remoteness in judge's discretion); 1 Wigmore, Evidence, § 143.

6. Browner v. Royal Indemnity Co., 246 Fed. 637, syl. 1 (C.C.A.Fla. 1917) (declarations several years before death when evidence showed that insured at time of death was subject to same depressing influence); Smith v. National Beneficial Society, 123 N.Y. 85, 25 N.E. 197, syl. 2 (1890) (declarations evincing intent to take out insurance and then kill himself admissible as res gestae); Klein v.

cases have either refused to receive them[7] or have hedged their admission with over-strict conditions.[8] Even more reluctance has been manifest in accepting in criminal cases threats of a third person to commit the act with which the accused is charged as evidence that the crime was committed by the third person, not the accused. While some cases seem to exclude such threats altogether,[9] the more acceptable practice is to admit them when the trial judge in his discretion finds that there is sufficient accompanying evidence of motive, overt acts, opportunity or like confirming circumstances to give substantial significance to the threats.[10]

In will cases it is now generally established that when the issue is, what were the acts of the decedent, his previous declarations of in-

tention are received as evidence of his later conduct.[11] Accordingly such declarations come in on the issues of forgery,[12] alteration,[13] contents of a last will[14] and as to whether acts of revocation were done by the testator.[15]

In homicide and assault cases when the accused claims self-defence, threats of the victim known to the accused are proveable to evidence his apprehension of danger and the reasonableness thereof.[16] For these purposes they have no hearsay element. When we pass to evidence of threats against the accused by the victim, of which the accused did not know, "uncommunicated threats," we find them relevant for quite a different purpose. They are declarations of intention to attack the accused, received as hearsay state-

Knights and Ladies of Security, 87 Wash. 179, 151 Pac. 241, syl. 1 (1915) (statements shortly before death); Note, Admissibility against Beneficiary of Declarations of Insured, 86 A.L.R. 146 at 157. As to admissibility of declarations to rebut the defense of suicide see Note, 93 A.L.R. 413 at 426.

7. See, e. g., Comm. v. Felch, 132 Mass. 32 (1882) and State v. Punshon, 124 Mo. 448, 457, 27 S.W. 1111, syl. 2 (1894) both overruled by decisions in their respective states cited in note 5, supra. Other excluding holdings are collected in 6 Wigmore, Evidence § 1726, note 4.

8. See, e. g., Greenacre v. Filby, 276 Ill. 294, 114 N.E. 536, syl. 2, 3 (1916) (A widow sued under the Dram Shop Act, to recover from persons who sold liquor to her husband, for his death. She alleged that due to intoxication he wandered on the railway track and was killed by a train. The defendants offered evidence that the husband had expressed the intention, at various times, to commit suicide. The court held them inadmissible and said that declarations of intention would be receivable only when accompanying an act, e. g., as when, on leaving the saloon, he declared his intention "to go home, kiss his wife and babies, and go to sleep.").

9. People v. King, 276 Ill. 138, 114 N.E. 601, 607, syl. 15 (1916) (hearsay and misleading); Buel v. State, 104 Wis. 132, 80 N.W. 78, syl. 5 (1899) and cases cited in 1 Wigmore, Evidence, § 140.

10. Alexander v. United States, 138 U.S. 353, 356, 357, 11 Sup.Ct. 350, 34 L.Ed. 954 (1891). And see the holding in Dubose v. State, 10 Tex.App. 230,

248, 252, syl. 3 (1881) that motive, threats and opportunity are admissible.

11. 6 Wigmore, Evidence, § 1735.

12. Atherton v. Gaslin, 194 Ky. 460, 239 S.W. 771 (1922), (able opinion by Clay, J.); State v. Ready, 78 N.J.L. 599, 75 Atl. 564 (Ct. of Errors and Appeals, 1909) (Gummere, C. J. reviews the cases); Johnson v. Brown, 51 Tex. 65, 67, 80 (1879) (testator declared that the purported legatees "should never have any of his property"). A leading case to the contrary, Throckmorton v. Holt, 180 U.S. 552, 21 Sup.Ct. 474, 45 L.Ed. 663 (1901) is disapproved in the first two opinions, supra, and is generally discredited. See Notes, Testator's declarations on the issue of genuineness, 62 A.L.R. 698, 119 A.L.R. 1366. But evidence of such declarations weighs lightly when put in the balance with evidence of expert document-examiners. See Re Creger's Estate, 135 Okl. 77, 274 Pac. 30, 62 A.L.R. 690, 693, 697, 1929, and compare J. P. McBaine, op. cit. 19 Calif.L.Rev. at 385, 1931.

13. Doe d. Shallcross v. Palmer, 16 Q.B. 747, 117 Eng.Rep. 1067 (1851).

14. Sugden v. Lord St. Leonards, 1 Prob.Div. 154 (Ct.App. 1876) (admissible to corroborate other evidence of contents).

15. Stuart v. McWhorter, 238 Ky. 82, 36 S.W.2d 842, syl. 5 (1931), and see Notes, Testator's Declarations as to Revocation, 79 A.L.R. 1493, 115 A.L.R. 713.

16. Jarrard v. State, 206 Ga. 112, 55 S.E.2d 706, syl. 7, 8 (1949); 2 Wigmore, Evidence, § 247; Dec.Dig. Homicide, ☞190(8).

ments to show the intention, and hence to ground the inference that the threatener carried out his purpose by committing the first act of aggression in the altercation with the accused.[17] Probably all courts would admit them for this purpose, but with varying qualifications.[18] The most liberal and reasonable of these qualifications is the requirement that there must be some additional evidence—and the testimony of the accused will be sufficient—that the victim was the first aggressor.[19] Some courts announce stricter views, such as a requirement that the other evidence, apart it seems from the defendant's own testimony, must not clearly show that the defendant was himself the first attacker, but must leave the question in doubt or conflict, before uncommunicated threats may be proved.[20] Another such limitation, espoused by a different group of courts, is the condition that there must have been evidence of eye-witnesses, seemingly other than the accused, that the victim committed the first hostile act.[21] These stricter views seem born of fear that the jury will feel that threats are a good ground for killing a man, or of a mistrust of the jury's capacity to weigh circumstantial inferences from threats in the balance with direct evidence of defendant's first aggression. Such fear and mistrust do not justify encroachment on the jury's function of passing upon conflicting testimony and inferences of fact.

Declarations of intention to show circumstantially the later conduct of the declarant are obviously subject, like all circumstantial inferences, to hazards of miscarriage. The declarant may change his mind or he may find it impossible to carry out his purpose. These hazards are increased when the plan requires joint action by another person, who may decline to cooperate. Where the declarant's intention is merely to find and be with the other person the latter's cooperation is at a minimum and admissibility presents little difficulty.[22] Even when the other person's part in the plan is more active, the courts have usually admitted the declaration.[23] This seems expedient. As showing

17. See the discriminating analysis of the relevancy on issues of the two kinds of threats in the able opinion of Lummus, J., in Comm. v. Rubin, 318 Mass. 587, 63 N.E.2d 344 (1945). It may be added, as pointed out in this case, that of course communicated threats are equally admissible for this purpose, but this use is usually ignored because of their stronger significance as showing reasonable apprehension by the accused.

18. The different views are discussed and the cases collected in 1 Wigmore, § 110, Dec.Dig. Homicide, ⚷190(7), and in a Comment, 18 U.Chi.L.Rev. 337 (1951). See also Notes, 49 Mich.L.Rev. 1234 (1951), 35 Minn.L.Rev. 315 (1951). The comment and notes deal with the interesting case of Griffin v. United States, reported at various stages, 164 F.2d 903; 336 U.S. 704, 69 Sup.Ct. 814, 93 L.Ed. 993; 183 F.2d 990 (1950). There accused was convicted of murder committed during a card game. The accused testified that the deceased attacked him first: all the other witnesses swore that the accused was the aggressor. Newly discovered evidence after the trial that an open pen knife was found in the pocket of the deceased though not in his hand, required, it was finally held, a new trial. Much of the discussion in the prevailing opinions dealt with the choice of varying views about the conditions of admitting uncommunicated threats. The equivalence of these facts with such threats may well be doubted.

19. Griffin v. United States, 183 F.2d 990, 992, syl. 2 (C.A.D.C.1950) (Edgerton, Circ. J. for majority); Comm. v. Rubin, 318 Mass. 587, 63 N.E.2d 344, syl. 4 (1945).

20. Comm. v. Peronace, 328 Pa. 86, 195 Atl. 57, syl. 6, 7 (1937) (threats properly excluded because evidence clearly showed accused first aggressor, though accused testified victim was aggressor).

21. State v. Carter, 197 La. 155, 1 So.2d 62, syl. 1, 2 (1941) (where only evidence of first aggression by deceased was from the accused and was not believed by judge, and all other evidence showed attack by accused, judge properly excluded evidence of threats under Code Cr.Proc. art. 482 making such threats inadmissible "in absence of proof" of overt acts by the victim).

22. See State v. Journey, in next note.

23. Mutual Life Ins. Co. v. Hillmon, 145 U.S. 285, 295, 296, 12 Sup.Ct. 909, 36 L.Ed. 706 (1892)

that the declarant probably carried out his share of the planned enterprise, his statement of intent is often a valuable and significant part of a larger matrix of circumstantial evidence. The possibility that the jury may use it as a hearsay report of the other person's intention, from which they will infer *his* conduct,[24] is safeguarded, first, by the adversary's right to an instruction limiting its use only to inferences as to declarant's intention and probable acts,[25] and second, by the necessity that the proponent produce independent and sufficient evidence of the other person's acts if they are material. Thus safeguarded, the risks of an unsanctioned hearsay use of the evidence are no greater than those we are accustomed to assume in other instances of evidence admis-

sible for one purpose, inadmissible for another.[26]

Whenever declarations of intention are offered as evidence of the declarant's subsequent conduct the question of admissibility of the evidence should be clearly discriminated from its sufficiency to support a finding that such conduct occurred. Standing alone such declarations would in the usual situation manifestly be insufficient to warrant such a finding,[27] and accordingly it is frequently said that declarations of intention are admitted in corroboration of other evidence to show such acts.[28] Insufficient as they frequently are, separately considered, they nevertheless may be significant contributions to an aggregation of evidence sufficient to establish the act and the identity

---

(letters of Walters expressing an intention of going on a trip with Hillmon, competent as evidence that he went, "and that he went with Hillmon"); People v. Alcalde, 24 Cal.2d 177, 148 P.2d 627, syl. 4, 5 (1944) (murder: the body of the victim, a woman of thirty, was found in a plowed field near city where accused lived; held, evidence that victim said to friend the day before her body was found, that she was going out with "Frank" (defendant's name) that evening properly received: excellent discussion of principle and decisions by Shenk, J.: able dissent by Traynor, J.); State v. Journey, 115 Conn. 344, 161 Atl. 515, syl. 6 (1932) (murder: victim's body found in burned barn, but death caused by shot-gun wounds; declarations of victim on morning of homicide that he was going to work for defendant properly admitted); State v. Perelli, 125 Conn. 321, 5 A.2d 705, syl. 3, 121 A.L.R. 1357, 1939, 128 Conn. 172, 21 A.2d 389, syl. 6, 1941 (murder: victim's declarations to wife of intended trip to meet defendants admissible, but his statements as to plan of himself and defendants for him to drive them to New Haven where the defendants would murder a third person, improperly received); Hunter v. State, 40 N.J.L. 495, 534, 536–538 (1878) (murder: statements of victim, shortly before leaving home, that he was going on business trip with accused properly received as *res gestae*); State v. Farnam, 82 Ore. 211, 161 Pac. 417, syl. 9–11 (1916) (murder of girl, whose body, on which abortion had been performed, was found in burned barn, five miles from girl's home; evidence that on same day, when invited to a friend's home, victim said she could not, because she thought Roy (accused) was coming down, properly received: defendant would

have been entitled to a limiting instruction if he had requested; extensive discussion and review of cases).

24. This danger is discussed and the prevailing practice of admitting such declarations is questioned in Maguire, The Hillmon Case, 38 Harv.L. Rev. 709, 717, 718 (1925).

25. Sometimes the courts require cautionary instructions which limit the probative use of the declarations too severely. See, e. g., State v. Phillips, 68 N.D. 113, 277 N.W. 609, syl. 4 (1938) (murder by abortion; declarations of deceased that she intended to go to defendant for abortion received with instruction that jury could consider it as tending to show her "design and plan" and merely for the purpose of showing that the abortion was probably done as planned; held, error, jury should have been told that such evidence could be considered only to show willingness of woman to have the abortion and the opportunity of defendant to perform it; Burr, J. dissenting). A critical note appears in 86 U.Pa.L. Rev. 904.

26. Compare the cases discussed in the fifth paragraph of the next preceding section, and see § 59.

27. The distinction between sufficiency and admissibility is clearly drawn by Clay, J. in Atherton v. Gaslin, 194 Ky. 460, 239 S.W. 771, 772 (1922). It is applied in Pritchard v. Harvey, 272 Ky. 58, 113 S.W.2d 865, syl. 3 (1938) (declarations insufficient standing alone to rebut presumption of revocation of lost will).

28. See the first opinion referred to in next preceding note, and see the cases cited in note 10, supra.

of the actor, and as such they will generally be admitted.

271. Declarations of State of Mind to Show Previous Conduct.

The estimate of the wisdom of the general policy excluding hearsay was higher thirty or forty years ago than it is today. Thus it is not surprising to find a commentator [1] of that era criticising the Hillmon holding [2] that declarations of intention are receivable to show later acts. He thought that its implications carried us too far, since they would logically require us to accept declarations of memory and belief to show the truth of the facts believed, which would undermine the hearsay principle itself. This warning, however, was heeded by the same court that decided Hillmon. It has declined to admit in a case of wife-murder by poisoning, the declaration of the wife while suffering from the dose, "My husband has poisoned me," offered to rebut the defense of suicide.[3] The evidence could not effectively be limited to proving her state of mind, Cardozo, J., said. "It will not do to say that the jury might accept the declarations for any light that they cast upon the existence of a vital urge, and reject them to the extent that they charged the death to some one else. Discrimination so subtle is a feat beyond the compass of ordinary minds. The reverberating clang of those accusatory words would drown all weaker sounds." [4] And of Hillmon he declared: "The ruling in that case marks the high-water line beyond which courts have been unwilling to go. It has developed a substantial body of criticism and commentary. Declarations of intention, casting light upon the future, have been sharply distinguished from declarations of memory, pointing backwards to the past. There would be an end, or nearly that, to the rule against hearsay if the distinction were ignored." [5]

Doubtless this theoretical position would currently be generally maintained by the courts. Nevertheless, the odor of sanctity of the general prohibition of hearsay is steadily weakening, and the stream of decision reveals the urge to admit declarations of persons deceased about previous happenings, where the needs of justice seem to require it.[6] It shows likewise the difficulty of an-

---

1. Seligman, An Exception to the Hearsay Rule, 26 Harv.L.Rev. 146 (1912). This commentary is itself discussed in E. W. Hinton, States of Mind and the Hearsay Rule, 1 U.Chi.L.Rev. 394, 403–423, 1934; Hutchins and Slesinger, State of Mind to Prove an Act, 38 Yale L.J. 283, 1929, and 13 Minn. L.Rev. 674; J. M. Maguire, The Hillmon Case— Thirty-three Years After, 38 Harv.L.Rev. 709, 1925.

2. Mutual Life Ins. Co. v. Hillmon, 145 U.S. 285, 12 Sup.Ct. 909, 36 L.Ed. 706 (1892), extensively discussed in next preceding section herein.

3. Shepard v. United States, 290 U.S. 96, 54 Sup.Ct. 22, 78 L.Ed. 196 (1933).

4. 290 U.S. 104.

5. 290 U.S. 105, 106.

6. Examples: Lloyd v. Powell Duffryn Steam Coal Co., Ltd., L.R. [1914] App.C. 733 (House of Lords) (proceeding under Workmen's Compensation Act by infant as illegitimate child of deceased coal-miner; held, declarations of deceased that he knew of mother's pregnancy and that he intended to marry her, admissible to prove (a) paternity and (b) dependency, i. e., probability that he would have supported the child: see analysis by Morgan (1948), 62 Harv.L.Rev. 209–213); Lee v. Mitcham, 69 App. D.C. 17, 98 F.2d 298, 117 A.L.R. 1427, syl. 4, 5, 1938 (Deceased with his own money paid the amount of a note of an orphan asylum of which he was treasurer, and receives from the holder possession of the note which was secured by a real estate mortgage; his heirs claim that the note was not paid, but was transferred to the deceased, and offer in evidence the notation to that effect made on the back of the note by the deceased as soon as he returned home; held, admissible); and Yarborough v. Prudential Insurance Co. of America, 99 F.2d 874, on rehearing, 100 F.2d 547, C.C.A.Ga., 1939 (Hutcheson, Circ. J., dissenting) comment 37 Mich. L.Rev. 966 (suit on life insurance policy by widow, defense, supported by evidence of insurance agent, that policy though reciting payment of premium, had not been paid for and was handed over for inspection only; widow allowed to testify that her husband, a few hours later, handed her the policy and told her to keep it, it was hers and paid for). See also People v. Weatherford, 27 Cal.2d 401, 164 P.2d 753, syl. 10, 11, 1945; noted 19 So.Calif.L.Rev.

swering this need within the trammels of accepted theory.

But in one field the courts have not waited for the advance of general hearsay theory. In wills cases the special need for the hearsay use of the testator's declarations to show his previous acts is apparent. The testator is dead and is usually the one who best knew the facts, and is often the only one who had any knowledge of them. The special reliability, though it is arguable that he may often want to deceive his relatives, is strongly supported by his first-hand knowledge and by his lack of selfish interest.[7] Accordingly, by the preponderance of recent decisions, the testator's declarations made after the alleged event are received to show that he has or has not made a will, or a will of a particular purport, or has or has not revoked his will.[8] Some courts reach these results by announcing a special exception to the hearsay rule for retrospective declarations in wills cases.[9] Others look upon the testator's declarations as statements of the mental condition of belief or memory, and hence coming within the present exception for declarations

---

449 (murder; declarations of deceased made to third persons of her intent to sell cafe and to go to mountains, held admissible as evidence that these intentions were known to defendant).

7. A powerful judicial argument for admissibility is that of Jessel, M.R. in Sugden v. Lord St. Leonards, L.R. [1876] 1 Prob.Div. 154, 241 (Ct.App.). After reviewing some other hearsay exceptions he says: "Now I take it the principle which underlies all these exceptions is the same. In the first place, the case must be one in which it is difficult to obtain other evidence, for no doubt the ground for admitting the exceptions was that very difficulty. In the next place the declarant must be disinterested; that is, disinterested in the sense that the declaration was not made in favour of his interest. And, thirdly, the declaration must be made before dispute or litigation, so that it was made without bias on account of the existence of a dispute or litigation which the declarant might be supposed to favour. Lastly, and this appears to me one of the strongest reasons for admitting it, the declarant must have had peculiar means of knowledge not possessed in ordinary cases.

"Now, all these reasons exist . . . in the case of a testator declaring the contents of his will."

The contrary argument is urged by Whelpley, J. in Boylan v. Meeker, 28 N.J.L. 274, 283 (1860): "No such motive [of self-interest] operates to secure truth in the declarations of a devisor. He may, to secure his own peace and comfort during life, to relieve himself from unpleasant importunities of expectant heirs, conceal the nature of his testamentary dispositions, and make statements calculated and intended to deceive those with whom he is conversing. He has neither the sanctity of an oath or the strong bond of self-interest to secure his adherence to the truth. The experience of every one must satisfy him that an inquiry made of a testator, as to the contents of his will, rarely elicits the truth."

McCormick Evidence HB—37

8. Gilliland v. Dobbs, 234 Ala. 364, 174 So. 784, syl. 13 (1937) (declaration by testator after date of alleged will, that she made no will, admissible to corroborate other evidence of forgery); Eder's Estate, 94 Colo. 173, 29 P.2d 631, syl. 16, 17 (1934) (declarations admitted as evidence that he had not revoked lost will); Saliba v. Saliba, 202 Ga. 791, 44 S.E.2d 744, syl. 11 (1947) (declarations admissible to support or rebut presumption of revocation, though not accompanied by any act); Loy v. Loy, 246 S. W.2d 578, syl. 2–5 (Ky.1952) (admissible, but not sufficient to establish contents of lost will); In re Roeder's Estate, 44 N.M. 429, 103 P.2d 631, syl. 2, 4 (1940) (declarations before and after alleged alteration of will by testator, received: liberal discussion of hearsay problem by Bickley, C. J.); Compton v. Dannenbauer, 120 Tex. 14, 35 S.W.2d 682, syl. 2, 79 A.L.R. 1488 (1931) (testator's statements after making will, that he made no other will, admissible on issue of revocation).

Contra: Barger v. Barger, 221 Ind. 530, 48 N.E.2d 813, syl. 2, 3 (1943) (post-testamentary declarations inadmissible as evidence of contents); Hickey v. Beeler, 180 Tenn. 31, 177 S.W.2d 277, syl. 7 (1943) (issue as to whether will propounded had been revoked by later inconsistent will, not found, or whether earlier will revived; held, declarations before and after alleged revocation inadmissible unless part of res gestae).

The problems are discussed and the cases classified in 6 Wigmore, Evidence § 1736. See also Dec.Dig. Wills, ⌐297; Notes, Declarations as Evidence of genuineness or due execution, 62 A.L.R. 698, 710, 119 A.L.R. 1366, 1368; on issue of revocation, Notes, 79 A.L.R. 1493, 115 A.L.R. 713, and see Managle v. Parker, 75 N.H. 139, 71 Atl. 637, 24 L.R.A.,N.S. 180, Ann.Cas.1912A, 269, syl. 1, 1908; May v. Brown, 144 Tex. 350, 190 S.W.2d 715, 165 A.L.R. 1180, syl. 6, 1945 (declarations of dissatisfaction with will admitted as evidence of revocation).

9. E. g., Loy v. Loy, Ky., and In re Roeder's Estate, N.M., in next preceding note.

of mental state, and raising the circumstantial inference that the belief must have been prompted by facts.[10] Or again the declarations may be looked on, not as statements, but as conduct evincing a belief circumstantially, and from this the inference as to the previous acts is derived.[11]

As the courts become further accustomed to the hearsay use of retrospective declarations in this important field of wills, it seems likely and desirable that this practice will serve as the core for a wider exception to the hearsay rule. This, by analogy, could take the following shape. The declarations of a person, now unavailable as a witness from death or other cause, as to facts within his knowledge, made under circumstances of apparent sincerity, will be received to evidence these facts.[12]

TOPIC 3

EXCITED UTTERANCES

272. Excited Utterances (Spontaneous Exclamations).[1]

From the mists of *res gestae*[2] there has emerged, under Wigmore's discerning analysis,[3] an exception to the hearsay rule for statements uttered under stress of excitement produced by a startling event and made before the declarant has had time or opportunity to reflect or contrive.[4] The factor of

---

10. See, e. g., Hannen, J. in Keen v. Keen, L.R. [1873] 3 P. & D. 105, 107 ("A statement by the testator that he has altered his mind as to the disposition of his property, and that he has therefore destroyed his will, although it may not be evidence of the fact of the destruction of the will, is evidence of intention, from which the fact of destruction may be inferred, there being other circumstances leading to the same conclusion."); 6 Wigmore, Evidence, § 1736.

11. See, e. g., Hannen, J., in Sugden v. Lord St. Leonards, L.R. [1876] 1 Prob.Div. 154, 202: ". . . Believing as I do, the testator made these statements [describing provisions in will] shewing a belief in his mind that the will was in existence at a time subsequently to that at which he could have revoked it, I am led to the conclusion that he had not, in fact, revoked it . . ."; Wigmore, Evidence, §§ 271, 1736, and compare the less liberal treatment generally of conduct offered for this purpose, see § 229, herein, and 1 Wigmore, Evidence, § 267.

12. Such a development is advocated in Hutchins & Slesinger, State of Mind to Prove an Act, 38 Yale L.J. 283, 289–295 (1929). The rule suggested in the text above is similar to the provisions of the Massachusetts Hearsay Statute (Gen.L.[Ter.Ed.] c. 233, § 65) the Model Code of Evidence, R. 503, and Uniform Rules of Evidence, R. 63(4) (c). See § 304, herein.

1. 6 Wigmore, Evidence, §§ 1745–1764; Hutchins and Slesinger, Spontaneous Exclamations, 28 Col. L.Rev. 432 (1928); Notes, Spontaneous Exclamations, 22 Minn.L.Rev. 391, 1938 (an illuminating treatment distinguishing this from the other branches of "res gestae" and suggesting the line of future development); Res Gestae in Accident Cases,

163 A.L.R. 15, a comprehensive note; and see Decennial Digests, Evidence, ☞118–128½, Criminal Law, ☞363, 366, 368.

Discussions focussed on local law: Notes, 25 Ill. Bar J. 288 (1937), 32 Corn.L.Q. 115 (1946) (New York); 6 Oh.St.L.J. 6 (1939); 13 Temp.U.L.Q. 242 (1939) (Pennsylvania); Hardman, Spontaneous Declarations, 54 W.Va.L.Rev. 93 (1952).

The principle is embodied in Uniform Rules of Evidence, R. 63(4), which admits "A statement (a) which the judge finds was made while the declarant was perceiving the event or condition which the statement narrates, describes or explains, or (b) which the judge finds was made while the declarant was under the stress of a nervous excitement caused by such perception. . . ."

2. See the discussion of "res gestae" in § 274, herein.

3. 6 Wigmore, Evidence, §§ 1745–1747.

4. "A res gestae declaration may be defined as a spontaneous declaration by a person whose mind has been suddenly made subject to an overpowering emotion caused by some unexpected and shocking occurrence, which that person has just participated in or closely witnessed, and made in reference to some phase of that occurrence which he perceived, and this declaration must be made so near the occurrence both in time and place as to exclude the likelihood of its having emanated in whole or in part from his reflective faculties." Maxey, J., in Allen v. Mack, 345 Pa. 407, 28 A.2d 783, 784 (1942). For other able formulations, see the opinions of Goodrich, J. in Trouser Corp. v. Goodman & Theise, 153 F.2d 284, 287 (C.C.A.Pa.1946); Carter, J. in Showalter v. Western P. Ry. Co., 16 Cal.2d 460, 106 P.2d 895, 899 (1940); Hallam, J., In Lambrecht v. Schreyer, 129 Minn. 271, 152 N.W. 645, 646 (1915).

special reliability is thought to be furnished by the excitement which suspends the powers of reflection and fabrication. Again, as in the other cases of "spontaneous" statements in this chapter, this factor of special reliability serves to dispense also with any requirement that the declarant be unavailable as a witness, on the view that even his testimony on the stand would be less reliable than the statements made under the excitement of the event.[5] Psychologists would probably concede that excitement stills the voice of reflective self-interest but they might question whether this factor of reliability is not over-borne by the distorting

effect which shock and excitement have upon observation and judgment.[6] But they might well conclude that contemporaneous statements both excited and unexcited are so valuable for the accurate reconstruction of the facts that the need is not to narrow the use of excited statements but to widen the exception to embrace as well unexcited declarations of observers near the time of the happening.[7]

At any rate, excitement flowing from a startling event is the key requirement now. Under prevailing practice the declaration itself seems to be taken as evidence of the fact of the happening of the startling event.[8]

This ground of admissibility is often resorted to when the statement of a driver or other employee after an accident is sought to be used against his employer but does not qualify as a vicarious admission. See, e. g., Hinton v. Dixie Ohio Exp. Co., 188 F.2d 121, syl. 1–3 (C.A.Ky.1951); MacDonald v. Appleyard, 94 N.H. 362, 53 A.2d 434, syl. 13 (1947).

5. Mobile & Montgomery R. Co. v. Ashcraft, 48 Ala. 15, 31 (1872) (declarations of passenger jumping off car, received. "We regard these declarations as a part of the res gestae and more convincing . . . than the testimony to that effect of the persons themselves some time after the occurrence"); 6 Wigmore, Evidence, § 1748.

6. "One need not be a psychologist to distrust an observation made under emotional stress; everybody accepts such statements with mental reservation. M. Gorphe cites the case of an excited witness to a horrible accident who erroneously declared that the coachman deliberately and vindictively ran down a helpless woman. Fiore tells of an emotionally upset man who testified that hundreds were killed in an accident; that he had seen their heads rolling from their bodies. In reality only one man was killed, and five others injured. Another excited gentleman took a pipe for a pistol. Besides these stories from real life, there are psychological experiments which point to the same conclusion. After a battle in a classroom, prearranged by the experimenter but a surprise to the students, each one was asked to write an account of the incident. The testimony of the most upset students was practically worthless, while those who were only slightly stimulated emotionally scored better than those left cold by the incident." Hutchins and Slesinger, Spontaneous Exclamations, 28 Col.L.Rev. 432, 437 (1928) (footnote references omitted).

7. See Hutchins & Slesinger, op. cit. at p. 439.

8. The cases are mostly suits upon life or accident insurance or death-claims for workmen's compensation, where there was no eye-witness to the accident. Often there are corroborative circumstances to aid the declaration. Travelers' Insurance Co. v. Mosley, 8 Wall. 397, 408, 19 L.Ed. 437 (1869). But the cases are numerous where the only direct evidence of the exciting event is the declaration itself. See, e. g., Collins v. Equitable Life Ins. Co., 122 W.Va. 171, 8 S.E.2d 825 (1940), noted in 47 W.Va.L.Q. 340, 130 A.L.R. 287; Stewart v. Baltimore & Ohio R. Co., 137 F.2d 527, syl. 4 (C.C.A.N.Y. (1943); Preferred Accident Ins. Co. of New York v. Combs, 76 F.2d 775, syl. 2 (C.C.A.Neb.1935); Johnston v. W. S. Nott Co., 183 Minn. 309, 236 N.W. 466, syl. 1, 2 (1931); National Life & Accident Ins. Co. v. Hedges, 233 Ky. 840, 27 S.W.2d 422, syl. 1, 2 (1930); Industrial Commission v. Diveley, 88 Colo. 190, 192, 193, 294 Pac. 532 (1930). Sometimes, however, the foundation for the declaration collapses because the circumstances fail to show that the time-interval was sufficiently brief. Aetna L. Ins. Co. v. Ryan, 255 Fed. 483, syl. 1 (C.C.A. 2, 1918). This practice of receiving the declaration to show the startling event and then justifying its admission under an exception to the hearsay rule because it is the product of the startling event—the declaration thus lifting itself by its boot-straps—may be explained on the ground that the trial judge in passing upon issues of fact preliminary to the admission of evidence is not bound by the jury-trial rules of exclusion. See 5 Wigmore, Evidence, § 1385. This sensible view, however, is hardly borne out by the practice of American courts generally on such issues, Maguire and Epstein, Rules of Evidence in Preliminary Controversies as to Admissibility, 36 Yale L.J. 1100 (1927), but is surely salutary in its present application. Or

Whether the declaration alone would be sufficient to prove these preliminary facts is not made clear by the decisions.[9] While the declarant is usually a participant in the exciting event—the driver of a colliding automobile,[10] the victim of the accident [11] or murderous assault,[12] or the rape-complainant [13]—, this is not essential and the declaration of a by-stander may qualify.[14] The declaration must, however, relate to the immediate facts of the startling occurrence.[15]

The test to be applied by the judge is: was the declaration spontaneous, excited, or impulsive, or was it the product of reflection and deliberation? This attempt to reconstruct the state of another man's mind and emotions as of a moment in the past is so complex and individualized a judgment that the trial judge must be given considerable lee-way of decision.[16]

The most important factor is the time-element. If as is frequently the case, the declaration occurs while the startling event is still in progress, it is easy to find that excitement prompted the utterance.[17] But

this straining for admission of decedent's declarations in these solitary-death cases may be thought of as a step toward the recognition of an exception for all declarations if the declarant is unavailable and had no motive for fabrication when the statement was made. See the remarks of the commentator in the Note, 163 A.L.R. at p. 203, where the cases on this problem are collected.

9. The declarations were received with a minimum of confirmatory evidence in Stewart v. Baltimore & Ohio Ry. Co., 137 F.2d 526, syl. 4 (C.C.A.N.Y.1943) and Armour & Co. v. Industrial Comm., 78 Colo. 569, 243 Pac. 546, syl. 4 (1926).

10. See, e. g., Lane v. Pacific Greyhound Lines, 26 Cal.2d 575, 160 P.2d 21, syl. 9 (1945); Duncan v. Rhomberg, 212 Iowa 389, 236 N.W. 638, syl. 5 (1931).

11. E. g., Kansas City Southern R. Co. v. Clinton, 224 Fed. 896, syl. 4 (C.C.A. 8, 1915); Chief Consol. Min. Co. v. Industrial Comm., 70 Utah 333, 260 Pac. 271, syl. 2 (1927).

12. E. g., State v. McCarthy, 160 Ore. 196, 83 P.2d 801, syl. 3 (1938); Giddings v. State, 130 Tex.Crim. 406, 94 S.W.2d 1168, syl. 1 (1936); Dec.Dig. Crim. Law, ⊂⟩366.

13. E. g., State v. McCrady, 152 Kan. 566, 106 P.2d 696, syl. 1–3 (1940); McCann v. Comm., 174 Va. 429, 4 S.E.2d 768, syl. 2 (1939); Dec.Dig. Crim.Law, ⊂⟩366. For other theories on which evidence of complaints may be received, see 6 Wigmore, Evidence, §§ 1760, 1761, and Dec.Dig. Rape, ⊂⟩48.

14. Vescio v. Penn. Elec. Co., 336 Pa. 502, 9 A.2d 546, 550, syl. 12 (1939) (dictum); Bennett v. City of Seattle, 22 Wash.2d 455, 156 P.2d 685, syl. 2 (1945) (injury to pedestrian in collision with bus; statement by bus passenger just after collision that pedestrian walked into bus, admissible); 6 Wigmore, Evidence, § 1755. But the disinterestedness of the casual bystander may be a factor influencing the court to find that he was not excited. Schendel

v. Chicago, M. & St. P. Ry. Co., 158 Minn. 378, 197 N.W. 744, 746 (1924). And a few courts, clinging to an outmoded "verbal acts" analogy, insist that the declarant must have been an actor in the transaction. Indianapolis, St. Ry. Co. v. Whitaker, 160 Ind. 125, 66 N.E. 433, 434, syl. 2 (1903) ("must be the act speaking through the witness"); Note, 163 A.L.R. 179–181.

15. Cook v. Hall, 308 Ky. 500, 214 S.W.2d 1017, syl. 2 (1948) (son's statement after collision that he had father's permission to drive truck, excluded: "must elucidate the act"); Bagwell v. McLellan Stores Co., 216 S.C. 207, 57 S.E.2d 257, syl. 5, 6 (1949) (after plaintiff's fall, bystander said, "The floor has just been oiled and she fell," excluded, does not "characterize the event"); 6 Wigmore, Evidence, §§ 1750(c), 1754. As applied in these cases the restriction seems to have little relevance to trustworthiness. It is a borrowing from the verbal act doctrine (see 6 Wigmore, Evidence, § 1752, and § 274 herein) and has no place here. The purport of the statement and its relation to the exciting event should be merely matters to be considered in determining whether the declaration was probably spontaneous or was reflective.

16. Hartford Accident & Ind. Co. v. Olivier, 123 F. 2d 709, syl. 2 (C.C.A.Tex.1941) (application of standard of spontaneity largely left to judge's discretion); Webber v. E. K. Larimer Hardware Co., 234 Iowa 1381, 15 N.W.2d 286, syl. 15, 16 (1944) (discretionary but here a clear abuse to exclude); Henry Chevrolet Co. v. Taylor, 188 Okl. 380, 108 P.2d 1024, syl. 5 (1940) (judge's discretion reviewable only for abuse, not here shown); Dec.Dig., Evidence, ⊂⟩118b. It has been suggested that the question of spontaneity be left wholly to the trial judge. 6 Wigmore, Evidence, § 1750.

17. See, e. g., Schwam v. Reece, 213 Ark. 431, 210 S.W.2d 903, syl. 9 (1948) (Bus passenger's exclamation to driver, "Throw on your brakes," and driver's reply, "I have no brakes," just before colli-

when the statement follows the event, the length of the interval between the startling event and the declaration is often crucial.[18] Whether this period affords opportunity for contrivance will be much affected by the declarant's physical condition during the interval, and shock, pain, unconsciousness and

like stresses will tend to postpone that opportunity.[19]

It is sometimes, under the lingering spell of the "res gestae" metaphor, held that a declaration which is a "mere narrative" of a past event,[20] or one made in answer to a question,[21] or one which is "self-serving" in

sion); Lambrecht v. Schreyer, 129 Minn. 271, 152 N.W. 645, syl. 4 (1915) (girl's exclamation as she fell from surrey); New York, C. & St. L. Ry. Co. v. Kovatch, 120 Oh.St. 532, 166 N.E. 682 (1929) (exclamation while train still passing at crossing, that train had run over child); Chief Consol. Min. Co. v. Industrial Comm., 70 Utah 333, 260 Pac. 271, syl. 2 (1927) (declaration while rocks were falling that declarant had been hit by one); Note, 163 A. L.R. 46–58.

18. Elapsed time in some recent cases follows. Declarations excluded: Alabama Power Co. v. Ray, 249 Ala. 568, 32 So.2d 219, syl. 3 (1947) (5 minutes); Everett v. State, 213 Ark. 470, 210 S.W.2d 918, syl. 5 (1948) (15 minutes); Brown v. United States, 80 App.D.C. 270, 152 F.2d 138, syl. 3 (1945) (3 hours); Bennett v. Bennett, 92 N.H. 379, 31 A.2d 374, syl. 15–20 (1943) (4 hours); Ebeling v. Harmon, 83 Oh.App. 519, 80 N.E.2d 704, syl. 3 (1948) (5–10 minutes); State v. Smith, 200 S.C. 188, 20 S.E.2d 726, syl. 8 (1942) (statements during period from 30 minutes to 1½ hours after homicidal act). Declarations admitted: Standard Accident Ins. Co. v. Heatfield, 141 F.2d 648, syl. 3, 4 (C.C.A.Wash., 1944) (statements one hour, and 1½ hours, respectively); Maynard v. Hall, 61 Ariz. 32, 143 P.2d 884, syl. 3, 150 A.L.R. 618 (1946) (1½–3 minutes); State v. Sucik, 217 Minn. 556, 14 N.W.2d 857 (1944) (2–3 minutes); State v. Godwin, 51 N.M. 65, 178 P.2d 584, syl. 5 (1947) (one-half hour); Meyers v. Hagert Const. Co., 74 N.D. 435, 23 N.W.2d 29, syl. 1 (1946) (one or two minutes); Comm. v. Logan, 361 Pa. 186, 63 A.2d 28, syl. 5 (1949) (7 minutes); Lusk v. Monongahela Water Co., 164 Pa.Super. 354, 64 A.2d 670, syl. 2–6 (1949) (about ½ hour); Taylor v. State, 149 Tex.Cr. 530, 196 S.W.2d 925, syl. 3 (1946) (5 minutes). See also notes collating time-intervals, 24 Wash.U.L.Q. 273 (1939), 130 A.L.R. 302–306.

State v. Stafford, 237 Iowa 780, 23 N.W.2d 832, syl. 3–5 (1946), noted 37 J.Crim.L. 419, is extreme and questionable. There a wife, who had been cruelly beaten and injured by her husband, after wandering all night came to her sister's house, in a desperate physical condition, and declared that her husband tried to kill her. This declaration was held to have been properly received in the judge's discretion, though made 14 hours after the beating.

19. Standard Accident Ins. Co. v. Heatfield, 141 F.2d 648, 651, syl. 3, 4 (C.C.A.Wash., 1944) (statements

made 1 hour and 1½ hours respectively after overexertion constituting the accident claimed; suffered severe pain and nausea during interval and died within 12 hours; held no abuse of discretion to admit; "such anguish negatives the existence of reflective thought"); Clark v. Davis, 153 Minn. 143, 190 N.W. 45, syl. 2 (1922) (solitary fatal accident; statement to sister "well within 2 hours" after accident, and to mother ½ hour later: before statements deceased had leg amputation, under ether, and had suffered "extreme agony"; held, properly admitted in discretion); Suhr v. Lindell, 133 Neb. 856, 277 N.W. 381, syl. 7–13 (1938) (truck driver fatally injured in night collision was taken to hospital with arm crushed, suffering from shock and loss of blood; statement to doctor and nurses "at least 30 minutes" after crash held properly received; statement shortly after to employer that he was not to blame held erroneously admitted). Compare Sconce v. Jones, 343 Mo. 362, 121 S.W.2d 777, 782, syl. 1–7 (1938) (Injured truckdriver lay with both legs broken, not conscious all the time for 1¼ hours and made statements to those who came up. "We cannot find that plaintiff's evidence shows that he was under such influence of shock or pain as to be unable to reflect or reason . . ."). See also Note, 130 A.L.R. 308–310.

20. Such phraseology seems to be employed in some jurisdictions to impose requirements that declarations must be actually, or nearly, concurrent with the event and exclamatory, not narrative or descriptive in form. See, e. g., Barnes v. Rumford, 96 Me. 315, 52 Atl. 844, syl. 7 (1902); Rankin v. Brockton Public Market, 257 Mass. 6, 153 N.E. 97; syl. 3 (1926); Simon v. Dixie Greyhound Lines, 179 Miss. 568, 176 So. 160, syl. 2, 3 (1937); Greener v. General Electric Co., 209 N.Y. 135, 102 N.E. 527, 528 (1913); Ingersoll v. Liberty Bank, 278 N.Y. 1, 14 N.E.2d 828, syl. 4 (1938): see criticism, 6 Wigmore, Evidence, § 1756. Other states, formerly having this stricter view, have yielded to the general trend toward the more liberal view which admits statements narrative in form and made after a brief interval under persisting excitement. See the review by states in Note, 163 A.L.R. 60–89. Examples of expressions of the liberal view are given in note 4, this section, above.

21. Excluded on this ground. Itzkowitz v. P. H. G. Ruebel & Co., 158 Ark. 454, 250 S.W. 535, syl. 2 (1923) and see Greener v. General Electric Co., 209

the sense of favoring the declarant's interest,[22] are automatically excluded. The currently prevailing view, however, is that these are merely factors for consideration of the judge in deciding whether the declaration was spontaneous or contrived.[23]

Must the declarant be shown to have met the tests of competency for a witness? In general, it seems not. The declarant is not usually before the court to be examined as to his competency, and the declarations furthermore come in only under special safeguards—here, the requirement of *excited utterance*—which diminish the need for further caution. Consequently, it is held that evidence of spontaneous declarations of infants is admissible despite the incompetency of the child as a witness.[24] Such is also the rule in the case of an insane declarant,[25] or one incompetent by reason of conviction of a felony,[26] or where the declaration was made by the husband or wife of the ac-

cused in a criminal case.[27] In a modified way, however, the knowledge qualification is applied. If a startling event and an excited utterance about it are shown and the circumstances are consistent with knowledge by the declarant, this is sufficient without direct qualifying proof of knowledge.[28] If there is doubt the question is for the jury.[29] If, however, the attendant circumstances show without reasonable dispute that the declarant had no opportunity to know the facts declared, the declaration will be excluded.[30]

The opinion rule, which prefers the concrete form of statement to the general or inferential form,[31] is defensible as a rule about examining witnesses in court, where a new question may be asked if the first is found to call for an opinion. But applied to out-of-court declarations admitted under the hearsay exceptions the rule would run counter to the way people naturally talk, and it should not have a place there.[32] In the field

---

N.Y. 135, 102 N.E. 527 (1913). Held merely **a** factor for consideration. Meyer v. Travelers' Ins. Co., 130 Minn. 242, 153 N.W. 523, syl. 1 (1915); McGowan v. Peter Doelger Brewing Co., 10 N.J.Super. 276, 77 A.2d 46, syl. 2 (1950); and see Lucchesi **v.** Reynolds, 125 Wash. 352, 216 Pac. 12, syl. 3 (1923); Note, 163 A.L.R. 167–171.

22. Fischer v. Chicago & N. W. Ry. Co., 193 Minn. 73, 258 N.W. 4, syl. 3, 4 (1934) (motorist injured at crossing allowed to testify to his own reproaches to trainman, shortly after he "came to" after accident, held, should have been excluded as self-serving). But by the prevailing view this aspect is not conclusive but merely a factor in passing on spontaneity. Bennett v. Bennett, 92 N.H. 379, 31 A.2d 374, syl. 20 (1943); Notes, 22 Minn.L.Rev. 391, 402, 403 (1938), 163 A.L.R. 128, 129.

23. See notes 20–22, above.

24. New York C. & St. L. Ry. Co. v. Kovatch, 120 Oh.St. 532, 166 N.E. 682, 684 (1929) (girl 5 years old); City of Houston v. Quinones, 142 Tex. 282, 177 S.W.2d 259, syl. 9 (1944) (girl 3 at time of injury, under 5 at time of trial, held not ground of exclusion, "if the child possesses sufficient intelligence to render . . . her statements reliable"); 6 Wigmore, Evidence, § 1751.

25. Wilson v. State, 49 Tex.Cr.R. 50, 90 S.W. 312, syl. 11 (1905) (murder-victim's declaration admitted, and held it was not necessary to submit to the jury the

question whether he was conscious and sane at the time).

26. Blocker v. State, 118 Tex.Cr.R. 202, 40 S.W.2d 803, syl. 2, 3 (1931).

27. Robbins v. State, 73 Tex.Cr.R. 367, 166 S.W. 528, syl. 2 (1914) (murder; declarations of defendant's wife "Poor man! He lost his life trying to protect me," offered by state held admissible).

28. New York, C. & St. L. Ry. Co. v. Kovatch, 120 Oh. St. 532, 166 N.E. 682, 684 (1929) (evidence of scream immediately after accident to boy, "the engine runned over David," while the train was passing, apparently by little girl seen nearby but not subsequently identified, properly received, citing and describing like cases); and see 6 Wigmore, Evidence, § 1751(a), Notes, 24 Iowa L.Rev. 558 (1939), 127 A.L.R. 1030, 163 A.L.R. 185, 186.

29. See § 10, herein.

30. Commonwealth v. Fugmann, 330 Pa. 4, 198 Atl. 99, syl. 1–10 (1938) (victim who received "infernal machine" in mail declares after explosion, "F. done this"); Lavender v. Kurn, 355 Mo. 168, 195 S.W.2d 460, syl. 2, 3 (1946) (spontaneous statement that H "was supposed" to have been struck by **something** protruding from car, inadmissible).

31. See §§ 11, 12, herein.

32. See § 18, herein.

of excited utterances, however, as in other areas of hearsay admissible under exceptions, the courts have ignored the practical differences between the conditions of courtroom testimony and of out-of-court speech, and have usually said that the opinion rule will be applied.[33] There is some support, however, for the contrary view,[34] and it is believed that all courts would apply the rule more leniently to out-of-court declarations than to testimony in court.[35] The question arises most frequently in respect to those excited utterances wherein the speaker places blame or responsibility upon himself or upon another person. Here most courts do apply the opinion-restriction,[36] presumably on the view that the declaration is likely to be given exaggerated weight by a jury,[37] but it is believed that the need for the knowledge or impression about the facts which such a

statement conveys ordinarily outweighs this danger, and a considerable number of decisions have approved their admission.[38]

As appears in the foregoing discussion the trend is toward the widening of the admission of spontaneous statements under the vague rubric of *res gestae*.[39] There is need for further progress in this direction. Two deficiencies in existing practice are apparent. First, the tendency of a few courts to narrow admissibility to statements strictly concurrent with the startling event.[40] Second, even when excitement rather than concurrence in time is accepted as the standard, the limits of admissibility are still so narrow as to lead to one-sided and unjust results in the cases of fatal accidents where the declarations of the victim are the only evidence available to his survivors. Examples are the fatal accident to the solitary workman [41] or the col-

---

[33]. See, e. g., Hitchman v. H. S. Kerbough Co., 242 Pa. 282, 89 Atl. 669, syl. 2 (1914); Field v. North Coast Transp. Co., 164 Wash. 123, 127–132, 2 P.2d 672, syl. 3, 76 A.L.R. 1114, 1120 (1931) and cases cited in Notes, 163 A.L.R. 186–191, 42 L.R.A.,N.S., 938, and in Dec.Dig., Evidence ⊂⇒118f.

[34]. In Cromeenes v. San Pedro, L. A. & S. L. R. Co., 37 Utah 475, 109 Pac. 10, 19–21 (1910) the defendant's engine ran over a boy. M, a bystander, immediately went over to the engineer and said, "You have done a damn fine job. Why didn't you stop before you ran over him?" The majority held that this was properly received, and that the fact that the declaration is in opinion form is not a ground of exclusion. The opinion of Straup, C. J. cites an extensive array of decisions, civil and criminal, to like effect.

[35]. See, e. g., Houston Oxygen Co. v. Davis, 139 Tex. 1, 161 S.W.2d 474, 477, 140 A.L.R. 868 (1942). There the defendant in a collision case offered evidence that an occupant of a car which was passed by car in which plaintiff was riding, shortly before the collision, exclaimed that "they must have been drunk, that we would find them . . . wrecked if they kept that rate of speed up." The court held that it was error to exclude this declaration as "the witness was alluding to an occurrence within her own knowledge in language calculated to make her 'meaning clearer to the jury' than would a mere expression of opinion as to the speed. . . ."

[36]. Whitney v. Sioux City, 172 Iowa 336, 154 N.W. 497, syl. 1, 2 (1915) (by passenger in automobile, "We

were going too fast"); Gray v. Boston Elev. R. Co., 215 Mass. 143, 102 N.E. 71, syl. 5 (1913) (sudden start case, by spectator, "it was his own fault"); Bowers v. Kugler, 140 Neb. 684, 1 N.W.2d 299, syl. 1–8 (1941) (by driver fatally burned, "Oh, my God! It might have been my fault"); Neisner Bros v. Schaefer, 124 Oh.St. 311, 178 N.E. 269, syl. 1 (1931) (by clerk in store, "I am sorry I caused it; I should not have dropped the paper on the floor"); Notes, 163 A.L.R. 188, 189, 13 U.Detroit L.J. 231 (1950).

[37]. See comment in Note, 163 A.L.R. 188.

[38]. Cross Lake Logging Co. v. Joyce, 83 Fed. 989, syl. 1 (C.C.A. 8, 1897) (by plaintiff, "I wouldn't have lost my leg if you had done as you agreed to and put another man in his place"); Atlantic Coast Line Ry. Co. v. Crosby, 53 Fla. 400, 43 So. 318, 331, syl. 18 (1907) (child hurt on train, statement of mother, "it was all my fault"; one judge dissenting on this point); State v. Sloan, 47 Mo. 604, 610 (1871) (murder, statement of deceased to surgeon dressing his wound, "Sloan was not at fault, that he had drawn on the difficulty by attacking him and that if his pistol had not hung he would have killed him").

[39]. Travelers' Insurance Co. v. Mosley, 8 Wall. 397, 408, 19 L.Ed. 437 (1869); Texas Employers' Ins. Ass'n v. Shiffette, 91 S.W.2d 787, 790 (Tex.Civ.App. 1936); Heg v. Mullen, 115 Wash. 252, 197 Pac. 51, 52 (1921).

[40]. See note 20, supra.

[41]. See cases cited in note 43, below.

lision resulting in the death of the driver of one car though the occupants of the other car may have survived.[42] Some courts have said that there should be a wider latitude for the admission of spontaneous statements in workmen's compensation cases,[43] and the Minnesota court has held in a fatal accident case that a statement by the victim as to a fall made unexcitedly about 45 minutes later, uttered before he could have believed that his injury would be serious and when he had no motive to misrepresent, was admissible under "a liberal interpretation of the *res gestae* rule." [44] This is the kind of judicial enlargement of existing evidence law to meet emerging needs that offers the best promise of survival of the common law system. In states where judges have a more restricted view of their responsibilities,[45] the legislature, it seems, should move in the direction signalled by the Massachusetts hearsay statute admitting declarations of deceased persons when the judge finds that the statement was made before suit in good faith upon personal knowledge.[46]

TOPIC 4

DECLARATIONS OF PRESENT SENSE IMPRESSIONS

273. Unexcited Declarations of Present Sense Impressions.

The creative recognition by Wigmore of excitement as the source of special trustworthiness for declarations following a startling event has gone far to clarify the murky mist of res gestae and to give a rational basis for admission of excited utterances incident to a crime or an accident.[1] Another brilliant generalization by Morgan has led to an advance in clear thinking about statements accompanying non-startling events or relating to a condition which the declarant is observing. Such statements though unexcited usually possess a high degree of trustworthiness. If a person observes some situation or happening which is not at all startling or shocking in its nature, nor actually producing excitement in the observer, the observer may yet have occasion to comment on what he sees (or learns from other senses) *at the very time that he is receiving the impression*. Such a comment, as to a situation then before the declarant, does not have the safeguard of impulse, emotion, or excitement, but as Morgan points out [2] there are other safeguards. In the first place, the report at the moment of the thing then seen, heard, etc., is safe from any error from defect of *memory* of the declarant. Secondly, there is little or no *time* for calculated misstatement, and thirdly, the statement will usually be made to another (the witness who reports it) who would have equal opportunities to observe and hence to check a misstatement. Consequently, it is believed that such comments, limited to reports of *present* sense-

---

42. See, e. g., Suhr v. Lindell, 133 Neb. 856, 277 N.W. 381 (1938).

43. Jacobs v. Village of Buhl, 199 Minn. 572, 273 N.W. 245, 247, syl. 1 (1937) ("In every small city and hamlet there is a policeman working alone at night. Night watchmen work alone. Other employees work alone. These employees are subject to numerous possibilities of accidents which may cause conditions that may bring about their death. They do not have a witness with them to furnish proof as to the happening of an accident if the injuries they receive close their lips in death. The number of compensation cases which reach the courts of last resort where the only proof of the accident is the declaration of the injured employee give weighty proof of the truth of the declaration of the Pennsylvania court that to give a strict application of the res gestae rule in compensation cases would defeat the intent of the Workmen's Compensation Law."); Thompson v. Conemaugh Iron Works, 114 Pa.Super. 247, 254, 175 Atl. 45, 48, syl. 2 (1934).

44. Jacobs v. Village of Buhl, next preceding note.

45. See, e. g., the opinion of Simmons, C. J., in Hamilton v. Huebner, 146 Neb. 320, 19 N.W.2d 552, 559 (1945), rejecting the view that any liberalization is called for in cases of workmen's compensation for solitary fatal accidents.

46. See Note, 22 Minn.L.Rev. 391, 407–9 (1938) and the discussion of this statute and of proposals for liberalization of the hearsay rule in § 303, herein.

1. See next preceding section.

2. See Morgan, A Suggested Classification of Utterances Admissible as Res Gestae, 31 Yale L.J. 229,

impressions, have such unusual reliability as to warrant their admission under a special exception to the hearsay rule for declarations of present sense-impressions. At least one court [3] has clearly accepted this view, and others have admitted evidence of declarations of this sort under the benison of the res gestae phrase.[4]

236–239, 1922. See also Hutchins and Slesinger, Spontaneous Exclamations, 28 Col.L.Rev. 432, 439 (1928), and the excellent Note, Spontaneous exclamations in the absence of a startling event, 46 Col.L.Rev. 430 (1946) ("the best evidence of all is a statement made in immediate response to an external stimulus which produces no shock or nervous excitement whatever. . . . With emotion absent, speed present, and the person who heard the declaration on hand to be cross examined, we appear to have an ideal exception to the hearsay rule."); Morgan, Res Gestae, 12 Wash.L.Rev. 91, 94 (1937).

Ground was cleared for the new insights of Wigmore and Morgan by Thayer's historic essay, Bedingfield's Case—Declarations as a Part of the Res Gestae, Legal Essays, 207 (1908), 14 Am.L.Rev. 817, 15 Am.L.Rev. 1, 71 (1880–81).

3. Houston Oxygen Co. v. Davis, 139 Tex. 1, 161 S.W. 2d 474, 476, syl. 5, 6, 140 A.L.R. 868 (1942) (automobile collision case; declaration of observer before the collision, while car in which plaintiff was riding was passing that "they must have been drunk, that we would find them somewhere on the road wrecked . . ." held admissible as declaration of present sense-impression). The case is noted in 21 Tex.L.Rev. 298, 306, and in 140 A.L.R. 874.

4. Decisions pro: Kelly v. Hanwick, 228 Ala. 336, 153 So. 269, syl. 22 (1934) (bystander's statement that he heard automobile coming and that at speed at which it was traveling driver could not make curve); Tampa Elec. Co. v. Getrost, 151 Fla. 558, 10 So.2d 83, syl. 3 (1942) (statement of lineman before he was electrocuted and before he anticipated harm, that circuit was open); Sellers v. Montana-Dakota Power Co., 99 Mont. 39, 41 P.2d 44, syl. 10 (1935) (remarks by persons in burning building as to smell of smoke as indicating that the fire came from gas); Hornschurch v. Southern Pac. Co., 101 Ore. 280, 203 Pac. 886, syl. 1 (1921) (bystander called to those in automobile to stop, just before collision); Marks v. I. M. Pearlstine & Sons, 203 S.C. 318, 26 S.E.2d 835, syl. 2, 3 (1943) (declaration before collision, "trucks are going to kill somebody yet," while trucks were racing by). Contra: Wrage v. King, 114 Kan. 539, 220 Pac. 259, syl. 1 (1923) (exclamation of bystander, "See that fellow

TOPIC 5

RES GESTAE

274. Res Gestae.[1]

The use of the term *res gestae* seems to have first come into common use in the discussion of questions of admissibility of declarations accompanying material acts or sit-

jump in front of that car," excluded, no shock or excitement); Shadowski v. Pittsburgh Rys. Co., 226 Pa. 537, 75 Atl. 730 (1910) (bystander's declaration before accident, "Look at that damn fool: he will run over that little girl up there"; excluded as not emanating from the litigated act, the accident itself); Barnett v. Bull, 141 Wash. 139, 250 Pac. 954, syl. 3, 4 (1926) (statement of bystanders before accident and more than a mile away that party was driving in careless manner, excluded, distinguishing earlier local cases admitting, as being statements nearer in time and space to accident). Cases pro and con are collected and analyzed in Notes, 46 Col.L.Rev. 430 (1946), 163 A.L.R. 38–58. See also Uniform Rules of Evidence, R. 63(4), which admits "A statement (a) which the judge finds was made while the declarant was perceiving the event or condition which the statement narrates, describes or explains. . . ." See also Model Code of Evidence, R. 512(a), which widens the time-requirement slightly by admitting statements made while the declarant was perceiving the event, etc., "or immediately thereafter."

If this principle is accepted, it is arguable that it should operate to admit statements of a bystander reciting the license number of an automobile leaving the scene of an accident. They were excluded however in Neusbaum v. State, 156 Md. 149, 143 Atl. 872, syl. 18, 19 (1928), and Athas v. Fort Pitt Brewing Co., 324 Pa. 313, 188 Atl. 113, syl. 3 (1936). They frequently come in when promptly embodied in a memorandum. Rathbun v. Brancatella, 93 N.J.L. 222, 107 Atl. 279, syl. 1, 2 (1919); Chalmers v. Anthony, 8 N.J.Misc. 775, 151 Atl. 549 (1930); State v. Sacavone, 85 N.H. 207, 155 Atl. 701, syl. 6 (1931).

1. 6 Wigmore, Evidence, §§ 1745, 1767 (history and meaning), 1768, 1769 (doctrines to which the phrase is applied); Morgan, A Suggested Classification of Utterances Admissible as Res Gestae, 31 Yale L.J. 229 (1922), Res Gestae, 12 Wash.L.Rev. 91 (1937); Hinton, States of Mind and the Hearsay Rule, 1 Univ.Chi.L.Rev. 394, 400, note 20 (1934) (a pithy description of the uses of the term); Note, Res Gestae and Hearsay in Illinois, 42 Ill.L.Rev. 88 (1947); Slough, Res Gestae, 2 Kan.L.Rev. 41, 121, 246 (1953–4); Dec.Dig., Evidence, ☞118–128. Crim.Law, ☞362–368.

uations, in the early 1800s.[2] It was employed as a convenient escape from the hearsay objection, before the understanding of what is and what is not hearsay was as precise as it is today, and before the various exceptions were fully developed and clearly defined. In the preceding sections of this chapter, four exceptions to the hearsay rule are discussed, which today have become fairly well recognized as distinct exceptions, with different indicia of special trustworthiness. These are (1) Declarations of present bodily condition, (2) declarations of present mental states and emotions, (3) excited utterances, and (4) declarations of present sense-impressions. Admission of all these classes of declarations was, in the early stages, usually explained in terms of *res gestae* and this usage still lingers with some courts, especially in respect to excited utterances.

In addition, the phrase *res gestae* is likewise frequently employed to explain the admission of declarations which are not hearsay at all and this duality of usage indicates the indiscriminate coverage of the term. Thus, when an operative transaction, such as a sale, a gift, a bailment, or a loan or payment of money, consists both of acts of delivery and accompanying words which express and define the transaction, the words are sometimes said to come in as part of the *res gestae*.[3] The words as well as the acts are part of the conduct to which the law attaches the operative effect of a sale, or other

particular kind of shift in legal relations. Then again there are transactions whose operative effect hinges under the law upon the doing of an act with a particular state of mind or intent. Examples are the revocation of a will or the change of a domicile. Here the actor's words accompanying the act are used not as part of the operative conduct itself but as evidence of the inner intention. Unless the words happened to be a direct statement of intention ("I intend to revoke," "I mean to make a new home here") they would not be hearsay. Usually they are such as to indicate only circumstantially the requisite intention. Instances are the testator who as he tears the will curses the legatee or who tells his wife as they move into the new house, "This is God's country." The latter, i. e., the non-hearsay type of declarations as well as the former type are frequently let in under the aegis of *res gestae*.[4]

If there is any common element or concept present in all these variegated uses of the term *res gestae* it is a very rudimentary one, namely the notion that evidence of a concededly relevant act or condition may bring in likewise the words which accompanied it. This represents a broadening of the original employment of the term which denoted words accompanying the *principal litigated fact,* such as the murder, collision or trespass, which is the subject of the action. This older meaning is still often reverted to, and serves to narrow the usefulness of the doctrine without perceptible gain.[5] The general notion of words accom-

---

2. Thayer, Bedingfield's Case, Legal Essays 207, 238 15 Am.L.Rev. 5, 81 (1881) quoted in 6 Wigmore, Evidence, § 1767.

3. National Bank of the Metropolis v. Kennedy, 17 Wall. 19, 20, 21 L.Ed. 554, 556 (1873) (where cashier makes loan, and question is whether for himself or bank, held conversation between parties was part of res gestae of loan); Hood v. French, 37 Fla. 117, 19 So. 165, syl. 3 (1896) (declaration of payor at time of making payment); Morgan, op. cit. 31 Yale L.J. 229, 232.

4. Shapiro v. United States, 166 F.2d 240, syl. 2, 3 (C.C.A.2nd, 1948) (declarations of insured when he

delivered form for change of beneficiary, admitted to resolve ambiguity, as evidence of his intent: exemplifies the principle, but opinion does not refer to evidence as res gestae); Matzenbaugh v. People, 194 Ill. 108, 62 N.E. 546, syl. 1 (1901) (declarations as to intentions in moving to another state on question of domicile); Blackett v. Zeigler, 153 Iowa 344, 133 N.W. 901, syl. 10 (1910) (declarations at time of destroying will as evidence of intention as to reviving an earlier will); Morgan, op. cit., 31 Yale L.J. 229, 233.

5. As in the cases which exclude utterances made in the train of events leading up to a collision, because

panying an act or situation involves also some requirement of concurrence, or close relationship, *in time* between the words and the act or situation. Here again the narrowness or liberality in the application of this requirement is a measure of the scope of the usefulness of *res gestae* in the particular jurisdiction.

Perhaps we may discern two main policies or motives in the recognition of *res gestae* as a pass-word to the admission of evidence. Surely one is a desire to permit the witness to tell his story in a natural way by telling all that happened at the time of the narrated incident including those details which give life and color to the story. Truth is a seamless web and the naturalness with which the details fit each other gives confirmation to the whole account.[6] The other policy, most emphasized in the last generation under the leadership of Wigmore, is the recognition of spontaneity as the source of special trustworthiness. This quality of spontaneity characterizes in greater or less degree nearly all the types of declarations which have been labeled *res gestae*.

The writers [7] and, less frequently, the courts [8] have criticized the use of the phrase, *res gestae*. Its vagueness and imprecision are apparent. Moreover, as we have said, some of the traditional limitations on the doctrine have restricted its usefulness.[9] We may agree, however, that in the last century the preponderant need has been for the expansion of the scope of admissibility. Predominantly the use of the phrase *res gestae* has been as a reason for admitting, not for excluding evidence. Manifestly, too, the very vagueness of the term has been beneficial, as making it easier to widen the application of the doctrine into new fields. Perhaps the time has now come when this policy of widening admissibility will be even better served by striving for a clearer analysis of the different classes of evidence coming in under the phrase *res gestae* and of the justifying reasons for the admission of each class, as a basis for pointing out the need for further liberalization. If so, we could well jettison the ancient phrase, with due acknowledgment that it has well served its era in the evolution of evidence law.

---

they do not emanate from the principal fact, the collision, see note 4, next preceding section, which cites cases pro and con on the question.

6. ". . . however classified, the admissibility of the proofs as res gestae has as its justifying principle that truth, like the Master's robe, is of one piece, without seam, woven from the top throughout, that each fact has its inseparable attributes and its kindred facts materially affecting its character, and that the reproduction of a scene with its multiple incidents, each created naturally and without artificiality and not too distant in point of time, will by very quality and texture tend to disclose the truth." Case, J., in Robertson v. Hackensack Trust Co., 1 N.J. 304, 63 A.2d 515, 519 (1949).

7. See, e. g., 6 Wigmore, Evidence, § 1767 ("The phrase 'res gestae' is, in the present state of the law, not only entirely useless, but even positively harmful. It is useless, because every rule of evidence to which it has ever been applied exists as a part of some other well-established principle and can be explained in the terms of that principle. . . . It should never be mentioned."); Morgan, op. cit.,

31 Yale L.J. 229 ("The marvelous capacity of a Latin phrase to serve as a substitute for reasoning, and the confusion of thought inevitably accompanying the use of inaccurate terminology, are nowhere better illustrated than in the decisions dealing with the admissibility of evidence as "res gestae." It is probable that this troublesome expression owes its existence and persistence in our law of evidence to an inclination of judges and lawyers to avoid the toilsome exertion of exact analysis and precise thinking.") Compare the defence of the phrase in Note, 163 A.L.R. 15, 20.

8. See, e. g., the witty comment of Bleckley, C. J., in Cox v. State, 64 Ga. 374, 410 (1879) ("The difficulty of formulating a description of the 'res gestae' which will serve for all cases seems insurmountable. To make the attempt is something like trying to execute a portrait which shall enable the possessor to recognize every member of a numerous family."), quoted in Wigmore, ubi supra.

9. Especially the insistence in England and a few states upon strict concurrence in time of word and act, see § 272, note 20, above.

TOPIC 6

SELF-SERVING DECLARATIONS

275. Self-Serving Declarations.[1]

The doctrine that a party's out-of-court declarations or statements cannot be evidence in his favor, because "self-serving," seems to have originated as a counter-part and accompaniment[2] of the rule, now universally discarded, forbidding parties to testify.[3] When this latter rule of disqualification for interest was abrogated by statute, the accompanying rule against "self-serving" declarations should have been regarded as abolished by implication. Unfortunately it has lingered in the language of many opinions as a sweeping rule of exclusion.

Actually the appropriate rule for the exclusion of a party's declarations offered in his own behalf as evidence of the truth of the facts declared[4] is the hearsay rule.[5] Correspondingly, when such declarations fall within the exceptions to the hearsay rule, which are designed to admit hearsay statements when specially needed and unusually trustworthy,[6] they should be admitted though made by a party and offered in his behalf. This result would usually be accepted today as to most of the established exceptions, such as the exceptions for business records,[7] for excited utterances,[8] and for spontaneous declarations of present bodily feelings or symptoms.[9] As to the excep-

---

1. 6 Wigmore, Evidence, § 1732; 31 C.J.S., Evidence, § 216; 20 Am.Jur., Evidence, § 558; Dec.Dig., Crim. Law, ⟷413, Evidence, ⟷271. Whether a declaration is "self-serving" is to be tested by whether an interest existed at the time the statement was made, Cowen v. C. J. Stewart Lumber Co., 177 Okl. 266, 58 P.2d 573, 574 (1936). And if it was not favorable "in any contingency which was then foreseeable" it is not self-serving. Lebrun v. Boston & M. R. R., 83 N.H. 293, 142 Atl. 128, 132 (1928) (able discussion by Snow, J.). Contra: Stone v. Union Fire Ins. Co., 106 Colo. 522, 107 P.2d 241, 244 syl. 6 (1940).

2. See Phipson, Evidence, 231 (9th ed. 1952).

3. See § 65, herein.

4. Of course, if not offered for a hearsay purpose, but relevant and competent for another purpose, "self-serving" is no ground of exclusion. Thus, declarations admissible under the rule of "completeness" (see § 56, herein) come in though self-serving. Lowber v. State, 6 Boyce (Del.) 353, 100 Atl. 322, 2 A.L.R. 1014 (1917) (on proof of alleged oral confession, defendant entitled to give evidence of his exculpatory statements on same occasion); Charles G. Clapp Co. v. McCleary, 89 N.H. 65, 192 Atl. 572, syl. 4 (1937) (letter, to complete correspondence). See also the excellent discussion by Branch, J., in Caplan v. Caplan, 83 N.H. 318, 142 Atl. 121, 127, 128, syl. 32–34 (1928), examining the relation of "self-serving" to "hearsay," and holding that evidence of conduct to show state of mind is not hearsay and hence not subject to attack as "self-serving."

5. The rule against self-serving declarations is said to be included in the hearsay rule. Caplan v. Caplan, next preceding note; Cowen v. T. J. Stewart Lumber Co., 177 Okla. 266, 58 P.2d 573, 577, syl. 2 (1936).

6. Goodale v. Murray, 227 Iowa 843, 289 N.W. 450, 461, 126 A.L.R. 1121 (1940); 5 Wigmore, Evidence, §§ 1420–1422.

7. See, e. g., Taylor v. Martin, 292 Ky. 780, 168 S.W. 2d 8, syl. 4 (1943).

8. Excited exclamations favorable to the declarant's interest are constantly received in civil cases. See, e. g., Suhr v. Lindell, 133 Neb. 856, 277 N.W. 381, syl. 11 (1938) (chauffeur of truck involved in collision stated while under pain in hospital that he had been struck by an automobile which was on wrong side of road); Missouri, K. & T. R. Co. of Texas v. Schilling, 32 Tex.Civ.App. 417, 75 S.W. 64, syl. 7 (1903) ("self-serving" objection overruled). And in criminal cases. See, e. g., Tindall v. State (Tex.Cr. 1929) 20 S.W.2d 765, syl. 1 (defendant's statement to his wife within ten minutes after homicide that he had tried to make friends with deceased and deceased would not let him and that deceased had tried to cut him with a knife). The very hypothesis upon which evidence of these declarations is admitted is that whatever motive or interest to falsify may exist, the excitement of the moment has so seized the mind of the declarant as that the truth will uncontrollably be uttered. But the fact that the declaration is favorable to the declarant may be considered by the court in determining whether it actually was spontaneous. Suhr v. Lindell, supra, syl. 12 (truck driver's statement to employer that collision was not his fault, excluded); Semprini v. Boston & M. R. Co., 87 N.H. 279, 179 Atl. 349, syl. 5, 6 (1935) (statement of fireman to mother of child killed by train, shifting blame to engineer, excluded: lucid exposition by Woodbury, J.).

9. Hartford Accident & Ind. Co. v. Baugh, 87 F.2d 240, syl. 2 (1936); Smith v. Wilson, 296 S.W. 1036, syl. 8 (Mo.App.1927).

tion for another type of spontaneous declarations, namely, the declarant's declarations of his present state of mind or emotion,[10] some influential courts have adhered to the view that the self-serving character of a declaration is not of itself a ground of exclusion,[11] though in applying the requirement that the declarations must have been made under circumstances of apparent sincerity the fact of self-interest would be weighed in the balance.[12] Other courts, however, have applied here a supposed general rule of exclusion of self-serving statements.[13] This has been especially marked in an area where exclusion creates the greatest danger of injustice, namely, in the exclusion of the declarations of the accused, in homicide and assault cases, made before or after the event, of his peaceful intentions, or of his fear of the other party.[14] If made under circumstances of seeming sincerity they should come in to show the state of mind or emotion of the accused, as a third party's declaration would when material to show his state of mind. The courts which exclude assume that because made by a party and offered on his behalf the declarations are so likely to be dishonest as not to be worth hearing. This is the same discredited assumption that interested testimony is to be purged not weighed, on which rested the ancient rule that parties could not testify.

---

10. See § 268, herein.

11. Lee v. Mitcham, 98 F.2d 298, syl. 4 (C.A.D.C.1938) (decedent's statement of intention to purchase rather than to pay off a note owed by an orphanage of which he was trustee, admitted); United States v. Matot, 146 F.2d 197, syl. 3 (C.C.A. 2, 1944) (misapplication of money of bank; defendant's declarations to president of bank showing want of intention to defraud, though "self-serving" should have been admitted; opinion by L. Hand, J.); Rogers v. Manhattan Life Ins. Co., 138 Cal. 285, 71 Pac. 348, 350 (1903) (declaration of intention to commit suicide); Kelly v. Bank of America, 112 Cal.App.2d 388, 246 P.2d 92, 96, syl. 3 (1952) (grantor's declarations after deed made as to intent to deliver, citing previous decisions); Caplan v. Caplan, 83 N.H. 318, 142 Atl. 121, 126, syl. 21 (1928) (alienation of affection, plaintiff's declaration as to affection for husband); Worth v. Worth, 48 Wyo. 441, 49 P.2d 649, syl. 9 (1935) (alienation of affections: defendant's statement to third party of desire that husband and wife be reconciled; held error to exclude as self-serving).

12. Caplan v. Caplan, next previous note.

13. See the cases collected in the references, note 1, above, and the cases cited in note 14, below.

14. Moss v. State, 208 Ark. 137, 185 S.W.2d 92, syl. 4 (1945) (declaration five minutes after the killing, "I had to kill him"); People v. Smith, 8 Cal.2d 502, 104 P.2d 510, syl. 8 (1940) (wife-murder, letters of accused to wife expressing affection, several days before killing, self-serving and remote); State v. Barnett, 156 Kan. 746, 137 P.2d 133, syl. 9 (1943) (statement before shooting tending to show fear); State v. Gadwood, 342 Mo. 466, 116 S.W.2d 42, syl. 8 (1937) (statement showing peaceful intentions, before killing); Woods v. State, 115 Tex.Cr. 111, 28 S.W.2d 554, syl. 6 (1930) (appeal made on day before homicide for police protection).

Contra: Deeb v. State, 131 Fla. 362, 179 So. 894, syl. 22 (1938) (accused asked sheriff and others for advice as to making up with deceased and expressed fear); Parsons v. Comm., 138 Va. 764, 121 S.E. 768, syl. 5 (1924) (defendant's statement before killing that he was afraid of deceased; able opinion by Prentis, J.).

Decisions are collected in 6 Wigmore, Evidence, § 1732, and in Dec.Dig., Crim.Law, ⊗➞413.

CHAPTER 31

RECORDS OF PAST RECOLLECTION

276. History and Theory.[1]

We have already discussed in the chapter on Examination of Witnesses,[2] the practice of permitting a witness to refresh his memory by looking at a written memorandum, and then to testify from his memory thus revived. This was accepted custom by the middle 1600s.[3] It often happened, however, that the witness, though an inspection of the writing did not bring back to memory the facts recorded, yet was able to recognize that the writing was made by him, and on the basis of the writing was willing to testify that the facts recited were true. By the 1700s this practice also had become accepted, acceptance at first being made easier by speaking of this new process by the old name of "refreshing recollection,"[4] which of course does not fit the new situation. Beginning with the early 1800s[5] the courts have come generally to distinguish sharply the two situations,[6] instead of discussing them as two ways of refreshing recollection.

Moreover, they have developed requirements[7] as to the time of making the record of past recollection, and as to the necessity that the witness vouch for its correctness, which are usually not imposed on the process of refreshing memory.

This voucher of correctness, as we shall see, need not be founded on present memory, but is usually based on the faith of the witness in the writing. Most courts, moreover, admit the writing as evidence of the facts recited. Looked at from this point of view, the writing being a statement made out of court and used as evidence of the facts recited is hearsay evidence and since it comes in, does so under an exception to the rule against hearsay.[8] This seems the more realistic classification. On the other hand, from the traditional point of view, the situation is viewed as one where the writing is incorporated by reference in the testimony when the witness adopts it as correct, and thus

---

1. See Wigmore, Evidence, §§ 734–757; Decennial Digests, Evidence, ☞355, 356, 377, Criminal Law, ☞435, Witnesses, ☞253–260; Notes, Past Recollection Recorded, 28 Ia.L.Rev. 530 (1943) (excellent), Recollection on the Witness Stand, 15 Wash.L.Rev. 257 (1940) (good summary of rules as applied in local cases), Note, 125 A.L.R. 19 (extensive collection of cases on memoranda of present and past memory).

2. See § 9, herein.

3. 3 Wigmore, Evidence, § 735.

4. Ibid.

5. Ibid.

6. See, e. g., Acklen's Exec. v. Hickman, 63 Ala. 494, 498 (1879); State v. Easter, 185 Iowa 476, 170 N.W. 748, syl. 3 (1919); State v. Legg, 59 W.Va. 315, 53 S.E. 545, syl. 2 (1906).

7. See the next section.

8. Thomes v. Atkins, 52 F.Supp. 405, 411, syl. 9 (D. Minn.1943, Nordbye, D.J.). Morgan seems to suggest this view in Hearsay and Preserved Memory, 40 Harv.L.Rev. 712, 718, 719 (1927).

comes in evidence as a part of the oral testimony.[9]

277. Requirements: Knowledge, Time of Making, and Absence of Present Memory.

The usual requirement for witnesses [1] and for hearsay declarants [2] that they must have had first-hand knowledge of the facts is enforced here.[3] But the most distinctive requirement is designed to guarantee that this knowledge must have been clearly and accurately remembered by the witness who tenders the writing, as of the time that he made or recognized the correctness of the writing. An older, strict formula, still commonly used, is that the writing must have been made or recognized as correct "at or near the time" [4] of the events recorded. This limitation has some support in psychological findings.[5] More liberal is the standard often found in the opinions [6] and pre-

ferred by Wigmore,[7] namely, at a time when the events were "fairly fresh" in the memory of the witness. The last test seems the more practical and it should be flexibly administered. It is true that the nearer to the event the more reliable the statement is likely to be, but it is equally true that all statements made substantially nearer to the event than the trial itself suffer less from errors of memory than the testimony of witnesses from purported present recollection on the stand.

The testimony preliminary to the admission of the memorandum, when the writing is one written or signed by the witness who observed the facts recorded, must include a voucher by the witness of the accuracy of the writing.[8] This may of course be a statement that he remembers that he correctly recorded the facts. But if his memory does

9. See, e. g., Ettelson v. Metropolitan Life Ins. Co., 164 F.2d 660, 667, syl. 12 (C.C.A.N.J.1947) ("This record, which he verified and adopted, thus became . . . a present evidentiary statement. . . ."); Cogswell v. Frazier, 183 Md. 654, 39 A.2d 815, 818, syl. 8 (1944); 3 Wigmore, Evidence, § 754. Compare the penetrating discussion of the two theories by Hamersley, J. in Curtis v. Bradley, 65 Conn. 99, 31 Atl. 591, 595 (1894).

1. See § 10, herein.

2. See §§ 253, 262, 286, herein.

3. United States v. Keppler, 1 F.2d 315, syl. 1 (C.C.A. 3, 1924) (witness testified to information contained in memorandum of another of facts not known to witness); Town of Norwalk v. Ireland, 68 Conn. 1, 35 Atl. 804, syl. 4 (1896) (witness identified inventory as made partly from his own inspection, partly from information given by assistants: inadmissible); People v. Zalimas, 319 Ill. 186, 149 N.E. 759, syl. 1, 2 (1925) (druggist testifies to his sale of arsenic to Mrs. Z., but had no knowledge of her identity).

4. Maxwell's Execs. v. Wilkinson, 113 U.S. 656, 658, 5 S.Ct. 691, 28 L.Ed. 1037 (1885) ("at or shortly after the time of the transaction, and while it must have been fresh in his memory"; twenty months after, too late); Halsey v. Sinsebaugh, 15 N.Y. 485 (1857); and see State v. Bradley, 361 Mo. 267, 234 S.W.2d 556, 560 (1950) ("at the time or so near the time of the event that, *in the circumstances*, it could be

safely assumed his recollection . . . was sufficiently fresh to enable him to correctly record it," second day afterward, timely).

5. See Hutchins and Slesinger, Memory, 41 Harv.L. Rev. 860, 866, 870 (1928) who point out that the curve of forgetting starts with a sharp rise and begins to flatten at the end of two or three days, and as the time interval increases errors creep into what is remembered. See also the enlightening discussion in Gardner, Perception and Memory of Witnesses, 18 Corn.L.Q. 391, 393 (1933).

6. Paige v. Carter, 64 Cal. 489, 2 Pac. 260, 261 (1884) ("at any time when the fact was fresh in his memory"); Chamberlin v. Ossipee, 60 N.H. 212, 213 (1880) (doctor's memorandum 3 days after examination was "made at a time when the facts . . . were fresh in the mind of the witness"). See also Cal.Code Civ.Proc. § 2047 ("at the time when the fact occurred, or immediately thereafter, or at any other time when the fact was fresh in his memory"); Model Code of Evidence, Rule 504 ("at a time when the matter was recently perceived and the recollection of it by the witness was clear").

7. 3 Evidence, § 745.

8. Brown v. Provident Loan Soc., 282 N.Y. 453, 26 N.E.2d 965, syl. 2 (1940); Hodas v. Davis, 203 App. Div. 297, 196 N.Y.S. 801, syl. 1, 2 (1922) (excellent discussion by H. T. Kellogg, J., quoting the formulas of verification approved in the New York cases); 3 Wigmore, Evidence, § 747.

not serve so far, it is sufficient if he says that he knows it is correct because it was his habit or practice to record such matters accurately.[9] Or even short of this, it is acceptable if he states that he is satisfied that it is correct because he recognizes the handwriting or signature as his own, and believes that he would not have written or signed it unless it were true.[10] If the writing was not made or signed by the witness he must give evidence that when the matter was fresh in his memory he read the memorandum and then knew that it was correct.[11]

There are many cases, especially the earlier ones, in which the court in explaining the new theory of the admissibility of records of past recollection, draws the contrast between using the writing to stimulate present memory and using it as a record of past memory, when "the memorandum fails to refresh and revive the recollection."[12] This phrase was employed as describing the usual condition in which the record was needed, without considering the question whether the record could be admitted when the witness did retain some recollection of the facts. Earlier cases in New York[13] (now shaken by a later holding[14] which seems to weaken the underpinning of the doctrine) and the federal courts,[15] with occasional dicta or holdings in other jurisdictions,[16] have set up the requirement that, before the record can be used the

---

9. Hancock v. Kelly, 81 Ala. 378, 2 So. 281, 286 (1887) ("When an original memorandum is produced, and a witness testifies that he made it in the usual course of business, and that at the time he made it he knew its contents to be true, this is equivalent to an affirmation of the truth of the contents, and lets in both the testimony of the witness and the memorandum."); St. Louis S. W. Ry. Co. v. White Sewing Machine Co., 78 Ark. 1, 93 S.W. 58, syl. 1, 2 (1906); and see Koehler v. Abey, 168 Mich. 113, 133 N.W. 923, syl. 5 (1911).

10. Martin v. Good, 14 Md. 398, 410 (1859) (witness stated "from the paper being in his own, he had no doubt it did contain the true terms of the agreement made in his presence," held sufficient; if more were required would defeat the ends of justice since few men could relate the particulars, independently of the paper).

11. Alabama Trunk & L. Co. v. Hauer, 214 Ala. 473, 108 So. 339, syl. 3 (1926); Mercantile Trust & Deposit Co. v. Rode, 137 Md. 362, 112 Atl. 574, syl. 10 (1921); Wigmore, Evidence, § 748.

12. See Acklen's Executors v. Hickman, 63 Ala. 494, 498 (1879), and other opinions quoted in 3 Wigmore, Evidence, pp. 68, 69.

13. E. g., National Ulster County Bank v. Madden, 114 N.Y. 280, 21 N.E. 408, syl. 1 (1889); People v. McLaughlin, 150 N.Y. 365, 44 N.E. 1017, 1025, syl. 4 (1896).

14. People v. Weinberger, 239 N.Y. 307, 146 N.E. 434, 435, syl. 1, 3 (1925) (prosecution for staging immoral play: trial judge rejected transcript of play which witness testified performances followed exactly; held, ruling cannot be sustained on ground that witness has general present memory of words used by actors: Lehman, J.: "The rule that the present recollection of a witness must be exhausted before a record of his past recollection may be admitted in evidence, though applied in New York and the federal courts, has not been universally accepted or approved. There are times when the record of a past recollection, if it exists, is more trustworthy and desirable than a present recollection of greater or less vividness (Wigmore on Evidence [2d Ed.] § 738), and that is clearly the case here. . . . No reasonable man could suppose that the exact words could be obtained from a witness' recollection as well as they could be obtained from a transcript of the play checked up by the witness at some performance. To ask the witness whether he can remember the exact words of a whole play would be either a useless formality or result in obtaining evidence less reliable than could be obtained from the introduction of the transcript. As well might we refuse to receive in evidence a copy which has been compared with a lost document until the person who testified to the comparison has first exhausted his memory as to the contents of the lost document." Two judges dissented.).

15. Vicksburg & Meridian R. R. v. O'Brien, 119 U.S. 99, 102, 7 S.Ct. 118, 30 L.Ed. 299 (1886) (attending physician's memorandum about patient's injury held wrongly admitted: Harlan, J.: ". . . it does not appear here, but that at the time the witness testified he had, without even looking at his written statement, a clear, distinct recollection of every essential fact stated in it. If he had such a present recollection, there was no necessity whatever for reading that paper to the jury").

16. See, e. g., Bendett v. Bendett, 315 Mass. 59, 52 N.E.2d 2, 5, syl. 7 (1943); Guardian Depositors' Corp. v. Keller, 286 Mich. 403, 282 N.W. 194, syl. 11 (1938); Jackson v. Pioneer Adhesive Works, 132 N.J.L. 397, 40 A.2d 634, syl. 2–5 (S.Ct.1945) (memorandum produced by plaintiff, a workman, of his

witness must be shown to have no adequate recollection, after looking at the writing, of the "essential facts" recorded. This requirement is highly inexpedient and it is to be hoped that most courts, if the question were squarely presented, would reject it. The practice of securing witnesses to write down facts when fresh in their memory is commendable and generally serves the interest of the perpetuation of truth. Memoranda of facts, made nearer to the event than later oral testimony, are more reliable than such testimony from later memory.[17] Moreover, when both the memorandum and the testimony come in you have a far better opportunity to use the test of cross-examination, than when you have only the one or the other.

278. The Writing Itself is Evidence.

The memorandum used to refresh memory, and for that purpose alone, is looked on merely as an outside stimulus to the witness, and the proponent cannot introduce it into evidence.[1] When the rules about records of

past recollection sprang by cellular division from the old practice of refreshing memory, a few courts, not clearly distinguishing the two, nor seeing the inapplicability to records of past recollection of the old rule that refreshing memoranda are not evidence, still say that records of past recollection are not evidence.[2] But the majority properly hold that such records are receivable in evidence,[3] and this conclusion seems the only justifiable one, whether we base it on the view, as most courts do, that the writing is adopted by reference as part of the testimony of the witness,[4] or on the probably more realistic analysis, that the writing comes in, like other writings admitted under exceptions to the hearsay rule (such as business entries or dying declarations), as an out-of-court statement of special reliability received as evidence of the truth of the matters recited.[5]

A corollary of this view that the memorandum itself is evidence is that the Best Evidence Rule, requiring that the original writing if procurable[6] be produced to show its

---

overtime hours, excluded because (1) he had present recollection of the facts and (2) because self-serving); State v. Gross, 31 Wash.2d 202, 196 P.2d 297, 304, syl. 4 (1948).

17. In Fisher v. Kyle, 27 Mich. 454 (1873), it appeared that the trial court refused to permit an attorney to read to the jury the minutes taken by him of testimony given on a former trial. The court, speaking by Cooley, J., said: "Had Draper testified to any present recollection of what these witnesses swore to, he would have been allowed to state what it was. But clearly his minutes, taken at the time, and which he swore were correct, were much less liable to err than any recollection he might have could possibly be. His minutes embodied his understanding of the evidence at the time, and would remain the same, and not become varied in the lapse of time; but his recollection, which would start with the same understanding, was constantly liable to be more or less perverted and changed, or in material parts obliterated from the memory. It could not possibly, therefore, be more certain than the minutes, and, as every variation from the minutes must render it more uncertain and unreliable, any rule of evidence which would admit the recollection and exclude the minutes must obviously be illogical and unsound."

1. See § 9, herein.

McCormick Evidence HB—38

2. Bendett v. Bendett, 315 Mass. 59, 52 N.E.2d 2, 6, syl. 9 (1943); Hoffman v. Chicago M. & St. P. Ry. Co., 40 Minn. 60, 41 N.W. 301, 302 (1889) (dictum). But the witness may read the memorandum to the jury, and even show it to them, and the difference between this and introducing the writing is merely "technical." Bendett v. Bendett, supra.

3. Grossman v. Del. Electric Power Co., 155 Atl. 806, 811, syl. 7 (Del.Super.1929); State v. Brady, 95 Iowa 410, 69 N.W. 290, 292, syl. 5 (1896) ("The modern doctrine, at least in this country, seems to be that such documents are admissible in evidence, and that the court will not go through the useless ceremony of having the witness read a document relating to a fact of which he had no present recollection, except that he knew it was correct when made."); Graves v. Boston & M. R. R., 84 N.H. 225, 149 Atl. 70, syl. 2 (1930); Ft. Worth & D. C. Ry. Co. v. Garlington, 92 S.W. 270, syl. 1 (Tex.Civ.App.1906) (semble).

4. See cases cited in § 276, note 9, supra.

5. See authorities cited in § 276, note 8, supra.

6. Clark v. Holmes, 71 Conn. 749, 43 Atl. 194, syl. 2 (1899) (stenographer may not read from transcript of notes taken at former trial, without producing original notes); Amor v. Stoeckele, 76 Minn. 180, 78

terms, is applicable and only when the writing is shown unavailable may resort be had to a copy or other secondary evidence.[7]

279. Co-operative Records and Reports.

The typical and classic record of past recollection was a one-man affair. The verifying witness was the man who originally observed the facts and the man who wrote them down in the memorandum. One deviation from this pattern, however, we have already mentioned.[1] This is the situation where the written statement is made by someone other than the witness, but the witness verifies it for admission by testifying that when his own memory of the facts was fresh, he read the memorandum and knew that it was true.[2] Here only the witness who recognized the truth of the memorandum need be called.

A second instance of co-operative reports occurs when a person, who may be known as R, reports orally the facts known to him, and another person, W, writes down a memorandum of the oral report. In commercial practice, this is familiarly seen when the salesman or time-keeper reports sales or time to the book-keeper. Here the record comes in when R swears to the correctness of his oral report (though he may not remember the detailed facts) and W testifies that he faithfully transcribed the oral report.[3]

A third and much debated question arises when W, to whom R has reported orally, does not write down the facts, but trusts to his unaided memory in testifying to what R reported. Again R appears and vouches for the correctness of what he reported. May the testimony of the two be received as evidence of the facts, of which R perhaps now has no memory, originally reported by R? It certainly does not rise to the height of a record of past recollection, for W's memory is no record, and it is the existence of this written memorial that has been one of the chief elements in the recognition of the reliability of such records. Accordingly, some courts have excluded this combination of testimonies.[4] On the other hand, since both R and W vouch for their respective fact-contributions and submit themselves to at least a limited cross-examination thereon, it may well be urged that when the report of R was

N.W. 1046, syl. 2 (1899) (similar to last); Donner v. State, 72 Neb. 263, 100 N.W. 305, 306, syl. 1 (1904) (stockyard record copied from original entries, excluded); 3 Wigmore, Evidence, § 749. But where the official stenographer makes a transcript of his notes as part of his duty, this comes in as an official statement without producing the original notes. Smith v. Scully, 66 Kan. 139, 71 Pac. 249, syl. 4 (1903).

7. Cowley v. State, 18 Okl.Cr. 224, 194 Pac. 284, syl. 2 (1921) (copy of transcript of testimony permitted to be read, when proof made that original could not be found).

1. See § 277, note 11, herein.

2. Some courts in rejecting particular memoranda vouched for but not prepared by the witness have given weight to the fact that the memorandum was prepared by or on behalf of one of the parties. Rice v. Fidelity & Cas. Co., 250 Mich. 398, 230 N.W. 181, syl. 7 (1930) (memorandum of conversation prepared four months later); O'Neale v. Walton, 1 Rich. (S. C.) 254 (1845); 3 Wigmore, Evidence, p. 88. This danger of partisan suggestion, however, seems a matter rather to be considered on credibility than as a ground of exclusion.

3. Curtis v. Bradley, 65 Conn. 99, 31 Atl. 591, syl. 2 (1894) (instructive opinion by Hamersley, J.). And it is no objection to the final memorandum thus verified by both participants that the original reporter gave his information with the aid of temporary slips or memoranda not produced. Johnson's Adm'r v. Pigg, 242 Ky. 631, 47 S.W.2d 63, syl. 3 (1932); Miller v. Shay, 145 Mass. 163, 13 N.E. 468 (1887); Lawn v. Prager, 67 Wash. 568, 121 Pac. 466 (1912).

4. Mallinger v. Sarbach, 94 Kan. 504, 146 Pac. 1148 (1915) (W testifies that R reported to him a conversation with defendant: R testifies that he does not remember talking to R, but has no doubt he did, and whatever he told R was true: all excluded, extensive discussion by Porter, J.); Gillotti v. State, 135 Wis. 634, 116 N.W. 252, syl. 3 (1908) (robbery: identity of robbers in issue: testimony of sheriff and of prosecuting witness that latter informed sheriff shortly after robbery, of particulars of description of one of the robbers, excluded, three judges dissenting). See Neusbaum v. State, 156 Md. 149, 143 Atl. 872, syl. 18 (1928) (testimony that eyewitness immediately after accident called out the license number of car, excluded as hearsay, the eyewitness not being produced).

made at a time when the facts were fresh in his memory and the facts reported are relatively simple so that an ordinary man might be expected to remember them, the combined evidence should come in.[5]

280. The Overlapping Principles of Past Recollection Recorded and Business Records.

The admission under a special exception to the rule against hearsay for Business Records (also called Book Entries and Business Entries) is treated in another chapter.[1] At common law such records were received to show the facts recorded, provided the entrant were shown to be unavailable. If someone else, such as a salesman or weigher, reported the facts to the entrants, he also must be shown to be unavailable. But suppose one or more of these participants is available.

Clearly, when the person who new the facts at first-hand made the entry and is produced as a witness and testifies that he made the record correctly upon personal knowledge and at a time when the transaction was fresh in his memory though he now has no recollection as to the facts recorded, the book or entry is admissible. The entries then come in under the principle applicable to records of past recollection[2] without the necessity of resort to any special rules relating to book entries.[3]

Where both the entrant and the reporter are produced and the entrant swears to the correctness of his transcription of the report and the reporter swears that he correctly reported the facts (though he may not now remember them) the entry is clearly admissible as a combined record of past recollection,[4] without the need of resorting to the Business Records principle, though seemingly that should be available as an alternative theory.[5]

[5.] Shear v. Van Dyke, 17 N.Y.S.Ct.Rep. 528, 10 Hun 528 (1877) (suit for services in loading hay; to prove the amount loaded plaintiff offered R, who aided in the loading, and asked him how many loads there were: he answered that he could not remember, but knew at the time and told plaintiff: the plaintiff then testified that the number of loads reported by the first witness was 14; held, not hearsay and properly admitted, one judge dissenting); Hart v. Atlantic Coast Line Ry. Co., 144 N.C. 91, 56 S.E. 559, syl. 1 (1907) (number of cords of wood in yard, similar to last case); see Morgan, Hearsay and Preserved Memory, 40 Harv.L.Rev. 712, 722–732 (1927). See also cases admitting evidence of reports of bystanders as to the license number of a car involved in a collision, under circumstances which may or may not involve this problem. Rathbun v. Brancatella, 93 N.J.L. 222, 107 Atl. 279, syl. 1, 2 (Ct. Errors and App. 1919) (exhaustively analyzed in Morgan's article, cited above); Chalmers v. Anthony, 8 N.J.Misc. 775, 151 Atl. 549 (1930).

[1.] See ch. 32, herein.

[2.] Ettelson v. Metropolitan Life Ins. Co., 164 F.2d 660, 667, syl. 11 (C.C.A.3, 1947) (doctor producing records, testifies that they correctly reflected the facts as to patient's statements to him: judge admitted them under Federal Business Records Act; held, they could have come in as records of past recollection without need to resort to the Act); Shokuwan v. Higeyoshi, 140 F.2d 13, syl. 5 (Ct.App.D.C.1944) (plaintiff verifies his record of loans made).

[3.] Of course, entries so made may also be used by a witness as memoranda to refresh his present recollection (see § 9, herein) when the examination of the entry by the witness actually has that effect, but in such event the entries themselves need not be introduced in evidence, though presumably they could be received in evidence as book-entries, if desired.

[4.] International & G. N. Ry. Co. v. Startz, 42 Tex.Civ. App. 85, 94 S.W. 207, 212 (1906) (quoting with approval Greenleaf's text to above effect).

[5.] See Missouri Pac. R. Co. v. Johnson, 7 S.W. 838, syl. 1 (Tex.1888) where a "scale book" was held admissible where plaintiff and his clerk testified that one or other of them weighed all the wheat, and made the entries, and to the correctness of both.

CHAPTER 32

BUSINESS RECORDS

281. Alternative Grounds for Admission of Business Records: Basis for the Hearsay Exception.[1]

As will appear from the following discussion, entries in business books may be offered in evidence in many different aspects. They may come in, if the entries are made by a party to the suit, against him as admissions.[2] Or if the entrant is produced as a witness the entries may be used to refresh his memory,[3] or may come in as records of past recollection.[4] Sometimes they may come in as declarations against interest.[5] None of these uses require resort to any distinctive principle peculiar to business records. Such principle is only involved when the business record is it-

---

1. 5 Wigmore, §§ 1517–1520 (general), 1521–1533 (regular entries), 1536–1561 (Parties' books); Morgan, et al., The Law of Evidence, Some Proposals for Its Reform, ch. 5 (1927); Notes, Business Entry Statutes, 48 Col.L.Rev. 920 (1948), Business Entries before the Court, 32 Ill.L.Rev. 334 (1938), Ginsburg, Business Records, 29 Neb.L.Rev. 60 (1949). See also Tracy, Introduction of Business Records, 24 Iowa L.Rev. 454, 1939; Whittier, Account-books in California, 14 Calif.L.Rev. 263, 1926; Kinnare, Account-books as Evidence in Illinois, 11 Chi.-Kent Rev. 278, 1933; Notes, Chadwell, Business Records, 38 Ill.Bar J. 440 (1950); The Business Entry Exception, 35 Calif.L.Rev. 434, 1937; Business Entries in Mississippi, 16 Miss.L.J. 266, 1944; Business Entries in Virginia, 24 Va.L.Rev. 814, 1938, Decennial Digests, Evidence, ☞350, 354, 361, 376, 383(8), Criminal Law, ☞434; 32 C.J.S., Evidence, §§ 682–696, 699–702.

2. Parker v. Priestley, 39 So.2d 210, 215 (Fla. 1949) (party's account book admitted against him as admission despite statute providing such books shall be admissible in his favor); Wentz v. Guaranteed Sand & Gravel Co., 205 Minn. 611, 287 N.W. 113, syl. 1 (1939) (corporation's books); Utilities Ins. Co. v. Stuart, 134 Neb. 413, 278 N.W. 827, syl. 11 (1938) (firm books admissible against individual partners); Dec.Dig. Evidence ☞354 (18)(24); 32 C.J.S. 584, and see ch. 27, herein.

3. Lowe v. Swafford, 209 Ind. 514, 199 N.E. 709, syl. 10, 103 A.L.R. 1222 (1936); Dec.Dig. Witnesses ☞255(7)(8), and see § 9, herein.

4. Ettelson v. Metropolitan Life Ins. Co., 164 F.2d 660, syl. 12 (C.C.A.N.J. 1947); Dec.Dig. Evidence, ☞355(5) (6), and see § 280, herein.

5. Gus Dattilo Fruit Co. v. Louisville & N. R. Co., 238 Ky. 322, 37 S.W.2d 856, syl. 3 (1931); 32 C.J.S., Evidence, § 695, and see § 253, herein.

self offered as evidence of the truth of its terms without the production of the person who made the entry. In such aspect the evidence is clearly hearsay, and some exception to the Hearsay Rule must be appealed to if the evidence is to come in. The exception which admits regular entries in the books of a business is justified by the following reasons: First, the element of *unusual reliability* is furnished by the fact that in practice regular business records have a comparatively high degree of accuracy (as compared to other memoranda) because such books are customarily checked as to correctness by systematic balance-striking, because the very regularity and continuity of such records is calculated to train the record-keeper in habits of precision, and because in actual experience the entire business of the country constantly functions in reliance upon such entries. Secondly, the *necessity* for resort to such hearsay statements appears from the requirement that the entry be admitted under this exception (i. e. in the absence of the testimony of the person or persons who made the entry) only when the person or persons who made the entry and upon whose knowledge it is based, are unavailable as witnesses because of death, insanity, disappearance or other reason.

282. The Distinctive Practice in Respect to the Admission of the Books of a Party in His Own Behalf, Known as the Shop-Book Rule.[1]

By the 1600's in England a custom had emerged in the common law courts of receiving the "shop-books" of tradesmen and craftsmen as evidence of debts for goods sold or services rendered on open account. It was manifestly convenient to do so, especially in a day of small businesses when the shop-keeper was customarily his own book-keeper also. But convenience ran counter to the prevailing legal philosophy which regarded self-interest as a ground for disqualifying witnesses. Accordingly, in 1609 a statute was passed limiting the use of such

books to the period of one year after the debt was created except where a bill of debt was given or where the transaction was between merchants and tradesmen.[2] Thereafter the higher courts frowned on the use of such books which in practice was retained only in the petty courts for small claims.

The same need and the same suspicion of self-interest were felt in the American colonies, but in most of the colonies the need prevailed and enabling laws letting in the books were adopted, or the practice was sanctioned under local decisions. This development was doubtless influenced by the example of the Dutch procedure accepting such books of account in proof of debts.

Nevertheless, these laws and judicial customs were limited by restrictions born of the hostility to the party's "making evidence for himself." Thus in addition to the requirement of the broader exception for business records generally, namely that the entries be regularly made at or about the time of the transactions, as a part of the routine of the business,[3] other restrictions were imposed in one or another colony. Among them were these:[4] (1) the party using the books must not have had a clerk, (2) he must file a "suppletory" oath to the justness of the account, (3) the books must bear an honest appearance, (4) each transaction recorded must not exceed a certain limited value, (5) witnesses must testify from their experience in deal-

---

1. The summary of the history of the shop-book rule given herein is mainly derived from the account in 5 Wigmore, Evidence, § 1518, and from the extensive opinion of Harris, J., in Radtke v. Taylor, 105 Ore. 559, 210 P. 863 (1922). For a comprehensive survey of the American decisions down to 1900 see Note, A party's books of account as evidence in his own favor, 52 L.R.A. 545. See also Morgan et al., The Law of Evidence, Some Proposals for Its Reform, 51–58 (1927).

2. St. 7 Jac. I, ch. 12, summarized 5 Wigmore, Evidence, § 1518.

3. See the next section, herein.

4. See 5 Wigmore, Evidence, §§ 1538–1557; Radtke v. Taylor, 105 Ore. 559, 210 P. 863, 872, syl. 11 (1922).

ing with the party that the books are honest, (6) the use is limited to the proof of open account for goods or services furnished the defendant, thus excluding loans, goods and services furnished under special contract, or furnished to third persons on defendant's credit, and (7) other proof must be made of the actual delivery of some part of the goods sued for.

By the latter 1800's two developments had occurred which have removed the need for these special enabling laws and customs permitting on conditions the use of this particular class of business records, parties' shop-books. These developements were, first, the emergence of the wider doctrine of the admissibility generally of all regular business records,[5] and second, the abolition of the interested party's disqualification as a witness which removed the special necessity for the use of his books by enabling him to testify as his own witness to the facts.[6] The tradition, however, especially in the older states, of special treatment by legislatures and courts of parties' books dies hard, and special statutes regulating such "shop-books," with fragments of the primitive restrictions, listed above, linger in many states,[7] and current ju-

dicial traditions in some jurisdictions are still influenced by earlier customs.[8]

There is little harm in such clinging to earlier usage, when the courts merely look on the shop-book rule and statutes (when the terms allow it) as a permissible alternative to the general business records doctrine, either of which the party may pursue if he chooses.[9] But a most archaic impediment would be placed upon the just enforcement of claims if the party, wishing to use his books were confined to the shop-book route, instead of being free to use them under the regular business records doctrine, or as refreshing or recording recollection. Most courts, indeed, would today it is believed disregard the special nuances of the shop-book rule, and test the party's books offered in his own behalf, under the wider standards developed by the modern decisions for business records generally.

283. The Common-Law Doctrine Admitting Business Records Generally: Regular Entries in the Course of Business as an Exception to the Hearsay Rule: The Duty Element: Oral Reports.

The suspicion attaching to a party's books used in the party's favor did not extend to

---

5. See the following sections, herein.

6. In most states, however, the common law disqualification of parties is retained (see § 65, herein) in actions brought by or against a decedent's estate in respect to testimony about transactions with the dead man. Fortunately, however, in one guise or another the tradition deriving from the shop-book rule permitting the use of the party's books on his own behalf, with a "suppletory" oath by the party which was not regarded as "testimony" subject to the prohibition, has been generally maintained under these "dead man" statutes. Rath v. Headlee, 238 Iowa 1340, 29 N.W. 2d 923, syl. 6 (1947) (party's testimony to correctness of his books not testimony to transaction with decedent); Fidelity & Columbia Trust Co. v. Lyons, 302 Ky. 839, 196 S.W.2d 605, syl. 2 (1946) (specific statutory provision permits use of books); Wilson v. Prudential Ins. Co., 276 Mich. 232, 267 N.W. 824, syl. 4–6 (1936), and see In re Winslow's Will, 146 Iowa 67, 124 N.W. 895, 896 (1910) (administrator's introduction of decedent's books is not testifying so as to waive adverse party's dis-

qualification—dictum). Contra: Tipps v. Landers, 182 Cal. 771, 190 P. 173, syl. 3 (1920) (in suit against estate, plaintiff cannot testify to correctness of books). For discussion and authorities, see 5 Wigmore, Evidence, §§ 1554, 1559; 20 Am. Jur., Evidence, § 1076; Note, 6 A.L.R. 756.

7. See the statutes compiled in 5 Wigmore, Evidence, § 1519.

8. See, e. g., Hopkins' Exec'x v. Osborne, 278 Ky. 229, 128 S.W.2d 575, syl. 2–4, 142 A.L.R. 1403 (1939) (decedent's account-book with alterations unexplained should not have been admitted). Bendett v. Bendett, 315 Mass. 59, 52 N.E.2d 2, syl. 3 (1943) (entries in plaintiff's book inadmissible as shop-book under local common law because items exceeded $6.66, the limit for items provable by book account).

9. Thus in Bendett v. Bendett, next preceding note, the court assumed that it was proper to admit the plaintiff's account book if it could qualify either under the shop-book rule or the statute regulating the admission of business records generally.

the use of book-entries made by other persons. When used to prove the facts recorded they were hearsay, of course, and it might be impossible to produce the recorder to give his knowledge of the facts first-hand. But by the early 1700's the special trustworthiness of an entry made by a clerk of a party "in the usual way of . . . trading" had come to be recognized and was allowed as proof of delivery of the goods, when the drayman reporting delivery was shown to be dead and thus unavailable as a witness.[1] From this seed grew the modern common law doctrine that regular entries made in the routine of a business, upon the personal knowledge of the recorder or of some employee reporting to him, and entered at or near the time of the transaction recorded, as a record of original entry, is admissible to prove the facts recited, upon a showing that the recorder or his informant is unavailable.[2] The customary accuracy of business records, vital to the survival of the business and backed by the usual training

and experience of book-keepers furnishes the special reliability, and the unavailability of the participants guarantees the need for the use of this kind of hearsay.

In this context, a "business" means any on-going enterprise or institution, which need not be commercial.[3] Nor is it requisite by the American view that the entry or the report on which it is based be made in the course of duty to another.[4] Thus the entries or reports made by the owner in the course of the business will satisfy the rule.[5]

What of *oral* reports regularly made in the course of business? They cannot come within the terms of a doctrine of admissibility of business records, the reliability of which is largely based on prompt reduction to writing, but the oral business reports do satisfy the other guaranty of trustworthiness which comes from being part of the system on which the operation of the business depends. Some courts, therefore, have admitted them on the basis of this partial analogy to business records.[6]

1. Price v. Earl Torrington, 2 Ld.Raym. 873, 92 Eng. Rep. 84 (1703) (clerk's entry of beer delivered, upon report of the drayman on the day of delivery, held by Holt, C. J., "good evidence to charge the defendant").

2. Among recent opinions recognizing the rule and explaining the basis for it are Edsall v. Rockland Paper Co., 194 A. 115, syl. 2–4 (Del.Super.1937) (distinguishing it from the party-book rule); Gus Dattilo Fruit Co. v. Louisville & N. R. Co., 238 Ky. 322, 37 S.W.2d 856, syl. 3, 4 (1931); Missouri Forged Tool Co. v. St. Louis Car Co., 205 S.W.2d 298, syl. 2–5 (Mo.App.1947); Lebrun v. Boston & M. R. Co., 83 N.H. 293, 142 A. 128, syl. 3–8 (1928).

3. Ford v. State, 82 Tex.Cr. 639, 200 S.W. 841 (1918) (church's register of birth and baptism); Leach v. State, 80 Tex.Cr. 376, 189 S.W. 733 (1916) (Sunday school's record of attendance, to prove an alibi); 5 Wigmore, Evidence § 1523.

4. Hutchins v. Berry, 75 N.H. 416, 75 A. 650, 652, 653 (1910); Lebrun v. Boston & M. R. Co., 83 N.H. 293, 142 A. 128, syl. 11 (1928) (dictum); 5 Wigmore, Evidence § 1524. But the English and Canadian cases require a duty. Smith v. Blakey, [1867] L.R. 332; Dominion Tel. Securities Ltd. v. Minister of Nat. Rev., [1946] 4 D.L.R. 449, 463.

5. This is implicit in the early cases under the shop-book rule which admitted the entries when the party had no clerk, see next preceding section, and is assumed in the modern cases. But many decisions seem too strict in excluding wholesale the party's memoranda, entries, and check-stubs dealing with his personal financial affairs, as distinguished from his business. See, e. g., In re Cummings' Estate, 226 Iowa 1207, 286 N.W. 409, syl. 2 (1939) (plaintiff's memorandum-book of loans made by him, excluded because he was not in the loan business); Dec.Dig. Evidence, ☞354(3) (7). Rather the test should be whether the records were so regularly and systematically kept as to be reasonably trustworthy. See Creighton v. Creighton, 6 Cal.App.2d 270, 43 P.2d 1104, syl. 1–3 (1935) (question of fact for the judge); Valentine v. Valentine, 31 Wash.2d 650, 198 P.2d 494, syl. 1 (1948) (account book kept by plaintiff's sister showing money advanced to plaintiff's wife, admitted); 5 Wigmore, Evidence § 1623.

6. Geralds v. Champlin, 93 N.H. 157, 37 A.2d 155, syl. 1–6 (1944) (in compensation proceeding for alleged injury necessitating amputation of leg, superintendent allowed to testify to oral reports of deceased foreman, made as part of check-up system, as to continual complaints of plaintiff of trouble

284. Must be an "Original" Entry: Type of Record: Preliminary Slips: Day-Book or Journal: Ledger: Carbons and Duplicates, Loose Sheets and Punch-Cards.

The entries to be admissible must be "original" entries, and not mere transcribed records or copies.[1] This restriction is based upon the assumption that the original entries are likely to be more accurate than subsequent copies or transcriptions. In many businesses, however, it is customary for the daily transactions such as sales, or services, to be noted upon slips, memorandum-books or the like, by the employee concerned, such as a salesman, clerk, foreman, weigher, or workman, and thereafter these slips or memoranda are regularly and promptly collected and entries made therefrom in a permanent book such as a journal or ledger. In such event, the entries in the permanent book sufficiently comply with the requirement that the entries be "original,"[2] and would certainly be admissible if the slips or memoranda have disappeared,[3] and would seem, since they are held to be original entries, to be independently admissible without any proof as to the unavailability of the first tentative memoranda.[4] Under this principle, the cash-book, and the day-book or journal, recording the transactions in chronological order and made up either from original entries or from entries taken from temporary slips or memoranda, would be admissible as the first permanent record.[5] Upon the same basis, a ledger or other similar book, wherein the items of debit and credit are arranged under the names of the parties concerned, when made up day by day from memory or directly from the original slips or memoranda, would also be admissible.[6] And where the ledger is made, not from memory or from the original slips, but from the journal, day-book and cash-book which are, in turn, based on the original slips, but is regularly, promptly, and systematically kept and is used and relied on in the operation of the business, it would seem that there could still be no sound reason against the ledger's ad-

with his legs; admission approved in lucid opinion by Marble, C. J.); Notes, 93 U.Pa.L.Rev. 101, 8 U. Detroit L.J. 42; Williams v. Walton & Whann Co., 9 Houst. (Del.) 322, 32 A. 726, syl. 3 (1892) (oral reports admissible if made regularly); The Sussex Peerage, 11 Cl. & Fin. 85, 113 (H.L.1844); Regina v. Buckley, 13 Cox C.C. 293 (1873); but cf. Dawson v. Dawson, 22 T.L.R. 52 (P.1905); Tucker v. Oldbury Urban Council, 81 L.J. (N.S.) 668 (K.B.1912). Wigmore advocates their admission if made in course of duty (§ 1528).

1. Stark v. Burkitt (1910) 103 Tex. 437, 440 (syl. 3), 129 S.W. 343; 5 Wigmore, Evidence, §§ 1532, 1558; Dec.Dig. Evidence, ☞354(2–10, 13); Note, What Constitutes Books of Original Entry, 17 A.L.R.2d 235.

While under the principle above discussed the books or entries as to which evidence is offered must have been "original," i. e. current books or entries made in the course of the business, yet in some instances where it is impossible to produce such books or entries, secondary evidence, i. e. copies or oral descriptions of them, may be admitted under the rules obtaining as to secondary evidence generally. Barclay v. Deyerle (1909) 53 Tex.Civ.App. 236 (syl. 3), 116 S.W. 123.

2. Plummer v. Struby, etc. Co., 23 Colo. 190, 47 P. 294, syl. 1 (1896) (The fact that the charges were made in the first instance upon slips of paper, and the same day transferred to a day-book, does not keep the day-book from being "original"); Miller v. Shay, 145 Mass. 162, 13 N.E. 468 (1887) (A small account-book, in which the plaintiff, who was unable to write, entered by marks the number of loads of sand delivered to defendant, is admissible even though the marks were transferred by him to the book from marks on his cart.).

3. Mahoney v. Hartford Investment Co., 82 Conn. 280, 73 A. 766, syl. 7 (1909).

4. Banner Grain Co. v. Burr Farmers' Elev. & Supply Co., 162 Minn. 334, 202 N.W. 740, syl. 1 (1925) (books based on "trading cards," production of cards not required); Corkran v. Taylor, 77 N.J.L. 195, 71 A. 124, syl. 2 (1908) (books made up from time-slips admissible "with or without" the slips).

5. Scruggs v. E. L. Woodley Lumber Co., 179 S.W. 897, syl. 3 (Tex.Civ.App.1915).

6. Rocky Mt. Beverage Co. v. Walter Brewing Co., 107 Colo. 63, 108 P.2d 885, syl. 2 (1941); State v. Stephenson, 69 Kan. 405, 76 P. 905, syl. 1–3 (1904); Green v. Woods, 325 Mich. 649, 39 N.W.2d 317, syl. 2 (1949). Edgewood Lumber Co. v. Hull, 32 Tenn. App. 577, 223 S.W.2d 210, syl. 1, 2, 17 A.L.R.2d 228, 1949, cert. den.

missibility.[7] It is far more convenient for use in evidence than the slips or the journal, when the purpose is to reveal the whole state of an account. Furthermore, if prepared promptly and regularly, e. g. when posted daily or weekly, it is an "original" entry-book in the sense that the entries are made while the transactions recorded are still fresh in the memory of the participants.

Furthermore, it would seem that the first slips or memoranda made at the time of the transaction would likewise be admissible as regular entries since the books compiled from them are admissible.[8] Under the now widely prevailing practice of "loose-leaf" book-keeping, by the use of carbon copies, multiple slips are made for each transaction, each an exact copy of the others, one of which is used as an invoice, another as the basis for a receipt, and another as a journal entry, later posted in the ledger. It seems that under this practice each of the duplicate slips should be admissible as an "original" entry.[9]

The still more recently devised systems of accounting by the use of punched cards will probably present little difficulty as to proof. Doubtless the punched holes in the cards would be acceptable as regular entries when accompanied by testimony explaining their meaning under the code used in the particular system employed.

285. Time: Record Must Have Been Made Shortly after the Transaction.[1]

Obviously the reliability of any system of business records depends largely upon the promptness with which transactions are recorded. Accordingly, cases and text-writers formulate the requirement that the entry must be "at or near the time of the transaction recorded,"[2] or "at the time or nearly so of the principal fact,"[3] or "at or reasonably near the time of the transaction."[4] It is believed that these necessarily vague statements as to time should not be too rigidly applied and that the entries should be admitted if they are such as business men would regard as current entries, i. e. made while the matter is sufficiently fresh as to be still verifiable by the memory of the participants.

---

7. Givens v. Pierson's Adm'x, 167 Ky. 574, 181 S.W. 324, 327, syl. 2 (1916); H. F. Shepherdson Co. v. Central Fire Ins. Co., 220 Minn. 401, 19 N.W.2d 772, syl. 10 (1945). But see Campanella v. Bono, 120 N.J.L. 435, 200 A. 544, syl. 2 (1938) where a ledger sheet was said to be inadmissible, "not being accompanied by the day-book."

8. Southwestern Telegraph & Telephone Co. v. Pearson (1911, Tex.Civ.App.) 137 S.W. 733 (call-tickets made by telephone operators showing time of calls held admissible, but exclusion of evidence held not shown to be harmful).

9. Lake v. Jones Lumber Co., (1921, Tex.Civ.App.) 233 S.W. 1011 (syl. 4) (slips held admissible as original entries).

Cases on loose-leaf books are collected in 32 C.J.S., Evidence, § 685c, note 43.

1. 5 Wigmore, Evidence, §§ 1526, 1550; Dec.Dig. Evidence, ☞354(12); 32 C.J.S. Evidence, § 690.

2. 5 Wigmore, Evidence, § 1526. See Dameron v. Harris, 281 Mo. 247, 219 S.W. 954, syl. 11, 12 (1920) (manager of farm, with office in town, made entries about farm as soon as he returned to office, some-

times from memory, sometimes from memoranda, held, admissible; extensive discussion of time-requirement). This standard was held not to have been proved to be met in Lane v. May & Thomas Hdw. Co., 121 Ala. 296, 25 So. 809 (1899). The Uniform Business Records Act (see § 289, infra) requires that the record be made "at or near the time of the act, condition or event."

3. Anchor Milling Co. v. Walsh, 108 Mo. 277, 18 S.W. 904, 906 (1892). The Model Act on Business Records (see § 289, infra) requires that the entry be made in the regular course of business, "and that it was the regular course of such business to make such memorandum or record at the time of such act . . . or within a reasonable time thereafter." This requirement was held not shown to be met in Roge v. Valentine, 280 N.Y. 268, 20 N.E.2d 751, syl. 5 (1939).

4. Kamm v. Rees, 177 F. 14, 23 (C.C.A.Ore., 1910) (charges for machinery made to order sufficiently contemporaneous when made during progress of work); Hembree v. Von Keller, 189 Okl. 439, 119 P.2d 74, syl. 11 (1941) (dictum).

286. First-Hand Knowledge.[1]

The chief foundation of the special reliability of business records is the requirement that they must be based upon the first-hand observation of someone whose job it is to know the facts recorded.[2] This is the general requirement for hearsay declarants [3] as it is for witnesses who are offered to testify to facts on the stand.[4] But obviously under the complex and specialized division of labor in modern business,[5] it is not required that the person or persons, the clerks, book-keepers and accountants, who do the recording, must know the facts at first hand. It is sufficient that their records be based upon the reports of informants, salesmen, time-keepers, mechanics and the like, who know the facts [6] and report them orally or by temporary memoranda to those who will make the record. In respect to a particular record, it may not be possible to prove specifically that the particular informant actually observed the facts, or indeed who the informant was.[7] As evidence that he did, it will be prima facie sufficient to show that it was someone's job, or his business duty in the firm's routine or system, to observe them.[8] But if the evidence in the particular case discloses that the record was not based upon the report of an informant having the business duty to observe and report, then the record is not admissible under this exception, to show the truth of the matter reported to the recorder.

The Model Act [9] after providing that the record must have been made in the regular course of business, recites that "all other circumstances of the making of such writing or record, including lack of personal knowledge by the entrant or maker, may be shown to affect its weight but shall not affect its admissibility." This could be interpreted as abolishing the requirement of first-hand knowledge by one whose job is to know the facts. The more reasonable interpretation, however, is to read "entrant or maker" as meaning the recorder only, and thus merely making clear that one who makes the record on reports of others need not know the facts, without broadening (beyond the probable intent of the drafters) the content of this hearsay exception to embrace records founded on reports by one who has no business duty to know the facts.[10] Thus, the statements of

---

1. 5 Wigmore, Evidence, §§ 1530, 1530a, 1555.

2. Chaffee v. United States, 18 Wall. 516, 541–543, 21 L.Ed. 908 (1873) (collector's entries based on bills of lading or captain's verbal reports, where neither collector nor captains saw the goods, inadmissible); Conn. Mut. Life Ins. Co. v. Schwenk, 94 U.S. 593, 597, 24 L.Ed. 294 (1876) (entry by lodge-secretary of member's age entered before he became a member); McDonald v. Carnes, 90 Ala. 147, 7 So. 919, syl. 1 (1890) (entries admissible "to prove the correctness of all items within the knowledge of the person making them").

3. See, e. g., §§ 253, 262, 277, herein.

4. See § 10, herein.

5. For description of the system of operations and records involved in handling a mixed order by a leading manufacturer of linoleum, see Morgan et al., The Law of Evidence, 57–61 (1927).

6. Pittsburgh C. C. & St. L. R. Co. v. City, 242 Ill. 178, 89 N.E. 1022, syl. 10, 14 (1909) (car-records kept by clerk on basis of reports, held admissible);

State v. Shinborn, 46 N.H. 497, 88 Am.Dec. 224 (1866), and cases collected in Notes, 52 L.R.A. 597, 27 A.L.R. 1439.

7. Morgan, op. cit., preceding note.

8. Thus, in listing the requirements for business records, the court included, "That the entries were made by one who was authorized to do so, and that he did the acts so recorded himself or that he made the record upon information derived from one who was authorized to do so." Stark v. Burkitt, 103 Tex. 437, 129 S.W. 343, 344, syl. 2 (1910).

9. Upon which the Federal, New York, Massachusetts, Maryland, Connecticut, Michigan and Rhode Island legislation is based, see § 289, herein.

10. "These acts were intended to make admissible records which, because made pursuant to a regular business duty, are presumed to be reliable. The mere fact that recordation of third party statements is routine, taken apart from the source of the information recorded, imports no guaranty of the truth of the statements themselves. There is no reason for supposing an intention to make admis-

by-standers recorded in a policeman's report of accident or the "history" given by an accident-victim or other patient, and recorded by an attendant, upon being received at a hospital, would be denied admission as business records to show the facts reported,[11] though they might come in on other theories.[12]

The provision of the Uniform Act[13] requires for admissibility that "in the opinion of the court, the sources of information, method and time of preparation were such as to justify [the record's] admission." Under this provision, likewise, there is little doubt that the courts will require generally that the "source of information" be first-hand knowledge of someone whose job it is to know, unless in the particular case the volunteer informant's report appeared to be so especially trustworthy as in the judge's opinion to justify admission.

287. Regularity: Reports as to Matters Not of Constant Recurrence: Doctor's Reports and Employee's Accident Reports.

As we have seen, the doctrine of the admissibility of business records originated in the recognition of the need for using parties' shop-books, later extended into the area of entries in the account-books of third persons.[1] "Regular entries" became the accepted phrase and, like many such catch-phrases, this one tends to shape and narrow the developement of the doctrine. Thus, the earlier cases tend to restrict the evidence to book-keeping entries of debit and credit.[2] Recently, however, it has become apparent that any written statement made as a part of a continuing job, occupation or business duty furnishes adequately the guaranty of special reliability which the rule supposes. While it is said that the statement must not be a "casual

---

sible hearsay of this sort. So to construe these statutes would make of them almost limitless drag-nets for the introduction of random, irresponsible testimony beyond the reach of the usual tests for accuracy." Note, Business Entry Statutes, 48 Col. L.Rev. 920, 927 (1948).

11. So held as to police reports of accidents based on bystanders' statements. Johnson v. Lutz, 253 N.Y. 124, 170 N.E. 517 (1930). As to hospital records of "histories" given by patient or others of events outside the hospital. Valenti v. Mayer, 301 Mich. 551, 4 N.W.2d 5, syl. 7–10 (1942); Kelly v. Ford Motor Co., 280 Mich. 378, 273 N.W. 737, syl. 9 (1937); Geroami v. Fancy Fruit & Produce Corp., 249 App. Div. 221, 291 N.Y.S. 837, syl. 1, 2 (1931). An exception, however, to this requirement is recognized in Pekelis v. Transcontinental & Western Air, 187 F.2d 122, syl. 5, 6 (C.A.2d 1951) where in an action for death in an airplane accident, it was held that the report of a board set up by defendant to investigate and report on the cause of the accident was admissible as evidence of the cause under the Federal Business Records Act because such report was within the scope of duty of the Board though based in part on information supplied by persons having no business duty to give it.

12. The business records exception lets in the recorder's entry to prove that the statement or history was made to him, when such recording is part of his regular routine. Thus, it proves the making of the volunteer's statement, and if that is legally

significant, or if it comes in under another exception to the hearsay rule to prove its truth, it will be admissible. This is clearly brought out in Kelly v. Ford Motor Co., 280 Mich. 378, 273 N.W. 737, 739, 741, where the recorded "history" given by deceased to doctors was rejected as a business entry to prove the facts of the accident, but it was recognized that if it qualified as a party's admission, or if his making of a claim were legally significant, it could come in. See also Pekelis v. Transcontinental & Western Air, 187 F.2d 122, syl. 3, 4 (C.A.2d 1951) (reports of investigating boards set up by defendant to investigate accident admissible as adoptive admission); Freedman v. Mut. L. Ins. Co., 342 Pa. 404, 413, 21 A.2d 81, 86 (1941) (statement to doctor of bodily condition); Comm. v. Harris, 351 Pa. 325, 332, 41 A.2d 686, 692 (1945) (similar to last); Brock, Hospital Records under the Federal Act, 23 Tex. L.Rev. 178, 187 (1944); Note, Business Entry Statutes, 48 Col.L.Rev. 920, 927, 928 (1948).

13. See § 289, herein.

1. See §§ 281–283, herein.

2. See, e. g., Paine v. Meier & Frank Co., 146 Ore. 40, 27 P.2d 315, syl. 4 (1933) (notations on back of ledger sheets as to requests for payment, etc., excluded; two judges dissenting); Barley v. Byrd, 95 Va. 316, 28 S.E. 329, 330, syl. 6 (1897) (memorandum by Bushrod Washington, attorney for James Wilson, as to lands conveyed to Wilson inadmissible as business entry). See also Note, Admissibility of Books, Reports and the like, other than Books of Account, 125 Am.St.Rep. 841.

and isolated" one,[3] it no longer is restricted to standardized commercial entries in books of account, and extends to statements and reports made in the course of business duty or the routine of a job or profession about particular matters not of daily or regular recurrence.[4] This is recognized in the Model Act[5] which admits "any writing or record, whether in the form of an entry in a book or otherwise" and the Uniform Act[6] which speaks comprehensively of "a record of an act, condition or event," made in the course of business.

Accordingly, well-reasoned modern decisions have admitted in accident cases the written reports of doctors of their findings from an examination of the injured party, when it appears that it is the doctor's professional routine or duty to make such report.[7] Similarly, it would seem that the report of an employee, such as a bus or truck driver, or a locomotive engineer of an accident in the course of the business, when such report is required by the employer's instructions and

routine should qualify as a business record, and should be evidence of the facts recited, at least so far as it is based on the reporter's first-hand knowledge. When offered against the employer, however, such reports have usually been discussed on the footing of admissions of a party,[8] and the possible application of the doctrine of business records has been generally overlooked.[9] Moreover, when an engineer's report of a crossing accident was sought to be used by the defendant railroad company, the engineer having died before trial, the Federal Supreme Court held it was properly rejected under the Federal statute which follows the Model Act.[10] The court's reasoning leading up to the conclusion that the report was not made in the regular course of business was to the effect that the report was made with a view to litigation, rather than "for the systematic conduct of the enterprise as a railroad business."[11] Commentators have questioned the notion that accident-reporting is not a regular and necessary part of railroad operations.[12]

---

3. 5 Wigmore, Evidence, § 1525.

4. See, e. g., Reynolds v. McNeil, 218 Ark. 453, 236 S.W.2d 723, syl. 1 (1951) (well driller's report to oil and gas commission as to initial production of well); Walker v. Curtis, 116 Mass. 98, 101 (1874) (surveyor's memorandum of results of examination). But compare Baltimore & O. R. Co. v. Zapf, 192 Md. 403, 64 A.2d 139, syl. 5 (1949) (X-ray report of radiographer to referring physician, excluded; reporter should be called for cross-examination on his interpretation) and see Gilbert v. Gulf Oil Corp., 175 F.2d 705, syl. 8 (C.C.A.Va.1949) (letter written by chief and member of fire department giving opinion to one of the litigants as to cause of fire, inadmissible under Federal Business Records Act, 27 U.S.C.A. § 1732, not in the regular course of business).

5. See the Act, set out in § 289, herein.

6. Described in § 289, herein.

7. Korte v. New York N. H. & H. R. Co., 191 F.2d 86, syl. 6–8 (C.A.N.Y.1951), noted 37 Corn.L.Q. 290, 5 Vand.L.Rev. 651 (doctor's letter to railway which employed him to make examination admissible against railway as a business record made in course of doctor's business: lucid opinion by Clark, J.; Chase, J., dissenting); Lebrun v. Boston & M. R.

Co., 83 N.H. 293, 142 A. 128, syl. 2–14 (1928) (railway surgeon's report offered by railway admissible after his death as business record, over objection that it was self-serving and mere isolated memorandum; learned opinion by Snow, J.).

8. See §§ 244, 78, herein.

9. Notes, Statutes on Business Records as Applicable to Reports of Accidents, 144 A.L.R. 727, 729; Accident Reports as Business Records, 4 Stan.L. Rev. 288 (1952).

10. Palmer v. Hoffman, 318 U.S. 109, 63 S.Ct. 477, 87 L.Ed. 645, 144 A.L.R. 719 (1943).

11. A somewhat analogous theory was advanced in Clainos v. United States, 163 F.2d 593, syl. 3, 4 (C.A.D.C.1947) to support the view that police records showing convictions of a person are not admissible under the Federal Business Records Act which are limited to records of the internal operations of the police. It seems that the result could have been more securely grounded on the best evidence rule. Note, 26 Tex.L.Rev. 669.

12. Morgan, Evidence 1941–1945, 59 Harv.L.Rev. 481 at 566 (1946); Maguire, Evidence: Common Sense and Common Law, 156 et seq. (1947). But there is an approving Note, 43 Col.L.Rev. 392 (1943).

They have considered that it was the court's fear of the self-serving use of such statements that was the probable motivation of the decision.[13] On this supposition it has been held that the decision does not stand in the way of receiving *against* the employer as a business record the report of an accident-investigating board set up by such employer.[14]

288. The Necessity Element: Requirement of Unavailability of the Makers of the Record: Undue Inconvenience as a Modern Equivalent of Unavailability.

The rules and doctrines thus far discussed in this chapter have, in the main, been those relating to the first general requirement for exceptions to the Hearsay Rule, namely, the circumstantial guaranty of special *reliability* of the evidence received under the exception. The requirement under discussion in the present section relates to the policy demanding that the facts show a special *need* for the particular hearsay.

The common law rule implementing this policy requires that before business records may be received as evidence of their truth, under this particular exception to the hearsay rule, the entrant, or in the case of a co-operative entry based on information given by other employees, both the entrant and the informant or informants who reported the facts recited in the record, must be proven to be unavailable for production as witnesses.[1] Illness,[2] death,[3] disqualifying insanity,[4] and absence from the jurisdiction[5] are the common grounds, but any facts which in the particular situation render it impractical for the party to produce the person as a witness should suffice.

When the record was made upon the personal knowledge of the entrant, and the entrant is produced as a witness, he may give his testimony independently of the record, if he remembers the facts, or he may use the record to refresh his memory.[6] If he does not recollect the facts, the record should be usable as a business record, under the present exception or as a record of past recollection.[7] If the entrant is unavailable but the informant is produced, or the informant is unavailable but the entrant is produced, then a combination of theories may be used. The admissibility of the entry may be supported under the present exception, as far as it reflects the past knowledge and the former statement of the absent participant. In so far as it reflects the past knowledge and statement of the present witness, it may come in either on the theory of business records, or that of past recollection recorded.

---

13. Note, Business Entry Statutes, 48 Col.L.Rev. 920, 925 (1948). This motive-to-misrepresent basis was the ground of the brilliant and exhaustive opinion in the court below, which evoked a forcible dissent by Clark, J., 129 F.2d 976. See the penetrating criticism by Professor Maguire, 56 Harv. L.Rev. 458 (1942).

14. Pekelis v. Transcontinental & Western Air, 187 F.2d 122, 130 (C.A.N.Y.1951).

1. Missouri Forged Tool Co. v. St. Louis Car Co., 205 S.W.2d 298, syl. 2, 3 (Mo.App.1947) (unavailability of recorders not shown); Rathborne v. Hatch, 80 App.Div. 115, 80 N.Y.S. 347, syl. 1 (1903) (absence of informant telephone clerk not accounted for); Clayton v. Metropolitan Life Ins. Co., 96 Utah 331, 85 P.2d 819, syl. 5, 120 A.L.R. 1117 (1938) (hospital record, failure to produce nurse who made rec-

ord); 5 Wigmore, Evidence, § 1521; 20 Am.Jur., Evidence, §§ 1069–1072.

2. Griffin v. Boston & M. R. Co., 87 Vt. 278, 89 A. 220, syl. 21 (1913).

3. Robinson v. Puls, 28 Cal.2d 664, 171 P.2d 430, syl. 6, 7 (1946) (under Uniform Act, dispensing with proof of time of making entry, when entrant dead); Dec.Dig., Evidence, ☞376(8).

4. Bridgewater v. Roxbury, 54 Conn. 213, 6 A. 415, syl. 1 (1886); Dec.Dig. Evidence ☞354(22½).

5. Gus Dattilo Fruit Co. v. Louisville & N. R. Co., 238 Ky. 322, 37 S.W.2d 856, 857 (1931) (where absent from state or whereabouts unknown); Dec. Dig. Evidence, ☞354(22½).

6. See § 9, herein.

7. See §§ 276, 280, herein.

The requirement of production of all entrants and informants or proof of their physical unavailability was imposed in an era of small business units. It has not worked well in a time when large organizations have taken over a great part of industry and commerce. In such an organization, dealing with complicated problems of manufacturing, finance, transportation, or the like, records are kept by many hands of data furnished from many sources. It is impracticable, especially in this day of typewritten records, to ear-mark each entry so as later to ascertain which employee made it. It is almost impossible, oftentimes, to ascertain who reported the information upon which the entry was based. Furthermore, even if upon the offer of the entry as evidence, it may be possible to identify the entrants and reporters, they may be very numerous as to any particular account, as to which a different set of witnesses might be required for each entry. Finally, if such witnesses are produced, they will in such a business almost invariably have no recollection about the particular transaction, and their evidence will be merely a routine repetition of the formulas that they correctly reported and recorded the matters in question.

Accordingly in this situation many courts, under the guidance of Wigmore,[8] have come to the view that common sense requires a relaxation of the strict rule of production.

Consequently they recognize a discretion in the trial judge to dispense with the production of the entrants and informants, and to permit the records to be verified by a supervising officer who can testify that they have been regularly kept, when it appears that the inconvenience of producing the participants, in the light of their number and probable lack of present knowledge, outweighs the value of producing them for examination and cross-examination.[9]

Thus far and no farther have the courts gone through the decisional development of common law principles to ease the heavy burden of preliminary proof necessary to the use of business records in court. The next section deals with the work of the legislatures in meeting this problem.

289. Modernizing the Law of Business Records: The Model Act, the Uniform Act, the Texas Act.[1]

The inherited law of business records is archaic as a system regulating the use of such records as proof. There are gaps such as the unavailability of a party's books of account to prove cash transactions.[2] There are lingering uncertainties. How far does the common law of regular entries apply in a particular case, how far a narrower shopbook rule, usually statutory? How far does a report on a particular transaction, not a matter of day-to-day recurrence, qualify as a business record?[3] But as we have suggested the most

---

8. Evidence, § 1530. Judges too had pointed the way. Fielder v. Collier, 13 Ga. 499 (1853) (Lumpkin, J.); Mississippi River Logging Co. v. Robson, 69 F. 773, 781, syl. 4 (C.C.A.Iowa, 1895) (Thayer, J.).

9. Massachusetts Bonding & Ins. Co. v. Norwich Pharmacal Co., 18 F.2d 934, syl. 3, 4 (C.C.A.N.Y.) (leading opinion by L. Hand, J.); Jennings v. United States, 73 F.2d 470, syl. 10 (C.C.A. 5th, 1934); Continental Nat. Bank v. First Nat. Bank, 108 Tenn. 374, 68 S.W. 497, 499 (1912); Heid Bros., Inc. v. Commercial Nat. Bank, 240 S.W. 908, syl. 5, 6, 24 A.L.R. 904 (Tex.Comm.App.1922); French v. Virginian Ry. Co., 121 Va. 383, 93 S.E. 585, syl. 2 (1917); Willett v. Davis, 30 Wash.2d 622, 193 P.2d 321, syl. 11 (1948); State v. Larue, 98 W.Va. 677, 128 S.E. 116, syl. 6 (1925).

1. 5 Wigmore, Evidence, § 1520; Ray, Business Records—A Proposed Rule, 5 Southwestern Law J. 33 (1951) (an illuminating survey); Note, Business Entry Statutes, 48 Col.L.Rev. 920 (1948); Note (by Roscoe L. Barrow), Business Entries before the Court, 32 Ill.L.Rev. 334 (1938) (somewhat local in treatment, but valuable, with careful draft of statute). See also Ginsberg, Business Records, 29 Neb.L.Rev. 60 (1949) (discussing new Nebraska version of Model Act); Note, Engstrand, Business Entry Exception, 35 Calif.L.Rev. 434 (1947) (discusses California cases under Uniform Act); Note, Business Records Legislation, 47 Harv.L.Rev. 1044 (1934) (discusses the Model Act).

2. See § 282, above.

3. See § 287, above.

burdensome feature of this archaic system is the requirement that each participant, whether entrant or informant, in the making of the record, be produced or at least identified and shown to be dead, out of the state or otherwise unavailable.[4] This showing of the identity and unavailability of absent informants where the records are those of a large and wide-spread business imposes a burden of preliminary proof which may be so expensive as to be impractical. We have seen that forward-looking courts have permitted trial judges to relax these requirements in their discretion.[5] The main task of legislation has been to lighten these burdens of producing or accounting for an undue number of unneeded witnesses by permitting the records to be verified by anyone who knows that they were made in the regular course of the business.

The provisions of the Model Act [6] designed to meet these problems and to simplify and reform the archaic doctrines regulating the admission of business records, are as follows:

"Any writing or record, whether in the form of an entry in a book or otherwise, made as a memorandum or record of any act, transaction, occurrence or event shall be admissible in evidence in proof of said act, transaction, occurrence or event, if the trial judge shall find that it was made in the regular course of any business, and that it was the regular course of such business to make such memorandum or record at the time of such act, transaction, occurrence or event or within a reasonable time thereafter. All other circumstances of the making of such writing or record, including lack of personal knowledge by the entrant or maker, may be shown to affect its weight, but they shall not affect its admissibility. The term business shall include business, profession, occupation and calling of every kind." [7]

Using the Model Act as a starting-point the Commissioners on Uniform State Laws promulgated in 1936, the Uniform Business Records as Evidence Act as follows:

"§ 1. Definition.—The term 'business' shall include every kind of business, profession, occupation, calling or operation of institutions, whether carried on for profit or not.

"§ 2. Business Records.—A record of an act, condition or event, shall, in so far as relevant, be competent evidence if the custodian or other qualified witness testifies to its identity and the mode of its preparation, and if it was made in the regular course of business, at or near the time of the act, condition or event, and if, in the opinion of the court, the sources of information, method and time of preparation were such as to justify its admission." [8]

4. See § 288, above.

5. See § 288, above.

6. This Act was prepared by a distinguished Committee constituted by the Commonwealth Fund to propose specific reforms in the law of evidence. The members of the committee were Charles M. Hough, United States Circuit Judge, William A. Johnston, Chief Justice Kansas Supreme Court, Professors E. M. Morgan, Harvard, J. H. Wigmore, Northwestern, Z. Chafee, Jr., Harvard, R. W. Gifford, Columbia, E. W. Hinton, Chicago, and E. R. Sunderland, Michigan. The results of their research upon the business practice and legal doctrines respecting business records and the reasons for the proposed Act are set out in Morgan, et al., The Law of Evidence: Some Proposals for Its Reform, Ch. V (Yale Univ. Press, 1927).

7. Morgan, et al., op. cit. next preceding note at p. 63.

This Act has been the model for the Federal Business Records Act, 28 U.S.C.A. § 1732 and for statutes in the states as follows: Conn.Gen.St.1949, § 7903; Md.Ann.Code Gen.Laws, art. 35, § 68 (1939), Code 1951, art. 35, § 68; Mass.G.L.(Ter.Ed.) c. 233, § 78; Mich.Comp.Laws 1948, § 617.53; Nebraska, Laws 1949, L.B. 309; N.M.1941 Comp. § 20–219; (Supp. 1947); New York, Civ.Prac.Act, § 374a, adopted by N.Y.Laws 1928, c. 532; R.I.Gen.Laws 1938, c. 538, § 1. See Note, 48 Col.L.Rev. 920, 922, notes 11–13.

8. 9 Uniform Laws Ann. 387 (1951). As appears on p. 385 of the same volume the Uniform Act, with or without modifications, has been adopted as follows: California, St.1941, p. 1788, Code Civ.Proc. §§ 1953e–1953h; Delaware, Laws 1945, c. 252, 10 Del.C. §

What are the distinctive features and respective merits of these two widely adopted Acts? Both of them supply the gaps and remove the uncertainties mentioned above as to cash transactions, special treatment of parties' books, and admissibility of special reports. The Uniform Act in addition makes clear that non-commercial records are covered and specifies that the record may be used to prove a "condition" which opens the way for reports of diagnoses in hospital records.[9] As to the burden of production of participants and preliminary proof of unavailability of absent participants, the Model Act undoubtedly is intended to dispense with these requirements by omitting them and merely requiring that the trial judge shall find that the record was made in regular course, etc. The Uniform Act is more satisfactorily specific in its handling of this problem in providing that all the necessary preliminary proof may be made "by the custodian or other qualified witness." Both Acts fail to give a clear answer to the question whether business records of information furnished by one who has no business duty to give it are admissible in proof of the facts so volunteered.

The Uniform Act in its last clause introduces the element of discretion of the trial judge to admit or exclude the record according to his "opinion" as to whether the sources of information, etc. were "such as to justify its admission."[10] This affords a flexibility which may be valuable in particular cases but it may be questioned whether predictability of admission when certain fairly objective standards for the offered record are met is not a more useful aim.

This is the view reflected in an Act drafted by Professor Roy R. Ray, after a thorough reconsideration of the subject.[11] This Act, adopted in Texas in 1951, and omitting formal clauses, is as follows:

"Section 1. A memorandum or record of an act, event or condition shall, in so far as relevant, be competent evidence of the occurrence of the act or event or the existence of the condition if the judge finds that:

"(a) It was made in the regular course of business;

"(b) It was the regular course of that business for an employee or representative of such business with personal knowledge of such act, event or condition to make such memorandum or record or to transmit information thereof to be included in such memorandum or record;

"(c) It was made at or near the time of the act, event or condition or reasonably soon thereafter.

"Sec. 2. The identity and mode of preparation of the memorandum or record in accordance with the provisions of paragraph one (1) may be proved by the testimony of the entrant, custodian or other qualified witness

4310; Florida, Laws 1949, c. 25111, F.S.A. § 90–25; Hawaii, Laws 1941, Act 218, Rev.Laws 1945, § 9902; Idaho, Laws 1939, c. 106, I.C. § 16–401A; Minnesota, Laws 1939, c. 78, M.S.A. §§ 600.01 to 600.04; Missouri, Laws 1949, p. 275, V.A.M.S. §§ 490.660 to 490.690; Montana, Laws 1937, c. 59; R.C.M.1947, §§ 93–801–1 to 93–801–4; New Jersey, Laws 1949, c. 124, N.J.S.A. 2A:82–34 to 2A:82–37; North Dakota, Laws 1937, c. 194, NDRC 1943, 31–0801; Ohio, Laws 1939, No. 317, R.C. §§ 2317.40 to 2317.41; Oregon, Laws 1941, c. 414, ORS 41.680 to 41.710; Pennsylvania, Laws 1939, p. 42, No. 35, 28 P.S. §§ 91a–91d; South Dakota, Laws 1939, c. 226, SDC 36.1001; Vermont, Laws 1939, No. 48, V.S. §§ 1753–1756; Washington, Laws 1947, c. 53, RCW 5.44.100 to 5.44.120; Wyoming, Laws 1941, c. 82, W.C.S.1945, §§ 3–3122 to 3–3125.

The Uniform Rules of Evidence, R. 63(13) is a simplified version of the Uniform Act. It admits "Writings offered as memoranda or records of acts, conditions or events to prove the facts stated therein, if the judge finds that they were made in the regular course of a business at or about the time of the act, condition or event recorded, and that the sources of information from which made and the method and circumstances of their preparation were such as to indicate their trustworthiness."

9. See § 290, infra.

10. That the clause does confer discretion is clear. Choate v. Robertson, 31 Wash.2d 118, 195 P.2d 630, syl. 6 (1948).

11. See Ray, Business Records—A Proposed Rule of Admissibility, 5 Southwestern L.J. 33 (1951).

even though he may not have personal knowledge as to the various items or contents of such memorandum or record. Such lack of personal knowledge may be shown to affect the weight and credibility of the memorandum or record but shall not affect its admissibility.

"Sec. 3. Evidence to the effect that the records of a business do not contain any memorandum or record of an alleged act, event or condition shall be competent to prove the non-occurrence of the act or event or the non-existence of the condition in that business if the judge finds that it was the regular course of that business to make such memoranda or records of all such acts, events or conditions at the time or within reasonable time thereafter and to preserve them.

"Sec. 4. 'Business' as used in this Act includes any and every kind of regular organized activity whether conducted for profit or not." [12]

This retains the most valuable clauses of the two preceding Acts, settles clearly the question as to records based on "volunteer" reports, minimizes the area of discretion, and further clarifies for the trial lawyer the requisites of preliminary proof. In addition it has the useful feature, not touched in the

previous Acts, of providing that the absence of the record of a transaction may be received as evidence of its non-occurrence.[13]

290. Hospital Records.[1]

As we have seen the recognition of the special reliability of regular entries was an outgrowth of the needs of merchants and shop-keepers for the use in evidence of their books and records.[2] Some of the courts have been slow to extend the principle to such non-commercial establishments as hospitals,[3] thus forcing resort in some instances to the hearsay exception for official statements to let in the records of public hospitals [4] or hospital records required by law.[5] Many states have special statutes regulating their admission.[6] The safeguards of trustworthiness, however, of the records of a modern hospital are at least as substantial as the guaranties of reliability of the records of business establishments.[7] With the progress in the science and skills of medicine and surgery goes a corresponding improvement and standardization of the practice of recording the facts about the patient—facts upon which the treatment of the patient, and hence his health and often his life, may depend. The scope of such records is shown by the Manual of Hos-

12. Laws 1951, ch. 321.

13. Uniform Rules of Evidence, R. 63(14) is substantially identical. The Michigan Business Records Act has a like provision. Comp.Laws § 14207. See In re Atkinson's Estate, 297 Mich. 15, 296 N.W. 864, syl. 1–3 (1941). Without a statute, the decisions are divided on the question whether such an application of the regular entries principle is allowable. See, e. g., Zurich v. Wehr, 163 F.2d 791, syl. 1 (C.C.A. 3d 1947) (pro); Shreve v. United States, 77 F.2d 2, syl. 5 (C.C.A. 9th 1935) (apparently contra, but with qualifications). Wigmore argues strongly for this application. 5 Evidence, § 1531. See also 32 C.J.S., Evidence § 687.

1. 6 Wigmore, Evidence, § 1707; Hale, Hospital Records as Evidence, 14 So.Cal.L.Rev. 99 (1941); Medina, Current Developements, 30 Corn.L.Q. 449, 454 (1945) (discussing New York decisions); Braham, Case Records of Hospitals and Doctors under Business Records Act, 21 Temp.L.Q. 113 (1948)

McCormick Evidence HB—39

(discussing Pennsylvania statutes and decisions); Notes, 75 A.L.R. 378, 120 A.L.R. 1124.

2. See §§ 281, 282, supra.

3. See, e. g., Mutual Ben. Health & Acc. Ass'n v. Bell, 49 Ga.App. 640, 176 S.E. 124, 130 (1934) ("purely hearsay"); Levy v. J. L. Mott Iron Works, 143 App.Div. 7, 127 N.Y.S. 506, syl. 2–4 (1911).

4. Galli v. Wells, 209 Mo.App. 460, 239 S.W. 894, syl. 1, 2 (1922) (city hospital); Dallas Coffee & Tea Co. v. Williams, 45 S.W.2d 724, syl. 11 (Tex. Civ.App. 1931) (same), noted 10 Tex.L.Rev. 510.

5. Kirkpatrick v. Wells, 319 Mo. 1040, 6 S.W.2d 591, syl. 4, 5 (1928) (private hospital).

6. These are compiled in 6 Wigmore, Evidence, § 1707.

7. Globe Indemnity Co. v. Reinhart, 152 Md. 439, 446, 137 A. 43, 46 (1927); Schmidt v. Reimenschneider, 196 Minn. 612, 265 N.W. 816, 817 (1936).

pital Standardization of the American College of Surgeons.[8]

In the light of these developements most courts would concede today that hospital records will be received upon the same conditions of meeting the requirements of regularity, personal knowledge, contemporaneousness, production of participants and the like, as are prescribed for business records. This result is made easier by the Model Act with its broad definition of "business"[9] and the Uniform Act which broadens the definition still further by adding "whether carried on for profit or not."[10] A growing realization by lawyers of the importance of hospital records in personal injury and life and accident insurance litigation and in trials for homicide has resulted in a deluge of decisions in the last two decades upon the admissibility of such records. Only a few of the problems raised in these cases can be touched upon here.

Preliminary proof. Production of a witness, having knowledge of the facts, to testify to the making of the record in the regular course of the hospital routine, and that it was the practice to make the records accurately and promptly is properly insisted on,[11] as in the case of commercial records.[12] Unfortunately, the additional common law requirement for business records that each entrant and reporter who participated in the record be produced or accounted for[13] is likewise often imposed.[14] It operates in the same way here as an impractical impediment on the use of such records unless the liberal doctrine[15] is here applied that a showing of undue inconvenience is a sufficient accounting for non-production,[16] or the still more liberal practice under modern statutes dispensing with the production of entrants and reporters[17] is followed.[18]

---

8. The detailed requirements for such records (and the information to be covered in them) as then prescribed by the Manual are set out in Hale, Hospital Records as Evidence, 14 So.Calif.L.Rev. 99 at pp. 113, 114 (1941). At p. 99 of the same article Dean Hale gives an excellent description of the make-up of such records. A later version of the Manual was issued by the American College of Surgeons (40 E. Erie St., Chicago) in 1946. It deals with records at p. 28.

9. See next preceding section.

10. See next preceding section.

11. Williams v. Williams, 87 N.H. 430, 182 A. 173, syl. 5 (1935) (hospital record sought to be verified by nurse properly excluded because "she disclosed no knowledge . . . as to the system or method in accordance with which the hospital records were kept" or the identity of the persons who kept it or their duties); State v. Guaraneri, 59 R.I. 173, 194 A. 589, syl. 2 (1937) (must appear that it was matter of duty to keep record in regular course of the business of the hospital); Hale, Hospital Records, 14 So.Cal.L.Rev. 99, 101, 102 (1941).

12. See §§ 283–287, above.

13. See § 288, above.

14. Wright v. Upson, 303 Ill. 120, 135 N.E. 209, syl. 5 (1922) (one of two nurses who participated in entries produced, other unaccounted for; inadmis-

sible); Clayton v. Metropolitan Life Ins. Co., 96 Utah 331, 85 P.2d 819, syl. 5, 120 A.L.R. 1117 (1938) (nurse who made entry not produced or accounted for; record excluded); Osborne v. Grand Trunk Ry. Co., 87 Vt. 104, 88 A. 512, syl. 7 (1913) (similar); Hale, op. cit., 14 So.Cal.L.Rev. at 102.

15. See § 288, above.

16. St. Louis v. Boston, & M. Ry. Co., 83 N.H. 538, 145 A. 263, 264, syl. 1 (1929) ("There were 31 pupil nurses in the hospital during the time the plaintiff was there. Under such circumstances proper verification by the record clerk would doubtless have rendered the bedside notes admissible."). See also Lund v. Olson, 182 Minn. 204, 234 N.W. 310, syl. 3, 75 A.L.R. 371 (1931) where a hospital chart was seemingly held admissible upon the verification of a surgeon without producing the nurses who made the record. Accord: Gearhart v. Des Moines Ry. Co., 237 Iowa 213, 21 N.W.2d 569, syl. 2 (1946).

17. See § 289, above.

18. The court in Weis v. Weis, 147 Oh.St. 416, 72 N.E. 2d 245, 250, 169 A.L.R. 668 (1947) stated as the purpose of the Uniform Act "as applied to hospital records, to avoid the necessity and thereby the expense, inconvenience and sometimes the impossibility of calling as witnesses the attendants, nurses and physicians who have collaborated to make the hospital record of a patient."

History.[19] Under standard hospital practice a trained attendant enters upon the record a "Personal History" identifying the patient and giving an account as recited by the patient or those accompanying him, of the present illness or injury and of the events and symptoms leading up to the present condition.[20] This information, of course, is sought for its bearing upon the diagnosis and treatment of the patient's injury or disease. In considering the admissibility of the recorded "history," two questions need to be clearly distinguished. First, is the record when duly authenticated and when it purports to embody the statement of the patient (or of some other named person) receivable as evidence that the statement was actually made by that person? When the accompanying proof shows that the taking and recording of statements such as the one offered is in the regular course of hospital practice and in the regular course of the business of the attendant who took and recorded it, the business records exception seems to support the admissibility of the record as evidence that the purported narrator actually made the statement.[21] This result is subject to the qualification that the matters asserted in the statement must fall within the broad range of facts which under hospital practice are considered relevant to the diagnosis or treatment of the patient's condition.[22] The second question is this: having established the making of the statement by the patient (or other person) by proving the making of the record in regular course, is such statement receivable as evidence of the truth of the facts stated? It seems clear that such use of the statement cannot be supported under the business records exception to the hearsay rule, since the patient or other person accompanying him did not make the statement in the course of a business duty or routine.[23] However, it may still be receivable to prove the facts stated, if it can qualify under any other exception to the rule against hearsay.[24] Of these, the most frequently available would be the exception for the admissions of a party-opponent, as when the patient is plaintiff and his statements are sought to be used against him by the defendant.[25] Other possibilities are the exceptions for spontaneous exclamations,[26] dying declarations[27] and declarations against interest.[28]

---

19. See Notes, 48 Col.L.Rev. 920, 928 (1948), Brock, 23 Tex.L.Rev. 178, 187, 188 (1944), 47 Mich.L.Rev. 124 (1948).

20. See regulations referred to in note 8, above.

21. See, e. g., Watts v. Delaware Coach Co., 58 A.2d 689, syl. 6, 7 (Del.Super.1948) (patient's "history" received as admission, under Uniform Act).

22. Watts v. Delaware Coach Co., 58 A.2d 689, syl. 6, 7 (Del.Super.1948) ("Patient states he twisted ankle while walking along street"; held, sufficiently related to injury and diagnosis and treatment thereof to be admissible as evidence that patient, now the plaintiff, made the statement); Scott v. James Gibbons Co., 192 Md. 319, 64 A.2d 117, syl. 5 (1949) ("history" provable to show the patient was hurt in automobile accident but not the particulars of such accident); Green v. City of Cleveland, 150 Oh. St. 441, 83 N.E.2d 63, syl. 3, 4 (1948) (statement in "history" "fell off street-car, caught heel," not admissible against patient as admission because "not incident to treatment," also because not here sufficiently identified as made by the patient himself;

here the "history" was offered to negate plaintiff's present claim that his fall was due to sudden starting; whether due to tripping or to sudden starting may not be material to treatment, but a description of the accident is needed for treatment and "tripped" is an inevitable part of such description); Comm. v. Harris, 351 Pa. 325, 41 A.2d 688, syl. 4 (1945) (statement entered by doctor in hospital record stating that patient (murder victim) said he had been shot by "a white man" inadmissible on behalf of accused, a negro; the color of the man who shot not material to patient's condition, mere bit of "gratuitous reporting").

23. See § 283, above.

24. See Notes, 48 Col.L.Rev. at 928, 23 Tex.L.Rev. at 187.

25. See, e. g., the Watts and Green cases, supra n. 4.

26. See § 272, herein.

27. See ch. 29, herein.

28. See ch. 28, herein.

It should be pointed out also that the declarant's words or statements in the recorded "history" might

Diagnostic statements.[29] Professional standards for hospital records contemplate that entries shall be made of diagnostic findings by attending physicians at various stages,[30] and such entries are clearly in the regular course of the operations of the hospital and of the duties of the doctors and recorders. As in the case of expert opinions given on the witness-stand, the qualifications of the declarant should appear,[31] but it would seem that if it is proven or judicially noticed that the hospital from which the records come is a reputable institution of high standards this would justify the inference that what purport to be diagnoses made by physicians are made by doctors duly qualified to give such opinions.[32] The admissibility of ordinary diagnostic findings customarily based on objective data and not usually presenting more than average difficulty of interpretation, is generally conceded.[33] Even when the diagnosis embodies a conclusion which must be based upon data unusually difficult of interpretation, or upon "subjective" symptoms, as in the case of some psychiatric diagnoses, most courts will still receive the findings in evidence.[34] However, in one noteworthy federal opinion the court considered that such a "conjectural" conclusion is likely to be overvalued by a jury where the declarant is not presented for cross-examination, and that the recorded opinion should be rejected.[35] Against this view the provision in the Federal Act, under which the case was decided, may be urged, to the effect that "all other circumstances of the making of such writing or record . . . may be shown to affect its weight, but they shall not affect its admissibility."[36] Perhaps a discretion to admit or exclude such an opinion might be spelled out of the condition on admissibility in the Uniform Act, "if in the opinion of the court the sources of information were such as to justify its admission."[37]

come in, having been proven by the record, for any relevant non-hearsay purpose, for example as an inconsistent statement offered to impeach. Maguire, Evidence: Common Sense and Common Law, 158 (1947).

29. Hale, Hospital Records, 14 So. Cal.L.Rev. 99, 107 (1941); Notes, 48 Col.L.Rev. 920, 929, 930 (1948), 54 Yale L.J. 868 (1945), 8 Intramural L.Rev. (N.Y.U.), 259 (1953).

30. See regulations referred to in note 8, supra.

31. See, e. g., Paxos v. Jarka Corp. 314 Pa. 148, 171 A. 468, syl. 7, 8 (1934) (reports of internes or students as to fractured vertebra rejected because of want of showing of qualification).

32. See Hale, op. cit., 14 So.Cal.L.Rev. at 108.

33. Findings admitted: Reed v. Order of United Commercial Travelers, 123 F.2d 252, syl. 1, 2 (C.C.A. 2d 1941) ("well under the influence of alcohol"); Ulm v. Moore-McCormack Lines, 117 F.2d 222, syl. 1, 2 (C.C.A.2d 1941) ("he does not appear acutely ill"); D'Amato v. Johnston, 140 Conn. 54, 97 A.2d 893, syl. 1–8 (1953) (entries by interne and roentgenologist that accident-patient was intoxicated: whether relevant to diagnosis and treatment was for trial judge preliminarily: able opinion by Inglis, J.); Wickman v. Bohle, 173 Md. 694, 196 Atl. 326, syl. 6 (1938) ("a fractured right clavicle two weeks prior to his admission"); Cowan v. McDon-

nel, 330 Mass. 148, 111 N.E.2d 759 (1953) ("impression, odor of alcohol"); and cases cited in Notes, 38 Mich.L.Rev. 219, 226, 227 (1939), 54 Yale L.J. 868, 874 (1945), 27 Temp.L.Q. 223 (1953).

34. Buckminster's Estate v. Commissioner of Int. Rev., 147 F.2d 331, syl. 2 (C.C.A.2d 1944) (hospital record made at the time when taxpayer's decedent was stricken with a cerebral hemorrhage, admitted, seemingly for diagnostic findings); People v. Kohlmeyer, 284 N.Y. 366, 31 N.E.2d 490, syl. 1, 4, 7 (1940) (records of daily observation of patient's mental and physical condition including physician's diagnoses of "manic depressive insanity," admissible).

35. New York Life Ins. Co. v. Taylor, 79 App.D.C. 66, 147 F.2d 297, syl. 8, 9, 12–18 (1945) (claim on life policy for double indemnity for accidental death: defense, suicide, held in powerful majority opinions by Arnold, J., that trial judge properly excluded, under Federal Business Records Act, hospital records showing diagnostic report by psychiatrist, "phychoneurosis, hysteria, conversion type"; persuasive dissenting opinion by Edgerton, J.). The case is commented on in 33 Geo.L.J. 349, 18 So.Calif.L. Rev. 60, 19 id. 67, 23 Tex.L.Rev. 178, 9 Detroit L.J. 32, 94 U.Pa.L.Rev. 112, 31 Va.L.Rev. 702, 54 Yale L.J. 868.

36. See § 289, supra.

37. See § 289, supra.

A court might reasonably conclude in such case that if the declarant-physician were unavailable the record should be admitted, but that if he were available the proponent should be required to call him to authenticate the record, and thus afford the adversary the safeguard of cross-examination. On the whole, however, it is believed that, even as to these controversial diagnoses, the majority view favoring admission is the more expedient one. It works for simplicity by making it unnecessary to draw a difficult line, itself provocative of doubt and dispute; it serves the modern policy of the free use of organizational records; and is not too burdensome on the adversary who may himself call the declarant and thus bring out, if he can, any weaknesses of the diagnosis.

Privilege.[38] As we have seen, about two-thirds of the states, by statutes of widely varying phraseology have given to patients a privilege against the disclosure by physicians of information acquired in attending the patient and necessary for diagnosis and treatment.[39] The policy motivating such statutes is probably unsound and a literal

reading of them might not give a privilege against the use in evidence of hospital records embodying information so secured. The legislative purpose, however, would so manifestly be frustrated by such a result, that the courts have generally held that hospital records are within the privilege to the extent that they incorporate the statements made by the patient to the doctor and the physician's diagnostic findings.[40] As to whether other information recorded by nurses or attendants, such as the history given to an attendant and the nurses' charts and progress notes showing diet, treatment, temperatures and condition of the patient, the cases are divided. For denial of the privilege as to this kind of data is the argument that privilege-statutes are strictly construed, and that most privilege-statutes do not mention nurses or attendants.[41] For granting, the theory is available that the information is gathered and recorded by the nurse as an agent for the physician to aid him in treatment.[42] Solving any specific problem of the application of this privilege requires consideration of the wording and history of the particular governing statute.

---

38. Hale, Hospital Records, 14 So.Cal.L.Rev. 99, 108 (1941); 8 Wigmore, Evidence, § 2382, no. 10; Notes, 48 Col.L.Rev. 920, 930 (1948); 75 A.L.R. 393, 120 A.L.R. 1140, 169 A.L.R. 678.

39. See ch. 11, herein.

40. Weis v. Weis, 147 Oh.St. 416, 72 N.E.2d 245, 252, syl. 14, 169 A.L.R. 668 (1947) (able opinion by Hart, J.). See also Kaplan v. Manhattan Life Ins. Co., 71 App.D.C. 250, 109 F.2d 463, 465 (1939) (hospital records of "diagnosis and treatment" privileged, but not other records).

41. Weis v. Weis, 147 Oh.St. 416, 72 N.E.2d 245, syl. 11–13, 169 A.L.R. 668 (1947) (privilege strictly construed and does not extend to records of entrance, physician's directions, analyses of blood and urine, and day to day charts); Leusink v. O'Donnell, 255 Wis. 627, 39 N.W.2d 675, syl. 2, 3 (1949) (to be strictly construed, does not cover nurses' and technicians' notes and records, but if it applied at all would be "to the medical reports of the attending physician"). A few statutes do specifically include nurses, e. g., in Arkansas and New York, see 8 Wigmore, Evidence, § 2380, note 5.

42. See cases excluding the testimony (not records) of hospital nurses on this theory, e. g., Culver v. Union Pacific R. R., 112 Neb. 441, 450, 199 N.W. 794, 797 (1924); Meyer v. Russell, 55 N.D. 546, 214 N.W. 857, syl. 6 (1926).

CHAPTER 33

OFFICIAL WRITTEN STATEMENTS

291. The General Rule.[1]

The admission of Official Written Statements, sometimes referred to as Public Records and Documents, under an exception to the hearsay rule is a subject of major importance. It is so largely governed by statutes, which in each state minutely and variously regulate the admissibility of particular kinds of records and documents that a comprehensive treatment in a brief text would be impractical. Accordingly only a summarized and selective discussion will be attempted.

Where the statute is silent about admissibility, the decisions seem to announce as a common law doctrine [2] that a written statement of a public official which he had a duty [3] to make, and which he has made upon first-hand knowledge,[4] is receivable as evidence of the facts recited.[5] The official duty and the habit of honesty and accuracy in the performance of such duties supply the element

[1] 5 Wigmore, Evidence, §§ 1630–1684; Model Code of Evidence, Rules 515–522; Uniform Rules of Evidence, Rules 63 (15–22), 64; 32 C.J.S., Evidence, §§ 626–675; 20 Am.Jur., Evidence, §§ 984–1042; Dec.Dig., Evidence, ⊂⊃333–349, 383(3, 4), Crim.Law, ⊂⊃429, 430.

[2] "But as Wigmore points out, the 'official statements' exception to the rule excluding hearsay is 'good common law,' though, as he adds, 'the numerous petty statutory rules have made the Bar suppose that they must always find a statute.' 5 Wigmore on Evidence, 3d Ed. 1940, § 1638a. Actually this exception is recognized because of necessity or the inconvenience which would result from always requiring the testimony of the official in person to the facts he has recorded; and his official duty supports the requirement that there be found some circumstantial probability of trustworthiness. Id. §§ 1630–1633". Clark, Circ. J., in Vanadium Corp. v. Fidelity & Deposit Co., 159 F.2d 105, 109 (C.C.A.N.Y.1947).

[3] 5 Wigmore, Evidence, §§ 1632, 1633.

[4] The official duty usually extends only to the recording of facts within his personal observation, and as a general rule only records so founded are admissible. But there are exceptions. A principal officer, such as a court clerk, may certify facts reported by his deputies. And in some instances, an officer is required by law to ascertain and report facts from an investigation which may include the sifting of information received from others (see § 294, herein). 5 Wigmore, Evidence, § 1635.

[5] The general rule is codified in Uniform Rules of Evidence. One of the exceptions to the rule excluding hearsay is the following: Rule 63(15): "Subject to Rule 64 written reports or findings of fact made by a public official of the United States or of a state or territory of the United States, if the judge finds that the making thereof was within the scope of the duty of such official and that it was his duty (a) to perform the act reported, or (b) to observe the act, condition or event reported, or (c) to investigate the facts concerning the act, condition or event and to make findings or draw conclusions based on such investigation".
This is subject to the important qualification in Rule 64, as follows: "Any writing admissible under exceptions (15), (16), (17), (18), and (19) of the Rule 63 shall be received only if the party offering such writing has delivered a copy of it or so much thereof as may relate to the controversy, to each adverse party a reasonable time before trial unless the judge finds that such adverse party has not been unfairly surprised by the failure to deliver such copy."
For examples of comprehensive codifications of the principle see Vernon's Tex.Civ.St. art. 3731a; Wis.St.1951, § 327.18.

of special trustworthiness. The need for the use of the record instead of summoning the recorder in person rests on the fact that to require such officials to attend as witnesses for this purpose would unduly interrupt public business, and upon the fact that the official written statement, made contemporaneously, will usually be more reliable than present recollection. Consequently, there is no requirement here that the person who made the record be shown to be unavailable as a witness.

292. No General Common Law Authority to Give Certificates: Certified Copies.

The common-law practice admitted without difficulty any regular and continuous record of official acts, such as the records of the acts of a legislature or of the judgments of a court or the record of receipt and discharge of prisoners in a jail, and admitted also certain kinds of special and occasional reports, such as a sheriff's return upon a writ, or a surveyor's report. But no general authority was recognized at common law for officers to give to private persons on demand a certificate as to past official happenings.[1]

Nevertheless, one kind of such special certificate has come into general use, and in this country may be said to have common-law sanction, even apart from innumerable particular enabling statutes, that is, the certificate of the official custodian of a public record or document, to the correctness of a copy.[2] The usual requirement for the production of the original document is not applied to official records.[3] Such certified copies have accordingly become the most usual and convenient means of proving the purport of records of official acts, and the contents likewise of those private documents, such as deeds and chattel mortgages, which under our registration systems have been recorded or deposited in a public office.[4] But a mere paraphrase of the records by the custodian or a statement interpreting their effect, e. g., a recital that "our records show

thus-and-so," will not be admitted under this principle, nor without specific statutory authority.[5]

293. Relaxations of Requirement of Official Duty: Marriage and Death Certificates.

The courts have been willing to interpret liberally the requirement that the record must have been made under the countenance of "official" duty. The clergyman's return upon a marriage license, certifying his performance of the ceremony, is usually admitted, and so likewise the report of an attending physician as to the fact and date of birth or death.[1] Such duties, though special and occasional, being limited to members of a profession recognized by law are easy to look upon as "official" and are guaranteed by a similar warrant of accuracy and responsibility. Where the law places upon the parent the duty to report the birth or death of a child, the duty is statutory but hardly "official" and the courts are divided upon whether the record founded on such report may come in to evidence the fact reported,[2] but the first-hand knowledge and the disinterestedness of the reporter, and the need for this source of proof, furnish impelling common-sense grounds for the use of such records by the courts. On the other hand, the reports required by statute from manufacturers, or motorists, in respect to accidents, manifestly lack the voucher of disinterestedness, and the requirement of the "official"

1.   5 Wigmore, Evidence, § 1674.

2.   5 Wigmore, Evidence, § 1677.

3.   See § 204, herein.

4.   5 Wigmore, Evidence, §§ 1677–1684.

5.   In re Kostohris' Estate, 96 Mont. 226, 29 P.2d 829, syl. 17, 20, 21 (1934) (custodian's certificate that records show certain listed payments to veteran, excluded). Wigmore, Evidence, § 1678, where the requirement is criticized as "too strict for practical convenience."

1.   Wigmore, Evidence, §§ 1642–1646.

2.   Wigmore, Evidence, § 1646.

character of the report may here be sensibly insisted on.[3]

More difficulty is encountered, and a stricter insistence upon traditional standards is manifest, in applying the requirement of first-hand knowledge. Thus, the statutes usually require the attending physician to certify facts relating to the circumstances and the cause of death. It has been held that his statement as to the time of origin of the fatal disease, where the sickness began before he was called in, is inadmissible on this ground.[4] Moreover, this strictness has been carried even further. A medical officer examined the body of a deceased person, and stated in his certificate as the cause of death, "suicide by firearm." In a suit upon an insurance policy the defendant offered the certificate to show suicide, and relied upon the statute which made it prima facie evidence of the "facts" therein stated. The court held, however, that the particular statement was not one of "fact," but was a mere inference from observed facts or from hearsay report.[5] Thus the rigors of the hearsay and opinion rules are added to the requirement of first-hand knowledge, and all are read into the statute as conditions upon admissibility.

294. Reports of Official Investigations.[1]

There are doubtless instances where the statutes provide for the gathering of data by officials by inquiry from other persons, where the results are valuable for statistical purposes, but where no high degree of accuracy of information may be expected. Such are the data gathered by the census-takers by questioning the heads of families. The specific answers recorded in such inquiries may be thought too unreliable for use in litigation.[2] But from early times, certain officials have been vested with the duty to make thorough-going inquests or investigations, by formal or informal examination of witnesses acquainted with the facts, and to report their conclusions as the basis for official action. If these same facts later become material in private litigation, should not such official reports, though founded upon inquiry and not upon first-hand official knowledge, be received not as conclusive, but as matter for consideration? Wigmore argues convincingly that they should,[3] and shows that as to some such reports of inquiry, notably the inquisition of escheat, and the inquisition of lunacy, the common law admitted the reports upon this basis.[4]

3. Wigmore, Evidence, § 1633a, and see, e. g., Ezzo v. Geremiah, 107 Comm. 670, 142 Atl. 461 (1928) (automobile driver's report of accident).

4. Williams v. Metropolitan Life Ins. Co., 116 S.C. 277, 108 S.E. 110 (1921). Contra: Meth v. United Benefit Life Ins. Co., 198 F.2d 446, syl. 4–6 (C.A. Pa.1952) (attending physician's statement admissible not only as to time and cause of death but as to time of onset of illness, though this occurred before the physician attended him: lucid opinion by McLaughlin, Circ. J.).

5. Backstrom v. New York Life Ins. Co., 183 Minn. 384, 236 N.W. 708 (1931), comment, 16 Minn.L.Rev. 209. To like effect is Carson v. Metropolitan Life Ins. Co., 156 Oh.St. 104, 100 N.E.2d 197, syl. 8 (1951). Compare, however, Branford Trust Co. v. Prudential Ins. Co., 102 Conn. 481, 129 Atl. 379, 1929, 42 A.L.R. 1450, a liberal decision admitting the medical examiner's conclusion that death was "suicidal." The conflict has continued in later cases, which are interestingly discussed in Morgan, Evidence, 1941–1945, 59 Harv.L.Rev. 481, 560 (1946).

See also Note, Report of public officer on cause of injury to person or property, 153 A.L.R. 163.

1. 5 Wigmore, Evidence, §§ 1670–1672; Yates, Evaluative Reports by Public Officials, 30 Tex.L.Rev. 112 (1951). The last writer discusses police reports, fire reports, and reports by special investigative boards, chemists, and government physicians, and autopsy reports, coroners' reports and death certificates. Cases are collected in Dec.Dig., Evidence, ⬤⟼333(1); Note, Admissibility of Report of Public Officer on Cause of Injury to Person or Property, 153 A.L.R. 163.

2. Campbell v. Everhart, 139 N.C. 503, 52 S.E. 201, syl. 13 (1905); 5 Wigmore, Evidence, § 1671(7), note 12. But the last reference cites a greater number of decisions to the contrary, e. g., Priddy v. Boice, 201 Mo. 309, 99 S.W. 1055, 1059, syl. 4 (1906) (extensive discussion).

3. 5 Wigmore, Evidence, §§ 1671, 1672.

4. 5 Wigmore, Evidence, §§ 1670, 1671. But in a more familiar instance, the coroner's inquest, the

The principle is accepted in the Uniform Rules which would admit the report when it was the duty of the reporting official "to investigate the facts . . . and to make findings or draw conclusions based on such investigation." [5] Most courts have been reluctant to go so far. Reports on narrow states of fact, founded on first-hand knowledge, such as those of an official chemist [6] or seed analyst,[7] are readily admitted. But when the report, such as a police report upon an accident or a fire-marshal's report on a fire, is based partly on observation, and partly on statements of others, and draws conclusions as to cause or fault, the majority of courts seem currently to exclude the conclusions, as "hearsay," or "opinion on the issue" or on grounds of want of first-hand knowledge or of expert qualifications.[8] Others have said—and this seems a reasonable

courts have usually refused to receive the jury's report as evidence of the cause of death. Wigmore, Evidence, § 1671(6). Doubtless this may be attributed to a distrust of the reliability of the findings of such juries, acting without the supervision of a professional judge. See Aetna Life Ins. Co. v. Milward, 118 Ky. 716, 82 S.W. 364, 368, 68 L.R.A. 285, 4 Ann.Cas. 1092 (1904). But the result has impeded the acceptance generally of the suggested principle.

5. Uniform Rules of Evidence, R. 63(15), quoted in full in § 291, note 5, above. An interesting case applying this principle to the reports of Congressional committees of investigations into subversive activities is Stasiukevich v. Nicolls, 168 F.2d 474, syl. 7–10 (C.C.A.1, 1948).

6. Comm. v. Slavski, 243 Mass. 605, 140 N.E. 465, 467–9, syl. 4, 5 (1923) (statute making report of analysis admissible in liquor prosecution, constitutional; Rugg, C. J.: "The principle . . . is that a record of a primary fact made by a public officer in the performance of official duty is or may be made by legislation competent prima facie evidence as to the existence of that fact, but that records of investigations and inquiries conducted, either voluntarily or pursuant to requirement of law, by public officers concerning causes and effects and involving the exercise of judgment and discretion, expressions of opinion, and making conclusions are not admissible as evidence as public records.")

7. E. K. Hardison Seed Co. v. Jones, 149 F.2d 252, syl. 7–9 (C.C.A.6, 1945).

8. Police reports. Davis' Adm'x v. Gordon, 309 Ky. 121, 216 S.W.2d 409, syl. 4 (1949) (error to admit, where contained diagram based partly on personal knowledge of officer and partly on hearsay); Hadley v. Ross, 195 Okl. 89, 154 P.2d 939, syl. 4 (1939) (report based on information given the officers by undisclosed persons, inadmissible); Jacobson v. Bryan, 244 Wis. 359, 12 N.W.2d 789, syl. 2, 6, 7 (1944) (report containing statements made from officer's observation of scene, and also conclusion that collision due to "sideswipe," admissible as to former, not as to latter; but admission here not prejudicial and objector disabled to complain because he did not specify objectionable part). Similarly, the official report of an army investigating board on an airplane crash was held inadmissible as "containing expressions of opinion or the exercise of judgment and discretion." Barnes v. Northwest Airlines, 233 Minn. 410, 47 N.W.2d 181, 193, syl. 21 (1951).

Fire marshal's reports. Gilbert v. Gulf Oil Co., 175 F.2d 705, syl. 9–11 (C.C.A.Va.1949) (letters from chief of fire department and inspector to defendant giving their opinions as to cause of fire, inadmissible). See Kansas City Stock Yards Co. v. A. Reich & Sons, 250 S.W.2d 692, 790, syl. 18, 19 (Mo.1952) (report of fire prevention chief, required by ordinance, "Cause of fire, careless use of welding torch," where officers had no personal knowledge, and based report presumably on statements of others, properly excluded as hearsay and opinion on the very issue); Cawley v. Northern Waste Co., 239 Mass. 540, 132 N.E. 365, syl. 6 (1921) (entry by fire department chief as to cause, properly excluded). See also the decisions cited in note 9, below.

The statutes authorizing reports frequently provide that they shall be admissible. See, e. g., Comm. v. Slavski, note 6, above, and In re Mundy, 97 N.H. 239, 85 A.2d 371 (1952) (petition by state for committal of respondents as "sexual psychopaths"; statute authorizing court in such proceeding to admit report of examining board that respondents were sexual psychopaths held constitutional). Occasionally such statutes provide that the reports shall be inadmissible. See, e. g., 49 U.S.C., § 581 providing "that no part of any report . . . of . . . the Civil Aeronautics Board relating to any accident, or the investigation thereof, shall be admitted as evidence or used in any suit or action for damages growing out of any matter mentioned in such report or reports." This provision was held inapplicable to a report which consisted wholly of statements of personal observation, not based on hearsay or containing conclusions, in Lobel v. American Airlines, 192 F.2d 217, syl. 5–7 (C.C.A.2, 1951). See also as to statutory privileges for such reports made by private individuals, § 149, herein.

middle ground—that such evaluative official reports, based on the duty to draw conclusions, are admissible in the judge's discretion.[9] This view will permit the judge to weigh such factors as the personal knowledge and expertness of the reporter, or the want of them, the concrete or inferential character of the findings, and the availability or not of the reporter or of other persons who could testify to the facts. Thus he would base his ruling upon an appraisal of the relative needs for and dangers of admitting the evidence.

295. Judgments in Previous Cases: Evidence in Civil Cases of Judgments of Conviction.[1]

The judgments of the courts determining issues of fact, though they are in some sense the reports of the findings of official investigations, have not been received as a general practice as evidence in other suits of the facts so found.[2] Their use in court has been guided by a different principle, that of *res judicata,* and in consequence the findings are received only where the parties to the earlier suit are the same as in the present, or where the present parties are claiming under them, and the earlier findings then come in, not as evidence merely but as conclusive determinations of the issues. But the rule was that if the judgment could not come in as a conclusive adjudication, because the parties on both sides were not the same or claiming in the same interest, the previous finding upon the same issue would not even be received as evidence of the fact found. The question most often arises in respect to judgments of conviction of crime offered against a party in a civil action.[3] Upon the subordinate issue of a witness' character, a judgment of conviction has always been received to show the criminal act.[4] When, however, in a suit on a fire policy the defendant offers the plaintiff's conviction upon a prosecution for arson for setting fire to the house, or in a suit for personal injuries the plaintiff offers the defendant's conviction for reckless driving on the same occasion, the majority of courts have excluded the evidence.[5] They have banned such evidence as mere opinion and have invoked the argument of reciprocity, namely, that the person prosecuted could not if he had been acquitted, have used the judgment of acquittal in the civil case, and a distinguished commentator has suggested that the jury in the civil case cannot measure the value of the finding "but must either blindly accept the conclusion of the first jury or ignore it because there is no rational alterna-

---

9.   Franklin v. Skelly Oil Co., 141 F.2d 156, 153 A.L.R. 156, 162 (C.C.A.Okl.1944) (letter from Inspector to State Fire Marshal, giving writer's opinion that cause of fire in residence was installation of improper piping for butane gas; held, with careful discussion by Murrah, Circ. J., that trial judge, in view of the opinion-character of the report, had a discretion which he properly exercised by excluding it).

1.   4 Wigmore, Evidence, § 1346a, 5 id. § 1671a; Dec. Dig., Judgment, ☞648.

2.   5 Wigmore, Evidence, § 1671a.

3.   An able article reviews briefly the state of the American law, and discusses critically the English and Commonwealth decisions. Cowen, The Admissibility of Criminal Convictions in Subsequent Civil Proceedings, 40 Calif.L.Rev. 225 (1952). A Note, 39 Va.L.Rev. 995 (1953) ably reviews the literature and the decisions. For collections of cases see Notes, 31 A.L.R. 261, 18 A.L.R.2d 1287; Dec.Dig., Judgment, ☞648.

4.   See § 43, herein.

5.   Hollington v. F. Hewthorn & Co. [1943] K.B. 587 (Ct.App.) (plaintiff offered in death action defendant's conviction for careless driving: held, inadmissible); General Exchange Ins. Co. v. Sherry, 165 Md. 1, 165 Atl. 809 (1933) (reckless driving); Girard v. Vermont Mutual Fire Ins. Co., 103 Vt. 330, 154 Atl. 666 (1931) (arson). A recent writer criticises the conservatism of the English and Canadian decisions. Note, 21 Can.Bar Rev. 653 (1943).

But a plea of guilty to a criminal charge of conduct material in the present case comes in against the party as an admission. Weiss v. Wasserman, 91 N.H. 164, 15 A.2d 861, syl. 7 (1940) (speeding); Note, 18 A.L.R.2d 1307. And a conviction admitted to impeach the party as a witness may have a strong substantive side-effect.

tive." [6] Nevertheless, a growing minority of courts has become discontented with this reasoning and has insisted that common sense and consistency of adjudication require that a judgment of conviction, offered against the person convicted in a later civil case involving some of the same issues, be admitted as evidence of the facts on which the judgment was based.[7] This view was embodied in the Model Code,[8] and has been sanctioned by the Uniform Rules with the important limitation to convictions for felony.[9]

Probably the trend of evolution will be toward the admission generally against a present party of any judgment or finding in a former civil or criminal case if the party had an opportunity to defend. The principles on which is founded the hearsay exception for official written statements would justify this extension.

6. E. W. Hinton, Judgment of Conviction: Effect on a Civil Case, 27 Ill.L.Rev. 195, quoted Wigmore, Evidence, § 1671a.

7. Fidelity Phenix Fire Ins. Co. v. Murphy, 226 Ala. 226, 146 So. 387, syl. 18 (1933) (suit on insurance policy for indemnity against liability due to loss of ship: conviction for conspiracy to defraud by destroying ship, admissible, distinguishing judgment of acquittal); North River Ins. Co. v. Militello, 100 Colo. 343, 67 P.2d 625, syl. 3 (1937) (arson). See Schindler v. Royal Insurance Co., 258 N. Y. 310, 179 N.E. 711, 80 A.L.R. 1142 (1932) (arson), a leading liberal decision. See also Notes, 41 Harv.L.Rev. 241 (1927), 6 N.C.L.Rev. 333 (1928); 41 W.Va.L.Q. 396 (1935); 10 Rocky Mt.L.Rev. 282 (1938); 18 A.L.R.2d 1299. But even these courts have not sanctioned the admission for the civil defendant of a prior acquittal, viewing it as a mere holding that guilt was not proved beyond a reasonable doubt. See the dicta in the Alabama and New York cases, supra.

One court has gone even further and allowed the arson conviction as conclusively establishing the defence in the action on the fire policy. Eagle, Star, and British Dominions Ins. Co. v. Heller, 149 Va. 82, 140 S.E. 314, 323, syl. 7 (1927), noted 12 Minn. L.Rev. 546, 12 Va.L.Rev. 546.

8. Model Code of Evidence, Rule 521.

9. Uniform Rules of Evidence, Rule 63(20) makes admissible "evidence of a final judgment adjudging a person guilty of a felony, to prove any fact essential to sustain the judgment." The reason for the limitation is disclosed by the following excerpt from the commentary, ". . . there is widespread opposition to opening the door to let in evidence of convictions particularly of traffic violations in actions which later develop over responsibility for damages. In other words, trials and convictions in traffic courts and possibly in misdemeanor cases generally, often do not have about them the tags of trustworthiness as they often are the result of expediency or compromise. To let in evidence of conviction of a traffic violation to prove negligence and responsibility in a civil case would seem to be going too far. . . ." A like view is taken in Note, Admissibility of Traffic Convictions, 50 Col.L.Rev. 529 (1950).

CHAPTER 34

VARIOUS OTHER EXCEPTIONS TO THE HEARSAY RULE

296. Treatises.[1]

An expert witness may give his opinion, though it is founded not upon personal observation but upon knowledge gained from books and treatises in his field.[2] Moreover, on cross-examination of an expert who states that his opinion given on direct was wholly or partly based upon such authority, the cross-examiner may read from standard treatises, and examine him upon them, in order to test the soundness of his statements.[3] Again, a judge may freely consult any reference works, books or journals that he chooses, in informing himself as to facts that are in the realm of judicial notice.[4] But these practices fall short of a hearsay use of the treatises. In a few instances, certain books and reports of narrow scope do seem to be received as evidence of the truth of the matters recited. Among these are market reports of current prices in journals used by the trade,[5] recognized business registers

---

[1] 6 Wigmore, Evidence, §§ 1690–1708; Decennial Digests, Evidence, ☞318(6), 360–365, 381.

[2] Boswell v. State, 114 Ga. 40, 39 S.E. 897, syl. 3 (1901) (doctors testified from book-knowledge that bluestone is poison, though they had no personal observation of its effect); 2 Wigmore, Evidence, § 665b, 3 id. § 687.

[3] Reilly v. Pinkus, 338 U.S. 269, 70 Sup.Ct. 110, syl. 3, 4, 94 L.Ed. 63 (1949) (administrative order reversed because examiner refused to allow such cross-examination); People v. Feldman, 299 N.Y. 153, 167, 85 N.E.2d 913, syl. 3, 4 (1949); Bowles v. Bourdon, 148 Tex. 1, 219 S.W.2d 779, 783, syl. 5 (1949) (passages may be read by cross-examiner not as evidence of their truth but solely to discredit witness); Notes, 41 J.Crim.L. 192 (1950); 34 Va. L.Rev. 718 (1948); 82 A.L.R. 440. But a substantial minority of the courts (including those of Illinois, Iowa, Massachusetts, Michigan and North Carolina) seem to forbid cross-examination upon the statements in scientific treatises except when the witness specifically purports, in his direct examination, to rely upon such authority. See Note, 82 A.L.R. 440, 448; Decennial Digests, Evidence, ☞558(11). This seems to give an undue advantage to the ignorant and unscrupulous expert over the honest and well trained one.

As to the technique of examination and cross-examination of medical witnesses, see Goldstein and Shabat, Medical Trial Technique, Ch. I, 1942.

[4] See Ransom, Judge's Right of Private Examination, 36 Mich.L.Rev. 610 (1938), and see generally Ch. 37, herein.

[5] Virginia v. West Virginia, 238 U.S. 202, 212, 35 Sup.Ct. 795, 800, 59 L.Ed. 1272 (1914) (Hughes, J.: "It is unquestioned that, in proving the fact of market value, accredited price-current lists and market reports, including those published in trade journals or newspapers which are accepted as trustworthy, are admissible in evidence." [citing many cases]); 6 Wigmore, Evidence, § 1704. The Uniform Rules of Evidence, Rule 63(30) (following Model Code R. 528) admits: "Evidence of statements of matters of interest to persons engaged in an occupation contained in a list, register, periodical, or other published compilation to prove the truth of any relevant matter so stated if the judge finds that the compilation is published for use by persons engaged in that occupation and is generally used and relied upon by them".

The admissibility of polls or surveys of public opinion may, in some circumstances, be argued for on the analogy of this exception for trade reports. Many aspects of this topic are ably dealt with in Sorenson and Sorenson, The Admissibility and Use of Opinion Research Evidence, 28 N.Y.U.L.Rev. 1213 1953), and in Notes, Public Opinion Surveys as Evidence, 66 Harv.L.Rev. 498 (1953), Admissibility of Public Opinion Polls, 37 Minn.L.Rev. 385 (1953).

and city directories,[6] and mortality and annuity tables used by life insurance companies.[7] The disinterestedness and reliability of standard scientific treatises or authoritative works in any field of scholarship would seem equally to warrant their use before a jury as evidence of the truth of their statements.[8] One court has accepted this view,[9] and statutes in a few states authorize the use of treatises to evidence "facts of general notoriety and interest." [10] Rule 63(31) of the Uniform Rules adopts the principle.[11] The courts generally, however, have declined to sanction a broad exception to the hearsay rule for standard treatises as such.[12]

297. Statements and Reputation as to Pedigree and Family History.[1]

One of the oldest hearsay exceptions admits, subject to certain conditions, statements about matters of family history, such as the date and place of birth and death of members of the family and facts about marriage, descent, and relationship. Not only are individual statements of members of the family received,[2] but evidence of the tradi-

---

6. Williams v. Campbell Soup Co., 80 F.Supp. 865, syl. 6 (W.D.Mo.1948) (city directory), comprehensively noted, Raulston, 2 Baylor L.Rev. 104; Louisville & N. R. Co. v. Kice, 109 Ky. 786, 60 S.W. 705, syl. 3 (1901) (American stud books to show pedigree of horse); State v. McInerny, 163 Wyo. 280, 182 P. 2d 28, syl. 4 (1947) (telephone and city directories to show whether signers of petition were residents of city); 6 Wigmore, Evidence, § 1706.

7. Avance v. Thompson, 387 Ill. 77, 55 N.E.2d 57, syl. 6, 7 (1944) (personal injury: admissible where injury permanent but jury must be instructed as to their use); Mitchell v. Arrowhead Freight Lines, 117 Utah 224, 214 P.2d 620, syl. 8–10 (1950) (combined mortality and annuity table); 6 Wigmore, § 1698; Dec.Dig., Evidence, ⊜364.

8. See the convincing arguments in 6 Wigmore, Evidence, §§ 1690–1692, and in a Note, 19 St. Louis L.Rev. 353 (1934).

9. City of Dothan v. Hardy, 237 Ala. 603, 188 So. 264, syl. 3 (1939).

10. See statutes compiled in 6 Wigmore, Evidence, § 1693. But the limitation prevents the use of medical and scientific treatises. See Gallagher v. Market Street R. Co., 67 Cal. 13, 6 Pac. 869, 51 Am.Rep. 680, note, (1885); Note, 65 A.L.R. 1111.

11. *"Learned Treatises.* A published treatise, periodical or pamphlet on a subject of history, science or art to prove the truth of a matter stated therein if the judge takes judicial notice, or a witness expert in the subject testifies, that the treatise, periodical or pamphlet is a reliable authority in the subject." The Uniform Rules of Evidence, Rule 63(31), adapted from the Model Code of Evidence, Rule 529.

12. See, e. g., Mississippi Power & Light Co. v. Whitescarver, 68 F.2d 928, syl. 8, (C.C.A.Miss.1934), and cases cited in 6 Wigmore, Evidence, § 1696, and in Notes, Medical Books as Evidence, 65 A.L.R. 1102, Medical treatises, 12 So.Calif.L.Rev. 424 (1939); Scientific books, 26 Marq.L.Rev. 43 (1941); 1945 Wis.L.Rev. 455.

1. See Wigmore, Evidence, §§ 1480–1503, 1602–1606; Hale, Proof of Facts of Family History, 2 Hastings L.J. 1 (1950); Note, 5 Ark.L.Rev. 58 (1951); Dec. Dig., Evidence, ⊜285–297. These matters are elaborately regulated in Model Code, Rules 524 and 525, and in Uniform Rules, R 63 (23–27), see later footnotes in this section.

2. See, e. g., Pollock v. Metropolitan Life Ins. Co., 138 F.2d 123, syl. 4 (C.C.A.N.J.1943) (declaration of deceased as to his own age and birth, admitted: lucid discussion by Goodrich, Circ.J.); Ellis v. Dixon, 294 Ky. 609, 172 S.W.2d 461, syl. 1, 2 (1943) (stating rule); and see Note, Admissibility of parent's hearsay declarations on paternity, 32 Iowa L. Rev. 779 (1947). Uniform Rules, R. 63 (23–25) admit:

"(23) A statement of a matter concerning a declarant's own birth, marriage, divorce, legitimacy, relationship by blood or marriage, race-ancestry or other similar fact of his family history, even though the declarant had no means of acquiring personal knowledge of the matter declared, if the judge finds that the declarant is unavailable;

"(24) A statement concerning the birth, marriage, divorce, death, legitimacy, race-ancestry, relationship by blood or marriage or other similar fact of the family history of a person other than the declarant if the judge (a) finds that the declarant was related to the other by blood or marriage or finds that he was otherwise so intimately associated with the other's family as to be likely to have accurate information concerning the matter declared, and made the statement as upon information received from the other or from a person related by blood or marriage to the other, or as upon repute in the other's family, and (b) finds that the declarant is unavailable as a witness;

"(25) A statement of a declarant that a statement admissible under exceptions (23) or (24) of this rule was made by another declarant, offered as tending to prove the truth of the matter declared by both declarants, if the judge finds that both declarants are unavailable as witnesses".

tional reputation in the family [3] and even, according to one view, the reputation in the community as to the fact,[4] will come in. Likewise, the contemporary records of family history, such as the entries in the family Bible, or the entry on a tombstone, though authorship is not further identifiable, are admitted.[5] As to individual statements the conditions designed to guarantee special reliability are that the declarant must be shown to have been a member of the family of the person or persons whose pedigree or

history is being investigated,[6] or (under a more liberal view) intimately associated with the family,[7] and it must further be proved that the declaration was made before the origin of the present controversy [8] and without an apparent motive to deceive.[9] It need not be shown that the declarant had first-hand knowledge of the facts of birth, death, kinship or the like. It suffices that by living with the family as a member he had the means of knowing the family tradition.[10] The declarant, however, must be proven to be

---

3. Kelly's Heirs v. McGuire, 15 Ark. 555, 604 (1855) ("general repute in the family"); Geisler v. Geisler, 160 Minn. 463, 200 N.W. 742, syl. 2 (1924); Duncan v. Adams, 210 S.W.2d 180, syl. 13, 14 (Tex.Civ.App. 1948) (when proved by member of family); Dec. Dig., Evidence, ☞288. Uniform Rule 63(26) admits: "Evidence of reputation among members of a family, if the reputation concerns the birth, marriage, divorce, death, legitimacy, race-ancestry or other fact of the family history of a member of the family by blood or marriage".

4. As to one fact, the fact that persons living together were married, community reputation is universally admitted. Wigmore, Evidence, § 1602. As to other matters of family-history, some decisions, especially the earlier ones, received it. Ringhouse v. Keever, 49 Ill. 470, 471 (1869); Stillie v. Stillie, 119 Kan. 816, 244 Pac. 844 (1926); Daniels v. Johnson, 216 Ark. 374, 226 S.W.2d 571, syl. 10, 15 A.L.R.2d 1401 (1950) (able opinion by Leflar, J.). But there is substantial authority which rejects it. See, e. g., Ashe v. Pettiford, 177 N.C. 132, 98 S.E. 304, 305, syl. 1 (1919); In re Hurlburt's Estate, 68 Vt. 366, 35 Atl. 77, 35 L.R.A. 794 (1896). Decisions pro and con are collected in Note, 15 A.L.R.2d 1432–14, and in Dec.Dig., Evidence, ☞288. Wigmore argues for a discretionary power to receive it, in proof of facts for which it is appropriate, where other evidence is meager. Wigmore, Evidence, § 1605. Uniform Rule 63(27) admits "Evidence of reputation in a community as tending to prove the truth of the matter reputed if . . . (c) the reputation concerns the birth, marriage, divorce, death, legitimacy, relationship by blood or marriage, or race-ancestry of a person resident in the community at the time of the reputation, or some other similar fact of his family history or of his personal status or condition which the judge finds likely to have been the subject of a reliable reputation in that community".

5. In re Hennion's Estate, 131 N.J.Eq. 293, 25 A.2d 35, syl. 2 (1942); 5 Wigmore, Evidence, §§ 1495, 1496.

6. Under the stricter view, statements by non-relatives, even family servants or family doctors, are excluded. 5 Wigmore, Evidence, § 1487. See the next footnote, for the contrary view. But relatives by birth or marriage, however remote, are within the rule. Id., Section 1489. It has been held that where a claim of inheritance of property owned in the Black family rests upon the assertion that White, under whom the claim is made, was related to the Blacks, the declarant whose statements are offered must first be shown to be related to the Blacks, and proof of his kinship to White will not avail. Aalholm v. People, 211 N.Y. 406, 105 N.E. 647, L.R.A.1915D, 215, Ann.Cas.1915C 1039. Wigmore argues convincingly for the contrary view. 5 Wigmore, Evidence, § 1491. So also Hinton, Changes in the Exceptions to the Hearsay Rule, 29 Ill.L.Rev. 422, 437 (1934), and Reid, C.J. in Hines v. Donaldson, 193 Ga. 783, 20 S.E.2d 134, 143 (1942).

7. Daniels v. Johnson, 216 Ark. 374, 226 S.W.2d 571, syl. 8, 15 A.L.R.2d 1401 (1950). Wigmore supports this extension. 5 Evidence, §§ 1486, 1487, and it is adopted in Uniform Rule 63(24), see n. 1, above.

8. 5 Wigmore, Evidence, § 1483.

9. Byers v. Wallace, 87 Tex. 503, 29 S.W. 760 (1895) (declaration that declarant had a nephew who was killed in the Texas war for independence, excluded because declarant would be sole heir); 5 Wigmore, Evidence, § 1484.

10. See Grand Lodge, A. O. U. W. v. Bartes, 69 Neb. 631, 96 N.W. 186, 98 N.W. 715, 111 Am.St.Rep. 577 (1904) (wife allowed to testify to age of deceased husband, where she had lived in family circle for twenty years and had become acquainted with family history); 5 Wigmore, Evidence, § 1486. Similarly, a person is allowed to testify to his own age, is, in effect, a statement of family tradition. Kreitz v. Behrensmeyer, 125 Ill. 141, 185, 17 N.E. 232, 8 Am.St.Rep. 349 (1888); 5 Wigmore, Evidence, § 1493.

dead or for other cause unavailable as a witness,[11] whence arises the special need for this kind of hearsay.

298. Recitals in Ancient Writings.

In an earlier section[1] we have considered the exceptional status of ancient documents in respect to authentication. The American courts have frequently held, as if it were merely an application of the rule about authentication, that the statements in an ancient document or record, authenticated as such, come in as evidence of the truth of the recitals.[2] Manifestly this is not a logical consequence of the authentication at all. Is the result a just and practical one? The requirements for authentication are that the writing must be shown to be thirty years old, and to have come from proper custody, and it must be free from suspicion in appearance. Likewise, in case of deeds, some jurisdictions require a showing that possession was given under the instrument. The age-requirement of itself limits the use to cases where the existence of a special need for the use of hearsay would usually be clear. The dearth of other sources of proof of the facts, and the usual unavailability of the writer as a witness, whether from death or forgetfulness, would both point to this need. But as to special truthworthiness, the other foundation for exceptions to the hearsay rule, it is argued that the mere age of the writing af-

fords no ground for credence.[3] Lying was as common thirty years ago as today. The defenders of the exception[4] concede this, and concede that no adequate substitute for cross-examination exists in this situation. They contend, however, that standards of reliability must be fixed with regard to the scarcity of sources of proof, and that thus gauged, there are sufficient guaranties of trustworthiness. First, the danger of fabrication, or mistransmission, so apparent in all cases of oral declarations, is here reduced to a minimum by the requirements for authentication. Second, the recital by its very age must have been made at a time before the beginning of the present controversy, and consequently uninfluenced by that source of partisanship. Almost never is there reason to believe that the declarant had any other motive to misrepresent. Moreover, the usual qualification for witnesses and out-of-court declarants, that of personal knowledge, would be insisted upon here so far as practicable, i. e., the recital would be excluded if it appeared that the writer did not have an opportunity to know the facts at first hand.[5] A final question arises. The exception has gained surest foothold in cases of ancient deed-recitals. Deed-recitals of the contents and execution of an earlier instrument, of heirship, and of consideration are nearly everywhere received to evidence these facts.[6] In cases at least where possession is taken

---

11. The courts frequently specify death as the requirement, e. g., Ellis v. Dixon, 294 Ky. 609, 172 S.W.2d 461, syl. 2 (1943). But presumably most courts today, in line with the holdings in respect to the other exceptions, would accept other grounds of unavailability, such as absence from the jurisdiction. See, e. g., Paulsen's Estate, 179 Cal. 528, 178 Pac. 143, syl. 5, 6 (1919); 5 Wigmore, Evidence, § 1481; Uniform Rule 63 (23–25), quoted in n. 1, above.

1. § 190.

2. See, e. g., Thompson v. Buchanan, 195 N.C. 155, 141 S.E. 580, 583 (1928). Decisions are collected in Wickes, Ancient Documents and Hearsay, 8 Tex.L. Rev. 451 (1930) (the leading discussion) and in a careful note, 83 U.Pa.L.Rev. 247 (1934). See also Note, 26 Harv.L.Rev. 544 (1913) and Dec.Dig., Evi-

dence, ☞372(1). All of the foregoing writers advocate the recognition of the exception, but point out that the judicial opinions have failed to articulate it in general terms, and that in most instances where the recitals in ancient instruments other than deeds have been received, they could have been admitted under other established exceptions, e. g., as declarations against interest, as business entries, or as official statements.

3. See an able criticism of the theory of a general exception for ancient recitals, Note, 33 Yale L.J. 412, 417 (1924).

4. See Wickes, op. cit., n. 2, supra.

5. See, as to this, the interesting case of Budlong v. Budlong, 48 R.I. 144, 136 Atl. 308, syl. 5–10 (1927).

6. Wilson v. Snow, 228 U.S. 217, 33 Sup.Ct. 487, syl. 1. 57 L.Ed. 807 (1913) (deed of executrix reciting that

under the deed, such recitals certainly have unusual reliability. Other ancient entries and records, and recitals in wills, letters and the like, will usually have less publicity and less likelihood of challenge if untrue. But many courts have ignored such a limitation and have accepted ancient recitals in other writings as evidence of their truth.[7] Certainly, when great judges have advocated that all statements of deceased persons should come in as evidence of the facts stated[8] and Massachusetts has had such a rule on its statute-book for half a century,[9] the acceptance of a general exception for ancient written recitals seems a desirable and conservative position. The Uniform Rule, however, limits the exceptions to recitals in deeds, wills or other documents purporting to transfer land or personal property.[10]

299. Reputation.[1]

The existence of a reputation, or general manifestation of belief of a large group of people as to a particular fact, may be material, apart from the correctness of the belief. This is true, for example, when reputation that a fact exists is offered not to show the fact but to show that someone in the range of the reputation probably had knowledge of the reputed fact.[2]

When reputation is offered to show the truth of the fact reputed the general approach is that the hearsay rule excludes it, unless it falls within one of those particular classes of fact which by tradition are permitted to be evidenced by reputation.[3] This practice of using such evidence in these particular areas harks back to a time when jurors looked to neighborhood repute, rather than to testimony in court, as their source of knowledge, and long antedates the hearsay rule itself.[4] We have already considered its use as evidence of personal character,

---

it was given under power of sale in will held admissible as evidence that she had qualified); Anderson v. Cole, 234 Mo. 1, 136 S.W. 395, syl. 4 (1911) (recital of payment of consideration); Rollins v. Atlantic City Ry. Co., 73 N.J.L. 64, 62 Atl. 929, syl. 1, 2 (1906) (heirship: requirements of pedigree exception not imposed when recital is ancient); 5 Wigmore, Evidence, § 1573; Dec.Dig., Evidence, ⬌372(1).

7. E. g., State v. Taylor, 135 Ark. 232, 205 S.W. 104, syl. 2 (1918) (recital of sale of land in "plat books" of state land office); Whitman v. Shaw, 166 Mass. 451, 44 N.E. 333, syl. 1 (1896) (map to show boundaries); Weiner v. Zweib, 128 S.W. 699, syl. 12 (Tex. Civ.App.1910), affirmed 105 Tex. 262, 141 S.W. 771, 147 S.W. 867 (entries in minutes of lodge to show fact and time of member's death); Bruni v. Vidaurri, 140 Tex. 138, 166 S.W.2d 81, syl. 15 (1942) (recital in certificate of public official, setting out copy of agreement of partition). Contra: King v. Watkins, 98 Fed. 913, 917, syl. 1, (C.C.Va.1899), reversed on other grounds 118 Fed. 524; Hurlburt v. Bussemy, 101 Conn. 406, 126 Atl. 273, syl. 6 (1924) (map).

8. See the statements of Mellish, L. J., Cockburn, L. C. J., Appleton, C. J., and Learned Hand, Circ. J., quoted in 5 Wigmore, Evidence, § 1576.

9. The Massachusetts Hearsay Statute is discussed in § 303, herein.

10. Rule 63(29) admits: "Evidence of a statement relevant to a material matter, contained in a deed of conveyance or a will or other document purporting to affect an interest in property, offered as tend-

ing to prove the truth of the matter stated, if the judge finds that the matter stated would be relevant upon an issue as to an interest in the property, and that the dealings with the property since the statement was made have not been inconsistent with the truth of the statement;". This is an adaptation of Model Code, Rule 527.

1. 5 Wigmore, Evidence, §§ 1580–1626; 20 Am.Jur., Evidence, §§ 461–476; Dec.Dig. Evidence, ⬌322, 324; Uniform Rules 63(26–28).

2. See, e. g., Fake v. Addicks, 45 Minn. 37, 47 N.W. 450, syl. 2, 22 Am.St.R. 716 (1890) (reputation of dog as vicious, admitted to show owner's knowledge); Guedon v. Rooney, 160 Ore. 621, 87 P.2d 209, 120 A.L.R. 1298, 1309, 1315 (1939) (driver's reputation for recklessness evidence of knowledge of owner of car of his incompetence); Alexander v. Ritchie, 132 W.Va. 865, 53 S.E.2d 735, syl. 8 (1949); 20 Am.Jur., Evidence, § 462.

3. See, e. g., Brown v. Brown, 242 Ala. 630, 7 So.2d 557, syl. 3, 4 (1942) (repute as evidence of ownership of cow, excluded, stating general rule); Coleman v. Lewis, 183 Mass. 485, 67 N.E. 603, syl. 2 (1903) (one's financial standing not provable by repute); Re Nelson, 210 N.C. 398, 186 S.E. 480, 105 A.L.R. 1441 (1936), annotated on this point (business ability not to be proved by reputation, stating general rule of exclusion); 5 Wigmore, Evidence, § 1609; 20 Am.Jur., Evidence, § 461, note 18.

4. 5 Wigmore, Evidence, § 1580.

particularly to prove the character of a witness for veracity,[5] and the character of an accused for the trait involved in the crime on trial,[6] and earlier in the present chapter we have mentioned the use of reputation in a family group, and in the community, to prove facts of family history.[7]

In addition, reputation as a means of proof of reputed facts is customarily received in two other classes of cases. First, as to the location of the boundaries of land,[8] reputation in the district is admitted when the reputation is ancient, that is, goes back to a past generation,[9] and antedates the beginning of the present controversy.[10] Second, as to

facts loosely defined as matters of public or general interest.[11] Presumably, the fact inquired into must be ancient, that is, must date back to a former generation,[12] and while the doctrine sanctions proof of reputation, the question usually presented is whether a particular historical treatise shall come in as evidence of the existence of such reputation.[13]

Furthermore, in particular states, by local tradition or statute, reputation may be received to prove other matters,[14] among them, ownership of property,[15] financial standing,[16] and the maintenance of a house as an establishment for liquor-selling or prostitution.[17]

---

[5] See § 44, herein.

[6] See § 158, herein.

[7] See § 297, above.

[8] In England the use of the evidence is limited to public boundaries or other public rights. Nichols v. Parker, 14 East 331n., 104 Eng.Rep. 629 (N.P.1805). But in this country, except in a few states, it extends to private boundaries also. Hail v. Haynes, 312 Ky. 357, 227 S.W.2d 918 (1950); Hemphill v. Hemphill, 138 N.C. 504, 51 S.E. 42 (1905); 5 Wigmore, Evidence, § 1587; Dec.Dig., Boundaries, ⊙=35(2).

[9] Peltz v. Burgess, 196 N.C. 395, 145 S.E. 781, syl. 1 (1928) (reputation must have "its origin at a time comparatively remote"); 5 Wigmore, Evidence, § 1582. But the Uniform Rule seems to dispense with this requirement. Rule 63(27) admits: "Evidence of reputation in a community as tending to prove the truth of the matter reputed, if (a) the reputation concerns boundaries of, or customs affecting, land in the community, and the judge finds that the reputation, if any, arise before controversy. . . ." To like effect is the statement of the rule in Ames v. Empire Star Mines Co., 17 Cal.2d 213, 110 P.2d 13, syl. 21 (1931).

[10] Peltz v. Burgess, 196 N.C. 395, 145 S.E. 781, syl. 1 (1928); 5 Wigmore, Evidence, § 1588(1).

[11] 5 Wigmore, Evidence, §§ 1586, 1597–1599. Uniform Rule 63(27) admits "Evidence of reputation in a community as tending to prove the truth of the matter reputed, if . . . the reputation concerns an event of general history of the community or of the state or nation of which the community is a part, and the judge finds that the event was of importance to the community. . . ."

[12] 5 Wigmore, Evidence, § 1597.

McCormick Evidence HB—40

[13] See, e. g., Montana Power Co. v. Fed. Power Comm., 185 F.2d 491, syl. 13, 14 (C.A.D.C.1950) (in ascertaining navigability of upper Missouri River Commission properly admitted and considered newspaper accounts and histories describing use of river in 19th century, citing judicial admission of this kind of hearsay); Trustees of Pencader Church v. Gibson, 26 Del. 375, 22 A.2d 782, syl. 12–14 (1951) (statement in history of particular Presbyterian church properly excluded, when offered to show proceeds of former church building applied to erection of present building; book not shown to be so widely accepted as to represent community repute, nor were facts of sufficient community-wide interest). As to judicial notice of historical facts, see § 325, herein.

[14] 5 Wigmore, Evidence, §§ 1620–1626.

[15] Chicago & Eastern Ill. R. Co. v. Schmitz, 211 Ill. 446, 71 N.E. 1050, syl. 12 (1904) (personal injury to pedestrian by train: reputation that particular railway company owns track, sufficient evidence of ownership) and see statutes cited 5 Wigmore, Evidence, § 1626(4).

[16] Lucas v. Swan, 67 F.2d 106, 110, syl. 21 (C.C.A. W.Va.1933) (insolvency of indorsers of demand note); Ellis v. State, 138 Wis. 513, 119 N.W. 1110, 1114, syl. 6 (1909) (dictum). This is probably the majority view. 5 Wigmore, Evidence, § 1623; 20 Am.Jur., Evidence, § 465. Contra: Coleman v. Lewis, 183 Mass. 485, 67 N.E. 603, syl. 2 (1903).

[17] Elder v. Stark, 200 Ga. 452, 37 S.E.2d 598, syl. 2 (1946) ("blind tiger"); State v. Mauch, 236 Iowa 217, 17 N.W.2d 536, syl. 18 (1945) (keeping a house of ill-fame, reputation of premises and of defendant); People v. Lee, 307 Mich. 743, 12 N.W.2d 418, syl. 2, 20 (1943) (similar to last); Dec.Dig., Disorderly House, ⊙=16, and see decisions and statutes collected in 5 Wigmore, Evidence, § 1620. Such evidence though admissible may not be sufficient. Johnson v. State, 102 Tex.Cr. 409, 278 S.W. 210 (1925).

CHAPTER 35

CHANGES AND PROPOSALS FOR CHANGE IN THE RULES ABOUT HEARSAY

300. Weaknesses of the Present Rules.

The great characteristic feature of the common law of evidence is the group of rules requiring that testimony be limited to statements in court of witnesses who observed the facts at first hand and are produced for cross-examination. This demand for the best, reduced to a rule, voices a high ideal, but manifestly one that in the every-day world must constantly be compromised. First-hand observers die and move away; their letters and declarations must be accepted as second-best. When will the second-best be good enough? It now seems strange that the courts should have attempted to answer this by defining in sharp categories the special situations when the secondary proof would be allowed. But the urge for certainty prevailed, and the particular situations where the second-hand evidence seemed most needed in the first half of the eighteen hundreds were crystallized into exceptions to the hearsay rule. These now number from ten to twenty, depending on the minuteness of the classification. The exceptions were struck off in the heat of trial as improvisations intended to be played by ear, but they fail of that purpose because the classes are grown so many and the boundaries so meandering that no one can carry any large part of this hearsay-exception-learning in his head. Moreover, the values of hearsay declarations or writings, and the need for them, in particular situations, cannot with any degree of realism be thus minutely ticketed in advance. Is it realistic, for instance, to say in advance that when an injured person consults his physician the patient's descriptions of his pain and symptoms will be receivable, but his statements to the doctor of how he got hurt will not?[1] Or that a dying declaration is worth hearing in a prosecution for killing the declarant, but not in any other kind of case, civil or criminal?[2] Much worthless evidence will fit the categories, much that is vitally needed will be left out.[3] A broader and more practical method is needed.

301. Some Factors to be Appraised in Planning a Change.

When we first come to discuss the need for reform of our hearsay rules we tend to start

---

1. See Aetna Life Insurance Co. v. Quinley, 87 F.2d 732 (C.C.A.Neb.1937); Wise v. State Industrial Accident Commission, 148 Ore. 461, 35 P.2d 242 (1934).

2. See § 260, herein.

3. Professor Hinton in Changes in the Exceptions to the Hearsay Rule, 29 Ill.L.Rev. 422, 427 (1934), commented: "Probably no phase of the law of evidence has presented more difficulties and more inconsistencies than this field. . . . If a given item of evidence was recognized as hearsay, it had to be excluded unless it clearly fell within the scope of some recognized exception. But what was the scope of the exception? That was a matter settled by precedent and frequently by some accidental or casual circumstance involved in an early case rather than the fundamental reason for the exception."

with the assumption that hearsay is all more or less alike and can be dealt with in a simple uniform manner. In fact, types of hearsay are as numerous and variegated as the types of communication. The trustworthiness of hearsay ranges from the highest reliability to utter worthlessness. Among the kinds of hearsay, i. e., un-cross-examined statements offered to prove the facts stated in them, are the following: history books, newspapers, business records, official records and certificates, affidavits, letters and other written statements, simple oral hearsay (A reports that B said), multiple hearsay (A reports that B said that C said, and so on), reputation, and gossip or rumors. Our daily life is guided and directed in largest part by hearsay information, and survival of existence and protection of possessions depends upon skill in gauging the probable truthfulness of hearsay. In doing this we commonly are guided by habit and practice rather than by formulated principles and standards.

If such principles and standards need to be formulated as the basis for improving the judicial handling of hearsay, the following, it seems, are some of the factors for consideration. As bearing on the *need* for the use of the particular hearsay statement, we may ask: is the declarant dead or otherwise unavailable as a witness? Are there other sources of information, better than the hearsay statement, which enable us to make a satisfactory investigation of the facts, without resorting to the particular statement? Are the facts which the declaration is offered to prove genuinely disputed, so that well-tested evidence may be required, or is the issue merely a perfunctory one, as to which slighter proof, such as a letter or an affidavit, ought practically to be enough?

As bearing on the reliability with which the statement is *transmitted* to the tribunal, we ask: is the statement in *writing* and, if so, is it satisfactorily authenticated? If the out-of-court statement is oral, the witness who reports it is subject to cross-examination as to the accuracy of his reporting, but we may still ask the questions about the reliability of his report that we ask below about the declarant and his hearsay statement.

In respect to these latter, we may inquire: did the declarant have first-hand knowledge of the facts declared, or did he base his statement on others' reports? Was the statement made near in time to the facts related, so that his memory was fresh, or was it remote? Was there an inducement of interest, emotional or pecuniary, for him to make such a statement? Was the statement made before or after the present controversy began?

Some general policy questions remain. Should a reformatory statute or rule retain the long present list of specific exceptions to the hearsay rule [1]—liberalized, of course, in detail—with the addition of one or more wider exceptions? Or, on the other hand, should the attempt be made to find a few general exceptions which should displace the entire present galaxy? The former solution would preserve the fruits of two centuries of experience as to when hearsay can safely be used, the latter would answer the great need for making evidence law simple and workable if its vitality is to endure.

A second policy question is whether a freer use of hearsay should be permitted in trials before a court than in trials to a jury.[2] Indeed, it seems that the hearsay rule could well be discarded altogether in trials to a judge. His general power to exclude cumulative evidence or evidence of so little value as not to be worth consuming the time of the court,[3] and his duty to rest his findings only on substantial evidence would prevent abuses. If administrative boards can be trusted with

[1]. See chs. 26–34, herein.

[2]. See the interesting Comment, Exclusionary Rules of evidence in Non-Jury Proceedings, 46 Ill.L.Rev. 915 (1952); Davis, Administrative Law, §§ 141, 142 (1951).

[3]. See § 152, herein.

this responsibility for hearing and evaluating hearsay,[4] judges can even more safely be trusted with it.[5] It is true that in "law" cases either party may demand a jury, and a difference in the rules of evidence to be applied might sometimes lead a party to demand a jury who otherwise would not do so. If this is a substantial objection, which may be doubted, it could be met by limiting the freedom to admit hearsay to judge-tried cases in which a jury is not demandable.

Finally, there arises for consideration the question how far the constitutional provisions entitling the accused to be confronted with the witnesses against him prevent the extension to criminal cases of new and wider exceptions to the hearsay rule.[6]

302. Judicial and Other Pronouncements of the Need for Change.[1]

Judicial opinions and learned discussions furnish many forcible expressions of the need for reform of the system of rules about hearsay. Examples follow.

Mellish, L. J.: "I have not the least hesitation in saying that I think it would be a highly desirable improvement in the law if the rule was that all statements, made by persons who are dead, respecting matters of which they had a personal knowledge, and made 'ante litem motam,' should be admitted. There is no doubt that by rejecting such evidence we do reject a most valuable source of evidence." [2]

James Bradley Thayer: "I beg to submit to you the following 'formulated suggestion' for an amendment of the law of evidence, viz.,

"No declaration of a deceased person, made in writing *ante litem motam,* shall be excluded, as evidence, on the ground of hearsay, if it appear to the satisfaction of the judge to have been made upon the personal knowledge of the declarant." [3]

Learned Hand, Circ. J.: "When a witness is not available at all or available only with a disproportionate expense of time, let us hear what he has said on the matter, just as we do in every other concern of life, even in affairs which may involve our lives or the safety of the state. You will perhaps, with the instinct of lawyers, recoil at what seems so far-reaching an innovation. I do not complain; I agree that it involves chances, but in answer I argue that, as the law now stands, the party who has only such proof is deprived of any chances at all. It would of course be undesira-

---

4. See the masterly analysis and evaluation of the practice of administrative boards and commissions in admitting evidence which would be incompetent under the judicial rules of evidence, in Davis, Administrative Law, §§ 143–149 (1951).

5. In United States v. United Shoe Machinery Corp., 89 F.Supp. 349, 356 (D.Mass.1950), a civil anti-trust case tried without a jury, Wyzanski, D. J., in discussing a hearsay question, cogently said: "It is difficult to imagine any satisfactory ground for deciding that evidence which is admissible before the Federal Trade Commission is inadmissible before a judge sitting without a jury in a civil anti-trust case brought by the government. . . . In a *civil* anti-trust case the Government has the unfettered choice of going before a Commission or before a court without a jury. . . . The Commission's hearing officer may be no more experienced or skillful than a District Judge in sifting the reliable hearsay from the untrustworthy hearsay. . . . One other consideration deserves mention. Recent years have seen a marked increase in the number of

social and economic controversies which have been removed from the courts to administrative agencies for adjudication. . . . To preserve their own jurisdiction the courts must in this type of controversy relax the rigidity of the hearsay rule."

6. See § 231, herein, and 5 Wigmore, Evidence, § 1397.

1. See the compilation of such expressions in 5 Wigmore, Evidence, § 1576.

2. Sugden v. Lord St. Leonards, L.R. [1876] 1 P.D. 154, 250.

3. Thayer, Legal Essays, 303, note (1908). The quotation in the text is from a letter dated December 22, 1896, to a Committee of the Suffolk Bar Association, and contains the further statement: "In support of this suggestion I may submit the remark of Lord Justice Mellish [quoted in the text above]. . . . It will be observed that my suggestion falls much inside the scope of Lord Justice Mellish's suggestion, for I limit the proposed change to statements *in writing.*"

ble to open the doors to hearsay evidence when better was available, but I ask you whether Baron Gilbert was not right in saying that men should use in their disputes the best means they can get to reach the truth?" [4]

Royal Commission on the Dispatch of Business at Common Law, 1934–36 (a commission composed of the Master of the Rolls and five eminent barristers):

"228.—(2) *Relaxation in Rules of Evidence.*—English law starts from the general principle that facts should be proved by a witness produced in court and subjected to cross-examination. Evidence by written declaration or affidavit is distrusted. We do not question the soundness of this principle. On an important point seriously disputed it is highly unsatisfactory to be obliged to act on evidence which is not given in court and subjected to cross-examination. But in most cases there are points which a judge could decide with confidence on an affidavit, a certificate from a public body, company or officer, or even on an unsworn declaration or a statement in a book of reputation.

"229. The above relates to written evidence of witnesses, *i. e.*, evidence brought into existence 'ad hoc' for the trial. But English law equally rejects as inadmissible (except as against the writer) letters and documents which came into existence before any dispute had arisen. Nevertheless, such documents may be more convincing than the writer's assertion on oath at the trial. It is high time that this principle should be reconsidered. So long as all questions of fact were decided by juries it was reasonable to exclude types of evidence which juries are not well qualified to understand and to weigh. But in civil cases questions of fact are now for the most part decided by judges.

"230. The calling of witnesses where written evidence would suffice is a great source of delay and expense, and we are in favour of a very substantial relaxation in this respect. We consider that the judges should have a discretion to admit *all documents and records* relating to the matters in question *which came into existence before the dispute arose.* This would put the judge in the same position as the ordinary commercial arbitrator, who is usually given power to receive and act upon all such evidence as he chooses to admit. . . .

"231. Similarly we consider that the Court should have power to admit affidavit evidence or *even unsworn declarations*, without limitation. The opposite party should not have an absolute right to require the production of the deponent for cross-examination; but where the subject matter of the affidavit is important and seriously disputed, or it is desirable to compel a witness to submit himself to cross-examination, leave would no doubt in practice be granted in proper cases.

"232. The above observations relate only to the admissibility of evidence and not to its weight. The judge will give to the evidence what weight he thinks it deserves and no more.

"Further, these remarks do not apply to trials with a jury, nor do they apply to any criminal cases." [5]

Persuasive statements of the need for the reformation of the complex restrictions upon the use of hearsay may likewise be found in the writings of Wigmore,[6] Morgan,[7] Maguire,[8] James,[9] and Baker.[10]

4. The Deficiencies of Trials to Reach the Heart of the Matter, 3 N.Y. City Bar Asso. Lectures on Legal Topics, 1921–22, p. 99 (pub. 1926).

5. Report, pp. 78, 79.

6. Wigmore, Evidence, vol. I, § 8c, pp. 277–280, vol. V, §§ 1427, 1476.

7. Model Code of Evidence, 217–224 (1942) (Introductory note to chapter on Hearsay).

8. Evidence: Common Sense and Common Law, 147–165 (1947).

9. The Role of Hearsay in a Rational Scheme of Evidence, 34 Ill.L.Rev. 788 (1940).

10. The Hearsay Rule (circa 1950).

303. Legislation: The Massachusetts and English Acts.

Prompted by a suggestion from James Bradley Thayer,[1] the Massachusetts Hearsay Statute of 1898 was enacted as follows: "A declaration of a deceased person shall not be inadmissible in evidence as hearsay if the Court finds that it was made in good faith before the commencement of the action and upon the personal knowledge of the declarant."[2]

It has since been amended by striking out the requirement that the declaration must have been made before the commencement of the action, and in other minor particulars, but the elements of the original reform remain in effect.[3]

Seemingly the judicial interpretation of the act has been for the most part in keep-ing with its purpose of opening the door to trustworthy statements of decedents.[4] After a quarter century of experience under the Act a questionnaire was addressed by a responsible committee to the lawyers and judges of the state, to ascertain their views as to the merits of the Act, and 638 answers were received. Of those having experience with the operation of the Act, 71 percent thought that its effects were wholesome and only 19 percent were of the opposite opinion.[5] Thus the extensive available evidence indicates that the Act has worked well.[6] The American Bar Association in 1938 recommended a liberalized version of the Act for adoption by the states.[7]

The only other instance of a legislative creation of an important new exception to the hearsay rule is the English Evidence Act of 1938.[8] The chief promoter of the bill was

---

1. See next preceding section.

2. Mass. Acts 1898, ch. 535. Rhode Island has a similar statute. Gen.Laws 1938, c. 538, § 6.

3. The present version of the Act is as follows: "In any action or other civil judicial proceeding, a declaration of a deceased person shall not be inadmissible in evidence as hearsay or as private conversation between husband and wife, as the case may be, if the court finds that it was made in good faith and upon the personal knowledge of the declarant." Mass. G.L.(Ter.Ed.) c. 233, § 65, as amended 1941 and 1943.

4. See the decisions collected in the Annotated Laws, cited next previous note, and in 5 Wigmore, Evidence, § 1576, note 11. The court in In re Keenan, 287 Mass. 577, 192 N.E. 65 (1934) held the statute applicable in disbarment proceedings and said that was to be given a liberal interpretation because of its remedial purpose. By contrast, the only decision under the Act which seems to have been generally criticised is Brady v. Doherty, 253 Mass. 518, 149 N.E. 198 (1925), which, surprisingly, held the Act inapplicable to the trial of issues framed by the Probate Court in a will case. See Morgan and Maguire, Cases on Evidence, §§ 772, 773 (3d ed. 1951). See also Larimore v. Dobbs, 74 S.D. 635, 57 N.W.2d 750, syl. 1–3 (1953), critically noted 52 Mich.L.Rev. 611, holding that a statute somewhat similar to the Massachusetts Act was inapplicable in a death action.

5. Morgan et al. (constituting the Commonwealth Fund Committee), The Law of Evidence: Some Proposals for Its Reform, Yale University Press, 39–49 (1927).

6. For other approving expressions, see Vanderbilt, C. J. in Robertson v. Hackensack Trust Co., 1 N.J. 304, 318, 63 A.2d 515, 522 (1949) ("This sensible statute"); Maguire, Evidence, Common Sense and Common Law, 153–155 (1947); Terwilliger and Effland, Legislative Comment, 1938 Wis.L.Rev. 587, 592; 5 Wigmore, Evidence, § 1576.

7. "That declarations of a deceased or insane person should be received in evidence if the trial judge shall find (1) that the person is dead or insane, (2) that the declaration was made and (3) that it was made in good faith before the commencement of the action and upon the personal knowledge of the declarant." Vanderbilt, Minimum Standards of Judicial Administration, 321, 338 (1949).

8. 1 & 2 Geo. 6, c. 28 sec. 1. The pertinent parts of the Act are set out in 5 Wigmore, § 1576, note 4, and in a Comment, Hearsay and the English Evidence Act, 1938, 34 Ill.L.Rev. 974, note (1940). Lord Maugham, the sponsor of the Act, gives an illuminating account of the reasons for its enactment in an article, Observations on the Law of Evidence, 17 Can.Bar Rev. 469 (1939). See Phipson, Evidence, ch. 22 (9th ed., Burrows, 1952), and Baker, The Hearsay Rule, 145–152 (1950) (lucid expositions of the effect and interpretation); Cowen and Carter, The Interpretation of the Evidence Act, 1938, 12 Mod.L.Rev. 145 (1949) (acute analysis of the decisions).

Lord Maugham, Lord Chancellor at the time of its enactment. The Act is long and detailed, and only the salient features of its liberalization of the existing restrictions on the use of hearsay can here be summarized.

It applies only to *written* hearsay statements and provides that

1. The maker must have had personal knowledge of the facts or, if not, he must have made it as a part of a continuous record in the course of duty, on information supplied by one who had knowledge.

2. The maker must be called as a witness, or must be shown unavailable, or if available the judge in his discretion may dispense with his attendance if undue delay or expense would be entailed.

3. The maker must not be "a person interested at a time when proceedings were pending or anticipated involving a dispute as to any fact which the statement might tend to establish."

4. In trials before a jury, statements which satisfy the requirements of the Act may nevertheless be rejected by the Court in its discretion, if it appears "inexpedient in the interests of justice" to receive them.

5. The part of the Act here summarized does not apply to criminal trials.

The principal planner of the English Act was unaware of the existence of the important Massachusetts Act and the extensive experience under it, when the English Act was drafted.[9] In one respect the English Act is much narrower, namely in its application to written statements alone.[10] While written statements as a class are far more reliable than oral, due to the greater certainty that they were actually made, there has been little tendency in this country among the proponents of reform to give them special treatment, and the English Act has been criticised for its failure to include oral statements,[11] and is probably to be regarded as too restrictive in this respect, in view of the fact that it is limited to civil proceedings which are nearly always tried in England without a jury. In another aspect, the English Act is far wider than the Massachusetts law, which limits admission to the situation where the declarant is dead, whereas the English Act lets in the statement when the maker is unavailable for any reason, as well as when he is called as a witness, and when the judge in his discretion dispenses with the requirement of unavailability. The widening of the grounds of unavailability is characteristic of the proposals for reform in this country also.[12]

304. The Principal Proposals for Hearsay Reform: The Model Code and the Uniform Rules.

The drafters of the Model Code of Evidence of the American Law Institute took a bold course about hearsay. They drafted a sweeping new exception to the hearsay rule as follows:

Rule 503: "Evidence of a hearsay declaration is admissible if the judge finds that the declarant

    "(a) is unavailable as a witness, or

    "(b) is present and subject to cross-examination."

This rule, however, was qualified and safeguarded by other rules which (1) limited its application to declarations by persons with personal knowledge and excluded hearsay upon hearsay,[1] and (2) empowered the trial

---

9. Maugham, op. cit., 17 Can.Bar Rev. 460, 482.

10. "It guards against that great source of error, the fallibility of human memory in the reporting of oral statements and conversations. While it may afford but little assurance of the correctness of the original statement itself, it does give almost complete assurance that the statement is faithfully transmitted to the court." Comment, 34 Ill.L.Rev. 974, 983 (1940).

11. Helman, The Reform of the Law of Hearsay, 17 Can.Bar Rev. 302 (1939) and in Baker, The Hearsay Rule, 151, 152 (1950).

12. See § 304, below.

1. R. 501(3).

judge to exclude such hearsay whenever its probative value was outweighed by the likelihood of waste of time, prejudice, confusion or unfair surprise.[2] The traditional exceptions, in addition to the new sweeping one, were retained in general, but liberalized by dispensing with the requirement, which obtained as to most at common law, that the declarant be unavailable.[3]

The drafters of the sweeping rule were ahead of their time. This liberalizing of the use of hearsay was a chief ground of opposition to the Model Code in professional discussion. This opposition, together with a sort of cyclical apathy which succeeded a period of successful activity in procedural reform, has accounted for the failure of the Model Code to be adopted in any jurisdiction.

Nevertheless, the controversy over the Model Code, awakened a new interest in many enlightened lawyers in the improvement of evidence law, and it is widely believed that the time is at hand for another attempt, on more conservative lines, to modernize the rules of evidence. Accordingly, the Commissioners on Uniform State Laws, in cooperation with the American Law Institute and building on the foundation of the Model Code, have drafted and adopted a more modestly reformative code, styled the Uniform Rules of Evidence.[4] The American Bar Association has approved this action.[5]

Instead of admitting, as the Model Code does, practically all first-hand hearsay when the declarant is unavailable, the drafters of the new Rules hedged the extension with careful safeguarding restrictions. The relevant rules are the following:

"Rule 63. Evidence of a statement which is made other than by a witness while testifying at the hearing offered to prove the truth of the matter stated is hearsay evidence and inadmissible except:

"(1) A statement previously made by a person who is present at the hearing and available for cross examination with respect to the statement and its subject matter, provided the statement would be admissible if made by declarant while testifying as a witness;

. . .

"(4) A statement (a) which the judge finds was made while the declarant was perceiving the event or condition which the statement narrates, describes or explains, or (b) which the judge finds was made while the declarant was under the stress of a nervous excitement caused by such perception, or (c) if the declarant is unavailable as a witness, a statement narrating, describing or explaining an event or condition which the judge finds was made by the declarant at a time when the matter had been recently perceived by him and while his recollection was clear, and was made in good faith prior to the commencement of the action;"

As in the Model Code the other traditional exceptions are retained and liberalized,[6] and the judge may exclude hearsay (as other evidence) when its value is outweighed by the danger of prejudice, confusion, surprise and waste of time.[7] As in the Model Code prior statements of a witness on the stand

2. R. 303.

3. Rules 504–529.

4. Published in pamphlet form by the National Conference of Commissioners on Uniform State Laws, 1419 First National Bank Building, Omaha 2, Nebraska.

5. 39 A.B.A.J. 1029 (1953).

6. Rule 63, subsecs. 1–31.

7. Rule 45: "Except as in these rules otherwise provided, the judge may in his discretion exclude evidence if he finds that its probative value is substantially outweighed by the risk that its admission will (a) necessitate undue consumption of time, or (b) create substantial danger of undue prejudice or of confusing the issues or of misleading the jury, or (c) unfairly and harmfully surprise a party who has not had reasonable opportunity to anticipate that such evidence would be offered."

come in as substantive evidence (subs. 1) and declarations of present perception (subs. 4(a)) are received as many courts do under existing law.[8] The significant restrictive provision is sub. 4(b), which instead of letting in all declarations on personal knowledge of unavailable declarants requires the judge's finding (1) that the statement was made within a brief period after the matter was perceived ("recently"), (2) while memory was clear, (3) in good faith, and (4) before the commencement of the action. All this includes the safeguard that the judge, if he does not believe that the statement was made at all, cannot make the necessary findings for admission and will exclude it.

This treatment of hearsay, while it opens the door more narrowly than the Model Code, will nevertheless empower the judges to admit much needed and highly reliable evidence, particularly in the cases of fatal accidents to solitary workmen and in many cases involving transactions with persons since deceased, which would now have to be excluded. It is believed that this is an enlightened and conservative measure of hear-

say reform, and that the profession generally will approve it. The Uniform Rules on hearsay probably are the longest step forward which is now feasible by legislative action.

305. The Future of Hearsay.

Beyond the modest liberalization of hearsay restrictions which the Uniform Rules would accomplish,[1] what other improvements may be foreseen, either in the near future, or as later stages in the progression?

1. Occasionally, judges in their opinions will present the issue of admissibility of a particular hearsay statement, not merely as stopping with the inquiry whether the statement meets any one of the specific exceptions to the hearsay rule, but as whether under the circumstances it satisfies the *reasons* which lie behind the exceptions. Do the facts show that there is a special need for the use of the statement? Are the circumstances such as to afford a reasonable assurance of the truthfulness of the statement? The guidance of these beacon decisions,[2] if generally followed, would in a measurable

---

8. See § 273, herein.

1. See § 304, above.

8. Goodale v. Murray, 227 Iowa 843, 289 N.W. 450, 126 A.L.R. 121 (1940) (in proceeding for probate of lost will, a subscribing witness who heard banker-draftsman read will to testator was allowed to testify to purport of the reading; held, in able opinion by Bliss, J., properly received; "the essential of necessity is fully met. The same is true of the circumstantial guarantee of trustworthiness. What good reason can there be to suspect the sincerity or the truth or reliability of what either the testator or Scholz did or said on that occasion? . . . In this case there was no basis or occasion for either inaccurate perception or faulty memory, for neither memory nor perception were called into action. Scholz merely read what he had just written. And as already stated there was no reason for untruthfulness. It is our judgment that the testimony met every essential requisite justifying its admission as an exception to the hearsay rule."); Gagnon v. Pronovost, 97 N.H. 500, 92 A.2d 904, 906 (1952) (trial judge admitted memorandum books of predecessor in title stating that she and another had con-

tributed certain amounts to the purchase of the land; on appeal, Blandin, J., after finding the entries did not fall with the exceptions for business entries or declarations against interest, said: "However, we believe the sensible test to determine whether this evidence should have been admitted was suggested by Peaslee, Jr., many years ago in Hutchins v. Berry, 75 N.H. 416, 75 A. 650, 653, where he said when speaking of a record kept in a memorandum book, 'Is this account so lacking in apparent truthworthiness that it must be wholly rejected, or should it be admitted, and the objections to it be used to detract from its weight? The latter course seems the more reasonable.' 75 N.H. 419, 75 A. 650. We agree with this statement and so apparently do influential modern authorities."

Notable opinions discussing and approving the modern legislation and the proposals for legislation liberalizing the admission of hearsay are those of Vanderbilt, C. J., concurring, in Robertson v. Hackensack Trust Co., 1 N.J. 304, 318, 63 A.2d 515, 522 (1949), and of Van Winkle, Advisory Master, in In re Petagno, 24 N.J.Misc. 279, 48 A.2d 909 (Ch.1946).

time accomplish even more than the proposals for legislation discussed in the preceding section.

2. The admission of hearsay evidence in trials without a jury, subject to the limitation that the judge may exclude evidence of trivial value in the interest of time and can base a finding only upon evidence of substantial probative worth, may come at a day not too distant.

3. If the present hearsay system of exclusion subject to exceptions continues in jury trials, a new exception, wider still than the Model Code rule or the Uniform Rule, will need to be formulated so that the judge may use the greatest resource we have for justice in these matters of evidence—his responsible judgment. I suggest this: a hearsay statement will be received if the judge finds that the need for and the probative value of the statement render it a fair means of proof under the circumstances.

4. Still further beyond the horizon, we may anticipate that, like other exclusionary rules, the rule excluding hearsay will eventually disappear,[3] and we shall adopt the practice which, subject to variations, prevails in the leading countries of Europe,[4] that is, the system of receiving hearsay and evaluating it.

[3.] Among the writers who discern a trend in this direction are Baker, The Hearsay Rule, 169 (1950); Davis, Administrative Law, § 140 (1951); Leflar, Statements Made out of Court, 2 Ark.L.Rev. 26, 51 (1948).

[4.] Hammerman, Hearsay Evidence, A Comparison, 67 L.Q.Rev. 67 (1951). The writer surveys the practice in France, Italy, Switzerland and Germany and concludes that in these countries no general rule against the admission of hearsay exists, even for jury trials (p. 77). He points out, however, that the conducting of the examination of witnesses by the judge under the inquisitional system minimizes the need for cross-examination by the parties, whereas under our adversary system cross-examination looms larger as a safeguard, and in planning reform, this fact must be kept in mind. (pp. 78–80). The Continental practice in respect to hearsay seems to prevail also in the modern Canon Law. Martin, Hearsay at Common Law and at Canon Law, 11 Jurist 58, 226 (1951).

CHAPTER 36

THE BURDEN OF PRODUCING EVIDENCE, PRESUMPTIONS AND THE BURDEN OF PERSUASION [1]

306. "Burden of Proof" in the First Sense: The Burden of Producing Evidence.[2]

"Proof" is an ambiguous word. We sometimes use it to mean evidence, such as testimony or documents. Sometimes, when we say a thing is "proved" we mean that we are convinced by the data submitted that the alleged fact is true. Thus, "proof" is the

---

[1.] See 9 Wigmore, Evidence, §§ 2483–2498 (general theory); 2499–2550 (burdens and presumptions in specific issues); Jones, Evidence, vol. 1, ch. 2, vol. 2, ch. 4 (2 ed. rev. 1926); Model Code of Evidence, Rules 1(2, 3), 701–704; Uniform Rules of Evidence, Rules 1(4), 13–16; Morgan, Some Observations Concerning Presumptions, 44 Harv.L.Rev. 906, 1931, Presumptions, 12 Wash.L.Rev. 255, 1937, Techniques in the Use of Presumptions, 24 Iowa L.Rev. 413, 1939; Evidence 1941–1945, 59 Harv.L.Rev. 481, 491, 495, 1946; How to Approach Burden of Proof and Presumptions, 25 Rocky Mt.L.Rev. 34 (1952); McCormick, Charges on Presumptions, 5 N.C.L.Rev. 291 (1927), What Shall the Trial Judge Tell the Jury about Presumptions? 13 Wash.L.Rev. 185 (1938); Hanbury, Burden of Proof, 61 Juridical Re-

view 121 (1949); Reaugh, Presumptions and the Burden of Proof, 36 Ill.L.Rev. 703, 819, 1942; Helman, Presumptions: A Review, 22 Can.Bar Rev. 118, 1944; Ray, Burden of Proof and Presumptions, 13 Tex.L.Rev. 33, 1934; Laughlin, In Support of the Thayer Theory of Presumptions, 52 Mich.L.Rev. 195 (1953); Gausewitz, Presumptions in a One-Rule World, 5 Vand.L.Rev. 324 (1952); Taintor, Presumptions in Pennsylvania, 17 Pa.B. A.Q. 89, 193, 1945–6. Decisions are collected in 31 C.J.S., Evidence, §§ 103–157, 20 Am.Jur.Evidence, §§ 131–244, Decennial Digests, Evidence, ☜53–98, Trial, ☜205, 234(7), 237, Criminal Law, ☜305–336, 778, 789.

[2.] The two meanings of "burden of proof" were pointed out by certain nineteenth century judges,

end-result of conviction or persuasion produced by the evidence. Naturally, the term "burden of proof" shares this ambivalence. In one sense—the one discussed in this section—it means the necessity of producing evidence, satisfactory to the judge, of a particular fact in issue. This burden is usually cast first upon the party who has pleaded the existence of the fact, but as we shall see, the burden may shift to the adversary when the pleader has discharged his initial duty. The duty of proceeding with evidence on an issue means the liability to an adverse ruling (a non-suit or a directed verdict) if evidence on the issue has not been produced.

Let us suppose that the plaintiff, claiming an estate in land for another's life, had the burden of pleading, and has pleaded, that John Smith was alive at the time the action was brought. He seeks to fulfill the duty of first producing evidence of this fact.

To do this he may offer *direct* evidence, e. g., of witness Jones, that he saw Smith alive in the clerk's office while the writ in the action was being issued. From this the inference of the truth of the fact to be proved depends only upon the truthfulness of Jones. Or, he may offer *circumstantial* evidence, which requires a weighing of probabilities as to matters other than merely the truthfulness of the witness. For example, he may secure the testimony of Jones to the effect that he, Jones, received a letter in the mail which was signed "John Smith" one month before the action was brought. Patently in this latter case, the tribunal may be satisfied

that Jones is speaking the truth, and yet the tribunal may decline to infer the fact of Smith's being alive when the action began.

How strongly persuasive must the offered evidence be to satisfy the duty? Obviously it must be such that a reasonable man could draw from it the inference of the existence of the particular fact to be proved. In case of direct evidence no difficulty occurs. It is sufficient, though given by one witness only, however negligible a human being he may be. But if the evidence be circumstantial, forensic disputes as to its sufficiency to warrant a jury to draw the desired inference often arise. Ordinarily the judge when called upon to rule on this question[3] must do so in the light merely of his own common sense and experience of human affairs. In the last analysis his ruling then rests on his individual opinion as to the limits of reasonable inference from the facts proven. However, certain situations constantly recur and give rise repeatedly to litigation, and a given judge, in his desire for consistency and the consequent saving of time and mental travail, will rule alike whenever the same situation is proved and its sufficiency to warrant a certain inference is questioned. Other judges follow suit and a standardized practice, ripening into a rule of procedure, results. Most of these rules are positive rather than negative. They announce that certain types of fact-groups are sufficient to enable the person who has the first duty to go forward with evidence to fulfill that duty, i. e., they enable him to rest

---

e. g., Shaw, C. J. in Powers v. Russell, 30 Mass. (13 Pick.) 69, 76 (1832), and Brett, M. R., in Abrath v. N. E. Ry. Co., 11 Q.B.D. 440, 452 (1883), but the distinction and its consequences were first emphasized and elaborated by James Bradley Thayer in his Preliminary Treatise on Evidence, ch. 9 (1898). Modern cases making the distinction are collected in Dec. Dig.Evidence ☜90.

What we have called here the burden of producing evidence is sometimes termed the "burden of evidence" (31 C.J.S., Evidence, § 103) or "the duty of going forward." Thayer, op. cit., 355.

3. The test of sufficiency of circumstantial evidence is thus announced by Wigmore (Evidence, sec. 2494): "Are there facts in evidence which if unanswered would justify men of ordinary reason and fairness in affirming the question which the plaintiff is bound to maintain?" This is approved in Lawrence v. Yadkin River Power Co., 190 N.C. 664, 130 S.E. 735, 738 (1925) holding evidence as to origin of a field-fire sufficient to warrant inference that it was due to defendant's negligent maintenance of its power-line and right of way.

after proving them without being subject to the penalty of an adverse ruling. Examples of such enabling fact-groups, as given in a recent North Carolina decision, are: delivery of goods to a carrier in good condition and delivery by the carrier in a damaged state, to show negligence; injury to neighboring property by fire set from passing locomotives, also to show negligence; and injury to passengers in a wreck or derailment, likewise to show negligence.[4]

Suppose the one who had the initial duty of offering evidence in support of the alleged fact, on pain of an adverse ruling, does produce evidence barely sufficient to satisfy that duty, so that the judge can just say, "A reasonable jury *could* infer that the fact is as alleged, from the circumstances proved." If the proponent then rests what is the situation? Has the duty of going forward shifted to the adversary? Not if we define that duty (as we did before) as the liability to a peremptory adverse ruling on failing to give evidence, for if at this juncture the original proponent rests and the adversary offers no proof, the proponent will not be entitled to the direction of a verdict in his favor on the issue, but rather the court will leave the issue to the decision of the jury. But it is frequently said that in this situation the duty of going forward has shifted to the adversary [5] and this is unobjectionable if we bear in mind that the penalty for silence is very different here from that which was applied to the original proponent. If he had remained silent at the outset he would have irrevocably lost the case on this issue, but the only penalty now applied to his adversary is the risk, if he remains silent, of the jury's finding against him, though it may find for him. Theoretically he may have this risk still, even after he has offered evidence in rebuttal. It is simpler to limit "duty of going forward" to the liability, on resting, to an adverse ruling, and to regard the stage just discussed (where the situation is that if both parties rest, the issue will be left to the jury) as one in which neither party has any duty of going forward.

In the situation just discussed the party who first had the duty, i. e., the necessity, of giving proof, has produced evidence which requires the judge to permit the jury to infer, as it chooses, that the fact alleged is or is not true. It is a permitted, but not a compulsory, inference. Is it possible for the original proponent of evidence to carry his proof to the stage where if he rests, he will be entitled to a directed verdict, or its equivalent, on the issue? Undoubtedly, with a qualification to be noted, this is possible, and when it occurs there is a shifting to the adversary of the duty of going forward with the evidence, in the strictest sense. Such a ruling means that in the judge's view the proponent has not merely offered evidence from which reasonable men could draw the inference of the truth of the fact alleged, but evidence from which (in the absence of evidence from the adversary) reasonable men could not help but draw this inference. Thus, Lord Mansfield, in Rex v. Almon,[6] told the jury that upon the issue of whether defendant had published a libel, proof of a sale of the book in defendant's shop was, being unrebutted, "conclusive," and Nash, J., in State v. Floyd,[7] said: "Prima facie evidence is a rebuttable presumption of law, and if not rebutted, *the jury is bound in law to find their verdict in accordance with it, and if they refuse to do so, they violate their duty.*" Thus, in the case first supposed, if the plaintiff brought

---

4.   See Austin v. Seaboard Air Line R. Co., 187 N.C. 7, 121 S.E. 1, 3 (1923). No doubt some of these examples would be treated by some courts as cases of mandatory presumptions and not mere permissible inferences.

5.   For example, see Hunt v. Eure, 189 N.C. 482, 127 S.E. 593 (1925) especially p. 597 (presumption of consideration from recital of value in nonnegotiable note); and Austin v. Ry. Co., supra, note 4.

6.   5 Burr. 2686 (K.B.1770).

7.   35 N.C. 382, 386.

forward the *direct* evidence of Jones that Smith was alive when the writ was issued, and there is no contrary evidence at all, or if he brings forward circumstantial evidence (that is, evidence that Smith was seen alive in perfect health ten minutes before the writ was issued) which is, in the absence of contrary circumstances, irresistibly convincing, the jury should no more be left to refuse at will to draw the only rational inference, than they should be permitted to draw an inference from insufficient data, where the proponent has failed to sustain his initial duty of producing evidence enough to support the inference desired. Here again the ruling, from repeated occurrence of similar facts, may become a standardized one. The statement that one who has the duty of going forward can go forward far enough not merely to escape an adverse peremptory ruling himself, but to subject his opponent to one if the latter declines to take up the gage by producing evidence, has however the following qualification. Obviously if the testimony were conflicting as to the truth of the facts from which the inference of the fact in issue is desired to be drawn, and the judge believes the inference (conceding the truth of the premise) is irresistible to rational minds, he can only make a conditional peremptory ruling. He directs the jury, if you believe the evidence that fact A is so then you must find fact B, the fact in issue. And in some jurisdictions, if the party seeking the ruling has the ultimate burden of persuasion on the issue, meaning usually the party who has pleaded the fact, he can only get

such a conditional ruling, though his witnesses are undisputed and unimpeached.[8] But, in either event, if the inference is overwhelming, the judge does not permit the jury to cogitate over that, but only over the truthfulness of those who testify to the basic data.

We have seen something of the mechanics of the process of "proceeding" or "going forward" with evidence, viewed from the point of view of the *first* party who is stimulated to produce proof under threat of a ruling foreclosing a finding in his favor. He may in respect to a particular issue pass through three stages of judicial hospitality (a) where if he stops he will be thrown out of court (b) where if he stops and his adversary does nothing, his reception will be left to the jury, and (c) where if he stops and his adversary does nothing, his victory (so far as it depends on having the circumstantial inference he desires drawn) is at once proclaimed. Obviously, whenever the first producer of proof stops, the adversary may go forward with evidence in turn, and he again may in his turn pass through the same three stages. *His* evidence again may be (a) insufficient to warrant a finding in his favor, (b) sufficient to warrant a finding, or (c) irresistible, if unrebutted.

307. "Burden of Proof" in the Second Sense: The Burden of Persuasion.[1]

The burden of producing evidence is apportioned to one party—as to most issues, to the plaintiff in the first instance—and is enforced by the judge during the course of the presentation of evidence. It is a critical

---

8. Giles v. Giles, 204 Mass. 383, 90 N.E. 595 (1910); Anniston Nat. Bank v. School Committee of Durham, 121 N.C. 107, 28 S.E. 134 (1897) (construing C.S. 564). In a majority of jurisdictions no such restriction exists, except as to instructions against the defendant in criminal cases. 9 Wigmore, Evidence sec. 2495.

1. Wigmore terms this "the risk of non-persuasion." 9 Evidence, § 2485. "Thayer in A Preliminary Treatise on Evidence at the Common Law, Chapt. 9,

p. 353, said: 'The term "burden of proof" . . . imports the duty of ultimately establishing any given proposition . . . this phrase, "the burden of proof," . . . marks . . . the peculiar duty of him who has the risk of any given proposition on which parties are at issue,—who will lose the case if he does not make this proposition out, when all has been said and done.' " Se-Ling Hosiery v. Margulies, 364 Pa. 45, 70 A.2d 854, 856 (1950).

and important mechanism in a jury trial,[2] as it empowers the judge to decide the case without jury consideration when a party fails to sustain the burden.

In a case, however, where the parties have sustained their burden of producing evidence upon the given issue and the issue comes to be submitted to the jury, the necessity arises, under the common law tradition, of instructing them how they shall decide the issue if their minds are left in doubt by the evidence. Theoretically a similar problem is presented when the facts are tried to the judge, but in such cases it does not loom so large as in jury cases where the apportionment of the burden of persuasion may be raised on appeal, though it does not appear that the jury was left in such doubt as made the instruction applicable.

Usually the party who has the duty of pleading a fact has also the first burden of producing evidence of the fact.[3] This burden as we have seen he may satisfy and may even shift to the adversary.[4] Likewise the pleader will ordinarily be found at the close of the evidence to have this ultimate burden of persuasion.[5] The courts frequently say that this burden does not shift[6] but this statement is somewhat misleading since there is no occasion for it to shift during the course of the presentation of the evidence. The burden of persuasion simply does not come into play until the end of the proofs, when the judge charges the jury, or when in a judge-tried case he finds himself in doubt on the facts.

308. Presumptions, Permissive and Mandatory.[1]

One ventures the assertion that "presumption" is the slipperiest member of the family of legal terms, except its first cousin, "burden of proof," of whom more anon. Agreement can be secured to this extent, however: a presumption is a standardised practice, under which certain oft-recurring fact groupings are held to call for uniform treatment whenever they occur, with respect to their effect as proof to support issues. Admittedly, as we have seen, proof of one class of type-situation (e. g., delivery of a shipment in good condition to a carrier, and its delivery by the carrier at destination in a damaged state) may by a rule of practice be recognized as calling for a ruling that the producer of the proof has gone forward far enough to "get to the jury" on the inference (damage by acts of the carrier) which is desired. Every judge in every case should so rule, and he is relieved of the usual necessity of critically considering the rational permissibility of the inference. But we have also seen that in another class of fact-groupings (e. g., the facts of the mailing of a letter properly stamped and addressed offered to show receipt by the addressed) the standardized practice to be automatically applied by the judge is to rule that the proof of the particular recognized group of facts is compulsory, that is, the inference is not to be weighed by judge or jury, but if the circumstantial facts are undisputed, or if disputed are found to be true, the conclusion follows as a matter of

---

2. In the writer's view this mechanism has far more influence upon the final outcome of cases than does the burden of persuasion, which has become very largely a matter of the technique of the wording of instructions to juries. This wording may be chosen in the particular case as a handle for reversal, but will seldom have been a factor in the jury's decision. See § 322, below.

3. See § 306, above.

4. See § 306, above.

5. Reliance Life Ins. Co. v. Burgess, 112 F.2d 234, syl. 1–3 (C.C.A.Mo.1940) (citing cases); Cohen v.

Swanson Petr. Co., 133 Neb. 581, 276 N.W. 190, syl. 1 (1937) (existence of written contract sued on); Dec.Dig.Evidence, ☞91.

6. Clapper v. Lakin, 343 Mo. 710, 123 S.W.2d 27, syl. 5 (1938); Fitzsimons v. Frey, 153 Neb. 124, 43 N.W. 2d 531, syl. 7 (1950); In re Atkinson's Will, 225 N. C. 526, 35 S.E.2d 638, syl. 7 (1945) (contestant's burden to establish undue influence does not shift); Dec.Dig.Evidence, ☞91.

1. 9 Wigmore, Evidence, §§ 2490, 2491; 1 Jones, Evidence, §§ 23–28 (2d ed. rev. 1926); Thayer, Preliminary Treatise on Evidence, ch. 8 (1898); Model Code of Evidence, ch. 8.

law provided no counter-proof is offered.[2] Does a "presumption" give its beneficiary the right to the first of these rulings, the *permission* to the jury to infer, or to the second, the *compulsion* to find (in the absence of contrary proof) without weighing the inference? Very few of the decisions discuss this distinction, because very seldom does the adversary fail to produce some counter-proof so that the effect of the stark fact-groups, standing alone, seldom comes in issue. Thayer,[3] Wigmore,[4] and the Uniform Rules of Evidence [5] unite in attributing to the "presumption" the (provisionally) compulsory effect. Many judicial definitions are in accord.[6] On the other hand, many decisions which hold merely that the group of facts considered was *sufficient* to warrant the de-

sired inference, describe the result as a "presumption." In this latter sense a presumption is the same as a "prima facie case." [7] Probably the best practical treatment of the problem of nomenclature is to recognize the word "presumption" as a collective term embracing both varieties of procedural rules, but to distinguish the two as permissive presumptions, and mandatory presumptions.[8] The recognition of permissive presumptions as true presumptions is a departure from the language of the text-books, but accords with much actual judicial usage, and signalizes that the permissive presumption, such as the rule of *res ipsa loquitur,* is just as much a rule of law about the effect of proof as is the mandatory presumption. The use of presumptions as a collective term to include

2. Bragaw v. Supreme Lodge, 124 N.C. 154, 32 S.E. 544 (1899) (presumption of receipt of letter duly mailed; the conflicting evidence raised a doubt only as to whether it was actually mailed. Held: a charge which left to the jury whether it was *received* was error; only the question whether it was *mailed* was for their consideration); cf. Standard Trust Co. v. Bank, 166 N.C. 112, 81 S.E. 1074 (1914). The expression "conclusive presumption" means something different. It means that when fact A is proven, fact B is to be taken as true, and the adversary is not allowed to dispute this at all. Obviously, the result is that the existence of fact B has become legally immaterial. Frequently, this is an end-result of a process of evolution. Thus, long continued possession of land, may at an earlier era if challenged have the benefit of a rebuttable presumption of a lost grant, and later by a veiled change of substantive law, the presumption becomes conclusive, that is, the long-time possession itself confers ownership. See 9 Wigmore, Evidence, § 2492; Thayer, Preliminary Treatise on Evidence, 317–319 (1898).

3. Preliminary Treatise on Evidence, pp. 317, 321, 326.

4. Evidence, sec. 2490.

5. Rule 13: "A presumption is an assumption of fact resulting from a rule of law which requires such fact to be assumed from another fact or group of facts found or otherwise established in the action."

6. Walker, J., in Cogdell v. R. R., 132 N.C. 852, 44 S.E. 618 (1903): "The Court was requested to charge that there was a presumption that the deceased had exercised care, which the Court refused to give, but charged the jury that there was an inference that due care was exercised. The presumption has a

technical force or weight, and the jury, in the absence of sufficient proof to overcome it, should find according to the presumption; but, in the case of a mere inference, there is no technical force attached to it. The jury, in the case of an inference, are at liberty to find the ultimate fact one way or the other as they may be impressed by the testimony. In the one case the law draws a conclusion from the state of the pleadings and evidence, and in the other case the jury draw it. An inference is nothing more than a permissible deduction from the evidence, while a presumption is compulsory and cannot be disregarded by the jury." In re Bauer's Estate, 79 Cal. 304, 307, 21 Pac. 759, 760 (1869): "A presumption (unless declared by law to be conclusive) may be controverted by other evidence, but unless so controverted, the jury are bound to find according to the presumption."

7. White v. Hines, 182 N.C. 275, 109 S.E. 31, 38 (1921): "In some of our decisions the expressions *res ipsa loquitur*, prima facie evidence, prima facie case, and presumption of negligence have been used as practically synonymous. As thus used, each expression signifies nothing more than evidence to be considered by the jury." Hunt v. Eure, 189 N.C. 482, 127 S.E. 593, 597 (1925): "A presumption of negligence, when establishing a prima facie case, is still only evidence of negligence for the consideration of the jury, and the burden of the issue remains on the plaintiff." See also Dudley's Adm'r v. Fid. & Dep. Co., 240 S.W.2d 76, syl. 4 (Ky.1951). In older usage permissive presumptions were sometimes termed "inferences" and "presumptions of fact."

8. Permissive and mandatory, that is, as respects its effect on the jury.

them both recognizes that they have in common the most important advantage that a presumption, however defined, could give, namely, they enable the proponent to "get to the jury."

309. Reasons for the Creation of Presumptions:[1] Classification of Particular Presumptions.[2]

The reasons for the recognition of presumptions by the courts are various. First and foremost is the reason of probability. In certain recurring fact-situations it becomes accepted by the judges that the proof of fact A renders the inference of the existence of fact B so probable that it is sensible and time-saving to assume the truth of fact B until the adversary disproves it. A second ground is procedural convenience. In a criminal case it is convenient to require the accused, if he wishes to raise the question of sanity, to produce evidence of his insanity. This saves the state the fruitless trouble of proving sanity in the great number of cases where the question will not be raised. The vehicle for accomplishing this saving of time is the presumption of sanity.[3] A third consideration is that of fairness in allocating the burden of first producing evidence upon the party who has superior means of access to the proof. The stock example is the presumption that as between connecting carriers the damage occurred on the line of the last carrier.[4] Fourth, notions, usually implicit rather than expressed, of social and economic policy incline the courts to favor one contention by giving it the benefit of a presumption, and correspondingly handicapping the disfavored adversary. A classic instance is the presumption of ownership from possession,[5] which tends to favor the prior possessor and to make for the stability of estates. In addition we shall see from the examples which follow that most presumptions are based not on one of these grounds alone, but upon a combination of several of them.

It would be inappropriate to attempt to list the hundreds of recognized presumptions, but they are such an important part of the tactical resources of the lawyer who is planning the task of making out a prima facie case or defense that it is worthwhile to name and attempt to classify some of the presumptions most frequently employed. The classifications, according to whether permissive or mandatory, and according to reasons, are based in most instances merely on the opinion of the writer, as the courts seldom have occasion to make such characterizations.

Official actions by public officers, including judicial proceedings, are presumed to have been regularly and legally performed.[6] Probably mandatory.[7] Reason: probability.

1. See Morgan, Presumptions, 12 Wash.L.Rev. 255, 257 (1937); Morgan and Maguire, Cases on Evidence, 76 (3d ed. 1951); Chafee, The Progress of the Law 1919–1921, 35 Harv.L.Rev. 302, 310 (1922).

2. Particular presumptions are listed in 9 Wigmore, Evidence, §§ 2499–2540; 1 Jones, Evidence, ch. 2 (2d ed. rev. 1926); 31 C.J.S.Evidence, §§ 120–157; Dec.Dig.Evidence, ⊂⇒55–83.

3. Davis v. United States, 160 U.S. 469, 16 Sup.Ct. 353, syl. 2, 40 L.Ed. 499 (1895); 9 Wigmore, Evidence, § 2501(1).

4. When the shipper proves that he delivered the goods to the first carrier in good condition and received them from the last in bad condition, the damage is presumed to have occurred on the line of the last carrier. Chicago & N. W. Ry. Co. v. C. C. Whitnack Prod. Co., 258 U.S. 369, 42 Sup.Ct. 328, syl. 2,

McCormick Evidence HB—41

3 (1922) (not changed by the Carmack Amendment making initial carrier liable); 13 C.J.S. 950, note 35.

5. Oklahoma R. Co. v. Guthrie, 175 Okl. 40, 52 P.2d 18, 23 (1935) (railway premises); Guyer v. Snyder, 133 Md. 19, 104 Atl. 116, syl. 3 (1918) (personal property); 9 Wigmore, Evidence, § 2515.

6. Thompson v. Consol. Gas Utilities Corp., 300 U.S. 55, 57 Sup.Ct. 364, syl. 3, 81 L.Ed. 510 (1937) (regulations of administrative board, purporting to be made under delegated authority, presumed to be supported by justifying facts); Lewis v. City of South Hutchinson, 162 Kan. 104, 174 P.2d 51, syl. 15, 16 (1946) (mayor and city council, action in respect to bond issue); Rains v. Mercantile N. Bank, 144 Tex. 490, 191 S.W.2d 850, syl. 2 (1946) (officers issuing county warrants); State v. Burke, 253 Wis. 240, 33

7. See Note 7 on following Page.

When a condition, ordinarily continuing, is shown to exist it is presumed to continue as long as is usual for such a condition.[8] This notion is applied frequently to the continuance of the life of a person,[9] insanity,[10] ownership,[11] possession,[12] agency,[13] and residence.[14] Usually permissive. Reason: probability.

A letter properly addressed, stamped and mailed is presumed to have been duly delivered to the addressee.[15] Mandatory. Reason: probability.

When the plaintiff has been injured by the negligent operation of a vehicle, then upon the proof of further facts he has the benefit of a presumption that the person driving the vehicle (not being the defendant himself) was doing so in the scope of his employment, and in the course of the business of the defendant.[16] In the majority of states the plaintiff secures the advantage of this presumption by proof that the defendant was the owner.[17] In a substantial minority, however, the plaintiff to gain the benefit of the presumption must not only prove ownership, but also that the driver is regularly employed by the defendant.[18] Probably most courts would treat this

---

7. City of Montpelier v. Town of Calais, 114 Vt. 5, 39 A.2d 350, syl. 17 (1944).

8. Kelly v. Laclede Real Estate & Inv. Co., 348 Mo. 407, 155 S.W.2d 90, syl. 1, 138 A.L.R. 1065 (1941); 9 Wigmore, Evidence, §§ 2530, 2531; Dec.Dig.Evidence, ⊂‒67.

9. Allen v. Mazurowski, 317 Mass. 218, 57 N.E.2d 544, syl. 2 (1944) (intestate's widow and children, heard from within three years, presumed to be still living though they were last heard from in enemy-held Poland).

10. Turley v. Turley, 374 Ill. 571, 30 N.E.2d 64, syl. 1 (1940) (when insanity of a continuing rather than temporary kind shown—here "manic depressive phychosis"—presumed to continue).

11. Collins v. Streitz, 95 F.2d 430, syl. 10 (C.C.A. Ariz., 1938) (land).

12. Tesar v. Bartels, 149 Neb. 889, 32 N.W.2d 911, syl. 3, 4 (1948) (replevin: defendant's possession presumed to continue until date of action). Compare, however, Mr. Justice Jackson's characterization of this presumption as a mere inference allowable or not according to the recency of the proved possession and other surrounding circumstances. Maggio v. Zeitz, 333 U.S. 56, 65, 66, 68 Sup.Ct. 401, 92 L.Ed. 476 (1948), comments, 61 Harv.L.Rev. 1240, 46 Mich. L.Rev. 933, 34 Va.L.Rev. 707.

13. Gudger v. Manton, 21 Cal.2d 537, 134 P.2d 217, 226 syl. 22 (1943).

14. Price v. Price, 156 Pa. 617, 626, 27 Atl. 291, syl. 1 (1893).

15. Franklin Life Insurance Co. v. Brantley, 231 Ala. 554, 165 So. 834, syl. 4 (1936); 9 Wigmore, Evidence, § 2519; Dec.Dig.Evidence, ⊂‒71.

16. 9 Wigmore, Evidence, § 2510a.

17. See, e. g., Peoples v. Seamon, 249 Ala. 284, 31 So.2d 88, 93, syl. 8 (1940); White v. Keller, 188 Ore. 378, 215 P.2d 986, 989, syl. 5 (1950); Van Court v. Lodge Cab Co., 198 Wash. 530, 89 P.2d 206, 211, syl. 2 (1939); Hollen v. Reynolds, 123 W.Va. 360, 15 S.E. 2d 163, syl. 1 (1941); Laurent v. Plain, 229 Wis. 75, 281 N.W. 660, syl. 1 (1938), and see decisions collected. Dec.Dig. Automobiles, ⊂‒242(5), 242(6), d. Notes, 42 A.L.R. 900, 74 A.L.R. 951, 96 A.L.R. 635, 1953 U.Ill.L.F. 121. Similar rules have been embodied in statutes, see, e. g., Fla.F.S.A. 51.12; Conn.Gen. St.1949, § 7905, held constitutional in Koops v. Gregg, 130 Conn. 185, 32 A.2d 653, syl. 4 (1943). Proof, in turn, that a business vehicle bore defendant's name raises a "presumption" of ownership, and hence of agency and scope of employment, under this view. Murphy v. Wolverine Express, 155 Pa.Super. 125, 38 A.2d 511, syl. 2 (1944); Cappello v. Aero Mayflower Transit Co., 116 Vt. 64, 68 A.2d 913, syl. 4 (1949), noted 30 B.U.L.Rev. 284. So also as to proof that the car bore a license number issued to defendant. Frew v. Barto, 345 Pa. 217, 26 A.2d 905, syl. 1 (1942).

It is sometimes said that the proof that the car bore defendant's name is a mere "inference," i. e., a permissive presumption, of ownership, and consequently that if the defendant offers no evidence, the question of ownership goes to the jury. Walker v. Johnston, 236 S.W.2d 534 (Tex.Civ.App.1951). As forcibly argued, "the sense of fair play rebels against allowing the defendant to withhold his information and try his luck with the jury. Rather, it requires that the defendant be forced to come forward to produce his evidence under the threat of a peremptory charge." Golden, Note, 30 Tex.L.Rev. 127, 129.

18. Manion v. Waybright, 59 Idaho 643, 86 P.2d 181, syl. 2 (1938) ("operated by one in the general employ of defendant"); Brooks v. Bale, 198 Ark. 17, 127 S.W.2d 135, syl. 2 (1939); Galloway Motor Co.

N.W.2d 242, syl. 2 (1948) (habeas corpus after judgment of conviction; judge presumed to have informed accused of right to counsel); 9 Wigmore, Evidence, § 2534; Dec.Dig.Evidence, ⊂‒82, 83.

presumption as mandatory.[19] Reasons: Probability, Fairness in the light of defendant's superior access to the evidence, and the Social Policy of promoting safety by widening the responsibility in border-line cases of owners for injuries caused by their vehicles.[20]

When a violent death is shown to have occurred and the evidence is not controlling as to whether it was due to suicide or accident, there is a presumption against suicide.[21] Probably permissive. Reasons: The general probability in case of a death unexplained, which flows from the human revulsion against suicide, and, probably, a social policy which inclines in case of doubt toward the

fruition rather than the frustration of plans for family protection through life insurance.

A rule of law precipitated from customary judicial practice in submitting cases to juries is known by the phrase, *res ipsa loquitur*— "the situation speaks for itself." This rule is to the effect that when the plaintiff in a negligence case proves that he has been injured (a) by a casualty of a sort which usually does not occur in the absence of negligence, (b) by an instrumentality within the defendant's exclusive control, (c) under circumstances indicating that it was not caused by any voluntary act or neglect of the plaintiff, an inference that it was due to the defendant's negligence is allowable.[22] In nearly all jurisdic-

v. Huffman's Adm'r, 281 Ky. 841, 137 S.W.2d 379, syl. 4 (1940); Collins v. Leahey, 347 Mo. 133, 146 S. W.2d 609, syl. 3 (1941); Claxton v. Page, 190 Okl. 422, 124 P.2d 977, syl. 3 (1942); Broaddus v. Long, 135 Tex. 353, 138 S.W.2d 1057, syl. 1, 2 (1940); Dec. Dig.Automobiles, ☞242(6), f; Notes, 96 A.L.R. 641, 74 A.L.R. 962, 42 A.L.R. 915.

North Carolina seems to espouse an even more restrictive view, requiring the plaintiff to produce specific evidence that the driver was acting in the scope of employment on the particular occasion. Carter v. Thurston Motor Lines, 227 N.C. 193, 41 S.E.2d 586, syl. 2, 5 (1947) (three judges dissenting), noted adversely, Harkey, 30 N.C.L.Rev. 491.

19. A few courts speak of an "inference" or of "prima facie" evidence which merely makes a case for the jury. See, e. g., Montgomery v. Hutchins, 118 F.2d 661, 665, syl. 4 (C.C.A.Calif.1941) (jury may but not compelled to draw inference); Bunnell v. Parelius, 166 Ore. 174, 111 P.2d 88, 90, syl. 4, 5 (1941) (inference not a presumption). But usually it is described as a "presumption" which places on the adversary the duty of going forward. Martin v. Burgess, 82 F.2d 321, syl. 1 (C.C.A.Ala.1936); Dep't of Water & Power v. Anderson, 95 F.2d 577, 584, syl. 21 (C.C.A.Nev.1938) (if defendant introduces no evidence inference conclusively presumed to be true); Amento v. Mortensen, 130 Conn. 682, 37 A.2d 231, syl. 2 (1944) (statutory presumption conclusive if not rebutted); Galloway Motor Co. v. Huffman's Adm'r, 281 Ky. 841, 137 S.W.2d 379, syl. 3 (1940); Broaddus v. Long, 135 Tex. 353, 138 S.W.2d 1057, syl. 1, 2 (1940); Dec.Dig.Automobiles, ☞242(6), d, f. Where the presumption is based on proof of ownership alone, the argument that the presumption should be mandatory is persuasive, see note 17, above. But when both ownership and regular employment are required to be proved, the argument

that it should be conclusive in the absence of substantial opposing evidence seems irresistible.

20. This policy underlies those statutes which take the next step beyond our presumption, and make the owner liable for negligent operation by a member of his family, or anyone, using the vehicle with his consent. See, e. g., Calif. Sec. 402(a), Vehicle Code, St.1937, p. 2353; Michigan, Comp.Laws 1948, § 256.29, and New York Consol.Laws, Book 62–A, Vehicle and Traffic Law, art. 5, § 59. The kinship in policy between these statutes and the common law presumptions is pointed out by Brandeis, J., in Young v. Masci, 289 U.S. 253, 259, 53 Sup.Ct. 599, 77 L.Ed. 1158, 88 A.L.R. 170 (1933) (sustaining validity of New York statute as applied to an accident in New York involving a car lent by the owner in New Jersey).

21. Grola v. Industrial Comm., 388 Ill. 114, 57 N.E. 2d 373, syl. 4 (1944); Wellisch v. John Hancock Mut. Life Ins. Co., 293 N.Y. 178, 56 N.E.2d 540, syl. 2, 3 (1944); 31 C.J.S., Evidence, § 135b; Dec.Dig. Evidence ☞59, 60e.

This presumption not being based on specific facts proven, but constituting rather a make-weight consideration where the circumstantial inferences are in doubt, can seemingly have little practical usefulness except as an admonition to the jury in the instructions. The practice of instructing on the presumption is approved in Wellisch v. John Hancock Mut. Life Ins. Co., supra, and in Wyckoff v. Mut. Life Ins. Co., 173 Ore. 592, 147 P.2d 227 (1944). Contra: Ryan v. Metropolitan Life Ins. Co., 206 Minn. 562, 289 N.W. 557 (1939).

22. It has been applied in a suit by a passenger injured when a bus skidded and overturned. Lachman v. Pennsylvania Greyhound Lines, 160 F.2d 496, syl. 4 (C.C.A.4, 1947). To an airplane crash. Bratt

tions its effect is merely permissive,[23] and under the classification adopted in this chapter it would thus be classed as a permissive presumption. Reasons: (1) probability and (2) fairness in that defendant will usually have superior access to the proof of causative circumstances.

v. Western Air Lines, 169 F.2d 214, syl. 1, 2 (C.C.A. 10, 1948). To death of a patient in a minor operation under anaesthetic. Cavero v. Franklin Gen. Ben. Soc., 36 Cal.2d 301, 223 P.2d 471, syl. 5–7 (1950) (Traynor and Edmonds, JJ., dissenting). To injury caused when automobile parked downhill left curb and struck plaintiff. Lewis v. Wolk, 312 Ky. 536, 228 S.W.2d 432, syl. 3 (1950). To the derailment of a train. Fink v. New York Central R. Co., 144 Oh.St. 1, 56 N.E.2d 456, syl. 7 (1944).

The statement of the doctrine in the text is based on Prosser, Torts, § 43 (1941). See also 9 Wigmore, Evidence, § 2509(A) which discusses the problems rather summarily but has a valuable collection of illustrative decisions, and see Dec.Dig., Negligence, ⬅121(2) (3). Two recent cases in our highest court raise questions as to requirements (b) and (c) in the text. Johnson v. United States, 333 U.S. 46, 68 Sup. Ct. 391, syl. 1, 3–6, 92 L.Ed. 468 (1948) (fellow-servant with whom plaintiff was working at coiling rope, dropped block of rope on plaintiff), Notes, 34 Iowa L.Rev. 137, 27 Tex.L.Rev. 100; Jesionowski v. Boston & M. R. Co., 329 U.S. 452, 67 Sup.Ct. 401, syl. 1–4, 91 L.Ed. 416 (1947) (brakeman killed while working on switch at which cars were derailed, where derailment could have been caused by the fault of deceased brakeman). Prosser, supra, cites the periodical literature. Subsequent references: Shain, Res Ipsa Loquitur, 17 So.Cal.L.Rev. 187 (1944); McLarty, Res Ipsa in Airline Passenger Litigation, 35 Va.L.Rev. 55 (1951); Prosser, Res Ipsa in California, 37 Calif.L.Rev. 183, Shife, The Iowa Doctrine, 35 Iowa L.Rev. 393 (1950); S. T. Morris, Res Ipsa in Texas, 26 Tex. 257, 761 (1948).

23. Sweeney v. Erving, 228 U.S. 233, 33 Sup.Ct. 416, 418, 57 L.Ed. 815 (1913) (injury to patient from x-ray machine; held, no error to refuse charge that placed burden of persuasion on defendant; "res ipsa loquitur means that the facts of the occurrence warrant the inference, not that they compel such an inference"); Levine v. Union & New Haven Trust Co., 127 Conn. 435, 17 A.2d 500, syl. 2 (1941); Marsh v. Henriksen, 213 Minn. 500, 7 N.W.2d 387, syl. 2 (1943); Prosser, The Procedural Effect of Res Ipsa, 20 Minn.L.Rev. 241 (1936).

Even under this view as to the normal procedural effect of the doctrine, it is recognized that the circumstances in the particular case may make the inference irresistible, and entitle the plaintiff to a directed verdict when his evidence is not refuted by

When a bailor proves delivery of the property to the bailee in good condition and return in a damaged state, or a failure to return after due demand, a presumption arises that the damage or loss was due to the negligence or fault of the bailee.[24] This presump-

counter-proof. Alabama & V. Ry. Co. v. Groome, 97 Miss. 201, 52 So. 703, 704, syl. 6 (1910); Prosser, Torts, 304 (1941).

It has been said that a minority of jurisdictions go further and attribute generally to the res ipsa maxim the effect of a mandatory presumption, entitling the plaintiff to an instructed verdict on the issue, if the inference is unrebutted. Prosser, Torts, 304 (1941), Notes, 53 A.L.R. 1500, 1504. It is believed, however, that the cases cited, in using the term "presumption", intend it in the sense of a permissive presumption, (see Note, 167 A.L.R. 663) and in most instances in which they say it is conclusive if not rebutted such intimations are dicta since that situation was not actually before them. See, e. g., Chicago City Ry. Co. v. Eick, 111 Ill.App. 452, 454 (1903), Lewis v. Wolk, 312 Ky. 536, 228 S. W.2d 432, syl. 4 (1950), and Brown v. Consol. Light, Power & Ice Co., 137 Mo.App. 718, 109 S.W. 1032, 1036 (1909). Cases like Moglia v. Nassau Elec. Ry. Co., 127 App.D.C. 243, 111 N.Y.S. 70 (1908), where the trial judge actually directed a verdict for plaintiff and was sustained, are believed to be rare. Prosser argues that the mandatory effect should be accorded only in cases such as those of carriers and bailees where policy justifies imposing special responsibility. Prosser, Torts, 306 (1941).

Whether in the instructions the burden of persuasion in a res ipsa case may be cast on defendant is discussed in § 317, herein.

24. 9 Wigmore, Evidence, § 2508; Notes, Hart, 4 Baylor L.Rev. 327 (1952), 7 Oh.St.L.J. 250 (1941), 14 Temp.L.Q. 261 (1940); 8 C.J.S., Bailments, § 50, Dec.Dig., Bailment, ⬅31(1).

The presumption casts the burden on the bailee of proceeding with evidence (a) of the cause of the loss, e. g., fire, theft, damage from collision. Some cases hold that, if the facts thus disclosed are consistent with due care, e. g., a fire of unknown origin, the bailee has satisfied the burden. Commercial Molasses Corp. v. New York Tank Barge Corp., 314 U.S. 104, 62 Sup.Ct. 156, syl. 13, 14, 86 L.Ed. 89 (1941) (barge sinks in calm water); Exporters' & Traders Compress & Warehouse Co. v. Schulze, 265 S.W. 133, syl. 3 (Tex.Comm.App.1924) (fire); Goodwin v. Georgian Hotel Co., 197 Wash. 173, 84 P.2d 681, syl. 6 (1938). But other cases, more soundly it seems, require the bailee to go further and give evidence of facts from which the jury could reasonably find that the loss was not caused by the bailee's negli-

tion is mandatory.[25] Reason: fairness in the light of the superior access of the bailee to the evidence of the facts surrounding the loss.

Proof that a person has disappeared from his home and has absented himself therefrom for at least seven years and that during this time those who would be expected to hear from him have received no tidings from him and after diligent inquiry have been unable to find his whereabouts, raises a presumption that he died at some time during the seven year period.[26] The rule though not very ancient [27] is already antiquated.[28] Its probable effect is that of a mandatory presump-

gence. Downey v. Martin Aircraft Service, 96 Cal. App.2d 94, 214 P.2d 581, syl. 2 (1950) (fire); Gen. Exch. Ins. Corp. v. Service Parking Grounds, 254 Mich. 1, 235 N.W. 898, syl. 2 (1931) (damage to car while stolen). It is generally held that the plaintiff carries throughout the burden of persuasion as to negligence. Commercial Molasses Corp. v. New York Tank Barge Corp., supra, and cases cited in 8 C.J.S. 344, note 90. Nevertheless, it is apparent that this fission of burden of proof into the two burdens is here especially hard to maintain consistently. A burden phrased in terms of explaining or exculpating is difficult to distinguish from a burden of persuading. Accordingly, a minority of cases frankly place the burden of persuasion upon the bailee to show that there was no causative negligence. This practice has simplicity and expediency to commend it. The risk of failure of convincing proof is thus placed on the bailee. Agricultural Ins. Co. v. Constantine, 56 N.E.2d 687, syl. 8 (Oh. App.1944), affirmed 144 Oh.St. 275, 58 N.E.2d 658; Brown, Personal Property, 333, 334 (1936). It has been suggested that a similar imposition of this burden may be accomplished by suing, not in tort, but upon the bailment contract, in which case loss without negligence would be an affirmative defence. U Drive & Tour v. System Auto Parks, 28 Cal.App. 2d 782, 71 P.2d 354, syl. 3 (1937); Smith v. Noe, 159 Tenn. 498, 19 S.W.2d 246, syl. 10 (1929); Notes, 14 Temp.L.Q. 261, 262, note 6, 151 A.L.R. 730. And occasionally a statute allocates the burden of persuasion on the bailee. See, e. g., Mich.Comp.Laws 1948, § 443.8 (". . . the burden shall be upon the warehouseman to establish the existence of a lawful excuse . . ."), construed in Price & Pierce v. Jarka Great Lakes Corp., 37 F.Supp. 939, syl. 2, 3 (W.D.Mich.1941) (fire).

25. Bowman v. Vandiver, 243 Ky. 139, 47 S.W.2d 947, 948 (1932) (plaintiff entitled to instructed verdict in absence of rebutting proof by defendant); Hogan v. O'Brien, 212 App.D. 193, 208 N.Y.S. 477, syl. 3 (1925) ("in default of such proof, the bailor is entitled, as a matter of law to a verdict in his favor"—dictum); Trammell v. Whitlock, 150 Tex. 500, 242 S.W.2d 157, syl. 6 (1951) (where bailee of trailer gives explanation of damage to trailer inadequate to exculpate him of negligence, bailor entitled to instructed verdict on that issue).

26. Green v. Royal Neighbors, 146 Kan. 571, 73 P.2d 1, syl. 3, 114 A.L.R. 244 (1937); Donea v. Massachu-

setts Mut. Life Ins. Co., 220 Minn. 204, 19 N.W.2d 377, syl. 1–15 (1945); 9 Wigmore, Evidence, § 2531a; 25 C.J.S., Death, § 6; Dec.Dig., Death, ⊙2. Some jurisdictions dispense with the requirement of search and inquiry. See, e. g., Banks v. Metropolitan, 142 Neb. 823, 8 N.W.2d 185, syl. 2 (1943) (applying R.S.1943, § 30–1901).

It is often stated, moreover, as if it were one of the required facts of the presumption that the absence must be "unexplained." Butler v. Mutual Life Ins. Co., 225 N.Y. 197, 121 N.E. 758, syl. 2 (1919); 31 C.J. S. 1057, note 39. It is believed, however, that this is misleading. The more reasonable view, it seems, is not that the proponent of the presumption must show that the absence is "unexplained," but that explanatory circumstances (e. g., that the person was a fugitive from justice) whether brought out by the proponent or the opponent, are to be considered by the jury in rebuttal of the presumption. See, e. g., Shaw v. Prudential Ins. Co., 158 Wash. 43, 290 Pac. 694 (1930); Ewing v. Metropolitan Life Ins. Co., 191 Wis. 299, 210 N.W. 819 (1926).

Under the majority view, there is no presumption as to the time of death within the seven years. Mutual Life Ins. Co. of N. Y. v. Hamilton, 143 F.2d 726, syl. 2 (C.C.A.Fla.1944); Ferril v. Kansas City Life Ins. Co., 345 Mo. 777, 137 S.W.2d 577, syl. 2 (1940). But a minority, in aid of the settlement of controversies over succession, recognize a presumption that the death occurred at the end of the seven years. In re Chicago & N. W. Ry. Co., 138 F.2d 753, syl. 1–4 (C.C.A.Ill.1943) (presumption of continuance of life controls for period up to the end of seven years, when person is first accounted for). Edwards v. Equitable Life Assur. Soc., 296 Ky. 448, 177 S.W.2d 574, syl. 3 (1944). But under either view the circumstances of the disappearance may be sufficient evidence that the death occurred at or about the time of disappearance. Hefford v. Metropolitan Life Ins. Co., 173 Ore. 353, 363, 144 P.2d 695 (1944), noted 43 Mich.L.Rev. 217.

Interesting practical questions are discussed in Note, Cox, The Presumption of Death as Affecting the Statute of Limitations and the Non-Payment of Premiums, 14 Wash.L.Rev. 319, 1939. See also as to limitations, Glassman, Note, 20 B.U.L.Rev. 148 (1940).

27. Thayer traces it to an English case of 1804. Doe d. George v. Jesson, 6 East 80, 102 Eng.Rep. 1217.

28. See Note 28 on following page.

tion.[29] Reasons: (1) probability, and (2) the social policy of enforcing family security provisions such as life insurance, and of settling estates.[30]

Proof that a child was born to a woman during the time when she was married creates the presumption that the offspring is the legitimate child of the husband.[31] Despite the controversy over whether presumptions generally shift the burden of persuasion upon the opponent,[32] it is universally agreed that in the case of this presumption, the adversary contending for illegitimacy does have the burden.[33] This burden, moreover, is usually measured not by the normal standard for civil cases of preponderance of the evidence,[34] but rather by the requirement of clear, convincing, and satisfactory proof, as most courts say,[35] or even by the criminal

But the period of seven years seems to derive from the Bigamy Act of 1604 and from a statute of 1667 which provided "in the case of estates and leases depending upon the life of a person who should go beyond the seas, or otherwise absent himself within the kingdom for seven years, that where the lessor or reversioner should bring an action to recover the estate, the person thus absenting himself should 'be accounted as naturally dead,' if there should be no 'sufficient and evident proof of the life,' and that the judge should 'direct the jury to give their verdict as if the person . . . were dead.' " Preliminary Treatise on Evidence, 319–324 (1898).

28. As Wigmore points out, the seven year period is too long. It was fixed in a time when communication and transportation were infinitely slower than now. Again, it is unwise to apply any single arbitrary rule as the measure of different problems and situations. He advocates the adoption of the Uniform Absence as Evidence of Death and Absentees' Property Act, which has been enacted (with or without modifications) in Maryland, Tennessee and Wisconsin. 9 Wigmore, Evidence, § 2531b; 9 Uniform Laws Ann. 5 (1951).

29. Though the question can seldom arise as to the judge's function when there is no rebutting evidence—since there almost always is—the judges talk in terms of a presumption which is conclusive in the absence of rebutting evidence. See Meyer v. Madreperla, 68 N.J.L. 258, 53 Atl. 477, 479, syl. 2 (1902); Bonanno v. Prudential Ins. Co., 62 R.I. 78, 3 A.2d 249, 250, syl. 6 (1938); Simpson v. Simpson, 162 Va. 621, 175 S.E. 320, syl. 11, 12, 94 A.L.R. 909 (1934); 25 C.J.S. 1063, note 92. See also Tyrrell v. Prudential Ins. Co., 109 Vt. 6, 192 Atl. 184, 192, syl. 22, 115 A.L.R. 392 (1937). But in McLean v. A. O. U. W. Grand Lodge, 59 S.D. 17, 238 N.W. 126 (1931) it was treated as permissive.

30. See Robb v. Horsey, 169 Md. 227, 181 Atl. 348, 351 (1935).

31. Matter of Findlay, 253 N.Y. 1, 170 N.E. 471, 473 (opinion by Cardozo, C.J., tracing the history and limits of the presumption); In re Jones' Estate, 110 Vt. 438, 8 A.2d 631, 128 A.L.R. 704 (1939); 9 Wigmore, Evidence, § 2527; Notes, 33 Harv.L.Rev. 306 (1920), 23 So.Cal.L.Rev. 538 (extensive: emphasis lo-

cal), 25 Corn.L.Q. 598 (1940); 7 Am.Jur.Bastards, §§ 14–19, 43–48; Dec.Dig., Bastards, ☞2–4.

The presumption applies even when the child was conceived before, and born after, marriage. McCulloch v. McCulloch, 69 Tex. 682, 7 S.W. 593, 5 Am.St. Rep. 96 (1888). As to the interesting problems of presumptions which arise when a child is conceived while the wife is married to husband number one and is born after she married number two, see Notes, 26 Neb.L.Rev. 127 (1947), 25 Tex.L.Rev. 428 (1947).

Presumptions have often developed into rules of substantive law. Here, however, the course of evolution has been from a rule of substantive law into a rebuttable presumption. But the strictness of an older day when if the husband was not beyond the four seas, the child was conclusively assumed to be his, lingers in modified form. Thus, for example, the court in Haugen v. Swanson, 219 Minn. 123, 16 N.W.2d 900, 902 (1944) the court held that where husband and wife were living under the same roof at the time of conception, the presumption would be conclusive unless there were "proof of miscegenation, or of his impotency, or of the negative results of reliable blood tests by impartial physicians."

32. See § 317, herein.

33. See the opinion of Sturdevant, J., in In re Jones' Estate, 110 Vt. 438, 8 A.2d 631, syl. 1, 128 A.L.R. 704 (1939) recognizing this allocation of the burden of persuasion, but characterizing this apportionment of the burden as a "rule of substantive law" —an analysis that may be questioned, see §§ 317, 322, herein. Cases are collected in Note, Degree of Proof Necessary to Overcome Presumption of Legitimacy, 128 A.L.R. 713.

34. Though a few courts have used this standard. See In re Walker's Estate, 180 Cal. 478, 181 P. 792, syl. 9 (opinion by Olney, J.); Wright v. Hicks, 12 Ga. 155, 160 (1854) (antenuptial conception); Note, 128 A.L.R. 723.

35. The variations in phraseology are wide. Re Davis, 169 Okl. 133, 36 P.2d 471, syl. 1 (1934) ("strong, satisfactory and conclusive"); State ex rel. Walker v. Clark, 144 Oh.St. 305, 58 N.E.2d 773, syl. 7 (1945) ("clear and convincing"); Hale v. State,

formula, beyond a reasonable doubt.[36] In addition, as pointed out elsewhere in this work, the contender for illegitimacy is further handicapped by a rule rendering incompetent the testimony or declarations of the spouses offered to show non-access, when the purpose is to bastardize the child.[37] Manifestly, this is a mandatory presumption. Reasons: (1) social policy, to avoid the visitation upon the child of the sins of the parents caused by the social stigma of bastardy and the common law rules (now generally alleviated by statutes) as to the incapacities of the *filius nullius,* the child of no one; (2) probability.

In the tracing of titles to land there is a useful presumption of identity from name. Thus, when the same name appears in the chain of title first as grantee or heir and then as grantor, it will be presumed that it was the same person in each case.[38] The courts sometimes describe the rule in terms of "prima facie evidence," [39] sometimes in terms of a presumption,[40] but it seems that the more practical view is that it is a mandatory presumption.[41] If permissive, it seems the jury would be allowed to guess upon insufficient data. Reasons: (1) procedural convenience, enabling the court and the parties to rely upon the regularity of the apparent chain of title, until this is challenged by evidence contesting identity, and (2) the social policy of quieting claims based on the face of the record.

The presumption of innocence.[42] This phrase, taken over from continental usage, was merely a general rule that in absence of contrary facts it was to be assumed that any person's conduct upon a given occasion was lawful.[43] So stated, the assumption doubtless has a fair basis in probability. But when it came to be employed, in argument and in instructing juries, in criminal trials under the common law, it became a source of mysticism and confusion. As applied to the accused, any assumption, or "presumption" of innocence, in the popular sense of an inference based on probability, is absurd. The probability is the reverse.[44] The assumption of innocence which is reasonable in the absence

---

175 Md. 319, 2 A.2d 17, syl. 1 (1938) ("clear, satisfactory and convincing"); Note, 128 A.L.R. 718–722.

36. Taylor v. Whittier, 240 Mass. 514, 138 N.E. 6, 7 (1922); In re Jones' Estate, 110 Vt. 438, 8 A.2d 631, syl. 4, 6, 128 A.L.R. 704 (1939); Note, 128 A.L.R. 717; Wis.Laws 1947, July 10, c. 399.

37. See § 67, herein.

38. Huston v. Graves, 213 S.W. 77, syl. 1, 5 A.L.R. 423 (Mo., 1919), with note, Presumption of identity of persons from identity of names in chain of title. See also 9 Wigmore, Evidence, § 2529; Dec.Dig., Evidence, ☞55, Names, ☞14. Distinguish questions whether in a particular situation evidence of name would be admissible as evidence of identity, and whether such evidence would be sufficient, standing alone, to sustain a finding of identity. See Wigmore, cited above.

39. See cases collected in Note, 5 A.L.R. 429.

40. Note, 5 A.L.R. 431.

41. See e. g., Gitt v. Watson, 18 Mo. 274, 276 (1853) (sameness of names makes it incumbent on adversary "to show" not the same person).

42. 9 Wigmore, Evidence, § 2511, Thayer, The Presumption of Innocence in Criminal Cases, printed as Appendix B, in his Preliminary Treatise on Evidence, 551 (1898); 21 C.J.S., Crim.Law, § 581, 23 C.J.S. Crim.Law, § 1221, 31 C.J.S., Evidence, § 130, Dec.Dig., Crim.Law, ☞308, 778(3).

43. Thayer, op. cit. 552, 553.

"In the first place, the so-called presumption of innocence is not, strictly speaking, a presumption in the sense of an inference deduced from a given premise. It is more accurately an assumption which has for its purpose the placing of the burden of proof upon anyone who asserts any deviation from the socially desirable ideal of good moral conduct." Alexander, J., in Carr v. State, 192 Miss. 152, 4 So.2d 887, 888 (1941).

44. " 'Law presumes that the prisoner is innocent until he is found guilty, but it were well to wager four to one that the jury will be satisfied of his guilt. In 1883 there were 11,347 persons found guilty against 2,723 found not guilty.' Maitland, Justice and Police. Macmillan & Co., 1885." quoted, Thayer, op. cit. 562, note. In the Report of the Director of the Federal Bureau of Investigation, 1944, pp. 25, 26, a tabulation based on reports from 118 cities indicates that of those charged by the police with certain serious offenses 78.9 percent were found guilty by the courts. Percentages for particular offenses,

of contrary facts becomes quite unrealistic when we include in the picture the facts that the person has been officially charged with the crime and has been brought to trial. Nevertheless, the phrase "presumption of innocence" has been adopted by judges as a convenient introduction to the statement of the burdens upon the prosecution, first of producing evidence of the guilt of the accused and, second, of finally persuading the jury or judge of his guilt beyond a reasonable doubt.[45] But the popular meaning of presumption as an inference from probability has lent a false connotation, and defense counsel have naturally used the phrase in argument and in requests for instructions, as if it meant that there was an inherent probability that one officially charged and tried for a crime is innocent. Thus, some courts have been persuaded to charge that the presumption is "evidence," [46] and that "it remains with the accused to the end of the trial." [47] These flourishes have now been widely discredited.[48] Most courts however still insist that the phrase "presumption of innocence" must be distinctly included in the charge.[49] It is said that this insistence is justified as the charge on the presumption will convey the needed admonition that guilt should not be inferred from the indictment or from mere suspicion.[50]

---

however, ranged from 48.7 for negligent manslaughter to 81.5 for larceny. Similar results appear in 22 Unif.Crim.Rep. 53, 54(1951). The Report of the Director of the Administrative Office of the United States Courts, 1951, p. 153, shows that in the year ending June 30, 1951, the cases of 44,901 criminal defendants were terminated in the district courts. Convictions were 39,975.

45. The language of Texas, Vernon's Ann.P.C. art. 9 is representative: "Every person accused of an offense shall be presumed to be innocent until his guilt is established by legal evidence beyond a reasonable doubt."

46. This heresy was first given currency by Greenleaf in his treatise on Evidence, sec, 34 (1842) when he said: "This legal presumption of innocence is to be regarded by the jury in every case as matter of evidence, to the benefit of which the party is entitled. It was reinforced by the elaborate opinion of White, J., espousing the same view in Coffin v. United States, 156 U.S. 432, 15 Sup.Ct. 394, 401, 39 L.Ed. 481 (1896). A few courts still seem to cling to this fallacy. Williams v. State, 241 Ala. 348, 2 So.2d 423, syl. 2 (1941); Behrens v. State, 140 Neb. 671, 1 N.W.2d 289, syl. 3 (1941); 22 C.J. S. 895, note 57.

47. People v. Long, 407 Ill. 210, 95 N.E.2d 461, syl. 7 (1950); Jones v. State, 13 Tex.App. 1, syl. 2 (1882); 22 C.J.S. 896, notes 71–75.

48. Thus the "evidence" dictum in Coffin v. United States, supra n. 46, was criticized in the lecture by Thayer cited n. 42, supra, and the theory was abandoned in Agnew v. United States, 165 U.S. 36, 51, 17 Sup.Ct. 235, 41 L.Ed. 624 (1897), followed in Holt v. United States, 218 U.S. 245, 31 Sup.Ct. 2, 6, 54 L.Ed. 1021 (1910), and see to like effect the opinion of Brogden, J., in State v. Boswell, 194 N. C. 260, 139 S.E. 374, syl. 1 (1927). See also Notes, Presumption of Innocence as Evidence, 34 A.L.R.

938, 94 A.L.R. 1042. And see Tyrrell v. Prudential Ins. Co., 109 Vt. 6, 192 Atl. 184, 115 A.L.R. 392 (1937). The following notable passages show the trend:

". . . the statements that it is evidence in behalf of the accused, and that it always abides with him until the verdict is reached, are both judicial innovations, never heard of anywhere, and not found in any textbook or report until after the beginning of the nineteenth century. Such statements wholly ignore the history of the presumption. They are at variance with the reason and philosophy of it, and they involve the subject in such mysticism and inexplicable confusion that it becomes impossible of application or even comprehension." Richardson, J., in Culpepper v. State, 4 Okl.Cr. 103, 111 Pac. 679, 685 (1910).

"There seems to be no reason why this assumption, although it may be conceded that it 'enters the trial with the defendant,' should 'go throughout' the trial despite its early or complete liquidation by overwhelming proof. . . . The force of the 'presumption' as a valuable right available to the defendant is not conserved by tolerating its expression in the fantastic phrases accepted as appropriate adjuncts to trial eloquence, whence, indeed, its bombast was borrowed." Alexander, J. in Carr v. State, 192 Miss. 152, 4 So.2d 887, 888, 889 (1941).

49. A leading case is Comm. v. Madeiros, 255 Mass. 304, 151 N.E. 297, syl. 12, 47 A.L.R. 962 (1926) (refusal to instruct on presumption reversible error though judge instructed that indictment and custody were not to be taken against him and that they should not decide on suspicion). See also People v. Leavitt, 301 N.Y. 113, 92 N.E.2d 915, syl. 3 (1950) and cases collected in 21 C.J.S., Crim.Law § 1221; Dec.Dig.Crim.Law ⊕⇒778(3).

50. 9 Wigmore, Evidence, p. 407, Thayer, op.cit. 565.

It seems, however, that the standard instruction on the state's burden of proving the crime beyond a reasonable doubt amply covers these points. If not they should be covered specifically, and not by a phrase which can only suggest to a juror that there is some inherent probability that a person tried for a crime is innocent. The instruction on "presumption of innocence" should, it seems, be regarded merely as a traditional but unnecessary amplification of the instructions on the prosecution's burdens of evidence and of persuasion beyond a reasonable doubt.[51] The supposed presumption of the innocence of an accused, in fine, is not in any common usage of the term a presumption at all. It is not a presumption in the popular sense of an inference from probability, nor is it a presumption in the legal sense of a rule as to the effect of facts proven as requiring or permitting other facts to be taken as true.

The notion of a "presumption of innocence" is frequently employed in opinions in civil cases where misconduct or crime is charged[52] and in criminal cases as to alleged crimes collaterally involved. Here there is more of a backing of probability than in "presuming" the innocence of a man on trial for crime, but the cases do not make it clear whether the expression is intended to denote a legal rule of presumption permitting or requiring the inference, or a mere maxim based on human experience employed by the courts to justify or explain their conclusions from the evidence. Probably it is sometimes used in one sense, sometimes in the other. So far as it may be regarded as a presumption, it is believed that it would more often be given a permissive than a mandatory effect.[53] Reasons: probability [54] and the social policy of protecting the *status quo* from being lightly disturbed.

310. A Presumption Takes the Issue to the Jury.

The foregoing discussion of particular presumptions may leave the reader with some concern as to why the courts have left doubtful, in respect to most presumptions, whether they are permissive merely or mandatory if not rebutted. This vagueness results from the fact that in practice the need for making the distinction seldom arises, because the opponent seldom fails to come forward with rebutting evidence. From the viewpoint of the lawyer planning a case or defense, the great value of presumptions is that when he finds that facts which he can prove give him the benefit of a presumption that other facts essential to his case are true, then he knows that as to these essential inferences (e. g., death of the insured, receipt of a mailed letter, negligent maintenance of a machine) he can "get to the jury." The practice which permits the adversary to call for a preliminary ruling from the judge as to its suffi-

---

51. This realistic view is followed in at least two states. Cranford v. State, 156 Ark. 39, 245 S.W. 189, syl. 8 (1922); Johnson v. Comm., 297 Ky. 760, 181 S.W.2d 262, syl. 4 (1944); C.J.S. Crim.Law § 1221, n. 33.

52. See, e.g., British America Assur. Co. v. Bowen, 134 F.2d 356, syl. 1 (C.C.A.Okl.1943) (suit on fire insurance policy, defense arson: presumption held applicable but conclusively rebutted by contrary evidence); Cass v. Blake, 98 Colo. 381, 56 P.2d 42, syl. 1 (1936) (president's gift to corporation presumed genuine rather than fictitious and fraudulent); Berkey v. Gay, 244 N.Y. 84, 155 N.E. 58, syl. 4, 5 (1926) (parent street railway will not be presumed to intend to operate line of subsidiary in violation of penal statute, where acts equally compatible with innocence: opinion by Cardozo, J.);

and cases cited 31 C.J.S. Evidence, § 130; Dec. Dig. Evidence, 59.

53. Perhaps under varying circumstances it may be given either effect. "[The presumption of innocence] is not only a technical presumption, one 'of law,' but is also . . . a presumption 'of fact,' which means that an inference that conduct is of that sort is warranted even when not required." Lummus, J., in Moroni v. Brawders, 317 Mass. 48, 57 N.E.2d 14, 18 (1944).

54. "It has often been said that there is a 'presumption' that the conduct of a person is lawful, regular, proper, innocent, honest and in good faith, and this because most human conduct is of that sort." Lummus. J., in Moroni v. Brawders, supra.

ciency as soon as the proponent rests his case, is a rigorous one, and a presumption which will take the proponent over this hurdle is an important element of his case.

311. Value as Circumstantial Evidence of the Facts upon Which the Presumption Rests: Presumption Met by Uncontradicted Evidence Disputing the Presumed Facts.

We have seen in a previous section [1] that most presumptions have a strong footing in probability. By this we mean that the basic facts of the presumption not merely give the proponent the benefit of a rule of law permitting or requiring the assumption of certain inferred facts, but they also constitute circumstantial evidence raising a logical probative inference that such facts exist. It often happens that the adverse party, by himself or other witnesses, gives testimony denying the existence of these presumed facts. This rebuttal obviously "overcomes" the presumption in the sense that if the presumption is a mandatory one the adversary escapes the directed verdict which would follow if he were unable to produce rebutting evidence. Assume further, however, that the party resting on the presumption is unable to produce any witnesses who will directly contradict the adversary's rebutting evidence denying the presumed facts. Is the adversary entitled to a directed verdict or other form of peremptory ruling by the judge that the presumed facts do not exist? Or does the conflict between the circumstantial inferences— for the inference remains though the "presumption" has "disappeared"—and the direct testimony call for a determination by the jury?

Let us suppose that a party proves due mailing of a letter, properly addressed, bearing a return address, and that it was never returned. Not only does this create a technical, legal presumption, conclusive if contrary evidence is not adduced, that the letter was duly delivered to the addressee, but if the evidence is believed, it creates a probability which measured by experience makes the odds overwhelming in favor of due delivery. We may certainly assume that the class of letters, of which all we know is that they have been duly mailed, correctly addressed and not returned, will have been duly delivered in the ratio of one thousand delivered to one miscarried. But suppose this is not all we know. Suppose the addressee takes the stand and testifies unequivocally that he did not receive the letter. Here we have traveled outside the range of familiar current experience. We cannot generalize with confidence upon the odds against miscarriage in the group defined as cases where the sender swears to due mailing and addressing and no return, and the addressee swears to non-delivery. On the one hand, the addressee may be lying or mistaken about delivery. On the other, the sender may be lying or mistaken about the mailing; or the postal service, by remote chance, may have miscarried. The latter possibility still seems a minor factor in the equation. The testimony of the addressee that he did not receive the letter is not disputed, we assume, by any direct testimony of anyone who asserts that he did receive it. Is it for this reason to be accepted as conclusive by all reasonable men, and must the judge accordingly direct the jury to find, contrary to the presumption, that the letter was not received? Despite some early cases when mails were less regular, and others where the balancing factors were not recognized, the answer today is clear. The issue is ordinarily for the jury.[2] It seems that the need

---

1. See § 309, supra.

2. Rosenthal v. Walker, 111 U.S. 185, 4 Sup.Ct. 382, 386, 28 L.Ed. 395 (1884); American Surety Co. v. Blake, 54 Idaho 1, 27 P.2d 972, 91 A.L.R. 153, 164 (1933); Standard Trust Co. v. Commercial Nat. Bank, 166 N.C. 112, 81 S.E. 1074, syl. 2, 3 (1914) (time of delivery); Southland Life Ins. Co. v. Greenwade, 138 Tex. 450, 159 S.W.2d 854, 857, syl. 4 (1942) (Taylor, C.: "We agree . . . that a presumption as such is not evidence and that it vanished as such in view of the opposing evidence; but we do not agree that the evidentiary facts upon which

here is imperative for an instruction upon the presumption, preferably one which explains the presumption, and the probabilities on which it rests, and advises the jury that the addressee's testimony, though not directly contradicted, is not conclusive.

In another situation, now frequently recurrent, the circumstantial inference behind the presumption, and the direct testimony, again meet head-on. The plaintiff sues for injury caused by an automobile. To establish the defendant's responsibility, the plaintiff proves that the automobile was owned by the defendant, and that at the time of the injury, it was driven by an employee of the defendant. These facts are usually not controverted. They raise a presumption, and an inference from experience, that at the time of the accident, the car was being used in the course of the owner's business. But the defendant and the driver testify that the driver at the particular moment was using the car against orders and upon a private errand. If there is no direct contradiction, and no evidence of other circumstances bearing on the probable truth of the stories of the owner and driver, should the issue go to the jury? It would seem that in these circumstances reasonable

men could usually find either way. True; the regularity of chauffeurs in sticking to business is much less invariable than the regularity of the mails. The chances of deviation are greater, but even so, the odds are very heavy on regularity. Moreover, the foundation-facts of ownership and employment (unlike the letter-mailing) are easily checked, and usually admitted. In addition, the situation would be pregnant with temptation to safe and successful perjury if there were a rule that the owner's and driver's testimony, though against the grain of experience as evidenced by the presumption, must be believed. Similar problems arise with respect to the presumption of authority when based, as it is in many states, upon mere proof of ownership of the vehicle,[3] and also in connection with the statutory presumption of consent from proof that the vehicle was being used by a member of the owner's family.[4]

In all these vehicle-presumption cases, the courts have tended to test the allowability of a directed verdict for the opponent by a formula requiring that his evidence must be "undisputed, clear and convincing and not inherently improbable."[5] Results of the use

it was established, could no longer be considered by the trier of facts"); Goodwin Co. v. Schwaegler, 147 Wash. 547, 266 Pac. 177 (1928); 91 A.L.R. at 157. Contra: Grade v. Mariposa County, 132 Cal. 75, 64 Pac. 117 (1901) and see Dunn v. Goldman, 111 N.J.L. 249, 168 Atl. 299, syl. 3, 4 (1933) (presumption of genuineness of purported reply letter).

3. See, e. g., Curry v. Stevenson, 58 App.D.C. 162, 26 F.2d 534, syl. 4 (1928) (defendant entitled to directed verdict); Cruse-Crawford Mfg. Co. v. Rucker, 220 Ala. 101, 123 So. 897, syl. 2 (1929) (similar). When ownership only is relied upon, obviously the circumstantial inference of authority is obviously weaker than when the proponent shows also that the driver was in the owner's employ.

4. See, e. g., O'Dea v. Amadeo, 118 Conn. 58, 170 Atl. 486, syl. 6 (1934) (whether defendant's car operated by son, was operated under defendant's "general authority," was for jury despite denial of defendant and son, and absence of evidence from plaintiff on issue); Cebulak v. Lewis, 320 Mich. 710, 32 N.W.2d 21, 5 A.L.R.2d 186, 194 (1948) (own-

er has burden of producing clear, positive and credible proof; here for jury).

5. Pollard v. Grimes, 202 Okl. 118, 210 P.2d 778, syl. 2 (1949) (presumption from ownership and employment: defendant entitled to directed verdict) and see Nicosia v. Marangi, 13 N.J.Super. 550, 81 A.2d 20, syl. 2 (1951) (only where opponent's evidence is "contradictory or reasonably subject to contradictory interpretations," that the question is for jury: directed verdict sustained). Cases are collected in Notes, Overcoming Inferences of Driver's Agency for Owner, on Latter's Consent, 5 A.L.R.2d 196, Notes, Conclusiveness of uncontradicted testimony of interested witness opposed to presumption, 72 A.L.R. 94, Glenn, Effect of uncontradicted evidence rebutting presumption of respondeat superior in automobile accidents, 8 N.C.L.Rev. 298, 1930 (excellent discussion) and see Dec.Dig. Automobiles, ☞245(30).

Other instructive cases on vehicle presumptions faced by counter-evidence: (1) cases for directed verdict for opponent: Koops v. Gregg, 130 Conn. 185, 32 A.

of this and similar formulas seem usually to be just and reasonable, but it is suggested that the formula is somewhat one-sided in testing the matter solely upon the appraisal of the opponent's evidence. The weight, greater or less, of the circumstantial inference from the proponent's facts, should be equally recognized as a part of the equation.[6] The circumstantial force of these facts has not "vanished" on the appearance of the counter-evidence. Not only in respect to the vehicle-presumptions but as to other presumptions having more or less of a grounding in probability,[7] the question of the allowability of an instructed verdict for the opponent upon evidence not directly contradicted should be left, as the question of directing a verdict is usually left, for individualized handling by the trial judge in the exercise of his trained and responsible judgment. The prob-

lem will then be seen as one of assessing all the evidence and inferences, including the inference behind the presumption, and including the discounting effect of any interest which a witness may have, to determine whether minds could reasonably differ as to the conclusion to be reached.

312. Conflicting Presumptions: Presumption of Validity of Second Marriage.

W, asserting that she is the widow of H, the deceased, claims her share of his property, and proves that on a certain day she and H were married. The adversary then proves that three or four years before her marriage with H, the alleged widow married another man. How should the case be decided on these facts?

The problem can be formulated as a clash of conflicting presumptions. W's proof gives

---

2d 653, syl. 8, 9 (1943); Frick v. Bickel, 115 Ind. App. 114, 54 N.E.2d 436, syl. 8 (1944); Fiocco v. Carver, 234 N.Y. 219, 137 N.E. 309 (1922) (proponent's own showing fortified the rebutting evidence: opinion by Cardozo, J.); Judson v. Bee Hive Auto Service Co., 136 Or. 1, 294 Pac. 588, 297 Pac. 1050, 74 A.L.R. 944 (1931); Empire Gas & Fuel Co. v. Muegge, 135 Tex. 520, 143 S.W.2d 763 (1940), Comment, 21 Tex.L.Rev. 302–306; Bradley v. S. L. Savidge, Inc., 13 Wash.2d 28, 123 P.2d 780, syl. 6–13 (1942) (changing former Washington rule that directed verdict could not be given on testimony of interested witnesses: exhaustive collection and discussion of cases); (2) cases for jury: Standard Coffee Co. v. Trippet, 108 F.2d 161, syl. 2–4 (C.C.A. Tex.1940) (jury could disbelieve driver's story that he was making 40 mile trip to get his razor); Beach v. Richtmyer, 275 App.Div. 466, 90 N.Y.S.2d 332, syl. 3, 4 (1949); Jeffrey v. Osage Mfg. Co., 197 N.C. 724, 150 S.E. 503 (1929); McFadden v. Pennzoil Co., 336 Pa. 301, 9 A.2d 412, syl. 4 (1939) (inference from ownership carries case to jury despite owner's rebutting evidence); Davis v. Browne, 20 Wash.2d 219, 147 P.2d 263, syl. 9–12 (1944) (presumption from ownership of family purpose agency); Weismantle v. Petros, 124 W.Va. 180, 19 S.E.2d 594, syl. 7, 8 (1942).

6. See the instructive opinion of Traynor, J., in Blank v. Coffin, 20 Cal.2d 457, 126 P.2d 868, 870, 871 (1942) ("In most cases . . . the jury is free to disbelieve the evidence of the non-existence of the fact and to find that it does exist on the basis of the inference"; here, inference that employee driving employer's car after hours had em-

ployer's consent, under Sec. 402(a) of Calif.Vehicle Code, St.1937, p. 2353, rendering owner liable where driven with his consent). See Comment, McBaine, 31 Calif.L.Rev. 108.

7. Thus the problem has arisen, for example, in connection with the following presumptions (in addition to those of receipt from due mailing, and liability from ownership of a vehicle) which I should rank in a descending scale as to strength of probabilities. Payment of premium, from delivery of policy to insured. Beggs v. Metropolitan Life Insurance Co., 219 Iowa 24, 257 N.W. 445, 95 A.L.R. 863 (1934) (for jury). Presumption in death-action of due care of deceased. Reinhart v. Ore.-Wash. R. & N. Co., 174 Wash. 320, 24 P.2d 615 (1933) (for jury). Presumption of sanity of accused in criminal case. Commonwealth v. Clark, 198 N.E. 641 (Mass.1935) (for jury). Statutory presumption that statement secured from injured person within thirty days after injury was fraudulently procured. Cosgrove v. McConagle, 196 Minn. 6, 264 N.W. 134 (1935) (presumption created no issue for jury, in face of undisputed contrary credible evidence). Presumption that plaintiff in libel suit bore good reputation. Luna v. Seattle Times Co., 186 Wash. 618, 59 P.2d 753, 105 A.L.R. 932 (1936) (for jury). Many presumptions have so weak a backing of probability as to yield readily to contrary proof, see, e. g., State ex rel. Northwestern Development Corporation v. Gehrz, 230 Wis. 412, 283 N.W. 827, syl. 4–8, 1939 (presumption of continuance of situation proved to have existed); Scullin v. Cities Service Oil Co., 304 Mass. 75, 22 N.E.2d 666, syl. 12, 1939 (regularity of official action).

her the benefit of the presumption of the validity of a marriage. The adversary's proof gives rise to the general presumption of the continuance of a status or condition once proved to exist, and a specific presumption of the continuance of a marriage relationship. The presumed facts of the claimant's presumption and those of the adversary's are contradictory. How resolve the conflict?

One solution is to consider that the presumptions in this situation have disappeared and the facts upon which the respective presumptions were based shall simply be weighed as circumstances with all the other facts that may be relevant, giving no effect to the presumptions.[1] When the conflicting presumptions involved are of the same type, or when on both sides they are merely presumptions based upon probability or upon procedural convenience, this solution seems a fairly practical one.[2]

The particular presumptions involved in the case supposed at the outset, however, were not of that description. On the one hand, the presumption of the validity of a marriage is founded not only in probability, but in the strongest social policy favoring legitimacy and the stability of family inheritances and expectations.[3] On the other hand, the presumptions of continuance of lives and marriage relationships are based chiefly on probability and trial convenience, and the probability, of course, varies in accordance with the length of time for which the continuance is to be presumed in the particular case. It is this special situation of the questioned validity of a second marriage that has been the principal area in which the problem of conflicting presumptions has been discussed by the courts. They have not been willing here to follow Thayer's suggestion of disregarding both of the rival presumptions and leaving the issue to the indifferent arbitrament of a weighing of circumstantial inferences. They have often preferred to formulate the issue in terms of a conflict of presumptions and to hold that the presumption of the validity of marriage is "stronger" and should prevail.[4] This doctrine that the weightier presumption prevails should probably be available in any situation which may reasonably be theorized as one of conflicting presumptions, and where one of the presumptions is grounded in a predominant social policy. In the type-situation of the claim based on the second marriage it furnishes a suitable basis for decision in favor of the second marriage where its possible bigamous character is genuinely in doubt on all the

---

1. See Thayer, Preliminary Treatise on Evidence, 346 (1898) followed in 9 Wigmore, Evidence, § 2493; Model Code of Evidence, R. 701(3), 704(2). For a convincing exposition of the contrary view that as between conflicting presumptions the one founded on the stronger policy should prevail, see Morgan, Some Observations Concerning Presumptions, 44 Harv.L.Rev. 932, note (1931).

2. See for example City of Montpelier v. Town of Calais, 114 Vt. 5, 39 A.2d 350, syl. 20–22 (1944) where each side invoked the presumption of official regularity in respect to the acts of its own officers, and the court held that the case would be determined without regard to the presumptions.

3. State v. Rocker, 130 Iowa 239, 106 N.W. 645, 649 (1906) ("where necessary to sustain the legitimacy of children or in making disposition of property interests. . . ."). See Nixon v. Wichita Land & Cattle Co., 84 Tex. 408, 19 S.W. 560, 561 (1892), where Gaines, J. quotes the following from Bishop,

Marriage and Divorce (6th ed.) sec. 457: "It being for the highest good of the parties, of the children, and of the community that all intercourse between the sexes in form matrimonial should be such in fact, the law, when administered by enlightened judges, seizes upon all probabilities, and presses into its service all things else, which can help it in each particular case to sustain the marriage, and repel the conclusion of unlawful commerce."

4. Murchison v. Green, 128 Ga. 339, 57 S.E. 709, syl. 2, 11 L.R.A.,N.S., 702 (1907); Smith v. Fuller, 138 Iowa 91, 115 N.W. 912, syl. 2, 16 L.R.A.,N.S., (1908); Greensborough v. Underhill, 12 Vt. 604, 607 (1839); Note, 14 A.L.R.2d 42, 43; Dec.Dig. Marriage, ⊕ 40(9). So also Unif.Rules of Evidence, R. 15: "If two presumptions arise which are conflicting with each other the judge shall apply the presumption which is founded on the weightier considerations of policy and logic. If there is no such preponderance both presumptions shall be disregarded."

facts. In a jury-tried case, where such doubt on the facts exists, a directed verdict in favor of the presumption of validity could not be justified, and it seems that to give practical effect to the predominant policy it would be desirable to instruct the jury as to the prevailing presumption and to charge them that, as in the case of the presumption of legitimacy, it should control unless the opponent should persuade them to the contrary beyond a reasonable doubt.[5]

As an outgrowth of these perplexing problems of weighing the rival considerations of social policy and probability in civil controversies based on questioned marriages, most courts have now developed a wider formula which side-steps the theory of conflicting presumptions. A new presumption has evolved which embraces in its terms the basic facts of the older rival presumptions. Under this view, where a person has been shown to have been married successively to different spouses, there is a presumption that the earlier marriage was dissolved by death or divorce before the later one was contracted.[6] While of course the presumption is rebuttable, many courts place a special burden of persuasion upon the party attacking the validity of the second marriage by declaring that the presumption can only be overcome by clear, cogent and convincing evidence.[7]

313. The Validity of Statutory Presumptions.

How far the legislature, state or national, can go in creating presumptions [1] is a troublesome question, particularly in criminal cases. The urge for simplifying the task of the prosecutor in certain cases by requiring the defendant to go forward with evidence on some of the issuable facts is balanced by the fear that if we go too far in this direction we shall find some day that we have substituted an inquisitorial procedure for our traditional accusatory system.[2] Several ap-

---

5. See the argument for this result in Chafee, The Progress of the Law, 1919–1921, 35 Harv.L.Rev. 302, 315, 316 (1922).

6. J. J. Cater Furn. Co. v. Banks, 152 Fla. 377, 11 So.2d 776, syl. 1–3 (1943); Nicholas v. Idaho Power Co., 63 Idaho 675, 125 P.2d 321, syl. 5 (1942); Holman v. Holman, 288 S.W. 413, syl. 1 (Tex.Comm. App.1926) and cases collected in 9 Wigmore, Evidence, § 2506; Notes, Barron, 1 Baylor L.Rev. 203 (1948), Sprogell, 82 U.Pa.L.Rev. 508, 510–12 (1934), 14 A.L.R.2d 7; 55 C.J.S. Marriage, § 43(3); Dec.Dig. Marriage, ☞40(5, 6). It is not sufficient for the adversary to prove that the former spouse was living at the time of the later marriage. He must go further and make the difficult proof that the earlier marriage had not been dissolved by divorce. Roberts v. Roberts, 124 Fla. 116, 167 So. 808, syl. 6, 7 (1936); Nelson v. Jones, 245 Mo. 579, 151 S.W. 80, syl. 9 (1912); Holman v. Holman, supra; Parker v. American Lumber Corp., 190 Va. 181, 56 S.E.2d 214, syl. 2–6, 14 A.L.R.2d 1 (1949); Note, 14 A.L.R.2d 24.

Since the policy reasons are absent, the presumption is held inapplicable in prosecutions for bigamy. Fuquay v. State, 217 Ala. 4, 114 So. 898, 56 A.L.R. 1264 (1927) (when first spouse shown living at time of second marriage accused has burden of producing evidence first marriage dissolved by divorce); Fletcher v. State, 169 Ind. 77, 81 N.E. 1083, syl. 1 (1907); Note, 56 A.L.R. 1273.

7. Kolombatovich v. Magma Copper Co., 43 Ariz. 314, 30 P.2d 832, syl. 4, 5 (1934); Re Jubala's Estate, 40 N.M. 312, 59 P.2d 356, syl. 2 (1936); Note, 14 A.L.R. 2d 45–47; Dec.Dig., Marriage, ☞40(10, 11).

1. Among the more significant discussions are the following: Brosman, The Statutory Presumption (1930) 5 Tul.L.Rev. 17, 178 (the most comprehensive treatment); Keeton, Statutory Presumptions—Their Constitutionality and Legal Effect (1931) 10 Texas Law Review 34; Morgan, Federal Constitutional Limitations upon Presumptions Created by State Legislation, Harvard Legal Essays (1934) 323, reprinted in 2 Select Essays on Constitutional Law (1938) 1500; Rottschaeffer, Constitutional Law (1939) 798; (1934) 48 Harv.L.Rev. 102; Comment (1940) 38 Mich.L.Rev. 366.

Decisions are collected in Cen. and Dec.Dig., Const. L. ☞266; 16 C.J.S. 1183, Const.Law § 589, n. 54–59; Notes 51 A.L.R. 1139, 86 id. 179, 162 id. 477.

2. Martin, The Burden of Proof as Affected by Statutory Presumptions of Guilt (1939) 17 Can.Bar Rev. 37, 48, suggests such a misgiving. See also O'Toole, Artificial Presumptions in the Criminal Law (1937) 11 St.John's L.Rev. 167. But see Esmein, History of Continental Criminal Procedure (1913) Ch. I, § 1, which emphasizes publicity and confrontation as the essentials of the accusatory system. Neither of these features would be threatened by an expansion of the scope of presumptions.

proaches to the problem have been advocated, and various tests and formulas have been used at various times by the Supreme Court of the United States, which upon some of the most critical issues involved has the last say.

One approach is simply and directly that "the sky is the limit." This is advocated by Wigmore, whose influence in shaping the law in the field of evidence in the last generation has certainly not been less than that of the Supreme Court. He says:

> "(a) A rule of presumption is simply a rule changing one of the burdens of proof, i.e., declaring that the main fact will be inferred or assumed from some other fact until evidence to the contrary is introduced. There is not the least doubt, on principle, that the Legislature has entire control over such rules, as it has (when not infringing the Judiciary's prerogative) over all other rules of procedure in general and Evidence in particular—subject only to the limitations of the rules of Evidence expressly enshrined in the Constitution. If the Legislature can abolish the rules of disqualification of witnesses and grant the rule of discovery from an opponent, it can shift the burden of producing evidence.
>
> "Yet this elementary truth has been repeatedly questioned, and Courts have repeatedly vouchsafed an unmerited attention to the question, chiefly through a hesitation in appreciating the true nature of a presumption and a tendency to associate in some indefinite manner the notion of conclusively shutting out all evidence and that of merely shifting the duty of producing it. . . .
>
> "(b) It has occasionally been suggested that these legislative rules of presumption, or any legislative rules of Evidence, must be tested by the standard of *rationality*, and are invalid if they fall short of it. But this cannot be conceded. . . . All that the Legislature does in such an event is either to render admissible a fact which was before inadmissible, or to place the burden of producing evidence

on the opposite party. When this has been done, the jury is free to decide; or, so far as it is not, this is because the party has voluntarily failed to adduce contrary evidence. There is here nothing conclusive, nothing prohibitive. So long as the party may exercise his freedom to introduce evidence, and the jurors may exercise their freedom to weigh it rationally, no amount of irrational legislation can change the result." [3]

A second approach is the widely accepted "rational connection" test, as declared by Lurton, J., in the Turnipseed case:

> "That a legislative presumption of one fact from evidence of another may not constitute a denial of due process of law or a denial of the equal protection of the law it is only essential that there shall be some rational connection between the fact proved and the ultimate fact presumed, and that the inference of one fact from proof of another shall not be so unreasonable as to be a purely arbitrary mandate." [4]

A third approach may be termed "the greater includes the less" solution. In Ferry v. Ramsey [5] a Kansas statute was challenged. It imposed liability upon bank directors who, knowing of their bank's insolvency, assented to the reception of deposits, and further provided that proof of the bank's insolvency should be prima facie evidence of the directors' knowledge and assent. Said Holmes, J.:

> "It is said that the liability is founded by the statute upon the directors' assent to the deposit and that when this is the ground the assent cannot be proved by artificial presumptions that have no warrant from experience. But the short answer is that the statute might have made the directors person-

3. 4 Wigmore, Evidence (3d ed.1940) 724, § 1356.

4. Mobile, J. & K. C. R. R. v. Turnipseed, 219 U.S. 35, 43, 31 Sup.Ct. 136, 138, 55 L.Ed. 78 (1910).

5. Ferry v. Ramsey, 277 U.S. 88, 48 Sup.Ct. 443, 72 L.Ed. 796 (1928).

ally liable to depositors in every case, if it had been so minded, and that if it had purported to do so, whoever accepted the office would assume the risk. The statute in short imposed a liability that was less than might have been imposed, and that being so, the thing to be considered is the result reached, not the possibly inartificial or clumsy way of reaching it. If without any mention of assent or presumptions or prima facie evidence the statute had said: 'Every director of a bank shall be personally liable to depositors for every deposit accepted by the bank after it has become insolvent,' all objections would be met by the answer, 'You took the office on those terms.' The statute would be none the worse if it allowed a defence in the single case of the defendants having made an honest examination and having been led to believe that the bank was solvent." [6]

A fourth test seems to be suggested in the Henderson case,[7] though the decision is not an easy one to evaluate. It appears to gauge the validity of the presumption there involved by the effect given to it at the trial. As in the Turnipseed case, the question involved was the validity of a statute making proof of injury inflicted by the operation of railway trains the basis of a presumption of negligence. The statute in question was construed to give the presumption the effect of evidence which the jury could weigh against railroad's testimony of due care, and also to place the burden of persuasion upon the railway to show due care. Butler, J., for the court said:

"The mere fact of collision between a railway train and a vehicle at a highway grade crossing furnishes no basis for any inference as to whether the accident was caused by negligence of the railway company or of the traveler on the highway or of both or without fault of any one. . . . Appellee relies principally upon Mobile, J. & K. C. R. v. Turnipseed, 219 U.S. 35, 31 S.Ct. 136. . . . That case is essentially different from this one. Each of the state

enactments raises a presumption from the fact of injury caused by the running of locomotives or cars. The Mississippi statute created merely a temporary inference of fact that vanished upon the introduction of opposing evidence. . . . That of Georgia as construed in this case creates an inference that is given effect of evidence to be weighed against opposing testimony, and is to prevail unless such testimony is found by the jury to preponderate. The presumption raised by § 2780 is unreasonable and arbitrary, and violates the due process clause of the Fourteenth Amendment." [8]

Finally, the court has recognized another element in the equation, namely, the peculiar knowledge of the defendant of the fact presumed, and has said that this element of superior access to the proof may, according to its weight, right the balance if the "rational connection" is weak or absent altogether. In the Morrison case,[9] a California statute was weighed in this balance and found wanting. A landowner and a tenant were charged with conspiring to violate the Alien Land Law by placing the tenant, who was alleged to be a Japanese ineligible for citizenship, in the possession of land. Both were convicted, merely on proof that the tenant had gone on the land under an agreement with the landlord, by the application of a provision in the statute that upon proof of taking possession, any defendant alleged to be an ineligible alien, should have the burden to prove citizenship or eligibility thereto. In reversing the convictions, Cardozo, J., for the court said:

"What is proved must be so related to what is inferred in the case of a true presumption as to be at least a

6. 277 U.S. at 94.

7. Western & Atlantic R. R. v. Henderson, 279 U.S. 639, 49 Sup.Ct. 445, 73 L.Ed. 884 (1929).

8. 279 U.S. at 642, 643, 644.

9. Morrison v. California, 291 U.S. 82, 54 Sup.Ct. 281, 78 L.Ed. 664 (1934).

warning signal according to the teachings of experience. . . . There are, indeed, 'presumptions that are not evidence in a proper sense but simply regulations of the burden of proof.' . . . Even so, the occasions that justify regulations of the one order have a kinship, if nothing more, to those that justify the others. For a transfer of the burden, experience must teach that the evidence held to be inculpatory has at least a sinister significance, . . . or, if this at times be lacking, there must be in any event a manifest disparity in convenience of proof and opportunity for knowledge, as, for instance, where a general prohibition is applicable to every one who is unable to bring himself within the range of an exception. Greenleaf, Evidence, vol. 1 § 79. The list is not exhaustive. Other instances may have arisen or may develop in the future where the balance of convenience can be redressed without oppression to the defendant through the same procedural expedient." [10]

With this array of available theories developed in its previous experience, the court faced the task of passing on the validity of a presumption contained in the Federal Firearms Act.[11] The statute is one of unusual consequence in the repression of crime and the presumption seems to have been considered a material aid to its administration. The Act makes it "unlawful for any person who has been convicted of a crime of violence to receive any firearm . . . which has been shipped . . . in interstate . . . commerce," and further provides that "the possession of a firearm . . . by any such person shall be presumptive evidence that such firearm was . . . received . . . by such person in violation of this Act." [12] It was conceded that the Act penalized only the direct receipt by the offender of the firearms in interstate commerce, and not a subsequent acquisition after the article had been transported interstate. The Act became effective June 30, 1938.

Two defendants, Tot and Delia, were separately convicted under the Act. As to the former, the Government proved possession on September 20, 1938, of a nineteen-year-old revolver. As to the latter, possession was proved on September 5, 1941, of a twenty-year-old pistol. Both were manufactured in other states than the state where possession was shown. In each instance the defendant took the stand. Tot testified that he bought his pistol before the Act became effective and Delia swore that he picked up the revolver found in his possession, when it was dropped by a person who attacked him—an intrastate acquisition. The Government produced no testimony in either case (beyond the "presumptive evidence") tending to show that defendant received the firearm in interstate commerce.

A way was open, it seems clear, to set aside the convictions without deciding the constitutional question. If the presumption be given no greater effect than that attributed to it by Thayer, Wigmore, and many later decisions of the court,[13] namely, that of casting the burden on the defendant of producing evidence to the contrary that a jury *could* believe, then the defendants fully sustained their burden. Having done so, they were no longer faced with the presumption, and the Government was obliged to produce evidence of the fact of interstate receipt after the effective date of the Act, failing which, the defendants were entitled to directed verdicts.

Nevertheless, the court ignored this ground, which was fully discussed in the court below,[14] and turned the decision solely

10.   291 U.S. at 90, 91.

11.   Tot v. United States: United States v. Delia, 319 U.S. 463, 63 Sup.Ct. 1241, 87 L.Ed. 1519 (1943).

12.   52 Stat. 1252 (1938), 15 U.S.C.A. § 900 (1941).

13.   See New York Life Insurance Co. v. Gamer, 303 U.S. 161, 170, 58 Sup.Ct. 500, 502, 503, 82 L.Ed. 726 (1938) and authorities cited therein.

14.   United States v. Tot, 131 F.2d 261, 267, 268 (C.C.A.3d, 1942).

on the invalidity of the statutory presumption. Speaking through Roberts, J., it said:

> "Under our decisions, a statutory presumption cannot be sustained if there be no rational connection between the fact proved and the ultimate fact presumed, if the inference of the one from proof of the other is arbitrary because of lack of connection between the two in common experience. This is not to say that a valid presumption may not be created upon a view of relation broader than that a jury might take in a specific case. But where the inference is so strained as not to have a reasonable relation to the circumstances of life as we know them it is not competent for the legislature to create it as a rule governing the procedure of courts.
>
> "The Government seeks to support the presumption by a showing that, in most states, laws forbid the acquisition of firearms without a record of the transaction or require registration of ownership. From these circumstances it is argued that mere possession tends strongly to indicate that acquisition must have been in an interstate transaction. But we think the conclusion does not rationally follow. Aside from the fact that a number of states have no such laws, there is no presumption that a firearm must have been lawfully acquired or that it was not transferred interstate prior to the adoption of state

regulation. Even less basis exists for the inference from mere possession that acquisition occurred subsequent to the effective date of the statute—July 30, 1938. . . . It is not too much to say that the presumptions created by the law are violent, and inconsistent with any argument drawn from experience." [15]

Thus, the opinion dismisses the alternative tests of the earlier cases, and sets up "rational connection" as the sole criterion of validity. The Government had urged that the "greater includes the less" theory of Holmes, J., in Ferry v. Ramsey [16] was applicable. This contention was based on the bold claim that the power of Congress under the commerce clause extends to the outright prohibition of possession of firearms within the states by persons who have been convicted of violent crimes.[17] Accepting this premise, it seems strongly arguable that Congress would have the power to make the same prohibition with an exception in defendant's favor that he shall be acquitted if he gives evidence that he did not acquire the firearm in interstate commerce after the Act, and produces a reasonable doubt on these facts.[18]

The answer given in the opinion is, first, that this argument does not sustain the presumption of acquisition after the effective date of the Act. But why not, if the premise

---

15. 63 Sup.Ct. at 1245.

16. See note 5, supra.

17. See the brief for the United States in Delia's case, pp. 33–38.

18. My former colleague, Professor K. C. Davis, suggests that the greater power does not always embrace the less. The exception in favor of a particular class of defendants might constitute an unreasonable discrimination and thus a denial of equal protection or it might infringe some other specific constitutional privilege as where a defense is given which can only be asserted by an accused who takes the stand. Compare People v. Hoogy, 277 Mich. 578, 269 N.W. 605 (1936), in which a parking ordinance, providing that any owner of a vehicle was presumed to be the one who parked it unless he submitted himself to examination as to the identity of the operator or voluntarily revealed such identity,

was held invalid. Nevertheless the "greater includes the less" argument seems to me a persuasive counter to the general charge of unfairness implicit in the "rational connection" attack. Thus the holding in Sandstrom v. California Horse Racing Board, 31 Cal.2d 401, 189 P.2d 17, syl. 4, 8–11 (1948) that a regulation may validly impose strict liability for expulsion upon a trainer if tests show that his horse raced under influence of stimulants, suggests that a statute or regulation basing liability upon knowledge or negligence, but presuming negligence or knowledge if the presence of stimulants is shown by the tests, would be valid. See, however, Mahoney v. Byers, 187 Md. 81, 48 A.2d 600 (1946) where a statute to like effect with the California regulation but phrased in the form of a conclusive presumption was held unconstitutional.

be accepted that any possession of a firearm by a convicted person after the effective date could be prohibited altogether? Such possession here was concededly established. Secondly, "Congress, for what ever reason, did not seek to pronounce general prohibition of possession . . . but dealt only with their future acquisition." [19] This is the same argument with which Sutherland, J., dissenting, sought to answer Holmes, J., in Ferry v. Ramsey, when he said: "I should have supposed the liability of the director must be measured by what the state has enacted and not by what it had the power to enact." [20] Measured by what is enacted, certainly; that is just what the supporter of the statute in each case is contending for. It is only the defendant who is seeking to avoid what is "enacted." In looking to the power of the legislature to enact the supposed statute, one is not seeking to measure present "liability" by such imaginary statute, but merely, by comparison, to shed light on the question whether what was actually enacted was in the scope of power.

It seems that if the argument is to be given a satisfactory answer, it is the premise and not the conclusion that must be attacked. Is there such relationship in fact between the possession of firearms by persons convicted of violent crimes, and the prevention of the transport of firearms and the passage of criminals across state lines for unlawful ends, that Congress might reasonably consider that prohibiting possession by such persons altogether is an appropriate means of accomplishing this authorized purpose? [21] This

---

[19]. 63 Sup.Ct. at 1247.

[20]. 277 U.S. at 97.

[21]. That the question is at least debatable is indicated by the tenor of the government's argument as shown by the following excerpts:

"The power to prohibit even intrastate possession or acquisition rests here on a well-founded congressional judgment of a probable dangerous interstate movement of the men themselves, 'a reasonable fear upon the part of Congress' that the intrastate act of possession will 'probably and more or less constantly' form part of a pattern which has a deleterious interstate effect. Stafford v. Wallace, 258 U.S. 495, 521, 42 Sup.Ct. 397, 403, 404. This judgment of potential interstate crime on the part of ex-convict possessors of guns is in turn deeply rooted in the facts. . . . The hearings before the Special Committee dealt extensively with the problem of the roving gunman, his transit from state to state, his tendency to use one state as a base of operation for crimes committed in another, and the inability of the state of commission to cope with him; and the witnesses who brought these situations to the Committee's attention all recommended rigid federal firearms control. This testimony on successful criminals is confirmed by statistics on unsuccessful criminals, showing that possessors of guns move from state to state far more readily than the remainder even of the criminal population. [Footnote: Department of Commerce, Bureau of the Census, The Prisoner's Antecedents (1929), pp. 11–17, 54–58, covering federal and state commitments for the first six months of 1923. . . .]

"Since the explicit overruling of Hammer v. Dagenhart, 247 U.S. 251, 38 Sup.Ct. 529, by United States v. Darby, 312 U.S. 100, 115, 61 Sup.Ct. 451, 457, 458, there is no longer any doubt that the multiform power of Congress to legislate on intrastate subject matter to the extent necessary or even desirable to effectuate control of an interstate traffic includes prohibition of intrastate acts deemed preparatory to probable interstate movement. . . .

"A congressional prohibition of the possession of guns by people of demonstrated tendency to violent crime is thus a proper exercise of the commerce power not merely over the gun in past transit from Connecticut to Michigan but over the gunman in prospective transit from Michigan to some other state, based upon the judgment supported by the record before the Special Committee and confirmed by the statistics, that it is probable that as a member of the gunmen class he will so move. If gunmen operated in plain sight, from known addresses and with regular methods, some action short of the prohibitory presumption might be sufficient to control them in the interest of destination states. But the fugitive and clandestine nature of the traffic requires as it justifies the stringency of the control method from the viewpoint both of the commerce clause and of substantive due process. . .

We submit that the presumption of Section 2(f) does not offend the due process clause, because it is something less than a flat prohibition of possession of guns and ammunition by ex-convicts, and a flat prohibition would be an appropriate preventative against movement of guns in commerce on the part of a class deemed by Congress particularly likely so to move them to the harm of the destination

seems a highly pertinent and necessary inquiry to be answered before striking down the statutory presumption in the Firearms Act, an inquiry which involves the weighing of national and individual interests quite as significant as those which the court did discuss. The proposed means is one that has effects so much wider than the supposed end, that the court after considering the question might well have been unwilling to concede the existence of the power.

Perhaps the heart of the case is the insistence on "rational connection" as the invariable criterion as expounded in the passage quoted. The opinion likewise rejects "comparative convenience of producing evidence" as an alternative test, and characterizes it as a mere "corollary" of the rational connection standard. The meaning of this standard requires examination. The judicial opinions content themselves with general phrases which contrast those presumptions based on "experience" with those which are merely "arbitrary." But there are two degrees of "rational connection" between a fact proven and a fact to be inferred, and these vague expressions fail to make clear which is intended to be required. Perhaps the vagueness indicates an uncertainty in the minds of the courts themselves. These two are first, relevancy, and second, probative sufficiency. The first is satisfied if the fact proven tends to prove the fact to be established, that is, if it renders the inference more probable than it would be without the fact proven.[22] The second is more rigorous and requires that the fact (or facts) proven render the inference more probable than not. Doubtless, upon analysis, the courts which demand "rational connection" for the statutory presumption

would be driven to decide that it is the second quality, probative sufficiency in the sense of something more than a fifty-fifty chance, that they are demanding.

It has been suggested that a statutory presumption founded on such a probability is needless, for the inference would always be recognized as a permissible one without the statute.[23] It is believed, however, that this is an unfounded assumption and that judges would often differ as to the sufficiency of similar groups of facts, and that consequently a statutory rule which codifies the presumption may well be useful. Who shall judge then of the sufficiency, in this sense of 51 per cent probability, of the facts proven to warrant the inference which the particular presumption-statute authorizes? Presumably, the legislature in the first place and the court, passing on due process, only secondarily. Thus in the great number of cases where no one has the information which would enable him to say with assurance that the inference authorized is more probable than not, the court has only to ask: in the light of our experience and the data brought before us, can we say—and the attacker has the burden —that the legislature could not reasonably have believed that this inference is more probable than not? Thus "reasonable connection," even in the stricter sense, becomes merely a requirement that the legislature must not appear to have lacked a reasonable basis for considering the facts proven enough to support the inference.

Even when thus watered down, does the "rational connection" formula offer a feasible test for all cases of statutory presumptions, to determine their compliance with due process? As to statutes regulating civil liability

---

states. Brooks v. United States, 267 U.S. 432, 437, 45 Sup.Ct. 345, 346." Brief in Supreme Court in Delia's case, pp. 34–38.

22. See James, Relevancy, Probability and the Law (1941) 29 Calif.L.Rev. 689, 699, an illuminating discussion of relevancy, one of the most often used and most rarely analyzed terms of the law.

23. Compare the following passage: "Plainly, if the evidence which raises the presumption made a conclusion in the bailor's favor rationally permissible, there would be no need for it at all; its existence presupposes the opposite." Learned Hand, Circuit Judge, in Alpine Forwarding Co. v. Pennsylvania R. Co., 60 F.2d 734, 736 (C.C.A.2d, 1932).

only, it seems clear that the answer must be no. The distribution in civil cases of the burden of pleading, as between plaintiff and defendant, carrying with it usually the burden of proceeding with evidence and the burden of persuasion, was not governed by considerations of probability alone. The fact that one party would normally have better access to the evidence, or the desire to handicap a particular kind of claim on social grounds, were often the controlling considerations.[24] The same variety of motives actuated the courts in evolving the common-law presumptions, with their lesser burdens, and a substantial number of common-law presumptions are founded on convenience and not upon the greater probability of the inference.[25] Since there is no reason for special protection of one party to the civil cause rather than the other as there is in criminal cases, and since the presumption always leaves open the door to all the adversary's proofs, it is inconceivable that the courts at this date will strait-jacket within the limits of "rational connection" the legislature's power to create presumptions.

In a civil case, then, we may concede that the legislature, or the court through its rule-making power, could validly provide that the defendant should have both the burden of evidence and the burden of persuasion to disprove all averments in the plaintiff's statement of claim. Presumably this would not militate against a fair hearing, and would be due process. These burdens have to be placed upon one party or the other, and there is little basis for preference. In the realm of criminal prosecutions, however, the case is quite different. The traditional common law procedure emphasized the general rule that the burden of evidence and the burden of persuasion are upon the government to establish the guilt of the accused.[26] True, this rule was not quite universal because a few facts, such as self-defense, insanity, and license, were treated as defenses, rather than elements of the case for the prosecution, and the burden of first producing evidence to raise the issue is placed on the defendant.[27] However, even as to these in most states he does not carry the burden of persuasion, but will win if he raises a reasonable doubt on the issue.[28] And the range of these facts which the defendant must prove has always been narrower than in civil cases.

Moreover, this rule that the prosecution has the burden of proving all facts necessary to show the crime and of establishing guilt beyond a reasonable doubt is not merely a happen-so of procedure. It embodies a policy which, in the last one hundred and fifty years at least, has been considered an important safeguard of the individual citizen against injustice and oppression.[29] This policy is given form and color by the paradoxical maxim, that one who is accused of crime is presumed

---

24. See 9 Wigmore, Evidence, §§ 2485, 2486 (3d ed. 1940).

25. Chafee, The Progress of the Law, 1919–1921: Evidence (1922) 35 Harv.L.Rev. 302, 311, 312. "Some rebuttable presumptions have no logical core, but rest on some policy of that particular branch of the substantive law with which they are connected. Thus, since many promissory notes are given for accommodation, the presumption of consideration rests on no great probability that a note was given for value, but on the policy of the law of negotiable instruments that the enforcement of a note should be made a simple matter. Again, the presumption that if goods are handled by several carriers, damage in transit was caused by the last carrier is obviously based on the justice of relieving the shipper

of the initial burden of investigation and putting it on some one who has facilities for doing it."

26. "Throughout the web of the English Criminal Law one golden thread is always to be seen, that it is the duty of the prosecution to prove the prisoner's guilt. . . ." Lord Chancellor Sankey, in Woolmington v. Director of Public Prosecutions [1935] A.C. 462, 481.

27. Wigmore, op.cit.supra note 24, § 2512.

28. Ibid.

29. See Thayer, Preliminary Treatise on Evidence (1898), App. B, 551–560 and compare 1 Stephen, Hist.Crim.Law of England (1883) 397, 437–442.

to be innocent. In the light of this traditional policy, it may be arguable that in criminal cases there is a deprivation of due process if the legislature goes too far in transferring to the accused by means of a presumption the initial burden of producing evidence, so that the accused before there is any substantial showing of guilt is required to prove his innocence.

There are other arguments, also, for a stricter rule in curbing statutory presumptions in criminal cases than in civil, but they are less impressive. Thus it has been thought that the presumption may violate the constitutional privilege against self-incrimination.[30] The presumption, however, though it places on the defendant the necessity of producing answering evidence, and it may happen that his own testimony is all he has, says nothing about the kind of rebutting evidence. It no more compels him to be a witness than does the case made out by the prosecution without the aid of presumption.[31] Nor can the challenge of the statutory presumption as an infringement of jury trial[32] guaranteed by the constitution be sustained. If the presumption does no more than create

a permissible inference it can hardly be thought that the judge's direction that the jury *may* convict is an invasion of the jury's function. Even if, exceptionally, the presumptions should be construed to cast the burden of persuasion upon the defendant so that the judge would direct them to convict unless the defendant has proved by a preponderance the facts in rebuttal he would not, by instructing them upon the burden of proof, be departing from his traditional function. If, tested by the requirements of due process, this allocation of the burden of persuasion is proper, there is no basis for complaining that the jury's province is infringed.

Conceding, however, that due process may reasonably be thought to place some limits upon legislative power to create presumptions in criminal cases,[33] we revert to the question, should "rational connection" be accepted as the universal test? With deference, it is submitted that it should not,[34] and that the Supreme Court in the opinion—not in the actual decision—in the cases of Tot and Delia went too far. The proof in those cases so clearly rebutted the presumption that the defendants were entitled to directed verdicts. It well

---

30. Brosman, supra note 1, says at 182, that this objection "from a technical standpoint seems to have much of soundness in it," but he states that the decisions "uniformly dismiss the objection."

31. See Yee Hem v. United States, 268 U.S. 178, 185 45 Sup.Ct. 470, 472, 69 L.Ed. 904 (1925)—in discussing a Federal Act making possession of opium "sufficient evidence" of knowledge that it was illegally imported, the Court said: "The point that the practical effect of the statute creating the presumption is to compel the accused person to be a witness against himself may be put aside with slight discussion. The statute compels nothing. . . . It leaves the accused entirely free to testify or not as he chooses. If the accused happens to be the only repository of the facts necessary to negative the presumption arising from his possession, that is a misfortune which the statute under review does not create but which is inherent in the case. The same situation might present itself if there were no statutory presumption and a prima facie case of concealment with knowledge of unlawful importation were made by the evidence."

32. See Brosman, supra note 1, at 180, n. 126, citing numerous decisions; Watson (1940) 38 Mich.L.Rev. at 369.

33. The trend, however, at least in the cases of review of state action, seems to be in the direction of emphasis upon fundamental fairness rather than upon conformity with traditional criminal procedure. Garland v. State of Washington, 232 U.S. 642, 645, 34 Sup.Ct. 456, 457, 58 L.Ed. 772 (1914) ("Due process . . . does not require the state to adopt any particular form of procedure, so long as it appears that the accused has had sufficient notice of the accusation and an adequate opportunity to defend . . ."); Lisenba v. People of California, 314 U.S. 219, 236, 62 Sup.Ct. 280, 289, 290, 86 L.Ed. 166 (1941) ("As applied to a criminal trial, denial of due process is the failure to observe that fundamental fairness essential to the very concept of justice."

34. It is significant that nearly all of the text-writers and commentators (see note 1 supra) who have discussed the question, and notably Wigmore, Morgan, Brosman, and Keeton, have taken this view.

may be also that by any fair test the presumption in the Firearms Act would fall. But a rule that all criminal presumptions must be supported by a preponderance of probabilities is too inflexible to meet the varying needs of different fields of regulation. Cardozo, J., may prove to have had a truer insight when he said in the Morrison case, "The decisive considerations are too variable, too much distinctions of degree, too dependent in last analysis upon a common sense estimate of fairness or of facilities of proof, to be crowded into a formula." [35] Roberts, J., in the present case, in his laudable anxiety to protect the accused against oppression, feared that if considerations of convenience of proof were allowed to enter, there would be no stopping place in imposing on defendants the duty to produce exculpatory evidence at the outset.[36]

It is suggested, that a reasonable middle ground is offered in a combination of the most workable theories developed in the previous decisions of the Court which are discussed above. In this view, the statutory presumption in criminal cases would meet the requirements of due process (a) if there is a "rational connection," or (b) if the legislature could have imposed a liability not conditioned by the fact presumed—"the greater includes the less," or (c) if the facts are likely to be much more easily provable by the defendant than by the government, and the nature of the charge and of the facts on which the presumption rests make it fair to call on the defendant to produce evidence.

Since the decision in the Tot case the state courts have occasionally stricken down statutory presumptions in criminal cases as lacking the rational connection requirement laid down in that case.[37] On the other hand, both the Supreme Court of the United States [38] and several state courts [39] have since the Tot case continued to rely upon the more flexible formula of the Morrison case as a basis for upholding the validity in criminal cases of burden-shifting provisions.

314. Instructions on Presumptions—(a) In General.

May the judge in leaving fact-questions to the jury in his charge inform them of presumptions arising from the evidence, and under what circumstances may this be done? It is sometimes asserted that presumptions have no efficacy except to elicit or avoid peremptory rulings of non-suit or directed verdict, and that if the evidence in its shift-

35. 291 U.S. 82, 91.

36. 63 Sup.Ct. at 1246.

37. Garcia v. People, 121 Col. 130, 213 P.2d 387, syl. 2, 3 (1949) (statute providing that proof of failure by one who has butchered a neat animal to produce hide or give true explanation of its disposition is prima facie evidence of larceny); State v. Kelly, 218 Minn. 247, 15 N.W.2d 554, 162 A.L.R. 477 (1944) (statute providing that finding of intoxicating liquor in person's possession by means of search warrant is prima facie evidence of intent to sell; comprehensive discussion by Streissguth, J.).

See also Mantell v. Jones, 150 Neb. 785, 36 N.W.2d 115, syl. 3–6 (1949) sustaining, against attack under the Tot case, statute to effect that possession of motor vehicle with engine numbers removed or mutilated is prima facie evidence of theft.

38. United States v. Fleischman, 339 U.S. 349, 360–363, 70 Sup.Ct. 739, syl. 6, 7, 94 L.Ed. 906 (1950) (in prosecution for wilful failure to produce papers under subpoena: burden on defendant to prove excusing circumstances, if any).

39. People v. Pay Less Drug Store, 25 Cal.2d 108, 153 P.2d 9, syl. 7, 8 (1944) (statute enacting that proof of sale below cost is presumptive evidence of intent to injure competitors); People v. Scott, 24 Cal.2d 774, 151 P.2d 517, syl. 10–14 (1944) (possession of firearm whose marks of identification have been tampered with prima facie evidence that tampering was done by possessor: persuasive opinion by Traynor, J.); People v. Terra, 303 N.Y. 332, 102 N.E.2d 576 (1951) (statute making presence in room of machine gun presumptive evidence of its illegal possession by all occupants). See also Williams v. United States, 138 F.2d 81, syl. 2, 3 (C.A.D.C.1943) which uses the reasoning of the Morrison case to sustain an interpretation of the abortion statute placing upon the defendant the burden of showing that the operation was justified on therapeutic grounds.

ing course comes to an end at a stage where the conflicting inferences are for the jury that any presumptions which may have been available during the trial are now like spent balls, or, in the witty and oft-quoted phrase of a Missouri lawyer, like "bats of the law flitting in the twilight, but disappearing in the sunshine of actual facts." [1] In this view presumptions are simply rules directing the judge when to drop, or refuse to drop, the final curtain on the drama of the jury trial,[2] and they are nothing more. They would thus not need to be mentioned in the court's charge at all. This is an attractive solution and seems to be advocated as a general practice by Chamberlayne,[3] and by some modern opinions.[4] Thus, Judge Learned Hand recently said: "If the trial is properly conducted, the presumption will not be mentioned at all." [5]

Nevertheless, the writer submits that this practice of keeping silent about the relevant presumptions in a case, where the facts are disputed and must be submitted to a jury abandons one of the judge's useful opportunities for wise guidance of the trial, and runs counter to the traditions of the trial courts in most states.[6] As will appear in the two succeeding sections, there are some situations in which instructions on presumptions are essential and others in which the giving of such instructions may often be expedient.

315. Instructions on Presumptions—(b) When the Opponent's Evidence Is Limited to Contradicting the Basic Facts of the Presumption.

The proponent has given evidence proving the basic facts of a permissive presumption, such as *res ipsa loquitur* [1] or the pre-

---

1. Lamm, J., in Mockowik v. Ry. Co. (1906) 196 Mo. 550, 94 S.W. 256, 262, quoted in 5 Wigmore, Evidence, sec. 2491; compare Faris, J., dissenting, in Reynolds v. Casualty Co. (1918) 274 Mo. 83, 201 S.W. 1128: "The moment explanatory evidence comes into the case the presumption dissolves into thin air and becomes as wholly non-existent as though it never had had existence." Quoted in 23 Mo.Law Bulletin, 43.

2. Swoboda v. Nowak (1923) 213 Mo.App. 452, 255 S.W. 1079; McCune v. Daniels (1923, Mo.App.) 251 S.W. 458; Railway v. Wise (1917) 186 Ind. 316, 116 N.E. 299.

3. 3 Modern Law of Evidence, v. 2, § 1085 (1911).

4. A leading case is Ryan v. Metropolitan Life Ins. Co., 206 Minn. 562, 289 N.W. 557 (1939) (error to instruct on presumption against suicide where circumstantial evidence of suicide strong). See extensive approving Note, 24 Minn.L.Rev. 651. Other decisions disapproving the practice of informing the jury of this presumption. Reliance Life Insurance Co. v. Burgess, 112 F.2d 234, syl. 8, C.C.A.Mo., 1940; Kirschbaum v. Metropolitan Life Insurance Co., 133 N.J.L. 5, 42 A.2d 257, 158 A.L.R. 743, syl. 4, 1945. See also the able opinion of Knutson, J., in Te Poel v. Larson, 236 Minn. 482, 53 N.W.2d 468 (1952) (error to tell jury of presumption of due care in death action where defendant already had burden of establishing contributory negligence), noted 37 Minn. L.Rev. 629.
Invaluable discussions of the question of whether instructions on presumptions should be given and

if so in what form are Morgan, Instructing the Jury on Presumptions and the Burden of Proof, 47 Harv.L.Rev. 59, 1933; Techniques in the Use of Presumptions, 24 Ia.L.Rev. 413, 1939; Further Observations on Presumptions, 16 So.Calif.L.Rev. 245, 1943; Falknor, Notes on Presumptions, 15 Wash.L. Rev. 71, 82, 1940; Reaugh, Presumptions and the Burden of Proof, 36 Ill.L.Rev. 819, 830, 1942.

5. Alpine Forwarding Co. v. Pennsylvania R. Co., 60 F.2d 734, 736 (1932).

6. Persuasive opinions sanctioning instructions on presumptions: Wyckoff v. Mutual Life Ins. Co., 173 Ore. 592, 147 P.2d 227 (1944) (Belt, J.: presumption against suicide), Comment, Morgan, 23 Ore.L.Rev. 269; Worth v. Worth, 48 Wyo. 441, 49 P.2d 649, 103 A.L.R. 107 (1935) (Worth, J.: presumption, in alienation suit against parents, that defendants' advice was given in good faith). See also Hamilton v. Southern R. Co., 162 F.2d 884, 888, 889, syl. 6, 7, C.C.A.Va., 1947 (presumption of negligence); Wellisch v. John Hancock Mutual Life Insurance Co., 293 N.Y. 178, 56 N.E.2d 540, 542, 1944 (quoting judge's instruction on presumption against suicide with seeming approval); Karp v. Herder, 181 Wash. 583, 44 P.2d 808, syl. 6, 1935 (presumption of due care, opposed by direct testimony of negligence, instruction that presumption continues "until overcome by evidence" approved by five to four) commented on by Morgan, 12 Wash.L.Rev. 255, 269, 1937, Falknor, 15 id. 71, 1940.

1. See § 309, note 22, above.

sumption in criminal cases of theft from possession of stolen property.[2] The adversary confines his defence in the *res ipsa* case to testimony denying that the injurious happening occurred, or that the appliance was under his control, or in the theft case denies that the property found in his possession was the property stolen. Here it seems that to give due effect to the presumptions the judge would be required to instruct the jury that, if they find the disputed facts to be true then they *may* find therefrom, that the alleged facts-to-be-inferred, of causative negligence or theft respectively, are true.[3]

Even clearer is the need for a conditional instruction on the presumption when it is one of those which is classed in the particular jurisdiction as mandatory in the absence of facts rebutting the inference.[4] Thus, in a jurisdiction where seven years' disappearance without news creates a mandatory presumption of death, upon proof of disappearance seven years before trial and no subsequent tidings,[5] the adversary might offer evidence only that the first witnesses are mistaken, and that the person left home only six years ago. In such event, the judge should direct the jury that if they find seven years' disappearance without tidings, they must find the person to be dead. A like example would be presented by the application of the presumption of receipt of a letter from the fact of due mailing.[6] If the opponent offers evidence to the effect only that the letter was not mailed, it seems that the jury should be instructed that if they find that the letter was duly mailed then they must find that it was duly received, there being no evidence in denial of that conclusion.

316. Instructions on Presumptions—(c) When the Presumption Has Been Met by Counter-Evidence Disputing the Presumed Fact.

We are now brought to a second problem. Shall the judge be free to inform the jury in the charge of the existence of a presumption when the opponent has produced evidence direct or circumstantial denying or rebutting the presumed fact? The answer here seems to be unaffected by the question whether the presumption involved was mandatory or permissive or by the fact that the opponent may have produced evidence contradicting the basic facts, as well as evidence disputing the facts-to-be-inferred.

The problem is a difficult and important one, of which there is little discussion in the decisions (so far as I have read them) which pierces through the particular problem to considerations of general application. In the first place, can we settle the question at once by banishing all such mention of presumptions from the charge, as a forbidden[1] comment on the weight of evidence? This is Chamberlayne's view.[2] There are supporting expressions in the decisions, but it is believed that the prevailing view is that merely advising the jury of the existence of the presumption as a rule which *warrants or authorizes* them to find in accord with it, does not violate the statute.[3] Certainly the

---

[2] See Johnson v. State, 190 Ark. 979, 82 S.W.2d 521 (1935); Decennial Digests, Larceny, ⊜77.

[3] I find no case precisely in point, but the implications of the following cases lend support: Johnson v. Marshall, 232 Iowa 299, 4 N.W.2d 369, syl. 5 (1942) (presumption of ownership, and continuance thereof, from possession): Beardsley v. Suburban Coach Co., 83 Ga.App. 381, 63 S.E.2d 911, syl. 11 (1951) (presumption of concealment from failure to produce evidence); Venditti v. St. Louis Pub. Service Co., 360 Mo. 42, 240 S.W.2d 921, syl. 8 (1951) (res ipsa loquitur sustains plaintiff's burden if you find de-

fendant's busses collided causing injury to plaintiff passenger).

[4] 9 Wigmore, Evidence, §§ 2490, 2498a, sub-sec. 20.

[5] See § 309, note 26, supra.

[6] See § 309, note 15, supra.

[1] Under the rule obtaining in most states but not in England nor in the Federal Courts.

[2] 2 Modern Law of Evidence, sec. 1085.

[3] See Austin v. Seaboard Air Line, 187 N.C. 7, 121 S.E. 1, 3 (1923), where Hoke, J., said: "And in

practice of apprising the jury of presumptions is followed constantly in many states.[4] Moreover, it seems not to offend the intention of the "comment" statutes for they are designed to prevent the particular judge's individual view of the fact-inferences to be drawn from the testimony from being known to the jury. This objection does not apply to the expression by the judge of presumptions which are legal rules to be announced in all similar cases, assessing the sufficiency of certain standard fact-groups as evidence of certain conclusions. A frequent error is the statement in the charge that from certain facts a certain presumption arises, when in truth no such presumption, i.e., standar-

dized, regularized inference, is recognized for the particular fact-group by the courts of that jurisdiction. The so-called presumption is likely to be nothing more than an allowable inference from the particular facts selected by the judge, and his direction of the jury's attention to them and the possible inferences from them is regarded as an expression of the individual judge's opinion on the weight of the evidence, and hence as error.[5] This is an error very difficult for a trial judge to avoid, for it is often nearly impossible to determine when the allowable fact-inference has crystallized into a judicially accepted permissive presumption. A group of facts may be treated in one state as mere-

cases of the kind suggested on an issue of negligence of defendant, the burden of the issue is upon the plaintiff; but where it appears that goods have been shipped with a common carrier in good condition and have been lost or delivered in an injured condition, or where claimant's property has been destroyed or injured by fire communicated from defendant's engine or train, or where one a passenger or employee has been killed or injured by a collision or derailment of trains, and these basic facts are established by the greater weight of the evidence, a proper charge would be that they constitute or present a prima facie case, carrying the burden of liability to the jury on the issue and without more justifying the inference of negligence if the jury so find."

4. Examples of such charges are seen in the following cases: Pooler v. Smith, 73 S.C. 102, 52 S.E. 967 (1905), presumption of legitimacy; Patterson v. Campbell, 136 Ga. 664, 71 S.E. 1117 (1911), presumption of payment from lapse of time; McMahon v. Flynn, 154 Minn. 326, 191 N.W. 902 (1923), presumption of due care of victim of fatal accident. And see Reid's Branson, Instructions to Juries, (3d ed. 1936) Index, title "Presumptions."

5. These non-standardized fact-inferences were called in an older and now largely abandoned terminology, "presumptions of fact," as distinguished from "presumptions of law," i. e., true presumptions. See Jones, Evidence (Civil Cases), 3rd Ed., sec. 10, and Lockhart, Handbook of Evidence for North Carolina, sec. 228, approved in Austin v. Ry. Co., 187 N.C. 7, 121 S.E. 1, 3 (1923). Presumptions proper were to be enforced by the charge, but the bastard presumptions "of fact," or mere allowable inferences, were not to be mentioned in the instructions. People v. Carrillo, 54 Calif. 63 (1879) (instruction that failure by tax collector to pay over money collected raised a presumption of felonious appropriation, unwar-

ranted); Herkelrath v. Stookey, 63 Ill. 486 (1872): "In that instruction the jury are told, 'if the mortgage was made by a father to two of his sons, in the night time, under suspicious circumstances, and at the same time the father transferred to said sons all his land and personal property, and the property in the chattel mortgage was subject to be consumed or destroyed in its use by the mortgagor, these are circumstances from which the jury may infer that the transaction was a fraudulent one.' . . . Another and fatal objection is, that while the circumstances named in the instruction may be suspicious, they do not raise a legal presumption of fraud. They are to be considered in connection with all the other evidence, and it is for the jury to determine, from the entire evidence, what inference is to be drawn, without being instructed by the court as to what weight they are to attach to any particular portion of it. When the court says that a certain inference may be drawn from certain facts, if proven, most juries would understand the instruction as meaning that it was their duty to draw such inference;" Life Ins. Co. v. Buchanan (1884) 100 Ind. 63, 81; Mitchell v. Stanton (1911 Tex.Civ.App.) 139 S.W. 1033, 1036; Stooksbury v. Swan (1893) 85 Tex. 563, 22 S.W. 963, 966, 967, charge that acts of public officers are presumed to be regular, held an improper comment. The opinion has an unusually extended and pertinent discussion of the limits of the judge's power to charge on presumptions: "It has been frequently held in this state that a charge which, in effect, informed the jury that the law presumes the existence of some fact from the existence of others, is a charge upon the weight of evidence, and therefore improper, unless it be in those cases in which the presumption is said to be one of law, and therefore conclusive, or one of fact, required by positive law, but rebuttable"; White v. McCullough (1909) 56 Tex.Civ.App. 383, 120 S.W. 1093, 1095.

ly the basis for a fact-inference, in another as creating a permissive presumption or *prima facie* case, and in still another as a full-fledged mandatory presumption.

A more fashionable objection now to the practice of charging on presumptions, when the inferred fact is met by counter-evidence, is based on the dogma derived from Thayer [6] that the *only* effect of presumptions is to place on the adversary the burden of producing such counter-evidence through the threat of a peremptory ruling. Accepting this premise, if the opponent does produce such evidence, then the presumption is spent and disappears. Accordingly, if it has disappeared it is error for the judge to raise the ghost by charging on a vanished presumption. This is a mechanistic rather than a pragmatic solution, which has been questioned by eminent scholars,[7] but it has been sanctioned by Wigmore,[8] adopted in the Model Code [9] and approved by many modern decisions.[10]

Nevertheless, it seems that as to some presumptions, the custom of informing the jury in some fashion of the rule of presumption, is well-nigh universal. *Res ipsa loquitur*,[11] and the presumption of receipt of a letter from due mailing are instances. In criminal cases, this is especially true of those presumptions which look to a general rather than to a specific inference, and might be called "hortatory" presumptions, such as the presumption of innocence, the presumption that one intended the consequences of his acts, and the presumption against one who suppresses evidence, that it would have made against him.[12] The form books are replete with instructions on presumptions,[13] and the digests give abundant evidence of the widespread and unquestioning acceptance of the practice of informing the jury of the presumption despite the fact that countervailing evidence has been adduced upon the disputed inference.[14]

6. Preliminary Treatise on Evidence, ch. 8, passim, and especially pp. 314, 336 (1898).

7. See, e. g., Morgan, Instructing the Jury upon Presumptions and Burden of Proof, 47 Harv.L.Rev. 59, 82 (1933); Reaugh, Presumptions and the Burden of Proof, 36 Ill.L.Rev. 819, 833 (1942).

8. Evidence, § 2491(2). See, however, the apparent modification of his views as expressed in Evidence, § 2498a, sub-sec. 21, set out in § 317 note 8, infra.

9. Rule 704(2) (". . . when the basic fact . . has been established . . . and evidence has been introduced which would support a finding of the non-existence of the presumed fact . . . the existence or non-existence of the presumed fact is to be determined exactly as if no presumption had ever been applicable . . .," and Comment, "A presumption, to be an efficient legal tool must . . (2) be so administered that the jury never hear the word presumption used since it carries unpredictable connotations to different minds. . . .")

10. See, e. g., Orient Ins. Co. v. Cox, 218 Ark. 804, 238 S.W.2d 257, syl. 8 (1951); Ammundson v. Tinholt, 228 Minn. 115, 36 N.W.2d 521, syl. 9 (1949) and cases collected in Dec.Dig. Evidence, ☞89(a), Trial,' ☞205.

11. It is held in a leading case that in a *res ipsa loquitor* situation a mere general submission to the

jury of the issue of negligence, placing the usual burden of proof on the plaintiff, is insufficient. The plaintiff is entitled to instructions which "present the rule in respect to the *prima facie* case." Gleeson v. Virginia Midland R. Co., 140 U.S. 435, 444 (1891). The practice of instructing upon the *res ipsa loquitor* rule is reflected in Windos v. Galston & Sutton Theatres, 35 Cal.App.2d 533, 96 P.2d 170 syl. 1 (1939); Ryan v. George L. Lilley, 121 Conn. 26, 183 Atl. 2, syl. 8 (1936) (court should, in proper case, explain if requested); Potts v. Armour & Co., 183 Md. 483, 39 A.2d 552, syl. 11 (1944); Thompson v. Kansas City Pub. Service Co., 232 Mo.App. 1124, 114 S.W.2d 145, syl. 4 (1938); George Foltis, Inc. v. City of New York, 287 N.Y. 108, 38 N.E.2d 455, syl. 25, 153 A.L.R. 1122 (1942) and in the cases cited in Note, 53 A.L.R. 1494, Decennial Digests, Negligence, ☞138(2).

12. For numerous instances of the giving of instructions upon these and other presumptions in criminal cases, see Decennial Digests, Criminal Law, ☞778; Reid's Branson, Instructions to Juries (3d ed.1936).

13. See for example the title Presumptions in the indexes of Randall, Instructions to Juries (1922); Brickwood's Sackett on Instructions to Juries (3d ed.1908).

14. Decennial Digests, Trial, ☞205, 234(7).

It seems to me that the practice is wise and indeed almost necessary.[15] In most of our states, the trial judge has lost his common law power of summing up the testimony orally and informally in language the jury can understand, and advising them as to the way of judging the credibility of conflicting witnesses and the persuasiveness of rival inferences from the facts. Instead, he must often give his charge in writing, and as a practical matter he must use abstract language, preferably culled from appellate opinions in past cases, so as to avoid the danger that, in fitting the instructions to the particular case, he may be held to have violated the prohibition against commenting on the evidence. Instructions upon presumptions, whether permissive or mandatory, since they announce judicial custom crystallized into rules, escape as we have seen the imputation of being the judge's individual opinion or comment.

They can give the jury substantial aid in avoiding mistakes in difficult cases. A presumption is a rule which has the effect that from certain circumstances a certain inference may be drawn. Persons unaccustomed to weighing evidence and particularly persons of limited intelligence are notoriously suspicious of circumstantial inferences. Such persons, on the other hand, are prone to be overcredulous of direct testimony. If a party having the burden of persuasion, then, must rest upon circumstantial evidence

to prove an issuable fact, there is danger that the jury reading the burden-of-proof charge will mistakenly suppose that the circumstantial inference, especially if countered by direct testimony, could not be "a preponderance of the evidence." If the counsel can find a presumption upon which to rely, and can secure a charge upon it, he can use it in his argument as a basis for an explanation which may prevent the case from being decided upon this mistaken notion.

317. Instructions on Presumptions—(d) Form of Instructions, When the Presumption Is Met by Counter-Evidence Disputing the Presumed Fact.

The needs and demands for instructions which will inform the jury of a presumption arising on the facts, though the presumption be faced by evidence supporting a contrary inference, are strong enough to guarantee the continuance of the practice in most states, as long as juries continue to sit and judges continue to instruct them. We must face, then, a second and more difficult question: What is to be the form and purport of such an instruction? What shall the jury be told about the presumption, and their use of it? I assume that some standard approach, good for all presumptions except for occasional deviation, should be sought. To attempt to handle them differently, according to a classification based upon their varying origins in trial convenience, in experimental probability, in superiority of access of one party to

---

15. Illuminating discussions of the question and collections of pertinent cases appear in E. M. Morgan, Instructing the Jury upon Presumptions and Burden of Proof, 47 Harv.L.Rev. 59 (1933) and the scholarly opinions of Blume, J. in Worth v. Worth, 48 Wyo. 441, 49 P.2d 649, 103 A.L.R. 107 (1935), and of Belt, J., in Wyckoff v. Mutual Life Ins. Co., 173 Ore. 592, 147 P.2d 227 (1944).

The Uniform Rules of Evidence lend their weight to the view favoring instructions on presumptions, but with the reasonable limitation that the presumption must be one having a basis in probability. R. 14: "Subject to Rule 16, and except for presumptions which are conclusive or irrefutable under the rules of law from which they arise, (a) if the facts from

which the presumption is derived have any probative value as evidence of the existence of the presumed fact, the presumption continues to exist and the burden of esablishing the non-existence of the presumed fact is upon the party against whom the presumption operates, (b) if the facts from which the presumption arises have no probative value as evidence of the presumed fact, the presumption does not exist when evidence is introduced which would support a finding of the non-existence of the presumed fact, and the fact which would otherwise be presumed shall be determined from the evidence exactly as if no presumption was or had ever been involved." See also the Comment appended to the rule.

proof of the fact, or in external considerations of policy, seems impractical. The ingredients are too mixed for the trial judge to detect by offhand taste the predominant flavor, or to admit of agreement to any useful extent, upon a predetermined grouping founded on this scheme of analysis.[1]

The baffling nature of the presumption as a tool for the art of thinking bewilders one who searches for a form of phrasing with which to present the notion to a jury. In a matter where intuition and conjecture play so large a part, it is dangerous to be dogmatic, but certain formulas seem likely to be of little use to the jury. For example, judges have occasionally contented themselves with a statement in the instructions of the terms of the presumption, without more. This leaves the jury in the air, or implies too much.[2] The jury, unless a further explanation is made, may suppose that the presumption is a conclusive one, especially if the judge uses the expression, "the law presumes."

Another solution, formerly more popular than now, is to instruct the jury that the presumption is "evidence," to be weighed and considered with the testimony in the case.[3] This avoids the danger that the jury may infer that the presumption is conclusive, but it probably means little to the jury, and certainly runs counter to accepted theories of the nature of evidence.

More attractive theoretically, is the suggestion that the judge instruct the jury that the presumption is to stand accepted, unless they find that the facts upon which the presumed inference rests are met by evidence of equal weight, or in other words, unless the contrary evidence leaves their minds in equipoise, in which event they should decide against the party having the burden of persuasion upon the issue.[4] It is hard to phrase such an instruction without conveying the impression that the presumption itself is "evidence" which must be "met" or "balanced,"[5] The overriding objection, however, is the impression of futility that it con-

---

1. Interesting attempts to classify particular presumptions according to their origins in policy, experience and convenience may be found in the opinions of Maltbie, C. J., in O'Dea v. Amodeo, 118 Conn. 58, 170 Atl. 486 (1934) and Maxey, J., in Watkins v. Prudential Insurance Co., 315 Pa. 497, 173 Atl. 644 (1934), and in Morgan, Presumptions, 12 Wash.L. Rev. 255, 257 (1937) and Chafee, 35 Harv.L.Rev. at pp. 310–313 (1922).

2. See the criticism of such a charge in Garrettson v. Pegg, 64 Ill. 111 (1872). But an instruction merely directing the jury to consider the presumption against suicide without explaining its effect was thought sufficient in Radius v. Travelers Ins. Co., 87 F.2d 412 (C.C.A.Cal., 1937).

3. A few states seem to retain the notion that presumptions generally, or some presumptions, are evidence. See, e. g., Mutual Life Ins. Co. v. Maddox, 221 Ala. 292, 128 So. 383, syl. 1, 2, 5 (1930) (presumptions against suicide); Smellie v. Southern Pac. Co., 212 Cal. 540, 299 Pac. 529, syl. 2–10 (1931) (based on construction of provisions of Code of Civil Procedure), see criticisms, McBaine, 26 Calif.L.Rev. 519 (1938), Verleger, 31 id. 105 (1942), Note, 2 Stanford L.Rev. 559 (1950); Wyckoff v. Mutual Life Ins. Co., 173 Ore. 592, 147 P.2d 227, syl. 5 (1944) (under similar Code provisions); Bryan v. Aetna Life Ins. Co., 174 Tenn. 602, 612, 130 S.W.2d 85, syl. 9, 10 (1939) (no er-

ror to refuse to instruct that presumption against suicide is not evidence).

The abstraction that a presumption is evidence is hard to justify analytically and in consequence, most courts, even those that formerly accepted it, now reject the notion. See, e. g., Wilson v. Grace, 273 Mass. 146, 153, 173 N.E. 524, syl. 12 (1930) (presumption of innocence); Tyrrel v. Prudential Ins. Co., 109 Vt. 6, 23, 192 Atl. 184, syl. 22, 115 A.L.R. 392 (1938) (presumption of death from seven years absence) and see cases collected in Notes, Presumptions as Evidence, 95 A.L.R. 878, Presumptions against Suicide as Evidence, 103 A.L.R. 185, Presumption of Death as Evidence, 115 A.L.R. 404; 31 C.J.S. Evidence, § 119.

It will be observed that the notion that presumptions are, or are not, evidence is used to solve two quite distinct practical questions: (1) does the presumption when met with uncontradicted counter-evidence create a conflict requiring submission to the jury, see § 311, supra, and (2) is it proper to call the presumption "evidence" in the charge.

4. This form of instruction seems to be adopted in Ohio. Klunk v. Hocking Valley R. Co., 74 Oh.St. 125, 77 N.E. 752 (1906); Tresise v. Ashdown, 118 Oh.St. 307, 160 N.E. 898, 58 A.L.R. 1476 (1928).

5. Such an instruction was disapproved on this ground in Bollenbach v. Blumenthal, 341 Ill. 539, 173

veys. It prescribes a difficult metaphysical task for the jury, which they would only attempt to perform if they were hesitant and doubtful as to how to proceed, and having performed it, if the doubt remains, the reward is the instruction to disregard the presumption. It seems to me that it is more calculated to mystify than to help the average jury.

There are some forms of instruction that might give genuine aid toward an intelligent consideration of the issue. Usually, where a presumption is faced with adverse circumstantial evidence, if there is an issue to go to the jury at all, it is because the facts on which the presumption rests create a general probability that the presumed fact exists. The judge might mention these foundation facts, and point out the general probability of the circumstantial inference, as one of the factors to be considered by the jury.[6] As has already been pointed out, however, the trial judges in most states must tread warily to avoid an expression of opinion on the facts.

In some of these the practice frowns on any explanation of the allowable circumstantial inferences from particular facts, as being "on the weight of the evidence."[7] Where, however, the judge retains his full common law powers, or short of that, is authorized to explain the allowable inferences, this form of instruction may serve most of the useful purposes of a charge upon the presumption itself.[8]

Most, but perhaps not all. The mind abhors the vacuum of uncertainty. The trial must end in a verdict, a truth-saying. But there are many controversies where certainty about the truth is really impossible. An airplane falls from the sky, a locomotive crashes into an automobile at midnight, a trawler sinks without a trace. Liability hinges upon "fault." There are no survivors who witnessed the crucial happenings preceding the disaster. Still the jury must reach, if possible a "finding" upon the "facts." The principal agency which is provided to enable them to simulate certainty

---

N.E. 670, 673 (1930). Compare Hildebrand v. Chicago, B. & Q. Ry. Co., 45 Wyo. 175, 17 P.2d 651, syl. 3 (1933).

6. Thus, in a recent Federal case, in disapproving a charge on the presumption against suicide, the court said: "Ordinarily, it is not necessary to refer to the presumption against suicide in the charge to the jury. If the basic fact of death by violence is admitted, or proved, the presumption arises, and in the absence of countervailing evidence, the judge should direct a verdict for the plaintiff. If such evidence is produced, the judge should charge the jury in the usual fashion. He may of course refer in his discretion to the improbability of suicide as an inference of fact, based on the common experience of mankind, but the jury should be permitted to give the inference such weight as it deems best, undisturbed by the thought that the inference has some sort of artificial probative force which must influence their deliberation." Soper, Circ. J., in Jefferson Standard Life Insurance Co. v. Clemmer, 79 F.2d 724, 103 A.L.R. 171, 180 (C.C.A., Va., 1935). It will be observed, however, that in the "usual fashion" of instructing a jury in the Federal court, the judge is free to follow the common law tradition of explaining the allowable inferences from the particular circumstantial evidence.

7. Pridmore v. Chicago, R. I. & P. R. Co., 275 Ill. 386, 114 N.E. 176, syl. 6 (1916); Kennedy v. Phillips, 319 Mo. 573, 5 S.W.2d 33, syl. 7 (1928); 64 C.J. 527, n. 4.

8. Compare a suggestion, somewhat similar, embodied in proposals for improvement in the practice, in 9 Wigmore, Evidence, § 2498a, subsec. 21: "But if the opposing party has offered some evidence of the ultimate fact contrary to the effect of the presumption (§ 11), and has later received from the judge a ruling that there is such sufficient evidence and that the presumption therefore does not control the jury, then the judge by the traditional practice in some jurisdictions may instruct the jury as follows: 'You are bound by no rule of law in reaching your belief; but you may give special weight, if you think fit, to the course of experience as embodied in the maxim [here stating the fact that formed the basis of the presumption]; however, you are to decide the issue on all the evidence from both sides, having regard to the burden of proof.'

"This instruction may be termed, 'Instruction on the Evidential Value of Experience.'"

See also Arnold, Note, Instructions on Res Ipsa Loquitur, 13 Mo.L.Rev. 217, 221 (1948) setting forth and discussing a form for such a charge, in California Jury Instructions, No. 206O (3d ed.1943).

is the notion of burden of proof in the sense of burden of persuasion. The judge is to instruct them that if they are uncertain upon an issue, they nevertheless shall make a "finding of the facts" against the party having this burden. This unlucky burden is fixed largely with reference to the rules regulating the duty of pleading. But the principal object of pleading is the conveying of fair notice to an adversary of the scope of one's claim. This secondary effect of apportioning the risk of uncertainty, when tied strictly to the regulation of pleading, seems to lead occasionally to unsatisfying results. The general effect of the pleading rules is to place most of the burden upon the plaintiff, and as to certain particular groups of facts the result of this allotment of the burden of persuasion is felt to be harsh and inexpedient.

Many courts have found escape by the use of presumptions. The presumption has a closer kinship with the burden of persuasion than the rules of pleading have. The burden of persuasion is a fiction by which a feeling of uncertainty may be converted into a finding of facts. The presumption, as an instrument of reasoning, is but a mild and ingrati-

ating form of the same fiction.[9] The mind when beset with difficulties does not steam continuously straight ahead to its goal. It tacks across from point to point. Or like a swimmer making his way toward a safe and distant shore, it seeks a reef on which to rest until it may be shown that it can move on with safety. So in reasoning toward a difficult decision we are prone to look for some rational hypothesis, some "working assumption"[10] on which we can stand until lured away by the attraction of a more inviting theory or conclusion. The hypothesis is not a goal, but a station on the journey. Consequently, the mere mention of the presumption to the jury, or the instruction as to the allowable circumstantial inference, without more leaves us with an unsatisfied feeling, with a fear that the jury may wish to know. Where do we go from there?

Accordingly, the custom has persisted in many states, with surprisingly tough resistance to the criticisms of the text-writers, of charging the jury as to certain presumptions having a substantial backing of probability, that the presumption stands until overcome in the jury's mind by a preponderance of evidence to the contrary.[11] In other words, the

9. For an enlightening discussion of the fictional element in presumptions, see L. L. Fuller, Legal Fictions, 25 Ill.L.Rev. 363, 393 (1930).

10. Del Vecchio v. Bowers, 296 U.S. 280, 286, 56 S. Ct. 190, 193 (1935).

11. See Morgan, Presumptions, 12 Wash.L.Rev. 255, 265 (1937); Bohlen, The Effect of Rebuttable Presumptions of Law upon the Burden of Proof, 68 U.Pa.L.Rev. 307 (1920). Recent American decisions espousing this view are Page v. Phelps, 108 Conn. 572, 581, 143 Atl. 890, 893 (1928) (presumption in will contest that legatee in confidential relation exerted undue influence will stand unless jury believes from preponderance that legacy not so obtained); O'Dea v. Amodeo, 118 Conn. 58, 170 Atl. 486, syl. 3, 4 (1934) (statutory presumption that car driven by member of owner's family was being operated as a family car; able opinion by Maltbie, C.J., apportioning for this presumption a limited burden of persuasion; "the presumption shall avail the plaintiff until such time as the trier finds proven the circumstances of the situation with

reference to the use made of the car and the authority of the person operating it to drive it, leaving the burden then upon the plaintiff to establish, in view of the facts so found, that the car was being operated at the time as a family car."); Wyckoff v. Mutual Life Ins. Co., 173 Ore. 592, 147 P.2d 227, syl. 8 (1944) (presumption against suicide); Lewis v. New York Life Ins. Co., 131 Mont. 151, 124 P.2d 579, syl. 11, 12 (1942) (same: semble); Karp v. Herder, 181 Wash. 583, 44 P.2d 808, syl. 6, 1935 (presumption of due care, opposed by direct testimony of negligence, instruction that presumption continues "until overcome by evidence" approved by five to four). A recent English case approving this practice is Winnipeg Electric Co. v. Geel [1932] A.C. 690 (Privy Council).

The courts sometimes seem to adopt the practice without realizing that they have done so. See e. g., Krisher v. Duff, 331 Mich. 699, 50 N.W.2d 332, 339, syl. 19 (1951) (under statutory presumption that member of family using car is doing so with owner's consent, error to refuse to charge the jury that the adversary must come forward with evidence

presumption is a "working" hypothesis which works by shifting the burden to the party against whom it operates of satisfying the jury that the presumed inference is untrue. This often gives a more satisfactory apportionment of the burden of persuasion on a particular issue than can be given by the general rule that the pleader has the burden. One looks rather to the ultimate goal, the case or defense as a whole, the other to a particular fact-problem within the case. Moreover, an instruction that the presumption stands until the jury are persuaded to the contrary, has the advantage that it seems to make sense, and so far as we may judge by the other forms thus far invented of instructions on presumptions by that name, I think we can say that it is almost the only one that does.[12]

Accordingly, while the judge should be conceded a reasonable discretion whether or not to instruct the jury upon a given presumption arising in the case, it seems that the normal form of such instruction if one is given should place the burden on the opponent of overcoming the presumption by the preponderance of evidence.[13] It must be acknowledged that the weight of recent orthodoxy rejects this last conclusion.[14]

Professor Morgan argues persuasively for endowing the presumption with the effect of shifting the burden of persuasion, but suggests that this may best be done by the charge on the burden of proof, without mentioning the presumption to the jury at all.[15] As I have indicated earlier in this paper, I am inclined to think that it is a more natural practice, especially under the American tied-judge system, to mention the presumption, so that the jury may appreciate the legal recognition of a slant of policy or probability as the reason for placing on the party this particular burden. If this is true when the presumption operates (as it usually would) in favor of the plaintiff, who has the general burden of proof, so that the presumption would result in an issue being singled out and the burden thereon placed on the defendant, much more is it true when the presumption operates in favor of the defendant. In such case under the orthodox view the presumption would be swallowed up in the larger instruction that the plaintiff has the burden on everything that he has pleaded. This smothers any hint of the recognized policy or probabilities behind the particular presumption.

318. The Burden of Persuasion—(a) The Basis of Allocation of the Burden.[1]

As to every fact which is material to the establishment of an enforcible claim, one

---

of a "clear, positive and credible nature" to refute the presumption), Note, 65 Harv.L.Rev. 1077.

In respect to one presumption, the presumption that a child born during wedlock is legitimate, the courts agree that the adversary has the burden of persuasion. In re Jones's Estate, 110 Vt. 438, 8 A.2d 631, 128 A.L.R. 704, syl. 3, 1939, Note, 25 Corn.L.Q. 598; see also Note, 128 A.L.R. 713; Wigmore, Evidence, § 2527; and authorities cited § 309, note 33, supra.

12. Compare the words of Larson, C.J., in discussing the effect of a statutory presumption of negligence: "To rebut is to overcome, to contradict, to persuade or convince to the contrary. Unless the employer carries this burden of persuasion, of convincing the jury he was not negligent, the verdict must be for the employee who has met the requirements of proof necessary to invoke the presumption." Buhler v. Maddison, 109 Utah 267, 176 P.2d 118, 124 (1947).

13. This view is supported by the Uniform Rules of Evidence, R. 14 (quoted § 316, note 15, supra) in respect to presumptions based on probability.

14. American Insurance Co. v. Naylor, 101 Colo. 34, 70 P.2d 349, syl. 1–9 (1937) (vehicle-presumption); McCloskey v. Koplar, 329 Mo. 527, 46 S.W.2d 557, syl. 3–7, 92 A.L.R. 641 (1932) (res ipsa loquitur: three justices dissenting); Plumb v. Richmond Light & R. Co., 233 N.Y. 285, 135 N.E. 504, syl. 3, 25 A.L.R. 685 (1922) (res ipsa); In re Atkinson's Will, 225 N.C. 526, 35 S.E.2d 638 (1945) (presumption of undue influence from confidential relation); 9 Wigmore, Evidence, § 2489; 20 Am.Jur.Evidence, § 133; 31 C.J.S., Evidence, § 111; Dec.Dig., Trial, ⟜234(7).

15. 12 Wash.L.Rev. 281.

1. 9 Wigmore, Evidence, § 2486; 31 C.J.S. Evidence, §§ 103–105; Dec.Dig., Evidence, ⟜90–97.

party or the other will have three distinct burdens. This trio consists of (1) the burden of pleading the fact, (2) the initial duty of producing evidence of the existence of the fact, and finally (3) the burden of persuading the jury or judge of the existence, or non-existence of the fact. Usually, the party who had the burden of pleading the fact when he comes to the trial must carry likewise the other two burdens in respect to this fact,[2] and looking to the pleadings is the common guide for apportioning the duties of producing evidence and of ultimate persuasion.

We have seen, however, that the burden of first producing evidence is not an unvarying echo of the pleadings. The party who pleaded the fact may have the benefit of a presumption which will enable him to satisfy the burden of producing evidence of

the fact pleaded, e.g., the death of an insured, by furnishing evidence of other facts, namely, seven years disappearance without tidings.[3] Or the presumption, as in the case of the presumption of sanity in a will-contest in some jurisdictions, may relieve the proponent of the burden of introducing evidence of sanity at the outset, though he may have been required to plead sanity.[4]

The burden of persuasion, however, i. e. the burden of persuading the trier by evidence and argument of the truth of the fact, is much more closely hitched to the burden of pleading. In civil cases, almost the only useful general rule which will aid you in ascertaining who has the burden of persuasion of a particular fact or group of facts is this, that if the fact is one that is required to be "affirmatively" pleaded by the defendant,[5] he

2. Reliance Life Ins. Co. v. Burgess, 112 F.2d 234, syl. 2, 3 (C.C.A.Mo.1940) ; In re Ewing's Estate, 234 Iowa 950, syl. 3 (1944) ; Dec.Dig. Evidence, ⊜ 91.

3. See § 309, above, note 26.

4. See, e.g., Sheehan v. Kearney, 82 Miss. 688, 21 So. 41, 45, syl. 3, 4 (1896). But there are variations from state to state. See 9 Wigmore, Evidence, § 2500(a).

5. For a representative list of affirmative defenses, see Federal Rules of Civil Procedure, Rule 8(c): "In pleading to a preceding pleading, a party shall set forth affirmatively accord and satisfaction, arbitration and award, assumption of risk, contributory negligence, discharge in bankruptcy, duress, estoppel, failure of consideration, fraud, illegality, injury by fellow servant, laches, license, payment, release, res judicata, statute of frauds, statute of limitations, waiver, and any other matter constituting an avoidance or affirmative defense. . ." For examples of, and references to, other similar rules and statutes, see Clark, Code Pleading, § 96 (2d ed.1947).

If a party mistakenly pleads a fact upon an issue which his adversary had the burden of raising by an affirmative pleading, the prevailing view is that the burden of persuasion will still be cast upon the party who had the burden of pleading. Fitchburg Ry. Co. v. Nichols, 85 Fed. 945, syl. 1 (C.C.A. 1, 1898) (plaintiff's unnecessary allegation that she was in exercise of due care, does not change rule that the burden of proof of contributory negligence is on the defendant) ; Bevis v. Vanceburg Tel. Co., 132 Ky. 885, 113 S.W. 811, syl. 1 (1908) (similar to

last) ; Steward v. C. M. Kopp Co., 134 Wash. 150, 234 Pac. 1053, syl. 1 (1925) (plaintiff sued for price of apples sold; defendant denied sale and alleged it was a consignment; plaintiff has burden of persuasion to show sale, not defendant to show consignment); 31 C.J.S. 715, note 87. This doctrine seems desirable as a guide for the trial judge and when he has allocated the burden of persuasion in accordance with the burden of pleading, disregarding the form of the particular pleadings, his action should be approved on appeal. If, however, he has mistakenly assigned the burden of persuasion of a fact to a party who has "affirmatively" pleaded it, it seems that this party has invited the error and has no ground of complaint. Vycas v. St. George Guard Society, 97 Conn. 509, 117 Atl. 692, 693 (1922) ("A defendant who unnecessarily elaborates a general denial by alleging facts inconsistent with the allegations denied is in no position to complain, in case the court takes him at his word and erroneously instructs the jury as to the burden of proof.") ; Hatch v. Merigold, 119 Conn. 339, 176 Atl. 266, 96 A.L.R. 1114, 1116 (1935) (plaintiff by pleading lack of contributory negligence waives benefit of statute placing burden of persuasion on defendant on this issue) ; Boswell v. Pannell, 107 Tex. 433, 440, 180 S.W. 593, 596 (1915) (defendant by pleading affirmatively voluntarily assumed burden of persuasion and cannot complain when assigned to him). Probably the greater number of cases would reject this qualification. See e. g., Schmitz v. Matthews, 133 Wash. 335, 336, 233 Pac. 660, 661 (1925) ("not an invitation . . . to commit error . . . merely an opportunity"). See Notes, Effect of Un-

will ordinarily have the burden of persuasion in establishing it, otherwise such burden will be cast upon the plaintiff. In criminal cases, in modern practice, the prosecution in most jurisdictions has the burden of persuasion upon all the material facts, and even as to so-called matters of defense the accused has only a burden of producing evidence.[6]

The rules of pleading which assign certain facts material to the enforcibility of the claim to the defendant owe their developement partly to merely traditional happen-so and partly to considerations of policy, convenience and fairness.[7] Thus the policy of handicapping a disfavored contention probably accounts for the requirement that the defendant must plead as affirmative defenses such matters as contributory negligence, fraud, statute of limitations, and truth in defamation. Convenience in following the natural order of story-telling may account for calling on the defendant to plead those matters which arise after a cause of action

has matured, such as payment, release and accord and satisfaction. The distinction between the constituent elements of the promise, or of the statutory command, which must be pleaded by the party who relies on the contract or statute, and matters of exception, which must be pleaded by his adversary,[8] has several roots. Even so far as it is due to a mere choice of forms by the draftsman, it still has the convenience of a recognizable guide to the burden of pleading and its concomitant burdens. Moreover, when the exceptions are numerous, fairness requires that the adversary give notice of the particular one which is the point of attack. Again, if the adversary is unable to adduce proof or to persuade the trier that he is within the exception, assigning him the burdens is fairer than placing these risks on the other party. Exceptions usually point to exceptional situations, and if proof of the facts is inaccessible, it is fairer to act as if the exceptional situation did not exist.[9]

necessary Affirmative Pleading upon the Burden of Proof, 39 Yale L.J. 117 (1929), Pleading want of contributory negligence as waiver of presumption of freedom from negligence, 98 A.L.R. 1116.

6. See § 321, note 27, herein.

7. See Clark, Code Pleading, § 96 (2d ed.1947) where these considerations and the relation of the pleading rules to the burden of proof are lucidly discussed.

8. Thus, in an action on a life insurance policy with an exception for death by suicide the defendant has the burden of pleading and persuasion on the issue of suicide. New York Life Ins. Co. v. Prejean, 149 F.2d 114, syl. 2 (C.C.A.La.1945); Pacific Mutual Life Ins. Co. v. Young, 40 Ariz. 1, 9 P.2d 188, syl. 1 (1932). But in a suit on an accident policy, or on the double indemnity provision of a life policy, since suicide is not an accident, the plaintiff pleading accident has the burden of persuasion on the issue of suicide. New York Life Ins. Co. v. Prejean, supra (double indemnity provision); Travelers' Ins. Co. v. Wilkes, 76 F.2d 701, 705, syl. 6, 7 (C.C.A.Fla.1935); Note, Burden of Proof of Excepted Clauses in Insurance Policies, 46 Col.L.Rev. 802, 810 (1946).

An interesting example of the application of the distinction to statutes is Williams v. United States, 138 F.2d 81, syl. 1, 153 A.L.R. 1213 (1943) (defendant

charged with abortion had burden of producing evidence that he was within clause excepting operations necessary to preserve patient's health). See also Nicoli v. Briggs, 83 F.2d 375, syl. 15–17 (C.C. A., 10, 1936).

9. See Stone, Burden of Proof and the Judicial Process, 60 L.Q.Rev. 262 (1944). The learned writer examines the opinions in Joseph Constantine Steamship Ltd. v. Imperial Smelting Corp. Ltd., [1942] A.C. 154 (H.L.) which determined the novel question whether upon the plea of frustration in an action on a contract, the defendant or the plaintiff has the burdens of producing evidence and of persuasion on the issue whether the frustration was contributed to by the fault of the defendant. The opinions in placing the burdens upon the plaintiff stress the formal distinction between an essential element of the defense and an exception to its operation, and purport to reach their conclusions mainly upon definitions, logic and analogy. The author urges that as to this new question, the judges might more fruitfully have grounded their decision upon considerations of justice and policy, such as the following: "Let it be assumed then that in the great majority of frustration cases no fault of the parties was operative; and let it be assumed that in these cases the impossibility of proof mentioned by the Lords is present. A rule requiring the defendant pleading frustration to negative fault will

The foregoing discussion relates to the basis for allocating the burden of pleading, which usually draws with it the other two burdens. There are additionally some traditional doctrines which purport to classify situations where the "burden of proof" of a fact may be assigned to one who did not have the burden of pleading it. These are not reliable guides. Thus it used to be said that a party making a negative averment was not required to prove it,[10] but this was probably to be understood as properly applying only to the denial by a party of an opponent's previous pleading, and now one who has the burden of pleading a negative fact as part of his cause of action generally has the accompanying burdens of producing evidence and persuasion.[11]

Another traditional doctrine often repeated by the courts is that where facts pleaded by one party lie peculiarly in the knowledge

of the adversary, the latter has the burden of proving it. We have seen that this consideration of easier access by one party to the proof has been a governing consideration in the creation of certain presumptions, which regulate the burden of producing evidence.[12] It is believed, moreover, that as a general doctrine, apart from specific presumptions, its effect is similarly limited to apportioning the burden of producing evidence without affecting the burden of persuasion.[13] Nor can it be taken as a general standard by which to explain the assignment to one party or the other of the burden of pleading, since as often as not one must plead matters as to which the adversary has superior access to the proof.[14]

There is, then, it seems, no key-principle which governs the apportionment of the burden of persuasion. In ascertaining the party who is to carry this burden, we can

---

then *ex hypothesi* do injustice to the great majority of defendants. While on the other hand, a rule requiring the plaintiff to prove fault will *ex hypothesi* do injustice to only a small minority of plaintiffs." (p. 278).

Compare also the suggestion in the Note, 46 Col.L. Rev. 802, 817 (1946) in discussing the incidence of the burden of persuasion on the issue of suicide in suits on accident policies, that "as between the insured and insurer the latter appears better able to anticipate and provide for bearing the loss in these cases."

10. See, e.g., Walker v. Carpenter, 114 N.C. 675, 57 S.E. 461 (1907) ("The first rule laid down in the books on evidence is to the effect that the issue must be proved by the party who states an affirmative, not by the party who states a negative"), and other cases cited 2 Jones, Evidence, § 491, note 7 (2d ed. rev.1926).

11. Saari v. George C. Dates and Associates, 311 Mich. 624, 19 N.W.2d 121, syl. 3 (1945) (wrongful discharge: defendant pleaded plaintiff's failure to perform, burden on defendant); Johnson v. Johnson, 229 N.C. 541, 50 S.E.2d 569, syl. 2, 7 (1948) (plaintiff alleging in replication that deed was forged had burden of establishing non-execution by purported grantor). It is sometimes said, however, the party pleading a negative need not prove it when the facts are peculiarly within the knowledge of the other party. New York Life Ins. Co. v. Beason, 229 Ala. 140, 155 So. 530, 531, syl. 1

(1934) (doctrine recognized but held inapplicable); Valles v. Peoples-Pittsburgh Trust Co., 339 Pa. 330, 336, 13 A.2d 19, 21 (1940) (similar). Or more mildly that as to the party pleading a negative that the law will be satisfied with a lesser quantum of proof, particularly when the facts are within the knowledge of the adverse party. In re Chicago Rys. Co., 175 F.2d 282, syl. 14 (C.A. 7, 1949). See 31 C.J.S., Evidence, § 105; Dec.Dig. Evidence, ☞ 92, 93.

12. See § 309, above.

13. Johnson's Ex'r v. Wilkerson, 294 Ky. 208, **171** S.W.2d 249, syl. 2 (1943); Wilson v. Moline, 229 Minn. 164, 38 N.W.2d 201, 205, syl. 4 (1949); H. P. Welch Co. v. State, 89 N.H. 428, 199 Atl. 886, syl. 21, 120 A.L.R. 282 (1938); Guaranty Life Ins. Co. v. Nelson, 187 Okl. 56, 101 P.2d 627, syl. 5 (1940); 31 C.J.S., Evidence, § 113; Dec.Dig. Evidence, ☞ 93.

14. Nearly all required allegations of the plaintiff in actions for tort or breach of contract relating to the defendant's acts or omissions describe matters peculiarly in the defendant's knowledge. An extreme example is the averment required of the plaintiff in malicious prosecution that the defendant acted without probable cause. Correspondingly, when the defendant is required to plead contributory negligence, he pleads facts specially known to the plaintiff.

only look to the practice which the courts in the light of tradition and of their notions of convenience, fairness and policy, have worked out in the particular type of case, for the burden of pleading and thus for the companionate burden of persuasion.[15]

319. The Burden of Persuasion—(b) the Measure of Persuasion in Civil Cases Generally.[1]

According to the customary formulas a party who has the burden of persuasion of a fact must prove it in criminal prosecutions "beyond a reasonable doubt," [2] in certain exceptional controversies in civil cases, "by

clear, strong and convincing evidence," [3] but on the general run of issues in civil cases "by a preponderance of evidence." [4] It will be noted that the "reasonable doubt" formula points to what we are really concerned with, the state of the jury's mind, whereas the other two divert attention to the evidence, which is a step removed, being the instrument by which the jury's mind is influenced.[5] These latter phrases, consequently, are awkward vehicles for expressing the degree of the jury's belief.[6]

What is the most acceptable meaning of the phrase, proof by a preponderance, or

---

15. See the opinions of Murrah, J. in Denning Warehouse Co. v. Widener, 172 F.2d 910, 13 A.L.R.2d 668, 680 (C.A.N.M.1949), of Heher, J., in Ocean County Nat. Bank v. Stillwell, 123 N.J.Eq. 337, 197 Atl. 286, 289 (1938), and of Blume, J. in Takahashi v. Pepper Tank & Contracting Co., 58 Wyo. 330, 131 P.2d 339, 351 (1942), all relying on 9 Wigmore, Evidence, § 2486.

A new area in which these considerations of fairness and policy are having to be determined and applied is the field of actions for declaratory judgments. If the plaintiff in such a suit is seeking the declaration as a basis for some further affirmative claim against the defendant, he is in no special case and the distribution of the burden of pleading and persuasion between him and the defendant will be as usual, with the major share going to the plaintiff. See, e. g., Jerry Vogel Music Co. v. Forster Music Publisher, 147 F.2d 614, syl. 2 (1945) (suit for declaration plaintiff owner of copyrighted song, plaintiff has burden to establish ownership, defendant to establish defence of joint ownership); see International Hotel Co. v. Libbey, 158 F.2d 717, syl. 5 (C.C.A.Ill.1947) (suit by lessee for declaration construing lease provision). Dec.Dig. Declaratory Judgment, ⊕⇒342. But when the plaintiff, usually an insurance company, sues for a declaration of non-liability in an anticipated suit by the defendant, then some judges hold that the defendant should have the burden of persuasion on the issues on which he would bear the burden in the anticipated suit. Travelers' Ins. Co. v. Greenough, 88 N.H. 391, 190 Atl. 129, 109 A.L.R. 1096 (1937) (suit to have non-coverage declared under a liability insurance policy); Preferred Acc. Ins. Co. v. Grasso, 186 F.2d 987, syl. 1, 4–6 (C.A.Conn. 1951) (similar to last, opinion by Clark, Circ. J.). Others seem to reject this allocation of the burden by reference to the anticipated suit and to place the burden generally on the plaintiff. Reliance Life Ins. Co.

v. Burgess, 112 F.2d 234, syl. 1–4 (C.C.A.Mo.1940, Sanborn, Circ.J. dissenting) (suit to declare non-liability on life and accident policy because death due to suicide); Metropolitan Cas. Ins. Co. v. Miller, 188 F.2d 702, syl. 1 (C.A.Ill. 1951) (suit by insurer to declare that liability policy was not validly issued); see Dec.Dig. Declaratory Judgment, ⊕⇒343. See Borchard, Declaratory Judgments, 404 et seq. (2d ed. 1941) and an excellent Note, Sauer, 1941 Wis.L.Rev. 513. See also Note, 109 A.L.R. 1099.

1. 9 Wigmore, Evidence, § 2498; Morgan, Instructing the Jury on Presumptions and Burden of Proof, 47 Harv.L.Rev. 59, 64 (1933); McBaine, Burden of Proof: Degrees of Belief, 32 Cal.L.Rev. 242 (1944); Note, Instructions Defining Preponderance, 93 A.L.R. 155; 32 C.J.S. Evidence, §§ 1021, 1022; Dec.Dig. Evidence, ⊕⇒598, Trial, ⊕⇒237.

2. See § 321, herein.

3. See the next section, herein.

4. Prof. McBaine, cited above note 1, cogently suggests, at p. 246, that these formulas are equivalent to statements that the trier must find that the fact is (a) almost certainly true, (b) highly probably true, and (c) probably true.

5. See Morgan, article cited, at p. 64.

6. This may be evidenced by the results of a questionnaire sent to jurors by Judge Walter B. Wanamaker, Akron, Ohio. In answer to the question, "What propositions of law were most difficult to understand?" the answers were

"a. Preponderance of the evidence, 232.

"b. Reasonable doubt, 136.

"c. Negligence, 110.

"d. Proximate cause, 203."

Trial by Jury (report of a conference), 11 U.Cin.L. Rev. 119, 192 (1937).

greater weight, of the evidence? A widely accepted definition is that evidence preponderates when it is more convincing to the trier than the opposing evidence. This is a simple common-sense explanation which will be understood by jurors and could hardly be misleading in the ordinary case. It may be objected, however, that it is misleading in a situation where, though one side's evidence is more convincing than the other's, the jury is still left in doubt as to the truth of the matter.[7] It is said, moreover, to be inconsistent with the practice under which a party's evidence may be held to be sufficient to go to the jury, but not entitling him to a directed verdict, though his adversary offers no opposing evidence.[8] It is somewhat strained to say that sufficient evidence versus no evidence is not a preponderance, yet the jury is allowed to find against it.

The most acceptable meaning to be given to the expression, proof by a preponderance, seems to be proof which leads the jury to find that the existence of the contested fact is more probable than its non-existence.[9] Thus the preponderance of evidence becomes the trier's belief in the preponderance of probability. Some courts have boldly accepted this view.[10]

Other courts have been shocked at the suggestion that a verdict, a truth-finding, should be based on nothing stronger than an estimate of probabilities. They require that the trier must have an "actual belief" in, or be "convinced of" the truth of the fact by this "preponderance of evidence." [11] Does

---

7. See discussion by Wolfe, J., in McDonald v. Union Pac. R. Co., 109 Utah 493, 167 P.2d 685, 689 (1946) (". . . I can conceive of a case where the jury might be *more* convinced that the evidence of one side is nearer the truth than that of the other side and yet not feel that the evidence satisfied them as to the right to recover." See McBaine, article cited note 1, above, at p. 248, and Trickett, Preponderance of Evidence and Reasonable Doubt, 10 The Forum, Dickinson School of Law (1906) quoted 9 Wigmore, Evidence, § 2498.

8. Morgan, article cited note 1, above, at p. 64.

9. See Model Code of Evidence: Rule 1 (3): "'Burden of persuasion of a fact' means the burden which is discharged when the tribunal which is to determine the existence or non-existence of the fact is persuaded by sufficient evidence to find that the fact exists."; (5): "'Finding a fact' means determining that its existence is more probable than its non-existence. A ruling implies a supporting finding of fact; no separate or formal finding is required."; Morgan, article cited note 1, above, at p. 66. Compare Uniform Rules of Evidence, R. 1(8): "'Finding of fact' means the determination from proof or judicial notice of the existence of a fact."

10. Murphy v. Waterhouse, 113 Cal. 267, 45 Pac. 866, syl. 3 (1896) (error to charge that jury must be "convinced"; "preponderance of probability" is sufficient): Beckwith v. Town of Stratford, 129 Conn. 506, 29 A.2d 775, syl. 1 (1942) (standard in civil cases is proof which produces a reasonable belief of probability of the existence of the material facts); Moffie v. Slawsby, 77 N.H. 555, 94 Atl. 193, syl. 2 (1915) (a finding that the trans-

---

feree probably knew that the note was usurious is a finding that the party having the burden had satisfied the trier of fact); Livanovich v. Livanovich, 99 Vt. 327, 328, 131 Atl. 799, (1926) ("If . . . you are more inclined to believe from the evidence that he did so deliver the bonds . . . even though your belief is only the slightest degree greater than that he did not, your verdict should be for the plaintiff," approved; "a bare preponderance is sufficient though the scales drop but a feather's weight"), and see Mutual Life Ins. Co. v. Springer, 193 Ark. 990, 104 S.W. 2d 195, syl. 5 (1937) (court said in approving sufficiency of evidence that leukemia was caused by blow, ". . . as between man and man, where a loss must fall upon one or the other, it is right that the law should cast upon him who is shown to have been the cause of the loss, by proof establishing the reasonable probability of the fact."; Northwest States Utility Co. v. Ashton, 51 Wyo. 168, 65 P.2d 235, syl. 6 (1937); 32 C.J.S. 1053, n. 99.

11. See the remarks of Lummus, J. in Sargent v. Massachusetts Accident Co., 307 Mass. 246, 29 N. E.2d 825, 827 (1940) ("It has been held not enough that mathematically the chances somewhat favor a proposition to be proved; for example, the fact that colored automobiles made in the current year outnumber black ones would not warrant a finding that an undescribed automobile of the current year is colored and not black, nor would the fact that only a minority of men die of cancer warrant a finding that a particular man did not die of cancer. . . . After the evidence has been weighed, that proposition is proved by a preponderance of the evidence if it is made to

this mean that they must believe that is certainly true? Hardly, since it is apparent that an investigation by fallible men based upon the testimony of other men with all their defects of veracity, memory and communication, cannot yield certainty. Does it mean a kind of mystical "hunch" that the fact must be true? This would hardly be a rational requirement. What it would most naturally be understood to mean by the jury (in the unlikely event that they should carry analysis so far) is that they must be persuaded that the truth of the fact is not merely more probable than not, but highly probable. This is more stringent than our tradition or the needs of justice warrant, and seems equivalent to the standard of "clear, strong and convincing proof," hitherto thought to be appropriate only in exceptional cases.[12]

When it is customary in instructing on the burden of persuasion in the particular jurisdiction to include a reference to the effect of the evidence on the jury's mind, e. g., "if you find and believe from a preponderance of the evidence," [13] or "the plaintiff must satisfy you by the greater weight of the evidence," [14] there is much insistence upon the cabalistic word. In this bemusement with word-magic, "satisfy" has been the center of debate.[15] It is the customary expression in some states and is a convenient one, but some courts with more logic than realism condemn its use as equivalent to proof beyond a reasonable doubt.[16] In Alabama they have hit upon the compromise, "to the reasonable satisfaction of the jury" and have discarded the "preponderance of evidence" appendage altogether.[17] This simplification has much to commend it.

A court may properly advise the jury that the preponderance of evidence does not necessarily mean the greater number of witnesses,[18] but that if the witnesses are of equal credibility, the number of witnesses is one factor to be considered in determining the convincing power of the evidence adduced by the respective parties.[19]

---

appear more likely or probable in the sense that actual belief in its truth, derived from the evidence, exists in the mind or minds of the tribunal notwithstanding any doubts that may still linger there.") See also Lampe v. Franklin American, 339 Mo. 361, 96 S.W.2d 710, 723, syl. 24, 107 A.L.R. 465 (1936) (no error to refuse charge, "If you find and believe that it is more probable," etc., since a verdict must be based on "what the jury finds to be facts rather than what they find to be 'more probable' "); Anderson v. Chicago Brass Co., 127 Wis. 273, 106 N.W. 1077, 1079, syl. 4 (1906) (not only must charge require that party with burden produce evidence of greater convincing power but that "it must be such as to satisfy or convince . . . the jury of the truth of his contention").

12. See the next section, herein.

13. This is the customary phrasing in Texas.

14. This is the usual expression in North Carolina.

15. See the unbelievable number of decisions referred to in Note, Use of the word "satisfaction" in instructions relating to degree of proof, 147 A.L.R. 380–439, and in Dec.Dig., Trial, ⊄237(6). Examples of recent decisions: Abrahamian v. Nickel Plate Ry. Co., 343 Ill.App. 353, 99 N.E.2d 153, syl. 4 (1951) (condemning); McDonald v. Union

Pac. Ry. Co., 109 Utah 493, 167 P.2d 685, syl. 4 (1946) (permitting).

16. Torrey v. Burney, 113 Ala. 496, 21 So. 348, 351 (1897) ("Before it can be said that the mind is 'satisfied' of the truth of a proposition, it must be relieved of all doubt or uncertainty, and this degree of conviction is not required even in criminal cases"); Powell v. J. J. Newman Lbr. Co., 174 Miss. 685, 165 So. 299, syl. 2 (1936).

17. Nelson v. Belcher Lbr. Co., 232 Ala. 116, 166 So. 808, syl. 9 (1936) (usual statement, "reasonably satisfies the jury by the evidence").

18. Louisiana & A. Ry. Co. v. Muldrow, 181 Ark. 674, 27 S.W.2d 516, syl. 4, 5 (1930); Verdi v. Donahue, 91 Conn. 448, 99 Atl. 1041, syl. 1 (1917); Note, 93 A.L.R. 166, 167; Dec.Dig. Evidence, ⊄598(1), Trial ⊄237(5).

19. City of Lake Forest v. Janowitz, 295 Ill.App. 289, 14 N.E.2d 894, syl. 5 (1938); Abraham v. Wilson & Co., 121 N.J.L. 530, 3 A.2d 576, syl. 3 (1939). And some courts hold that if such instructions are given, they should include statement of tests by which value of testimony of witnesses must be appraised. Rice v. City of Cleveland, 144 Oh.St. 299, 58 N.E.2d 768, syl. 3 (1944). As an invariable requirement, this last seems unduly burdensome.

There has been much waste of time in the appellate courts over the metaphysics of "preponderance." Of the types of instructions customary in different states, it is hard to believe that the variations in language lead to any differences in jurors' attitudes in the different states or in the course of verdicts. Probably the courts that deal most successfully with the matter are those that emphasize it least and handle it most casually. The chief time-waster is the definition of "preponderance of evidence." Most courts sensibly hold that the phrase is one of common knowledge, and that it is not necessary to define it.[20] Where this is true, and no request is made by the jury, it seems the part of a wise trial judge not to define it. If local practice demands a definition, then since appellate courts have a sharp distaste for variations from the traditional formula, the practical thing is to search out the locally accepted phraseology and adhere to it.

320. The Burden of Persuasion—(c) Requirement of Clear and Convincing Proof.[1]

While we have seen that the normally required measure of persuasion in civil cases is by a preponderance of evidence,[2] there is a limited range of claims and contentions which the party is required to establish by a more exacting measure of persuasion. The formula varies from state to state, but among the phrases used are the following: "by clear and convincing evidence," [3] "clear, convincing and satisfactory," [4] "clear, cogent and convincing," [5] and "clear, unequivocal, satisfactory and convincing." [6] The phrasing within most jurisdictions has not become as standardized as is the "preponderance" formula, but even here the courts sometimes are surprisingly intolerant of slight variations from the approved expression.[7] No high degree of precision can be attained by these groups of adjectives. It has been persuasively suggested that they could be more simply and intelligibly translated to the jury if they were instructed that they must be persuaded that the truth of the contention is "highly probable." [8]

The requirement of proof more than usually convincing for certain types of contentions seems to have had its origins in the standards prescribed for themselves by the chancellors in determining questions of fact in equity cases,[9] but it has now been extended

20. Brunton v. Stapleton, 65 Colo. 576, 179 Pac. 815, syl. 2 (1919); Chicago City Ry. Co. v. Kastrzewa, 141 Ill.App. 10, syl. 5 (1908); Arnold v. State Bank & Trust Co., 218 N.C. 433, 11 S.E.2d 307, syl. 1 (1940) (in absence of appropriate prayer); Martin v. St. Louis S. W. Ry. Co. of Texas, 56 S.W. 1011 (Tex.Civ.App.1900); Note, 93 A.L.R. 155, 156, Dec. Dig. Trial, ⊕219.

1. 9 Wigmore, Evidence, § 2498, par. 2(3); 32 C.J.S. Evidence, § 1023, 20 Am.Jur. Evidence, §§ 1252, 1253; Dec.Dig. Evidence, ⊕596(3), Trial, ⊕237(3).

2. See next preceding section.

3. Lynch v. Lichtenthaler, 85 Cal.App.2d 437, 193 P.2d 77, syl. 2 (1948) (agreement for reciprocal wills).

4. In re Williams' Will, 256 Wis. 338, 41 N.W.2d 191, syl. 1 (1950) (mental incapacity and undue influence).

5. Frazier v. Loftin, 200 Ark. 4, 137 S.W.2d 750, 752 (1940) (claim of fraud inducing signing of contract, leases and deed).

6. Capps v. Capps, 110 Utah 468, 175 P.2d 470, 473 (1946) (oral trust).

7. See, e. g., Williams v. Blue Ridge Building & Loan Ass'n, 207 N.C. 362, 177 S.E. 176, syl. 2 (1934) ("We are constrained to hold that when his honor, in explaining the meaning of the words 'clear, strong and convincing proof,' told the jury that the plaintiffs 'must . . . satisfy you to a moral certainty,' he required of the plaintiffs an intensity of proof not warranted . . ."); Molyneux v. Twin Falls Canal Co., 54 Idaho 619, 35 P.2d 651, 94 A.L.R. 1264, syl. 11–14, 1934 ("clear, positive, and unequivocal" imposes too heavy a burden).

8. McBaine, Burden of Proof: Degrees of Belief, 32 Cal.L.Rev. 242, 246, 253, 254 (1944).

9. See Henkle v. Royal Exchange Assurance Co., 1 Ves.Sen. 317, 319, 27 Eng.Rep. 1055, 1056 (Ch.1749) (suit to reform insurance policy: relief denied for insufficiency of proofs; Lord Ch. Hardwicke: "There ought to be the strongest proof possible"); Marquis Townshend v. Stangroom, 6 Ves.Jun. 328,

to certain types of actions at law tried before juries, and the chancellors' cautionary maxims are now conveyed to the jury in the form of instructions on the burden of persuasion.[10]

Among the classes of cases to which this special standard of persuasion has been applied are the following: (1) charges of fraud[11] and undue influence,[12] (2) suits on oral contracts to make a will,[13] and suits to establish the terms of a lost will,[14] (3) suits for the specific performance of an oral contract,[15] (4) proceedings to set aside, reform or modify written transactions[16] or official acts[17] on grounds of fraud, mistake or incompleteness, and (5) miscellaneous types of claims and defenses,[18] varying from state to state, where there is thought to be special

---

333, 31 Eng.Rep. 1076 (Ch.1801) (similar); Carpenter v. Providence Washington Ins. Co., 45 U.S. (4 How.) 185, 224 (1846) (Suit in equity to require the defendant insurance company to indorse an acknowledgment of notice on the policy; held, claim of fraud fails because such a charge should be strengthened "by very satisfactory auxiliaries though not perhaps by so strong evidence as is necessary in reforming contracts" (citing earlier cases). American equity cases on the degree of proof necessary in reforming contracts are collected in 3 Pomeroy Equity Jurisprudence, § 859a (5th ed., Symons, 1941).

In Iowa the requirement of "clear, satisfactory and convincing" proof is limited to cases in equity. Provident Mutual Life Ins. Co. v. Bennett, 58 F.Supp. 72, syl. 17 (N.D.Iowa, 1944); Jamison v. Jamison, 113 Iowa 720, 84 N.W. 705, syl. 4 (1900).

10. See, e. g., Minton v. Farmville-Woodward Lbr. Co., 210 N.C. 422, 187 S.E. 568, syl. 1 (1936) (suit to establish oral trust); Ziegler v. Hustisford Farmers' Mut. Ins. Co., 238 Wis. 238, 298 N.W. 610, syl. 1 (1941) (defense of arson in action on fire insurance policy); Dec.Dig. Trial, ⊗—237(3).

In Texas, however, where, as in North Carolina, the facts in equity as well as law issues are tried to a jury, the "clear and convincing" standard may not be prescribed in the instructions. The trial judge, moreover, may not direct a verdict if he considers the evidence not "clear and convincing," but he may use the test, in appropriate cases, to set aside a verdict. Sanders v. Harder, 148 Tex. 593, 227 S.W.2d 206, syl. 7–11 (1950), critically noted, T. Smith, 28 Tex.L.Rev. 988.

11. Holley Coal Co. v. Globe Ind. Co., 186 F.2d 291, syl. 12 (C.A.W.Va.1950) (suit on employees' fidelity bond, defence that plaintiff's officers colluded with embezzlers); Jewell v. Allen, 188 Okl. 374, 109 P.2d 235, syl. 1 (1941) (action for damages for deceit); Dec.Dig., Fraud, ⊗—58(1)c. The policy of placing such a special burden on one who claims to be the victim of fraud seems debatable. Compare Rice-Stix Dry Goods Co. v. Montgomery, 164 Ark. 161, 261 S.W. 325, 329 (1924) where the court said: "While fraud at law, as well as in equity, is never to be presumed and must be proved, yet in actions at law one who has the burden of proof

to establish fraud meets the requirements of the rule when he proves the fraud only by a preponderance of the evidence. The same rule likewise prevails in equity, except in those cases where the rescission, cancellation, or reformation of a writing for fraud of one party and mistake of the other, or mutual mistake, is the relief sought, in which latter case, as we have stated, the proof of fraud or mistake must be clear, unequivocal, and decisive." To like effect: In re Delligan's Estate, 111 Vt. 227, 13 A.2d 282, 287, syl. 6 (1940) and cases cited 14 Am.Jur. 119, notes 12, 13.

12. In re Mazanec's Estate, 204 Minn. 406, 283 N.W. 745, 748, syl. 5 (1939).

13. Jensen v. Housley, 297 Ark. 742, 182 S.W.2d 758, syl. 2 (1944). And so of an oral gift asserted after the donor's death. St. Louis Union Trust Co. v. Busch, 346 Mo. 1237, 145 S.W.2d 426, syl. 3 (1940).

14. Coddington v. Jenner, 57 N.J.Eq. 528, 41 Atl. 874, syl. 1 (1898); 7 Wigmore, Evidence, § 2106.

15. Steketee v. Steketee, 317 Mich. 100, 26 N.W.2d 724, 726 (1947) (terms of agreement must be established by convincing proof).

16. Cox v. Tayman, 182 Md. 74, 32 A.2d 368, syl. 2 (1943) (suit to set aside a deed for fraud); Phillipine Sugar Estates D. Co. v. Government of Phillipine Islands, 247 U.S. 385, 38 Sup.Ct. 513, syl. 6, 62 L.Ed. 1177 (1918) (reformation of written contract for mutual mistake); Carlisle v. Carlisle, 225 N.C. 462, 35 S.E.2d 418, 421 (1945) (to establish an oral trust in land taken by deed absolute); Gillock v. Holdaway, 379 Ill. 467, 41 N.E.2d 504, syl. 4 (1942) (to show that deed was intended as mortgage); Dec.Dig. Mortgages, ⊗—38(2).

17. Deering v. Winona Harvester Works, 155 U.S. 286, 301, 15 Sup.Ct. 118, 39 L.Ed. 153 (1894) (showing of prior use to invalidate a patent must be made "by evidence so cogent as to leave no reasonable doubt in the mind of the court"); Bernstein v. Bernstein, 398 Ill. 52, 74 N.E.2d 785, syl. 2 (1947) (proof to impeach the correctness of a notary's certificate of acknowledgment of a deed).

18. E. g., Reed v. Reed, 202 Ga. 508, 43 S.E.2d 539, syl. 6 (1947) (invalidity of marriage); Lewis v.

danger of deception, or where the court considers that the particular type of claim should be disfavored on policy grounds.

The appellate court, under the classical equity practice, tried the facts *de novo,* upon the deposition-testimony in the record, and thus it was called on to apply anew the standard of clear and convincing proof in its study of the evidence. But in the modern system there are usually restrictions upon appellate review of a judge's findings of fact, even in equity issues. Thus, in the federal courts under Rule 52(a) such findings will only be reversed when "clearly erroneous." And in jury-tried cases the verdict will be reviewed only to the extent of determining whether there was evidence from which reasonable men could have found the verdict. Will the appellate court, then, today, if there was substantial evidence from which the judge or jury could have made the findings it did, consider the question whether the evidence

met the "clear and convincing" standard, in a case where it applies? On the one side is the argument that the judge or jury, seeing the witnesses, had superior opportunities to assess their convincingness,[19] and on the other the view that rules should be so shaped as to free the courts of last resort to employ most effectively their wisdom and sense of justice.[20]

321. The Burden of Persuasion—(d) Proof beyond a Reasonable Doubt.[1]

The consequences to the life, liberty and good name of the accused from a conviction of crime may be much more serious than the effects of a judgment in a civil case. Accordingly, it is just and reasonable to require a greater degree of confidence by the trier in the truth of the charge in a criminal than in a civil case. This demand for a higher degree of persuasion in criminal cases was recurrently expressed from ancient times,[2] but

---

Blumenthal, 395 Ill. 588, 71 N.E.2d 36, syl. 3 (1947) (to establish that a deed has been forged or altered); Krisher v. Duff, 331 Mich. 699, 50 N.W.2d 332, syl. 5, 10–12 (1951), noted 65 Harv.L.Rev. 1077 (statutory presumption that member of owner's family was driving it with his consent can be overcome only by testimony that is clear, positive and credible and plaintiff entitled to have jury instructed to that effect: see discussion § 311, above.); Taylor v. Hamrick, 134 S.W.2d 52, syl. 5 (Mo.1939) (to establish oral contract of adoption); Wells v. Tietge, 143 Neb. 230, 9 N.W.2d 180, syl. 6 (1943) (to prove adverse possession); Craswell v. Biggs, 160 Ore. 547, 86 P.2d 71, syl. 3 (1938) (subsequent oral agreement discharging or modifying a writing); Wilson v. Wilson, 145 Tex. 607, 201 S.W.2d 226, syl. 3 (1947) (presumption that property acquired during marriage is community property can only be overcome by clear and satisfactory evidence); King v. Prudential Ins. Co., 13 Wash.2d 414, 125 P.2d 282, syl. 3 (1942) (services by daughter in father's shop presumed gratuitous and presumption could not be overcome except by clear and convincing evidence).

19. See, e. g., Beeler v. American Trust Co., 24 Cal. 2d 1, 147 P.2d 583, syl. 2 (1944) (review of judge's findings); Davis v. Pursel, 55 Colo. 287, 134 Pac. 107, syl. 2 (1913) (review of findings of judge and jury). In both of these cases the lower court found that deeds were intended as mortgages and on

appeal it was held that, there being substantial evidence, it was for the trial court alone to decide whether the evidence was clear and convincing.

20. This view is urged in Note, Appellate Review in Federal Courts of Findings Requiring More than a Preponderance, 60 Harv.L.Rev. 111, 118 (1946) and see Comment, Bennett, Clear and Convincing Proof: Appellate Review, 32 Calif.L.Rev. 74 (1944); and see cases where appellate courts have imposed their own measure of "clear and convincing proof" to reverse the finding below: Zolintakis v. Orfanos, 119 F.2d 571, syl. 7–9 (C.C.A.Utah 1941) (oral trust). Equitable Life Assur. Soc. v. Aaron, 108 F.2d 777, syl. 4–6 (C.C.A.Ohio 1940) (reformation of policy); Langford v. Sigmon, 292 Ky. 650, 167 S.W.2d 820, syl. 1, 3 (1943) (oral trust in land conveyed), and cases cited by Traynor, J. in his dissenting opinion in Beeler v. American Trust Co., next preceding note.

1. 9 Wigmore, Evidence, § 2497; Morgan, Instructing the Jury on Presumptions and Burden of Proof, 47 Harv.L.Rev. 59, 63 (1933), McBaine, Burden of Proof: Degrees of Belief, 242, 255 (1944), Note, Degrees of Proof, 691 U.S.L.Rev. 169, 171 (1935); C.J.S. Crim.Law, v. 22, §§ 566–578, v. 23, §§ 1267–1284; Dec.Dig. Crim.Law, ☜326–336, 789.

2. Thayer, Preliminary Treatise on Evidence, 558, 559 (1898) quotes passages in Corpus Juris, dating from the fourth century, and from Coke's 3d Institute, to this effect.

its crystallization into the formula "beyond a reasonable doubt" seems to have occurred as late as 1798.[3] It is now accepted in common law jurisdictions as the measure of persuasion by which the prosecution must convince the trier of all the essential elements of guilt.[4] A simple instruction that the jury will acquit if they have a reasonable doubt of the defendant's guilt of the crime charged in the indictment would ordinarily be sufficient.[5]

Courts, however, frequently paint the lily by giving the jury a definition of "reasonable doubt." A famous early instance was the oft-echoed statement of Chief Justice Shaw in the trial of Prof. Webster for the murder of Dr. Parkman: "It is that state of the case, which, after the entire comparison and consideration of all the evidence, leaves the minds of jurors in that condition that they cannot say they feel an abiding conviction, to a moral certainty, of the truth of the charge."[6] It is an ancient maxim that all definitions are dangerous and this one has been caustically criticised as raising more questions than it answers[7] and as giving an instrument to adroit defense counsel with which to play upon the fanciful doubts and exaggerated scruples of susceptible jurors.[8] Other definitions, often more carefully balanced to warn against the over-stressing of merely possible or imaginary doubts, have become customary in some jurisdictions.[9] Reasonable doubt is a term in common use almost as familiar to jurors as to lawyers. As one judge has said, it needs a skilful definer to make it plainer by multiplication of words,[10] and as another has expressed it, the explanations themselves often need more explanation than the term explained.[11] A def-

---

3. "Its first appearance, so far as we have been able to determine, was in the high-treason cases tried in Dublin in 1798, as reported by MacNally [Rules of Evidence on Pleas of the Crown; Dublin, 1802], who was himself counsel for the defense. 'It may also,' he says, 'at this day, be considered a rule of law, that, if the jury entertain a reasonable doubt upon the truth of the testimony of witnesses given upon the issue they are sworn well and truly to try, they are bound' to acquit." May, Reasonable Doubt in Civil and Criminal Cases, 10 Am.L.Rev. 642, 656–7 (1876) quoted in Note, 69 U.S.L.Rev. 169, 172 (1935).

4. The jury is not required to believe each fact in an aggregate of circumstantial evidence. People v. Klinkenberg, 90 Cal.App.2d 608, 204 P.2d 47, 62, syl. 18–20 (1949), State v. Barry, 93 N.H. 10, 34 A.2d 661, 663, syl. 3 (1943) (not essential that each fact bearing on identity be established beyond reasonable doubt). Nor facts unrelated to guilt, such as venue. Barragan v. State, 141 Tex.Cr. 12, 147 S.W.2d 254, 256, syl. 3 (1941).

5. See, e. g., People v. Russell, 34 Cal.App.2d 665, 94 P.2d 400, 403, syl. 13 (1939).

6. Comm. v. Webster, 59 Mass. (5 Cush.) 295, 320 (1850).

7. Prickett, Preponderance and Reasonable Doubt, 10 The Forum, Dickinson School of Law, 76 (1906) quoted, 9 Wigmore, Evidence, § 2497.

8. May, Reasonable Doubt in Civil and Criminal Cases, 10 Am.L.Rev. 642 (1876) quoted 9 Wigmore, Evidence, § 2497.

9. They are set out by the hundreds in Dec.Dig. Crim.Law, ⊂⇒789 and in 36 Words and Phrases, 297–348 (Perm.Ed.1940).

10. Newman, J. in Hoffman v. State, 97 Wis. 576, 73 N.W. 51, 52 (1897).

11. Mitchell, J. in State v. Sauer, 38 Minn. 438, 38 N.W. 355 (1888) referring to the definition, "a doubt for which you can give a reason," said, "Like many other definitions of the term which have been given, it does not define, but itself requires definition. The most serious objection to it is that it is liable to be understood as meaning a doubt for which a juror could express or state a reason in words. A juror may, after a consideration and comparison of all the evidence, feel a reasonable doubt as to the guilt of a defendant, and yet find it difficult to state the reason for the doubt. The term 'reasonable doubt' is almost incapable of any definition which will add much to what the words themselves imply. In fact it is easier to state what it is not than what it is; and it may be doubted whether any attempt to define it will not be more likely to confuse than to enlighten a jury. A man is the best judge of his own feelings, and he knows for himself whether he doubts better than any one else can tell him. Where any explanation of what is meant by a reasonable doubt is

inition, of course, in terms locally approved is proper, but if not requested by accused is not required.[12] Whether if so requested it is the judge's duty to define the term, is matter of dispute,[13] but the wiser view seems to be that it lies in his discretion,[14] which should ordinarily it seems be exercised by declining to define, unless the jury itself asks for a fuller explanation.

There are certain excuses or justifications allowed to the defendant, which although proveable for the most part under the plea of not guilty, are spoken of for some purposes as "affirmative defenses."[15] Among these are self-defence,[16] duress,[17] insanity,[18] intoxication[19] and claims that the accused is within an exception or proviso in the statute defining the crime.[20] Some courts have even so classified the defence of alibi,[21] though analytically it seems a mere form of denial of participation in the criminal act. The older decisions[22] and treatises[23] placed the "burden of proof" upon matters of justification or excuse upon the accused, without discrimination between the two meanings, of producing evidence and of persuading, and many statutes still retain this form of expression.[24] A few states as to some of these defenses actually place upon the defendant not only the burden of first producing evi-

---

required, it is safer to adopt some definition which has already received the general approval of the authorities, especially those in our own state."

12. Epple v. State, 190 Ind. 87, 129 N.E. 403, syl. 3 (1921); People v. Spears, 241 Mich. 67, 216 N.W. 398, syl. 7 (1927); Comm. v. Berney, 262 Pa. 176, 105 Atl. 54, syl. 2 (1918) and cases collected 23 C.J.S. 945, note.

13. Recognizing such a duty are Mundy v. United States, 176 F.2d 33, syl. 3 (C.A.D.C.1949) (here waived by failure to request); Blatt v. United States, 60 F.2d 481 (C.C.A. 3, 1932) (reversal for refusal to define); Davis v. State, 46 Fla. 137, 35 So. 76, syl. 5 (1903) (same as last).

No such duty: People v. Buzan, 351 Ill. 610, 184 N.E. 890, syl. 7 (1933); State v. Ransom, 340 Mo. 165, 100 S.W.2d 294, 299, syl. 12 (1936); Mott v. State, 94 Okl.Cr. 145, 232 P.2d 166, 177, syl. 7 (1951); Gallegos v. State, 215 S.W.2d 244, syl. 7 (Tex.Cr.1948) (does not appear whether request made); State v. Velsir, 61 Wyo. 476, 159 P.2d 371, 161 A.L.R. 220, 231 (1945). For cases pro and con see 23 C.J.S. 838, Dec.Dig. Crim.Law, ☞789(3).

14. State v. Herring, 201 N.C. 543, 160 S.E. 891, 895, syl. 1 (1931).

15. 9 Wigmore, Evidence, §§ 2512, 2514; 22 C.J.S. Criminal Law, §§ 572, 577; Dec.Dig. Crim.Law, ☞329–333.

16. Comm. v. Troup, 302 Pa. 246, 153 Atl. 337, 340, syl. 11 (1931). See Note, Burden of Proof of Self-Defence, 39 J.Crim.L. 189 (1948).

17. State v. Sappienza, 84 Oh.St. 63, 95 N.E. 381 (1911).

18. State v. George, 108 N.J.L. 508, 158 Atl. 509, syl. 2 (1932).

19. State v. Johnson, 211 Iowa 874, 234 N.W. 263, syl. 5 (1931).

20. State v. McLean, 157 Minn. 359, 196 N.W. 278, syl. 2 (1923) (separate proviso clause); State v. Rosasco, 103 Ore. 343, 205 Pac. 290, syl. 4–7 (1922) (exceptions and provisos separate from the definition of the crime).

21. Porter v. State, 200 Ga. 246, 36 S.E.2d 795, syl. 4 (1946) (defendant must establish to reasonable satisfaction of the jury); People v. Silvia, 389 Ill. 346, 59 N.E.2d 821, syl. 9, 10 (1945) (alibi is "affirmative defense": defendant must produce evidence of it sufficient to raise reasonable doubt).

22. See, e. g., Rex v. Greenacre, 8 Car. & P. 35, 42, 173 Eng.Rep. 388 (1837) ("where it appears that one person's death has been occasioned by the hand of another, it behooves that other to show from evidence, or by inference from the circumstances of the case, that the offence is of a mitigated character, and does not amount to the crime of murder").

23. See, e. g., Foster, Crown Law, 255 (1762) ("In every charge of murder, the fact of killing being first proved, all the circumstances of accident, necessity, or infirmity are to be satisfactorily proved by the prisoner, unless they arise out of the evidence produced against him; for the law presumeth the fact to have been founded in malice, until the contrary appeareth.")

24. See, e. g., Calif.Pen.Code, § 1105: "Upon a trial for murder, the commission of the homicide being proved, the burden of proving circumstances of mitigation, or that justify or excuse it devolves upon him . . ."; Tex.Vernon's Ann.P.C. art. 46, "When the facts have been proved which constitute the offense, it devolves upon the accused to establish the facts or circumstances on which he relies to excuse or justify the prohibited act or omission."

dence but also cast upon him the burden of persuasion by a preponderance of the evidence.[25] This practise is most prevalent in respect to the defence of insanity,[26] a plea which many courts evidently feel is to be disfavored on policy grounds. But as to all these claims for exoneration their truth goes in final analysis to the guilt,—to the rightness of punishing the accused. Thus it seems inconsistent to demand as to some elements of guilt, such as an act of killing, that the jury be convinced beyond a reasonable doubt, and as to others, such as duress or capacity to know right from wrong, the jury may convict though they have such doubt. Accordingly, the recent trend both in English and American decisions is to treat these so-called matters of defence as situations where-

in the accused will usually have the first burden of producing evidence in order that the issue be raised and submitted to the jury, but at the close of the evidence the jury must be told that if they have a reasonable doubt of the fact on which the justification is based they must acquit.[27]

When a charge of crime is at issue in a civil action, the threatened consequences of sustaining the accusation, though often uncommonly harmful to purse or prestige, are not generally as serious as in a prosecution for the crime. Accordingly the modern American cases have come around to the view that in the interest of justice and simplicity the civil measure of preponderance should apply to these issues.[28] Nevertheless, the doctrine that "clear and convincing"

---

25. The cases cited in notes 16–19 above, this section, so hold.

26. Examples of recent cases placing burden of persuasion on the accused: Barker v. State, 188 Ga. 332, 4 S.E.2d 31, syl. 4 (1939) (to jury's "reasonable satisfaction, by a preponderance"); State v. Lynch, 130 N.J.L. 253, 32 A.2d 183, syl. 3 (1943) (satisfaction and preponderance); State v. Swink, 229 N.C. 123, 47 S.E.2d 852, syl. 3 (1948) (to the satisfaction of the jury). This practice stems from the classic McNaghten's Case, 10 Cl. & Fin. 200, 8 Eng.Rep. 718 (1843) ("the jurors ought to be told that every man is presumed to be sane and to possess a sufficient degree of reason to be responsible for his crime until the contrary be proved to their satisfaction"). Twenty-two states are cited as placing the burden on defendant in some form, in 9 Wigmore, Evidence, § 2501. Oregon, by an extraordinary statute (ORS 136.410, 136.390, 136.-400) requires the accused to establish his sanity beyond a reasonable doubt, and this was sustained as due process in Leland v. Oregon, 343 U.S. 790, 72 Sup.Ct. 1002, syl. 2–10, 96 L.Ed. 1302 (1952).

The Federal courts and a strong contingent of states place the burden of persuasion (not of evidence) on the prosecution, beyond a reasonable doubt, unless otherwise stated. Davis v. United States, 160 U.S. 469, 16 Sup.Ct. 353, 40 L.Ed. 499 (1895); Corbin v. State, 129 Fla. 421, 176 So. 435, syl. 6 (1937); People v. Patlak, 363 Ill. 40, 1 N.E.2d 228, syl. 5, 6 (1936); Brattain v. State, 61 N.E.2d 462, syl. 4 (Ind.1945); People v. Nino, 149 N.Y. 317, 43 N.E. 853, 856 (1896) (by a preponderance). See Dec.Dig. Crim.Law, ☞331.

27. See, e. g., Woolmington v. Director of Public Prosecutions, 1935 Appeal Cases 462, 481 (murder by

shooting, claim of accident: "Throughout the web of the English Criminal Law one golden thread is always to be seen, that it is the duty of the prosecution to prove the prisoner's guilt subject to what I have already said as to the defence of insanity and subject also to any statutory exception."); Tatum v. United States, 190 F.2d 612, syl. 5–10 (C.A.D.C.1951) (insanity); People v. Hardy, 33 Cal.2d 52, 198 P.2d 865, syl. 13 (1948) (murder: accused claims he was unconscious); State v. Strawther, 342 Mo. 618, 116 S.W.2d 133, syl. 8, 9, 120 A.L.R. 583 (1938) (murder, defense of another, error to place "burden of proof" on defendant, as misleading); Jones v. Comm., 187 Va. 133, 45 S.E. 2d 908, syl. 6 (1948) (murder, self-defense, holding similar to last). See Jenkins v. State, 80 Okl.Cr. 328, 161 P.2d 90, syl. 20 (1945) where the court approved an instruction which told the jury that if the killing is proved or admitted and self-defense is pleaded, "it then devolves upon the defendant to show any circumstances to excuse or justify it by some proof strong enough to create in your minds a reasonable doubt" as to whether accused acted in self-defense.

28. Stone v. Union Fire Ins. Co., 106 Colo. 522, 107 P.2d 241, syl. 8 (1940) (arson by insured); Atlanta Journal v. Mayson, 92 Ga. 640, 18 S.E. 1010 (1893) (libel charging forgery, plea of truth); Sundquist v. Hardware Mut. Fire Ins. Co., 371 Ill. 360, 21 N.E.2d 297, syl. 1, 124 A.L.R. 1375 (1939) (suit on fire policy, defense, false statement by assured; abandoning earlier rule in Illinois, and reviewing similar shift of decisions elsewhere); Hyder v. Hyder, 215 N.C. 239, 1 S.E.2d 540, syl. 3 (1939) (divorce action, defense of wilful abandonment); State v. Gray, 141 Tex. 604, 175 S.W.2d

proof is required for charges of fraud [29] is often applied in these civil cases where crime is charged,[30] and a few courts have said that the "clear and convincing" standard applies generally as to charges of crime.[31]

It seems to be generally agreed that, while the measure of persuasion "beyond a reasonable doubt" must guide the jurors in their deliberations, it is not a test to be applied by the trial judge in ruling on a motion for directed verdict, nor by the appellate court in passing on the sufficiency of the evidence.[32] Doubtless they do [33] and should [34] apply their standard more strictly in view of the gravity of the consequences, but their professed criterion is simply whether the evidence will rationally support a finding of guilt,[35] not whether the evidence "should satisfy reasonable men beyond a reasonable doubt."[36]

322. Exaggeration of the Importance of the Burden of Persuasion.

The "burden of proof" has been classed as a matter of "substance" rather than one of procedure, in the application of the principle that state "substantive" law governs in suits in the federal courts under the diversity jurisdiction.[1] On the other hand, results have been variable in deciding whether it is "substance" or "procedure" under the conflict of laws when suit is brought in one state upon

224, syl. 2 (1943) (suit for order for destruction of machines, issue whether used as gambling devices). Most courts seem to reject the reasonable doubt standard or charges of crime in disbarment proceedings, but are divided upon whether "preponderance" or "clear and convincing" is the measure. 7 C.J.S. Attorney and Client, § 33(3).

Cases are collected in 9 Wigmore, Evidence, § 2498, notes 3–12; Groom, Proof of Crime in a Civil Proceeding, 13 Minn.L.Rev. 556 (1929); Note, Degrees of Proof, 69 U.S.L.Rev. 169, 174 (1935); Note, Reasonable Doubt in Civil Cases, 124 A.L.R. 1378; Dec.Dig., Evidence, ⊜596(2).

29. See § 320, note 11, above.

30. See, e. g., Ziegler v. Hustisford Farmers' Mut. Fire Ins. Co., 238 Wis. 238, 298 N.W. 610, syl. 2 (1941) (suit on fire policy, defense, arson by insured; court correctly placed burden on defendant by "clear and satisfactory preponderance," which is different from "beyond a reasonable doubt").

31. Dregner v. Civil Service Comm., 398 Ill. 219, 75 N.E.2d 303, syl. 3 (1947) (review of dismissal of officer for soliciting bribe); Truckers Exchange Bank v. Conroy, 190 Miss. 242, 199 So. 301, syl. 2 (1941); Ziegler v. Hustisford Farmers' Mut. Fire Ins. Co., next preceding note (fraud or crime).

32. Pierce v. United States, 252 U.S. 239, 251, 40 Sup.Ct. 205, 64 L.Ed. 542 (1920) ("There being substantial evidence in support of the charges, the court would have erred if it had peremptorily directed an acquittal upon any of the counts. The question whether the effect of the evidence was such as to overcome any reasonable doubt of guilt was for the jury, not the court, to decide."); United States v. Feinberg, 140 F.2d 592, syl. 1, 2 (C.C.A. 2, 1944) (acute discussion by L. Hand, J.); Hays v. United States, 231 Fed. 106, syl. 1 (C.C.A. 8, 1916)

(leading opinion by Amidon, D. J.); United States v. Spagnuolo, 168 F.2d 768, syl. 1–3 (C.C.A. 2, 1948) (Clark, J.). United States v. Sherman, 171 F.2d 619, syl. 1 (C.A. 2, 1948) (L. Hand, Ch. J.); State v. DeKraai, 276 N.W. 11, syl. 4, 5 (Iowa, 1937); State v. Linarducci, 122 N.J.L. 137, 3 A.2d 796, syl. 19 (1939); State v. Adams, 213 N.C. 243, 195 S.E. 822, syl. 11 (1938); State v. Salzman, 186 Wash. 44, 56 P.2d 1005, syl. 4 (1936); Dec.Dig. Crim.Law, ⊜741(1).

33. See Judge L. Hand's statement to this effect in United States v. Feinberg, supra, at p. 594.

34. Certainly the usual unwillingness of our apellate courts to review the facts or appraise the justice of the conviction is an abdication of their highest potential service. See Orfield, Criminal Appeals in America, 87, 88 (1939).

35. United States v. Sherman, 171 F.2d 619, 621 (C.A. 2, 1948).

36. United States v. Feinberg, 140 F.2d 592, 594 (C.C.A. 2, 1944).

1. Cities Services Oil Co. v. Dunlap, 308 U.S. 208, 60 Sup.Ct. 201, syl. 1, 2, 84 L.Ed. 196 (1939) (in diversity suit in Texas federal court, court is required to follow Texas rule that one attacking the legal title has burden of proof that legal holder took with notice or without paying value). The court relied on an earlier decision, Central Vt. Ry. Co. v. White, 238 U.S. 507, 512, 35 Sup.Ct. 865, 867, 59 L.Ed. 1433 (1915) on a converse situation. There it was held that in an action brought in the state court under the federal employers' Liability Act, the federal decisional rule that the defendant has the "burden of proof" of contributory negligence is controlling as matter of substance, though the state rule was to the contrary.

a cause of action arising in another.[2] And the federal courts in applying the principle first mentioned have recently developed a new criterion of "substance" as distinguished from "procedure," namely, does the choice of rule in this respect "significantly affect the result of a litigation."[3] Here we need to discriminate between the burden of first producing evidence upon an issue and the ultimate burden of persuasion. There are many cases where one party will fail to get to the jury upon an issue if he has the burden of evidence. His adversary would often equally fail if he had this burden, for the evidence one way or the other is inaccessible.[4] The allocation of the burden thus will often "significantly affect" the outcome.

This is much less true, it is believed, as to the burden of persuasion by itself. Occasionally a judge will rationalize his judgment as being based upon an equilibrium of mind, but he will do this infrequently and reluctantly, for it is a confession of defeat in the search for the truth and justice of the matter. In the absence of actual investigation, the assertion may be reckless, but the writer's observation of jurors leads him to believe that few of them ever give any weight in their deliberation to the charge on burden of proof, except possibly where absence of any other arguable contention leads some counsel to harp on it unduly in his speech.[5] Under the "outcome" test, then, it is believed that the mere allocation of the burden of persuasion should be regarded as a matter of procedure and one of subordinate consequence. Doubtless many of the cases classing "burden of proof" as "substance" are explainable as referring to the package of the two burdens, one of which as we have seen may well affect the outcome. Finally, in view of these considerations, it is submitted that a misdirection as to the burden of persuasion should be assumed by the upper court not to have influenced the verdict unless special reasons appear in the particular case to believe that it did.[6]

2. Thus, in Levy v. Steiger, 233 Mass. 600, 124 N.E. 477 (1919), an action in Massachusetts for an injury sustained in Rhode Island, the court held that the Massachusetts statute placing the burden of proving contributory negligence on the defendant was to be applied as matter of procedure. But in Southern Ry. Co. v. Robertson, 7 Ga.App. 154, 66 S.E. 635, syl. 3 (1909) the local Georgia statute placing the burden of disproving contributory negligence on the plaintiff was held inapplicable to an Alabama injury, since the Georgia requirement was substantive as being a condition precedent to the existence of a cause of action. See the lucid discussion of these and other authorities in Stumberg, Conflict of Laws, 137–141 (2d ed. 1951). See also Morgan, Choice of Law Governing Proof, 58 Harv. L.Rev. 153, 180–191 (1944) where he demonstrates the hollowness of the distinction sought to be taken by some courts and writers between a condition which is "part and parcel" of the cause of action and a "mere procedural" requirement placing the burden of proof upon plaintiff or defendant.

3. Guaranty Trust Co. v. York, 326 U.S. 99, 109, 65 Sup.Ct. 1464, 89 L.Ed. 1418 (1945) (holding that in a diversity case the applicable state statute of limitation is "substantive"). Recognizing that the line between "substance" and "procedure" may be differently drawn for different purposes (see Cook, The Logical and Legal Bases of the Conflict of Laws, 1942, ch. vi) the court fixed upon the "outcome" test so as to minimize the incentive to choose the federal forum instead of the state.

4. This is frequently true on the issue of which of two people died first in a collision, or on the issue of whether a person who is presumed dead after seven years disappearance, died before or after the time when a life policy lapsed, or whether a midnight fire in a warehouse was due to negligence. Whoever has this burden of producing evidence will lose.

5. For a similar view, see Morgan, op. cit., 58 Harv. L.Rev. at 191.

6. For an expression of an opposite point of view, see Fitzsimons v. Frey, 153 Neb. 124, 43 N.W.2d 531, 535 (1950) ("It should . . . be jealously guarded and rigidly enforced . . ."). Cases holding that minor imprecisions in instructions on burden of proof are not ground of reversal, are found in 5 C.J.S., Appeal and Error, § 1763(c), note 32. An example is Leaman v. Campbell 66 Express Truck Lines, 355 Mo. 939, 199 S.W.2d 359, syl. 2 (1947). Placing the burden of persuasion on the wrong party may be disregarded if the issue was not seriously disputed, or close on the facts. Kingsul Theatres v. Quillen, 29 Tenn.App. 248, 196 S.W. 2d 316, syl. 13 (1946); Costello v. Federal Life Ins. Co., 259 Ill.App. 321, syl. 8 (1930).

JUDICIAL NOTICE

323. The Need for and the Effect of Judicial Notice.[1]

The process of proving facts under the traditional Anglo-American system of trial demands rigorous guaranties of accuracy, with its insistence upon proof by witnesses having first-hand knowledge, its mistrust of hearsay, however reliable, except for narrow exceptions, and its insistence upon original documents and their authentication by witnesses. These requirements have their roots in the contentious or adversary system, where the party and not the judge is responsible for gathering and presenting facts, and in the method of jury trial. But this strict though scientific insistence upon proving everything at first hand is, like jury-trial itself, enormously costly in time, energy and money.

The principal effect of the use of the doctrine of judicial notice is to excuse the party having the burden of establishing a fact from the necessity of producing formal proof of the fact [2] by sworn witnesses and authenticated documents or objective evidence. Besides this important effect of dispensing at least provisionally with formal proof, which all courts and writers concede to be the primary effect of judicial notice, there are other possible consequences, sometimes disputed, which will be discussed in a later section.[3]

The requirement of formal proof by witnesses and documents under the restrictions of the preferential and exclusionary rules has thus far been assumed to be justified generally for the ascertainment of facts at judicial trials. But in some situations this cumbrous process of formal proof is plainly not needed at all. In other situations compliance with the process might conceivably give some enhanced accuracy, but the added assurance

[1] General references: 9 Wigmore, Evidence, secs. 2565–2583; Thayer, Preliminary Treatise on the Law of Evidence, c. 7 (1898); Morgan, Judicial Notice, 57 Harv.L.Rev. 269 (1944); Maguire, Common Sense and Common Law, 166–175 (1947); Davis, Official Notice, 62 Harv.L.Rev. 537 (1949); Strahorn, The Process of Judicial Notice, 14 Va.L. Rev. 544 (1928); Keeffe, Landis, and Shaad, Sense and Nonsense about Judicial Notice, 2 Stanford L. Rev. 664 (1950); York, Unjudicial Notes on Judicial Notice, 13 Rocky Mt.L.Rev. 374 (1941); Decennial Digests, Evidence, ☞1–52, Crim.Law, ☞304; 31 C.J.S., Evidence, §§ 6–102; 20 Am.Jur., Evidence §§ 16–130.

For good general statements of the doctrine see Porter v. Sunshine Packing Corp., 81 F.Supp. 566, 575 (W.D.Pa. 1948); Williams v. Comm., 190 Va. 280, 56 S.E.2d 537, 542, syl. 2 (1949).

[2] Varcoe v. Lee, 180 Cal. 338, 181 P. 223, 226 (1919) ("Judicial notice is a judicial short cut, a doing away . . . with the formal necessity of evidence because there is no real necessity for it," Olney, J.); Piechota v. Rapp, 148 Neb. 443, 27 N.W.2d 682, syl. 14 (1947) (only effect is to relieve one of the parties of the burden of resorting to usual forms of evidence).

[3] See § 330, infra.

would be marginal and clearly not worth what it would cost.

What are these situations?[4] First, where the fact in question is known at once with certainty by all the reasonably intelligent people in the community without the need of resorting to any evidential data at all. Second, where reasonably intelligent people might not have in mind the information in question, but where they would agree that the facts are verifiable with certainty by looking at authoritative books of reference. This principle of verifiability with certainty should prove to be the growth-principle in the evolution of judicial notice. Third, where the ascertainment of the matter falls within the special responsibility of the judge as a judge, such as the rules of law applicable to a case before him, and matters pertaining to the personnel, records, organization, and jurisdictional boundaries of the court-system to which his court belongs. Fourth, where questions arise as to other governmental facts, which the judge as an officer of government is considered to have special facilities and responsibility for learning and verifying. Fifth, where a judge is faced with the task of creating law, by deciding upon the constitutional validity of a statute, or

the interpretation of a statute, or the extension or restriction of a decisional rule, upon grounds of policy, and such policy is thought to hinge upon social, economic, political or scientific facts. Though the conclusions from these facts, or the facts themselves, may be debatable, the situation is close to class three, the lawfinding process, so that jury-trial is inappropriate, and the restrictions of formal proof almost equally so.

These situations are, of course, not mutually exclusive. For instance, the characteristic of the second situation, certain verifiability, obtains also in respect to situations three and four. All will be dealt with in the sections which follow.

Certain other circumstances, less specifically definable in effect, may also be suggested as apparently influencing the courts' willingness to apply the doctrine of judicial notice. A court is more willing to notice a general than a specific fact, as for example, the approximate time of the normal period of human gestation,[5] but not the precise maximum and minimum limits.[6] Again, it is obvious in reading the cases that the courts make a wider use of judicial notice in formulating arguments for conclusions of law than

---

4. Compare with the classification in the text Uniform Rules of Evidence, R. 9: *"Facts which Must or May Be Judicially Noticed.*

"(1) Judicial notice shall be taken without request by a party, of the common law, constitutions and public statutes in force in every state, territory and jurisdiction of the United States, and of such specific facts and propositions of generalized knowledge as are so universally known that they cannot reasonably be the subject of dispute.

"(2) Judicial notice may be taken without request by a party, of (a) private acts and resolutions of the Congress of the United States and of the legislature of this state, and duly enacted ordinances and duly published regulations of governmental subdivisions or agencies of this state, and (b) the laws of foreign countries, and (c) such facts as are so generally known or of such common notoriety within the territorial jurisdiction of the court that they cannot reasonably be the subject of dispute, and (d) specific facts and propositions of generalized

knowledge which are capable of immediate and accurate determination by resort to easily accessible sources of indisputable accuracy.

"(3) Judicial notice shall be taken of each matter specified in paragraph (2) of this rule if a party requests it and (a) furnishes the judge sufficient information to enable him properly to comply with the request and (b) has given each adverse party such notice as the judge may require to enable the adverse party to prepare to meet the request."

5. Equitable Trust Co. v. McComb, 19 Del.Ch. 387, 168 Atl. 203, syl. 6 (1933).

6. Comm. v. Kitchen, 299 Mass. 7, 11 N.E.2d 482, syl. 6 (1937). But it may so far take cognizance of the general limits as to find a particular birth to be probably within or beyond them. See Estate of McNamara, 181 Cal. 82, 183 P. 552, syl. 4, 7 A.L.R. 313 (1919); Compare Cronin v. Cronin, 234 Ky. 207, 27 S.W.2d 950, syl. 2 (1930); Harward v. Harward, 173 Md. 339, 196 A. 318, syl. 1, 2 (1938).

in deciding particular facts in issue. Moreover, it seems that the easy accessibility of reliable sources of information, and the experience and skill that the judge possesses in the particular field will influence him in his decision whether to take judicial notice. Another factor which seemingly should, and probably does have an influence, is the feeling that judicial notice may work beneficially in certain cases by withdrawing from jury consideration fact-questions of science and technology which a jury, because of its limitations and prejudices, is ill-adapted to handle.[7] Finally, the decisions of the upper courts manifest a willingness to extend the bounds of judicial notice for the purpose of sustaining a just judgment in the lower court,[8] and a corresponding tendency to restrict its application where the result would be to overturn a satisfactory disposition.

Judges have been prone to emphasize the need for caution in applying the doctrine of judicial notice.[9] The great writers on Evidence, on the other hand, having perhaps a wider view of the needs of judicial administration, advocate a more extensive use of the doctrine. Thus Thayer suggests: "Courts may judicially notice much that they cannot be required to notice. That is well worth emphasizing; for it points to a great possible usefulness in this doctrine, in helping to shorten and simplify trials. . . . The failure to exercise it tends daily to smother trials with technicality and monstrously lengthens them out."[10] And Wigmore says, "The principle is an instrument of usefulness hitherto unimagined by judges."[11]

324. Matters of Common Knowledge: Jury Knowledge.

The oldest and plainest ground for judicial notice is that the fact is so commonly known in the community as to make it unprofitable to require proof, and so certainly known as to make it indisputable among reasonable men.[1] Though this basis for notice is sometimes loosely described as universal knowledge, manifestly this could not be taken literally[2] and the modern opinions, more reasonably, speak in terms of the knowledge of "most men,"[3] or of "what well-informed persons generally know,"[4] or "the knowledge

---

7. See Jordan v. Mace, 144 Me. 351, 69 A.2d 670 (1949) where the court (without however alluding to judicial notice) set aside a verdict establishing paternity in a bastardy case on the ground of the scientific reliability of blood-tests showing non-paternity. See also Note, 163 A.L.R. at 949 collecting conflicting decisions on the courts' power to take judicial knowledge of the scientific validity or conclusiveness of such tests.

8. See Note, 45 Harv.L.Rev. 190 (1931).

9. See, e. g., Varcoe v. Lee, 180 Cal. 338, 345, 181 P. 223, 226 (1919); State v. Clousing, 205 Minn. 296, 285 N.W. 711, 123 A.L.R. 465, 470 (1939).

10. Thayer, Preliminary Treatise on Evidence, 300 (1898).

11. 9 Wigmore, Evidence, § 2583, p. 585.

1. Varcoe v. Lee, 180 Cal. 338, 181 P. 223, 227, syl. 11 (1919) ("The test, therefore, in any particular case where it is sought to avoid or excuse the production of evidence because the fact to be proven is one of general knowledge and notoriety,

is: (1) Is the fact one of common, everyday knowledge in that jurisdiction, which every one of average intelligence and knowledge of things about him can be presumed to know? and (2) is it certain and indisputable? If it is, it is a proper case for dispensing with evidence, for its production cannot add or aid."); Gulf C. and S. F. Ry. Co. v. State, 72 Tex. 404, 10 S.W. 81, 82 (1888) (quoting 1 Wharton, Evidence, § 329); Morgan, Judicial Notice, 57 Harv.L.Rev. 269, 272, 273 (1944).

2. In City of Topeka v. Stevenson, 79 Kan. 394, 99 P. 588 (1909) the court in taking judicial notice of the meaning of the initials R.M.L.D. (retail malt liquor dealer) said: "It is not necessary for courts to wait, before taking judicial notice of a thing, until everybody knows and understands it. The meaning of a term has become a part of our common knowledge when it is generally understood by persons familiar with the subject."

3. Porter v. Waring, 69 N.Y. 250, 253 (1877).

4. Brandon v. Lozier-Broderick & Gordon, 160 Kan. 506, 163 P.2d 384, 387, syl. 6 (1945).

that every intelligent person has." [5] These phrases progressively widen the circle of facts within "common knowledge." Moreover, though usually facts of "common knowledge" will be generally known throughout the country, it is sufficient as a basis for judicial notice that they be known in the local community where the trial court sits. [6] By analogy may the common knowledge concept be extended to knowledge common to those in a particular trade? There are some affirmative intimations, [7] but it seems the law has not yet gone so far, [8] and that most of the need for judicial knowledge of facts generally known in a trade or profession can be satisfied by resort to the formula

developed in the next section of facts ascertainable with certainty.

A famous colloquy in the Year Books shows that a clear difference has long been taken between what judges may notice judicially and the facts that the particular judge happens personally to know. [9] It is not a distinction easy for a judge to follow in application, but the doctrine is accepted that actual private knowledge by the judge is no sufficient ground for taking judicial notice of a fact as a basis for a finding or a final judgment, [10] though it may still be a ground, it is believed, for exercising certain discretionary powers, such as awarding probation

---

5. Strain v. Isaacs, 135 Oh.St. 495, 18 N.E.2d 816, 825 (1938).

6. Varcoe v. Lee, 180 Cal. 338, 181 P. 223, syl. 13 (1919) (that a certain portion of Mission Street is in a business district is well known to citizens of San Francisco); Randall v. Comm., 183 Va. 182, 31 S.E.2d 571, syl. 4 (1944) (in robbery prosecution trial judge will be assumed, in taking judicial notice that "half-way house", the place of the robbery, was located in county where venue laid, to have done so on basis of community knowledge). But "night club gossip and stories appearing in newspapers" are not equivalent to community knowledge. Berry v. Chaplin, 74 Cal.App.2d 669, 169 P.2d 453, syl. 11–14 (1946) (Los Angeles trial court in filiation case could not take judicial notice of extent of wealth of Charles Chaplin).
There are intimations that local customs may not be noticed. See, e. g., First National Bank v. Commercial Bank & Trust Co., 137 Wash. 335, 242 P. 356, syl. 6, 7 (1926). But, under the present principle, if generally and certainly known in the community, they should be.

7. See, e. g., United States v. Rappy, 157 F.2d 964, syl. 4 (C.C.A.2, 1946) (judicial notice taken of maritime practice as to the making up of manifests from bills of lading); United Carbon Co. v. Monroe, 92 F.Supp. 460, 465, syl. 6 (W.D.La. 1950) ("The court may also take notice of conditions in the Monroe Field, which were the common knowledge of those engaged in the gas industry to the effect that it was proven territory and in the particular area covered by this contract production could be had simply by drilling at a rather uniform cost . . . ."); Ritholz v. Johnson, 244 Wis. 494, 12 N.W.2d 738, 741, syl. 3, 4 (1944) (suggesting that the court might take notice of conditions, not known to it but ascertainable, in the railroad busi-

ness, but declining to do so as to conditions relating to optometry).

8. Kennedy v. General Geophysical Co., 213 S.W.2d 707, syl. 1 (Tex.Civ.App. 1948) (notice refused of scientific facts "known only by a specially informed class of persons," but why not resort to the principle of the next section herein?). And the courts say that they will not notice, as such, customs in a particular trade; Eluzis' Case, 292 Mass. 351, 198 N.E. 262, syl. 2 (1935); Usher v. Eckhardt, 176 Minn. 210, 222 N.W. 924, syl. 1 (1929), though there is no reason why, in a given case, such custom might not be a matter commonly known or certainly ascertainable.

9. Anon., Y.B. 7 Hen. IV, f. 41, pl. 5 (1406), from which the following is an excerpt: "Tirwhit: Sir, let us put the case that a man kills another in your presence and sight, and another who is not guilty is indicted before you and is found guilty of the same death, you ought to respite the judgment against him, for you know the contrary, and report the matter to the King to pardon him. No more ought you to give judgment in this case . . . Gascoigne, C. J. One time the King himself asked me about this very case which you have put, and asked me what was the law, and I told him just as you say, and he was well pleased that the law was so."

10. Gibson v. Von Glahn Hotel Co., 185 N.Y.S. 154, syl. 1 (1920) (issue, in suit for loss of personal effects, whether defendant's house was a hotel; held, error to rule on personal knowledge that it was a hotel); Darnell v. Barker, 179 Va. 86, 18 S.E.2d 271, syl. 3–5 (1942) (appeal from custody order in divorce: error for trial judge to consider facts of his private knowledge, not in record); Note, 113 A.L.R. 258.

in a criminal case, or granting a motion for new trial to avoid an injustice.

Jury knowledge. The jury has the power, analogous to the power of the judge, to consider as if proven, facts within the common knowledge of the community. Accordingly, the court may instruct them to take in account their knowledge and experience, common to the community generally, in weighing the evidence;[11] counsel may, without evidence, argue the truth of such facts;[12] and the courts in passing upon the sufficiency of the evidence to support the verdict, will give weight to this factor.[13] The other grounds, however, for judicial notice, discussed in succeeding sections, are not the basis for jury-knowledge but are available only for administration by the judge.

325. Facts Capable of Certain Verification.

The earlier and still the most familiar basis for judicial notice is "common knowledge." Not only has this conception widened with the progress of the law, as we have seen,[1] but a second and distinct principle has now come to be recognized. Matters of common knowledge would nearly always be matters that the judge would know off-hand without occasion for any investigation. But when asked to notice a fact not generally known, but which obviously could easily be ascertained by consulting materials in common use, such as the day of the week on which January 1 fell ten years ago, the judges resorted to the fiction that in consulting the calendar and taking judicial notice they were merely "refreshing memory" as to a matter of common knowledge.[2] More realistically, we have here an important extension of judicial notice to the new field of facts "capable of accurate and ready demonstration,"[3] "capable of such instant and unquestionable demonstration, if desired, that no party would think of imposing a falsity on the tribunal in the face of an intelligent adversary,"[4] or "capable of immediate and ac-

---

11. Marshall v. State, 54 Fla. 66, 44 So. 742, syl. 5 (1900) (Instruction, "You will bring to bear in consideration of the evidence . . . in addition, all that common knowledge of men and affairs, which you as reasonable men have and exercise in the everyday affairs of life," approved); Notes, 16 Tex.L.Rev. 403 (1938), 144 A.L.R. 932. In principle of course the knowledge of a juror about the facts of the particular case should not be considered. He should testify. Perhaps, in strictness, expertness of particular jurors about values, skills, or occupational knowledge should not be used by the jury, not being common to the jurors and shared by the community. Some courts have held that instructions on jury-knowledge which fail to make this clear are ground for reversal. Downing v. Farmers' Mutual Fire Ins. Co., 158 Iowa 1, 138 N.W. 917, syl. 2 (1912). But there is much force to the contrary view that this restriction sacrifices one of the chief values of jury trial, and is a restriction which jurors cannot and will not obey. Solberg v. Robbins Lumber Co., 147 Wis. 259, 133 N.W. 28, syl. 3 (1911) (instruction permitting jurors to pool their individual knowledge, approved).

12. State v. Marsh, 70 Vt. 288, 40 A. 837, syl. 12 (1898) (semble); Kuehl v. Hamilton, 136 Ore. 240, 297 P. 1043, syl. 6, 7 (1931).

13. Leary v. Fitchburg Ry. Co., 173 Mass. 373, 53 N.E. 817, 818 (1889) (common experience as to way of alighting from cars); Carlton v. Sley System Garages, 143 Pa.Super. 127, 17 A.2d 748, 749 (1941) (jurors' community knowledge about streets and traffic in Philadelphia); Shikany v. Salt Creek Transp. Co., 48 Wyo. 190, 45 P.2d 645, syl. 13 (1935) (common knowledge about value of rugs).

1. See § 324.

2. See, e. g., Friend v. Burnham & Morrill Co., 55 F.2d 150, 151 (C.C.A., 1, 1932) ("The District Court in this case was warranted, therefore, in taking judicial notice of any common or general knowledge relating to canning cooked foods, and to refresh his recollection by reference to standard publications. Brown v. Piper, 91 U.S. 37, 42, 23 L.Ed. 200; Luten v. Allen et al. (D.C.) 254 F. 587; King v. Gallun, 109 U.S. 99, 101, 3 S.Ct. 85, 27 L.Ed. 870; American Fibre-Chamois Co. v. Buckskin-Fibre Co. (C.C.A.) 72 F. 508; Clark Thread Co. v. Willimantic Linen Co., 140 U.S. 481, 11 S.Ct. 846, 35 L.Ed. 521; Ferro Concrete Const. Co. v. Concrete Steel Co. (C.C.A.) 206 F. 666; Wright v. Wisconsin Lime & Cement Co. (C.C.A.) 239 F. 534; 15 R.C.L. p. 1061.")

3. Note, 47 Col.L.Rev. 151 (1947).

4. 9 Wigmore, Evidence, § 2571, p. 548.

curate demonstration by resort to easily accessible sources of indisputable accuracy," [5] as variously stated.[6] In this realm fall most of the facts, theories, and conclusions which have come to be established and accepted by the specialists in the areas of natural science,[7] natural phenomena,[8] chronology,[9] technology,[10] history,[11] geography,[12] statistical facts,[13] and other fields of professional and scientific knowledge.

5. Uniform Rules of Evidence, R. 9(2) (d) quoted § 323, note 4, above.

6. See also In re Malcom, 129 F.2d 529, 533 (C.C.P.A., 1942) ("This doctrine does not require actual present knowledge on the part of the judicial authority. As was well stated in the case of Ball v. Flora, 26 App.D.C. 394, cited in the Solicitor's brief: 'The process of taking judicial notice does not necessarily imply that the judge at the moment actually knows and feels sure of the truth of the matter submitted; it merely relieves the party from offering evidence because the matter is one which the judge either knows, or can easily discover.' "); Nichols v. Nichols, 126 Conn. 614, 13 A.2d 591, 595 (1940) ("Most matters which the court may notice fall into one of two classes, those which come to the knowledge of men generally in the course of the ordinary experience of life, and are therefore in the mind of the trier, or those which are generally accepted by mankind as true and are capable of ready demonstration by means commonly recognized as authoritative."); State v. Schriber, 185 Ore. 615, 205 P.2d 149, syl. 6 (1949) (similar to last).

7. See, e. g., Electric Storage Battery Co. v. Shimadzu, 123 F.2d 890, syl. 3 (C.C.A. 3rd 1941) (that heated oxygen will combine with lead to form lead oxide); Russo v. Swift & Co., 136 Neb. 406, 286 N.W. 291, syl. 2 (1939) (nature and origin of disease of echinococcosis); State v. Schriber, 185 Ore. 615, 205 P.2d 149, syl. 8 (1949) (that Bang's disease is an infectious and contagious disease of cattle). See Note, Judicial Notice of Medical Facts, 36 Mich.L. Rev. 610 (1938). See also Buhrkuhl v. F. T. O'Dell Const. Co., 232 Mo.App. 967, 95 S.W.2d 843, syl. 4–8, (1936), where the court takes judicial notice that a barn taller than other buildings on an isolated farm was a place of special danger from lightning. Disagreements as to whether particular scientific questions are within the field of judicial knowledge are, naturally, not uncommon. See, e. g., Universal Granite Quarries Co. v. Industrial Commission, 224 Wis. 680, 272 N.W. 863, syl. 1, 1937, and Smith v. Harbison-Walker Refractories Co., 340 Mo. 389, 100 S.W.2d 909, syl. 16, 1936 (that some dust causes lung trouble); In re Swahn's Will, 158 Misc. 17, 285 N.Y.S. 234, 1936, and Commonwealth v. English, 123 Pa.Super. 161, 186 A. 298, syl. 7, 1936 (that blood-grouping tests are relevant on question of paternity); Cowan v. Georgia Railroad & Banking Co., 52 Ga.App. 677, 184 S.E. 635, 1936, and Wm. A. Smith Const. Co. v. Brumley, 88 F.2d 803, syl. 3, C.C.A.Okl. 1937 (whether rays of locomotive headlight crossing rays of automobile light would cut off latter light). The courts not infrequently will use the doctrine of judicial notice as a basis for determining that expert opinion testimony contrary to accepted knowledge, is not to be believed. See, e. g., Parton v. Phillips Petroleum Co., 231 Mo.App. 585, 107 S.W.2d 167, syl. 7, 1937 (testimony that it is not dangerous to pour kerosene on a fire).

Manifestly, a court may judicially notice general principles and limits where it cannot be certain of the particular application. See Muse v. Page, 125 Conn. 219, 4 A.2d 329, syl. 6–8, 1939 (distance within which a truck can be stopped).

8. McAffee v. United States, 111 F.2d 199, syl. 1 (App.D.C. 1940) (notice taken of maximum and minimum temperatures in the District of Columbia on a certain date); State v. Perkins, 342 Mo. 560, 116 S.W.2d 80, syl. 5 (1938) (the time of sunrise on a particular morning).

9. State v. Van Ness, 109 Vt. 392, 199 A. 754, syl. 10, 117 A.L.R. 415 (1938) (the days of the week on which certain dates fell).

10. Werk v. Parker, 249 U.S. 130, 132, syl. 1, 39 S.Ct. 197, 63 L.Ed. 514 (1919) (court by reference to encyclopedia and other authorities could take notice that long before present patent was issued the use of horse-hair mats in presses for the extraction of oil was well known in the art).

11. Unity Oil Co. v. Gulf Oil Corp., 141 Me. 148, 40 A.2d 4, syl. 5, 156 A.L.R. 297 (1944) (dates of declaration of World War II and of beginning of rationing); Miller v. Fowler, 200 Miss. 776, 28 So.2d 837 (1947), syl. 3–7 (that acts of warfare between Japan and the United States had not entirely ceased on Aug. 14, 1945).

12. See, e. g., Swarzwald v. Cooley, 39 Cal.App.2d 306, 103 P.2d 580, syl. 6 (1940) (meaning of phrase, "ordinary high tide," in the vicinity of Laguna Beach).

13. Groves v. Board of Com'rs, 209 Ind. 371, 199 N.E. 137, syl. 2 (1936) (Supreme Court will notice population of cities and towns of state shown by Federal census); Cox v. Polson Logging Co., 18 Wash.2d 49, 138 P.2d 169, syl. 6 (1943) (trial judge may inform jury of life expectancy from mortality tables without proof); Dec.Dig. Evidence, ☞12.

The judge is free to consult on his own motion any sources that he considers reliable,[14] but under our tradition of party-presentation, the extent of the judge's willingness to take the initiative in looking up the authoritative sources will usually be limited,[15] and it is the task of counsel to find and to present in argument and briefs such references, excerpts and explanations as will convince the judge that the fact is certain and demonstrable.[16] If on investigation he finds that the fact, theory or conclusion which he is asked to notice is one which the authorities in the field reveal as debatable, he will leave the question for resolution by expert testimony.

An able Minnesota judge has said that judicial notice of scientific facts can be taken only when such facts are "generally recognized" and not when such facts "are known, if at all, only by a specially informed class of persons."[17] It is suggested, however, that this limitation is a throw-back to the earlier view that common knowledge was a universal requirement, and is inconsistent with the later recognition that ready and indisputable verifiability is a distinct and sufficient basis for judicial notice. Such a restriction would stand as a bar to judicial notice in most of the areas of science, technology, and statistics, where it can be most usefully employed. It is true that the judge when asked to notice scientific facts will on examination of the data often conclude that the scientists do not agree or do agree that the supposed fact is doubtful or debatable, or he may conclude that he, the judge, is unable from his reading of the data to be sure that the fact *is* scientifically accepted. All these would be clear grounds for refusing notice. But to say that he can never notice a scientific fact if not commonly known assumes that judges having in view their general level of intelligence and training are not able, in a useful proportion of cases, to examine technical scientific materials and determine safely whether a given fact, theory or conclusion is accepted. Surely this is too modest an estimate of the capacity of our judges. Certainly the restriction is not the measure of what they actually do.[18]

In the progress of science facts and theories are constantly changing from the unknown or debatable to the realm of the accepted and established. Thus, the theories underlying the identification of the handwrit-

---

14. Brown v. Piper, 91 U.S. 37, 42 (1875) ("any means . . . which he may deem safe and proper"); Dwinell-Wright Co. v. National Fruit Product Co., 140 F.2d 618, 624, syl. 12 (C.C.A. 1st, 1944) (essays, magazine articles and brochures); People v. Mayes, 113 Cal. 618, 45 P. 860, 862, syl. 1 (1896) ("any source of information which he may deem authentic, either by inquiry of others, or by the examination of books, or by receiving the testimony of witnesses"); 9 Wigmore, Evidence, § 2568a; 31 C.J.S. 516, 517. Compare, however, the holding that the trial court should not rely on medical treatises on an issue on which evidence has been received, in Anderson v. Jersey Creamery Co., 278 Mich. 396, 270 N.W. 725, syl. 1 (1936), critically noted, 36 Mich.L.Rev. 610, 615 (1938). A favorite source, as might be expected, is the encyclopedia. See, e. g., Chiulla de Luca v. Board, 94 Conn. 7, 107 A. 611, 612 (1919) (propensities of lightning); Timson v. Manufacturers' Gas & Coal Co., 220 Mo. 580, 119 S.W. 565, 568 (1909) (that all coal mines generate gas, notice refused); Note, Notice of Scientific Facts from Encyclopedias and Dictionaries, 9 Kansas City L.Rev. 38 (1940).

15. Compare Russell v. Liberman, 71 R.I. 448, 46 A.2d 858, 860 (1946) ("In our judgment it is not reasonable to expect this court, by examining medical treatises that were not in evidence, to determine the cause or causes of acute hepatitis, and to substitute that information for the medical evidence that the trial justice adopted in making his decision."

16. Shapleigh v. Mier, 299 U.S. 468, 475, 57 S.Ct. 17, syl. 5, 81 L.Ed. 386 (1937) (question of validity of an expropriation under Mexican law; held, party having burden to prove invalidity fails, when the court is left without knowledge of invalidating rule, after exploring, in its function of judicial notice, every channel of information).

17. Lickfett v. Jorgenson, 179 Minn. 321, 229 N.W. 138, 139, syl. 3 (1930).

18. See the holdings described in notes 7–13, supra, and see Note, 36 Mich.L.Rev. 610, 611 (1938).

ing of a document by expert analysis, or of a person by his fingerprints, or of firearms by "ballistics-tests" were all once debatable but are now accepted.[19] The capacity of "lie-detector" tests, by measurements of blood-pressure interpreted by technicians, to reveal conscious lying is now considered debatable [20] but tomorrow may be viewed by the courts as scientifically established.[21] And even now, we probably are in transition from judicial scepticism to judicial acceptance of the certainty of conclusions to be drawn from biological tests showing non-paternity.[22] On the other hand innumerable scientific "certainties" of the past such as the fact of the flatness of the earth, or the efficacy of blood-letting as a remedy for disease, which could once have been judicially noticed under this principle, would today have to be noticed in reverse.

In the increasingly important practice of judicial notice of scientific and technological facts, some of the possibilities of error are, first, that the courts may fail to employ the doctrine of judicial notice in this field to the full measure of its usefulness,[23] second, that they may mistakenly accept as authoritative scientific theories that are outmoded or are not yet received by the specialists as completely verified, and third, that in taking judicial notice of accepted scientific facts, the courts, in particular cases may misconceive the conclusions or applications which are supposed to flow from them. Of these, it seems that the first has thus far been the most frequent shortcoming.

326. The Judge's Task as Law-Finder: Judicial Notice of Law.

One of the principal functions of the judge, for which he is specially qualified by professional equipment, is to find and interpret the law applicable to the issues in a trial, and in a jury case, to announce his findings of law to the jury for their guidance. The heavy-footed common law system of proof by witnesses and authenticated documents is too slow and cumbrous for the judge's task of finding what the applicable law is. Usually this law is familiar lore and if not he relies on the respective counsel to bring before him the statutes, reports, and source-books, and these every-day companions of judge and counsel are read from informally in discussion or cited and quoted in trial and appellate briefs. Occasionally the judge will go beyond the cited authorities to make his own investigation. In the ordinary process of finding the applicable law, the normal method, then, is by informal investigation of any sources satisfactory to the judge, that is, by judicial notice. We shall see that where this norm was departed from, it was in cases where the source-material was not easily accessible to the judge, as in case of "foreign" law, or "private" laws or city ordinances. We shall also see that as these materials become more accessible, the tendency is toward permitting the judges to do, what perhaps they should have done from the beginning, that is, to rely on the diligence of counsel to provide the necessary materials, and accordingly to take judicial notice of *all* law. This seems to be the goal toward which the practice is marching.

19. See §§ 172, 173, herein.

20. See People v. Forte, 279 N.Y. 204, 18 N.E.2d 31, syl. 2, 119 A.L.R. 1198 (1938) (court could not take judicial notice that the lie-detector is or is not effective for the discovery of truth). To like effect is State v. Cole, 354 Mo. 181, 188 S.W.2d 43, syl. 12, 13 (1945). See § 174, herein.

21. See Smallwood, Lie-detectors: Discussions and Proposals, 29 Corn.L.Q. 535 (1944), and § 174, herein.

22. Contrast Berry v. Chaplin, 74 Cal.App.2d 652, 169 P.2d 442, syl. 22–28 (1946) (jury may rely on mother's testimony and reject result of test) with Jordan v. Mace, 144 Me. 351, 69 A.2d 670, syl. 1–3 (1949) (verdict contrary to result of tests, authorized by statute, cannot stand).

23. The holding in Loth v. Loth, 227 Minn. 387, 35 N.W.2d 542, syl. 16, 6 A.L.R.2d 176 (1949) declining to notice the value of stocks presumably quoted on the market, seems to be an instance.

Domestic law. As to domestic law generally, the judge is not merely permitted to take judicial notice but required to do so,[1] at least if so requested, although in a particular case a party may be precluded on appeal from complaining of the judge's failure to notice a statute where his counsel has failed to call it to the judge's attention.[2] This general rule that judicial notice will be taken of domestic law means that state trial courts will notice Federal law,[3] which is controlling in every state, and has been held to mean that in a Federal trial court the laws of all the states, not merely of the state where it is sitting, are domestic and will be noticed.[4] Similarly all state-wide, or nation-wide, executive orders and proclamations,[5] which are legally effective, and all state or national administrative regulations,[6] having the force of law, will also be noticed. When such documents are included in the Federal Register it is provided that their contents shall be judicially noticed.[7] Under this principle the laws of antecedent governments will be noticed.[8] Exceptions to the principle, however, are recognized for private laws [9] and municipal ordinances.[10]

1. Strain v. Isaacs, 135 Oh.St. 495, 18 N.E.2d 816, 825 (Oh.App.1938) (dictum); Randall v. Comm., 183 Va. 182, 31 S.E.2d 571, 572, syl. 1 (1944) (dictum); 20 Am.Jur. Evidence, § 23; Uniform Rules of Evidence, Rule 9 (2) quoted § 323, note 4, supra.

2. Great American Ins. Co. v. Glenwood Irr. Co., 265 F. 594, syl. 3–5 (C.C.A.Colo.1920) (in action for damage from fire trial court's failure to charge that, under Colorado statute, leaving fire unextinguished would impose liability regardless of negligence, could not be complained of because plaintiff failed to call statute to judge's attention). See, however, an illuminating comment, Overlooking Statutes, 30 Yale L.J. 855 (1921) which surveys the cases and concludes that, generally, errors arising from ignorance of a statute should be corrected on appeal.

3. State v. Superior Court, 205 Ind. 355, 186 N.E. 310, syl. 12 (1933) (constitution and statutes); Mangum v. Atlantic Coast Line Ry. Co., 188 N.C. 689, 125 S.E. 549, syl. 1 (1924) (Federal Employers' Liability Act); Dec.Dig. Evidence, ⟨key⟩34.

4. Lamar v. Micon, 114 U.S. 218, 223, 5 S.Ct. 857, 29 L.Ed. 94 (1885) (on appeal from Federal Court in New York, proper for trial and appellate courts to notice Georgia law); Lane v. Sargent, 217 F. 237, syl. 1 (C.C.A.N.H.1914). This rule of judicial notice being a matter of procedure rather than substantive law it seems that the controlling force of state substantive law, under Erie R. Co. v. Tompkins, 304 U.S. 64, 58 S.Ct. 817, 82 L.Ed. 1188 (1938), is inapplicable. Wm. J. Lemp Brewing Co. v. Ems Brewing Co., 164 F.2d 290, syl. 4 (1947) (semble); but see Keeffe et al., Judicial Notice, 2 Stanford Law Review 664, 686 (1950). Compare Eliscu v. Fiber, 157 F.2d 136, syl. 1 (C.C.A.N.J.1946), which purports to rely on the New Jersey Uniform Act as a ground for noticing New York law. On appeal, however, from a state court, the Federal Supreme Court will not notice the law of another state unless the state court below could have done so. Hanley v. Donoghue, 116 U.S. 1, 6, 6 S.Ct. 242, 29 L.Ed. 535 (1885).

5. U. S. ex rel. Crow v. Mitchell, 89 F.2d 805, syl. 1, 67 App.D.C. 61 (1937) (Presidential orders relating to Civil Service); Hamilton v. James, 231 Ala. 668, 166 So. 425, syl. 4 (1936) (President's and Governors' proclamations declaring moratorium); Heyward v. Long, 178 S.C. 351, 183 S.E. 145, syl. 8, 114 A.L.R. 1130 (1936) (Governor's proclamation declaring highway department in state of insurrection); Parker v. Anderson, 112 Vt. 371, 25 A.2d 41, syl. 7 (1942) (President's order requiring Navy to use force to protect lives and property endangered by hostile power); Dec.Dig. Evidence, ⟨key⟩46.

6. Tucker v. Texas, 326 U.S. 517, 66 S.Ct. 274, syl. 2, 90 L.Ed 274 (1946) (regulations of Federal Public Housing Authority); United States v. Bradford, 160 F.2d 729, syl. 4 (C.C.A.2d 1947) (regulations of Federal administrative agencies); Milwaukee Mechanics' Ins. Co. v. Oliver, 139 F.2d 405, syl. 4 (C.C.A.Tex.1943) (regulations of state fire insurance board); Powell v. Anderson, 147 Neb. 872, 25 N.W.2d 401, syl. 4 (1946) (Federal regulations); 9 Wigmore, Evidence, § 2572, note 6; Dec.Dig. Evidence, ⟨key⟩47. For a comprehensive discussion, see Note, 59 Harv.L.Rev. 1137 (1946).

7. 44 U.S.C.A. § 307.

8. Ponce v. Roman Catholic Church, 210 U.S. 296, 309, 28 S.Ct. 737, 52 L.Ed. 1068 (1908) (Spanish laws in Puerto Rico); Martinez v. Gutierrez, 66 S.W.2d 678, syl. 8 (Tex.Comm.App.1933).

9. Courts do not notice private acts. Bolick v. City of Charlotte, 191 N.C. 677, 132 S.E. 660, syl. 1 (1926). Chambers v. Atchison, T. & S. F. Ry. Co., 32 Ariz. 102, 255 P. 1092, syl. 1 (1927) (private Acts of Congress). The same has been held as to local laws. Caldwell v. Crosser, 20 S.W.2d 822, syl. 2 (Tex.Civ.App.1928, error refused). And Special Acts. Brodsky v. Fine, 263 Mass. 51, 160 N.E. 335,

9. See Note 10 on following Page.

In terms of practical expediency under modern conditions these last mentioned limitations seem indefensible.[11]

The law of sister states. It is easy to see how the difference of languages and inaccessibility of source-books should have led the English courts to develope the common law rule that the laws of foreign nations would not be noticed but must be pleaded and proved as facts.[12] The assumption in the earlier cases in this country [13] that the courts of one state must treat the laws of another state as foreign for this purpose is less understandable and to the after-view seems a deplorable instance of mechanical jurisprudence. Yet it remains today, in nearly every state which has not yet adopted a

reformatory statute, the common law rule that notice will not be given to the laws of sister states.[14] This is probably the most inconvenient of all the limitations upon the practice of judicial notice. Notice here could certainly be justified on the principle of certainty and verifiability,[15] and the burden on the judge could be minimized by casting the responsibility upon counsel either to agree upon a stipulation as to the law or to produce on each side for the benefit of the court all materials necessary for ascertaining the law in question.

Under the present practice when pleading and proof of the foreign law has been overlooked, or has been unsuccessfully attempted, the resulting danger of injustice is somewhat

---

syl. 3 (1928). But all such Acts are readily accessible nowadays, and the rule refusing notice is archaic. Half the states have abrogated it by statute. 9 Wigmore, Evidence, § 2572, n. 14.

10. Gardner v. Capital Transit Co., 80 App.D.C. 297, 152 F.2d 288, syl. 5 (1945) (District Court in District of Columbia properly declined to notice speed ordinance of the District); Page v. Weiland, 137 Oh.St. 198, 38 N.E.2d 583, syl. 2 (1940); Dec. Dig. Evidence, ☞32. This needlessly burdensome practice has been reformed by statute in a few states only. 9 Wigmore, Evidence, § 2572, note 15. And in New Hampshire, by decision the enlightened result has been reached that the court may in its discretion notice ordinances. Walsh v. Public Service Co., 92 N.H. 331, 30 A.2d 494, syl. 3, 4 (1943). However, a municipal court will notice the ordinances of the city, and by what seems the better view, on appeal the reviewing court will do the same. Orose v. Hodge Drive-It-Yourself Co., 132 Oh.St. 607, 9 N.E.2d 671, syl. 1, 2, 111 A.L.R. 954 (1937), Notes, 11 U.Cin.L.Rev. 535, 4 Oh.St.L.J. 131, 111 A.L.R. 954. A city charter, granted by public law, will of course be noticed. Grant v. Aldermen, 316 Mass. 432, 55 N.E.2d 705, syl. 4 (1944).

11. They are discarded in the provisions of the Uniform Rules of Evidence, Rule 9 (2) (3) (judge may, and if furnished by the party with sufficient information, must notice private acts, and ordinances and regulations of governmental divisions).

12. See, e. g., Freemoult v. Dedire, 1 P.Wms. 431, 24 Eng.Rep. 458 (1718), Mostyn v. Fabrigas, 1 Cowp. 161, 174, 98 Eng.Rep. 1021 (1774). This view had wide support in continental law also. Nussbaum,

The Problem of Proving Foreign Law, 50 Yale L.J. 1019, n. 2 (1941).

13. See, e. g., Brackett v. Norton, 4 Conn. 517, 520 (1923).

14. See, e. g., United Merc. Agencies v. Bissonnette, 155 Fla. 22, 19 So.2d 466, syl. 4, 5, 155 A.L.R. 916 (1944) (must be pleaded and proved); Mason v. Pelkes, 57 Idaho 10, 59 P.2d 1087, syl. 8 (1936); Hillmer v. Grondahl, 109 Vt. 388, 199 A. 255, syl. 5 (1938). In New Hampshire, however, the court found that this rule was so wanting in "logical support" and "practical merits" that the court's continuing responsibility for developing a reasonable procedure justified it in abandoning the outmoded practice and in taking judicial notice of the law of sister states. Saloshin v. Houle, 85 N.H. 126, 155 A. 47, syl. 11, 14, 15 (1931). If such a common-sense attitude toward the rules of proof were more widespread the law of evidence would soon be freed from many of its archaic rigidities.

The burden of the requirement of technical proof is somewhat mitigated by statutes and judicial holdings admitting as evidence printed copies of statutes and decisions when they profess to be official copies. 5 Wigmore, Evidence, § 1684. Or privately printed reports of cases when proved to be commonly used in the courts of the state where the cases were decided. 6 id. § 1703. Or even legal treatises of recognized credit. 6 id. § 1697. The practice as to statutes has been codified in the Uniform Proof of Statutes Act, now in effect in twenty-three states and territories. 9A Unif.Laws Ann. 246, 247.

15. See § 325, above.

mitigated by the presumption that the law of the sister state is the same as that of the forum,[16] or more simply the practice of applying local law if the law of the other state is not invoked and proven.[17] But this presumption-tool is too rough for the job in hand,[18] particularly when the materials for ascertaining the laws of sister states are today almost as readily accessible as those for local law, and in any event counsel as officers of the court are available to find and present those materials to the judge in just the same informal and convenient fashion as if they were arguing a question of local law. In 1936 the Conference of Commissioners on Uniform Laws accepted this view and drafted the Uniform Judicial Notice of Foreign Law Act [19] which has now in substance been adopted

16. Where the question is one which would be governed at the forum by a rule of common law, it is presumed that the same common law rule prevails in the sister state. Vartan Garapedian Inc. v. Anderson, 92 N.H. 390, 31 A.2d 371, syl. 1 (1943). But it has been held that this presumption does not obtain as to the law of Louisiana, which was not regarded as a common law state. Kennard v. Illinois Central Ry. Co., 177 Tenn. 311, 148 S.W.2d 1017, syl. 5, 134 A.L.R. 770 (1941). Where the matter is governed by statute in the forum state, the majority of courts will presume that a similar statute exists in the sister state. Hall v. Proctor, 242 Ala. 636, 7 So.2d 764, syl. 12 (1942); Buhler v. Madison, 105 Utah 39, 140 P.2d 933, syl. 14 (1943). The minority will in these circumstances presume that the common law of the forum before it was modified by statute prevails in the sister state. Stern v. Lieberman, 307 Mass. 77, 29 N.E.2d 839, syl. 1 (1940); Zwirn v. Galento, 288 N.Y. 428, 43 N.E.2d 474, syl. 2 (1942). See 9 Wigmore, Evidence, § 2536; Stumberg, Conflict of Laws, 176 et seq. (2d ed. 1951); Parker, Note, 12 Tex.L.Rev. 333 (1934); Decennial Digests, Evidence, ☞80; 31 C.J.S., Evidence, § 133; Restatement, Conflict of Laws, §§ 622, 623.

17. Bollinger v. Gallegher, 144 Pa. 205, 22 A. 815, syl. 3 (1891); Blethen v. Bonner, 93 Tex. 141, 53 S.W. 1016, syl. 1 (1899).

18. See, e. g., Dixie Ohio Exp. Co. v. Butler, 179 Tenn. 358, 166 S.W.2d 614, syl. 1–3 (1942), noted 17 Tenn.L.Rev. 877, where the plaintiff sued in Tennessee for a death injury which occurred in Kentucky. The Kentucky Death Act was neither pleaded nor proved, but a verdict and judgment for damages was rendered for plaintiff. The Supreme Court, though in previous decisions it had presumed that statutory law in other states was the same as in Tennessee, declined, "in view of the well known differences between statutes of this kind [Death Acts] in the different states" to presume the identity of the Kentucky statute with that of the forum, but recognizing that the failure to plead and prove the Kentucky statute was a mere oversight, it did not dismiss the suit but remanded it with leave to the plaintiff to amend her declaration. It called attention, however, to the Uniform Judicial Notice of Foreign Law Act, and doubtless as a result of this intimation, the legislature adopted the Act.St.1943, Feb. 11, c. 137.

19. Its substantive provisions follow:
"Section 1. (Judicial Notice.) Every court of this state shall take judicial notice of the common law and statutes of every state, territory and other jurisdiction of the United States.
"Section 2. (Information of the Court.) The court may inform itself of such laws in such manner as it may deem proper, and the court may call upon counsel to aid it in obtaining such information.
"Section 3. (Ruling Reviewable.) The determination of such laws shall be made by the court and not by the jury, and shall be reviewable.
"Section 4. (Evidence as to Laws of other Jurisdiction.) Any party may also present to the trial court any admissible evidence of such laws, but, to enable a party to offer evidence of the law in another jurisdiction or to ask that judicial notice be taken thereof, reasonable notice shall be given to the adverse parties either in the pleadings or otherwise.
"Section 5. (Foreign Country.) The law of a jurisdiction other than those referred to in Section 1 shall be an issue for the court, but shall not be subject to the foregoing provisions concerning judicial notice." 1936 Handbook Nat'l. Conference of Commissioners on Unif. State Laws, 355–359; 1945 id. 124; 9 Uniform Laws Ann. 401, 1954 suppl. 132; Notes, 26 Corn.L.Q. 502 (1941); 46 Harv.L.Rev. 1019 (1933); 32 Mass.L.Q. no. 2, p. 20. As to the requirement of pleading or notice, see Note, 134 A.L.R. 576. It has been said that where contrary statutes or decisions of the sister state have not been called to the court's attention, the presumption of identity will prevail. Strout v. Burgess, 144 Me. 263, 68 A.2d 241, syl. 20, 21, 12 A.L.R.2d 939 (1949); Knych v. Trustees, 320 Mass. 339, 69 N.E.2d 575, syl. 1 (1946), but compare Heater v. Mittendorf, 72 Oh.App. 4, 50 N.E.2d 559, syl. 4 (1943) (court required to inform itself of statutes of sister state). In ascertaining the sister state's law, it is proper for the court to consider an affidavit of an attorney of that state setting out statutes and passages from court-opinions claimed to be pertinent. Franzen v. Equitable Life Assur. Soc., 130 N.J.L. 457, 33 A.2d 599, syl. 7 (1943).

by more than half the states.[20] It has been suggested with much persuasiveness that Congress could and should, under the powers conferred by the Full Faith and Credit clause of the Constitution prescribe this practice for the courts of all the states.[21]

The law of foreign countries.[22] Statutes in four of our states[23] provide that the court must take judicial notice of the law of foreign countries, and two states, New York[24] and Michigan,[25] permit the court to do so in its discretion. Maryland requires its courts to notice the laws of foreign jurisdictions "having a system of law based on the common law of England."[26] The Uniform Act, however, contains no provision for notice of the law of other nations. Accordingly in the Federal courts and in all the states, except the seven referred to above, the common law practice of refusing judicial notice to the law of foreign countries prevails.[27] Accordingly in these jurisdictions the burden of strict proof

must be undertaken. When the foreign law is in the form of a statute or decree, it is generally held at least in the earlier cases in this country that an authenticated copy must be produced.[28] This would require, in strictness, a sworn or officially certified copy,[29] but (as in respect to the laws of sister states[30] this has been ameliorated by statutes or decisions permitting the use of a copy in a book purporting to be printed by authority of the foreign state or proved to be commonly recognized in its courts.[31] Ordinarily the written text must be interpreted in the light of the applicable decisions, treatises and commentaries, and this under common-law proof must be accomplished by taking the testimony in person or by deposition of an expert in the foreign law.[32] The adversary of course is free to take the testimony of other experts if he can find such on his side, and the cross-examination of conflicting experts is likely to accentuate the disagreements.[33] This

---

20. See statutes and court rules compiled in 9 Wigmore, Evidence, § 2573, and suppl., and statutes referred to in 9 Uniform Laws Ann. 1954 suppl. p. 132.

21. Hartwig, Congressional Enactment of Uniform Judicial Notice Act, 40 Mich.L.Rev. 174 (1941). See also Field, Judicial Notice of Public Acts, 12 Minn. L.Rev. 439 (1928); Simpson, Note, 14 Wash.L.Rev. 222 (1939).

22. For valuable discussions, see Nussbaum, The Problem of Proving Foreign Law, 50 Yale L.J. 1018 (1941); Keeffe, Landis, and Shadd, Sense and Nonsense about Judicial Notice, 2 Stanford L.Rev. 664, 673 (1950); Wachtell, 69 U.S.L.Rev. 526, 580 (1935).

23. Mass.G.L. (Ter.Ed.) c. 233, § 70; Miss.Code 1942, § 2168; North Carolina, G.S. § 8–4; West Virginia, Code 57–1–4.

24. Civ.Prac.Act, § 344a.

25. Comp.Laws 1948, §§ 617.25, 617.27.

26. Code 1951, art. 35, § 56.

27. See, e. g., U. S. ex rel. Jelic v. District Director of Immigration, 106 F.2d 14, syl. 11 (C.C.A.2d 1939); Rowan v. Commissioner of Int. Revenue, 120 F.2d 515, syl. 3 (1941); Groome v. Freyn Eng. Co., 374 Ill. 113, 28 N.E.2d 274, syl. 4 (1940); Greer v. Paust, 202 Minn. 633, 279 N.W. 568, syl. 2 (1938); Dec. Dig. Evidence, ⬅37.

28. See e. g. Pierce v. Indseth, 106 U.S. 546, 551, 1 S.Ct. 418, 27 L.Ed. 254 (1882). Cases pro and con are cited in 4 Wigmore, Evidence, § 1271 n. 4. In England an expert was permitted to testify to the effect of the foreign statute, and indeed the statute's terms were not sufficient to prove the foreign law without the expert's opinion. Baron de Bode's case, 8 Q.B. 208, 115 Eng.Rep. 854 (1845); 7 Wigmore, Evidence, § 2090a.

29. Emery v. Berry, 28 N.H. 473, 485 (1854); see 4 Wigmore, Evidence, § 1273.

30. See Note 14, supra.

31. See Uniform Proof of Statutes Act, 9 Uniform Laws Ann. 609, 1951 suppl. 286, and statutes and decisions collected 5 Wigmore, Evidence § 1684, 6 id. § 1703.

32. A case illustrating this practice is In re Neilson's Estate, 118 Mont. 304, 165 P.2d 792 (1946) (deposition of legal counselor of Danish Legation discussing legal treatises and giving opinion as to inheritance rights of aliens under Danish law).

33. "It is the writer's impression that under the present practice of the courts, skillful advocates may succeed in developing confusing divergencies between experts on purely verbal matters in situations where coherent and well-substantiated written opinions would eliminate all difficulties." Nussbaum, op. cit., 50 Yale L.J. 1018, 1029.

method of proof seems to maximize expense and delay and hardly seems best calculated to ensure a correct decision by our judges on questions of foreign law. It could be vastly improved by pre-trial conferences [34] in which agreements as to undisputed aspects of the foreign law could be secured, and by the appointment by the court of one or more experts on foreign law as referees [35] or as court-chosen experts [36] to report their findings to the court. In any event the adoption by the Federal courts and by the states which have not yet adopted it, of the flexible procedure of judicial notice, whereby the court is free to get its information from any convenient source, seems the path of justice and common sense. The courts could then accept, as they should, the opinions of experts submitted by letters instead of being limited to cross-examined testimony.[37]

The unwillingness of the courts to notice the laws of other countries creates difficulties where the party whose case or defense depends, under conflicts rules, upon foreign law and he fails to prove that law as a fact. There are several solutions. First, the court may decide the issue against him for failure of proof.[38] This is often a harsh and arbitrary result. Second, the court may simply apply the law of the forum on the ground that no other law is before it,[39] especially if the parties have tried the case as if local law were applicable.[40] Third, the court may presume that the law of the other country is the same as that of the forum,[41] thus reaching the same result as under the second theory but raising intellectual difficulties because the presumption is so frequently contrary to fact. When the doctrine involved is one of common law, but the other nation is not a common law country, some courts will decline to apply the presumption.[42] On the other hand, when the common law rule invoked is a part of the common fund of all civilized systems,

---

34. As provided, for example, by Rule 12, Federal Rules of Civil Procedure.

35. As to extent of court's common law powers in this direction, see Ex parte Peterson, 253 U.S. 300, 40 S.Ct. 253, 64 L.Ed. 919 (1920).

36. See Wigmore, Evidence, § 563; Buescher, Use of Experts by the Courts, 54 Harv.L.Rev. 1105 (1941); Uniform Rules of Evidence, R. 59. See also Usatorre v. The Victoria, 172 F.2d 434, 443 (C.A.2d 1949), where in reversing a lower court decision for the judge's failure to make a finding as to Argentine law, the court said: "Perhaps [such a finding] can be made without further testimony on the subject. It may be that, if he considers it desirable, some arrangement will be agreed upon which will enable the judge to summon an expert of his own choosing."

37. See the enlightening Comment by Prof. Nussbaum, Proving the Law of Foreign Countries, 3 Am. J.Comp.Law 60 (1954), in which he describes the cost, delay and consequent injustices resulting from the common law requirements of proof, and from the unwillingness of those courts which are empowered by legislation to take judicial notice, to use and rely on the simple informal methods of ascertaining foreign law which are in use in civil law countries.

38. Compare Cuba Railroad v. Crosby, 222 U.S. 473, 32 Sup.Ct. 132, 23 L.Ed. 190 (1912) (the plaintiff, an employee of the defendant, lost his hand in an accident due to a defect in machinery which the defendant had promised to repair; the plaintiff having failed to prove the Cuban law, the Supreme Court in an opinion by Holmes, J., reversed a judgment below for the plaintiff for this failure).

39. See, e. g., Burgess v. Western Union Telegraph Co., 92 Tex. 125, 46 S.W. 794, syl. 1 (1899).

40. Watford v. Alabama & Florida Lumber Co., 152 Ala. 178, 44 So. 567, syl. 4 (1907).

41. See, generally, the illuminating discussion in Nussbaum, op. cit., 50 Yale L.J. 1018, 1035 et seq. (1941). See also Stumberg, Conflict of Laws, 177 2d ed. 1951). Cases are collected in Dec.Dig. Evidence, ☞81.

42. Cuba R. Co. v. Crosby, 222 U.S. 473, 479, 32 S. Ct. 132, 23 L.Ed. 190 (1912) (law of Cuba as to responsibility of employer for injury to employee); Commissioner of Internal Revenue v. Hyde, 82 F. 2d 174, syl. 9 (C.C.A.2d 1936) (court cannot presume that French civil law same as local common law in respect to validity of contract made in France for creation of trust by husband for wife); In re Everett's Estate, 112 Vt. 252, 23 A.2d 202, syl. 6, 7 (1942) (Italy not presumed to have common law rule requiring seal on power of attorney to execute a bond).

such as the binding force of ordinary commercial agreements, the presumption is applied though the foreign country is not a common law country.[43] Moreover, by what is probably the prevailing and more convenient view, if the question would be governed locally by a statute, a like statute in the foreign country may be presumed.[44]

International and maritime law. The rules, principles and traditions of "international law," or "the law of nations," or the maritime law common to Western nations generally, will be noticed in the Federal [45] and state courts.[46] Sometimes this is a mere noticing of the international sources of the court's local law, sometimes it may constitute the noticing of the law regulating transactions in a foreign country. But as to the latter there are limitations which narrow the inviting possibilities in the international field

of the process of informal proof and free investigation, which we call judicial notice. If the maritime rules [47] or the prize rules [48] of the foreign country have been published here by governmental authority as the authentic foreign law they will be noticed. Or if the foreign maritime rules are embodied in a widely-adopted international convention, they may be considered as having passed into general maritime law, and noticed as such.[49] But even in this last case, it was held that the court could not notice the subsurface effect and interpretation of such rules, but would leave this to formal proof.[50] Specific rules of maritime law obtaining in the foreign state, not claimed to be part of the common fund of international rules will not be noticed.[51] Even the presumption of identity of the foreign law with the local law, which would seem to be unusually convenient and

43. Cuba R. Co. v. Crosby, 222 U.S. 473, 478, 32 S. Ct. 132, 23 L.Ed. 190 (1912) (dictum); Parrot v. Mexican Cent. R. Co., 207 Mass. 184, 93 N.E. 590, syl. 7 (1911) (presumption that defendant would be liable in Mexico on agreement made there by its general passenger agent, under "universally recognized fundamental principles of right and wrong").

44. Wickersham v. Johnston, 104 Cal. 407, 38 P. 89, syl. 1 (1894) (sale of note by English executors, powers of executors presumed to be limited as under California statute); Murphy v. Murphy, 145 Cal. 482, 78 P. 1053, syl. 3 (1904) (California statutory rate of interest presumed to prevail as to amount due on English judgment). Contra: Parrot v. Mexican Cent. R. Co., 207 Mass. 184, 90 N.E. 590, syl. 5 (1911) (dictum).

45. The Paquete Habana, 175 U.S. 677, 20 S.Ct. 290, 299, syl. 6, 44 L.Ed. 320 (1899) (question of what was the international rule as to whether warring nations would abstain from seizing coastal fishing vessels of the enemy country; elaborate opinion by Gray, J.).

46. McFeena's Adm'r v. Paris Home Telephone, etc., Co., 190 Ky. 299, 227 S.W. 450, syl. 3 (1921) (dictum).

47. The New York, 175 U.S. 187, 20 S.Ct. 67, 70, 44 L.Ed. 126 (1899); The Scotia, 14 Wall. 170, 20 L. Ed. 822 (1872) (British orders in council as to the "rules of the road" at sea, later adopted by Congress).

48. Talbot v. Seeman, 1 Cranch 1, 38, 2 L.Ed. 15, 27 (1801) (French decree law as to condemnation of prizes).

49. Black Diamond S. S. Corp. v. Robert Stewart and Sons, Ltd., 336 U.S. 386, 396, 397, 69 S.Ct. 622, syl. 7, 8, 93 L.Ed. 754 (1949).

50. Such holding rests on a supposition that conflicting partisan expert testimony will reveal more accurately the right foreign interpretation than will the submission of informal opinions and briefs —a most debatable assumption.

51. Black Diamond S. S. Corp. v. Robert Stewart & Sons, Ltd., 336 U.S. 386, 396, 397, 69 S.Ct. 622, 628, 93 L.Ed. 754 (1949) ("It is true that this Court has on several occasions held international rules which had passed into the general maritime law to be subject to judicial notice. . . . But where less widely recognized rules of foreign maritime law have been involved, the Court has adhered to the general principle that foreign law is to be proved as a fact."); Yang-Tsze Ins. Ass'n v. Furness Withy & Co., Ltd., 215 F. 859, syl. 4 (C.C.A.2d 1914) (though local laws of two countries to which colliding vessels belong may coincide, such laws cannot notice such laws nor apply them unless pleaded and proved); Usatorre v. The Victoria, 172 F.2d 434, syl. 4 (C.C.A.2d 1949) (where crew of torpedoed Argentine vessel abandoned ship and then volunteered to return to the drifting derelict, their duty to return to vessel and hence their right to salvage, determinable by Argentine law which must be

realistic in the maritime field, has been narrowly restricted.[52]

327. Facts Relating to the Personnel, Operation and Records of the Court.[1]

There is an area of facts relating to the court of which he is the principal officer that the judge has an official duty to know or to ascertain, and the judge obviously has special facilities for learning these facts. Moreover, many of the facts about the court, such as its jurisdiction, are regulated by domestic law, and many of them if not of general professional knowledge are readily and certainly verifiable. These bases for judicial notice apply to the trial judge who is asked to notice facts about his own court, and to the appellate judges as grounds for noticing facts re-

lating to their own court and those pertaining to the courts over which they have appellate supervision. Thus, the judges take notice of the identity of the officers of their courts, such as the other judges,[2] the sheriffs,[3] clerks,[4] and attorneys;[5] of the duration of the terms and sessions,[6] and of the rules of court.[7] It would seem obvious that the judge of a court would take notice of all the records of the institution over which he presides, but the courts have been slow here to give the principles of judicial notice their full reach of logic and expediency. It is settled of course that the courts, trial and appellate, take notice of their own respective records in the present litigation, both as to matters occurring in the immediate trial,[8] and in pre-

proved as a fact; but judge not bound to follow the opinion of the only expert produced).

52. Ozanic v. United States, 165 F.2d 738, syl. 17, 18 (C.C.A.2d 1948) (in libel for damage to Yugoslavian vessel on high seas libellant has burden to prove Yugoslav law as fact; "However it might be in respect to British maritime law, we cannot assume that the law of Yugoslavia, a civil law country and not even a great maritime power, is the same in respect to the measure of damages as that of the United States."); Sonnesen v. Panama Transport Co., 298 N.Y. 262, 82 N.E.2d 569, syl. 4 (1948) (court would not notice Panama law as to seaman's right of maintenance and cure, under Civ.Prac.Act, § 344a, nor would it assume Panama maritime law same as ours).

1. See 9 Wigmore, Evidence, §§ 2578, 2579; 31 C.J. S., Evidence, §§ 44–50; Dec.Dig. Evidence, ☞40–43.

2. Payne v. Williams, 47 Ariz. 396, 56 P.2d 186, syl. 4 (1936) (Supreme Court notices names of superior court judges, their counties and terms); State ex rel. Nickerson v. Rose, 351 Mo. 1198, 175 S.W.2d 768, syl. 9 (1944) (similar). See also Comm. v. Keenan, 347 Pa. 574, 33 A.2d 244, syl. 5, 6 (1943) where, in mandamus proceeding to compel judges of a common pleas court to decide certain cases long pending, the Supreme Court took judicial notice that "illness" pleaded by the president judge as excuse for his neglect of duty was of such self-inflicted nature as to afford no excuse for his failure to perform his duties.

3. Sowers-Taylor Co. v. Collins, 14 S.W.2d 692 (Mo. App.1929) (names of officers authorized to serve process).

4. Favre v. Louisville & N. R. Co., 180 Miss. 843, 178 So. 327, syl. 2 (1938).

5. Squire v. Bates, 132 Oh.St. 161, 5 N.E.2d 690, syl. 4 (1937) (persons who have been admitted and dates of their admission).

6. Vance v. Harkey, 186 Ark. 730, 55 S.W.2d 785, syl. 1 (1933) (Supreme Court knows that term at which decree entered has elapsed); Roberts v. Turk, 225 Ky. 100, 7 S.W.2d 849, syl. 5 (1928) (Court of Appeals knows its own terms).

7. A trial court, of course, knows its own rules without formal proof. Wallace v. Martin, 166 So. 874, syl. 1 (La.App.1936). And on general principles an appellate court knows judicially what the trial court judicially knew. See § 330, note 22, infra. Nevertheless, many appellate courts have refused to notice trial court rules, unless embodied in the bill of exceptions. See, e. g., Scovill v. Cassidy, 275 Ill. 462, 114 N.E. 181, syl. 17 (1916) (where municipal court rules not in bill of exceptions, appellate court erred in ordering the rules certified to them and considering them when certified); and cases cited 31 C.J.S. 617, n. 86. This inconvenient formalism has been repudiated by statute in Illinois, see Boettcher v. Howard Engraving Co., 389 Ill. 75, 58 N.E.2d 866, syl. 2 (1945) (applying S.H.A. ch. 51, § 48b). And elsewhere by decision, see e. g., Hudson v. Hoster, 47 N.E.2d 637, syl. 3, 4 (Ct.App. Ohio, 1942) (Court of Appeals will notice rules and customary practices of the Common Pleas Court).

8. Nichols v. Nichols, 126 Conn. 614, 13 A.2d 591, syl. 8, 12 (1940) (superseded pleading claimed to constitute admission, will be noticed but must be

vious trials or hearings.[9] The principle seemingly is equally applicable to matters of record in the proceedings in other cases in the same court, and some decisions have recognized this,[10] but the majority thus far have adhered to the needless requirement of formal proof, rather than informal presentation, of recorded proceedings in other suits in the same court.[11] Matters of record in other courts are usually denied notice but one decision blazes the trail for such notice on the ground that they are public documents.[12]

328. Other Governmental Facts.

Not only is the judge a judicial officer with the special functions of knowing or informing himself about the law and about the operations of his branch of the court-system, but he is an officer as well of the general state or Federal government and has duties and facilities of knowledge about the powers and operations of such general government.[1] Not only does this principle serve to justify the practice of noticing governmental facts, but other principles we have discussed often offer additional bases for judicial notice in respect to particular governmental facts. Thus, the location of a state capital is a matter of common knowledge and will usually also be designated as such in some domestic law, and furthermore, such location would be a matter verifiable as certain and indisputable. Accordingly, in considering a question of notice of governmental facts, not only the present principle but the foregoing alternative possibilities should be canvassed.

International Affairs. The courts, state and Federal, take judicial notice of treaties entered into by the United States with foreign nations, as part of the national law.[2] Similarly, as a governmental fact, the courts notice the recognition by the executive department of a particular foreign government.[3] The making of pacts and treaties between foreign governments would not, seemingly, be noticed under this last theory, but important facts of international relations, such as the Munich pact of 1938,[4] may be

---

9.   Collins v. Leahy, 347 Mo. 133, 146 S.W.2d 609, syl. 5 (1941) (where city map was part of record of prior appeal to Supreme Court, court would take notice of it on subsequent appeal though not introduced in evidence at later trial). But compare In re Aughenbaugh, 125 F.2d 887, syl. 1, 2, 5, 6 (C.C. A.2d 1941) (referee in hearing on contested claim not entitled to consider, without notice to parties, facts shown by papers previously filed in the same bankruptcy proceedings).

10.   Willson v. Security-First Nat. Bank, 21 Calif.2d 705, 134 P.2d 800, syl. 3 (1943) (dictum: exceptionally, court will notice proceedings in another case in interest of justice); Fox v. Schaeffer, 131 Conn. 439, 41 A.2d 46, syl. 16, 157 A.L.R. 132 (1944) (right to notice judgment in another case does not mean that court can give weight to conclusions embodied in judgment); Johnson v. Marsh, 146 Neb. 257, 19 N.W.2d 366, syl. 3 (1945) (may notice where other case interwoven with present).

11.   Gray v. Bradford, 194 Ga. 492, 22 S.E.2d 43, syl. 10 (1942); People v. McKinlay, 367 Ill. 504, 11 N.E. 2d 933, syl. 6 (1938); Naffah v. City Deposit Bank, 339 Pa. 157, 13 A.2d 63, syl. 3 (1940); Dec.Dig. Evidence, ⊜43(3).

called to trial court's attention); Branch v. Branch, 194 Ga. 575, 22 S.E.2d 124, syl. 2 (1942).

12.   Zahn v. Transamerica Corp., 162 F.2d 36, 48, note 20 (C.C.A.Del.1947).

1.   See, e. g., State v. Sims, 132 W.Va. 826, 54 S.E.2d 729, 741 (1949) (". . . we are not required to close our eyes to things in plain view, especially in matters which concern the government of the state, of which we are a part.").

2.   Allen v. Markham, 156 F.2d 653, syl. 9 (C.C.A.Calif. 1946); Munich Reinsurance Co. v. First Reinsurance Co., 6 F.2d 742, syl. 4 (C.C.A.Conn.1925); Seaboard Trust Co. v. Topken, 130 N.J.Eq. 46, 20 A.2d 709, syl. 4 (Ch.1941); Dec.Dig. Evidence, ⊜ 39.

3.   Oetjen v. Central Leather Co., 246 U.S. 297, 38 S. Ct. 309, syl. 1, 62 L.Ed. 726 (1918) (recognition of Carranza government in Mexico first as de facto and later as de jure government); United States v. Belmont, 301 U.S. 324, 330, 57 S.Ct. 758, 81 L.Ed. 1134 (1937) (recognition of Soviet government); 9 Wigmore, Evidence, §§ 2566, 2574.

4.   United States ex rel. Reichel v. Carusi, 157 F.2d 732, syl. 1 (C.C.A.3d) (court took notice of treaty between Germany and Czechoslovakia and its terms); Fox River Paper Corp. v. United States, 65 F. Supp. 605, syl. 4 (E.D.Wis.1946) (making of

noticed as a matter of common knowledge or as a matter of readily verifiable current history. Our declaration of war with a foreign power would be noticed as a governmental fact,[5] as would the making of an armistice or formal termination of hostilities, but a court has also noticed as a matter of current history the fact of continued fighting in remote areas after the Japanese surrender in September, 1945.[6] In like manner, the existence of a state of war between foreign countries may be noticed as a notorious fact.[7]

Facts as to the Territory of the Government.[8] Under the present principle the state courts take judicial notice of the boundaries of the nation,[9] of the location of the states and territories,[10] and the location and boundaries of the state in which the court is sitting[11] and of the counties,[12] districts[13]

and townships[14] thereof, as well as the location of the capital of the state and the location and identity of the county seats.[15] Similarly, the location and boundary of any incorporated city, as a subdivision of the state should be noticed.[16] The location of governmental buildings[17] and institutions[18] is likewise noticed.

Identity of Officials and Other Facts about Them.[19] All courts would presumably notice the identity of the principal officers of the national government.[20] Courts whether state or Federal sitting in a state would notice the identity of incumbents of principal state offices.[21] Similarly trial courts are entitled to notice the incumbency of particular persons as officers of the county or district in which the court is sitting.[22] Similarly, the dates of the beginning and end of their periods of

Munich treaty in September 1938 and its effect on world anticipation of peace, noticed).

5. See Johnson v. Biddle, 12 F.2d 366, syl. 3 (1926) (courts take judicial notice whether United States is or is not engaged in war); Dec.Dig. Evidence, ⊕ 11f. Compare Gara v. United States, 178 F.2d 38, syl. 9 (C.A.6th, 1949) (noticing existence of "cold war" necessitating enactment of Selective Service Act of 1948).

6. Miller v. Fowler, 200 Miss. 776, 28 So.2d 837, syl. 3–7 (1947).

7. The Austvard, 34 F.Supp. 431, syl. 9, 10 (D.Md. 1940).

8. 9 Wigmore, Evidence, § 2575, Dec.Dig. Evidence, ⊕25, 31 C.J.S., Evidence, § 33b.

9. Reese v. Cobb, 135 S.W. 220, syl. 2 (Tex.Civ.App. 1911) (boundary line between United States and Mexico, as recognized by their governments).

10. Curtis v. Sexton, 252 Mo. 221, 159 S.W. 512, syl. 11 (1913) (sister states); Swofford v. State, 3 Tex. App. 76, 84 (Indian Territory) (1877).

11. Watson v. Western Union Co., 178 N.C. 471, 101 S.E. 81, syl. 4 (1919).

12. State v. Armstrong, 315 Mo. 298, 286 S.W. 705, syl. 1 (1926) (location of city and county of St. Louis); Elmore County v. Tallapoosa County, 221 Ala. 182, 128 So. 158, syl. 1 (1930) (area and boundaries).

13. Board of Education v. State, 222 Ala. 70, 131 So. 239, syl. 2 (1930) (school district).

14. Nelson v. Thomas, 103 Cal.App. 108, 283 P. 982, syl. 2 (1930).

15. Bunten v. Rock Springs Grazing Assn., 29 Wyo. 461, 215 P. 244, syl. 26 (1923).

16. Rosenau v. Lansing, 113 Ore. 638, 234 P. 270, syl. 2 (1925).

17. Times-Mirror Co. v. Superior Court, 3 Cal.2d 309, 44 P.2d 547, syl. 7 (1935).

18. Murphy v. Daly, Warden, 206 Ind. 179, 188 N.E. 769, syl. 6 (1934) (state prison).

19. See 9 Wigmore, Evidence, § 2576; Dec.Dig. Evidence, ⊕44; 31 C.J.S. Evidence, § 37.

20. United States v. Phelps, 40 F.2d 500, syl. 1 (C. C.A.2d 1930) (assistants to the Secretary of Labor); Lyman Flood Prevention Ass'n v. City of Topeka, 152 Kan. 484, 106 P.2d 117, syl. 1 (1940) (time of retirement of Woodring as Secretary of War); In re Son-se-grah's Will, 78 Okl. 213, 189 P. 865, syl. 3 (1920) ("heads of departments of the federal government and their chief subordinates," here the Assistant Secretary of the Interior).

21. See, e. g., Picking v. Pennsylvania R. Co., 151 F. 2d 240, syl. 3 (C.C.A.Pa.1945) (that named defendants were officials of Pennsylvania and New York); Patten v. Miller, 190 Ga. 123, 8 S.E.2d 757, syl. 2 (1940) (chairman, State Highway Board).

22. See, e. g., Prudential Insurance Co. v. Calvin, 227 Ala. 146, 148 So. 837, syl. 4 (1933) (that certain person was health officer and death certificate issued by him as registrar); Rockford v. Mower, 259 Ill. 604, 102 N.E. 1032, syl. 4 (1913) (persons

service [23] and the amount of their salaries [24] will be noticed as to officers of these classes. But as to officers not within these descriptions, and generally as to officers in inconspicuous or subordinate posts the courts, though judicial knowledge could often be justified on grounds of verifiability, are inclined to refuse to notice their identity.[25]

Official Documents. Within limits similar to those prescribed in the preceding paragraph, the courts have judicially noticed the existence and contents of documents issued by the classes of officers indicated above as their public, written acts.[26] This doctrine

dispenses with formal authenticating proof of the genuineness of the documents, but this does not mean that if the document is a statement of facts, such facts are themselves judicially noticed.[27] A similar result of dispensing with formal authentication may be attained by doctrines to the effect that signatures of such officers may be "noticed" as genuine, or that their seals will be "noticed." [28] Wigmore has suggested that a more supportable theory is that the purported signatures and seals are themselves accepted as sufficient evidence of the genuineness of the document.[29]

---

holding office as city clerk in the various cities in the county in which court is sitting).

23. People v. Neary, 113 Colo. 12, 154 P.2d 48, syl. 1 (1945) (end of term of state District Attorney); Lyman Flood Prevention Ass'n v. City of Topeka, 152 Kan. 484, 106 P.2d 117, syl. 1 (1940) (time of retirement of Secretary of War).

24. Pink v. State, 105 S.W.2d 265, syl. 4 (Tex.Civ.App. 1937), affirmed 133 Tex. 82, 124 S.W.2d 981 (1939) (in passing upon receiver's fee court could notice salaries of state offices held by him).

25. See, e. g., Crawford v. State, 155 Ind. 692, 57 N.E. 931, syl. 2 (1900) (deputy attorney general); Ward v. Henry, 19 Wis. 76, 81 (1865) (deputy marshal).

A classic instance of illiberality in denying notice is People v. Schmitz, 153 Cal. xviii, 94 P. 419, syl. 5 (1908) (indictment for extortion defective in failing to allege that defendants Schmidt and Ruef were mayor and political boss of San Francisco though both of those facts were notorious), criticised in 9 Wigmore, Evidence, § 2583.

26. See, e. g., Fletcher v. Jones, 70 App.D.C. 179, 105 F.2d 58, syl. 5 (1939) (records and reports of Home Owners' Loan Corporation); General Hosp. Soc. v. New Haven County, 127 Conn. 53, 14 A.2d 746, syl. 3 (1940) (returns of county commissioners as printed by comptroller); State v. Couch, 139 Fla. 353, 190 So. 723, syl. 2 (1939) (bill filed in office of Secretary of State); Stankus v. New York Life Ins. Co., 312 Mass. 366, 44 N.E.2d 687, syl. 5 (1942) (President's reports to Congress under Lease-Lend Act); and cases cited Dec.Dig. Evidence, ⬦48.

But the practice is limited to public transactions of general interest. Carson Cadillac Corp. v. Birmingham, 232 Ala. 512, 167 So. 794, syl. 3 (1936); 20 Am.Jur. 67.

All public transactions which are embodied in the Federal Register, "shall be judicially noticed." The Federal Register Act, 44 U.S.C.A. § 307.

As to notice of proclamation, orders, regulations, etc., in their aspect as laws, see § 326, above.

27. See the illuminating opinion of Magruder, Circ. J., in Stasiukevich v. Nicolls, 168 F.2d 474, 479, syl. 7–12 (C.C.A.1st, 1948). That was a naturalization proceeding where the applicant's "attachment" was disputed on the ground of membership in an alleged communist affiliated organization. Reports on this organization by state and Federal legislative investigating committees were considered by the trial court. On appeal the court said: ". . . The court could properly take judicial notice of the report, without its formal introduction in evidence. But though the court may receive the report in evidence, or may take judicial notice of its existence and contents, this does not mean that the court must accept the findings in the report as indisputable truth; the findings are merely evidence of the facts asserted. See United States v. Aluminum Co. of America, 2 Cir. 1945, 148 F.2d 416, 445, 446; Morgan, The Law of Evidence, 1941–1945, 59 Harv. L.Rev. 481, 485–86 (1946)."

28. See, e. g., Atlantic Industrial Bank v. Centonze, 130 Conn. 18, 31 A.2d 392, syl. 1 (1943) (seals and signature of heads of department of state government); Kuhnhausen v. Stadelman, 174 Ore. 290, 148 P.2d 239, 149 P.2d 239 (1944) (statute requiring notice of succession in office and signatures and seals of "principal" officers not limited to most exalted); Dec.Dig. Evidence, ⬦49, 31 C.J.S., Evidence § 38.

29. 7 Wigmore, Evidence, § 2161. For the scope and limits of the rule as applied to official documents, see ibid. §§ 2161–2167.

329. Social and Economic Data Used in Judicial Law-Making: "Legislative" Facts.[1]

Under modern views, the judge has not only the task of finding what the law is, but between the gaps of existing doctrines to create new law.[2] In doing this, he will be guided as a legislator would be [3] by considerations of expediency and public policy. In doing so he must act either upon knowledge already possessed or upon assumptions, or upon investigation of the pertinent general facts, social, economic, political, or scientific. Under the older tradition the custom was to rationalize the result solely in terms of analogy to old doctrines leaving the considerations of expediency unstated. In recent decades the trend is toward a wider use by the judges in their opinions of explicit statements of their policy-judgments and of the factual grounds therefor. These latter have been helpfully classed as "legislative facts," as contrasted with "adjudicative facts" which are the facts about the particular parties to the controversy and their specific interests and transactions.[4] How are these legislative facts to be presented to the court?

"Where the existence of a rational basis for legislation whose constitutionality is attacked depends upon facts beyond the sphere of judicial notice, such facts may properly be made the subject of judicial inquiry, Borden's Farm Products Co. v. Baldwin, 293 U.S. 194, 55 S.Ct. 187, and the constitutionality of a statute predicated upon the existence of a particular state of facts may be challenged by showing to the court that those facts have ceased to exist. Chastleton Corporation v. Sinclair, 264 U.S. 543, 44 S.Ct. 405." [5]

The usual resort, however, for ascertainment of legislative facts is not through formal proof by sworn witnesses and authenticated documents but by the process of judicial notice. Is judicial notice here trammeled by the usual requirement that the facts noticed must be certain and indisputable? [6] Such a requirement seems inappropriate here where the facts are often generalized and statistical and where their use is more nearly argumentative, or as a help to value-judgments, than conclusive or demonstrative.

In cases where the validity of a statute is attacked for want of due process the nature of the issue narrows sharply the need for certainty. The court is asking not whether the social facts support the statute, but only whether the legislature had reasonable

---

1. See Davis, Administrative Law, ch. 12 esp. §§ 153, 154 (1951), an unusually original and enlightening discussion; Davis, Evidence in the Administrative Process, 55 Harv.L.Rev. 364, 404 (1942); Morris, Law and Fact, 55 Harv.L.Rev. 1303, 1318–1325 (1942); Morgan, Judicial Notice, 57 Harv.L.Rev. 269, 287–291 (1944); Fuchs and Freedman, Wagner Act Decisions and Factual Technique in Public Law Cases, 22 Wash.U.L.Q. 510, 1937; Manoff and Sarcia, Pleading and Proof of Constitutional Facts, 15 Conn.Bar.J. 227, 1941; Biklé Judicial Determination of Questions of Fact Affecting Constitutional Validity, 38 Harv.L.Rev. 6 (1924); 1 Wigmore, Evidence, § 4*l*, 9 id. § 2555(d). See also Notes, Social and Economic Facts—Appraisal of Suggested Techniques for Presenting Them to the Courts, 61 Harv.L.Rev. 692 (1948); Consideration of Facts in Due Process Cases, 23 Ind.L.J. 176 (1948); The Presentation of Facts underlying the Constitutionality of Statutes, 49 Harv.L.Rev. 631 (1936); The Consideration of Facts in Due Process Cases, 30 Col.L.Rev. 360 (1930); Consideration of

Extrinsic Evidence on Constitutionality, 82 L.Ed. 1244 (1938).

2. Cardozo, The Nature of the Judicial Process, 113, 114 (1921).

3. Cardozo, op.cit., 120.

4. Davis, Administrative Law, § 153 (1951).

5. United States v. Carolene Products Co., 304 U.S. 144, 153, 58 S.Ct. 778, 784, 82 L.Ed. 1234 (1938). And this practice obtains in a majority of state courts. Ritholz v. Johnson, 244 Wis. 494, 12 N.W. 2d 738, syl. 7 (1944); Note, 82 L.Ed. at 1246. A minority hold that the court is limited in its consideration of "legislative" facts to those of which it can take judicial notice. Note, 82 L.Ed at 1250. Upon such "judicial inquiry" by formal proof, the decision since it concerns the ascertaining of law is for the judge, not the jury. 9 Wigmore, Evidence, § 2555(d).

6. See §§ 323, 325, above.

grounds for believing that they do.[7] On this issue, the court considers such data as reports of legislative committees,[8] investigating commissions,[9] and administrative bureaus,[10] compilations of legislation in the various states and countries,[11] encyclopedias,[12] dictionaries,[13] and scientific books and articles.[14] In this context, when the courts state that they take judicial notice of such writings, they mean merely that they take notice that such sources are authentic and suffi-

ciently reliable for the legislature reasonably to give weight to their statements[15]—not that they take notice of the truth of the statements.[16] A similarly restrictive use may be made when such fact-reports are noticed for the purpose of aiding in the interpretation of a statute. Committee reports and other sources reciting social facts may often be used not to show what the facts were, but what was reported to the legislature,[17] or what was so widely or authorita-

---

7. Thus in repelling an attack on the Filled Milk Act as wanting in due process, the court said: "When Congress exercises a delegated power such as that over interstate commerce, the methods which it employs to carry out its purposes are beyond attack without a clear and convincing showing that there is no rational basis for the legislation; that it is an arbitrary fiat." Carolene Products Co. v. United States, 323 U.S. 18, 31, 65 S.Ct. 1, 8, 89 L. Ed. 15 (1944).

8. Carolene Products Co. v. United States, 323 U.S. 18, 28, 65 S.Ct. 1, 6, 89 L.Ed. 15 (1944); Everard's Breweries v. Day, 265 U.S. 545, 561, 44 S.Ct. 628, 632, 68 L.Ed. 1174 (1924).

9. Levy Leasing Co. v. Siegel, 258 U.S. 242, 245, 42 S.Ct. 289, 290, 66 L.Ed. 595 (1922) (reports of Governor's and Mayor's committees on housing emergency); McLean v. Arkansas, 211 U.S. 539, 549, 29 S.Ct. 206, 208, 209, 53 L.Ed 315 (report of Industrial Commission authorized by Congress to show need for state miners' wage regulation).

10. Parker v. Brown, 317 U.S. 341, 363, 63 S.Ct. 307, 319, 87 L.Ed. 315 (1943) (reports of U.S. Tariff Commission and publications of U.S. Department of Agriculture, notice as supporting economic need for raisin proration program under state act).

11. Hutchinson Ice Cream Co. v. Iowa, 242 U.S. 153, 157, 158, 37 S.Ct. 28, 61 L.Ed. 217 (1916) (butterfat requirements for ice-cream); Muller v. Oregon, 208 U.S. 412, 419, 28 S.Ct. 324, 325, 52 L.Ed. 551 (1908) (compilation in the famous "Brandeis brief" of laws regulating working hours of women); State v. Main, 69 Conn. 123, 135, 37 A. 80, 83 (1897) ("peach yellows").

12. Jacobson v. Massachusetts, 197 U.S. 11, 31, 25 S.Ct. 358, 363, 49 L.Ed. 643 (1905) (showing experience of other countries with compulsory vaccination).

13. State v. Main, 69 Conn. 123, 135, 37 A. 80, 83 (1897) ("peach yellows").

14. Jacobson v. Massachusetts, 197 U.S. 11, 33, 25 S.Ct. 358, 364, 49 L.Ed. 643 (1905) (text on vaccination); Parker v. Brown, 317 U.S. 341, 363–368, 63 S.Ct. 307, 319–322, 87 L.Ed. 315 (1943) (reports, bulletins, articles and books on the economics of the grape industry).

15. See Muller v. Oregon, 208 U.S. 412, 420, 28 S. Ct. 324, 326, 52 L.Ed. 551 (1908) ("The legislation and opinions referred to in the margin may not be, technically speaking, authorities, and in them is little or no discussion of the constitutional question presented to us for determination, yet they are significant of a widespread belief that woman's physical structure, and the functions she performs in consequence thereof, justify special legislation restricting or qualifying the conditions under which she should be permitted to toil."); Carolene Products Co. v. United States, 323 U.S. 18, 31, 65 S.Ct. 1, 8, 89 L.Ed. 15 (1944) (quoted in note 42, above).

16. See the quotation from Stasiukevich v. Nichols, in § 328, note 27, supra.

The court may also take judicial notice of "legislative" facts for the opposite purpose of finding the statute invalid. Thus in Jay Burns Baking Co. v. Bryan, 264 U.S. 504, 517, 44 Sup.Ct. 412, 415, 68 L.Ed. 813, 32 A.L.R. 661 (1924), in holding a state statute fixing the size of bread-loaves wanting in due process, said "There is no evidence in support of the thought that purchasers have been or are likely to be induced to take a nine and a half or ten ounce loaf for a pound (16 ounce) loaf . . . and it is contrary to common experience and unreasonable to assume that there could be any danger of such deception." See Davis, Administrative Law, 489 (1951). It seems that due respect for legislative authority demands that judicial notice for this purpose be limited to facts which the court believes to be certain and indisputable.

17. And hence the probable purpose and scope of the statute. See Note, Legislative Materials to Aid Statutory Interpretation, 50 Harv.L.Rev. 822, 826 (1937).

tively believed that it was probably considered by them.[18]

Situations remain, however, where these discriminations are inapplicable and where the judge as law-maker must search for the social facts as they are in truth, and not merely for what the legislature could reasonably have supposed them to be. Shall the court in a state where the question is new, accept or reject, in the light of the social and economic consequences, the traditional doctrine that in letting a dwelling-place the landlord has no duty to repair defects that are dangerous to the life of the occupant?[19] In fixing common-law liability for injury to a pedestrian shall an automobile be classed as a "dangerous machine"?[20] At a time when the tests were relatively new should the court admit evidence of the results of a blood-test for paternity?[21] The courts today are coming more and more to bring into the open such policy questions as the basis for making law by a choice of doctrines. On some such questions, particularly those of scientific cast as in the paternity-test example, the court might be willing to hear formal expert testimony, but its normal reliance is judicial notice. Under this process the social, economic and scientific data can be con-

veniently and cheaply presented in the briefs, or can be found by the research of the judge or his assistants. And here again, it is believed, the usual requirements for judicial notice of certainty and indisputability should not be insisted on. The reports, statistics and professional opinions which the judge relies on will be those which he thinks most trustworthy, but they will not usually be indisputable.[22] Nor should the ultimate fact-conclusions of the judge on which his policy-judgment is based be required to be certain. In the realm of basic "legislative" facts, as in respect to policy-valuations themselves, certainty "is not the destiny of man."

Judicial notice in the field of "legislative" facts is an important avenue for a more informed consideration by our courts in policy-making of the contributions of the social, economic, and physical sciences. No rigid requirement of certainty should curb it, but appropriate safeguards should be developed. Among these are the giving of notice to the parties, (perhaps in some cases accompanied with proposed findings)[23] affording them opportunity to furnish materials, or supplementary materials, when such notification is needed,[24] and in exceptional cases the resort to expert referees or masters to ascertain the facts.[25]

---

18. See H. J. Heinz Co. v. National Labor Relations Board, 311 U.S. 514, 523–526, 61 Sup.Ct. 320, 324–326, 85 L.Ed. 309 (1941), where the court in determining whether refusal to sign a written agreement was an unfair labor practice under the Act, referred to materials outside the record including textbooks on the history of labor relations, articles, official and unofficial bulletins and other materials.

19. See Morris, Law and Fact, 55 Harv.L.Rev. 1303, 1318 (1942).

20. See Southern Cotton Oil Co. v. Anderson, 80 Fla. 441, 86 So. 629, 16 A.L.R. 255 (1920), where the court, on the basis of statistics of deaths and injuries due to automobiles taken from Census Bureau reports and of opinions expressed in publications of the National Safety Council concludes that they are "dangerous machines." See also Davis v. Co-operative Equity Co., 262 U.S. 312, 316, 43 S.Ct. 556, 557, 558, 67 L.Ed. 996 (1923). There the court struck down as a "burden on inter-

state commerce" a Minnesota statute permitting a summons to foreign railroad corporations to be served on a soliciting agent in the state. In reaching that conclusion it relied on statistics as to the numbers of suits against such railroads in Minnesota courts, as recited in a proclamation of the Governor.

21. See § 178, herein.

22. See Davis, Administrative Law, § 153 (1951); Davis, Evidence in the Administrative Process, 55 Harv.L.Rev. 364, 403–407 (1942).

23. This suggestion is made in Note, 61 Harv.L.Rev. 692, 698 (1948). Compare the "proposed report" of administrative agencies as described in Davis, Administrative Law, § 154 (1951).

24. Note, 61 Harv.L.Rev. 692, 697 (1948).

25. For discussion of these and similar aids to the court see Note, 61 Harv.L.Rev. 692, 700 (1948);

330. Procedural Incidents.[1]

Some of the practical requirements and effects of judicial notice should be briefly discussed.

First, the distinction should again[2] be mentioned between taking judicial notice of sources, documents and materials,[3] without formal proof of authenticity, and taking notice of facts recited in such materials.[4] The court in noticing the materials may intend to notice the facts also, but the court's statement that it takes notice of the particular source must be shown to have had the wider intent before it can be persuasively cited as a precedent for that effect.

Fairness will ordinarily require that the court before making a final ruling that judicial notice will be taken of a given fact should notify the parties of his intention to do so and afford them an opportunity to present information which might bear upon the propriety of noticing the fact, or upon the truth of the matter to be noticed.[5] The need for such opportunity would be more frequent in respect to adjudicative than as to legislative facts, and even as to the former there are many routine matters of common knowledge which the judge would notice as a matter of course. Common sense demands a reasonable discretion for the judge to determine whether fairness requires such notification.

In some instances it will be apparent to the court that the matter is one which the parties are expecting him to notice. The tenor of domestic law, common and statutory, and facts of universal knowledge are examples.[6] In a wide range of other matters, however, such expectation would not be obvious.[7] As to facts of this kind, and as to

---

Buescher, The Use of Experts by the Courts, 54 Harv.L.Rev. 1105, 1107, 1118 (1941), quoting from the English Rules of the Supreme Court, Ord. 55, r. 19 (taken from the Chancery Act, 1852) which provides that "The Judge in chambers may, in such way as he thinks fit, obtain the assistance of accountants, merchants, engineers, actuaries, and other scientific persons the better to enable any matter at once to be determined, and he may act upon the certificate of any such person."

1. I acknowledge with gratitude the benefit of valuable suggestions of Prof. K. C. Davis, some but not all of which I have been able to adopt, about the questions discussed in this section.

2. See note 27, § 328, and notes 15, 16, § 329, above.

3. Examples: People v. Stralla, 14 Cal.2d 617, 96 P.2d 941, syl. 1 (1939) (for determining whether gambling ship was operated in a "bay," may examine historical data and maps); Schultz v. Winston & Newell Co., 68 N.D. 674, 283 N.W. 69, syl. 5 (1938) (mortality tables); McClain v. Comm., 189 Va. 847, 55 S.E.2d 49, syl. 4 (1949) (official map).

4. The distinction is taken in Stasiukevich v. Nichols, 168 F.2d 474, 479, syl. 9 (C.C.A. 1st 1948) and in Morgan, The Law of Evidence 1941–1945, 59 Harv.L. Rev. 481, 485–86 (1946). See also Fox v. Schaeffer, 131 Conn. 439, 41 A.2d 46, syl. 16, 157 A.L.R. 132 (1944) (right of the court to notice a judgment appearing in a file in another case in same court does not mean that it will give it conclusive effect at to facts found).

5. Uniform Rules of Evidence, R. 10(1) provides: "The judge shall afford each party reasonable opportunity to present to him information relevant to the propriety of taking judicial notice of a matter or to the tenor of the matter to be noticed." R. 12(4) contains a similar provision governing the case when judicial notice of a fact not formerly noticed is to be taken on new trial or appeal. See also § 4 of the Uniform Judicial Notice of Foreign Law Act, which provides, in part, "to enable a party to offer evidence of the law in another jurisdiction or to ask that judicial notice be taken thereof, reasonable notice shall be given to the adverse parties either in the pleadings or otherwise."

6. As to these, R. 801, Model Code of Evidence provides that the judge "shall of his own motion take judicial notice." See Mills v. Denver Tramway Corp., 155 F.2d 808, syl. 6 (C.C.A.Colo.1946) where the trial court, though not requested to do, was reversed for failure to take notice, in the absence of evidence to the contrary, that the street car involved in the accident was equipped with a warning bell. See critical Note, 60 Harv.L.Rev. 299. See also Lilly v. Grand Trunk Western R. Co., 317 U.S. 481, 488, 63 S.Ct. 347, 352, syl. 10, 87 L.Ed. 411 (1943) (appellate court reversed for failure to notice a rule of the I. C. C. having the force of law, though the rule was not called to the attention of the trial court whose holding was consistent with it).

7. "So there are many classes of things of which the courts take judicial notice, or have judicial knowledge. Some of these are so self-evident as to be ever

materials, records and sources of information sought to be noticed the party seeking notice must ordinarily request such notice and present such materials at the trial, if he is to complain later of the court's failure to notice such facts or materials.[8]

Assuming that the requirement of a request is satisfied or that a case is presented where request is unnecessary, is the court bound to take judicial notice wherever the fact is proper for it? It seems to be agreed that in some cases it is mandatory as for example in respect to domestic law and facts universally known.[9] In another range of cases it is discretionary whether the court will take judicial notice or will leave the matter to formal proof.[10] It has been said

with much generality that the exercise of discretion "depends on the nature of the subject, the issue involved, and the apparent justice of the case." [11]

If the trial judge takes judicial notice of a fact, how far is this fact thereafter open to dispute? Certain situations should be distinguished. First, it is clear that fairness often requires that the judge before he notices a fact apprise the parties of the possibility and give them an opportunity to bring forward, not formal proof, but informal data (books of authority, calendars, scientific articles, government bulletins, etc.) to convince him that the matter is not clear and hence not proper for notice, or that the

present in the mind, so that they naturally enter into a decision of any point to which they have application, as, for instance, knowledge of the order of succeeding days of the week or months or seasons of the year, of the familiar laws of nature, etc. But there are other things, which, from motives of policy, the law requires a court to judicially notice, or have knowledge of, but of which, in reality, it is ignorant. It is the duty of a litigant desiring the advantage of that knowledge to suggest it to the court and to assist the court in examining at the proper sources for actual information." Ellison, P. J., in Christy v. Wabash R. Co., 195 Mo.App. 232, 191 S.W. 241, 245 (1917).

8. Shapleigh v. Mier, 299 U.S. 468, 57 S.Ct. 261, 264, 81 L.Ed. 355, 113 A.L.R. 253 (1937) (particular Mexican constitutional provisions, laws, etc.); Goodhall v. Cox, 129 Conn. 79, 26 A.2d 551, syl. 3 (1942) (public documents); Knych v. Trustees, 320 Mass. 339, 69 N.E.2d 575, syl. 1 (1946) (laws of New York); Line v. Line, 119 Md. 403, 86 A. 1032, syl. 5 (1913) (that certain date fell on Sunday); Christy v. Wabash R. Co., 195 Mo.App. 232, 191 S.W. 241, syl. 14 (1917) (I.C.C. rule, but cf. Lilly v. Grand Trunk Western R. Co., note 6, supra); Russell v Kniffin, 118 Misc.R. 808, 194 N.Y.S. 792, syl. 2 (1922) (that date was Sunday); Amundson v. Wilson, 11 N.D. 193, 91 N.W. 37, syl. 4 (1902) (previous judgment); Mogul Transportation Co. v. Larison, 181 Ore. 252, 181 P.2d 139, syl. 3 (1947) (O.P.A. regulations); 9 Wigmore, Evidence, § 2568; Note, 113 A.L.R. 258, 259; 31 C.J.S. Evidence, § 13c. See extensive Comment, Judicial Notice by Appellate Courts of Facts and Foreign Laws not Brought to the Attention of the Trial Court, 42 Mich.L.Rev. 509 (1943).

9. Uniform Rules of Evidence, R. 9(1) (3) quoted in § 323, note 4, above. Power v. Bowdle, 3 N.D. 107, 54

N.W. 404, syl. 6 (1893) (trial court reversed for failure to notice that under general usage of state, abbreviated symbols on tax rolls were insufficient descriptions of the land taxed). See 20 Am.Jur. Evidence § 23.

10. Thayer, Preliminary Treatise on Evidence, 309 (1898) ("Courts may judicially notice much which they cannot be required to notice."); Burkuhl v. F. T. O'Dell Const. Co., 232 Mo.App. 967, 95 S.W.2d 843, syl. 6. (1936) (that barn higher than other buildings more likely to be struck by lightning, discretionary, notice taken); Walsh v. Public Service Co., 92 N.H. 331, 30 A.2d 494, syl. 3–5 (1943) (municipal ordinance, discretionary, notice not taken, but party did not tender "proof" of its terms); Kraus v. Kraus, 183 Misc. 667, 51 N.Y.S.2d 886, syl. 1 (1944, by Pecora, J.) (notice of foreign law, discretionary, under sec. 344a, C.P.A.); Randall v. Comm., 183 Va. 182, 31 S.E.2d 571, 572 (1944) (trial court properly in its discretion noticed that certain well known house was in the county). Of course, the wording of particular statutes regulating judicial notice in terms of "may" or "shall" will often control. See, e. g., Kraus v. Kraus, supra. The Model Code of Evidence provides for Compulsory Notice without Request (R. 801, domestic common law and public statutes and indisputable "propositions of generalized knowledge"); Discretionary Notice without Request (R. 802, private Acts, ordinances and regulations; specific notorious facts; specific and generalized facts, capable of certain verification; law of sister states), and Compulsory Notice on Request (R. 803, matters mentioned in R. 802 must be noticed if the party requests notice and furnishes adequate information, and has notified the adversary).

11. Hunter v. New York, O. & W. Ry. Co., 116 N.Y. 615, 23 N.E. 9, 10 (1889).

fact he proposes to find is not true.[12] That is part of the investigative process which is judicial notice. Second, as we have seen, the courts often take judicial notice of the authenticity and general trustworthiness of particular *sources* of information, such as legislative committee reports, or government bulletins, but not of the facts asserted therein.[13] When this is so, even though the authenticity of the source may not be attacked by formal proof, the facts asserted can be freely disputed by evidence.[14] Again, the court may take judicial notice of a fact, not as constituting part of the issue, but merely as circumstantial evidence, raising an inference of some other ultimate fact in issue. At the same time the court may rule that the fact noticed does of itself give rise to a permissible inference, or an *ad hoc* presumption, of the ultimate fact. In such event, even though the fact noticed could not be contradicted by evidence, of course evidence would be allowable to rebut the inference.[15]

This brings us to the crucial question, if the judge after due investigation with opportunity for the parties to assist therein, makes his deliberate ruling that he takes judicial notice of a given material fact, may the opposing party dispute by formal evidence the truth of the fact noticed, and in a jury-tried case, ask that the question of fact be submitted to them? Thayer suggests qualifiedly an affirmative answer [16] and Wigmore more sweepingly follows in his train.[17] However, it seems that even these great writers and judges equally great,[18] in advocating this view lose sight of the reasons for judicial notice and its purpose and function. As we have seen the conditions of judicial notice are that the fact to be noticed must either be (a) *in the special competence of the judge,* such as a conclusion about the content of a legal rule or of "legislative" fact, or (b) *indisputable,* because it is universally known to be true or because it can be readily and certainly verified upon reference to unimpeachable sources. As to the first it is apparent that the judge is specially equipped to go to reliable sources, that testimony would be a waste of time, and that the jury has no function to play. As to the second, the obvious policy is that parties shall not be permitted to dispute by proof what the judge has found to be a moot or sham issue, not

---

12. See, e. g., Ohio Bell Telephone Co. v. Pub. Utilities Comm'r, 301 U.S. 292, 300–303, 57 S.Ct. 724, 729, syl. 4–6, 81 L.Ed 1093 (1937) (where Commission, after rate-hearing, considered additional sources of information without notifying the utility nor embodying the sources in the record, and state reviewing court considered only the record and took "the word of the Commission as to the outcome of a secret investigation," due process denied). Uniform Rules of Evidence, R. 10(1) provides "The judge shall afford each party reasonable opportunity to present to him information relevant to the propriety of taking judicial notice of a matter or to the tenor of the matter to be noticed."

13. See notes 2, 4, supra.

14. United States v. Aluminum Co. of America, 148 F.2d 416, 446, syl. 42 (C.C.A.2d 1945), explained in Morgan, The Law of Evidence 1941–1945, 59 Harv. L.Rev. 480, 482–6 (1946).

15. In Harper Furniture Co. v. Southern Express Co., 144 N.C. 639, 57 S.E. 458, 459, syl. 1 (1907), an action for delay in dispatching a broken crank shaft from Erie, Pa., to plaintiff at Lenoir, N. C. the court held

that it would take judicial notice of the existence of railroad lines between the two cities and of the nature of the express business and said, "The court taking judicial notice of these facts, it must follow, as a fair and reasonable inference, that 14 days is too long a time for the transportation of freight by express between the two points, Lenoir, N. C., and Erie, Pa., and that, prima facie, there has been actionable negligence in the performance of the contract of carriage."

16. Preliminary Treatise on Evidence pp. 308–309, par. (3) (1898).

17. Evidence, § 2567.

18. See the expressions of Cardozo, J., and Learned Hand, J., respectively, in Ohio Bell Tel. Co. v. Public Utilities Comm'r, 301 U.S. 292, 300–03, 57 Sup.Ct. 724, 728–730, syl. 4–6, 81 L.Ed. 1093 (1937); and United States v. Aluminum Co. of America, 148 F.2d 416, 446, syl. 42 (2d Cir.1945). The weight of these holdings as supporting the general position seems limited, as appears from the cogent critique in Morgan, op. cit., 59 Harv.L.Rev. 482–486.

susceptible of reasonable dispute. Thus judicial notice of indisputable facts rests on the same policy as the practice of summary judgments. Accordingly the weight of reason [19] and the prevailing authority [20] support the view that a ruling that a fact will be judicially noticed precludes contradictory evidence and requires that the judge instruct the jury that they must accept the fact as true.

This view recognizes the process of judicial notice as a distinct level of investigation, confined to a limited range of facts, in which informal unprescribed data are used. Investigation on this level should include a liberal opportunity, before and after the taking of judicial notice is first announced, for the party aggrieved to bring in *his* informal data, his briefs and arguments, and his requests for reconsideration. At some point, however, the judge must call the investigation to a halt and announce his final conclusion that he will or will not notice the fact. This conclusion may be freely reviewed, and new data may be marshaled for the court, on appeal. If he decides for notice, then it seems duplicative and wasteful to allow the adversary to launch a new investigation of the same question on the other level of formal proof, and to start a new procession of proof and counterproof, authenticated documents, exclusionary rules, and examination and cross-examination.

The action of the trial judge taking notice of a fact or directing the jury to find it, or refusing to take judicial notice should be embodied in the record for appellate review, with references to its sources when appropriate.[21] If the fact was one proper for judicial notice by the trial court, as for exam-

19. Most convincingly expounded in Morgan, Judicial Notice, 57 Harv.L.Rev. 269, esp. 273–287 (1944), and by the same author in The Law of Evidence 1941–1945, 59 Harv.L.Rev. 481, 482–487 (1946).

20. See. e. g., Lane v. Sargent, 217 F. 237, syl. 1 (C.C.A.N.H.1914) (Federal court in New Hampshire will notice Massachusetts law and properly excluded evidence of Massachusetts decisions); State v. Main, 69 .Conn. 123, 37 A. 80, syl. 3 (1897) (in passing on validity of statute providing for destruction of infected trees court should take judicial notice of prevalence of belief in danger of "peach yellows" and not submit reasonableness of the law to jury); Beardsley v. Irving, 81 Conn. 489, 71 A. 580, syl. 2 (1909) (party entitled to have the court take notice whether date fell on Sunday and instruct jury accordingly rather than leave question to them); State ex rel. Landis v. Thompson, 121 Fla. 561, 164 So. 192, syl. 6 (1935) (judicial notice of legislative journals precludes contradictory evidence); Nicketta v. National Tea Co., 338 Ill.App. 159, 87 N.E.2d 30, syl. 1 (1949) (trial court properly took notice on pleadings that trichinosis cannot be contracted from eating properly cooked pork, and dismissed complaint; evidence thereon unnecessary); Comm. v. Marzynski, 149 Mass. 68, 21 N.E. 228, syl. 2 (1889) (court will take notice that tobacco and cigars are not medicine and exclude testimony to contrary); Stocker v. Boston & M. R. Co., 83 N.H. 401, 143 A. 68, syl. 11 (1928) (railroad's knowledge of protective devices at crossings judicially noticed; evidence thereof unnecessary and fact cannot be contradicted; and see Calif. Code Civ.Proc. § 2102 ("the court is to declare such knowledge to jury who are bound to accept it") and other Western Codes cited in 9 Wigmore, Evidence, § 2567, note 4; Uniform Rules of Evidence, Rule 11 ("the judge . . . shall instruct the trier of the fact to accept as a fact the matter so noticed").

Contra: In re Bowling Green Milling Co., 132 F.2d 279, syl. 10 (C.C.A. 6th 1942) (dictum); Macht v. Hecht Co., 191 Md. 98, 59 A.2d 754, syl. 5 (1948) (refusal to take judicial notice on pleadings of a fact open to dispute: dictum that if notice taken, can dispute by evidence); Scheufler v. Continental Life Ins. Co., 350 Mo. 886, 169 S.W.2d 359, syl. 13 (1943) (in application for allowance of fee, judicial notice of prior proceedings does not cut off applicant's right to be heard on reasonableness of allowance); State ex rel. Attorney-General v. Norcross, 132 Wis. 534, 112 N.W. 40, syl. 1 (1907) (in proceeding to abate dam as nuisance court could not, on demurrer to complaint, take notice that stream was not navigable and thereby cut off contrary evidence); State v. Lawrence, 234 P.2d 600, syl. 7–9 (Utah, 1951) (error to instruct jury in prosecution for theft that a 1947 Ford sedan in good condition was of greater value than $50), noted critically in 32 Bost.U.L.Rev. 115, and see cases cited in notes 12 and 14, supra.

Cases pro and con are cited in Wickes, Book Review, 16 Tex.L.Rev. 204, 207, 208 (1938) and 31 C.J.S. 520, notes 61, 62.

21. See Nichols v. Nichols, 126 Conn. 614, 13 A.2d 591, syl. 13 (1940); Uniform Rules of Evidence, R. 11: "If a matter judicially noticed is other 'than the common law or constitution or public statutes of

ple a matter notorious in the local community, the upper court will likewise notice it,[22] and similarly if not within the power of the lower court, the upper court will hold itself within the same limit.[23] As we have seen above, the failure of the party to request judicial notice of a fact at the trial, is significant in determining the fairness of his complaint on appeal of the judge's failure to notice. In the absence of such request below will the upper court notice the matter? If the effect will be to sustain a satisfactory judgment, the court is much more likely to do so, than when the result is reversal of a judgment apparently just.[24] The matter is probably not reducible to rule.[25] The trial court's findings in the realm of judicial notice are not conclusive upon the upper court, which may make its own investigation and reach its finding independently.[26]

331. Trends in the Development of Judicial Notice.

All writers on the subject have been impressed by the importance and the latent possibilities for usefulness of the process of judicial notice. What trends in its past growth can we discern, which may be projected into the future? In the first place, the emphasis is shifting from the ancient and now comparatively less important basis of "common knowledge" to the more pregnant basis of verifiable certainty. This latter is a channel which easily brings to the court the abundant fruits of new scientific findings and discoveries as soon as they become professionally accepted and enables the court to translate these findings to the jury not tentatively but with authority. In the second place, this shift of emphasis, from what needs no proof to what can be verified with certainty by investigation, reveals that judicial notice is not merely a substitute for formal proof by witnesses but is itself another method of proof of certain kinds of facts, namely, the method of research into the professionally authoritative books and reports in the particular field. Viewed thus as a new system of proof of facts within a particular range it is apparent that judicial notice is still in a formative stage. To attain full usefulness, certain directions of growth may be looked for. Among these are the clearer acceptance of safeguards for the parties in the form of notice and opportunity to present materials on matters proposed to be noticed, the wider consciousness of the responsibility of counsel for the production of reliable sources for investigation, the realization by the judges of their primary responsibility for the adequacy of the research and the trustworthiness of the sources relied on, and finally the provision for the judges of expert and impartial assistants who can evaluate the data from the viewpoint of the particular science in cases when such evaluation is beyond the competence of the judges.

this state, the judge shall indicate for the record the matter which is judicially noticed . . ."

22. Varcoe v. Lee, 180 Cal. 338, 343, 181 P. 223, 225, syl. 7 (1919).

23. Thus the Supreme Court of the United States in reviewing lower Federal courts takes judicial notice as the lower courts may of the laws of all the states, but in reviewing state courts it takes notice of other states' laws, only when the particular state court under review has that power. Hanley v. Donoghue, 116 U.S. 1, 6, 6 S.Ct. 242, 245, 29 L.Ed 535 (1885).

24. See Comment, 42 Mich.L.Rev. 509, 513 (1943).

25. See discussion of Clark Circ. J., in American Legion Post v. First Nat. Bank, 113 F.2d 868, 872, syl. 4, 5 (C.C.A.2d, 1940).

26. 9 Wigmore, Evidence, § 2567(c). And the failure or refusal of the trial court to take notice of a fact does not preclude the upper court from noticing it. Rogers v. Cody, 8 Calif. 324, 38 P. 81, syl. 1 (1894) (that land foreclosed was outside county).

TABLE OF CASES

References are to pages

720

References are to pages

Cohn v. Chapman, 433
Cohn v. Kramer, 443
Coker v. State, 235, 248
Colbert v. Dallas Joint Stock Land Bank, 406
Colbert's Estate, In re, 497
Colburn v. Chicago, St. P., M. & O. Ry. Co., 118
Cold Metal Process Co. v. Aluminum Co., 209
Cole v. Andrews, 185
Cole v. Harvey, 541
Cole v. Lake Shore & M. S. Ry. Co., 20
Cole v. Lea, 402
Cole v. State, 165
Coleman v. Lewis, 624, 625
Coleman v. McIntosh, 126, 407
Coleman v. Southwick, 459
Coles v. Harsch, 153, 176
Coley v. Hall, 189
Colling v. Treweek, 416
Collings v. Northwestern Hospital, 148
Collins v. Collins' Estate, 117
Collins v. Commonwealth, 239
Collins v. Dorchester, 350
Collins v. Equitable Life Ins. Co., 124, 579
Collins v. Leahey, 643, 702
Collins v. Streitz, 127, 642
Columbia & P. S. R. Co. v. Hawthorne, 159, 543
Columbus, City of v. Ogletree, 403
Colvin v. Wilson, 108
Colwell v. Dyer, 217
Combs v. State, 483
Comer v. Comer, 419
Comer v. State, 556
Commander v. State, 463
Commercial Molasses Corp. v. New York Tank Barge Corp., 644, 645
Commercial Standard Ins. Co. v. Robinson, 565
Commission of Conservation of Department of Conservation v. Hane, 348
Commissioner of Internal Revenue v. Hyde, 699
Commonwealth v. Anderson, 529
Commonwealth v. Antonini, 549
Commonwealth v. Ball, 401
Commonwealth v. Beal, 334
Commonwealth v. Becker, 335
Commonwealth v. Belenski, 392
Commonwealth v. Berney, 683
Commonwealth v. Burke, 104
Commonwealth v. Carr, 313
Commonwealth v. Cavalier, 233
Commonwealth v. Chance, 391
Commonwealth v. Clark, 652
Commonwealth v. Clendinning, 312
Commonwealth v. Colangelo, 564
Commonwealth v. Congdon, 310
Commonwealth v. Crecorian, 513
Commonwealth v. Dana, 291
Commonwealth v. Dascalakis, 234
Commonwealth v. Dawn, 564
Commonwealth v. Del Giorno, 405
Commonwealth v. Descalakis, 393

Commonwealth v. Emery, 285
Commonwealth v. English, 692
Commonwealth v. Everson, 174, 175
Commonwealth v. Felch, 573
Commonwealth v. Fugmann, 582
Commonwealth v. Galavan, 13
Commonwealth v. Gallo, 484, 485, 493
Commonwealth v. Galvin, 60
Commonwealth v. Gantz, 146
Commonwealth v. Giacobbe, 533
Commonwealth v. Goldenberg, 533
Commonwealth v. Graham, 528
Commonwealth v. Grieco, 528
Commonwealth v. Griffin, 162
Commonwealth v. Haney, 559
Commonwealth v. Harris, 603, 611
Commonwealth v. Harvie, 337
Commonwealth v. Haywood, 235
Commonwealth v. Hebert, 528
Commonwealth v. Heller, 330
Commonwealth v. Hipple, 232
Commonwealth v. Ingraham, 107
Commonwealth v. Jenkins, 108
Commonwealth v. Jensky, 476
Commonwealth v. Johnson, 30
Commonwealth v. Jones, 228, 232
Commonwealth v. Keenan, 701
Commonwealth v. Kenney, 528, 530
Commonwealth v. Kitchen, 688
Commonwealth v. Kline, 329
Commonwealth v. Knable, 556
Commonwealth v. Kostan, 90
Commonwealth v. Lannan, 18
Commonwealth v. Lenousky, 483
Commonwealth v. Lettrich, 231, 537
Commonwealth v. Levine, 18
Commonwealth v. Logan, 581
Commonwealth v. McCue, 475
Commonwealth v. McDermott, 17
Commonwealth v. Mabey, 231
Commonwealth v. Madeiros, 648
Commonwealth v. Marzynski, 711
Commonwealth v. Meleskie, 560
Commonwealth v. Musto, 266
Commonwealth v. Nagle, 341, 342
Commonwealth v. Nolly, 404
Commonwealth v. Peronace, 574
Commonwealth v. Plubell, 559
Commonwealth v. Ponzi, 18
Commonwealth v. Powers, 471
Commonwealth v. Prince, 259
Commonwealth v. Ransom, 329
Commonwealth v. Regan, 344
Commonwealth v. Ricci, 464
Commonwealth v. Richardson, 286
Commonwealth v. Richmond, 278
Commonwealth v. Roller, 389
Commonwealth v. Rubin, 574
Commonwealth v. Santos, 572
Commonwealth v. Schaffner, 88

TABLE OF CASES

H

K

M

V

W

Waddell v. Trowbridge, 416
Wade v. King, 488
Waggoman v. Ft. Worth Well Machinery & Supply Co., 338
Wagner v. Jones, 120
Wagstaff v. Wilson, 520
Wahl v. Cunningham, 193
Wainwright v. Westborough Country Club, 467
Walker v. Anderson, 137
Walker v. Brautner, 549
Walker v. Carpenter, 675
Walker v. Curtis, 604
Walker v. Fields, 126, 127
Walker v. Great Atlantic & Pac. Tea Co., 564
Walker v. Herke, 538, 539
Walker v. Johnston, 642
Walker v. Prudential Ins. Co., 564
Walker v. Saricks, 438
Walker v. State, 85, 154
Walker v. Walker, 480, 499
Walker's Estate, In re, 646
Walker's Trial, 98
Walkerton v. Erdman, 490
Wallace v. American Toll Bridge Co., 116
Wallace v. Martin, 701
Wallace v. State, 88
Waller v. Sloan, 43
Waller v. State, 499
Waller v. Waller, 515
Walling v. Richmond Screw Anchor Co., 304, 308
Wallis v. Southern Pac. Co., 341
Walnut Ridge Merc. Co. v. Cohn, 554
Walsh v. Public Service Co., 696, 709
Walsh v. Walsh, 444
Walter Pratt & Co. v. G. W. Chaffin & Co., 454
Walthall v. State, 558
W. A. Manda, Inc. v. City of Orange, 123
Ward v. Henry, 704
Ward v. Martin, 281
Ward v. Morr Transfer & Storage Co., 18
Ward v. Oliver, 173
Ward v. Pittsburgh, City of, 9
Ward v. State, 175, 271
Ward v. Texas, 243
Ward v. Thompson, 48
Ware v. Allen, 450
Ware v. Boston & M. R. Co., 544
Ware v. State, 537
Warmke v. Commonwealth, 231
Warner v. Maine Central R. R., 160
Warickshall's Case, 155
Warren v. Greenfield, 551
Warren v. Pulley, 436
Warren's Estate, In re, 399
Warren Live Stock Co. v. Farr, 132
Wartell v. Novograd, 184, 192, 540
Washington & O. D. Ry. Co. v. Smith, 70
Wassenich v. City & County of Denver, 349

Watford v. Alabama & Florida Lbr. Co., 699
Watkins v. Prudential Ins. Co., 669
Watkins Salt Co. v. Mulkey, 433, 437
Watson v. Adams, 355
Watson v. Western Union Co., 703
Watts v. Delaware Coach Co., 611
Watts v. Indiana, 245
Watts' Estate, 448
Waugh v. The King, 279
Wausau Sulphate Fibre Co. v. Commissioner, 403
Weathered v. State, 131
Weaver v. United States, 99
Webb v. Biggers, 134
Webb v. Francis J. Lewald Coal Co., 205
Webb v. Lewald Coal Co., 220
Webb v. State, 558
Webber v. E. K. Larimer Hardware Co., 580
Weber v. Chicago, R. I. & P. R. Co., 27, 548, 549, 554
Webster v. Moore & Son, 476
Weeks v. United States, 294
Weibert v. Hanan, 137
Weigel v. Powers Elevator Co., 17
Weightnovel v. State, 530
Weiner v. Zweib, 624
Weinshenk v. Sullivan, 194
Weis v. Weis, 215, 610, 613
Weisenborn v. Rutledge, 137
Weismantle v. Petros, 652
Weiss v. United States, 299
Weiss v. Wasserman, 618
Weisser v. Preszler, 197
Weissman v. Wells, 219
Welborn v. Rigdon, 537
Welch v. State, 316
Wellisch v. John Hancock Mut. Life Ins. Co., 643, 664
Wells v. Burton Lines, 507
Wells v. Niagara Land & Timber Co., 450
Wells v. State, 474
Wells v. Tietge, 681
Wells v. Toogood, 310
Welsh v. Gibbons, 534
Welshire v. Bruaw, 148
Wentworth v. Crawford, 43
Wentworth v. Lloyd, 164
Wentz v. Guaranteed Sand & Gravel Co., 596
Werk v. Parker, 692
Werner, In re, 260
Werner v. State Bar, 489, 492, 500
West, In re, 259
West v. Cashin, 540
West v. Houston Oil Co., 407
West v. Louisiana, 483
West v. Redmond, 146
Westberry v. State, 558
West Chicago St. Ry. v. Kennelly, 477
Western States Grocery Co. v. Mirt, 537
Western Twine Co. v. Wright, 405
Western & Atlantic R. R. v. Henderson, 656
Westgate Oil Co. v. McAbee, 83
Westinghouse Co. v. Tilden, 419

INDEX